Y0-EBW-897

THE
History *and* Antiquities
OF THE
EXCHEQUER
OF THE
KINGS OF ENGLAND,

IN TWO PERIODS:

TO WIT,

From the NORMAN CONQUEST, to the End of the Reign of K. JOHN;

AND

From the End of the Reign of K. JOHN, to the End of the Reign of K. EDWARD II.

TAKEN FROM RECORDS.

TOGETHER WITH

A Correct Copy of the ANCIENT DIALOGUE concerning the Exchequer, generally ascribed to GERVASIUS TILBURIENSIS.

AND

A DISSERTATION concerning the most ancient GREAT ROLL of the Exchequer, commonly styled The Roll of QUINTO REGIS STEPHANI.

BY THOMAS MADOX, ESQ.

THE SECOND EDITION.
With a Full and Compleat INDEX.

VOLUME II.

GREENWOOD PRESS, PUBLISHERS
NEW YORK

Originally published in 1769
by William Owen & Benjamin White

First Greenwood Reprinting, 1969

Library of Congress Catalogue Card Number 70-75579

SBN 8371-1076-9

PRINTED IN UNITED STATES OF AMERICA

THE TABLE of CONTENTS TO THE SECOND VOLUME.

CHAP. XX.

Of the Exchequer *of the Kings of* England, *from the End of the Reign of King* John, *to the End of the Reign of King* Edward II.

I. *Of its Declensions from its antient grandeur.* p. 1
II. *Of the* Duo Scaccaria. p. 2
III. *Of certain inferiour Exchequers.* p. 3
IV. *Of the Times of Session at the Exchequers.* p. 5
V. *Of the Place where the Exchequer was holden.* p. 7
VI. *That the King sometimes sat and acted in Person at the Exchequer.* p. 10
VII. *Of the Privilege of Barons, Residents, and Ministers of the Exchequer.* p. 11
VIII. *That the Exchequer was a Court of great Power, and a Repository of Records.* p. 23

CHAP. XXI.

Of the Persons that sat and acted at the Exchequer *during the second Period.*

I. *Of the King's Chief Justicier, his Chancellor and his Council, acting at the Exchequer.* p. 26
II. *Of the Treasurer and his Lieutenant.* p. 33
III. *Of the Chancellor and Barons of the Exchequer.* p. 51

CHAP. XXII.

Of the Business *and* Proceedings *in the* Exchequer-*during the second Period.*

I. *Of Affairs relating to the Revenue.* p. 63
II. *Of Pleas.* p. 73
III. *Of Business of various Kinds. Of Conventions, Recognitions,* &c. *made in the Exchequer.* p. 86
IV. *Of the Presentation and Admission of Officers.* p. 87
V. *Of the Presentation of Mayors, Sheriffs.* p. 92
VI. *Of Fealty done and Rents paid at the Exchequer.* p. 99
VII. *Of Affairs relating to the Government and Defence of the Realm.* p. 102
VIII. *Of the Records and Judgments of the Exchequer.* p. 112
IX. *Of Messages or Letters sent to the Exchequer by the King, Queen, and Prince.* p. 121

CHAP. XXIII.

Of Accounts *rendered at the* Exchequer.

I. *A Specification of some of those Accounts.* p. 128
II. *Of the Office and the Accounts of Sheriffs.* p. 137
III. *Certain Assises or Rules of the Exchequer touching the King's Debtors and Accountants:* viz. *the immediate Baillee was to render the Account.* p. 175

The Table of Contents.

IV. *Accounts were to be rendred in Course.* p. 176
V. *In Person.* p. 177
VI. *Upon Oath.* p. 182
VII. *The King's Debt was to be paid first.* p. 183
VIII. *The King might betake himself, for Payment, to one indebted to his Debtor.* p. 189
IX. *The Heir of the King's Debtor was not to be distrained, if the Debtor's Chattels were sufficient.* p. 190
X. *Nor Lands holden in Dower, if the Heir had sufficient.* p. 191
XI. *Nor Sureties, if the Principal had sufficient.* p. 192
XII. *The King's Debtors were wont to have Writs of Aid.* p. 192
XIII. *Sheriffs, who had levied or received the King's Debt, were to acquit the Debtor at the Exchequer.* p. 194
XIV. *Sheriffs were to notify the Time of their accounting to Bailiffs of Liberties and other Persons concerned.* p. 197
XV. *The King's Debtors were to find Sureties for Payment, if required.* ibid.
XVI. *Of Writs of the Great and Privy Seal that were sent to the Exchequer.* p. 199
XVII. *Of Allowances made to Accountants* per breve Regis, *or otherwise.* ibid.
XVIII. *Of Atterminations.* p. 208
XIX. *Of Respites.* p. 213
XX. *Of Discharges and Pardons.* p. 220
XXI. *Of Surplusage.* p. 231
XXII. *Of the Punishments for Default of accounting:* viz. *of Amercements and Issues, of Seizure of Lands, of Arrests, of Seizure of Liberties.* p. 234
XXIII. *Of distraining of Clerks.* p. 249
XXIV. *Of Accountants sitting at the Exchequer.* p. 251
XXV. *Of Accounts rendered* in Camera Regis. ibid.
XXVI. *Of the Method of putting Debts in Charge* p. 253
XXVII. *Of the Original, and other Estreats.* p. 254
XXVIII. *Of Tallies.* p. 258
XXIX. *Of Counters.* p. 261

CHAP. XXIV.

Of the Officers *or* Ministers *of the* Exchequer.

I. *Introduction.* p. 263
II. *Of the two Remembrancers.* p. 264
III. *Of the Ingrosser of the Great Roll, and of the Comptroller.* p. 269
IV. *Of the Usher.* p. 271
V. *Of the Constable.* p. 281
VI. *Of the Marshall.* p. 284
VII. *Of the Auditours.* p. 290
VIII. *Of the Clerks of Estreats.* p. 293
IX. *Of the* Clericus Brevium. p. 294
X. *Of the Chamberlains.* p. 295
XI. *Of the Treasurers Clerks.* p. 303
XII. *Of the Tellers.* p. 307
XIII. *Of the Pesour.* ibid.
XIV. *Of the Fusour.* p. 309

CHAP. XXV.

A List of Barons *of the* Exchequer, *from the* Conquest *to the End of the Reign of K.* Edward II. p. 312
Antiquus Dialogus de Scaccario, Gervasio de Tilbury *vulgo adscriptus.* Præmittitur Dissertatio Epistolaris ad Perillustrem Carolum Dominum Halifax. p. 331

Disceptatio Epistolaris de Magno Rotulo Anni quinti R. Stephani, ad Perillustrem Johannem Dominum Somers. p. 455

A Complete Index to the whole Work.

THE HISTORY and ANTIQUITIES OF THE EXCHEQUER.

CHAP. XX.

Of the EXCHEQUER *of the Kings of* ENGLAND, *from the End of the Reign of King* John, *to the End of the Reign of King* Edward II.

I. *Of its Declension from its antient Grandeur.*
II. *Of the* Duo Scaccaria.
III. *Of certain Inferiour Exchequers.*
IV. *Of the Times of Session at the Exchequer.*
V. *Of the Place where the Exchequer was holden.*
VI. *That the King sometimes sat and acted in Person at the Exchequer.*
VII. *Of the Privilege of Barons, Residents, and Ministers of the Exchequer.*
VIII. *That the Exchequer was a Court of great Power, and a Repository of Records.*

I. WE may observe, that at the Beginning of this Second Period, and for some time afterwards, the Exchequer continued in much the same State that it was in during the First Period; bateing the Change made by the Separation of Common Pleas from the *King's Court* and it (of which I have spoken in Chap. XIX): I say, for some time after the Beginning of this second Period, it was, as before, a great and solemn Court, frequented by the King's great Officers, and guided for the most part by the antient

ent Rules, Affizes, and Cuftoms. Before the End of K. *Henry* the Third's Reign, it fell in great meafure from its ancient Grandeur; and from thence forward continued in a State of Declenfion; infomuch that about the End of this fecond Period, it was in many Refpects different from what it had been in former Ages. This, I fuppofe, will appear from the hiftorical Deduction contained in thefe Volumes; and particularly, by comparing the State of the Exchequer during the firft Period, with the State of it during the latter Part of the fecond (to fay nothing now of the next fucceeding Times). I who propofe to deliver Matters of Fact, do not think my felf concerned to engage in fo abftrufe a Theme, as to enquire what were the efpecial Caufes of this Declenfion: nor am I willing to amufe the Reader with my Conjectures.

II. In the King's Exchequer, there ftill continued the Diftinction of the two notable Terms in the Year, called the *Duo Scaccaria*. The Reafon why thefe two Terms were at firft inftituted and afterwards obferved in the Exchequer, is (with great Probability of Truth) affigned by the worthy Author of the Dialogue (*a*); to whom the Reader is referred. But let us now, if you pleafe, fhew in fome Inftances the Continuance of the *Duo Scaccaria* during this fecond Period. And that will appear in the Cafe of *Robert Marmiun* (*b*), of the Men of *Fecham* (*c*), of *R.* Bifhop of *Chichefter* (*d*), *Laurence de Wenlefwurth* (*e*), *Nicholas del Caftle* (*f*), and *John Longynou.*

(*a*) *Dial. in Append. L.* 2. *cap.* 1. Audivi jamdudum; & *L.* 2. *cap.* 2. Magnum tuæ.

(*b*) Termini, Ad feftum S. Trinitatis anno fecundo Regis H. tertij C marcæ, & ad feftum S. Michaelis proximo fequens C marcæ, & ad Pafcha proximo fequens C marcæ; Et fic de Scaccario S. Michaelis ad Scaccarium Pafchæ de anno in annum, C marcæ ad utrumq; Scaccarium donec quingentæ libræ Regi fuerint perfolutæ. *Mag. Rot.* 2. *H.* 3. *Rot.* 5. *b. War. & Leic.*

(*c*) Reddendo per annum ad Scaccarium xx l, fcilicet ad Scaccarium S. Michaelis x l, & ad Scaccarium Pafcæ x l. *Mag. Rot.* 14. *H.* 3. *Wygornia.*

(*d*) Refpondendo inde Regi & hæredibus fuis fingulis annis, per manum fuam, ad Scaccarium, quamdiu vixerit de C l; Ad Scaccarium Pafchæ de xx l, & ad Scaccarium S. Michaelis de quater xx libris; pro omni fervitio & demanda ad idem Manerium pertinente. *Mag. Rot.* 15. *H.* 3. *Effex & Hertf.*

(*e*) Rex conceffit Laurencio de Wenlefwurth, quod de xl marcis ad quas amerciatus fuit pro tranfgreffione, reddat ei per annum octo marcas, videlicet ad Scaccarium Pafchæ anno xxix° quatuor marcas, & ad Scaccarium S. Michaelis quatuor marcas, & fic de anno in annum octo marcas, donec &c. Et ideo &c. B e in f M. Et mandatum eft Vicecomiti. *Hil. Commun.* 29. *H.* 3. *Rot.* 5. *a.*

(*f*) Rex commifit Nicholao de Caftello Hundreda de Humilierd, Blafeld, Taverham, & Walfham, cuftodienda quamdiu Regi placuerit; Reddendo inde per annum ad Scaccarium xx libras, videlicet unam medietatem ad Scaccarium S. Michaelis, & aliam medietatem ad Scaccarium Pafchæ. Per R. Bathonienfem & Wellenfem Epifcopum Cancellarium,

Chap. XX.   *of the Kings of* England.   3

nou (*g*). To thefe, more Inftances need not be added; in regard the fame Diftinction hath continued all along in the following Ages, and is well known at this Day in the *Receipt* of Exchequer. The Diftinction of the *Duo Scaccaria* was likewife ufed in *Normandy* (*h*).

III. Befides the great or principal Exchequer, there were feveral inferiour Receipts or Treafuries that were called by that Name. There was an Exchequer to be made in the King's Manour-houfe at *Woodftock* (*i*). K. *Henry* III. gave towards the Fabrick of *Weftminfterchurch* Two thoufand Five hundred and Ninety Pounds; and appointed a private Exchequer [or Cheft] for the Receipt and Management thereof; and made two Perfons Treafurers of that Exchequer (*k*). There was an Exchequer of *Wolvefey* belonging to the Bifhoprick of *Winchefter* (*l*).
There

Cancellarium, Thefaurarium, & Barones. Datum xxiiij die Aprilis anno Decimo. *Paf. Commun.* 9 *&* 10. *E.* 1. *Rot.* 4. *a.*

(*g*) — Reddendo inde Regi per annum quatuor libras; unam inde medietatem ad Scaccarium S. Michaelis, & aliam medietatem ad Scaccarium Pafchæ. *Hil. Commiſſiones* 1. *E.* 2. *Rot.* 9. *a.*

(*h*) *Ante, Cap.* 4. *fect.* 4. *ad ann.* 2 *Joh.* Rex &c. G. de Glappion. *& ib. alibi.*

(*i*) Rex Cuftodi Manerij de Wudeftoke falutem. Præcipimus tibi, quod fine dilatione fieri facias quoddam Trellicium ferreum in gradu noftro coram Camera noftra verfus herbarium noftrum, & quoddam laticium ligneum in duabus feneftris coram camera Reginæ noftræ, & appenticium fupra illas feneftras plumbo cooperiri facias; Aperturas etiam duorum appenticiorum inter Aulam noftram & Cameram Reginæ noftræ & Capellam noftram verfus herbarium noftrum bordiri, & duas feneftras de albo vitreo in eifdem borduris fieri facias; Duas etiam veruras fieri facias in gabulo aulæ noftræ, & feneftras ejufdem aulæ verfus orientem fimiliter cum pictura ejufdem aulæ emendari facias; Quoddam etiam Scaccarium fieri facias in eadem aula, quod contineat hunc verfum,

Qui non dat quod amat, non accipit ille quod optat.

Omnes etiam domos utriufq; Curiæ noftræ, & fontes, & muros, qui reparatione indigent fimiliter emendari facias: Et cuftum quod ad hoc pofueris computabitur tibi ad Scaccarium T. Rege apud Wudftoke vj die Novembris. *Rot. Liberat.* 25. *H.* 3. *m.* 23.

(*k*) Rex dedit & conceffit Deo & Beato Edwardo & ecclefiæ Weftmonafterij ad fabricam ipfius Ecclefiæ duo mille quingentas xx iiij xj libras in quibus Regi tenetur Licor [icia] quæ fuit uxor David de Oxonia Judæi. Et Rex vult quod pecunia illa reddatur ad Novum Scaccarium quod Rex ad hoc conftituit apud Weftmonafterium, Archidiacono Weftmonafterij & Edwardo de Weftminftre, quos ejufdem Scaccarij Rex thefaurarios affignavit, ad terminos in Rotulo Cancellar[iæ] de Finibus contentos, donec pecunia illa plene reddatur ficut prædictum eft. In cujus &c; T. Rege apud Windefore xxij die Aprilis. *Pat.* 30. *H.* 3. *m.* 5.

(*l*) Rex omnibus &c falutem. Sciatis quod de confilio Magnatum qui funt de Confilio noftro, conceffimus dilecto nobis in Chrifto Andreæ Priori S. Swithuni Wintoniæ, qui electus eft in Epifcopum Wintonienfem, duo milia marcarum fingulis annis percipienda ad Scaccarium de Woluefeye apud Wintoniam, de exitibus Epifcopatus Wintoniæ vacantis & in manu noftra exiftentis, quamdiu lis pendeat fuper negocio electionis prædictæ, videlicet mille marcas ad Scaccarium S. Michaelis & ad Scaccarium Pafchæ mille marcas. Et de ifta folutione loco & terminis fupradictis facienda,

Of the Exchequer — Chap. XX.

There was an Exchequer in the *Cambium* of *London* (*m*), the Exchequer of *Durham* (*n*), the Exchequer of *Chester* (*o*), of *Carlisle* (*p*), and of *Berwick* (*q*). There was also an Exchequer of *Kaernarvan* (*r*): At which Exchequer, the King had his Chamberlain (*s*); and his

cienda, Nicholaum de Handlou Custodem prædicti Episcopatus juramentum præstare fecimus corporale. Et hoc idem jurare faciemus singulos Custodes ejusdem Episcopatus dum in manu nostra fuerit, quod solutionem illam simili modo facient non obstante aliquo mandato nostro eis super hoc dirigendo. In cujus &c; T. Rege apud Westmonasterium ij die Augusti. Ista littera præcepta fuit præsentibus R. Comite Gloucestriæ, Petro de Sabaudia, H. le Bigod Justiciario Angliæ, Philippo Basset, & Johanne Mansell Thesaurario Ebor[acensi]; & liberata cuidam Monacho Wintoniensi per W. de Merton apud Windesore x die Augusti. *Pat.* 43. *H.* 3. *m.* 4.

Et in pergameno empto ad Scaccarium de Wolvese & canabo ad idem, iij s. *Mag. Rot.* 52. *H.* 3. *Rot.* 1. *b. in compoto Walteri de Burges de exitibus Episcopatus Wintoniæ.*

(*m*) Et pro panno ad cooperiendum Scaccarium Cambij, & pro linea tela ad fenestras, v s & vj d. *Mag. Rot.* 17. *Joh. Rot.* 6. *b. m.* 1. *in compoto Cambij Londoniæ.*

Et in stipendijs hostiar[ij] ejusdem Cambij [of *London*] per idem tempus, dimidia marca: Et in uno panno ad Scaccarium in eodem Cambio xj s: Et in incausto & pergameno tallijs cultellis filo & saccis & alijs minutis expensis in Cambio v s, per idem tempus. *Mag. Rot.* 49. *H.* 3. *Rot.* 11. *a.*

Et in uno panno ad Scaccarium ejusdem Cambij, x s. *Ib. m.* 1. *a. in Rotulo Compotorum.*

(*n*) Mandatum est Episcopo Dunolmensi quod si Petrus Saracenus quondam Civis Romanus consuevit percipere feodum xl l ad Scaccarium Dunolmi, & quod idem feodum —*Memor.* 42. *H.* 3. *Rot.* 18. *a.*

(*o*) —quia compotus Abbathiarum, Prioratuum, Custodiarum, & Eschaetarum de Comitatu Cestriæ ad Scaccarium Cestriæ, & non ad Scaccarium Londoniæ redditur—. *Ryl. Plac. P. p.* 97. anno 20. *E.* 1.

(*p*) — & quod Præpositus dicti Roberti de Ros de Cargaue solvit quolibet anno xxxij den. de Cornagio ad Scaccarium Domini Regis apud Karliolum pro prædicta Sapientia—. *Estaet.* 3. *E.* 1. *n.* 81.

(*q*) Rex mittit Baronibus quandam Cedulam præsentibus interclusam Regi per Thesaurarium Scaccarij Berewici nuper missam, in qua quædam videre poterunt contineri quæ idem Thesaurarius usq; Berewyck pro ordinatione Scaccarij ejusdem mitti petit. Et quia Rex vult quod idem ordo per omnia qui est in Scaccario Westmonasterij, in dicto Scaccario Berewici de cætero habeatur, Mandat Baronibus, quod visa diligenter Cedula supradicta, ea quæ continentur in eadem & de quibus pro ordinatione dicti Scaccarij Berewici viderint opus esse, dicto Thesaurario Scaccarij ejusdem ad citius quod fieri poterit transmittant, ut hiis habitis idem ordo in dicto Scaccario Berewici valeat ordinari, qui in prædicto Scaccario Westmonasterij observatur. Teste Rege apud S. Edmundum xvj die Novemb. anno xxiiij. Cedula est annexa huic brevi in custodia Marescalli. *Mich. Record.* 24. *E.* 1. *D.*

(*r*) Rex commisit Watero de Huntercombe Castrum de Bere cum Armaturis & omnibus alijs in munitione Castri illius existentibus; custodiendum quamdiu Regi placuerit: Et concessit eidem ducentas marcas annuatim, pro custodia ejusdem Castri ad Scaccarium Regis de Kaernarvan, per manus Camerarij Regis qui pro tempore fuerit percipiendas &c. T. R. apud Kaernarvan 21 die Octobris. *Rot. Walliæ* 12. *E.* 1. *m.* 2.

(*s*) Rex concessit Johanni de Beuclare Castrum de Herdelagh &c; & concessit eidem septies viginti & novem libras & decem denarios singulis annis, pro custodia ejusdem Castri, ad Scaccarium suum Kaernarvan, per manus Camerarij sui &c. *Rot. Wall.* 13. *E.* 1. *m.* 2.

Chap. XX.   *of the Kings of* ENGLAND.   5

Treasurer (*t*) : And the Writ of Summonce was used there (as in the Superiour Exchequer) for levying of the King's Debts arising in those Parts. The Principal Exchequer was sufficiently distinguishable from these or other inferiour ones. However, when the former and any one of the latter are mentioned together, there has been commonly a Name or Character of Distinction used. With reference to the Exchequer of *Chester*, the principal Exchequer has been called *Scaccarium de Londonia* (*u*) With respect to the Exchequer of *Berwick*, it has been called *Scaccarium Westmonasterij* (*w*) : With reference to the Exchequer of the *Receipt* (*x*), and likewise to the Exchequer of the *Jews* (*y*), *Magnum* or *superius Scaccarium*.

IV. The principal Times of Session at the Exchequer were the two Terms of *Easter* and St. *Michael*. At which Times the Process that issued *pro Rege* was returnable, and many Acts became necessary to be done there in consequence thereof. The Exchequer was also holden during the other two Law-Terms, to wit of St. *Hilary* and of the *Trinity*. But it seemeth, that the Treasurer and Barons sometimes sat if there was Occasion, at other Times not comprized within the Limits of the Four Terms above mentioned; and sometimes on Sundays. In the 11th year of K. *Henry* III, *William Pippard* was summoned to be

---

(*t*) Rex dilectis & fidelibus suis Roberto de Staundon Justiciario suo Northwalliæ, & Magistro Roberto de Belvero Thesaurario Scaccarij sui de Karnarvan, salutem. Sciatis quod de gratia nostra speciali perdonavimus Mariæ quæ fuit uxor Manasseri le Fosseur de Carnarvan viginti & tres solidos & octo denarios, in quibus prædictus Manasserus quondam vir ipsius Mariæ nobis tenebatur de arreragijs compoti sui de tempore quo fuit Ballivus noster in Karnarvan, & qui per Summonitionem ejusdem Scaccarij exiguntur ab eadem: Et ideo vobis mandamus, quod ipsam Mariam de prædictis viginti & tribus solidis & octo denarijs quietam esse faciatis. T. R. apud Westm. 28 die Maij. *Rot. Wall.* 14. *& seq. E.* 1. *m.* 3. *viz. anno* 21. *E.* 1.

(*u*) *Hic supra*, Sect. 3. Quia compotus.
(*w*) *Hic supra*, Sect. 3. Rex mittit.
(*x*) Edwardus Dei gratia &c; Fratri Joseph de Chauncy Thesaurario suo, salutem. Sciatis quod commisimus dilecto Clerico nostro Radulpho de Besages officium illud quod Adam de Stratton nuper habuit ad Scaccarium nostrum, videlicet tam ad Magnum Scaccarium quam ad Scaccarium nostrum de Recepta, & quod nuper cepimus in manum nostram ex certa causa, custodiendum quamdiu nobis placuerit, respondendo inde nobis sicut ei injuximus : Et ideo vobis mandamus, quod eidem Magistro Radulpho officium illud, cum clave & alijs ad officium illud pertinentibus, liberetis, custodiendum sicut prædictum est ; T. &c xxij° die Maij anno r n sexto. *Pas. Commun.* 6. *E.* 1. *Rot.* 5. *b.*

(*y*) Baronibus, pro Johanne de Burgo. Rex dedit respectum eidem J. de omnibus debitis quæ ei debet, tam de Magno Scaccario suo quam de Scaccario Judæorum, quamdiu fuerit cum eo in servicio suo in partibus Wasconiæ — *Hil. Communia* 27. *H.* 3. *Rot.* 6. *a.*

— ad Thesaurarium & Barones Superioris Scaccarij———. *Ante, cap.* 7. *sect.* 7. *ad ann.* 13 *&* 14. *E.* 1. Præfati vero,

at the Exchequer on the Sunday next before Ascension-day (z). In the 52d Year of that King, the Exchequer was shut up on the Morrow of St. *Peter ad Vincula* (a). In the 26th Year of K. *Edward* I, in regard the Treasurer was obliged to attend on certain Affairs which the King had entrusted him with, so that he could not be at the Exchequer to dispatch the Businesses there, the King, by Writ of Privy Seal, orders the Chancellour and Barons to continue Sitting at the Exchequer this present *August*, to levy Moneys to his Use, to receive the Accompts, and to dispatch the other Business there, in the best Manner they could (b). So also K. *Edward* II, (*anno Regni* 2º), by Writ of the Privy Seal commanded the Treasurer and Barons to sit longer than the usual time, for dispatch of such Business as was urgent (c). In the 5th Year of K. *Edward* II, upon the Friday next before Whitsontide, the Exchequer was shut-up for that Term, And the Exchequer-Seal laid up in the Treasury (d). In the same 5th Year,

(z) Walterus Pippard debet L 1 Bl. de firma de Hintlesdon. Summoneatur Willelmus hæres ejus; sit ad Scaccarium, inde responsurus, Dominica proxima ante Ascensionem. Hugo le Tailur serviens ipsius Willelmi cepit in manum, quod habebit Dominum suum ad Scaccarium dicto die. *Ex Memor.* 11. *H.* 3. *Rot.* 5. *a. Norf. Suff.*

(a) Baronibus, pro Hominibus de Bruges; Allocate eisdem in firma ejusdem villæ———. Ista duo brevia sunt in bursa ubi ponitur Sigillum Scaccarij, & duo brevia quæ venerunt Baronibus pro Willelmo de Grey & Ricardo de Grey filio suo. Quia clausum erat Scaccarium quando recepta fuerunt dicta brevia per Thesaurarium & Barones in crastino S. Petri ad Vincula. *Ex Memor.* 52. *H.* 3. *Rot.* 12. *a.*

Another Writ issued pro Waltero de la Naperye. Breve est in Bursa cum Sigillo Scaccarij; quia Scaccarium fuit clausum quando breve venit. *Ib. Rot.* 12. *b.*

(b) Edward par la Grace de Dieu Roi Dengleterre &c, Au.. Chanceler e as.. Barouns del Escheqer Salutz. Pur ceo qe il covient qe Levesqe de Cestre nostre Tresorier voit precheinement a Loundres, pur aucunes busoignes dont nous lui avoms enchargie, par quey ney porra mie orendreit entondre pur delivrez les busoignes del Escheqier: Nous vous prioms, qe vous demoergez sour Lescheqer ceste seison Daugst, & qe vous metez pein pour levex deners a nostre oes, e pur rescivre les Accountes sour les busoignes qe touchent meisme Lescheqer, si avant come vous porrez. E ceo ne soit en nule manere lessez. Donez souz nostre Prive seal a Temple Liston, le xx jour de Juyl, lan de nostre regne xxvj. *Trin. Brevia* 26. *E.* 1. *Rot.* 88. *b. in bund.* 25 & 26. *E.* 1.

(c) Edward par la grace de Dieu &c, Au Tresorer, e as Chaumberleyns de nostre Escheqer, salutz. Nous vous maundoms & chargeoms, qe vous demorgez adessement de nostre Escheqier en ceste vacacion, por ordener e faire taunt par totes les maneres qe vous porrez, qe nous seyoms covenablement servy de deners en nostre guerre Descore, & qe totes nos autres bosognyes seyent sy ben ordenez come vous saverez & porrez. Done souz nostre Prive Seal a Wyndesore, le xx jour de Joyl, lan de nostre regne secound. *Trin. Brevia* 1. *E.* 2. *Rot.* 67. *a.*

(d) De Sigillo Scaccarij liberato in Thesauraria. Memorandum quod modo, die Veneris proximo ante festum Pentecostes, videlicet duodecimo die Maij, quo die Scaccarium fuit clausum pro hoc Termino, liberatum fuit Ricardo de Crombwell & Petro le Blund Camerar[arijs] &c Sigillum hujus

Chap. XX.   *of the Kings of* ENGLAND.   7

Year, the Barons of the Exchequer and several Persons of the King's Council sat at the Exchequer on Sunday the 23d Day of *July* (*e*). The Day of the *Liberate* was counted the Time of their Rising. The King commands the Treasurer's Lieutenant, the Barons, and Chamberlains, to certify him in what State Things would be at the *Receipt* of Exchequer, after their *Liberate*, now at their [next] Rising (*f*). In the Archive of *Corpus Christi* College in *Cambridge*, there is a Manuscript that contains a Calendar made for the Use of the *Auditores compotorum* and others residing at the Exchequer. It is entitled there, *Kalendarium de Scaccario*. The Beginning of it gives Rules for finding the Dominical Letter and Holy Days (*g*).

V. Albeit the Exchequer was generally held at *Westminster* during this second Period, yet it was sometimes by the King's special Commandment held elsewhere. In *Michaelmass* Term in the 6th Year incipient of K. *Edward* I, the Exchequer was held at *Shrewsbury* (*h*). In the 11th Year of the same King the Common-Bench was also removed to *Shrewsbury* upon occasion of the King's being at that Time engaged in his Expedition against *Wales* (*i*). In the 13th Year of K. *Edward* I,

jus Scaccarij custodiendum salvo & secure donec aliud &c, sub sigillis W. de Norwyco, Magistri J. de Everdon, & Johannis Abel, Baronum de eodem Scaccario. *Pas. Commun.* 5. *E.* 2. *Rot.* 46. *a.*

(*e*) Suhampton. Manucaptio de debitis Johannis de Berewyk. Willelmus de Heyghton de Comitatibus Dorsetæ & Suhamtoniæ, Walterus de Buttesthorn de Comitatu Suhamtoniæ & Adam Barnard de Comitatu Leycestriæ, venerunt coram Baronibus ad Scaccarium, die Dominico vicesimo tertio die Julij, Præsentibus venerabili Patre J. Bathoniensi & Wellensi Episcopo, A de Valencia Comite de Penebrok, H. le Dispenser, J. de Benstede, Justic. & alijs de Consilio Regis, & concesserunt se esse Executores testamenti Johannis de Berewyco defuncti &c——. *Trin. Commun.* 5. *E.* 2. *Rot.* 65. *a. inter Fines &c.*

(*f*) R. au Lieu tenant le Tresorer, as Barons & as Chaumberleyns de nostre Eschequer salutz. &c——. *'Tis a Privy Seal importing, that the King sends* Roger de Wyngefeld *to the Exchequer, to see that the Justices of the one Bench and the other deli-* vered their *Estretes at the Exchequer, and commanding the Barons to issue them and other Estretes in the presence of the said* Roger, pur faire lever noz dettes a tote la Haste com hom purra &c. Dautrepart vos mandoms, que vous mustre au dit Roger tout lestat de nostre receite, & en quel point elle serra apres voster Liberate ore a voster lever, Issint quil nous en puisse certefier a son returner a nous. Done souz nostre Prive seal a Everwyk, le quarte jour de Feverer lan quint. *Hil. Brevia* 5. *E.* 2. *Rot.* 30. *b. in imo.*

(*g*) *Ex antiq. Cod. MS. J.* 2. [*it is in a hand of temp.* E. 2. *or* 3. *circiter*] *in Bibl. Corp. Christi Cantab.*

(*h*) Adventus Vicecomitum ad Scaccarium apud Salopiam, in crastino S. Michaelis anno v° Regis E. incipiente Sexto. *Ex Memorand.* 5. *& 6. E.* 1. *Rot.* 1.

(*i*) Rex Thesaurario & Camerarijs suis salutem. Liberate de thesauro nostro dilecto Clerico nostro Eliæ de Bekingham, Custodi Rotulorum & Brevium nostrorum de Banco, viginti solidos quos ei concessimus pro misis & expensis, quas fecit circa cariagium rotulorum & brevium prædictorum

de

Edward I, the Exchequer was held (as it seems) at *Westminster*, in the King's *Parliament* (*k*). And in the 26th and 27th Year of the same King, *Robert de Coleshull* came before *Walter* Bishop of *Coventry* the Treasurer and *William de Carleton* a Baron of the Exchequer, in the King's Parliament, and there made Fine to the King for the Cause hereunder mentioned (*l*). The Exchequer was likewise holden in the King's Parliament at *Westminster* (as it seems) in the 2d Year of K. *Edward* II. For it is said, that an Ordinance or Indenture concerning the King's Mines in *Devonshire*, was made by the Treasurer, Chancellour, and Barons of the Exchequer, and others of the King's Council, at his Parliament, in the Term of St. *Michael*, in the second Year of the King's Reign. It is dated at *Westminster*. And one Part of the Indenture was under the Exchequer Seal (*m*). Let it be considered,

de Westmonasterio usq; villam nostram Salopiæ, ubi Bancum prædictum teneri fecimus anno regni nostri undecimo, nobis tunc existentibus in expeditione nostra Walliæ. T. R. apud Westmon. primo die Julij. *Lib.* 13. *E.* 1. *m.* 3.

(*k*) Baronibus pro hæredibus & executoribus testamenti Stephani nuper Waterfordensis Episcopi. Cum idem Stephanus Regi teneretur in magna summa pecuniæ, de arreragijs Compoti sui quem reddidit ad Scaccarium apud Westmonasterium in Parliamento Regis post Pascha anno tertio decimo, de toto tempore quo fuerat Justiciarius Regis & Thesaurarius in Hiberniæ—&c ; de quibus forsan secundum Vigorem recti Compoti & aliquorum Judicium, allocanciam non haberet, Rex præfato Episcopo, ipsius aliunde pensatis meritis, totam pecuniam prædictam & omnia arreragia illa, de gratia sua speciali, perdonaverit, & ipsum inde acquietaverit—&c. *Ex Pas. Memorand.* 34. *E.* 1. *Rot.* 29. *a. inter Brevia.*

(*l*) Berk. Robertus filius Heliæ de Coleshulle venit coram Venerabili Patre W. Coventrensi & Lich. Episcopo Thesaurario, & Willelmo de Carleton Barone de Scaccario, xix° die Marcij hoc anno, in Parliamento Regis apud Westmonasterium, & finem fecit cum Rege per quinquaginta marcas, pro habenda licentia Regis super ingressu Maneriorum de Aldermanston & Spersholt, quæ fuerunt Roberti Achard qui ea de Rege tenuit in Capite: De quibus L. marcis habuit diem ad solvendum Regi ad Pascha tunc proximo futurum x marcas, & ad festum Nativitatis S. Johannis Baptistæ proximo sequens xx marcas, & ad festum S. Michaelis proximo post xx marcas; Per Plegiagium Warini de Insula & Eliæ de Coleshulle. Postea solvit prædictas L marcas per duas Tallias. *Pas. Fines* 26 & 27. *E.* 1. *Rot.* 66. *b.*

(*m*) Devonia. Ordinatio pro Minera Regis. Fait a remembrer, qe ordene est par Loneurable Piere en Dieu sire Wauter par la grace de Dieux Evesq; de Wirecestre Tresorer nostre Seignur le Roy, en la presence sire Johan de Sandale Chanceler, sire William de Carleton, sire Thomas de Cantebrugg, sire Roger de Hegham, Mestre Richard de Abydon, Mestre Johan de Everesdon, Barons de Lescheker, & plusurs autres del Consail du dit nostre seignur le Roy a son Parlement, en le Terme de seint Michel, lan de son regne secund, Qe Robert de Thorp Clerk soit Gardein de la Minere le Roy en Byrelond en Deveneshire, & des autres Mineres qe il purra faere cerchier es parties de Deveneshire, ou il entendra faere le proffit le Roy, Et qe Johan de Repple Clerk soit Controlleur des dites Mineres a surveer controlleur & tesmoigner la Mine trete laendroit——&c——. En tesmoignnance de queu chose a la partie de ceste Endenture demorant devers les ditz Gardein & Controuller, le Roy ad faet mettre son seal de son Escheker, E a la partie demorant devers le Roy, les ditz Gardein & Contrerouller

sidered, how these Instances are to be understood. Shall we say, that the Exchequer was not holden in the same Place where the Parliament was held, but only at the same Time? But the Words of these Records seem to import more than that, and to mean the same Place. However, let the Antiquaries (who have a Notion of the Communication there anciently was between the King's Courts after the Division of them) determine, if they please, this Matter. Further. K. *Edward* I, in the 18th Year of his Reign, commanded the Barons to transfer the Exchequer to the *Husting* of *London*, and to hold it there (*n*). The same King, in the 26th Year of his Reign, caused his Exchequer, with the Receipt and Bench, to be removed to the City of *York*; and commanded the Sheriff of *York*, forthwith to provide a large convenient Hall within the King's Castle of *York*, for holding the Pleas of the said Bench, with other Conveniencies for Seats for the Justices, Barons, and others; and to fit-up the Castle-Hall for the Exchequer, with a square Chequer-board, and Seats about it for the Treasurer, Barons, Clerks, and Ministers there, and with a Bar for those who plead and attend there; And also to fit-up the Tower of the Castle for the Receipt of the Exchequer, and furnish it with Doors, Bars, Locks, and other Things necessary for Security of the King's Treasure to be lodged there: And to do all these Things according to the Directions which should be given him by *John Dymmok* Usher of the Exchequer: And the Expences thereof were to be allowed the said Sheriff upon his Accompt (*o*). And soon afterwards, the King commanded the several Sheriffs of the Counties lying in the Road from *London* to the City of *York*, to take care, within their respective Bailywicks, about the safe conveying of the King's Rolls, Writs, and Treasure, to the said City of *York* (*p*). K. *Edward* II, in the 12th Year of his Reign, commanded the Exchequer and the Bank to be transferred to *York*, and to be held there on the Morrow of St. *Michael* then next; and ordered the Treasurer and Barons to transfer the Exchequer accordingly, with the Rolls, Tallies, Memoranda, and other Things necessary, at the King's Charges: This was

rouller unt mys leurs seaux. Ceste Endenture fust faete a Westmonster le xij jour de Decembre lan avantnomee. *Mich. Recorda* 2. *E.* 2. *Rot.* 41. *a*.

(*n*) Baronibus de Scaccario transferendo. Quia Rex certis de causis vult quod Scaccarium suum usq; Hustengum Londoniæ transferatur, & ibidem teneatur, usq; aliud inde duxerit ordinandum: Rex mandat Baronibus, quod Scaccarium prædictum ibidem teneant in forma prædicta. T. Rege apud Wyntoniam vicesimo die Aprilis anno decimo octavo. *Pas. Commun.* 18. *E.* 1. *Rot.*—C.

(*o*) *Pas. Brevia Irretornab.* 26. *E.* 1. *Rot.* 78. *a.* Et vid. Ryl. Plac. Parl. *p.* 225. *ad ann.* 26. *E.* 1.

(*p*) *Pas. Brev. Irret.* 26. *E.* 1. *Rot.* 79. *a.*

done

done by Letters Patent; which are printed in *Ryley's* Appendix (*q*), and are also entered in the Records of the Exchequer (*r*). The Letters Patent for removing the Bank are likewise printed by *Ryley* (*s*.) K. *Edward* II, in the 15th Year of his Reign, commanded the Exchequer to be removed to and to be held at *York* on the Morrow of the Close of Easter, by his Writs of the Great and Privy Seal hereunder recited. Accordingly, the Vice-treasurer, the Archbishop of *Canterbury*, the Chancellor of the Exchequer, two Justices of the King's Bench, two Justices of the Common Bench, and others of the King's Council, being assembled at the Exchequer at *Westminster*, concerted and ordered the Manner of removing it; particularly as to the Number of the Carriages to be used upon that Occasion, and the Stages or Days-journeys upon the Road, &c (*t*). And about the same Time, the King by Writs of the Great Seal, notified to the Sheriffs of the several Counties the said Transferment of the Exchequer to *York*; and commanded them to be personally at *York* at the Time appointed, to pay their Profers and return their Writs there; and to give Notice to Bailiffs, Fermours, and other Persons, concerned, to appear there likewise at the said Time (*u*).

VI. As in the first Period, so also in the second, the King, if he pleased, sat and acted in Person at the Exchequer. K. *Henry* III. sat and acted in the Exchequer, in the 25th Year of his Reign (*w*), in the 31st Year of his Reign (*x*), in the 35th Year (*y*), in the

---

(*q*) *Plac. Parl. p.* 564.
(*r*) *Trin. Brevia* 12. *E.* 2. *Rot.* 104. *b.*
(*s*) *Ryl. Plac. Parl. Append. p.* 564.
(*t*) *Hil. Communia* 15. *E.* 2. *Rot.* 17. *a.*
(*u*) *Hil. Brev. Retorn.* 15. *E.* 2. *Rot.* 86. *b.*
(*w*) Consideratum est coram Domino Rege & consilio suo & Baronibus, quod Episcopus Londoniensis & Canonici S. Pauli non habeant amerciamenta de Itinere Justiciariorum, nec de se ipsis nec de hominibus suis; quia in Cartis suis quas habent de Regibus Angliæ, non continetur quod eas habere debeant. Et quod de Justiciarijs Itinerantibus intelligitur, & de Justiciarijs de Banco intelligatur. *Ex Memor.* 25. *H.* 3. *Rot.* 1. *b.*
(*x*) Loquendum cum Domino Rege de quibusdam præstitis factis Galfrido de Mandevill & W. filio suo tempore Regis Johannis, de quibus contentio est inter Comitem Herefordiæ & Johannem filium Galfridi. Postea consideratum est coram Domino Rege & Consilio suo, quod illa præstita quæ fuerunt facta prædictis G. & W. filio suo in exercitibus pro defensione terræ quam de Rege ten[ebant] & occasione expeditionis, sint super prædictum Comitem qui est hæres ipsorum, & alia præstita quæ fuerunt facta prædicto Galfrido extra expeditionem & non occasione defensionis prædictæ terræ in exercitu, sint super Johannem filium Galfridi. *Hil. Communia* 31. *H.* 3. *Rot.* 4. *a.*

(*y*) Provisio Domini Regis. Thomas Corbet & Henricus de Colne responderunt de proficuo Comitatuum qui fuerunt in custodia eorum ita insufficienter, quod de toto proficuo vix potuerint perfici corpora eorundem Comitatuum. Et ideo Dominus Rex coram Consilio suo & Baronibus de Scaccario providit, quod ipsi T. & H. responderent eodem modo quo alij qui proximo ante eos tenuerunt Comitatus illos responderunt. *Ex Memor.* 35. *H.* 3. *Rot.* 8. *a.*

Chap. XX.   *of the Kings of* ENGLAND.

37th Year (*z*), in the 39th Year (*a*), in the 49th Year (*b*), in the 51st Year (*c*), and in the 52d Year of his Reign (*d*).

VII. From the moſt ancient Times, the Perſons employed in the King's Service at his Exchequer were wont to enjoy ſeveral Privileges; ſome of which will be ſpecified by and by. The Records of the firſt Period, that relate to this Subject, are not ſo clear and full as thoſe of the ſecond Period. However, in the former, we find, the Barons and Officers of the Exchequer had then divers Immunities allowed to them *per libertatem ſedendi ad Scaccarium*, in reſpect of their Attendance there. Some of theſe Caſes are mentioned by the Dialogue (*e*).

(*z*) Dominus Rex ſedens ad Scaccarium perſonaliter, præcepit & injunxit † Theſaurario & Baronibus de Scaccario, quod manuteneant & conſervent illæſa omnia quæ tangunt Libertates Abbatiæ Weſtmonaſterij. *Mich. Communia* 37. *H.* 3. *Rot.* 4. *Pars* 2.
† *'Tis written in the Roll,* junxit.

(*a*) Memorandum, pro R. de Quency Comite Wintoniæ, Quod ſedente Domino Rege in Scaccario in craſtino Purificationis B. Mariæ, perdonavit R. de Quency Comiti Wintoniæ amerciamentum ad quod debuit amerciari per ipſum Dominum Regem, pro defalta quam fecit coram Juſticiarijs Itinerantibus in Comitatu Bedefordiæ, occaſione Communis Summonitionis. *Ex Memor.* 39. *H.* 3. *Rot.* 8. *b*.

In this year the King ſat in the Exchequer and heard the Cauſe concerning a Royal Fiſh which was taken on the Land of an Infant who was the Biſhop of Norwiches *Ward. Hic, Cap.* 20. *ſect.* 7. Sedente Domino Rege.

(*b*) Cives Londoniæ venerunt coram Rege ſedente in Scaccario, & præſentaverunt Thomam filium Ricardi quod ſit Major Londoniæ hoc anno. Et ad hoc admiſſus eſt, & præſtitit ſacramentum &c. *Mich. Commun.* 49. *H.* 3. *Rot.* 2. *b*.

Communis reſpectus; Idem reſpectus conceſſus eſt per Dominum Regem & Juſtic[iarium] uſque in quindenam S. Michaëlis. *Paſ. Communia* 49. *H.* 3. *Rot.* 8. *b*.

Thomas filius Otonis venit coram Rege præſente in Scaccario, & Baronibus, & petijt quod veteres Cunei fracti de Cambio Londoniæ qui fuerunt in Theſaur[aria] ſibi redderentur tanquam pertinentes ad jus & hæreditatem ſuam, & quos Anteceſſores ſui prius habere conſueverunt: Et Rex inquiſita & comperta ſuper hoc veritate, præcepit quod dicti Cunei ſibi redderentur. *Hil. Commun.* 49. *H.* 3. *Rot.* 6. *b*.

Londonia. Quia conſideratum fuit coram Domino Rege & Conſilio ſuo præſentibus in Scaccario, quod Vicecomites Londoniæ de anno xlviij° reddant Eymerico Sykard Mercatori xxviij l pro xxviij dolijs vini captis in manum Regis tanquam eſcaëta Regis, & poſtea adjudicatum fuit quod eſcaëta non eſſent; præceptum eſt eiſdem Vicecomitibus, quod reddant eidem Eymerico prædictas xxviij l, loco xxviij l quæ eis allocantur in Rotulo ejuſdem anni in corpore Comitatus. *Hil. Commun.* 49. *H.* 3. *Rot.* 8. *a*.

(*c*) Memorandum quod die Sabbati proximo poſt feſtum S. Hilarij, præcepit Dominus Rex, in pleno Scaccario, Theſaurario & Baronibus ejuſdem Scaccarij, quod ſi aliquis Vicecomes vel Ballivus, qui in aliquo debito Regi tenetur, veniat ad Scaccarium, non recedat inde donec totum debitum perſolverit; Et ſi idem Dominus Rex poſtea mittat Breve ſuum de prædicto debito reſpectuando vel perdonando, non faciant aliquid pro hujuſmodi Brevi, quouſq; Dominus Rex ſuper hoc conſulatur. *Ex Mem.* 51. *H.* 3. *Rot.* 4. *a*.

(*d*) — De quibus omnibus idem Robertus [de Nevil, Conſtabularius Caſtri de Hamburg] reddidit compotum coram Rege & Conſilio ſuo, & in præſencia Viſorum Operationum Caſtri prædicti ad hoc juratorum. *Ex Mem.* 52. *H.* 3. *Rot.* 6. *a*.

(*e*) *Dial. L.* 1. *c.* 8. Sic eſt. Sed proſequamur.

The

The Records of the subsequent Times speak more distinctly. They mention the Privilege of impleading and being impleaded in the Exchequer only; Freedom from Toll, for Things bought for their own use; Freedom from Suit to County-Courts, Hundred Courts, &c.; and other Privileges. It is also to be understood, that several of the Residents at the Exchequer had Privilege not only for themselves, but also for their Clerks and their Men. I will produce some Instances of these Things; not pretending to enumerate all the Officers and Residents who were in those Times privileged, nor all the Privileges to which they were entituled. In the 38th Year of K. *Henry* III, a Writ was sent to the Sheriff of *Norfolk*, reciting that whereas by the ancient Custom and Assise of the Exchequer, no Baron of the Exchequer, or other Officer in Fee attending there, ought to plead or be impleaded in any other Place besides the Exchequer; and commanding the Sheriff to remove a Plea which depended in the County-Court between Master *Roger de Gosebec*, who resided at the Exchequer for the Marshal of *England*, and *William de Eys* and others, into the Exchequer, and to summon the Parties Defendants to be there to answer in the Premisses (f). The same K. *Henry* III, in the 39th Year of his Reign, granted and confirmed to the Barons that sat at the Exchequer, all the ancient Liberties and Freedoms which the Barons of the Exchequer had in the Time of his Predecessors Kings of *England*, and which the Barons then living had in his own Time, as well in Pleas moved, and Exactions made for their Lands, Rents, Tenements, Fees, and Possessions, as also in respect of Trespasses and Injuries done to them and their Men: And granted, that they should enjoy the said Liberties as fully as any Barons of the Exchequer in

---

(f) Norf. Quia secundum antiquam consuetudinem & assisam Scaccarij Regis, nullus Baronum Regis ibidem per præceptum Regis residentium, vel eorum qui in ministerio Regis pro feodis quæ de Rege tenent Regi ibidem deservire & assidere tenentur, inplacitari debent vel alibi placitare quam in ipso Scaccario Regis, postquam ibidem inceperint residere, & conpotis Vicecomitum & Baillivorum Regis intendere, eo quod sine dampno Regis inde recedere non possunt: Mandatum est Vicecomiti Norfolciæ, quod loquelam quæ est in Comitatu Suffolciæ inter magistrum Rogerum de Gosebec qui residet in Scaccario Regis pro Marescallo Angliæ, & Willelmum de Eys, Johannem Snod, Henricum personam de Eys, Willelmum de Furlang, & Adam servientem personæ de Eys, de averijs ipsius Magistri Rogeri per ipsum Vicecomitem .., quæ prædicti W. J. H. & A. ceperunt injuste ut dicit, ponat coram Baronibus &c a die S. Michaelis in tres septimanas; Et summoneat per bonos summonitores dictum Willelmum & alios prænominatos, quod tunc sint ibi, responsuri quare ceperunt averia prædicti Magistri, & illa retinuerunt contra vadium & plegium. Et habeat summonitores & hoc breve. *Trin. Commun.* 38. *H.* 3. *Rot.* 19. *a.*

Chap. XX. *of the Kings of* ENGLAND.

Times paft had enjoyed the fame *(g)*. The King's Treafurer had the Privilege of suing and being fued only in the Exchequer. As in the Cafe of *Hugh de Patefhull* (*h*); and *Philipp Lovell* (*i*). *Alexander,* Treafurer of St. *Paul's London*, Baron of the Exchequer (*k*), and *Nicolas de Crioll*, Baron of the Exchequer (*l*), had the like Privilege. *Robert de Fulham* Conftable of the Exchequer fued the Priour of *Michelham* and another Perfon, in the Exchequer, for a Debt (*m*).

John

(*g*) Rex Baronibus de Scaccario; Attendentes utilitatem fidelis Obfequij quod nobis impenditis, Volumus & vobis ac alijs qui ex mandato noftro vobifcum affident in præfato Scaccario, & ibidem compotis Ballivorum noftrorum audiendis intendunt, concedimus, quod habeatis omnes Antiquas Libertates & liberas confuetudines quas Barones de eodem Scaccario habuerunt temporibus Prædeceſſorum noftrorum Regum Angliæ, & eciam quas vos noftro tempore habuiftis, tam in placitis motis & movendis, exactionibus factis & faciendis de terris, redditibus, tenementis, feodis, poffeffionibus, & rebus veftris, quam in tranfgreffionibus & injurijs vobis & hominibus veftris factis & faciendis; Et quod prædictis Libertatibus & liberis confuetudinibus, a tempore quo inceperitis federe in dicto Scaccario, & compotis prædictis intendere, libere poffitis uti, ficut aliqui Barones de eodem Scaccario, temporibus Prædeceſſorum noftrorum Regum Angliæ, melius & liberius uſi fuerunt, & vos noftro tempore uſi eftis. *Memor.* 39. *H.* 3. *Rot.* 7. *a.*

(*h*) Effex & Hertford. Rex Vicecomiti; Quia fecundum antiquam confuetudinem & affifam Scaccarij noſtri, nullus Baronum noftrorum ibidem per præceptum noftrum refidencium, vel eorum qui in Minifterio fuo pro feodis quæ de nobis tenent, nobis ibidem defervire & affidere tenentur, implacitari debet vel implacitare alibi quam in ipfo Scaccario noftro, poftquam ibidem refidere & compotis Vicecomitum & Ballivorum noftrorum intendere, Eo quod fine dampno noftro inde recedere non poffunt: Tibi præcipimus, quod loquelam quæ eft in Comitatu Hertford, inter dilectum & fidelem noftrum Hugonem de Patefhull Thefaurarium noftrum, & Ricardum de Argentem, de averijs ipfius Thefaurarij noftri per te replegiatis, quæ idem Ricardus cepit injufte in terra ejufdem Thefaurarij noftri ut dicit, ponas coram prædictis Baronibus de Scaccario apud Weftmonafterium a die S. Johannis Baptiftæ. Et fummone per bonos fummonitores dictum Ricardum quod tunc fit ibi, refponfurus quare cepit averia dicti Thefaurarij noftri, & illa retinuit contra vadium & plegium. Et habeas tunc ibi fummonitores & hoc breve. Tefte A. Archidiacono Salopiæ xxj die Junij. *Memor.* 22 *H.* 3. *Rot.* 9. *b.*

(*i*) War. & Leyc. Mandatum eft Vic. ad refpondendum Philippo Lovell Thefaurario &c, de hoc quod ceperunt columbas de columbari fuo &c, contra pacem &c. *Ex Memor.* 40. *H* 3. *Rot.* 1. *b. Et ibid Rot.* 5. *a. Norf.*

(*k*) Effex & Hertford. Mandatum eft Vicecomiti, quod habeat coram Baronibus in octabis S. Michaelis Henricum le Lechin & alios nominatos in brevi, ad refpondendum A. Thefaurario S. Pauli Londoniæ Baroni de Scaccario, de hoc quod foffatum fuum proftraverunt in Andebury, & arbores fuas ibidem exftirpaverunt, contra pacem Regis, ut dicitur———. T. J. Francigena xxvj die Julij. *Trin. Commun.* 29 *H.* 3. *Rot.* 11. *b.*

(*l*) Effex. Mandatum eft Vicecomiti, quod venire &c in craftino Cinerum Magiftrum Stephanum de Sandwico, ad refpondendum Nicholao de Crioll Baroni de Scaccario, de xviij l quas ei debet &c. *Hil. Communia* 49 *H.* 3. *Rot.* 7. *a.*

(*m*) Mandatum eft Vicecomiti, quod diftringat Priorem de Michelham & Robertum le Huf. per terras & catalla, ad reddendum Roberto de Fuleham Clerico de Conftabelaria Scaccarij Regis xl s, quos debuit ei folviffe in Octabis Apoftolorum Petri & Pauli.

John Peverel Constable of the Exchequer impleaded *Osbert Wynd,* and others, for beating and wounding [his Servant] *Eudo Haddoc* (*n*). *Robert de Exton* was summoned into the Exchequer, to answer *William de Meburne* a Chamberlain of the Exchequer, for beating, wounding, and evil-intreating his Men (*o*). *Richard le Later* was summoned to appear in the Exchequer, to answer *Richard de Oxhay* a Chamberlain of the Exchequer, for beating *Simon de Mikelfield,* his Man (*p*). *Roger de la Grene* was summoned into the Exchequer, to answer *Baldwin de Lisle* a Chamberlain of the Exchequer, for a Trespass done to him in his Manour belonging to the said Chamberlainry (*q*). And *Herbert le Mercer* and his Man were summoned in like Manner, to answer *William Mauduit* a Chamberlain of the Exchequer, for a Trespass (*r*). Two Persons were summoned into the Exchequer, to answer *Richard de Oxey* Chamberlain of the Exchequer, for breaking his Mew, and taking thence a Hawk (*s*). *Stephen de Elcost* and others were summoned to appear in the Exchequer, to answer to *James* Earl of *Albemarle* Chamberlain of the Exchequer and *John Samson* (the Earl's Constable of

---

Pauli, sicut recognovit coram Baronibus de Scaccario, ita quod idem Robertus habeat prædictos denarios a die S. Johannis Baptistæ in tres septimanas. *Memor.* 33 *H.* 3. *Rot.* 8. *a.*

(*n*) Essex. Mandatum est Vicecomiti, quod venire &c in xv Michaelis, Osbertum Wynd. (*and others*) ad respondendum Johanni Peverel Constabulario de Scaccario, de hoc quod Eudonem Haddoc verberaverunt, vulneraverunt &c. *Memor.* 51. *H.* 3. *Rot.* 7. *a.*

(*o*) Leic. Mandatum est Vicecomiti quod venire faciat in octabis S. Martini Robertum de Exton, ad respondendum Willelmo de Meburne Camerario de Scaccario, quare verberavit homines suos, vulneravit, & viliter tractavit, contra pacem nostram. *Ex Memor.* 28. *H.* 3. *Rot.* 2. *b.*

— ad respondendum Willelmo de Medburne, residenti in officio Camerariæ de Scaccario. *Ib. Rot.* 11. *b.*

(*p*) Hertford. Mandatum est Vicecomiti, quod ingrediatur Libertatem S. Albani, & venire faciat &c in octabis S. Martini Ricardum le Later de la Westwode & Ricardum filium ejus, ad respondendum Ricardo de Oxhay Camerario de Scaccario, de hoc quod verberaverunt & male tractaverunt Simonem de Mikelfeud hominem suum, contra pacem &c; Et habeat breve. *Memor.* 39. *H.* 3. *Rot.* 3. *b.*

(*q*) Mandatum est Vicecomiti Hertfordiæ, quod venire faciat coram &c Rogerum de la Grene de Sebrithwerth, ad respondendum Baldwino de Insula Camerario de Scaccario, de hoc quod parcum suum in prædicto Manerio pertinente ad predictam Camerariam fregit, Et averia capta pro servicio ei debito & in prædicto parco inclusa inde fugavit contra pacem &c. *Ex Memor.* 42. *H.* 3. *Rot.* 10. *a.*

(*r*) Mandatum est Vicecomiti Glouceftriæ, quod ingrediatur libertatem Burgi Glouceftriæ, & venire faciat coram &c a die —, Herbertum le Mercer de Glouc. & Gilbertum hominem suum, ad respondendum Willelmo Mauduit Camerario de Scaccario, de hoc quod equum suum cum victualibus suis arestaverunt, & per octo dies &c, & Radulfum carectarium suum verberaverunt &c, contra pacem —. *Ib. Rot.* 11. *a.*

(*s*) Mandatum est Vicecomiti Hertfordiæ, quod venire faciat coram &c in crastino Animarum, G. P. & D. de Jarpenvile, ad respondendum Ricardo de Oxeya Camerario de Scaccario, de hoc quod fregerunt mutam suam in villa de H, & quendam Osturum suum inde asportaverunt, contra pacem &c. *Memor.* 42. *H.* 3. *Rot.* 1. *b.*

Skipton

Chap. XX.   *of the Kings of* ENGLAND.

Skipton Castle) for an Assault and Battery (*t*). *Amicia* Countess of *Devon* was summoned to appear there, to answer to *Isabell* Countess of *Albemarle* Chamberlainess of the Exchequer, for the Issues of certain Lands (*u*). Afterwards the King having commanded the Barons to transfer into the Common Bench, all Plaints depending before them, except such as concerned the Ministers of the Exchequer, the Barons thereupon were about to transfer into the Common Bench, the Plaints depending before them between *Amicia* Countess of *Devon*, and *Isabell* Countess of *Albemarle*: But in regard the said *Isabell* was by her Attorney's constantly attending on the King's Service, in the Office of Chamberlain of the Exchequer, the King commands the Barons to adjudge in the Exchequer upon all Plaints wherein she was concerned, as according to Right and Usage they ought to do (*w*). *John de Matham*, a Person employed in the Chamberlain's Office, sued *William le Sumeter* and another in the Exchequer, for driving away and ill-treating his Cattle (*x*). *Taylefer* the Usher sued *Walter Wam*

in

(*t*) Ebor. Mandatum est Vicecomiti, quod venire faciat &c, a die S. Trinitatis in xv dies, Stephanum de Elcoft, Willelmum le Waleys, Johannem de Seleye Majorem Eboraci, Johannem le Especer, Serlonem de Steyngrine, Willelmum de Seleby, & Andream de Seleby, ad respondendum Jacobo Comiti Alberm. & Camerario de Scaccario, & Johanni Samson Constabulario Castri de Schipton, de hoc quod ipsum Johannem insoltaverunt, verberaverunt, vulneraverunt, & maletractaverunt, contra pacem &c. *Pas. Communia* 52 & 53. *H.* 3. *Rot.* 10. *a.*

(*u*) Suthamton. Mandatum est Vicecomiti, quod venire faciat &c, a die S. Trinitatis in xv dies Amiciam Comitissam Devoniæ, ad respondendum Isabellæ de Fortibus Comitissæ Alberm. Camerar. de Scaccario, de exitibus terrarum suarum quas recepit de annis xlv, vj, vij, viij, una cum exitibus terrarum Margaretæ Comitissæ Devoniæ tunc in manu prædictæ Isabellæ existencium ut eadem Isabella dicit; sicut rationabiliter &c. *Ib. Rot.* 11. *a.*

(*w*) Baronibus, pro Isabella de Fortibus Comitissà Devoniæ [*legendum*, Albemarliæ] Monstravit Regi eadem Isabella Cameraria de feodo ad Scaccarium, quod cum nuper Rex mandaverit eisdem Baronibus, quod omnia Placita ad Scaccarium existencia, coram Justiciarijs de Banco præfigerent, exceptis placitis Ministros ejusdem Scaccarij contingentibus. [Mand. ejusdem quod (*these three words are superfluous*)], loquelam quæ est coram eis ad Scaccarium prædictum, inter ipsam Comitissam & Amiciam Comitissam Devoniæ, de debitis & quibusdam aliis, & omnes alias loquelas prædictam Comitissam Albemarliæ ibidem contingentes usq; ad Bancum transferre proponunt & partes inde adjornare. Et quia ipsam Comitissam Albemarliæ, quæ per suos Attornatos jugiter intendit obsequijs Regis in Officio Camerariæ Scaccarij prædicti, libertatibus suis aut usu earum prætextu mandati Regis non debet defraudari; Mand. dictis Baronibus, quod omnes loquelas ipsam contingentes coram eis deduci faciant, prout de jure fuerit faciendum, & sicut fieri consuevit. T. &c. *Hil. Communia* 56. *H.* 3. *Rot.* 5. *a.*

(*x*) Buck. Rex Vicecomiti; Pone per vad. & salvos plegios Willelmum le Sumeter & Willelmum de Ycheburne, quod sint coram Baronibus &c, in crastino Ascensionis, ad respondendum Johanni de Matham qui est in servicio nostro in Officio Camerariæ, quare ceperunt averia predicti Johannis in libera pastura sua de Tiscote, & duxerunt

in the Exchequer, for not mowing his Meadow, and gathering in the Hay in due Time; whereby the Hay was all spoiled; to his Damage Half a Mark. *Walter* came and pleaded, that he duly mowed the said Meadow and got-in the Hay; and that the Hay was not spoiled by his Neglect, but by a Flood which carried away great Part of it. Upon this an Issue was joined, to be tried by the Neighbourhood. And a *Venire facias* was awarded to the Sheriff of *Surrey*'s Clerk, to summon four of the Neighbours to try the Issue [at the Exchequer] on the Morrow of the Ascension (*y*). *Thomas Malbraunch* and others were summoned into the Exchequer, to answer to the King, for assaulting and beating the King's Messenger who carried the King's Summonce (*z*). Two Persons were summoned into the Exchequer, to answer for a Trespass in beating *Hugh de la Grave* a Servant of the Treasurer (*a*): And, it seems, the Treasurer had the Fine which was incurred by that Trespass (*b*). *John de E* and others were summoned into the Exchequer, to answer for a Trespass in beating and imprisoning the Treasurer's Men (*c*). *Ralf de Bosco* and others were summoned

erunt usq; Wengrave, homines ipsius Johannis male tractantes, & dicta averia vexantes, occasione cujus quædam eorum mortua sunt; unde dicit se dampnificatum ad valenciam xl solidorum & amplius; Et habeas ibi nomina plegiorum & hoc breve. T. J. quarto die Aprilis anno r n xiiij⁰. *Pas. Commun.* 18. *H.* 3. *Rot.* 6. *a.*

(*y*) Surreia. Taylefer Hostiarius de Saccario conqueritur de Waltero Wam, de hoc quod cum idem Walterus recepisset ab eodem Taylefer unam acram prati, ad falcandum tempore oportuno, & fænum inde proveniens salvo adunandum; Idem Walterus pratum prædictum tempore oportuno non falcavit nec salvo adunavit; Ita quod per negligenciam & defectum ipsius perijt totum fænum prædictum, ad dampnum ipsius Taylefer dimidiæ marcæ. Et prædictus Walterus venit & dixit, quod prædictum pratum bene falcavit, & fænum Salvo adunavit; & quod ipsum fænum non perijt propter defectum ipsius, sed propter superundationem aquæ, quæ dictum fænum in majori parte asportavit; & hoc petit verificar. per Viciniam: & Taylefer similiter. Et præceptum est Willelmo Norman clerico Vicecomitis, quod venire &c die Veneris proximo post ascensionem Domini, quatuor vicinos, per quos &c, ad certificandum &c. *Pas. Communia* 49. *H.* 3. *Rot.* 11. *a.*

(*z*) Mandatum est Vicecomiti Norhamton, quod venire faciat coram &c in crastino ——, Thomam Malebraunch de Norhamton, Symonem Fabrum, & Johannem Fabrum de eadem, ad respondendum Regi, de hoc quod verberaverunt Thomam Nuncium Regis deferentem Summonitionem Regis &c, & ipsum maletractaverunt &c ——. *Ex Memor.* 42. *H.* 3. *Rot.* 15. *b.*

(*a*) Buk. & Bed. Mandatum est Vicecomiti, quod habeat coram Baronibus de Scaccario die Lunæ post festum S. Nicholai corpora Eliæ & Roberti fil[iorum] Rogeri de Wimbervill, ad respondendum quare verberaverunt Hugonem de la Grave servientem Thesaur[arij] Regis &c ——. *Ex Memor.* 25. *H.* 3. *Rot.* 2. *b.*

(*b*) Bed. & Buk. Mandatum est Vicecomiti, quod distringat Rogerum de Wimbervill, ad reddendum W. de Havershull Thesaurario xl s pro uno dolio vini de fine pro transgressione filiorum suorum; ita quod habeat denarios ad Scaccarium in crastino Ascensionis ——. *Ib. Rot.* 6. *a.*

(*c*) Cant. & Hunt. Mandatum est Vicecomiti, quod venire faciat coram Baronibus in crastino Animarum, Johannem de E——, ad

summoned into the Exchequer, to answer to the Abbot of *Westminster*, a Baron of the Exchequer, for beating and wounding his Men (*d*). *Richard de Curton* Valet of *Philipp Lovell* the King's Treasurer sued *Henry* Son of *Fulcher* for taking and detaining his Catell (*e*). *William de Welton* and others were summoned into the Exchequer, to answer *Peter de Horepol* Valet of *W. Mareschall* a Baron of the Exchequer in a Plea of Debt *(f)*. *John le Butiler* Valet to the Treasurer sued *Walter le Fuller* for wounding *William Herbert* the said *John's* Man, and taking away some of *John's* Goods from the said *William* (*g*). Master *Everard* Clerk to *P. de Rivalle* Baron of the Exchequer sued *John Sewale* there for a Debt of x Marks (*h*). The Abbot of *Westminster*, a Baron of the Exchequer, sued *Geoffrey le Despenser* and others in the Exchequer for beating *G. de Pulla* his Man (*i*). Herbert

ad respondendum W. de Haverhull Thesaurario, quare incarceraverunt homines suos, verberaverunt, & viliter tractaverunt, contra pacem Regis ut dicitur—. *Ex Memor.* 28. *H.* 3. *Rot.* 1. *a.*

(*d*) Hertford. Mandatum est Vicecomiti, quod venire faciat coram Baronibus in crastino S. Michaelis Radulfum de Bosco, Robertum fratrem ejus & alios nominatos in brevi, ad respondendum Abbati Westmonasterij Baroni de Scaccario, de hoc quod homines suos vulneraverunt, verberaverunt, & viliter tractaverunt, contra pacem Regis, ut dicitur. Et habeat tunc breve. T. E. filio Odonis vj die Augusti. *Trin. Commun.* 29. *H.* 3. *Rot.* 12. *b.*

(*e*) Notingeham. Quia secundum antiquam consuetudinem & assisam Scaccarij, nullus Baronum de Scaccario ibidem per præceptum Regis residentium vel eorum qui in Ministerio suo pro feodis quæ de Rege tenent Regi ibidem deservire & assidere tenentur, implacitari debent vel alibi placitare quam in ipso Scaccario, postquam ibidem inceperint residere, & compotis Vicecomitum & Ballivorum Regis intendere, eo quod sine dampno Regis inde recedere non possunt : Mandatum est Vicecomiti, quod venire faciat &c in crastino Animarum, Henricum filium Fulcheri de Hirton, ad respondendum Ricardo de Curton Valetto P. Lovell Thesaurarij Regis, quare cepit averia & catalla ipsius Ricardi in Regali chimino, & ea detinuit contra vadium &

plegios ; Et habeat breve. *Memor.* 39. *H.* 3. *Rot.* 3. *a.*

(*f*) Norhamton. Mandatum est Vicecomiti, quod ve. a die Paschæ in xv dies Willelmum de Welton, Willelmum le Mercer, & Willelmum de Burcote, ad respondendum Petro de Horepol vadletto W. Marescalli Baronis de Scaccario, de xl s quos ei debent &c. *Hil. Commun.* 49. *H.* 3. *Rot.* 7. *a.*

(*g*) Staff. Præceptum est Vicecomiti, quod venire &c in crastino S. Margaretæ Walterum le Fulir de Tresl. ad respondendum Johanni le Butiler vallecto Thesaurarij, de hoc quod Willelmum Herbert hominem ipsius vulneravit & male tractavit, & bona ipsius Johannis in custodia ejusdem Willelmi existentia ad valenciam xx s asportavit &c. *Ex Memor.* 52. *H.* 3. *Rot.* 11. *a.*

(*h*) Mandatum est Vicecomiti Midd. quod venire faciat coram &c, die —, Jo. Sewale —, ad respondendum Magistro Everardo Clerico P. de Rivalle Baronis de Scaccario, de x marcis quas &c. *Ex Memor.* 42. *H.* 3. *Rot.* 11. *b.*

(*i*) Glovernia. Mandatum est Vicecomiti, quod distringat Galfridum le Despenser, Willelmum de Kerdif, Johannem le Serjaunt, & Radulfum Armigerum prædicti W, per terras & catalla sua, Ita quod habeat corpora eorum coram Baronibus in crastino Cinerum ad respondendum Abbati de Westmonasterio Baroni de Scaccario, de hoc quod verberaverunt G. de Pulla hominem

bert Parson of *Hadley*, a Clerk of the Exchequer, sued *Richard de Ewell* there for a Debt (*k*). *Richard de Hereford*, a Clerk of the Exchequer, sued *Thomas le D* and others in the Exchequer, for beating *Maurice de Tywing Richard*'s Man (*l*). *Richard Chamberlain* a Clerk of the Exchequer, sued *Goldhofe* in the Exchequer, for beating *Robert Williamfon* the said *Richard*'s Man (*m*). *Hugh de Clahale* Valet of *E. de Weftminftre*, Clerk of the Exchequer, brought his Action in the Exchequer againſt certain Perſons for taking and carrying away his Fiſh (*n*). *John de Ely* a Servant in the Exchequer brought his Suit there againſt one for taking and detaining his Swans (*o*). *Richard de Chefterford* a Clerk of the *Receipt* sued *Nicolas Poynz* and another in the Exchequer for Debt (*p*). A Plea was alſo moved in the Exchequer between the ſaid *Richard de Cheftreford* and *Bonenfaunt* a *Jew*, for contumelious Words ſpoken by the *Jew* againſt *Richard*. The Proceſs and Judgment in that Plea may be ſeen in *Prynn* (*q*). *Robert* Dean of *Gildeford* was attached to anſwer *Hugh de Oldebuf* a Clerk of the Exchequer, for a Treſpaſs. *Hugh*, and others the

nem ſuum, & maletractaverunt contra pacem &c, ut dicitur. *Ex Memor.* 35. *H.* 3. *Rot.* 7. *a.*

(*k*) Mandatum eſt Vicecomiti Eſſexiæ, quod venire faciat coram &c, in octabis S. Johannis Baptiſtæ, Ricardum de Ewell, ad reſpondendum Hereberto Perſonæ de Hadlega Clerico de Scaccario de xx s, ſicut rationabiliter &c. *Memor.* 40. *H.* 3. *Rot.* 17. *a.*

(*l*) Midd. Mandatum eſt Vicecomiti, quod venire faciat coram Baronibus in craſtino —, xij de legalioribus & probioribus hominibus de viſneto de Totenham, qui nulla affinitate attingant Ricardum de Hereford, nec Thomam le D, S D, nec P P, & qui tales ſint quod ad eos capere nos poſſimus ſi in aliquo deliquerint, ad certificandum prædictos Barones, ſi predictus Thomas verberavit & male tractavit Mauricium de Tywing hominem prædicti Ricardi, & utrum hoc fecit per præceptum prædictorum Simonis & Petri vel non. *Ex Memor.* 35. *H.* 3. *Rot.* 14. *a.*

(*m*) Buk. Mandatum eſt Vicecomiti ſicut alias, quod habeat coram Baronibus in craſtino Animarum, corpora Roberti Goldhoſe & Johannis Garin, ad reſpondendum Ricardo Camerario Clerico de Scaccario, de hoc quod verberaverunt & male tractaverunt Robertum filium Willelmi hominem prædicti Ricardi, contra pacem Regis ut dicitur —. *Memor.* 35. *H.* 3. *Rot.* 1. *a.*

(*n*) Mandatum eſt Vicecomiti Hertfordiæ, quod venire faciat coram Baronibus —, ad reſpondendum Hugoni de Clahale valeto E. de Weſtminſtre Clerici de Scaccario, de hoc quod ipſi ceperunt piſcem ſuum in libera piſcaria ſua in villa de Staundon, & inde aſportaverunt—. *Ex Memor.* 42. *H.* 3. *Rot.* 1. *a.*

(*o*) Mandatum eſt Vicecomiti Cantebrigiæ, quod habeat coram &c die —, ad reſpondendum Johanni de Ely ſervienti de Scaccario, de hoc quod cepit tres cignos ſuos, & illos detinet, contra pacem —. *Memor.* 42. *H.* 3. *Rot.* 10. *b.*

(*p*) Sumers & Dors. Mandatum eſt Vicecomiti, quod venire faciat &c a die S. Trinitatis in xv dies Nicholaum Poynz, ad reſpondendum Ricardo de Ceſtreford Clerico de Recepta de iiij marcis. Venire etiam faciat ibidem ad eundem diem Henricum de Cokinton, ad reſpondendum eidem Ricardo de x s quos ei debet ut dicit &c ſicut &c. *Memor.* 52. *H.* 3. *Rot.* 9. *b.*

(*q*) *Ex Memorandis* 51. *H.* 3. *Rot.* 4. *a. Vid.* Prynne *on* 4 *Inſtit. p.* 58.

King's

King's Bailiffs, who by the King's Command or Writ had arrested *Robert*, were prosecuted for it in the Ecclesiastical Court before *John de Barton* Official to the Bishop of *Worcester*. The Official was commanded by a Writ of *Prohibition*, not to proceed to execute a Sentence which he had pronounced for the said Cause against *Hugh* and the Bailiffs. Notwithstanding, the Official did again denounce them excommunicated. Hereupon, the Official was summoned to appear at the Exchequer, to answer why he had acted in that Manner, in Contempt of the King, and in Elusion of the Liberties belonging to the Residents of the Exchequer (*r*). Add hereto, that the King's Chaplain (*s*), his Mason (*t*), and others that were in his Service, had, as it seemeth, the Privilege of being sued in the Exchequer.

Again; the Residents of the Exchequer were, by the ancient Custom of the Exchequer, to be quit of Toll for Things bought to their own Use (*u*). *Ralf de Leicestre* a Clerk of the Exchequer was exempted from paying Toll for Goods bought by his Servants for his Use in *Eton*-Fair (*w*). K. *Edward* I. remitted to *Roger de Northwod* and

---

(*r*) Vicecomiti Suthamtoniæ, pro Rege. Præceptum est Vicecomiti, quod venire faciat coram Baronibus de Scaccario apud Westmon. in crastino S. Jacobi, Magistrum Johannem de Barthon Officialem Wigorniensis Episcopi, ad respondendum Regi quare postquam inhibuit ei quod ab executione Sententiæ quam in Hugonem de Oldebuf Clericum de eodem Scaccario, & quosdam alios Ballivos Regis, eo quod per præceptum ipsius Regis pro quadam transgressione eidem Hugoni facta contra pacem prædicti Regis, Robertum Decanum de Gudeford attachiaverunt, detulerat, omnino desisteret, prædictos Hugonem & alios Ballivos Regis iterum denunciat excommunicatos, in Regis contemptum, & in elusionem Libertatum & Consuetudinum Residentibus in eodem Scaccario concessarum, & in grave dampnum prædictorum Hugonis & aliorum Ballivorum Regis; Et habeat ibi tunc breve. Teste &c. *Memor*. 1. *E*. 1. *Rot*. 8. *b*.

(*s*) Surr. & Suffex. Mandatum est Vicecomiti quod venire &c faciat &c, die Jovis proximo post diem S. Petri ad Cathedram, Aliciam Cokerel de Suwerk, ad respondendum Thomæ de Lewes Capellano Capellæ nostræ Westmonasterij, de vj s x d & obolo quos ei debet &c, sicut &c. Et habeas ibi tunc hoc breve &c. *Memor*. 51. *H*. 3. *Rot*. 5. *b*.

(*t*) Mandatum est Vicecomiti Surreiæ quod venire faciat coram &c die Lunæ proximo post festum S. Johannis Baptistæ, Robertum Vinetarium & alios in brevi, ad respondendum Magistro Johanni Cæmentario Regis, de hoc quod verberaverunt, vulneraverunt, & maletractaverunt Mauricium servientem suum contra pacem &c. *Memor*. 40. *H*. 3. *Rot*. 17. *a*.

(*u*) Buk. Quia per antiquam consuetudinem Scaccarij omnes ex præcepto Regis residentes in eodem Scaccario quieti debent esse de Teloneo, de omnibus Emptionibus factis ad opus suum proprium; Mandatum est Vicecomiti, quod si Willelmus Lambert & Walterus de Hogeshawe Ballivi de Aylesbirie, ceperunt aliquod Teloneum de Hominibus Abbatis Westmonasterij, ex præcepto Regis residentis in prædicto Scaccario, de Emptionibus factis ad opus prædicti Abbatis, tunc illud Teloneum prædicto Abbati sine dilatione reddi faciat. *Memor*. 39. *H*. 3. *Rot*. 14. *b*.

(*w*) Warrewich. Rex Vicecomiti; Questus est nobis Radulfus de Leycestre Clericus de Scaccario, quod cum servientes sui emerent ad opus suum in nundinis de Eton,

and *John de Cobeham* Barons of the Exchequer the Service due to the King in the Army of *Wales*, for Lands which they held of the King in Chief; viz. the King remitted it *hac vice* of his special Grace, in respect of their Attendance at the Exchequer (*x*).

Moreover, the Residents of the Exchequer were privileged to be free from Suit to County-Courts, Hundred-Courts, &c. and from the Common Amercements of the Counties or Hundreds wherein their Lands lay. In the Reign of K. *Richard* I. *William Marefchall* and *Geoffrey Fitz-Pierre* were, by reason of their Session at the Exchequer, exempted from the common Amercement of the County for a Murder (*y*). The like Privilege or Exemption was allowed to *Roger Fitz-Renfrey* (*z*), to *Geoffrey Fitz-Pierre* again (*a*), to *Warin Fitz-Gerold* (*b*), the Bishop of *London* (*c*), the Bishop of *Ely* (*d*),

the

Prior de Eton & ballivi sui extorserunt ab eis theloneum, ut dicitur; licet servientes sui prætenderent Libertatem suam de Scaccario. Et quia Clerici residentes in eodem Scaccario, ratione Sessionis suæ ibidem quieti sunt & esse debent de tholoneo quamdiu ibidem resederint ———, Tibi præcipimus, quod venire facias ———. *Memor.* 28. *H.* 3. *Rot.* 10. *b.* & *ib. Rot.* 12. *a.*

(*x*) *Kancia.* De Servicio Rogeri de Northwod & J. de Cobeham remisso per Regem. Memorandum quod cum die Sabbati proxima post festum Ascensionis Domini, facta esset mencio coram Domino Rege, de servicio quod Rogerus de Northwode & Johannes de Cobeham Barones de Scaccario, ipsi Domino Regi facere tenentur in exercitu Walliæ, pro terris & tenementis quæ de Rege tenent in Capite, idem Dominus Rex, de gracia sua speciali, concessit præfatis Rogero & Johanni, quod sint quieti hac Vice de servicio suo prædicto; Ita quod intendant Compotis & alijs negocijs Regis expediendis in Scaccario suo prædicto, modo consueto. *Pas. Communia* 5. *E.* 1. *Rot.* 5. *a.* in bund. 4 & 5. *E.* 1.

(*y*) Idem Vicecomes r c de iiij s & vj d, de Hikeshelle hundredo, pro Murdro; In perdonis per Libertatem sedendi ad Scaccarium, Willelmo Marescallo iiij s & vj d; Et Q. e. Idem Vicecomes r c de v s & iiij d, de Burnham hundredo, pro Murdro; In Perdonis per prædictam Libertatem Galfrido filio Petri v s & iij d, Et Q. e. *Mag. Rot.* 2. *R.* 1. *Rot.* 11. *b. Buk.* & *Bedef.*

(*z*) Idem Vicecomes r c de ij mareis, de Louedon wapentaco, pro murdro: In thesauro xij s vj d. Et in Perdonis, per Libertatem Cartæ Regis Militibus de Templo xiij d, Et Monialibus de Simplingeham xvij d, Et Episcopo Lincoliensi iiij s, Et Rogero filio Renfridi iiij s per Libertatem sedendi ad Scaccarium: Et debet iij s & viij d. *Mag. Rot.* 5. *R.* 1. *Rot.* 4. *b. Lincoll.*

(*a*) N. P. & N. C. per Ricardum Londoniensem Episcopum, & Walterum filium Roberti, & Willelmum de Warenna, & Otonem filium Willelmi, & Reginaldum de Argentem: Idem Vicecomes [sc. Galfridus filius Petri] r c de xx s, de Dunmawe hundredo pro Murdro; In thesauro vj s & viij d, Et in Perdonis per Cartam Regis Monialibus de Cadomo iij s, Et Galfrido filio Petri x s & iiij d, per Libertatem Scaccarij, Et Q. e. *Mag. Rot.* 5. *R.* 1. *Rot.* 1. *a. Essexa* & *Hurtf.*

(*b*) Idem Vicecomes r c de xl s, de Hundredo de Umiliard; In thesauro xx s, Et in perdonis Warino filio Geroldi iiij s & iiij d, per Libertatem quam habet de Scaccario; Et Abbati de Hulmo ij s per Cartam: Et debet xiij s & viij d. *Mag. Rot.* 7. *R.* 1. *Rot.* 6. *b. Norf.* & *Sudf.*

(*c*) Idem Vicecomes r c de j marca de Esseburn hundredo pro murdro; In thesauro xij s & xj d; Et in perdonis Episcopo Londoniæ v d per Libertatem sedendi ad Scaccarium, Et Q. e. *Mag. Rot.* 7. *R.* 1. *Rot.* 18. *b. Sudsexx.*

(*d*) Idem Vicecomes r c de dimidia marca

de

Chap. XX. *of the Kings of* ENGLAND.

the Bishop of *Norwich*, and Earl *Roger* (*e*), [Earl *Roger* was at this time one of the King's Justiciers *(f)*, and an Assessour or Baron of the Exchequer (*g*)], to the Bishop of *London* (*h*), to *Alexander de Luci* and to others. In the Reign of K. *Henry* III. Privilege or Exemption of one or other of the kinds aforementioned was allowed to the Persons hereunder named (*i*); *viz.* To *John de Windlesore* (*k*), and *Thomas de Windlesore* (*l*), who were *Ponderatores* of the Exchequer; to the Knights and Freeholders of *Falk de Breaute* belonging to the Fee which he held by the Service of the Chamberlainry of the Exchequer (*m*); to *Matthew de Eston* Tenant to *Margaret de Riparijs*, of the Fee which she held by the Service of the King's Chamberlainry (*n*); to *Richard de Oxehay*, Chamberlain of the Exchequer (*o*);
to

de Grimesho hundredo, pro murdro: In Perdonis Episcopo Elyensi ij s & iij d, per Libertatem quam habet de Scaccario; Et debet iiij s & v d. *Mag. Rot.* 7. *R.* 1. *Rot.* 6. *b. Norf. & Sudf.*

(*e*) Idem Vicecomes r c de xl s, de Galcho hundredo pro murdro; In thesauro xx s, Et in Perdonis Comiti Rogero ij s & viij d, per Libertatem sedendi ad Scaccarium, Et Episcopo Norwicensi xviij d per Libertatem de Elmeham quam habet; Et debet xv s & x d. *Ib. Rot.* 6. *b.*

(f) De Placitis Rogeri le Bigot & Sociorum ejus in Norfolchia. *Mag. Rot.* 7. *R.* 1. *Rot.* 6. *a.*

(*g*) *Capt. Ult. sect.* 6.

(*h*) Cives Londoniæ, Constantius filius Alulfi & Robertus le Bel pro eis, r c de CCCl Bl; In thesauro *So much*; And in *Allowances, Such and Such summs; amongst other summs This*, Et in quietantia terræ Episcopi Londoniensis, per Libertatem sedendi ad Scaccarium, C s. *Mag. Rot.* 10. *R.* 1. *Rot.* 12. *a.*

(*i*) Comitatus de Cumberland, præter Copland & quinq; Villatas, reddunt compotum de Lxij marcis & dimidia, ut sint quieti de Communi Misericordia: In Thesauro xlj l & vij s & ix d: Et in Perdonis, Alexandro de Luci v s & v d, per Libertatem Sedendi ad Scaccarium & per breve Regis. *Mag. Rot.* 4. *Joh. Rot.* 18. *b. tit.* Cumberland.

(*k*) Dorset. Mandatum est Vicecomiti quod pacem habere permittat Johanni de Windlesore de demanda quam ei facit ad reddendum partem Finis ducentarum marcarum, quem Comitatus Dorsetæ fecit pro habendo Vicecomite ad electionem suam, quia idem Johannes quietus [esse] debeat ex hac demanda per officium suum ad Scacarium. *Memor.* 6. *H.* 3. *Rot.* 2. *b.*

(*l*) Suthamton. Mandatum [est] Vicecomiti, quod permittat Thomam de Windlesore pacem habere de demanda quam ei facit de sectis, de quibus debet habere quietanciam per libertatem sedendi ad Scaccarium Regis. Et averia &c. *Ex Memor.* 25. *H.* 3. *Rot.* 2. *a.*

(*m*) Suffok. Rex Vicecomiti; Præcipimus tibi quod non exigi permittas a Militibus & libere tenentibus de Falcasio de Breaute, de Feudo quod ipse tenet per servicium Camerariæ de Scaccario nostro, sectam Comitatus & hundredi; quoniam ipsi facere non debent nec solent. *Memor.* 6. *H.* 3. *Rot.* 3. *a.*

(*n*) Oxon. Mandatum est Vicomiti, quod non exigat vel exigi permittat a Mathæo de Eston, qui tenet de Margareta de Riparijs de feudo Camerariæ Regis, quam eadem M. tenet de Rege per liberum servicium prædictæ Camerariæ, exactiones vel consuetudines quas facere non debet nec facere consuevit—. *Ex Pas. Memor.* 11. *H.* 3. *Rot.* 3. *b.*

(*o*) Ballivo Libertatis S. Albani. Quia Ricardus de Oxehay Camerarius de Scaccario Regis fuit ibidem in Servicio Regis die Mercurij proxima post festum S. Andreæ
Apostoli

to the menial Men of *Baldwin de Lisle*, Chamberlain of the Exchequer (*p*); to *Roger* Usher of the Exchequer (*q*); to *Robert de Fulham* Constable of the Exchequer, touching Suit before Justices Itinerant, upon the common Summons, and Suit to the Hundred of *Berdestaple* (*r*); to *William de Stebbinges* a Minister resident in the Exchequer (*s*); to *Ralf Sumer* a Minister of the Exchequer (*t*); to *Richard Alswick* one of the Keepers of the King's Palace at *Westminster*, who was attending on the Barons (*u*); and to *Adam de Stratton* a Clerk

Apostoli per præceptum Regis, ita quod eo die coram Ballivo Libertatis S. Albani in Curia Abbatis S. Albani apud S. Albanum, occasione sectæ Curiæ prædictæ, esse non potuit: Mandatum est eidem Ballivo &c, quod prædictus Ricardus &c non ponatur &c. *Memor.* 39. *H.* 3. *Rot.* 6. *a. The like writ,* Justiciarijs Itinerantibus in Com. Heref. pro Ricardo de Oxehaye. *Ib. Rot.* 6. *b.*

(*p*) Quia secundum consuetudinem antiquam Scaccarij, omnes residentes in eodem Scaccario debent esse quieti de omnimodis sectis Comitatuum & hundredorum, Mandatum est Vicecomiti, quod de demanda quam facit hominibus spectantibus ad Camer. Baldewini de Insula Camerarij de eodem Scaccario, de sectis Comitatuum suorum & hundredorum pacem habere permittat; Et averia &c. Eodem modo mandatum est Vicecomitibus Norf. Essex. & Hertf. Oxon. Berk. & Norhamtoniæ. *Trin. Commun.* 41. *H.* 3. *Rot.* 16. *b.*

(*q*) Custodi Honoris Waligfordiæ. Mandatum est eidem, quod quia Rogerus Hostiarius quietus est de sectis Comitatuum & hundredorum & Curiarum, ratione custodiendi Hostium de Scaccario, eidem de secta Curiæ de Waligford pacem habere permittat. *Memor.* 14. *H.* 3. *Rot.* 10. *b.*

(*r*) Gilberto de Preston & Socijs suis Justiciarijs Itinerantibus in Comitatu Essexiæ. Quia Robertus de Folleham Clericus de Constabularia Scaccarij fuit in servitio Regis ad idem Scaccarium diæ Lunæ proxima post festum S. Lucæ Ewangelistæ, ita quod coram Gilberto de Preston & socijs suis Justiciarijs Itinerantibus in Comitatu Essexiæ apud Chelmarford occasione Communis Summonitionis [&c]: Mandatum est eisdem Justiciarijs, quod prædictus Robertus propter Absenciam suam non ponatur in defalta nec in aliquo sit perdens; Quia Dominus Rex warantizat ei diem illum quoad hoc. Eodem modo mandatum est Magistro Simoni de Bauton & socijs suis Itinerantibus in Comitatu Buk., pro Ricardo de Gatesden. *Memor.* 39. *H.* 3. *Rot.* 3. *a.*

Essex. Quia Robertus de Fuleham Constabularius de Scaccario fecit Regem securum per Walterum de Godichestre & Robertum de Ghilgate de Comitatu Essexiæ, Mandatum est Vicecomiti, quod venire faciat &c a die S. Trinitatis in unum mensem Willelmum Giffard ad respondendum præfato Roberto, quare distringit eum ad faciendum sectam ad Hundredum de Berdestaple, contra libertatem a Domino Rege & Prædecessoribus suis concessam Baronibus de Scaccario & alijs ibidem residentibus, per quam inde quietas esse debet, ut dicit; Et habeat Breve. *Memor.* 39. *H.* 3. *Rot.* 12. *b.*

(*s*) Quia secundum antiquam consuetudinem Scaccarij omnes Residentes in eodem Scaccario & eorum Ministri ibidem residentes quieti sunt de omnimodis sectis; Et Willelmus de Stebbingges sit minister residens in eodem Scaccario: Mandatum est G. de Rocheford, quatinus de districtione quam ei facit occasione sectæ ad hundredum de Tendr. ei pacem habere permittat. &c. *Memor.* 40. *H.* 3. *Rot.* 20. *b.*

(*t*) Quia secundum antiquam consuetudinem Scaccarij, residentes in Scaccario sunt quieti de omnimodis sectis: Mandatum est Senescallo Abbatis Westmonasterij, quod de demanda quam facit Radulfo Sumer servienti in prædicto Scaccario de secta Curiæ prædicti Abbatis, ei pacem &c, Et averia &c. *Trin. Commun.* 41. *H.* 3. *Rot.* 16. *b.*

(*u*) Quia secundum antiquam consuetudinem Scaccarij, Custodes Domorum Regis Westmo-

Clerk of the Exchequer (*w*). There was also, as I take it, a sort of Privilege allowed to Persons who were Suitors or Accomptants at the Exchequer: namely, If they were to appear in any inferior Court or Place upon a certain Day, in case they were that Day attending at the Exchequer, they were not to be put in Default below. This Privilege was allowed to *John* Son of *Osbert* Citizen of *Lincoln* (*x*).

VIII. The Exchequer was a Court greatly concerned in the Conservation of the Prerogatives as well as the Revenue of the Crown. It was the Care of the Treasurer and Barons and the King's Council at the Exchequer, to see that the Rights of the Crown were not invaded by such as claimed Liberties or Exemptions; and to allow or disallow of Liberties or Exemptions claimed, as Reason and Justice should require. It is true, the Allowance or Disallowance of Liberties had some relation to the Regal Revenue: inasmuch as Men were wont to be punished by Amercements, Seisures, and Fines, for undue Usurpations of Liberties; and were obliged or induced to fine for Confirmation or Improvement of their Liberties, if they desired the same. However, many Affairs of this Nature were wont to be examined and regulated at the Exchequer: and therein great Care was taken, to preserve the Rights of the Crown inviolate. Upon this Ground, probably, it became the usual Method, for Charters of Liberties to be read and enrolled at the Exchequer. So that commonly, when the King granted or confirmed Liberties by his Letters Patent, a close Writ, directed to the Treasurer and Barons, was wont to issue, reciting the Substance of such Grant or Confirmation, and commanding the Barons to allow thereof. The Records both of the Chancery and the Exchequer are full of Instances of these Matters. Let me add, that the Authority and Dignity of the Court of Exche-

---

Westmonasterij qui sunt intendentes Baronibus &c, quieti sunt de sectis Comitatuum & hundredorum: Mandatum est Vicecomiti Hertfordiæ, quod de demanda quam facit Ricardo Alswik Custodi &c, de prædictis sectis, ei pacem &c; & averia &c. *Memor.* 41. *H.* 3. *Rot.* 14. *a.*

(*w*) Ballivo Abbatis de Westmonasterio pro Ada de Stratton. Quia Clerici & alij ministri de Scaccario Regis, quamdiu negoeijs Regis intendunt, quieti esse debent de sectis Comitatuum Curiarum & hundredorum: Præceptum est eidem, quod de demanda quam facit eidem Adæ Clerico de eodem Scaccario, & ibidem in servicio Regis commoranti, de secta facienda ad Curiam ejusdem Abbatis & Conventus Westmonasterij de Wathamsted & Harpedene, ei pacem habere permittat. *Memor.* 1 & 2. *E.* 1. *Rot.* 5. *a.*

(*x*) Lincoln. Rex Decano & Capitulo: Sciatis quod Johannes filius Osberti Civis Lincolniæ fuit coram Baronibus de Scaccario die Mercurij proximo ante festum S. Lucæ, & ideo non potuit tunc coram vobis esse illo die; & nos diem illum ipsi warantizamus. *Memor.* 6. *H.* 3. *Rot.* 5. *b.*

quer was esteemed so great, that the Acts thereof were not to be examined or controlled (if I take the Matter right) in any other of the King's ordinary Courts of Justice. For Example: In the 26th Year of K. *Edward* I. upon the Occasion set forth hereunder in the Margin, a Writ issued under the Great Seal, *Teste Rogero le Brabanzon* Chief Justice of the Court holden before the *King himself*, directed to the Treasurer and Barons; commanding them to certifie to the King *ubicunq*; &c. under the Seal of the Exchequer, the Record and Process of a certain Recognisance made in the Exchequer. This Writ, by Assent of the Treasurer and Barons, was retorned or indorsed thus; *viz.* " Upon this Writ nothing ought to be done; because a Record
" of such Things as are done in the Exchequer ought not, nor was
" ever from the first Foundation of the Exchequer wont, to be sent
" any whither out of the same Exchequer before any Justices what-
" ever; but if any Justices whatever, for the Explanation of any Pleas
" depending before them, have a necessary Occasion to be certified
" concerning any Matters transacted or done in the Exchequer, they
" ought to come to the Exchequer, and there, at the Request of the
" said Justices, to be certified by the Treasurer and Barons touching
" the Premisses, in such manner as the Treasurer and Barons shall
" judge meet on the King's Behalf (*y*)."

The

(*y*) Breve directum Baronibus pro Galfrido filio Warini. Rex mandavit breve suum de Magno Sigillo Thesaurario & Baronibus de Scaccario in hæc verba. Edwardus Dei gratia &c Thesaurario & Baronibus suis de Scaccario salutem, Cum nuper præceperimus Vicecomiti nostro Surreiæ, quod scire faceret Thomæ de Jarpenvill per duos liberos & legales homines de Comitatu suo, quod esset coram nobis in Octabis Sancti Hillarij ubicunq; tunc fuerimus in Anglia, ad ostendendum si quid pro se haberet seu dicere sciret, quare Centum marcæ de terris & catallis suis fieri non deberent, ad reddendum Galfrido filio Warini in partem solutionis octies viginti marcarum, quas idem Thomas in Curia nostra coram nobis cognovit se debere prædicto Galfrido, solvendas eidem ad Terminos dudum præteritos, & nondum solvit, ut dicit; Idem Vicecomes nobis retornavit ad eundem Terminum quod scire fecit eidem Thomæ; qui venit & dixit, quod alias præsentatum fuit coram vobis, quod prædictus Galfridus fugam fecit de Ecclesia de Watford, per quod omnia bona & catalla sua confiscata fuerunt in manum nostram pro fuga prædicta, Et quia vobis datum erat intelligi, quod ipse Thomas tenebatur prædicto Galfrido in prædicta pecunia, eundem Thomam coram vobis venire fecistis ad pecuniam prædictam cognoscendam; qui venit coram vobis & cognovit quod debuit prædicto Galfrido pecuniam prædictam per prædictam recognitionem coram vobis factam, & ea occasione assignati fuerunt ei Termini coram vobis ad prædictam pecuniam nobis solvendam; & de hoc posuit se super Recordo Rotulorum de Scaccario nostro, & pecijt quod non distringatur ad prædictam pecuniam prædicto Galfrido solvendam, quousq; discussum fuerit, utrum ad nos vel ad prædictum Galfridum prædicta pecunia reddi debeat: Et ideo vobis mandamus, quod Recordum & processum Recognitionis prædictæ coram vobis factæ, cum omnibus ea tangentibus, nobis sub sigillo Scaccarij nostri a die Purificationibus Beatæ Mariæ in quindecim dies
ubicunq;

Chap. XX.   *of the Kings of* ENGLAND.

The Exchequer was a great Repository of the King's Records. Thither the Records of the Court holden before the King, of the Court of Common Bench, and of the Justices in Eire were brought, to be laid up in the Treasury there (z). But I need not go about to prove by ancient Records, that the Treasury of the Exchequer was a Repository for the Rolls and Records of the several Courts abovementioned. That Matter is evident of it self. For at this Day we find the ancient Rolls and Records of the Court held before the King, of the Common Bench, and of the Justices Itinerant for Common Pleas and for the Forest, reposited and still remaining in that Treasury, under the Custody of the Treasurer and Chamberlains of the Exchequer.

ubicunq; tunc fuerimus in Anglia mittatis, & hoc breve. T. R. le Brabanson apud Westm. xxv° die Januarij anno Regni nostri vicesimo sexto. Et indorsatur per assensum Thesaurarij & Baronum sic. Per istud breve nichil debet fieri; quia Recordum de hijs quæ fiunt in Scaccario non debent alicubi coram quibuscumq; Justiciarijs extra idem Scaccarium mitti, nec unquam a fundatione Scaccarii mitti consuevit; sed si Justiciarij quicunq; ad explanationem placitorum quæ coram eisdem justiciarijs placitantur super hijs quæ in Scaccario pertractantur seu fiunt necesse habeant certiorari, debent ad Scaccarium venire, & ibidem ad requisitionem Justiciariorum illorum per Thesaurarium & Barones debent super præmissis certiorari, prout ijdem Thesaurarius & Barones pro Rege viderint fore faciendum. *Hil. Communia* 25 *&* 26. *E.* 1. *Rot.* 49. *b.*

(z) De Rotulis de Banco liberatis ad Scaccarium. *Mich. Communia* 18. *E.* 1. *Rot.* 4. *b.*

De Rotulis Johannis de Luvetot liberatis ad Scaccarium. *Ib. Rot.* 5. *a.*

De Rotulis Willelmi de Saham liberatis ad Scaccarium. *Ib. Rot.* 5. *a.*

And the like of several others; *Ib. Rot.* 5. *b. Rot.* 6. *b. Rot.* 7. *a.*

De multis Rotulis liberatis ad Scaccarium ibidem reservandis. *Mich. Commun.* 17. *finiente Edw.* 1. *b. & Rott. seqq. And Hil.* 18. *Edw.* 1. *Rot.* — . *b.*

CHAP. XXI.

Of the Perſons that ſat and acted at the EXCHEQUER *during the ſecond Period.*

I.   *Of the King's Chief Juſticier. his Chancellor, and his Council, acting at the Exchequer.*
II.   *Of the Treaſurer and his Lieutenant.*
III.   *Of the Chancellor and Barons of the Exchequer.*

I. IN the Beginning of this ſecond Period, and for a ſhort Time after, the King's Chief Juſticier continued to preſide and act at the Exchequer, as he had before uſed to do. Afterwards, when he ceaſed to preſide there, the Power of the Treaſurer encreaſed. Then, the Affairs of the Exchequer were guided and ordered by the Treaſurer and Barons of the Exchequer. To them may be added the King's Council. For in the Beginning of K. *Henry* the third's Reign, and in the ſucceeding Times, we often find the King's Council acting both in the Superiour Court and in the Exchequer. Of them, during the Nonage of K. *Henry* III, *William Mareſchall*, Rector of the King and Kingdom, was Chief. Inſomuch that Letters Patent and other Acts running in the King's Name were ſealed with *William's* Seal; as appears by many Inſtances in the Patent and cloſe Rolls. Some Examples may be here produced of the Treaſurer, Barons, and Council acting at the Exchequer. In the ſecond Year of K. *Henry* III, *William Mareſchall* Earl of *Pembroke* Guardian of the King and of the Realm, *Peter* Biſhop of *Wincheſter*, *Hubert de Burgh* Chief Juſticier, and the King's Council, were preſent at the Exchequer, and adjudged *Nicolas de Verdun* to be diſcharged of D L j l, which had been arbitrarily and without Judgment charged on him by the Suggeſtion of *Reginald Baſſet* (*a*). In the 2d and 3d Year of K. *Henry* III, the King's
Council

(*a*) Nicholaus de Verdun [debet] CC marcas, Ut ſit quietus de D & Lj l de Auxilio Militum de Honore Leiceſtriæ quæ exigebantur ab eo de tempore quo pater ſuus fuit Vicecomes Warewic. & Leirceſtr., qui remanſit quietus de tempore illo: Et quia nec pater ſuus nec Thomas frater ſuus primogenitus inventi fuerunt in prædicto debito in Rotulis H. Regis Avi Regis, nec in Rotulis Regis Ricardi; ſed per ſuggeſtionem Reginaldi Baſſet voluntate & ſine Judicio tempore Regis J. poſitum fuit debitum illud ſuper ipſum Nicholaum; Judicatum eſt per W. Mariſcallum Comitem de Pembroc

Chap. XXI. *of the* EXCHEQUER. 27

Council at the Exchequer made an Order touching the Corrody of *David* the *Lardiner* (*b*). In the 6th Year of K. *Henry* III, there were present at the Exchequer, the Justicier, the Treasurer, and Barons (*c*); in the 8th Year of the same King, the Justicier, and Barons of the Exchequer (*d*); in the 9th Year, *Hubert de Burgh* Justicier, R. Bishop of *Chichester* the King's Chancellor, R. Bishop of *Saresbury*, J. Bishop of *Bathe*, B. Bishop of *Rochester*, and other Barons of the Exchequer (*e*); in the 11th and 12th Years, *Hubert de Burgh* Justicier, and the Barons of the Exchequer (*f*). In the 14th Year of the same King, there were present at the Exchequer, before the King, H. *de Burgh* Justicier, R. of *Chester*, R. of *Cornwall*, G. of *Gloucester*, W. of *Warenne*, W. of *Albemarle*, H. of *Hertford*, J. of *Huntendon*, Earls, with others of the King's Barons (*g*). In the same 14th Year, there were present at the Exchequer, W. Bishop of *Carlile*, J. Bishop of *Bathe*, and others of the King's Barons of the Exchequer (*h*). In the

---

broc Rectorem Regis & Regni, & per P. Wintoniensem Episcopum, & H. de Burgo Justiciarium, & Consilium Regis, quod de prædictis D & Lj l sit quietus. Et debet prædictas CC marcas pacare a Pascha anni tertij infra tres annos proximo sequentes. *Mag. Rot.* 2. H. 3. *Rot.* 4. *b. tit.* Residuum Comitatus Warewiksiræ & Leircesiresiræ.

(*b*) Provisum est per Consilium Domini Regis ad Scaccarium, in crastino S. Valentini, quod David Lardinarius recipiet Liberationem suam de Civitate Ebor., de firma ejusdem Civitatis. *Ex Memorand.* 2. *&* 3. *Hen.* 3. *Rot.* 1. *b.*

(*c*) Hugo de Nevill recognovit ad Scaccarium, die Lunæ post octabas S. Trinitatis, coram Justiciario, & Thesaurario, & alijs Baronibus de Scaccario, quod non tradidit Henrico de Braybrok nisi quatuor acras ad assartandum in Bosco de Coreby, nec amplius voluit ei tradere. *Ex Mem.* 6. H. 3. *Rot.* 2. *b. Norhamtescira.*

(*d*) Cornubia. Die Sanctorum Fabiani & Sebastiani, coram Justiciario & alijs Baronibus de Scaccario, præceptum fuit Vicecomiti, quod pacem habere permittat Waltero filio Willelmi nepoti Roberti de Cardigan, de demanda xx marcarum pro defalta Justiciariorum Autumpnalium. *Ex Mem.* 8. H. 3. *Rot.* 3. *a.*

(*e*) Willelmus de Abrincis r c de xxix l & j marca, de duobus Scutagiis de tempore Regis J, In thesauro xviij l & j marcam per ij taleas ante guerram, pacatas per G filium Petri, & allocatas per H. de Burgo Justiciarium, coram R. Cicestrensi Episcopo Regis Cancellario, R. Saresberiensi, J. Bathoniensi, B. Roffensi Episcopis, & alijs Baronibus de Scaccario: Et debet xj l. *Mag. Rot.* 9. H. 3. *Rot.* 12. *b. Kancia.*

(*f*) Hamo de Blachamton r c de Lxj s & iiij d, pro transgressione patris sui. In Thesauro liberavit per unam Taleam de ante guerram, allocatam præcepto H. de Burgo Justiciarij, coram Baronibus de Scaccario; Et Q. e. *Mag. Rot.* 11. H. 3. *Wiltesire.*

The like in the case of Philipp de Aura; *Mag. Rot.* 12. H. 3. *Glovernia.*

(*g*) Consideratum est die Mercurij proximo ante Purificationem B. Mariæ anno regni Regis Henrici tercij xiiij, apud Westmonasterium, coram Rege, per H. de Burgo Justiciarium, R. Cestriæ, R. Cornubiæ, G. Governiæ, W. Warannæ, W. Albemarliæ, H. Hertfordiæ, J. Huntedoniæ, Comites, & alios Domini Regis Barones, tunc ibidem præsentes, quod talliæ factæ ante Guerram quæ recognitæ fuerint esse de Scaccario, & non fuerunt hucusque allocatæ, allocentur. *Hil. Commun.* 14. H. 3. *Rot.* 4. *b.*

(*h*) Die Sabbati proximo post festum S. Johannis ante Portam Latinam, protulit R. Dunel-

the same Year, the King and several of his great Men were expected to be present at the Exchequer (*i*). About the 25th Year, it was adjudged by the Archbishop of *York* and the King's Council at the Exchequer, that the Heir of *Peter de Maulay* should answer to the King certain Debts hereunder mentioned, whereof the said *Peter* had been discharged in the great Roll (*k*). About the 27th Year, the Archbishop of *York* and others of the King's Council sat and acted at the Exchequer (*l*); in the 55th Year, the King's Council, and the Treasurer and Barons (*m*).

In the first Year of K. *Edward* I. there were present at the Exchequer, *Philipp de Eye* Treasurer, *Hervicus de Borham* and *Roger de la Leye* Barons of the Exchequer (*n*); in the 9th Year of K. *Edward* I. the King's Chancellor, and others of his Council (*o*); in the 9th and 10th Years, the King's Chancellor, the Treasurer, and Barons (*p*); in the 10th Year, the King's Council (*q*); in the 25th Year the Barons of the Exchequer, the King's Chancellor, and the Keeper of his Wardrobe (*r*); in the 25th or 26th Year, the Treasurer and Barons, *W.* Bishop of *Ely*, *R.* Bishop of *London*, and others of the

Dunelmensis Episcopus' cartam Regis Ricardi (& Confirmationem Regis J), coram W. Karl. & J. Bathon. Episcopis, & alijs Baronibus Domini Regis de Scaccario tunc ibi existentibus—. *Pas. Commun.* 14. *H.* 3. *Rot.* 6. *b.*

(*i*) Sudhamton. *An Award, concerning the Men of* Awelton, *which was entered on the Roll, is cancelled there, with the Reason of it in these Words,* Quia expectatur adventus Regis & aliorum Magnatum. *Mich. Commun.* 14. *H.* 3. *Rot.* 3. *b.*

(*k*) Hæres Petri de Malo lacu [debet] C s pro Roberto de Turnham quos idem Robertus recepit de Abbate de Fiscampo ; Et Lxxiij l x s de Scutagio Walliæ & Scociæ, Et x l pro ij Palefridis, pro habenda feria iij dierum apud Donecastriam, Et vij l et x s de firma de Stok de iij partibus anni quinti Regis Ricardi : Quæ omnia requirebantur de Petro de Malo lacu in Rotulo xvj in Ebor.; & unde per Recordum ibidem fuit Quietus : Et modo per Archiepiscopum Eboracensem—& Consiliarios Regis consideratum est, quod hæres prædictus respondebit : Sed non debet inde summoneri usque ad legitimam ætatem ejusdem hæredis. *Mag. Rot.* 25. *H.* 3. *Ebor.*

(*l*) *Trin. Communia* 27. *H.* 3. *Rot.* 11. *a.*
(*m*) *Ex Memor.* 55. *H.* 3. *Rot.* 4. *b.*
(*n*) *Memor.* 1 *E.* 1. *Rot.* 6. *b.*
(*o*) *Hil. Commun.* 18. *E.* 1. *Rot.*—*b.*
(*p*) Memorandum quod injunctum est Thesaurario & Baronibus per R. Bathoniensem & Wellensem Episcopum Regis Cancellarium, quod ponant in visum super Compotum Willelmi de Redham quodam Vicecomitis Norf. & Suff. Lx libras, usque post festum S. Michaelis. *Pas. Commun.* 9. *&* 10. *E.* 1. *Rot.* 4. *b.*

(*q*) Memorandum quod provisum est per Consilium Regis, quod allocentur R. Bathoniensi & Wellensi Episcopo, Regis Cancellario, in Compoto suo de Receptis & Expensis suis de denarijs Regis antequam esset Rex, pro expensis suis & misis quas fecit circa custodiam terrarum & aliarum rerum Regis antequam esset Rex, & pro negocijs Regis expediendis in diversis locis, a festo S. Michaelis anno regni Regis H. Liiijo finiente, usque ad idem festum anno Primo Domini Regis nunc finiente, scilicet per tres annos, DC libræ ; videlicet per annum CC libræ. *Pas. Commun.* 9 *&* 10. *E.* 1. *Rot.* 4. *b.*

(*r*) *Trin. Memor.* 25. *E.* 1. *Rot.* 24.

King's Council (*s*); in the 26th Year, the Archbishop of *Dublin*, the Bishop of *Ely*, the Bishop of *London*, the Bishop of *Coventry* and *Lychfeld* the King's Treasurer, the Chancellor of *England*, the Barons of the Exchequer, the Justices of both Benches, and several others of the King's Council (*t*); in the same 26th Year, *J. de Langeton* Chancellor of *England*, *R. Brabazun* Justicier of the King's Pleas, *W. de Berford* Justicier of the Common Pleas, the Treasurer, Barons, and others of the King's Council (*u*); in the 26th and 27th Year, the Treasurer and Barons, *Roger Brabazoun* and *Gilbert de Roubiry* Justices of the King's Bench, *John de Metingham*, and his Companions, Justices of the Common Bench (*w*); in or about the 27th Year, the Treasurer, the King's Chancellor, and others [of his Council] (*x*); and in the 35th Year, *Walter* B. of *Coventry* and *Lichfield* the King's Treasurer, *William de Carleton*, *Roger de Hegham*, Master *Richard de Abyndon* Barons of the Exchequer, and others of the Council (*y*).

In the first Year of K. *Edward* II. there were present and acted at the Exchequer, the Treasurer, Barons, and others of the King's Council, together with *Amadeo* Earl of *Savoy* (*z*); at another Time, the Treasurer and Barons, *J.* Bishop of *Chichester* Chancellor of *England*, *Roger le Brabanzon* Justice of the King's Bench, *Ralph de Hengham* Justice of the other Bench, *John de Benstede* Keeper of the King's Wardrobe, and others of the King's Council (*a*); at another Time

---

(*s*) *In the Case of* Richard de Lue, *a Chamberlain of the Exchequer*; Postea die sabbati in festo S. Clementis, praesente ipso Ricardo [de Luda] coram Thesaurario & Baronibus, & recitato processu isto in praesentia ipsorum Thesaurarij & Baronum, necnon Venerabilium Patrum W Eliensis & R. Londoniensis Episcoporum, & aliorum de Consilio Regis in Scaccario tunc sedencium, Consideratum est quod praedictus Johannes [de Cobeham, *a Baron of the Exchequer*] pro contemptu praedicto sibi facto per praedictum Ricardum, dampna sua versus eum recuperet, quae per Thesaurarium & Barones taxentur; & quod idem Ricardus, pro contemptu per ipsum facto Regi & huic Curiae, adeat prisonam; & quod ab officio Camerarij quo in Scaccario intendebat, amoveatur donec aliud &c. Postea die Lunae in festo S. Katerinae, praedictus Ricardus venit hic, & in praesentia Thesaurarij & Baronum & praedictorum Episcoporum eis affidentium, & vadiavit praedicto Johanni, pro contemptu sibi per ipsum facto, quingentas libras, solvendas eidem Johanni ad voluntatem suam. Et idem Johannes remisit eidem Ricardo omnem rancorem quem erga eum habuit occasione dicti contemptus. *Mich. Commun.* 25. *&* 26. *E.* 1. *Rot.* 22. *b.*

(*t*) *Hil. Communia* 26. *E.* 1. *Rot.* 44. *b.* Tit. Provisio facta per Consilium Regis, de Clericis Vicecomitum puniendis. *This Record is printed for a Statute, in Tot. Stat. Vett. P.* 1. *fol.* 159. *a.*

(*u*) *Pas. Commun. in bund.* 25. and 26. *E.* 1. *Rot.* 71. *b.*

(*w*) *Hil. Commun. in bund.* 26. *&* 27. *E.* 1. *Rot.* 16. *a.*

(*x*) *Mich. Commu.* 26. *&* 27. *E.* 1. *Rot.* 11. *b.*

(*y*) *Trin. Commun.* 35. *E.* 1. *Rot.* ——*a.* Vasconia.

(*z*) *Hil. Communia* 1. *E.* 2. *Rot.* 40. *b.*

(*a*) *Pas. Recorda* 1. *E.* 2. *Rot.* 56. *a.*

in the same Year, the Treasurer, the Bishop of *Chichester* Chancellor of *England*, *John de Sandale* Chancellor of the Exchequer, *J. de Benstede* Keeper of the King's Wardrobe, and the Barons of the Exchequer (*b*); at another Time in the same Year, *J. de Langeton* Bishop of *Chichester* Chancellor of *England*, *W*. Elect of *Worcester* the Treasurer, *R. le Brabanzoun* Justice of the King's Bench, *J. de Drokenesford* Chancellor of the Exchequer, *J. de Benstede* Keeper of the King's Wardrobe, *William de Carleton*, *Roger de Heghham*, Master *R. de Abendon*, and Master *J. de Everdon*, Barons of the Exchequer, and *William de Bereford* Justice of the Common Bench (*c*); at another Time in the same Year, *W*. Elect of *Worcester* the King's Treasurer, *J. de Langeton* Bishop of *Chichester* the King's Chancellor, *John de Sandale* Chancellor of the Exchequer, and *John de Drokesford*, *William Inge*, and others of the King's Council (*d*); at another Time in the same Year, the Treasurer and Barons, and *H. de Lacy* Earl of *Lincoln* (*e*); and at another Time in the same Year, the Treasurer and Barons, *A*. Earl of *Savoy*, *John de Drokenesford* (*f*). In the second Year of the same King, there were present at the Exchequer *J*. Bishop of *Chichester* Chancellor of *England*, the Treasurer and Barons, *John de Britaigne* Earl of *Richmund*, *Hugh le Despenser*, and others of the King's Council (*g*); at another Time in the same Year, the Treasurer and Barons, the Chancellor of *England*, and others of the King's Council (*h*); at another Time, the Chancellor of *England*,

---

(*b*) Hil. Brevia Irretor. 1. E. 2. Rot. 82. a.
(*c*) Trin. Recorda 1. E. 2. Rot. 69. a & b.
(*d*) Memor. 1. E. 2. Rot. 71. b.
(*e*) Norf. *In a case of one John de Rothing:* Et Thesaurarius & Barones tractatum inde habentes, assidente eis H. de Lacy Comite Lincolniæ, concordarunt quod præfatus Johannes de Rothing habeat allocationem de x marcis pro expensis funeralibus prædicti defuncti — &c. Trin. Commun. 1. E. 2. Rot. 76. b. inter Fines &c.

(*f*) Kancia. *A Writ to the Sheriff for Frere* William de la More *Master of the Temple, and Two Brothers of the same Order, to give them Liberty (being then in Custody) to take the Air and refresh themselves;* Teste Thesaurario, xiiij die Marcij. Et memorandum, quod forma hujusmodi mandati concordata fuit per Thesaurarium & Barones, in præsentia A. Comitis Sabaudiæ, & Johannis de Drokenesford &c. Hil. Brevia Irretornab. 1. E. 2. Rot. 81. a.

(*g*) Lincolnia. Dominus Rex mandavit hic Breve suum———. Et prætextu hujus brevis, tractato isto negocio coram J. Episcopo Cicestrensi Cancellario Angliæ, Thesaurario & Baronibus, Johanne de Britannia Comite Richemundiæ, Hugone le Despenser, & alijs de Consilio Regis, modo xxj die Januarij, concordatum est per idem Consilium, quod —. Hil. Commun. 2. E. 2. Rot. 55. a.

(*h*) Wygornia. — Et petit idem Frater Willelmus (*a Monk of* Evesham, *Proctor or Attorney for that House to act in this Affair*) admitti ad Finem faciendum cum Domino Rege super præmissis. Et habito inde tractatu per Thesaurarium & Barones, assidentibus eis Venerabili patre J. Cicestrensi Episcopo Cancellario Angliæ, & alijs de Consilio Regis, concordatum est quod admittatur ad præsens ad Finem &c, pro proxima futura Vacatione tantum—. Hil. Memor. 2. E. 2. Rot. 54. b.

H. Earl

Chap. XXI.   *of the* Exchequer.

H. Earl of *Lincoln,* H. *le Defpenfer,* J. *de Sandale* the Treafurer's Lieutenant, the Barons of the Exchequer, and others of the King's Council (*i*). In *Hilary* Term in the 5th Year of K. *Edward* II. there were prefent at the Exchequer *Walter de Norwich* the Treafurer's Lieutenant, J. *de Merkyngfeld* Chancellor [of the Exchequer], *John Foxle,* Mafter *Richard de Abindon,* Mafter *John de Everdon,* Barons of the Exchequer, *John de Clavering* and other Lieges (*k*); at another Time, *John de Merkyngfeld* Chancellor, and Mafter *John de Everdone* Baron of the Exchequer, *L. de Trikingham* and J. *de Benftede* Juftices of the Bank (*l*); at another Time in the fame Year, J. Bifhop of *Bathe* and *Wells,* A. *de Valentia* Earl of *Penbrok,* H. *le Defpenfer,* J. *de Benftede,* and others of the King's Council (*m*); at another Time, the Chancellor of *England,* the Bifhop of *Coventry* and *Lichfield,* and others of the Council (*n*); in the fame Year, *Adomar de Valence* Earl of *Pembroke,* the Chancellor of *England,* the Treafurer and Barons of the Exchequer, the Juftices of both Benches, *Hugh le Defpenfer,* and others of the Council (*o*); in the 9th Year of the fame King, the Treafurer and Barons and others of the King's Council (*p*). In the 8th Year of the fame King, the Office of the Sheriff of *Devonfhire* was granted to *Thomas de Pyn* by the King's Chancellor and his Council at the Exchequer (*q*). In the 5th Year

(*i*) Londonia.——Prædictus Johannes de Puntoife modo xij die Junij venit hic ad Scaccarium coram J. Ciceftrenfi Epifcopo Cancellario Angliæ, H. Comite Lincolniæ, H. le Defpenfer, J. de Sandale Tenente locum Thefaurarij, Baronibus de Scaccario, & alijs de Confilio Regis ——. *Trin. Fines &c.* 2. *E.* 2. *Rot.* 91. *a.*

(*k*) *Hil. Commun.* 5. *E.* 2. *Rot.* 31. *b.*

(*l*) *Ib. Rot.* 34. *a.*

(*m*) Suhamton. Willelmus de Heyghton de Comitatu Dorfetæ Subamtonæ, Walterus de Butterfthorn de Comitatu Suhamtonæ, & Adam Bernard de Comitatu Leyceftriæ, venerunt coram Baronibus ad Scaccarium die Dominica xxiij die Julij, Præfentibus Venerabili Patre J. Bathon. & Wellenfi Epifcopo, A. de Valencia Comite de Penebrok, H. le Defpenfer, J. de Benftede Juftic. & alijs de Confilio Regis, & concefferunt fe effe Executores teftamenti Johannis de Berewyco defuncti——. *Trin. Commun.* 5. *E.* 2. *Rot.* 65. *a. inter Fines &c.*

(*n*) *Mich. Commun.* 5. *E.* 2. *Rot.* 18. *b.*

(*o*) Electio de Vicecomitibus xviij° die Octobris, præfentibus Adomaro de Valencia Comite Pembrochiæ, Cancellario Angliæ, Thefaurario & Baronibus de Scaccario, Jufticiarijs de utroque Banco, Hugone le Defpenfer, & alijs de Confilio. *Mich. Commun.* 5. *E.* 2. *in Cedula annexa Rotulo* 20. *a.*

(*p*) Edwardus &c, Dilecto & fideli fuo Willelmo Truffel Vicecomiti Warwici & Leyceftriæ falutem. Mandamus vobis firmiter injungentes, quod omnibus alijs prætermiffis veniatis ad Scaccarium noftrum apud Weftmonafterium cum omni celeritate qua poteritis, cum Thefaurario & Baronibus de eodem Scaccario & alijs de Confilio noftro ibidem exiftentibus, fuper quibufdam arduis negocijs nos fpecialiter tangentibus tractaturi, & ulterius facturi quod vobis ibidem injungetur ex parte noftra. Et hoc nullo modo omittatis. Et habeas ibi hoc breve. T. Thefaurario xxiiij die Aprilis. Per ipfum Thefaurarium. *Paf. Brevia Retornab.* 9. *E.* 2. *Rot.* 167. *b.*

(*q*) *Paf. Memoran.* 8. *E.* 1. *Rot. a.*

of the same King, the Bishop of *Worcester* (the King's Chancellor) declared at the Exchequer, that it was the King's Pleasure, that *W.* Bishop of *Coventry* and *Lichfield* should be admitted one of the King's Council at the Exchequer. Accordingly the Bishop of *Coventry* and *L.* was called out, and placed amongst the King's Council there (*r*). In the 12th Year of the same King, Master *John Waleweyn*, lately the King's Treasurer, having been removed from that Office, the King by his Writ commands the Barons, that in respect of the said Master *John*'s former good Services done to the King, they should give him an honourable Place amongst them at the Exchequer whenever he should come thither, and should communicate with him in the King's Business there (*s*).

From these Instances it appears that the King's Council frequently sat and acted at the Exchequer. And it is likely they did not sit there only occasionally; because it is found, that Men were sometimes summoned to appear before the King's Council there on set Days. As in the Case of *Walter de Kelk* (*t*), *John de Limbury* (*u*), and others.

In or about the Reign of K. *Edward* II. the Persons who were of the King's Council, were sworn according to the Articles hereunder written (*w*).

II.

(*r*) Anglia. De Episcopo Cestrensi admisso ad Consilium Regis. Idem etiam Cancellarius [W. Wygorniensis Episcopus] dicit se habere mandatum a Rege, quod Dominus Rex vult quod W. Coventrensis & Lich. Episcopus sit de Consilio suo, & quod admittatur inter alios Consiliarios &c, in quibuscunque consulendis pro ipso Rege &c; & quod ipse Cancellarius hoc nunciaret Consilio Regis nunc hic. Et statim super hoc idem Episcopus evocatus, assessus est inter alios de Consilio Regis &c. *Mich. Commun.* 5. *E.* 2. *Rot.* 18. *b.*

(*s*) Honori Regis convenit, personas fideliter obsequencium & bene meritorum favoribus condignis attollere, & Regijs affectibus specialius conjungere, & si se ab officijs onerosis separaverint, eo nichilominus tanquam fideles in cæteros consiliarios collocare: Cum itaq; dilectus Clericus Regis Magister Johannes Waleweyn nuper Thesaurarius Regis, in officio illo dum eidem intendebat, ac alijs officijs & negocijs sibi per Regem pluribus vicibus commissis, fideliter & laudabiliter servierit ac gratanter. Rex ipsius fidelitatem & circumspectionem providam, suis exigentibus meritis, commendans, ac inde specialiter confidens, sperando juxta experientiam præteritorum per ipsius maturitatem consilij negocia sua effectualiter prosperari, Vult & mandat Baronibus, quod præfatum Magistrum Johannem, cum ipsum ad Scaccarium prædictum, vel ad alia Consilia ipsum Regem ad dictum Scaccarium suum tangencia, accedere contigerit, tunc ipsum inter eos honorifice collocent, & de dictis negocijs suis communicent cum eodem. T. Rege apud Eboracum v die Decembris anno duodecimo. Per ipsum Regem. *Pas. Brevia* 12. *E.* 2. *Rot.* 99. *b.*

(*t*) *Mich. Commun.* 34 & 35. *E.* 1. *Rot.* 19. *b.* & *Rot.* 22. *b.*

(*u*) *Mich. Commun.* 34 & 35. *E.* 1. *Rot.* 20. *a.*

(*w*) Celi qe serra jurez du Conseil le Roi, soit chargez des pointz desoutz escriptz; & sil deiue estre Justice, soit chargez du drain point.

Vous

Chap. XXI.   *of the* Exchequer.

II. I will now shew in some Instances within this second Period, in what Manner the Treasurer and his Lieutenant, the Chancellor of the Exchequer, and the Barons, were appointed to their Offices. First, of the Treasurer; then of the others in Order. K. *Henry* III. (*Anno Regni* 16) by his Charter granted his Treasury of his Exchequer of *England* to *Walter de Mauclerc* Bishop of *Carlile*, to hold during his Life; with all the Liberties and Appurtenances to the said Treasury belonging: So that he should have and keep the said Treasury at the King's Exchequer, in his own Person, or by some discreet and fit Person his Assignee or Vicegerent; which Assignee should be sworn to serve faithfully in his Office; and if such Assignee should die, or become professed in Religion, or for reasonable Cause should be removed by the King or the Treasurer, or should himself be unwilling to serve any longer, then the said Treasurer should substitute some other discreet and fit Person in the room of such Assignee; and the Person so substituted was to be likewise sworn to serve faithfully (*x*). In the next

---

Vous jurez, qe bien & loialment consaillerez le Roi, selonc vostre sen & vostre poair.

Et qe bien & loialment son consail celerez.

Et qe vous ne accuserez autre de chose quil dirra a conseil, qe touche le conseil le Roi.

Et qe vostre peine eide & conseil e tot vostre poair dorrez & mettrez, as dreitures le Roi e la Corone garder & meintenir sauuer & repeller, per la ou vous porrez. saunz tort faire, & selonc ce qil affert a son office.

Et la ou vous saverez le choses de la Corone & le droitz le Roi concelez ou atort alienez ou sustretez, qe vous le freez adresser a vostre poer, ou qe vous le freez saver au Roi ou a son Conseil, en la manere qe a vous appent.

Et qe la Corone acrestrez a vostre poair & en loial manere.

Et qe vous ne serrez en lien ne a conseil ou le Roy se decresse de chose qe a la Corone appent, si ceo ne soit chose qe vous conneigne faire.

Et qe vous ne lerrez pur nulli, pur amour ne haour, pur bone gre ne pur mauveis gre, qe vous ne facez faire a chescun, de quel estat ou condicion quil soit, droiture & reson, selonc vostre poair & a vostre escient, e qe de nulli rien ne prendrez pur tort faire ne droit delaier.

Et qe en Jugement ou droiture faire la ou vous serrez assignez, vous nespernierez nulli pur hautesce ne pur pouerte ne pur richesse qe droit ne soit fait a vostre poer.

Et si vous eez fait alliaunce a Seignurage ou a autre par quei vouz ne puissez ceste chose faire ou tenir saunz celle alliaunce enfreindre, qe vous le dirrez ou frez saver au Roi.

Et qe desormes alliaunce de serment ne frez a nulli saunz Conge le Roi.

Et qe rien ne prendrez de doun de nulli pur plede ne pur autre chose quil eit a faire devant vous si ceo ne soit manger & beiuer a la journee. *Lib. Rub. Scacc. fol. sive membr.* 15. *a. This Oath may be seen also in Tott. Stat. Vett. P.* 1. *fol.* 165. *a.*

(*x*) H. Rex &c, Salutem. Sciatis nos concessisse & hac Carta nostra confirmasse venerabili Patri W. Carleolensi Episcopo Thesaurariam nostram Scaccarij nostri Angliæ, habendam toto tempore vitæ suæ, cum omnibus pertinentijs, libertatibus, & consuetudinibus, ad prædictam Thesaurariam pertinentibus; Ita quod Thesaurariam illam habeat & custodiat in propria persona sua ad Scaccarium nostrum, quamdiu voluerit, vel per aliquem virum discretum, Sufficientem,

&

next Year, the King by Patent committed the Treasury of his Exchequer [of *London*] with the Appurtenances, to *Peter de Rivall*, to hold during the King's Pleasure. Hereupon *Walter* Bishop of *Carlile*, the King's Treasurer, was commanded to deliver (by View and Testimony of true Men) the Keys of the Treasury, with the Treasury and all Things belonging to it by Inventory, to *Peter de Rivall*, or to *Robert Passelewe* his Attorney, nominated by him for that Purpose before the King. Afterwards the King commanded S. *de Segrave* his Justicier to give Possession of the Treasury to *Peter*, or to *Robert* his Attorney, in case the Bishop of *Carlile* refused to deliver it (*y*). And the Barons and Chamberlains of the Exchequer were commanded to be intendent and respondent to *Peter* as the King's Treasurer, and to *Robert* as his Deputy (*z*). K. *Henry* III. (*Anno Regni* 18) committed to *Hugh de Pateshull* the Treasury of his Exchequer of *London*, with the Ap-

& idoneum, Assignatum suum vices suas ibidem gerentem; Qui quidem Assignatus nobis fidelitatem faciet de fideli servitio, & de prædicta Thesauraria nostra loco suo fideliter custodienda, antequam custodiam prædictæ Thesaurariæ recipiat; Et si forte idem Assignatus suus decesserit, vel vitam suam mutaverit, vel ob causam rationabilem per nos vel per ipsum Thesaurarium nostrum amotus fuerit, vel ipse assignatus Thesaurariam illam ulterius custodire noluerit, idem Thesaurarius noster loco illius assignati sui, alium virum discretum, sufficientem, & idoneum substituat, Ita quod fidelitatem nobis faciat de fideli servitio, & de prædicta Thesauraria nostra loco suo fideliter custodienda, antequam custodiam prædictæ Thesaurariæ recipiat, sicut prædictum est. Quare volumus &c, quod prædictus W. Carleolensis Episcopus prædictam Thesaurariam nostram Scaccarij nostri Londoniæ habeat toto tempore vitæ suæ, cum omnibus pertinentijs, Libertatibus, & Consuetudinibus, ad prædictam Thesaurariam pertinentibus; Ita quod Thesaurariam illam custodiat in propria persona sua, ad dictum Scaccarium nostrum, quamdiu voluerit &c, per omnia ut superius ante Quare Volumus. Hijs Testibus, H. de Burgo &c, W. de Cantilupo, G. de Craucumbe, Johanne filio Philippi, Amaurico de Sancto Amando, G. Dispenser, G. de Cauz, Barth. Pech, Ricardo filio Hugonis, H. de Capella, & alijs. Dat. per manum nostram apud Burgum ij° die Julij. *Cart.* 16. *H.* 3. *m.* 4.

(*y*) De Thesauraria Scaccarij Londoniæ. Rex Thesaurariam Scaccarij sui cum pertinentijs commisit Petro de Rivall, custodiendam quamdiu Regi placuerit, Et mandatum est W. Carleolensi Episcopo Thesaurario Regis, quod per visum & testimonium proborum & legalium hominum, ipsi Petro, vel Roberto Passelewe quem idem Petrus ad hoc loco suo coram Rege attornavit quamdiu ei placuerit, claves ipsius Thesaurariæ, cum ipsa Thesauraria, & omnibus ad ipsam pertinentibus, distincte & aperte in scriptum redactis, liberet. T. Rege apud Wudestok vj die Jan. Postea mandatum fuit S. de Sedgrave Justiciario, quod si ipse Episcopus eandem Thesaurariam reddere noluerit sicut prædictum est, ipse eam reddat prædicto Petro, vel Roberto Attornato suo. *Pat.* 17. *H.* 3. *m.* 7.

(*z*) Rex commisit Petro de Rivall Thesaurariam Scaccarij sui cum omnibus pertinentijs, custodiendam quamdiu Regi placuerit: Et mandatum est Baronibus & Camerarijs ejusdem Scaccarij, quod eidem Petro tanquam Thesaurario Regis & Roberto Passelewe quem loco suo ad hoc posuit quamdiu eidem P. placuerit, intendentes sint & respondentes sicut prædictum est. T. P. Winton. Episcopo apud Westmon. xix° die Januarij. *Ib. m.* 7.

purtenances,

purtenances, during his Pleasure; and commanded the Barons and Chamberlains of the Exchequer, to be intendent and respondent to him in all Things relating to the Treasury: *Peter de Rivall* and *Robert Paffelewe* were commanded to deliver to him, as to the King's Treasurer (by View and Testimony of the Justices of the *Bank*, and Constable of the Tower of *London*, and of *Andrew Bukerel* Mayor of *London*, and *Richard Reynger*) the Keys of the Treasury, with the Treasury and all Things belonging to it by Inventory: And the Justices of the *Bank*, the Constable of the Tower of *London*, and *Andrew Bukerel* Mayor, and *Richard Reynger* were commanded to be present at delivering Possession of the said Treasury (*a*). And in the same Year, the King granted to the said *Hugh de Pateshull* his Treasurer, One hundred Marks, payable to him yearly at his Exchequer, for his Support in the said Office of Treasurer, till the King should otherwise provide for him [by some ecclesiastical Benefice] (*b*). In the 36th Year of K. *Henry* III. *Philipp Lovell* was constituted the King's Treasurer, during Pleasure, by the Patent hereunder recited (*c*):

(*a*) De Thesauraria Scaccarij Londoniæ. H. Rex Angliæ &c; Dilectis & fidelibus suis Baronibus & Camerarijs Scaccarij sui Londoniæ salutem. Sciatis quod commisimus dilecto & fideli nostro Hugoni de Pateshull, Thesaurariam Scaccarij nostri Londoniæ cum pertinentijs suis, custodiendam quamdiu nobis placuerit. Et ideo vobis mandamus, quod eidem Hugoni, in omnibus quæ ad dictam Thesaurariam pertinent, intendentes sitis & respondentes, sicut prædictum est. In c r t &c, T. Rege apud Glouc. primo die Junij.

H. Rex Angliæ &c, Dilecto & fideli suo Petro de Rivall salutem. Sciatis quod commisimus dilecto & fideli nostro Hugoni de Patteshull, Thesaurariam Scaccarij nostri Londoniæ cum pertinentijs suis, custodiendam quamdiu nobis placuerit: Et ideo vobis mandamus, quod per visum & testimonium Justiciariorum nostrorum de Banco & Constabularij Turris nostræ Londoniæ, & dilectorum & fidelium nostrorum Andreæ Bukerel Majoris Londoniæ & Ricardi Reynger, eidem Hugoni tanquam Thesaurario nostro Claves ejusdem Thesaurariæ, cum ipsa Thesauraria, & omnibus ad ipsam pertinentibus distincte & aperte in scriptum redactis, sine dilatione liberari faciatis. In c r t &c, T. Rege, ut supra.

Eodem modo scribitur Roberto Passelewe & per eadem verba, T. Rege, ut supra.

Et mandatum est Justiciarijs de Banco, & Constabulario Turris Londoniæ, & Andreæ Bukerel Majori Londoniæ & Ricardo Reynger, quod intersint liberationi prædictæ Thesaurariæ &c. *Pat*. 18. *H*. 3. *m*. 11.

(*b*) Rex omnibus ad quos præsentes literæ pervenerint salutem. Sciatis nos concessisse dilecto & fideli nostro Hugoni de Pateshull Thesaurario nostro, Centum marcas singulis annis percipiendas ad Scaccarium nostrum, ad se sustentandum in Officio prædictæ Thesaurariæ; donec ei alias providerimus. In cujus rei testimonium &c. Teste Rege apud Westmonasterium, 21 die Octobris. *Pat*. 18. *H*. 3. *m*. 2.

(*c*) Rex Baronibus & Camerarijs suis de Scaccario Salutem. Sciatis quod constituimus dilectum & fidelem nostrum Philippum Luvel Thesaurarium nostrum quamdiu nobis placuerit. Et ideo vobis mandamus, quod eidem tanquam Thesaurario nostro, de omnibus quæ ad prædictum Thesaurariam pertinent, sitis intendentes. In cujus &c. Teste Rege apud Sanctum Albanum 27 die Augusti. *Pat*. 36. *H*. 3. *m*. 3.

And

And thereupon a close Writ was issued to *Edward de Westminstre*, commanding him to go (together with *Philipp Luvel*) to the King's Treasury; and having searched to see what Monies *W. de Haverhull* the late Treasurer had received to the King's Use, to deliver to *Philipp* the Rolls, the lesser Seal, and all other Things belonging to the said Office (*d*). The same King (*Anno Regni* 43) by Advice of the Nobles of his Council, constituted *John de Crachale*, Archdeacon of *Bedford*, his Treasurer; commanding him to receive his Treasure, and the Rolls, Keys, and other Things belonging to that Office, of *Philipp Luvel* late Treasurer, in whose Custody they were: And a Writ was also issued to *Philipp Luvel* to deliver the same to the said *John* accordingly (*e*). In the 49th Year of K. *Henry* III. *H.* Prior of St. *Radegund* was presented before the Barons as the King's Treasurer by two Noblemen (*f*).

K. *Edward* I. in the 12th Year of his Reign, committed to *John de Kirkeby* the Office of Treasurer of his Exchequer, with all Things thereto belonging, during the King's Pleasure. And thereupon, two Writs were issued; one to the Executors of *R*. Abbot of *Westminster* the last Treasurer, commanding them to deliver to the said *John* the Keys and all other Things which they had in their Custody belonging to the said Office; and another Writ to the Chamberlains and Barons of the Exchequer, commanding them to put the said *John* into Possession of the said Office (*g*). The same King, in the 18th Year

---

(*d*) De Rotulis & parvo Sigillo Scaccarij liberandis Philippo Luvel. Cum Philippum Luvel Rex constituerit Thesaurarium suum quamdiu Regi placuerit; Mandatum est Eduuardo de Westminstre, quod una cum ipso Philippo accedat ad Thesaur[ariam] Regis, & scrutatis diligenter omnibus quæ W. de Haverhull quondam Thesaurarius Regis recepit, quando Rex Thesaurarium suum constituit, Rotulos una cum parvo Sigillo & alijs omnibus ad officium illud pertinentibus, eidem Philippo liberet custodienda, sicut prædictum est. T. Rege apud Dytton xx die Septembris. Per Regem, procurante P. Luvel. *Cl.* 36. *H.* 3. *m.* 4.

(*e*) Rex dilecto & fideli suo Johanni de Crachale Archidiacono Bedfordiæ Thesaurario suo, Salutem. Cum de Consilio Procerum de Concilio nostro, constituerimus vos Thesaurarium nostrum: Vobis mandamus, quod Thesaurum nostrum, Rotulos, Claves, & alia ad dictum Officium pertinentia, quæ sunt in Custodia Philippi Luvel nuper Thesaurarij nostri, recipiatis ab eodem Philippo, cui mandavimus quod ea vobis sine dilatione liberet. In cujus &c; Teste Rege apud Westm. ij° die Novembris.

Et mandatum est Philippo Luvell, quod Thesaurum Regis, Rotulos, Claves, & alia ad dictum Officium pertinentia, quæ sunt in Custodia sua, eidem Johanni sine dilatione liberet. Teste ut supra. *Pat.* 43. *H.* 3. *m.* 15.

(*f*) In crastino Animarum venerunt Episcopus Londoniensis & H. le Despenser Justiciarius, & præsentaverunt coram Baronibus H. Priorem de Sancta Radegunde Thesaurarium Domini Regis. *Mich. Commun.* 49. *H.* 3. *Rot.* 3. *b.*

(*g*) Rex commisit Johanni de Kirkeby Officium Thesaurarij Scaccarij Regis, cum omnibus

Chap. XXI.   *of the* EXCHEQUER.

Year of his Reign, by his Letters Patent committed to *William de Marche*, the Office of Treasurer of his Exchequer, during his Pleasure, to hold in the same Manner as *J.* Bishop of *Ely*, late Treasurer, or as other Treasurers held the same. And thereupon two Writs issued, one to the Chamberlains of the Exchequer, commanding them to deliver to *William* the Keys and all other Things in their Custody belonging to the said Office: And another to the Barons of the Exchequer, commanding them to admit him to the said Office (*h*). The Writ that was sent in this Case to the Barons, is entered in the Rolls of the Exchequer according to the Tenour set forth hereunder (*i*). The same King, in the 23d Year of his Reign, by Letters Patent committed to *Walter de Langeton* the Office of the Treasury of his Exchequer, during his Pleasure, to hold in like Manner as other Treasurers held it. And Writs were made forth to the Chamberlains and Barons in like Form as above in the Case of *William de Marche* (*k*).

K. *Edward*

omnibus quæ ad Officium illud pertinent, custodiendum quamdiu Regi placuerit. In cujus &c, Teste Rege apud Crideling. 6° die Januarij.

Et mandatum est Executoribus testamenti R. Abbatis Westm. nuper Thesaurarij ibidem, quod eidem Johanni Claves, & omnia alia dictum Officium contingentia, quæ fuerunt in custodia præfati Abbatis, per Cyrographum &c, liberet &c, custodienda in forma prædicta. Teste ut supra.

Et mandatum est Camerarijs & Baronibus de Scaccario per Brevia clausa, quod præfato Johanni Officium prædictum cum omnibus ad illud pertinentibus liberent, custodiendum in forma prædicta. Teste ut supra. *Pat.* 12. *E.* 1. *m.* 19.

(*h*) Rex omnibus ad quos &c, Salutem. Sciatis quod commisimus dilecto Clerico nostro Magistro Willemo de Marchia Officium Thesaurariæ Scaccarij nostri cum pertinentijs, custodiendum quamdiu nobis placuerit, eodem modo quo bonæ memoriæ J. quondam Elien. Episcopus & Thesaurarius noster, ac alij Thesaurarij ibidem, custodire consueverunt. In cujus &c, Teste Rege apud Wodestoke 6° die Aprilis.

Et mandatum est Camerarijs de Scaccario prædicto, quod eidem Willelmo Claves, & omnia alia Officium illud tangentia, quæ sunt in Custodia sua, liberent, custodienda sicut prædictum est. Teste ut supra.

Et mandatum est Baronibus de eodem Scaccario quod ipsum Willelmum ad hoc admittant. Teste ut supra. *Pat.* 18. *E.* 1. *m.* 33.

(*i*) Cum Rex commiserit Magistro Willelmo de Marchia Officium Thesaurarij Scaccarij cum pertinentijs, custodiendum quamdiu Regi placuerit; prout in Literis Regis patentibus eidem Willelmo inde confectis plenius continetur: Rex mandat Baronibus, quod eundem Willelmum ad hoc admittant. T. Rege apud Wodestok vj die Aprilis anno xviij. *Pas. Commun.* 18. *E.* 1. *Rot.*—. *a.*

(*k*) Rex omnibus ad quos &c, Salutem. Sciatis quod commisimus dilecto & fideli nostro Waltero de Langeton, Officium Thesaurariæ Scaccarij nostri cum pertinentijs, custodiendum quamdiu nobis placuerit, prout Venerabilis Pater W. Bathoniensis & Wellensis Episcopus nuper Thesaurarius noster, & alij Thesaurarij nostri ibidem, Officium illud custodire consueverunt temporibus retroactis. In cujus &c, Teste Rege apud Wyngeham xxviij° die Septembris.

Et mandatum est Camerarijs Regis de Scaccario, quod Claves & omnia alia Officium prædictum contingentia, præfato

Waltero

K. *Edward* II. in the firſt Year of his Reign, by Letters Patent (hereunder recited) committed to *Walter Renaud* the Office of Treaſurer of his Exchequer, during Pleaſure; and commanded the late Treaſurer to deliver to him the Keys and all other Things belonging to the ſaid Office (*l*). K. *Edward* II. in the third Year of his Reign committed to *John de Sandale* the Office of Treaſurer of his Exchequer, during his Pleaſure. And a Writ was ſent to the late Treaſurer, commanding him to deliver to the ſaid *John* the Keys and all other Things in his Cuſtody relating to the ſaid Office (*m*). The ſame King, in the 5th Year of his Reign, by his Letters Patent committed to *Walter* Biſhop of *Coventry* and *Lichfield* the Office of Treaſurer of his Exchequer, to hold till the next Parliament; and commanded the Barons to be intendant and reſpondent to him in all Things relating to that Office (*n*). The ſame King (*Anno Regni* 8) committed to *Walter de Norwich* the Office of Treaſurer of his Exchequer, during his Pleaſure. And *John de Sandale* was commanded by Writ to deliver to *Walter* by Indenture all Things in his Cuſtody

Waltero liberent, cuſtodienda in forma prædicta. In cujus &c, Teſte ut ſupra.

Et mandatum eſt ſimiliter, per breve clauſum, Baronibus de Scaccario, quod eundum Walterum ad hoc admittant ſicut prædictum eſt. Teſte ut ſupra. *Pat.* 23. *E.* 1. *m.* 6.

(*l*) Rex omnibus ad quos &c, Salutem. Sciatis quod commiſimus dilecto Clerico noſtro Waltero Reginaldi, Officium Theſaurarij Scaccarij noſtri, cum omnibus quæ ad Officium illud pertinent, cuſtodiendum quamdiu nobis placuerit. In cujus &c; Teſte Rege apud Comenok 22º die Auguſti. Per Breve de privato Sigillo.

Et mandatum eſt Venerabili Patri W. Coventrenſi & Lich. Epiſcopo, quod præfato Waltero Claves, & omnia alia dictum Officium contingentia, quæ ſunt in Cuſtodia ejuſdem Epiſcopi, per Cirographum inter ipſos inde conficiendum, liberet, cuſtodienda in forma prædicta. Teſte Rege ut ſupra. Per Breve de Privato Sigillo. *Rot. Pat.* 1. *E.* 2. *p.* 1. *m.* 21.

(*m*) Rex omnibus ad quos &c. Salutem. Sciatis quod commiſimus dilecto Clerico noſtro Johanni de Sandale Officium Theſaurarij Scaccarij noſtri cum omnibus quæ ad Officium illud pertinent habendum quamdiu nobis placuerit. In cujus &c. Teſte Rege apud Weſtm. 6º die Julij.

Et mandatum eſt Venerabili Patri W. Wigorn. Epiſcopo quod eidem Johanni Claves & omnia alia Officium illud tangentia quæ ſunt in Cuſtodia ſua per Cirographum inter ipſos inde conficiendum liberet cuſtodienda in forma prædicta. Teſte Rege ut ſupra. *Pat.* 3. *E.* 2. *m.* 3.

(*n*) Baronibus & Camerarijs de Scaccario, per Regem. Cum Rex nuper commiſerit Venerabili patri Waltero Conventrenſi & Lichefeldenſi Epiſcopo officium Theſaurariæ Scaccarij, habendum uſq; ad proximum parliamentum Regis; prout in Literis patentibus eidem Epiſcopo inde confectis plenius continetur: Mandat Baronibus ſicut alias mandavit, quod eidem Epiſcopo tanquam Theſaurario ſuo in omnibus quæ ad officium prædictum pertinent intendentes ſint & reſpondentes; Et hoc ſicut indignationem Regis vitare voluerint nullatenus omittant. T. Rege apud Novum Caſtrum ſuper Tinam xij die Aprilis anno quinto. Per ipſum Regem. *Paſ. Brevia* 5. *E.* 2. *Rot.* 42. *b. in imo.*

Chap. XXI.   *of the* Exchequer.

that belonged to the said Office (*o*). The same King (*Anno Regni* 10) committed to *J*. Bishop of *Ely* the Office of Treasurer of his Exchequer, with all Things belonging to it, during his Pleasure. And *Walter de Norwich* was commanded to deliver to the Bishop of *Ely* the Keys, Rolls, *Memoranda,* and all other Things in his Custody relating to that Office (*p*). The same King (*Anno Regni* 11) committed to *John Walewayn* the Office of Treasurer of his Exchequer, in like Form (*q*). The same King (*Anno Regni* 12) committed to *John* Bishop of *Winton* the Office of Treasurer of his Exchequer, to hold during his Pleasure (*r*). The same King, in the 13th Year of his Reign, committed to *W*. Bishop of *Exeter* the Office of Treasurer of his Exchequer. And *Walter de Norwich, Custos* of the King's Treasury, was commanded to deliver to him the Keys, Rolls, Memoranda, and all other Things in his Custody belonging to the said Office (*s*). The same King, in the 15th Year of his Reign, committed

---

(*o*) Rex omnibus ad quos &c. Salutem. Sciatis quod commisimus dilecto & fideli nostro Waltero de Norwico Officium Thesaurarij Scaccarij nostri habendum cum omnibus ad Officium illud spectantibus quamdiu nobis placuerit. In cujus &c. Teste Rege apud Ebor. 26 die Septembris, per ipsum Regem & Concilium.

Et mandatum est Johanni de Sandale quod eidem Waltero omnia Officium illud tangentia quæ sunt in custodia sua per Indenturam inter ipsos inde conficiendam liberet habenda in forma prædicta. Teste ut supra. Pat. 8. E. 2. p. 1. m. 21.

(*p*) Rex omnibus ad quos &c salutem. Sciatis quod commisimus Venerabili patri J. Eliensi Episcopo officium Thesaurar. Scaccarij nostri, habendum cum omnibus ad officium illud spectantibus, quamdiu nobis placuerit. In cujus &c, T. Rege apud Westmon. xxvij die Maij. Per ipsum Regem.

Et mandatum est Waltero de Norwyco, quod eidem Episcopo, claves, rotulos, memoranda, & omnia alia officium illud tangencia quæ sunt in custodia sua liberet, custodienda in forma prædicta. T. ut supra. Pat. 10. E. 2. pars 2. m. 10.

(*q*) Rex omnibus ad quos &c. Salutem. Sciatis quod commisimus dilecto Clerico nostro Magistro Johanni Walewayn Officium Thesaurarij Scaccarij nostri habendum cum omnibus ad officium illud spectantibus quamdiu nobis placuerit. In cujus &c. Teste Rege apud Westm. 10 die Junij. Per ipsum Regem.

Et mandatum est J. Elien. Episcopo quod eidem Johanni Claves Rotulos Memoranda & omnia alia Officium illud tangentia quæ sunt in Custodia sua liberet custodienda in forma prædicta. In cujus &c. Teste ut supra. Per ipsum Regem. Pat. 11. E. 2. p. 2. m. 10.

(*r*) Anglia. De Johanne de Sandale Episcopo Wynton. admisso ad Officium Thesaurarij. Edwardus Dei gratia Rex Angliæ Dominus Hiberniæ & Dux Aquitaniæ, Omnibus ad quos præsentes litteræ pervenerint, salutem. Sciatis quod commisimus Venerabili patri Johanni Wynton. Episcopo Officium Thesaurarij Scaccarij nostri, habendum cum omnibus ad Officium illud spectantibus quamdiu nobis placuerit. In cujus r t, h L n f f p. T. me ipso apud Ebor. xvj die Novembris anno r n duodecimo. Per ipsum Regem & Consilium. Mich. Communia 12. Edw. 2.

(*s*) Rex omnibus ad quos &c. Salutem. Sciatis quod commisimus Venerabili Patri W. Exon: Episcopo Officium Thesaurarij Scaccarij nostri habendum cum omnibus ad Officium illud spectantibus quamdiu nobis placuerit.

mitted the said Office to the said *W.* Bishop of *Exeter*, in the same Form as he had done in the 13th Year (*t*). The said King, in the said 15th Year of his Reign, at the instant Request of *Walter* Bishop of *Exeter*, discharged him the said *Walter* from the Office of Treasurer of his Exchequer, which he had for some Time held by the King's Commission; and committed the Custody of the said Office to *Walter de Norwich*, one of the Barons of the said Exchequer, till such Time as the King should dispose of the said Treasury. And the said Bishop was commanded to deliver to the said *Walter* the Keys, and all other Things that were in his Custody, relating to the said Office (*u*). In this Year there was a *Custos officij Thesaurariæ Regis* (*w*): Probably *Walter de Norwich*, who at this Time was stiled *Guardian of the Treasury* (*x*). The same K. *Edward* II, in the 18th Year of his Reign,

placuerit. In cujus &c. Teste Rege apud Westm. 18 die Februarij. Per ipsum Regem.

Et mandatum est Waltero de Norwico Custodi Thesaurariæ Regis quod eidem Episcopo Claves Rotulos memoranda & omnia alia ad Officium illud spectantia quæ sunt in custodia sua liberet custodienda. Teste ut supra, per ipsum Regem. *Pat.* 13. *E.* 2. *m.* 19.

(*t*) Rex commisit venerabili Patri W. Exoniensi Episcopo Officium Thesaurarij Scaccarij Regis, habendum cum omnibus ad Officium illud spectantibus, quamdiu Regi placuerit. In cujus &c. Teste Rege apud Ebor. 9° die Maij. Per ipsum Regem.

Et mandatum est Waltero de Norwico Custodi Officij Thesaurariæ prædictæ, quod eidem Episcopo Claves Rotulos memoranda & omnia alia ad dictum Officium spectantia, quæ sunt in custodia sua, liberet, custodienda in forma prædicta. Teste ut supra. *Pat.* 15. *E.* 2. *p.* 2. *m.* 16.

(*u*) Rex omnibus ad quos &c, Salutem. Sciatis quod ad instantem requisitionem venerabilis patris Walteri Exoniensis Episcopi, ipsum ab Officio Thesaurarij Scaccarij nostri quod aliquamdiu habuit ex commissione nostra, duximus exonerandum, & custodiam Officij prædicti dilecto & fideli nostro Waltero de Norwico uni Baronum de dicto Scaccario commisimus, habendam quousque de Thesauraria duximus providendum. In cujus &c. Teste Rege apud Turrim Londoniæ xxv° die Augusti. Per ipsum Regem, nunciante Rogero de Northburgh.

Et mandatum est præfato Episcopo, quod eidem Waltero Claves & alia officium prædictum tangentia liberet, custodienda in forma prædicta. Teste Rege ut supra. Nunciante R. de Northburgh. *Pat.* 15. *E.* 2. *p.* 1. *m.* 19.

(*w*) Mandatum est Clariciæ quæ fuit uxor Rogeri le Sauwage executrici testamenti ejusdem Rogeri defuncti, quod omnes Extractas quas penes se habet de tempore quo prædictus Rogerus fuit Justiciarius Regis tam ad diversas transgressiones in diversis Comitatibus Regni Regis Angliæ audiendas & terminandas & ad diversas Gaolas deliberandas assignatus quam aliunde, habeat ad Scaccarium Regis in crastino clausi Paschæ, . . Custodi Officij Thesaurarij Regis & . . Camerarijs de eodem Scaccario, ibidem liberandas. T. J. de Foxle primo die Marcij. *Hil. Brevia Retornab.* 15. *E.* 2. *Rot.* 86. *b.*

(*x*) Edward par la grace de Dieu &c, A nostre cher & foial Wauter de Norwyz Gardeyn de nostre Tresorie salutz. Nous vous mandoms, qe vouz facez ordeiner en tien manere de la sustenaunce de noz estalons & jumentz qe sont en le garde nostre bien amez frere Johan de Redemere Gardein daucuns nos haraz, & auffint de noz poleyns qe serront tretz ore ceste sefon, & demorront en la garde Hugh de Beaurepeyr, qil neient nulle defaute. Donne souz nostre Prive Seal a Porcestre, le viij jour Doctobre lan de nostre regne quinzisme. *Mich. Brev.* 15. *E.* 2. *Rot.* 40. *b.*

committed

Chap. XXI.   *of the* Exchequer.

committed to *W.* Archbishop of *York*, Primate of *England*, the Office of Treasurer of his Exchequer, during his Pleasure. And *Walter* Bishop of *Exeter* was commanded to deliver to him the Keys and other Things that belonged to the said Office (*y*).

Some Persons have been inclined to think, that the Office of *The King's Treasurer* (or, as we now call it, *Treasurer of England*) and the Office of *Treasurer of the Exchequer*, were two distinct Offices. As to that Matter, I shall here refer Precedents to the Reader's Consideration. *Walter* Bishop of *Carlile* is stiled, *Treasurer of the King's Exchequer of England*, and *The King's Treasurer*: *Peter de Rivall* is styled, *Treasurer of the King's Exchequer [of London]*, and *The King's Treasurer*: *Hugh de Pateshull, Treasurer of the Exchequer*, and *The King's Treasurer*. *William de Marche* was, by his Patent, to hold the Office of *Treasurer of the King's Exchequer*, in the same Manner as *J.* Bishop of *Ely*, late *the King's Treasurer*, and other *Treasurers there* held the same. And *Walter de Langeton*'s Patent was in like Form. All which Cases are set forth above in this Section. *Walter de Norwich* is stiled the King's Treasurer (*z*); and he is also styled Treasurer of the Exchequer (*a*). I suppose, the Instances of this Kind need not be multiplied. For whoever will compare Things together, may find most of the Treasurers during the Reigns of KKK. *Henry* III, *Edward* I, and *Edward* II, styled, sometimes *The King's Treasurer,* and sometimes *Treasurer of his Exchequer.*

It doth not appear to me, what Fee or Appointment the Treasurer in the most ancient Times was wont to receive of the King for the Execution of his Office. In the 4th Year of K. *Richard* I, *Richard Fitz-Neal* the Treasurer had xx *l* by Tale in Rent assigned to him in *Essenden* and *Beiford* (*b*): Which xx *l* was also paid to *William de Ely*

(*y*) Rex omnibus ad quos &c, Salutem. Sciatis quod commisimus Venerabili Patri W. Eboracensi Archiepiscopo Angliæ Primati, Officium Thesaurarij Scaccarij nostri, habendum cum omnibus ad officium illud spectantibus quamdiu nobis placuerit. In cujus &c; Teste Rege apud Westmon. tertio die Julij. Per ipsum Regem.
Et mandatum est W. Exoniensi Episcopo nuper Thesaurario Regis, quod eidem Archiepiscopo Rotulos Claves memoranda ac omnia alia Officium illud tangentia, quæ sunt in Custodia sua, liberet, custodienda in forma prædicta. Teste ut supra. *Pat.* 18. *E.* 2. *p.* 2. *m.* 5.

(*z*) Edward par la grace de Dieu &c, A nostre chier & foial Monf. Wauter de Norwiz nostre Tresorier, saluz. *Trin. Brevia* 9. *E.* 2. *Rot.* 60. *a.*

(*a*) Hereford. Idem [Gilbertus de Aylesford Miles] venit coram Waltero de Norwico Thesaurario hujus Scaccarij xxx die Marcij, & recognovit —. *Hil. Recognit.* 9. *E.* 2. *Rot.* 73. *a.*

(*b*) Et Ricardo Thesaurario Episcopo Lond[oniensi], xx l numero, in Essenden & in Beiford. *Mag. Rot.* 4. *R.* 1. *Rot.* 1. *a. Essex & Hurtf. inter Terras datas.*

a suc-

a succeeding Treasurer (*c*). But I am not sure that this yearly Sum of xx *l* was the Treasurer's Salary, or Part of it. In the Reign of K. *Henry* III, the yearly Fee or Salary allowed by the King to his Treasurer for the Execution of his Office, was C Marks (*d*). The said Salary of C Marks a Year was paid to *J*. Bishop of *Ely*, Treasurer, in the 15th Year of K. *Edward* I (*e*), to *W*. Bishop of *Coventry* and *Lichfeld*, Treasurer, in the 27th Year (*f*), to the same Treasurer in the 31st Year (*g*). But at that Time the King used to make other Provision for the Treasurers, by some beneficial Grant or ecclesiastical Preferment. K. *Henry* III granted to *Thomas de Wimondham* his Treasurer the first Wardship in *England* that fell next, and was worth fifty Pounds a Year, together with the Marriage of the Heir; unless the King should in the mean time provide for the said *Thomas* in some Dignity, Prebend, or ecclesiastical Benefice worth two hundred Marks a Year (*h*). In like Manner the Kings in those Times used to provide for their Chancellors and other Officers who were ecclesiastical Persons, by some Dignity or Benefice in the Church. K. *John*, in the ninth Year of his Reign, whilst the Bishoprick of *Exeter* was void and in the King's Hands, gave to *W. de Grey* his Chancellor, the Prebend which *Gilbert Basset* Archdeacon of *Tottenese* lately held (*i*);

and

(*c*) Et Willelmo Thesaurario, in Esenden & Beiford, xx l. *Mag. Rot.* 2. *Joh. Rot.* 3. *a*. *Essex & Hurtf.*

(*d*) *Paul. sup. ad ann.* 18. *H.* 3. Rex omnibus ad.

(*e*) *Lib.* 15. *E.* 1. *m.* 1. *& m.* 3.

(*f*) Rex Thesaurario & Camerarijs suis salutem. Liberate de thesauro nostro Venerabili patri W. Coventrensi & Lych. Episcopo Thesaurario nostro quadringentas marcas, videlicet de Terminis Paschæ & S. Michaelis de annis regni nostri vicesimo quarto, vicesimo quinto, vicesimo sexto, & vicesimo septimo, de annuo feodo suo Centum marcarum quod ei concessimus percipiendum in Officio prædicto. T. R. apud Westm. xvj die Octobris. *Lib.* 27. *E.* 1. *m.* 3.

(*g*) Rex Thesaurario & Camerarijs suis salutem. Liberate de thesauro nostro Venerabili Patri W. Coventrensi & Lych. Episcopo Thesaurario nostro Centum & quinquaginta marcas, videlicet de terminis Paschæ & S. Michaelis de anno regni nostri tricesimo Centum marcas, & de termino Paschæ anno regni nostri tricesimo primo quinquaginta marcas, de annuo feodo suo Centum marcarum, quod ei concessimus percipiendum in officio prædicto. T. Rege apud Villam S. Johannis de Perth xxx die Junij. *Lib.* 31. *E.* 1. *m.* 2.

(*h*) Rex omnibus &c salutem. Sciatis quod concessimus dilecto Clerico nostro Magistro Thomæ de Wimundham Thesaurario nostro, primam Custodiam quæ nobis accidet in Regno nostro, quæ valeat per annum quinquaginta libras cum maritagio hæredis ejusdem Custodiæ sine disparagatione, nisi eidem Thomæ prius providerimus in dignitate præbenda vel beneficio Ecclesiastico, quæ vel quod valeat annuatim ducentas marcas, quod ei bona fide facere promittimus quamcito facultas se optulerit; Salva provisione quam ad instantiam Edwardi primogeniti nostri concessimus Roberto Burnel Clerico filij nostri prædicti &c. T. R. apud Westmonasterium iiij die Aprilis. *Pat.* 50. *H.* 3. *m.* 20.

(*i*) Rex Capitulo Ecclesiæ Exoniensis &c. Sciatis quod concessimus, & quantum

ad

Chap. XXI.   *of the* EXCHEQUER.   43

and in the fame Year (whilft the Honour of *Eye* was in the King's Hands) prefented him to the Church of *Stradbroc,* upon the Refignation of *Eudo Martell* (*k*): Upon which Occafion *Eudo* had the perpetual Vicarage of that Church allotted to him, and was to pay *Walter de Grey* one Befant yearly *nomine penfionis* (*l*). K. *John* granted to *Ralf de Nevill* (then his Vice-chancellor or Keeper of his Seal) the Church of *Lutegarfhal,* and the Church of *Stratton,* to hold during his Life (*m*).

Some other mifcellaneous Things relating to the Treafurer may be here fet down. The Treafurer fometimes fat and acted in the *King's Court*. A final Concord was made in the King's Court at *Weftminfter* on the Morrow of St. *John Baptift* in the third Year of K. *Henry* III, before *Euftace de Faucumberg* the King's Treafurer, *Martin de Patefhull, Robert de Nevill, Geoffrey Gibewin* Juftices, and other the King's Liegemen, between *Alice de Holewell* Demandant, and *William* Abbot of *Weftminfter* Deforciant, concerning the Advowfon of the Church of *Holewell* (*n*). In the 18th Year of K. *Edward* I, the Treafurer

was

ad nos pertinet, dedimus dilecto Cancellario noftro W. de Gray, præbendam in Ecclefia veftra quæ fuit Gilleberti Baffet quondam Archidiaconi Tottenefiæ, & vacat & ad noftram fpectat donationem ratione Epifcopatus Exonienfis vacantis & in manu noftra exiftentis; Ipfumq; ad eam vobis præfentamus, rogantes quatenus eum in corporalem ejus poffeffionem, fecundum confuetudinem Ecclefiæ veftræ, mittatis. T. Domino Wintonienfi Epifcopo apud Wudeftok vij die Augufti. *Pat.* 9. *J. m.* 5.

(*k*) Dominus W. de Gray Cancellarius habet Literas patentes de præfentatione ad Ecclefiam de Stradebroc, ad refignationem Eudonis Martell perfonæ ejufdem Ecclefiæ, quæ eft de donatione Domini Regis ratione Honoris de Heya exiftentis in manu fua. Et diriguntur Litteræ ad Dominum Norwicenfem. *Pat.* 9. *J. m.* 1.

(*l*) Idem Eudo habet literas patentes directas eidem Epifcopo, de perpetua vicaria ejufdem Ecclefiæ, reddendo inde annuatim prædicto W. j bifantium nomine penfionis. *Ib. juxt. m.* 1.

(*m*) J. Dei gratia Rex Angliæ &c, Omnibus Chrifti fidelibus præfentem cartam infpecturis falutem. Noveritis nos intuitu Dei, conceffiffe & quantum ad nos pertinet dediffe & hac carta noftra confirmaffe, dilecto Clerico noftro Radulfo de Nevill Ecclefiam de Lutegarefhal cum omnibus pertinentijs fuis quæ de noftra eft advocatione: Habendam & tenendam toto tempore vitæ fuæ, adeo bene libere quiete & integre ficut aliquis prædecefforum fuorum eam umquam melius liberius quietius & integrius tenuit. T. Domino W. Burdigalenfi Archiepifcopo, W. Comite de Ferrarijs, R. Comite Ceftriæ, Hugone de Gornaco, Brieno de Infula, Roberto de Roppele, Henrico filio Comitis, Hugone de Berneval. Datum per manum ipfius Radulfi de Nevill apud Niort. fexta die Maij anno regni noftri fextodecimo. *Chart.* 16. *J. m.* 11.

J. Dei gratia Rex Angliæ &c Omnibus &c. Noveritis nos intuitu Dei conceffiffe & quantum ad nos pertinet dediffe & hac carta noftra confirmaffe dilecto Clerico noftro Radulfo de Nevill Ecclefiam de Stratton cum omnibus pertinentijs fuis quæ de noftra eft advocatione: Habendam & tenendam toto tempore vitæ fuæ, adeo bene libere quiete & integre, ficut aliquis prædeceforum fuorum eam umquam melius liberius quietius & integrius tenuit. T. ut prox. fupra. Data eadem. *Ib. juxt.*

(*n*) Hæc eft Finalis Concordia facta in

Curia

was associated to the Justices of the Bank to determine Causes. As in the Case of *William de Wasthull* (*o*). Sometimes the Treasurer acted as the King's Almoner; as in the Cases cited hereunder (*p*). Further: A Manucaption having been entered into before the King's Treasurer at St. *Edmunds*, for securing certain Debts due to the King; the Treasurer, by his Letter to the Barons, directs them to cause the said Manucaption to be duly enrolled at the Exchequer (*q*). *William Trussell*, late Sheriff of *Kent*, appointed *Elyas de Morton* his Clerk, to render for him an Account of the Goods and Chattels taken by the said Sheriff in the Manors of the Archbishop of *Canterbury* in that County. *Elias* came and offered to pass the said Account. But in regard the Treasurer would have it passed in his Presence, and he was then going in all Haste to the King in *Scotland*, *Elias* had Day given him till the Treasurer's Return to pass the said Account (*r*). K. *Edward*

Curia Domini Regis apud Westmon. in crastino S. Johannis Baptistæ anno regni Regis Henrici filij Regis Johannis tercio, coram Eustacio de Faucumberg Domini Regis Thesaurario, Martino de Pateshull, Roberto de Nevill, Gaufrido Gibewin Justic. & alijs Domini Regis fidelibus tunc ibi præsentibus, Inter Aliciam de Holewell petentem per Thomam Malhore positum loco suo ad lucrandum vel perdendum, & Willelmum Abbatem de Westmonasterio deforciantem, de advocatione Ecclesiæ de Holewell, unde assisa ultimæ præsentationis summonita fuit inter eos in præfata Curia, scilicet quod, *the Abbot released the said Advowson to* Alice *and her Heirs, saving to the Abbot and his Successours the Pension anciently wont to be paid to the Abbey for the said Church of* Holewell. *Ex autogr. pede Finis inter archiva Eccl. B. Petri Westmon.*

(*o*) Et dictum est eis [Justiciarijs de Banco] quod associato sibi Thesaurario & vocatis partibus faciant quod de jure fuerit faciendum. Et Mathæus postea coram Thes. & Justic. &c venit, & bene cognoscit
Ryl. Pl. Parl. p. 16. 17. *anno* 18. E. 1.

(*p*) Robertus la Waite r c de xiij d de j virgata terræ, sicut continetur in Rot. viij° Regis J, qui debent dari in elemosina per manum Thesaurarij pro Rege, Et dati fuerunt; Et quietus est. *Mag. Rot.* 2. *H.* 3. *Rot.* 7. *a.*

Hertford. Stephanus le Wayte reddit ad Scaccarium xiij d distribuendos pauperibus per manum Thesaurarij, pro quadam terra quam de Rege tenet in Capite in Rindewell. *Mich. Commun.* 29. *H.* 3. *Rot.* 1. *a.*

(*q*) W. de Langeton Domini Regis Thesaurarius Socijs & Amicis suis Dominis P. de Wylegby & Baronibus de Scaccario Domini Regis prædicto, salutem & dilectionem sinceram; Quia Venerabilis Pater Dominus W. Eliensis Episcopus, manucepit coram nobis apud Sanctum Edmundum *such a Day*, pro omnibus debitis Simonis de Elefwurth nuper defuncti in quibus Domino Regi tenebatur — : Vobis mandamus, quatinus negotium & formam manucapcionis supradictæ, una cum circumstancijs & condicionibus ipsam contingentibus, debito modo irrotulari faciatis — &c. Bene valete. Datum apud S. Edmundum, 22 die Novembris supradicto, anno regni Regis E. xx. *Mich. Commun.* 25. E. 1. *inter Manucaptiones.*

(*r*) Kancia. Willelmus Trussel nuper Vicecomes Kanciæ ponit loco suo Elyam de Morton Clericum suum, ad reddendum pro eodem Willelmo compotum suum de bonis & Catallis captis per eundem Vicecomitem in Comitatu Kanciæ, de Manerijs Venerabilis patris R. Archiepiscopi Cantuariensis anno xxiiij° & xxv°, per quandam billam Baronibus hic directam nunc quarto die Julij, per Johannem de Insula Baronem Scaccarij sub Sigillo ejusdem, quæ invenietur
inter

ward I, sent a Writ of the Privy Seal to the Barons of the Exchequer, for raising of Foot-soldiers in the Counties of *Chester* and *Lancaster* to serve against the *Scots*; and a Letter which had been sent to the King by *Reginald de Grey* upon the same Affair. The Treasurer sent a Letter to the Chancellor of *England* under his (the Treasurer's) Privy Seal, by the Hand of Master *Richard de Havering*, with both those Letters inclosed in it; and desired the Chancellor to cause Letters Patent to be made to the said *Reginald de Grey* for levying of Foot-soldiers according to the Tenor of the said inclosed Letters, and to deliver them to the said *Richard de Havering*, who was intrusted to get the said Business dispatched, and to pay the Wages of the said Soldiers (*s*). In the 26th Year of K. *Edward* I, the Treasurer by his Letter signified to the Barons of the Exchequer, that he had given Day to *John de Lytegreynes*, late *Custos* of the Archbishoprick of *York sede vacante*, till the Morrow of the *Trinity*, to account for the Issues of that Archbishoprick, and of other Escheats hereunder mentioned. And thereupon the Barons ordered it to be entered in the *Memoranda* of the Exchequer, that the said *John* should account for the said Issues at that Day (*t*). The same King by Writ commanded the Treasurer and

inter petitiones de anno xxvj°. Et idem Elyas modo venit, offerens se ad reddendum compotum prædictum. Et quia Thesaurarius vult eundem compotum fieri & audiri in sua præsentia, & ipse instanter iturus est ad partes Scotiæ ad Dominum Regem agentem ibidem, datus est dies præfato Elyæ essendi hic, ad reddendum compotum prædictum ad reditum præfati Thesaurarij a partibus prædictis. Et super hoc idem Elias liberavit hic duas cedulas, per quas asserit prædictum compotum reddere debere, quæ sunt in custodia Rememoratoris Thesaurarij. Postea computavit; sicut contineatur in magno Rotulo xxv°, in Kancia. *Trin. Fines* 26. *Ed.* 1. *Rot.* 94. *a. in bund.* 25 & 26. *E.* 1.

(*s*) Baronibus, pro Peditibus eligendis pro Scotia. *A Letter or Writ of Privy Seal from the King to the Barons, reciting a Letter from* Reginald de Grey *to the King, and the same Letter from* Reginald de Grey, *are here enrolled one after another. Then it follows thus*, Postea mandavit Thesaurarius Cancellario in hæc verba. Salutem quam sibi: Mittimus vobis per Magistrum Ricardum de Haveringg, litteras quas Dominus Rex nobis misit sub privato sigillo suo, & litteras Domini Reginaldi de Gray directas Domino Regi dictis litteris regijs interclusas, quas penes vos custodire velitis usq; ad adventum nostrum apud Eboracum; vos rogantes quatinus Litteras patentes sub magno Sigillo Regis fieri faciatis dicto Domino Reginaldo, pro hominibus peditibus de Comitatibus Cestriæ & Lancastriæ eligendis, juxta tenorem litterarum prædictarum, & dictas Litteras Patentes dicto Magistro Ricardo de Haveringe tradatis, cui injunximus sequi negotium prædictum cum omni festinatione qua poterit & effectu; Tradi enim fecimus eidem magistro Ricardo denarios pro vadijs prædictorum peditum, juxta tenorem prædictarum literarum. Bene valete. Datum apud Westmonasterium xiiij die Maij, mane. Et sciendum quod literæ Domini Regis mittebantur sub privato sigillo Thesaurarij interclusæ, per magistrum Ricardum de Haveringg. *Pas. Communia* 26. *E.* 1. *Rot.* 75. *b. in bund.* 25 & 26. *E.* 1.

(*t*) Litera Thesaurarij missa Baronibus. Quia dedimus diem Johanni de Lytegreynes nuper

and Barons, to make Allowances or Assignments to several Persons to whom the King was indebted for Prices or Captures of Wools, Leathers, and other small Things taken of them to his Use, and likewise for Moneys and Moneys-worth taken in Abbeys and religious Houses to his Use, in Satisfaction of such their respective Debts. And the Treasurer and Barons agreed, that the same should be done accordingly, although the Treasurer happened to be absent at the Time of doing it (*u*). *Walter*, Bishop of *Coventry* and *Lichfeld*, Treasurer, sent the Letter hereunder recited to the Barons of the Exchequer, with a Letter from the King directed to the said Treasurer and Barons inclosed in it, directing the Barons to put the King's said Letter in Execution (*w*). *Walter Renaud*, Treasurer, having received a Writ from

nuper Custodi Archiepiscopatus Eboracensis sede vacante, ad computandum de exitibus ejusdem Archiepiscopatus in crastino Trinitatis apud Eboracum; dedimus eciam eidem eundem diem, ad computandum de exitibus Escaetriæ Honoris de Tikehull, aliarumq; terrarum quæ sunt in custodia ejusdem : Vobis mandamus, quod demandam quam facitis eidem Johanni de compoto reddendo de exitibus terrarum Alani de Aldefeld & Willelmi de Chauncy de Monketon, de quibus Petrus de Lound debet ipsum acquietare ut dicit, sicut idem Petrus recognovit in Scaccario, per Rotulum in Memorandis de termino Sancti Michaelis anno decimo octavo incipiente; Et similiter demandam quam facitis eidem Johanni, de hoc quod acquietet Jordanum Foliot de x l versus Dominum nostrum Regem, de quibus habuit diem ad computandum in crastino clausi Paschæ, ponatis in respectum usq; in crastinum S. Trinitatis. Datum apud Stocfeld xº kl. Maij anno Regni Domini nostri Regis xxvjº. Et ponitur in Memorandis, quod idem Johannes respondebit de omnibus exitibus suprascriptis ad prædictum diem crastinum S. Trinitatis. *Pas. Communia* 26. E. 1. *Rot.* 74. *a. in bund.* 25 & 26. E. 1.

(*u*) *Anglia.* Memorandum quod cum Dominus Rex mandaverit Thesaurario & Baronibus hic per Brevia sua de Magno Sigillo, irrotulata alibi inter recorda hujus termini, quod cum ipse rex teneatur diversis hominibus de regno Angliæ, de prisis de ipsis factis ad opus Regis de lanis corijs & alijs minutis rebus, ac eciam de denarijs & de narratis captis ad opus Regis, per Scrutinium in Abbathijs & alijs domibus Religiosis & alibi in Regno Angliæ dudum factum; de quibus Rex nondum satisfecit; præfati Thesaurarius & Barones satisfaciant omnibus illis quibus Rex tenetur in forma prædicta, per allocationem debitorum quæ ipsi creditores Regis Regi debent, aut per assignationem debitorum quæ Regi debentur eisdem creditoribus faciendam : W. Coventrensis & Lichfeldensis Episcopus Thesaurarius, Magister Ricardus de Abyndon & Humphridus de Waleden Barones &c, modo præsentes concordarunt, quod de omnimodis debitis quæ debitores Regis debent Regi hic ad Scaccarium, exceptis firmis & redditibus & finibus factis cum Rege hoc anno, fiat assignatio predictis creditoribus Regis super præmissis, & quod assignacio hujusmodi & similiter allocacio debitorum in forma superius annotata, fiant secundum discrecionem Baronum &c, non expectata præsencia præfati Thesaurarij, si ipsum aliquociens abesse contigerit cum assignacio & allocacio hujusmodi fuerint faciendæ. Postea J. de Benstede Cancellarius & W. de Carleton Baro &c, concordarunt præmissa fieri ut prædictum est. *Trin. Communia* 35. E. 1. *Rot.* 59. *b. in bund.* 34 & 35. E. 1. *b. parte* 1.

(*w*) Socijs suis & amicis karissimis Baronibus de Scaccario Domini Regis, W. permissione divina Coventrensis & Lich. Episcopus, ipsius Regis Thesaurarius, salutem & sinceram in Domino caritatem. Directas nobis

from the King, sent it inclosed, in the Letter hereunder written, to *William de Carleton*, one of the Barons of the Exchequer, desiring him to get it executed with all Speed (*x*). The Treasurer and some of the Barons being absent from the Exchequer at such a Time, the other Barons would not then proceed in a certain Business that came before them (*y*). K. *Edward* II, in the first Year of his Reign, intending to have *Walter de Langeton* Bishop of *Chester*, late Treasurer, called to an Account before Justices assigned, for certain Misdemeanors which he had committed in his Office of Treasurer, commanded the Barons of the Exchequer, by the Writ of Privy Seal hereunder cited, to find out by the best Means they could, and to set down in Writing all the Trespasses and Damages which the said late Treasurer had committed, as well in wrongful Allowances, false Enrollments, and false Judgments, in taking Champert for the King's Debts, in converting to his own Use a great deal of the King's Treasure, and causing the same to be paid at his own House or elsewhere at his Pleasure, in acquitting Accomptants unduly, in setting Ferms at an Undervalue for Bribes, and for other Misdemeanors; and to certify the same to Monsieur *William de Bereford*, whom the King had appointed to hear and determine the Complaints made against the said late Treasurer: and herein the Barons were to act with Diligence and Fidelity, as they tendered their Oaths and Allegiance (*z*). The Bishop of *Worcester* Chancellor of *England* came to the Exchequer, and declared to the Barons and Chamberlains there, that it was the King's Pleasure, that *John de Sandale* the King's Treasurer should act no longer in that Office till further Order; and that he brought his Mes-

nobis & vobis Literas Domini nostri Regis, quas aperuimus & inspeximus, vobis mittimus præsentibus interclusas; Rogantes ut vice nostra & vestra ipsarum execucionem fieri faciatis. In Christo feliciter & perpetue valeatis. Datum apud Karliolum xj die Februarij. *Pas. Brevia* 35. *E*. 1. *Rot*. 39. *b*.

(*x*) A soen cher amy Sire Willem de Carleton Baroun del Escheker nostre Seignur le Roi, Gauter Renaud Treforer nostre Seignur le Roi salutz & chiers amistes. Joe vous envoy enclos denz cestes un Bref que me vint de par nostre Seignur le Roi icoe Lundy a Totenham, & vous pri que hastivement vues cestes Lettres, facez execucion de meismes le Bref en touz poins, solom le maundement nostre seignur le Roi, & solom quil est contenu en meismes le Bref. Nostre seignur vous gard. Escrit a Totenham icest Lundy au vespre. *Mich. Brevia* 1. *E*. 2. *Rot*. 16. *b*.

(*y*) Londonia. De quodam tenemento in vico Tamisiæ capto in manum Regis. *Process was had in this Affair*. Et quia Thesaurarius & quidam Barones modo absentes sunt, sine quorum præsencia Cancellarius & Barones modo præsentes nolunt ulterius procedere in præmissis, datus est dies ex præfixione Curiæ, prædictis Magistro [Hospitalis S. Bartholomæi Londoniæ] & Nicholao [de Rokesle], usq; a die Paschæ in unum mensem, eo statu quo nunc; Et idem dies datus est prædicto Ricardo [de Stanlowe] qui sequitur pro Rege ———. *Hil. Communia* 25 & 26. *E*. 1. *Rot*. 58. *b*.

(*z*) *Mich. Brevia* 1. *E*. 2. *Rot*. 21. *a*.

sage

sage by the King's Command (*a*). In fine: by ancient Right and Usage the King's Treasurers for the Time being, used to receive of the Sheriff of *Oxfordshire* and *Berkshire* yearly, one Ship-load of Wood for Fuel, or else Lx*s*. in lieu of it. In the 51st Year of K. *Henry* III. Master *Thomas de Wymondeham* Treasurer received it (*b*); in the 9th Year of K. *Edward* II. *Walter de Norwich* Treasurer had it (*c*); and others in other Years. This Wood was what they called *Busca*, or *Mortuus Boscus*, dry Wood for Fuel (*d*).

Sometimes there was at the Exchequer an Officer called the Treasurer's Lieutenant; which might be the same with the Treasurer's Assignee or Attorney, as he is called above in Sect. 2. in the Case of *Walter de Malclerc* and *Peter de Rivall*. This Lieutenant acted for the Treasurer in his Absence, or, if there was no Treasurer, executed the Treasurer's Office *par interim*. He was in effect the Treasurer's Deputy, or Vice-treasurer; for *Locum tenens* signified a Deputy, or a Person that acted in another's stead, and was used in many other Cases besides this: that is to say, there were Lieutenants to Officers of divers Kinds. For Example: there was a *Locum tenens* of the King's Chancellor (*e*); of the Archbishop of *York* (*f*); of a Sheriff

(*a*) Memorandum quod Venerabilis Pater W. Wygorniensis Episcopus Cancellarius Angliæ venit hic die Sabbati videlicet xxiij° die Octobris, & convocatis Baronibus & Camerarijs, nunciavit eisdem ex parte Regis, quod certis de causis non est voluntatis Regis ad præsens, quod Johannes de Sandale Thesaurarius Regis se intromittat amplius de eodem officio, donec Rex aliud inde &c; asserens se habere mandatum ad hoc quod ipse nunciaret hoc eidem Johanni ex parte Regis. *Mich. Commun. 5. E. 2. Rot. 18. b.*

(*b*) Oxon. & Berk. Scias quod Thesaurarij Regis qui pro tempore fuerint residentes in Scaccario, ex antiqua consuetudine percipere consueverunt singulis annis, per manus Vicecomitis Berk. unam bonam navatam Buscæ, vel Lx s pro eadem Busca: Et ideo Rex mandat, quod ipsam Buscam vel prædictos denarios habeat ad Scaccarium in octabis S. Martini, Magistro Thomæ de Wimundeham nunc Thesaurario Regis solvendos. *Ex Memor. 51. H. 3. Rot. 2. b.*

(*c*) Memorandum quod computante Ricardo de Wyndesore Vicecomite Oxoniæ & Berk. hic ad Scaccarium die Veneris proximo ante festum Apostolorum Simonis & Judæ Loc Anno, videlicet de anno octavo, W. de Norwico Thesaurarius recognovit sibi satisfactum esse per ipsum Ricardum Vicecomitem, de una Navata Buscæ de dicto anno octavo, quam ad Thesaurarium qui pro tempore fuerit singulis annis spectat habendam de Vicecomite dictorum Comitatuum qui pro tempore fuerit, præter firmas Regi debitas de dictis Comitatibus, & temporibus Progenitorum Regis spectabat &c. *Mich. Communia 9. E. 2. Rot. 89. b.*

(*d*) De busca data. Mandatum est H. de Nevill, quod habere faciat Priori Hospitalis S. Thomæ de Stamford xx carectatas de mortuo bosco in bosco de Dodinton ad focum suum. *Cl. 14. H. 3. m. 20.*

(*e*) —veut le Roy qe celes soient returnez au Chaunceler ou a son lieu tenaunt, & qil pregne resnable Fin sur ceo selom la quantite de la chose—. *Pas. Commun. 26 & 27. E. 1. Rot. 24. b.*

Et missa est eadem Inquisitio sub sigillo Thesaurarij, W. de Hamilton tenenti locum Cancellarij; & mandatum est eidem, quod dicto Priori habere faciat Literas Patentes Regis super Licentia prædicta, per Finem prædictum. *Ib. Pas. Fines, Rot. 67. a.*

(*f*) A *Writ directed* Archiepiscopo Ebor. vel ejus locum tenenti. *Trin. Brevia pro Rege 20. E. 1. Rot. 38. a.*

and

and Hundredor (*g*); of the Earl Marshal of *England* (*h*); of the Constable of the Tower of *London* (*i*); and of the Dean of *London* (*k*): There hath also been Mention made of the *Vices gerentes* of the Treasurer and Barons of the Exchequer (*l*). In the 35th Year of K. *Edward* I. *Walter de Langeton*, Bishop of *Coventry* and *Lichfield*, Treasurer of *England*, made *William de Carleton* his Lieutenant by his Letter. Whereupon, on the Morrow of St. *Hilary*, *Walter de Norwic*, in the Presence of *John de Benstede*, Chancellor of the Exchequer, *Roger de Hegham*, Master *Richard de Abingdon*, and *H. de Waleden*, Barons of the Exchequer, *&c.* declared to the said *William de Carleton* on the Treasurer's Behalf, that it was the Treasurer's Pleasure, that in his Absence he should hold his Place for him here in the Exchequer, and should do all Things belonging to the Office of Treasurer, which the Treasurer himself might do if he were present in Court, except only as to the admitting of gross Fines in the Exchequer; and that the said *William* should not intermeddle in any thing relating to the Receipt of the Exchequer (*m*). King *Edward* II. in the

(*g*) *Trin. Commun.* 1. *E.* 2. *Rot.* 74. *b.*

(*h*) A toutz qi cestes Lettres verront ou orront, nous Johan Botetourte Conestable en la Cumpaignie le Counte de Garenne assigne parmy le Counte de Hereford Conestable Dengleterre, & Johan de la Huse Marefchal assigne a meisme la Cumpaignie par Monsieur Johan Lovel lieu tenaunt le Counte Marefchal Dengleterre, salutz en Dieu —. Done a Dunlaverdyn 34 Edw. I. *Mich. Commun.* 2. *E.* 2. *Rot.* 36. *a.*

(*i*) —— Et in continenti liberatus est Eliæ Puger Tenenti locum .. Constabularij Turris Londoniæ præsenti in Curia custodiendus in eadem Turri &c. *Trin. Communia* 2. *E.* 2. *Rot.* 89. *a.*

(*k*) —— Ac jam ex parte tenentis locum dicti Decani & Capituli loci prædicti, Rex acceperit, quod —: *So the King commands the Barons*, quod audita querela tenentis locum Decani & Capituli, eis in præmissis faciant debitum & festinum justitiæ complementum. *Mich. Brevia* 12. *E.* 2. *Rot.* 67. *a.*

(*l*) Baronibus, ad certificandum [Regi] de debitis Archiepiscopi Cantuariensis. Rex Thesaurario & Baronibus suis de Scaccario vel eorum vices gerentibus salutem. *Mich. Commun.* 25. *E.* 1. *Rot. notato G. a.* The Return made to this Writ is, Excellentissimo Principi Domino suo Reverendo, Domino E Dei gratia Regi Angliæ illustri, Domino Hiberniæ, et Duci Aquitaniæ, Devoti sui Barones de Scaccario suo fidele semper servicium cum omni reverencia & honore. Sciat vestra Magestas reverenda, quod —. *And concludes*, Valeat Excellencia vestra per tempora diuturna. Scriptum in dicto Scaccario apud Westmonasterium prædicto xiiij die circa horam nonam. *Ib.*

(*m*) Memorandum pro W. de Carleton. Walterus de Langeton Coventrensis & Lich. Episcopus Thesaurarius Angliæ, mandavit Litteram suam Willelmo de Carleton Baroni hujus Scaccarij in hæc verba. Salutem quam sibi; Quia nuper in recessu nostro de Londonia oblivioni dedimus vobis tetigisse quod locum nostrum in Scaccario in absencia nostra teneretis; de fidelitate & industria vestra plurimum confidentes, ut locum nostrum in Scaccario prædicto tenere velitis, prout Dominus Walterus de Norwyco vobis dicet ex parte nostra, dum nos abesse contigerit, petimus & rogamus; feliciter in Christo valeatis. Scriptum apud Wynch. viij die Januarij. Et prædictus Walterus modo in crastino S. Hillarij, coram J. de Benstede Cancellario hujus Scaccarij, R. de Hegham

the 5th Year of his Reign, by Writ of the Great Seal constituted *Walter de Norwich* (one of the Barons of the Exchequer) Lieutenant of the Treasurer of the said Exchequer, until the King should appoint a Treasurer there, or order otherwise; whereupon he was sworn and admitted to that Office, before the Chancellor of *England*, the Bishop of *Coventry*, and others of the King's Council, at the Exchequer (*n*). Afterwards the King made the Bishop of *Coventry* and *Lichfield*. Treasurer; and the Bishop being by some other Affairs hindered from executing the Office of Treasurer for the present, the King continued *Walter de Norwich* in the Place of the Treasurer's Lieutenant, with Instructions for him to act therein till the King should order otherwise (*o*). The same King, in the 6th Year of his Reign, constituted *John de Sandale* Lieutenant of his Treasurer in the Exchequer, during his Pleasure. And *Walter de Norwich* was commanded to deliver to the said *John* the Keys, and all other Things belonging to the said Office that were in his Custody, by Chirograph

Hegham, Magistro Ricardo de Abyndon, & H. de Waleden, Baronibus Scaccarij &c, dixit eidem Willelmo ex parte dicti Thesaurarij, quod idem Thesaurarius vult quod teneat locum suum hic in Scaccario, & faciat omnia quæ ad Officium Thesaurarij pertinent &c, & quæ idem Thesaurarius faceret si præsens esset in Curia &c, dum ipsum Thesaurarium abesse contigerit, grossis finibus faciendis in Scaccario duntaxat exceptis; Et quod de aliquibus tangentibus receptam Scaccarij in nullo se intromittat. *Hil. Commun.* 35. *E.* 1. *Rot.* 31. *a. Parte* 2.

(*n*) Anglia. Cum Rex per Breve suum de Magno Sigillo datum apud Langele xxiij die Octobris hoc anno quinto, quod est inter Communia de eodem anno, mandaverit Baronibus hic, quod cum ipse Rex dilectum & fidelem suum Walterum de Norwyco unum Baronum de Scaccario constituerit Tenentem locum Thesaurarij de eodem Scaccario, quousq; Rex providerit de Thesaurario ibidem, vel duxerit aliud inde &c, quod Barones eidem Waltero tamquam Tenenti locum Thesaurarij intendant &c, idem Walterus præsens &c die Lunæ xxv die Octobris, præsentibus W. Wygornienfi Episcopo Cancellario Angliæ, W. Coventrensi & Lich. Episcopo, & alijs de Consilio, admissus est &c, & præstitit sacramentum coram eis de bene & fideliter se habendo in eodem officio &c. *Mich. Commun.* 5. *E.* 2. *Rot.* 18. *b.*

(*o*) Baronibus & Camerarijs. Cum Rex nuper assignaverit dilectum & fidelem suum Walterum de Norwyco unum Baronum de Scaccario suo Locum tenentem Thesaurarij Regis in eodem Scaccario quousq; Thesaurarium ibidem fecisset Rex vel aliud inde duxisset ordinandum, & postmodum Rex commisisset Venerabili Patri W. Coventrensi & Lich. Episcopo officium Thesaurarij in Scaccario prædicto usq; ad proximum Parliamentum, ac præfatus Walterus pro eo quod idem Episcopus super executionem officij illius quibusdam de causis fuit impeditus, prædictum officium Locum Thesaurarij tenentis hucusq; continuaverit in Scaccario supradicto: Rex continuationem illam acceptans, vult quod idem Walterus locum Thesaurarij sui in eodem Scaccario ulterius teneat & ea quæ ad officium illud pertinent faciat & exequatur, quousq; Rex duxerit aliud ordinandum; prout in Literis suis patentibus eidem Waltero inde confectis plenius continetur. Et ideo Rex mandat quod eidem Waltero in hijs quæ ad officium Thesaurariæ prædictæ pertinent intendentes sitis & auxiliantes sicut prædictum est. T. Rege apud Ebor. xvij die Maij anno quinto. *Trin. Brevia* 5. *E.* 2. *Rot.* 52. *a.*

to be made between them: And the Barons of the Exchequer were commanded to be Intendant to the said *John* as the King's Lieutenant in his Exchequer (*p*). In the 19th Year of the same King, the Archbishop of *York*, the King's Treasurer, went into the North by the King's Command to dispatch some Business of the King's and of his own there, and was to stay in those Parts for some Time. Hereupon the King appointed *Roger Beler* to hold the Place of the said Treasurer in the Exchequer during his Absence; provided that the Archbishop, when he returned to the Exchequer, should hold the Office of Treasurer, as he held the same before his late Recess (*q*).

III. As to the Chancellor of the Exchequer, he seems to have been an Officer appointed to be a Controul or Check upon the Treasurer. In the 18th Year of K. *Henry* III. *John Mansell* was appointed to execute a certain Office at the Exchequer. I cannot tell what Office it was, unless it was that of Chancellor. The Appointment was by close Writ, in this Manner: The King, by the Writ directed to *Hugh de Pateshull* Treasurer, sent *John Mansell* to reside at the Exchequer of *Receipt*, and to have a Counter-roll of all Things pertaining to the said *Receipt*; and commanded the Treasurer to admit him accordingly (*r*). In the 32d Year of K. *Henry* III. *Ralph de*

(*p*) Rex omnibus ad quos &c. Salutem. De fidelitate circumspectione & industria dilecti Clerici nostri Johannis de Sandale plenius confidentes, ipsum Johannem tenentem locum Thesaurarij nostri in Scaccario nostro quamdiu nobis placuerit constituimus per praesentes. Teste Rege apud Wyndefore 4° die Octobris. Per ipsum Regem, nunciante .. Comite Pembrochiae.

Et mandatum est Waltero de Norwyco, quod eidem Johanni Claves & omnia alia Officium illud tangentia quae sunt in Custodia sua per Cyrographum inter ipsos inde conficiendum liberet, custodienda in forma praedicta. Teste ut supra.

Et Mandatum est Baronibus Regis de Scaccario, quod eidem Johanni tanquam locum tenenti Regis in Scaccario praedicto sint intendentes. Teste ut supra. *Pat.* 6. *E.* 2. *p.* 1. *m.* 14.

(*q*) Rex dilecto & fideli suo Rogero Beler Salutem. Cum venerabilis pater W. Eboracensis Archiepiscopus Thesaurarius noster, pro quibusdam negotijs nostris & suis in partibus borialibus expediendis de mandato nostro versus easdem partes se divertat, ibidem per aliquod tempus moraturum; volumus quod vos locum ipsius Thesaurarij nostri in Scaccario nostro dum sic absens fuerit teneatis: Et ideo vobis mandamus, quod ad ea quae ad dictum Officium pertinent in Scaccario praedicto, dum idem Archiepiscopus sic absens fuerit, intendatis; Ita tamen quod praefatus Archiepiscopus cum a partibus praedictis ad dictum Scaccarium redierit, Officium Thesaurarij nostri teneat, prout illud tenuit ante recessum suum ab eodem. In cujus &c. Teste Rege apud Havering atte Boure 9° die Augusti. Per ipsum Regem. *Pat.* 19. *E.* 2. *p.* 1. *m.* 31.

(*r*) Rex dilecto & fideli suo Hugoni de Patteshull Thesaurario suo salutem. Mittimus ad vos dilectum clericum nostrum Johannem Maunsel ad residendum loco nostro [*or*, vestro] ad Scaccarium nostrum de Recepta, & ad habendum Rotulum unum de hijs quae ad praedictam Receptam pertinent: Et ideo vobis mandamus, quod ipsum Johannem ad hoc admittatis. T. R. apud Keninton v die Julij. *Cl.* 18. *H.* 3. *m.* 16.

Leicestre

Leiceſtre with the King's Leave ſurrendered to the King the Office of Chancellor of the Exchequer (*s*); and the King committed the Exchequer-Seal to *Edward de Weſtminſtre* (*t*). The ſame King, by his Writ, commanded *Albric de Fiſcamp* to execute the Office of Chancellor in his Exchequer (*u*). K. *Henry* III. gave Leave to Maſter *Godfrey Giffard*, Chancellor of the Exchequer (*w*), to ſubſtitute a fit Perſon to execute his Office, as often as his Affairs ſhould give him Occaſion to withdraw from the Exchequer (*x*). The King, by his Writ, commanded the Treaſurer to deliver the Seal of the Exchequer to *Roger de la Leye*, to be kept by him during the King's Pleaſure. The Seal was delivered accordingly; and *Roger* was ſworn *de Sigillo fideliter cuſtodiendo* (*y*). In the ſame Record, *Roger* is ſtiled Chancellor of the Exchequer (*z*). K. *Edward* I. (*Anno Regni* 5°) made *Geoffrey de Neubaud* Chancellor of the Exchequer during Pleaſure (*a*). K.
Edward

(*s*) Rex mandat Baronibus, quod Radulphus de Leyceſtria de Licentia Regis remiſit Regi Officium Cancellarij de Scaccario, in quo Regi laudabiliter eſt obſecutus; Pro quo Rex ipſum habet ſpecialiter commendatum; & Barones habeant ſimiliter ipſum recommendatum. B e in f M. *Trin. Commun.* 32. *H.* 3. *Rot.* 8. *b.*

(*t*) Rex Baronibus; Volumus quod Edwardus [de] Weſtminſtre habeat Cuſtodiam Sigilli noſtri Scaccarij, & quod Magiſter Nicholaus de Sancto Albano ſit Rememorator noſter in eodem Scaccario. *Ib. Rot.* 8. *b.*

(*u*) Albrico de Fiſcampo. Rex mandat eidem, Cum de Conſilio noſtro providerimus, quod vos moram faciatis in Officio Cancellarij in Scaccario noſtro, Vobis mandamus quod eidem Officio diligenter intendatis, Et hoc nullatenus omittatis. T. &c. *Mich. Commun.* 49. *H.* 3. *Rot.* 1. *a.*

(*w*) Sumerſet. Præceptum eſt Vicecomiti, quod venire &c in craſtino S. Andreæ Robertum Frankeleyn, ad reſpondendum Magiſtro Thomæ de Sutton clerico Magiſtri G. Giffard Cancellarij de Scaccario, de iiij marcis quas ei debet ut dicit &c. *Memor.* 51. *H.* 3. *Rot.* 2. *b.*

(*x*) Baronibus, pro Magiſtro Godefrido Giffard. Cum Rex conceſſerit eidem, quod quocicns opus habuerit pro negocijs ſuis, a Scaccario prædicto poſſit recedere, cum aliquem virum ydoneum ad officium ſuum explendum ibidem, pro quo reſpondere velit, loco ſuo ſubſtituat: Ideo Rex mandat eiſdem, quod prædictum Magiſtrum, quociens opus habuerit & ab ipſo requiſiti fuerint, a Scaccario prædicto libere recedere permittant, & ipſum quem loco ſuo ibidem ſubſtituere voluerit ſine dilatione admittant; ſicut prædictum eſt &c. *Ib.* Rot. 1. *b.*

(*y*) Magiſtro Thomæ de Wymundeham Theſaurario, pro Rege. Rex mandat eidem, quod Sigillum Scaccarij liberet dilecto Clerico ſuo Rogero de la Leye, cuſtodiendum quamdiu Regi placuerit. Teſte &c. Breve eſt in forulo Mareſcalli. Et idem Magiſter Thomas liberavit eidem Rogero in craſtino S. Nicholai prædictum Sigillum, cuſtodiendum in forma prædicta. Et idem Rogerus recepit Sigillum prædictum eodem die, & præſtitit ſacramentum de eodem Sigillo fideliter cuſtodiendo. *Memor.* 52. *H.* 3. *Rot.* 4. *b.*

(*z*) Berk. Mandatum eſt Vicecomiti, quod venire &c a die Paſchæ in xv dies, Bartholomæum Capellanum de Silamſted, ad reſpondendum Johanni de Offinton Capellano Rogeri de la Leye Cancellarij de Scaccario, de ix marcis quas ei debet &c. *Ib.* Rot. 7. *b. Et ib.* Rot. 8. *b.*

(*a*) Tenor brevis Regis directi Theſaurario & Baronibus. Edwardus Dei gratia &c. Sciatis quod commiſimus dilecto Clerico Galfrido de Neubaud officium Cancellarij Scaccarij noſtri, cuſtodiendum quamdiu
nobis

Edward II. made *John de Sandale* Chancellor of his Exchequer during Pleasure; and commanded the Treasurer and Barons to admit him to that Office (b): and after him *John de Drokenesford* during Pleasure (c). The same King, by his Letters Patent, committed to *Hervicus de Staunton* the Office of Chancellor of the Exchequer during his Pleasure; and commanded the Barons to admit him to the said Office (d). Afterwards, *Hervicus de Staunton* being made Chief Justice of the King's Bench, the King committed during his Pleasure the Custody of his Seal of the Exchequer to *W*. Bishop of *Exeter* his Treasurer (e); and afterwards granted the Office of Chancellor of the

nobis placuerit. Et ideo vobis mandamus, quod prædictum Galfridum ad hoc recipiatis, sicut prædictum est. In cujus rei t, h L n fieri fecimus. T. me ipso in Castro prope Basingewerc, xx die Augusti anno rn quinto. *Mich. Commun.* 5 & 6. *E.* 1. *Rot.* 2. *a.*

(b) Rex omnibus ad quos &c, Salutem. Sciatis quod commisimus dilecto Clerico nostro Johanni de Sandale Officium Cancellarij de Scaccario nostro, habendum cum omnibus ad Officium illud pertinentibus, quamdiu nobis placuerit, eo modo quo dilectus Clericus noster Johannes de Benstede, nuper Cancellarius ibidem, officium habuit antedictum. In cujus &c; Teste Rege apud Commenok 20° die Augusti. Per Breve de privato Sigillo.

Et mandatum est Thesaurario & Baronibus de Scaccario, quod ipsum Johannem de Sandale ad officium illud admittant in forma prædicta; Teste ut supra. *Rot. Pat.* 1. *E.* 2. *pat.* 1. *m.* 19.

Cum Rex commiserit Johanni de Sandale Officium Cancellarij de Scaccario, Habendum cum omnibus ad officium illud pertinentibus quamdiu Regi placuerit, eo modo quo Johannes de Benstede nuper Cancellarius ibidem officium habuit antedictum, prout in Literis Patentibus eidem inde confectis plenius continetur: Rex mandat Baronibus, quod ipsum Johannem de Sandale ad Officium illud admittant in forma prædicta. T. Rege apud Commenok, xx die Augusti anno primo. Per breve de Magno Sigillo. *Mich. Commun.* 1. *E.* 2. *Rot.* 16. *a.*

(c) Cum Rex commiserit dilecto Clerico suo Johanni de Drokenesford Officium Cancellarij Scaccarij prædicti ('*tis in the same Words*, mutatis mutandis, *as above to* John de Sandale). T. Rege apud Westmon. xx° die Maij anno primo. *Pas. Brevia* 1. *E.* 2. *Rot.* 52. *b.*

(d) Cum Rex commiserit dilecto & fideli suo Hervico de Staunton Officium Cancellarij Scaccarij sui, habendum cum omnibus ad Officium illud spectantibus quamdiu sibi placuerit, prout in Literis suis patentibus eidem Hervico inde confectis plenius continetur; Mandat Baronibus, quod ipsum Hervicum ad Officium prædictum admittant. T. Rege apud Westmon. xxij die Junij anno nono. *Trin. Brevia* 9. *E.* 2. *Rot.* 51. *a.*

(e) Rex omnibus ad quos &c. Salutem. Sciatis quod cum dilectus Clericus & fidelis noster Henricus de Staunton Cancellarius Scaccarij nostri, de mandato nostro intendat Officio Capitalis Justiciarij nostri ad placita coram nobis tenenda, per quod dicto Officio Cancellarij ad præsens intendere non potest, Custodiam Sigilli nostri Scaccarij prædicti Venerabili Patri W. Exoniensi Episcopo Thesaurario nostro commisimus, habendam quamdiu nobis placuerit, percipiendo pro Custodia prædicta feodum consuetum. In cujus &c, Teste Rege apud Skergill xxvij° die Septembris. Per Breve de privato Sigillo. *Pat.* 17. *E.* 2. *p.* 1. *m.* 9. & *iterum m.* 16.

Dominus Rex mandavit W. Exoniensi Episcopo Thesaurario per breve suum de Privato Sigillo suo, cujus data est apud Skergil xvij die Septembris hoc anno, quod quia Hervicus de Staunton Capitalis Justiciarius de Banco Regis, qui habuit custodiam Sigilli de Cancellar[ia] hujus Scaccarij, de cætero ad custodiam officij Cancellar[ij] intendere non potest, quod idem
Thesaurarius

the Exchequer to *Robert de Ayleston* during Pleasure, who was sworn and admitted *(f)*. K. *Edward* I. gave a Licence to *Philip de Wylugby*, that he might attend at the Exchequer with the other Barons, as often as he had Leisure and Convenience *(g)*. The Chancellor of the Exchequer, upon entering into his Office, took an Oath to this Effect, *viz :* That he should well and truly serve the King in the Office of Chancellor of the Exchequer: That he should well and truly do what pertained to that Office : That he should dispatch the King's Business before all other : And that he should seal with the Exchequer-seal no judicial Writ of any other Court besides the Exchequer, whilst the Chancery [or Chancellor] was within twenty Miles of the Place where the Exchequer was holden *(h)*.

Concerning the Constituting of the Barons, in brief K. *Henry* III. (*Anno Regni* 18) assigned *William de Beauchamp, Alexander de Swereford* Treasurer of St. *Paul*'s in *London*, and *Richard de Muntfichet*, to reside at the Exchequer as Barons, for dispatching the Business of the Exchequer (*i*) ; and the King granted to the said *Alexander de Swereford*,

Thesaurarius custodiam dicti Sigilli recipiat de præfato Hervico, & dictum Sigillum debito modo uti faciat, quousq; Rex aliud &c. Prætextu cujus mandati, idem Thesaurarius custodiam dicti Sigilli admisit in forma prædicta, sicut idem Thesaurarius præsens hic vij die Octobris hoc anno recognovit. *Mich. Commun.* 17. *E.* 2. *Rot.* 1. *b.*

(*f*) Memorandum quod die Jovis in Vigilia S. Jacobi Apostoli, anno Regis hujus vicesimo incipiente, Hervicus de Stanton præstitit sacramentum, coram Venerabilibus patribus W. Archiepiscopo Eboracensi Angliæ Primate Thesaurario, W. Exoniensi Episcopo, Magistro R. de Baldok Cancellario Regis, & Baronibus de Scaccario, & Justiciarijs de Communi Banco, de bene & fideliter se habendo in officio Capitalis Justiciarij de Banco, prout moris est.

Et eodem die Magister R. de Ayleston præstitit sacramentum de bene & fideliter se habendo in officio Cancellarij de Scaccario Domini Regis. *Trin. Commun.* 19. *E.* 2. *Rot.* 11. *b.*

Dominus Rex mandavit hic breve suum de Magno Sigillo suo quod est inter Communia de hoc anno in hæc verba. Edwardus Dei gratia Rex Angliæ D. H. & D. A, Thesaurario & Baronibus suis de Scaccario salutem. Cum commiserimus dilecto Clerico nostro Magistro Roberto de Ayleston officium Cancellarij Scaccarij prædicti, Habendum quamdiu nobis placuerit, prout in Literis nostris patentibus inde confectis plenius continetur : Vobis mandamus, quod ipsum ad officium prædictum admittatis. T. me ipso apud Westmon. xviij die Julij anno r n vicesimo. Prætextu cujus brevis, prædictus Magister Robertus admittitur ad officium prædictum, & præstitit sacramentum de bene & fideliter &c. *Trin. Commun.* 19. *E.* 2. *Rot.* 7. *b.*

(*g*) *Mich. Communia* 30. *E.* 1. *Rot.* 35. *a. ex parte Remem. Reg.*

(*h*) Vous jurrez, qe bien & loialment servirez a Roy en loffice de Chaunceller del Escheqer, & bien & loialment frez quanq; atient a celle office, & lez bosoignez le Roy esploiterez devaunt toutz auters, & nulle bref de Juggement dautre place forsque del Eschequer mesme enfealerez du seal del Eschequer, tant come Chaunc. serra vint leukes emviron on leschequer demurt. Si &c. *Lib. Rub. Scacc. fol.* 14. *b. tit.* Sacramentum Cancell. Scaccarij.

(*i*) De Justic. ad Scaccarium. Rex Thesaurario & Baronibus suis de Scaccario salutem. Sciatis quod assignavimus dilectum & fidelem nostrum Willelmum de Bello Campo vobis socium ad residendum ad Scaccarium

ford the Salary of forty Marks a Year, until the King did otherwise provide for him (*k*). The same King (*Anno* 37) made *Peter de Ryvall* a Baron of the Exchequer (*l*). The same King, on the first Day of *November*, in the 48th Year of his Reign, by Writ of the great Seal commanded Master *John de Chishull*, Archdeacon of *London*, Chancellor of the Exchequer, and the rest who were resident there, that they should keep the Exchequer open, as it was formerly wont to be; and because there was at present no Baron resident there, as the King was informed, he assigned *Roger de la Leye*, a Remembrancer of the Exchequer, to execute the Office of a Baron there; and ordered, that for the future, they should write to all the Sheriffs of *England* concerning all Business pertaining to the Exchequer, as they formerly used to do: And the King commanded as well the said Chancellor and Residents to admit *Roger*, as also the said *Roger* to execute the Office of a Baron till further Order (*m*): And on the 30th Day of *November* aforesaid, the King sent out a close Writ, importing that he had not yet appointed a Treasurer and a Chancellor to reside at the Exchequer, and therefore he commanded *Roger de la Lye* to execute the Offices of Treasurer and Chancellor in the usual Manner, till he should receive further Orders from the King (*n*). This desolate State

of

carium nostrum tanquam Baro, pro negocijs nostris quæ ad idem Scaccarium pertinent. Et ideo vobis mandamus, quod ipsum Willelmum ad hoc admittatis, & agenda Scaccarij nostri eidem communicetis. T. R. apud Kingeston vj die Julij.

Eodem modo mandatum est eisdem, de Alexandro de Swereford Thesaurario S. Pauli Londoniæ & de Ricardo Muntfichet. *Cl.* 18. *H.* 3. *m.* 16. *Dors.*

(*k*) Rex omnibus ad quos &c. Sciatis nos concessisse dilecto & fideli nostro Magistro Alexandro de Swereford Thesaurario Sancti Pauli Londoniæ, Quadraginta Marcas singulis annis percipiendas ad Scaccarium nostrum, ad se sustentandum in servitio nostro ad Scaccarium ubi residet per præceptum nostrum, donec ei aliter providerimus. In cujus rei testimonium &c. Teste Rege apud Westm. 21º die Octobris. *Pat.* 18. *H.* 3. *m.* 2.

(*l*) De Petro de Rivall sedendo ad Scaccarium. Rex Thesaurario & Baronibus suis de Scaccario salutem. Sciatis quod associavimus vobis dilectum & fidelem nostrum Petrum de Ryvall: Et ideo vobis mandamus, quatinus eundem P. tamquam Socium vestrum & Baronem Scaccarij nostri admittatis. T. R. apud Wintoniam xvjº die Junij. *Cl.* 37. *H.* 3. *m.* 8.

(*m*) Mandatum est Magistro J. de Chishull Archidiacono Londoniæ Cancellario Scaccarij sui, & cæteris residentibus in eodem Scaccario, quod Scaccarium Regis apertum teneant, prout temporibus retroactis teneri consuevit. Et quia Rex Baronem in eodem Scaccario ad præsens non habet ut intellexit, assignavit Rogerum de la Lye Rememoratorem Scaccarij prædicti, ad officium Baronis in Scaccario supradicto explendum; Mandans eisdem quod ipsum ad hoc admittant. Cæterum, de cætero scribant Vicecomitibus Regis per Angliam, de omnibus Scaccarium prædictum contingentibus, sicut antea facere consueverunt. Teste Rege apud Oxon. primo die Novembris.

Et mandatum est præfato Rogero quod Officio Baronis in eodem Scaccario intendat, donec Rex inde aliud Mandaverit; Teste ut supra. *Claus.* 48. *H.* 3. *m.* 10.

(*n*) Quia Rex nondum providit de Thesaurario

of the Exchequer was occasioned by the Troubles which were then in the Realm; by means whereof there were no Barons resident at the Exchequer at Easter in the 48th Year of the King, and his Rents and Ferms due at that Term were not paid in (*o*). The same King (*Anno Regni* 49) by Writ appointed *Roger de la Leye* to be a Baron of the Exchequer, and likewise to execute the Office of Treasurer there, till further Order (*p*); and *William le Marescal* (*q*) and Master *Alexander le Seculer* (*r*) to be two other Barons there.

K. *Edward* I. constituted *John de Cobeham* a Baron of his Exchequer during his Pleasure, and commanded the Barons to admit him to that Office (*s*). In the 23d Year of K. *Edward* I. *Walter de Langeton*, the Treasurer, declared to the Barons at the Exchequer, that the King ordered them to admit *John de Lisle* a Baron there, to hold that Office during the King's Will; and thereupon *John* was admitted and sworn a Baron (*t*). K. *Edward* I. in the 34th Year of his Reign,

saurario & Cancellario ponendis ad Scaccarium Regis: Mandatum est Rogero de la Lye, quod Officio tam Thesaurarij quam Cancellarij, prout hactenus fieri consuevit, intendat, donec aliud a Rege receperit in mandatis, & aliter super hoc ordinaverit. Teste Rege apud Roff. xxx die Novembris, per Regem, Hugonem le Bigod & J. de War. *Clauf.* 48. *H.* 3. *m.* 8.

(*o*) Bedford. & Buk. pro Rege. Quia perturbationem in Regno habitam non fuerunt Barones residentes in Scaccario ad Pascha anno xlviij°, propter quod redditus assisi Regis & firmæ suæ de eodem termino nondum sunt Regi persoluti. Et ideo mandatum est Vicecomiti, quod fieri faciat omnes redditus & res assisas spectantes ad firmam dictorum Comitatuum de eodem termino, & inde omnes denarios provenientes habeat ad Scaccarium in octabis S. Hilarij Regi reddendos & breve. *Mich. Commun.* 49. *H.* 3. *Rot.* 5. *a.*

(*p*) Rogero de la Leye. Rex mandat eidem, quod quia de Consilio Regis provisum est, quod moram faciat in Officio Baronis in Scaccario Regis, quod Officio illi intendat, Et similiter Officio Thesaur. ibidem intendat, donec aliud inde fuerit ordinatum. Et hoc, sicut Regem diligit, nullatenus omittat, &c. *Mich. Commun.* 49. *H.* 3. *Rot.* 1. *a.*

(*q*) Rex Baronibus; Quia de Consilio Regis provisum est, quod Willelmus de Marescal moram faciat ad Scaccarium Regis in Officio Baronis ibidem, [Rex mandat] quod eundem Willelmum ad hoc admittant, & hoc nullatenus omittant. *Ib. Rot.* 5. *a.*

(*r*) Baronibus, pro Rege. Rex eisdem; Mittimus ad vos dilectum Clericum nostrum Magistrum Alexandrum le Seculer, de cujus providencia & fidelitate confidimus, quod ad residendum Baro una vobiscum ad Scaccarium nostrum nobis sit necessarius: Vobis mandantes, quod ipsum Baronem & Socium in eodem Scaccario admittatis. *Pas. Commun. ib. Rot.* 7. *b.*

(*s*) Rex mandat Baronibus de Scaccario suo, quod constituit dilectum & fidelem suum Johannem de Cobeham Baronem suum ejusdem Scaccarij; ita quod officium Baronis ibidem exerceat quamdiu sibi placuerit: Et ideo mandat eisdem, quod ipsum Johannem in Baronem ejusdem Scaccarij ad hoc admittant in forma prædicta. T. meipso apud Westmon. viij die Junij anno regni sui quarto. *Trin. Communia* 4. *E.* 1. *Rot.* 8. *b.*

(*t*) Memorandum quod vicesimo die octobris anno xxiij finiente, dilectus & fidelis Regis Walterus de Langetone ipsius Domini Regis Thesaurarius, exposuit hic Baronibus ex parte Regis, quod ipsi Johannem de Insula in conbaronem suum ad officium Baronis hic in Scaccario exercendum ad

Reign, by Writ Patent of the Great Seal, appointed *Humphrey de Waleden* to be a Baron of the Exchequer, during Pleasure (*u*); and accordingly he was sworn and admitted (*w*).

K. *Edward* II. in the first Year of his Reign constituted *William de Carleton, Roger de Hegham*, and *Thomas de Canterbrugg*, Barons of the Exchequer, during Pleasure, by Letters Patent (*x*). In the same Year that King, by Letters Patent, constituted Master *Richard de Abyndon* a Baron of the Exchequer during Pleasure; and gave him the same Place or Precedency there, that he had in the Time of K. *Edward* I. (*y*). And in the next Year the King gave *William de Carleton* (in Consideration of his ill Health and long Service in the Exchequer) special Leave to reside at his own House as often and as long as his Health

ad voluntatem Regis admitterent; & eo exposito, idem Johannes admissus est ad officium Baronis in forma prædicta; & in continenti præstitit sacramentum de fideliter se habendo in officio prædicto. *Mich. Commun.* 24. *E.* 1. *Rot.* 7. *a. in bund.* 23 & 24. *E.* 1.

(*u*) Rex dilecto & fideli suo Humfrido de Waleden salutem. Sciatis quod constituimus vos unum Baronem nostrum de Scaccario nostro, ad ea quæ ad Officium illud pertinent, quamdiu nobis placuerit, facienda: Et ideo vobis mandamus, quod ad ea quæ ad dictum Officium pertinent intendatis in forma prædicta: Mandavimus enim Thesaurario & Baronibus nostris de dicto Scaccario, quod vos ad hoc in Socium admittant sicut prædictum est. In cujus &c. T. Rege apud Lanrecost xix die Octobris. Per breve de Privato sigillo. Et mandatum est Thesaurario & Baronibus de Scaccario, quod ipsum Humfridum ad hoc admittant in forma prædicta. Teste ut supra. Per breve de Privato sigillo. *Rot. Pat.* 34. *Edw.* 1. *m.* 3.

(*w*) Memorandum quod vij die mensis Novembris nunc, Humfridus de Waleden coram W. Coventrensi & Lich. Episcopo Thesaurario & Baronibus de Scaccario, admissus est in Baronem de Scaccario, & præstitit sacramentum de bene & fideliter se habendo in Officio illo. Postea dictus Humfridus liberavit hic Breve Regis Patens de Magno Sigillo, datum apud Lanercost xix die Octobris anno xxxiiij, per quod Rex mandavit Thesaurario & Baronibus, quod dictum Humfridum ad Officium Baronis in Scaccario admittant &c. *Mich. Communia* 34 & 35. *E.* 1. *Rot.* 17. *a.*

(*x*) Cum Rex per Literas suas Patentes constituerit Willelmum de Carleton, Rogerum de Hegham, & Thomam de Canterbrugg, Barones de Scaccario quamdiu Regi placuerit; & mandaverit eis, quod ipsi ad cicius quod poterunt, ad idem Scaccarium accedant, ibidem coram Thesaurario & Willelmo de Bereford de officijs illis bene & fideliter faciendis sacramentum præstaturi †: Mandat Thesaurario, quod capto a præfatis Willelmo de Carleton, Rogero, & Thoma, hujusmodi Sacramento, liberent eisdem litteras Regis antedictas. T. Rege apud Clipston xx die Septembris anno primo. per Breve de Magno Sigillo. *Mich. Commun.* 1. *E.* 2. *Rot.* 16. *a. inter Brevia.*
† *rectius*, præstituri.

(*y*) Cum Rex per Literas suas Patentes, constituerit dilectum & fidelem suum Magistrum Ricardum de Abyndon Baronem suum de Scaccario, quam diu Regi placuerit, Ita quod in eodem Scaccario habeat eundem locum quem habuit tempore Domini E. quondam Regis Angliæ Patris Regis nunc, prout in litteris Regis prædictis plenius continetur: Rex mandat Baronibus quod capto ab eodem Magistro Ricardo sacramento de hijs quæ ad officium prædictum &c, admittant in forma prædicta. T. Rege apud Dover. xx die Januarij anno primo per ipsum Regem, nunciante W. de Inge. *Hil. Brevia* 1. *E.* 2. *Rot.* 32. *a.*

and

and private Business should require, and to attend at the Exchequer in his Place there when he should think fit (z). And at the same Time the King granted to *Thomas de Cantebrigg*, then a Baron of the Exchequer, that, in the Absence of *William de Carleton*, he should have the Place in the Exchequer which *William*, if present, had; and when *William* was there, *Thomas* should sit next to him (a). The same King, in the second Year of his Reign, constituted by Letters Patent *John de Foxle* a Baron of the Exchequer, in the room of *Roger de Hegham* deceased, during Pleasure, with the Fee usually assigned for that Office (b). The same King, in the 5th Year of his Reign, by Letters Patent constituted *Walter de Norwich* a Baron of the Exchequer, during Pleasure, in the room of *Roger Stoter* de-

(z) Rex omnibus ad quos &c. Quantumcunq; obsequencium nobis servicia sint utilia & accepta, pietas tamen suadet & debitum humanitatis exposcit, ut ad personas emeritas quæ in obsequijs nostris diucius laborarunt respectum condignum habentes, hijs benivole faveamus quæ quietem illorum respiciunt & salutem: Ideoq; dilecti & fidelis nostri Willelmi de Carleton Baronis de Scaccario nostro qui nobis tam in dicto Scaccario nostro quam alibi diu laudabiliter & utiliter & sine intermissione servivit precibus annuentes, ut de cætero proprijs negocijs intendere ac in domo sua propria residere, quociens & quam diu pro sui corporis quiete seu recreatione suorumve negociorum expeditione sibi videbitur expedire, nec non & ad nos & ad Scaccarium prædictum redire, & ibidem pro voluntate sua possit morari, prout antea facere consuevit, sibi tenore presencium licenciam concedimus specialem, ac eciam liberam facultatem. In cujus rei testimonium, has litteras nostras fieri fecimus patentes. T. me ipso apud Westmonasterium xxiiij° die Octobris, anno regni nostri secundo, per ipsum Regem. *Mich. Commissiones* 2. *E.* 2. *Rot.* 6. *b.*

(a) Cum Rex concesserit & licenciam dederit Willelmo de Carleton Baroni de Scaccario suo, quod ipse causa recreationis suæ, vel alia pro suæ voluntatis libito, ad propria declinare, & ad idem Scaccarium redire & ibidem in obsequio Regis morari possit; Et Rex voluerit quod Thomas de Cantebrigg Baro de eodem Scaccario, quocienscunq; ipsum Willelmum abesse contigerit, locum quem Willelmus in eodem Scaccario habet cum presens fuerit, teneat; & in præsentia ipsius Willelmi ibidem, eidem Willelmo propinquius sedeat in Scaccario antedicto; prout in literis Regis patentibus inde confectis plenius continetur: Rex mandat Baronibus quod ipsum Thomam, in absencia prædicti Willelmi, locum quem idem Willelmus in eodem Scaccario habet cum presens fuerit tenere, & in presencia ipsius Willelmi eidem propinquius sedere permittant, juxta tenorem litterarum prædictarum. T. Rege apud Westmonasterium, xxiiij° die Octobris anno secundo. *Mich. Brevia* 2. *E.* 2. *Rot.* 26. *a.*

(b) Cum Rex constituerit dilectum & fidelem suum Johannem de Foxle, Baronem suum de Scaccario suo, loco Rogeri de Hegham nuper Baronis ejusdem Scaccarij defuncti, quamdiu Regi placuerit, Ita, quod in officio illo percipiat feodum consuetum; prout in litteris Regis patentibus eidem Johanni inde confectis plenius continetur: Mandat Baronibus, quod ipsum Johannem loco præfati Rogeri, ad officium illud in socium admittant in forma prædicta. T. Rege apud Westmonasterium, xxviij° die Februarij anno secundo. Et prædictus Johannes præstitit Sacramentum coram Thesaurario & Baronibus &c. die Sabbati primo die Marcij de fideliter se habendo in officio prædicto. *Hil. Brevia* 2. *E.* 2. *Rot.* 50. *a.*

ceased;

Chap. XXI.   *of the* EXCHEQUER.   59

ceased (*c*); and *John Abel* in like Manner; appointing him to have the same Place in the Exchequer which *Walter de Norwich*, then a Baron of the Exchequer, lately had there (*d*). The same King (*Anno Regni* 10) constituted *Ingelard de Warle* a Baron of the Exchequer, during his Pleasure, in the room of *Hervicus de Staunton* (*e*); and *John de Okham* in like Manner, in the room of *Richard de Abyndon* (*f*). In this Year *Walter Norwich*, who had served K. *Edward* I. and the present King in several Posts in the Exchequer, and was now Treasurer of the Exchequer, made his humble Suit to the King to be discharged from his Office. Hereupon the King discharged him (with a great *Elogium*) from his Office of Treasurer, and made him chief Baron of his Exchequer during his Pleasure; commanding that he should be made privy to the King's Counsels, both secret and other, when he was able to attend [at the Exchequer] (*g*). The same King made

(*c*) Cum Rex per Litteras suas Patentes, loco Rogeri Stoter nuper unius Baronum Regis de Scaccario defuncti, constituerit Walterum de Norwico unum Baronem de dicto Scaccario, quamdiu Regi placuerit; prout in Literis Regis prædictis plenius continetur: Rex mandat Baronibus, quod ipsum Walterum loco dicti Rogeri ad officium illud admittant in forma prædicta. T. Rege apud Ebor. tercio die Marcij anno quinto. Per ipsum Regem. *Pas. Brevia* 5. *E.* 2. *Rot.* 39. *a.*

(*d*) Cum Rex per Literas suas Patentes, constituit Johannem Abel [Baronem] de Scaccario, quamdiu Regi placuerit; ita quod habeat eundem locum in Scaccario quem Walterus de Norwico nunc Baro de Scaccario Regis prædicto prius habuit in eodem; prout in Literis prædictis plenius continetur: Rex mandat Baronibus, quod accepto ab eodem Johanne sacramento Regi debito in hac parte, ipsum ad hoc admittant. Teste Rege apud Ebor. viij die Marcij anno quinto. Per ipsum Regem. *Pas. Brevia* 5. *E.* 2. *Rot.* 39. *a.*

(*e*) De Barone Scaccarij constituto. Rex omnibus ad quos &c. salutem. Sciatis quod loco dilecti Clerici nostri Hervici de Stanton nuper unius Baronum de Scaccario nostro, jam Cancellarij de eodem Scaccario, constituimus dilectum Clericum nostrum Ingelardum de Warle, Baronem de eodem Scaccario, quamdiu nobis placuerit. In cujus &c; T. Rege apud Not. xxix die Decembris. Per ipsum Regem. Et mandatum est Thesaurario & Baronibus de Scaccario, quod ipsum Ingelardum loco ipsius Hervici ad hoc in Socium admittant. T. ut supra. *Pat.* 10. *E.* 2. *P.* 2. *m.* 35.

(*f*) Rex omnibus ad quos &c. salutem. Quia dilectus Clericus noster Ricardus de Adyndon, unus Baronum nostrorum de Scaccario, adeo impotens sui existit, quod ea quæ ad officium illud pertinent non potest commode exercere; loco ipsius Ricardi dilectum Clericum nostrum, Johannem de Okham, constituimus unum Baronum nostrorum de Scaccario prædicto, quamdiu nostræ placuerit voluntati, percipiendo per annum feodum consuetum. In cujus &c. T. Rege apud Padyngton xviij die Junij. Per Breve de Privato sigillo.

Et mandatum est Thesaurario & Baronibus de Scaccario, quod eundem Johannem ad hoc in Socium admittant. T. ut supra. *Pat.* 10. *E.* 2. *pars* 2. *m.* 4.

(*g*) Rex omnibus ad quos &c. salutem. Regiam decet Magestatem fideliter obsequentes & Regijs obsequijs utiliter insistentes affectibus intimis conjungere, & condignis honoribus venerari; set quantum cumq; ipsorum obsequia utilia sunt & accepta, tanto ipsorum immunitati est diligencius providendum. Cum itaq; dilectus & fidelis

made *Robert de Wodehouse* a Baron of the Exchequer in the room of *Ingelard de Warlee*: And by Writ of the Privy Seal commanded the Treasurer and Barons, to give *Robert* the Estate of a Baron, and the same Place that *Ingelard* lately had there (*h*). The same King made *Roger Beler* a Baron of the Exchequer during his Pleasure, in the room of *John de Foxle*; and by a close Writ of the Great Seal commanded the Treasurer and Barons to admit *Roger* as their Companion (*i*). In the 4th Year of K. *Edward* I. one of the Keys of the King's Treasury was delivered to *Philipp de Wileby*, Baron of the Exchequer, by the Hand of *Giles de Audenard* (*k*). In pursuance of a Provision lately made at the Parliament of *York*, the King, by a Writ of Privy

noster Walterus de Norwyco, a tempore quo potuit deservire, Domino E. genitori nostro & nobis postmodum in diversis officijs in Scaccario nostro, ac nobis ultimo in officio Thesaurarij Scaccarij nostri, a jamdiu bene fideliter & laudabiliter deservierit, labores indefessos sustinendo, & hujusmodi laboribus nimium fatigatus, eosdem labores absq; corporis sui detrimento & quasi exinanitione nequiens ulterius sustinere, nobis supplicaverit ut de ipsius exoneratione in hac parte providere curaremus: Nos ad laudabilia obsequia ipsius Walteri nobis utili & pervigili diligentia multipliciter impensa, quæ de ipso, sicut & de cæteris nobis fideliter obsequentibus, ad ipsorum honorem & laudis præconium manifestari cupimus, nostrum intuitum convertentes, ad requisitionem ipsius Walteri & aliorum Magnatum de Consilio nostro, eundem Walterum ab onere officij illius exonerare duximus, taliter requisiti: Ac nolentes obsequijs fructuosis tam utilis & tam fidelis Ministri, ac Regijs affectibus, suis exigentibus meritis, conjuncti carere, set ipsum in nostro servicio, ubi cum moderamine laborum nobis gratum locum-tenere possit, modis omnibus affectantes retinere, eundem Walterum Capitalem Baronem Scaccarij nostri constituimus, quamdiu nobis placuerit, Volentes quod idem Walterus cum potens fuerit laborare, nostris consilijs tam secretis quam alijs intersit & intendat, prout & quociens pro nostro Honore & commodo viderit expedire. In cujus &c. Teste Rege apud Westmon. xxx die Maij. Per ipsum Regem. *Pat.* 10. *E.* 2. *p.* 2. *m.* 11.

(*h*) Edward &c. Au Tresorier & a son Lieutenant, & as Barons de nostre Escheqier salutz. Come nous eoms establi nostre cher Clerk Robert de Wodehouse un des Barons de nostre dit Escheqier, en lieu Ingelard de Warlee (qest a Dieu comande) nadgaires Baroun dycel: Vous mandoms, qe au dit nostre Clerk facez avoir lestat de Baroun, & le lieu qe le dit Ingelard tint par cele reson taunt come il vesquit en nostre Escheqier avandit. Et ce en nulle manere ne lessez. Done souz nostre Prive Seal a Burstwyk, le xiiij jour Doctobre lan de nostre regne douzisme. *Mich. Brevia* 12. *E.* 2. *Rot.* 64. *a.*

(*i*) Rex Thesaurario & Baronibus suis de Scaccario, salutem. Cum loco dilecti & fidelis nostri Johannis de Foxle, nuper unius Baronum de Scaccario nostro prædicto, constituerimus dilectum & fidelem nostrum Rogerum Beler Baronem de eodem Scaccario, quamdiu nobis placuerit; Percipiendo in officio illo feodum consuetum; prout in Literis nostris patentibus eidem Rogero inde confectis plenius continetur: Vobis mandamus, quod ipsum Rogerum loco ipsius Johannis in Socium admittatis. T. me ipso apud Ebor. xx die Julij anno r n xvj. Per ipsum Regem. *Trin. Brevia* 15. *E.* 2. *Rot.* 63. *b.*

(*k*) Memorandum quod Philippus de Wyleby Baro de Scaccario recepit unam clavem de domo Thesaur[ariæ] Domini Regis, viij° die Junij, per manum Egidij de Audenard Clerici. *Trin. Commun.* 4. *E.* 1. *Rot.* 8. *b.*

Chap. XXI. *of the* EXCHEQUER.

Seal, commanded the Treasurer, that, if the Barons of the Exchequer were found to be too numerous, he should advise which of them might best be spared, and should do therein as should be accorded; provided that *Robert de Wodehouse* and *John de Okham* do still continue to be Barons (*l*). The same King constituted *Edmund de Passele* a Baron of the Exchequer, in the room of *Walter de Friskeney*: Commanding the Treasurer and Barons, to admit him *in Socium*; and him, to attend at the Exchequer on the Morrow of St. *Michael* (*m*). In or about the Reign of K. *Edward* II. a Baron of the Exchequer, upon entering into his Office, took an Oath to the Effect hereunder set forth (*n*). In the 8th Year of K. *Edward* I. the Chancellor of the Exchequer and the Barons hereunder named, had each of them xx *l*. a Year

(*l*) Edward par la grace de Dieu &c. Al honorable Piere en Dieu J. par la meisme grace Evesq; de Wyncestre nostre Tresorier, salutz. Il vous doit sovenir, coment a Everwyk a nostre darrein Parlement, fut nadgaires assentuz, qe les Barouns de nostre Escheqier deyvent estre suffisaunz, & nient plus qe ne covenent pur la place governer: Par quoi vous mandoms, qe si vous voiez qe la Place soit trop chargez, adonqes avisez vous des queux des Barons de nostre dit Escheqier hom se purra mielz suffrer, & facez ce qest acordez, issint totes foitz qe noz chers Clercs Robert de Wodehous & Johan de Okham, queux nous tenoms suffisaunz & necessaires pur cele place, y demoergent en pees en lour estatz. Donez soutz nostre Prive Seal a Beverle le Secound jour de Janevoir, lan de nostre Regne douzisme. *Hil. Brevia* 12. *E.* 2. *Rot.* 81. *a.*

(*m*) Rex omnibus ad quos &c. Salutem. Sciatis quod loco dilecti & fidelis nostri Walteri de Friskeney nuper unius Baronum nostrorum de Scaccario, constituimus dilectum & fidelem nostrum Edmundum de Passele Baronem nostrum de eodem Scaccario quamdiu nobis placuerit, percipiendo in Officio illo feodum consuetum. In cujus &c. Teste Rege apud Kyrkeby Malesart xx° die Septembris. Per ipsum Regem.

Et mandatum est Thesaurario & Baronibus de Scaccario quod ipsum Edmundum loco præfati Walteri ad hoc in Socium admittant, Teste ut supra. Per ipsum Regem.

Et mandatum est præfato Edmundo, quod ad Scaccarium prædictum apud Westm. jam existens se transferat, & ibidem Officio illi in crastino Sancti Michaelis proximo futuro cum cæteris Baronibus de dicto Scaccario intendat. Teste ut supra. Per ipsum Regem. *Pat.* 17. *E.* 2. *p.* 1. *m.* 16.

(*n*) Vous jurrez, qe bien & loialment servirez au Roy en loffice de Baroun de leschequer; & qe loialment chargerez & deschargerez les gentz qont acompter devant vous; & droiture frez as totes gentz auxi bien as pouers come as riches; & qe pur hautesse ne pur richesse, ne pur haour ne pur estat de nuly person, ne pur bienfait, doun, ne promesse de nulli, qe fait vous soit ou vous purra estre fait, ne pur arte, ne pur engyn, droiture le Roy ne autry destourberez ne respiterez countre les leys de la terre; ne les dettes le Roy metterez en respite per la ou eles purront bonement estre levez; & qe les busoignes le Roy esploiterez devant touz autrez; & pur doun ne pur autre lower ne bienfait, ne celerez ne destourberez le profit & lavantage le Roy, en avantage dautry ne de vous meismes; Et qe vous ne preignez fee ne robe de nulluy sinoun de Roy mesmez; & qe rien ne prendrez de nully pur tort faire ou droiture delaier, ou pur deliverer ou pur delaier les gentz qont affaire devant vous, mes a plustoft qe vous poez deliverer [ez]; & qe per la ou vouz poez savoir tort ou prejudice estre fait au Roy, vous metterez tout vostre poiar & diligence de ceo redresser, & si vous ne poez ceo fair qe vous le dirrez au Roy ou a ceux de son Conseil qe le purront dire au Roy, si vous ne poez a lui venir; & qe le counsel

a Year Stipend, *Nicolas de Castle*, one of the Remembrancers, xl *l*. for himself and his Clerks, and *Odo de Westminstre*, the other Remembrancer xx *l*. for him and his Clerks (*o*). And in the 31st of K. *Edward* I. *Philipp de Wylgheby*, Chancellor of the Exchequer, and *William de Carleton* and *Peter de Leycestre*, Barons there, had each of them xl Marks a Year Salary (*p*).

counsel le Roy celerez en toutes choses. Si Dieu vous eide & les Seintz. *Lib. Rub. Scacc. fol.* 14. *b. tit.* Sacramentum Baronum.

(*o*) Rex Thesaurario & Camerarijs suis salutem. Liberate de Thesauro nostro di & fi nostris, Galfrido de Neubaud Cancellario Scaccarij nostri, Rogero de Norwod, Johanni de Cobeham, & Philippo de Wyleby Baronibus ejusdem Scaccarij quaterviginti marcas, videlicet unicuiq; eorum viginti marcas de Termino S. Michaelis proximo præterito, de annuo feodo quadraginta marcarum, quod cuilibet eorum concessimus percipiendum ad Scaccarium prædictum in officio prædicto, Et Nicholao de Castello uni Rememoratorum ejusdem Scaccarij viginti marcas de Termino prædicto de annuo feodo suo quadraginta marcarum quod ei concessimus percipiendum ad sustentationem suam & Clericorum suorum secum existencium in officio prædicto, Et Magistro Odoni de Westmonasterio alteri rememoratorum ejusdem Scaccarij decem libras de eodem termino de annuo feodo suo viginti librarum, quod similiter ei concessimus percipiendum ad sustentationem suam in officio prædicto. T. R. apud Westm. xxiiij die Octobris. *Lib.* 8. *E.* 1. *m.* 3. [Philipp de Wyleby *was also at this time Keeper of the fourth Key of the Treasury, at* x *l. yearly Fee*; *Lib.* 8. *E.* 1. *m.* 5.]

The like Writ as above verbatim *issued for Payment of their Salary due at Easter. Ib. m.* 6.

(*p*) Rex Tenenti locum Thesaurarij & Camerarijs suis salutem. Liberate de Thesauro nostro, dilectis & fidelibus nostris Philippo de Wylgheby Cancellario Scaccarij nostri, Willelmo de Carleton, & Petro de Leycestr., Baronibus ejusdem Scaccarij, Centum & quaterviginti marcas, videlicet cuilibet eorum quadraginta marcas de terminis Paschæ & S. Michaelis, de anno regni nostri tricesimo, & cuilibet eorum viginti marcas de termino Paschæ de anno regni nostri tricesimo primo, de annuis feodis suis quæ eis concessimus percipienda in officiis supradictis. T. Rege apud Villam S. Johannis de Perth, xxvj die Julij. *Lib.* 31. *E.* 1. *m.* 2.

CHAP.

CHAP. XXII.

Of the BUSINESS *and* PROCEEDINGS *in the* EXCHEQUER, *during the second Period.*

I.   *Of Affairs relating to the Revenue.*
II.   *Of Pleas.*
III.   *Of Business of various Kinds. Of Conventions, Recognitions, &c. made in the Exchequer.*
IV.   *Of the Presentation and Admission of Officers.*
V.   *Of the Presentation of Mayors, Sheriffs, &c.*
VI.   *Of Fealty done and Rents paid at the Exchequer.*
VII. *Of Affairs relating to the Government and Defence of the Realm.*
VIII. *Of the Records and Judgments of the Exchequer.*
IX.   *Of Messages or Letters sent to the Exchequer by the King, Queen, and Prince.*

WHEN we considered (*a*) the Business transacted at the Exchequer during the first Period, we ranked it under three general Heads; *viz.* I. Affairs of Revenue; II. Causes; III. Business of various Kinds: and we will here assume the same Heads.

I. As to Affairs of Revenue and Things incident to Revenue. There was in the Exchequer a great Variety of Business springing from that Root. The Reader will not expect, I should treat at large of each Sort of that Business. However some Instances must be given.

Fines of divers Kinds were imposed or set at the Exchequer. K. *Edward* I. in the 27th Year of his Reign, ordered, that all Persons, who desired to amortise Lands or Tenements, or to purchase Lands holden of the King in chief, Letters of Protection or general Attorney, Parks, Fairs, Markets, and other Franchises, should go to the Exchequer, that reasonable Fines might be there set for the same (*b*). *Richard de Pontfrait* lay imprisoned above three Years in

Wor-

(*a*) Vol. I. *Chap.* 6.
(*b*) Ordinatio facta per Dominum Regem, de Finibus Religiosorum & aliorum recipiendis in Scaccario, pro Licentia ingrediendi feodum Regis &c.
Fet a Savoir que le Roys ordena a Westmonster,

Worcester Gaol, for fishing without Leave in the King's Pond of Fekingham. He offered to make Fine for that Trespass. And thereupon a Writ of *Duci facias* was awarded to the Sheriff of Worcestershire, to bring him before the Treasurer and Barons of the Exchequer. By virtue of which Writ, he was brought up, and before them made Fine to the King for the said Trespass in xx *s*. But in regard he had been so long imprisoned, the Fine was remitted, and he was set at large (*c*). Sir *Thomas de Bavent*, *Walter de Bernham*, and *Edmond de Mikle-*

monster, le primer jour Daurel Ian de sen regne vint & septime, qe ceux qe voudront purchacer Noveal Park, & Gentz de Religion qui voudront terre & tenement amorter, eent Bref de la Chauncelerie pur enquerre solom les pointz acoustumez, e teles choses, e qe les enquestes de terre ou de tenement que vaille par an pleus de xx Soultz par extente, soient retournez al Escheqier, & la ceo face la fin pur la mortissement, ou pur le park avoir, si les enquestes eenrent pur ceux qe les purchacent. E deloeqes soit maunde au Chauncelier ou au Lieutenant, ceo quil en deura faire. E des enquestes faire pur amorter terre au tenement, qui namontera par an outre vint Soutz par extente, & de vint soutz en aual, veut le Roy qe celes soient returnez au Chauncelier ou a son lieutenant, e qil pregne resnable Fin sur ceo, selom la quantite de la chose, & puis les delivre. En meisme la manere soit fait, qe ceux qui voudront purchacer terres ou tenementz que sont tenuz du Roy en cheif. Item gentz demoraunt la outre qui ont terre ou Rente en Engleterre, sil voillent purchacer Lettres de protection, ou de Generaux Attornez, soient envoiez al Escheqier, e la facent lur Fyn. E deloeqes soit maunde au Chaunceler ou a son Lieutenant, qil en deura faire. En mesme le manere soit fait de ceux qui voudront purchaser Faire, Marche, Garenne, ou autre Merchandise. E item ceux qe voudrent purchaser atterminement de lur dettes, seent envecz al Escheqier. E item Gentz de noun poer a travailler, & gentz des Countez loinz temps de la Chauncelerie, qui pledent ou sont enpledez eient Bref de la Chauncelerie a aucun suffisaunt home qui receive les attornez quant mestres est. E pur remembraunce de cestes choses, est Endenture faite en trois partis, don lun demoert on Chauncelerie, lautre en Lescheqier, & la tierce en Garderobe : Et memorandum quod die Sabbati in Crastino Apostolorum Philippi & Jacoby anno supradicto, Venerabilis Pater W. de Langeton Coventrensis & Lich. Episcopus Thesaurarius tulit hic videlicet in Scaccario apud Eboracum, unam partem Indenturæ prædictæ, quæ est in custodia Marescalli inter Communia de anno xxvij°. *Pas. Communia* 26. & 27. *E.* 1. *Rot.* 24. *b.*

(*c*) Vicecomiti Wigorniæ ; Quia Ricardus de Ponte fracto, pro eo quod in Vivario nostro de Fekingham sine licentia & voluntate nostra piscatus fuit & piscem cepit & asportavit, jam per triennium & amplius in prisona nostra Wigorniæ extiterit, & finem nobis facere optulerit pro transgressione prædicta : Tibi præcipimus, quod sub salvo & securo conductu ipsum Ricardum sumptibus suis proprijs duci facias coram Thesaurario & Baronibus nostris de Scaccario, ad finem suum faciendum pro transgressione prædicta, Ita quod eum habeas coram eisdem Thesaurario & Baronibus in Crastino Ascensionis Domini prox. futuro apud Eboracum, ad faciendum & recipiendum ibidem coram eis, tam super deliberatione sua quam reductione ad prisonam nostram prædictam, quod per ipsum Thesaurarium & Barones ordinabitur tunc ibidem. Et habeas ibi tunc hoc breve, Teste me ipso apud Westmon. xxij° die Aprilis anno regni nostri xxvij°. per petitionem de Consilio.

Prætextu hujus brevis prædictus Vicecomes Wygorniæ xxij° die Junij hoc anno duci fecit prædictum Ricardum coram prædictis

Miklefeud, were convicted, before Justices assigned to hear and determine in *Norfolk* and *Suffolk,* of maliciously procuring *John le King* to be indicted for the Death of *Isabell le Shapestere;* and *Hugh Tyrel* of divers Conspiracies. The said Justices were commanded by Writ, to transmit into the Exchequer the Records and Processes touching the Convictions of the said four Persons, together with their Advice concerning the Sums proper to be taken of them by way of Fine for their several Trespasses. The Records and Processes were accordingly transmitted together with the Advice of the Justices touching the Fines. The said four Persons, who were Prisoners in the Tower of *London* for their said Trespasses, being brought up to the Exchequer, and the Treasurer and Barons having inspected the said Records and Processes, Sir *Thomas de Bavent* fined in xxx l. *Walter de Bernham* in xx Marks, *Edmond de Miklefeud* in xl l. and *Hugh Tyrel* in C Marks *(d)*. *John de Winton,* a Clerk of the Wardrobe, came to the Exchequer, and produced the King's credential Letter; which being delivered to the Treasurer, *John* notified on the King's Behalf, that the King willed the Treasurer to cause *Simon de Segrave,* who was convicted of certain Trespasses before *Peter de Maulay,* and other Justices in *Lincolnshire,* and remained Prisoner in the Tower of *London* for the same, to be brought before him the said Treasurer and the Barons of the Exchequer, and to set him at large out of the said Prison, when they had taken of him a Fine for the said Trespasses. *Simon* was brought up to the Exchequer; and the Causes of his Commitment to the Tower of *London* (which were certified by one of the said Justices) being seen and examined by the Treasurer and Barons, he fined before them, for his said Trespasses, in D Marks *(e)*. *John le Goldsmyth,* imprisoned at *Canterbury* for a Redisseisine, was brought up, by Writ of *Duci facias,* before the Treasurer and Barons, to make Fine; and he made Fine before them in Half a Mark *(f)*.

The Treasurer and Barons were wont to set and affeer Amercements. An Amercement set upon a Sheriff was affeered by the Treasurer's Lieutenant and the Barons. But afterwards, in Consideration of the Sheriff's good Service, the Treasurer pardoned him the Amercement *(g)*.

Richard

dictis Thesaurario & Baronibus. Et eodem die prædictus Ricardus Finem fecit cum Rege pro Transgressione prædicta per xx s. Qui quidem xx s condonantur eidem propter diuturnam moram quam sustinuit in prisona prædicta videlicet per Triennium & amplius. Et sic deliberatur a prisona. *Trin. Communia* 26. & 27. *E.* 1. *Rot.* 26. *b.*

(d) Pas. Fines 33. & 34. *E.* 1. *Rot.* 34. *b. Parte* 1.
(e) Mich. Communia 34. & 35. *E.* 1. *Rot.* 23. *b. Parte* 1.
(f) Mich. Commun. 2. *E.* 2. *Rot.* 44. *a. Inter Fines.*
(g) Ebor. *The Sheriff is amerced for an insufficient Return of a Writ.* Ipse Vicecomes

Richard de Keston, Clerk, was appointed to affeer Estreats of Amercements in several Counties, by Oath of Jurors. And *John de Cobham* and other Barons of the Exchequer were appointed to affeer divers other Amercements (*h*). Fifty Rolls of Amercements set in the Common Bench were brought to *John de Foxlee*, a Baron of the Exchequer, to be affeered. *John* was commanded to affeer the same; and to have them (being so affeered) at the Exchequer with all Speed. He did affeer them. And thereupon the same were sent out in Summonce (*i*).

But sometimes others of the King's Justices affeered Amercements; and sometimes Commissioners were appointed to do it. *Thomas de Weyland* (Chief Justice of the Common Bench) was allowed by the King xl l. for the Expences he had been at in going several Times through several Counties of the Realm, to take Assises and Enquests, and to tax Amercements (*k*). Four Justices of the Common Bench had C Marks allowed them by the King, to be distributed amongst them and their Clerks at the Discretion of the Treasurer and Barons, for their Charges in taxing the Amercements in divers Counties which had been set in the Common Bench (*l*). *Richard de Kestane* was assigned to affeer the Estreats in the Counties of *Lincoln*, *Northampton*, *Bedford*, and *Buckingham* (*m*). Commissioners were appointed (whereof some were Barons of the Exchequers) to affeer Amerciaments, to enquire of Forfeitures, and of the Behaviour of Taxors and Collectors, to hasten the levying of the King's Debts, to survey the King's Castles and Manors, and to do other Things for the King's Service (*n*). *William de Chesterfeild* was sent into divers Counties of the Realm at divers Times, to affeer Amercements for the King's Behoof; and was allowed his Expences for that Service (*o*).

The

mes videlicet Willelmus de Honk in misericordia. Et afforatur in continenti per . . Tenentem locum Thesaurarij, Willelmum de Carleton, & Magistrum Ricardum de Abyndon Barones, ad Decem libras. Postea in adventu W. Coventrensis & Lich. Episcopi Thesaurarij, pro eo quod dictus Vicecomes diligenter se habuit circa alia debita Regis levanda, sicut ipse Thesaurarius testatur, Amerciamentum prædictum per eundem Thesaurarium condonatur. *Hil. Commun.* 34. *Edw.* 1. *Rot.* 20. *a*.

(*h*) *Trin. Communia* 26. *E.* 1. *Rot.* 87. *b*.
(*i*) *Trin. Commun.* 12. *E.* 2. *Rot.* 31. *a*.
(*k*) Rex Thesaurario & Camerarijs suis salutem. Liberate de thesauro nostro di & fi nostro Thomæ de Weyland xl l, quas ei concessimus in subventionem expensarum suarum, quas fecit per diversas vices in eundo per diversos Comitatus Regni, tam ad Assisas & Inquisitiones per præceptum nostrum capiendas, quam pro amerciamentis taxandis, annis regni nostri decimo & undecimo. T. Rege apud Rothelan xxij die Junij; ad mandatum Cancellarij. *Lib.* 11. *E.* 1. *m.* 6.

(*l*) *Liberate* 12. *E.* 1. *m.* 4.
(*m*) *Hil. Communia* 25. *&* 26. *E.* 1. *Rot.* 50. *b.*
(*n*) *Trin. Commun.* 1. *E.* 2. *Rot.* 75. *a.*
(*o*) Supplicavit Regi Willelmus de Chestrefeld, quod cum ipse annis regni sui octavo nono & duodecimo, in obsequium
suum

Chap. XXII. *of the* EXCHEQUER.

The Barons of the Exchequer sometimes surveyed the King's Manors, and committed or devised the same. They also sometimes (by the King's Command or Assent) committed the Counties of the Realm to Sheriffs, and upon Occasion removed Sheriffs from their Bailywicks. *William de Carleton,* a Baron of the Exchequer, was appointed to survey the Works in the King's Castle of *Norwich* (*p*). *John de Foxlee, W. de Carleton, W. de Norwich,* and other Barons of the Exchequer, were assigned to survey the King's Castles and Manors in the several Counties of *England* (*q*). *John de Foxlee,* a Baron of the Exchequer, is appointed to survey the King's Manor of *Keninton* (*r*). The Treasurer and Barons committed the Manor of *Selveston* to *Thomas del Brok,* and *Henry Wade* and others, with the Assent of the King's Council, at the yearly Rent of xiiij l (*s*). The County of *Cumberland* was delivered to *Robert de Viepont,* by *Walo* the Legate, the Chief

suum missus fuisset ad diversos Comitatus regni sui, pro amerciamentis ad opus Regis assurendis, velit sibi de rationabilibus expensis suis in obsequio suo tunc appositis satisfacere, prout decet: Rex volens —— *So the King commands the Barons to make him due Satisfaction accordingly.* Pas. Brevia 12. E. 2. Rot. 100. a.

Et prætextu hujus mandati, Thesaurarius & Barones, præsente Willelmo de Bereford Capitali Justiciario de Banco, per informationem & avisamentum ejusdem, habita plenius consideratione ad præmissa, concordarunt quod prædictus Willelmus de Cestrefeld percipiat de Rege, pro labore suo & expensis per ipsum appositis in forma prædicta, decem libras. Pas. Commun. 12. E. 2. Rot. 27.

(*p*) Norf. De Operationibus factis in Castro Norwici tempore W. de Rothing Vicecomitis supervidendis per W. de Carleton Baronem Scaccarij. *'Tis a Commission to him to enquire concerning those Works, and the Expence of them, and to certify the Treasurer and Barons thereof.* Hil. Commissiones 26. & 27. E. 1. Rot. 49. b.

(*q*) Anglia. De Castris & Manerijs Regis supervidendis, & Inquisitione facienda super diversis articulis per singulos Comitatus Angliæ. *The King assigns John de Foxlee, for the Counties of* Surr. Sussex. Midd. Oxon. & Berk. Teste xxiiij die Julij: W. de Carleton & W. de Norwyco, *or one of them,* *for other Counties:* Roger de Hegham, *for other Counties:* Walter de Bedewynde, *for* York: *Master* J. de Everdon, *for other Counties:* Master Richard de Abyndon, *for other Counties:* Adam de Herwynton, *for other Counties:* Adam de Eglesfeld, *for other Counties:* Master Adam de Agmodesham & Elias Puger, *for other Counties.* Trin. Commiss. & Lit. Pat. 1. E. 2. Rot. 15. a.

(*r*) De supervidendo defectus Manerij de Kenynton. Rex dilecto & fideli suo Johanni de Foxle Baroni de Scaccario salutem. —— *'Tis a Commission to him to survey the Premisses.* Teste &c xx die Januarij. Per breve de Privato sigillo directum eidem Thesaurario. Hil. Commission. & Lit. Pat. 9. E. 2. Rot. 5. a.

(*s*) Memorandum quod die Jovis proxima ante festum S. Edmundi Regis & Martiris, commiserunt Thesaurarius & Barones de Scaccario, de assensu Magnatum qui sunt de Consilio Regis, Thomæ del Brok & Henrico Wade & alijs hominibus Regis de Selveston, prædictum Manerium, custodiendum quamdiu Regi placuerit; reddendo inde per annum ad Scaccarium xiiij l, videlicet unam medietatem ad Scaccarium Paschæ, & aliam medietatem ad Scaccarium S. Michaelis. Et custodient Domos Regis ibidem sumptibus suis proprijs, ita quod in reparatione & sustentatione earundem de suo nihil apponent. Mich. Commun. 56. H. 3. Rot. 2. b.

Justicier,

Justicier, the Bishop of *Winchester*, and *Falk de Breaute*, in Recompence for the Castle and Honour of *Tikehill* (*t*). *Henry de Bathe* and *Philip Lovell* came before the Barons of the Exchequer, and acknowledged, that they on the King's Behalf had committed the County of *Cumberland* and Castle of *Carlile* to the Earl of *Albemarle*, to hold during the King's Pleasure, rendering C l. at the Exchequer for the *Proficuum* of that County. The same Persons committed the County of *Lancaster* to *John de Cokerinton* (*u*). The King removed *Simon de Houcton* from his Sheriffdom of *Cambridge* and *Huntendon*; and by a close Writ commanded the Barons of the Exchequer, to put another Sheriff in his Place (*w*). The Treasurer and Barons committed *Wiltshire* to Sir *Richard de Worcester*, during the King's Pleasure (*x*). *Reginald de Acle* was commanded by Writ of the Exchequer to take the Office of Sheriff of *Gloucestershire* into the King's Hand, and commit it to a trusty Person till the King should give further Orders; and in the mean time to repair to the Exchequer, to receive the King's Commands from the Barons there (*y*). At the End of K. *Edward*
the

(*t*) Comitatus de Cumberlaunde traditus fuit Roberto de Veteri Ponte per Legatum Walonem, Justiciarium, Episcopum Winton., & per Falconem, die Dominica proxima ante festum S. Petri ad vincula anno iij° regni Regis H. iij, pro Castro de Tikehull quod traditum fuit Comiti Augi, & pro expensis quas idem Robertus in dicto Castro fecerat; Ita quod prædictus Robertus non responderet ad Scaccarium de firma neque de proficuo dicti Comitatus, quousque Curia Domini Regis ei teneret Justiciam de jure quod dicebat se habere in Castro & Honore de Tikehull. Debuit autem dictus Robertus respondere ad Scaccarium de Eschaetis, wardis, finibus, & itinere Justiciariorum, & debitis alijs de Summonitione Cumberlaundiæ, a die qua recepit Comitatum usque in unum mensem post diem S. Hyllarij anno vj Regis ejusdem. *Memor.* 6. *H.* 3. *Rot.* 3. *b.*

(*u*) Henricus de Bathonia & Philippus Lovell venerunt coram &c, & recognoverunt quod ipsi ex parte Domini Regis commiserant Domino Comiti Albemarliæ custodiam Comitatus Cumbriæ & Castri Karlioli, Tenenda quamdiu Regi placuerit, pro C l reddendis ad Scaccarium pro proficuo prædicti Comitatus. Et habebit omnia quæ prædecessor suus habebat in prædicto Comitatu. *Memor.* 42. *H.* 3. *Rot.* 1. *b.*

The same Persons committed the County of Lancaster, ex parte Regis, *to* John de Kokerinton. *Ib. Rot.* 2. *a.*

(*w*) Mandatum est Baronibus de Scaccario, quod loco Simonis de Houcton, quem Rex amovit ab officio Vicecomitis Cantebrigiæ & Huntendoniæ, fieri faciant unum Vicecomitem qui, præstito sacramento sicut fieri solet, Regi de exitibus eorundem Comitatuum respondeat ad Scaccarium Regis. T. Rege apud Portesmuth iiij die Julij. *Cl.* 37. *H.* 3. *m.* 7.

(*x*) Thesaurarius & Barones de præcepto Domini Regis commiserunt Ricardo de Wygornia Militi Comitatum Wiltesiæ, custodiendum quamdiu Regi placuerit, reddendo per annum pro proficuo ejusdem Comitatus quater xx marcas, sicut Radulfus de Aungers; Et perficiet corpus Comitatus, & reddet elemosinas constitutas, sicut alij Vicecomites prius reddere consueverunt. *Memor.* 51. *H.* 3. *Rot.* 6. *a.*

(*y*) Reginaldo de Acle pro Rege. Mandatum est eidem, quod statim visis Literis Regis capiat in manum Regis Officium Vicecomitis Comitatus Gloucestriæ, & illud alicui fideli Regis committat, custodiendum
donec

the First's Reign, Measures were taken at the Exchequer for removing several Sheriffs from their Offices, and putting others in their room (z). K. *Edward* II. by Privy Seal commanded the Treasurer's Lieutenant and the Barons, to remove *Walter de Gedding* from the Sherivalty of *Surrey* and *Sussex*, and to put *William de Henlee* into that Sherivalty, if he was fit for it, or, if he was not fit for it, to put in some other fit Person (a). The same King, *Anno Regni* 2, sent a Writ to the Barons of the Exchequer for removing the several Sheriffs of *England*, and placing other fit Persons in their room (b). At another Time, by Privy Seal, he commanded the Treasurer's Lieutenant and the Barons, to put *Nicolas de Teukesbury* into the Bailywick of Sheriff of *Devonshire*, to hold during the King's Pleasure (c). And in the 5th Year of his Reign, *John de Wylughby*, Sheriff of *Northampton*, being so engaged in certain Affairs, that he could not attend to execute his Sherivalty: The King by Privy Seal commands the Treasurer and Barons to discharge him from that Office, and put another fit Person into it (d). In the 12th Year of that King, the Commons of *Hantshire* petitioned the King, shewing that the King and his Council had lately ordered, that all Sheriffs in the Realm and their Ministers, who had been in Office since the King began to reign, should be put out of Office, that so the People, who had been wronged or oppressed by

donec Rex inde aliud præceperit. Et ipse in propria persona sua sit ad Scaccarium, ad audiendum & faciendum præceptum Regis ei per Barones exponendum. Teste &c. *Mich. Communia* 1. *&* 2. *E.* 1. *Rot.* 3. *a.*

(z) De Vicecomitibus si expediens fuerit removendis & alijs subrogandis. *Trin. Commun.* 35. *E.* 1. *Rot.* 49. *a. in band.* 34. *&* 35. *E.* 1. *parte* 2.

(a) Edward par la grace de Dieu &c, Au Lieutenant nostre Tresorier & as Barons de nostre Escheker Salutz. Pur aucunes resons nous vous maundoms, qe Wauter de Gedding qui ad demore nostre Visconte de Surrie & de Sussex facetz remuer de cel Office, & y facetz mettre William de Henlee si vous veetz quil soit pur meme Loffice covenable, suffisaunt, & profitable pur nous & nostre people. Et si il ne soit mye a ceo suffisaunt, adonqes y mettet autre qe a ceo soyt suffisaunt, & profitable pur nous & nostre people de la dite Balye. Done soutz nostre prive Seal a Langele, le xij jour Daveril lan secund. *Pasc. Brevia* 2. *E.* 2. *Rot.* 65. *a.*

(b) Baronibus pro Rege. *Mich. Brevia* 8. *E.* 2. *Rot.* ——— *a.*

(c) Edward par la grace de Dieu &c, Au Leu tenaunt nostre Tresorier & as Barons de nostre Eschekier salutz. Nous vous maundoms, qe a nostre bien amez Nicholas de Teukesbury facetz aver la Balye de nostre Visconte de Devenischyre, a tenir la taunt come il nous plera. Done souz nostre prive seal a Langele, le xvj jour de Juyn lan secund. *Trin. Brevia* 2. *E.* 2. *Rot.* 81. *b.*

(d) Edward par la grace de Dieu &c, Au lieu tenaunt du Tresorier & as Barons de nostre Escheqer salutz. Por ceo qe Mon[sieur] Johan de Wylughby nostre Visconte de Norhamton est tant occupez de diverses busoignes, quil ne peust entendre a la dite Viscuntee: Vous maundoms, qe le dit Johan facez descharger del dit Office, & facez mettre un autre en mesme loffice qi soit ben covenable & suffisaunt pur nous e pur nostre people. Don souz nostre Prive Seal a Brustewyk, le xx jour de Juyn lan de nostre regne quint. *Trin. Brevia* 5. *E.* 2. *Rot.* 53. *b.*

such Sheriffs or their Ministers, might the more easily obtain Relief against them; and that *James de Norton*, who was Sheriff of *Hantshire* before the said Ordinance, still continued in that Office, whereby Men could not easily get Redress against him for Wrongs done them: and praying that he might be removed. Hereupon the King commanded the Barons, that if the Fact was so, they should remove *James* from the Office of Sheriff of that County, and commit it, on the King's Behalf, to some other whom they should judge to be a fit Person (*e*).

In fine; it was the Business of the Treasurer and Barons to speed the levying and getting-in of the King's Debts, and to manage the Crown Revenue to the best Advantage. This was their incessant Care, and the principal Scope to which their Acts and Proceedings tended; as all the Records of the Exchequer do evince. Nevertheless, if the King thought them remiss, or if he wanted Money very urgently, he would send Writs or Messages to them, to hasten the getting-in of Money in such Manner as he directed. There are several Things of this Kind remarkable enough to be here inserted. K. *Henry* III. with the Advice of his Council, ordered the Amercements of the Exchange of *London*, and the Mulcts of *Caworsini* and *Tramontani* residing in *London* to be levied, viz. CC Marks of each Society: and now by his Writ commands the Barons to cause the same to be levied with all Speed (*f*). The King by his Writ commanded the Barons to cause his Escuage for the Army of *Wales*, viz. xl s. *per Scutum*, to be levied of all Fees holden of the King *in Capite*, or of his Wardships; except the Fees of such Persons as had Writs *de Scutagio suo habendo* (*g*). The King, being in great Want of Money, commanded the Barons to send to him the Summons of the Exchequer under Seal, for Debts contained in the Estreats of the Chancery, and for Fines and other clear Debts, to the Value of Ten

---

(*e*) Trin. Brevia 12. E. 2. Rot. 106. a.

(*f*) Quia ante recessum Regis ab Anglia, per ipsum Regem & Consilium suum fuit provisum, quod Amerciamenta Cambij de hijs qui Cambium in Civitate Londoniæ contra præceptum Regis vel contra statuta Cambij, & eciam de Kaworsinis & Ultramontanis in eadem Civitate commorantibus, scilicet de qualibet Societate eorundem, ducentæ marcæ levarentur, & illud idem oretenus injunxit dilecto Fratri & Fideli Regis Ricardo Comiti Cornubiæ, & dilecto Clerico Magistro Willelmo de Kilkenny Archidiacono Coventrensi: Mandat Rex Baronibus, quod amerciamenta prædicta cum festinatione levari faciant. Breve est in f. M. Et mandatum est Vicecomitibus Londoniæ. Memor. 38. H. 3. Rot. 17. a.

(*g*) Rex mandavit Baronibus, quod levari faciant Scutagium suum, videlicet de Scuto xl s, pro exercitu Walliæ, de omnibus feodis Militum quæ tenentur de Rege in Capite, vel de Wardis in manu Regis existentibus; exceptis feodis illorum qui brevia Regis habuerunt de Scutagio suo habendo. Ex Memor. 42. H. 3. Rot. 4. b.

thousand

thousand Marks, that the King might cause the same to be levied for his Use (*h*). The King sent to the Barons certain Estreats of Fines and Amercements, commanding them to levy the Money contained therein without Delay (*i*). K. *Edward* I. commanded the Barons both by Message and by Writ of the Privy Seal, in very urgent Terms, to cause Money to be levied for him with all Speed, as well out of the Customs of Wool and Leather, as also out of the Issues of his Realm, and otherwise, for his present Supply (*k*). The same King commanded the Barons, both by Message and by Writ of Privy Seal, to use their utmost Diligence to supply him with Money for the Expences of his Houshold (*l*). K. *Edward* II. by Writ of Privy Seal, com-

(*h*) Baronibus, pro Rege. Quia Rex ad urgentissima negocia sua inde expedienda, ad præsens quamplurimum indiget, Mandat quod scrutatis rotulis Scaccarij sui, tam de extractis Cancellariæ quas Rex eis mittit, quam de finibus & claris debitis suis, mittant Regi Summonitiones sigillo Scaccarij signatas usque ad decem millia marcarum, ut Rex pecuniam illam ad opus suum, ut melius expedire viderit, levari faciat. Teste &c. *Memor.* 51. *H.* 3. *Rot.* 4. *a.*

(*i*) Baronibus pro Rege. Rex mittit eis extractas Finium & Amerciamentorum factorum coram Gilberto de Preston & socijs suis, in ultimo Itinere suo in Comitatu Notinghamiæ: Mandans eis, quatinus totam pecuniam in eisdem extractis contentam sine dilatione levari faciant; ita quod eam habeant ad Scaccarium suum ad festum Purificationis B. Mariæ proximo futurum. Et hoc nullatenus omittant. T. &c. *Hil. Commun.* 52. & 53. *H.* 3. *Rot.* 8. *a.*

(*k*) Baronibus, pro Rege. Edward par la grace de Dieu &c. Entre totes les autres choses qui nous vous fesoms savoir par nostre cher Clerk Johan de Drokenesford Gardein de nostre Garderobe, dont nous li avoms enchargez, vous mandoms e chargoms en la foy qe vous nous devez, e sicome vous amez honur de nous & de nostre Reaume e de nos amis ausint, qe vous metez tote la peyne e la diligence qe vous porrez, coment deniers seient levez a nostre oes ove tote faison e le haste qe vous porrez, ausi bien de la Custume de Leyne e de quirs come des issues de nostre Reaume, e par totes les autres voies par out levees se porront fere.

Car si nous pussoms conforter nos amisdaukuns deniers par temps, nous esperons qe nos busoignes par tot iront bien ove laide e la grace de nostre Seignour. Por la queu chose nous vous chargoms derechief fermement enjoignantz, qe vous eez ceste chose au quoer, qe nous pussoms aparcevoir qe vous y aurez mis diligeaument vostre entente. Donees de souz nostre Prive Seal a Merinton, le vij jour Doctobre lan de nostre Regne xxiiij. *Mich. Commun.* 24. & 25. *E.* 1.

(*l*) Edward par la grace de Diu &c, A nos chers Clerks William de Carleton, e Mester Richard de Abyndon Barons de nostre Escheqer, salutz. Pur ceo qe nous avoms retenuz noster cher Clerk Johan de Drokenesford gardeyn de nostre Garderobe es parties ou nous somes, pur acunes certeynes busoignes que nous avoms afaire de lui, jusqes a cest Venderdy en la primere semeyne de quareme avenir, ou le Lundy procheyn suyant: Vous mandoms, qe vous ne remuez nule part de noster Escheqer ne les autres que sunt mesme la place, eynz y demorgez jusqes a sa venue, pur sere espleyter les busoignes qe tuchent la dite place; Et quant il serra venuz, ordinez issi entre ly e vous, e mettez voster poer qe nous puissoms estre servises deners, si soisonablement come mester nous serra, pur les despenses de noster Hostel, solum ceo que il vous avisera plus pleynement de par nous; & ceo ne lessez. Don souz noster Prive Prive Seal a la Hyde pres de Wyncestre, le xxj jour de Feverer lan xxxiiij. *Hil. Brevia* 34. *E.* 1. *Rot.* 19. *b.*

mands

mands and charges the Barons very urgently, to cause all the Debts due to his Father at the Time of his Death, and all that are now due to himself, to be speedily levied and paid into the Exchequer; and to forbear respiting or estalling any Debt whatsoever, without special Order from him (*m*). The same King issued several Precepts touching the speedy collecting and answering of a triennial Disme imposed by the Pope on the Clergy (*n*). The same King, by Writ of the Privy Seal, commanded the Treasurer and Barons to send to him without Delay all the Money they had at the Exchequer, for the Expences of his Houshold; and to borrow Money for him in the best Manner they could, to the Value of Two thousand Pounds, or thereabouts, for the Expences of his said Houshold (*o*). And a few days after he sent them another Writ of the Privy Seal, charging them to raise all the Money they could, as well by Chevisance as otherwise, to supply the Expences aforesaid (*p*). The same King, by Writ of Privy Seal,
commanded

(*m*) Edward par la grace de Dieu &c, Au Treforer & as Barons de noftre Efcheker, falutz. Pur ceo qe nous avoins molt graundement a faire de deniers ore apermeifmes, por moltz des groffes bofoignes qe nous touchent, & qe nous cherront fure procheinement: Vous maundoms fermement enjoignanz, & chargeoms en la foi qe vous nous devez, qe vous nous facez haftivement levoir & paier a noftre Efcheqer, totes les dettes qe furent dues a noftre cher pere, qi Dieus affoille, avaunt fa mort, & totes celes qe funt dues a nous aufint pur queuque caufe qe ce foit; & ne refpitez ne eftallez nule dette qe foit due a noftre Piere ne a nous, faunz efpecial maundement de nous, fur noftre greve forfeture. Et metiez fi diligeaument peine & entente de nous bien fervir de deniers a noftre befoign, dore que nous puiffoms & devoms prifer voftre peniblere & voftre diligence en cele partie. Don fouz noftre Prive Seal a Redinges, le fecond jour de Decembre, lan de noftre [Regne] primer. *Mich. Brevia* 1. *E.* 2. *Rot.* 21. *a.*

(*n*) *Mich. Brevia Retornab.* 5. *E.* 2. *Rot.* —— *b.*

(*o*) Baronibus per Regem. Come nous mandoms par Bref de noftre Grant Seal, au Lieutenant de Treforier & as Chamberleyns de noftre Efcheqiere, qil enveent a nous fanz delay toutz les deners qil ount a noftre Efcheqier, pur les defpens de noftre Houftel, & nous eoms trefgrant fuffrete de deners en noftre Garderobe pour noftre dit defpens, ficome le portur de cefte Lettre vous faura plus pleinement dire de bouche: Vous mandoms & chargeoms fur tote laffiance qe nous avoms de vous, qe vous mettez voftre peine & diligence de faire cheviffance de deners a noftre oeps, en queuque manere qe vous puiffet mielz; iffint qe nous puiffoms eftre ferviz a cefte foiz de deux Mille livers, ou a plus pres de cele fumme qe vos unqes poerez, pur les defpens de noftre Houftel avantdit. Et cefti noftre maundement eez fi a quer & li menez a fi bon effect, qe nous puiffoms apercever la diligence qe vous y averet mis. Don fouz noftre Prive Seal a Everwyk le xxx jour de May, lan de noftre regne quint. *Trin. Brevia* 5. *E.* 2. *Rot.* 53. *a.*

(*p*) Baronibus pro Rege. Edward par la grace de Dieu &c, Au Liutenant dou Treforer & as Barons de noftre Efcheqier falutz. Nous vous mandoms & chargeoms ficome autrefoiz vous avoms mandez, qe vous mettez peyne & diligence de purchacer & affembler a noftre oeps la forfon des deners qe vous porrez, auffibien par cheviffance come en autre manere, pur les defpens del Houftiel; Car nous avoms trefgrant fuffrete de deniers en noftre Garderobe pur les defpens

commanded the Treasurer and Barons, to cause all the Debts due at the Exchequer, as well in the Time of his Ancestors as in his own Time, to be levied with all possible Speed, without sparing or respiting any body (notwithstanding any Commandment for Respites sent to them before this Time) till further Order from the King (*q*) Another Writ of Privy Seal, of the like Import and Urgency, was sent to the Treasurer and Barons, for levying of Debts due by Imprests made at the Exchequer and Wardrobe (*r*).

II. Secondly, As to Pleas or Causes. In the xviiith Chapter of the first Volume we have spoken concerning the Division of the King's Courts of Law, and the Separation (that followed thereupon) of Common Pleas from the King's Court and Palace: whereby great Alteration was made in the Court of Exchequer, as far as related to the Holding of Common Pleas there. Nevertheless, let us consider now how the Case stood, under this second Period, in that Respect. For although it was forbidden, first, by the great Charters of K. K. *John* and *Henry* III, and afterwards by a Statute or Ordinance (which will be mentioned by and by) made by the King, and the Prelates and Barons of the Realm, to hold Common Pleas in the Exchequer: yet in fact some Common Pleas were still holden there. This gave Occasion to the issuing of several Writs, directed to the Treasurer and Barons of the Exchequer, some of which are hereunder set forth. In the 56th Year of K. *Henry* III. divers Pleas were moved in the Exchequer by original Writs, for Debts of divers Persons; the discussing of which Pleas was a great Hindrance to the Sheriffs and others accompting at the Exchequer: whereupon the King by his Writ commanded the Treasurer and Barons to atterminate all Pleas then depending before them (except such Pleas as concerned the Ministers of the Exchequer) before the Justices of the *Bank*; and to transmit, under the Exchequer Seal, the said original Writs, and the Records of the said Pleas, to the said Justices; whom the King had commanded to receive and determine the same according to Law (*s*). In the 5th

Year

---

spens avantdiz: Et mettez y si diligaument voftre entente, qe nous puissoms apperceveir qe nous ferroms du miels serviz par le bon consail qe vouz y averez miz. Done souz nostre Prive Seal a Houeden le xij jour de Jayn, lan de nostre Regne quint. *Trin. Brevia* 5. *E.* 2. *Rot.* 53. *a. in imo.*
(*q*) *Pasf. Brevia* 15. *E.* 2. *Rot.* 56. *a.*

(*r*) *Trin. Brevia* 15. *E.* 2. *Rot.* 61. *a.*
(*s*) Memorandum de Placitis Scaccarij prohibitis. H. Dei gratia &c, Thesaurario & Baronibus suis de Scaccario suo salutem. Quia constat nobis, quod per Placita mota coram vobis per brevia nostra Originalia, de debitis diversorum, & ibidem pendencia, impediuntur negocia nostra, ita quod Compotus

Year of K. *Edward* I, a Writ was sent to the Barons of the Exchequer. It recites, that according to the Law and Custom of the Realm, and the Tenor of *Magna Charta*, Pleas ought not to be holden before the Barons in the King's Exchequer, unless for the Debts of the King, or of his Ministers of the Exchequer: that nevertheless *John de Mucheldene*, who was not a Minister of the Exchequer, impleaded *Agnes Ash* before the Barons there for a Debt of xiij l: wherefore it commands the Barons not to hold the said Plea, or any other Common Plea in the Exchequer (*t*). Other Writs (not unlike in Form) issued for *John de Cokefeld, Roger le Taverner* and his Wife, and *Robert Fitz-Hugh* (*u*); for *Roger Baynard* (*w*); for *Nicolas de Hastyng*, and others, in

potus Vicecomitum & aliorum Ballivorum & Ministrorum nostrorum de Ballivis suis & exitibus earum audiri non potest, in nostri grave dampnum, quod sustinere nolumus sicut nec debemus: Vobis mandamus, quod omnia Placita quascumque personas tangencia, Exceptis ministris ejusdem Scaccarij, atterminetis coram Justiciarijs nostris de Banco ad certos dies, prout melius videritis expedire: Et Brevia nostra Originalia, & recorda Placitorum illorum eisdem Justiciarijs sub Sigillo ejusdem Scaccarij transmittatis, Quibus mandavimus quod ea a vobis recipiant, & Placita illa terminari faciant, prout secundum Legem & consuetudinem Regni nostri fuerit faciendum. Teste me ipso apud Westmon. xx die Octobris anno &c Lv°. *Mich. Communia* 56. *H.* 3. *Rot.* 1. *b*.

(*t*) Baronibus, de Placitis non tenendis. Cum Placita coram Baronibus in Scaccario Regis, secundum legem & consuetudinem Regni sui, teneri non debeant, nisi de debitis Regis proprijs & Ministrorum de Scaccario prædicto: Ac Johannes de Mucheldene, qui non est Minister Regis in Scaccario prædicto ut dicitur, Agnetem de Fraxino implacitet coram eis in Scaccario, de debito xiij l in quibus idem Johannes dicit præfatam Agnetem sibi teneri, & eam multipliciter inquietet occasione prædicta, sicut ex ipsius Agnetis gravi querimonia Rex accepit: Rex nolens sustinere hujusmodi Placita, contra tenorem Magnæ Cartæ de Libertatibus Angliæ, alibi quam suis locis proprijs & debitis placitari, mandat eisdem, quod Placitum illud vel aliud placitum commune ulterius coram eis non teneant in Scaccario prædicto: Quia Rex singulis de Regno suo, cum sibi in Curia sua perquirere voluerit, paratus est communem justiciam exhibere, prout de jure &c. *Hil. Commun.* 4. & 5. *E.* 1. *Rot.* 3. *b*.

(*u*) Baronibus, pro Johanne de Cokefeld. Cum secundum Legem & Consuetudinem Regni, communia placita coram Baronibus ad Scaccarium placitari non debeant, nisi placita illa Regem aut Ministros suos ejusdem Scaccarij specialiter tangant: Et Rex jam ex insinuatione Johannis de Cokefeld acceperit, quod Robertus Peverel qui Minister ejusdem Scaccario non est, ipsum implacitet coram Baronibus in Scaccario prædicto per Breve Regis, de eo quod idem Johannes reddat præfato Roberto quoddam Dolium Vini precij v marcarum: Rex mandat Baronibus, quod si ita est, tunc de placito illo coram eis ulterius tenendo se non intromittant, set præfato Roberto dicant, quod Breve Regis versus prædictum Johannem alibi, sicut fieri solet, placitandum sibi impetret, si sibi viderit expedire. T. Rege apud Westmon. xxv die Aprilis anno xxxiij. *Mich. Communia* 34. & 35. *E.* 1. *Rot.* 10. *a. Pars* 1. A like Writ to the Barons (reciting as above, mutatis mutandis) was awarded for Roger le Taverner and his Wife; *Pas. Brevia* 34. *E.* 1. *Rot.* 26. *b*. And the like Writ for Robert Fitz Hugh. *Trin. Brevia* 6. *E.* 2. *Rot.* 54. *b*. For Henry de Calverd de Eboraco; *Hil. Brevia* 5. *E.* 2. *Rot.* 30. *b*; for Geoffrey de Matham senior; *Pas. Brevia* 1. *E.* 2. *Rot.* 46. *b*; for Thomas Gryk; *Pas. Brevia* 2. *E.* 2. *Rot.* 65. *b*; and others.

(*w*) Baronibus, pro Rogero Baygnard. Cum

Chap. XXII.   *of the* Exchequer.

in purfuance of the Ordinance made by the Prelates, Earls, and Barons in the Reign of K. *Edward* II (*x*); and for Mafter *John de Blebury*, in purfuance of the fame Ordinance (*y*). *Gilbert Peche* had by his Charter granted to K. *Edward* I. and *Alianor* then Queen Confort, and their Heirs, the Homages and Services of *John Peche* and others (who held of the faid *Gilbert in Capite*) and of their Heirs: A *Scire facias* iffued out of the Exchequer to the faid *John* and others, to appear there, and fhew Caufe why they fhould not attorn to the King for their faid Homages and Services: afterwards the Treafurer and Barons, confidering that the faid Affair ought to be profecuted before the Juftices of the *Common Bench,* according to the Direction of the *Great Charter,* ordered (for that and other Reafons mentioned in the Record cited hereunder) that *Nicolas de Warwick* the King's Serjeant fhould profecute the fame in the Common Bank (*z*).

Cum fecundum Confuetudinem in Regno Angliæ approbatam hactenus & obtentam, Communia placita coram Baronibus de Scaccario placitari non debeant, nifi placita illa Regem aut aliquem Miniftrorum fuorum de eodem Scaccario fpecialiter tangant; Et Rex jam acceperit, quod Robertus Benedicite de Norwyco, qui Minifter Regis de eodem Scaccario non eft ut dicitur, Rogerum Baygnard de debito C s implacitat coram Baronibus in Scaccario prædicto, contra Confuetudinem prædictam: Rex mandat Baronibus, quod fi ita eft, tunc placito illo coram eis in eodem Scaccario ulterius tenendo fuperfedeant. T. Rege apud Lanrecoft xxij die Novembris anno xxxv. *Mich. Commun.* 34. *&* 35. *E.* 1. *Rot.* 10. *b. Parte* 1.

(*x*) *Mich. Brevia* 9. *E.* 2. *Rot.* 11. *a.*

(*y*) *Trin. Brevia* 9. *E.* 2. *Rot.* 51. *b.*

(*z*) Memorandum, quod cum prætextu Cartæ quam Gilbertus Peche fecit Domino Regi qui nunc eft & Alianoræ quondam Reginæ conforti fuæ & hæredibus fuis, de Homagijs & fervicijs Johannis Peche, Reginaldi de Brokedyfh, & aliorum diverforum Tenencium qui tenuerunt de ipfo Gilberto in Capite, & hæredum fuorum, quæ quidem Carta ad plenum inferitur in Rotulo Memorandorum de Termino Pafchæ anno vicefimo quarto, Barones alias, videlicet Termino & anno eifdem, concordaffent, quod hic in Scaccario profequeretur verfus illos vel eorum hæredes, quorum fervicia & homagia dictus Gilbertus Regi & Reginæ dederat per Cartam prædictam, quod venirent hic oftenfuri fi quid fcirent dicere, quare fe attornaffe non debuiffent Domino Regi de Homagijs & fervicijs fuis, juxta formam Domini prædicti, & verfus eos profecutum fuerit hic, ficut continetur in Rotulis placitorum pro Rege de anno vicefimo quinto: Thefaurarius & Barones modo perpendentes, quod dictum negocium profequi debet coram Jufticiarijs in Banco, maxime propter innovationem Magnæ Cartæ, quæ exigit quod Communia Placita in certo loco videlicet coram ipfis Jufticiarijs exequantur, & eciam pro eo quod idem negocium exigit exequi fecundum Communem Legem qua coram præfatis Jufticiarijs plenarie utitur, Concordarunt quod hic non fequatur inde ulterius &c; fed quod Nicholaus de Warrewik ferviens Regis, ad negocia Regis coram præfatis Jufticiarijs exequenda deputatus, profequatur coram eifdem prout juftum fuerit, verfus illos quorum Homagia & Servicia ad Regem pertinere debent per Cartam prædictam; & hoc tam occafionibus fupradictis, quam pro eo quod quædam Nota cujufdam Finis refidet in Banco prædicto de hijs quæ continentur in Carta prædicta. Et in continenti tranfcribitur eadem Carta & tranfcriptum inde prædicto Nicholao liberatur, ad profequendum inde in Banco pro Rege, quod fuerit profequendum, Videlicet quarto decimo die Februarij. *Hil. Recorda* 25 *&* 26. *E.* 1. *Rot.* 48. *b.*

But

But although it was forbidden by the Great Charters of K. K. *John* and *Henry* III. to hold Common Pleas in the Exchequer: yet the King sometimes gave Leave to particular Persons to bring their Suits and recover their Debts there. For Example: King *Henry* III. by his Writ commanded the Barons, that as soon as the Executors of *Ralf* late Bishop of *Chichester* had certified to them the Names of all Persons who were indebted to the Bishop, and the Sum of each Debt, they should distrain all the said Debtors in each County of *England*, to pay their respective Debts to the Bishop's Executors at the Exchequer (*a*). King *Edward* I. gave Leave to the Executors of *John* Earl of *Warenne*, to implead his Debtors at the Exchequer (*b*). K. *Edward* II. by Writ of Privy Seal commanded the Barons to let the Merchants *Friskobalds* sue before them in the Exchequer for their Debts (as there should be Occasion) and to levy the same for them like as the King's own Debts, according to the Law and Usages of the Exchequer (*c*). The same King by Writ of Privy Seal granted to Master *James Despaigne*, that he might plead at the Exchequer, to recover all the Debts due to him, and commanded the Barons to receive him thereto, as often as he would sue before them for his said Debts (*d*). The like Writ issued for *Gerard de Ozum* (*e*), *William de Otefwyche* (*f*), *Nicolas de Haluford* (*g*), the Executors of *John* Earl

---

(*a*) Baronius, pro executoribus testamenti R. quondam Cycestrensis Episcopi. Rex eisdem; Quia debita quæ debebantur eidem Episcopo non soluta [sunt] ipsius executoribus, sicut animæ ipsius expediret, & nos volentes eidem animæ in hac parte subvenire, quia prædictus Episcopus nobis fuit specialiter dilectus: Vobis mandamus, quod in singulis Comitatibus regni nostri distringi faciatis omnes debitores ejusdem Episcopi, ad reddendum executoribus ipsius vel eorum assignato ad Scaccarium omnia debita prædicta, ex quo prædicti executores nomina prædictorum debitorum & quantitates cujuslibet debiti vobis scire fecerint. B. e. in f. M. *Pas. Commun.* 29. *H.* 3. *Rot.* 9. *a*.

(*b*) *Ryl. Plac.* P. *p.* 277. 33. *E.* 1.

(*c*) Baronibus, pro Mercatoribus de Societate Friskebaldorum. *The King commands*, — qe vous lour retenetz a ce totes les feez [*or* feitz] quil averont a faire (*as often as they shall have Occasion*) a recoverir lour dettes, & lor dettes facez lever ausi come les noz dettes propres, solonc la ley & les usages de nostre Escheqer. Donne souz nostre Prive Seal &c, lan de nostre regne primer. *Mich. Brevia* 1. *E.* 2. *Rot.* 20. *b*.

(*d*) Baronibus, pro Johanne de Ispannia. Edward par la grace de Dieu &c. Au Tresorier e as Barons de nostre Escheqier salutz. Pur ceo qe de nostre grace especiale, avome grante a nostre Cher Clerk & Cosyn Meistre James Despaigne, quil puisse pleder a nostre Escheqier, Vous mandoms qe vouz rescevez a ceo le dit Meistre James, totes lez foiz qil voudra suire devaunt vous, por pleder por ses dettes avauntdites. Done souz nostre Prive Seal a Wyndesore le xxvij jour de May lan de nostre Regne premier. *Pas. Brevia* 1. *E.* 2. *Rot.* 53. *a*.

(*e*) *Trin. Brevia* 1. *E.* 2. *Rot.* 62. *a*.
(*f*) *Mich. Brevia* 2. *E.* 2. *Rot.* 23. *a*.
(*g*) *Mich. Brevia* 2. *E.* 2. *Rot.* 25. *a*.

Chap. XXII.   *of the* Exchequer.   77

of *Warenne* (*h*), and the Executors of *Walter* late Bishop of *Coventry* and *Lichfield* (*i*).

Sometimes, after a Plea had been commenced in the Exchequer, the King (if he thought fit) would command the Barons not to proceed therein. K. *Edward* I. having granted to *Tecla Amadour*, and other Merchants of *Florence*, Leave to recover their Debts in the Exchequer, according to the Course of the Exchequer; and the Barons having summoned before them the Prior of *Mountague*, to answer the said Merchants for C Marks: the King by his Writ (issued in Favour of the Merchants, but for what Reasons it does not here appear) commands the Barons to proceed no further in the Exchequer upon the said Plea (*k*). The King commanded the Barons, that no Writ should be granted to *Roger la Zuche* or *Helene la Zuche*, against the Earl of *Warwick*, before the Feast of St. *Hilary* next (*l*).

Again; sometimes Common Pleas have been commenced and prosecuted in the Exchequer, between Persons who were not (as it seemeth) Residents or Accomptants at the Exchequer; and where there was no particular Leave (for ought that appears) given to either of the Parties to sue there. For Example: The Abbot of *Lavendene* appeared at the Exchequer, in a Plea between him and *James* the *Jew* of *Northampton*, and others (*m*). *Sibyll*, Daughter and Heir of *Ralf de Iclesham*, came into the Exchequer and complained, that *Sibyll de*

(*h*) *Trin. Brevia* 2. *E.* 2. *Rot.* 81. *a.*

(*i*) Edward par la grace de Dieu &c, Au Treforier & as Barons de noftre Efcheqier, falutz. Come pur le bon fervife qe Wauter jadis Evefque de Ceftre fift a noftre chier Piere, qi Dieux affoille, & puis a nous, tant come il vefquift, & aufint pur aucunes bountees qe nous avoms trovez en les executours du teftament le dit Wauter, eoms grantez de noftre grace efpeciale, a meifmes les executours, quil puiffent enpleder les dettours le dit Wauter a noftre dit Efcheqier, & recoverer illoqes les dettes qe lour fount detenues: Vous mandoms, qe a ce les receviez, & lour facez aver fi haftif recoverir come vous porrez, folonc ley & ufage de cele Place. Don fouz noftre Prive Seal a Everwik, le xiiij jour de Maij lan de noftre regne xv. *Paf. Brevia* 15. *E.* 2. *Rot.* 56. *a.*

(*k*) Baronibus pro Tecla Amadour & focijs. Cum nuper conceffserit Rex Teclæ Amadour & Loter Bonawik & Socijs fuis Mercatoribus Florentinis, quod debitores fuos coram eis venire faciant, ita quod debita fua in Scaccario fecundum confuetudinem ejufdem Scaccarij recuperare poffent, ac priorem de Monte acuto coram eis venire fecerint, ad refpondendum præfatis Mercatoribus de C marcis: Rex mandat Baronibus, quod placitum illud de decætero non teneant ibidem &c. *Mich. Communia* 4 & 5. *E.* 1. *Rot.* 1. *a.*

(*l*) De Inhibitione facta ex parte Domini Regis, per Radulphum de Sandwyco. Memorandum quod inhibitum eft per Regem Baronibus, quod nullum breve concedatur Rogero la Zuche, aut Helenæ quæ fuit uxor Alani la Zuche, fuper Comitem War., citra feftum S. Hillarij proximo futurum. *Mich. Commun.* 4 & 5. *E.* 1. *Rot.* 1. *b.*

(*m*) Buk. Abbas de Lavendene optulit fe ad Scaccarium, in craftino S. Hyllarij & per tres dies fequentes, contra Jacobum Judæam de Norhamton, & alios adverfarios fuos; & nullus adverfariorum fuorum comparuit. *Memor.* 11. *H.* 3. *Rot.* 2. *a.*

Dene,

Dene, Mother of *Ralf de Iclesham*, permitted *Robert de Dene*, Brother of the said *Ralf*, to receive the Homages of the Tenants of certain Land in her Tenure, in Disherison of her [*Sibyll*] the Complainant; and prayed Justice might be done her in the Case (*n*). In the 14th Year of K. *Henry* III, *Roger le Champenois* was Attorney for one of the Parties litigant in a Plea of Debt depending in the Exchequer (*o*). A Plea was moved in the Exchequer between the Bishop of *Exeter* and the Knights of *Devonshire* concerning the Fine paid to the King for de-afforesting of *Cornwall* (*p*). The Abbot of *Cerne*, by *Hugh le Brun* and *William de Cerne*, made an Essoign *de Malo lecti* before the Barons of the Exchequer against the Prior of St. *Swithin*, in a Plea of Land (*q*). A Writ issued to summon *Hugh* Son of *Oliver* to appear before the Barons of the Exchequer, to warrant to *Peter de Cruket* and *Joan* his Wife one Virgate of Land in *Stanebrugge*, which the King claimed in his Court against them as belonging to his Serjeantry of *Stanburg*; the said *Peter* and *Joan* having in the same Court before the King vouched the said *Hugh* to Warranty against the King (*r*). *Richard de Mucegros* appeared at the Exchequer before the Barons three Weeks after the *Purification*, against *Hugh le Tanur* and *Juliana* his Wife, and *Isabell* her Sister, in a Plea of *Land* (*s*). A Writ of *Venire facias* issued to the Sheriff of *Cambridgeshire*, to summon

(*n*) Suffex. Sibilia filia & hæres Radulfi de Iclesham uxor Nicholay Haringot conqueritur, quod Sibilla de Dene uxor Ricardi de la Cumbe & Mater Radulfi de Iclesham patris sui, permittit Robertum de Dene fratrem dicti Radulfi recipere Homagia de terra quam ipsa tenet, in ipsius Sibillæ conquerentis exæreditationem ut dicit. Et petit sibi justitiam exhiberi. *Memor.* 11. *H.* 3. *Rot.* 1. *b.*

(*o*) Surreia. Rogerus le Champenois est atornatus Roberi de Mikelham, de placito debiti versus hæredem Willelmi de [Tylle]broc, ad lucrandum vel perdendum. *Mich. Commun.* 14. *H.* 3. *Rot.* 1. *a.*

(*p*) Devonia. Dies datus est Episcopo Exoniensi & Militibus Devoniæ, de contentione inter illos mota de Fine pro deafforestatione Cornubiæ, in octabis S. Johannis Baptistæ, sine essonio. *Trin. Commun.* 14. *H.* 3. *Rot.* 7. *a.*

(*q*) Dorf. Abbas de Cerne essoniavit se coram Baronibus, die Sabbati proximo post festum S. Hyllarij, versus Priorem S. Swithuni de Malo lecti, de placito Terræ, per Hugonem le Brun & Willelmum de Cerne. *Hil. Commun.* 27. *H.* 3. *Rot.* 6. *a.*

(*r*) Bed. & Buk. Mandatum est Vicecomiti, quod ponat per vadium & salvos plegios Hugonem filium Oliveri, ita quod sit coram Baronibus in octabis S. Trinitatis, ad warantizandum Petro de Cruket & Johannæ uxori ejus unam virgatam terræ cum pertinentijs in Stanebrugge, quam Rex in Curia sua versus eosdem clamavit de Serjantia sua de Stanburg; & unde ijdem P. & J. in eadem Curia Regis coram Rege vocaverunt ad warantum prædictum Hugonem versus Regem. Et habeat &c. *Memor.* 35. *H.* 3. *Rot.* 11. *b.*

(*s*) Wigorn. Ricardus de Mucegros optulit se ad Scaccarium coram Baronibus a die Purificationis B. Mariæ in tres septimanas, versus Hugonem le Tanur & Julianam uxorem suam & Isabellam sororem ejusdem Julianæ de placito terræ. *Memor.* 35. *H.* 3. *Rot.* 8. *a.*

a Jury

Chap. XXII. *of the* EXCHEQUER. 79

a Jury of twelve Men, to find whether *Gilbert Taillard* imprisoned and commanded to be imprisoned *John de Heltesley* (t). *William Wymer* appointed (in the Exchequer) one to be Attorney for him, in a Plea depending between the King and him touching a Vivary (u). A Writ issued to the Sheriff of *Hampshire,* commanding him to go in Person to *William de Micheldover,* and see whom he would make his Attorney in a Plea of Debt depending between him and *John de Wintereshull,* and that he should receive the Attorney, and certify his Name to the Barons on the Morrow of *Candlemass* (w): a like Writ issued for the Prior of *Bridlington* (x). An Issue was joined in the Exchequer in the 45th Year of K. *Henry* III. in a Plea of Trespass and Rescusse, together with the *Postea* and Verdict thereupon. I have set it down *verbatim* as it standeth in the Plea-Roll (y). *John de Bayliol* constituted before the King two Persons to be his Attorneys,

(t) Cantebr. Mandatum est Vicecomiti, quod venire faciat &c in crastino animarum xij probos &c, & qui nulla affinitate attingant Gilbertum Taillard nec Johannem de Heltesleg, & qui electi sint in pleno Comitatu de consensu utriusq; partis, Si prædictus G. inprisonavit & inprisonari præcepit prædictum Johannem——. *Memor.* 40. *H.* 3. *Rot.* 1. *b.*

(u) Willelmus Wymer ponit loco suo Radulfum Wymer filium & hæredem suum, ad lucrandum &c, in loquela quæ est inter Dominum Regem & ipsum, de quodam vivario in Strafford. *Ex Memor.* 40. *H.* 3. *Rot.* 2. *b.*

(w) Mandatum est Vicecomiti Suthamptoniæ, quod in propria persona sua accedat ad Willelmum de Micheldover, & videat quem loco suo attornare voluerit, in Placito Debiti quod est inter ipsum & Johannem de Wintereshull, & illum recipiat, & scire faciat Baronibus &c in Crastino Pur. B. M. quem loco suo ad hoc attornaverit, & hoc breve. *Ex Memor.* 42. *H.* 3. *Rot.* 9. *a.*

(x) *Ib. Rot.* 11. *b. Ebor.*

(y) Somerset. Nicholaus le Pestur, Johannes filius Adæ le Marescal, Walterus Falc, Johannes Orri, Rogerus de Mutford, Johannes le Someter, Willelmus de Welleye, Willelmus le Feure, Willelmus le Brun, & Willelmus Pine, attach[iantur] ad respondendum Domino Regi, de hoc quod vi & injuste inpediverunt Philippum de Cerne Vicecomitem Regis in Comitatu prædicto, & ballivos suos, quo minus potuerunt facere districtionem pro debitis Domini Regis in Civitate Bathoniæ; & averia capta pro prædictis debitis rescusserunt; contra pacem &c. Venerunt & hoc dediderunt de verbo ad verbum. Et de hoc pon[unt] se in inquisitionem patriæ. Et Robertus Senescallus Prioris Bathoniæ pro Rege dicit quod sic; & de hoc petit patriam. Fiat inquisitio in pleno Comitatu &c, per xij &c, qui nulla affinitate &c. Et Vicecomes habeat eam hic in crastino S. Andreæ &c. Præceptum est Vicecomiti &c; & Vicecomes distringat Johannem Miles Willelmum le Res & Robertum le Neyr per terras &c; ita quod possit &c, & quod habeat corpora &c, ad prædictum diem. Postea venit inquisitio; quæ dicit, quod Nicholaus Pistor, Johannes le Marescal, Rogerus de Mutford, Johannes le Sumeter, & Willelmus le Brun, vi & injuste rescusserunt prædicta; prout continetur in ipsa inquisitione ut prædictum est. Et prædictus Johannes le Sumeter fuit præsens. Ideo adjudicata fuit ei prisona; & finivit pro redemptione per xx solidos, per plegium Johannis Budde. Et mandatum est Vicecomiti, quod alios supradictos qui se posuerunt in ipsam inquisitionem distringat per terras &c, ita &c, & quod habeat corpora eorum hic in crastino S. Illarij ad audiendum &c. *Trin. Placita* 45. *H.* 3. *Rot.* 12. *a. ex parte Remem. Thes.*

ad

ad lucrandum vel perdendum, in a Plea depending before the Barons, between the said *John* and *John de Somerleton* and others named in the original Writ, for a Debt of xl *l.* which the said *John de Bayliol* demanded of them: therefore the King commands the Barons, that they do admit the said Persons, or either of them (if both of them cannot be present) to be Attorneys for the said *John de Bayliol* (*z*). In the 56th Year of K. *Henry* III. there was a Plea pending in the Exchequer by virtue of the King's Writ, between *William Giffard* and *Gundrede* his Wife Demandants, and *William de Munchenesey* and others named in the same Writ Deforciants, touching Suit of Frankpledge, *&c:* which Plea the Barons had not determined, saying they would not determine it without consulting with the King: hereupon, the King by his Writ commands the Barons, that in the Presence of the Justices of the *Bank*, they should in the Exchequer consider the said Plea, and with the Advice of the said Justices determine it in due Manner, doing full Justice to the said Parties according to the Law and Custom of the Exchequer without further Delay (*a*). In the 5th Year of K. *Edward* I. an Essoign was taken before the Treasurer and Barons of the Exchequer at *Westminster*, on *Friday* next after the Quinzime of *Easter*; viz. *Agnes* Wife of *Nicolas de Creton* essoigned against *Richard del Auney*, in a Plea of Land, by *Richard de Bikele* and *Walter de Lynton* [her Attorneys] (*b*). There was a Plea of

(*z*) Baronibus pro Johanne de Balliolo de attornatis suis. Rex mandat quod idem Johannes attornavit coram Rege loco suo Johannem de Huche & Nicholaum de Carro, ad lucrandum vel perdendum, in loquela quæ est coram eisdem Baronibus per breve Regis, inter ipsum Johannem & Johannem de Somerleton & alios in brevi Regis originali contentos de debito xl l, quod idem Johannes de Balliolo a prædicto Johanne de Somerleton & alijs prædictis exigit. Et ideo Rex mandat, quod prædictos Johannem de Huche & Nicholaum, vel alterum eorum si ambo interesse non possunt, loco ipsius Johannis de Balliolo ad hoc recipiant. Teste &c. *Ex Memor.* 52. *H.* 3. *Rot.* 4. *a*.

(*a*) Baronibus pro Willelmo Giffard & Gundreda uxore ejus. Cum Rex pluries mandaverit eisdem Baronibus, quod loquelam quæ est coram eis per breve Regis, inter Willelmum Giffard & Gundredam uxorem ejus petentes, Et Willelmum de Monte Caniso & alios in eodem brevi nominatos deforciantes, De secta Franci plegij, Wardis, Wardepenyes, & sede loci, de Hundredo Regis de Berdestaple, & quibusdam alijs quæ idem Willelmus & Gundreda de Rege tenent ad feodi firmam pro xxv marcis per annum, secundum Legem & consuetudinem Scaccarij terminarent, & partibus plenam Justiciam exhiberent; & ijdem Barones nichil inde hucusq; fecerint, sed se excusaverint, & dixerint se non velle hoc facere sine Consilio Regis: Rex nolens dictam loquelam ulterius contra justiciam protrahi aut prorogari, Mandat Baronibus, quod in præsentia Justiciariorum de Banco, quibus Rex scribit, quod dictæ loquelæ una cum eis a die S. Hillarij in xv dies, quem diem dictis partibus præfixerunt, intendant in Scaccario, & de eorum Consilio dictam loquelam debito modo terminent, & partibus plenam Justiciam secundum Legem & consuetudinem Scaccarij sine dilatatione faciant. T. &c. *Hil. Communia* 56. *H.* 3. *Rot.* 4. *b*.

(*b*) Essonia de malo lecti capta coram Thesaurario

of Debt pending before the Barons between *Robert le Baker* and *Roger de Cantok*, a Burgess of *Bristol*: the King by his Writ commanded the Barons to continue that Plea till next St. *Edward*'s Day (*c*). A Plea being moved in Court Christian before the Bishop of *Chichester* concerning Sepulture in old *Winchelsey*; and the said Plea being in Derogation of the King's Right and Prerogative; the King by his Writ commands the Bishop of *Chichester* to put the said Plea in Respite, and to warn the Parties to appear before the Treasurer and Barons of the Exchequer on the Morrow of *All-Souls*, to receive Judgment therein: accordingly, the Parties and the Bishops Official appeared at the Exchequer: but the Court adjourned the Proceedings therein, till such Time as the Treasurer should send one of the Barons to view the Place in question (*d*). *William Noel* was attached to answer to the King in the Exchequer in a Plea of Trespass. *John Dimmok*, who sued for the King, declared against *William*; for that when *Garsias de Ispania* the King's Equerry was leading some of the King's Colts along the Town of *St. Alban* towards *Raleigh*, the said *William* assaulted the said *Garsias*, and did beat and evil-intreat him, in Contempt of the King and against his Peace, to the Damage of *Garsias* C Marks. *William* came and pleaded, that the said *Garsias* met him riding along in the said Town, and by the Rencounter of his Horse threw him the said *William* to the Ground, whereupon he struck *Garsias* twice with a Scourge, *viz*. once upon the Face (by which Blow he drew Blood) and again upon the Shoulders of *Garsias*. And in regard *William* by this Plea acknowledged, that without Judgment or Warrant of Law he had taken Revenge for the Injury done him by the said *Garsias*, and thereby had committed a Trespass against the King's Peace; it was adjudged by the Court of Exchequer, that he should be imprisoned. Afterwards he found Sureties, to appear before the Treasurer and Barons in *Easter* Term, to satisfy the King for the said Contempt, and the said *Garsias* for the said Trespass (*e*). Upon

---

Thesaurario & Baronibus de Scaccario apud Westmonasterium, die Veneris proxima ante quindenam Paschæ Anno R. Regis E. quinto.

Devonia. Agnes uxor Nicholai de Creton apud Heyen in Comitatu Devoniæ essoniat se versus Ricardum del Auney, de placito Terræ, per Ricardum de Bikele & Walterum de Lynton.— *Communia de Termino Clausi Paschæ* 5. *E*. 1. *Rot*. 3. *b*. *in bund. anni* 4 & 5. *E*. 1.

(*c*) Rex mandat Baronibus, quod loquelam quæ est coram eis inter Robertum Pistorem & Rogerum de Cantok Burgensem Bristollæ de quodam debito viginti & quatuor librarum vj s viij d quod præfatus Robertus ab eodem Rogero exigit continuent usq; ad diem S. Edwardi proximo futurum &c. *Mich. Commun*. 4 & 5. *E*. 1. *Rot*. 1. *a*.

(*d*) Breve Regis directum Episcopo Cicestrensi pro Rege——&c. *Mich. Brevia* 20. *E*. 1. *Rot*. 8. *a*.

(*e*) *Hil. Communia* 21. *E*. 1. *Rot*. 2. *a*.

Complaint

82 *Of the* BUSINESS Chap. XXII.

Complaint made before the Barons of the Exchequer at *York*, by *Asculph de Whytewell*, that one *Walter Campion* privily cut his Purse in the Presence of the Barons, and took away his Money; the said *Walter* was attached in Court. And though he was not caught in the Fact, yet being accused as well by the By-standers as by the said *Asculph*, he was committed to Prison. Afterwards he found Sureties for his good Behaviour, and was set at large *(f)*. *Walter de Maideston* was arrested for making use of certain counterfeit Bulls; and *Robert le Harpur* for being of Assent with him therein. Ten Persons came into the Exchequer, and undertook, Body for Body, at the Will of the King and of the Treasurer and Barons, to have the said *Walter* before the said Barons from Day to Day, and from Term to Term. In like manner seven Persons came and undertook to have the said *Robert* before the Barons, or where-ever else the King pleased. And *Robert* was thereupon released from his Imprisonment in *Ludgate* *(g)* *Adam Frere* was attached to answer to the King; for that whereas *John Sparrow*, Bailiff of *Norwich*, had taken into the King's Hands at *Norwich* Ten Quarters of Malt in Part of the Purveyances for the King's Liege-men, who were in his Service in *Scotland*, the said *Adam* broke the Attachment so made for the King, and carried away the said Malt. *Adam* pleaded, that he did not break the said Attachment, nor carry away the Malt. An Issue was joined upon that, between him and *John Sparrow*, who followed *pro Rege*. A *Venire facias* was awarded for trying the Issue. But the King dying before Trial and Judgment, the Plaint was discontinued *(h)*. *Jordan*, Son of *Gilbert de Pestour*, and two others, were attached to appear in the Exchequer, to answer the King in a Plea of Trespass. *Henry de Say Pincerna Regis qui sequitur pro Rege*, declares against them. It was for meeting the foreign Merchants before they came to their Ports, and buying up such of their Wines as they liked best; whereby they forestalled the said Wines, to the Damage of the King and his People. An Issue is joined; but no Judgment given therein *(i)*. *William de Whitewey*, late Parker of *Stansted Park* in *Sussex*, was accused before the Treasurer and Barons of the Exchequer, of certain Trespasses by him committed in the said Park, whilst the same was in the Hands of K. *Edward* I. by reason of the Infancy of *Edmund de Arundel*, Son and Heir of *Richard Fitz-Alan*, late Earl of *Arundel*, and being con-

(f) *Trin. Fines* 25 & 26. E. 1. *Rot.* 93.
(g) *Mich. Commun.* 25 & 26. E. 1. *Rot.* 33. a.
(h) *Hil. Commun.* 35. E. 1. *Rot.* 33. b. *Parte* 1.
(i) *Trin. Record.* 1. E. 2. *Rot.* 70. b. *Kancia*.

victed

victed thereof by Verdict of the Country, he was by Judgment of the said Court [of Exchequer] committed to the Tower of *London*, and had lain there in Prison for above four Years, and was still there: Now in regard the Judgment given against the said *William* was not fully executed, the King by his Writ commands the Barons, that upon View and Examination of the Record and Process of the said Plea, which was had before the Treasurer and Barons of the Exchequer, they should without Delay, notwithstanding the Death of K. *Edward* I. cause the said Judgment to be finally executed (*k*). About the End of the Reign of K. *Edward* I. *Roger Ughtred* had impleaded *Walter de Kelk* before the King's Council in the Exchequer, for a Contempt done to the King and a Trespass done to the said *Roger*; and before Judgment given the Plea was discontinued by the King's Death: So K. *Edward* II. by his Writ commands the Barons, that having called to them in the Exchequer some of the King's Council, they should proceed therein according to Right and Law (*l*). In the first Year of K. *Edward* II. an Issue was joined between *William de Billingleye* Clerk, and *Thomas de Gardinis* late Sheriff of *Gloucestershire*, about providing of Corn for the Use of K. *Edward* the First's Army in *Scotland*. It was tried at the Exchequer by Jurors summoned from the Town of *Bristol* and Parts next adjacent. The Verdict was in favour of *Thomas de Gardinis* (*m*). In the 2d Year of K. *Edward* II. *Philipp Balun* came into the Exchequer and prayed Relief upon his Case. The Barons of the Exchequer, before they would proceed in the Matter, ordered an Inquisition to be taken, Whether *Roger le Bygod* died seised of a Tenement mentioned in a Charter which *Philipp* now vouched *&c.* The Sheriffs of *London* were commanded by Writ to summon before *Thomas de Cantebrigge* and *Roger de Hegham*, Barons of the Exchequer, or either of them, at *St. Martin* in *London*, on the *Saturday* next before the Octaves of the Purification, xxiiij lawful Men of *London* of the Visnue of *Brokenwharf* (where the said Tenement stood) *per quos &c, Et qui nulla affinitate &c.* An Inquisition was accordingly taken before *Thomas de Cantebrigge* at *St. Martin*. And the Matters alleged by *Philipp* were found by the Jurors (*n*). In the same Year, in the Case of *James de Lamburne*, who prayed to have Execution of certain Writs sent to the Treasurer and Barons, recited here in the Record, the Court ordered

(*k*) *Trin. Brevia* 2. *E.* 2. *Rot.* 86. *b.*
(*l*) *Mich. Brevia* 5. *E.* 2. *Rot.* 5. *a.*
(*m*) Glouc. De Thoma de Gardinis. *Paf, Commun.* 1. *E.* 2. *Rot.* 71. *a.*
(*n*) *Hil. Commun.* 2. *E.* 2. *Rot.* 56. *a.*

the Sheriff of *Essex* to summon twelve of the Visnue of *Estmeresey*, twelve of the Visnue of *Colne Quency*, twelve of the Visnue of *Aumfreton*, and twelve of another Visnue, as well Knights as other lawful Men, *per quos &c. & qui nulla &c.* to appear at the Exchequer in the Octaves of St. *Michael*, or before *W. de Norwich*, Remembrancer *Si prius &c.* to enquire into the Truth of the Matter, and certify the Barons thereof. The Process was continued *pro defectu juratorum* to the Quinzime of *Easter*. At that Day it was delayed *pro defecta Militum gladio cinctorum*. And a *pluries Distringas* was awarded, to have the Jurors who were named in the Panel, before *William de Carleton*, Baron of the Exchequer at *Colchester*, on *Monday* next after the Feast of St. *John* Baptist, and likewise other Knights (*tot & tales tam Milites gladio cinctos, &c*). And the Record and Process sealed with the Exchequer-seal (*consignata pede Sigilli Scaccarij*) were delivered to *James de Lamburne*, to be carried to the said *William de Carleton* at the said Day, for the taking of the said Inquisition. And in the Octaves of St. *John* Baptist, *William de Carleton* transmitted into the Exchequer under his Seal an Inquisition taken before him *super præmissis* (*o*). In the 9th Year of K. *Edward* II. an Information was brought before the King's Council in the Exchequer by *Philipp le Viroler*, against *Robert le Messager*, for speaking irreverent and indecent Words of the King. *Robert* pleaded, Not guilty. The Jury found him guilty of speaking certain Words which are set forth here in the Record. Afterwards, at the Instance of *Isabell* Queen Consort, the Archbishop of *Canterbury* became Manucaptor for *Robert*, that he should appear before the King *ad recipiendum &c.* whenever his Majesty pleased. And upon that Manucaption *Robert* was delivered out of Prison (*p*). In the same Year, *Johanne*, late Wife of *John Shench*

(*o*) *Trin. Commun. 2. E. 2. Rot. 90. b.*

(*p*) Philippus de Viroler de Newenton exhibuit Consilio Domini Regis hic, quandam Cedulam per quam ipse suggessit, quod Robertus le Messager de Newenton nuper protulit inreverenter plura verba indecentia de Domino Rege, in contemptum Domini Regis, offerens se hoc velle verificare pro Domino Rege contra eundem Robertum.

Robert, *being present in Court*, & allocutus inde defendit quicquid &c; & dicit quod ipse nulla verba protulit quæ redundare possent ad dedecus Domini Regis vel derogationem Honoris Domini Regis &c; & hoc offert verificare qualitercumq; &c. *The issue was directed to be tryed* hic coram Consilio, die Veneris proximo post festum omnium Sanctorum. *The Jury found certain words, which are herein mentioned, to have been spoken by Robert.* Postea die Sabbati in vigilia S. Andreæ Apostoli, ad instantiam Isabellæ Reginæ Angliæ Consortis Regis, W. Archiepiscopus Cantuar. manucepit prædictum Robertum, de habendo illum coram Domino Rege ad voluntatem ipsius Regis &c, ad recipiendum quod &c. Et prætextu hujus manucaptionis idem Robertus deliberatur &c. *Mich. Communia 9. E. 2. Rot. 89. b.*

deceased,

Chap. XXII.   *of the* EXCHEQUER.

deceased, who held of the King in Chief the Serjeanties of the Custody of the King's Palace of *Westminster* and of his Prison of *Flete*, married *Edmund de Cheney* without Licence obtained from the King in that Behalf. Whereupon, the said Serjeanties were taken into the King's Hands. And straitway the Treasurer and Barons committed the Custody of the Palace to *Richard Abbot*, who was sworn *de fideliter &c.* and the Custody of the *Flete Prison* to *John Dymmok*, Usher of the Exchequer, who was sworn in like Manner. Afterwards the said *Edmund* made Fine for the said Trespass; and the said Serjeanties were restored (*q*). In the same Year, *Thomas de Tynwell* was accused in the Exchequer, of having spoken at *Oxford* irreverent Words of the King. *Thomas* pleaded, Not guilty. The Issue was tried at the Exchequer, by lawful Men of the Town of *Oxford*, who found him not guilty (*r*). K. *Edward* II. by his Writ (for the Reasons therein contained) commanded the Barons to proceed judicially against *John de Wengave*, Mayor of *London*, upon the Presentments exhibited against him at the Eire at the Tower of *London* (*s*).

In Suits moved between Parties in the Exchequer, sometimes the King granted Preference to one Person; namely, that he should be

(*q*) De Serjantia Custodiæ Palacij Westmonasterij & Prisonæ de Flete capta in manum Regis. *Mich. Communia* 9. *E.* 2. *Rot.* 89. *a.*

(*r*) Oxon. de Thoma de Tynwell occasionato de Transgressione. Præsens in Curia quidam Robertus de Malton suggessit Curiæ, quod quidam Thomas de Tynwell Clericus, nuper apud Oxoniam die Veneris proximo ante festum Sancti Thomæ Apostoli hoc anno, infra Portam Borealem Oxoniæ, in præsentia Johannis de Necton, Edmundi le Barber, *and four others by name*, & aliorum, locutus est irreverenter de Domino Rege, parvipendendo ipsum per verba indecentia, & dicendo ipsum non esse Filium Domini E. nuper Regis Angliæ, in contemptum Domini Regis &c; Et pecijt quod idem Thomas qui præsens est &c, respondeat inde Domino Regi, protestans se velle sequi pro Domino Rege versus eundem Thomam & verificare præmissa &c. Et idem Thomas allocutus inde, modo die Mercurij proximo post quindenam Paschæ, defendit quicquid est in Contemptum Domini Regis &c; & dicit quod ipse in nullo præmissorum est culpabilis &c; & hoc offert verificare qualitercunque &c. Ideo fiat inde inquisitio. Et præceptum est Vicecomiti quod venire faciat hic in Crastino Ascensionis Domini, xij probos & legales homines de Villa Oxoniæ, de Visneto juxta portam Borealem, per quos &c, & qui nulla affinitate &c, ad certificandum Baronibus &c; Et idem dies datus est prædicto Roberto ad sequendum pro Rege &c. *After several Continuances*, Et quia Robertus non venit ad sequendum pro Rege, Concordatum est, quod Johannes de Notton *and the six others*, in quorum præsentia dicitur dictum Thomam locutum fuisse irreverenter de Domino Rege &c, veniant hic ad certificandum &c, simul cum Juratoribus. Et præceptum est Vic. quod distringat eos, &c, Ita quod habeat Corpora——*The Inquisition came*——. Et prædicti Edmundus le Barber & Thomas de Tannere venerunt; quibus juratis & associatis Juratoribus Inquisitionis prædictæ——; *He was found not Guilty.* Ideo consideratum est, quod prædictus Thomas de Tynwelle super præmissis eat sine die. *Pasc. Communia* 9. *E.* 2. *Rot.* 100.

(*s*) *Mich. Brevia* 15. *E.* 2. *Rot.* 42. *a.*

paid

paid before other Creditors. This was done in the Case of *Pontius de Mora*. The Merchants of *Luka* sued the Executors of *John le Gros* in the Exchequer for Money borrowed of them by *John*; who at the Time of his Death was also indebted to *Pontius de Mora* in several Debts: The King by his Writ commanded the Barons to call before them the said Executors, and to assist *Pontius* in recovering his Debts of them, and as soon as the said Merchants had recovered their said Debts, to let *Pontius* be preferred before the other Creditors of the Deceased (*t*). The like Preference was granted by the King to *John Bardun* (*u*).

III. Under the Head of Business of *various Kinds* we may place Conventions and Recognitions made at the Exchequer; Presentations and Admissions of Officers of the Exchequer, and of the Exchange &c; Presentations of Mayors and Sheriffs; Payment of Rents; and other miscellaneous Business. Of these, in Order. Conventions and Recognitions were frequently made in the Exchequer. *John de Bosell* came before the Barons of the Exchequer, and in their Presence put *Robert Gardman* into full Seisin of certain Houses and Lands in *Lincoln*; and acknowledged before the Barons, that *Robert* had satis-

(*t*) Baronibus pro Poncio de Mora. Rex mandat eisdem, quod quam cito mercatores sui de Luka recuperaverint coram eis ab executoribus testamenti Johannis le Gros, debita quæ idem Johannes eisdem Mercatoribus debuit die quo objit, tam de mutuo ab eisdem mercatoribus per eundem Johannem capto de denarijs suis, quam de denarijs mercatorum suorum, & unde placitum est in Scaccario inter eosdem executores & mercatores prædictos, vocatis coram eis eisdem executoribus, sint in auxilium Poncio de Mora, cui idem defunctus in pluribus debitis tenebatur die quo objit, ad recuperanda debita illa, prout ea sibi deberi rationabiliter monstrare poterit coram eis, Ita quod idem Poncius in hujusmodi debitis suis recuperandis cæteris creditoribus dicti defuncti præferatur, T. &c. *Trin. Commun.* 7. *E.* 1. *Rot.* 4. *a.*

(*u*) *A Writ issued to the Barons, setting forth, That the King had commanded the Sheriff of* Norfolk, *to levy of the Goods of* John le Gross *late Merchant, in his Bailywick, a certain Sum due to the Merchants of* Luka; *and then of the Residue to levy* 89 *l.* 12 *s. due from the Defunct to* John Bardun, & eidem Johanni Bardun habere faceret; Ita quod idem Johannes soluta prius prædictis mercatoribus pecunia quam dictus defunctus eis debebat, sicut prædictum est, cæteris creditoribus ejusdem defuncti in solutione hujusmodi præferetur; & jam per eundem Vicecomitem acceperit, quod id facere non potest propter alia mandata sua sibi pro alijs mercatoribus diversis directa, ipse eidem Johanni Bardun gratiam facere volens, Mandat eisdem Baronibus, quod cum pecunia dictis mercatoribus de Luka, ab eodem defuncto debita, De bonis & catallis prædictis levari & eisdem habere fecerint, dictas quaterviginti ix l xij s de residuis bonis & catallis dicti defuncti levari, & præfato Johanni Bardun habere faciant, prout ipse pecuniam illam sibi debere rationabiliter monstrare poterit coram eis; proviso quod idem Johannes Bardun cæteris creditoribus dicti defuncti in prædicti debiti solutione præferatur. *Pas. Commun.* 7. *E.* 1. *Rot.* 4. *b.*

fied him Lx Marks for the said Houses (*w*). *Robert le Lozeng* came before the Barons, and acknowledged that he had made a Charter of Obligation to Master *Robert de Kadenay*, for *John de Bosell*, importing that the said *Robert de Lozeng* and his Heirs would warrant to the said Master the said Land and Houses, in case the said *John* could not warrant them (*x*). *Rosamund de Erlham* tendered before the Barons of the Exchequer xxvij l x s, which was payable to *William de Somerfeld*, upon a Bond entered into by her before the Justices of the *Jews*. No body came to receive the Money. So she *stetit parata* (to pay the said Money *modo prædicto*) on St. *John* Baptist's Nativity, *& per tres dies proximo sequentes* (*y*). A Tender of Money was made in the Exchequer *in præsentia Baronum*, by *John de Hotoft*, on behalf of *Henry de Leyburn* Knight, for *John le Latymer* to receive it, according to Covenants contained in an Indenture : But *John le Latymer* did not come (*z*). In fine, the ancient Rolls of the Exchequer abound with Conventions and Recognitions.

IV. Of the Presentation and Admission of Officers of the Exchequer, we shall speak hereafter in Chapter xxiv. In this Section something may be said concerning the Officers of the Coinage and some others. Several Officers of the Exchange and Coinage of Money have been, from time to time, presented and sworn in the Exchequer. *Ilger*, the Goldsmith, and several other Officers of the Mint were sworn before the High Justicier there (*a*). The King's

---

(*w*) Johannes filius Theobaldi de Bosel venit coram Baronibus, & in præsencia eorundem posuit Magistrum Robertum Gardman in plenam seisinam domorum & terrarum quæ fuerunt prædicti Theobaldi patris sui in Lincolnia ; & recognovit coram eisdem Baronibus, quod idem Magister Robertus satisfecit ei de Lx marcis pro eisdem domibus in Lincolnia. *Ex Memorand.* 28. *H.* 3. *Rot.* 2. *a.*

(*x*) Robertus le Lozeng. venit coram Baronibus, & recognovit se fecisse quandam Cartam Obligationis Magistro Roberto de Kadenay, pro Johanne filio Theobaldi de Bosell, scilicet quod dictus Robertus le Lozeng. & hæredes sui warantizabunt dicto Magistro dictam terram & domos, si prædictus Johannes warantizare non poterit, sicut in Obligatione quam idem Magister inde habet plenius continetur. *Ib. Rot.* 2. *a.*

(*y*) Suthampton. De Proffero Rosamundæ de Erlham facto. *Trin. Communia* 56. *H.* 3. *Rot.* 7. *a.*

(*z*) *Mich. Communia* 34 *&* 35. *E.* 1. *Rot.* 14. *a. Parte* 1. *tit.* Kancia ; Recordum Baronum pro Henrico de Leyburn.

(*a*) London. Custodes Monetæ. Ilgerius Aurifaber, *and three others.* Jurati.

Custodes Cuneorum. Adam Blundus, *and seven others.* Jurati.

Reparator Cuneorum. Michael de Sancta Elena. Juratus.

Assaiatores Monetæ. Robertus de Grettone & Galfridus de Frowe. Jurati.

In Crastino Cinerum anno v° Regis, traditi fuerunt prædictis viij Cunei ad obulos & qua-

King's *Cuſtos Cunei* for *Canterbury* was preſented and ſworn in the Exchequer (*b*). *Otho Fitz William,* Keeper in Fee of the King's Mint, preſented at the Exchequer *Richard Abel,* Goldſmith, to be Maker and Cutter of the Dyes till Candlemaſs next (*c*). At another time the Bailiffs of *Canterbury* preſented to the Barons an Aſſayer of the the Mint; who was ſworn and admitted (*d*). The Mayor and Sheriffs of *London* preſented an Aſſayer and a *Cuſtos Cuneorum,* who were ſworn and admitted (*e*). The Mayor and Sheriffs of *London* were commanded to chooſe, by the Oath of twelve good Men of their City, one of the moſt approved Men of their ſaid City, to be the King's *Cuſtos Cunei* in the room of *Walter de Flemeng* deceaſed, and to have him before the Barons of the Exchequer on the Morrow of the Cloſe of *Eaſter* (*f*). And *John Hardell,* being accordingly choſen to that Office, and preſented at the Exchequer by the Sheriffs of *London,* he was there admitted and ſworn (*g*). The King commanded

& quadrantes rotundos faciendos, & ipſis eadem die juratis in præſentia Juſticiarij ad Scaccarium; Poſtea traditi fuerunt eiſdem, die Jovis ante Paſcha, viij Cunei ad denarios, & viij Cunei ad obolos, & viij Cunei ad quadrantes, præter primos viij Cuneos. *Memor.* 6. *H.* 3. *Rot.* 3. *b.*

(*b*) Die Lunæ proximo poſt feſtum Apoſtolorum Petri & Pauli, venerunt ad Scaccarium Thomas Mareſcallus (*and five others*) Burgenſes Cantuariæ, & præſentaverunt ibidem, ex parte Civitatis Cantuariæ, Lambinum Dravet electum per ſacramentum xij, ydoneum ad cuſtodiendum Cuneum Domini Regis in Cantuaria, quem cuſtodivit Adam Mercerus, ſicut eis mandatum fuit per Litteras Regis. Et receptus eſt idem Lambinus, & Juravit. Et mandatum eſt Cuſtodi Cambij, quod eum ad hoc recipiat. *Memor.* 22. *H.* 3. *Rot.* 10. *b.*

(*c*) De Factore Cuneorum. Otto filius Willelmi præſentavit coram Baronibus Ricardum Abel Aurifabrum, ad faciendum & incidendum Cuneos Monetariorum, uſque ad feſtum Purificationis B. Mariæ. *Mich. Commun.* 27. *H.* 3. *Rot.* 4. *a.*

(*d*) Bailivi Civitatis Cantuariæ præſentaverunt coram Baronibus ad Scaccarium Galfridum Rikeward quem ad mandatum Domini Regis elegerunt Aſſaiatorem in Cambio Cantuariæ; Qui præſtito ſacramento ad idem officium eſt admiſſus. *Trin. Commun.* 32. *H.* 3. *Rot.* 8. *b.*

(*e*) De Aſſaiatore Cambij Londoniæ. Ricardus Bonaventure præſentatus eſt ad Scaccarium per Majorem & Vicecomites Londoniæ ad Officium Aſſaiatoris. Præſtito ſacramento, ad idem Officium eſt admiſſus.

De Cuſtode Cuneorum ejuſdem Cambij. Walterus de Mora præſentatus eſt ad Scaccarium per prædictos, ad cuſtodiendos Cuneos. Præſtito juramento, ad idem officium eſt admiſſus. *Paſ. Commun. ib. Rot.* 8. *b.*

(*f*) Londonia. Mandatum eſt Majori & Vicecomitibus, quod per Sacramentum xij proborum & legalium hominum de Civitate Londoniæ elegi faciant unum de probioribus & legalioribus hominibus ejuſdem Civitatis ad cuſtodiendum Cuneum Regis loco Walteri le Flemeng defuncti, & ipſum venire faciant coram Baronibus in craſtino Clauſi Paſchæ, ad audiendum & faciendum præceptum Regis; Et habeant tunc breve. *Hil. Commun.* 31. *H.* 3. *Rot.* 5. *a.*

(*g*) Johannes Hardell electus per Cives Londoniæ per Breve Regis ad cuſtodiendum Cuneum Cambij Londoniæ, & præſentatus coram Theſaurario & Baronibus per Vicecomites Londoniæ, præſtito juramento de fideli ſervitio ad idem officium admiſſus

Chap. XXII.   *of the* EXCHEQUER.   89

manded the Bailiffs and Men of *Walingeford*, that in full Town-Court they should chuse (by the Oath of four and twenty good Men) four Persons of the most trusty and prudent of their Town, for the Office of Moneyors in that Town, and other four like Persons for the keeping of the King's Mints there, and two fit and prudent Goldsmiths to be Assayors of the Money to be made there, and one fit and trusty Clerk for the keeping of the Exchange; and to send them to the Treasurer and Barons at the Exchequer, to do there what by ancient Custom and Assize was to be done in that Case. The like Commandment was given to the Bailiffs and good Men of *Bristol*, *Ivecester*, *Hereford*, *Newcastle upon Tyne*, *Nottingham*, *Carlile*, *Shrewsbury*, and *Wilton* (*h*). *Peter Delveday*, chosen an Assayor by the Mayor and Citizens of *Winchester*, was admitted and sworn at the Exchequer (*i*). *John Juvenal*, chosen by the Mayor and Citizens of *London* to be Keeper of the Mint, was sworn and admitted at the Exchequer (*k*). *Reginald*, Son of *Henry*, being presented by the Abbot of St. *Edmund* to the Office of a Moneyor at St. *Edmunds*, was admitted and sworn in the Exchequer to that Office (*l*). One *William*, the King's Goldsmith, was sworn in the Exchequer into the Office of the King's *Custos Cambij* for *London* and *Canterbury* (*m*). The Sacrist of St. *Edmund* presented at the Exchequer a Moneyor, an Assayor, and a *Custos Cunei*, who were sworn into their Offices (*n*). *William le Shrub* was sworn a *Custos Cunei* in the Town of St. *Edmund*, at the Presentation of the Sacrist of the Abbey there (*o*). *Richard le Espee* was sworn Moneyor of *Canterbury*, being presented by the Archbishop of *Canterbury*'s Steward (*p*). *Ralf le Blund* was sworn Cutter of the Dyes in the King's Mint (*q*). *Bartholomew de Brauncestre* was sworn
Assayor

---

admissus est ab ipsis Thesaurario & Baronibus. *Pas. Commun.* 31. *H.* 3. *Rot.* 5. *b.*

(*h*) *Memor.* 33. *H.* 3. *Rot.* 1. *a.*

(*i*) Petrus Delveday electus ad Assayatorem per Majorem & Cives Wintoniæ, præstito sacramento admissus est. *Memor.* 33. *H.* 3. *Rot.* 1. *b.*

(*k*) Johannes Juvenal electus per Majorem & Cives Londoniæ ad custodiam Cunei, præstito sacramento ad idem Officium est admissus. *Memor.* 33. *H.* 3. *Rot.* 4. *a.*

(*l*) Abbas de Sancto Eadmundo essoniatus de malo lecti fecit fratrem Rogerum de Neketon Monachum attornatum suum per literas patentes, ad præsentandum nomine suo & Ecclesiæ suæ unum monetarium ad officium monetariæ apud Sanctum Eadmundum. Qui quidem Monachus præsentavit Reginaldum filium Henrici Aurifabrum ad idem officium; qui admissus fuit coram Baronibus, & præstitit sacramentum de fidelitate; Et hoc de gratia eorundem Baronum; quia dictus Abbas non per attornatum sed personaliter debuit eundem R. vel alium ydoneum præsentasse. *Memor.* 42. *H.* 3. *Rot.* 18. *a.*

(*m*) *Memoranda* 42. *H.* 3. *Rot.* 1. *b.*

(*n*) *Hil. Commun.* 49. *H.* 3. *Rot.* 6. *b.*

(*o*) *Memor.* 52. *H.* 3. *Rot.* 2. *b.*

(*p*) *Memor.* 52. *H.* 3. *Rot.* 8. *b.*

(*q*) Idem Thomas [filius Otonis] venit coram Baronibus die Martis proximo post festum S. Hillarij, & præsentavit Radulfum
le

Assayor of the Money (*r*). *Jocee*, the Goldsmith, was sworn *Custos Cunei* for the Abbot of St. *Edmund* (*s*). *Richard de Bentley* was sworn Assayor of the Money in the Town of St. *Edmund* (*t*). The Dyes for the new Money were delivered to the Keepers of the Mint at *London*, who (together with other Ministers of the Exchange) were sworn at the Exchequer (*u*). In the 14th Year of K. *Edward* I, a Writ issued to the Treasurer and Barons, commanding them to deliver the *Pixes* of the *Exchanges* of *London* and *Canterbury* to *John de Caturco* and *Gerald Mauhan*, in order to coin Money, and to administer to them the Oath requisite upon that Occasion (*w*). K. *Edward* II (*Anno Regni* 2°) by Writ of Privy Seal granted to *John de Puntoise* the Office which *John le Porcher* lately held in the King's Exchange at the Tower of *London*, to hold during Pleasure. Whereupon *John de Puntoise* came to the Exchequer before the Chancellor of *England*, H. Earl of *Lincoln*, H. *le Despenser*, *J. de Sandale* the Treasurer's Lieutenant, the Barons of the Exchequer, and others of the King's Council, and undertook to pay to the King, as long as he should hold the said Office, one Farthing for every Pound of Silver which was delivered to him to coin, more than had been hitherto answered to the King for the like Quantity of Silver, by way of *Proficuum*; and found Pledges for his true answering the same, and for his good Abearance in his said Office (*x*). *W. Trente* was sworn the King's *Custos Cambij* for *London* (*y*). *Lapine Rogers* was sworn in the Exchequer into the Office of Master-Moneyor, during the King's Pleasure; provided, that if he was removed from that Office, he should be restored to the Offices of Assayor of the King's Money, and Exchanger in the

le Blund Civem Londoniæ ad Officium Incisionis Cuneorum Domini Regis; qui admissus fuit eodem die, & sacramentum præstitit de fideliter se habendo in Officio prædicto. *Mich. Commun.* 52, *incipien.* 53. H. 3. *Rot.* 5. *b.*

(*r*) De Assaiatore monetæ præsentato. Bartholomæus de Castello Custos Cambij Londoniæ præsentavit ad Scaccarium iiij° die Junij Bartholomæum de Braunceftre, ad faciendum Assaiam monetæ in Cambio prædicto; Qui eodem die admissus fuit, & sacramentum præstitit de fideliter se habendo in Officio prædicto. *Memor.* 1 & 2. E. 1. *Rot.* 8. *a.*

(*s*) *Mich. Commun.* 4 & 5. E. 1. *Rot.* 1. *b.*

(*t*) *Pas. Commun.* 5. E. 1. *Rot.* 5. *a.*

(*u*) Memorandum quod xvij die Maij liberati fuerunt Cunei Novæ monetæ Gregorio de Rokesle Majori Londoniæ & Rolandino de Podio Custodibus Cambij; Qui præstiterunt sacramentum coram Baronibus de Scaccario, una cum alijs Ministris de eodem Cambio, de fideliter se habendo in Officio suo prædicto. *Pas. Commun.* 7. E. 1. *Rot.* 6. *a. Et Trin. Commun.* 7. E. 1. *Rot.* 6. *b.*

(*w*) *Trin. Commun.* 14. E. 1. *Rot.* 12. *b.*

(*x*) *Trin. Fines &c.* 2. E. 2. *Rot.* 91. *a.*

(*y*) London. De W. Trente jurato ad Custodiam Cambij Regis. *Hil. Commun.* 8. E. 2. *Rot.* 3. *a.*

Exchange

Exchange of *Canterbury*, which were lately before granted to him for Life (z).

Some others, who were Officers at large, were also sworn at the Exchequer. For instance: *John de Preston* and *John Hauteyn*, Customers in the Port of *London*, were sworn in the Exchequer (a). By virtue of a Writ directed to the Treasurer, *John de Blakethorn* and *Walter de Dertford*, by the Oath of xij Goldsmiths of *London*, were chosen to keep and repair St. *Edward*'s Shrine (b). The King appointed *Richard Bonaventure* to keep the Key of the House where St. *Edward*'s Shrine lay; and by his Writ commanded the Treasurer that the said Key, which *Robert de la Leye*, Chancellor of the Exchequer, then had in Custody, be straitway delivered to the said *Richard* (c). *John de Lidegreynz* came before the King's Chancellor and the Barons of the Exchequer, and took his Oath for the Office of a Justice [in Eire] (d). *William Howard* took his Oath in the Exchequer, for the Office of Justice of the Common Bank (e). Commissioners for Per-

---

(z) *Trin. Commun.* 12. *E.* 2. *Rot.* 35. *b.*

(a) Rex omnibus ad quos &c. Sciatis quod cum officium custodiæ Custumæ lanarum pellium lanutarum & coriorum in portu nostro Londoniæ, quod Willelmus de Hedersete & Willelmus de Rude nuper habuerunt, tenendum ad vitam eorundem, certis de causis capi fecerimus in manum nostram nomine Districtionis: comisimus idem officium dilectis nobis Johanni de Preston & Johanni de Hauteyn civibus nostris civitatis nostræ Londoniæ, custodiendum quamdiu nobis placuerit; Ita quod de exitibus inde provenientibus nobis respondeant ad Scaccarium nostrum, videlicet de quolibet Sacco lanæ dimidiam marcam, de quibuslibet trescentis pellibus lanutis dimidiam marcam, & de quolibet lasto coriorum unam marcam: Et ideo vobis mandamus, quod eisdem Johanni & Johanni, tamquam Collectoribus Custumæ prædictæ, in hijs quæ ad eandem collectionem pertinent, intendentes sitis & respondentes. In cujus rei testimonium has literas nostras fieri fecimus patentes. T. W. Exoniensi Episcopo Thesaurario, xxv die Augusti.

Et prædicti Johannes & Johannes, præsentes hic coram Baronibus, præstiterunt Sacramentum de bene & fideliter se habendo in officio prædicto. Et Sigillum quod dicitur Coket liberatur eisdem; videlicet una pars Sigilli uni, & altera pars Sigilli alteri. Et mandatum est prædicto Willelmo de Hedersete & Willelmo de Rude, quod omnes res Regis ad eandem Custumam pertinentes, prædictis Johanni & Johanni liberent per Indenturam inter eos inde conficiendam &c. T. ut supra. *Trin. Commissiones* 16. *E.* 2. *Rot.* 5. *a.*

(b) *Pas. Communia* 52 & 53. *H.* 3. *Rot.* 11. *b.*

(c) *Trin. Communia* 52 & 53. *H.* 3. *Rot.* 11. *b.*

(d) Sacramentum Johannis de Lidegreynz Justiciarij. Memorandum quod Johannes de Lidegrenz venit coram R. Bathoniensi & Wellensi Episcopo Cancellario Domini Regis & Baronibus de Scaccario, quinto die Julij anno xviij, & præstitit sacramentum quod bene & fideliter se habebit in officio Justiciarij. *Trin. Communia* 18. *E.* 1. *Rot.— a.*

(e) Willelmus Howard xj die octobris anno prædicto venit coram Baronibus de Scaccario, & in præsencia Johannis de Langeton tunc Cancellarij Regis & eorundem Baronum præstitit sacramentum ad idem Scaccarium, quod fideliter se habebit in Officio Justiciarij de Banco, quamdiu steterit in Officio illo ibidem, in forma sacramenti Officij Justiciarij per Consilium Regis provisi. *Mich. Commun.* 25 & 26. *E.* 1. *Rot.* 14. *b.*

ambulation

ambulation of Forests were sworn in the Exchequer for their good Abearance in executing that Commission *(f)*. In the 9th Year of K. *Edward* II. whereas *John de Sandale* the King's Chancellor, Bishop Elect of *Winchester*, was coming towards *London* to be confirmed; the King commands the Treasurer, that as soon as he should be confirmed, and the Archbishop of *Canterbury* by his Patent Letters had certified his Confirmation, he should receive, in the King's Name, the Oath of the Fidelity of the said Bishop Elect, and certify the King thereof *(g)*.

V. Next, Of the Presentation which was wont to be made at the Exchequer of Mayors and Chief Officers of Towns, Escheators, *&c.* The Citizens of *London*, after they had chosen a Mayor, used to present him yearly on the Morrow of SS. *Simon* and *Jude* before the Treasurer and Barons of the Exchequer, who swore and admitted him into his Office. They used also yearly, when they had chosen their Sheriffs, to present them at the Exchequer before the Treasurer and Barons, on the Morrow of St. *Michael*, in the Manner hereunder set forth. In the 28th Year of K. *Henry* III. the Citizens of *London* presented to the Treasurer and Barons of the Exchequer *Nicholas Batt* their Mayor, who was sworn and admitted (*h*). In the 40th Year of the same King, the Citizens presented *Ralf Hardell* their Mayor, who was sworn and admitted (*i*). In the 55th Year of the same King, the Citizens of *London* came before the Barons on *Thursday* next after the Feast of SS. *Simon* and *Jude*, and presented their Mayor *John Adrien*, who the same Day was admitted, and took an Oath to behave himself faithfully towards the King and his Heirs, and to keep the City of *London* faithfully to the Use of the King, of *Edward* his eldest Son, of *John* Son of the said *Edward*, and the other Heirs of [the Kingdom of] *England* that should happen to come after them. The Case was this: The Citizens of *London* having this Year chosen *John Adrien* for their Mayor, who with the King's Admittance and Consent had been Mayor the foregoing Year, the King by his Writ ordered the Barons to admit him, and to give him an Oath in due Form, that

---

(*f*) *Mich. Commun.* 25 & 26. *E.* 1. *Rot.* 23. *b.*

(*g*) *Trin. Brevia* 9. *E.* 2. *Rot.* 60. *a.*

(*h*) Cives Londoniæ præsentarunt Thesaurario & Baronibus de Scaccario Nicholaum Batt Majorem suum Londoniæ in crastino Apostolorum Simonis & Judæ; Qui, præstito sacramento, ab eisdem est admissus. *Memor.* 38. *H.* 3. *Rot.* 2. *a.*

(*i*) Cives Londoniæ præsentaverunt coram Baronibus Radulfum Hardell Majorem Londoniæ; Qui præstito sacramento ad idem admissus est. *Mich. Memor.* 40. *H.* 3. *incipiente* 41. *Rot.* 3. *b.*

he would constantly during his Life adhere to the King, and would keep the said City well and truly for the Security of the King and his Liege-men; that if the King died, *Edward* his eldest Son living, he would bear true Faith to the said *Edward*; that if the King and the said *Edward* died, living the said *John* Son of *Edward*, he would bear like Faith to *John* before all others, and after his Decease to the right Heirs of the Crown of *England*; that he would cause his Fellow-Citizens and the whole Community of the City to take the same Oath at the Exchequer; that he would cause the Gates of the City to be kept Day by Day by Men sufficiently armed, and to be safely shut every Night; that he would suffer no Arms, nor any Horse of One hundred Shillings Price or above, to be bought and carried out of the City, unless by Persons approved by the King, nor any Meeting of suspected Persons to be holden; nor would let any Horses of Value with any Arms enter into the City, unless they belonged to the King's known Friends: and this under Pain of forfeiting all the Lands and Chattels he had in the King's Dominions (*k*). In the 5th Year of

---

(*k*) Præsentatio Civium Londoniæ. Iidem Cives venerunt coram Baronibus die Jovis proximo post festum Apostolorum Simonis & Judæ, & præsentaverunt Johannem Adryen Majorem suum; qui eodem die fuit admissus, & præstitit sacramentum de fideliter se habendo erga Dominum Regem & hæredes suos, & quod fideliter custodiet prædictam Civitatem Londoniæ ad opus ipsius Domini Regis, Edwardi Primogeniti sui, Johannis filij ejusdem Edwardi, & aliorum hæredum Angliæ quos post ipsos esse contigerit. *Memor*. 55. *H*. 3. *Rot*. 3. *a*.

De Majore Londoniæ admisso, & sacramento ejusdem & tocius Communitatis Civitatis ejusdem præstito. Baronibus, pro Rege. Cum Cives Londoniæ Johannem Adrien Concivem suum, qui anno præterito Major ejusdem Civitatis extitit de assensu & admissione Regis, adhuc iterato sibi elegerunt in Majorem, sicut ijdem Barones per Literas suas Regi significaverunt: Placet Regi quod ipsum admittant, recepto ab ipso sacramento in forma debita, Quod fidei Regis suo perpetuo constanter adhærebit; & quod Civitatem prædictam ad securitatem Regis & fidelium suorum fideliter & bene conservabit: Adicientes in sacramento illo; Quod si vivente Edwardo Primogenito Regis de Rege humanitus contigerit, ipsi Edwardo tanquam Domino suo firmam fidem portabit; & si vivente Johanne filio ipsius Edwardi Rex & ipse Edwardus in fata concesserint, ipsi Johanni præ cæteris mortalibus eandem fidem portabit; & post ejus decessum rectis hæredibus Coronæ Angliæ; & quod Concives suos & totam Communitatem ejusdem Civitatis illud idem sacramentum coram Thesaurario de Scaccario infra dictam Civitatem, ad diem certum [quem] † per consilium ipsius Thesaurarij præstare faciet: Et similiter, quod portas Civitatis prædictæ cum hominibus sufficienter armatis de die in diem custodiri & noctibus secure claudi faciet; & quod arma aut aliquem equum precij centum solidorum vel ultra emi & extra eandem Civitatem abduci, nisi specialibus Regi hactenus expertis & approbatis, aut aliquod collogium hominum de quibus aliqua sinistra suspicio haberi possit, vel equos de precio cum armis nisi eorum qui amici Regis notorij sint dictam Civitate intrare minime permittant, super forisfacturam terrarum & omnium bonorum quæ habet in Regno Regis. T. Rege apud Windesore xxix die octobris anno &c Lv. *Ib*. *Rot*. 3. *b*. † quem, *is superfluous*.

K. *Edward*

K. *Edward* I. on the Morrow of SS. *Simon* and *Juae*, the Citizens of *London* presented at the Exchequer *Gregory de Rokesle* their Mayor, who was sworn before the Barons to keep the said Town faithfully, and to perform the King's Commands (*l*). In the 7th Year of the same King they presented *Gregory de Rokesle* their Mayor, who was sworn to behave himself faithfully (*m*). In the 5th Year of K. *Edward* II. the Aldermen and other Citizens of *London*, on the Morrow of SS. *Simon* and *Jude*, presented before the Barons *John Gisors*, chosen Mayor of the said City by the said Aldermen and the Community of the said City, praying the Barons to assent on the King's Behalf to their Choice, and to admit the said *John* to the said Office in the usual Manner; and he was admitted and sworn (*n*). The same King manded the Barons not to receive *John le Taverner*, Mayor of *Bristol*, who was presented to them; but to order the Townsmen to chuse another (*o*).

Moreover, in the 6th Year of K. *Henry* III. the Mayor and Citizens of *London* attorned, at the Exchequer, *Richard Rengier* and *Thomas Lambert* their Sheriffs, to do to the King what Sheriffs ought to do (*p*). In the 8th Year of K. *Henry* III. the Citizens of *London* assigned *Andrew Bukerell* and *John Travers* their Sheriffs, to answer

(*l*) Præsentatio Civium Londoniæ. Cives Londoniæ venerunt coram Baronibus in crastino Apostolorum Simonis & Judæ, & præsentaverunt Gregorium de Rokesle Majorem suum; Qui præstitit sacramentum coram eisdem Baronibus de fideliter custodiendo prædictam villam, & ad faciendum præceptum Regis. *Mich. Communia* 4 & 5. *E.* 1. *Rot.* 1. *b.*

(*m*) Cives Londoniæ venerunt coram Baronibus & præsentaverunt Gregorium de Rokesle Majorem suum; qui præstitit sacramentum de fidelitate. *Mich. Commun.* 6 & 7. *E.* 1. *Rot.* 1. *b.*

(*n*) Aldermanni Londoniæ & alij Cives ejusdem Civitatis venerunt hic, modo die Veneris in crastino Apostolorum Simonis & Judæ, & præsentaverunt coram Baronibus Johannem Gisors Concivem suum, per ipsos Aldermannos & Communitatem dictæ Civitatis in Majorem Civitatis ejusdem electum, & petierunt quod ipsi Barones adhibito ex parte Regis assensu &c ut est moris ipsum Johannem ad dictum officium admittant &c. Et idem Johannes admissus est. Et præstitit sacramentum de bene & fideliter se habendo &c. *Mich. Commun.* 5. *E.* 2. *Rot.* 26. *b. inter Præsentationes.*

(*o*) Au Tresorier & as Barons de nostre Escheqier salutz. Pur ce qe nos avoms entendu qe les gentz de la Comunaute de la Ville de Bristeud ount eslutz en Meire de mesme la ville Johan le Taverner le quel il vient procheinement presenter devant vous a nostre dit Escheqier: Vous mandoms, por ce qe nous ne nous paioms mye de lui, qe vous ne le resceivez mye, a ce, einz facez maunder par lettres desoutz le seal de nostre dit Escheqier a ceux de la dite Comunaute, qil elisent un autre en leur Meire qe soit profitable & suffisiaunt por nous & por eus. Done souz nostre Prive Seal a Weymoustre, le xxiiij jour Doctobre lan de nostre Regne secund. *Mich. Brevia* 2. *E.* 2. *Rot.* 25. *a.*

(*p*) Major Londoniæ & alij Barones Londoniæ attornaverunt ad Scaccarium Vicecomites hujus anni sexti Ricardum Rengier & Thomam Lamberti, ad faciendum Domino Regi quod alij Vicecomites facere debent. *Ex Memor.* 6. *Hen.* 3. *Rot.* 5. *a.*

to the King at the Exchequer for the City (*q*): and in the 39th Year two others (*r*). In the 40th Year (or 41st), the King commanded the Barons of the Exchequer not to admit the new Sheriffs or Mayor whom the Citizens of *London* should present before them, until the said Citizens had satisfied *Luke de Luca* and his Companions, Merchants, for the Arrears of certain Money which they owed them. The Mayor and Citizens came and presented at the Exchequer, ... *Assewy*, Draper, and *Richard de Ewell*: and the said Mayor and Sheriffs bound themselves in the Penalty of xx Marks of Gold to satisfy the said Merchants before the Feast of *All Saints*. And soon afterwards the said *Luke de Lukes* came and acknowledged, that he and his Companions were satisfied the said Debt [which was a Debt of D *l*. due to them from the King by his Charter; and *Luke* delivered up the said Charter to the Treasurer and Barons, who caused it to be cancelled] (*s*). In the 51st Year the King, at the Supplication of the *Londoners*, granted to them, that they might chuse from amongst themselves two Bailiffs, faithful to the King and to the City, to have the Custody of the City and the County of *Middlesex*, until the King should give further Orders therein; and commanded the Barons of the Exchequer to admit the said Bailiffs, when the Citizens should present them at the Exchequer in the usual Manner. Afterwards, on on the Morrow of St. *Martin*, the Citizens came and presented for the said Custody *John Adrien* and *Luke de Bathencurt* their Bailiffs; who were the same Day admitted, and took an Oath to behave them-

---

(*q*) Cives Londoniæ assignaverunt Vicecomites, Andream Bukerell & Johannem Travers, ad respondendum Domino Regi ad Scaccarium pro Civitate. *Memor*. 8. H. 3. *Rot*. 1. *a*.

(*r*) Major & Cives Londoniæ venerunt coram Baronibus de Scaccario, & præsentaverunt Robertum de Lincon. & Willelmum Eswy Vicecomites Londoniæ, ad faciendum Præceptum Regis, & ad respondendum pro eis de Firma & Summonitionibus. *Mich. Commun*. 39. H. 3. *Rot*. 1. *a*.

(*s*) Rex mandat Baronibus, quod novos Vicecomites vel Majorem, quos Cives Londoniæ præsentaverint coram eis, non admittant, donec satisfecerint Lucæ de Luca & Socijs suis Mercatoribus, de arreragijs pecuniæ in qua eis tenentur. Breve est in forulo Marescalli. *Ex Mich. Memor*. 40 H. 3. *incip*. 41. *Rot*. 1. *a*.

Major & Cives Londoniæ venerunt coram Baronibus, & præsentaverunt ... de Assewy Draperium & Ricardum de Ewell Vicecomites suos, ad faciendum præcepta [Baronum de] Scaccario hoc anno. Et idem Major & Vicecomites manuceperunt sub pœna xx marcarum auri ...., quod satisfiet Lucæ de Lukes & socijs suis Mercatoribus Luc....., citra festum Omnium SS. *Ib. Rot*. 1. *a*.

Memorandum, quod Lucas de Lukes venit coram Baronibus, & recognovit, quod Major & Cives Londoniæ satisfecerant ei & socijs suis Mercatoribus Lukensibus, de Quingentis marcis, quas Rex eis debebat per Cartam suam, & eandem Cartam liberavit Philippo Lovell Thesaurario & Baronibus, qui eam fecerunt cancellari. *Ib. Rot*. 6. *b*.

selves faithfully in the said Custody towards the King and the City (*t*). In the 55th Year the Mayor and Citizens presented for Sheriffs *Henry le Waleys* and *Gregory de Rokesle*; provided that the said Sheriffs should answer to the King for CCCxv *l.* the old Ferm, and the Citizens for fourscore and five Pounds of new Increment (*u*).

They presented their Sheriffs at the Exchequer in the first Year of King *Edward* I. (*w*); in the second Year incipient of the same King (*x*); in the 5th Year incipient (*y*); in the 17th Year (*z*); and in the 25th Year (*a*). They also presented their Sheriffs in the first

(*t*) Baronibus, pro Civibus Londoniæ; Cum Rex, precibus Civium suorum Londoniæ annuere volens, concesserit eisdem Civibus, quod duos Ballivos de se ipsis, Regi & eidem Civitati fideles, eligere possint ad custodiam Civitatis prædictæ & Comitatus Middelsexæ, donec Rex de Consilio suo aliud inde providerit: Rex mandat Baronibus, quatinus cum Cives prædicti prædictos Ballivos, prout moris est, eis præsentaverint, ipsos ad hoc admittant, sicut prædictum est: Ita tamen quod de firma eorundem Regi respondeant ad Scaccarium, sicut fieri consuevit. T. &c. *Ex Memor.* 51. H. 3. *Rot.* 2. *b.*

Præsentatio Civium Londoniæ. Postea venerunt Cives prædicti in crastino S. Martini, & præsentaverunt ad Custodiam prædictam Johannem Adrien & Lucam de Bathencurt Ballivos suos, qui eodem die admissi fuerunt, et sacramentum præstiterunt, quod fideliter se habebunt in Custodia prædicta erga Dominum Regem & Civitatem prædictam, sicut prædictum est. *Ibid. juxt.*

(*u*) Major & Cives Londoniæ venerunt coram Baronibus, & præsentaverunt Henricum le Waleys & Gregorium de Rokesle Vicecomites suos ad faciendum præceptum Regis & Baronum de Scaccario, & ad respondendum pro Civitate & Comitatu Middelsexæ de hijs quæ ad Vicecomites pertinent; Ita scilicet, quod prædicti Vicecomites respondebunt Regi de CCCxv l de Veteri firma, & prædicti Cives respondebunt Regi de quater xx, v l de novo cremento. *Memor.* 55. H. 3. *Rot.* 1. *a.*

(*w*) Major [&] Cives Londoniæ venerunt coram Baronibus, & præsentaverunt Walterum le Poter & Johannem Horn Vicecomites suos, ad faciendum præceptum Regis & Baronum de Scaccario, & ad respondendum pro Civitate & Comitatu Middelsexæ, de hijs quæ ad Vicecomites pertinent. *Ex Memor.* 1. *E.* 1. *Rot.* 1. *a.*

(*x*) Major & Cives Londoniæ venerunt coram Baronibus, & præsentaverunt Petrum Cosin & Robertum de Meldeburn Vicecomites suos, ad faciendum præceptum Regis & Baronum de Scaccario, & ad respondendum pro Civitate & Comitatu Middelsex quæ ad Vicomites pertinent; Qui postea pro Magna transgressione quam fecerunt fuerunt amoti; Et loco eorum præsentaverunt Henricum de Coventre & Nicholaum de Wintonia. *Ex Memor.* 1 *&* 2. *E.* 1. *Rot.* 1. *a.*

(*y*) Major & Cives Londoniæ venerunt coram Baronibus de Scaccario, & præsentaverunt Robertum de Araz & Radulphum Fabrum Vicecomites suos, ad faciendum præcepta Domini Regis & Baronum prædictorum, & ad respondendum pro Civitate & Comitatu Midd. de hijs quæ ad Vicecomites pertinent. *Mich. Commun.* 4 *&* 5. *E.* 1. *Rot.* 1. *a.*

(*z*) Cives Londoniæ venerunt coram Baronibus, & præsentaverunt Fulconem de Sancto Albano & Salomonem le Cuteler Vicecomites suos, ad respondendum pro Civitate prædicta & Comitatu Middelsexiæ, de hijs quæ ad Officium Vicecomitum pertinent. Et ad hoc fideliter faciendum, præstiterunt sacramentum coram eisdem Baronibus. *Mich. Commun.* 17. *E.* 1. *Rot.*—*a.*

(*a*) Johannes le Bretun Custos Civitatis Londoniæ, & Cives ejusdem Civitatis, venerunt coram Philippo de Wilugby Cancellario de Scaccario Tenente locum Thesaurarij,

first (*b*) and other Years of K. *Edward* II. In the 9th Year of that King, *John Gysors*, Mayor, the Aldermen, and other Citizens, came before the Treasurer and Barons on the Morrow of St. *Michael*, and presented *Hamon Godchep* and *William de Buddele* their Sheriffs. And when the Treasurer and Barons required the said *Hamon* and *William* to take the Oath for their good Behaviour in their Office, the said Mayor and Aldermen, *&c.* say, that the said *Hamon* and *William*, or others whom the Citizens of *London* presented to that Office, are not bound, nor ought to take an Oath touching the Exercise of their Office, any where save before the Mayor and Aldermen of their City; and that since the Time that the King's Progenitors granted to the Citizens of *London* the Power of choosing and making whom they pleased Sheriffs of *London* and *Middlesex*, and of putting them out of Office at their Pleasure, it was never known that any such Oath had been taken, except once, when the said City was in the Hands of King *Edward* I: and they pray, that the said *Hamon* and *William* may be admitted to the said Office upon their Presentation, as had been accustomed aforetime. To this it was answered for the King, that although it belonged to the Citizens by their Charters to choose or make Sheriffs of *London* and *Middlesex*, and to present them at the Exchequer; yet the Persons whom they should so choose or make Sheriffs were not by that exempt from taking the aforesaid Oath, unless particular Exemption in that Behalf was granted by the King or his Progenitors: wherefore the said Citizens were told by the Treasurer and Barons, that unless the said *Hamon* and *William* took the Oath, they the said Treasurer and Barons do by no Means accept or admit them for Sheriffs, nor will accept or admit them without the King's Privity; albeit they do not hereby impeach or make void the said Election: but that if the said Persons would execute an Office under the King, such as the Office of Sheriffs is, before they had been sworn thereto at the Exchequer, it would be at their Peril (*c*). In the 12th Year of the same King, the

saurarij, & Baronibus ibidem, & præsentaverunt Thomam de Suffolk & Adam de Fulham Vicecomites suos, ad respondendum pro Civitate Londoniæ & Comitatu Middelsexiæ, in hijs quæ ad officium Vicecomitum pertinent, & ad faciendum præceptum Domini Regis, Thesaurarij, & Baronum de Scaccario. *Mich. Memor.* 25. *E.* 1.

(*b*) Johannes le Blund Major Civitatis Londoniæ & Cives ejusdem Civitatis, venerunt coram Thesaurario & Baronibus hic, ultimo die Septembris, & præsentarunt Nicholaum Pycot & Nigellum Drury Vicecomites suos Civitatis prædictæ & Comitatus Middelsexiæ, ad respondendum pro ipsis Civibus in hijs quæ ad Officium Vicecomitum in Civitate & Comitatu prædictis pertinent, & ad faciendum præcepta Domini Regis, & Thesaurarij, & Baronum de Scaccario. *Mich. Commun.* 1. *E.* 2. *Rot.* 29. *a.* inter *Præsentationes.*

(*c*) Johannes Gysors Major, . . Aldermanni

the Mayor, Aldermen, and Citizens of *London* came before the Treasurer and Barons at the Exchequer on the Morrow of St. *Michael*, and presented *John Poynz* and *John de Dallyng* Sheriffs. And when the said Sheriffs were required to take the Oath of their Office, the said Mayor and Aldermen asserted, that the Persons chosen by them for Sheriffs ought not to take such Oath before the Treasurer and Barons at the Exchequer (*d*). In the 15th Year of the same King, *Hamon de Chigewell*, Mayor of *London*, with the Aldermen and Citizens, came before the Barons on the Morrow of St. *Michael*, and presented *Richard Constantyn* and *Richard de Hakeneye* for their Sheriffs, praying to have them admitted. The Barons required the said Sheriffs to be sworn. And the Mayor and Aldermen alleged (as above in the

manni & alij Cives Londoniæ venerunt coram Thesaurario & Baronibus, modo die Martis in crastino S. Michaëlis, & præsentaverunt Hamonem Godchep & Willelmum de Buddele Vicecomites suos Civitatis Londoniæ & Comitatus Middelsexiæ, ad respondendum pro eisdem Civibus in hijs quæ ad Officium illud pertinent. Et exacto per prædictos Thesaurarium & Barones ab eisdem Hamone & Willelmo sacramento de bene & fideliter se habendo in Officio prædicto &c, prædicti Major & Aldermanni &c dicunt, quod ipsi Hamo & Willelmus, aut alij quos Cives Londoniæ præsentaverint ad prædictum Officium, non tenentur nec debent præstare sacramentum super eodem Officio exercendo, alibi quam coram Majore & Aldermannis &c, nec aliter visum fuit aliquo tempore a quo concessum fuit per Progenitores Domini Regis, quod Cives Londoniæ eligerent & facerent Vicomites Londoniæ & Middelsexiæ quos vellent &c, & eos amoverent ad voluntatem suam quociens &c, nisi tantummodo aliquo tempore quando dicta Civitas fuit in manu Domini Regis E. Patris Domini Regis nunc. Et petunt, quod præfati Hamo & Willelmus admittantur ad Officium prædictum, ad præsentationem eorundem .. Majoris & Aldermannorum & Civium prædictorum, prout hactenus &c. Et dictum est pro Rege, quod quamvis ad dictos Cives per Libertatem Cartarum suarum pertineat eligere sive facere Vicecomites &c, Et eos præsentare &c, non tamen per hoc erunt nec esse debent illi sic electi vel præfecti Vicomites &c, exempti a præstando sacramento de bene &c, nisi aliqua specialis mentio inde habeatur de Concessione Regis aut Progenitorum Regis &c; propter quod dictum est eisdem Civibus per eosdem Thesaurarium & Barones, quod nisi dicti Hamo & Willelmus præstiterint sacramentum &c, ipsi Thesaurarius & Barones non acceptant nec admittunt de plano ipsos Hamonem & Willelmum tanquam Vicecomites &c, nec ipsos ad hoc acceptare vel admittere volunt Domino Rege inconsulto; nec tamen electionem ipsorum Vicecomitum infirmant &c; sed si Regale Ministerium quod ad Officium Vicecomitum &c exercuerint, antequam sacramentum præstiterint ad Scaccarium &c, hoc sit sub periculo quod incumbit. *Mich. Præsentationes* 9. *E.* 2. *Rot.* 118. *a.*

(*d*) Johannes de Wengrave Major, .. Aldermanni & alij Cives Londoniæ venerunt coram præfatis Thesaurario & Baronibus hic ad prædictum crastinum S. Michaelis, & præsentaverunt Johannem Poynz & Johannem de Dallyng Vicecomites suos Civitatis prædictæ & Comitatus Middelsexiæ, ad respondendum pro eisdem Civibus in hijs quæ ad Officium illud pertinent &c. Et exacto a præfatis Johanne & Johanne sacramento de bene & fideliter se habendo in officio prædicto, præfati Major & Aldermanni asserunt prædictos Johannem & Johannem nec aliquos quos elegerint Vicecomites suos debere præstare sacramentum hujusmodi coram præfatis Thesaurario & Baronibus; Super quo alias facta fuit calumpnia, sicut continetur in Memorandis anni decimi, inter Præsentationes de Termino S. Michaelis. *Mich. Præsent.* 12. *E.* 2. *Rot.* 49. *a.*

12th

12th Year) that they ought not to be sworn in the Exchequer (*e*). In the 17th Year of the same King, *Nicolas de Farendon* Mayor, the Aldermen, and other Citizens of *London*, came before the Treasurer and Barons on the Morrow of St. *Michael*, and presented *Adam de Sarcsbury* and *John de Oxford* for Sheriffs; praying they might be admitted to that Office. They were admitted; and were sworn to behave themselves well and truly, &c. *(f)*.

If a Sheriff of *London*, being chosen, did not come to the Exchequer at the King's Command, to take upon him the Office of Sheriff, he was to be amerced for the Contempt. So it was in the Case of *Philipp le Taylur* (*g*).

The Mayors or chief Officers of *Oxford, Northampton, Ipswich,* and other Towns, were also wont in ancient Times to be presented at the Exchequer. But I omit them.

Sometimes Sheriffs of Counties, Under-sheriffs to hereditary Ones, Escheators, and Sub-escheators, were sworn in Person at the Exchequer, for their good Abearance in their Office. Of which Matters I must not stay to give particular Instances.

VI. Several of the King's Tenants in *Capite* by Knight's Service did their Fealty in the Exchequer. *John Dyve* did Fealty before the Treasurer and Barons for the hundredth Part of a Knight's Fee holden

---

(*e*) *Mich. Præsentat.* 15. *E.* 2. *Rot.* 33. *a.*

(*f*) Nicholaus de Farendon Major, Aldermanni, & alij Cives Civitatis Londoniæ, venerunt coram Thesaurario & Baronibus hic modo in crastino S. Michaelis, & præsentarunt Adam de Sarum & Johannem de Oxonia, concives suos, Vicecomites Civitatis prædictæ & Comitatus Middelsexæ; supplicantes ipsos ad officium Vicecomitatus in Civitate & Comitatu prædictis exercendum admitti. Et admissi sunt; & præstiterunt sacramentum de bene & fideliter se habendo &c. *Mich. Commun.* 17. *E.* 2. *Rot.*—*a. inter Præsentationes.*

(*g*) Baronibus, pro executoribus testamenti Philippi le Taylur. Cum Philippus le Taylur quondam Civis Londoniæ defunctus, nuper in vita sua coram Johanne de Kirkeby tunc Thesaurario Regis & Baronibus, amerciatus fuerit ad L l, pro contemptu quem fecit non veniendo ad Scaccarium ad mandatum Regis, ad Officium Vicecomitis in Civitate Londoniæ, ad quod electus fuit, recipiendum: Ac Rex tam amerciamentum illud, quam quantitatem & modum delicti prædicti, ponderans, Visum est Regi idem amerciamentum nimis grave esse & onerosum, maxime cum Dominus H. quondam Rex Angliæ Pater Regis per literas suas Patentes concesserit pro se & hæredibus suis, præfato Philippo, quod toto tempore vitæ suæ hanc haberet libertatem, videlicet quod non fieret Vicecomes aut alius Minister prædicti H. Regis vel hæredum suorum, contra voluntatem ejusdem Philippi: Rex mandat Baronibus, quod ad tenorem Concessionis prædictæ, & quantitatem delicti ipsius, considerationem habentes, amerciamentum illud juxta discrecionem suam amensurare, & executores testamenti prædicti Philippi de eo quod per eos per hujusmodi amensurationem de prædictis L l fuerit abstrahendum, exonerari faciant. T. Rege apud Westm. xxiij die Martij anno xxvij°. *Pas. Brevia* 26 & 27. *E.* 1. *Rot.* 18.

of the Honour of *Albemarle* (*h*). The Widows of Persons, who held of the King in Chief by Knight's Service, came into the Exchequer, and made Oath before the Barons there, that they would not marry without the King's Licence, nor to any but such as were in Ligeance to the King. An Oath of that Kind was made at the Exchequer by *Agnes*, late Wife of *William de Lancaster* (*i*); by *Margaret*, late Wife of *Thomas de Moleton* (*k*); *Margaret*, late Wife of *John de Cameys* (*l*); and *Joan*, late Wife of *Bertun de Oughtretsate* (*m*).

Some Persons, who held of the King *in Capite* by Rent-service, paid their Rent at the Exchequer. *Walter le Brun*, Farrier at the *Strand* in *Middlesex*, was to have a Piece of Ground in the Parish of St. *Clement*, to place a Forge there, he rendering yearly six Horse-shoes for it (*n*). This Rent was anciently wont to be paid at the Exchequer every Year; for Instance, in the 1st Year of K. *Edward* I (*o*), in the 2d Year of K. *Edward* I (*p*), in the 15th Year of K. *Edward* II (*q*); and afterwards. It is still rendered at the Exchequer to this Day by the Mayor and Citizens of *London*, to whom in Process of Time the said Piece of Ground was granted. Again; *Nicolas*

(*h*) Johannes Dyve filius & hæres Willelmi Dive venit coram Thesaurario & Baronibus xx die Februarij, & fecit fidelitatem Regi pro Centesima parte feodi unius Militis quam tenet de Honore de Albemarle qui nunc est in manu Regis tamquam Eschaeta sua. *Hil. Commun.* 13 & 14. *E.* 1. *Rot.* 6. *b.*

(*i*) Memorandum quod die Lunæ post diem Paschæ in tres septimanas, in præsentia Thesaurarij & Baronum ad Scaccarium, præstitit Agnes quæ fuit uxor Willelmi de Lanc. sacramentum, quod se non maritabit sine assensu Domini Regis; Et fecit fidelitatem Regi & Reginæ & Edwardo filio eorum Primogenito, sicut Dominus Rex mandavit per breve suum. *Pas. Commun.* 31. *H.* 3. *Rot.* 6. *a.*

(*k*) Cumbr. & Linc. Margareta quæ fuit uxor Thomæ filij Lamberti de Moleton defuncti, qui de Rege tenuit in Capite, venit coram Baronibus xxviij die Aprilis anno xxij, & præstitit sacramentum quod non se maritabit sine licentia & voluntate Regis, nec alicui qui non sit ad fidem ejusdem Domini Regis. *Pas. Commun.* 22. *E.* 1. *Rot.* 1. *a.*

(*l*) *Trin. Fines &c.* 26. *E.* 1. *Rot.* 93. *b.*

(*m*) Cumbria. Sacramentum Johannæ quæ fuit uxor Bertun. de Oughtretsate. *She took the Oath of Fealty before* William de Carleton, *Baron of the Exchequer, who was appointed by Writ of the Great Seal to administer it.* Et similiter fecit sacramentum, quod se non maritabit sine licentia Regis, nec alicui quin ad Fidelitatem Regis existat. Et idem Willelmus [de Carleton] eodem die remisit breve prædictum Domino Cancellario sub Sigillo suo. *Mich. Commun.* 26 & 27. *E.* 1. *Rot.* 7. *a.*

(*n*) Walterus le Brun Marescallus de Stranda r c de vj ferris equorum, pro habenda quadam placea in parochia S. Clementis, ad fabricam ibidem locandam, sicut continetur in Originali; In th. liberavit, Et Q. e. *Mag. Rot.* 19. *H.* 3. *Lond. & Midd.* m. 2. *b.*

(*o*) Middlesex. Redditus. Walterus Marescallus ad Crucem lapideam reddit sex ferra equorum cum clavibus, pro quadam fabrica quam de Rege tenet in Capite ex opposito Crucis lapideæ. *Memor.* 1. *E.* 1. *Rot.* 1. *a.*

(*p*) *Mich. Communia* 1 & 2. *E.* 1. *Rot.* 1. *b.*

(*q*) *Mich. Commun.* 15. *E.* 2. *Rot.* 29. *a.*

de Mora rendered at the Exchequer two Knives, one good, the other a very bad one, for certain Land which he held *in Capite* in *Shropshire* (r). *Roger de Ros*, the King's Taylor, rendered at the Exchequer a silver Needle, for certain Land which he held of the King *in Capite* in *Essex* (s). In the 56th Year of K. *Henry* III, *Robert de Bruweys* rendered at the Exchequer his Rent of one *Modium* of Wine, and two hundred Pearmains, for certain Land which he held of the King *in Capite* in *Runham* (t). The said Rent was paid again in the 14th Year of K. *Edward* I (u). In the 9th Year of K. *Edward* II, *Rannulph de Helebek* rendered at the Exchequer two hundred Pearmains, and two *Modiums* of Wine, for the Manor of *Ronneham*, which he held of the King *in Capite*, in the County of *Norfolk*. The Pearmains were delivered to *John de Eggemere*, Usher of the Exchequer, to be sent to the Treasurer's Wife, and the Wine was delivered to the same Person, to be kept by him till the Treasurer came to the Exchequer (w). The same Rent was paid at the Exchequer in the 15th Year of K. *Edward* II (x). In the 2d Year of K. *Edward* I, *John de Audeley* rendered a mewed Hawk at the Exchequer for the Manor of *Echemendon*, which he held of the King *in Capite* (y). In the 12th Year of K. *Edward* II, *Robert de Dunstaple* paid or rendered at the Exchequer three Pilches of Grey, each having seven Fesses, *viz.* for the 8th, 9th, and 10th Year of the present King, due for a Tenement in the City of *Winchester*, which he held of the King *in Capite*. And the said three Pilches were delivered to *John de Stokesby*, one of the Ushers of the Exchequer, to be carried to *Ralph de Stokes*, Clerk

---

(r) Salopsire. Nicholaus de Mora reddit ad Scaccarium ij Cultellos, unum bonum & alterum pessimum, pro quadam terra quam de Rege tenet in Capite in Mora. *Mich. Commun.* 29. H. 3. Rot. 1. b.

(s) Essex. Rogerus de Ros Scissor Domini Regis reddit ad Scaccarium j acum argenti, pro quadam terra quam de Rege tenet in Capite in Hallingebury; & unum acum de anno præterito. *Hil. Commun.* 29. H. 3. Rot. 7. a.

(t) Norfolcia. Redditus. Robertus de Brweys reddit ad Scaccarium unum modium vini & ducenta pyra permannorum, pro quadam terra quam de Rege tenet in Capite in Runham *Mich. Commun.* 56. H. 3. Rot. 1. b.

(u) *Mich. Commun.* 14. E. 1. Rot. 1. a.

(w) Norfolcia. Redditus. Rannulphus de Helebek reddit ad Scaccarium ducenta Piremanna & duo Modia Vini, pro Manerio de Ronneham quod de Rege tenet in Capite in Comitatu Norfolciæ. Et memorandum quod Piremanna prædicta liberantur Johanni de Eggemere Hostiario ad mittendum Consorti Thesaurarij per præceptum J. de Foxle, & Vinum prædictum liberatur prædicto Johanni de Eggemere, custodiendum usq; ad Adventum dicti Thesaurarij. *Mich. Fines &c.* 9. E. 2. Rot. 109.

(x) *Mich. Commun.* 15. E. 2. Rot. 29. a.

(y) Salopsire. Redditus. Jacobus de Audithele reddit ad Scaccarium j Spervarium mutarium, pro Manerio de Echemendon quod de Rege tenet in Capite. *Mich. Commun.* 1 & 2. E. 1. Rot. 2. a.

of the King's great Wardrobe (*z*). In the great Wardrobe (*a*). In the 15th Year of K. *Edward* II, *William de Kerdyff*, who held the Manor of *Queenhull*, in *Worcestershire*, of the King, by the Service of rendering yearly a Dog *de mota*, rendered at the Exchequer six Dogs *de mota* for six Years past. Which were delivered to Sir *David de Betoigne* to be carried to the King who was then in *Kent* (*b*).

VII. During this second Period (as well as during the first) the Chief Justicier, the Treasurer and Barons, and Council, at the Exchequer, did sometimes act in Affairs relating to the publick Peace, and to the Government and Defence of the Realm. For Example: K. *Henry* III, in the 34th Year of his Reign, came with his Council to the Exchequer, and there with his own Mouth commanded all the Sheriffs of *England* who were at that time there present, First, That by all means they keep and maintain the Liberties of the Holy Church, and likewise protect Infants, Orphans, and Widows, and do them speedy Justice; and if they found any one blaspheming the Name of *Jesus*, that they straitway attach him, to answer for it at such Day and Place as the King should appoint: Item, That no Rustick be distrained for the Debts of his Lord, so long as his Lord hath whereby he may be distrained; and that they diligently enquire, how the great Men carry themselves towards their Tenants, and if they find them trespassing, that they amend the Trespasses as far as they are able; and if perchance they are not able fully to amend them, that they shew the Trespasses to the King: Item, That no Sheriff do put Hundreds, Wapentakes, or other Bailywicks to Rack-ferms, nor let them to any but such as would deal justly with the People: Item, That they diligently enquire what

---

(*z*) Suhamton. Robertus de Dunstaple, tenens terrarum quæ fuerunt Willelmi le Taillour, reddit ad Scaccarium xxviij die Julij, tria pellicia de Griseo, quorum quodlibet est de vij sessis, pro tribus annis, videlicet pro annis octavo nono & decimo Regis nunc, pro quodam tenemento quod de Rege tenet in Capite in Civitate Wyntoniæ. Et memorandum quod prædicta tria pellicia liberantur Johanni de Stokesby uni Hostiar. de Scaccario eodem die, ad deferendum Radulpho de Stokes Clerico Magnæ Garderobæ Regis. *Trin. Redditus* 12. *E.* 2. *Rot.* 48. *a*.

This Rent was also paid at the Exchequer, anno 26. & 27. E. 1. *by* William de Dunstapele. *Pas. Fines, &c.* 26. & 27. *E.* 1. *Rot.* 66. *a*.

(*a*) *Trin. Redditus* 12. *E.* 2. *Rot.* 48. *a*.
(*b*) Wygornia. Redditus. Willelmus filius & hæres Paulini de Kerdyff qui tenet Manerium de Quenhull in Comitatu Wygorniæ per servicium reddendi Domino Regi per annum unum Canem de Mota, reddidit hic ad Scaccarium xxix° die octobris sex Canes de mota pro sex annis præteritis. Et memorandum quod prædicti canes liberantur eodem die David de Betoygne Militi, ad ducendum Domino Regi existenti in Comitatu Kanciæ in partibus de Ledes. *Trin. Visores* 15. *E.* 2. *Rot.* 28. *a*.

Markets

Chap. XXII.   *of the* EXCHEQUER.   103

Markets are held without Warrant, or to the Nuisance of the neighbouring Markets, and certify the King thereof: Item, That they safely keep all the Rights and Prerogatives of the King, and do not make Return of the King's Writs to any one, nor do suffer any one to have a View of Frankpledge, or Sheriffs Turn, or Sheriffs Aid, or other Liberties which belong to the King's Crown, without Warrant; except such Persons as have the King's Charters for those Liberties, or such whose Ancestors had obtained them of ancient Time (c). In the 14th Year of K. *Edward* I, there being then certain Affairs to be settled between the King and the Earl of *Flanders*, relating to Traffick, the King by his Writ commands the Barons, that when the said Earl should send over Commissioners to treat upon the said Affairs, the Barons should postpone other Business, and dispatch those Affairs; taking Care withal that due Justice be done to the *English* Merchants, according to a Composition or Convention entered into by the King and the Earl (d). And in the same Year *John Duraunt* was commanded by the King's Writ, to appear before the Treasurer and Barons in the Quinzime of St. *Hilary* at furthest, to treat concerning some Affairs of the Merchants of *England* and of *Flanders*, as the said Barons should direct (for which Purpose the Earl of *Flanders* was to send his Commissioners thither too) (e). The like Writs were sent to some other Persons to be there to treat as aforesaid (f). And about the same time an Account was made up at *Westminster* [in the Exchequer] between the Procurator or Commissioner of the Earl of *Flanders*, and the *English* Merchants (g). In the 23d Year of K. *Edward* I, a Writ

(c) *Ex Memor.* 35. H. 3. Rot. 2. a. *A Copy of this Record is already published in* Prynne *on the* 4th *Instit. p.* 53.

(d) Baronibus, de forma Compositionis initæ inter Regem & Comitem Flandriæ. Supplicavit Regi G. Comes Flandriæ, quod cum Plegij sui in carcerem jam se posuerunt apud Monstroll., juxta formam Compositionis dudum initæ inter Regem & ipsum, Rex plegios illos mandaret liberari a carcere, dum aliqui ex parte Regis & sua Londoniam transmittendi mutuum haberent tractatum de negocio quod inter Regem vertitur in hac parte, adiciens quod de suis aliquos ad octabas Omnium Sanctorum ad Civitatem prædictam transmittet, qui pro parte sua plenariam super hoc habeant potestatem. Quocirca Rex mandat Baronibus, quod cum dictus Comes de suis aliquos ad diem & locum prædictos transmiserit ad tractandum de negocio supradicto, eidem negocio, dimssiis alijs, intendant, taliter providentes quod Mercatoribus Terræ Regis Angliæ quorum interest, juxta tenorem Compositionis prædictæ tunc fiat justiciæ complementum; Ita quod non oporteat Regem amplius de negocio vexari. Rex enim mandavit Johanni Bek, quod die & loco prædictis intersit, & quod ibidem secum habeat omnia quæ negocium memoratum contingunt. *Mich. Communia* 14. E. 1. *Rot.* 3. *a. in bund.* 13 & 14. E. 1.

(e) *Hil. Brevia* 14. E. 1. *Rot.* 25. *a.*
(f) *Ib. juxt.*
(g) *Hil. Commun.* 13 & 14. E. 1. *Rot.* 7. *b.*

issued

issued out of the Exchequer to the Sheriff of *Rutlandshire*, commanding him to warn all Persons within his County, as well Knights as others, who had forty Pounds a Year or more in Land and Rents, so to provide themselves, that they might be ready with Horse and Arms to march in the King's Service, and to continue at the King's Wages as he pleased, whensoever they should, on the King's Behalf, by the Space of Three Weeks, be thereunto forewarned: The Sheriff was also commanded to warn all Persons who had not forty Pounds a Year in Land and Rents, but under that Sum, in case they had Horses and Arms, to come, if they would, upon such Forewarning, as is aforesaid, into the King's Service, and to remain at his Wages: The King likewise commandeth the Sheriff to cause all the said Persons who had forty Pounds a Year or more, to come before him the said Sheriff to be mustered, &c. The like Writs or Commissions were sent to the other Sheriffs of *England* (h). In the 25th Year of K. *Edward* I, the Lieutenant of the Treasurer, and the Barons of the Exchequer, sent to the King by the Hand of *Robert Dyvelyn*, Usher of the Exchequer, a Letter under the Exchequer-Seal, notifying that the Earl *Mareschall*, the Earl of *Hereford*, and others, came to the Bar of the Exchequer on the Thursday before the Feast of St. *Bartholomew* at Three o' Clock; and that the Earl of *Hereford*, on behalf of the Earl *Mareschall* and the others there present, and of the whole Commonalty of the Realm, both Clergy and Lay (as he alleged) did let them know, that they and the said Commonalty found themselves aggrieved in two Things: The one related to certain Points which they had already remonstrated to the King, their Liege Lord, in certain Articles; the other related to certain Things done by the Barons and Officers of the Exchequer without the King's Knowledge, particularly, the levying of the Utime and the taking of Wools; and that in the Writs issued for levying the Utime it was contained, that the Earls, Barons, Knights, and Commonalty of the Realm had granted the said Utime as they and their Ancestors had done in former Times, whereas the said Utime was not granted by them nor by the said Commonalty. In fine, that the Tallage of the Utime and the taking of

---

(h) Rex Vicecomiti Rotelandiæ salutem. Cum sexto die Maij proximo præterito—. Et hoc, sicut indignationem nostram vitare & te indempnem servare volueris, nullatenus omittas. Et habeas ibi tunc hoc breve. Teste W. de Langeton Thesaurario nostro apud Westmonasterium xix die Octobris anno r n xxiij. Consimili modo mandatum est Vicecomitibus subscriptis videlicet, Cumberlandia, Norhumberlandia, *and of the other Counties of* England. *Memor.* 23 & 24. E. 1. *Mich. Commun. viz. inter brevia missa pro Rege, Rot. numerato* 10. h. *This Writ is printed in Maynards Edward II, in the Appendix, p.* 36.

Wools was not to be endured, and they would not endure it. Hereupon the Barons of the Exchequer defire to know the King's Pleafure. The King fends them a Privy Seal, dated the 23d of *Anguft*, and another, dated the 24th of *Auguft*: By the former he commands them to proceed to tax and levy the Utime in fuch Manner as had been appointed, and to caufe Proclamation to be made in the Counties where the Taxation was to be made, declaring that the fame fhould not turn to the Prejudice or Servage of the People, nor be drawn into Ufe in Time to come, fo as the King might now have the Benefit of it for his prefent moft urgent Occafions, and for the Salvation of himfelf, and of them and the whole Realm : And directs, that the Chancellor fhould make out fuch Letters of the Great Seal, and the Barons fuch Letters under the Seal of the Exchequer, as they upon mutual Advifement fhould think would be proper and effectual; and that, if they fhould have Occafion to defire further Direction about this or any other urgent Affair, they fhould make it known to the Prince and his Council ; and that the Council, with the Advice of the Barons of the Exchequer, fhould do what appeared fit to be done. By the latter Privy Seal, he commands them to advife with the Prince and his Council, fo that upon Deliberation had amongft them all, the beft Meafures might be taken. The King likewife fent to the Prince a Privy Seal, dated on Shipboard the 24th of *Auguft*, with Inftructions for his Conduct in this Affair, and another Privy Seal to the Chancellor, commanding him to make forth, by the Advifement of the Barons of the Exchequer, fuch Letters as fhould be thought expedient, for taxing the Utime in the Realm, fo that it might not turn to the Prejudice or Difheritance of the People or their Heirs, nor be drawn into Ufage in Time coming (*i*). K. *Edward* I, in the 26th Year

(*i*) De Adventu Comitum, Marefcalli & Herefordiæ, in Scaccario. Tenens locum Thefaurarij & Barones de Scaccario miferunt Domino Regi quafdam Litteras fub figillo dicti Scaccarij in hæc verba. Sire, y ceft Joedi procheyn devaunt la Fefte Seinte Bertelmeu a houre de Tierce vindrent a voftre Efchekier a la barre le Count Marefchal e le Count de Hereford, Monf. Sire Robert Le Fitz-Roger, Sire Aleyn la Zouche, Sire Johan de Segrave, Sire Henry de Tyeys, Sire Johan Lovel, e plufours autres Banerez & Bacheliers. E le Counte de Hereford dit, quil feuft charge a dire de par le Count Marefchal e les autres qe illioques furent, & par tute la Comounaute du Reaume auxibien Clers com Lais, qe de deus chofes fe fentirent eaux e la dite Comounaute grevez ; Lune Daukunes grevaunces dount il aveient fait monftrer les Articles a vous come a leur Lige Seignour, e lautre quil entendirent qe feuft fait par nous dil Efchekier, Sauntz voftre feu com endreit dil utime lever e des leines prendre ; e dit, qen les briefs que funt iffuz pur lever le utime, eft contenu, qe Countes, Barouns, Chivaliers & la Comounaute du Reiaume, unt graunte le utime, ficom a eux e leur Aunceftres unt fait cea en ariere, la ou le dit utime par eux ne par la dite Comounaute unqes ne feut graunte; e dit outre, qe nule chofe ne met plu tot homme en fervage, qe rechat de faunc, e eftre taille a volunte ; e qe fi le utime feuft iffi levee,

Year of his Reign, sent his Letters of the Privy Seal to the Treasurer and Barons, with a Letter enclosed therein from *Reginald de Grey*, about raising of Foot in the War with *Scotland*. The Treasurer thereupon writes to the Chancellor, desiring him to cause Letters Patent under the King's Great Seal to be made forth to *Reginald de Grey*, for raising of Foot in *Cheshire* and *Lancashire*, according to the Tenor of the said Letters, and to deliver the said Letters Patent to *Richard de Haveringe*, who was enjoined by the Treasurer to look after and dispatch that Affair, and had Money delivered to him to pay the Wages of the Foot Soldiers to be raised as aforesaid (*k*). In the 26th or 27th Year of K. *Edward* I, the Chancellor and Barons of the Exchequer enjoined the Sheriff of *Nottingham* and *Derby* (then present in the Court) to cause, by himself and his Bailiffs, the King's Peace to be kept at the *Lenton* Fair which was then near at hand, so that the Peace might not be broken through the Neglect of him or his Bailiffs (*l*). In the 27th Year of K. *Edward* I, on St. *Vincent*'s Day there were delivered in the Exchequer to *John Byroun*, Sheriff of *Yorkshire*, three Letters sealed with the Treasurer's Seal, one of them directed to the King, another to *Robert de Clifford*, Commander of the King's Garrison against the *Scots* in the Borders of *Cumberland*, and the third to *Walter de Huntercombe* and the Sheriff of *Northumberland*, about certain Affairs relating to the said Garrison: And because the sending of the said Letters required quick Dispatch, the Treasurer and Barons enjoined the said *John*, the Sheriff, to transmit the said Letters forthwith by riding Messengers to the King and the said other

ceo turnereit a dereceiteson de eaux e de leur heirs ; E dit apertement, e toutz les autres apres, qe tiel taillage e prise de leines ne furent mie suffrables, ne il ne suffreint en nule manere ; E nous prierent qe cestes choses feissoms redrescier ; e ataunt sen partirent sauntz nule respounse atendre. E pur ceo, Sire, nous voillez maunder, si vous plest, sur ceste chose vostre volunte. Sire, nostre Seignour vous doint bone vie e longe, e acresse vos honours. Escrit a Westmonstre, le Joedi avaunt dit, a houre de noune. Ista littera missa fuit Domino Regi per Robertum Dyvelyn Hostiarium de Scaccario ad prædictam horam nonæ.

Littera missa Baronibus per Regem—. *This Record is too long to be inserted* verbatim. *Trin. Recorda* 25. *E*. 1. *Rot*. 28. *b*. & *seqq*.

(*k*) Baronibus, pro Peditibus eligendis pro Scocia. *Pas. Communia* 26 & 27. *E*. 1. *Rot*. 5. *b*.

(*l*) Notingham. Præceptum factum Vicecomiti Notingamiæ pro Pace servanda. Memorandum quod die S. Leonardi Abbatis, præsente hic Radulpho de Schirlegh Vicecomite Notingamiæ & Derbiæ, Injunctum est eidem Vicecomiti per Cancellarium & Barones de Scaccario Regis, quod per se & Ballivos suos, custodiri faciat Pacem Domini Regis in Nundinis de Lenton quæ erunt ad instans festum S. Martini ; Ita quod Pax Domini Regis pro negligencia sua & suorum Ballivorum non lædatur ibidem ; maxime pro eo quod Prioratus Loci prædicti de Lenton in manu Domini Regis esse dinoscitur, eo quod Prior ejusdem Alienigena est & de Potestate Regis Franciæ. *Mich. Communia* 26 & 27. *E*.1. *Rot*. 5. *b*.

Per-

Persons (*m*). K. *Edward* I, in the 31st Year of his Reign, sent his Writ under the Exchequer-seal to *Thomas de Furnivall*; commanding him to repair in Person to *York* (where the Exchequer was then holden) with all possible Speed, to confer and treat with the King's Treasurer and Barons and others of his Council, concerning the Estate of the Nobility and others whom the King had ordered to serve in his Army against the *Scots*, and further to do what the King's Council should ordain in his Name touching the Premisses. The like Writs were sent to *William le Vavassour, Brian Fitz-Alan*, and six or seven other Barons of the northern Parts (*n*). In the 34th Year of that King, several foreign Merchants were brought before the Treasurer, the Chancellor of *England*, the Barons, the Justices of both Benches, and others of the King's Council at the Exchequer, and were examined on the King's Behalf, what and how many Merchants of their respective Societies were at present in these cismarine Parts. The Merchants gave in their Answer. Whereupon, they were enjoined by the said Council on the King's Behalf, that under Pain of forfeiting their Liberty and Chattels, no one of them do go out of the Realm, or export any Thing without the King's special Leave; and that each Society do on the Morrow find Security to do accordingly; and that they do lay a distinct and true Account, of all the Goods and Chattels they had in the Realm in Money or Monies-worth, before the said Council on the Monday following. The next Day the Merchants came before the Barons and Council; but not being able to find

---

(*m*) Hil. Commun. 26 & 27. E. 1. Rot. 14. a.

(*n*) Rex dilecto & fideli suo Thomæ de Furnivall salutem. Quia propter quosdam rumores quos audivimus jam de novo, volumus & necessario expedit, quod Thesaurarius & Barones de Scaccario nostro & cæteri de Consilio nostro apud Eboracum existentes, vobiscum & quibusdam alijs fidelibus nostris partium illarum, colloquium habeant & tractatum, super statu Magnatum & aliorum quos in exercitum nostrum contra Scotos inimicos & rebelles nostros nuper destinavimus, in partibus illis secundum quod ordinavimus moraturos: Vobis mandamus, in fide & dilectione quibus nobis tenemini firmiter injungentes, quatinus sicut honorem nostrum & tranquilitatem regni nostri diligitis, usq; ad Scaccarium nostrum apud Eboracum, visis præsentibus, cum omni celeritate qua poteritis personaliter accedatis, cum dictis Thesaurario & Baronibus ac alijs de Consilio nostro ibidem, super præmissis specialiter tractaturi, & ulterius facturi quod de dicto Consilio nomine nostro fuerit ordinatum; Ita quod sitis ibidem die Mercurij proximo ante festum S. Gregorij jam instantis, sine dilatione ulteriori. T. P. de Willugby tenente locum Thesaurarij nostri apud Eboracum, ij die Martij anno regni nostri xxxj. Consimili modo mandatum est Willelmo le Vavassour &c, Et Briano filio Alani, Et Radulfo filio Willelmi, Et Petro de Malo Lacu, Et Jerardo Salveyn, Radulfo filio Ran[ulfi], Et Marmeduko de Twenge, Et Thomæ de Collevill, Et Johanni le Vavassour, Et . . . —. Hil. Brevia Retornab. 30 & 31. E. 1. Rot. 69. a.

Security

Security, as they had been enjoined to do, they were committed to the Custody of *Ralph de Sandwich*, Constable of the Tower of *London*. Afterwards they became Manucaptors for one another, and so were delivered out of Prison (*o*). In the same Year, Sir *Henry de Kyghele* having confessed, upon his Examination before the King, that he was the Person who brought the Bill [or Petition] from the Archbishop of *Canterbury* and the others who pressed the King outrageously at the Parliament of *Lincoln*, the King sends the said *Henry* to the Exchequer, and by his Privy Seal commands the Treasurer to cause him to be put into safe Custody in the Tower of *London*, there to remain till he should repent of what he had done, and till the King should give further Order about him; and the King directs, that he should be kept without Irons and mildly used, but in such Manner that the kind Usage might rather seem to be owing to the Treasurer's Curtesy than to the King's Orders (*p*). Accordingly, the said Sir *Henry* was brought by two of the King's Valets into the Exchequer, before the Treasurer, Barons, and Council there; and was committed to the Constable of the Tower of *London*, to be kept in the said Tower in such Manner as the King had directed. Afterwards, by virtue of the King's Writ of Privy Seal, the said *Henry* was brought into the Exchequer, and when he had taken a corporal Oath, not to offend for the future against the King, his Heirs, or his Crown, he was delivered out of Prison (*q*). In the same Year, some of the King's Serjeants at Arms brought before the Treasurer and Barons *Patrick de Graham*, a *Scots* Knight, who had rendered himself to the King's Peace, in order to stand to Right: And with him the King sent his Writ of Privy Seal to the Treasurer, commanding him to commit the said *Patrick* to some Castle in *England*, as he should find most convenient, where the Prisoner might be safely kept, and so that his Keepers might be

(*o*) *Pas. Recorda* 34. *E.* 1. *Rot.* 31. *b.*
(*p*) Thesaurario pro Rege. Edward par la grace de Dieu &c; Al Honorable Piete en Dieu Wautier par meisme la grace Evesqe de Cestre, nostre Tresorier, salutz. Nous envoions a vous par les porturs de ces Lettres, Monsieur Henry de Kyghele, qui ad este devant nous, & avoms bien trove par sa reconissance demeine, quil est celi qui nous porta la bille depar Lercevesqe de Canterbiris, & depar les autres qui nous presserent outraiousement au Parlement de Nichole, & le quel nous avons taunt fait serchier; Et vous mandoms, qe le dit Henri sacez mettre en sauve garde en la Tour de Loundres, a demorer y tanq; nous puissoms saver qil soit repentant de ce quil en ad fait, & qe nous eons sur ce autrement ordene. Et sachez qe nous volons, qe le dit Henri soit curteisement & sauvement gardez en la dite Tour, hors des fers, mes qe cele curtesie & cele garde soit ensi ordence, quil puisse entendre qe ce viegne de vostre cortesie, & ne mye de nous. Don souz nostre Prive Seal a Thindene, le v jour de Juyn. *Trin. Brevia* 34. *E.* 1. *Rot.* 40. *b.*
(*q*) *Trin. Commun.* 34. *E.* 1. *Rot.* 44. *b. Trin. Brevia* 35. *E.* 1. *Rot.* 50. *b.*

charged

Chap. XXII. *of the* EXCHEQUER. 109

charged to anfwer for him Body for Body: Hereupon the faid *Patrick* was delivered to the Conftable of the Tower of *London*, who was then prefent in Court, to be by him fafely kept Body for Body (*r*). About the fame time *Malculm de Innerpeffry*, a *Scotfman*, was committed by the Treafurer to the Tower of *London* much after the fame Manner (*s*). And by another Privy Seal the King commands the Treafurer, to let the faid *Malcolm* make his Profit or do his Pleafure with two of his Horfes (*t*). In the 35th Year of K. *Edward* I, the Conftable of *Dovor Caftle* arrefted *Adam de Swilington* Knight, for going beyond Sea to the Turnaments, contrary to the King's Inhibition: A Valet of the Conftable's brought *Adam* before the Treafurer and Barons, who committed him to the Conftable of the Tower of *London* (*u*). In the fame Year, it was ordered by the Treafurer and Barons, that fuch Sheriffs throughout *England* as were found unfit to execute that Office, fhould be removed, and other fit Perfons put into their Places; and that the Barons might do this by themfelves, without ftaying for the Treafurer's Prefence, in cafe he happened not to be at the Exchequer, when it was to be done (*w*). K. *Edward* II, by his Writ of Privy Seal, commanded the Barons of the Exchequer to fend fpeedily towards the Coaft of *Scotland* two Ships and two Barges, well and fufficiently manned and victualled, to act againft the *Scots* (*x*). In the

(*r*) De Patricio de Graham liberato Turri Londoniæ. *Mich. Communia* 34 & 35. *E.* 1. *Rot.* 17. *a. parte* 1.

(*s*) De Malculmo de Innerpeffry Scoto liberato Turri Londoniæ. *The King fends a Writ of Privy Seal to the Bifhop of* Chefter, *Treafurer, commanding him to fend* Malcolm *to fome ftrong Caftle to be there fafely kept* hors de fers, *and the Keeper to anfwer for him Body for Body*, Donne fouz noftre Prive feal a Lanrecoft, le xxiiij jour de Novembre lan de noftre regne xxxv. Et incontinenti, videlicet vij die Decembris, prædictus Malculmus liberatur Radulpho de Sandwyco Conftabulario Turris Londoniæ, cuftodiendus in forma prædicta. *Mich. Commun.* 34 & 35. *E.* 1. *Rot.* 19. *a.*

(*t*) Thefaurio per Regem, pro equis dicti Scoti. *Ibid. juxt.*

(*u*) *Mich. Commun.* 34 & 35. *E.* 1. *Rot.* 19. *b. pars* 1.

(*w*) De Vicecomitibus fi expediens fuerit removendis, & alijs fubrogandis. Item concordatum eft per præfatos Thefaurarium & Barones, quod ad Proffrum S. Michaelis proximo futurum, & ex tunc Barones quos contigerit tunc effe præfentes hic, habito inter eofdem confilio & tractatu de Vicecomitibus Angliæ; fi videlicet aliquis eorum idoneus vel fufficiens non fuerit, fecundum difcrecionem eorum ad officium Vicecomitis exercendum, ipfum vel ipfos quem vel quos in hoc effe minus fufficientem vel minus fufficientes decreverint, licet dictus Thefaurarius præfens non fuerit, ab Officio Vicecomitis faciant ammoveri; & loco ipforum fic ammotorum alios quos ad Officium Vicecomitis fufficientes & idoneos fore viderint, fubrogari, præfencia præfati Thefaurarij ad hoc nullatenus expectata. *Trin. Communia* 35. *E.* 1. *Rot.* 59. *b. parte* 1. citat. Cap. 22. *fect.* 1.

(*x*) Baronibus per Regem. *The King commands the Barons to caufe to be fent*, haftivement vers les parties Defcoce, dieux Nief & deux Barges bien & fuffifaument efkypez de gentz & de vitailles ———, a damager nos enemys Defcoce———. Don fouz noftre Prive Seal a Everwik, le quart jour de Juyn lan de noftre regne quint. *Trin. Brevia* 5. *E.* 2. *Rot.* 53. *a.*

12th

12th Year of K. *Edward* II, Complaints were made to the Treasurer, Barons, and Council at the Exchequer, that divers Murders, Robberies, and other Outrages had been lately committed in *London*; particularly, the Pope's Nuncio informed them, that on last Midsummer-day, at the Time of Vespers, four or five hundred Malefactors came into St. *Paul*'s Church armed, and there insulted a certain *Lumbard* and others of his Company with drawn Swords, &c. The Mayor and Aldermen of *London* were ordered to appear before the Treasurer, and Barons and Council, to answer touching the Premises. *John de Wengrave*, the Mayor (who had been in that Office a Year and three Quarters) came before the Treasurer and Barons, in the Presence of the Archbishop of *Canterbury*, the Bishop of *Exeter*, *Humfrey* Earl of *Hereford*, Master *J. Waleweyn*, and others of the Council; and with him came several Aldermen and the Sheriffs. The Mayor was examined touching the Matters complained of, and was chidden; in regard he had been several Times questioned at the Exchequer on the like Occasions. Upon the Whole, the Court enjoined the Mayor, Aldermen, and Sheriffs, to take Inquisitions concerning the said Malefactors, and bring them to Punishment; particularly, the Mayor was enjoyned so to behave himself in his Office, that the King might have no Cause to set a *Custos* over the City; and the Inquisitions which he should take, he was to get ready against such a Time, under Pain of forfeiting the Liberties of the City. Afterwards the Mayor and Aldermen came again to the Exchequer; and being spoken to by the Council, they said they had made solemn Inquisitions, and would so behave themselves in the Custody of the City and Conservation of the Peace, that there should hereafter be no Cause of Complaint through their Default (*y*). In the same Year the King, intending to send a Fleet to guard the Sea and annoy the *Scots*, commands the Treasurer and Barons by his Privy Seal, to order, in his Name, *John Mot* and *Richard Golde* to make Haste, with the Mariners and Ships they had got ready, towards *Kingston upon Hull*, and to stay there and do according to the Directions which the King had given to *Simon de Dryby* (*z*). About the same time he commands

(*y*) *Trin. Communia* 12. E. 2. *Rot.* 31. *b.*
(*z*) Edward par la grace de Dieu, &c, Al honurable piere en Dieu J. par la meisme grace Evesqe de Wyncestre nostre Treforier falutz. Pur ceo qe nous avoms ordinez denvoier navie pur la garde de la meer devers le Est, & pur grever nos enemys Defcoce: Vous maundoms, qe vous facetz charger fanz delay depar nous Johan Mot & Richard Golde noz mariners, qil se treent haftivement od noz niefs qil ount en garde vers Kyngeston fur Hull, e demoergent y felonc ce qe noftre cher vallet Simon de Dryby vous avysera depar nous, & lour facet trover lour coutages tantqe illoqes. Done foutz noftre Prive Seal a Everwyk, le xj jour de Marz lan de noftre regne douzifme. *Paf. Brevia* 12. E. 2. *Rot.* 94. *b.*

the

Chap. XXII. *of the* EXCHEQUER.

the Barons, to cause Corn and Victuals and other Stores to be provided by the Sheriffs of Counties, and carried to proper Ports, there to be embarked, and afterwards landed near the Marches of *Scotland*, for the Use of the King's Army (*a*). The same King, *Anno Regni* 15, by Privy Seal commands the Keeper of the Office of Treasurer and the Barons and Chamberlains of the Exchequer, to take Care that his Castles be sufficiently victualled and stored (*b*). In the 16th Year of K. *Edward* II, a Commission issued out of the Exchequer to *Geoffrey de St. Quyntyn* and *John de Hasthorp*, ordering them to raise speedily, in every Town and Place in the Wapentake of *Dykryng* as well within the Franchises as without, all the defensible Men that were between the Age of Sixteen and Sixty, as well of *Gentz darmes* as of Foot, each Man being duly arrayed according to his Estate, and to put the said Men in Array by Hundreds and Twenties, and being so arrayed to lead them to the King at *York* by such a Day, to act against the *Scots*. The like Commissions issued out of the Exchequer, to *John de Belkthorp* and *Geoffrey Stull* for the Wapentake of *Buckros*, and to other Persons for other Wapentakes, as hereunder particularly appeareth (*c*).

VIII. In

(*a*) Trin. Brevia 12. E. 2. Rot. 105. a.
(*b*) Hil. Brevia 15. E. 2. Rot. 49. a.
(*c*) Edward par la grace Dieu Roi Dengleterre Seignour Dirlaund & Ducs Daquitaigne, a ses feals & loials Geffrey de seint Quyntyn & Johan de Hasthorp salutz. Por ce qe noz enemys & noz rebeals Descoce sount ja a graunt force entre nostre Roialme Dengleterre, & leinz demoerent ardaunt & destruyant de jour en autre seint Eglise & le poeple de nostre dit Roialme. Et toux ceux de nostre ligeance sount tenuz par tutes les voies qils saverent ou purront a lever & aparer ove tut lour poer en eide de nous & de eux & pur la sauvete de seint Eglise & du Roialme, a arester, refreyndre, & destruyre ove tute la haste qil unque purront les enemys avantditz: Vous avoms assignez jointement & severaument affere lever denz le Wapentak de Dykryng, sans nul delai ou excusacion, de vile en vile, de lieu en lieu, auffi bien de denz fraunchise com de hors, touz les hommes defensables qui sount entre les ages de sesze & seisaunte annz, auffi bien les gentz darmez com gentz a pee chescun homme duement araie solom son estat, & vous meismes affere mettre tutes celes gentz en aray en centeignes & vynteignes & ensi araez mener a nous a Everwyk, issi qe vous & eux soiez a nous a Everwyk y ce Mekresdy en la velle des Apostles seint Simen & seint Jude prest a oier & affere ce qe par nous & les grauntz de nostre Roialme qore y sount & adonque serrount serra ordyne sur lespleit de la busoigne avantdite sur quantqe chescun de eux puisse a nous forfere. Par quoi vous mandoms & chargeoms a la foi & ligeance qe vous nous devez & sur tut ce qe vous nous purrez forfere, qe tutes les choses susditez facez & fournissez en la manere susdite. Et ce en nule manere ne lessez sicom vous amez la sauuete de nous & de vous & de nostre Roialme & com vous volez eschure qe vous ne checez en la forfeture desusdite. Nous avoms auffi maunde a nostre Viscounte de Everwyk qil soit entendant a vous en les choses susdites a tutes les soitz que vous lui freez assavoir. En tesmoignance de queu chose cestes noz lettres avoms fet fere patentes. Tesmoigne Lonourable piere Wauter Evesqe Dexcestre nostre

VIII. In general, the Business and Acts of the Court of Exchequer were wont to be entered or recorded in several Rolls: The principal whereof were these; viz. *The Rotulus Annalis* or Great Roll of the Pipe, the *Memoranda*, and the *Plea Rolls*. Amongst the Records of the Exchequer the *Great Roll* of the *Pipe* must be placed first, by reason of its pre-eminent Dignity. It was and is the most stately Record in the Exchequer, and the great Medium of Charge and Discharge, of Rents, Farms, and Debts due to the Crown. Into it the Accounts of the royal Revenue entered through divers Channels, as Rivers flow into the Ocean. The worthy Author of the Dialogue concerning the Exchequer (*d*) giveth some Account of the *Great Roll*; whose Words I need not here repeat (*e*). In the 4th Year of K. *Edward* I, it was stiled *Primus Rotulus Scaccarii* (*f*). And the Authority

nostre Tresorer a Everwyk le vyntisme jour Doctobre lan de nostre regne seszisme.

Meisine tieles commissions sount fetez a les gentz & lieux desouz nomez cest assavoir: A Johan de Belhthorp & Geffrey Stull en le Wapentak de Buckros; William Twyer, Robert de la More, en le Wapentak de Holdernesse; William Malebys, Henry de Munketon, en le Wapentak de Aynsty; Johan Mauleverer, Peres de Middelton, en le Wapentak de Clarhowe; Adam de Swylyngton, William de Stargill, en le Wapentak de Skyryk; Robert de Raygate, Johan de Lacy, en le Wapentak de Barkeston; Thomas de Furnivall Leyne, Edmund de Wasteneys, William Clarell, en le Wapentak de Strafford; William de Anne, en le Wapentak de Tykhill; Adam de Wannervill, Geffrey de Staynton, Esmon Butiller, en les Wapentaks de Osgotecros & Stayncros; Johan de Eland, William de Weston, en le Wakentak de Morley; Robert de Beaumont, Thomas de Tothill, en le Wapentak de Agbrig; William de Ponteburg, Robert de Weston, en le Wapentak de Knaresburg; Roger de Nonewyk, William de Clotherom, en le Wapentak de Rypoun; Johan de Walkyngham, Johan Waxand, en le Wapentak de Brudeford; William Darel, Johan de Hamby, en le Wapentak de Alverton; Johan de Thorneton de Stowesby, Hwe Gryvell, en le Wapentak de Bulmer; Johan de Faburn, Henry de Moreby, en les Wapentaks de Ouse & Derewent; Homme trovera plus de cestes Commissions en le doos de cest roule; Robert le Conestable, Roger de Somervill, en le Wapentak de Herthill; Robert de Colvill, Robert Capoun, en le Wapentak de Langebrug; Thomas de Bolton, Symon Lovell, en le Wapentak de Rydale; Johan Druell, William de Yekand, en le Wapentak de Pykeryng; Alisaundre Cock, Johan atte See, en le Wapentak de Ravenesere; Richard de la Pole, Geffrey le Fitz Hwe, en le Wapentak de Kyngeston sur Hull; Rychard Roce, William de Rolleston, en le Wapentak de Beverle; Robert Wawayn, Rey[mun] le Carter, en le Wapentak de Scardeburgh; Johan de Wykham, William Payne, en le Wapentak de Whiteby; Nichol de Portyngton, William de Lincoln, Roger Deyvill, en le Wakentak de Houeden. *Mich. Commissiones & Lit. Pat.* 16. *E.* 2. *Rot.* 1. *a & b.*

(*d*) *Dial. L.* 1. *cap.* 5. Quid ad scriptorem Thesaurarij; *& alibi.*

(*e*) Et. vid. *Dissert. de Mag. Rot.* 5. Ste.

(*f*) Rex Thes. & Camerarijs suis salutem. Liberate de thesauro nostro dilecto clerico nostro Rogero de la Leye Cancellario Scaccarij nostri viginti libras, Johanni de Sancto Valerico Baroni ejusdem Scaccarij nostri viginti libras, Rogero de Northwode Baroni dicti Scaccarij viginti libras, Ricardo

rity of it was so great, that when Debts had been put in Charge there, they could not be discharged, unless by Judgment or Award of the Chief Justicier, or of the Treasurer, the King's Chancellor, or his Council, or the Barons of the Exchequer. The *Great Roll* was written and settled with an exact Care. Each single Roll of the ancient Bundles is commonly marked at the Bottom; viz. in a spare Place on the Dorse, *Emendatus, iterum emendatus,* &c. Every County was written by itself. So it was also where two Counties were conjunct, or committed to one Sheriff. If a single Roll would not contain a whole County, the Residue of that County was written upon another Roll or Part of a Roll, and so forward till the whole was finished. The first Roll of every County, to wit, that which contained the *Corpus Comitatus,* was in that Case usually called *Rotulus principalis* (g); and was marked or intituled, for Example, *Kancia*; the next Roll or Part of a Roll, *Item Kancia,* or *Residuum Kanciæ*; the next, *Adhuc Item Kancia,* or *Residuum,* according as the Case was; and so forward. The particular Rolls were not wont to be numbered. And it is likely the Accounts were digested in this Manner, and written upon Parts of Rolls where there was Room for them, that Parchment might not be spent unnecessarily, and likewise that the Rolls might not have in them many or large blank Spaces. The Great Roll, as I take it, is properly the Treasurer's Roll. This is intimated in the Dialogue (h). But as the Chancellor of the Exchequer seems to have been an Officer appointed to be a Check upon the Treasurer; so it seemeth that the Chancellor from ancient Time caused a Counter-roll of the Treasurer's great Rool to be made up every Year: Which Counter-roll was the same *verbatim* with the other great Roll, and was called *Rotulus Cancellarij*. There are many of these *Rotuli Cancellarij* of the Reign of K. *Henry* III, and of subsequent Kings, to be seen in the Repository

---

Ricardo de Hereford Clerico ejusdem Scaccarij decem libras, Nicholao de Castello Clerico ejusdem Scaccarij decem libras, Magistro Odoni Custodi Memorandorum nostrorum ejusdem Scaccarij viginti & quinque marcas, & Ricardo de Stanford Scriptori primi Rotuli Scaccarij nostri prædicti decem marcas, in subventionem expensarum suarum in servicio nostro. T. R. apud Turrim Londoniæ xxiiij de Novembris. *Lib.* 4. *E.* 1. *m.* 11.

(g) Idem R. Vicecomes debet xxvl ix s ob. Bl[ancos] & Cxxiiij l v s numero, de remanente firmæ Comitatus, sicut continetur in Rotulo Principali post Corpus Comitatus. *Mag. Rot.* 49. *H.* 3. *Item Kancia m.* 1. *b.* Rogerus de Leyburn Vicecomes.

Idem R. Vicecomes debet xxv l ix s ob. Bi[ancos] de remanente firmæ Comitatus, sicut supra continetur, Et Cxxiiij l v s de remanente firmæ numero, sicut continetur ibidem. Et respondet post Item Kancia. *Ib. in eod. bundello tit.* Kancia. *m.* 1. *b.*

(h) *Dial. L.* 1. *cap.* 5. Scriptoris qui proximus est; & *L.* 2. *cap.* 4. Gratulor te memorem.

of the *Pipe* at *Weſtminſter*. In Truth, there are extant ſome Duplicaments of great Rolls more ancient (but not in a continued Series) than the Reign of K. *Henry* III. This Obſervation may ſerve to reſolve a Doubt, which the Antiquaries have hitherto lain under. For Example: There is in the Record-office in the Tower of *London* a Duplicate great Roll of the ſixth Year of K. *Richard* I, and another of the 7th Year of K. *John*. And there is another of the 3d Year of K. *John* in the Cuſtody of the Treaſurer and Chamberlains of the Exchequer. The great Rolls of which ſeveral Years are alſo extant in the Repoſitory of the *Pipe*. And in the ſame Repoſitory of the *Pipe* there are two great Rolls of the 4th Year of K. *John*; which are (for I have compared them in Part) of one and the ſame Tenor. All theſe Duplicate great Rolls I take to be *Rotuli Cancellarij*.

The Records or Bundles made up by the two Remembrancers of the Exchequer have been uſually called *Memoranda*, the *Memorands* or *Remembrances*. A *Remembrance* was anciently wont to be made for every Year in each of the Remembrancer's Offices. On the Part of the Treaſurer's Remembrancer, each yearly Bundle was wont to contain ſeveral Heads or Titles, ſuch as, *Communia*, the common or ordinary Buſineſs; *Compota* or *Compoti*, Accounts; *Viſus*, Views; *Adventus*, the Advents of Accountants to the Exchequer; and other Titles. For Example: The Titles or Heads ſet forth hereunder in the Margin, are found in the 11th Year of K. *Henry* III (*i*), in the 28th Year (*k*), in the 42d Year (*l*); in the 7th Year of K. *Edward* I (*m*); in the 16th Year of K. *Edward* II (*n*); and the like in other

---

(*i*) Item Communia; *Memor*. 11. *H*. 3 *Rot*. 1: Adventus; *Ib. Rot*. 2. Item Communia; *Ib. Rot*. 3. Viſus; *Ib. Rot*. 4. & 5; Compotus; *Ib. Rot*. 6. *ad finem*.

(*k*) Communia; *Memor*. 28. *H*. 3. *Rot*. 1, *compriſing* 14 *Rolls*; Compotus; *which takes up four Rolls*; Viſus compotorum, *one Roll*; *and* Adventus, *one Roll*.

(*l*) Communia; Memo. 42. *H*. 3. *Rot*. 1; *this Title containeth nineteen Rolls*; Compota; *beginning Rotulo* 20, *and ending Rot*. 27; Adventus [viz. in craſtino S. Michaelis *and* in craſtino clauſi Paſchæ], *Rot*. 28. *a*; Dies dati; *Rot*. 28. *b*; Communis reſpectus; *Rot*. 29.

(*m*) Communia de Termino S. Michaelis anno Regis E. ſeptimo incipiente: *And* Communia *of the other three Terms*.

Affidationes de Termino S. Michaelis anno R. R. E. ſeptimo incipiente. *Under this Head there are*, Viſus, Dies dati, Polo's.

Recognitiones de Termino S. Michaelis anno R. E. ſeptimo incipiente: *And* Recognitiones *of the other three Terms*.

Brevia pro Rege de Termino S. Michaelis anno R. E. ſeptimo incipiente: *And* Brevia *for the other three Terms*.

Præcepta facta ſuper compota.

Viſus Vicecomitum de primo dimidio anno ſeptimo.

Adventus Vicecomitum ſuper Puroffrum ſuum ad Scaccarium, in craſtino Clauſi Paſchæ anno vij°.

Dies dati.

Adventus. *Ex Bundell. Memorandor*. 7. *E*. 1. *ex parte Remem. Theſ*.

(*n*) Adventus Vicecomitum ad Scaccarium

Chap. XXII.   *of the* EXCHEQUER.

other Years of the said Kings. So also the *Memoranda* on the Part of the King's Remembrancer have, in the Reigns of the said Kings, the like Heads or Titles. Of the Originals of the Chancery, which have been wont to be reposited in the Treasurer's Remembrancer's Office, I speak elsewhere (*o*). In the *Memoranda* of the Exchequer there was entered great Variety of Business. For Instance: The King's Writs and Precepts of many Kinds, relating to Revenue, Tenures, and other Matters agitated in the Exchequer; Commissions of Bailywicks, Custodies, Ferms, &c; Presentations and Admissions of Officers of the Exchequer, and other Officers; Pleadings and Allegations of Parties; Judgments and Awards of the Justicier, the Treasurer and Barons, and the King's Council; Recognitions of Debts, and Conventions of divers Kinds; Accounts, and Views of Accounts, with several Acts relating to Accountants; Inquisitions of Sheriffs, Escheators, &c; Advents of Sheriffs, Escheators, and others; and in general, all those Things which were comprized under the Term *Communia*, or common Business. Many Instances of these and other Kinds, cited out of the *Memoranda* of the Exchequer, may be seen in these Volumes; so that more need not be subjoined here. There were also many *Memorandums* entered in these Rolls *pro commodo Regis*, to controll Accountants, or to save the King's Rights; either by way of *Memorandum pro Rege*, or of *Loquendum cum Rege*, or *Loquendum cum Justiciario*, or *cum Concilio Regis*, &c. Of which latter I would here give some Instances, because there are not many Things of that Sort cited elsewhere in these Volumes: Thus, a *Loquendum* was entered for the King, touching certain Money imprested

rium in crastino S. Michaelis Anno regni Regis E. filij Regis E. xvj.

Dies dati Vicecomitibus ad computandum post proffrum S. Michaelis anno xvj.

Adventus Vicecomitum ad Scaccarium in crastino Clausi Paschæ anno regni Regis E. filij Regis E. xvj.

Dies dati Vicecomitibus ad computandum post proffrum Paschæ anno R. Regis E. filij E. xvj.

Commissiones & Literæ Patentes de Termino S. Michaelis anno xvj; *and* Commissiones & L. P. *of the other Terms.*

Communia de Termino S. Michaelis anno R. R. E. filij R. E. sextodecimo: Fines, Manucaptiones, Redditus, Affidationes, & Visores : *The like for the other Terms.*

Brevia directa Baronibus de Termino S. Michaelis anno sextodecimo ; *and for the other Terms.*

Recognitiones de Termino S. Michaelis anno R. R. E. f. R. E. sextodecimo ; *and for the other Terms.*

Brevia Irretornabilia de Termino S. Michaelis anno R. R. E. f. R. E. sextodecimo; *and for the other Terms.*

Brevia Retornabilia ; *as above.*

Status & Visus Compotorum de Termino S. Michaelis, *as above, for the several Terms.*

Præcepta facta super Compota. *Ex Memor.* 16. *E.* 2.

(*o*) *Cap.* 23. *sect.* 27.

to the Archbishop of *York* (*p*); *Loquendums* were also entered touching the Fair at St. *Ive* belonging to the Abbot of *Ramsey* (*q*); and in the Case of *Robert de Ros* and *Peter Fitz-Herbert* (*r*); concerning the Debts due to the King in *Richmondshire* (*s*); concerning a Debt demanded of the Earl Marshal by Summonce of the Exchequer (*t*); concerning certain Charters produced at the Exchequer on Behalf of *Walter de Esseleye* (*u*); concerning a Fine made by *Alan de Lindon*, which was mis-entered in the Original (*w*); and concerning the Town of *Bedford* not being tallaged when the King's other Demesnes were tallaged (*x*). Again; *Peter de Chacepork*, Keeper of the Wardrobe, had charged himself with a greater Sum of Money than was contained in the Writ of *Liberate* that was issued for impresting Money to him. A *Memorandum* thereof was made in the Rolls of the Exchequer (*y*).

And

(*p*) Loquendum, De Archiepiscopo Ebor. de quingentis marcis de præstito antequam iter arriperet versus Consilium Romanum. *Ex Memor.* 1 *&* 2. *H.* 3. *Rot.* 1. *b.*

(*q*) Loquendum cum Justiciario de x marcis promissis ab Abbate de Rameseie, per sic quod Nundinæ Sancti Yvonis durarent per viij dies ultra quam consueverant. Vicecomes dicit quod Nundinæ non fuerunt elongatæ, quia hoc esset contra Libertatem Hominum Domini Regis de Huntedonia. *Memor.* 2 *&* 3. *H.* 3. *Rot.* 2. *a.*

(*r*) Loquendum cum Radulfo de Nevill, De Servicio de Wichtone, quod Robertus de Ros & Petrus filius Herberti tenent. Summoneantur. *Memor.* 1 *&* 2. *H.* 3. *Rot.* 1. *b. Ebor.*

(*s*) Loquendum de multis debitis in Richemundesire, ad quæ Vicecomes non extendit manum. *Memor.* 6. *H.* 3. *Rot.* 11. *a.*

(*t*) Idem exequtores [testamenti W. Comitis Marescalli] habent superplusagium in Compoto suo CCxlij libras xiij solidos ix den. ob.
Loquendum cum Rege de L marcis quæ exiguntur de Comite Marescallo per Summonitionem Scaccarij quas exequtores Comitis Marescalli senioris petunt sibi allocari in superplusagio suo superius notato. *Memor.* 14. *H.* 3. *Rot.* 10. *b.*

(*u*) Glovernia. Walterus de la Grave Miles Walteri de Esseleye profert cartam Regis Henrici de xiiij libratis terræ in Cherton, quousque Rex ei dederit garisonem suam, & cartam Regis Ricardi quæ sessat eum de xiiij libratis terræ & nominat Cleton, per servicium dimidij Militis. Et non invenitur quod fecerit servicium. Et quia diversa nomina in cartis prædictis apponuntur: Ideo loquendum est de hoc cum Dominis Cancellario & S. de Segrave. Habet diem in octabis Trinitatis, & ad audiendum judicium super cartis suis. *Pas. Commun.* 14. *H.* 3. *Rot.* 5. *a.*

(*w*) Loquendum cum Cancellario pro Alano de Lindon, De decem marcis quas, ut habetur in Originali, Alanus de Lindon promisit pro licentia essartandi viij acras de bosco suo de Eston in Northamton; Quia Dominus Dunelmensis dicit, quod illas promisit pro illo bosco claudendo, & quod erratum est in scriptura de Originali, & quod Cancellarius illius erroris memor est, & illum faciet emendari. *Pas. Commun.* 14. *H.* 3. *Rot.* 6. *b.*

(*x*) Loquendum cum Rege. Homines Bedfordiæ non fuerunt talliati anno xxx^{o}, quando Rex talliavit alia Dominica sua. *Memor.* 31. *H.* 3. *Rot.* 9. *b.*

(*y*) Memorandum quod P. Chacepor onerat se de MMMD & Lxiij l xiiij s & v d receptis de Scaccario in crastino S. Edwardi anno xxvj: Et breve de Liberate, cujus data est xviij die Augusti anno eodem, non continet nisi 5 Mille & C marcas: Et sic onerat se de C Lxiij l xiiij s & v d, præter dictam receptam. Inquirendum unde recepit

Chap. XXII. *of the* Exchequer.

And whereas *Peter*, in his Account of the Wardrobe, did not charge himself with Cloth and Furs, a *Memorandum* is made of that (*z*). A *Memorandum* is also made as well of the Sums imprested to *William Hardell*, *John de Colemere*, and *Richard Rufus*, for the Liveries of Knights, Serjeants, and Mariners, as likewise of the Provisions delivered to the said *Richard*, and the Money paid to him out of the Wardrobe; in order, probably, to charge them with the same upon their Accounts (*a*). The Bishop of *Lincoln* claimed to have the Chattels of his Men who were Fugitives or hanged. An Entry of *Loquendum* is made touching that Claim (*b*). In fine, many other Entries by way of *Loquendum* or *Memorandum* appear upon Record: as in the Case of the Knights of *Wiltshire* owing Ward to the Castle of *Devises* (*c*), of *Robert de Dacres*, touching Distress for the King's Debts within the Bishoprick of *Carlile* (*d*), of the Executors of *William de Vaux* concerning the Issues of the Honour of *Knaresburgh* (*e*), of

pit dictos denarios. *Ex Memor.* 29. *H.* 3. *Rot.* 11. *in Ced. adnexa.*

Item memorandum quod die Veneris proximo post annunciacionem B. Virginis anno xxvij°, recepit idem P. apud Burd. xij mille marcas de Scaccario Londoniæ per manum Nicholai de S. Edmundo & servientum Baronum de Scaccario, & breve de Liberate cujus data est anno eodem viij die Februarij, non continet nisi x mille marcas. *Ib. in alia Ced. annexa ad Rot.* 11.

(*z*) Memorandum quod Petrus Chaceporc non onerat se de panno & pellura. *Trin. Commun.* 29. *H.* 3. *Rot.* 11. *b.*

(*a*) Memorandum quod Willelmus Hardell, Johannes de Colemere, & Ricardus Rufus Clericus, debent respondere de denarijs eis liberatis ad liberationes Militum servientum & marinellorum. *Trin. Commun.* 29. *H.* 3. *Rot.* 11. *b.*

Memorandum quod summa totalis Ricardi Rufi est Centum xix panni, Mille octingenta xvj quarteria frumenti, Mille DCCC Lxxiiij quarteria & j bussellum avenæ, sexies xx xv Bacones, & omnium denariorum quos idem Ricardus recepit de Garderoba anno xxvj, xxvij, xxviij, & xxix, usque ad diem Martis post Translationem S. Thomæ Martiris anno xxix, xv mille xx l x s vij d ob. *Trin. Commun.* 29. *H.* 3. *Rot.* 11. *b.*

(*b*) Loquendum de Episcopo Lincolniensi.

Memorandum de Episcopo Lincolniensi, qui clamat habere catalla hominum suorum fugitivorum & suspensorum; & de C s quos similiter clamat pro Escapio. *Memor.* 38. *H.* 3. *Rot.* 2. *b.*

(*c*) Loquendum cum Domino Rege seu Consilio suo de Militibus Wiltesiæ qui debuerunt wardas ad Castrum de Devises, qui eas subtraxerunt per xx annos & amplius. *Ex Memor.* 38. *H.* 3. *Rot.* 26. *b. tit.* Compotus Com. Wyltes.

(*d*) Loquendum. Robertus de Dacre venit coram Baronibus, & protestatus est quod non est ausus distringere pro debitis quæ debentur Domino Regi in Episcopatu Karliolensi, de tempore quo idem Episcopatus fuit vacans & in manibus Domini Regis, propter Sententiam Episcopi Dunolmensis in Comitatu Northumberlandiæ, & propter Sententiam Officialis Electi Carliolensis in Comitatu Cumberlandiæ. Et ideo loquendum cum Domino Rege. *Memor.* 39. *H.* 3. *Rot.* 13. *b.*

(*e*) Ebor. De debito quod Johannes de Vallibus filius & hæres Willelmi de Vallibus defuncti, & Burga quæ fuit uxor ejusdem Willelmi, Executores testamenti ejusdem Willelmi, debent de remanente compoti sui de exitibus Castri & Honoris de Knaresburgh, sicut continetur in Rotulo proximo præcedente; ponuntur in visu CLxj l x s, quos

of the Sheriff of *York* and *William de St. John*, touching certain Sums of Money with which they were to be charged *(f)*, of the City of *Winchester* and Town of *Porchester* touching Tallage (*g*), of *William de Canteloup* (*h*), in relation to a Rent or Ferm in *Duneslie*, which was escheated to the Crown (*i*), in the Case of the Priory of *Thetford*, touching Money imprested (*k*), of *Geoffrey* the Almoner (*l*), of the Abbot of *Tychesield* (*m*); and in many other Cases.

The Judgments and Awards of the Chief Justicier, and of the Treasurer and Barons of the Exchequer, were commonly entered in the Rolls in the Terms, *Consideratum est*, or *Concordatum est, per Justiciarium*, or *per Thesaurarium & Barones*; and sometimes *Provisum est*, and *Adjudicatum est*. But other Words were also sometimes used, as *Ordinarunt, præceperunt*, &c. And these or the like Terms were also used in other Judicatures. In *Glanvill* it is said, the Tenant or Defendant should be discharged by Judgment of the Court, *per Con-*

quos dictus Willelmus de exitibus ballivæ suæ habere facit viginti hominibus ad arma & quindecim balistarijs in munitione Castri prædicti commorantibus—, *and several other Sums*—. Et debent de claro Cxxj l xij s iiij d ob.; qui respectuantur usque crastinum Sanctæ Margaretæ, & interim *loquendum cum Rege de præsenti negocio*, & de eo quod dictus Willelmus de Vallibus objit in servicio Regis &c. Postea solvuntur inde per unam talliam xlvij l v s vij d ob.; Et remanent Lxxiiij l vj s ix d. *Hil. Stat. & Visus Comp.* 9. *E.* 2. *Rot.* 140. *a.*

(*f*) Vicecomes debet de Tallagijs Maneriorum quæ recepit $^{xx}_{iiij}$ & xviiij l; Idem de Scutagijs quæ recepit, C & j l ij s & vj d ob. de primo Scutagio Regis hujus; Idem de Totalibus de Itinere Justiciariorum C & $^{xx}_{iiij}$ & iij l xv s ix d, præter xx l de Malgero Wavasor; Idem de Parcialibus ejusdem Itineris xxxix l & xx sol. ix d; Cum xx l quas recepit de Malgero Wavasor. *Memor.* 2 & 3. *H.* 3. *Rot.* 1. *b. Ebor.*

Willelmus de Sancto Johanne debet respondere de proficuo Comitatus de dimidio anno xv°, & de anno xvj° & de tribus partibus anni xvij. *Ib. Rot.* 3. *a.*

(*g*) Memorandum de Suhamtesire, quod Civitas Wintoniæ & Villa de Porceestria fuerunt talliatæ tempore Regis hujus, & non plures Villæ. *Memor* 2. & 3. *H.* 3. *Rot.* 3. *a.*

(*h*) Leycestria. Dominica proxima post festum S. Lucæ Ewangelistæ, reddidit Willelmus de Cantilupo in manus Domini Regis xl solidos terræ in Medburn, quæ est Dominicum Regis, & quam tenuerat sine waranto. *Memor.* 8. *H.* 3. *Rot.* 1. *a.*

(*i*) In Rotulo xix° Regis Henrici, invenitur quod Dunesleh est escheita Domini Regis, & ideo non debent allocari in corpore Comitatus x s in Duneslie pro terra Willelmi Pollard. *Ex Memor.* 11. *H.* 3. *Rot.* 9. *b. Essex.*

(*k*) Norf. & Suff. Memorandum quod Prior Monachorum de Teford debet Regi xl marcas, quas W. Hardel ei liberavit de præstito, sicut continetur in brevi ipsius Domini Regis quod est in f. M. *Memor.* 22. *H.* 3. *Rot.* 8. *b.*

(*l*) Dunolm. Memorandum quod CCC libræ de tricesima Regis quas J. filius Philippi liberavit fratri Galfrido elemosinario, non sunt ei allocatæ, quia Willelmus de Londonia Clericus qui reddidit compotum pro eo non oneravit se in recepta sua. *Memor.* 25. *H.* 3. *Rot.* 6. *b.*

(*m*) Memorandum quod data Cartæ Abbatis Tychefeldiæ de Manerio de Tychefeld est vicecesimo die Septembris anno r. R. H. xvj. *Mich. Commun.* 31. *H.* 3. *Rot.* 3. *b.*

siderationem

Chap. XXII. *of the* EXCHEQUER. 119

fiderationem Curiæ (n). In the 8th Year of K. *Richard* I, *Geoffrey de Mandevill* gave C Marks to have the Judgment of the King's Court, *Confiderationem Curiæ Regis* (o). In the 14th Year of K. *Henry* III, Judgment was given in the Exchequer, in a Cafe relating to the Abbot of *Weftminfter* and Prior of *Derhurft* ; *Confideratum eft coram Baronibus de Scaccario* (p). The Prior of *Bernewell* and his Men of *Chefterton* were acquitted of Tallage by the Judgment of the King's Courts, *per Confiderationem Curiæ Regis* (q). *Hugh de Cancelles* was obliged, by Judgment of the Court of Exchequer, to warrant the Mill of *Upton* to the Abbey of St. *James* without *Northampton*, and to acquit the Abbey againft the King of a yearly Payment of L s. hereunder mentioned ; *Confideratum eft in Curia Regis coram Baronibus de Scaccario, quod* —— (r). *Gilbert Blundel, William Jofeberd*, and others, were attached to anfwer to the King; for that they, being Taxors of the King's Quinzime in the Town of *Meffendoun*, levied Money, and retained it to their own Ufe, and concealed it from the King. They plead, that they made their Taxation faithfully, *& nichil inde detinuerunt*. The Iffue was tried at the Exchequer; and the Jury acquitted the Parties. The Judgment is, *Ideo confideratum eft, quod* (s). In the 27th Year of K. *Edward* I, in the Cafe of *Milifent de Monte alto* the

(n) Tunc quidem per Confiderationem Curiæ dimittetur ipfe quietus a clameo petentis. *Glanv. L.* 2. *c.* 18.

(o) De Placitis & Conventionibus & Finibus & Oblatis factis Regi poft reditum fuum ab Alemannia : Galfridus de Mandevill debet C marcas, pro habenda confideratione Curiæ Regis——. *Mag. Rot.* 8. *R.* 1. *Rot.* 18. *a. Dorf. & Sumerf.*

(p) Londonia. Confideratum eft coram Baronibus de Scaccario, die Martis proxima poft Purificationem B. Mariæ, quod Abbas Weftmonafterij participet cum Priore de Derhurft, in ammerciamento murdri & aliis ammerciamentis in eodem hundredo, & quod Rex remaneat in eadem faifina in qua inventus eft, & Abbas purchaciet fe fi velit. *Ex Memor.* 14. *H.* 3. *Rot.* 10. *a.*

(q) Baronibus, pro Priore de Bernewell. Rex conceffit eidem, quod ipfe & homines fui de Ceftretun de cætero quieti fint de taillagio fecundum quod invenitur in Rotulo Regis J. xvj; non obftante folutione taillagij facti ad Scaccarium anno octavo & nono ejufdem Regis J; & de quo taillagio idem Prior & homines fui de Ceftretun quieti funt per Cartam fuam quam Rex infpexit, & per Confiderationem Curiæ Regis. *Memor.* 25. *H.* 3. *Rot.* 7. *b.*

(r) Norhamton. Confideratum eft in Curia Regis coram Baronibus de Scaccario apud Weftmonafterium, quod Hugo de de Cancellis debet warantizare Abbati & Conventui S. Jacobi extra Norhamton Molendinum de Upton cum omnibus pertinentijs in tali ftatu quantum ad fectam Molendini quo fuit tempore quo Robertus filius Sweyn predeceffor prædicti Hugonis dedit prædicto Abbati Molendinum prænominatum & pratum quod vocatur Tatholm, & eos acquietare verfus Regem de L s annuis, per quos idem Abbas finem fecit Regi pro prædictis Molendino & prato quæ funt de Serjantia quam idem Hugo tenet de Rege in Upton. *Memor.* 35. *H.* 3. *Rot.* 12. *a.*

(s) Ideo confideratum eft quod prædicti Willelmus Jofeberd & focij fui prædicti recedant inde quieti fine die. *Hil. Recorda* 22. *E.* 1. *Rot.* 12. *a.*

Entry

Entry is, *Concordatum eſt per Theſaurarium & Barones, quod* —— (*t*). In the firſt Year of K. *Edward* II, in the Caſe of the *Templars, Concordatum eſt per Theſaurarium & Barones & alios de Conſilio, quod* — (*u*). In the ſame Year, in the Caſe of *John de Rothing, Theſaurarius & Barones concordarunt, quod* —— (*w*). In the 16th Year of K. *Edward* II, in the Caſe of *Nicolas Gentil*, Sheriff of *Surrey* and *Suſſex* (*x*). The Word *Concordatum* was likewiſe ſometimes uſed in Judgments given in other Courts or Places (*y*). *William le Mareſchal*, by adhering to *Simon de Montfort* and his Accomplices, forfeited to the King the Manor of *Haſelberg:* the King (*viz. Henry* III.) granted that Manor to *Alan Plukenet*. *John Mareſchal*, Son and Heir of the ſaid *William*, came into the King's Court *coram Rege*, and prayed to have it reſtored to him according to the *Dictum de Kenelworth*. The King granted he ſhould have Reſtitution thereof accordingly. Afterwards, in the Court holden before the Juſtices Itinerant at *Wilton*, the King recovered the ſaid Manor againſt *John Mareſchal* as his Right and Eſcheat, by Judgment of the ſaid Court. And the Record and Proceſs of that Judgment, being at the Inſtance of the ſaid *John Mareſchal* removed into the Court holden before the King himſelf, it was there adjudged, *Concordatum fuit*, that the ſaid Judgment given before the Juſtices Itinerant was given duly, and according to the Law and Cuſtom of the Realm (*z*). Sometimes the Words *Concordatum* and *Conſideratum* were both uſed together in a Judgment, as in the Caſe of *Richard Oyſel* (*a*). The like in Parliament, in the Caſe of *John de Haſtinges* (*b*). Sometimes the Words *Proviſum eſt* were uſed in Judgments or Awards. It was adjudged or ordered (*Proviſum eſt*) by the King's Council at the Exchequer, that *Ralf Dayrel* and *Robert*

(*t*) *Cap.* 23. *ſect.* 18. Manucaptio pro debitis.

(*u*) *Cap.* 21. *ſect.* 1.

(*w*) *Ib. cap.* 21. *ſect.* 1.

(*x*) Poſtea in adventu Theſaurarij, deliberatum eſt inde per Theſaurarium & Barones, & habito reſpectu ad cauſam prædictam, concordatum eſt quod dictum amerciamentum adnulletur, & quod idem Nicholaus pro defalta prædicta decætero non occaſionetur nec moleſtetur. *Mich. Commun.* 16. *E.* 2. *Rot.*—*a. & b.*

(*y*) *Ryl. Plac. Parl. p.* 349, *anno* 35. *E.* 1. *& p.* 351, *p.* 354, *p.* 361. *& alibi paſſim.*

(*z*) Cujus quidem Judicij recordum & proceſſum poſtmodum ad querimoniam ipſius coram nobis venire fecimus; Quo coram nobis & Conſilio noſtro recitato audito & intellecto, Concordatum fuit, Judicium illud modo debito & ſecundum legem & conſuetudinem Regni noſtri eſſe factum. *Mich. Commun.* 26 *&* 27. *E.* 1. *Rot.* 7. *a.*

(*a*) *Ebor.* De Ricardo Oyſel.——Concordatum eſt & conſideratum per Theſaurarium & Barones, quod prædictus Ricardus de prædictis quaterviginti marcis in compoto ſuo prædicto totaliter exoneretur, & dictus Willelmus Perſone pro eodem Ricardo inde oneretur. *Mich. Commun.* 34 *&* 35. *E.* 1. *Rot.* 20. *b.*

(*b*) Concordatum eſt & conſideratum per Regem & Conſilium, quod ——. *Ryl. Pl. P. p.* 220. *anno* 23. *E.* 1.

Chap. XXII.   *of the* Exchequer.   121

de Haringee should have each of them viiid. *per* Day for their Wages (*c*). And it was adjudged (*Provisum est*) by the King's Council, that R. Bishop of *Bathe* and *Wells*, should be allowed upon his Account certain Sums for his Expences (*d*). When Judgment was given in the Exchequer for the Party against the King, it was entered with a *Salvo jure Regis*, as in the Case relating to the Seizure of a Tenement in *Scardeburg* (*e*), in the Case of the Abbot of *Nuttely* (*f*), *David de Flettywyk* (*g*), the Abbess of *Shafton* (*h*), and others. Many Judgments in Parliament were also entered with the like *Salvo jure*; as in the Case of *William de Fyens* (*i*), of *John* and *Reginald de Ingeham* (*k*), and others.

IX. In the Business of the Exchequer (with respect both to Pleas and Accompts) there was frequent Use of Writs or Letters sent from the King to the Treasurer and Barons, signifying to them his Pleasure about Matters depending before them. These Writs or Letters passed under the Great or the Privy Seal; most commonly under the latter. And sometimes Messages or Instructions were brought by living Messengers from the King to the Treasurer and Barons upon the like Occasions. More particularly, in regard three Sorts of Writs

---

(*c*) Provisum est per Dominum Eboracensem & alios de Consilio Domini Regis, quod &c. *Pas. Communia* 27. *H.* 3. *Rot.* 10. *b. citat. cap.* 21. *sect.* 1.

(*d*) Memorandum quod provisum est per Concilium Regis, quod allocentur R. Bathoniensi &c. *Pas. Commun.* 9 & 10. *E.* 1. *Rot.* 4. *b. citat. cap.* xxi. *sect.* 1.

(*e*) Ebor. De tenemento in Scardeburg deliberato a manu Regis.—— Et Thesaurario & Baronibus non constat, quod dicta domus capta fuit in manum Regis alia de causa, quam pro eo quod dictus Adam [Gomer] fuit decapitatus. Et quia per Inquisitionem prædictam compertum est, quod non fuit decapitatus, pro Felonia, Concordatum est per eosdem Thesaurarium & Barones, quod præcipiatur Vicecomiti quod manum Regis inde ammoveat, & prædicto Simoni cum exitibus inde perceptis a tempore quo idem Vicecomes eam cepit in manum Regis, & eam Simoni fratri prædicti Adæ liberet; Salvo tamen Regi jure suo cum alias inde loqui voluerit, & jure alterius cujuscumque. *Trin. Commun.* 26 & 27. *E.* 1. *Rot.* 28. *a.*

(*f*) ——Ideo consideratum est, quod Abbas [de Nuttele] ad præsens quoad hoc recedat quietus; Salva semper Regi actione sua in præmissis, cum de jure suo sibi plenius constare poterit. *Trin. Commun.* 26 & 27. *E.* 1. *Rot.* 28. *a.*

(*g*) David de Flettewyk *was attached to answer for not being at* Carlile *to do his Service in the King's Army. Upon Search of the Rolls it was not found that he held in Chief.* Ideo idem David inde ad præsens [eat] sine die, Salvo semper statu Regis cum alias inde loqui voluerit. *Mich. Communia* 34 & 35. *E.* 1. *Rot.* 16. *a.*

(*h*) ——Et ideo consideratum est, quod prædicta Abbatissa inde ad præsens eat sine die, Salvo semper Jure Regis cum alias inde loqui voluerit. *Mich. Commun.* 2. *E.* 2. *Rot.* 37. *b.*

(*i*) Salvo semper jure Domini Regis & hæredum suorum cum inde loqui voluerint. *Ryl. Plac. P. p.* 122. *anno* 21. *E.* 1. Et *ib. p.* 133. 21. *E.* 1.

(*k*) Salvis semper ipsi Domino Regi & hæredibus suis actione & jure suo. *Ib. p.* 312. 35. *E.* 1.

or Messages sent to the Treasurer and Barons were (as I remember) most frequent and numerous, I will here subjoin some Instances of them. They were Writs or Messages to do Right to Litigants or Accomptants, or to shew them Favour, or to give them Dispatch.

First, Of the Writs or Messages, to do Justice or Right to Parties. The Rolls of the Exchequer abound with these Writs. They were, for their Kind or Form, such as follow: that is to say, Writs of this Sort were issued for the Countess of *Ou* (*l*), for the Men of the Hundreds of *Brokeswor* and *Grimeswrosn* (*m*), for *John Thorpe* (*n*), the Men of *Ripton* (*o*), *Hugh Veer* (*p*), *William de Welleby* (*q*), *Alyne Lovel* (*r*), *Hugh de Veer* (*s*), and others.

Secondly, Of the Writs or Messages, to shew Favour to Parties. I have not observed these to be so numerous as the former. Some of this Sort follow hereunder: that is to say, Writs of Favour were issued respectively, for *Ralf de Leicestre* (*t*), for certain Abbots (here named) who had complied with the King's Demands of Money towards the

---

(*l*) Baronibus pro Comitissa Augy. Mandamus vobis, quod assumptis vobiscum Justiciarijs nostris de Banco, videatis demandam quam facitis Aliciæ Comitissæ Augi per summonitionem Scaccarij nostri, de Servitio Willelmi de Chaurces, & de Scutagio de Kery; & secundum legem & consuetudinem ejusdem Scaccarij nostri prædictæ Comitissæ judicium suum inde habere faciatis. *Ex Memor.* 22. *H.* 3. *Rot.* 10. *b.*

(*m*) Pro hominibus hundredorum de Brokeswor & Grimeswrosn. Rex mandat Baronibus, quod vocato coram eis Willelmo de Sancto Omero quondam Vicecomite Herefordiæ, audiant transgressiones & injurias quas idem Willelmus intulit hominibus hundredorum de Broksesse & Grimeswrosne, & inde eis celerem faciant justiciam, & ipsum W. castigent secundum quantitatem delicti. B. e. in f. M. *Memor.* 38. *H.* 3. *Rot.* 14. *b.*

(*n*) ⸺ Dominus Rex eciam per Breve suum, quod est inter Communia de anno xxxiij°, mandavit Thesaurario & Baronibus super hoc, quod eidem Johanni de Thorpe fieri faciant quod justicia suadebit; jure psius Regis in omnibus semper salvo ⸺. *Mich. Communia* 33. *E.* 1. *Rot.* 8. *a.*

(*o*) *Mich. Brevia* 34. *E.* 1. *Rot.* 1. *b.*

(*p*) Baronibus pro Hugone Veer. *'Tis a Writ to them*, quod fieri faciant (*upon his Case*) debitum & festinum justitiæ complementum, prout de jure fore viderint faciendum. T. Rege apud Carledecotes xxviij die Junij anno xxxv. *Trin. Brevia* 35. *E.* 1. *Rot.* 54. *a.*

(*q*) *Trin. Brevia* 1. *E.* 2. *Rot.* 67. *b.*

(*r*) Edward &c. Au Treforier & as Baruns &c; Nous vous mandoms, que a Alyne Lovel de Clahangre, sur les busoignes que lui tuchent devant vous a nostre Escheqier, faciez fere hastive Droiture, solum la lei & les usages de nostre roialme. Done souz nostre Prive Seal a Clipston le xxiij jour ⸺. *Mich. Brevia* 1. *E.* 2. *Rot.* 20. *a.*

(*s*) *Hil. Brevia* 2. *E.* 2. *Rot.* 47. *b.*

(*t*) Rex mandat Baronibus, quod Radulphus de Leycestre Clericus per multa tempora ei servivit ad Scaccarium, propter quod in agendis suis uberiorem graciam debet invenire coram &c: Et quod idem Radulpho de debitis suis recuperandis versus quosdam debitores suos quos eis nominabit, ac de alijs negocijs suis omnem quam poterunt mediante Justicia favorem & graciam inpendant, sicuti vellent eis fieri in casu consimili. *Ex Mem.* 42. *H.* 3. *Rot.* 11. *b.*

Ranſom of *John de St. John* (*u*), for *Joan de Wake* (*w*), *Aline de Bonele* (*x*), *Joan de Lovetot* (*y*), *Nicolas de Halghford* (*z*), *Robert Romayn* (*a*), and the Merchants of *Barde* (*b*).

Thirdly, Of the Writs or Meſſages, to give Diſpatch to Parties. Some of this Sort were ſent to the Treaſurer and Barons for the following Perſons : namely, for *Richard de la Lade* (*c*) for the Keepers

(*u*) Baronibus per Regem. Edward par la grace de Dieu &c ; A honurable Piere en Dieu W. par meſme la grace Eveſque de Ceſtre e de Lichefeld noſtre Treſorer, Nous vous enveoms par Monſieur Thomas Paynel les nouns des Abbez Dengleterre qui nous reſqueiſmes ne ad guerres for la boſoigne Monſieur Johan de Seint Johan, ſicome bein Savez. E vous maundoms, qe a ceux qui ont bien reſponduz feez auſi gracious favorable e deboneires, en totes les beſoignes quil averont a fere de vers vous, come vouz porrez par reſon. E as autres volums qe vous facez dreit Saunz nule grace du munde. Done ſous noſtre Privee Seel a Culeford, le xj iour de May lan de noſtre regne vinteſiſme.

Les nons des Abbez qui ont reſpondu a la volunte le Rey, e as quieux veut le Rey faire tote manere de grace, ce eſt aſſavoir, Labbe de Glaſtinbury, Labbe de Weyminſter, Labbe de Burgh Seint Pieres, Labbe de Eveſham, e Labbe de Seint Edmun.

Les nouns dez Abbez qui ne voillent en nule manere faire la voluntes le Rey, endreit de la deliveraunce de Sire Johan de Seint Johan, as queux le Rey ne voet faire qe commune ley ; ceſt aſſavoir, Labbe de Rammeſeye, Labbe de Abindon, Labbe de Wautham, Labbe de Seint Auban, e Labbe de la Hide. *Paſ. Communia* 26. *E*. 1. *Rot*. 77. *b. in bund*. 25 & 26. *E*. 1.

(*w*) Baronibus pro Johanna de Wak. Edward par la grace de Dieu &c ; nous vous enveons les Peticions noſtre bein amee Johanne Wake dame de Lydel ci dedenz encloſes, E vous mandoms qe examinees meiſmes les Peticions, facez a la dite Johanne endreit des dites Peticions le grace qe vous puvez en bone manere, & felonc ce qe vous veirez qe face a faire par reiſon. Don ſouz noſtre Prive Seal a Lanrecoſt, le xxx iour de Septembre, lan de noſtre Regne xxxiij. *Mich. Brevia directa Baronibus* 34. *E*. 1. *Rot*. 1. *in dorſo*.

(*x*) Baronibus. Edward par la grace de Dieu &c. Nous vous mandoms, qe vous haſtez la boſoigne qe Aline de Bonele ad a faire devaunt vous, le plus favourablement qe vous porretz, ſolome la ley & les uſages de noſtre Realme. Done ſouz noſtre Prive Seal a Wy, le xj iour de Janever lan de noſtre [regne] primer. *Hil. Brevia* 1. *E*. 2. *Rot*. 32. *a*.

(*y*) Edward par la grace de Dieu &c ; Nous vous mandoms, qe en les boſoignes qe touchent noſtre ben amee Johane de Lovetot devant vous, li facez le favour qe vous porrez bonement ſauntz offendre dreit. Done ſous noſtre Prive Seal a Langele, le iiij iour de Juyn lan de noſtre regne premer. *Trin. Brevia* 1. *E*. 2. *Rot*. 63. *b*.

(*z*) *The like Writ to the Barons, for him.* Nous mandoms qe four les choſes contenues en ſa Peticion, la facez faire tote la grace e la favour qe noſtre Court purra bonement ſoufrir. Done ſouz noſtre Prive Seal a Wyndeſor, le xxvj iour de May lan de noſtre regne primer. *Ib. Rot*. 63. *b*.

(*a*) *Hil. Brevia* 1. *E*. 2. *Rot*. 88. *a*.

(*b*) *Trin. Brevia* 12. *E*. 2. *Rot*. 117. *a*.

(*c*) H. Theſaurario, pro Ricardo de Lada. Rex eidem ; Mandamus vobis, quod una cum Johanne filio Roberti & alijs vobiſcum præſentibus, audiatis compotum Ricardi de la Lade, non expectatis pluribus Baronibus. *Memor*. 22. *H*. 3. *Rot*. 10. *a*.

of the King's Works at the Tower of *London* (*d*), *William de Luda* (*e*), *John de Shefeld* (*f*), and *Simon Warde* (*g*).

And sometimes Messages or Writs were sent by the Queen and Prince to the Treasurer and Barons, touching Things depending before them. For Example: The Queen sent her Writ to the Barons of the Exchequer, importing, that she had given Respite to *John Lestrange* for a Debt which he owed to *John* Son of *Philipp*, and desiring them to give him their Assistance in that Affair (*h*). The Queen sent her Writ to the Barons, desiring them to respite a Debt due to the King from *William del Garden*; she undertaking to pay it for him (*i*). The Queen, by her Writ, prayed and required the Treasurer and Barons to respite all the Debts, demanded at the Exchequer, of *Thomas Bardolf*, till the Utas of St. *Michael*, and to search and certify her by the Bearer, how much the said *Thomas* owed the King at his Exchequer (*k*). A Writ or Letter on Behalf of Dame *Margaret Hereward*

was

(*d*) Baronibus, de compoto Turris Londoniæ. Rex eisdem; quod antequam Scaccarium hac vice claudatur, audiant compotum custodum operationum Turris Regis Londoniæ. *Ex Memor.* 25. *H.* 3. *Rot.* 10. *a.*

(*e*) Rex mandat Baronibus, per breve suum de Magno Sigillo quod est in forulo Marescalli, quod compotum prædicti Magistri Willelmi de Luda, de anno xj° & xij°, de Garderoba sua, de tempore prædicto, sine dilatione audiant. Postea computavit. *Paf. Commun.* 14. *E.* 1. *Rot.* 8. *a.*

(*f*) The King commands the Barons of the Exchequer, to hear the Accompt of John de Shefeld, quam cicius ad hoc vacare poterint———. *Trin. Brevia* 8. *E.* 2. *Rot.* 45. *a.*

(*g*) Edward par la grace de Dieu &c, Au gardein de nostre Tresorie & as Barons de nostre Escheqier salutz. Nous vous mandoms, qe ceux qe nostre cher & foial Simon Warde nostre Viscounte Deverwyk ad assignez a rendre son acounte devant vous en son noun au dit Escheqier, facez espleiter si en haste come vous porrez; & si le dit Viscounte soit trovez en nules arrerages sur son dit acounte, Nous certifiez distinctement & apertement en queus arrerages, & par quele reson, & ne facez a lui ne a ses attornez nul empeschement par cele encheson, tanqe vous en ciez autre mandement de nous.

Donne souz nostre Prive Seal a Eltham, le xx jour Doctobre lan de nostre regne quinzisme. *Mich. Brevia* 15. *E.* 2. *Rot.* 45. *a.*

(*h*) Breve Reginæ pro Johanne Extraneo. Regina Baronibus; Sciatis quod dedimus respectum eidem Johanni super debito in quo tenetur Johanni filio Philippi, usque ad xv Paschæ: Quapropter vos rogamus, quatinus ipsum & ballivos suos interim deliberantes, consilium & juvamen eidem velitis impendere ad perquirendum pecuniam illam de Ballivis suis, qui sub ipso terram dicti Johannis custodiebant, per quorum infidelitatem dicit se tale dampnum incurrisse. *Ex Memor.* 35. *H.* 3. *Rot.* 5. *b.*

(*i*) Regina rogat Barones, quod demandam quam faciunt Willelmo de Gardinis, de L marcis debitis Regi pro warda & maritagio filij & hæredis Thomæ de la Haye, ponant in respectum; quia ipsa wlt inde Regi satisfacere. Breve Reginæ est in forulo Marescalli. Et mandatum est Vicecomiti Norfolciæ & Suffolciæ, quod dictam demandam ponant in respectum usque ad festum Omnium Sanctorum. *Trin. Commun.* 42. *H.* 3. *Rot.* 18. *b.* Another like Writ from the Queen; *Ib. juxt.*

(*k*) Thesaurario & Baronibus per M. Reginam. Margarete par la grace de Dieu &c; Nous vous prioms & requeroms especiaument,

Chap. XXII.   *of the* EXCHEQUER.   125

was sent to the Treasurer by the Queen; and the like Letters by the Princes *Thomas* and *Edmond* (*l*). *Edward* Prince of *Wales* sent his Letters of Privy Seal to the Treasurer, desiring him to be gracious and friendly to *Richard de Lue* (who had lately been put out of his Office of Chamberlain of the Exchequer for a Misdemeanor), in *Richard*'s Business then depending in the Exchequer (*m*). The same Prince, by Letters of his Privy Seal, commanded and prayed the Treasurer and Barons, to dispense with the Sheriff of *Cumberland*'s Attendance at the Exchequer at the Day prefixed to him, the Prince having Occasion for his Service in the Marches of *Scotland* (*n*). The same Prince sent two Letters or Writs to the Barons of the Exchequer on Behalf of *Stephen de Stone*, upon certain Business of *Stephen*'s depending before them (*o*). These Writs of the Great Seal and of the Privy Seal, used in these and other Cases, were very numerous; and indeed they were often issued in Cases wherein there was, as it seemeth, no necessary Occasion for them, or wherein the Treasurer and Barons might have acted *ex officio* or *Rege inconsulto*. For Example: The Writs, or many of them, commanding the Treasurer and Barons to do Justice, or to give Dispatch to Litigants or Accountants, might, as it seemeth, have been spared. But it was the Manner or Custom

eiaument, por nostre cher & bien ame Monsieur Thomas Bardolf, qe totes les demandes qe li touchent en lescheker avanedit, voillez mettre en respit, tant qe a les utaves de la Seint Michel prochein avenir. E si nule destresce li seit faite par cele acheison, tant dementers li facez estre deliures. Oustre ce vous prioms, qe cerchez com bien de dett le dit Monsieur Thomas est tenuz a nostre Seignour le Rei en lescheker susdit, nous voillez par le Portour de cestes Lettres por lamour de nous. Nostre Seignour vous gard. Don a Wolveseye le xxvij jour de May. *Trin. Brevia* 34. *E.* 1. *Rot.* 37. *a.*

(*l*) *A Writ or Letter from the Queen to the Treasurer, desiring him to estall, at the Request of her and her Sons* Thomas *and* Edmund, *the Debt of* Ma Dame Margarete Hereward. Donez a Norhamton, le xvj jour de mous de Juin.

Al Honorable Piere en Dieu Wauter per la grace de Dieu Evesk de Cestre, e Tresorer nostre Seignour le Rey e pere, Edmon filz au dit Rei, saluz e bon amour. Come nostre chere Dame Madame la Reyne vous riet requise, qe vous vossislez graunter a noftre ben ame ma dame Margarete, qe fust la femme Mounsieur Roberd Hereward, de estaller la dette ———. *He desires the same Thing.* Escrit a Norhamton, le xvj jour de Juin.

Al Honorable Peire en Dieu Wauter per la grace de Dieu Evesk de Cestre e Tresorer nostre Seignour le Rey e pere, Thomas [filz] au dit Rey ———. *He desires the same Thing.* Escrites a Norhamton le xvj jour de Juin. *Trin. Brevia* 35. *E.* 1. *Rot.* 52. *a.*

(*m*) *Trin. Brevia* 33 & 34. *E.* 1. *Rot.* 41. *a. parte* 1.

(*n*) *Trin. Brevia* 34. *E.* 1. *Rot.* 42. *b.*

(*o*) Baronibus, pro Stephano de Stone, Edward fiuz au Noble Roy Dengletere, Prince de Gales &c, a ses bien ames les Barons del Escheqier nostre Seygnour le Roy, saluz e bon amour ———. Donez sous nostre Prive Seal a Lamheth, le ters jours de July. *Trin. Brevia* 35. *E.* 1. *Rot.* 53. *a.*

Baronibus per Principem Walliæ, pro Stephano de Stone. *This is another Writ from the Prince for the said* Stephen. *Ib. juxt.*

of those Times to use them. For then most or very many of the judicial and other Acts of the King's Ministers moved from the Throne. So that the Kings, notwithstanding the Trust which they reposed in their judicial Ministers, seem to have reserved unto themselves the supreme Direction of Affairs transacted in their Exchequer. If the learned Reader thinks this Observatum not to be just and well-grounded, it is not my Meaning to obtrude it on him, but barely to leave it under his Consideration. In Process of Time, this Correspondence between the Palace and the judicial Courts, or, if you please, the Practice of sending Writs of the Great and Privy Seal, or other Messages to the Judges of the King's Courts, was, in many Cases, forbidden by Statute. Which Restriction, in regard it happened after the Period where the present History ends, must not be treated of here.

CHAP.

CHAP. XXIII.

Of Accounts rendered at the Exchequer.

I. *A Specification of some of those Accounts.*
II. *Of the Office and the Accounts of Sheriffs.*
III. *Certain Assises or Rules of the Exchequer touching the King's Debtors and Accountants; viz. The immediate Baillee was to render the Account;*
IV. *Accounts were to be rendered in Course;*
V. *In Person;*
VI. *Upon Oath;*
VII. *The King's Debt was to be paid first;*
VIII. *The King might betake himself, for Payment, to one indebted to his Debtor;*
IX. *The Heir of the King's Debtor was not to be distrained, if the Debtor's Chattels were sufficient;*
X. *Nor Lands holden in Dower, if the Heir had sufficient;*
XI. *Nor Sureties, if the Principal had sufficient;*
XII. *The King's Debtors were wont to have Writs of Aid;*
XIII. *Sheriffs, who had levied or received the King's Debt, were to acquit the Debtor at the Exchequer;*
XIV. *Sheriffs were to notify the Time of their accounting to Bailiffs of Liberties, and other Persons concerned.*
XV. *The King's Debtors were to find Sureties for Payment, if required.*
XVI. *Of Writs of the Great and Privy Seal that were sent to the Exchequer.*
XVII. *Of Allowances made to Accountants per breve Regis, or otherwise.*
XVIII. *Of Atterminations.*
XIX. *Of Respites.*
XX. *Of Discharges and Pardons.*
XXI. *Of Surplusage.*
XXII. *Of the Punishments for Default of accounting; viz. Of Amercements and Issues; of Seizure of Lands; of Arrests; of Seizure of Liberties.*
XXIII. *Of distraining of Clerks.*
XXIV. *Of Accountants sitting at the Exchequer.*

XXV.   Of *Accounts rendered* in Camera Regis.
XXVI.   Of *the Method of putting Debts in Charge.*
XXVII. Of *the* Original, *and other Eſtreats.*
XXVIII. Of *Tallies.*
XXIX.   Of *Counters.*

I. IN this Chapter I muſt treat of the Accounts rendered at the Exchequer; which I ſhall do with all convenient Brevity. And in regard one cannot eaſily diſcover the Manner of accounting there, during the firſt Period, I am obliged to put both firſt and ſecond Period together; that what is obſcure or wanting in the former, may be ſupplied out of the latter. During the firſt Period, the moſt conſiderable Accountants to the Crown were the Sheriffs of the ſeveral Counties. A great Part of the Land-Revenue went through their Hands; that is, was collected by them, and anſwered either in Specie, or by ſufficient Warrant of Diſcount, according to the Uſage of thoſe Times. Their Accounts were not ſummary, nor could be. Several Months commonly paſſed between their laſt *Profer* and their *Sum*. For their Accounts did not conſiſt purely of Receipt and Payment. The Property of the King's Subjects was often concerned and mixed therein. Many Things were neceſſary to be taken in Charge by Sheriffs, and to be made Parcel of their Accounts, upon which ſometimes certain Doubts or Queſtions aroſe, that could not well be diſcuſſed and reſolved on the ſudden: of which Sort were Seizures of Lands and Rents, Levies of Deodands, forfeited Chattels, and divers other Kinds of Debts. In fine, the Sheriffs accounted to the King every Year. And the Method of their Account was regular and exact. For which Reaſon, whilſt I am treating of Accounts, I ſhall draw moſt of my Inſtances from the Accounts of Sheriffs; following therein the famous Author of the *Dialogue* concerning the Exchequer, who taketh that Courſe. It is true there were, during the firſt and the ſecond Period, ſeveral other ſtated Accountants, beſides Sheriffs of Counties. Such were the Eſcheators (or *Cuſtodes Eſcaëtarum*) the Fermers or *Cuſtodes* of ſuch Towns and Burghs as were not Part of the *Corpus Comitatus,* nor within the Sheriffs Receipt, the *Cuſtodes Cambij*, the Cuſtomers, the Keepers of the Wardrobe, and others. But it is to be underſtood, that all Perſons who held any Bailywick from the King, or received any of his Treaſure or Revenue by Impreſt or otherwiſe, were obliged to render an Account thereof. I will be conciſe in what I offer concerning the Accountants laſt above-mentioned; and therefore will ſpeak of them here in the Beginning of this Section, and ſo diſmiſs them.

them. In the 19th Year of K. *Henry* III, *Walter de Kirkham*, Keeper of the King's Wardrobe, accounted at the Exchequer for his Receipts in that Office, from the *Wednesday* before the Feast of St. *Dunstan* in the 18th Year of the King, until *Saturday* the Invention of the H. *Cross* in the 20th Year, by the View and Testimony of *William de Haverhull* (a): and in the 20th Year, the said *Walter* accounted in like Manner, from the said *Invention of the H. Cross*, until the Eve of the Apostles *Simon* and *Jude* in the 21st Year incipient, by View and Testimony of the said *William* (b). In the 33d of K. *Henry* III, *Walter de Bradele*, Keeper of the Queen's Wardrobe, accounted from the Feast of the Apostles *Philipp* and *James* in the 33d Year of the King, until the Feast of St. *John Baptist* in the 34th Year, by the Testimony and Controll of *Robert de Chaury* Clerk (c). In the 35th Year of K. *Henry* III, *Peter Chaceporc*, Keeper of the Wardrobe, rendered an Account of his Receipts for that Office, from the Feast of St. *John Baptist* in the 29th Year of the King, till Sunday next after St. *Valentine* in the 36th Year. He accounted, for the Time ending on *Thursday* next after *Michaelmass* in the 33d Year, by the View and Testimony of *William Watthamsted*, who was appointed by the King's Writ, instead of *William Hardel*, for Part of the Time, and of Master *William de Kyrkenny* for the Residue of the Time. He renders an Account of thirty-three thousand seven hundred twenty-seven Pounds and odd, which he had received out of the King's Treasury within the Time aforesaid, by the Hands of *William de Haverhull* Treasurer, by virtue of fourscore and fourteen Writs of *Liberate* (d).

In

(a) Compotus Walteri de Kyrkham, per Visum & testimonium Willelmi de Haverhull, de Receptis ejusdem, a die Mercurij ante festum S. Dunstani anno xviij°, usq; ad diem Sabbati in Inventione S. Crucis anno xx°, utraq; die computata. *Mag. Rot. 19. H. 3. in Rot. Compotor. b. m. 1.*

(b) Compotus Walteri de Kyrkham, per Visum & testimonium Willelmi de Haverhull, de Receptis ejusdem, ab Inventione S. Crucis anno xx°, usq; ad Vigiliam Apostolorum Simonis & Judæ anno incipiente xxj°, utraq; die computata. *Mag. Rot. 20. H. 3. in Rot. Compotor. b. m. 1.*

(c) Compotus Walteri de Bradele Custodis Garderobæ Reginæ, per testimonium & contrarotulum Roberti de Chaury Clerici, a festo Apostolorum Philippi & Jacobi anno xxxiij, usq; ad festum S. Johannis Baptistæ anno xxxiiij° ———. *Mag. Rot. 33. H. 3. in Rotulo Compotor. m. 2. a.*

(d) Compotus P. Chaceporc per visum & testimonium Willelmi de Watthamsted, loco Willelmi Hardel, assignati per Breve Regis usq; ad diem Jovis proximam post festum S. Michaelis anno R. R. Henrici xxxiij°, & Magistri Willelmi de Kyrkenny ab illo die usq; ad diem Dominicam proximam post festum S. Valentini anno r ejusdem Regis xxxvj° ; De receptis ejusdem P. in Garderoba Regis ; a festo S. Johannis Baptistæ anno xxix, usq; ad diem Dominicam proximam post festum S. Valentini anno xxxvj, prædicto die non computato. Idem reddit compotum de xxxiij Mille DCC xxvij l xvj s iiij d ob., receptis de Thesauro Regis per supradictum tempus, per manum Willelmi de Haverhull Thesaurarij,

130   *Of* ACCOUNTS   Chap. XXIII.

In the 49th Year of K. *Henry* III, *Hugh de la Penne* accounted for the Queen's Wardrobe, from the Feaſt of SS. *Philipp* and *James* in the 41ſt Year of the King, till the Feaſt of SS. *Simon* and *Jude* in the 49th Year incipient, by the Teſtimony and Controll of *Alexander de Bradeham* Chaplain. His Receipts amount to eleven thouſand fifty-eight Pounds and odd. The Expences were of this Sort. In the Queen's Houſhold, to wit, in the Panetry, Butlery, Kitchen, Scullery, Salſary, Hall, in feeding the Poor, in Liveries of Garſons, Mareſ-chalcie, and ſhoeing of Horſes, ſix thouſand eight hundred ſixteen Pounds and odd: in Oblations on Holidays, and Alms diſtributed daily and by the Way, one hundred fifty-one Pounds eighteen Shillings: in Silk, Mantles, upper Garments, Linnen, Hoſe for the Ladies, and other ſmall Expences belonging to the Wardrobe, a hundred four-ſcore and eleven Pounds: in Horſes bought, in Robes for the Queen's Family, in mending of Robes, in Shoes, Saddles, Reins, Almonds, Wax, and other Neceſſaries for the Wardrobe: in Gifts given to Knights, Clerks, and Meſſengers coming to the Queen, three hundred ſixty-eight Pounds and odd: in ſecret Gifts and private Alms, four thouſand and ſeventeen Pounds ten Shillings and three Pence: in Electuaries, divers Spices, Apples, Pears, and other Fruit, two hundred fifty-two Pounds ſixteen Shillings nine Pence Halfpenny: in Jewels bought for the Queen's Uſe, to wit, for eleven rich Garlands, with Emeralds, Pearls, Sapphires, and Granates, of the Value of a hundred forty-five Pounds four Shillings and four Pence: and in many other Things. The Total of the Expences was twenty-one thouſand nine hundred and four Pounds thirteen Shillings ſeven Pence Halfpenny. And the Accountant, upon the Foot of his Account, was in Surpluſage ten thouſand eight hundred forty-ſix Pounds three Shillings and three Pence (*e*). In the 19th Year of K. *Edward* I, Maſter *William*

rarij, per quater xx & xiiij Brevia Regis de Liberate —— &c. *Mag. Rot.* 35. *H.* 3. *Rot. penult.* m. 1. *a*.

(*e*) Compotus Hugonis de la Penne de Garderoba Reginæ, a feſto Apoſtolorum Philippi & Jacobi anno xl primo, uſq; ad feſtum Apoſtolorum Simonis & Judæ incipiente anno xlixº, per teſtimonium & contrarotulum Alexandri de Bradeham Capellani. *Then follow the Receipts,* Summa, xj Mille Lviij l x s iiij d ob.: In theſauro nichil: Et in expenſis factis in Hoſpicio ejuſdem Reginæ, videlicet Paneteria, boteleria, coquina, ſcuteleria, ſalſaria, aula, pauperibus paſcendis, liberationibus garcionum, Mareſcalcia & ferura equorum, per totum prædictum tempus, vj. Mille DCCC & xvj l iiij s ix d ob.: Et in oblationibus feſtivis, & elemoſinis diurnis & per viam, CLj l xviij s per idem tempus: Et in ſerico, peplis, coepertinis, linea tela, ſotularibus dominarum, & alijs minutis expenſis neceſſarijs ad eandem garderobam per prædictum tempus C $\genfrac{}{}{0pt}{}{xx}{iiij}$ xj l xij d ob.: Et in equis emptis, robis ad familiam Reginæ, robis conſuendis, calciamentis, ſellis, lorenis, amigdalis, cera, & alijs neceſſarijs ad eandem warderobam per prædictum tempus, vj Mille

C

Chap. XXIII.   *and* ACCOUNTANTS.   131

liam de Luda, Keeper of the King's Wardrobe, accounted at the Exchequer, from the Feast of St. *Edmund*, King and Martyr, in the 13th Year incipient, until the same Feast in the 14th Year incipient, by the Comptrol of Master *William de Marchia*, Comptroller in the same Wardrobe (*f*).

In the 18th Year of K. *Henry* II, *Robert Mantell* and *William Fitz-Ralf* rendered an Accompt at the Exchequer, of the Paunage of the King's Forests throughout *England* for the Year past, and likewise for the present Year; to wit, of vij *l*. xij *s*. for *New-Forrest*, xxxviij *s*. for the Forest of *Northumberland*; and so for the rest. They accounted also for the Perquisites and small Events of the King's Forest throughout *England*, arising both in the present and past Year; to wit, for v*s*. for a Dog that was not expedated [or lawed] for viij *s*. the Chattels of *Randulf* who perished in the [Judgment of the] Water, xvij*s*. the Chattels of *Ralf de Burbeche* who perished also at the Water, Liij *s*. iiij *d*. the Chattels of *Alured de Keteleſtan* who perished in the Judgment of Water, and other Sums for Bark, Wax, Honey, and Chattels of Persons that became Fugitives for the Forest (*g*). In the

C $^{xx}_{iij}$ xj l xv s iij d ob.: Et in donis datis Militibus, clericis, & nuncijs venientibus ad Reginam per idem tempus, CCCLxviij l xj s x d: Et in quibusdam donis secretis & elemosinis privatis MMMMxvij l x s iij d: Et in electuarijs, speciebus diversis, pomis, piris, & alijs fructibus, CCLij l xvj s ix d ob. per idem tempus— : Et pro Jocalibus emptis & opus Reginæ, videlicet pro xj garlandis de precio, cum smaragdinibus, perlis, saphiris, & granatis, precij de Cxlv l iiij s iiij d ——— : Summa Misarum, xxj Mille DCCCCiiij l xiij s vij d ob.: Et habet de superplus. x Mille DCCCxlvj l iij s iij d. *Mag. Rot.* 49. *H.* 3. *Rot.* 11. *b*.

(*f*) Compotus Magistri Willelmi de Luda Custodis Garderobæ Regis, a festo S. Edmundi Regis & Martiris anno xiij Regis incipiente, usq; ad idem festum anno xiiij incipiente, per contrarotulum Magistri Willelmi de Marchia tunc Contrarotulatoris in eadem Garderoba. *Mag. Rot.* 19. *E.* 1. —*Rot. Compotor.* m. 2. *a*.

(*g*) Robertus Mantel & Willelmus filius Radulfi r c de Pasnagio Forestarum Regis per Angliam de anno præterito; Scilicet, de xxxij s & ij d de Scardeburc, Et de xv s de Pikering, Et de xij l & iiij s & iiij d de Cumberland, *And of other Forests in several Counties:* Summa, Lvj l & iiij s; In thesauro liberaverunt in xiij tallijs, Et Q. s.

Idem r c de vj l & xv s de Windlesora de Pasnagio de anno præterito; In th. l. & Q. s.

Robertus Mantellus & Willelmus filius Radulfi r c de Pasnagio Forestarum Regis per Angliam de hoc anno, scilicet de vij l & xij s de Nova Foresta, Et de xxxviij s de Norhumbreland, *And for other Forests*; Summa, xvij l & xix s & viij d; In th. l. in viij tallijs, Et Q. s.

Idem r c de vj l de Pasnagio de Windresora de hoc anno; *And of other Forests*; Summa, xxij l & x s & vij d; in th. l. in viij tallijs, Et Q. s.

Robertus Mantellus & Willelmus filius Radulfi r c de perquisitionibus & minutis eventibus Forestarum Regis per Angliam tam de hoc anno quam de anno præterito; Scilicet de v s pro cane non expedato, Et de viij s de cattalis Radulfi qui perijt in aqua, Et de xvij s de cattalis Radulfi de Burbeche qui perijt ad aquam, Et de cattalis Willelmi filij Evæ fugitivi, Et de Liij s & iiij d de cattalis Aluredi de Keteleſtan qui perijt in Judicio aquæ, Et de vij s de cortice vendito, Et

the 31ft Year of K. *Henry* II, *Geoffrey Fitz-Pierre* accounted for the Pafnage of all the Forefts of *England* (*h*). In the 7th Year of K. *Richard* I, *Geoffrey Fitz-Pierre* accounted for the Paunages of divers Forefts (*i*).

In the tenth Year of K. *Richard* I, *William de Wroteham* accounted at the Exchequer for the Ferm and Iffues of the Mines of *Devonfhire* and *Cornwall*, and for feveral Receipts as well in Money as in Tin, for one whole Year (*k*). In the 14th Year of K. *John*, *William de Wrotham* accounted for CC Marks the Ferm of the Stannary of *Cornwall*, for the 13th and 14th Years of that King; and for CC *l.* the Ferm of the Stannary of *Devonfhire* for the fame Space of Time; and for Dxlij *l.* v *s.* for the Marks proceeding from the Tin of *Cornwall* and *Devon* for the 13th Year, and for DCLxviij *l.* xij *s.* ix *d.* for the like for the 14th Year (*l*).

In the 3d Year of K. *Richard* I, *Henry de Cornhill* rendered an Account of the Profit of the *Cambium* (or Mint) of all *England*, except *Winchefter*. He was charged with One thoufand Two hundred Pounds, which he had received out of the King's Treafure, to fupply the *Cambium*, and for the Liveries of Knights and Serjeants that were in the King's Service; and with Four hundred Pounds, the Profit of the

---

Et de iiij d de Cera apum Regis, Et de iiij d de Melle, Et de x s pro ij canibus non expedatis, Et de iij s & iiij d de Melle Haiarum de Clipfton; Summa, viij l & xix s & vj d; In thefauro liberaverunt in xiij tallijs, Et Q. f.

Idem r c de xvj s de catallis Willelmi Warini fugitivi, Et de ij s & vj d de catallis Ricardi de Crec fugitivi, Et de iiij d de Cera Apum de Galtris; Summa, xviij s & x d; In th. l. in iij tallijs, Et Q. f.

Idem r c de catallis fugitivorum pro forefta; fcilicet de xv s de catallis Arturi de Crec &c; Summa, xxxviij s & vj d; In th. l. Et Q. f. *Mag. Rot.* 18. *H.* 2. *Rot.* 2. *a. Not. & Derb.*

(*h*) Pafnagium Foreftarum totius Angliæ; hic; Quia non erat ei locus in Norhantefcira: Galfridus filius Petri r c de vij l & ij s & vij d, de Pafnagio Foreftæ de Cumberland, Et de x l & xiij s & iiij d, de Pafnagio Foreftæ de Galtris in Everwicfcira, Et de . . . . . . de Forefta de Pikeringa in eodem Comitatu, Et de xiij l & vj s & iiij d de Pafnagio Foreftæ de Notingehamfcira, Et de Lij s de Pafnagio de Roteland. *And the like in feveral other Counties:* Summa, Lxij l & xv s & xj d: In Thefauro liberavit in xiiij talleis Et Q. e. *Mag. Rot.* 31. *H.* 2. *Rot.* 2. *b.*

(*i*) Compotus Galfridi filij Petri de Pannagijs diverfarum Foreftarum: Galfridus filius Petri, Lifiardus Clericus pro eo, r c de xj l & xviij s & viij d, de Pafnagio de Norhamtefcira de uno anno, Et de viij l & viij s & viij d, de Pafnagio Novæ Foreftæ pro uno anno. *And for the Forefts in other Counties.* *Mag. Rot.* 7. *R.* 1. *Rot.* 8. *a. in imo.*

(*k*) Compotus Willelmi de Wroteham de firma & exitu Minariæ de Devenefcira & de Cornubia, & de pluribus receptis tam in denarijs quam in Stanno, de anno integro. *Mag. Rot.* 10. *R.* 1. *Rot.* 12. *b.*

(*l*) Willelmus de Wrotham r c de CC marcis, de firma Staminis Cornubiæ de anno præterito & de hoc anno: Et de CC libris, de firma Staminis Devoniæ de prædicto tempore. Et de D & xlij l & v s, de marcis provenientibus de Stanno Cornubiæ & Devoniæ de anno præterito. Et de DC & Lxviij l & xij s & ix d de hoc anno. Summa, M & D & xliiij l & iiij s & x d. *Mag. Rot.* 14. *J. Rot.* 8. *b. poft Devenefciram.*

Cambium

Chap. XXIII. *and* ACCOUNTANTS.

Cambium for one whole Year. Whereout he paid divers Sums of Money, in Liveries of Knights and Serjeants employed in several Parts of *England,* and in other Appointments (*m*). In the 3d Year of K. *John, Hugh Oisel* rendered an Account of the *Cambium* of *England* for the second and third Year of the King. He accounted for MDCC Marks for the Ferm of the *Cambium* of all *England.* Whereof, he paid C *l.* at the *Receipt,* and M Marks, by virtue of the King's Writ, to *Oto* King of *Almaigne* (*n*). In the 4th Year of K. *John, Guy de Vou* stood charged with MLxvj *l.* viij *s.* iiij *d.* for the Ferm of the *Cambium* of *London* for the Time mentioned in the Great Roll of the first Year of K. *John* (*o*). In the 5th Year of K. *John, Hugh Oisel* owed the King L Marks, that he might have the *Cambium* of *England* at the same Rate and upon the same Terms as *Reginald de Cornhull* held the same (*p*). At the same time, he accounted for CCCCLxiij *l.* and odd, the Profit of the *Cambium* of *England* in his Time, and for the Money which he received for the Use of the *Cambium,* and for Lx *l.* received by him of *Reginald de Cornhull* (*q*). King *Henry* III, in or about the 13th Year of his Reign, committed to *Richard Reinger* the *Cambium* or Mint of *London* and *Canterbury,* with the Dies and Appurtenances, together with MCCCCxx *l.* x *s.* viij *d.* paid to him by the Hand of *Alexander de Dorsete* to negociate therewith. *Richard* was to hold, from Midlent in the 13th Year, for the Term of four Years; and to render to the King yearly DCC Marks. Provided, that the King was to have the

---

(*m*) Compotus de Proficuo Cambij totius Agliæ præter Wintoniam: Henricus de Cornhill r c de M & CC l, quas recepit de Thesauro per breve Cancellarij, ad sustinendum Cambium totius Angliæ, & ad faciendas liberationes Militum & Servientum qui fuerunt [in] servicio Regis, Et de CCCC l de proficuo Cambij de anno integro. Summa M & DC l. In Thesauro xiiij s. Et in Liberationibus Militum & Servientum qui fuerunt in Servitio Regis per Angliam, DLij l & iiij s & viij d, per breve Cancellarij, & per visum Baldwini Wach & Willelmi filij Ricardi: *And to others for like Services. Mag. Rot.* 3. *R.* 1. *Rot.* 12. *b.*

(*n*) Compotus Hugonis Oisel de Cambio Angliæ de anno præterito, & de hoc anno. Idem H. reddit compotum de M & DCC marcis de firma Cambij totius Angliæ: In Thesauro C libras per manum Reginaldi de Cornhull, Et Otoni Regi Alemanniæ M marcas, per breve Regis. *Mag. Rot.* 3. *J. Rot.* 19. *b.*

(*o*) Wido de Vou debet M & Lxvj l & viij s & iiij d, de firma Cambij Londoniæ, de tempore quod annotatur in Rotulo primo. *Mag. Rot.* 4. *J. Rot.* 20. *b. Lond. & Midd.*

(*p*) Hugo Oisel debet L marcas, pro habendo Cambio Angliæ, per idem forum & easdem consuetudines per quas Reginaldus de Cornhull illud tenet de Rege. *Mag. Rot.* 5. *J. Rot.* 1. *b. Lond. & Midd.*

(*q*) H. Oisel r c de CCCC & Lxiij l & ix s & iiij, de proficuo Cambij Angliæ de tempore suo, & de denarijs quos recepit ad sustentandum Cambium, Et de Lx l quas recepit a Reginaldo de Cornhull; In thesauro nichil, Et in Perdonis ipsi Hugoni CC marcas per breve Regis quod est in forulo Marescalli; Et debet CCCC marcas & Lxiij l & ix s & iiij d, & Lx l. *Ibid.*

MCCCCxx *l.*

MCCCCxx *l.* x *s.* viij *d.* at the End of the four Years; and that *Richard* do give the King Security, that he will safely keep the said *Cambium* in the mean time, according to the Assise of the *Cambium*; and that at the End of the Term he will answer to the King, as well for the said yearly Sum of DCC Marks, as likewise for other Monies which he should receive with the *Cambium*, And the Constable of the Tower of *London* was commanded to take Security of *Richard* for the Purposes above-mentioned, and to certify the King thereof (*r*). In the 29th Year of K. *Henry* III, *William Hardell* rendered an Account, as *Custos*, of the *Cambium* of *London* and *Canterbury*, for eight Years six Months and three Days past: He accounted for CCLxxj *l.* vj *s.* x *d.* for the Issues of the *Cambium* of *London* for the first Year; and for CCLxxvj *l.* vj *s.* j *d.* the Issues of the *Cambium* of *Canterbury* in the same Year, besides the Portion belonging to the Archbishop, which was three Parts out of eight: And he accounteth in like Manner for the Issues of the rest of the said Years (*s*). In the 7th Year of K. *Edward* I, *Bartholomew de Castell* accounted for the

(*r*) Rex commisit Ricardo Reinger Cambium Londoniæ & Cantuariæ, cum cuneis & pertinentijs suis, una cum mille & quadringentis & xx l & x s & viij d, quos recepit cum eodem Cambio per manum Alexandri de Dorsete ad negotiandum inde; pro Septingentis marcis annuis Regi reddendis, a Media quadragesima anni xiij usq; ad terminum quatuor annorum; Ita quod prædictæ M & CCCC & xx l & x s & viij d salvi sint Regi in fine quatuor annorum prædictorum; Et quod idem Ricardus Regem securum faciat & salvos plegios Regi inveniat de prædicto Cambio salvo interim custodiendo secundum Assisam Cambij; Et quod ram de prædictis septingentis marcis annuis, quam de denarijs alijs recipiendis cum prædicto Cambio, in fine prædicti termini Regi respondebit. Et mandatum est Constabulario Turris Londoniæ, quod ab eodem Ricardo securitatem recipiat de prædicto Cambio salvo custodiendo secundum Assisam Cambij, Et nomina illorum qui plegij sui esse voluerint de prædictis septingentis marcis annuis, & de alijs denarijs in fine prædicti termini Regi reddendis, inbreviari & Regi scire faciat. *Mag. Rot.* 13. *H.* 3. *tit.* Londonia & Midilsessia.

(*s*) Compotus Cambij Londoniæ & Cantuariæ, a festo S. Petri in Cathedra anno xxij, usq; ad viij diem Aprilis anni xxx^{mi}, per viij annos vj septimanas & iij dies. Willelmus Hardell ut Custos r c de CCLxxj l vj s x d de exitu Cambij Londoniæ: Et de CCLxxvj l vj s j d de exitu Cambij Cantuariæ, de portione Regem contingente, præter portionem contingentem Archiepiscopum de viij cuneis de quibus Archiepiscopus percipit exitus de iij cuneis de primo anno; Et de CCxxxviij l vij s ix d de Cambio Londoniæ; & de CC$^{xx}_{iiij}$ & iij l xvj s de cambio Cantuariæ de secundo anno, præter portionem Archiepiscopi; Et de Dxxxix l viij s iij d de Cambio Londoniæ; Et de CCCCLj l xv s vij d de Cambio Cantuariæ de tercio anno, præter portionem Archiepiscopi & Custodum Archiepiscopatus, quia ijdem Custodes debent respondere de exitibus ejusdem de tempore vacationis ejusdem [Archi]episcopatus: *And so for other sums for the rest of the Years:* Summa summarum, vij mille & C & Lx l v s xj d ob.: In thesauro, MM & DCC $^{iiij}_{xx}$ & viij l xv s x d ob., per xxx tallias; Et in iiij Baneris faciendis ad opus Regis xxxvj s j d, per breve Regis; *And in divers other expences. Mag. Rot.* 29. *H.* 3. *Rot. ult. a. m.* 1. & 2.

Issues

Chap. XXIII.   *and* ACCOUNTANTS.

Issues of the *Cambium* of *London*. The *Onus* of his Account was, MCCL *l.* xvij *s.* Whereof, there was put to him in View, M *l.* which he delivered in Silver by Weight to *Gregory de Rokesle* and the Merchants of *Luka*, Keepers of the said *Cambium*, and xx Marks paid by him to *Nicolas de Castell*. So he was indebted to the King in CCxxxvij *l.* x *s* iiij *d.* For which Sum he was committed to the Custody of the Marshal (*t*).

In the 19th Year of K. *Edward* I, *Stephen* Bishop of *Waterford*, the King's Treasurer in *Ireland*, accounted at the Exchequer of *England*, for his Receipts out of the King's Treasure at the Exchequer of *Dublin*, from the Feast of St. *Michael* (including *Michaelmass-day*) in the sixth Year finient, by a Counter-roll of Master *John de Kenle*, then Chamberlain [of the Exchequer of *Dublin*] exhibited at the Exchequer [of *England*] by the Hands of *John de Glaston*, Chaplain to the said Master *John*, now Chancellor of the Exchequer of *Dublin*, until the 28th Day of *October* in the seventh Year (*u*). K. *Edward* I, in the 21st Year of his Reign, commanded that for the future, the Accounts of *Gascony* and of *Ireland* should be rendered yearly at the Exchequer of *England* before the Treasurer and Barons there, *viz.* the former by the Constable of *Bourdeaux*, and the latter by the Treasurer of *Ireland* (*w*). In the 22d Year of K. *Edward* I, *William de Estdene*, the King's Treasurer in *Ireland*, accounted for the Monies he had received in the Treasury of the Exchequer of *Dublin*, from *Monday* the tenth Day of *June*, in the 20th Year of the King, till *Friday* the fourteenth Day of *June* in the 22d Year; by the Counter-roll of *Henry de Ponte*, one of the Chamberlains, exhibited at the Exchequer by *William de Meones* under the Seal which the King useth in *Ireland*, from the said *Monday*, until *Thursday* the first Day of *May*, in the 21st Year, before the said *Henry* was put out of that Office for certain Trespasses whereof he was accused;

(*t*) Londonia. Audito compoto Bartholomæi de Castello de exitibus Cambij Londoniæ, Debet MCCL l xvij s; De quibus ponuntur ei in Visu M l quas liberavit in argento per pondus Gregorio de Rokesle & Mercatoribus Luk. custodibus Cambij prædicti per Litteras Regis patentes, & xx marcæ quas liberavit N. de Castello per breve Regis; Et debet CCxxxvij l xs iiij d; Pro quibus liberatur Marescallo. *Trin. Commun.* 7. *E.* 1. *Rot.* 6. *b.*

(*u*) Compotus fratris Stephani Waterfordensis Episcopi, Thesaurarij Regis in Hybernia, de Receptis suis de Thesauro Regis ad Scaccarium Dubliniæ, a festo S. Michaelis anno sexto finiente, termino ejusdem festi computato, per contrarotulum Magistri Johannis de Kenle tunc Camerarij ut dicitur, exhibitum ad Scaccarium per manus Johannis de Glastonia, Capellani ipsius Magistri Johannis nunc Cancellarij de Scaccario Dubliniæ, usq; xxviij diem octobris anno vij &c. *Mag. Rot.* 19. *E.* 1. *in Rot. Compotor. m.* 1. *a.*

(*w*) *Ryl. Plac. Parl. p.* 128.

and by the Counter-roll of the said *William de Meones*, to whom *William de Vescy*, the King's Chief Justicier in *Ireland*, and others of the King's Council there, committed the Office of Chamberlainship in the room of *Henry*, from the said *Thursday* until *Friday* the fourth Day of *June*, in the 22d Year: The Counter-roll of *Geoffrey le Brun*, the other Chamberlain, from the said *Monday* till the Close of *Easter*, in the 22d Year, before the said *Geoffrey* was amoved from his Office for his Weakness in Body, and the Counter-roll of *Ralf de Stanes*, to whom the said Treasurer and Barons of the Exchequer of *Dublin* committed that Office, until the *Friday* abovesaid, remaining in the said Exchequer of *Dublin*, as was certified to the Exchequer of *England* by the King's Writ (*x*). Then follows the Account (in like Form) of *Nicolas de Clere*, the King's Treasurer of *Ireland* (*y*). In the 15th Year of K. *Edward* II, *Walter de Istlepe*, Treasurer of *Ireland*, passed his Account in the Exchequer of *England* for the Issues and Receipts of the Land of *Ireland*, by the Counter-rolls of the Exchequer of *Dublin* (*z*).

(*x*) Compotus Willelmi de Estdene Thesaurarij Regis in Hibernia, de Receptis suis in Thesauraria Regis ad Scaccarium Dublini, a die Lunæ proximo post Octabas S. Trinitatis, videlicet ix° die Junij, anno R. R. Edwardi vicesimo per breve Regis Patens, usq; ad diem Veneris proximam ante festum Pentecostes, videlicet xiiij^{tum} diem Junij anno R. R. E. prædicti vicesimo secundo, utroq; die conputato, per Contrarotulum Henrici de Ponte unius Camerariorum exhibitum ad Scaccarium per manus Willelmi de Meones sub sigillo Regis quo utitur in Hibernia, a prædicto die Lunæ usq; diem Jovis videlicet primum diem Maij anno xxj, antequam prædictus Henricus amotus esset ab officio illo pro quibusdam transgressionibus de quibus rettatus fuit, & per contrarotulum prædicti Willelmi de Meones, cui Willelmus de Vescy tunc Capitalis Justiciarius Regis in Hibernia & alij de Consilio Regis ibidem commiserunt officium Camerariæ loco ipsius Henrici, a prædicto die Jovis usq; supradictum diem Veneris videlicet quartum diem Junij anno xxij: Contrarotulo Galfridi Brun alterius Camerarij a prædicto die Lunæ usq; Paschæ clausum anno xxij, antequam idem Galfridus amotus esset ab officio illo propter corporis debilitatem, & Contrarotulo Radulfi de Stanes, cui prædictus Thesaurarius & Barones de Scaccario Dublini officium illud commiserunt, usque diem Veneris supradictum, residentibus in prædicto Scaccario Dublini per breve Regis. *Then follows the Accompt.* Msg. Rot. 22. E. 1. *In Rot. Compotor. m.* 2. *a.*

(*y*) Ibid.

(*z*) Hibernia. Audito Compoto Magistri Walteri de Istelep nuper Thesaurarij Regis in Hibernia de exitibus & receptis ejusdem Terræ, a quintodecimo die Aprilis anno septimo usq; festum S. Petri ad vincula anno quartodecimo finiente: Debet MCCCCLiiij l xvj s iij d ob. q: De quibus computaturus est in Garderoba Regis de Cj l xiiij s j d quos posuit in emptione undecim equorum &c. *Hil. Status & Visus* 15. *E.* 2. *Rot.* 97.

Walter de Istlep Thesaurarius Hiberniæ *had Day Here to Accompt. The Chamberlain of the Exchequer of* Dublin *was to come Here with the Counter-rolls of That Exchequer, to charge the said* Walter super compotum suum ibidem. Ad quem diem venit & incepit computare. Postea percomputavit. *Mich. Commun.* 15. *E.* 2. *Rot.* 36. *a.*

In

Chap. XXIII.   *and* ACCOUNTANTS.   137

In the 9th Year of K. *Edward* I, *Bonricini Giudiconi*, for himself and his Companions the Merchants of *Luca*, rendered an Account of Monies received for the new Custom of Wools, Skins, and Leathers in *England*, from *Easter* in the 9th Year till *Easter* in the 10th Year. He accounted for CCCxxiij *l.* iij *s.* 9 *d.* the Custom of DCCLxxj Sacks and vij Stone and a half of Wool, eleven thousand a hundred fourscore and two woolled Skins, and fourscore Lasts and twelve Dackers of Leathers, at the Port of *Newcastle upon Tyne*; to wit, for every Sack of Wool half a Mark, for a Last of Leathers a Mark, and for three hundred woolled Skins half a Mark; as appeared by a Roll of Particulars now exhibited. He accounted for One thousand fourscore and six Pounds ten Shillings and eight Pence received for the usual Customs in the Port of *Hull*; and in other Ports (*a*).

In the 15th Year of K. *Edward* II, *Henry de Shirokes*, Chamberlain of *North Wales*, accounted for the Issues of his Chamberlainship, to wit, from *Easter* in the 12th Year, to *Michaelmas* in the 14th Year (*b*).

II. Next, concerning the Accounts of Sheriffs. But before I come to treat of Sheriffs as Accountants, it may be proper to say something in brief of their Office. In ancient Times the Sheriffs of Counties were usually Men of high Rank and great Power in the Realm; they had the several Counties committed to them respectively by the King at his Pleasure, either in Custody or at Ferm certain. To them the King usually committed (together with the Counties) his Castles and his Manors lying within their Bailywick. They provided the Castles with Ammunition and other Necessaries, and they stocked and improved the Manors. In fine, the King usually intrusted the Sheriffs with the collecting of his Revenue, and with divers other Powers and

---

(*a*) Compotus Bonricini [*or* Bonruncini] Gidicon pro se & socijs suis Mercatoribus de Luka, de denarijs receptis de Nova Custuma Lanarum pellium & coriorum in Anglia, a Pascha anno ix° usq; ad Pascham anno decimo. Idem r c de CCCxxiij l iij s ix d, de Custuma DCCLxxj saccorum & vij petrarum & dimidiæ lanæ, xi mille C quater xxij Pellibus lanat. & quater xx lastis & xij dacr. coriorum de Portu Novi Castri super Tynam per idem tempus; videlicet de quolibet sacco lanæ dimidia marca, de lasto Coriorum j marca, Et DCCC pellibus lanat. dimidia marca; sicut continetur in Rotulo de particulis quem prædicti Mercatores liberaverunt in Thesauro: Et de M quater xx vj l x s viij d ob. receptis de consueta custuma in Portu de Hul—. *And the like* mutatis mutandis *for several other Ports.* Summa, viij mille CCCCxj l xix s xj d ob. *Out of this Money there was paid to* Geoffrey de Vesano *the* Pope's *Nuncio in* England MMMM marks de x [*or* ix] marcis annuis *which the King paid to the* Pope *nomine* census. *Mag. Rot.* 9. *E.* 1. *Rot.* 1. *b. m.* 2. *in imo.*

(*b*) *Hil. Status & Vis.* 15. *E.* 2. *Rot.* 97. *a.*

Juris-

Jurisdictions. Of which Points some Instances will be given by and by. Earl *Cospatrick* bought the County [or Sherifrick] of *Northumberland* of K. *William* I (*c*). *Maud*, the Empress, made an ample Convention with *Geoffrey* Earl of *Essex*. Amongst other Things contained in it, she granted to him all the Tenements which his Grandfather, his Father, or himself had held in Lands, Castles, and Bailywicks; namely, the Tower of *London*, and the Sheriffwick of *London* and *Middlesex* at CCC *l*. yearly Ferm, as his Grandfather *Geoffrey* held the same, and the Sheriffwick of *Hertfordshire* at Lx *l*. as his Grandfather held it. She granted also to Earl *Geoffrey* the Justiceship of *London* and *Middlesex*, and of *Essex* and *Hertfordshire*, so that no Justice should hold Pleas in those Counties, but with the Consent of him or his Heirs. This Convention was ratified by the Empress's Oath, and the Testimony of several great Lords. For the Performance of it, several Barons of *England* and *Normandy* were to be Hostages *per Fidem*, and the Clergy of that Part of *England* which was under her Obedience were likewise to confirm it (*d*). K. *Stephen*, by his Charter, granted or rendered to *Robert* Earl of *Leicester* and his Heirs, the Burgh of *Hereford* and the Castle there, and the whole County of *Herefordscyre*, to hold by hereditary Right; except the Lands belonging to the Bishoprick, to the Abbey of *Rading*, and to other Churches and Abbies which held of the King *in Capite*; and except some other Fees mentioned in the Charter (*e*). K. *Richard* I. gave the Sheriffwick of *Yorkshire* to the highest Bidder. For whereas

William

(*c*) Comes Cospatricius Comitatum Northumbriæ pretio assecutus a Willelmo I Rege. Houed. P. 1. p. 452. n. 30.

(*d*) M. Imperatrix H. Regis filia & Anglorum Domina, Archiepiscopis &c. Sciatis me reddidisse & concessisse Comiti Gaufredo Essexæ, omnia tenementa sua, sicut Gaufridus avus aut Willelmus pater ejus aut ipsemet postea unquam melius vel liberius tenuerunt aliquo tempore, in feodo & hæreditate sibi & hæredibus suis, ad tenendum de me & de hæredibus meis; viz. in Terris & turribus, in Castellis & Baillijs; & nominatim Turrim Lundoniæ cum castello quod subtus est, ad firmandum & essorciandum ad voluntatem suam; & Vicecomitatum Lundoniæ & Middelsexiæ per CCC libras, sicut Gaufredus avus ejus tenuit; & Vicecomitatum de Hertfordscire per Lx libras, sicut avus ejus tenuit.

Et præter hoc do & concedo eidem Gaufredo quod habeat hæreditabiliter Justitiam Lundoniæ & Middelsexæ, & Essexæ, & de Hertfordscire; ita quod nullus alius Justitia placitet in hijs supradictis Comitatibus nisi per eos—&c. *Ex Collectann. MSS. Willelmi Dugd. Equ. Aur. in Mus. Ashmol. Oxon. viz. in Libro* L. *fol.* 19. *a & b.*

(*e*) Stephanus Rex Anglorum, Archiepiscopis &c salutem. Sciatis nos reddidisse hœreditarie Roberto Comiti Legrecestriæ & hæredibus suis Burgum Herefordiæ & Castellum, & totum Comitatum de Herefordscyre; præter terram Episcopatus & terram Abbathiæ de Rading, & aliarum Ecclesiarum.& Abbathiarum qui tenent de me in Capite; Et excepto feodo Hugonis de Mortuomari, & feodo Osberti filij Hugonis, & feodo Willelmi de Braiosa, & feodo Gotsonis de Dinan quod fuit Hugonis de Laci;

Et

William Bishop of *Ely*, the Chancellor, had offered to give the King, for the Sherifdome of the several Counties of *York*, *Lincoln*, and *Northampton*, a thousand and five hundred Marks in Hand, and a hundred Marks Increment [above the usual Ferm] every Year for each of those Counties: *Geoffrey*, Archbishop of *York*, offered the King, for the Sherifdome of *Yorkshire*, three thousand Marks, and the yearly Increment of a hundred Marks: And upon that Profer the Archbishop was made Sheriff of *Yorkshire* (*f*). K. *John*, by Letters Patent, granted the Sheriffwick of *Lincolnshire* to *Gerard de Canvill*, to hold during the King's Pleasure: And commanded all the Men of that County to be intendant and obedient to *Gerard* as Sheriff (*g*). The same King, by Letters Patent, constituted *William de Botterells* Sheriff of *Cornwall* for so long as he should serve the King well in that Office; and commanded the Men of that County to be intendant to him as Sheriff (*h*). The same King, by Letters Patent, committed the County of *Southampton* to *William Briwer*, to hold it during the King's Pleasure; and commanded the Men of that County to be intendant to him as Sheriff (*i*). The same King committed the Counties of *Somerset* and *Dorset* to *William Briwer* in like Form during Pleasure (*k*): And the County

Et hac conditione, quod si Comes Legrecestriæ poterit facere versus præfatum Gotsonem, quod ipse voluerit feodum illud prædictum tenere de eo, bene concedo. Quare volo &c. Testibus, Roberto de Gant Cancellario, & Willelmo Comite de Warenna, & Willelmo Comite Lincolniæ, & Willelmo Comite de Albemarle, & Comite Simone, & Willelmo Martel, & Turgiseo de Abrincis, & Willelmo de Albenni Britone, apud Niwetonam. *Ex Collectan. MSS. Will. Dug. Mil. in Museo Ashmol. Oxon. viz. in Libro L. fol.* 51. *b.*

(*f*) Cum Cancellarius conventionasset se daturum Regi pro Vicecomitatu Eboracensis sciriæ, & pro Vicecomitatu Lincolniensi, & pro Vicecomitatu Nordhamptesciriæ, mille & quingentas marcas in principio conventionis, & singulis annis de unoquoq; prædictorum Comitatuum centum marcas de incremento: Gaufridus EboracensisArchiepiscopus obtulit Regi tria millia marcarum pro Vicecomitatu Eboracensi, & singulis annis centum marcas de incremento; & sic abjecto Cancellario, Eboracensis Archiepiscopus obtinuit Vicecomitatum Eboracensem. *Houed. P.* 2. *p.* 736. *n.* 50.

(*g*) Rex &c Episcopis &c, & omnibus &c de Comitatu Lincolniæ &c. Sciatis quod concessimus dilecto & fideli nostro Girardo de Canvilla Vicecomitatum Lincolniæ, Habendum quamdiu nobis placuerit. Et vobis mandamus, quod ei sicut Vicecomiti nostro sitis in omnibus intendentes & obedientes. T. me ipso apud Roth. xvj die Junij. *Pat.* 5. *J. m.* 8.

(*h*) Rex &c Omnibus Hominibus Cornubiæ &c. Sciatis quod constituimus Willelmum de Boterell. Vicecomitem Cornubiæ quamdiu ipse nobis bene servierit. Et ideo vobis mandamus, quod ei tanquam vicecomiti meo sitis intendentes. T. &c G. filio Petri &c v die Aprilis anno r n v. *Pat.* 5. *J. m.* 2.

(*i*) Rex omnibus de Comitatu Suhamtoniæ &c. Sciatis quod commisimus dilecto & fideli nostro Willelmo Briwer Comitatum Suhamtoniæ, custodiendum quamdiu nobis placuerit. Et ideo vobis mandamus, quod ei tanquam Vicecomiti nostro sitis interim intendentes & respondentes. T. me ipso apud Dunstapol. ij die Novembris anno r n ix. *Pat.* 9. *J. m.* 4.

(*k*) Rex &c Omnibus de Comitatibus Sumersetæ & Dorsetæ &c. Sciatis quod commisimus

County of *Wiltsire*, in like Form during Pleasure, to *Geoffrey de Nevill* (*l*). The same King, by Letters Patent, constituted *Richard de Muscengros* Sheriff of *Gloucestershire*, and committed that County to him, to hold for so long as he should serve the King well (*m*). K. *Henry* III, by his Letters Patent, committed the Counties of *Norfolk* and *Suffolk* to *Hubert de Burg*, Chief Justicier of *England*, to hold during the King's Pleasure: And commanded all Persons within those Counties to be intendant and respondent to *Hubert* as to the King's Bailiff and Sheriff (*n*). And the same King, by Letters Patent, committed the County of *Southamton*, with the Appurtenances both by Sea and Land, to *Peter* Pishop of *Winchester*, to be kept by him during the King's Pleasure: Commanding all Persons to suffer the Bishop and his Bailiffs to enjoy quietly that Bailywick (*o*); and in the third Year of that King, *Peter* Bishop of *Winchester* accounted as Sheriff of *Hamshire* (*p*). The same King granted, for himself and

commisimus dilecto & fideli nostro Willelmo Briwer Comitatus Sumersetæ & Dorsetæ, custodiendos quamdiu nobis placuerit. Ideo vobis mandamus & firmiter præcipimus, quod ei sicut Vicecomiti vestro sitis in omnibus intendentes & respondentes. T. me ipso apud Frigidam Mantellam iij die Decembris anno r n ix. *Pat.* 9. *J. m.* 4.

(*l*) Rex omnibus Comitibus Baronibus Militibus & libere tenentibus in Comitatu Wiltesiræ, salutem. Sciatis quod commisimus dilecto & fideli nostro Gaufrido de Nevill Comitatum Wiltesiræ, custodiendum quamdiu nobis placuerit. Et ideo vobis mandamus, quod ei interim tanquam Vicecomiti nostro & ballivo nostro sitis intendentes. T. Willelmo Briwer apud Broc, xxij die Julij anno r n ix°. *Pat.* 9. *J. m.* 5.

(*m*) Rex &c Omnibus &c. Sciatis nos constituisse dilectum & fidelem nostrum Ricardum de Muscengros Vicecomitem nostrum Glouceltriæ, & Comitatum illum ci commisisse; Habendum & tenendum quamdiu ipse nobis bene servierit. Et in hujus rei testimonium, has litteras nostras patentes ei inde fecimus. T. me ipso apud Gillingham, xxiiij die Julij. *Pat.* 9. *J. m.* 5.

(*n*) Rex Archiepiscopis, Episcopis, Abbatibus, Comitibus, Baronibus, Militibus, libere tenentibus, & alijs, de Comitatibus Norfolcia & Suffolcia salutem. Sciatis quod commisimus dilecto & fideli nostro Huberto de Burgo Justiciario nostro Angliæ, Comitatus Norfolciæ & Suffolciæ; custodiendus quamdiu nobis placuerit. Et ideo vobis mandamus, quod eidem Huberto, tanquam Ballivo & Vicecomiti nostro, in omnibus sitis intendentes & respondentes. Et in hujus rei testimonium &c, T. Comit[e] apud Certesiam x die Septembris anno regni nostri primo. *Pat.* 1. *H.* 3. *m.* 3.

(*o*) Rex omnibus has Literas inspecturis Salutem. Sciatis quod commisimus Venerabili in Christo Patri nostro Domino P. Wintoniensi Episcopo Comitatum nostrum Suthantoniæ, cum omnibus pertinentijs suis tam per mare quam per terram, custodiendum quamdiu nobis placuerit. Et ideo vobis mandamus firmiter præcipientes, quod ipsum Dominum Episcopum & Ballivos suos quos ad custodiendum ipsum Comitatum assignaverit, ballivam suam pacifice tenere & custodire permittatis, nullam manum ad eam extendentes vel in eam mittentes, nec per terram nec per aquam. Et in hujus rei testimonium, has literas nostras patentes &c. Teste ipso Comite [W. Marescallo] apud Glouceltriam vj° die Julij anno r n primo. *Pat.* 1. *H.* 3. *m.* 5.

(*p*) Petrus Wintoniensis Episcopus, Willelmus de Schorewell pro eo, reddit compotum de DC & vj l & iij s Bl. de firma Comitatus. *Mag. Rot.* 3. *H.* 3. *Rot.* 3. *a. Suhantescira.*

his

Chap. XXIII. *and* ACCOUNTANTS.

his Heirs, unto *Godfrey de Craucumbe*, the Custody of the County and Castle of *Oxford*, with the Meadow and Mill belonging to the Castle, and with other Things pertaining to the Sherivalty: To have and to hold of the King and his Heirs during *Godfrey*'s Life: Rendering yearly the ancient and due Ferm, which was wont to be rendered in the Time of K. *John*; and xx Marks more every Year, as *proficuum* (*q*). The same King committed the Counties of *Surrey* and *Sussex* to *Ralf de Cameys*, at the same Ferm at which *Gregory de Brodehamme* and *Philipp de Croft* held them (*r*). The King committed the County of *Lincoln* to *Andrew Lutterel*, during his Pleasure, at xx Marks more for the *proficuum Comitatus* than *William de Curtun* used to give (*s*). The King committed his Castle and County of *Northampton*, with the Honor of *Peverell*, to *William de Lisle*, to keep during the King's Pleasure. *William* was to pay Cxx *l.* for the *proficuum* of the County, and to keep the Castle at his own Cost, and to make good the *Corpus Comitatus*; and he was to have the Issues of the Honour (*t*). The King committed to *Hugh de Akor* the Counties of *Salop* and *Stafford*, with the Castles of *Shrewsbury* and *Bruges*, to keep during the King's Pleasure. *Hugh* was to render Cxxvj *l.* yearly for the *proficuum* of the Counties; and was to keep the said Castles at his own Cost; he was also to be allowed for certain Hundreds which were let out in Ferm, and was to make up the *Corpora Comitatuum* (*u*).

The

(*q*) Idem Vicecomes [Godefridus de Craucumb] r c de xx marcis, pro proficuo Comitatus [Oxoniæ]; per Breve Regis; In quo continetur quod Rex concessit pro se & hæredibus suis, Godefrido de Craucumb, Custodiam Comitatus & Castri Oxoniæ cum prato & molendino ad prædictum Castrum pertinente, & omnibus alijs quæ ad Vicecomitem pertinent: Habenda & tenenda de Rege & hæredibus suis toto tempore vitæ suæ: Reddendo inde singulis annis debitam & antiquam firmam quæ de eodem Comitatu reddi solet tempore Regis J. ad Scaccarium, & præterea xx marcas singulis annis nomine proficui ejusdem Comitatus pro omnibus quæ ad Vicecomitem pertinent. *Mag. Rot.* 16. *H.* 3. *tit.* Oxenfordeschira.

(*r*) Baronibus pro Radulfo de Cameys. Rex commisit eidem Comitatus Surreiæ & Sussexiæ, ad firmam ad quam Gregorius de Brodehamme & Philippus de Croft eos tenuerunt. Breve est in f M. *Trin. Commun.* 27. *H.* 3. *Rot.* 20. *a.*

(*s*) Baronibus, pro Andrea Lutterel Vicecomite Lincolniæ. Rex commisit Andreæ L Comitatum Lincolniæ, custodiendum quamdiu Regi placuerit, pro xx marcis reddendis per annum, ultra quod Willelmus de Curtun dare consuevit pro conficuo Comitatus. *Memor.* 35. *H.* 3. *Rot.* 12. *b.*

(*t*) Rex commisit Willelmo de Insula Castrum & Comitatum suum Northamtoniæ, cum custodia Honoris Peverelli in eodem Comitatu, custodienda quamdiu Regi placuerit; Et reddet pro proficuo Comitatus Cxx l, & custodiet Castrum ad custum suum proprium, & perficiet Corpus Comitatus, & habebit exitus prædicti Honoris. *Memor.* 40. *H.* 3. *Rot.* 4. *a. Orig.* 40. *H.* 3. *m.* 1.

(*u*) Rex commisit Hugoni de Akor Comitatus suos Salopiæ & Staffordiæ, cum Castris de Salopia & de Bruges, Custodienda

The King committed the County of *Lincoln* to *Roger Beler*, during his Pleafure, rendering CCvj *l*. and a Mark for the *proficuum* of the County. *Roger* was to make good the *Corpus Comitatus* (*w*). The King committed the County of *Lancafter*, with the Caftle of *Lancafter*, to *Patric de Holuefby*. *Patric* was to keep the Caftle at his own Coft. *William Hayrun* was his Pledge (*x*). K. *Henry* III, in the 42d Year of his Reign, committed all the Counties of *England* to the refpective Sheriffs (*y*): And again in the 44th Year (*z*). Sometimes the Barons of the Exchequer appointed Perfons to be Sheriffs, or, if you pleafe, letted the Counties at Ferm. The Barons of the Exchequer committed the Counties of *Salop* and *Stafford* to *Hugh de Mortimer*. He was to render yearly fourfcore Pounds for the *proficuum* of thofe Counties, to make good the *Corpus Comitatuum*, and to anfwer to the King for the reft of the Ferms as other Sheriffs ufed to do (*a*). At another time (in the Reign of K. *Edward* I) the Barons of the Exchequer, by virtue of a Writ of the Great Seal, committed to *Matthew de Egglefhey* the County of *Devon*, during the King's Pleafure (*b*). In the 13th or 14th Year of that King, the Treafurer and Barons made an Order for raifing the Sheriff of *Somerfet* and *Dorfets* Ferm (*c*). *Robert de Woddeton* was commanded by Writ to come with all Speed before the Treafurer and Barons of the Exchequer, to

enda quamdiu Regi placuerit. Et reddet pro proficuo Comitatuum fingulis annis Cxxvj l. Et idem cuftodiet Caftra prædicta ad cuftum proprium. Et debent allocari eidem Vicecomiti in firma fua.... percipit de Hundredarijs qui habuerunt quædam hundreda ad firmam tempore quo Robertus de Grendon fuit Vicecomes in Comitatibus prædictis. Et idem Vicecomes perficiet corpora Comitatuum. *Orig. de anno* 40. *H.* 3. *in Ced. ad m.* 1.

(*w*) *Ib.*
(*x*) *Ib. juxt.*
(*y*) Omnes Comitatus Angliæ commiffi. *Pat.* 42. *H.* 3. *m.* 1.
(*z*) Rex commifit diverfis Vicecomitibus omnes Comitatus Angliæ. *Memor.* 44. *H.* 3. *Rot.* 4. *b.* & *Rot.* 5. *a.*
(*a*) Memorandum quod die Jovis in craftino Apoftolorum Simonis & Judæ commiffi fuerunt per Barones de Scaccario Hugoni de Mortuo Mari Comitatus Salopfiræ & Staffordiæ, reddendo inde ad Scaccarium per annum $\frac{xx}{iiij}$l pro proficuo eorundem Comitatuum, & perficiet corpus Comitatuum & refpondebit Regi de alijs firmis ficut alij Vicecomites refpondere confueverunt, Et tenebit eofdem Comitatus per talem firmam a Pafcha anno Lv°, quando Rex primo commifit ei eofdem Comitatus, ufq; ad terminum fibi per ipfum Regem conceffum. *Mich. Communia* 56. *Hen.* 3. *Rot.* 1. *b.*

(*b*) Memorandum quod xv die Januarij, venit coram Baronibus Mathæus de Egglefhey, & ijdem Barones, per Breve de Magno figillo directum eifdem, commiferunt eidem Mathæo Comitatum Devoniæ, cuftodiendum quam diu Regi placuerit; reddendo per annum pro proficuis Comitatus prædicti C marcas, ficut Johannes Wyg & Thomas de Pyn prius Vicecomites prius reddere confueverunt; & perficiet corpus Comitatus &c. *Hil. Communia* 5. *E.* 1. *Rot.* 2. *b. in bund.* 4 & 5. *E.* 1. *The Pipe-award is,* In Ro.

(*c*) *Mich. Commun.* 13 & 14. *E.* 1. *Rot.* 6. *a.*

do

Chap. XXIII. *and* ACCOUNTANTS. 143

do what they should enjoin him on the King's Behalf. He came. And the King committed to him the County of *Devon* during his Pleasure (*d*). Moreover, the same K. *Edward* I, *Anno Regni* 15°, committed the County of *Hereford* and the Castle to *Henry de Solarijs*, during Pleasure, rendering at the Exchequer *so much, de remanente firmæ post terras datas,* and *so much de firma pro proficuo*. *Henry* was commanded to be manful and diligent in keeping the King's Peace, and not to let any suspected Persons lodge or hold Conventicles in the City of *Hereford* or elsewhere in his Bailywick; and if any such were found, to arrest and imprison them (*e*). The Counties of *Somerset* and *Dorset*, with the Castle of *Shireburne*, were committed to *Richard de Burghunte*, to be kept during the King's Pleasure, rendering yearly as much as *John de Sancto Laudo*, late Sheriff, used to render (*f*). The Counties of *Oxon* and *Berk*, with the Castle of *Oxford*, were committed during Pleasure to *William de Grenvill*, upon the like Terms: The Counties of *Cambridge* and *Huntendon*, with the Castle of *Cambridge*, to *Hugh de Babington*; and the County of *Southampton*, with the Castle of *Winton* and Town of *Winton*, to *Ingeram le Waleys*, upon the like Terms (*g*). The County of *Southampton*, with the Castle of *Winchester*, was committed to *Thomas de Warblington* during

(*d*) Roberto de Woddeton. Mandatum est eidem Roberto, quod veniat coram Baronibus cum omni festinatione qua poterit, ad faciendum quod Barones de Scaccario ei injungent ex parte Regis; Et hoc sicut seipsum & omnia bona sua quæ habet in Regno suo diligit nullo modo omittat. Ad quem diem venit, & Rex commisit ei Comitatum Devoniæ custodiendum quamdiu sibi placuerit, sicut continetur in Memorandis. *Pas. Brevia* 14. *E*. 1. *Rot.* 26. *a*.

(*e*) De fidelitate & industria Henrici de Solarijs Rex confidens ad securitatem Comitatus Herefordiæ & parcium adjacencium, commisit eidem xxj die Aprilis anno regni sui xv° Comitatum prædictum, & castrum Herefordiæ cum pertinentijs, custodiendum qamdiu Regi placuerit; reddendo inde per annum ad Scaccarium xlix l xviij d ob. Bl. de remanente firmæ Comitatus post terras datas, & L marcas de firma pro proficuo, Et ideo Rex mandat eidem, quod custodiæ prædictæ intendat in forma prædicta: Mandavit enim Rex Rogero de Burghull nuper Vicecomiti prædicti Comitatus, quod Comitatum & castrum prædicta, cum omnibus quæ ad custodiam illam pertinent, simul cum armaturis & instauro in eodem castro existentibus, ei liberet per cirographum inde inter eos conficiendum &c. Et mandatum est eidem Henrico, quod circa pacis Regis conservationem in partibus illis viriliter laboret, non permittens quod aliqui sinistræ suspicionis in civitate Herefordiæ, seu alibi in balliva sua hospitentur vel conventicula faciant; & si quos tales invenerit, eos arrestari & salvo custodiri faciat, donec aliud inde habuerit in mandatis; T. &c. *Pas. Brevia pro Rege* 15. *E*. 1. *Rot.* 22. *b*.

(*f*) De Comitatibus Somersetæ & Dorsetæ commissis. Rex xxv die octobris commisit Ricardo de Burghunte prædictos Comitatus & Castrum de Shyreburne cum pertinentijs, custodiendos quamdiu Regi placuerit; Reddendo inde per annum tantum quantum Johannes de Sancto Laudo nuper Vicecomes ibidem reddere consuevit. *Mich. Commun.* 18. *incip*. *E*. 1. *Rot.* 1. *a*.

(*g*) *Ib. juxt.*

Pleasure,

Pleasure, and with the like Provisoes (*h*). The King committed the County of *Gloucester* to *John de Langlegh*, during his Pleasure, rendering as much by the Year as *Thomas de Gardinis*, late Sheriff, was wont to render for the same. All Persons were commanded to be intendant and respondent to *John de Langlegh* in Things pertaining to his Office. And *Thomas de Gardinis* was commanded to deliver to the said *John* the Writs, Summonses, Rolls, and other Things relating to the said County by Chirograph to be made between them (*i*). Several Counties and Castles were committed by the King to several Persons, *quamdiu Regi placuerit* (*k*). K. *Edward* II. committed the County of *York*, with the Castle of *York*, to *John de Crepping*, to hold during Pleasure, rendering yearly as much as *William de Houk*, late Sheriff, rendered. And *William de Houk* was commanded to deliver the said County to *John de Crepping*, with the Rolls, Writs, &c. by Indenture (*l*). The King (30 *die Octob. anno* 1º) committed the Counties of *Norfolk* and *Suffolk*, together with the Castle of *Norwich*, to *Thomas de Sancto Omero* in like Form during Pleasure; the Counties of *Surrey* and *Sussex* to *Walter de Geddyngg*, during Pleasure, in like Form (*m*); and other Counties to others (*n*). The King, by Writ of Privy Seal, commanded the Treasurer to commit the Castle of *Norwich*, together with the Office of Sheriff of that Country, to *Monsieur Henry de Segrave*, after he had taken such Oath as was proper upon that Occasion (*o*). The King committed to *Thomas de la Hyde* the County of *Cornwall*, with the Appurtenances, and the Castles of *Tintagel*, *Restormel*, and *Tremeton*, and all his Lands and

---

(*h*) *Pas. Commissiones* 24 & 25. *E.* 1.
(*i*) *Mich. Commissiones* 26 & 27. *E.* 1. *Rot.* 45. *b.*
(*k*) *Mich. Communia* 26 & 27. *E.* 1. *Rot.* 45. *a* & *b.* *Rot.* 46. *a.* *Rot.* 74. *a.*
(*l*) Rex xxiij die Octobris anno primo commisit Johanni de Creppingg Comitatum Eboraci una cum Castro Eboraci cum pertinencijs, Custodiendum a festo S. Michaelis proximo præterito quamdiu Regi placuerit; Reddendo inde Regi per annum tantum quantum Willelmus de Houk nuper Vicecomes &c Regi reddere consuevit. T. Thesaurario die & anno præscriptis.
Et eodem die mandatum est eidem Willelmo, quod Comitatum prædictum, una cum Rotulis, brevibus, summonicionibus &c per indenturam liberet &c; T. &c. ut supra. *Mich. Commission.* 1. *E.* 2. *Rot.* 3. *b.*
(*m*) *Mich. Commiss. ib. Rot.* 3. *b.*
(*n*) *Ib. Rot.* 4. *a. Rot.* 5. *a. Rot.* 6. *a. Rot.* 7. *a.*
(*o*) Edward par la grace de Deu &c ; A nostre cher Clerk a seal, Gauter Renaud nostre Tresorer, saluz. Nous vous maundoms, qe vous facez avoir a notre cher e feal Monsf. Henri de Segrave, la garde de nostre Chastel de Norwyz ove les apurtenaunces, ensemblement ove le office du Viscunte de meisme le pays, a respoundre ent a nous en due manere. Et lui facez avoir sour ce nos Lettres en due fourme, quant il avera fet devaunt le serment qe y apent. Done souz nostre Prive Seal a Walingford, le xxix jour de Marz, lan de nostre regne primer. *Hil. Brevia* 1. *E.* 2. *Rot.* 36. *b.*

Tenements,

Tenements, and the Stannary and Coinage in the said County; to keep the same during Pleasure. And the King commanded Archbishops and all others to be intendant to the said *Thomas* as Sheriff of the said County, and Keeper of the Castles, Lands, Stewardship, Stannary, and Coinage aforesaid, in Things relating to the said Sherifrick and Custody (*p*). The King appointed *Walter Hakelut* to be Sheriff of *Herefordshire* during his Pleasure, rendering yearly at the Exchequer as much as other Sheriffs used to render; and gave him Power to depute one to execute for him the Office of Sheriff for so long as he should continue in the King's Service in his Houshold (*q*).

In the most ancient Times the Justiciers and other great Officers of the King's Court were frequently made Sheriffs of Counties. Many Instances of this may be seen in several Parts of the present History (*r*); so that I need not add many others here. In the 5th Year of K. *Stephen*, *Richard Basset* and *Alberic de Ver* (great Lords) were Sheriffs of the Counties of *Essex* and *Hertford* (*s*), and of several other Counties (*t*); they were also at the same time Justices Errant for many of the Counties of *England* (*u*). In the second Year of K. *Henry* II, *Richard de Luci* was Chief Justicier, or at least one of the King's Justiciers that sat and acted at the Exchequer. The Sum of sixty-six

(*p*) Cornubia. De Comitatu & Senescalcia commissis. Rex xxv die Junij commisit Thomæ de la Hyde Comitatum Cornubiæ cum pertinentijs, nec non Castra de Tintagel, Restormel, & Tremeton, & omnes terras & tenementa, ac Stagnariam & Cunagium in eodem Comitatu: Custodienda quamdiu Regi placuerit: ita quod de exitibus inde provenientibus Regi respondeat ad Scaccarium Regis. Et mandatum est Archiepiscopis &c, quod eidem Thomæ tamquam Vicecomiti Comitatus prædicti & Custodi Castrorum terrarum & tenementorum Senescalciæ, Stagnariæ & Cunagij prædictorum in hijs quæ ad officium Vicecomitis & Custodiam illam pertinent intendentes sint &c. Teste Thesaurario &c. *Trin. Commission.* 1. *E.* 2. *Rot.* 14. *b. in imo.*

(*q*) Thesaurario per Regem. Edward par la grace de Dieu &c; A nostre cher Clerk Wauter Reynaud nostre Tresthorier, saluz. Por ceo qe nous voloms, qe nostre cher Bacheler e seal Wauter Hakelut le suiz, seit nostre Vicont de Hereford, Rendaunt attaunt per an pur le dit office a nostre Eschequer, come altres Vicountes ont fait avaunt ces houres, & avoms graunte al dit Wauter, qi demoert en nostre hostel en nostre service par nostre comaundement, quil puisse mettre en son lieu, a faire loffice de Viscounte en dit Counte, un tieu loiaux homme & sage, por qi il meismes voudra respoundre en son peril: Vous maundoms, qe vouz faces avoir au dit Wauter tiel Commission come appent, pur la dite Baillie de Viscounte, a tenir taunt come il nous plerra en la forme avauntdite. Don sur nostre Prive Seal a Blith le xv jour de Septembre, lan de nostre Regne primer. Et prætextu hujus brevis Comitatus committitur prædicto Waltero; sicut continetur alibi inter Commissiones de hoc termino. *Mich. Brevia* 1. *Edw.* 2. *Rot.* 17. *b.*

(*r*) *Chap.* 3. *sect.* 12. *Vol.* 1. &c.

(*s*) Ricardus Basset & Albericus de Ver r c de firma de Essexa & Heortfordscira; In thesauro CCCC & xx l & iij s ad pensum &c. *Mag. Rot.* 5. *Ste. Rot.* 6. *a.*

(*t*) Vid. *Dissert. de* Magno Rot.

(*u*) *Cap.* 3. *sect.*

Shillings

Shillings and eight Pence was paid by an Accountant to *Salomon* the Queen's Clerk, and allowed at the Exchequer by the Precept of *Richard de Luci* (*w*). At that Time *Richard de Luci* was Sheriff of *Essex* and *Hertfordshire* (*x*). *Anno* 20 *Hen.* 2, *Robert Mantel* was Sheriff of *Essex* and *Hertfordshire*, and a Justicier Itinerant in those Counties (*y*). *Godfrey de Luci* and the Sheriff of *Cumberland* held Pleas in that County (*z*). In the Reign of K. *Richard* I, it was ordained, that no Sheriff should be Justicier in his own County, or in any other County whereof he had been Sheriff since the King's first Coronation. This was one of the *Capitula placitorum Coronæ Regis* (or Instructions given by the King to the Justices Errant) as may be seen in *Houedene* (*a*). But I think this Order was not observed punctually, or for any long Time after. For in the 8th Year of K. *Richard* I, the Sheriff of *Dorset* and *Sumerset* acted as a Justicier Itinerant in those Counties (*b*). In the 12th Year of K. *John*, *Engelard de Cigony*, Sheriff of *Gloucestershire*, acted as a Justice Itinerant in that County (*c*). In the third Year of K. *Henry* III, *Hubert de Burgh* was Sheriff of *Norfolk* and *Suffolk* (*d*), and a Justicier Itinerant in those Counties (*e*). In the same Year he was Sheriff of *Kent* (*f*), and the

(*w*) Et in Donis, Salomoni Clerico Reginæ, Lxvj s viij d, præcepto Ricardi de Luci. *Mag. Rot.* 2. *H.* 2. *Rot.* 2. *a.*

(*x*) Ricardus de Luci r c de firma Essexæ. Et idem r c de firma de Hurtfordscira. Winlesor: Idem Ricardus de Luci r c de firma de Winlesor —; Et de Censu Forestæ de Windresora & de firma de Weregrava —, Et de firma de Cocham & de firma de Brai. *Mag. Rot.* 2. *H.* 2. *Rot.* 3. *a.*

(*y*) Robertus Mantel r c de Veteri firma de Essexa & Hurtfordscira; Et idem de Nova firma. *Mag. Rot.* 20. *H.* 2. *Rot.* 6. *a.* Nova Placita & Novæ Conventiones, De Nova Assisa facta super Dominia Regis per ipsum Vicecomitem & Walterum de Hadfeld. *Ib. Rot.* 6. *a.* *Essex & Hurtf.*

(*z*) Nova Placita & Novæ Conventiones, per Godefridum de Luci, & Ipsum Vicecomitem, & Socios suos. *Mag. Rot.* 31. *Hen.* 2. *Rot.* 12. *b.* *Cumb.*

(*a*) Nullus Vicecomes sit Justiciarius in Vicecomitatu suo, nec in Comitatu quem tenuerit post primam Coronationem Domini Regis. *Houed. P.* 2. *p.* 744. *n.* 40.

(*b*) Amerciamenta Hominum in Dorsette, per Robertum Gerbert, & Reginaldum de Penton, & Vicecomitem de Dorietta. *Mag. Rot.* 8. *R.* 1. *Rot.* 16. *b.* Amerciamenta in Sumersette per prædictos. *Ib. juxt.*

(*c*) Engelardus de Ciconiaco, Ricardus Burgis ut Custos pro eo r c de firma Comitatus. *In this Account one of the Titles is*, Amerciamenta Justiciariorum Itinerantium coram Engelardo de Cigoni: Idem Vicecomites r c de xxij l & vj s & viij d de Misericordijs hominum quorum nomina annotantur in Rotulo quem prædicti liberaverunt in Thesauro. *Mag. Rot.* 12. *J. Rot.* 13. *b. Gloec.*

(*d*) Hubertus de Burgo r c de DCC & quater xx & x l & ij s Bl. de firma Comitatuum. *Mag. Rot.* 3. *H.* 3. *Rot.* 4. *a. Norf. & Suff.*

(*e*) De Amerciamentis factis per H. de Burgo. *Ib. Rot.* 4. *b. Norf. & Suff.*

(*f*) Hubertus de Burgo, Hugo de Windlesores pro eo, r c de DCCC & xxiiij l & xv s Bl., Et de CCC & xxxj l & vj s & viij d Numero de firma Comitatus de anno præterito & hoc anno. *Ib. Rot.* 12. *a. Kent.*

King's Chief Jufticier (*g*). In the fourth Year he was Sheriff of *Norfolk* and *Suffolk* (*h*), and a Juftice Itinerant in thofe Counties (*i*).

Whether the Sheriffs of *England* in the moft ancient Times took an Oath to the King upon entering into their Office, I cannot fay with Certainty; or (if they did) in what Form of Words. It appears that K. *Henry* III, in or about the 42d Year of his Reign, caufed the feveral Sheriffs of *England* to take an Oath in this Form: that he would ferve the King faithfully; that he would do Right to all Men equally, according to the Power vefted in him by his Office; and would not fail, for Love nor for Hate, nor for Fear of any one, nor for Defire of Gain, to do Right as well and as foon as he could both to the Poor and to the Rich; that he would not take any thing, by himfelf, or by another, or by any Art or Device, by reafon of his Bailywick, except only Meat and Drink, fuch as was wont to be brought to the Table, and but for one Day at moft; that he would not have above five Horfes at the Place where he lodged with any one by reafon of his Bailywick, nor would lodge with any body that had lefs than forty Pounds a Year in Land, nor with any Houfe of Religion that had lefs than a hundred Marks a Year in Land or Rents, nor would lodge with any of the Perfons abovefaid oftener than once in the Year, or at moft than twice, nor then unlefs at their Defire or with their Confent, and would not draw it into Example; and if he was obliged to lodge there oftener or longer, that he would take no Prefent nor other Thing of greater Value than twelve Pence; and that he would have with him no more Serjeants than were needful for the fafe-keeping of his Bailywick; that he would take fuch Serjeants as could give him Security upon their Fees, fo that the Country be not overmuch charged with their eating or drinking; and that they, whilft they continued in their Bailywicks, fhould not demand nor receive of any Man, Clerk or Lay, Free or Villain, nor of any Religious Houfe, or any Town, Lamb, Corn, Grain, Wool, or other Moveable, nor Money or Money's-worth. (This the Sheriff was to caufe the Serjeants to fwear, when he put them into their Bailywick.) At the fame time the King ordered, that Counties, Hundreds, Wa-

---

(*g*) Et H. de Burgo Jufticiario CC & L marcas, per breve Regis J. Patens quod eft in Thefauro, quas idem H. recognovit fe recepiffe. *Ib. Rot.* 12. *a. Kent. tit.* De Oblatis.

(*h*) Hubertus de Burgo r c de DCC & quater xx & x l & ij s Bl. de firma Comitatuum. *Mag. Rot.* 4. *H.* 3. *Rot.* 4. *a. Norfulk & Suff.*

(*i*) De Amerciamentis factis per H. de Burgo. Hubertus de Burgo debet C & quater xx & xiij marcas & xij d, quos recepit de totalibus Amerciamentorum de Itinere fuo, ficut recognovit. *Mag. Rot.* 4. *H.* 3. *Rot.* 4. *b. Norf. & Suff.*

pentacks,

pentacks, or other Bailywicks of the Realm, ſhould not be let to Ferm; that if Sheriffs or other Bailiffs were convicted of taking, by reaſon of their Bailywick, any thing more than what is above ſpecified, they, both the Giver and Taker, ſhould be puniſhed for it. And the King alſo commanded, that no Perſon, Man or Woman, ſhould offer, promiſe, or give any thing to any of his Bailiffs, under Pain of being puniſhed for it; declaring, that when the Sheriff came to account at the Beginning of the Year, the King would allow him for the reaſonable Expences of keeping his Bailywick both for himſelf and the Reward of his Serjeants; and that the King gave him of his own, to the Intent he ſhould take nothing of any one elſe. At the ſame time alſo the King ordered, that none of his Bailiffs which he put into Office in his Realm, neither Sheriff nor other, ſhould continue in his Bailywick longer than one Year; and that if any Wrongs had been done by the aforeſaid Bailiffs, the ſame ſhould be redreſſed (*k*). In the

(*k*) Henri par la grace Deu Rey de Engleterre, Seigneur de Irelande, Duc de Normandie & de Aquien, & Cunte de Anjou, a tutte gent del Cunte de Rotelande ke ceſtes Lettres verrunt, Saluz. Pur ce ke nous deſirons & volons ke haſtive dreiture ſeit fete par tute noſtre Reaume auſi al poure cum al Riche, nus volons & comandons, ke les torz Kunt eſte fet de noſtre tens en voſtre Cunte, ki kunkes les cit fet, ſeent muſtre a quatre Chevalers ke nus avons a ce atturne, ſi einz ne lur eent eſte muſtre, & nus al plus haſtivement ke nus purrons les frons amender & adreſcer, meſſi nus ne poons ſi haſtivement ceſte choſe fere cum nus voudrions & cum meſter ſerreit & a nus & a vus, ne vus devez pas marveiller ke la choſe eſt ſi longement mal alee a noſtre damage & a voſtre, kele ne puet mie ſi toſt eſtre amendee; mes par les premereins amendemenz ke ſerrunt fez es primers Cuntez v nus enverzuns noſtre Juſtice, & de nos autres prodes Hommes pur ce ſere, purrez aver certeine eſperance kanſi fra lein a vus al plus toſt ke lein purra. Et ſachez qe nus avuns fet jurer cheſcun de noz Viſcuntes icel Serement: Kil nus ſervira leaument, & tendra a ſun poer ce keſt deſuz eſcrit, ceſt aſaver, Kil fra dreiture communaument a tute gent ſolonc le poer kil a de ſun Office & ce ne lerra pur amur ne pur haine ne pur pour de nuli ne pur nule coveitiſe kil auſi ben & auſi toſt ne face haſtive dreiture al poure cum al Riche ne de nul ne de nule ren ne prendra ne par li ne par autri ne par nule manire dart ne dengin par acheſun de ſa baille fors ſolement mangers & beivres ke lein acoſtome de porter as tables auſi cum a un Jurnee al plus ne kil navra ke cinc Chevaus en leu v il herberge oveke autre par acheiſun de ſa Baille, noveke nuli ne herbergera keit meins de Quarante liveree de terre nen nule meiſun de Religion ke meins eit de la value de Cent mars cheſcun an de terres v de Rents noveke les deſuſdit ne herbergera kune feiz denz lan v deu feiz al plus & ke ce ne fra for par lur prere v par lur volunte & qe ce acuſtume ne trerra, & ſil covient kil i herberge plus kil ne prendra de preſenz ne dautre choſe qe plus vaille de duzze deners, & ke de Serianz naura fors tant cum il covendra beſoinablement pur garder ſa baillie, & qe Serjanz prendra de queis il ſeit ſi ſeur kil puiſſe reſpondre de lur fez, & quele pais ne ſoit trop greve par lur manger ne par lur beivre, & ceus tant cum il ſunt en baillie, de nul homme, Clerc ne Lay, franc ne vilein, de meiſun de Religiun ne de Ville, ne demandrent ne prendrent Aignel, garbe, ne ble, ne laine, nautre manere de moeble, ne dener, ne ke le vaille, ſicum pluſurs unt acuſtomez

the 26th or 27th Year of K. *Edward* I, *Guy* Earl of *Warwick*, Sheriff in Fee of *Worcestershire*, upon his entering on that Office, took the Oath hereunder set forth (*kk*). A Sheriff's Oath, as it stood in the 5th Year of K. *Edward* II, may be seen in *Ryley* (*l*). In the 12th Year of K. *Edward* II, a Commission was sent to the Abbot of *Malmsbury*, to receive of the Sheriff of *Wiltshire* his Oath for his good Behaviour in his Office, with the Tenor of the said Oath as it is set down in the red Book (*prout annotatur in rubeo Libro*) (*m*).

If the King required it, the Sheriff found Pledges for his good Service in his Office, and for true Payment of his Ferm and other Issues of his County. *Walter de Lascy, Hugh de Mortimer, John de Monemouth*, and *Walter de Clifford*, became Sureties to K. *Henry* III. for *Walter de Beauchamp*, to wit, that *Walter de Beauchamp* should serve the King faithfully for the future, and should not at any Time withdraw from his Service. And the King committed to *Walter de Beauchamp* the Castle and County of *Worcester*, upon Condition that

acustomez za en ariere. Ce lur face jurer le Viscunte quant il les mettra en Baillie. Et qe Cuntez, Hundredz, Wapentaks, ne nule autre Baillie ne nostre Reaume ne baudra a ferme a nuli. Et seent certeins Viscuntes, & tutte autre manere de Bailliez, ke si nul est ateint de nule manere dautre prise ke desus est escript, par achesun de sa Baillie, kil serra reint, & ausi le donur cum le pernur, kar nus avums purveu par le Cunseil de noz hauz Homez, ke tuz jurz mes seit fete plenere & hastive dreiture a tuz sanz nule manire de luer. E pur ce nus comandons & defendons a tuz & a tuttes, ka nuls de noz Bailliz ren neffrent, ne premettent, ne donient sur peine destre reint, kar qant le Viscunte vend al chef del an sur sun acunte, lein li alivera ses covenables despens, kil aura set pur sa baillie garder, & pur li & pur le luer de ses Serjanz ; Et pur ce lur donuns le nostre, ke nus ne volons kil eent achesun de ren prendre dautri ; & nus volons ke nul de noz Bailliz ke nuz mettons en nostre terre, ne Viscunte nautre, ne demuerge en sa Baillie plus dune anee ; & pur ce vus fesuns assaver, ke si durestes u torz vus seent fet par les avantdite Bailliz, ke vus meinz le detez & plus seurement lor tortz mustrez. Tesmoin mei meimes a Westmoster, le vintime jur de Octobre, lan de nostre Regne Quarante Secund. *Pat.*

42. *H.* 3. *m.* 1.

(*kk*) —— & instanter in Scaccario sedebat, & sacramentum præstitit quo ad Officium Camerarij quod secreta Regis celaret ; & pro Officio Vicecomitis exercendo in dicto Comitatu præstitit sacramentum in forma subsequenti. Quil leaument servira le Roi en office de Viscounte en le Counte de Wyrcestre, e le preu le Roi ferra en tuttes choses qui a lui appendent a farre soulom son sen & son poeir & les dreitures e qant qe a la coronne appent loiament gardera, & nassentira a desores ne a concel[ser] des droitz ne des fraunchises le Roi, e par la ou il savera les droitz le Roi ou de sa Coronne, seit en terres franchises, rentes ou sieutes conceles ou soustreez, quil mettra peine a ceo repeller, e sil meismes ne puisse les amendes farre, il le dirra au Roi ou teil de son Counseil de qui il seit certein quil le die au Roi, e qe leaument tretera le poeple de sa ballie, e a chescun ferra droit, e quil ne suffra nul Baillif desoutz lui en le dit Counte forsqe des plus loiauxs del pais ou dautre pais, qui mieuz e plus leaument puissent le Roi servir e le poeple. *Mich. Communia* 26 & 27. *E.* 1. *Rot.* 4. *b.*

(*l*) *Plac. Parl. in append.* p. 533.

(*m*) *Hil. Brevia Irretornab.* 12. *E.* 2. *Rot.* 151. *a.*

Walter should hold them for fourteen Years after the King's full Age, and then should resign them to the King in as good Plight as he received them, if the King so pleased (*n*). *Matthew Bezill*, *Ralf de Wilinton*, Sheriff of *Devonshire*, and *Nicolas Burdon*, became Sureties for *William de Lassebergh*, Sheriff of *Gloucestershire*, that *William* should faithfully serve the King in the Office of Sheriff; and that if he was not sufficient, they would answer for him to the King in all Things relating to the said Office (*v*). *William de Swyneford* found six Sureties, to wit, *William de Beaumont* and five others, for his faithful Service in the Office of Sheriff of *Norfolk* and *Suffolk*, and for his true Payment of the Ferms and other Duties (*p*). The King committed his Counties of *Stafford* and *Salop*, and his Castles of *Shrewsbury* and *Bruges*, to *Hugh de Dacovre*, during his Pleasure. *Hugh* was to pay Cxxvj l and a Mark for the *Proficuum* of the Counties; and was to keep the said Castles at his own Charges, and to be allowed out of his Ferm so much as the King received for certain Hundreds which were lately fermed out. *Hugh* found two Sureties; and was to find four more the next Time he came to the Exchequer (*q*). Sir *Thomas de Snyterton*, Knight,

(*n*) Omnibus præsentem Cartam inspecturis, Walterus de Lascy, Hugo de Mortuomari, Johannes de Monemuthe, & Walterus de Clifford, salutem. Noverit universitas vestra quod nos manucepimus & plegios nos constituimus erga Dominum nostrum Henricum Regem Angliæ illustrem pro Waltero de Bellocampo, quod idem Walterus fideliter ei serviet a die Mercurij proxima post medium Quadragesimæ anno regni sui primo in antea; nec aliquo tempore a servitio suo recedet. Dominus autem Rex committit eidem Waltero Castrum & Comitatum Wigorniæ, sub tali conditione, quod idem Walterus ea teneat usque ad quartum decimum annum ætatis Domini nostri Regis completum, & tunc illa reddet Domino Regi in eodem statu quo illa recepit, si Domino Regi placuerit. Nec idem Walterus occasione illius Commissionis aliquod jus sibi vendicabit in prædictis Castro & Comitatu Wigorniæ, sed ea reddet sicut prædictum est Domino Regi si ei placuerit. Et in hujus rei testimonium, & ad majorem rei securitatem huic scripto sigilla nostra apponi fecimus. *Ex Collectan. MSS. Willelmi Dugd. Equ. Aur. in Mus. Ashmol. Oxon. viz. in Libro*, L, *fol*. 22. *a*.

(*o*) Plegij Willelmi de Lassebergh Vicecomitis Gloucestriæ. Mathæus Bezill, Radulfus de Wilinton Vicecomes Devoniæ, & Nicholaus Burdon manuceperunt &c, quod Willelmus de Lessebergh Vicecomes Gloucestriæ fideliter serviet Domino Regi in officio Vicecomitis; & quod ipsi plene pro eo respondebunt de omnibus rebus ipsum Dominum Regem ratione dicti officij tangentibus, si idem Vicecomes non sufficiat. *Pas. Commun*. 39. *H*. 3. *Rot*. 1. *a*.

(*p*) Memorandum quod Willelmus de Sywneford manucepit coram Baronibus, adducere coram eis in octabis S. Nicholai sex plegios sufficientes de fideli servicio faciendo in Comitatibus Norfolciæ & Suffolciæ quos Dominus Rex ei commisit, & tam de firmis quam omnibus alijs ad dictos Comitatus pertinentibus fideliter solvendis. *Memor*. 40. *H*. 3. *Rot*. 4. *a*. Accordingly, William de Bello monte, *and five others, came and were Pledges for him in that Behalf*. *Ib. Rot*. 4. *infra*.

(*q*) Rex commisit Hugoni de Dacovere Comitatus suos Staffordiæ & Salopiæ & Castra sua de Salopia & Bruges, custodienda quamdiu Regi placuerit; & dabit pro proficuo Comitatus Cxxvj l & j marcam, & custodiet

Knight, and five others, came to the Exchequer before the Treasurer's Lieutenant and the Barons, and mainprised for *Gilbert de Holm*, Sheriff of the Counties of *Bedford* and *Buckingham*, that he should behave himself well and truly in the Office of Sheriff, and should well and truly answer to the King for the King's Debts and the Ferms of the said Counties; and in the said Mainprise they bound themselves, their Lands and Tenements, Goods and Chattels (*r*).

Hitherto I have spoken of the Manner of constituting or appointing Sheriffs to their Office. The Duty of their Office should be considered next. And that I think may, upon a general Scheme, be reduced to three or four Heads. It was the Sheriff's Duty to do the Justice of his County, to keep the publick Peace, to stock and improve the King's Lands, and to collect the King's Revenue. There may perhaps be some other Things pertaining to his Duty; which, though not here mentioned, are not designed to be excluded. It is not my Business to speak of the Sheriff here as an Officer of Justice, or a Conservator of the Peace. I am to speak of him, as he was the King's Farmer or Bailiff, and his Collector of Rents and other Revenue. It was (I say) Part of the Sheriff's Duty to collect and bring in the King's Revenue. This appears from the Manner of the Sheriff's accounting, and from many Records cited in this History. It was also Part of the Sheriff's Duty to stock and improve the King's Manors and Lands within his Bailywick. In the second Year of K. *Henry* II, *Richard de Luci*, Sheriff of *Hertfordshire*, had Allowance made to him for viij l, which he had disbursed in stocking the King's Manors in that County (*s*). *Robert de Stafford*, Sheriff of *Staffordshire*, was

allowed

---

custodiet Castra prædicta ad custum suum proprium, & debet allocari in firma prædicta quantum Dominus Rex percipit de quibusdam hundredis positis ad firmam tempore quo Robertus de Grendon fuit Vicecomes in Comitatibus prædictis. Et invenit hos plegios, Hugonem de Bucles, Stephanum de Irton ; & adhuc inveniet quatuor alios plegios in proximo adventu suo ad Scaccarium. *Memor.* 40. *H.* 3. *Rot.* 4. *a.*

(*r*) Thomas de Snyterton Miles, *and the five other Persons*, venerunt ad Scaccarium coram Tenente locum Thesaurarij & Baronibus, die Jovis proxima post festum S. Hilarij, & Manuceperunt pro Gilberto de Holm Vicecomite Bedfordiæ & Buckinghamiæ, quod idem Gilbertus bene & fideliter se habebit in officio prædicto, quam diu ipsum tenere continget officium Vicecomitatus prædicti, & quod bene & fideliter respondebit Domino Regi, & eidem plene satisfaciet de omnibus receptis suis, de debitis Regis, & firmis Comitatuum prædictorum, de tempore prædicto, & de toto tempore quo ipse Gilbertus fuerit Vicecomes ibidem &c. Et nisi fecerit, ijdem Thomas (*and the rest*) concesserunt se debere satisfacere pro eodem Gilberto super præmissis, & ad hoc obligant se terras & tenementa bona & catalla sua ad quorumcunque manus devenerint. *Hilar. Commun.* 1. *E.* 2. *Rot.* 43. *a. inter Fines &c.*

(*s*) Ricardus de Luci r c de firma de Hurtfortscira. In Thesauro Lvj l & xvij s Bl.

allowed xxix l xviij s, which he had laid out in stocking the King's Manors in that County (*t*). And in the same Year other Sheriffs had Allowance for the like Disbursements in their Counties. So it was in other Years. *Wimar le Chapelein*, Sheriff of *Norfolk* and *Suffolk*, stocked the Manor of *Wick* with xviij Oxen, two hundred fourscore and two Sheep, nine Cows, &c (*u*). *Alan de Valeines*, Sheriff of *Kent*, stocked the Manor of *Mapelescamp* and other Lands in his County (*w*). *Hugh de Bosco*, Sheriff of *Hanteshire*, stocked the King's Lands of *Mienes* with Cattle; to wit, with twelve Oxen, each Ox at iij *s* Price; an hundred Sheep, each Sheep at iiij *d* Price, &c (*x*). *William de Cantilupe* had ix *l* and ij *s* discounted to him for a Deficiency of Stock in the Town of *Fekeham*, which was Part of his *Corpus Comitatus* (*y*). *Thomas de Cirencestre*, Sheriff of *Somerset* and *Dorset*, stocked the King's Manors within his Bailywick with Cattle, Seed-corn, and other Things (*z*). When a Sheriff committed his County to another, that was to be done with the King's Leave and Consent. For Example: K. *Henry* III. committed the Counties of *Notingham*

Bl. Et in elemosina noviter constituta Militibus de Templo, xiij s & iiij d, Et in Liberationibus constitutis, xij l & xviij s & vj d & ob. Et in Restauratione Maneriorum viij l. Et in Soltis Mercator. Lx s, per Willelmum Cumin & Johannem Marescallum]. Et debet xix l & xv s & ix d Bl. *Mag. Rot.* 2. *H.* 2. *Rot.* 3. *a.*

(*t*) Robertus de Stafford r c de firma de Staffortscira; In thesauro xlvj l & xv s; Et in elemosina noviter constituta Militibus de Templo j marca argenti; *and in other Things so much*, Et in restauratione Maneriorum Regis totius Comitatus, xxix l & xviij s, Et Q. e. *Mag. Rot.* 2. *H.* 2. *Rot.* 6. *a.*

(*u*) Wimarus Capellanus r c de firma. In Thesauro *so much*; — Et ad perficiendum instaurum de Wicha, pro xviij bobus, & CC & quater xx & ij ovibus, & ix vaccis & j tauro, & iiij Capris & j Capro, & ij affris, ix l & iij s & vj d, per breve Regis. *Mag. Rot.* 22. *H.* 2. *Rot.* 5. *a. Nordfolch & Sudf.*

(*w*) Alanus de Valeinis r c de firma de Chent; In Thesauro nichil [*and in several Expences*]; Et ad perficiendum Instaurum de Mapelescamp, pro viij bobus & ij affris, L s, per breve Regis; Et pro xxxvij ovibus, xviij s & iiij d, per idem breve; [*and for stocking several other Lands*]. *Mag. Rot.* 32. *H.* 2. *Rot.* 13. *a.*

(*x*) Hugo de Bosco r c de firma. ——— Et pro instauranda terra de Mienes, quam Rex dedit Willelmo de Hundescote, pro xij bobus, xxxvj s, Bove computato iij s; Et pro C ovibus ij marcas & dimidiam, ove computata iiij d, per breve Regis; [*and for stocking other Lands*]. *Mag. Rot.* 9. *R.* 1. *Rot.* 2. *a. Sudhantesc.*

(*y*) Willelmus de Cantilupo, Walterus le Puiher pro eo, r c de firma; In thesauro *so much*; *and in several Expences so much*; Et in defalta instauri Villæ de Fekeham ix l & ij s. *Mag. Rot.* 10. *J. Rot.* 10. *Wirecestresc.*

(*z*) Et pro Semine & instauro ad Maneria Regis seminanda & instauranda, scilicet apud Camel xxxij boves ad quatuor carucas instaurandas, precium bovis viij s; Et ibidem xvj vaccæ, precium vaccæ dimidia marca; Et ibidem CCC oves, precium ovis xij d; Et in semine ibidem xlij quartera frumenti, precium quarteri iiij s; Et Lxxv quarteris avenæ, precium quarteri iij s; Et v quarteris fabarum, precium quarteri ij s & xj d; Et ibidem pro ij equis caretarijs emptis xvj s. *Mag. Rot.* 14. *H.* 3. *Sumersete & Dorsete m.* 1. *a.* Thomas de Cirencestre *Sheriff.*

and

Chap. XXIII.   *and* ACCOUNTANTS.

and *Derby* to *Walter* Archbishop of *York*. The Archbishop deputed *Hugh de Babington* to keep the said Counties under him. The King, by his Writ, signified to the Barons of the Exchequer, that he had accepted of the said Deputation, and willed that *Hugh* should answer at the Exchequer for the Archbishop (*a*). Next, of the Accounts or Sheriffs.

It is not easy to set forth particularly in what Manner the Accounts of Sheriffs were wont to be rendered during the first Period. But it seems likely, that the Method of accounting, which was used in the Beginning of the second Period, was in the main like to the Method used in the first Period. Let us essay upon the Subject. The Account of a Sheriff was wont to be divided into certain formal Parts. One was called the *Profer*; another the *Visus Compoti*; or *View* of the Account; another *Summa*, or the making of the *Sum*. The *Profer* was a Pre-payment made by the Sheriff out of the Issues of his Baily-wick, twice in the Year; as will be shewn hereafter (*b*). The *View* was the Entrance or Forepart of the Account; which stood *de bene esse*, whilst the Sheriff was purifying or liquidating his Account, by producing his *Waranta*, his Warrants and Vouchers, by virtue whereof he was to have an Allowance or Discharge of any Sums charged on him. Of the *View*, more is said in another Place (*c*). After the *View* was made, he proceeded to *make* or *cast* his *Sum* (*d*).

The Sheriff's Profer was a Pre-payment out of his Ferm and *Corpus Comitatus*, and out of his *Proficuum* and the Summonces. It was, probably, called *Profrum, a proferendo*. The King ordered the *Profers* of the *Judaism, quantum videlicet quilibet per se proferat & solvat*, to be written in a certain Roll by themselves (*e*). In the 41st Year incipient of K. *Henry* III, a Provision or general Rule was made by

(*a*) Baronibus, pro W. Eboracensi Archiepiscopo Angliæ Primate. Cum Rex commiserit eidem W. Comitatus suos Notinghamiæ & Derbiæ custodiendos, Ita quod de exitibus inde provenientibus Regi respondeat ad Scaccarium Regis; Et idem Archiepiscopus Comitatus illos commiserit Hugoni de Babington, custodiendos sub ipso in forma prædicta: Rex commissionem illam acceptans, volens & concedens quod prædictus Hugo Regi respondere possit ad Scaccarium prædictum, sicut Simon de Heddon inde respondere consuevit, tempore quo fuit Vicecomes in eisdem Comitatibus; Et ideo Rex mandat, quod sic fieri & inrotulari faciant. T. &c. *Memor*. 55. H. 3. *Rot*. 9. *a*.

(*b*) *Vid. paul. infra*.
(*c*) *Vid. paul. infra*.
(*d*) *Vid. paul. infra*.
(*e*) Baronibus pro Rege.——Proffrum autem singulorum Vicecomitum de Extractis illis (sc. Judaismi), quantum videlicet quilibet per se proferat & solvat, & qua de causa, & ad quam summam profrum hujusmodi attingat, & de quo tempore, in quodam rotulo per se conscribi & irrotulari faciant——. *Pas. Communi*. 9 & 10. *E*. 1. *Rot*. 4. *a*.

the King, that all Sheriffs should come in Person to the Exchequer on the Morrow of St. *Michael,* and on the Morrow of the Close of *Easter,* to make their Profer according to the ancient Custom of the Exchequer; or otherwise should be amerced, *viz.* the first, second, third, and fourth Day, at C *s,* and the fifth Day at the King's Pleasure: and that all Fermers, who ought to answer *per manus suas,* as well for Burghs as for other Demesnes of the King, should come in Person at the said Terms, to answer for their Ferms and other Debts, or otherwise that every Mayor of a City, or Fermer of a Burgh or other of the King's Demesnes, should be amerced at five Marks for the first, second, third, and fourth Day; and that for the fifth Day's Default the City, Burgh, or other Demesne, should be taken into the King's Hand, not to be restored but at the King's Pleasure: and that every of the King's own Bailiffs or Fermers should be amerced for every Day within the fifth Day at C *s,* like as if he were a Sheriff: and for Disobedience to this Provision, the City of *York* was taken into the King's Hand *(f).* K. *Henry* III, in the 55th Year of his Reign, commanded the Barons to certify him forthwith, whether all the Sheriffs had made their Profer at the Exchequer or not, and who

---

(f) Provisum est per Dominum Regem, Quòd singuli Vicecomites Angliæ veniant ad Scaccarium in Crastino S. Michaelis & in Crastino Clausi Paschæ in propria persona sua, tam cum firmis suis quam summonitionibus, ad Profrum suum inde faciendum, sicut debent secundum antiquam consuetudinem Scaccarij. Et nisi veniant sicut prædictum est infra quintum diem prædictis terminis, amercientur primo die ad Centum solidos, secundo die ad Centum solidos, tercio die ad Centum solidos, quarto die ad Centum solidos, & quinto die ad voluntatem Domini Regis. Et præceptum est per ipsum Dominum Regem singulis Vicecomitibus quod clamari faciant, in singulis Comitatibus suis, quod omnes firmarij qui debent respondere per manus suas ad Scaccarium, tam de Civitatibus, Burgis, quam alijs Dominicis Domini Regis, sint ad dictum Scaccarium dictis Terminis in proprijs personis suis, ad respondendum tam de firmis suis quam de alijs Debitis Domini Regis, de quibus debeant respondere per manus suas, per libertatem eis a Domino Rege concessam. Et nisi sint sicut dictum est, quilibet Major cujuslibet Civitatis, & quilibet firmarius tam Burgorum quam aliorum Dominicorum Domini Regis, amerciatur primo die ad quinq; marcas, secundo die ad quinq; marcas, tercio die ad quinq; marcas, quarto die ad quinq; marcas, & quinto die capiatur Civitas Burgus sive aliud Dominicum in manu Domini Regis, illud nullatenus rehabendum sine gratia & voluntate Domini Regis. Et si quis sit Ballivus seu Firmarius Domini Regis, qui debeat respondere inde sicut prædictum est, amerciatur quolibet die infra quintum diem ad Centum solidos, sicut esset Vicecomes.

Quia Gacius de Calvo Monte Major Civitatis & Ballivi Eboraci, non venerunt in Crastino Sancti Michaelis cum firma ejusdem Civitatis, nec miserunt sicut debuerunt secundum Consuetudinem Scaccarij, nec aliquod responsum fecerunt de debitis quæ eis veniunt in summonitione Domini Regis infra Libertatem prædictæ Civitatis, præceptum est Vicecomiti quod capiat prædictam Civitatem in manu Domini Regis, & illam salvo custodiat, donec aliud præceptum inde habuerit. *Mich. Rec.* 40 & 41. *H.* 3. *Rot.* 1. *b.*

had

Chap. XXIII.   *and* Accountants.

had and who had not, and for how much each Sheriff had made his Profer out of the Ferms, the *Corpus Comitatus,* and the King's Debts, and how much thereof each Sheriff had paid into the Exchequer, and how much he was still to pay; that the King might be apprised what the whole Income of the Exchequer (arising from that Branch of the Revenue) for this Term amounted to (*g*). If Accountants did not come duly to make their Profer, they were to be amerced, or otherwise punished; according to the Provision or Order above-mentioned. *Wichard de Charun,* Sheriff of *Northumberland,* was amerced C *s,* for not making his Profer at the Exchequer (*h*). The several Sheriffs and Bailiffs of *England* were amerced before the Barons of the Exchequer, for not coming to make their Profer, as well out of the King's Ferms as out of the Summonces of the Exchequer, on the Morrow of the Close of *Easter* (*i*). *Osbert de Bereford* and *Thomas de Farendon,* Sheriffs, were severally amerced v Marks, for not coming in Person to make their Profer on the Morrow of St. *Michael* (*k*). *John de Bitterle,* Bailiff of the Liberty of *Havering,* being present at the Exchequer on the Morrow of St. *Michael,* to do his Profer there of the Ferm of his Bailywick, and neglecting to pay the Arrerages of his Ferm as he had before undertaken to do, was committed by the Treasurer and Barons to the Fleet-prison (*l*). In the 15th Year of K. *Edward* II, the several Sheriffs of *England* having lately made

(*g*) Baronibus, pro Rege. Rex mandat firmiter injungens eisdem Baronibus, quatinus per latorem præsencium significent Regi festinanter, utrum omnes Vicecomites Regi proferum suum fecerunt ad Scaccarium vel non; Et si non omnes, Qui fecerunt & qui non; Et quantum quilibet Vicecomes de profero suo fecit de Firmis & Corpore Comitatus sui, scilicet cujuslibet Comitatus per se, Et quantum de debitis Regis, Et quantum quilibet Vicecomes de balliva sua solvit in Scaccario, & quantum solvendus est: Ut de toto proficuo ejusdem Scaccarij de hoc Termino Rex possit ad plenum cerciorari. T. &c. *Memor.* 55. *H.* 3. *Rot.* 1. *a.*

(*h*) Norhumbria, pro Rege. Præceptum est Vicecomiti, quod de bonis & catallis Wichardi de Charun in balliva sua fieri faciat C s, quos Regi debet, & ad quos amerciatus fuit coram Baronibus de Scaccario, anno regni Domini H. Regis L v°, quia non venit ad proffrum suum faciendum; ita quod habeat denarios ad Scaccarium in crastino S. Michaelis Regi solvendos &c. *Memor.* 1. *E.* 1. *Rot.* 8. *b.*

(*i*) Vicecomites & Ballivi amerciati coram Baronibus de Scaccario, quia non venerunt coram eisdem in proprijs personis suis in crastino Clausi Paschæ anno Regni Regis E xviij°, ad faciendum Puroffrum suum, tam de firmis Regis quam de Summonitionibus ejusdem Scaccarij. *In Rot. ante Pas. Commun.* 18. *Edw.* 1. *Rot.* 8. *a. Each County and Town is amerced five Marks, and Master Henry de Bray Escheator on this Side Trent,* x *l.*

(*k*) Osbertus de Bereford quondam Vicecomes debet v marcas, quia non venit in propria persona super profrum suum, in crastino S. Michaelis anno xiij°. Thomas de Farendon quondam Vicecomes, debet v marcas pro eodem. *Mag. Rot.* 18. *E.* 1. *War. & Leic.* m. 1. *b.*

(*l*) *Mich. Communia* 26 & 27. *E.* 1. *Rot.* 3. *a.*

their

their Profers at the Exchequer deficiently, to the King's great Damage; the King now by Writs directed to the respective Sheriffs of *England* commands them, that on the Morrow of the Close of *Easter* next, they should make their Profer full and entire, as well of the Ferms as of the Summonces; or else the King would cause them to be grievously amerced, and otherwise punished in an exemplary Manner (*m*). It seemeth, that anciently the Sheriff used to make his Profer in Person. But his personal Appearance was often dispensed with. In the 26th Year of K. *Edward* I, the Treasurer granted to *Gilbert de Knovill*, Sheriff of *Devon*, Leave to make his Profer by one of his Clerks. And *Richard de Brantescumbe* made the Profer for him (*n*). In the 31st Year of K. *Edward* I, the Treasurer sent a Letter to the Barons, desiring them to admit *Thomas de la Funtaigne* to do the Profer for the Sheriffs of *London* (*o*). In the first Year of K. *Edward* II, *Alexander de Bastonthwait*, Sheriff of *Cumberland*, being so occupied in the King's Business within his Bailywick, *viz*. in helping to keep the Peace in the Marches of *Scotland*, that he could not come to the Exchequer, to make his Profer in Person on the Morrow of the Close of *Easter*: the King by Privy Seal commands the Treasurer and Barons to let him make his Profer by Attorney for this Time (*p*). The same K. *Edward* II, (*Anno Regni* 12) commanded the Barons of the Exchequer by his Writ, to receive such Person as Monsieur *William de Beauchamp*,

---

(*m*) Norf. Quia Vicecomes, & alij Vicecomites Regis per Regnum puroffros suos ad Scaccarium ultimo per duas vices factos minus plene fecerint, in dampnum Regis non modicum, quod licet hactenus Rex dissimulavit, id tamen de cætero fieri sustinere non wlt, sicut nec debet; Præceptum est Vicecomiti, quod puroffrum suum quem facturus est in Crastino Clausi Paschæ proximo futuræ, habeat tunc ibidem plenarium & integrum, tam de firma quam de denarijs, quæ ei veniunt in summonitionibus Regis: alioquin taliter Rex ipsum amerciari faciet, quod ipse & hæredes sui suo perpetuo senient se inde esse gravatos. T. &c decimo quarto die Februarij anno quinto decimo.

Consimile Breve mandatum est Vicecomitibus Cumbriæ, Northumbriæ, Ebor., Linc. Not. & Derbiæ, Warr. & Leyc., Salop. & Staff., Hereford., Wigorn., Glouc., Oxon. & Berk., Norhamtoniæ, Bed. & Buck., Cant. & Hunt., Essexiæ & Hertford., Kanc. Surr. & Sussexiæ, Suhamtoniæ. *Hil. Brevia* 15. E. 1. *Rot*. 22. *a*.

(*n*) *Hil. Communia* 26 & 27. E. 1. *Rot*. 15. *a*.

(*o*) *Pas. Commun*. 31. E. 1. *Rot*. 11. *a*. *ex parte Remem. Reg*.

(*p*) Edward par la grace de Dieu &c, Au Treforer e as Barons de nostre Escheqer salutz. Pur ce qe noster cher e feal Monsieur Alisaundre de Bastunthwayt nostre Viscunte de Cumbreland est tant occupez en nos busoignes deinz sa ballie, entour la garde de nostre pees [en] celes parties, entendaunt a nos gardeyns en cele Marche, qil ne poet venir en propre persone a faire sun proffre devaunt vous a nostre Escheqer, a cest procheyn terme de la Cluse Pasqe: Vous mandoms, qe vous resceivez le proffre du dit Viscunte par sun attorne a ceste foiz, par lenchesun desudite. Done souz nostre Prive Seal a Wyndesore, la xij jour Daveril lan de nostre regne primer. *Pas. Brevia* 1. E. 2. *Rot*. 46. *a*.

Sheriff

Chap. XXIII.   *and* ACCOUNTANTS.   157

Sheriff of *Worcestershire*, should put in his Place, to make his Profer on the Morrow of St. *Michael*, and to forbear putting him in Default for not coming in Person; he being then in the King's Service (*q*). The like Writs issued on Behalf of several other Sheriffs (*r*).

Of the View of an Account: In the 15th Year of K. *Henry* II, *Geoffrey de Ver* entered upon his Account for the Honour of the *Constabularia*; and this (saith the Record) was a *View* only, *per verum dictum ipsius*, and not an Account; because *Geoffrey* had not yet got his Warrants (or Writs) of Discount or Allowance for the *Terræ datæ*, and other Things (*s*). In the 16th Year he made a View of his Account for the same Honour for the said 16th Year, by *William* his Clerk, upon the said *William*'s *Verumdictum*. But the Sums which he claimed were not actually allowed to him, because he had not as yet obtained his *Warantum Regis* (*t*). In the 21st Year of the same King, *Robert de Stutevill*, Sheriff of *Yorkshire*, made a View of his Account for certain Prises and Perquisites arising from the King's Demesnes in that County and otherwise, *per Verumdictum suum* (*u*). In the 8th Year of K. *Richard* I, the Sheriffs of *England* made the Views of their Accounts at the Exchequer in *Easter* Term; as appeareth by the Entries remaining in a Cedule annexed to the *Great Roll* of that Year (*w*). In the 7th Year of K. *John*, the several Sheriffs of *England* made the Views of their Accounts at the Exchequer in *Easter*

(*q*) *Mich. Commun.* 12. *E.* 2. *Rot.* 59. *a.*
(*r*) *Ib. Rot.* 59. *a & b.*
(*s*) Visus Compoti Galfridi de Ver de Honore Constabulariæ de hoc anno & de anno præterito, scil. de DC & quater xx & x l, secundum verum dictum ipsius Galfridi. *Mag. Rot.* 15. *H.* 2. *Rot.* 8. *a. in cedula.* *These Words are contained in a Cedule annext to the Roll; afterwards in the great Roll itself it is thus entered,* Honor Constabulariæ: De hoc Honore non reddidit idem Galfridus de Ver compotum, sed Visum tantum per verum dictum ipsius, quia non habuit Guarantum Regis de terris datis & alijs exitibus ejusdem Honoris. *Mag. Rot.* 15. *H.* 2. *Rot.* 8. *a.*
(*t*) Visus Compoti ejusdem Honoris [Constabulariæ] de hoc anno per Willelmum Clericum Galfridi de Ver, scilicet de CCC & xlv l per Verumdictum ejusdem Willelmi, — Et debet C & Lxxvj l & viij s & j d, De quibus C & xliij l & iiij s iiij d sunt in terris datis ejusdem Honoris, qui non computantur ei propter Warantum Regis quod nondum habuit. *Mag. Rot.* 16. *H.* 2. *in Ced. post Rot.* 9.

(*u*) Compotus ejusdem Vicecomitis [Roberti de Stuttevilla], de Prisis & Perquisitionibus tam de Dominijs Regis quam de Terris inimicorum Regis, per verum dictum suum. *Mag. Rot.* 21. *H.* 2. *Rot.* 11. *a. Everwichscira.*

(*w*) Compotus Vicecomitum Angliæ factus in Termino Paschæ anni octavi Regni Regis Ricardi. Cumberland: Willelmus filius Aldelini de firma de Cumberland; In Thesauro Lv l & ij d numero, Et Quietus est. Norhantesira: Simon de Pateshill de firma de Norhantesira, In thesauro Lxv l & vij s & iij d, Et Q. e. Essex & Hurtfordsira: W. Elyensis Episcopus, Robertus de Laweshell pro eo, de firma de Essex & Hurtfordsira; In thesauro CC & vij l & ix s & iiij d Bl; Et debet xj l & ij s & vij d. *And the like for other Counties. Mag. Rot.* 8. *R.* 1, *in prima Ced. ad Rot. ult.*

Term.

Term. Memorandums thereof are entered in a Cedule annexed to the Great Roll of the Pipe remaining in the Tower of *London* (*x*). In the 31ſt Year of K. *Henry* III, *William de Liſle*, Sheriff of *Northamtonſhire*, had a View of his Account made. Upon the View he owed *de claro*, xxxix *l* v *s* viij *d* ob.: he ſwore to the Marſhal for it: and had Day over (*y*). In the 36th Year of the ſame King, Views were made of ſeveral Sheriffs Accounts in *Eaſter* Term; to wit, of *Herefordſhire*, *Norfolk*, *Suffolk*, and others (*z*). In the 42d Year of that King, a View was made of the Account of *William Herun*, late Sheriff of *Northumberland*. He was charged with certain Arrerages and Profits of *Iters*; and after due Allowances had been made to him, he remained in *Debet*, DCCiiij *l* xviij *s* (*a*). In the 49th Year, a View was made of the Account of *Ralf Ruſſel*, late Sheriff of *Wiltſhire*. He owed *de claro*, Lxv *l* and odd. Whereof he was to pay at the Exchequer, or in the King's Wardrobe, xxx *l* at Midlent; and the Reſidue when he made up his Sum. He had Day given him, *viz.* the Quinzime of *Eaſter*, to make his Sum (*b*). In the 1ſt Year of K. *Edward* I, *Hugh de Penne* entered upon his Account for the Queen's Wardrobe, by the Teſtimony and Controll of *Alexander de Bradeham* the Queen's Chaplain (*c*): and this (ſaith the Record) was only a View,

(*x*) Viſus Compotorum Vicecomitum totius Angliæ de Termino Paſchæ anni regni Regis Johannis vij^{mi}: Gloweceſtreſcira Willelmus Mareſcallus Ricardus de Huſſeburne pro eo de firma Gloweceſtreſiræ; In theſauro, Et Quietus eſt. Norhumberland; Robertus filius Rogeri de firma de Norhumberland, In theſauro, Et Quietus eſt. *The like for ſome other Counties.* In Ced. annexa ad Rot. ult. Rotuli Pipæ 7. Joh. in Turro Londoniæ.

(*y*) Facto Viſu compoti Vicecomitis, Debet de claro xxxix l v s viij d ob., pro quibus affidavit Mareſcallo. Poſtea habet diem in quindena S. Trinitatis ad reddendum xxx l. Memor. 31. H. 3. Rot. 27. a. in imo. Northamt. Willelmus de Inſula, Sheriff.

(*z*) Viſus Vicecomitum Angliæ de Termino Paſchæ anno R. Regis xxxvj^{o}: Hereford; Henricus de Bradele de firma Comitatus, In theſauro liberavit, Et Quietus eſt. Norf. & Suff.; Robertus le Sauvage de firma Comitatuum In th. l, Et Q. e. *And four Sheriffs more.* In Cedul. ad Rot. 1. Magni Rot. 35. H. 3.

(*a*) Memorandum quod facto Viſu compoti Willelmi Herun quondam Vicecomitis Norhumbriæ de anno xl^{o} & xlj^{o}, debet de arreragijs ſuis, prout continetur in Magno Rotulo, DCCLij l xj s iij d; Et de ultimo Itinere Juſticiariorum in eodem Comitatu DCl, ſicut Clerici & executores ſui recognoverunt; Et allocatis allocandis, Debet DCCiij l xviij s. Memor. 42. H. 3. Rot. 13. a.

(*b*) Facto Viſu Compoti Radulphi Ruſſel de anno xlvij & tribus partibus anni xlviij, Debuit idem Radulphus de claro Lxv l xv s & j d. De quibus reddet ad Scaccarium vel in Garderoba Regis, ad Mediam Quadrageſimam, xxx l; Et reſiduum ſuper Summam ſuam. Et datus eſt ei dies & Radulpho de Aungers, ad faciendam Summam ſuam in Quindena Paſchæ. Memor. 49. H. 3. Rot. 20. a. poſt Compot. Vic. Wilteſ.

(*c*) Compotus Hugonis de Penna de Garderoba Reginæ, a feſto Apoſtolorum Symonis & Judæ incipiente anno Liiij^{o}, uſq; ad feſtum S. Edmundi Confeſſoris anno Lvij, antequam Rex moreretur, ſcilicet de tribus annis integris & viginti diebus, per teſtimonium

View, and not an Account; becaufe the Accountant had not his proper Vouchers to produce (*d*). In the 18th Year of K. *Edward* I, a View was made of the Debts of *Thomas de Pin*, late Sheriff of *Devonſhire*. He was in *Debet*, MCCxj *l* and odd. There were put in View to him ſeven hundred fourſcore and four Pounds and a Mark, which were paid into the Exchequer by four Dividend Tallies, ten Pounds for Carriage of the Money ariſing by the Diſme of the Clergy; and other Sums (*e*). In the 5th Year of K. *Edward* II, upon the Account rendered at the Exchequer, of the Triennial Diſme impoſed by the Pope on the Clergy, a *View* was made in this Manner: The *Onus* was 62,491 *l* 10 *s*: whereof there was anſwered by Counter-tallies 38,992 *l* 6 *s*; put in View to the Accountants 10,451 *l* 13 *d*; delivered to *William Teſta* in Part of the *Fourth* reſerved to the Pope —— *&c (f)*. In the 15th Year of the ſame King, in *Eaſter* Term, upon a View made of the Account of *Humphrey de Baſſingburn*, Sheriff of *Northamtonſhire*, for the firſt half of this fifteenth Year, he charged himſelf with xlvj *s* xj *d*, the Remanent of the Blank Ferm of the County, which is valued by Tale after the *Terræ datæ* in the Great Roll; and with L Marks the Ferm of the *Proficuum* of the County; but he doth not charge himſelf with the Ferms of Serjanties and other ſmall Ferms, becauſe, he ſaith, they are to be levied at *Michael-maſs* (*g*). In *Eaſter* Term, in the ſame 15th Year, upon a View made of the Account of *John de Tychebourne*, late Sheriff of *Wiltſhire*, for the firſt half of this Year, he chargeth himſelf with Lxv *l* v *s* vij *d* q. for all the Blank Ferms of the County, and for the Ferm for the

nium & contrarotulum Alexandri de Bradeham Capellani ejuſdem Reginæ. *Mag. Rot.* 57. *H.* 3. *Rot.* 1. *m.* 1. *a.*

(*d*) Omnia ſuperius ſcripta de Garderoba Reginæ ad inſtanciam & petitionem ipſius Reginæ facta ſunt: Unde habentur pro Viſu Compoti & non pro Compoto: Quia licet ſint de tempore Regis, tamen viſus prædictus ſcribitur in ſeptimana proxima ante feſtum B. Petri ad Vincula, anno primo Regis Edwardi filij prædicti Regis, ſine brevi ſuo vel aliquo alio Waranto. *Ib. Rot.* 1. *m.* 2. *b.*

(*e*) Facto Viſu de debitis Thomæ de Pin quondam Vicecomitis Devoniæ, Debet MCCxj l xij s ob. q. De quibus ponuntur ei in viſu DCC quater xx iiij l j marca, quas ſolvit ad Scaccarium per quatuor dividendas, quæ remanent in cuſtodia Magiſtri Petri de Gildeford Clerici Rememoratoris in quadam burſa ſub ſigillo Hawiſæ quæ fuit uxor dicti Thomæ, Et x l pro cariagio denariorum proveniencium de Decima Clericorum in Epiſcopatu Exonienſi &c. *Mich. Commun.* 18. *E.* 1. *Rot.* 1. *a. in bund.* 17 & 18. *E.* 1. *parte* 1.

(*f*) *Mich. Stat. & Viſus Comp.* 5. *E.* 2. *Rot.* — *a. tit.* Anglia, Wallia.

(*g*) Norhamton. Facto Viſu Compoti Humfridi de Baſſingburn Vicecomitis de primo dimidio hoc anno xv°, onerat ſe de xlvj s xj d de remanente firmæ Comitatus Bl. poſt terras datas extenſæ numero; Et de L marcis de firma pro proficua de eodem dimidio anno; Et non onerat ſe de minutis firmis ſerjantiarum & alijs minutis firmis, quia ſunt levabiles ad feſtum S. Michaelis, ut idem Vicecomes dicit ——— ——— . *Paſ. Stat. & Viſ.* 15. *E.* 2. *Rot.* 99. *a.*

Proficuum

Proficuum, deducting the yearly Allowances; but he doth not charge himself with any minute Ferms, because they are not leviable till *Michaelmass*; he also chargeth himself with other Money levied by virtue of the Summonce: The Sum of the *Onus* or Charge put together is, Cxv *l* xviij *s* vij *d* ob.; whereof there were respited to him *such and such* Sums, &c (*h*).

Of the Sum: In the 22d Year of K. *Henry* III, the Sheriff of *Sussex* had Day given him to cast his Sum, and pay his Arrerages (*i*). In the 41st Year of K. *Henry* III, the Sheriff of *Devonshire* had Day given him to make his Sum; which he did make accordingly (*k*). In the 52d Year of the same King, upon making the Sum of *John de Oketon*, Sheriff of *York*, he was in *Debet* Lxxviij *l* iiij *s* j *d*, for the *Firma pro Proficuo*, and the *Remanens Firmæ* of his County, which he could not levy because of the Civil Wars, &c (*l*). In the 7th Year of K. *Edward* I, upon making the Sum of *William le Moyne*, Sheriff of the Counties of *Cambridge* and *Huntendon*, he was in *Debet* Cxlj *l* and odd. Against which there was put to him in View xxvij *s*, for carrying two Provers, one to *Bedford*, the other to *Newgate*; and xlvij *l* and odd, for so much set off for certain Liberties which were granted by K. *Henry* III, in the 43d Year of his Reign (*m*). In the same 7th Year, *Hugh de Stapelford*, Sheriff of *Bedfordshire*, accounted. His Sum was made. He had a Surplusage. He was charged to account for the King's Escheats. He did account for them. His Writs [for Allowances] and other his Demands were put in View.

(*h*) Wyltes. Facto Visu Compoti Johannis de Tycheburne Vicecomitis de primo dimidio hoc anno xv°, onerat se de Lxv l v s vij d q;, de omnimodis firmis Comitatus Bl., & firma pro proficuo de eodem dimidio anno, deductis allocationibus annalibus; set non onerat se de aliquibus minutis firmis, quia sunt levabiles ad festum S. Michaelis ut dicit [*and not sooner*]; Item onerat se de L l xiij s q; levatis de debitis plurium per summonitionem. Summa Oneris conjuncta, Cxv l xviij s vij d ob.; De quibus respectuantur ei ——— ———. *Pas. Stat. & Vis.* 15. *E.* 2. *Rot.* 99. *b.*

(*i*) Vicecomes habet diem ad Summam suam jactandam, & arreragia sua reddenda, in crastino Purificationis B. Mariæ. *Memor.* 22. *H.* 3. *Rot.* 18. *a. Sudsex.*

(*k*) Vicecomes haber diem ad festum S. Jacobi, ad faciendam Summam suam. Postea venit & fecit Summam. *Memor.* 41. *H.* 3. *Rot.* 28. *a. Devonia.*

(*l*) Facta summa Johannis de Oketon Vicecomitis, debet idem J. Lxxviij l iiij s j d, de firma pro proficuo, & remanente firmæ Comitatus quos non potuit levare propter turbationem regni, & de quibus dedit quædam stipendia quibusdam militibus ad conservationem pacis, per præceptum Domini Edwardi filij Regis, ut dicit. *Memor.* 52. *H.* 3. *Rot.* 19. *a. Item Ebor.*

(*m*) Cantabrigia & Hunt. Facta summa Vicecomitis, Debet Cxlj l ix s iij d ob. De quibus ponuntur ei in Visu pro cariagio duorum probatorum, videlicet unius usq; Bedefordiam, & unius usque Neugate, xxvij s; Et xlvij l xij s ij d. ob. per breve Regis & Inquisitionem inde factam, per idem breve, pro libertatibus concessis diversis per Regem H. anno xliij° ejusdem Regis H. *Præcepta super Compot. Willelmi le Moyne Vicecom. in Memor.* 7. *E.* 1. *Rot.* 20. *b.*

There-

Chap. XXIII.   *and* ACCOUNTANTS.

Thereupon he was in *Debet* xlv *s* x *d*. He paid it, and was quit (*n*). In the 13th and 14th Year of the same King, another Sheriff had his Sum made up. Upon it, he owed CLvj *l* xv *d* ob.; for which he was committed Prisoner to the Flete. Afterwards there was xx *l*. which he had paid by Dividend Tally, put to him in View. Then he owed Cxxxvj *l* xv *d* ob.; for which he was committed to the Marshal. Afterwards he had Day given him to pay it at his Profer; so that his Profer was not to be lessened by it (*o*). In the 18th and 19th Years of the same King, the Community of the City of *London* accounted [for the Citizens]. Upon making their Sum, they were indebted thirteen thousand two hundred and five Pounds three Pence Halfpenny. From which, deducting twenty thousand Marks, they were indebted Dxxxviij *l* vj *s* xj *d* ob. And because all the Aldermen of the said City were not present, Day was given them, to wit, the Octaves of St. *Michael*, to answer for the said Debts (*p*). On the Morrow of St. *Michael*, in the 9th Year of K. *Edward* II, *Stephen de Abyndon* and *Hamon de Chigwell*, Sheriffs of *London* and *Middlesex*, came to account. Upon their Sum, they were indebted xij *l* xiij *s* ij *d*. There was put to them in View xxix *s* ij *d*, which they had paid out of the Ferm of their City to *Peter Fabre* of *Montpelier*, Keeper of the King's Lion in the Tower of *London*, and for Maintenance of the King's Leopard there; and then they were indebted iij *d* (*q*). It is to be

understood,

(*n*) Facta summa, Vicecomes habet superplusagium. Sed debet computare de eschaetis Regis. Postea computavit de eisdem eschaetis. Et positis ei in Visu brevibus & calumpnijs suis, debet xlv s x d. Quos postea solvit. Et Quietus est. *Præcepta facta super compotum Hugonis de Stapelford Vic. Bed. 7. E. 1. Rot. 22. b.*

(*o*) Facta Summa, Vicecomes debet CLvj l xv d ob.; pro quibus liberatur prisonæ de Flete. Postea ponuntur ei in Visu xx l per quandam talliam dividendam, Et debet Cxxxvj l xv d ob.; Pro quibus liberatur Marescallo. Postea habet diem in crastino Clausi Paschæ super puroffrum suum, Ita quod prædicti denarij non cadant in puroffro suo prædicto. *In bund. Memor. 13 & 14. E. 1. Rot. 30. a.*

(*p*) De Die dato Communitati Londoniæ. Facta summa debitorum contingencium Communitatem Londoniæ, debent tredecim mille CCv libras iij d obolum. De quibus, subtractis viginti mille marcis, Debent Dxxxviij l vj s xj d ob. Et quia omnes Aldermanni ejusdem Civitatis non fuerunt ibi præsentes, datus est eis dies in octabis S. Michaelis, ad respondendum de eisdem debitis. *Trin. Communia 18 & 19. E. 1. Rot. 23. a. in bundello 17 & 18. E. 1. parte 1.*

(*q*) Londoniæ Middelsexa. Præcepta facta super Compotum Stephani de Abyndon & Hamonis de Chigewell nuper Vicecomitum Londoniæ & Middelsexæ, computantium hic modo in crastino S. Michaelis de toto anno octavo.

Facta summa prædictorum Stephani & Hamonis de dicto anno octavo, debent xij l xiij s ij d. De quibus ponuntur in Visu xxix s ij d, quos de firma Civitatis prædictæ habere fecerunt Petro Fabre de Monte Pessulano Custodi Leonis Regis in Turri Londoniæ existentis, a festo Paschæ videlicet septimo die Aprilis anno septimo, *and for*

Maintenance

understood, that the Sheriff's Sum was made at the End of his Account. No Sheriff (faith the Record cited hereunder) rendering his Account here, ought to offer at getting an Allowance of his Tallies, or to defire that the Sum of his Account, which is the End of his Account, may be made up, until he hath fully accounted for all the Summonces of the Exchequer relating to his County, and for all his Receipts. And fome Accountants were imprifoned for acting againft this Rule (*r*).

There is another Way of confidering the Manner or Form of a Sheriff's Account: and that is, as the Account ftands in the *Great Roll*. In which refpect it confifted (when he accounted *ut Firmarius*) of feveral Parts; namely, the *Corpus Comitatus*; the *Remanens Firmæ*, after the *Terræ datæ*; the *Crementum*, if there was any fuch; the *Proficuum* or *Firma de Proficuo*; the Iffues of Efcheats and Purpreftures; Fines, Oblatas, Amerciaments of divers Sorts; Efcuages, Aids, Tallages, and cafual Profits; Ferms or Iffues of Towns, Burghs, Gilds, or Lands which were within the Sheriff's Charge; and the like. The *Corpus Comitatus* confifted of feveral Manors and Lands, which being letten or committed together unto the Sheriff, made the Fund out of which the annual Ferm to the Crown arofe. Thofe Manors and Lands were fuch as lay within the Sheriff's County. It was fo in general. But (I cannot tell by what Accident) there were anciently certain Manors lying in *Cornwall*, which belonged to the Ferm of *Devonfhire*. For Example: In the fifth Year of K. *Henry* II (*s*), in the 18th Year of the fame King (*t*), in the 7th Year of King *Richard* I (*u*), and in the tenth Year of K. *Edward* I (*w*). In Procefs of Time, the Kings charged the Manors or Lands, which made up the

Maintenance of the King's Leopard in the faid Tower and their Keepers. Et debent iij d. Mich. Præcepta 9. *E.* 2. *Rot.* 148.

(*r*) — Et quia nullus Vicecomes reddens hic compotum, fe ad allocationem Talliarum fuarum optinendam debeat proferre, nec Summam Compoti, quæ eft Finis Compoti, fieri petere, quoufq; percomputaverit de omnibus Summonitionibus Scaccarij Comitatum fuum contingentibus, & omnibus receptis fuis; maxime cum forma Sacramenti prædicti, & omnis juris confonantia, illud exigit & requirit———. *Certain Accountants here mentioned were adjudged to be committed to Prifon for acting againft this Rule*. Paf. Commun. 26. *E.* 1. *Rot.* 71. *a.* in bund. 25 & 26. *E.* 1.

(*s*) Et in Terris datis Comiti Reginaldo C & xxij l & x s Bl. de Manerijs quæ pertinent ad firmam de Devenefcira. Mag. Rot. 5. *H.* 2. Rot. 6. *a. Devenefc.*

(*t*) Mag. Rot. 18. *H.* 2. Rot. 7. *b. Devenefcira.*

(*u*) Mag. Rot. 7. Ric. 1. Rot. 10. *a.*

(*w*) Devonia. Thomas del Pyn r c de CCCxij l & vij s Bl., de firma Comitatus; In Thefauro [nichil]; Et in Manerijs Cornubiæ quæ pertinent ad firmam Comitatus, Cxxij l & x s Bl.; De quibus Vicecomes Cornubiæ refpondere confuevit, dum Comitatus fuit in manu Regis; *and in other Deductions*. Mag. Rot. 10. *E.* 1. Devonia, m. 1. *a.*

Corpus

Corpus Comitatus, with certain Payments of Alms and Liveries, called *Eleemosynæ* and *Liberationes constitutæ*; and the Kings also granted away Part of the said Lands. Hence came the Distinction of the *Terræ datæ*. For when several of the Lands, out of which the Sheriff's Ferm should arise, were granted away, it was fit the Sheriff should have Allowance or Deduction, for so much as the *Terræ datæ* amounted to or bore in the *Corpus Comitatus*. Accordingly, it was the Usage to make such Deduction; and the Sum to be answered for by the Sheriff after that Deduction, was called *Remanens Firmæ post Terras datas*. For Example: In the 9th Year of K. Henry III, *William Earl of Warenne* accounted as Sheriff of *Surrey*. After a Deduction had been made for the *Terræ datæ*, his Sum or Debt was fourscore and five Pounds seventeen Shillings and six Pence Blank. This Sum was extended at fourscore and ten Pounds three Shillings and four Pence by Tale; and the said extended Sum is called there in the great Roll, the *Remanens Firmæ* or *Firmarum* (x). In the second Year of King Henry II, *Henry de Oilli* accounted for the Ferm of *Oxfordshire*. He paid Part of it into the *Receipt*; and had Allowance or Deduction of other Part, for constituted Alms, and Liveries or Pensions; and likewise for the *Terræ datæ*; to wit, to the Earl of *Flanders* Lxxvj *l* Blank in *Bentun*, with C s for *Wich*; to Hugh de Plugenoi xlij *l* x s Blank in *Hedendon*; to the Abbess of *Godstowe* C s Blank in *Hedendon*; to Henry de Oxinefort L s Blank in the same Town; to Richard de Luci xx *l* by Tale in *Blochesham*, &c. The Sum of the *Terræ datæ* was Cxxvj *l* Blank, and Lxxvij *l* viij *s* by Tale (y). The Lands thus granted away, were sometimes said to be *Missæ extra Comitatum*, put out of the County; that is, separated from the Sheriff's *Corpus Comitatus*; as in the Case of *Richard de Canvill*, Sheriff of *Berkshire* (z). Besides the *Terræ datæ*, there were several constant and settled Payments wont to be made by the Sheriff out of his *Corpus Comitatus*. Such were the

(x) Summa totius debiti, quaterviginti & v l & xvij s & vj d Bl., qui sunt ei extensi ad quaterviginti & x l & iij s & iiij d numero. De quibus respond[et] infra. *This was the Sum* post terras datas. *A little lower in the Roll, it follows thus,* —— De quibus, quaterviginti & x l & iij s & iiij d allocantur ei supra, in remanente firmarum suarum. *Mag. Rot.* 9. *H.* 3. *Rot.* 3. *a. m.* 1. *Surreia*.

(y) Henricus de Oilli r c de firma Oxinefortscira; In thesauro xxv l & xij d Bl.; *In Alms, Liveries and* Donis *so much*; Et in Terris datis: Comiti Flandriæ Lxxvj l Bl. in Bentum cum C s de Wich.; Et Hugoni de Plugenoi xlij l & x s Bl. in Hedendun; Et Abbatissæ de Godeftou C s Bl. in eadem villa; Et Henrico de Oxinefort L s Bl. in eadem villa; Et Ricardo de Luci xx l numero in Blochesham, &c. Summa Terrarum datarum, C & xxvj l Bl., Et Lxxvij l & viij s numero. *Mag. Rot.* 2. *H.* 2. *Rot.* 7. *a*.

(z) *Paul. infra, ad ann.* 2. *H.* 2.

Eleemosynæ constitutæ, the *Liberationes constitutæ* (as hath been said above) and the *Tertius denarius Comitatus*, &c. There were also some casual Payments: such as occasional Disbursements or Provisions of various Sorts, Maintenance of Approvers, and the like. As to the *Eleemosynæ* and *Liberationes constitutæ*, and as to the said occasional Disbursements, many Examples of all these may be seen in these Volumes. Omitting them, I will here only add a few Instances concerning the *Tertius denarius*, and the *Terræ datæ*. Earl *Patrick*, who was both Earl and Sheriff of *Wiltshire*, had xxij *l* xvj *s* vij *d* allowed to him upon his Account for the *Tertius denarius Comitatus* (*a*). *Richard* Earl of *Devon* had xviij *l* vj *s* and viij *d* by Tale paid to him for the *Tertius denarius*, by *William de Boterells*, Sheriff of *Devonshire* (*b*). Earl *Geoffrey* [*de Mandevill*] had xl *l* x *s* x *d*, and the Earl of *Clare* xxxiij *l* xx *d*, paid to them respectively for the third Penny of the Counties of *Essex* and *Hertford*, by *Maurice de Tiretai*, Sheriff of those Counties (*c*). Earl *William de Mandevill* had xx *l* v *s* v *d*, and the Earl of *Clare* xvj *l* x *s* x *d*, paid to them respectively for the third Penny of the Counties of *Essex* and *Hertford* for one half Year, by *Nicolas le Clerk*, Sheriff of those Counties (*d*). In another Year the said Earls of *Essex* and of *Clare* had their respective third Penny paid to them by the Sheriff of the same Counties (*e*). *Geoffrey Fitz-Pier*, Earl of *Essex*, had likewise his third Penny of that County paid him by the Sheriff (*f*): and the same Earl *Geoffrey* again (*g*): and *William*

(*a*) Wiltescira. Comes Patricius r c de firma de Wiltescira. —— Et Comiti Patricio de tercio denario Comitatus xxij l & xvj s & vij d. *Mag. Rot.* 5. *H.* 2. *Rot.* 6. *a.*

(*b*) Et Comiti Ricardo de Tertio denario Comitatus xviij l & vj s & viij d Numero. *Mag. Rot.* 5. *H.* 2. *Rot.* 6. *a. Devenescira.* Willelmus de Boterellis *Sheriff.*

(*c*) Et Comiti Gaufrido xl l & x s & x d in Tertio denario Comitatus de Essexa; Et Comiti de Clara xxxiij l & xx d in Tertio denario Comitatus de Hurtfort. *Mag. Rot.* 6. *H.* 2. *Rot.* 2. *a. Essexa & Hurtfortscira.* Mauricius de Tiretai *Sheriff.*

(*d*) Nicholaus Clericus r c de Veteri firma de Essexa & de Hurtfordscira: Et idem de Nova firma de dimidio anno —: *Deducted or allowed to the Sheriff out of his Ferm, viz.* In Decimis & in Liberationibus constitutis per duos Comitatus xviij l & ix s & iiij d de dimidio anno; Et Comiti Willelmo xx l & v s & v d in Tertio denario Comitatus; Et Comiti de Clara xvj l & x s & x d de Tertio denario Comitatus de Hurtfordscira. *Mag. Rot.* 15. *H.* 2. *Rot.* 9. *a.*

(*e*) Et Comiti Willelmo de Mandevilla xl l & x s & x d, de Tertio denario Comitatus de Essexa; Et Comiti de Clara xxxiij l & xx d, de Tertio denario Comitatus de Hurtfordscira. *Mag. Rot.* 31. *H.* 2. *Rot.* 2. *a. m.* 1. *Essex & Hurtf.*

(*f*) Et Galfrido filio Petri xl l & x s & x d in Tertio denario Comitatus. *Mag. Rot.* 5. *R.* 1. *Rot.* 1. *a. Essexa & Hurtfordscira.*

(*g*) Et Galfrido filio Petri xx l & v s & v d in Tertio denario Comitatus de Essexa. *Mag. Rot.* 9. *R.* 1. *Rot.* 5. *a. Essex & Hertf.* Hugo de Nevill, Unfridus de Barenton pro eo, Vicecomes de dimidio anno.

de

Chap. XXIII.   *and* ACCOUNTANTS.

de Vernun, Earl of *Devon*, in like Manner (*h*). So *Walter de Shelfhangre*, Sheriff of *Norfolk*, had Allowance made to him upon his Account, for the third Penny of that County payable to Earl *Roger le Bygot* (*i*). And *Isabell*, Sister and Heir of *Baldwin del Isle*, late Earl of *Devon*, had xviij *l* and half a Mark paid to her for [the Arrear of] the yearly Fee [or third Penny] of that County (*k*). If the *Tertius denarius* was withheld, or not duly paid by the Sheriff, the Earl to whom it was due might have a Writ, ordering Payment of it. K. *Henry* III, by his Writ, commanded the Barons of the Exchequer to cause the *third Penny* of the County of *Surrey* to be paid to *John de Warenne*, in like Manner as his Father and other Ancestors used to receive it (*l*). K. *Edward* I, by his Writ, commanded the Sheriff of *Lincolnshire* to pay to *Henry de Lacy*, Earl of *Lincoln*, the third Penny of that County, as the said Earl and his Ancestors were wont to receive the same (*m*). And the Treasurer and Barons awarded a Writ to the Sheriff of *Devonshire*, for paying the yearly Fee of that County to *Hugh de Courtney* (*n*).

The principal Part of the Sheriff's Ferm arose out of the *Corpus Comitatus*. The *Corpus Comitatus* consisted of several assised Lands or Rents, which, when put together, made the total Sum that was called

(*h*) Et Willelmo de Vernun Comiti xviij l & vj s & viij d de Tertio denario Comitatus. *Mag. Rot.* 5. *J. Rot.* 6. *a. Devenescira.*

(*i*) Manucaptio Walteri de Shelfhangre Vicecomitis Norfolciæ. Nicholaus de Wintonia Hostiarius de Scaccario manucepit, quod idem Walterus reddet Rogero le Bygot Comiti Norfolciæ L marcas sterlingorum ad festum Purificationis B. Mariæ proximo futurum. Quæ quidem L marcæ ei aretro sunt de Tercio denario Comitatus prædicti, & quæ allocatæ fuerunt eidem Vicecomiti in Compoto suo reddito ad Scaccarium in crastino S. Leonardi, & eas nondum solvit. *Mich. Commun.* 4 & 5. *E.* 1. *Rot.* 2. *b.*

(*k*) Et Isabellæ sorori & hæredi Baldewyni de Insula quondam Comitis Devoniæ, de annuo feodo suo ejusdem Comitatus, xviij l & dimidia marca. *Mag. Rot.* 13. *E.* 1. *Devon. m.* 1. *a.*

(*l*) Rex mandat Baronibus, quod faciant habere Johanni de Warenna tercium denarium provenientem de exitibus Comitatus Surriæ, sicut Willelmus de Warenna quondam Comes Surriæ pater ipsius Johannis cujus hæres ipse est, & alij antecessores sui illum denarium percipere consueverunt, tanquam pertinentem ad Comitatum suum Surriæ. *Memor.* 40. *H.* 3. *Rot.* 20. *a.*

(*m*) Lincolnia. Præceptum est Vicecomiti, quod habere faciat Henrico de Lacy Comiti Lincolniæ Tercium denarium Comitatus prædicti de tempore suo, sicut idem Comes & antecessores sui Comites Lincolniæ temporibus retroactis percipere consueverunt T. J. de Drokenesford Tenente locum Thesaurarij xxiiij die octobris anno xxv°. *Mich. Communia* 25 & 26. *E.* 1. *Rot.* 24. *a.*

(*n*) Petitio Hugonis de Courteney pro Annuo feodo suo Comitatus Devoniæ. *The Petition was allowed.* Et hijs compertis, Thesaurarius & Barones concordarunt, quod mandetur Vicecomiti Devoniæ, quod ipse præfato Hugoni filio Hugonis, de annuo feodo prædicto, a prædicto xx die Junij anno xxv, tanquam hæredi prædictæ Isabellæ, satisfieri faciat. *Trin. Commun.* 26. *E.* 1. *Rot.* 83. *a. in lund.* 25 & 26. *E.* 1.

by that Name. And they had a Way to compute the Value of the several Things that made up the *Corpus Comitatus,* whensoever Part thereof was granted away, and when thereupon a Deduction of so much came to be made out of the Sheriff's Ferm. In making this Valuation, they used to say, such a Manor or Land *portat in Corpore Comitatus* so much. Thus the Manor of *Hedindon* bore or amounted to L *l.* in the *Corpus Comitatus.* The L *l.* was divided thus. To the Abbess of *Godstowe* C *s.* to *Geoffrey le Flechier* L *s.* and to *Thomas Basset* xlij *l.* x *s.* (*o*). The Sheriff of *Somerset* and *Dorset* is commanded to enquire by Oath of lawful Men, how much the Town of *Brideport* beareth in the *Corpus Comitatus* at the Exchequer, and how much it used to bear in the Time of the King's Predecessors (*p*). And in another Case, it was judged upon Computation, that xv *l.* in *Gaynz* and xl *s.* in the foreign Hundred of *Rading* ought not to be allowed to the Sheriff of *Berkshire,* because he had, without them, enough in assised Lands to make up the full Sum of his *Corpus Comitatus,* with v *s.* over and above (*q*). If the King granted to any Man a Manor, Lands, or other Profits, which were Part of the *Corpus Comitatus,* or of the settled *Proficuum* of the County, the Sheriff was wont to have upon his Account an Allowance or Discount *de tanto.* *Richard de Canvill* had a Deduction made to him out of the Ferm of *Berkshire* for the *Terræ datæ,* the Lands granted away or put out of the *Corpus Comitatus,* to the Value of one hundred fourscore and sixteen Pounds Blank, and two hundred and twenty-six Pounds and a Mark by Tale (*r*). The Manor of *Writele* was Part of the *Corpus Comitatus* of *Essex.* The King granted some Franchises to *John Fitz*

(*o*) Manerium enim de Hedindon portat in Corpore Comitatus L 1; quæ sunt sic partitæ, Abbatissæ de Godestowe C sol., Galfrido Flechario L sol., Thomæ Basset xlij l & x s ; Summa, L l. *Memor.* 11. *H.* 3. *Rot.* 8. *b. Oxon.*

(*p*) Eidem [sc. Vicecomiti Sumersetæ & Dorsetæ]; Præcipimus tibi quod diligenter inquiras per liberos & legales homines &c, quid & quantum villa de Brideport portat in Corpore Comitatus tui ad Scaccarium nostrum, & quantum portare solebat in eodem Corpore temporibus prædecessorum nostrorum Regum Angliæ, & inquisitionem &c in crastino Purificationis &c. Et habeas ibi &c. T. J. vij die Decembris anno r n xiiij. *Mich. Commun.* 14. *H.* 3. *Rot.* 3. *a.*

(*q*) Satis probatum est, quod xv l in Gaynz & xl s in Forinseco hundredo de Rading non debent allocari Vicecomiti ; quia sine illis habet Vicecomes in terris assisis unde plene respondeat ad summam Corporis Comitatus, & v solidos plus. *Memor.* 11. *H.* 3. *Rot.* 10. *b. Berksire.*

(*r*) Ricardus de Chanvill r c de firma de Berchescira. In Thesauro xxiij l & xij d Bl. Et in terris missis extra Comitatum ; Ricardo de Luci, Brai, pro Lx l. Bl., De quibus idem Ricardus debet redere compotum ; Et eidem, Cocham, pro Lx l, de Dono Regis Bl. ; *And other Lands.* Summa terrarum datarum, Bl. C & quater xx & xvj l, Et CC & xxxvj l & xiij s & iiij d numero. *Mag. Rot.* 2. *H.* 2. *Rot.* 7. *a.*

William

Chap. XXIII. *and* ACCOUNTANTS. 167

William and *Walter de Hadfeld*; by which Means the said Manor decreased in its yearly Value. By Oath of twelve Knights of the County, and twelve Men of the Town of *Writele*, that Decrement was valued at vj *l.* vj *s.* v *d.* yearly. And the Sheriff of *Essex*, amongst the *Terræ dat*æ, was allowed after that Proportion upon his Account (*s*). When the King had granted to *Ralf Teisun* Quitance of Sheriff's Aids, Allowance or Discount was made to *Reginald de Cornhull*, Sheriff of *Kent*, of xv *s.* which were wont to be raised upon the Lands of *Ralf* for Sheriff's Aid; and the like Allowance was made for Quitance of Sheriff's Aid granted to the Earl of *Leicester* (*t*). K. *Henry* III. granted the Hundred of *Sumerton* to *Alienor*; Prince *Edward*'s Consort, during her Life. And therefore commanded the Barons, that if they found the said Hundred was *de Corpore Comitatus*, then they should allow the Ferm and Rent of it to the Sheriff of the County upon his Account, as of Right ought to be done (*u*). But if Lands were reputed to be Part of the *Corpus Comitatus*, and were not really so, the Sheriff was to have no Deduction or Allowance for such Lands (*w*). Or if Lands which had for a time been taken away or severed from the *Corpus Comitatus*, reverted to the Crown, then the Ferm or Profits of them were to be accounted for by the Sheriff, or else by the Escheatour or *Custos* (*x*). The Manor of *Bensenton* in *Oxfordshire* (which had been Part of the *Corpus Comitatus*) was extended or valued at C *l.* at the Time when it was granted out to *Robert de Harecurt*. And whereas that Extent was more by xlij *l.* xij *s. per Annum*

(*s*) Et in pejoramento Manerij de Writele; pro Libertate quam Dominus Rex concessit terræ Johannis filij Willelmi & Walteri de Hadfeld, xij l & xij s & x d de ij annis, per sacramentum xij Militum Comitatus & xij hominum ejusdem Villæ. *Mag. Rot.* 4. *R.* 1. *Rot.* 1. *a. Essex & Hurtf.*

(*t*) Et in quietantijs terrarum Radulfi Teisun de Auxilijs Vicecomitis xv s hoc anno, per breve Regis, Et in quietantia terrarum Comitis Leircestriæ iij s hoc anno, per idem breve. *Mag. Rot.* 4. *J. Rot.* 15. *b. Kent.*

(*u*) Baronibus pro Alenora Consorte Edwardi filij Regis. Cum nuper Rex concesserit eidem Alienoræ Hundredum de Sumerton cum firma, redditibus, exitibus, & omnibus alijs pertinentijs suis, Habendum ad sustentationem suam quoadvixerit, de gratia Regis speciali: Rex mandat, quod si eis constiterit quod Hundredum prædictum sit de Corpore Comitatus Sumersetæ ut de Corona, & tunc Vicecomiti nostro Sumersetæ firmam & redditum Hundredi prædicti in Compoto suo ad Scaccarium allocent, sicut de jure fuerit faciendum. T. &c. Breve e in f. M. *Mich. Commun.* 52, *incip.* 53. *H.* 3. *Rot.* 2. *a.*

(*w*) Probatum est quod Manerium de Derlinton, quod valet per annum x l, non debet allocari Vicecomiti in Corpore Comitatus; quia non est de Corpore Comitatus. *Memor.* 11. *H.* 3. *Rot.* 8. *a.*

(*x*) . . . . [debet] . . . de x libratis terræ, quas Abbas de S. Johanne aliquando tenuit in Derteford, Wylwyth, & Modingham, de Corpore Comitatus, nunc rejunctis Coronæ, sicut continetur in Memorandis anni xij. *Mag. Rot.* 18. *E.* 1. *Kancia. m.* 1. *a.*

than the Sum (viz. Lvij *l.* viij *s.*) which was wont to be allowed to the Sheriff in the *Corpus Comitatus* whilst the Manor was in the said *Robert*'s Hands: When the Manor reverted to the Crown, the Sheriff of *Oxfordshire* was charged for it upon his Account at the Rate of the said Extent (*y*). And K. *Henry* III. granted to *Walter* Bishop of *Worcester* Cognisance of Pleas *de vetito namio,* with the Profits arising from thence, which had been formerly Part of the *Proficuum Comitatus,* whereby the said *Proficuum* was lowered in Value iiij *l.* yearly. So the King by his Writ commanded the Barons to allow iiij *l.* yearly to the Sheriff of *Worcestershire* in his Ferm in respect to that Deduction (*z*). The Sheriff of *Essex* and *Hertfordshire* was discharged of the *Proficuum* of his Counties; because the *Res Assisæ*, Pleas, and Perquisites of the Counties were not sufficient to make up the Value of the *Corpus Comitatuum* (*a*).

There were in ancient Time two Ways of committing a County to the Sheriff, namely, either at Ferm or in Custody. This Difference in committing the County made a Difference in some Particulars in the Sheriff's Account. The Sheriff that was Fermer was charged absolutely with the Ferm of his County, and with the *Crementum,* if there was any, and if he accepted the County upon those Terms; and with a Ferm for the *Proficuum* of the County. But the Sheriff that was *Custos* was not absolutely charged to answer in the same Manner; for he was but a kind of a *Proficuarius,* or Bailiff. *John Bucuinte* had the Sherivalty of *London* and *Middlesex* committed to him upon this Condition, that he should have all those Sums allowed to him upon his Account at the Exchequer, which were deducted out of the Profits of the Counties by virtue of the King's Charters of Quitance made to

---

(*y*) Idem Vicecomes [Tomas Basset, Robertus de Aumari pro eo] debet C & xlix l & ij s de extensione Manerij de Bensenton, quod fuit extensum ad C l quando liberatum fuit Roberto de Harecurt, quæ Extensio est xlij l & xij s per annum ultra Lvij l & viijs, quæ solebant locari in Corpore Comitatus Vicecomiti quando idem Robertus habuit Manerium. *Mag. Rot.* 9. *J. Rot.* 5. *a. Oxenefordscira.*

(*z*) Rex mandat Baronibus, quod allocent, singulis annis Willelmo de Bello Campo Vicecomiti Wygorniæ, in firma sua ejusdem Comitatus, iiij l, quæ ei decidunt per annum de proficuo dicti Comitatus, occasione concessionis quam Rex fecit Waltero Wygornensi Episcopo de placito vetiti namij, cum proficuo de eodem placito proveniente, quod ad ipsum Willelmum pertinere consuevit, ut dicitur, sicut Rex accepit per dictos Barones & per Inquisicionem factam coram eis—. *Memor.* 42. *H.* 3. *Rot.* 12. *a.*

(*a*) Idem Vicecomes [debet *so much*] de proficuo Comitatuum, Et [*so much*] de eodem, de ultima quarta parte anni præteriti. Sed non debet inde summoneri, quia omnes res assisæ & placita & perquisita Comitatuum non sufficiunt ad perficiendum corpus Comitatus. *Mag. Rot.* 49. *H.* 3. *Rot.* 2. *a. Essex & Hertf.*

the

Chap. XXIII.   *and* ACCOUNTANTS.   169

the Clergy and the Barons (*b*). *Henry de Colevile*, Sheriff of *Cambridge* and *Huntendon*, was to account to the King at the Exchequer as *Cuſtos* of thoſe Counties and not as Fermer (*c*). *Hugh*, Son of *Otho*, *Robert de Cornhull*, and *Thomas de Baſing*, Sheriffs and Committees of the City of *London* whilſt it was in the King's Hands, accounted as *Cuſtodes* (*d*). A Sheriff who accounted as *Cuſtos* was to anſwer for the *Proficuum* of his County, and to be diſcharged of the Ferm (*e*). Again, *Henry de Audley*, Sheriff of *Shropſhire* (*Anno* 13. *H.* 3.) had the whole *Proficuum* of that County for that Year granted or allowed to him, for the Cuſtody of the County and of the Caſtles of *Shrewſbury* and *Bridges*: And the like for *Staffordſhire* (*f*). *Walter de Glouceſter*, late Sheriff and Improver of the Counties of *Somerſet* and *Dorſet*, was indebted to the King upon his Account, in certain Sums of Money *de remanenti firmæ*, and *de remanenti proficui*, and *de Auxilio Vicecomitis*. Theſe Sums the King, of his ſpecial Grace, remitted to him, in conſideration of his good Service, and of his Expences in his Office; and commanded the Barons to make him an Allowance thereof (*g*).

It being the ancient Courſe to write the King's Debts in the *Great Roll* afreſh every Year, in order to charge the Sheriff therewith: This became very burdenſome to the Officers of the Exchequer concerned

---

(*b*) Johannes Bucuinte r c de xxxvij l & ix s & vj d, de Veteri firma Comitatus: Ricardo & Henrico Converſis qui locuti fuerunt verſus Deuleſalt Judæum de proficuo Regis, v marcas, per breve Regis; & Joſeph & Rogero Clericis Regis de Scaccario Aaron, ij marcas & dimidiam de Dono, per breve Regis; Et in Perdonis, per breve Regis, ipſi Johanni xxxij l & ix s & vi d, Quia recognitum eſt coram Baronibus, quod habuit Balliam hac conditione, quod Quietantiæ per Cartas Regis factæ Eccleſijs & Baronibus debebant ei computari, Et Q. e. *Mag. Rot.* 3. *R.* 1. *Rot.* 11. *a. Lond. & Midd.*

(*c*) Rex conceſſit Henrico de Colevile, quod per Finem quem fecit cum Rege, reſpondeat Regi ad Scaccarium, a tempore quo Rex commiſit ei cuſtodiam Comitatuum Cantebrigiæ & Hunt., de exitibus eorundem Comitatuum per eundem Vicecomitem perceptis, tanquam Cuſtos & non ut Firmarius. *Memor.* 35. *H.* 3. *Rot.* 3. *a.*

(*d*) Hugo filius Ottonis, Robertus de Cornhull, & Thomas de Baſing, Ballivi ut Cuſtodes. r c de CCC xlvj l xiiij s vj d, de exitibus Civitatis Londoniæ de tribus partibus anni, ſecundum particulas annotatas in Rotulo Lij°, antequam reſtituerent dictam Civitatem. *Mag. Rot.* 54. *H.* 3. *Lond. & Midd.* m. 1. *a.*

(*e*) Memorandum quod ſi Rex concedat eidem Vicecomiti, quod reſpondeat ut Cuſtos, de annis 46°, 47°, & tribus partibus anni 48ⁱ, tunc debet reſpondere de proficuo Comitatus, & exonerari de firma. *Memor.* 52. *H.* 3. *Rot.* 22. *b.*

(*f*) Idem Vicecomes [Henricus de Alditheleya, Willelmus de Bromleya ut Cuſtos pro eo] non reſpondet de proficuo Comitatus de hoc anno; quia Rex conceſſit Vicecomiti totum proficuum hujus Anni pro Cuſtodia Comitatus & Caſtrorum de Salopebiria & de Briges; per breve ſuum quod eſt in forulo Mareſcalli. *Mag. Rot.* 13. *H.* 3. *Salopeſchir.* The like *Words* ut ſupra, *for the ſame* Henry de Audley *Sheriff of* Staffordſhire. *Ib. paul. infr.*

(*g*) *Liberat.* 22. *E.* 1. *m.* 1.

in that Service; especially where Debts were desperate or stood long in Charge: And was at the same time of little or no Advantage to the Crown. For Remedy of this Inconvenience, a Form of a Provision was drawn up by the Treasurer and Barons of the Exchequer, and presented to the King. On the Morrow of St. *Scholastica*, in the 54th Year of K. *Henry* III, that Form of a Provision was read, debated, and approved before the King, and his Council, to wit, *Richard* King of the *Romans*, *Walter* Archbishop of *York*, *Godfrey* Bishop of *Worcester*, Prince *Edward*, *William de Valencia*, the King's Brother, *Roger de Mortimer*, *Philipp Basset*, *Henry de Alemannia*, *Robert Aguillon*, *Robert Walerand*, and other *Magnates* of the King's Council. The Provision related chiefly to the Manner of entering the Sheriff's Account in the *Great Roll*, and of charging him with the King's Ferms and Debts. First (saith it) let the *Corpus Comitatus* be written [in the *Great Roll*] then the settled Alms and Liveries, and the Warrants for the Sheriff's Disbursements. Then charge the Sheriff with the Ferm for the *Proficuum* of his County, or with the *Proficuum*. Then write all the Ferms both great and small, and all attermined Debts, each in their proper Order. In like Manner write all great Debts or other known or clear Debts down to the usual Title, *Nova Oblata*. After that Title, charge the Debts contained in the Originals, which the Sheriffs take in Charge upon their Returns of Writs or their Apposals. Let the Sheriffs be diligently apposed concerning all other Debts. If the Sheriff hath levied no Part of them, let them stand in the Roll, and the Letter *D* be set against each Debtor's Name. At the End of the Sheriff's Account yearly, let this Title be written, The Debts of sundry Persons having the Letter *D* set before their Names in such a Roll; which are to go out in Summonce yearly. And afterwards let them go out in Summonce accordingly. If the Sheriff receive any Part of such Debts, then let the Letter *D* be taken away, and write, He [the Debtor] answereth in the *Great Roll*. And let such Debts be put in Charge there, and the Debtors be discharged. This was the Sum of the Provision. And the same, being ratified by the King and his Council, was sent to the Treasurer and Barons of the Exchequer, and they by a Writ of the Great Seal were commanded to act according to the Tenor thereof (*h*). This Provision was pursued,

---

(*h*) Rex Magistro Johanni de Chishull Decano S. Pauli Londoniæ Thesaurario, & Baronibus de Scaccario, salutem. Ex frequenti relatu vestro accepimus, quod propter longas & inutiles annuas scripturas diversorum debitorum nostrorum, compoti plurium Vicecomitum & aliorum Ballivorum nostrorum ad manum [*leg.* magnum] damp-num

sued, as appeareth by the Form used in the Great Roll of the three and fiftieth Year of K. *Henry* III, in the County of *Gloucester* (*i*), and in the rest of the Counties of *England*. The like Form was used in the 55th Year of that King, in the Counties of *Norfolk* and *Suffolk* (*k*), and the rest of the Counties: And in the 10th (*l*) and the 12th Years of K. Ed-

num nostrum remanent inauditi: propter quod quandam formam providistis, per quam correctio in hac parte fieri poterit in futurum: Quæ quidem forma in crastino Sanctæ Scolasticæ virginis anno regni nostri quinquagesimo quarto coram Nobis, Ricardo Rege Romanorum fratre nostro, Venerabilibus Patribus Waltero Eboracensi Archiepiscopo & Godefrido Wigornensi Episcopo, Edwardo Primogenito nostro, Willelmo de Valencia fratre nostro, Rogero de Mortuo mari, Philippo Basset, Henrico de Aleman[nia], Roberto Aguillon, Roberto Walerand, & alijs Magnatibus qui sunt de Consilio nostro, lecta fuit, exposita, examinata, & ab omnibus prædictis approbata; cujus formæ tenor talis est.

Primo scribatur Corpus Comitatus, deinde Elemosinæ constitutæ & Liberationes & Brevia de misis Vicecomitum, sicut semper fieri consuevit. Deinde oneretur Vicecomes de firma pro proficuo Comitatus vel de proficuo. Deinde scribantur omnes Firmæ tam majores quam minores, & omnia debita atterminata; in suis locis secundum ordinem Rotuli. Similiter scribantur omnia Magna debita & alia debita cognita usq; ad Titulum, NOVA OBLATA. Et post titulum prædictum exigantur debita contenta in Originalibus tam majoribus quam minoribus de quibus onerentur Vicecomites per suas responsiones. Omnia vero alia debita exigantur diligenter a Vicecomitibus coram assidentibus. Et si nulla fiat responsio de denarijs inde receptis, tunc remaneant in Rotulo in quo scripta sunt, et ultra nomina eorum qui debent eadem debita ponatur littera D. Finito autem compoto singulis annis scribatur titulus talis, DEBITA diversorum quorum nominibus præponitur litera D in tali Rotulo exigantur & summoneantur singulis annis; & postea fiat summonitio illa & mittatur Vicecomiti cum alijs summonitionibus. Et finito compoto

secundi anni, exigantur eadem debita sicut prius. Et si Vicecomes aliquid receperit de prædictis debitis, tunc deponatur Litera D, & scribatur, respondet in Rotulo Annali. Et ibi scribantur eadem debita, & inde acquietantur debitores. Et iste ordo de cætero servetur. Nos igitur prædictam formam concedentes & approbantes, vobis mandamus, quod in scripturis Rotulorum nostrorum & compotis prædictis audiendis, sicut nobis melius videritis expedire, secundum tenorem formæ prædictæ de cætero procedatis. In cujus &c; Teste Rege apud Westmonasterium, xij° die Februarij. *Rot. Pat.* 54. *H.* 3. *m.* 22.

(*i*) Debita diversorum, quorum nominibus supraponitur Litera D in Rotulo L°, singulis annis exigantur, & ea de quibus Vicecomes nichil inde reddit, summoneantur finito compoto. Et mittatur Summonicio Vicecomiti cum alijs Summonicionibus, sicut provisum est per Regem & ejus Consilium, & sicut continetur in Literis suis patentibus quæ sunt in Thesauro. *Mag. Rot.* 53. *H.* 3. *Item Glouc. The like Award is entered in the other Counties, at the foot of each Sheriffs Accompt.*

(*k*) Debita diversorum, quorum nominibus supraponitur Litera D in Rotulo Liij, singulis annis exigantur, & ea de quibus Vicecomes nichil inde reddit, summoneantur finito compoto, Et mittatur Summonicio Vicecomiti cum alijs Summonicionibus, sicut provisum est per Regem & ejus Consilium, & sicut continetur in Literis suis patentibus quæ sunt in Thesauro. *Mag. Rot.* 55. *H.* 3. *Item Norf. & Suff. The like Award in other Counties.*

(*l*) Debita diversorum, quorum nominibus supraponitur Litera D in Rotulo Lij°, singulis annis exigantur. Et ea de quibus Vicecomes nichil reddidit summoneantur finito compoto, & mittatur summonitio Vicecomiti una cum alijs summonitionibus, sicut

K. *Edward* I (*m*). In the 12th Year of K. *Edward* I, a Writ Patent under the Great Seal was sent to the Treasurer, Barons, and Chamberlains of the Exchequer, whereby it was ordered, that for the future, the *Corpus Comitatus* of each County should not be written every Year afresh in the *Great Roll* but in a particular Roll by itself, and out of that Roll should be read every Year to the Sheriff upon his Account. But that the *Remanens firmæ* after the *Terræ datæ* should be written in the *Great Roll* every Year, and the Sheriff charged therewith. That there should be a *View* in the Exchequer to settle the Allowances which were fit to be made to Sheriffs, and that after such *View* made, the Treasurer and Barons should make a Certificate to the King's Chancellor, upon which Certificate the Chancellor should cause Writs to issue for Allowances to be made to the Sheriff. That in the *Great Roll* there should be written the Sheriff's Ferm, the *Proficuum* of the County, the Ferms of Serjanties and Assarts, the Ferms of Cities, Burghs, and Towns, and other yearly Ferms. That in the same there should be written all Debts atterminated, all sperate and clear Debts. And when in writing the *Great Roll* they came to the Title of *Nova Oblata*, no Debts should be charged in the *Great Roll* of every Year, except those of which the Sheriff levied somewhat, or those which were found in the *Originals* and seemed to be clear Debts. But that for dead Ferms and desperate Debts, a particular Roll should be made for each County; which Roll should be read yearly upon the Sheriff's Account; and if the Sheriff levied any of those Debts, then the same should be written in the *Great Roll*, and there discharged. There are also in this Writ Patent several other Directions, touching the producing and Allowance of Tallies of Acquittance given by Sheriffs to the King's Debtors, touching Dividend-tallies to be made at the *Receipt*, and touching the holding of Common Pleas in the Exchequer (*n*). By virtue of this Writ, in the following Years

---

sicut provisum est per Regem H. & ejus Consilium, & sicut continetur in Literis suis Patentibus quæ sunt in Thesauro. Et eodem modo fiat de debitis diversorum quorum nominibus supraponitur Litera D in Rotulo Lvj°, sicut provisum est per illos qui tenent locum Regis qui nunc est. *Mag. Rot.* 10. *E.* 1. *Rot.* 1. *a. in imo. Northumb. Et in alijs Comitatt.*

(*m*) Debita diversorum quorum nominibus supraponitur litera D in Rotulo Lij in hoc Comitatu, singulis annis exigantur. Et ea de quibus Vicecomes nichil inde reddit summoneantur finitis compotis, & mittantur Summonitiones Vicecomiti una cum alijs summonitionibus, sicut provisum est per Regem H. & ejus consilium, & sicut continetur in Litteris suis patentibus, quæ sunt in Thesauro. Et eodem modo fiat de debitis contentis in Rot. de Corporibus & Rot. pullorum. *Mag. Rot.* 12. *E.* 1. *Item Sussex, m.* 2. *b. in ima ora Rotuli. Et in alijs Comitatt.*

(*n*) Breve Regis de Corporibus Comitatuum de Rotulis Annalibus amovendis &c; sicut

Chap. XXIII.   *and* ACCOUNTANTS.   173

Years of this King, the *Corpus Comitatus* of each County was written by itself in a separate Roll. And in that Roll the dead Ferms and desperate Debts were also entered. Thus in the 13th Year of K. *Edward* I, the *Corpus Comitatus* of *Notinghamshire* and *Derbyshire* is left out of the *Great Roll*, and referred to as entered in the separate Roll appointed for that Purpose. And then the Sheriff of those two Counties accounts for the *Remanens firmæ* of his Counties; and so goes on with his Account in the usual Manner (*o*). The like was done in this 13th Year, by the other Sheriffs of *England*. And the *Corpus Comitatus* of each County being left out of the *Great Roll*, the Account of each Sheriff begins, *Corpus hujus Comitatus annotatur* &c. And afterwards, *viz.* in the 22d Year of K. *Edward* I, the Sheriff's Account usually began with the *Remanens firmæ* after the *Terræ datæ*. So the Account of the Sheriff of *Gloucester* began (*p*); and the Account of the Sheriff of *Notingham* and *Derbyshire* (*q*); and the Accounts of other Sheriffs in that Year.

sicut patet infra. Rex mandavit Thesaurario & Baronibus suis de Scaccario ac Camerarijs suis, breve suum quod est in Thesauro, in hæc verba. Edwardus Dei gratia Rex Angliæ &c. Thesaurario & Baronibus suis de Scaccario ac Camerarijs suis salutem. Ut indempnitati———. In cujus rei testimonium has litteras vobis mittimus patentes. T. meipso apud Rothlan, xxiij die Marcij anno r n xij. Virtute cujus brevis, Corpora omnium Comitatuum scribuntur in quodam Rotulo qui intitulatur Rotulus de Corporibus Comitatuum. In quo quidem Rotulo firmæ mortuæ, & debita de quibus non est spes, similiter annotantur. *Mag. Rot.* 12. *E.* 1. *in Ced. ad Rot.* 1.

This Writ is printed as a Statute by Richard Tottell, *in his Collection of the Old Statutes, with this Title*, Statutum Novum de Scaccario, aliter dictum Statutum de Rotelande; *Tott. Stat. P.* 2. *fol.* 64, 65, 66. *In* Tothills *Copy it is*, Teste Rege apud Rotel. xxiiij die Maij anno decimo. *Whereas the Writ itself is*, T. meipso apud Rothlan xxiij die Marcij anno r n xij. *This mistake in the year and place of the* Teste *hath been propagated and continued by others who have published the Old Statutes. Vid.* Prynn. *on the* 4*th* Instit. *p.* 55.

This Writ is also enrolled in the Close-Roll *of the* 12*th Year of K.* Edward I. *Claus.* 12. *E.* 1. *m.* 7. *dorso.*

(*o*) Corpora horum Comitatuum annotantur in Rotulo de Corporibus Comitatuum, sicut continetur in Rotulo præcedente. *Then it goes on.* Gervasius de Clifton Vicecomes r c de vj l iiij s ob. numero, de remanenti firmæ Comitatuum tam Bl. quam numero, sicut continetur in Rotulo xij, & in Rotulis præcedentibus. In Thesauro nichil &c. *Mag. Rot.* 13. *E.* 1. *Rot.* 1. *a. Not. & Derb.*

(*p*) Thomas de Gardinis Vicecomes r c de xxxviij l xiiij s xj d Bl., de remanenti firmæ Comitatus post terras datas, sicut continetur in Rotulo x°. In thesauro xl l per j talliam. &c. *Mag. Rot.* 22. *E.* 1. *Glouc. m.* 1. *a.*

(*q*) Philippus de Paunton r c de vj l iiij s ob. numero, de remanenti firmæ Comitatuum tam Bl. quam numero; In thesauro nichil; Et in Elemosina &c.—. *Mag. Rot.* 22. *E.* 1. *Not. & Derb. m.* 1. *a.*

Ricardus de Afton Vicecomes non respondet de aliquo remanenti post terras datas; Quia habetur ibi superplusagium vij l iiij s ob.; Qui non debent ei allocari, quia excrescunt per extensionem Maneriorum, sicut continetur in Rotulo xj; Et in Elemosina &c. *Mag. Rot.* 22. *E.* 1. *m.* 1. *a.* Suthamt.

Some-

Sometimes the Sheriffs have craved Allowances to be made to them upon their Accounts, according to the Equity of their Cases. *Geoffrey le Rus*, who was Sheriff of the Counties of *Bedford* and *Buckingham*, in the 50th Year of K. *Henry* III, prayed to have Allowance made to him upon his Account of several Items, *viz.* For the *Res assisæ* of his Bailywick taken from him by the turbulent Barons; for the Horses and Arms he had bought, and other Expences he had been at in keeping the Peace by the Command of Prince *Edward*; for the Loss he sustained by reason of the King's Service in the burning of his Houses and Corn; for the Horses, Arms, Clothes, and other Goods, of which he was despoiled at his Manor of *Hendon* by *John de Eyville* and other Barons; for some of the King's Money then in his Hands, of which he was plundered by the said Barons; for the Defect in the Perquisites of the Counties, occasioned by the intestine War; and for so much Time as he wanted to make the Year of his Sherivalty complete (*r*).

The Sheriffs were wont to account for the whole Time that they held their Bayliwick, whether it was a Quarter of a Year, Half a Year, or a whole Year. In Process of Time, they generally accounted from *Michaelmass* in one Year, to *Michaelmass* in next Year. In the first Year of K. *Edward* II, *Thomas de Burnham*, Sheriff of *Lincolnshire*, accounted to the Crown for the Issues of his Office, *viz.* from the Feast of St. *Michael* in the 34th Year finient and 35th Year incipient of K. *Edward* I, until the 7th Day of *July*, to wit, the Day of the *Translation* of St. *Thomas* the Martyr in the said 35th Year; upon which Day K. *Edward* I. died, and upon which Day his Son and Heir K. *Edward* II. began to reign; and from the said Day of the *Translation* until the Feast of St. *Michael* then next following. And in that Year several other Sheriffs accounted in the same Manner (*s*). Hereditary

---

(*r*) Allocationes quas Galfridus le Rus Vicecomes petit de tempore quo fuit Vicecomes in Com. Bedef. & Buk. videlicet anno L°. Idem G. petit allocationem de xxxvij l vj s & v d de rebus assisis subtractis per potenciam Magnatum in eisdem Comitatibus. Item petit allocationem de xlij l in equis & armis emptis, expensis & alijs misis factis pro pace custodienda per præceptum Domini Eduuardi. Item petit allocationem de Lx l quas amisit occasione ballivæ suæ in cumbustione domorum suarum & bladi. Item petit allocationem de xxxij l vj s viij d de equis armis pannis & alijs bonis deprædatis apud Hendon Manerium suum, per Johannem de Eyville & alios Barones in itinere suo versus Londoniam. Item petit allocationem de xxij l x s ibidem deprædatis per prædictos Barones de denarijs Domini Regis. Item petit allocationem de hoc quod non habere potuit plene perquis[itiones] in Comitatibus prædictis, propter Gwerram tempore prædicto, unde posset respondere de proficuo Comitatuum. Item petit allocationem quod non habuit plene annum de placitis & perquisitis, quia defuit ei tempus a festo S. Michaelis usque ad festum S. Martini. *Memor.* 52. *H.* 3. *Rot.* 20. *in Ced. annexa.*

(*s*) Lincolnia. Thomas de Burnham Vicecomes a festo S. Michaelis anno regni Regis Edwardi filij Regis Henrici xxxiiijo finiente,

reditary Sheriffs accounted at the Exchequer in the same Manner as other Sheriffs did. *Thomas de Lancastre*, Earl of *Lancaster*, Son and Heir of *Edmund* Brother to K. *Edward* I, Sheriff in Fee of *Lancaster*, accounted for the King's Debts and the Ferm of the County of *Lancaster* in the usual Manner (*t*). The like was done by other Sheriffs in Fee.

K. *Edward* I. ordained, that the Sheriffs should be Escheators in their respective Counties. Accordingly, *Bogo de Knovile*, Sheriff of *Shropshire* and *Staffordshire*, accounted for the King's Escheats within those Counties (*u*). *Alexander de Kirketon*, Sheriff of *Yorkshire*, for the Escheats of his County (*w*); and other Sheriffs for the Escheats of their Counties.

III. It is to be known, that there were anciently several Assises or Rules observed in the Exchequer, touching the rendering of Accounts, and the levying and getting in of the King's Rights and Credits. Some of them do hereunder follow. For Example: If a Man held a Bailywick under the King, and executed it by Substitute, the immediate Baillee, and not the Substitute, was to pass the Account for the Issues of such Bailywick. *Alberic de Billingsgate* was charged with Lxxij *s* and iiij *d*, for the Customs of *Billingsgate*, *Botulfsgate*, and *Gracechurch* in *London*. But it was adjudged that *William de Haverhell* should account for the same; because *William* had that Bailywick from the King, and *Alberic* from *William* (*x*). *Gilbert Carbunel* stood charged

---

finiente, incipiente xxxv°, usque vij diem Julij videlicet diem Translacionis S. Thomæ Martiris eodem anno xxxv°, quo die idem Edwardus obijt, & quo die Edwardus filius & hæres ejusdem Edwardi filij Regis H. regnare incepit, & ab eodem die dictæ Translacionis usque festum S. Michaelis proximo sequens, reddit compotum de DCCCxxxvj l xx d Bl., Et de Cxl l numero de firma Comitatus, sicut continetur in Rotulo xj, & in Rotulis præcedentibus———. *Mag. Rot.* 35. *E.* 1. *Rot.* 1. *a. The same Words*; ibid. *Devonia. m.* 1. *a. & ib. Oxon. m.* 1. *a. & alibi ib.*

(*t*) Lancastria. Compotus Thomæ de Lancastre Comitis Lancastriæ filij & hæredis Edmundi fratris Regis Vicecomitis de feodo, Magistri Ricardi de Hoghton pro eo, de debitis Regis de hoc anno. Idem Vicecomes r c de CLxxiiij l vij s iiij d ob. de firma Comitatus Lancastriæ &c. *Mag. Rot.* 28. *E.* 1. *Lanc. m.* 2. *a.*

(*u*) Compotus Bogonis de Knovile de Eschaetis Regis in Comitatibus Salopiæ & Staffordiæ, per provisionem Regis quod Vicecomites sint Eschaetores in Comitatibus suis. *Mag. Rot.* 5. *E.* 1. *post Surr. & Suffex, m.* 2. *b.*

(*w*) Compotus Alexandri de Kirketon de exitibus Escaetarum Regis in Com. Eboraci, dum idem Alexander fuit Vicecomes in prædicto Comitatu & Escaetor, per provisionem factam per Regem quod Vicecomites essent Escaetores in ballivis suis. *Mag. Rot.* 9. *E.* 1. *Rot.* 2. *a. m.* 1.

(*x*) Albericus de Billingesgate [debet] Lxxij s & iiij d, de Consuetudinibus de Billingesgate & Botulvesgate & Garschierech, de tempore quo habuit Bailliam; sed consideratum est quod Willelmus de Haverhell

charged with xxv *l* Blank, an Arerage of the Ferm of *London* for a Year long since past. But in regard *Gilbert* was put into that Bailywick by Earl *William* [*de Mandevill*] who was the King's immediate Baillee; and in regard *Geoffrey Fitz-Pierre* did now enjoy Earl *William's* Land, the said Debt was set off from *Gilbert*, and charged upon *Geoffrey* (*y*). *John de Craft*, Bailiff or Receiver under *Almaric de St. Amand*, was charged as Debtor to the King for certain Money received by him: but in regard *John* was not the King's immediate Bailiff, the Heir of *Almaric* was ordered to account for the same (*z*). *Thomas de Camvill* came before the Barons to render an Account, as *Custos* of the Manor of *Wyham*. But forasmuch as he had not the Custody thereof immediately from the King, but from *Walter de Burgh*, the Barons ordered *Walter*, who was the King's immediate Baillee, to render the Account (*a*).

IV. The stated Accounts were wont to be rendered regularly in Course every Year, insomuch that sometimes, if an Account happened to be postponed, a *Memorandum* was made thereof, as well *pro commodo Regis,* as for preserving the usual Order of accounting. As in the Case of *William de Braiose* (*b*).

hell debet inde respondere, quia prædictus Albericus habuit Bailliam per ipsum. *Mag. Rot.* 7. *Ric.* 1. *Rot.* 9. *a. Lond. & Midd.*

(*y*) Galfridus filius Petri [debet] xxv l Bl. de Veteri firma de Londonia, quæ exigebantur a Gilberto Carbunel dum Comes Willemus habuit Custodiam Turris Londoniæ, per quem prædictus Gillebertus habuit Bailliam per Comitem, Cujus Comitis terram prædictus Galfridus filius Petri habet. *Mag. Rot.* 8. *R.* 1. *Rot.* 23. *b. Lond. & Midd.*

(*z*) Oxonia. — Et quia non est justum, quod de Recepta illa nos capiamus ad dictum Johannem [Craft, *who was the Sheriff's Bailiff or Receiver*], eo quod non fuit Ballivus noster in Capite, sed ad hæredem dicti Aumarici [de Sancto Amando] *late Sheriff of* Herefordshire] ——— &c. *Mich. Commun.* 27. *H.* 3. *Rot.* 5. *b.*

(*a*) Memorandum quod Thomas de Camvill venit coram Baronibus xxviij die Juny, & optulit se ad reddendum compotum de Manerio de Wyham quod habuit in custodia de ballio Walteri de Burgo a festo S. Barnabæ anno xxiiij° usq; ad festum S. Botulfi anno xxv°. Et quia non habuit prædictam Custodiam per Dominum Regem, set per Walterum de Burgo qui habuit custodiam plurimorum Maneriorum Regis, Barones distulerunt recipere compotum de ipso Thoma, & decreverunt audire compotum illum de W. de Burgo. *Memor.* 28. *H.* 3. *Rot.* 12. *b.*

(*b*) Herefordscira in Walia: Willemus de Braiose non reddidit compotum hoc anno de firma Comitatus neq; de Summonitionibus, quia Henricus de Longo Campo, qui anno proximo præcedente Comitatum tenuerat, propter Captionem suam compotum non reddidit: Cujus Compotus oportuit Compotum Willelmi præcedere. *Mag. Rot.* 4. *R.* 1. *Rot.* 10. *b.*

Herefordscira in Walia: Henricus de Longo Campo r c de firma de Herefordscira in Walia de anno tertio Regni Regis Ricardi, qui dilatus fuit propter Captionem ejusdem Henrici.

Willemus de Braiosa r c de firma de Herefordsira in Walia de anno præterito & de hoc anno. Cujus Compotus dilatus fuit propter Captionem prædicti Henrici. *Mag. Rot.* 5. *R.* 1. *Rot.* 7. *a.*

V. In general, Accountants were obliged to come in Person to render their Accounts. If they made an Attorney to account for them, it was usual to have the King's Leave for it. Sometimes the Accountant nominated his Attorney before the King: and thereupon the King by his Writ commanded the Treasurer and Barons to admit such Person as Attorney accordingly. But sometimes, especially towards the latter Part of the second Period, the Accountant's Attorney was admitted by Warrant or Leave of the Treasurer, Chancellor of the Exchequer, or Barons, or one of them. *John de Gatesden*, Sheriff of *Sussex*, attorned one before the King, to answer for him at the Exchequer touching his Sherivalty: and the King commanded the Barons to admit the Attorney thereto (*c*). The Abbot of *Waltham* having appointed, before the King, two Persons to be his Attorneys, to claim his Franchises in the Exchequer, the King by his Writ commands the Barons to receive them as such (*d*). The King commanded the Barons to receive *John de Shirewode*, as Attorney for the Mayor and Commonalty of *Notingham*, to claim for them at the Exchequer; they having deputed him so to do (*e*). So also the King by Writ commanded the Barons to admit Attorneys for the Persons hereunder named, to answer and act for them respectively: *viz.* For *Robert de Haye (f)*, the Sheriff of *Northumberland* (*g*), *Henry de Colne* (*h*), *William de Lancastre* (*i*), *John de Grey*, Justice of *Chester* (*k*),

Warin

(*c*) Rex eisdem [Baronibus]; Sciatis quod Johannes de Gatesden Vicecomes noster Sussexiæ attornavit coram nobis Philippum de Croft Vic. suum, ad respondendum pro eo ad Scaccarium nostrum, de hijs quæ pertinent ad idem Scaccarium de eodem Comitatu. Et ideo vobis mandamus, quod ipsum Philippum loco prædicti Johannis ad hoc recipiatis. Teste &c xxvij die Octobris anno xxij. *Memor.* 22. *H.* 3. *Rot.* 3. *a.*

(*d*) Sciant Barones, quod Ricardus Abbas de Waltham S. Crucis attornavit coram Rege loco suo, Petrum de Waltham & Laurentium de Bosco, ad Libertates suas coram Baronibus in Scaccario exigendas & calumpniandas. Et ideo Rex mandat Baronibus, quod ipsos Petrum & Laurentium vel alterum ipsorum (si ambo interesse non possint) loco ipsius Abbatis ad hoc recipiant. T. Rege apud Ditton xxiiij die Septembris anno Nono. *Mich. Brevia* 9. *E.* 2. *Rot.* 7. *a.*

(*e*) Quia Major & Communitas Villæ Notynghamiæ atturnaverunt coram Rege loco suo Johannem de Shirewode ad Libertates suas coram Baronibus hic in Scaccario prosequendas, calumpniandas, & defendendas: Rex mandat Baronibus, quod prædictum Johannem loco ipsorum Majoris & Communitatis ad hoc recipiant. Teste Rege apud Turrim Londoniæ xvj die Octobris anno xv. *Mich. Brevia* 15. *E.* 2. *Rot.* 46. *a.*

(*f*) Rex eisdem [Baronibus]; quod loco Roberti de Haya recipiant Johannem le Deveneis, ad respondendum pro eo coram eisdem, & ad compotum reddendum de Comitatibus Bed. & Buk., quamdiu idem Robertus fuerit in Itinere. *Memor.* 25. *H.* 3. *Rot.* 5. *a.*

(*g*) Vicecomes Norhumberlandiæ assignavit loco suo ad respondendum ad Scaccarium, Willelmum de C, per breve Regis quod est in forulo Marescalli. *Ex Memor.* 11. *H.* 3. *Rot.* 3. *a.*

(*h*) *Memor.* 28. *H.* 3. *Rot.* 4. *b.*

(*i*) *Ib. Rot.* 12. *a.*

(*k*) Rex Baronibus; Quoniam J. de Grey Justiciarius

Warin de Baffingburn (*l*), the Sheriff of *Hereford* (*m*), and *John de Cormayles*, Sheriff of *Sumerfet* and *Dorfet* (*n*). When *John de Chedney*, Sheriff of *Bukingham* and *Bedford*, came to account, *William* his Clerk, by virtue of the King's Writ, rendered the Account for him (*o*). *Robert Fitz-Roger* came before the Barons of the Exchequer, and prefented *Robert de Reynham* to anfwer for him, for all Debts due to the King, which went out in Summonce within the Liberty of the Hundred of *Clavering*, and for all other Things pertaining to his faid Mafter within the faid Liberty (*p*). A Monk of *Ely* came and produced in the Exchequer Letters of Proxy from the Prior of *Ely*, whereby he was affigned to replevy that Priory. But the Court told the Monk, that it was not the Courfe in the King's Court, for any one to attorn another by Letters of Proxy to profecute fuch a Bufinefs as this, or to admit Day of Adjournment in the King's Court, unlefs the King by his Writ gracioufly permit the Party fo to do; but the Party muft come in Perfon into the King's Court, or before fome Jufticier or other Officer having Record, and there make his Attorney. Whereupon the Monk withdrew *Re infecta* (*q*). The King commanded the Barons to receive as Attorneys of the Abbot of *Peterburgh*, to claim and defend for the Abbot in the Exchequer fuch Perfons as he fhould appoint for that Purpofe (*r*): and to admit *Geoffrey de Fencote* as Attorney for the Conftable of *Briftoll-Caftle*, to make his Profer for him on the Morrow of S. *Michael* (*s*). Whereas *Roger de Ingepenne*, Sheriff of *Cornwall*, could not go out of that County without Damage to the Earl of *Cornwall*, he being employed to make certain Purveyances for the Earl againft his coming into that County; fo that *Roger* could not appear before the Barons of the Exchequer on the

Jufticiarius nofter Ceftriæ a partibus Walliæ ob periculum imminens nequit elongari; Vobis mandamus quod Willelmum de Grey fratrem ejus ad compotum fuum pro eo reddendum recipiatis. Breve eft in f. M. *Hil. Commun.* 32. H. 3. Rot. 3. b.

(*l*) *Memor.* 51. H. 3. Rot. 7. a.

(*m*) *Mich. Communia* 4 & 5. E. 1. Rot. 1. a.

(*n*) Compotus Johannis de Cormayles Vicecomitis Somerfetæ & Dorfetæ, per Willelmum de Favelore clericum ejus & attornatum per breve Regis. *Mag. Rot.* 9. E. 1. Rot. 2. b.

(*o*) Buk. & Bedeford. Johannes de Chedny, Willelmus Clericus fuus pro eo per breve Regis, [r c de] CCCLxix l xix s xj d Bl. , Et de Cviij l numero, de firma Comitatuum. *Mag. Rot.* 10. E. 1. m. 1. a.

(*p*) Robertus filius Rogeri venit coram Baronibus, & præfentavit Robertum de Reynham, ad refpondendum pro eo de omnibus debitis Domini Regis quæ veniunt in Summonitione infra Libertatem Hundredi de Claveringg, & de omnibus alijs prædictum Dominum fuum tangentibus infra Libertatem prædictam. *Mich. Communia* 4 & 5. E. 1. Rot. 1. b.

(*q*) *Mich. Communia* 26 & 27. E. 1. Rot. 10. a.

(*r*) *Mich. Communia* 14. incip. E. 1. Rot. 1. a.

(*s*) Ib. Rot. 1. a.

Quinzime

Quinzime of St. *John Baptift*, to render his Account: therefore the King, *de Gratia fpeciali*, commands the Barons by his Writ, to receive for this Time, *John Hommeden* and *Gilbert de Berkhamfted*, or one of them, to render the faid *Roger*'s Account (*t*). *Gilbert de Knovill*, Sheriff of *Devonfhire*, being fick, the King by Privy Seal commanded the Treafurer and Barons, to receive an Attorney or Attorneys to account for *Gilbert* at the Exchequer: and he made Attorneys accordingly (*u*). The like Permiffion for a Sheriff to account by his Clerk was given by Writ of the Privy Seal, to *John de Nevill*, Sheriff of *Lincolnfhire*; he being then attending, by the King's Leave, upon certain Affairs of the Earl of *Warenne* (*w*). Nor is it to be wondered, that the Admiffion of Attorneys to act in Accounts, and other Bufinefs at the Exchequer, fhould be fo frequently regulated and directed by the King's Writs; for in feveral Cafes wherein the King was not (for what appears) any way concerned, namely in Pleas between Party and Party, Attorneys were many Times appointed or conftituted in the King's Prefence, or by his Permiffion. *Herbert de Venaifon* attorned one in his ftead *ad Lucrandum* and *Perdendum*, in a Plea of *Detinue* moved between him and *Richard le Avener* (*x*). This Cafe of *Herbert de Venaifon* being inferted in the *Norman* Roll of *Oblatas*, it is likely his Attorney was nominated by the King's Permiffion, and for a Fine paid to the King upon that Occafion. Mafter *William de Riparijs*, when he ftayed in *England* by the King's Leave, came before the King, and removed *John atte Merfh* (whom he had formerly attorned, together with *John Petipas*) from being one of his general Attorneys in *Ireland*; and in the room of *John atte Merfh* he fubftituted *Roger le Curtays*, together with the faid *John Petipas fub alternatione*, to be his Attorneys *ad Lucrandum*, &c. in all Pleas and

(*t*) Baronibus, pro Rogero de Ingepenne Vicecomite Cornubiæ. Quia idem Vicecomes a partibus Cornubiæ hijs diebus recedere non poteft abfq; dampno E. Comitis Cornubiæ, propter Providentias quas contra adventum ipfius Comitis ad partes Cornubiæ fieri ex præcepto ejufdem Comitis neceffario oportebit, per quod coram Baronibus in Scaccario in inftanti quindena S. Johannis Baptiftæ ad compotum fuum reddendum comparere non poteft, ficut ei fignificarunt: Rex mandat Baronibus, quod Johannem Hommeden & Gilbertum de Berkhamfted, vel eorum alterum quem præfentem effe contigerit, loco prædicti Rogeri ad compotum illum pro prædicto Vicecomite reddendum recipiant hac vice, de gratia Regis fpeciali. T. Rege apud Weftmon. viij die Junii anno xviij. *Trin. Commun.* 18. *E.* 1. *Rot.* — *a*.

(*u*) *Paf. Communia* 25 & 26. *E.* 1. *Rot.* 82. *a*.

(*w*) *By Privy Seal*; Donne a Clarindon le iiij jour de Janever lan de noftre regne difme. *Trin. Brevia* 12. *E.* 2. *Rot.* 117. *a*.

(*x*) Herbertus de Venatione ponit loco fuo ad lucrandum & perdendum, de loquela quæ eft inter ipfum & Ricardum le Avener, de Catallis fuis quæ ei injufte detinet ut dicit. *Rot. Oblat. Norm.* 2. *J. m.* 4. *dorfo*.

Suits in *Ireland*. This Letter of Attorney was to last until the Feast of St. *Calixtus*, and from thence for a Year complete. This Transaction was declared by duplicated Letters of the Great Seal (*y*). And, as I remember, some other Instances of the like Kind do occur in Records.

Sometimes also Attorneys were made by Accountants without any Writ or Precept from the King, for ought that appears. As in the Cases of the several Sheriffs and other Accountants hereafter named; to wit, in the Case of *William de Bickely* (*z*), *Robert de Meysey* (*a*), *John de Albernun* (*b*), *Alan la Zuche* (*c*), *W*. Archbishop of *York*, Sheriff of the Counties of *Notingham* and *Derby* (*d*), *Walter de Shelfhanger* (*e*), *Gregory de Rokesle* (*f*), *John de Kirkeby* (*g*), *Robert de Clifford* and *Idonea de Leyburne*, Sheriffs in Fee of *Westmerland* (*h*), *Edmund* Earl of *Cornwall* (*i*); and of *John de Montague*, Sheriff of *Somerset* and *Dorset* (*k*). Sometimes

---

(*y*) Magister Willelmus de Riparijs, qui de licentia Regis moratur in Anglia, amovit coram Rege Johannem atte Merssh, quem una cum Johanne filio Ricardi Petipas loco suo prius attornaverat ad lucrandum &c, pro ipso Willelmo vel contra ipsum in Hibernia; Et loco ipsius Johannis atte Merssh Rogerum le Curtays una cum praefato Johanne filio Ricardi, sub alternatione substituit, ad lucrandum &c in omnibus placitis & querelis praedictis; ita quod ijdem Rogerus & Johannes filius Ricardi vel eorum alter qui praesens fuerit loco ipsius Willelmi &c; In cujus &c; Duraturas usq; ad festum S. Kalixti Papae, scilicet quartum decimum diem Octobris proximo futurum, & ab eodem festo per unum annum proximo sequentem completum, Praes. &c T. R. apud Devyses, xxvj die Aprilis. Dupplicatur. *Pat.* 30. *E*. 1. *m*. 22.

(*z*) Willelmus de Bickel. Vicecomes Devoniae ponit loco suo Radulfum le Peytevin clericum suum, ad faciendum Visum pro eo de primo dimidio anno Lij°. *Memor*. 52. *H*. 3. *Rot*. 9. *a*.

(*a*) De Attornato Roberti de Meysey. Idem ponit loco suo Adam de Budeford ad reddendum compotum pro eo, de tempore quo fuit Vicecomes Herefordiae, usq; ad Summam. *Ib Rot*. 9. *a*.

(*b*) Johannes de Albernun ponit loco suo Walterum Dru ad reddendum compotum suum pro eo ad Scaccarium, de tempore quo fuit Vicecomes Regis in Comitatibus Surriae & Sussexiae, & ad ipsum onerandum & exonerandum usq; ad Summam. Postea atturnavit eundem ad Summam faciendam. *Memor*. 51. *H*. 3. *Rot*. 6. *b*.

(*c*) Idem Alanus [la Zuche] ponit loco suo Johannem de Oxinden vel Walterum le Butiller, ad percomputandum pro eo de exitibus Comitatus Norhamtoniae, & de foresta & castro de Rokingham; & ad ipsum onerandum de omnibus debitis quae recepit tempore quo fuit Vicecomes Norhamtoniae. *Memor*. 52. *H*. 3. *Rot*. 8. *b*.

(*d*) De Attornato W. Archiepiscopi Ebor. Idem ponit loco suo Hugonem de Stapilford Clericum, ad reddendum compotum suum pro eo, de tempore quo fuit Vicecomes Regis Comitatuum Notinghamiae & Derbiae, & ad onerandum & exonerandum eundem, acsi ipsemet esset praesens. *Mich. Commun*. 56. *H*. 3. *Rot*. 2. *b*. And Hugh *did accordingly pass the Account for the Archbishop*; *Ib. Rot*. 12. *a*. *inter Compotos*.

(*e*) *Mich. Commun*. 4 & 5. *E*. 1. *Rot*. 1. *a*.

(*f*) *Trin. Commun*. 4 & 5. *E*. 1. *Rot*. 6. *b*.

(*g*) *Trin. Fines &c* 26. *E*. 1. *Rot*. 94. *a*.

(*h*) *Trin. Praesentationes* 27. *E*. 1. *Rot*. 61. *a*.

(*i*) *Trin. Brevia* 26 & 27. *E*. 1. *Rot*. 29. *b*.

(*k*) Johannes de Monte acuto Vicecomes Somersetae

Sometimes Attorneys were admitted by Warrant or Order of the Treasurer, Chancellor, or Barons, or one of them: as in the Case of the Abbot of *Evesham,* and of *Reginald de Acle,* Sheriff of *Gloucestershire* (*l*), of *Philipp de Hoyvill,* Sheriff of *Hamshire* (*m*), *John de Metham,* Collector of the Vintisme and Quinzime (*n*), the Dean and Chapter of *Chichester,* Collectors of a Disme of the Clergy (*o*), the Abbot of *Abyndon,* a Collector of the same Disme (*p*), *John Howard,* Sheriff of *Norfolk* and *Suffolk* (*q*), *John de Dallingge,* one of the Sheriffs of *London* (*r*), and the Sheriff of *Norfolk* and *Suf-*

Somersetæ & Dorsetæ, qui diem habuit hic ad computandum nunc in crastino Ascensionis Domini, misit Thesaurario & Baronibus hic Literas suas Patentes in hæc verba; Dominis & amicis suis karissimis Thesaurario & Baronibus de Scaccario Domini Regis―――. *By reason of his own Infirmity of Body, he nominates (by this Letter) one* Richard de Byflet *to be his Clerk, to render his said Account for him at the Exchequer.* Et prædictus Ricardus de Byflet admissus est per Barones ad computandum pro eodem Vicecomite &c. *Pas. Commun.* 34. *E.* 1. *Rot.* 36. *a.*

(*l*) Idem Abbas [de Evesham] ponit loco suo coram Ricardo de Hereford Rememoratore de Scaccario, ad hoc assignato de præcepto Thesaurarij & Baronum de eodem Scaccario, Johannem le Esperun, ad respondendum pro eodem Abbate ad idem Scaccarium, de hijs quæ pertinent ad Libertatem suam, & ad calumpniandum pro eo omnes Libertates suas, sicut idem Abbas si præsens esset. *Pas. Communia* 56. *H.* 3. *Rot.* 6. *a.*

De Attornatis Reginaldi de Acle captis per Ricardum de Hereford.

Ricardus de Hereford Clericus de Scaccario de præcepto Thesaurarij & Baronum cepit Attornatos Reginaldi de Acle quondam Vicecomitis Gloucestriæ, videlicet Rogerum de Cheyny & Adam de Sandhurst ad reddendum Compotum pro eo de tempore quo fuit Vicecomes prædicti Comitatus. *Ibid. Pas. Communia* 56. *H.* 3. *Rot.* 6. *a.*

(*m*) *Philipp de Hoyvill, late Sheriff of* Southampton, qui habuit diem hic modo die Jovis post quindenam Paschæ, *to account, sent his Letters Patents to the Treasurer and Barons, signifying that* pro gravi infirmitate *he could not come at the Day assigned; and desiring that his Son and Heir* William, *whom he had put in his Place, might be by them admitted to pass his Account*; Datum apud Fontely undecimo die Aprilis, anno Regni Regis Edwardi tricesimo quinto. Prætextu quarum Literarum, & ex causa infirmitatis dicti Philippi, prædictus Willelmus filius & hæres ejusdem Philippi admittitur per Barones ad compotum prædictum reddendum pro eodem Philippo &c. *Pas. Præsentat.* 35. *E.* 1. *Rot.* 48. *a.*

(*n*) Ebor. Johannes de Metham unus Collectorum Vicesimæ & Quintædecimæ nuper Regi concessæ in Comitatu Eboraci, ponit loco suo Ricardum de Hothum ad reddendum Regi compotum de xx^a & xv^a antedictis. Per J. de Merkynfeld Cancellarium hujus Scaccarij. *Hil. Commun.* 5. *E.* 2. *Rot.* 36. *a.*

(*o*) Sussex. Decanus & Capitulum Cicestriæ Collectores Decimæ Regi a Clero in ultimo Parliamento Westmonasterij concessæ in Episcopatu Cicestrensi, ponunt loco suo Johannem le Sherer de Cicestria, ad reddendum pro eis Regi compotum de Decima prædicta. Per Hervicum de Stanton. *Hil. Attornati &c.* 9. *E.* 2. *Rot.* 123. *a.*

(*p*) *Ib. juxt.*

(*q*) Johannes Howard Vicecomes Norfolciæ & Suff., qui de præcepto Regis est profecturus ad Regem versus partes Boriales, ponit loco suo Galfridum de Ely clericum suum, ad reddendum Regi compotum pro eo, de officio Vicecomitatus prædicti de anno xj°. Per W. de Norwyco. *Mich. Commun.* 12. *E.* 2. *Rot.* 49. *a.*

(*r*) Johannes de Dallingge unus Vicecomitum Londoniæ, qui de licentia Thesaurarij

Suffolk (s). Several other Persons appoint their Attorneys (by the way of *ponit loco suo*) to act for them at the Exchequer. And they are allowed by the Barons (t).

VI. Accounts were to be rendered at the Exchequer upon Oath When the Accountant had been sworn *de fideli compoto reddendo*, he entered upon and went through his Account. In some Records Mention is made of the Accountants answering at the Exchequer *per Fidem*, or *per Verumdictum*. Whether this *Fides* and *Verumdictum* was the same with an Oath, or in what respect different from it, I am not prepared to determine. But I am inclined to think, it was rather a *Voire dire*, or a Declaration upon their Faith or Allegiance, than an Oath. The Sheriff of *Essex* and *Hertfordshire* accounted for the Escuage of the Honour of *Peverell* of *London*, *per Verumdictum suum* (u). The Sheriff of *Norfolk* and *Suffolk* answered at the Exchequer *per Fidem*, touching an Amercement of CC *l* set upon *William de Merlai* (w). The Sheriff of *Cumberland* answered *per Verumdictum*, touching an Escuage charged on *Lambert de Muleton*, who married the eldest Daughter and Heir of *Richard de Lucy* (x); and others in like Manner *mutatis mutandis*. Again, sometimes the Stewards of the Nobility were admitted to answer for their Lords at the Exchequer, *per Verumdictum*, or *per Fidem suam*, in their Accounts or Affairs depending there. For Example: *Randulf de Glanvill* made a View of his Ac-

saurarij est devillaturus & non rediturus citra festum S. Mariæ Magdalenæ, ponit loco suo Hugonem de Waltham, ad respondendum pro eo in omnibus quæ ipsum contingent, quoad Officium Vicecomitatus prædicti, citra festum prædictum, hic coram Thesaurario & Baronibus, & ad faciendum pro eo quod ijdem Thesaurarius & Barones eidem Hugoni, tamquam eidem Johanni si præsens esset, ducerent injungendum. Per ipsum Thesaurarium. *Trin. Commun.* 12. *E.* 2. *Rot.* 57. *b.*

(s) *Mich. Brevia Retornab.* 15. *E.* 2. *Rot.* 82. *a.*

(t) One, per W. de Norwyco; *another* per Walterum de Friskeneye; *a third* per R. de Wodehouse; *others* in pleno Scaccario. *Trin. Commun.* 15. *E.* 2. *Rot.* 39. *a.*

One, per W. de Friskeneie; *another* per Barones; *another* per L de Trikingham. *Mich. Recogn.* 15. *E.* 2. *Rot.* 69. *a.*

Again; per J. de Foxle; per R. de Wodehous. *Ib. Rot.* 69. *a. & b.* per R. de Everdon; *Ib. Rot.* 70. *b.*

(u) Idem Vicecomes r c de xxvij l & xv s & vj d, de xlj Militibus & dimidio & sexta parte Militis, de Honore Peuerelli de Lundonia in Baillia sua, per Verumdictum Vicecomitis. *Mag. Rot.* 14. *H.* 2. *Rot.* 3. *a. Esexa & Hertf.*

(w) Willelmus de Merlai debet CC marcas de misericordia. Sed de suo nichil invenitur extra septa Ecclesiæ, per Fidem Vicecomitis. *Mag. Rot.* 16. *H.* 2. *Rot.* 1. *a. Norfolch & Sudf.*

(x) Lambertus de Muleton, qui habet in uxorem Primogenitam filiam & hœredem Ricardi de Lucy, r c de xx s de j feodo de Veteri feffamento in Copland, secundum Veredictum Vicecomitis; In thesauro nichil, Et in superplusagio quod Vicecomes habet supra ibidem in debitis plurium, xx s, Et Q. e. *Mag. Rot.* 29. *H.* 3. *Cumb. m.* 1. *b.*

count

Chap. XXIII.   *and* ACCOUNTANTS.

count for *Weſtmerland* for three Years, by *Reiner* his *Dapifer:* and *Reiner* entered upon his Account *per Verumdictum ſuum* (*y*). The Earl of *Leiceſter*'s *Dapifer* anſwered at the Exchequer on his Lord's Behalf, *per Verumdictum*, concerning certain ſmall Fees of *Moreton* (*z*). This anſwering by *Dapifers* or Stewards was, I ſuppoſe, owing to the King's Favour (*a*). And as the Barons at the Exchequer, ſo the Sheriffs in their Counties uſed frequently to give Credit to the Stewards of great Lords, when they declared *per Fidem* on Behalf of their Lords, touching Debts which they owed to the King; as in the Caſe of *William de Areci* (*b*), and others. But in Proceſs of Time there was found to be ſome Inconvenience in that Practice. So it proved in a Caſe relating to *Robert de Tateſhal*. The King commanded the Sheriff of *Lincolnſhire* to levy upon *Robert*'s Chatells Lxx *l* xv *s*, which he owed to the King, and for the future not to believe the Steward of any Baron barely upon his *Fides*, where the King's Debts were concerned (*c*).

VII. Where one was indebted to the King, and likewiſe to other Perſons, the King's Debt was to be preferred in Payment; that is, the King was to be paid before any other Creditor of the Party. This was the Law and Aſſiſe of the Exchequer, as appeareth in the Caſe of the Executors of *R. de Chaucumb* and *Stephen Croc* (*d*), the Abbot of

---

(*y*) Viſus Compoti de Weſtmarieland per Reinerum Dapiferum Randulfi de Glanvill de tribus annis. Randulfus de Glanvill, Rinerus pro eo, reddit compotum de firma de Weſtmarieland per verumdictum Reineri Dapiferi ſui. *Mag. Rot.* 23. *H.* 2. *Rot.* 7. *b.*

(*z*) Anſketillus Mallor. & Robertus Capell. debent C & xiiij s & viij d de Scutagio Militum Comitis Legerceſtriæ de quibus xxxv s ſunt de parvis feodis de Moretonia, per verumdictum ipſius Dapiferi. *Mag. Rot.* 19. *H.* 3. *Rot.* 5. *b.*

(*a*) Rex Comiti Warenniæ. Mandamus vobis quod occaſione & dilatione poſtpoſitis, ſitis coram Baronibus noſtris de Scaccario in craſtino S. Lucæ Ewangeliſtæ, ad reſpondendum & ſatisfaciendum nobis de debitis noſtris. Et ſi venire non poteſtis, aliquem veſtrorum mittatis ad illud faciendum. *Mich. Commun.* 11. *H.* 3. *Rot.* 1. *a.*

(*b*) Willelmus de Areci debet j marcam, ut ſit quietus de hoc quod non fecit pacem ad Scaccarium de debito Domini ſui ſicut affidaverat in Comitatu. *Mag. Rot.* 10. *R.* 1. *Rot.* 4. *b. m.* 2. *Linc.*

(*c*) Lincolnia, pro Rege. Mandatum eſt Vicecomiti, quod de bonis & catallis Roberti de Tateſhal fieri faciat Lxx l xv s quos Regi debet de pluribus debitis, Ita quod habeat prædictos denarios ſuper compotum ſuum proximo ad Scaccarium; nec de cætero credat Seneſcallo alicujus Baronis per Fidem ſuam pro aliquibus debitis; Et habeat breve. *Paſ. Memor.* 41. *H.* 3. *Rot.* 15. *b.*

(*d*) Epiſcopo Lincolnienſi & alijs executoribus R. de Chaucumb. Rex eiſdem; Sciatis quod Robertus de Chaucumb debuit nobis die quo obijt C & xliij l viij s & iiij d de pluribus debitis, pro quibus areſtari fecimus omnia catalla quæ fuerunt ejuſdem R: Et ideo vobis mandamus, quod ad catalla illa manus non apponatis, donec de dictis debitis noſtris nobis fuerit plene ſatisfactum; Quia ſecundum conſuetudinem Regni noſtri

of *Forde* Executor of *Robert de Curtenay* (*e*), *Emery de St. Amand* (*f*), *Robert de Crepping* (*g*), the Executors of *Walter de Leyseton* (*h*); and in other Instances.

If one was indebted to the Crown, such Debtor could not make a Will to dispose of his Chatells to the King's Prejudice; nor could his Executor have Administration of his Chatells without Permission from the King, or from the Justicier, or Barons of the Exchequer. The Executors of *Thomas de Berkele*, the King's Debtor, were permitted to have Administration of his Goods, upon his giving Security to answer the King's Debts (*i*). In like Manner the Executors of *Saer*

nostri imprimis nobis debet de debitis nostris satisfieri. Teste xj die Octobris. *Memor.* 22. *H.* 3. *Rot.* 2. *a.* The like Writ mutatis mutandis *in the Case of* Stephen Croc, *concluding,* Cùm de consuetudine Regni nostri nobis debeat in primis satisfieri, Teste M. Belet &c. xxx die Jan. anno xxij. *Ib. Rot.* 5. *b.*

(*e*) Officiali Episcopi Exon. Rex eidem; Ostensum est nobis ex parte Abbatis de Forde executoris Roberti de Curtenay, quod cum idem Abbas teneatur nobis reddere xij l de debitis ipsius Roberti, vos citatis ipsum coram vobis autoritate ordinaria ad respondendum alijs quibus idem Robertus debuit debita. Et quia nos debemus præferri omnibus alijs donec debita nostra nobis persolvantur, præcipimus vobis quod non distringatis prædictum Abbatem ad reddendum alijs creditoribus debita quæ debuit, donec idem Abbas nobis satisfecerit de prædictis xij l, nisi vobis constiterit quod catalla prædicti Roberti quæ sunt prædicto Abbati satisfufficiant ad solutionem aliorum & nostrorum. *Ex Memor.* 28. *H.* 3. *Rot.* 4. *b.*

(*f*) Oxon. Rex Vicecomiti; Monstravit nobis Radulfus de Sancto Amando, quod distringis ipsum injuste ad reddendum nobis debita quæ Amaricus de S. Amando nobis debuit, videlicet—, desicut executores testamenti prædicti Amarici satis habent de bonis ejusdem A, unde nobis satisfacere possunt de prædictis debitis, ut idem R. dicit: Et quia debita quæ nobis debentur prius de bonis defuncti debent nobis reddi, quam satisfiat alijs creditoribus de debitis eorum, Tibi præcipimus, quod venire facias coram Baronibus de Scaccario in crastino S. Trinitatis Mathæum de C unum executorum testamenti prædicti A, ad respondendum nobis una cum alijs executoribus ejusdem A —; Et inhibeas eidem Mathæo ex parte nostra, ne alienet bona prædicti Amarici donec nobis satisfiat de prædictis debitis———. And hereupon *several like Writs were issued into several Counties against the several Executors. Ex Memor.* 28. *H.* 3. *Rot.* 10. *b.*

(*g*) Ebor. Mandatum est Vicecomiti, quod non permittat executores testamenti Roberti de Ayvill habere ullam administrationem de catallis quæ fuerunt ejusdem Roberti, quousq; prædicti executores reddiderint Roberto de Crepping ix l xij s ij d., qui ei aretro sunt de firma Molendini de Essingwald, sicut ostendere poterit quod ei aretro sunt, Ne pro defectu sui &c. Teste A Thes. S. Pauli Londoniæ xx die Oct. *Ex Memor.* 28. *H.* 3. *Rot.* 2. *b.*

(*h*) Prohibitum est Magistris J. Archidiacono & Willelmo de Newerk Officiali Ebor., ne Fratrem Gilbertum de Leyseton Monachum, & alios executores testamenti Walteri de Leyseton quondam Vicecomitis Lincolniæ, vexent occasione bonorum dicti Willelmi, neq; de eisdem bonis placitum in Curia Christianitatis teneant, quousq; per ipsos executores Regi fuerit satisfactum, de debitis quæ Regi debuit. *Memor.* 42. *H.* 3. *Rot.* 14. *a.*

(*i*) Rex eisdem [Baronibus]; Mandamus vobis, quod per rotulos nostros de Scaccario diligenter scrutari faciatis in quantis debitis nobis tenebatur Thomas de Berkele; & cum per prædictos rotulos inde certi fueritis, significetis Vicecomiti Gloucestriæ, quod accepta sufficienti securitate ab executoribus testamenti

Chap. XXIII.   *and* ACCOUNTANTS.

Saer Fitz-Henry were permitted to have Administration, upon giving Security for the King's Debts; and the Executors of several other Persons (*k*). The King granted to *William de Canteloup*, that he might make his Will, and that his Executors might administer his Goods: the King being content that *William*'s Heirs should pay his Debts, at the same Terms at which *William* was obliged to pay them (*l*). The King granted by his Patent to *William de Ferrers*, Earl of *Derby*, that although he happened to be indebted to the King, he might freely make a Will; and his Heirs should answer to the King his Debts (*m*). This Patent the King certified to the Barons, and commanded them to enroll and observe the same in the Exchequer. The like was done for the Executors of *William de Longespeye* (*n*). The King by his Writ

testamenti ipsius Thomæ de Berkele de prædictis debitis, eisdem executoribus plenam administrationem habere faciatis de omnibus rebus & catallis quæ fuerunt ipsius Thomæ — ; Et mandatum est Vic. Glouc. *Ex Memor.* 28. *H.* 3. *Rot.* 6. *a.*

(*k*) Plegij executorum Saeri filij Henrici. Maria quæ fuit uxor prædicti Saeri, Adam de Sumery Miles qui habet terras in Com. H. —, manuceperunt reddere Domino Regi omnia debita quæ idem Saerus Regi debuit, videlicet, Quilibet eorum in solidum & pro toto: Et mandatum est Vicecomiti Surreiæ, quod de catallis prædicti S. prædictæ Mariæ liberam habere administrationem faciat. *Ex Memor.* 35. *H.* 3. *Rot.* 12. *a.*

The like for the Executors of Geoffrey de Rokingham, *Ib. Rot.* 14. *a. The like for the Executors of* Margery de Echingeham, *Memor.* 42. *H.* 3. *Rot.* 5. *b. The like for the Executors of* Roger de Mohun, *Ib.* 42. *H.* 3. *Rot.* 12. *a. And for others, Ib. Rot.* 13. *b. & Rot.* 14. *a.*

(*l*) Rex concessit eidem Willelmo [de Cantilupo], quod libere & licenter posset condere Testamentum suum, & quod Executores sui habeant liberam administrationem de omnibus bonis & catallis ad executionem ejusdem Testamenti faciendam, sine impedimento Regis vel Ballivorum suorum: Quia Rex vult, quod hæredes ejusdem Willelmi solvant ei debita in quibus ipse Willelmus Regi tenetur, ad eosdem Terminos ad quos idem Willelmus eadem debita Regi reddere solebat. Breve est in f. M. *Memor.* 39. *H.* 3. *Rot.* 2. *a.*

(*m*) Breve Patens Comitis de Ferrariis. Rex concessit pro se & hæredibus suis W. de Ferrarijs Comiti Derbiæ, quod licet contingat ipsum Domino Regi in aliquo debito teneri, nichilominus libere possit condere testamentum suum absque impedimento Regis & Ballivorum suorum, ita quod occasione illius debiti Rex non capiet nec capi faciet terras, catalla, seu bona ipsius Comitis in manum suam; nec permittet quod aliquis ballivorum suorum de prædictis terris, catallis, seu bonis sus aliquatenus se intromittat; set hæredes dicti Comitis Domino Regi de dicto debito respondeant. In cujus r t &c; Teste Rege vij die Januarij anno xxxiij. *Memor.* 38. *H.* 3. *Rot.* 12. *a.*

(*n*) Rex mandat Baronibus Literas suas Patentes, per quas concessit dilecto quondam & fideli suo W. de Ferrarijs Comiti Derbiæ, ut libere possit condere testamentum suum absque impedimento Regis vel ballivorum suorum, teneri faciendas secundum tenorem earundem literarum. *Memor.* 40. *H.* 3. *Rot.* 3. *a.*

Rex mandat Baronibus, quod Literas Patentes per quas concessit executoribus testamenti quondam W. Comitis de Ferrarijs, quod habeant liberam administrationem de omnibus bonis &c quæ fuerunt prædicti Comitis, eo quod vivente prædicto Comite concesserat ei Dominus Rex, quod licet contingeret eum debere Domino Regi &c, libere possit condere testamentum &c, & quod hæredes sui responderent Regi de prædictis debitis, inrotulari & firmiter teneri &c. *Ib. Rot.* 9. *b. The like for the Executors*

Writ commanded, that *John de Steyngrine* should have Administration of his Brother *Peter*'s Goods; the said *John* giving Security to answer the King's Debts (*o*). The like Command (*mutatis mutandis*) was given for the Wife or Executors of *Robert de Lathun* (*p*), and the Executors of *John le Fraunceis* (*q*). The Heir and Executors of *John* Bishop of *Ely* came into the Exchequer, and prayed to have Administration of his Goods: which was granted to them upon these Terms; *viz.* that the Executors should pay the Debts due from the Deceased to the King as far as the Goods would extend; that the Goods should be sold to the King's best Profit; and out of the Money arising thereby, the King should be first paid. For the Performance of this, the Executors took an Oath, and found Sureties (*r*). The Executors of *Robert*, late Earl of *Oxford*, gave Security to pay unto the King the Debts due to him from their Testator; and thereupon

cutors of William de Longespye; *Hil. Record.* 41. *H.* 3. *Rot.* 9. *a.*

(*o*) Ebor. Quia Johannes de Steyngrine frater & hæres Petri de Steyngrine nuper defuncti fecit Regem securum per J. de O. & W. de N, ad reddendum Regi debita quæ idem Petrus Regi debuit, Mandatum est Vicecomiti quod de omnibus bonis & catallis quæ idem Petrus habuit in balliva sua die quo obijt, prædicto Johanni de Steyngrine plenam administrationem habere faciat, in partem solutionis prædictorum debitorum. Teste &c. *Memor.* 52. *H.* 3. *Rot.* 5. *a.*

(*p*) Baronibus, pro uxore & executoribus testamenti Roberti de Lathun. Rex mandat quod mandent Vicecomiti, quod si Johanna quæ fuit uxor prædicti Roberti, vel prædicti executores invenerint ad Scaccarium in xv Paschæ, sufficientem securitatem de debitis quæ Regi debuit reddendis, tunc eis de omnibus bonis & catallis quæ fuerunt ipsius Roberti plenam administrationem habere faciat. *Memor.* 52. *H.* 3. *Rot.* 6. *b.*

(*q*) Thomas de Wymundeham Præcentor Lichefeldiæ, Magister Petrus de Radenor Archidiaconus Salopiæ, executores testamenti Johannis le Frauenceys manuceperunt pro se & coexecutoribus suis reddere Domino Regi omnia debita quæ idem Johannes Regi debuit die quo obijt: Et mandatum est Vic. Linc. Bed. Ebor. Kanc. Westmerl. Cumbr. [quod] plenam administrationem eisdem executoribus habere faciant. *Memor.* 52. *H.* 3. *Rot.* 8. *a.*

(*r*) Memorandum quod die Sabbati proximo post octabas S. Trinitatis anno xviij°, venerunt coram Baronibus Willelmus de Kirkeby frater & hæres J. de Kirkeby nuper Elyensis Episcopi defuncti, Magister Guido de Tillebrok, & Philippus de Heverdon, executores testamenti prædicti defuncti, & petierunt administrationem bonorum & catallorum quæ fuerunt ejusdem defuncti; Et concessum est eis sub hac forma, videlicet quod prædicti Executores satisfaciant Domino Regi de debitis quæ idem defunctus ei debet, quatenus bona & catalla prædicta sufficiunt; unde summa est, v mille xxij l xviij s viij d; prout compertum est per Inventorium; & quod dicta bona & catalla de die in diem vendi facient, prout melius ad commodum Regis vendi poterunt; & quod de denarijs inde provenientibus nichil omnino alicui liberabitur, ante quam prædicto Domino Regi de debitis suis plenarie fuerit satisfactum. Et ad hoc fideliter faciendum præstiterunt Sacramentum coram præfatis Baronibus, Et insuper ad hoc invenerunt plegios subscriptos, videlicet Dominum R. Bathon. & Wellensem Episcopum, & Magistrum Willelmum de Luda Eliensem Electum. *Trin. Commun.* 18. *E.* 1. *Rot.*—*a.*

Chap. XXIII.   *and* ACCOUNTANTS.   187

Adminiſtration of the Earl's Goods was granted to them (*s*). In like Manner *(mutatis mutandis)* Adminiſtration was granted to the Executors of *Bartholomew Caſtle* (*t*); the Executors of *John de Somerſete* (*u*); the Executors of *Walter de Luveny* (*w*); the Executors of *Walter de Monci* (*x*); and the Executor of *Henry de Say* (*y*). It is true, from the Caſe of *William* and of *Mary de Brewoſe*, as it ſtands in *Ryley*, ſome may perhaps conjecture, that the Treaſurer and Barons of the Exchequer granted to *Mary* Adminiſtration of the Goods of *William de Brewoſe* deceaſed. But if I take the Matter right, that is to be underſtood thus; that the Treaſurer and Barons conſented to her having the Adminiſtration, which (in regard her late Huſband *William* was, at his Death, the King's Debtor) ſhe could not have had, without Conſent or Permiſſion of the King or the Court of Exchequer. The Caſe may be ſeen in *Ryley* (*z*). On the other Part: If the Debt demanded of a deceaſed Perſon on the King's Behalf was a doubtful Debt, the King would ſometimes command the Executors to retain in their Hands ſo much as the Sum amounted to, till the Matter was diſcuſſed in the Exchequer (*a*).

(*s*) Oxon. *Several Perſons become Sureties for the Executors of* Robert de Ver, *late Earl of* Oxon —; Et per manucaptionem prædictam conceſſa eſt eiſdem Executoribus adminiſtratio omnium bonorum *of the ſaid Earl*. *Memor.* 24 & 25. *E.* 1. *inter Mich. Manucaptiones.*

(*t*) *Mich. Manucaptiones* 25. *E.* 1.

(*u*) *Hil. Commun.* 25 & 26. *E.* 1. *Rot.* 48. *b.*

(*w*) Somerſ. & Dorſ. Johannes de Stafford Mareſcallus Scaccarij, manucepit reddere Regi omnia debita, quæ Walterus de Luveny nuper Vicecomes Somerſetæ & Dorſetæ defunctus Regi debet ad Scaccarium. Et per iſtam manucapcionem conceſſum eſt executoribus teſtamenti ipſius defuncti, quod habeant adminiſtrationem omnium bonorum & catallorum quæ fuerunt prædicti defuncti die quo obijt, ad executionem teſtamenti prædicti defuncti inde faciendam. *Mich. Fines* 26 & 27. *E.* 1. *Rot.* 64. *a.*

(*x*) Edward par la grace de Dieu &c, Au Treſorier & au Barouns de noſtre Eſcheqer ſalutz. Nus vous maundoms qe receue bone & ſuffiſaunte ſeurte des Executors du Teſtament Monſieur Wauter de Monci nadgaires noſtre Chaumberleyn, de nous reſpondre des totes maners de dettes qil nous deyt per queuque encheſon qe ceo ſeyt, ſuffretz meſmes les executours aver pleyne & due adminiſtracion des touz les biens qe furent au dit Wauter; & ſi noules de nos miniſtres y eient mis noſtre meyn, lour facetz maunder par Lettres de noſtre Eſcheker, quil en ouſtent noſtre meyn par la ſeurte avantdite. Done ſouz noſtre Prive Seal a Langele, le xxvij jour de Janever lan de noſtre regne Secund. *Hil. Brevia* 2. *E.* 2. *Rot.* 48. *a.*

(*y*) *Mich. Commun.* 5. *E.* 2. *Rot.* 20. *b.*

(*z*) *Plac. Parl. p.* 109. 20. *E.* 1.

(*a*) Executoribus J. Bathonienſis Epiſcopi. Rex eiſdem; quia non conſtat nobis utrum nos debeamus habere illas xx l, quas prædictus Epiſcopus recepit de Abbate Glaſtoniæ pro tranſgreſſione —, an idem Epiſcopus illas debeat habere per libertatem cartæ noſtræ quam habuit; Vobis mandamus, quatinus de catallis ejuſdem Epiſcopi retineatis uſque ad ſummam xx l, quouſque diſcutiatur coram Baronibus de Scaccario, utrum nos debeamus habere illas xx l, vel idem Epiſcopus. *Ex Memor.* 28. *H.* 3. *Rot.* 10. *a.*

If

If one died indebted to the King, and it was doubtful whether the Chatells of the Deceased would amount to satisfy the Debts due to the King [and to other Persons], it was usual for the King to seize into his Hands the Chatells of his Debtor deceased, in order to have Satisfaction of his Debt, before any other Creditor of the Deceased was paid, or the Chatells eloigned or applied to any other Use. This was done in the Case of the Earl of *Kent* (*b*). But when the King seized the Chatells of his Debtor deceased, he allowed out of the same a competent Part for the decent Funeral of the Deceased. As in the Case of *Malcolm de Harleigh*, Escheator on this Side *Trent*. The King by Writ of Privy Seal commanded the Treasurer's Lieutenant and the Barons of the Exchequer, that whereas upon *Malcolm's* Death they would probably seize his Goods and Chatells into the King's Hands, they should leave enough in the Hands of his Folks for the honourable Interrment of his Body: and that they should send some fit Person to all Places where he had any Goods, to make a true and exact Inventory of them, that the King, when he should be certified of the Affair in due Manner, might give such Orders therein as he thought meet. *Thomas de Boyvill* was assigned, by Letters Patent, to take an Inquisition concerning the Goods of *Malculm*. And the Treasurer's Lieutenant ordered, that out of the Goods of *Malcolm*, xlviij l xiiij s xj d should be delivered to *Richard de Harle* his Executor, for the Exequies and Burial of the Deceased (*c*).

VIII. If

(*b*) Essex. Rex Vicecomiti; Monstravit nobis Comitissa Kanciæ, quod tu distringis eam ad reddendum nobis quædam debita quæ Comes Kanciæ nobis debuit; Et quia catalla quæ fuerunt dicti Comitis Kanciæ sunt in manu nostra per præceptum nostrum, donec executores ejusdem Comitis nobis satisfecerint de debitis eisdem; Tibi præcipimus, quod dictæ Comitissæ pacem habere permittas de debitis prædicti Comitis, donec aliud inde præceperimus. *Ex Memor.* 28. *H.* 3. *Rot.* 6. *a.*

(*c*) Edward par la grace de Dieu &c; Au lieutenaunt le Treforer e as Baruns del Escheqer saluz. Por coe qe Macolum de Harlegh qe feu noster Eschetour de cea Trente, est a Dieu comaunde, a coe qe nus avoms entendu: Vous maundoms, qe de ses biens e ses chateux, qe vous prendrez par avienture en nostre mein par acheson de sa mort, leissez a ses gentz taunt dont le Corps porra bien e honorablement estre enseveli; E enveez par tot ou les biens e les chatteux sunt qe furunt au dit Maucolom, acun certeyn homme qui bien e loiaument face Lynventoire de totes les choses qe il trovera, & quil vous certifie de ceo quil avera fait, Issint qe quant nous en serroms certifiez en due Manere, nous en peussons comaunder ce qe nous verroms qe seit a faire. Done souz nostre Prive Seal a Harwe, la xx jour de Averil, lan de nostre regne xxvj. Postea prætextu brevis prædicti Thomas de Boyvill Clericus assignatur per Literas Regis patentes, ad inquirendum de omnibus bonis & catallis quæ fuerunt dicti defuncti, sicut continetur in rotulo Commissionum & Literarum Patencium hujus Termini.

Et per Philippum de Wylughby Tenentem locum Thesaurarij concessum est xxiiij° die Aprilis, quod de bonis quæ fuerunt dicti

VIII. If the King's Debtor was unable to satisfy the King's Debt out of his own Chatells, the King would betake himself to any third Person who was indebted to the King's Debtor, and would recover of such third Person the Debt he owed to the King's Debtor, in order to get Payment or Satisfaction of the Debt due to the Crown; and then, upon such Recovery had, the third Person was acquitted against the King's Debtor, and the King's Debtor was acquitted against the King, *de tanto*. This seems to be confirmed by the Case of *Henry de Cornhill* and *William* Earl of *Albemarle*, in the 5th Year of K. *Richard* I. *Henry de Cornhill* owed the King C *l*. for the Arerage of the *Cambium* of all *England* except *Winchester*, and vj *l*. for the Ferm of the Land of *Engelran de Muſtroil*. And *William* Earl of *Albemarle* acknowledged before the Barons of the Exchequer, that he owed so much to *Henry de Cornhill*. And thereupon *William* Earl of *Albemarle* was charged (as Debtor to the King) with the said respective Sums (*d*). However, this Usage appears plainly enough in the succeeding Times: For Example; in the Case of Persons indebted to *Herbert Fitz-Matthew*, Debtor to the King (*e*); in the Case of several Persons who had intermeddled with the Goods of *Ranulf Briton*, Debtor to the King (*f*); in the Case of *Beneit Aze* and others,

dicti defuncti liberentur Ricardo de Harle Executori testamenti ejusdem defuncti ad valenciam xlviij l xiiij s xj d, pro exeqrijs & sepultura ejusdem defuncti. *Pas. Cmmunia* 26. *E.* 1. *Rot.* 70. *a. in bund.* 25 & 26. *E.* 1.

(*d*) Willelmus de Forz Comes de Albem[arle] debet C l qui requirabantur ab Henrico de Cornhill de reragijs Cambij totius Angliæ præter Wintoniam. Quia idem Comes cognovit coram Baronibus de Scaccario, se prædictum debitum debere ipsi Henrico. Idem Willelmus debet vj l pro eodem Henrico de firma terræ Engelranni de Musterel; quia idem Comes cognovit coram Baronibus se prædictum debitum debere & debitorem constituit. *Mag. Rot.* 5. *R.* 1. *Rot.* 5. *b. Linc.*

(*e*) Summers. & Dorf. Mandatum est eidem, quod distringat debitores Herberti filij Mathæi, ad reddendum arreragia quæ ei debentur, de tempore quo idem Herbertus filius Mathæi fuit Vicecomes in ipsis Comitatibus, ne pro defectu &c. T. P. Grimb[aud] xxv die Novembris. *Ex Memor.* 25. *H.* 3. *Rot.* 3. *a.*

(*f*) Baronibus, pro Rannulfo Britone. Rex concessit eidem R, quod de debitis quæ Regi debet ad Scaccarium reddat Regi per annum sexies viginti libras —: Et ideo mandatum est eisdem Baronibus, quod accepta ab eo securitate de terminis prædictis servandis, omnes redditus ipsius Rannulfi in manu Regis captas ei deliberari faciant: Distringant etiam sine dilatione omnes illos qui pecuniam de bonis & catallis ipsius Rannulfi receperunt quamdiu in manu Regis exstiterunt, & ipsam pecuniam Regi nondum solverunt, quod pecuniam illam(omni dilatione & occasione postpositis)Regi reddant; & cum ipsa pecunia particulariter Regi fuerit soluta, in prædicto debito eidem Rannulfo particulariter allocari faciant; Et ad prædictam pecuniam perquirendam efficax consilium & auxilium ei impendant. *Memor.* 25. *H.* 3. *Rot.* 9. *a.*

Debtors to *John de la Bulehuſe*, Debtor to the King (*g*); in the Caſe of the Executors of *Edmund* Archbiſhop of *Canterbury*, Debtors to *William Talebot*, Debtor to the King (*h*); and of *Reginald de Wyme*, Debtor to *H.* late Earl of *Arundel*, Debtor to the King (*i*).

IX. The Heir of the King's Debtor was not to be diſtrained for the Debt due to the King, in caſe the Chatells of the King's Debtor were ſufficient to anſwer it; as may appear in the Caſe of *Ralf de St. Amand*, Heir of *Almaric* (*k*). In Truth, there was a Proviſion to this Purpoſe, made by the Great Charters of K. *John* (*l*), and K. *Henry* III (*m*). And *Walter de Avenbury*, Guardian of the Land and Heir of *Richard Aneſey*, had the like Privilege allowed to him (*n*).
But

(*g*) Suhamton. Rex Vicecomiti; Quia ſecundum conſuetudinem regni noſtri & aſſiſam Scaccarij, ubi debitores non ſufficiunt ad ſolvenda debita quæ nobis debent, capere nos conſuevimus ad debitores eorundem debitorum; & Benedictus Aze debeat Johanni de la Bulehuſe xviij l de j dolio vini, & alij nominati in brevi, ut Simon filius & hæres dicti Johannis dicit: Tibi præcipimus, quod intellecta ſuper veritate, diſtringas prædictos debitores ad reddenda nobis prædicta debita ad Scaccarium, in partem ſolutionis debitorum quæ idem Johannes nobis debuit, ita quod ea habeas ad Scaccarium per aliquem de tuis, a die———. *Ex Memor.* 28. *H.* 3 *Rot.* 12. *a.*

(*h*) B. Electo Cantuarienſi. Mandatum eſt eidem quod venire faciat coram Baronibus—executores teſtamenti E. bonæ memoriæ quondam Cantuarienſis Archiepiſcopi—, ad reſpondendum Regi de xx l quas idem E. reliquit Willelmo Talebot in ultima voluntate ſua, in parte ſolutionis debitorum quæ idem Willelmus Regi debuit—. *Memor.* 28. *H.* 3. *Rot.* 11. *b.*

(*i*) Mandatum eſt Vicecomiti Lincolniæ, quod venire faciat in craſtino S. Margaretæ Virginis, Reginaldum de Wyme, ad reſpondendum Regi de xxv libris, quas debuit H. de Albiniaco quondam Comiti Arundelliæ, in partem ſolutionis debitorum quæ idem Comes Regi debuit. Et habeat breve. *Memor.* 38. *H.* 3. *Rot.* 17. *a.*

(*k*) Oxonia. Rex Vicecomiti; Quoniam ſecundum leges & ſtatuta Scaccarij noſtri, hæredes illorum qui debita nobis debent, non conſueverunt diſtringi quamdiu catalla defunctorum ſufficiunt: Ad querelam Radulfi de Sancto Amando hæredis Almarici qui in debitis ſubſcriptis nobis tenebatur, venire facias coram Baronibus de eodem Scaccario Abbatem de Cyrenceſtria unum executorum teſtamenti dicti Almarici—. *Ex Memor.* 28. *H.* 3. *Rot.* 11. *a.*

(*l*) Nos vero vel Ballivi noſtri non ſeiſiemus terram aliquam nec redditum pro debito aliquo, quamdiu catalla debitoris præſentia ſufficiunt ad debitum reddendum, & ipſe debitor paratus ſit inde ſatisfacere. Nec plegij ipſius debitoris diſtringantur, quamdiu ipſe capitalis debitor ſufficiat ad ſolutionem debiti. *In Mag. Chart. R. Joh. cap.* 10. *ap. Brad. Hiſt. Angl.* P. I. *in Append. p.* 130. *& ap. Tyrell. Hiſt. Angl. Vol.* 2. *in Append. p.* 10.

(*m*) *The Clauſe runs in the ſame Words as above in K. John's Charter; ſave that for,* nec redditum, *this Charter has,* vel redditum. *Ex Mag. Chart. H.* 3. *inſpecta ab E. I.* (*viz. ex autogr. Regis E.* I.) *in archivo Eccleſ. Colleg. Weſtmon.*

(*n*) Rex Baronibus; Quia ut nobis videtur, non eſt æquum nec rationi conſonum, quod Walterus de Avenebury, qui finem fecit nobiſcum pro CCCC marcis, pro cuſtodia terræ & hæredis Ricardi de Aneſeye, diſtringatur pro fine xl marcarum quem idem Ricardus contraxit nobiſcum dum ſuperſtes

But if the Chatells of the King's Debtor deceafed were not fufficient to pay the King's Debt, the Debtor's Heirs were to be diftrained by their Lands for the fame. In the Reign of K. *Henry* III, *Simon de Heddon*, one of *Brian de Lifle*'s Executors, had not Affets in his Hands to fatisfy certain Debts due to the King from *Brian*. Therefore the Sheriff was commanded to diftrain *Brian*'s Heirs for the faid Debts (*o*). In the Reign of K. *Edward* II, in the Cafe of *Alan de Cherleton*, the Barons of the Exchequer were commanded by Writ, to apportion amongft Parceners a certain Debt due from their Anceftor to the King (*p*).

X. The Widow of the King's Debtor was not to be diftrained by her Dower to anfwer the King's Debt, in cafe the Heir had fufficient to anfwer it. *Maud de Beauchamp* was diftrained by the Dower which fhe had from her firft Hufband, to anfwer to the King for the Debt of her fecond Hufband. Upon Complaint, the King by his Writ commanded the Sheriff to forbear demanding that Debt from *Maud*, and to diftrain the Heirs of the fecond Hufband for it: Becaufe (faith the Writ) a Tenant in Dower ought not to be diftrained for Debts, whilft the Heir hath fufficient to anfwer the fame (*q*). *Juliana*, late Wife of *John de Cornhull*, likewife obtained Relief, upon her Cafe, by virtue of a Writ, reciting that by the Law and Cuftom of the Realm Women ought not to be diftrained in the Lands and Tenements which they hold in Dower, for the Debts of the King or of other Perfons, by the Summonce of the Exchequer or otherwife (*r*).

XI. The

---

perftes fuit pro quadam ferjantia, quamdiu bona & catalla quæ fuerunt ipfius R. fufficiant ad debitum illud acquietandum. Vobis mandamus, quod diftringatis executores teftamenti prædicti R. ad fatisfaciendum nobis de prædictis xl marcis prout bona & catalla illa fe extendere poffint —. *Memor.* 35. *H.* 3. *Rot.* 4. *a.*

(*o*) Mandatum eft Vicecomiti Notinghamiæ, quod quia Symon de Heddon unus executorum teftamenti Briani de Infula non habet in bonis quæ fuerunt ejufdem Briani, quod de demanda quam ei facit de debitis quæ idem B. Regi debuit ei pacem habere permittat——; & quod diftringat hæredes prædicti Briani ad reddendum Regi debita prædicta. *Memor.* 42. *H.* 3. *Rot.* 3. *a.*

(*p*) *Trin. Brevia* 12. *E.* 2. *Rot.* 112. *a.*

(*q*) Buk. & Bed. Rex Vicecomiti; Monftravit nobis Matilda de Bello Campo quæ fuit uxor Roberti de Turvill, quod tu diftringis eam per dotem fuam quam habet de Rogero de Bello Campo primo viro fuo, ad reddenda nobis debita quæ idem Robertus nobis debuit: Et quia Dos diftringi non debet pro debitis, dum hæres fufficit ad debita reddenda: Tibi præcipimus, quod eidem Matildæ de demanda quam ei facis de prædictis debitis pacem habere permittas, & diftringas hæredes dicti Roberti ad reddenda nobis debita quæ idem Robertus nobis debuit, ita quod fufficienter inde nobis refpondere poffis fuper compotum tuum &c; Tefte A. Archidiacono Salopiæ vij die Novembris. *Memor.* 22. *H.* 3. *Rot.* 2. *b.*

(*r*) Baronibus pro Juliana quæ fuit uxor Johannis

XI. The Sureties were not to be distrained so long as the principal Debtor had wherewith to answer the Debt. As in the Case of *Ralph Traer* (s); and *Walter de Berking* (t). This was also provided for by the Clause of K. *John's* Great Charter and K. *Henry* the Third's (u).

XII. By the ancient Usage of the Exchequer, the King's Debtors or Accountants were wont to have Writs of Aid, whereby to recover their Debts of such Persons as were indebted to them; in order to enable them to answer the Debts they owed to the King. For Example: *William de Horlesh* and *Richard de Redvers* were appointed to collect, in the Nortreding of *Yorkshire*, the Aid granted to K. *Henry* III. for marrying his Sister. And the Sheriff of the County was commanded by Writ to assist the said Collectors in distraining all Persons indebted to the King for that Aid (w). In like Manner, *mutatis mutandis*, Writs of Aid issued respectively, for *William de Lucy* and *Pauline Peivre* (x); for *William de Holwell* (y); for the Assessors and Col-

Johannis de Cornhull. Cum mulieres in terris & tenementis suis quæ tenent in dotem suam, pro debitis Regis aut aliorum per summonitionem Scaccarij aut alio modo distringi non debeant, nec hactenus secundum legem & consuetudinem Regni distringi consueverint: *She shewed, that she was distreined upon a Recognisance which her late Husband made in the Exchequer to* Peter de Huntingfeud *for x Marks: So the King commands the Barons to cease to demand, if it were so.* T. Rege apud Estry xv die Januarii *anno* xxij°, *Hil. Commun.* 22. *E.* 1. *Rot.* 1. *a.*

(s) Rex Baronibus; Quia consonum est rationi, ut fidejussores non distringantur quamdiu Principalis debitor habeat bona de quibus debitum suum reddere valeat; Vobis mandamus quod Radulpho Traer—. *This was in the King's Case; that is, the Party was Debtor to the King. Hil. Commun.* 32. *H.* 3. *Rot.* 6. *a.*

(t) Essex. Monstravit Regi Walterus de Berking, quod cum esset plegius Roberti de Badeford de dimidia marca, pro canibus habitis in Foresta Regis, vicecomes injuste distringit ipsum pro prædicta dimidia marca, desicut filius & hæres prædicti Roberti satis sufficit ad solutionem prædictæ marcæ, ut dicit: Et ideo mandatum est Vicecomiti, quod de demanda quam ei facit de prædicta dimidia marca ei pacem &c. *Memor.* 35. *H.* 3. *Rot.* 2. *b.*

(u) *Citat. hic paulo supra*; Nos vero vel.

(w) Ebor. Mandatum est Vicecomiti, quod sit in auxilium Willelmi de Horlesh & Ricardi de Ripariis, qui sunt assignati ad colligendum Auxilium Regi concessum ad maritandum Sororem suam, in Nortredhinga in Comitatu Ebor., ad distrinendos omnes illos qui aliquid inde debent Regi ibidem, ad reddendum eisdem Collectoribus id quod adhuc inde debent; Ne pro defectu &c. Teste ut supra [i. e. xiiij Oct.]. *Memor.* 22. *H.* 3. *Rot.* 2. *a.*

(x) War. & Leic. Mandatum est Vicecomiti, quod distringat omnes illos quos Willelmus de Lucy ei nominaverit, ad reddendum ei arreragia quæ ei debentur de tempore quo idem W. fuit Vicecomes Regis, sicut rationabiliter &c. Teste &c. *Memor.* 25. *H.* 3. *Rot.* 7. *b. The like for* Paulinus Peivre, *late Sheriff of* Buk. *and* Bed. *Ib. Rot.* 10. *b.*

(y) Buk. & Bed. Mandatum est Vicecomiti, quod distringat omnes illos quos
Willelmus

Chap. XXIII. *and* ACCOUNTANTS. 193

Collectors of the King's *Quadragesima* in *Middlesex*, and of the Aid *ad Sororem maritandam*, in *Cambridgeshire* (z) ; for the Assessors and Collectors of the King's *Tricesima* in *Suffolk* (a) ; for the Executors of *Hubert de Burgh*, who at the Time of his Death was indebted to the King (b) ; for the late Sheriffs of *London* (c) ; for *John de Baillol* and others (d) ; for the Executors of *P.* late Bishop of *Hereford* (e) ; for

Willelmus de Holewell ei nominabit, ad reddendum ei arreragia sua quæ ei aretro sunt de tempore quo fuit Vicecomes in Comitatibus suis sicut &c. ; Ne &c quin prædictus Willelmus sufficienter possit respondere de eisdem arreragijs. *Memor.* 35. *H.* 3. *Rot.* 15. *a.*

(z) Middlesex. Rex Vicecomiti ; Monstraverunt nobis Assessores & Collectores quadragesimæ nostræ in Comitatu tuo, quod villata de Stebhee debet eis vj s vj d de arreragijs prædictæ quadragesimæ (*and several other villates other arreres*); pro quibus arreragijs prædicti assessores non sufficiunt ad districtingendum : Et ideo tibi præcipimus, quod sis eis in Auxilium ad distringendum pro prædictis arreragijs ; Ne pro defectu &c ; T. &c. *Mich. Communia* 27. *Hen.* 3. *Rot.* 4. *a.*

Cauntebrugia. *The like Mandate to the Sheriff to be in Aid to the* Collectores Auxilij concessi ad Sororem nostram maritandam. *Trin. Commun.* 27. *H.* 3. *Rot.* 20. *b.*

(a) Norf. & Suff. Mandatum est Vicecomiti, quod distringat omnes illos quos assessores & collectores xxxæ ei nominaverint, ad reddendum eis arreragia quæ eis aretro sunt in Comitatu Suffolciæ de Libertate S. Eadmundi ; Ne pro defectu &c. *Memor.* 25. *H.* 3. *Rot.* 12. *a.*

(b) Et quia prædictus Comes [Kanciæ, Hubertus de Burgo] Regi tenebatur in pluribus debitis, Mandatum est Baronibus, quod distringi faciant omnes illos qui debita debebant prædicto Comiti, ad satisfaciendum prædictis Executoribus de debitis prædictis, ita quod de residuo debiti in quo prædictus Comes Regi tenebatur, plene Regi respondere possint. *Memor.* 35. *H.* 3. *Rot.* 15. *a.*

(c) Vicecomites habent diem ad arreragia sua reddenda die Lunæ proxima post festum S. Andreæ ; & Laurentius de Frowik habet eundem diem ut Priso pro arreragijs firmæ. Et præceptum est Vicecomitibus anni xxxij quod sint alijs Vicecomitibus anni xxxj in auxilium ad distringendum pro omnibus arreragijs prædictis. Et præceptum est Majori quod ipse habeat corpus Simonis filij Mariæ ad respondendum de arreragijs & de debitis proprijs ; alioquin Civitas capiatur in manum Regis. Et Major habet eundem diem ad reddendum omnia debita quæ veniunt in Summonitione super Communitatem Civitatis. *Memor.* 32. *H.* 3. *in fine Compoti Vicecomitum Lond. & Midd.*

(d) Cumbr. Præceptum est Vicecomiti, quod distringat omnes illos quos Johannes de Baillol sibi nominabit, ad reddendum sibi arreragia sua quæ ei aretro sunt de tempore quo fuit Vicecomes Cumberlandiæ, sicut rationabiliter monstrare &c. *Memor.* 40. *H.* 3. *Rot.* 3. *a. The like for* William de Engelfeud, *late Sheriff of* Devon. *And for* Peter le Templer. *Ib. juxt.*

(e) Cum P. quondam Herefordensis Episcopus Regi tenebatur in diversis debitis die quo obijt, ad quæ debita Regi solvenda bona ipsius defuncti non sufficiunt, nisi executores testamenti ipsius debita in quibus diversi homines eidem defuncto tenentur recuperent, ut Rex intellexit : Rex executoribus prædictis in hac parte gratiam facere volens specialem, mandat eisdem Baronibus, quod debitores ipsius defuncti ad debita in quibus ipsi præfato defuncto Episcopo tenebantur die quo obijt, præfatis executoribus solvenda distringant, prout ijdem Executores rationabiliter monstrare poterunt quod dicti debitores in præfatis debitis teneantur, & prout de jure fuerit faciendum. *Memor.* 55. *H.* 3. *Rot.* 4. *b.*

Hugh

Hugh de Gisors (*f*); for *Philipp de Paunton* (*g*); for *Walter de Watford* (*h*); for the Executors of *Robert la Ware* (*i*); for the Merchants of *Lucca* (*k*); and others.

XIII. When a Sheriff or other Officer, having the Summonce or Process of the Exchequer, had levied or received the Debt due from any Person to the King, such Sheriff or Officer was, by the Statutes and Custom of the Exchequer, to give such Debtor an Acquittance or Tally of Discharge, and afterwards to acquit the Debtor of such Debt at the King's Exchequer. But in regard Sheriffs, after they had levied or received the Debts due to the King, often neglected or failed to answer the same at the Exchequer, and thereupon to acquit the Debtors there: The Crown did sometimes, at the Complaint of the Parties grieved, issue Writs to enquire in the several Counties, what Persons had paid their Debts to Sheriffs, and what Sums, whereof the Sheriffs had not acquitted them at the Exchequer. And at length

(*f*) Baronibus, pro Hugone de Gisores. Rex mandat sicut alias firmiter injungens, quod Lx marcas quas Hugo de Gisorcio solvit Regi pro Civibus Londoniæ, ad quarum solutionem ijdem Cives obligarunt se præfato Hugoni, sub omni festinatione de bonis & catallis prædictorum Civium, secundum legem & consuetudinem Scaccarij levari & eidem Hugoni liberari faciant. *Memor.* 52. H. 3. *Rot.* 6. *b.*

(*g*) Lincolnia. Pro Rege & Philippo de Paunton. Præceptum est Vicecomiti, quod sine dilatione levari faciat res, redditus, assisos, & alia quæ ad Jacobum de Paunton quondam Vicecomitem Lincolniæ pertinent, & arreragia sua quæ ei debentur, & Turnum Vicecomitis de Termino S. Michaelis anno Regni Regis H. Li'ij^{ti}. Ita quod habeat omnes denarios provenientes de eisdem debitis, redditibus assisis, arreragijs, & Turno Vicecomitis, coram Baronibus de Scaccario apud Westmonasterium, a die S. Michaelis in xv dies, Regi solvendos in partem solutionis debitorum quæ idem Jacobus Regi debet. Teste &c. *Ex Memor.* 1. *E.* 1. *Rot.* 7. *b.*

(*h*) Baronibus, pro Waltero de Watford. Quia Walterus de Watford in diversis debitis Regi tenetur, ad quorum solutionem bona dicti Walteri non sufficiunt, nisi prius de debitis in quibus creditores [*ita in Rot.*] sui sibi tenentur satisfiat eidem: Rex mandat eisdem, quod ad certos dies creditores illos coram eis venire faciant, et Creditores illos ad debita illa quæ eidem Waltero debent sibi reddenda distringant, prout de jure & secundum legem & consuetudinem Scaccarij fuerit faciendum. *Trin. Communia* 7. *E.* 1. *Rot.* 6. *b.*

(*i*) *A Writ of Aid for the Executors of* Robert la Ware, *to enable them to answer to the King his Debts. Pas. Commun.* 14. *E.* 1. *Rot.* 8. *b.*

(*k*) Rex volens Mercatoribus suis Ricardo Giudichione, Orlandino de Podio, & socijs suis Mercatoribus Lucanis, in hijs quæ eorum commodum contingunt cum gratia subvenire, Mandat Baronibus, quod Debita in quibus Johannes nuper Elyensis Episcopus eisdem Mercatoribus die quo obijt tenebatur, & de quibus eis nondum est, ut asserunt, Satisfactum, de bonis ejusdem defuncti, ac si Debita Regis propria fuerint, sine dilatione secundum consuetudinem Scaccarij levari & præfatis Mercatoribus habere faciant, quatenus ijdem Mercatores debita illa sibi deberi & injuste detineri rationabiliter monstrare poterunt coram Baronibus. T. Rege apud Westm. vij die Junij anno xviij°. *Trin. Commun.* 18. *E.* 1. *Rot.* — *a.*

a Statute

a Statute was made for Punishment of Sheriffs and others offending in such Cases. In the 22d Year of K. *Henry* III, Whereas divers Persons in *Yorkshire* had paid (some of them to *John Fitz-Geoffrey*, others to *Brian de Isle*, others to *Philipp de Asseley*, others to *William de Stutevill*, and others to *Robert de Kokefeld*, or to their Bailiffs) divers Sums demanded of them for the King by the Summonce of the Exchequer; whereof the said Sheriffs had not acquitted the said Debtors at the Exchequer: The King, upon Complaint thereof made to him, sent a Writ to the present Sheriff, commanding him to make Proclamation, that all such Persons as had paid to the said Sheriffs or their Bailiffs any Debts due to the King, whereof they were not afterwards discharged at the Exchequer, should come before him (the present Sheriff) and the Coroners, at the Wapentacks in each Trehing wherein they dwelt, and bring their Tallies of Payment, and produce their Vouchers or Witnesses; whereupon the Sheriff was to view their Tallies, and examine their Witnesses, and to set down in a Roll to be made for that Purpose the Names of such as had paid as abovesaid, to whom, in whose Presence, when, where, and how much each Person had paid to each of the said *John, Brian, Philipp, William*, and *Robert*, or their Bailiffs, thereof they (the Debtors) were not discharged at the Exchequer; which Roll the Sheriff was to have before the Barons of the Exchequer upon his next Account, under his own Seal and the Seal of the Coroners (*l*). In the Reign of K. *Edward* I, *John de St. Valery*, Sheriff of *Somerset* and *Dorset*, was assigned to enquire in full County, what Debts several Sheriffs of those Counties and their Bailiffs had received of divers of the King's Debtors, which Debts still ran in Summonce. The Manner in which the Inquisition was to be made, is directed in the Writ hereunder recited (*m*). In the 27th Year of the same King, a Proclamation issued

(*l*) *Memor.* 22. *H.* 3. *Rot.* 11. *a. ad imum.*

(*m*) Vicecomiti Somerset & Dorf. Rex assignavit Johannem de Sancto Walerico Vicecomitem prædictorum Comitatuum, ad Inquirendum in plenis Comitatibus prædictis, quæ debita diversi Vicecomites Regis & eorum Ballivi receperunt in eisdem Comitatibus de diversis debitoribus Regis, Quæ quidem debita adhuc veniunt in Summonicione Regis: Et ideo Rex mandat eidem Johanni, quod in plenis Comitatibus Regis prædictam Inquisitionem capiat, & distringat prædictos Vicecomites & eorum ballivos, vel eorum hæredes si qui mortui fuerint, per terras & catalla & eorum corpora, ad veniendum coram eodem Johanne ibidem, ad recognoscendum vel dedicendum Tallias quas tunc coram eodem Johanne Rex wlt ostendi. Et debita in eisdem Tallijs recognita inrotulari faciat. Cui Rotulo prædictorum debitorum sigilla sua apponant. Veritatem itaq; Talliarum dedictarum similiter inquirat. Et si dedictores illarum super hoc fuerint attincti, habeat corpora eorum coram Baronibus de Scaccario apud Westmonasterium in quindena S. Michaelis, ad audiendum inde judicium suum. *Memor.* 1. *E.* 1. *Rot.* 6. *b.*

into

into *Yorkshire*, reciting that divers Persons of that County complained to the King, that the Sheriff distreined them for divers Debts due to the King, which they had paid to former Sheriffs, as appeared by Tallies of Payment given them by such Sheriffs, and commanded that Outcry be made, that all Men of the *Estriding*, having Tallies of Payment made to them by any Sheriffs during the present King's Reign, of Debts whereof they are not discharged, should bring or send their Tallies to the Exchequer at *York* at the Close of *Easter*, so that the Sheriffs and their Receivers might be sent for to come and discharge such Persons whilst the Exchequer continued in this County; and for sparing Men's Charges, it was directed, that one or two of the *Estriding* might be Attornies to bring the Tallies for all the rest. And the Debts running in Process were to be levied upon all such as did not come or send their Tallies. Those of the *Northriding* were to have Day in the Quinzime of *Easter*, and those of the *Westriding* three Weeks after *Easter*, in like Form respectively (n). Again, when Sheriffs had levied or distreined for the King's Debt, it was their Duty to sell or dispose of such Distress at a just and reasonable Price, so that the Owner was not aggrieved thereby. But in regard some Sheriffs had misbehaved themselves in that Behalf, it was provided by ancient Statute, that when the Sheriff had seized any Cattel for the King's Debt, certain Persons should be assigned to apprize the same, according to which Apprizement they were to be sold by the Sheriff, lest the Sheriff should sell them at Under-rates to the Wrong of the Owners. *Peter de Meuling* claimed to be hereditary Apprizer in this Case for the County of *Norfolk* or *Suffolk* (o).

(n) Ebor. Fôrma Proclamationis faciendæ per totum Comitatum, pro Tallijs Vicecomitum ostendendis ad Scaccarium. Pur ceo qe plusures gentz &c. *Hil. Communia* 26 & 27. *E*. 1. *Rot*. 15. *a*.

(o) Norf. Suff. Rex Vicecomiti; Datum est nobis intelligi; quod cum fuerit provisum & statutum antiquitus a Progenitoribus nostris Regibus Angliæ quod in quibusdam Comitatibus assignarentur quidam legales homines, qui justo precio & rationabili venderent averia capta pro debitis eorum, ne Vicecomites vel ballivi eorum illa pro voluntate propria, & forsitan in odium aliquorum qui debita debebant, minori precio quam valerent illa venderent, & ita debitores gravarent: Petrus de Meuling qui jure hæreditario, ut dicitur, in Comitatu tuo vendicat ad se hujusmodi vendiciones Animalium pertinere, Bovem quanticumque sit precij vel valoris pro ij s, Equum eciam pro eodem precio, Ovem pro iiij d vendit, quociens fuerint hujusmodi averia vendenda: propter quod valde gravantur debitores nostri in Comitatibus tuis. Et quoniam reputamus hujusmodi vendiciones valde iniquas & injuriosas, Tibi præcipimus, quod venire facias coram Baronibus dictum P. a die S. Johannis in xv dies, ad ostendendum quo jure vendicat sibi competere hujusmodi vendiciones facere, & precipue tali precio. T. &c. *Trin. Communia* 27. *H*. 3. *Rot*. 11. *a*.

XIV. When

Chap. XXIII. *and* ACCOUNTANTS. 197

XIV. When the Sheriff came to account, he was to warn all the Bailiffs of Liberties within his County, of the Time of his accounting, and likewise to make Proclamation thereof in his County, that all who had Tallies of the Exchequer (touching Things within his Account) might come forth and obtain Allowances thereupon. As in the Case of the Sheriff of *Surrey* and *Sussex* (*p*).

XV. The King's Debtors found Sureties (if they were required so to do) for their true Payment. The Sureties were usually called *Plegij*, *Obsides*, and *Manucaptores*. Sometimes the Pledges in these Cases were remarkably numerous. For example: *Hugh Cordele* fined to the King in fourscore and six Pounds and one Mark of Silver, that he might be let out of Prison, and might have his Land again. Hereof he paid into the King's Treasury xx Marks of Silver: and for the Remainder, *viz.* Cx Marks of Silver, he found the Pledges hereunder named; *Alberic de Ver* for xx Marks of Silver, *John*, Son of *Ulri*, for xij Marks of Silver, *Osbert Eight-pence* for v Marks, *Otho Alwynessune* for ix Marks, and other Persons for other Sums. The Pledges are in Number nineteen (*q*). *Ralf de Cornhull* owed the King MM Marks, that he might have again his Lands whereof he was dissaised, and the King's Favour. His Pledges for this Fine were the Earl of *Clare* for xl Marks, Earl

---

(*p*) Surr. Sussex. Licet Rex nuper dederit diem ad Scaccarium Vicecomiti Comitatuum prædictorum, crastinum videlicet Purificationis Beatæ Mariæ proximo futurum, essendi hic coram Baronibus, ad reddendum Regi compotum de exitibus Comitatuum prædictorum de tempore quo fuit Vicecomes, & compotum nondum reddidit. Quia tamen Rex reddicionem compoti prædicti certis de causis vult festinari, Præceptum est Vicecomiti, quod in propria persona sua sit hic in Craftino Sancti Martini proximo futuro, ad reddendum Regi compotum suum prædictum. Et præmunire faciat Ballivos libertatum &c. Et publice proclamare faciat in locis infra ballivam suam, quibus melius fore viderit faciendum, quod omnes & singuli qui tallias seu acquietancias alias habeant de dicto Scaccario, quod sint ad tunc ibidem ad prosequendum allocaciones suas, si sibi viderint expedire. T. J. de Foxle xxvj die Octobris. *Mich. Brevia Retornab.* 15. *E.* 2. *Rot.* 81. *b.*

(*q*) Hugo Cordele r c de quater xx & vj l & j marca argenti, ut exiret de captione & haberet terram suam; In thesauro xx marcas argenti; Et debet C & x marcas argenti; sed de istis sunt plegij, Albericus de Ver de xx marcis argenti, Johannes filius Ulri de xxij marcis argenti, Osbertus viij denar. de v marcis, Otho Alwinessune de ix marcis, Reginaldus Presbiter de x marcis, Radulfus de Oxenef. de xij marcis, Hugo filius Ulgeri de ix marcis argenti, Et Walterus frater suus de iiij Marcis, Wido filius Vlgeri de iij marcis, Willelmus Bucherellus de ij marcis, Anschet. Nepos Rogeri de v marcis argenti, Robertus filius Roberti de j marca argenti, Rogerus Nepos Deirel de ij marcis argenti, Radulfus de Winc. de iij marcis argenti, Willelmus pesnudus de iij marcis argenti, Thomas filius Odonis Bucherel de iij marcis argenti, Rannulfus filius Roberti de ij marcis argenti, Simon Lutro de iij marcis argenti, Raginaldus filius Morin. de ij marcis argenti. *Mag. Rot.* 5. *Steph. Rot.* 15. *a. Lond. & Midd.*

Alberic

Alberic for xx Marks, *Robert de Crevequoer* for xx Marks, *Richard de Muntfichet* for xx Marks, Earl *David* for xx Marks, *William de Warenne* for xv Marks, and fourteen Persons more for other Sums (*r*). *Fulk Fitz-Warin* found two and forty Sureties for a Debt which he owed to the Crown (*s*). *Hugh de Albiniaco* fined in 2,500 Marks, to have Seisin of his Lands, and found above thirty Sureties for the Fine (*t*). *W.* Bishop of *Exeter* fined in 2000 Marks, for the Custody of the Land and Heir of *W. de Abrincis* with his Marriage; he found above thirty Sureties for the Fine (*u*). And sometimes the King's Debtors bound their Lands for true Payment. In the 5th Year of K. *Henry* III, *Nicolas de Stutevill* stood charged to the King in M Marks for his Ransom. He had covenanted to pay it at four Terms; to wit, CCL Marks at Midlent in the second Year of the King, CCL Marks at Whitsontide, CCL Marks at St. *Peter ad vincula*, and CCL Marks at Martinmass in the third Year of the King; upon these Conditions, namely, If he did not make Payment at the first Term, he was to incur or forfeit upon his Manors of *Kirkeby*, *Moresheed* and *Lidel*, fifty Pounds in yearly Rent; if he failed at the second Term, fifty Pounds more; if at the third Term, fifty Pounds more; and if at the fourth Term, fifty Pounds more. If the said two Manors would not amount to make-up the said two hundred Pounds in yearly Rent, he was to supply it in his other Manors. *Robert de Stutevill* and *Walter de Soureby* became Manucaptors for this Fine; on condition, that if *Nicolas* did not keep his said Terms of Payment, all their Land was to be incurred or forfeited (*w*). Add, that the King's Debtor was

wont

(*r*) Radulfus de Cornhull debet MM marcas, Pro habendis terris suis unde dissaisitus fuit & benivolentia Regis. Sed in his computabuntur ei C marcæ pro his quæ capta sunt de terris illis postquam venerunt in manu Regis. Plegij ejus sunt Comes de Clara de xl marcis, Comes Albericus de xx marcis, Robertus de Crevequoer de xx marcis, Ricardus de Muntfichet de xx marcis, Comes David de xx marcis, Willelmus de Warenna de xv marcis, Gilebertus Basset de xx marcis, Willelmus de Bocland de x marcis, Robert de Mara de iij marcis, Derekinus del Acre de v marcis, Adam de Port de x marcis, Robertus de Curtenai de x marcis, Constabularius Cestriæ de x marcis, Henricus de Puteaco de v marcis, Rogerus de Sancto Edmundo de x marcis, Archidiaconus Cantuariensis de x marcis, Wiscardus Leidet de v marcis, Præcentor S. Pauli de x marcis, Robertus Parvus Clericus de Londonia de x marcis, Gilebertus de Lasci de x marcis. *Mag. Rot.* 9. *R.* 1. *Rot.* 11. *a. Londonia & Middlesexa.*

(*s*) Plegij Fulconis filij Warini: Radulfus de Bello Campo de xx marcis, Walterus de Wahull de x marcis; *and several others in several Sums; the Number of Pledges is in all forty two. Mag. Rot.* 9. *J. Rot.* 10. *b. post compotum de Abbatia de Rameseia.*

(*t*) Finis Hugonis de Albiniaco pro terris suis habendis. *Fin.* 18. *H.* 3. *m.* 11.

(*u*) De Fine Episcopi Exoniensis, pro habenda custodia terræ & hæredis W. de Abrincis. *Ib. m.* 10.

(*w*) Nicholaus de Stutevill [debet] M marcas pro Redemptione sua, quas debuerat
reddi-

wont to be summoned first in the County wherein he resided or had Lands; and if the Debt could not be levied in one County, it might be transferred and summoned in another. *Robert Fitz Bernard* owed the King Lxxij l Blank, and iiij l xix d by Tale, Areres of the Ferm of *Dovor*. The Debt was summoned in *Kent*. The Sheriff of *Kent* returned, that *Robert* was dead, and that his Heirs might be distreined in *Devonshire*. Hereupon the Debt was sent-out in Summonce in *Devonshire*; but the Sheriff of that County returned, that *Robert* had nothing in Demesne in *Devonshire* (x). Again; Distresses taken for the King's Debts were not replevyable, except by Precept from the King or Barons of the Exchequer. As in the Case of the Tenants of the Bishoprick of *London* (y). These are some of the Assises or Statutes of the Exchequer. There may be others, which, though omitted here, are not designed to be excluded.

XVI. Writs of the Great Seal and of the Privy Seal were frequently used, both in reference to Accounts, and other Business transacted at the Exchequer. Many Instances hereof may be seen in a foregoing Part of this History (z), and many other in this Chapter (a).

XVII. If the Sheriff or other Accountant was to have any Sum allowed or discounted to him upon his Account, such Allowance or Discount was usually made *per warantum*, to wit, either by virtue of the King's Writ in that Behalf (which was the most usual Way) or by Writ or Award of the Chief Justicier, or of some other Justicier

---

reddidisse ad quatuor terminos, scilicet ad Mediam Quadragesimam anno ij° Regis hujus CC & L marcas, & ad Pentecosten CC & L marcas, & ad festum S. Petri ad Vincula CC & L marcas, & ad festum S. Martini anno tercio ejusdem CC & L marcas, Ita scilicet quod si primum terminum non tenuerit, obligavit Maneria sua de Kirkeby & Moresheued & Lidel, sub hac forma: Quod de dictis Manerijs incurrantur L libratæ terræ; Similiter si Secundum terminum non tenuerit, incurrantur in eisdem Manerijs L libratæ terræ: Similiter si tercium terminum non tenuerit, incurrantur in eisdem Manerijs L libratæ terræ; similiter si Quartum Terminum non tenuerit, incurrantur in eisdem maneriis L libratæ terræ. Et si dicta duo Maneria non sufficiant ad CC libratas perficiendas, defectum illum supplebit in talijs Manerijs suis. Hunc Finem manuceperunt Robertus de Stutevill & Walterus de Soureby, hoc modo, quod si terminos non tenuerit, tota terra illorum incurratur. *Mag. Rot.* 5. *H.* 3. *Rot.* 9. *a. tit. Item Ebor.* m. 2.

(x) Robertus filius Bernardi debet Lxxij l Bl[ancas] & iiij l & xix d numero, de Veteri firma de Doura. Sed mortuus est, & hæredes ejus debent distringi in Devenescira, sicut Vicecomes dicit. Sed Vicecomes de Devenescira dicit, quod nichil habet in dominio in Devenescira. *Mag. Rot.* 9. *R.* 1. *Rot.* 3. *a. Kent.*

(y) Essex & Hertf. Rex Vicecomiti —; Et quia averia capta pro debitis nostris non sunt replegibilia, nisi per præceptum nostrum vel Baronum nostrorum de Scaccario nostro: Tibi præcipimus, quod averia quæ cepisti de hominibus dicti Episcopatus [viz. Londoniæ] in Wydernamium, deliberari facias ——. *Ex Memor.* 28. *H.* 3. *Rot.* 5. *b.*

(z) *Cap.* 22. *sect.* 9.

(a) *Cap.* 23. *sect.* 17, 18, 19, 20.

or Baron, or of the Treasurer. And it being usual for the King to order either the Whole or Part of such Monies as arose from his Ferms, or other Revenue, to be paid to such Persons as he was indebted to, there was by that Means a vast Number of Writs of *Allocate* and *Computate* issued from time to time, and directed to the Treasurer and Barons of the Exchequer, whereby they were impowered to allow to Accountants or Debtors the Monies which they had paid to others by virtue of Warrants or Precepts in that Behalf. Of this I must give some Instances. Allowance was made to an Accountant for redeeming certain Mortgages made to the *Jews*; it was made by virtue of the King's Writ *Teste Richard de Luci (b)*. Allowance was made to *Ralf Briton* by virtue of the King's Writ (c). Allowance was to be made, by virtue of the King's Writ, to *Robert de Stutevill* (d). Allowances were also made, by Force of the King's Writs in that Behalf, to *Roger de Herleberg* (e), *Ranulf de Glanvill*, accounting for the Honour of Earl *Conan (f)*, and for the County of *Westmerland* (g), one *Geoffrey* (h) *William Briewerre* (i), *Geoffrey Fitz-Pier* (k), *William Earl*

(b) Et pro vadijs eorum [Infirmorum Cantuariæ] redimendis de Judæis, xl l; per breve Regis, Teste Ricardo de Luci. *Mag. Rot. 13. Hen. 2. Rot. 13. a. Chent.*

(c) Idem [Radulfus Brito] non reddit compotum de terra Henrici de Essexa, neq; de terra Comitis Eustachij de hoc anno, per breve Regis quod attulit de Computando ei sicut computatum fuit annis præteritis, scilicet quod inde reddidit compotum Regi; Et Quietus est. *Mag. Rot. 17. H. 2. Rot. 8. b. tit.* Honor Boloniæ.

(d) Robertus de Stutevill non reddidit hoc anno compotum de firma Comitatus de Everwichsira, neq; de Debitis Regis in eodem Comitatu, quia nondum habuerat Warantum Regis de expensa quam fecerat tempore Werræ in servitio Regis. *Mag. Rot. 20. H. 2. Rot. 8. b.*

(e) In thesauro nichil; Et in terris datis Willelmo filio Walkel. xxij l & x s in Stembia de ij annis & dimidio, per breve Regis quod idem Rogerus [de Herleberga] attulit de computandis sibi omnibus terris quas Rex dederat. Et Quietus est. *Mag. Rot. 21. H. 2. Rot. 2. a. Lanc.* Roger de Herleberg *was Fermer of* Lancaster.

(f) Summa denariorum quos idem Rannulfus [de Glanvilla] misit in liberationibus Militum & Servientum Equitum & Peditum, de quibus liberavit in Thesauro breve continens nomina & numerum & terminos, DCCCC & xviij l & x s & j d; De quibus sibi conputandis attulit breve Regis. *Ib. Rot. 2. in Compoto de Honore Comitis Conani.*

(g) Et Fratribus Hospitalis S. Lazari de Jerusalem v marcæ, de Divisa Hugonis de Morevilla, per breve Regis quod prædictus Randulfus [de Glanvill] attulit, de conputandis sibi omnibus, in veritate sua, quæ posuit in Custodia Castellorum, & Waignerijs, & Instauramento terrarum, in Westmarieland. *Mag. Rot. 23. H. 2. Rot. 7. b.*

(h) Willelmus filius Galfridi [debet] ix l & xvij s & iiij d de reragio villæ de Chelardeston de duobus annis antequam ipse Galfridus perquisisset sibi breve Regis de Waranto de conputando sibi C s in eadem terra. *Mag. Rot. 10. R. 1. Rot. 8. a. Not. & Dereb.*

(i) Willelmus Briewerre r c de xx marcis pro Homagijs & Servitijs Roberti del Estre, sicut continetur in Rotulo præcedenti: In thesauro nichil, Et in Perdonis ipsi Willelmo CC marcas, per breve Regis quod attulit de conputandis CCL marcis in quocumq; debitorum suorum vellet; Et Q. e. *Mag. Rot. 6. J. Rot. 4. a. Cornewallia.*

(k) Et ipsi Regi in Camera sua xx marcas apud Bere, per manum Radulfi Camerarij, per

Chap. XXIII.   *and* ACCOUNTANTS.

Earl of *Sarefbery* (*l*), the Abbot of *Hammes* (*m*), the Abbot of *Strafford* (*n*), and the Sheriff of *Salop* (*o*). By virtue of the King's Writ the Men of *Rochefter* were allowed in their Ferm for the Maltolt of Perfons paffing through their Town towards the Holy-Land: and likewife vj *l* yearly for the Archbifhop of *Canterbury*'s Liberties in their Town (*p*). Allowance was made, by virtue of the King's Writ, to the Collectors of the Trentifme in *Cornwall*, for the Money they paid into the King's Wardrobe (*q*): and to *Pauline Peivre* for the like (*r*). By virtue of a Writ of *Allocate*, *Engelard de Cygoni* had xl *l*, which he owed the King, difcounted out of the yearly Fee he received at the Exchequer (*s*). The Barons were commanded, by Writ of *Computate*, to difcount to the Bailiffs of *Newcaftle* upon *Tine*, out of their Ferm, C *l* which they had laid-out upon the King's Engines, and in Seamens Wages, &c (*t*). The Barons were ordered, by a like Writ, to difcount to P. Bifhop of *Hereford*, out of the

per breve Regis quod attulit de conputandis fibi CC & xl marcis, pro pluribus pacamentis quæ pacavit in Camera Regis; Quod breve eft in forulo Marefcalli. *Mag. Rot.* 8. *J. Rot.* 4. *b.*

(*l*) Willelmus Comes Sarefberiæ debet DC & Lxxij l & ix s de pluribus debitis: Sed non debet inde fummoneri, quia prædictum debitum computatum ei fuit in feodo fuo de pluribus terminis de D l quas habet per annum de Rege, præcepto Regis, per record[um] P. Wintonienfis Epifcopi, & W. Briewerre, & aliorum Baronum de Scaccario; Et fic Q. e. *Mag. Rot.* 14. *J. Rot.* 16. *a. Wilt.*

(*m*) *Memor.* 2 & 3. *Hen.* 3. *Rot.* 3. *b.*

(*n*) *Ib. Rot.* 3. *b.*

(*o*) Idem Vicecomes r c de xxvij l de tallagio Maneriorum, ficut fupra continetur: In thefauro nichil: Et Roberto Lenfant & focijs fuis cuftodibus caftri de Salopefbiria xxvij l, ad operationem ejufdem caftri, per breve Regis quod attulit, de computandis fibi L l de tallagio affifo fuper Dominica Regis in eodem Comitatu, excepto tallagio Villæ de Salopefbiria. *Mag. Rot.* 7. *H.* 3. *Rot.* 11. *b. Salop.*

(*p*) Baronibus, pro hominibus Roffæ. Rex eifdem; Computate Ballivis noftris Roffæ, in firma Villæ fuæ Roffæ, quantum capi confuevit de Mala tolta a Crucefignatis tranfeuntibus per prædictam Villam Roffæ, antequam Rex Ricardus Advunculus nofter Malam toltam illam abolevit per Cartam fuam quam homines ejufdem villæ habent, ficut computari folet antequam Villam ipfam concederemus hominibus noftris prædictis ad feodi firmam. *Memor.* 22. *H.* 3. *Rot* 10. *a.*

Item computate Ballivis noftris Roffæ fingulis annis, vj l, pro Libertatibus Cantuarienfis Archiepifcopi in Villa Roffæ, ficut eis allocari confueverunt antequam Villam noftram Roffæ Civibus noftris Roffæ commifimus ad feodifirmam, per Cartam noftram quam eis inde fieri fecimus. *Ib. Rot.* 10. *a. juxt.*

(*q*) Rex eifdem [Baronibus]; Computate Roberto filio Willelmi & Henrico de B, collectoribus tricefimæ in Cornubia, D marcas, quas folverunt in Garderoba Regis. *Memor.* 25. *H.* 3. *Rot.* 6. *b.*

(*r*) Rex eifdem. Computate Paulino Peiure in exitibus Comitatuum Bed. & Buk. xl l, quas folvit in Garderoba, & Lxxviij s quos pofuit in reparatione Gaiolarum. *Ib. Rot.* 10. *b.*

(*s*) Rex Baronibus; Allocate Engelardo de Cygoni xl l quas nobis debet de firma Manerij de Odiham de duobus annis, fcilicet de anno xxvj° & xxvij°, in feodo fuo L l quod ei debemus de anno xxvij°. *Memor.* 28. *H.* 3. *Rot.* 5. *a.*

(*t*) *Mich. Communia* 29. *H.* 3. *Rot.* 1. *b.*

Debts

Debts he owed at the Exchequer, xxx Marks, laid-out by him in a Vestment and Mitre which the King had given to Cardinal *Hugh di San Caro* (*u*). By virtue of a Writ of *Allocate*, directed to the Treasurer and Barons, Allowance was made to *Peter Chacepork*, Keeper of the Wardrobe, of several Payments by him made, to wit, of x *l* to Master *Henry* the Poet, of Cix *l* to *Alexander* King of *Scots*, for his Corrody upon his Coming to the King of *England*'s Court, and returning back again, &c. and of other Sums to other Persons (*w*). In fine; Discounts or Allowances were made at the Exchequer, by virtue of particular Writs, to the Persons hereafter named, upon their respective Cases; *viz.* to *Gilbert de Preston* (*x*), to *Fulk Payforer*, Sheriff of *Kent* (*y*), *William de Engelby*, Sheriff of *Lincolnshire* (*z*), *Walter Hervy*, *John Adrian*, and others, late Bailiffs or *Custodes* of the City of *London* (*a*), *William de Wintreshull*

(*u*) Computate P. Herefordensi Episcopo, in debitis quæ nobis debet ad Scaccarium nostrum, xxx marcas, quas posuit per præceptum nostrum in uno vestimento decenti & in una mitra, emptis & datis Hugoni de Sancto Caro Cardinali Domini Papæ de dono nostro. *Memor.* 35. *H.* 3. *Rot.* 1. *b.*

(*w*) Et Magistro Henrico Versificatori, xl l —; Et Domino Alexandro Regi Scociæ percipienti per diem veniendo versus Curiam Domini Regis per præceptum ipsius, & redeundo C solidos, in Regno Angliæ, & perhendinando xxx s, pro liberationibus suis per xx dies, veniendo usq; ad Ebor., & redeundo, & per sex dies perhendinando ibidem C & ix l; Per breve Regis directum Thesaurario & Baronibus de Scaccario in hæc verba, Allocate Petro Chaceporc Custodi Garderobæ nostræ, in exitu ejusdem Warderobæ nostræ, omnes solutiones, liberationes, & pacationes, contentas in contrarotulis quondam Willelmi Hardel & Magistri Willelmi de Kylkenny, unde Compotus est reddendus ad Scaccarium nostrum sicut contrarotuli eorundem plenius testantur. *Mag. Rot.* 35. *in Rot. Compotor. m.* 1. *a.*

(*x*) Rex mandavit Baronibus, quod in debitis quæ Gilbertus de Preston ei debet, allocarent eidem Gilberto viginti libras de Termino Paschæ anno xxxix°, de annuo feodo suo quadraginta librarum quod concessit ei percipiendum ad Scaccarium. *Memor.* 39. *H.* 3. *Rot.* 15. *a.*

(*y*) Baronibus, pro Fulcone Payforer. Rex mandat, quod superchargium corporis Comitatus Kanciæ, de tempore quo idem Fulco fuit Vicecomes & approeator ejusdem Comitatus, a festo S. J. Baptistæ anno xlviij°, usq; ad festum S. Michaelis anno xlix°, scilicet per unum annum & unum quarterium, allocentur, sicut alijs Vicecomitibus ejusdem Comitatus firmarijs & approeatoribus allocari consuevit ad Scaccarium. *Memor.* 51. *H.* 3. *Rot.* 1. *b.*

(*z*) Baronibus, pro Willelmo de Engelby. Rex mandat quod audito compoto ejusdem Willelmi de tempore quo fuit Vicecomes Lincolniæ rationabiles expensas suas pro custodia dicti Comitatus de tempore prædicto, in exitibus dicti Comitatus, sibi faciant allocari, sicut alijs Vicecomitibus allocari fecerunt. *Memor.* 52. *H.* 3. *Rot.* 9. *b.*

(*a*) Memorandum de expensis Walteri Hervy & Sociorum suorum quondam Custodum Civitatis Londoniæ. Rex mandavit Baronibus de Scaccario, quod habere facerent Waltero Hervy, Johanni Adrian, & Willelmo de Dunolmo, Roberto de Cornhull, & Thomæ de Basing nuper Ballivis Civitatis Londoniæ, misas & expensas suas rationabiles quas fecerunt circa custodiam Civitatis prædictæ, tempore quo Civitas prædicta fuit in manu Regis, prout de jure fuerit faciendum. Thesaurarius igitur & Barones, vocatis coram eis prædictis Civibus & Vicecomitibus ejusdem Civitatis, & alijs

de

Chap. XXIII. *and* Accountants.

shull (*b*), *Richard de Holebrock* (*c*), *Ralph Paynel*, Sheriff of *Lincoln*, and other Sheriffs of other Counties (*d*), *Peter de Mauley* (*e*), *William de Nevill*, late Sheriff of *Warwick* and *Leicester* (*f*); and to other Persons without Number; as may appear both by the Records of the Exchequer, and by the *Liberate-Rolls* remaining in the Tower of *London*, which are full of Writs of *Allocate, Computate,* and *Liberate.* Again: Sometimes the King, by his Writ, would forbid the Barons to make Allowance, where it was not just and reasonable for Allowance to be made; as in the Case of the Bailiffs of *Staunford* (*g*). There were also some Cases wherein Allowance could not be made to Accountants, without the King's Writ. But in some of those Cases the Writs for Allowance were usually made of course. *John* Bishop of *Hereford* had laid out Money in Purveyances and other Necessaries for the King; which Money (faith the Record) could not without the King's Writ be

de discretioribus de prædicta Civitate, diligenter examinaverunt inter se, unde prædicti Custodes & eorum clerici majores & minores, et servientes diversi majores & minores, possent per annum sustentari, tam in victualibus quam robis stipendijs & alijs necessarijs, & invenerunt quod prædicti Custodes & alij possent sustentari rationabiliter per annum de Centum xlvj l & j marca. Unde provisum est, quod toto tempore quo fuerunt Custodes prædictæ Civitatis, allocetur eisdem per annum prædicta summa pecuniæ in debitis quæ Regi debent de remanente compoti sui de exitibus prædictæ Civitatis; scilicet cuilibet eorum prc rata temporis, & porcione ipsum contingente de eadem pecunia. Facta est postmodum Allocatio eisdem in Rotulo Liijº & Liiijº. *Ex Memor.* 55. *H.* 3. *Rot.* 6. *b.*

(*b*) Baronibus, pro Willelmo de Wintreshull. Rex mandat, quod allocent eidem Willelmo Vicecomiti Suthamptoniæ, in finibus & amerciamentis factis in Comitatu prædicto, coram Magistro Ricardo de Stanes Justiciario ad placita tenenda coram Rege, x marcas, quas per præceptum Regis liberavit Willelmo de Sancta Ermina, cui Rex concessit eas de dono suo ad expensas suas. *Memor.* 55. *H.* 3. *Rot.* 9. *a.*

(*c*) *Trin. Communia* 7. *E.* 1. *Rot.* 6. *b.*

(*d*) Baronibus, pro Radulpho Paynel nuper Vicecomite Lincolniæ. *This Writ commands the Barons to allow him upon his Account a great many Sums, laid out for Services of many Kinds*; *Pas. Brevia* 26 & 27. *E.* 1. *Rot.* 21. *a.*

Baronibus, pro Willelmo de Sutton nuper Vic. Essexiæ & Hertf.; *a like Writ to allow for Services and Expences of divers Kinds*; *Trin. Commun. ib. Rot.* 31. *a.*

Baronibus, pro Johanne de Kirkeby nuper Vic. Northumbriæ; *a like Writ to allow for warlike Provisions made by the said Sheriff. Ib. Rot.* 32. *a.*

The like Writ for Robert de Glamorgan nuper Vic. Surriæ & Sussex. *Ib. Rot.* 34. *a.*

(*e*) Baronibus, pro Petro de Malo lacu. Edward par la grace de Deu &c. Pour ceo qe nostre feial e loial Peres de Maulay est entendaunt a nostre service en office de Justice de la Pes; Vous maundoms, qe endreyt des dettis qe il nous deyt a nostre Escheker, ly facez allouaunce de ceo que il nous avera paez sy avaunt, cum il purra monstrer qe il en eyt sossisaunt aquitance——. Donez souz nostre Prive Seal a Cardoyl, le xxj jour de Mars le an de nostre regne xxxv. *Pas. Brevia* 35. *E.* 1. *Rot.* 41. *a.*

(*f*) *Trin. Brevia* 15. *E.* 2. *Rot.* 64. *a.*

(*g*) Baronibus pro Rege. Rex eisdem; —— Et ideo vobis mandamus, quod illas quaterviginti marcas in firma prædicta eisdem ballivis [de Staunford] amodo non allocetis——. *Ex Memor.* 28. *H.* 3. *Rot.* 5. *b.*

allowed

allowed to him in the Debts he owed at the Exchequer (*h*). *Henry de Bray*, an Escheator, had laid out divers Sums of Money in his Office of Escheatry, *viz.* in the Maintenance of the King's Wards, in the Custodies of Bishopricks, Abbeys, &c. Hereupon the King commands the Barons, that if by the Custom of the Exchequer, the Allowances which *Henry* prayed, could not be made without the King's Writ, then they should direct proper Writs to be made out for that Purpose (*i*). And in another Case, upon the Party's craving Allowance, he was directed by the Court to sue forth a Writ of *Allocate* (*k*).

There were also sometimes issued dormant Writs of *Allocate* or *Computate*; by virtue whereof Allowance was to be made to the Party from time to time. The Bailiffs of *Windsore* had a dormant Writ of *Allocate*, for xxvj s, which they paid yearly to the Canons of *Saresbury* for Tithes of Paunage in *Windsore* Forest (*l*). *John Silvester* had a Writ to be allowed ij *s per Diem* for his Expences, so long as he should continue in the Office of Keeper of the King's Mint (*m*). A dormant Writ

---

(*h*) Baronibus, pro J. Heref. Episcopo. Ostensum est Regi ex parte ejusdem J, quod cum Rex teneatur eidem in quadam pecuniæ summa, pro providentijs & alijs necessarijs quæ Regi habere fecit quando ultimo fuit apud S. Eadmundum; quam quidem pecuniæ summam eidem Episcopo in debitis quæ Regi debet ad Scaccarium sine præcepto Regis allocari non potest: Mandat Baronibus, quod venire faciant coram eis Rogerum de Colevill tunc Vicecomitem Norfolciæ & Suffolciæ, ad certificandum Regi quantum idem Johannes recepit ab eodem Rogero ad providentias illas faciendas, & quantum adhuc debetur de eisdem debitis diversis hominibus in Comitatibus prædictis: Et demandam quam eidem Episcopo faciunt occasione prædictorum debitorum interim relaxent. T. &c. *Trin. Commun.* 56. *H.* 3. *Rot.* 6. *b.*

(*i*) Rex vult & mandat Baronibus, quod allocent eidem Magistro Henrico [de Bray, Escaetori citra Trentam] omnia & singula quæ ipsi in compoto suo rationabiliter fuerint allocanda, una cum sumptibus Minorum infra ætatem existencium & educationibus eorundem, qui in Custodiam Regis inciderint dum idem Magister Henricus [curam] gessit ipsorum appositis, & eciam pro custodijs Episcopatuum, Abbatiarum, Prioratuum, Maneriorum, terrarum, & reddituum qui per Escaëtam in manum Regis pervenerunt, dum in custodia ejusdem Magistri Henrici fuerunt; quos legitime monstrare poterit se apposuisse circa præmissa. Et si ex consuetudine Scaccarij, sine Brevi Regis seu Brevibus non consueverint fieri allocationes hujusmodi, faciant fieri Brevia consueta super illis particulis quas viderint allocandas; Rex enim scribit Edmundo Comiti Cornubiæ Tenenti locum Regis in Anglia, ut talia Brevia per Barones facta faciat Sigillo Regis quo utitur in Anglia consignari. T. Rege apud Burdegalam xxviij° die Aprilis anno xv°. *Hil. Brevia in Bund.* 26 & 27. *E.* 1. *Rot.* 13. *b.*

(*k*) Et dictum est prædicto Willelmo, quod impetret breve clausum Domini Regis de Magno Sigillo, de Allocatione denariorum prædictorum. *Trin. Brevia in bund.* 26 & 27. *E.* 1. *Rot.* 29. *a.*

(*l*) Baronibus, pro Ballivis de Windsore. Rex eisdem; Allocate singulis annis eisdem ballivis in firma villæ suæ xxvj s, quos singulis annis reddunt per præceptum nostrum Ecclesiæ & Canonicis Saresb., pro decimis debitis prædictæ Ecclesiæ de pannagio forestæ de Windsore. *Ex Memor.* 28. *H.* 3. *Rot.* 8. *b.*

(*m*) Rex Baronibus; Allocate eidem J. [Silvestre]

Chap. XXIII. *and* Accountants.

Writ of *Allocate* iffued, for allowing vij *l* to the Sheriffs of *London*, upon their Account from Year to Year, in Deduction, for the Liberty of the Dean and Canons of St. *Paul* (*n*). The Men of *New Caftle* upon *Tine* had a dormant *Allocate*, for Difcount to be made out of the Ferm of their Town, till they fhould be reimburfed certain Monies which they had lent to the King (*o*).

Allowance was alfo fometimes made by the Writ or Award of the Chief Jufticier, or the Treafurer and Barons, or great Officers of the Exchequer. The Sheriff of *Suffolk*, by virtue of a Writ from Earl *Geoffrey* and *Richard de Luci*, Jufticiers, was allowed upon his Account x *s*, which he had paid to two Priefts for hallowing the Pits [that were for Juifes] at St. *Edmund* (*p*). The Sheriff of *Berkfhire* was allowed by the Writ of the Earl of *Leicefter*, a Jufticier, xx *l*, laid out in defraying Prince *Henry* (*q*). *William* Son of *Erenbald*, Fermer of the Mine of *Carlile*, was allowed upon his Account Money by him paid, by virtue of a Writ of *Richard de Luci*, Jufticier (*r*). The Sheriff of *Worcefterfhire* was allowed upon his Account, for the Livery or Subfiftence of certain Knights, by Writ of *Richard de Luci* (*s*): the Sheriffs of *London* and *Middelfex* for the Livery of cer-

[Silveftre] Cuftodi Cambij noftri, in exitibus ejufdem Cambij, ufq; ad feftum S. Vincentij anno xxxv°, fingulis diebus ad ij s ad expenfas fuas; & fic deinceps quamdiu habuerit Cuftodiam prædictam. *Memor*. 35. *H*. 3. *Rot*. 7. *b*.

(*n*) Rex conceffit per Cartam fuam Civibus fuis Londoniæ, quod pro Libertate S. Pauli Londoniæ allocentur eis fingulis annis ad Scaccarium feptem libræ, in compoto Vicecomitum ejufdem Civitatis. Et ideo mandat Baronibus, quod illas feptem libras, & de præterito unde funt in demanda, & de præfenti, & de futuro annuatim eis allocari faciant; Et Libertates quas eis de novo conceffit, & quas habent per Cartas prædeceflorum fuorum Regum Angliæ de cætero teneri faciant. *Memor*. 38. *H*. 3. *Rot*. 15. *a*.

(*o*) Cum probi homines Regis Villæ Novi Caftri fuper Tynam Regi mutuaverint Sexcentas triginta & tres libras fex folidos & octo denarios, ad negotia Regis inde expedienda; Ac Rex conceflerit eis, quod ipfi arreragia firmæ fuæ Villæ prædictæ in quibus Regi ad præfens tenentur, necnon & firmam ejufdem ex nunc penes eos retineant ufq; ad fummam Sexcentarum triginta & trium librarum fex folidorum & octo denariorum prædictorum; *the King commands the Barons to make Allowance accordingly*. Tefte Rege apud Dunelmum, primo die Augufti anno v. Per breve de Privato Sigillo. *Mich*. *Brevia* 5. *E*. 2. *Rot*. 6. *a*.

(*p*) Et duobus prefbiteris pro benedictione foffarum apud S. Ædmundum, x s; per breve Comitis Gaufridi & Ricardi de Luci. *Mag. Rot*. 12. *H*. 2. *Rot*. 2. *a*. *Norf. & Suthf*.

(*q*) Et in Corredio Henrici filij Regis, xx l, per breve Comitis Legerceftriæ. *Mag. Rot*. 13. *H*. 2. *Rot*. 2. *a*. *Berrochefcira*; Adam de Catmera, *Vicecomes*.

(*r*) Et Roberto de Vals xx l ad tenendos Milites in Caftello de Carleolo, per breve Ricardi de Luci; *and three other Sums*, per breve Ricardi de Luci. *Mag. Rot*. 19. *H*. 2. *Rot*. 11. *b*.

(*s*) Et in liberatione x Militum refidentium cum ipfo Vicecomite, xviij l & vj s & viij d, de Lv diebus; per breve Ricardi de Luci. *Mag. Rot*. 21. *H*. 2. *Rot*. 9. *a*. *Wireceftr*. Robertus de Luci *Sheriff*.

tain Knights Prisoners, by Writ of *Richard de Luci* (*t*): the Fermer of *Hanton* was allowed vij *l* x *s* (*u*), and the Sheriffs of *London* ninety-six Pounds and odd, upon Writs of the same *Richard de Luci* (*w*). The Fermer of the Honour of *Gloucester* had Allowance upon a Writ of *Ranulf de Glanvill* (*x*). The Sheriff of *Dorset* and *Somerset* had Allowance by Writ of *Ranulf de Glanvill* (*y*). *Hugh Bardulf* had Allowance by Writ of *Geoffrey Fitz-Pier*, of Lx *l.* which he paid to the *Flemings* (*z*). *Elias* the Engineer [or Architect] had x Marks, for Repairs of the King's Houses at *Westminster*, allowed to him by Writ of *Hubert*, Archbishop of *Canterbury*, Chief Justicier (*a*). The Sum of xl *l* x *s* and x *d* was allowed yearly to *Roger de Auntesey* and *Maud* his Wife by way of Discount (for the third Penny of *Essex*) by Precept or Award of *Hubert de Burgh*, Chief Justicier (*b*). In some Cases, Allowance was made to Accountants without any particular Writ directing it (for ought that appears). The *Custodes* or Committees of the Bishoprick of *Ely* (whilst it was void and in the King's Hands) had certain Allowances made to them, by Award of

(*t*) Et Jeremiæ de S. Nicolao Lxxij s, ad faciendam liberationem ij Militum prisonum, de CC & xvj diebus, per breve Ricardi de Luci. *Ib. Rot.* 3. *a. Londonia & Middilsexa.*

(*u*) Et in Passagio Esneccæ, In transitu Galfridi Lincolnensis Electi, & Johannis fratris sui, vij l & x s, per breve Ricardi de Luci, &c. *Mag. Rot.* 24. *H.* 2. *Rot.* 8. *a. Hantona.*

(*w*) Et in Soltis, per breve Ricardi de Luci, Deodato Episcopo Judæorum & Benedicto filio Saræ, & Mossi fratri suo, & Vivo, Judæis, quater xx & xvj l & xij s. *Mag. Rot.* 24. *H.* 2. *Rot.* 9. *b. Lond. & Midd.*

(*x*) Et Hugoni Bardul Senescallo Regis de Dono Regis, per breve Ranulfi de Gianvilla. *Mag. Rot.* 30. *H.* 2. *Rot.* 8. *b. tit.* Honor Comitis Gloecestriæ.

(*y*) Et pro j Nave locanda, ad portandum Rogerum Rastel & alios venatores, qui abierunt in Hyberniam cum equis & canibus suis, xxiij s, Per breve Rannulfi de Glanvilla; Et prædicto Rogero ij marcas, ad expendendum in ipso itinere, Per idem breve. *Mag. Rot.* 31. *Hen.* 2. *Rot.* 12. *a. Dorf. & Sumerf.*

(*z*) —— per breve G. filij Petri, quod idem Hugo [Bardulf] attulit de computandis sibi Lx l, quas prædictis Flandrensibus liberavit de prædictis feodis, Et Q. e. *Mag. Rot.* 10. *R.* 1. *Rot.* 11. *a. War. & Leic.*

(*a*) Et Elyæ Ingeniatori x marcæ, ad reparationem domorum Regis apud Westmonasterium, per breve H. Cantuarensis Archiepiscopi. *Mag. Rot.* 10. *R.* 1. *Rot.* 12. *a. Londonia & Midd.*

(*b*) Rogerus de Auntesye & Matildis uxor ejus r c de MMM & DC & quater xx & viij l xvij s & ij d, pro W. de Maundevill Comite Essexiæ: In thesauro xxxiiij *l* & vj s & ij d; Et in tercio denario Comitatus Essexiæ quem Comes W. de Maundevill cujus hæres ipsa M. est percipere consuevit, quem modo Vicecomes liberat in Thesauro Regis ad Scaccarium, Lxv l & xiij s & x d, videlicet xxv l & iij s a quintodecimo die Februarij anno Regis xij°, usque ad festum S. Michaelis anno eodem, Et xl l & x s & x d de toto hoc anno. Quæ quidem xl l x s & x d debent illi allocari singulis annis in prædicto debito, per præceptum H. de Burgo Justiciarij, donec totum prædictum debitum persolvatur; Et debent MMM & D & quater xx & viij l & xvij s & iij d. *Mag. Rot.* 13. *H.* 3. *in dorso. Essex & Hertf.*

the

Chap. XXIII.   *and* Accountants.

the Barons of the Exchequer (*c*). *Hervey Bagot* stood charged in the *Great Roll* with xviij *l* ix *s* vj *d* Escuage-money. It appeared to the Barons of the Exchequer, that *Hervey* was acquitted by the King's Writs both of the second and third Escuage [of *Normandy*]. And because by Mistake he paid to the second Escuage, whereas he ought to have paid to the first; they adjudged, that so much as he had paid should be discounted to him in the first Escuage (*d*). The Sheriff of *Lincolnshire* had xl Marks allowed to him for his Maintenance for the eleventh Year of K. *Henry* III, by Award of the Justicier (*e*). The King having lately granted the Town of *Oreford* with the Issues thereof to the Men of that Town in Fee-ferm, which had been formerly Part of the Sheriff's Ferm of the County; a Deduction was made of xxx *l*, in respect thereof, out of the Sheriff's Ferm, by Judgment of the Barons (*f*). Upon the Sheriff of *York*'s making the View of his Account in the Exchequer, the Treasurer and Barons ordered C Marks to be deducted for each Year out of the Sheriff's Ferm, in Consideration of his good Service to the King (*g*). *Bartholomew de Castle* was allowed the Wages of the Moneyors, Exchangers, Assayers, &c. in his Account of the Exchange of *Canterbury*, by Judgment of the King's Council at the Exchequer (*gg*). In Cases where the Allowances

were

(*c*) Et Inclusæ de S. Maria quæ solebat habere Discum Episcopi, viij s & viij d hoc anno, Consideratione Baronum; Et Rogero Nigro xx s hoc anno, Consideratione eorundem. *Mag. Rot.* 16. *H.* 2. *Rot.* 6. *b. tit. Episcopatus de Ely.*

(*d*) Herveius Bagot debet xviij l & ix s & vj d de Scutagio. Sed habet quietantiam per breve Regis Ricardi, Quia deprehensum est & per Barones recordatum, quod habuit quietantiam per brevia Regis tam de Secundo quam de Tercio Scutagio. Et quia per errorem ea quæ solvit de Secundo Scutagio debuit reddidisse de Primo, & ideo consideratum est quod ea quæ solvit computentur ei in primo Scutagio de quo non habuit quietantiam. *Mag. Rot.* 2. *J. Rot.* 18. *a. Staff.*

(*e*) Lincolnia. Provisum est per Justiciarium, quod Vicecomes habeat ad sustentationem suam anno Regis xj, xl marcas. *Memor.* 11. *H.* 3. *Rot.* 1. *b.*

(*f*) Consideratio de Oreford. Quia Rex concessit Willelmo de Swineford Comitatus Norf. & Suff., custodiendos quamdiu Regi placuerit, ita quod habeat omnes exitus quos Robertus le Sauvage habuit, Reddendo per annum C marcas plusquam idem Robertus reddidit pro eisdem Comitatibus: Et constat quod idem Robertus habuit Castrum de Oreford cum exitibus villæ de Oreford, quos Rex postea tradidit Hominibus ejusdem villæ ad feodi firmam pro xxx l annuis, de quibus respondere debent per manum suam: Consideratum est, quod prædictæ xxx l allocentur prædicto Vicecomiti in villa sua. *Memor.* 42. *H.* 3. *Rot.* 17. *b.*

(*g*) Ebor. Vicecomes fecit Visum per Henricum de Normanton Subvicecomitem suum —; & postea Provisum est quod pro laudabili servicio suo subtrahantur quolibet anno de eadem firma C marcæ —. Prædictus Visus & Provisio facta fuerunt præsentibus Fratre Josep tunc Thesaurario & Roberto Burnel. *Memor.* 1 & 2. *E.* 1. *inter Visus.*

(*gg*) Provisum est per Robertum Burnel & alios de Consilio Regis, quod stipendia Monetariorum Cantuariæ & Cambitorum ibidem, & stipendia Assaiatorum —, allocentur

were customary and known, there the Treasurer and Barons were wont to adhere to the Practice and Usage; taking due Care to prevent Innovation therein to the King's Prejudice. As in the Case of *John Giffard*, Keeper of the Castle of *Buelt*: he had Allowance made to him of more than was usual in like Cases: whereupon the Treasurer and Barons adjudged, that the former Allowance should be disallowed; and that a Deduction being made of what had been allowed more than was usual in like Cases, he should be allowed what had been customary, and no more (*h*).

XVIII. Atterminations were wont to be given by the Treasurer and Barons to the King's Debtors, by virtue of the King's Writs directed to them for that Purpose: and in like Manner Respites, and Discharges. By Attermination is meant, granting Men several Terms or Days for Payment of their Debt, where they were not able, or could not conveniently pay it at one entire Payment. *Ralf Fitz-Nicolas* owed the King CC *l*. The King, by Writ directed to the Barons, granted him Leave to pay it at xxx *l*. every Year; to wit, xv *l*. at the Exchequer of St. *Michael*, and xv *l*. at the Exchequer of *Easter*, till he had paid the whole Sum (*i*). The Debts due to the King from *P*. Bishop of *Hereford* were attermined at C Marks *per Annum*, by virtue of the King's Writ (*k*). The King commands the Barons, by his Writ, to attermine *William de Tykingcot*, for certain Amercements set on him for Trespasses, at so much a-Year, as it should be found by Inquisition he was able to pay, saving the Maintenance of himself, his Wife and Children (*l*). *Matthew de la Mare* and others had Attermination by a Message from the King, declared by the Treasurer, for certain Debts (*m*). The King by Writ commanded, that *Henry de Shotbrok* should

centur Bartholomæo de Castello Custodi ejusdem Cambij & Cambij Londoniæ, in compoto suo de eodem Cambio Cantuariæ anno l.vj. *Memor*. 1. *E*. 1. *Rot*. 6. *b*.

(*h*) *Hil*. Recorda 25 & 26. *E*. 1. *Rot*. 49. *a*.

(*i*) *Ex Memor*. 11. *H*. 3. *Rot*. 3. *a*.

(*k*) Baronibus, pro Episcopo Herefordensi. Rex eisdem; Sciatis quod de debitis quæ nobis debet P. Herefordensis Episcopus, de quibus aterminatus est per C marcas per annum per præceptum nostrum, perdonavimus ei Centum marcas; & concessimus ei quod de residuo illorum debitorum, & CCC l quas nobis debet de pluribus præstitis ei factis in Garderoba nostra, reddat nobis ad Scaccarium per annum C marcas, videlicet —. *Memor*. 28. *H*. 3. *Rot*. 4. *b*.

(*l*) Monstravit Regi Willelmus de Tykingcot, quod cum amerciatus esset ad xl marcas pro pluribus transgressionibus, Idem W. non habet in bonis, ut dicit, unde dictas xl marcas solveret aliquo modo terminis sibi statutis; Et ideo mandavit, quod facta diligenti inquisitione quantum inde Regi dare valeat per annum, salva sustentatione sua & uxoris suæ & liberorum suorum, tantum ab eo recipi & sic fieri faciant. *Ex Memor*. 40. *H*. 3. *Rot*. 5. *a*.

(*m*) Rex mandat Baronibus per Philippum

should have reasonable Estallment of his Debts, so that he might be able to pay them without being impoverished (*n*). The like Command was given in the Case of the poor Men of *Dodington*, that they might be able to pay their Debts to the King, saving their Contenement (*o*). In fine; Atterminations were granted by virtue of Writs, in the Case of *Simon le Lardener* (*p*), of *Milisent de Mohaut* (*q*), *Thomas Pridias* (*r*), *Roger de Chaundos* (*s*), and others. However, the Treasurer did sometimes give the King's Debtors Attermination, without any particular Writ, for ought that appears. And it has been said, that it was in that Case in the Power of the Treasurer only (exclusive of the Barons of the Exchequer) to grant Atterminations. In the 24th Year of K. *Edward* I, *John de Lockinton* prayed to have Attermination for certain Debts which he owed to the King. But the Barons of the Exchequer would not attermine him without the

pum Luvel Thesaurarium suum, quod de Lxxviij l xiiij d ob. quos Henricus de la Mare debuit Regi, concessit Mathæo de la Mare & alijs executoribus testamenti ipsius Henrici, quod reddant Regi per annum xx marcas, videlicet—. *Ex Memor.* 42. *H.* 3. *Rot.* 12. *b.*

(*n*) Quia Henricus de Shotbrok in officio Vicecomitis bene & fideliter servivit, Rege in partibus transmarinis existente, per quod Rex micius vult agere cum eodem; Rex mandat Baronibus, quod habita consideratione ad statum & facultates ejusdem Henrici, & servitium suum Regi sic impensum, eidem Henrico rationabiles terminos, ad quos debita quæ Regi debet ad Scaccarium, absq; status sui depressione, solvere valeat, assignent, de gratia Regis speciali. *Hil. Commun.* [13 &] 14. *E.* 1. *Rot.* 6. *b.*

(*o*) Cum de quibusdam pauperibus hominibus Villæ de Doddington, quorum quidam mortui sunt ut dicitur, diversa debita exiguntur; Rex mandat Baronibus, quod de nominibus mortuorum illorum sub sigillo Scaccarij ipsum certificent, ut viventibus residuis, de debitis in quibus Regi tenentur, competentes terminos, ad quos Regi [solvant] salvo contenemento suo, assignet. *Pas. Commun.* [13 &] 14. *E.* 1. *Rot.* 9. *a.*

(*p*) Baronibus, pro Simone le Lardener. Cum Barones ab hæredibus Roberti Hardel exigant xvj l xj s ix d, pro debitis ejusdem Roberti, ac debitum Simonis le Lardener & Johannæ Hardell uxoris suæ unius hæredum prædicti Roberti, inde aporcionatum sit ad xxxvj s iiij d, & præter hoc idem Simon Regi in xx s teneatur, ad quos amerciatus fuit coram H. Hautein, quia non fuit prosecutus: Rex mandat Baronibus, quod prædictum debitum taliter atterminent, quod contenementum suum non amittat. *Mich. Communia* 14. *E.* 1. *Rot.* 2. *a. in bund.* 13 & 14. *E.* 1.

(*q*) *Hil. Fines &c* 26 & 27. *E.* 1. *Rot.* 65. *b.*

(*r*) Baronibus, pro Thoma Pridias. Edward par la grace de Dieu &c; Por ceo qe nous avoms attermine & astalle a nostre cher & feal Thomas Pridias, les C livres quil fina en temps nostre cher Piere (qui Dieus assoille), a payer meismes les C livrs a nostre Escheqer en diz anz, cest a savoir &c; Vous maundoms qe—&c, & donqes facez enroller a nostre Escheqer cest Estallement, & le li facez garder en dite manere. Don souz nostre Prive Seal a Langele, le xij jour de Novembre, lan de nostre regne primer. *Mich. Brevia* 1. *E.* 2. *Rot.* 17. *b.*

(*s*) Et idem Rogerus [de Chaundo]s atterminatus est per Regem nunc de prædictis Centum marcis, per Breve Regis de Privato Sigillo, quod est inter Communia de hoc anno. *Mich. Commun.* 2. *E.* 2. *Rot.* 43. *a. inter Fines.*

Treasurer's Presence; to whose Office it belonged to attermine (*t*). *Robert le Faukener* fined to the King in x Marks, for Relief of certain Lands which he held of the King *in Capite*, by the Serjanty of keeping a Falcon from the Feast of St. *Martin* to Candlemas. The Treasurer granted him Terms of paying it, to wit, at two Marks a Year (*u*). The Treasurer granted Attermination to *John de Lokinton* (*w*), and to *John de Cormayles* (*x*).

If Men had Attermination granted to them, and did not keep their Terms by punctual Payment, they lost the Benefit of their Attermination. However, they were many times admitted to recover their Terms again, and be in the same or like State. *Damian*, the Clerk, fined in v Marks, for deteining x Marks due to the King longer than the Term at which he ought to have paid it (*y*). *Henry*, Son of *Hugh de Nevill*, was disseised of his Land, for not observing the Terms set him for Payment of his Fine (*z*). *Henry de Oili* accounted to the King for M and xv *l.* xvij *s.* xj *d.* a Debt of *Simon* the *Jew*, of *Oxford*, which was seized into the King's Hand. He paid L Marks of it to the King himself *in Camera sua*; and was attermined to pay the Remainder at the two Exchequers, at C Marks yearly; provided,

---

(*t*) Mayn. Edw. 2. inter Memor. Scacc. ib. de temp. E. 1. p. 37.

(*u*) Pas. Communia 15. E. 1. Rot. 5. a.

(*w*) Præceptum est Vicecomitibus Gloucestriæ & Wiltesiæ in pleno Scaccario, per Cancellarium, Tenentem locum Thesaurarij, & Barones, quod demandæ quam faciunt per Summonicionem Scaccarij, Johanni de Lokinton—, supersedeant donec aliud inde &c; Quia Thesaurarius in ultimo recessu suo versus partes transmarinas, concessit prædicto Johanni, quod cum redierit a partibus prædictis, ipsum Johannem atterminabit. Mich. Memor. 25. E. 1.

(*x*) Philippo de Wyleghby per Thesaurarium pro Johanne de Cormayles. Salutem quam sibi; Cum Johannes de Cormayles Domino Regi in quodam Patris sui debito teneatur, ac debitum illud ad Scaccarium Sibi atterminatum existat, Idemq; Johannes ratione moræ suæ cum Domino Rege in partibus Flandriæ, Terminum quemdam in dicta mora in Flandria transeuntem sibi per dictum Scaccarium super solutione portionis illius termini, videlicet C s, constitutum non observaverit, ut debebat; dictusq; Johannes labores & expensas in dicti Domini Regis obsequio sicut & alij sustinuerit in partibus memoratis, sicq; oporteat Dominum Regem facere ei gratiam in hac parte: Vobis mandamus, quod dictas C solidos qui aretro existunt pro mora Flandriæ ut prædictum est, ut ad persolutionem dicti debiti terminis ei concessis & etiam constitutis respectuare faciatis eidem; Ita tamen quod Terminos suos super dicta solutione venturos faciat debite observari, ac demum dictos C s quos dudum solvisse debuit, ut est dictum, solvat ad dictum Scaccarium, ut tenetur. Valete. Datum apud Novum Castrum super Tynam, die Dominica in festo Beati Clementis Papæ. Mich. Communia 26 & 27. E. 1. Rot. 2. b.

(*y*) Et de v marcis de Damiano Clerico, pro detentione x marcarum, quas debuit Regi, ultra terminum. Mag. Rot. 8. R. 1. Rot. 6. b.

(*z*) Henricus filius Hugonis de Nevill r c de xv marcis & j palefrido, Pro habenda saisina terræ unde dissaisitus fuit, eo quod non observavit terminos finis sui. Mag. Rot. 3. J. Rot. 2. b. Linc.

that

Chap. XXIII. *and* ACCOUNTANTS.

that if *Henry* did not keep his Terms of Payment, *Walter de Grai,* the King's Chancellour, was to restore to *Simon* the *Jew* the Charter by which that Debt was secured, and *Henry* was to lose all that he had paid before his Forfeiture incurred by breaking his Attermination (*a*). *Peter de Maillai* fined to the King in seven thousand Marks, that he might have to Wife *Isabell,* Daughter of *Robert de Turneham,* with all the Lands belonging to her by hereditary Right, whereof her Father *Robert* was seised on the Day of his Death. *Peter* was attermined to pay the Fine thus: in the first Year (to wit, the sixteenth of K. *John*) two thousand Marks, in the second Year one thousand Marks, and so in the third, fourth, fifth, and sixth Year a thousand Marks yearly. He found Pledges, to wit, *Ranulf* Earl of *Chester* for a thousand Marks, *William* Earl *de Ferrers* for a thousand Marks, and others. For the Residue of the Fine he put all the said Land in Counterpledge; on Condition, that if he did not observe his Terms of Payment, he should lose all that he had paid in any former Year (*b*). *William de Ferrers* Earl of *Derby* fined for and obtained an Attermination, though he did not punctually keep to the Terms granted him (*c*). *Thomas de Hemmegrave* had a fresh Attermination granted to him,

(*a*) Henricus de Oili r c de M & xv libris & xvij s & xj d de debito Simonis Judæi Oxenefordiæ capto in manum Regis, per breve ejusdem: In Thesauro nichil; Et ipsi Regi in Camera sua L marcas, per breve Regis; Et debet DCCCC & quater xx & ij l & xv d: De quibus debet reddere per annum ad Scaccaria C marcas, quousq; prædictum debitum fuerit persolutum: Ita quod si prædictus Henricus terminos suos non servaverit, W. de Grai Cancellarius, cui Carta prædicti Henrici de prædicto debito liberata est custodienda loco J. Norwicensis Episcopi per breve Regis, reddet prædicto Simoni Judæo cartam illam; & sit in perdito quicquid Regi inde solverit. *Mag. Rot.* 10. *J. Rot.* 16. *b. Oxenes.*

(*b*) Petrus de Maillai [debet] vij millia marcarum, Pro habenda in uxorem Ysabellam filiam Roberti de Turneham cum jure suo & omnibus terris ipsi Ysabellæ hæreditarie contingentibus, unde Robertus pater suus fuit vestitus die quo obijt: Termini, In primo anno scilicet anno Regis xvj° duo millia marcarum, Et in secundo anno scilicet xvij° mille marcas, Et sic in tercio, quarto, quinto, & sexto anno, per annum M marcas, donec prædictæ vij mille marcæ persolvantur: Plegij, Ranulfus Comes Cestriæ de millæ marcis, Willelmus Comes de Ferrarijs de M marcis, Savaricus de Malliun de M marcis, Reginaldus de Pontibus de M marcis, Willelmus Comes Saresberiæ de D marcis, Hubertus de Burgo de C marcis, Arnoldus de Avelent de C marcis, Walterus Episcopus Wignorensis de CC marcis: De residuo autem finis illius ponit prædictus P. in contraplegio totam terram suam prædictam; ita quod si Terminos suos non servaverit, amittetur quicquid inde in primo anno pacaverit. *Mag. Rot.* 16. *J. Rot.* 8. *h. Everwichsc.*

(*c*) Baronibus, pro Willelmo de Ferraijs Comite Derbiæ. Rex concessit eidem, quod finis ille quem fecit coram Domino Eboracensi Archiepiscopo dum fuit in partibus Wasconiæ, de reddendo Regi ad Scaccarium suum, de omnimodis debitis quæ ei debuit, L l per annum, stet donec totum debitum prædictum Regi persolvatur, non obstante eo si forte terminos suos non observaverit. *Ex Memor.* 28. *H.* 3. *Rot.* 6. *b.*

though

though he had not observed his former Terms (*d*). *Alexander de Hilton* was permitted to recover his Terms (*e*): And *Herbert Fitz-Matthew* (*f*) and *Reginald de Cornhull* were permitted to recover theirs (*g*). The Citizens of *Norwich* did not observe the Terms granted to them at the Exchequer for Payment of their Debts to the King. The Sheriff of *Norfolk* was commanded to enter their Liberty, and distrein twelve of the richer and more discreet Persons of the Community, to appear and answer in the Octaves of St. *Hilary*. The Citizens appeared, and were permitted to recover their Terms, and pay the said Debts at x *l. per Annum* (*h*). At another time, the Treasurer granted to *Roger de Presthope*, that he should recover his Terms; and he had a Writ of *Servat Terminos* thereupon (*i*). But after Atterminations had been granted, the King did sometimes, upon extraordinary Occasions, suspend or make void the same. Thus K. *Edward* II. commanded the Barons to cause to be levied all his Debts exceeding the Sum of xl *l.* notwithstanding any Atterminations granted by any others, except by the King himself or by his special

(*d*) Baronibus, pro Thoma de Hemmegrave. Rex concessit eidem, quod non obstante eo quod terminos suos non observavit, de fine quem fecerit reddendi ei xxx marcas per annum de debitis quæ Regi debet, reddat Regi viginti marcas ad festum S. Johannis Baptistæ anno xxviij, & xx marcas ad festum S. Michaelis proximo sequens, & x marcas ad Pascha anno xxix⁰, & decem marcas ad festum S. Michaelis anno eodem, & sic de anno in annum xx marcas ad eosdem terminos, donec &c; Et ideo &c. Breve est in forulo Mar. *Ex Memor.* 28. *H.* 3. *Rot.* 14. *a.*

(*e*) Norhumbria. Concessum est Alexandro de Hilton, quod recuperet terminos suos quos perdidit in anno xix⁰, quia plene pacavit. *Memor.* 22. *H.* 3. *Rot.* 9. *b.*

(*f*) Baronibus, pro Herberto filio Mathæi, Rex concessit eidem Herberto, quod non obstante eo quod duos terminos de fine quem fecit cum Rege non observavit, habeat amodo eosdem terminos quos ei prius inde concessimus. *Memor.* 25. *H.* 3. *Rot.* 9. *b.*

(*g*) Memorandum, quod concessum est Reginaldo de Cornhull, quod si solverit in quindena S. Michaelis ad Scaccarium xxj l x s, de Terminis suis transactis, de debitis quæ Regi debet, tunc recuperet terminos suos ei prius concessos de prædictis debitis. *Pas. Commun.* 41. *H.* 3. *Rot.* 15. *a.*

(*h*) Norfolcia. Quia Cives Regis Norwici non servaverunt terminos ad Scaccarium de diversis debitis de quibus Rex eos atterminaverat, præceptum est Vicecomiti quod non omittat propter Libertatem ejusdem Civitatis quin eam ingrediatur & distringat xij de dicioribus & discrecioribus hominibus ejusdem. Ita quod habeat corpora eorum &c in octabis S. Hilarij ad respondendum de eisdem debitis. Ad quem diem venerunt, & concessum est eis quod recuperent terminos, scilicet quod reddant per annum xl. *Mich. Brevia* 14 & 15. *E.* 1. *Rot.* 20. *a.*

(*i*) Midd. Viso statu debitorum Rogeri de Presthope. Rogerus solvit, per j talliam levatam xix die Septembris anno xvj⁰, Lxviij s iiij d, & per aliam talliam levatam xxv die Octobris anno xvij, xx s. Postea concessum est per Thesaurarium, quod non obstante quod dictus Rogerus fregit terminos suos, desicut solvit pro terminis elapsis, recuperet terminos suos. Et habet breve de *Servat terminos.* *Hil. Stat. & Visus* 15. *E.* 2. *Rot.* 96. *a.*

Command (*k*). And soon afterwards the King made void all the Atterminations granted to his Fermours (all over the Realm) touching their Ferms (*l*). But this was a singular Case.

XIX. In the next Place, Of Respites granted to the King's Debtors and Accountants. There seems to have been a like Method used in respiting as in attermining. Sometimes Respites were granted by virtue of the King's Mandates or Writs, and sometimes by the Treasurer and Barons without Writ. *Nicolas de Magena* had Respite for a Debt of CC Marks during the King's Pleasure, by virtue of the King's Writ (*m*). The Abbot of *Westminster* had Respite for xx *l*. Escuage, by virtue of the King's Writ or Command (*n*). *Alured de Wathamstede* had Respite for an Amerciament of Lx *l*. by virtue of the King's Writ, until the King should declare his Pleasure therein (*o*). A Debt of xvj *l*. upon *William Boterel* was respited by the King's Writ, till the King should declare his Pleasure therein (*p*). K. *John* by his Writ Patent commanded *Geoffrey Fitz-Pierre*, his chief Justicier, to let *Hugh de Malo Alneto* have Respite for xxij *l*. x *s*. Sterling which the King had lent to him in *Gascoigne*, and for Lx *s*.

(*k*) Rex mandat Baronibus firmiter injungens, quod omnia debita sua summam quadraginta librarum excedentia ad opus suum levari faciant, Non obstante atterminatione aliqua per alios quam per Regem & de mandato suo speciali inde facta. Et hoc nullo modo omittatis. T. Rege apud Ebor. xvij die Maij anno quinto. Per ipsum Regem. Nunciante Edmundo de Malo lacu. *Trin. Brevia* 5. *E.* 2. *Rot.* 52. *a*.

(*l*) Rex Vic. Norf. & Suff. salutem. *Tis a Writ to the Sheriff to make Proclamation, That all the King's Fermours should Pay-in their Ferms ; and that the King had made void the Atterminations of Debts ; he being in want of money for the expences of his Houshold and otherwise. The Sheriff was to Certify his execution of This Writ* in Quindena Nativitatis S. Johannis Baptistæ. T. W. de Norwyco Tenente locum Thesaurarij nostri apud Westmon., xij die Junij anno quinto.

Eodem modo mandatum est Vicecomitibus Cant. Hunt., Essex. Hertf., Kanc. Surr. Sussex., Suhamton., Wyltes, Oxon. Berk., Bed. Buk., Norhampton, Warr. Leyc., Wygorn. Glouc. Somers. Dors. Devon. Cornub. Heref. Salop. Staff. Not. Derb. Roteland. Lincoln. Ebor. Northumbr. Cumbr. Westmerl. Lancastr. *Trin. Brevia Retornab.* 5. *E.* 2. *Rot.*—*a*.

(*m*) Nicolaus de Magena debet CC marcas de Placitis Willelmi filij Johannis. Sed sunt in respectu per breve Regis quamdiu placuerit Regi, per Manesserum Biset. *Mag. Rot.* 9. *H.* 2. *Rot.* 1. *a*. *Herefordscira in Walijs*.

(*n*) Abbas de Westmon. debet xx l de Scutagio ; Sed sunt in respectu donec Rex inde loquatur. *Ib. Rot.* 2. *b*.

(*o*) Aluredus de Wathamsteda r c de Lx l de Misericordiâ. In thesauro Lxvj s & xj d, Et debet Lvj l & xiij s & j d. Et habet inde pacem per breve Regis, donec Rex ipse velle suum inde præcipiat. *Mag. Rot.* 12. *H.* 2. *Rot.* 10. *Essixa & Hurtf*.

(*p*) Willelmus de Boterel debet xvj l, sed sunt in respectu per breve Regis, donec Rex ipse præcipiat. *Mag. Rot.* 15. *H.* 2. *Rot.* 4. *a. Devenescira*.

Escuage-

Escuage-money, until the King gave further Command therein (*q*). K. *Henry* III, by the Writ Patent hereunder set forth, granted to *Hubert de Burgh*, Earl of *Kent* and Chief Justicier, Respite during his (the Earl's) whole Life, for a Debt of six hundred fourscore and three Pounds and half a Mark (*r*). *Engelard de Cicogny* had Respite for all his Debts given him by the King's Command until the Feast of St. *Michael*; and *Robert de Viepont* for his Debts till the Octaves of St. *Michael* (*s*). A Demand of several Tallages and other Debts of the Men of *Colchester* was put in Respite by vertue of the King's Writ, because of their Poverty (*t*). A Demand made upon

---

(*q*) Rex &c G. filio Petri &c. Mandamus vobis, quod respectum habere faciatis Hugoni de Malo Alneto de viginti duabus libris & x s sterlingorum, quas ei commodavimus in Wasconia, qui ab eo exiguntur ad Scaccarium nostrum, & de Lx s sterlingorum qui ab eo exiguntur ad Scaccarium nostrum de Scutagio de tempore R. Regis fratris nostri, quousq; aliud inde præceperimus. Et omnes terras & possessiones ipsius manuteneatis & defendatis; Nec permittatis quod Ricardus Foliot vel Willelmus de Langrin aliquam molestiam inferant ei aut gravamen. T. me ipso apud Rothomagum v die Februarij. *Pat.* 4. *J. m.* 5.

(*r*) Hubertus de Burgo debet DC & quater xx & iij l & dimidiam marcam de fine Beatriciæ de Warenna quondam uxoris suæ. Sed non debet summoneri; Quia idem H habet inde quietantiam ad totam vitam suam per breve Regis, quod est in forulo Marescalli; quod Tale est. H Dei gratia Rex Angliæ &c, Baronibus suis de Scaccario salutem. Sciatis nos pro nobis & hæredibus nostris concessisse dilecto & fideli nostro Huberto de Burgo Comiti Kanciæ Justiciario nostro, quod DC & quater xx & iij l & dimidia marca, quæ ab eo exiguntur per Summonitionem Scaccarij nostri, de fine quem Beatricia de Warenna quondam uxor ipsius Huberti, de qua pueros procreavit, fecit cum Domino J. Patre nostro, pro habendis terris & tenementis quæ fuerunt Willelmi de Warenna patris ipsius Beatriciæ, & quæ ipsam jure contingunt hæreditario; et pro se maritanda, et pro habenda rationabili dote sua de tenementis quæ fuerunt Dodonis Bardolf quondam viri sui, ab eodem Huberto Comite Kanciæ tota vita sua non exigantur, nec ad solucionem earum nobis faciendam distringatur; sed post decessum ipsius Huberti Comitis Kanciæ, cum hæres ipsius Beatriciæ recuperaverit secundum Legem & consuetudinem Regni nosti saisinam prædictarum terrarum & tenementorum quæ fuerunt ipsius Beatriciæ, & quæ ipsum hæredem jure contingunt hæreditario, nos ad ipsum hæredem de prædicto debito capiemus. Et ideo vobis mandamus quod sic fieri & inrotulari faciatis. Teste me ipso apud Westmon. xxij die Julij. anno R n undecimo. *Mag. Rot.* 11. *H.* 3. *tit. Norfolk & Sutfolk.*

(*s*) Engelardus de Ciconia habet respectum de omnibus debitis suis, per præceptum Domini Regis, usq; ad festum S. Michaelis. Mandatum est Vicecomiti. *Ex Memorand.* 11. *H.* 3. *Rot.* 3. *a.* Robertus de Veteri ponte habet respectum de omnibus debitis suis usq; ad octabas S. Michaelis per præceptum Domini Regis. Mandatum est Vic. *Ib. Juxt. Ebor.*

(*t*) Rex Vicecomiti; Pone in respectum demandam quam facis hominibus nostris de Coleceftria propter eorum paupertatem, de C & Lxviij libris et xvj den. de veteri talliagio, et de vij libris de quodam alio talliagio, et de xviij libris xij s iiij d de tercio talliagio, et de xx marcis de fine pro pannis venditis contra assisam, et de xj libris de quodam alio veteri talliagio, donec aliud præceptum inde habueris. T. ut supra [i. e. T. J. Bathon. v°. die Julij anno regni nostri xiiij°]. *Trin. Commun.* 14. *H.* 3. *Rot.* 8. *b.*

the

the Citizens of *London* was put in Respite by virtue of the King's Writ (*u*). *Griffin*, Son of *Wenunwen*, had Respite for a Debt by virtue of a Writ directed to the Barons (*w*). The Abbat of St. *Edmund* had Respite given him touching certain Franchises by him claimed, until the Octaves of the *Trinity*; it being the King's Pleasure, that Judgment should be given therein in his Presence (*x*). *William de Curton*, Sheriff of *Lincolnshire*, being busied in tallaging the King's Demeanes in that County, so that he could not as yet render his Account at the Exchequer, the King by his Writ commands the Barons to respite the same Account (*y*). K. *Henry* III, in the 51st Year of his Reign, by a general Writ ordered the Barons to grant common Respites to Persons claiming Liberties by his Predecessours Charters or his own (*z*). In short, Respites were granted by particular Writs for the Persons following: to wit, for *John de la Garston* (*a*) the Sheriff of *Cornwall* (*b*), the Dean and Chapter of St. *Martin*,

---

(*u*) Baronibus, pro Civibus Londoniæ. Mandatum est eisdem, quod ponant in respectum usq; in crastinum Animarum anno regni Regis xxij°, demandam ducentarum & xxv librarum quam eis facitis de tempore quo Petrus Neuelun & Willelmus Blundus fuerunt Vicecomites præfatæ Civitatis tempore Domini J. Regis; et interim scrutari faciant Rotulos & Memorias Scaccarij, si quæ solutio de prædictis ducentis & xxv libris in eis continetur, ita quod in adventu Regis ad Scaccarium inde possit certificari. *Memor*. 22. *H*. 3. *Rot*. 2. *b*.

(*w*) Baronibus, pro Girfino filio Wenunwen. Rex dedit respectum eidem usq; in quindenam S. Michaelis, de C libris de fine CC librarum, quem fecit cum Rege pro terra sua Walliæ. Breve est in forulo Marescalli. Et Mandatum est Vicecomiti Not. & Derb. *Pas. Commun*. 29. *H*. 3. *Rot*. 8. *b*.

(*x*) Baronibus, pro Abbate S. Edmundi Rex dedit respectum eidem usq; ad octabas S. Trinitatis, de murdro & catallis fugitivorum quæ tangunt Libertatem ipsius Abbatis; quia Rex wlt in presencia sua ut judicium reddatur, utrum prædictus Abbas debeat Regi de jure reddere ea quæ prædicta ratione ab eo exiguntur, vel non. *Pas. Commun*. 29. *H*. 3. *Rot*. 8. *b*.

(*y*) Pro Willelmo de Curton Vicecomite Lincolniæ. Quia idem intendit ad Dominica Regis tallianda in Comitatu Lincolniæ una cum Johanne Gubaud & Johanne de Sumercotes, quod coram Baronibus a die S. Hillarij in xv dies, ad reddendum compotum suum comparere non potest; Rex mandat eisdem, quantinus diem ad reddendum compotum suum in crastino clausi Paschæ eidem habere faciant. Breve est in f. M. *Memor*. 33. *H*. 3. *Rot*. 4. *a*.

(*z*) Baronibus, pro Communi respectu Concedendo. Rex mandat, quod omnimodos respectus qui concedi consueverunt ad Scaccarium, de Libertatibus & alijs, diversis hominibus Regni per Cartas prædecessorum suorum Regum Angliæ & suas concessis concedant eodem modo quo juxta mandata sua fieri consuevit temporibus retroactis. *Ex Memor*. 51. *H*. 3. *Rot*. 1. *b*.

(*a*) *Pas. Communia* 14. *E*. 1. *Rot*. 10. *b*.

(*b*) Rex mandat Baronibus, quod summonitionem quam fecerunt Vicecomiti Cornubiæ, ponant in respectum, donec Rex locutus fuerit cum eis ad octabas Purificationis B. Mariæ; Et tunc eis dicet plenius causam hujus: Sin autem summonitionem hujusmodi nondum ei fecerint, nullam interim faciant eidem. Per breve de Privato sigillo. *Hil. Commun*. 13. & 14. *E*. 1. *Rot*. 6. *b*.

London (c), *Theobald de Verdon* (d), *Bartholomew de Badelesmere* (e), *Richard de la Rivere*, Sheriff of *Gloucestershire* (f), the Bishop of *Ely* (g), *Peter Barde* (h), and others. The Treasurer and Barons of the Exchequer did sometimes grant Respites, without Writ for ought that appears. *Geoffrey de Ver*, Sheriff of *Shropshire*, did not account in his Year for the Aid due from several Knights Fees in his Bailywick; because the Barons of the Exchequer gave him Respite in that Case, till the King should declare his Pleasure (i). The Abbat and Monks of *Torre* had Respite given them at the Exchequer, touching a Market which they had held longer than the Time for which it was granted them; and in the mean time they might purchase of the King Acquittance for the Supertenure, if they thought fit (k). *Robert Fitz-Walter* had Respite for Escuage, by Writ of the Chief Justicier (l): and *Peter Mark* for a Debt of M l, by Writ of the Chief Justicier (m). For the better Conveniency to the Barons and the Accountants in the Exchequer, a general Writ for common Respite was in some Cases used. The King by his Writ commands the Barons, to grant all Manner of common Respites at the Exchequer, as they had been wont to do at the King's Command in Times past (n).

A Writ

(c) *Trin. Communia* 15. *E*. 1. *Rot*. 7. *a*.

(d) Rex volens eidem Theobaldo [de Verdoun] gratiam facere specialem, mandat Baronibus quod demandam quam ei faciunt per summonicionem Scaccarij de D marcis, ad quas nuper amerciatus fuit in Parliamento Regis, pro quadam transgressione Regi & suis illata, supersederi mandent omnino ad voluntatem Regis. Datum sub Privato sigillo apud Roubury, xxij die Junij anno xx°. *Pas. Commun*. 22. *E*. 1. *Rot*. 1. *a*.

(e) Teste Rege apud Karliolum, xxviij die Marcij anno xxxv. Per ipsum Regem nunciante Thesaurario. *Pas. Brevia* 35. *E*. 1. *Rot*. 39. *b*.

(f) *Hil. Commun*. 9. *E*. 2. *Rot*. 94. *a*.

(g) *Trin. Brevia* 15. *E*. 2. *Rot*. 60. *a*.

(h) *Mich. Communia* 15. *E*. 2. *Rot*. 41. *a*.

(i) Idem Vicecomes non reddidit compotum de feodis aliorum Militum de Ballia sua, de eodem Auxilio filiæ Regis; Quia est in respectu per Barones, donec Rex præcipiat. *Mag. Rot*. 14. *H*. 2. *Rot*. 6. *b*. *Salopes.* Gaufridus de Ver *Sheriff*.

(k) Devonia. Abbas & Monachi de Thorre habent respectum, usq; ad festum S. Michaelis, de demanda quæ eis fit, de hoc quod tenuerunt unum mercatum apud Wlinberge ultra ætatem Domini Regis, quod non habuerunt nisi usq; ad ætatem ejus, & tunc satisfacient de hac supertenura, nisi purchaciaverint quietantiam versus Dominum Regem. *Trin. Commun*. 14. *H*. 3. *Rot*. 7. *a*.

(l) Essex. Robertus filius Walteri solvit Centum marcas Domino Regi ad Scaccarium de hoc ultimo Scutagio; Et de residuo habet respectum usq; ad octabas Purificationis B. Mariæ, per Breve Justiciarij quod Johannes habet. *Mich. Commun*. 14. *H*. 3. *Rot*. 2. *a*.

(m) Notingham. Petrus Mark habet respectum de M l usq; ad octabas S. Hilarij, per Breve Domini Justiciarij. *Mich. Commun*. 11. *H*. 3. *Rot*. 1. *a*. Et vid. ib. *Rot*. 2. *a & b*.

(n) Baronibus, pro Communi respectu concedendo. Rex mandat, quod omnimodos respectus qui concedi consueverunt

ad

Chap. XXIII. *and* ACCOUNTANTS.

A Writ of common Respite was granted for the Abbat of *Wardon* at the Queen Mother's Instance (*o*).

When Men were in the King's Service, it was usual for the King, or the Chief Justicier, or the Treasurer, and Barons of the Exchequer, to put in Respite the Pleas, Debts, or Accounts of such Persons being in the King's Service. The Barons of the Exchequer respited a Debt of *William de Chainey*, he being in the King's Service (*p*). The Chief Justicier ordered a Debt due to the King from *William Basset* to be respited for so long as *William* was in the King's Service beyond Sea (*q*). Several Debts were put in Respite by the King's Writs for the several Persons following, who were in the King's Service; to wit, for *Hugh de Vivon, Raimund de Burgh, William de Vescy, Gilbert de Umframvill* (*r*), *Walter de Godarvill* (*s*), *Roger de Sumery* (*t*), and the Sheriff of *Wiltshire* (*u*). K. *Henry* III, having appointed

ad Scaccarium, de Liberatibus & alijs, diversis hominibus Regni per Cartas predecessorum suorum Regum Angliæ & suas concessis, concedant eodem modo quo juxta mandata sua fieri consuevit temporibus retroactis. *Memor.* 51. *H.* 3. *Rot.* 1. *b.*

(*o*) Abbas de Wardon habet breve de Communi respectu per Thesaurarium, ad instantiam A. Reginæ Angliæ Matris Regis, nunciante Guidone Ferre. *Trin. Commun.* 18. *E.* 1. *Rot.* —— *b. in imo.*

(*p*) Willelmus de Caisneio debet xv l & v s, de Veteri Exercitu Waliæ; Sed sunt in respectu per Barones, quia vadit cum filia Regis in Saxoniom. *Mag. Rot.* 13. *H.* 2. *Rot.* 3. *a. Norf. & Suthf.*

(*q*) Breve G. Filij Petri. G. Filius Petri &c, Vicecomiti: Præcipimus tibi, quod pacem habere permittas Willelmo Basset de Debito Domini Regis quod ab eo exigitur, quamdiu idem Willelmus fuerit in servicio Domini Regis ultra mare cum Equis & Armis. Teste me ipso apud Westmonasterium xvj die Octobris. *Ex fragm. Memorandor.* 1. *Joh. Rot.* 9. *a. Staffordescira.*

(*r*) Somerset. Hugo de Vyvonijs habet respectum quamdiu fuerit in servicio Domini Regis in partibus transmarinis, de xx marcis quas solebat reddere per annum de firma. T. R. Dunelmensi Episcopo xxiiij die Aprilis anno r n xiiij. *Pas. Commun.* 14. *H.* 3. *Rot.* 5. *a.*

The like respite for Raimund de Burgh, *for the same cause. Ib. Rot.* 5. *b.*

The like respite to William de Vescy, *for the same cause, for Imprests made to his Father* Eustace *in the time of K.* John. *Ib. Rot.* 5. *b.*

Northumbria. *The like respite for the same cause, to* Gilebert de Umfrinvilla *for xx marks,* de præstito facto Ricardo de Umframvilla patri suo tempore Regis J; Per breve de magno Sigillo. *Ib. Rot.* 5. *b. And for others, Ib. juxt.*

(*s*) Rex dedit respectum Waltero de Godarvill de debitis quæ Regi debet, de quibus consuevit reddere per annum x marcas & dimidiam, donec idem Walterus redierit de Hybernia, quo profectus est in Nuncium Regis. *Ex Memor.* 25. *H.* 3. *Rot.* 6. *a.*

(*t*) Pro Rogero de Sumery. *Because* Roger *was about to go with the King into* Gascoigne, *The King commands the Barons to respite his Account till the King's Return. Memor.* 38. *H.* 3. *Rot.* 3. *b.*

(*u*) Quia Vicecomes Regis Wiltesiæ intendit negotijs Regijs per præceptum Regis; mandatum est Baronibus de Scaccario, quod compotum suum ponant in respectum usq; in crastinum S. Michaelis. T. Rege apud Portesmuth xiiij die Julij. *Cl.* 37. *H.* 3. *m.* 6.

Peter

Peter de Montfort to go as his Ambassadour to *France,* commanded the Barons, either to give him speedy Dispatch touching a Demand made of him for the Aid pur faire Fitz Chivaler, or to put it in Respite till his Return into *England (w). Roger,* Abbot of *Glaston,* being gone as the King's Ambassadour or *Nuntius* to the Court of *Rome,* the King by Writ commanded the Barons to put in Respite, from Day to Day, all Pleas touching the Abbot and his Men, untill the King's Return to *London* (*x*). The same King commanded, that a Demand made upon *Robert de Beverley,* and others employed in the King's Works at *Westminster,* should be put in Respite as long as they continued in that Service (*y*). A Respite was also granted for *Robert Burnel,* of certain Demands made on him by Summonce of the Exchequer; he being to go as *Nuncius* or Agent for the King and Prince into *Ireland* (*z*). The King having provided in his Council, that all Pleas wherein such Persons as went forth with him in his Expedition against *Lewelin,* Son of *Griffin,* were concerned, except Pleas of *Darrein Presentment, Quare Impedit,* Dower *Unde nihil habet,* &c. should be suspended till the Quinzime of St. *Michael* then next: He commands the Barons by his Writ, that according to the said Provision they should forbear proceeding in a Plea depending before them between *Pontius de la More* and *Elyas de Rabayn* (*a*). Pleas and Accounts were also respited by virtue of the King's Writs, for Persons

(*w*) Rex mandat Baronibus, quod quia destinat P. de Monteforti in Nuncium suum in Franciam, de demanda quam ei faciunt de Auxilio ad Primogenitum filium Regis Militem faciendum, de feodis quæ tenet de Comite War. festinum judicium habere faciant, vel demandam illam ponant in respectum usq; reditum in Angliam. Breve est in forulo Marescalli. Et mandatum est Vic. War. *Ex Memor.* 40. *H.* 3. *Rot.* 9. *b.*

(*x*) Quia Rogerus Abbas de Glaston profectus est in Nuncium nostrum ad Curiam Romanam; Mandatum est Baronibus, quod omnes loquelas ipsum & homines suos coram eisdem tangentes, ponant in respectum de die in diem, usq; in Adventum Regis Londoniam, qui erit in festo S. Andreæ. *Memor.* 42. *H.* 3. *Rot.* 6. *a.*

(*y*) Hil. *Communia* 49. *H.* 3. *Rot.* 7. *a.*
(*z*) Trin. *Communia* 49. *H.* 3. *Rot.* 11. *b.*
(*a*) Baronibus pro Elya Rabayn. Edwardus &c; Cum nuper pro indempnitate illorum qui in expeditionem nostram contra Lewelinum filium Griffini & complices suos, inimicos & rebelles nostros, ad partes Walliæ jam profecti & adhuc nobiscum profecturi sunt, de Consilio nostro providerimus quod omnia placita tam in Curijs nostris quam aliorum quorumcunq; de Regno nostro, præterquam de ultima præsentatione, Quare impedit, Unde nichil habet, Attachiamentis super prohibitionibus nostris, & Assisis Novæ Disseisinæ, teneantur in suspenso usq; ad Quindenam S. Michaelis proximo futuram. Vobis mandamus, quod Placito quod est coram vobis inter Poncium de la More mercatorem, & Elyam de Rabayn, de debito viginti & unius libr. quinq; sol. & duorum den., quos idem Poncius a præfato Elya exegit ut dicitur, interim supersedeatis, juxta formam Provisionis prædictæ. *Pas. Communia* 5. *E.* 1. *Rot.* 5. *b.*

who

who were in the King's Service; *viz.* For *Richard de Aston* (b), *John de Erclave* (c), *Alexander de Kirketon* (d), *Gilbert Talebot* (e), *Richard de Weylaund* (f), and *John de Cambho* (g). The King's Chancellour granted to *John de Kyngeston* Respite of certain Debts, in regard he was in the King's Service in *Scotland* (h). The Knights, Esquires, and Commonalty of *Yorkshire* were warned to be at *Alverton* in the Octaves of *Candlemas* with Horse and Arms, as they were rated. Several of them alleged, that they did implead or were impleaded before the Barons of the Exchequer; and prayed the Treasurer, that their Pleas might be respited, and that they might not be damaged or put in Default before the said Barons: hereupon, the Treasurer sends a Letter to the Barons, praying that the Men of the said County might not be put in Default for not appearing before them at that Time (i). *John de Grey* being in the King's Service, the King commanded, that all the said *John*'s Affairs at the Exchequer should re-

(b) Præceptum est Magistro Ricardo de Clifford quondam Escaetori Regis citra Trentam, quod non exequatur aliquod breve versus Ricardum de Aston, de quodam Compoto reddendo de Escaetria, quia idem Ricardus habet Protectionem Domini Regis, & stat in servicio suo in Hibernia. *Pas. Commun.* 5. *E.* 1. *Rot.* 5. *b. Et Trin. Commun.* 5. *E.* 1. *Rot.* 6. *a.*

(c) Præceptum est eidem [Ricardo de Clifford], quod non exequatur aliquod breve versus Johannem de Erclave & Johannem filium Derij, qui sunt in servicio Regis in partibus Walliæ, quousq; redierint a partibus prædictis. *Pas. Commun.* 5. *E.* 1. *Rot.* 4. *a.*

(d) *Pas. Communia* 7. *E.* 1. *Rot.* 5. *b.*

(e) *Mich. Brevia* 25 & 26. *E.* 1. *Rot.* 16. *b.*

(f) Baronibus pro Ricardo de Weylaund. He being to go beyond Sea in obsequio Regis, the King by this Writ gives him Respite during his Pleasure of all Debts due to the King at his Exchequer. T. E. filio Regis apud Westmonasterium xxviij die Augusti anno xxv. Per testimonium Comitissæ Glouceftriæ. *Mich. Brevia* 25 & 26. *E.* 1. *Rot.* 19. *b.*

(g) *Mich. Communia* 26 & 27. *E.* 1. *Rot.* 2. *b.*

(h) Somerseta. Concessum est per Cancellarium Johanni de Kyngeston tenenti partem terrarum quæ fuerunt Osberti Giffard, quod habeat respectum donec aliud &c, de debitis prædicti Osberti. Quia idem Johannes moratur cum Rege in obsequio Regis in partibus Scotiæ. *Mich. Commun.* 34 & 35. *E.* 1. *Rot.* 25. *a.*

(i) Philippo de Wyleby & Baronibus per Thesaurarium. A ses chiers Amys & Compaignouns, Sire Philippe de Wylugby e les Barouns del Escheker nostre Seignour le Roy, Gautier par la grace de Dieu Evesq; de Cestre, salutz e chiers amytez; Bien savez, Seignurs, coment Chevaliers, Esquiers, e tote la Communeaute de Counte Deverwyk sont garniz de estre yceft Lundy as uctaves de la Chandeleur a Alverton, a chevaux e a armes, si com il sunt a sys, e plusurs de eaux dient quil empledent e sunt emple dez devant vous e nous ont priez qe lour pledez soyent respitez, e quil ne soient damagez ne mis en defaute devant vous, por ce qe il ne pouunt estre devant vous, e la a une foiz: Vous prioms, qe vous ne aillez a nule defaute vers nuly du Counte Deverwyk de coe a Vendredi prochein avenir: car avant ce jour ne porrount il ben venir devant vous; e adonqes vous ferroms a savoir les queux apparent le dit jour devant nous e quieux noun, si qe des adonqes en facez coe qui verrez qui soit afaire. A Dieux, sires, qui vous gard. Escrites a Alverton le Lundy avaunt dit. *Hilar. Brevia* 26 & 27. *E.* 1. *Rot.* 12. *b.*

main in the same State as now, till the Quinzime of *Easter* (*k*). And in many other Instances.

XX. Of Discharges granted to the King's Debtors, by virtue of Writs directed to the Barons of the Exchequer. The Men of *Ralf Taisson* were discharged of certain Amercements by virtue of the King's Writ (*l*). *William* the King's Brother was discharged of Lxij s iij d, by virtue of a Writ from the Queen (*m*); and *John de Bidun* of xl s, by Writ from the Queen (*n*). *Alan de Nevill* was charged with iiij l x s, the yearly Rent or Profit of the Forest of *Savernak*: but the King commanded by his Writ, that *Alan* should be discharged thereof (*o*). *Ralf*, Son of *Drogo*, was accountable for the Ferm of *Grimesby*. But in regard *Ralf*'s Sons had fined to the King in Hawks for the said Debt, the King by his Writ ordered *Ralf* to be discharged thereof (*p*). *Geoffrey Fitz-Pierre* fined in three thousand Marks, to have the Land of Earl *William*, which was the Inheritance of *Beatrice de Say*, *Geoffrey*'s Wife; provided that, according as *Geoffrey* should serve the King well, it was to be at the King's Pleasure, whether he would accept the whole Fine aforesaid or not. *Geoffrey* paid Part of the Fine. In the third Year of K. *Richard* I. he paid other Part of it (*q*). In the fifth Year of K. *Richard* I. there remained of the whole Fine five hundred Marks unpaid. In that Year, the King commanded by his

(*k*) *Mich. Brevia* 12. *E.* 2. *Rot.* 64. *a.*
(*l*) Gaufridus de Furnell. r c de xij marcis argenti & dimidia de Placitis Roberti Arundel de hominibus Radulfi Taisson de hominibus de Wnford: In Perdonis, per breve Regis, eisdem hominibus xij marcas argenti & dimidiam, quia non erant in Comitatu quando hæc placita placitata fuerunt; Et Q. e. *Mag. Rot.* 5. *Ste. Rot.* 16. *a. Devenescira.*
(*m*) In Perdonis Willelmo fratri Regis Lxij s & viij d, per breve Reginæ. *Mag. Rot.* 2. *H.* 2. *Rot.* 1. *b. Sudf.*
(*n*) Johannes de Bidun r c de xl s, de eisdem placitis [viz. de placitis Justic.]; In Perdonis, per breve Reginæ, eidem Johanni; Et Q. e. *Mag. Rot.* 2. *H.* 2. *Rot.* 4. *a. Buchingeham. & Bedef.*
(*o*) Alanus de Nevilla debet iiij l & x s, de Censu ejusdem Forestæ [de Savernac]. Sed Rex præcipit per breve suum, ne amplius exigantur ab eo per Rotulos de Scaccario. *Mag. Rot.* 9. *H.* 2. *Rot.* 4. *b. Wilt.*

(*p*) Radulfus filius Drogonis r c de C & Lxix l de Veteri firma de Grimesbi. Rex clamat eum inde quietum, & prohibet per breve suum ne amodo inde summoneatur; Quia filij ejusdem Radulfi, Walterus & Drogo, finierunt de eodem debito cum Rege per Aves. *Mag. Rot.* 14. *H.* 2. *Rot.* 5. *a. Linc.*
(*q*) Galfridus filius Petri r c de M & CCCC l, pro habenda terra Comitis Willelmi hæreditate Beatriciæ de Say uxoris suæ: Ita quod secundum quod Domino Regi servierit, in beneplacito Regis erit utrum velit accipere vel non: In Thesauro CCCC l per breve Regis: Et in soltis per breve Regis Gilleberto de Wascoil DCCC marcas, ad solvend[um] Mercatoribus Rom[anis] pro pecunia mutuata ab eis per Reginam & Archiepiscopum Roth[omagensem] ad opus Regis; Et Ricardo de Pec xl l ad custodiam Castri de Bolesoure: Et debet DC & xl marcas. *Mag. Rot.* 3. *R.* 1. *Rot.* 3. *a. m.* 2. *Essex & Hurtf.*

Writ,

Writ, that *Geoffrey* should be discharged of the said Fine, when he had paid the whole. He paid the said five hundred Marks; and was discharged accordingly (*r*). *Philipp* Bishop of *Duresine* was amerced D Marks, because *Hugh* his Predecessour held Plea in Court Christian touching the Advowson of a Church. But the King remitted to him the Debt, by Writ *de Ultra mare* sent to the Chief Justicier (*s*). *William Fitz-Geoffrey* was charged at the Exchequer with ix *l* and odd, for certain Chatells (apprized at that Sum) which were assigned to him when he was disseised of the Town of *Chelardeston*. Of which Debt (saith the Record) he could not be discharged without the King's Writ of Discharge. But when, afterwards, he brought a Writ of Discharge to the Justicier and Barons, they ordered him to be discharged accordingly (*t*). *Stephen de Turneham* fined to King *John* in M Marks. And thereupon, the King by his Letter or Writ, cited hereunder, and directed to the Barons of the Exchequer of *London*, quitclaimed *Stephen* of all Accounts, Rerages of Escheats and Wards for the whole Time that he had the Custody of them, as well in the Reign of K. *Richard* as of K. *John*, and of Ferms of Counties, and all other Fines, Tallages, and Receipts, wherewith he stood charged in the King's Rolls. The King released to *Stephen* CCC Marks, Part of this Fine of M Marks; and ordered, that out of the Residue *Stephen* should be allowed a Mark a-Day for the Custody of the King's Niece. Wherefore the King commanded the Barons to do accordingly (*u*). *Nicolas de Stutevill* was discharged by the King's Writ, of

(*r*) Galfridus filius Petri r c de D marcis, pro habenda terra Comitis Willelmi, hæreditate Beatricis de Say uxoris suæ; quæ remanserunt anno præterito de MMM marcis, quas idem Galfridus promisit Regi ab initio pro eadem terra habenda. De quibus Rex præcipit per breve suum, quod ipse quietus esset si prædictas MMM marcas plene reddidisset: In thesauro liberavit, Et quietus est. *Mag. Rot.* 5. *R.* 1. *Rot.* 1. *a. Essex & Hurtf.*

(*s*) Philippus Episcopus Dunelmensis r c de D marcis, quia H. antecessor ejus tenuit placitum de Advocatione Ecclesiæ in curia Christianitatis. In thesauro Nichil, Et in perdonis ipsi Episcopo Philippo D marcæ per breve Regis de Ultra mare, missum Galfrido filio Petri; Et Q. e. *Mag. Rot.* 10. *R.* 1. *Rot.* 3. *a. Everwic.*

(*t*) Willelmus filius Galfridi debet ix l & xvij s & iiij d de Reragio villæ de Chelardeston, sicut continetur in Rotulo præcedenti. Sed postea recordatum est per G. filium Petri & Barones de Scaccario, quod debitum illud fuit super eum propter catalla sua quæ ipse recepit quando diffaisitus fuit de villa de Chelardeston, quæ appreciata fuerunt ad prædictam summam; De quo debito non potuit quietus esse donec breve Regis attulisset de quietantia; Et quia, sicut per prædictos recordatum est, breve Regis attulit de prædicta terra sua cum omnibus catallis suis habendis, præceptum est per Justiciarium & Barones, ut de debito illo amplius non summoneatur; Et sic Quietus est. *Mag. Rot.* 2. *J. Rot.* 1. *b. Not. & Dereb.*

(*u*) *Mag. Rot.* 6. *J. Rot.* 7. *b. Wirecestrescira.*

a Fine

a Fine of M Marks demanded of him on the King's Behalf for his Ranfom (*w*). *Godfrey de Craucumbe*, Sheriff of *Oxfordſhire*, had a Writ dormant, to diſcharge him of rendering an Account ſeparately of the Manour of *Benſinton*, and of the Members thereof (*x*). *William de Cantilupe* was acquitted of fourſcore and odd Pounds by virtue of the King's Writ; by which Writ the King ordered, that if *William* was charged twice with the ſame Debts, he ſhould be diſcharged thereof according to Juſtice (*y*). *Griffin*, Son of *Wenunwen*, had a Writ to be diſcharged of Tallage demanded of him for his Manour of *Ahford* (*z*). *Nicolas de Lenham* fined in CCCC Marks, to have a Charter. He was acquitted of the ſaid Fine by virtue of the King's Writ, in Conſideration that he was to continue in the King's Service in *Gaſcony* for a whole Year, with three Knights more, at his own Charges (*a*). And other Writs were iſſued to the Barons of the Exchequer, for diſcharging the Perſons following: to wit, *Walter de Bath*, of his Impriſonment (*b*), *William le Cutiller* of Tallage aſſeſſed on

(*w*) Nicholaus de Stutevill debet M marcas pro redemptione ſua, ſicut continetur in Rotulo iiij°. Sed non debet ſummoneri, quia Rex mandavit per breve ſuum, quod proteſtatum eſt coram eo & conſilio ſuo, quod idem Nicholaus fecit finem illum cum W. Mareſc[allo] ſeniore pro redemptione ſua, ad opus ipſius Mareſcalli & non ad opus Regis, prout ſinguli priſones capti apud Linc., cum eis qui eos ceperant finem fecerunt: Et per idem breve prædictus Mareſcallus Quietus eſt. *Mag. Rot.* 7. *H.* 3. *Rot.* 11. *b. Everw. De Oblatis.*

(*x*) Breve Godefridi de Craucumbe de Allocatione Manerij de Benſinton. H. Dei gratia Baronibus de Scaccario. Sciatis quod conceſſimus dilecto & fideli noſtro G. de Craucumbe, quod ipſe & hæredes ſui proceſſu temporis non occaſionentur de compoto qui reddi ſolet de Manerio de Benſintone, uno videlicet per ſe de ipſo Manerio, & alio ut dicitur de membris ejuſdem Manerij, non obſtante eo quod talem compotum non reddidit nec reddet de Manerio prædicto & de membris ipſius ſeparatim, quamdiu extitit & futurus eſt Vicecomes noſter Oxoniæ. Et ideo vobis mandamus, quod id inrotulari & ipſum Godefridum & hæredes ſuos inde quietos eſſe faciatis, ſicut prædictum eſt. T. meipſo apud Geudeford xxj die Decembris anno r n xvj. Per ipſum Regem. *Mag. Rot.* 16. *H.* 3. *Oxenfordeſchir.*

(*y*) Willelmus de Cantilupo [debet] CC & Lij l vij s iiij d de pluribus debitis, ſicut ſupra continetur. Sed non debet ſummoneri de quater xx & ix l xvij s iiij d, per breve Regis, in quo continetur quod ſi inventum fuerit eundem W. bis honeratum fuiſſe eiſdem debitis, ſecundum juſticiam exoneretur; Quia conſtat per inſpectionem Originalium diverſorum præſtitorum de tempore Regis J, quod inde ſuperoneratus fuit Willelmus de Cantilupo pater ipſius, in hoc Comitatu & Comitatu Wigorniæ, in Rotulo xiij & xiiij; Et debet CLxij l & x s. *Mag. Rot.* 22. *H.* 3. *Rot.* —. *War. & Leirceſtr. m.* 2. *b.*

(*z*) *Trin. Commun.* 29. *H.* 3. *Rot.* 9. *b.*

(*a*) Nicholaus de Lenham r c de CCCC marcis pro habenda Carta; In theſauro nichil, Et in Perdonis eidem N CCCC marcæ per breve Regis, in quo continetur, quod idem N debuit morari in Waſconia in ſervicio Regis, ſe quarto Militum per unum annum ad cuſtum ſuum, Et Q. e. *Mag. Rot.* 35. *H.* 3. *Kancia. m.*2. *a.*

(*b*) Rex Baronibus; Mandamus vobis, quod

Chap. XXIII.   *and* ACCOUNTANTS.   223

on him (*c*), *Thomas Malemeyns* of an Amercement (*d*), *James Haunsard* of an Amercement (*e*), *John de Keyvill* of an erroneous Amercement (*f*), *William de Leyburn* of all Debts and Accounts (*g*), *Bogo de Knovill* of an undue Charge set on him (*h*), the Priour and Monks of the *Holy Trinity* of *Canterbury* of a Fine or Forfeiture for a Trespass (*i*), *Godfrey*, Bishop of *Worcester*, of an Overcharge of Relief for his Inheritance, being the third Part of a Barony (*k*), and *Elias Cotele* of a Debt (*l*). In the Reign of K. *Edward* I. a Writ was sent to the Barons on Behalf of *Geoffrey de Picheford*, Constable of *Windsor-Castle*, that they should not charge him with any Demands, but such as were right

quod Walterum de Bathonia Vicecomitem Devoniæ, arrestatum eo quod permisit malam monetam currere in Comitatu suo, quietum inde ad præsens permittatis abire. B. e. in f. M. *Pas. Commun.* 32. *H.* 3. *Rot.* 7. *a.*

(*c*) Rex Baronibus; Quia concessimus dudum Willelmo le Cutiller de Hoyland Mercatori Oxoniæ, quod ipse toto tempore vitæ suæ quietus sit de omnibus tallagijs: Vobis mandamus, quod de tallagio xl s nuper super eum assiso ipsum quietum esse faciatis. *Ex Memor.* 35. *H.* 3. *Rot.* 9. *a.*

(*d*) Baronibus, pro Thoma Malemeyns. Rex mandat, quod perdonavit eidem Thomæ xx s, ad quos amerciatus fuit coram Johanne de Cobham, quia sacramentum in quadam Jurata præstare recusavit: Rex mandat, quod ipsum Thomam de prædictis xx s quietum esse faciant, & sic fieri & inrotulari. *Memor.* 55. *H.* 3. *Rot.* 2. *b.*

(*e*) *Pas. Communia* 56. *H.* 3. *Rot.* 6. *a.*

(*f*) *Mich. Commun.* 9 & 10. *E.* 1. *Rot.* 2. *a.*

(*g*) *Mich. Commun.* 14. *E.* 1. *Rot.* 2. *a.*

(*h*) Baronibus, pro Bogone de Knovill. Cum Rex nuper præceperit eidem Bogoni tunc Vicecomiti Salopiæ, quod de Bancis ibidem reparatis ad Placita Regis ibidem tenenda commodum Regis faceret, & servientibus Regis ad placita prædicta curialitatem inde faceret, prout sibi visum esset faciendum, Ita quod de residuo Regi respondere posset ad Scaccarium; Et Justiciarij Regis Bancos prædictos præfatis servientibus, juxta consuetudinem inde hactenus usitatam liberaverint, Ita quod idem Bogo nichil inde recepit: Rex mandat Baronibus, quod eundem Bogonem de Venditione Bancorum prædictorum, unde oneratur ad Scaccarium, exonerent. T. Rege apud Westm. xviij° die Februarij anno xviij°. *Pas. Commun.* 18. *E.* 1. *Rot.* — *a.*

(*i*) *Trin. Commun.* 18. *E.* 1. *Rot.* — *a.*

(*k*) Ex parte Venerabilis Patris G. Wigorn. Episcopi Regi est ostensum, quod idem Episcopus tertiam partem unius Baroniæ tantum de nobis teneat in Capite, Barones ab eodem Episcopo pro relevio suo de prædicta tertia parte Baroniæ prædictæ tertiam partem Centum librarum exigunt per summonicionem Scaccarij prædicti, minus juste: Et quia juxta tenorem Magnæ Cartæ de Libertatibus Angliæ, centum marcæ tantum pro relevio de Baronia integra præstari debent, propter quod Rex eidem Episcopo injuriari non wlt in hac parte: Mandat Baronibus sicut alias, quod si prædictus Episcopus tertiam partem unius Baroniæ tantum de Rege teneat & non amplius, tunc recepta ab eodem Episcopo tercia parte C marcarum pro relevio suo dictæ terciæ partis, eundem Episcopum de eo quod ab ipso exigitur per summonicionem prædictam ultra dictam tertiam partem Centum marcarum pro eodem relevio exonerent, & ei de eadem tercia parte Centum marcarum rationabiles terminos, ad quos eam nobis commode solvere possit concedant. T. &c x° die Septembris anno &c decimo nono. *Ex Mich. Commun.* 20. *E.* 1. *Rot.* 4. *a. in imo.*

(*l*) Baronibus, per Regem pro Elia Cotele. Edward par la grace de Dieu &c; Comme Elys Cotele nostre Varlet nous feust tenuz en une dette, la quele il nous ad pleinement paie, se com il dit, & se com il vous porra plus apertement monstrer: Vous maundoms

right and reasonable (*m*). And in the same King's Reign, the Archbishoprick of *Canterbury* being void and in the King's Hands was committed by him, 8 *Junij anno regni* 34, to *Humfrey de Waleden*, during the King's Pleasure; and afterwards, 26 *Marcij anno* 35, at the Pope's Request, to *Magistro Guillelmo Testa Archidiacono Dran. in Ecclesia Couen. & Petro Amalm. Canonico Burdegalensi Clericis, & administratoribus Archiepiscopatus prædicti per dictum Dominum Summum Pontificem deputatis, vel eorum alteri ——, Custodiendum ad opus dicti Summi Pontificis:* hereupon K. *Edward* II. commands the Barons of the Exchequer by his Writ, that *Humfrey de Waleden* be acquitted of the Issues of the said Archbishoprick *a prædicto octavo die Junij usq; ad prædictum vicesimum sextum diem Marcij* (*n*).

But sometimes Men were discharged by the Chief Justicier, or by the Treasurer and Barons, without any especial Writ (for ought that appears) directed to them for that Purpose. *Ernald*, Son of *Fromond* of *Gepeswic*, was discharged, by Judgment of the Barons of the Exchequer, two Marks of Silver, an Amercement imposed by *Ralf Basset*, Justicier (*o*). *Ralf Musard* fined in C *l*, for Leave to marry as he should like. But the greater Part of this Fine was released to him by the Barons of the Exchequer, because he had before fined for the same with the Earl of *Moreton*, whose Tenant he was (*p*). *Gil-*

maundoms de ceo qe porra estre trove quil avera paie, lui facez aver due alouaunce, si kil en soit descharges. Done souz nostre Prive Seal a Estebenhithe, le xvij jour de Mai lan de nostre regne vint e setisme. *Trin. Brevia* 26 & 27. *E.* 1. *Rot.* 26. *b.*

(*m*) Edward par la grace de Dieu &c; Nous vous enveoms enclos denz ces lettres une mustrance, qe Monsieur Geffrey de Pichford nous ad faite bailler, par la quele nous avoms entendu qe lui faites aucunes damages du temps qil ad este Conestable du chastel de Wyndesore, e le charges a respondre des gardes apurtenantz au dit chastel, autrement qe les autres ont fait qui en ont est Constables avant lui: E pur ce nous vous mandoms, qe la dite Mustrance e totes les choses qe cele busoigne touchent examinez e avisez diligeaument, e ne suffrez qe nules demandes seient faites audit Geffrei en cele partie, fors qe celes qe sont dreitureles, e qe en deivent estre faites par reson. Donez sous nostre prive Seal a Impeton, le v jour de May lan de nostre regne vint sisime.

Littera directa Domino Regi per Galfridum de Picheford pro negotijs in brevi contentis atachiatur huic brevi, quod est in forulo Marescalli. *Pas. Brevia* 26. *Edw.* 1. *Rot.* 75. *a. in bund.* 25 & 26. *E.* 1.

(*n*) Baronibus, pro Humfrido de Waleden. — Teste Rege apud Westmon. xxviij die Novembris anno secundo. *Mich. Brevia* 2. *E.* 2. *Rot.* 31. *a.*

(*o*) Et idem Vicecomes r c de ij marcis argenti, de minutis hominibus, de placitis Radulfi Basset: Et in Perdonis, per considerationem Baronum de Scaccar[io], Ernaldo filio Fromundi de Gepeswic ij marcæ argenti; Et Q. e. *Mag. Rot.* 5. *Steph. Rot.* 10. *b. Sudfolc.*

(*p*) Radulfus Musard debet C l, pro se maritando ubi voluerit; & pro Fine terræ suæ. Sed consideratione Baronum relaxatæ sunt ei C marcæ; quia major pars terræ suæ est in terra Comitis Moritoniæ, cum quo finivit. *Mag. Rot.* 3. *R.* 1. *Rot.* 8. *a. Gloec.*

bert

Chap. XXIII.   *and* ACCOUNTANTS.   225

bert Fitz-Renfrey fined in xx Marks, for Earl *John*, to whom the Chancellor had committed CC *l*. But the Barons of the Exchequer adjudged, that *Gilbert* should not render the same for the Earl, because the Earl had not performed the Agreement made with him by *Gilbert*, in Consideration whereof *Gilbert* became charged therewith (*q*). *Robert de Gant* fined in DC Marks, to have Right for certain Lands which Earl *Simon* had given him. But the Barons of the Exchequer adjudged, that his Heir should not answer for the same till his full Age (*r*). *Reginald de Cornhill* was charged with C Marks Increment for the County of *Kent*. The King by his Writ declared, that *Reginald* had made Fine with him in a great Sum, for that Increment and other Matters together. Whereupon the Barons of the Exchequer adjudged, that *Reginald* should be discharged of the said C Marks Increment (*s*). *Robert de Gant* stood charged with a Debt of xxvj *l*. But by Judgment of the Barons he was acquitted thereof; and the Debt was set in Charge upon his Heir (*t*). *Robert de Turneham*, who married the Daughter and Heiress of *William Fossard*, was charged with Dx *l*. xiiij *s*. the Debts of *Aaron* the *Jew*. But it appearing to the Barons of the Exchequer, that *Aaron* by his Charter had quitclaimed *William Fossard* of the said Debt; the Barons adjudged, that *Robert de Turneham* should be discharged thereof (*u*). *William Briewerre*

(*q*) Gillebertus filius Renfredi debet xx marcas pro Comite Johanne, cui Cancellarius commendaverat CC libras. Sed consideratum est per Barones, quod prædictus Gillebertus non debet eas reddere pro Comite, quia Comes non tenuit ei Conventionem pro qua eas reddere debuerat, nec per eum stetit. *Mag. Rot.* 4. *R.* 1. *Rot.* 4. *b. Everwichsc.*

(*r*) *Ante*, vol. 1. *cap.* 12. *sect.* 1. *ad ann.* 4. *R.* 1. Robertus de Gant.

(*s*) Reginaldus de Cornhill promiserat Domino Regi C marcas de Cremento Comitatus de Kent. Sed Dominus Rex postea recordatus est per breve suum, quod est in forulo Marescalli, quod idem Reginaldus est quietus de illis C marcis unde Vicecomitatum accreverat, & de omnibus alijs demandis per finem de D marcis quem postea fecit cum eo. De quibus reddit compotum infra. Et ideo consideratum est quod de illis C marcis non debet amplius summoneri. *Mag. Rot.* 8. *R.* 1. *Rot.* 23. *a. Chent.*

(*t*) Robertus de Gant debet xxvj l super Yrneham & Liedes. Sed quia Yrneham & Liedes non sunt de hæreditate ipsius Roberti vel hæredis sui, Consideratum est per Barones, quod nulla debet fieri districtio super Yrneham & Liedes pro prædicto debito; Sed debet prædictum debitum exigi ab hærede ipsius Roberti. *Mag. Rot.* 9. *R.* 1. *Rot.* 7. *b. Linc. tit.* De debitis Aaron.

(*u*) Robertus de Turneham debet D & x l & xiiij s de Debitis Aaronis, quæ exigebantur a Willelmo Fossard, cujus filiam & hæredem prædictus Robertus habet uxorem. Sed quia recordatum fuit per Barones, quod Abbas de Mealse & Monachi attulerunt Cartam prædicti Aaron de quietantia prædicti debiti, quæ liberata fuit prædicto Willielmo coram Baronibus, in qua Carta continetur quod prædicti Monachi prædictum Willelmum acquietaverunt de prædicto debito pro Mille & CC & Lx marcis, sicut continetur in Rotulo Anni præcedentis: Consideratum est per Barones, quod Cartæ de prædictis debitis Aaron prædicto Roberto reddantur; & quod amplius nec ipse

werre stood charged with the Ferm of *Huiam*; and the Barons of the Exchequer adjudged him to be discharged thereof (*w*). *Peter de Schidimor*, Sheriff of *Dorset* and *Somerset*, was charged with L Marks and C Marks and L Marks more, as Increment of the said Counties for two half Years and one whole Year past. But it appearing, that *Peter*, when he became Sheriff, never consented to pay the said Increment, but always declared against it, and that accordingly he was admitted to fine with the Chief Justicier in x Marks, that the said Increments might not be demanded of him; he was acquitted thereof by Judgment of the Barons (*x*). *William de Albenni* was charged (as Fermour) with L *l*. under the Name of Increment. But in regard it appeared to the Chief Justicier and Barons, that *William* was to answer as *Custos*, they acquitted him of the said Increment (*y*). *Geoffrey de Mandevill* was charged with C Marks Fine, to have Right. But because *William* could not have Right by reason of the King's Prohibition, the Chief Justicier ordered him to be discharged of the said Fine (*z*). *Nicolas de Verdun* fined in CC Marks, that he might be quit of DLj *l*. which was demanded of him for the Aid of the Knights of the Honour of *Leicester*, for the Time wherein his Father had been Sheriff of the Counties of *Warwick* and *Leicester*. But forasmuch as his Father had his *Quietus* for those Years, and neither his said Father nor his eldest Brother *Thomas* were ever charged with the said Debt in the *Great Roll* of K. *Richard* I. but the said Debt was arbitrarily and

ipse nec hæredes ejus post ipsum pro hoc debito distringantur; Et ita Quietus est. *Mag. Rot.* 10. *R.* 1. *Rot.* 3. *b. Everwichscira.*

(*w*) Willelmus Briewerre debet xxvj s & viij d de firma de Huiam, quæ fuit Rogeri de Planes, de anno viij°. Sed recordatum est per Barones, quod terra illa de Huiam pertinet ad Baroniam de Doura, cujus custodiam cum pertinentijs & hærede Rex ei concessit; & ideo consideratum est quod non debet amplius inde summoneri. *Mag. Rot.* 10. *R.* 1. *Rot.* 14. *a. Kent.*

(*x*) Petrus de Schidimor debet L marcas de Cremento Comitatus de dimidio anno ix°, Et C marcas de anno præterito, Et L marcas de hoc dimidio anno. Sed postea finivit cum Justiciario per x marcas, ne prædicta Crementa exigerentur ab eo; quia quando recepit Comitatus, noluit ullo modo prædictum Crementum reddere, sed semper contradixit. Et ita consideratum est, quod amplius de prædictis Crementis non summoneatur. *Mag. Rot.* 1. *J. Rot.* 17. *a. Dorsete & Sumersete.*

(*y*) Idem W. [Willelmus de Albenni] debet L libras de novo cremento de dimidio anno ix°. Sed recordatum est per H. Cantuariensem Archiepiscopum & G. filium Petri, & per alios Barones, quod de hoc dimidio anno & de dimidio anno vij°, respondit sicut Custos: Et ideo consideratum est, quod de Cremento utriusq; prædicti anni sit quietus. *Ib. Rot.* 18. *a. Warewich & Leircestr.*

(*z*) Galfridus de Mandevil debet C marcas, sicut supra continetur: Sed recordatum est per Justiciarium, scilicet G. filium Petri, quod pro Prohibitione Regis non potuit habere Rectum; & ideo non debet summoneri. *Mag. Rot.* 8. *J. Rot.* 13. *a. Dorsete & Sumersete.*

without

without Judgment set upon the said *Nicolas* by the Suggestion of *Reginald Basset* in the Time of K. *John*, it was now adjudged by *William Mareschall* Earl of *Pembroke*, Governor of the King and Kingdom, by *Peter* Bishop of *Winchester*, *Hubert de Burgh* Chief Justicier, and by the King's Council, that *Nicolas de Verdun* should be discharged of the said DLj *l* (*a*). *Alan de St. George* was discharged of an Amercement of the Forest by Judgment of the Barons (*b*). The Abbot of *Barlinges* was pardoned, by the Justicier, an Amerciament of xx *s*, for the Soul of K. *John* (*c*). *William Hardel* was charged with xx *l*. for Wine. He came into the Exchequer before the Justicier, the Chancellor, the Bishops of *Bath* and of *Saresbiry*, the Earl of *Gloucester*, and other Barons there present, and made Oath that he did not owe the King the said xx *l*. And the Justicier ordered him to be discharged thereof (*d*). *Simon* Earl of *Huntendon* was charged with an hundred fourscore and sixteen Pounds for the Debts of *Aaron* the *Jew*. But in regard Earl *Simon* died without Heirs, the Barons of the Exchequer adjudged, that *John* now Earl of *Huntendon* ought not to be summoned for the said Debt; because he was not Heir to Earl *Simon*, nor had any Thing from him by hereditary Descent or otherwise (*e*). The

(*a*) Nicholaus de Verdun [debet] CC marcas, Ut sit quietus de D & Lj l de Auxilio Militum de Honore Leicestriæ, quæ exigebantur ab eo de tempore quo Pater suus fuit Vicecomes Warewici & Leircestriæ, qui remansit quietus de tempore illo. Et quia nec Pater suus, nec Thomas frater suus Primogenitus, inventi fuerunt in prædicto debito in Rotulo Regis Ricardi, set per suggestionem Reginaldi Basset, Voluntate & sine Judicio, tempore Regis J. positum fuit debitum illud super ipsum Nicholaum: Judicatum est per W. Mariscallum Comitem de Pembroc, Rectorem Regis & Regni, & per P. Wintoniensem Episcopum, & H. de Burgo Justiciarium, & Consilium Regis, Quod de prædictis D & Lj l sit Quietus. Et debet prædictas CC marcas pacare a Pascha Anni Tertij infra iij annos proximo sequentes. *Mag. Rot.* 2. *H.* 3. *Rot.* 4. *b. tit.* Residuum Comitatus Warewiksir. & Leirceftrescir.

(*b*) Suffex. Consideratum est quod Alanus de S. Georgio quietus sit de demanda v marcarum pro defalta in Comitatu de Wiltescira in placito Forestæ; quia protestatum est, quod dictus Alanus nunquam tenuit terram in illo Comitatu. *Memor.* 11. *H.* 3. *Rot.* 1. *b.*

(*c*) Lincolnia. Perdonati sunt Abbati de Barlinges xx s, quos debuit de Misericordia, pro Anima Regis Johannis, per Justiciarium. *Memor.* 11. *H.* 3. *Rot.* 1. *b.*

(*d*) Willelmus Hardel juravit coram Justiciario, & Cancellario, & Bathonensi & Sarreb. Episcopis, & Comite Gloverniæ, & alijs Baronibus, quod non debuit Domino Regi illas xx libras pro Vino: Et Quietus est per Justiciarium. *Memor.* 11. *H.* 3. *Rot.* 14. *a. in imo.*

(*e*) Comes Simon debet C & quater xx & xvj l de pluribus debitis Aaronis Judæi Lincolniæ. Set non habet hæredem. Et consideratum est per Barones de Scaccario, quod Johannes Comes Huntedoniæ non debet de debito prædicto summoneri, quia non est hæres ejusdem Simonis, nec habet aliquid quod ei de prædicto Simone descendat jure hæreditario vel alio modo. *Mag. Rot.* 13. *H.* 3. *Cauntebrig. & Huntedonescir.*

Citizens

Citizens of *London*, with *John Travers* and *Andrew Bukerel*, Bailiffs of the *Queen's Hithe*, were discharged of the Ferm of the *Queen's Hithe* for the 8th and 9th Years of the King's Reign, by Judgment of the Barons of the Exchequer *(f)*. *Hamon de Crevequor* was discharged of a Debt, by Judgment of the Barons; he having been doubly charged for one and the same Fact *(g)*. *John de Rocheford* was discharged by Judgment of the Barons, he having been also doubly charged for one and the same Fact *(h)*. The Abbot of *Vale Royal* was discharged by Judgment of the Court of Exchequer, of an Account and of certain Trespasses relating thereto, upon his making Fine with the King for the same *(i)*. A Debt of xx Marks was set-off from *William* Bishop of *Ely* by virtue of the King's Writ grounded upon a Recordation made at the Exchequer by *William Briewerre* and other Barons *(k)*. How-

(f) Lundonia. Consideratum est coram Baronibus de Scaccario, die Sabbati proximo post festum S. Nicholai, quod Cives Londoniæ cum Johanne Travers & Andrea Bukerell ballivis anni octavi & noni de Ripa Reginæ, quieti sunt de firma ejusdem Ripæ de eisdem annis octavo & nono. Et datus est dies Civibus Lundoniæ & Thomæ de Cyrencestria a die S. Hilarij in quindecim dies, ut tunc videatur, utrum dicti Cives aut dictus Thomas debeat respondere Domino Regi de viginti libris & decem solidis, qui exiguntur de firma ejusdem Ripæ de dimidio anno x°. Idem dies datus est eisdem Civibus & Radulfo de Dicton Ballivo Comitis Ricardi de eadem Ripa, coram Rege, de Navibus cum pisce quæ non applicant ad eandem Ripam, sicut debent & solent, ut idem ballivus dicit, Unde idem Cives vocant Dominum Regem in Warrantum, Qui dicunt quod Rex præcepit, quod Naves piscem deferentes applicarent ubi vellent. Et idem Thomas attornavit Henricum de Chansor Clericum suum loco suo. *Mich. Commun.* 14. *H.* 3. *Rot.* 3. *a.*

(g) Quia inventum est in Originali xxvij°, quod Hamo de Crevequor finem fecit cum Rege per x marcas pro transgressione Forestæ, & in eodem anno amerciatus est pro eodem facto ad x marcas, coram G. de Segrave Itinerante ad Placita Forestæ in Comitatu Essexiæ; Et sic honeratur bis pro uno & eodem facto: Consideratum est quod quietus sit per x marcas; De quibus respondet in Rotulo xxxix° & in Rotulis pendentibus. *Pas. Commun.* 41. *H.* 3. *Rot.* 15. *b.*

(h) —— Et Barones inspicientes Originale prædictum & Extractas prædictas, invenerunt quod una & eadem occasione dictus Johannes de xxx l in Originali & de alijs in extractis antedictis, Ubi onerari non debet nisi tantum de illis xxx l contentis in Originali prædicto, quia compertum est quod idem Johannes de illis xxx l, per quas fuit oneratus per Originale antedictum, dudum satisfecit: Consideratum est, quod idem Johannes deoneretur de illis xxx l, de quibus oneratur per extractas prædictas, & inde sit quietus. *Hil. Communia* 26 & 27. *E.* 1. *Rot.* 16. *a.* *The Pipe-award in the Margin of this Roll is,* In Rot. xxvj*to*.

(i) Cestria. *Mich. Communia* 26 & 27. *E.* 1. *Rot.* 9. *a & b.*

(k) Willelmus Elyensis Episcopus r c de CC & xx marcis, Pro habenda Custodia Stephani de Bello Campo cum hæreditate sua, & eo maritando ubi voluerit; In Thesauro CC marcas; Quæ fuerunt redditæ anno Regis Ricardi primo; In Perdonis ipsi Episcopo xx marcas per breve Regis; Quia recordatum est per Willelmum Briewerre & Hugonem Bardolf & alios Barones ad Scaccarium, quod non promisit prædictas xx marcas Regi, sed Bertrammo de Verdun qui prius finierat pro prædicta Custodia cum Rege pro CC marcis; Et sic Q. e. *Mag. Rot.* 7. *R.* 1. *Rot.* 9. *a.* *Cantebr. & Huntend.*

ever,

Chap. XXIII. *and* ACCOUNTANTS.

ever, in fome Cafes (as it feems) nobody but the King himfelf could grant a Difcharge. The following Cafe was one of that Sort. Certain Perfons became Manucaptors in the Exchequer for the Executors of *Gregory de Rokefley* an Accountant. The Executors came and accounted. And the Treafurer thereupon ordered, that the Manucaptors fhould be difcharged of their Manucaption, *quieti effent de Manucaptione fua prædicta, & quod fi quid Regi aretro effet &c, Rex fe caperet ad hæredes & tenentes terrarum prædicti Gregorij & ad executores teftamenti ejufdem.* Several Years afterwards this Matter coming to be reconfidered in Court, the Treafurer and Barons adjudged, that nobody befides the King himfelf could difcharge the faid Manucaptors of their faid Manucaption; and accordingly they annulled the faid Difcharge of the faid Manucaption, and ordered that the faid Manucaption fhould be in Force (*l*).

Sometimes both Debts and Accounts were difcharged by the King's Pardon. *Ralf Brito* paid a Fine of DCC *l* and odd, to be quit of rendering an Account of the Iffues of the Land of *Henry de Effex* and of the Honour of *Boloigne*, which had lately been in his Cuftody (*m*). K. *Henry* III. pardoned or remitted to the Heir of *William de Corneburh* M Marks and two Palfreys, being a Fine for obtaining the King's Favour; *William* having died in Imprifonment for that Debt (*n*). The fame King pardoned *William de Lund* C *s*, imprefted to him out of the King's Treafure at the Exchequer (*o*). For good Service done to the King by *Engelard de Cygony* in his Lifetime, the King granted to his Executors, that they fhould be quit of all Accounts to be rendered by them at the Exchequer, and of all Arerages of Accounts, and of all Debts and Imprefts (*p*). *Emme de Ely* iiij Marks and a half, Part of her Hufband's Quota of a Tallage fet upon the Citizens of *London* (*q*). The King quitted *Peter de Rivalle*, his Heirs and Executors,

---

(*l*) *Paf. Com.* 26 & 27. *E.* 1. *Rot.* 23. *a.*

(*m*) Radulfus Brito debet DCC & xxxiij l & vj s & viij d, Ut fit quietus de compoto fuo de exitibus terræ quæ fuit Henrici de Effexa & Honoris Comitis Boloniæ dum fuit in ejus Cuftodia. *Mag. Rot.* 29. *H.* 2. *Rot.* 3. *a. Effex & Hurtf.*

(*n*) Ebor. Mandatum eft Vicecomiti, quod Rex perdonavit hæredi Willelmi de Corneburh mille marcas & duos palefridos, quos idem Willelmus promifit Regi J. pro Benevolentia fua habenda; et qui mortuus fuit in prifona Regis J. pro prædicto debito: Et quod dictum hæredem pro prædicto debito non diftringat. *Ex Memor.* 11. *H.* 3. *Rot.* 3. *b.*

(*o*) Baronibus, pro Willelmo de Lunda. Rex perdonavit eidem Willelmo centum folidos, quos Regi debet de præftito ei facto ad Scaccarium Regis de Thefauro Regis. *Ex Memor.* 25. *H.* 3. *Rot.* 7. *b.*

(*p*) *Mich. Communia* 29. *H.* 3. *Rot.* 3. *b.*

(*q*) Rex Baronibus; Sciatis quod Perdonavimus Em. quæ fuit uxor Johannis de Ely iiij marcas & dimidiam, quæ nobis reftant reddendæ de xv marcis, ad quas prædictus J. talliatus fuit, in Tallagio quod affidere fecimus fuper Cives noftros Londoniæ. Breve eft in f. M. *Hil. Memor.* 32. *H.* 3. *Rot.* 3. *b.*

of all Debts, and all Accounts to be rendered to the King or his Heirs, for the Wardrobe (*r*). The King pardoned to the Master of the Hospital of *Ospreng* the last Tallage assessed upon him and his Tenants (*s*). It having been testified before the King, that *Nicholas de Bassingburn*, an Assessor and Collector of the Trentisme in *Cambridgshire*, had been maliciously robbed of xx *l* (the King's Money) arising out of the Trentisme, the King remitted to him the xx *l*, and commanded the Barons to discharge him of it (*t*). The Prior of *Luffeld* was attached to account. Because of the Poverty of that Priory, the Account, for a Fine paid to the King, was remitted to them (*u*). Mestre *Robert de Beuver*, an Accountant, had lost the Rolls and Remembrances, whereby he ought to render his Account to the King's Use: hereupon the King by Privy Seal commands the Barons to take of him some reasonable Fine for the same Account, and, that being done, to acquit him thereof (*w*). The King pardoned to the Earl of *Arundel* sundry Debts charged on him *de claro* at the Exchequer; and commanded the Barons to acquit him thereof (*x*). The King pardoned to *Cecill de Baquelle* four Marks, at which her Chatells were taxed in *London* to the Quinzime granted to the King in the first Year of his Reign by the Community of the said City; and commanded the Barons to acquit her thereof at the Exchequer (*y*). King *Edward* II. pardoned to *Ebulo de Montibus* CCL *l*, due upon his Account of the Issues of the *Templars* Lands, which *Ebulo* had in his Custody

---

(*r*) Pro Petro de Rivalle. Rex concessit eidem, quod ipse & hæredes sui & executores testamenti sui quieti sint ab omnibus debitis & demandis, compotis & ratiocinijs, Regi vel hæredibus suis reddendis, a tempore quo primo habuit custodiam Garderobæ Regis, usq; ad Natale Domini anno xxxv. *Ex Memor.* 35. *H.* 3. *Rot.* 8. *a.*

(*s*) Baronibus pro Magistro Hospitalis de Ospreng. Rex perdonavit eidem Tallagium super ipsum & Tenentes suos assessum in ultimo Tallagio, hac vice, de gratia sua speciali. *Pas. Commun.* 52 & 53. *H.* 3. *Rot.* 8. *b.*

(*t*) Quia testificatum est coram Rege, quod Nicholaus de Bassingburn, quem Rex nuper deputavit ad xxx^{am} in Comitatu Cantabrigiæ taxandam & colligendam, de xx l d e prædicta tricesima provenientibus nuper apud Costesheye maliciose extitit deprædatus; Rex perdonavit eidem Nicholao illas xx l; Et mandat Baronibus, quod ipsum Nicholaum inde quietum esse faciant. *Mich. Commun.* 14. *E.* 1. *Rot.* 4. *a.*

(*u*) *Mich. Memor.* 25. *Edw.* 1. inter *Fines.*

(*w*) *Trin. Brevia* 26 & 27. *E.* 1. *Rot.* 26. *a.*

(*x*) *Pas. Brevia* 35. *E.* 1. *Rot.* 42. *b.*

(*y*) Cum Rex de gratia sua speciali perdonaverit Ceciliæ quæ fuit uxor Johannis de Baquelle, illas quatuor marcas ad quas bona et catalla sua in Civitate Regis Londoniæ ratione Quintædecimæ Regi anno regni sui primo, per Communitatem ejusdem Civitatis concessæ, taxata fuerunt, et quæ ab ipsa Cecilia ad opus Regis exiguntur ratione Quintædecimæ supradictæ: Rex mandat Baronibus, quod ipsam Ceciliam de prædictis quatuor marcis quietam esse faciant. T. Rege apud Westmon. iiij° die marcij anno secundo. *Hil. Brevia* 2. *E.* 2. *Rot.* 52. *b.*

whilst

Chap. XXIII.   *and* ACCOUNTANTS.   231

whilst the same were in the King's Hands (*z*). The same King pardoned to the Earls, Barons, and all others, who served in Person in *Aquitany* in the War moved between K. *Edward* I. and the King of *France*, the Onzime and Disme granted to the said K. *Edward* I, payable out of the Goods of the said Persons who served in that War (*a*). But when the King had ordered certain Debts to be respited or pardoned, he sometimes countermanded such Order. K. *Henry* III, in the 51st Year of his Reign, commanded the Treasurer and Barons in full Exchequer, that no Sheriff or Bailiff, who owed the King any Debt, should depart from the Exchequer till he had fully paid it; and that if any Writ was afterwards sent to the Barons for respiting or pardoning such Debt, they should not do any Thing thereupon, without consulting the King himself (*b*).

XXI. If upon the Account viewed and stated, the Crown was found indebted to the Accountant, the Sum in which the Crown was so found indebted was called *Superplus* or *Superplusagium*; probably, because it was *so much* more than the Accountant's Receipts. *Pain*, Sheriff of *Surrey* and *Huntendonshire*, had a Surplusage in his Account for the County of *Surrey*: which was allowed to him in his Account for the County of *Huntendon* (*c*). *Henry de Cornhill*, accounting as Fermour of the Land late of *Henry de Essex*, had a Surplusage of xxx *s*, which was allowed to him in another Account (*d*).

William

(*z*) *Trin. Communia* 9. *E.* 2. *Rot.* 104. *a*.
(*a*) Baronibus, pro Comitibus & Baronibus. Sciant Barones, quod Rex de gratia sua speciali perdonavit Comitibus, Baronibus, & omnibus alijs nuper in guerra Domini E quondam Regis Angliæ patris Regis nunc inter ipsum patrem Regis & Regem Franciæ in Ducatu Aquitaniæ tunc mota exissentibus, Undecimam & Decimam eidem Patri Regis per communitatem Regni sui tunc concessas, ipsos sic in guerra sua prædicta existentes de proprijs bonis suis contingentes: Et ideo mandat Baronibus, quod omnes illos quos in obsequium ejusdem patris Regis in guerra sua prædicta eis constare poterit extitisse, de dictis Undecima & Decima ipsos de proprijs bonis suis contingentibus ad dictum Scaccarium exonerari & quietos esse faciant. T. R. apud Ebor. xx die Nov. anno xij. Per ipsum Regem. *Pas. Brevia.* 12. *E.* 2. *Rot.* 97. *b*.

(*b*) De præcepto facto Thesaurario & Baronibus per Dominum Regem. Memorandum quod die Sabbati proximo post festum S. Hilarij, præcepit Dominus Rex in pleno Scaccario Thesaurario & Baronibus ejusdem Scaccarij, quod si aliquis Vicecomes vel Ballivus, qui in aliquo debito Domino Regi tenetur, veniat ad Scaccarium, non recedat inde donec totum debitum persolverit; Et si idem Dominus Rex postea mittat breve suum de prædicto debito respectuando vel perdonando, non faciant aliquid pro hujusmodi brevi, quosq; dictus Dominus Rex super hoc consulatur. *Memor.* 51. *H.* 3. *Rot.* 4. *a*.

(*c*) Et habet de suo Superplusagio xlvij s & x d: Quod computatum est ei in firma Huntendonescira. *Mag. Rot.* 2. *H.* 2. *Rot.* 2. *a*. Et in suo superplusagio de Surreia xlvij s & x d. *Ib*.

(*d*) Et habet [viz. Henricus de Cornhill]
de

William de Briewerre, Sheriff of *Cornwall*, had a Surplusage of Lxxviij *s.* due to him upon his Account. He attorned the same to *William des Boterels*; who had it allowed to him upon his Account for the same County (*e*). *William de St. Oen* consented before the Barons, that Two several Surplusages which he had in his Accounts, should be allowed to the Sheriff of *Oxfordshire*, in any of his Debts that he should choose (*f*). *John de Gatesden* consented before the Barons, that L *s.* which *John de Selfhanger* owed to the King for an Escape, should be allowed to the said *John* in a certain Surplusage of his (*g*). *Henry de Penbroc* came before the Barons, and granted that a Surplusage which he had in *Gloucester*, in the Great Roll of the xlvjth Year of K. *Henry* III, should be allowed in the Debts of *Walter* Bishop of *Worcester* (*h*). The Mayor and Citizens of *London* came before the Barons, and granted that a certain Surplusage of ix *l.* and odd, which they had in the xlijth Year of K. *Henry* III, in a Tallage of MMM Marks, should be allowed to *Richard de Hereford*, a Clerk of the Exchequer, in any Debt that he pleased, for so much, which the Citizens owed to him (*i*). Q. *Alienor*, in the Presence of the Treasurer and a Remembrancer of the Exchequer, granted that out of a Surplusage which she had in the Roll of Accounts of the Expenses of her Wardrobe, there might be allowed 286 *l.* and odd to

de Superplus, xxx s; qui conputantur ei infra in firmis terrarum quas Willelmus de Piro saisivit. *Mag. Rot* 1. *R.* 1. *Rot.* 1. *b.*

(*e*) Willelmus des Boterels reddit compotum de — de firma Cornubiæ: Idem reddit compotum de eodem debito: In Thesauro nichil: Et in Superplusagio quod Willelmus Briewerre habet in anno præterito in firma de Cornewallia Lxxviijs; quos ipse Willelmus attornavit ad reddendos per Vicecomitem, coram Baronibus. *Mag. Rot.* 6. *Joh. Rot.* 4. *a. tit.* Cornewallia.

(*f*) Oxon. Willelmus de Sancto Audoeno venit coram Baronibus, & recognovit quod wlt & concedit quod xxx & vjs & iij **ob.**; quos habet de superplusagio in compoto suo in Rotulo xxxiiij, et vj l quas habet similiter in superplusagio in Rotulo xxxix, allocentur Vicecomiti Oxoniæ, ubicunq; ipse voluerit in debitis suis. *Memor.* 42. *H.* 3. *Rot.* 7. *a.*

(*g*) Memorandum de Johanne de Gatesden. Idem Johannes concessit coram Baronibus, quod L s, quos Johannes de Selfhanger Regi debet pro Evasione, allocentur eidem Johanni in superplusagio quod dictus Johannes habet. *Memor.* 42. *H.* 3. *Rot.* 2. *a.*

(*h*) Recognitio Henrici de Penbroc. Idem venit coram Baronibus, & concessit quod quoddam superplusagium quod habet in Glouceſtria in Rotulo xlvj°, allocetur in debitis Walteri Wygorniensis Episcopi. Postea allocatur eidem Waltero in debitis suis in Rotulo quinto. *Mich. Recogn.* 49. *H.* 3. *Rot.* 13. *b.*

(*i*) Major & Cives Londoniæ venerunt coram Baronibus in festo Sanctæ Margaretæ, & concesserunt quod ix libræ ij s & vij den. quos Cives Londoniæ habent de quodam superplusagio in Rotulo xlij°, in Tallagio MMM marcarum, allocentur in quo debito Ricardus de Hereford Clericus de Scaccario voluerit, pro quodam debito in quo dicti Cives ei tenebantur. *Trin. Communia* 56. *H.* 3. *Rot.* 7. *b.*

Edmund

Edmund Spigurnel in the Debts which he owed to the King (*k*). The Queen Mother sent a Message to the Barons by Frier *Joseph de Chauncy*, the Treasurer, granting that xv *l*. which she had in Surplusage in *Hugh de la Penne*'s Account for the Wardrobe, might be allowed to *Edmund Espigurnel* in any of his Debts at his own Choice (*l*). *John de Burstowe*, who was one of the Collectours of the Disme and the Sisme of the County of *Surrey* lately granted to K. *Edward* I. by the Layty, came before the Barons, and assigned to *John Daubernoun*, who was another of the Collectours of the said Disme and Sisme, viij *l*. xvj *d*. ob. being his (*John de Burstowe*'s) Contingent of xvj *l*. ij *s*. ix *d*. which the said *John* & *John* had in Surplusage in their Account entered in the *Rotulus Compotorum* of the xxxiijd Year of K. *Edward* I; and *John de Burstowe* granted for him, his Heirs and Executors, that the said viij *l*. xvj *d*. ob. should be allowed to the said *John Daubernoun* in the Debts he owed to the King in the Remanent of his Account of the Vintisme and Quinzisme for the County of *Surrey* lately granted to the King by the Laity (*m*). *John de Oddingseles* came before the Barons, and assigned to the Abbot of *Gracedieu* a certain Surplusage which he had in the Great Roll; and granted for him, his Heirs and Executors, that the same should be allowed to the Abbot in his Debts due to the Crown (*n*). *John de Wengrave* granted before the Barons, that out of a Surplusage of his of xxvj *l*. v *s*. there should be allowed C *s*. to *William Cosyn* upon his Account,

(*k*) Concessio A Reginæ Angliæ. Memorandum quod eadem Regina in præsencia Philippi de Eya Thesaurarij, & Ricardi de Hereford Rememoratoris de Scaccario, concessit quod de Superplusagio suo quod habet in Rotulo Liij° in Rotulo Compotorum, in Compoto de expensis Garderobæ suæ, allocentur Edmundo Spygurnel in debitis quæ Regi debet ad Scaccarium CC $_{iiij}^{xx}$ vj l x s iij d ob. *Memor.* 1. *E.* 1. *Rot.* 10. *a.*

(*l*) De Suplusagio Dominæ A Reginæ Matris Domini Regis concesso Edmundo Espigurnel. Memorandum quod eadem Regina mandavit Baronibus de Scaccario, per Fratrem Josep de Kauncy tunc Thesaurarium, quod xv l quas eadem Regina habet de superplusagio in Compoto Hugonis de la Penne de garderoba, allocentur eidem Edmundo in debitis suis ubicunque voluerit. *Mich. Communia* 3 & 4. *E.* 1. *Rot.* 3. *a.*

(*m*) *Hil. Communia* 9. *E.* 2. *Rot.* 93. *a.*

(*n*) Oxon. Memorandum quod Johannes de Oddinggeseles venit coram Baronibus xxx° die Junij, & assignavit .. Abbati de Gratia Dei vj l vj s viij d, quos habet de superplusagio in Magno Rotulo de anno octavo Regis nunc, in Item Oxonia; Et vult & concedit pro se hæredibus & executoribus suis, quod prædicti vj l vj s viij d allocentur præfato Abbati, in debitis quæ Regi debet hic de exitibus terrarum suarum forisfactis, sive aliunde. *Trin. Communia* 9. *E.* 2. *Rot.* 104. *a.* This is enrolled again inter *Trin. Commun.* 9. *E.* 2. *Rot.* 107. *a.*

and xx *l.* to *John Poyntel*, one of the Sheriffs of *London*, upon his Account (*o*).

XXII. If an Accountant did not come to render his Account, or did not pursue the same in due Manner, he was punished several Ways: namely, by Distress and Seisure of his Lands, and by Amercement. If he did not answer to the Crown the Debts or Sums wherewith he was charged, he was committed either to the Marshall, or to the *Fleet-Prison*, or to the Tower of *London*. In the 14th Year of K. *Henry* III, a Summonce *ad reddendum Compotum* was sent to *Walter de Beauchamp*, late Sheriff of *Worcestershire*, in the Terms *sicut te & omnia tua diligis* (*p*). In the 19th Year of the same King, *Simon*, Son of *Marie*, late one of the Sheriffs of *London*, was amerced xx *l.* for not coming to the Exchequer with his Consheriff, to render his Account (*q*). In other subsequent Years, *Walter de Rumesie* was amerced a Mark, for not paying into the Exchequer in due Time certain Money which he had received upon the Writ of Summonce (*r*); the Bailiffs and Citizens of *York* were amerced, for not paying the Ferm of their Town at the Exchequer, upon the Account of *John de Byron*, Sheriff of *Yorkshire* (*s*); a Writ of *Distringas* issued out of the Exchequer

(*o*) London. Johannes de Wengrave executor testamenti Willelmi de Trente defuncti, venit hic coram Baronibus primo die Augusti, & concedit quod de quater xx vj l v s quos idem Johannes habet de Superplusagio in compoto reddito pro prædicto Willelmo de exitibus Cambij Londoniæ & Cantuariæ, allocentur C s Willelmo Cosyn pro Elia Prodome & Isabella uxore ejus de debito Thomæ de Stodham. Et similiter concedit quod xx l de eodem superplusagio allocentur Johanni Poyntel uni Vicecomitum Londoniæ, in arreragijs compoti sui. *Trin. Commun.* 12. *E.* 2. *Rot.* 37. *b.*

(*p*) Wygornia. Rex Waltero de Bello Campo; Præcipimus tibi quod sicut te & omnia tua diligis, sis coram Baronibus de Scaccario nostro apud Westmonasterium in octabis Purificationis B. Mariæ, ad reddendum compotum tuum de tempore quo fuisti Vicecomes noster in Comitatu Wygorniæ anno regni nostri xiij; & ad ostendendum quare non fuisti coram eisdem Baronibus a die S. Martini in xv dies, ad reddendum compotum tuum de prædicto tempore, sicut tibi præceptum fuit per Vicecomitem nostrum ejusdem Comitatus. T.J. vj die Decembris anno xiiij. *Mich. Commun.* 14. *H.* 3. *Rot.* 3. *a.*

(*q*) Simon filius Mariæ [debet] xx l, quia non venit coram Baronibus de Scaccario ad compotum suum reddendum cum Socio suo. *Mag. Rot.* 19. *H.* 3. *Lond. & Midd.* m. 2. *b.*

(*r*) De Amerciatis ad Scaccarium: Walterus de Rumesie [debet] j marcam, quia recepit denarios per Summonitionem Scaccarij quos non solvit ad Scaccarium tempore debito. *Mag. Rot.* 20. *H.* 3. *Wilt.* m. 1. *a.*

(*s*) Quia super compotum Johannis Byrun Vicecomitis Eboraci redditum ad Scaccarium iiij° die Julij anno prædicto, compertum est quod Ballivi & Cives Eboraci non solverunt firmam villæ suæ de anno vicesimo quinto de temino Paschæ, Ideo consideratum est per Barones, quod sint in misericordia. *Trin. Commun.* 26. *E.* 1. *Rot.* 86. *b. in bund.* 25 & 26. *E.* 1.

against

Chap. XXIII. *and* ACCOUNTANTS.

against *Nicholas de Farindon* (*t*) and several others, Aldermen of several Wards in *London*, who had been Collectours within their several Wards of the Tallage assessed by *Roger de Hegham* and others in the City of *London*, to come and render an Account of the said Tallage; a Writ issued to the Justice of *Chester* to distrain the Sheriff of *Carnarvan* to come and account (*u*).

If Debtours did not keep their Terms or Days of Attermination, they were amerced; and sometimes by neglecting to make a second or third Payment, forfeited or lost the Sum which they had actually paid in for their first Payment. *John Wac* did not keep his Terms in Payment of CCC Marks. *Hugh de Nevill* (who was Pledge for him) was thereupon amerced xx Marks (*w*). If a Sheriff did not come to account at the Day prefixed to him, he was amerced at C*s*. for each Day wherein he made Default. *Ralf de Arden*, Sheriff of *Herefordshire*, was amerced Lxv *l*. for the Default of xiij Days (*x*); and *Alan de Valeines*, Sheriff of *Kent*, at the same Sum, for the Default of xiij Days (*y*); *William Fitz-Hervey*, Sheriff of *Norfolk* and *Suffolk*, was amerced at xx *l*. for four Days Default in not coming to the Exchequer, as he had been summoned (*z*). *William de Bocland*, Sheriff of *Cornwall*, was amerced at xxx *l*. for the Default of six Days, in not coming to the Exchequer,

---

(*t*) London. Præceptum est Vicecomitibus quod distringant Nicholaum de Farndon Aldermannum Wardæ de Farndon, Thomam de Kent executorem testamenti Johannis de Cantuatia quondam Aldermanni Wardæ Turris, Robertum de Armenteres & Johannem Tedmar Executores testamenti Johannis Darmenteres quondam Aldermani Wardæ de Langebourn, Richerum de Rofham Aldermannum Wardæ de Bassieshawe, Johannem le Blount Aldermannum Wardæ Flori, Johannem le Coroner Aldermannum Wardæ Vinetriæ, & Radulphum de Humilane Aldermannum Wardæ de Bredstret, per terras &c, Ita &c, Et quod de exitibus &c, & quod habeat corpora eorum &c in octabis Sancti Michaelis, ad reddendum Regi Compotem de tallagio Domini E. nuper Regis Angliæ Patris Regis nunc assesso in Civitate Londoniæ, per Rogerum de Hegham & socios suos Assessores ejusdem Tallagij, per prædictos Aldermannos collecto in Wardis prædictis. T. T. de Cantebrigia decimo quinto die Julij. Per Rotulum Memorandorum de anno primo, Trinit. Dies dati. *Trin. Brevia Retornabilia 2. E. 2. Rot. 124. a.*

(*u*) *Mich. Commun. 25 & 26. E. 1. Rot. 25. a.*

(*w*) Idem Hugo [de Nevill] debet xx marcas, quia Johannes Wac non servavit terminos suos de CCC marcis, cujus plegius fuit. *Mag. Rot. 12. J. Rot. 8. a.*

(*x*) Idem Vicecomes [Radulfus de Arden] r c de Lxv l de Misericordia; pro defalta xiij dierum quibus non venit ad Scaccarium, sicut summonitus fuit; In thesauro xx l, Et debet xlv l. *Mag. Rot. 1. R. 1. Rot. 8. b. Herefordscira in Walia.*

(*y*) Alan de Valeines, *Sheriff of* Kent, *was amerced in the same Summ; the Entry is in the same Words as above. Ib. Rot. 14. a.*

(*z*) Idem Vicecomes r c de xx l de misericordia iiij dierum quibus non venit ad Scaccarium sicut summonitus fuit: In perdonis, per breve Regis, ipsi Vicecomiti xx l; Et Q. e. *Mag. Rot. 1. R. 1. Rot. 3. b. Nordf. & Sudf. Willelmus filius Hervei Vic.*

as he was summoned (*a*). *William Fitz-Aldelm*, Sheriff of *Cumberland*, was amerced at Lx *l.* for the Default of twelve Days after Summonce (*b*). The Sheriff of *Hereford* was amerced at Lxv *l.* for the Default of thirteen Days after Summonce (*c*). *Roger de Glanvill*, Sheriff of *Northumberland*, was amerced Lx *l.* for the Default of xij Days (*d*). In the Reign of K. *Henry* III. the Course was, that if a Sheriff did not come to account at the Day prefixed to him, he was to be amerced the first Day C *s.* the second Day C *s.* the third Day C *s.* and the fourth Day at the King's Will. *Geoffrey Cross*, Sheriff of *Surrey* and *Sussex*, was amerced in that Manner (*e*); and so was *Gilbert de Cheyles*, Sheriff of *Lincoln* (*f*). *Nicolas de Hanred*, Sheriff of *Berk* and *Oxon*, was amerced at C*s.* for several Days together, until the 40th Day (*g*); and *William le Latimer*, *William de Bozal*, and *John de Oketon*, late Sheriffs of *Yorkshire* (*h*). *William de Mulcastre*, Sheriff of *Cumberland* (*i*), and the Sheriffs of *Westmerland* (*k*), and *Lancaster* (*l*), were acquitted of these Amercements, by reason of the

(*a*) Idem Vicecomes [debet] xxx l de Misericordia, pro defalta vj dierum quibus non venit ad Scaccarium, sicut summonitus fuit. *Ib. Rot.* 7. *a. Cornualia. Willelmus de Bochlanda Vic.*

(*b*) Idem Vicecomes [debet] Lx l de Misericordia, [pro] defalta xij dierum quibus non venit ad Scaccarium, sicut summonitus fuit. *Ib. Rot.* 8. *a. Cumb. Willelmus filius Aldelini Vicecomes.*

(*c*) Idem Vicecomes r c de Lxv l de Misericordia, pro defalta xiij dierum quibus non venit ad Scaccarium, sicut summonitus fuit: In thesauro xx l, Et debet xlv l. *Ib. Rot.* 8. *b. Heref. in Walia.*

(*d*) Idem Vicecomes [Rogerus de Glanvilla] r c de Lx l de Misericordia, pro defalta xij dierum quibus non venit ad Scaccarium, sicut summonitus fuit; In thesauro l, Et Q. e. *Ib. Rot.* 14. *b. Northumberland.*

(*e*) Galfridus de Cruce Vicecomes Surr. & Sufexiæ habuit diem in crastino S. Luciæ, ad respondendum Regi de debitis quæ Regi debet; & quia non venit ad dictum diem nec aliquis pro eo, sicut ei fuit præceptum, consideratum est, quod sit in misericordia primo die de C s, secundo die de C s, tercio die de C s, & quarto die ad voluntatem Regis. *Memor.* 40. *H.* 3. *Rot.* 7. *b.*

(*f*) Quia Gilbertus de Cheyles Vicecomes Lincolniæ non venit ad computandum in quindena S. Hylarij, sicut ei fuit statutum per breve Domini Regis: Consideratum est, quod primo die sit in misericordia C s, Et secundo die in misericordia C s, Et tercio die in misericordia C s, & quolibet die deinceps usq; ad xxj diem Febr., quo die primo venit ad computandum ad Scaccarium, in misericordia ad voluntatem Domini Regis. *Ib. Rot.* 11. *a.*

(*g*) Nicholaus de Hanred Vicecomes Berk. & Oxon. amerciatus est singulis diebus ad C s, usq; ad xl diem, quia non venit. *Memor.* 42. *H.* 3. *Rot.* 14. *b.*

(*h*) Ebor. Willelmus le Latimer, Willelmus de Bozal, & Johannes de Oketon habuerunt diem in crastino Animarum, ad reddendum compotum suum de tempore quo fuerunt Vicecomites Eboracisciræ, & ipsi non venerunt; Ideo amerciandi prima die, secunda, & tercia, & quarta die ad voluntatem Regis, secundum consuetudinem Scaccarij. *Memor.* 51. *H.* 3. *Rot.* 2. *b.*

(*i*) *Mich. Communia* 26 & 27. *E.* 1. *Rot.* 5. *b.*

(*k*) *Ib. Rot.* 5. *b.*

(*l*) Lanc. Radulphus de Mountjoye Vicecomes habuit diem hic ad computandum die Veneris proximo ante festum S. Augustini; Ad eundem diem non venit, nec

secundo,

the War with *Scotland*; which made it necessary for them to be present in their respective Counties. *Thomas de Ralegh*, Sheriff of *Devonshire*, was amerced for not coming to account; *viz.* for the Default of the first three Days xv *l.* and of the fourth Day at the King's Pleasure. And his Lands and Chatells were ordered to be seized (*m*). *Thomas de la Hyde*, Sheriff of *Cornwall*, was amerced for not accounting; and his Lands and Chatells were seized (*n*). *Nicolas de Clere*, Treasurer of *Ireland*, was amerced C *s.* for not accounting (*o*).

K. *John* seized the Barony and Regality of the Archbishop of *York*, for certain Debts due to the Crown, and for other reasonable Causes. And this the King did by the Judgment of his Court (*p*). The Bailiffs of *London* were commanded to have the Bodies of *John Adrien* and *Luke de Batencurt*, late Sheriffs, before the Barons such a Day; and to take the Chatells of *Luke* into the King's Hands, for certain Debts due to the King, and for not passing his Account (*q*). *Robert Malet,*

secundo, nec tercio sequentibus: Ideo amerciatur ad xv l, videlicet pro defalta cujuslibet diei C s secundum consuetudinem Scaccarij. *Pas. Commun. ib. Rot.* 24. *a.*

(*m*) *Trin. Commun.* 35. *E.* 1. *Rot.* 58. *b.*

(*n*) Thomas de la Hyde Vicecomes Cornubiæ habuit diem hic modo ad quindenam Nativitatis S. Johannis Baptistæ; & non venit primo die, secundo, nec tercio, quarto, nec deinceps. Ideo pro defalta cujuslibet illorum trium primorum dierum amerciatur ad C s; Unde summa est xv l; & pro defalta quarti diei & aliorum sequentium amerciandus est ad Voluntatem Regis. Et terræ & tenementa bona & catalla sua capiantur in manum Regis; & attachietur per corpus suum, Ita &c in crastino S. Michaelis ad reddendum compotum &c. *And a Writ issued to the Coroners accordingly. Afterwards it was testified in the Exchequer, that the said Sheriff could not appear by reason of his Sickness; In consideration whereof, and of his good Service rendered to the King in his said Office,* Concordatum est quod prædictæ defaltæ relaxentur eidem Thomæ; *And the Coroners were commanded to stay the Execution of the said Writs. Trin. Commun.* 5. *E.* 2. *Rot.* 60. *b. The Sheriff of* Surrey *and* Sussex, *for not coming to account, was amerced for the three first Days* C *s each Day, and for the fourth Day* amerciandus ad voluntatem Regis. *Hil. Communia* 12. *E.* 2. *Rot.*—*a.*

(*o*) Quia Nicholaus de Clere Thesaurarius Hiberniæ, qui incepit computare, non venit ad computandum die Lunæ proximo ante festum S. Nicholai, set se subtraxit a Compoto prædicto, Ideo amerciatur ad C s. *Mich. Commun.* 20. *E.* 1. *Rot.* 4. *a.*

(*p*) Rex S. Decano & Capitulo Ebor. Sciatis quod pro debitis quæ Eboracensis Archiepiscopus nobis debet, & pro defaltis & alijs causis rationabilibus, cepimus in manum nostram Baroniam & Regalia quæ Archiepiscopus Eboracensis de nobis tenet. Et hoc fecimus per judicium Curiæ nostræ. Nos autem contra eundem Archiepiscopum ad Dominum Papam appellavimus pro nobis & nostris & pro statu Regni nostri. T. G. filio Petri Comite Essexiæ apud Cunesburgum v. die Marcij. *Chart.* 2. *J. m.* 11. *dors.*

(*q*) Præceptum est Willelmo de Dunolmo & Waltero Hervy ballivis Civitatis Londoniæ, quod habeant coram Baronibus de Scaccario, die Mercurij proximo post clausum Paschæ, corpora Johannis Adrien & Lucæ de Batencurt, & quod omnia bona & catalla quæ idem Lucas habet in balliva eorum

Malet, late Sheriff of the Counties of *Bedford* and *Buckingham*, was behind in his Account. *James de Eggemere*, Usher of the Exchequer, was sent to *Robert*'s House to fetch him up to the Exchequer. *James* came back and said he could not find him. *Robert* was amerced for the Default of the four Days according to the Custom of the Exchequer. And afterwards the Sheriff was commanded to attach him by his Body, and to seize all his Lands and Chatells into the King's Hands (r), by a Writ of *Nomine districtionis* (s). *Richard Huceman* was committed Prisoner to the *Flete*, for Arerages due upon his Account. And all his Lands and Tenements, and Goods and Chatells were ordered to be seized into the King's Hands (t). *John atte Berwe* was committed to Prison, for not paying in the King's Money which he had received. And all his Lands and Chatells were ordered to be seized into the King's Hands (u). In like manner Amercements were set upon *Roger de Cheigny*, Sheriff of *Shropshire* and *Staffordshire*; whose Lands and Chatells were also ordered to be seized for the King, and his Body to be attached (w): And upon *John de Pabenham*, Sheriff of *Bedford* and *Buckingham*; whose Lands and Chatells were also ordered to be seized for the King, and his Body to be attached (x). *Robert de Horton*, Sheriff of *Devonshire*, was amerced the first, second, and third Day, &c. for not accounting. And the Coroners were commanded to attach his Body, and to seize his Lands and Chatells (y).

 Philipp de Staunton, late Sheriff of the Counties of *Cambridge* and *Huntendon*, was imprisoned in the Tower of *London*, for Arerages of Debts due to the Crown (z). *William de Hay*, Sheriff of *Oxfordshire*,

eorum capiant in manum Regis, pro diversis debitis in quibus dictus Lucas Regi tenetur, & pro compoto suo quod adhuc restat reddendum, de tempore quo fuit unus Vicecomitum Londoniæ & Midd. *Memor.* 52. *H.* 3. *Rot.* 8. *b.*

 (r) *Mich. Brevia pro Rege* 13 & 14. *E.* 1. *Rot.* 24. *b.*

 (s) *Mich. Communia* 14. *E.* 1. *Rot.* 4. *b.*

 (t) Notinham. Facto Visu Ricardi Huceman de Alto Pecco, debet ——. Postea, liberatur prisonæ de Flete. Et mandatum est Vicecomiti Notinghamiæ & Derbiæ, quod omnes terras & tenementa, & omnia bona & catalla sua capiat in manum Regis. *Mich. Memor.* 25. *E.* 1. *Rot.* ——.

(u) *Ib.*
(w) *Mich. Communia* 9. *E.* 2. *Rot.* 90. *b.*
(x) *Hil. Communia* 9. *E.* 2. *Rot.* 94. *a.*
(y) Devon. —— Et præceptum est Coronatoribus Comitatus prædicti quod attachient eum per corpus suum ubicunq; &c; Et omnes terras & tenementa &c. But he having been busied in the King's Affairs in Devonshire, *the said Default was released to him. Hil. Commun.* 9. *E.* 2. *Rot.* 94. *a.*

(z) Rex Baronibus; Mandamus vobis quod Philippum de Staunton quondam Vicecomitem Cant. & Hunt., detentum in prisona apud Turrim Londoniæ, pro arreragijs debitorum in quibus nobis tenetur, ab eadem prisona deliberari faciatis: ita tamen quod

was committed to the Marshall for the Arrerages of his Account (*a*). *Adam de Weston*, an Accountant (to wit, as Custos or Committee of the Lands late of *David*, Son of *Griffin*, a Felon) was committed by the Court of Exchequer to the Tower of *London* (*b*). Sir *Ralph de Wellewick*, an Accountant, was committed Prisoner to the Tower of *London* for Non-payment (*c*). *William de Rougate*, late Chamberlain of *Westwales*, was committed to Prison in the Tower of *London*, for the Arrerages of his Account of the said Chamberlainship (*d*). The Bailiffs of *Ipswich* were commanded by Writ to arrest certain Merchants of the Company of *Friscobalds*. They arrested *Andrew de Pistorio*, and brought him to the Exchequer before the Chancellour of *England*, and the Treasurer's Lieutenant and Barons. And thereupon he was by them committed Prisoner to *John de Crombwell*, Constable of the Tower of *London* (*e*). *Philipp*, late Mayor of *Grimesby*, was delivered to the Marshall for certain Areres of the Ferm of that Town; which he was to have paid *ut priso* on the Morrow of St. *Hilary*. Because he did not keep to his Day, he was sent Prisoner to the *Flete* (*f*). *John de Hoo*, Sheriff of *Essex*, was ordered to be attached, for not coming at his Day of Prefixion to account (*g*).

quod post festum S. Hyllarij veniat coram vobis, & inveniat ibidem sufficientem securitatem, quod secundum rationabilem extentam terrarum suarum faciendam, respondebit nobis de dictis debitis ad terminos eidem a vobis statuendos. *Ex Mem.* 35. *H.* 3. *Rot.* 5. *a.*

(*a*) Willelmus de Hay Vicecomes Oxoniæ liberatus est Marescallo, pro Lx l quas Regi debet de arreragijs conpoti sui. *Hil. Commun.* 29. *H.* 3. *Rot.* 6. *a.*

(*b*) *Hil. Commun.* 24. *E.* 1. *Rot.* 19. *b. in bund.* 23 & 24. *E.* 1.

(*c*) —— venit & nichil solvit. Et ideo ipse committitur Constabulario Turris Londoniæ, custodiendus quousq; &c. *Pas. Commun.* 34. *E.* 1. *Rot.* 31. *a. Linc.*

(*d*) Wallia. Memorandum quod cum Willelmus de Rougate Clericus, qui fuit Camerarius Westwalliæ tempore quo Dominus Rex nunc fuerat Princeps Walliæ, esset in prisona Regis in Turri Londoniæ pro arreragijs compoti sui de Cameraria prædicta: & idem Willelmus instetisset quod posset ad tempus deliberari ab eadem prisona ad tractatum habendum cum amicis suis in partibus suis, ut subveniatur ei per eosdem amicos suos ad satisfaciendum de arreragijs antedictis. *So* William *found Manucaptors for his Appearance at the Exchequer at a Day to be prefixed &c; and was delivered out of Prison* usq; crastinum clausi Paschæ. *Mich. Commun.* 1. *E.* 2. *Rot.* 27. *b.*

(*e*) *Mich. Communia* 5. *E.* 2. *Rot.* 20. *b.*

(*f*) Lincolnia. De Prisone misso usq; Flete. Misericordia. Memorandum quod Philippus quondam Major de Grimesby qui liberatus fuit Marescallo pro xvij l viij s, quos Homines ejusdem villæ Regi debuerunt de Firma sua, & quos solvisse debuit ut Priso in crastino S. Hilarij, sicut continetur in Memorandis in Termino S. Michaelis, missus est ad prisonam de Flete, quia diem suum prædictum non servavit. Postea fecit finem ut deliberetur a Prisona prædicta, per xl s. *Memor.* 1. *E.* 1. *Rot.* 7. *a.*

(*g*) De attachiando Johannem de Hoo Vicecomitem, quia non venit ad computandum ad diem præfixum. *Mich. Commun.* 8. *E.* 2. *Rot.* 1. *b. Essex.*

Nicholas

Nicolas de Tykehull, late Keeper of the King's Victuals in the Castle of *Dovor,* was committed Prisoner to the *Flete,* there to remain till he found sufficient Sureties for his accounting to the King (*h*). *Henry,* Parson of *Greneford,* was committed to the Marshall for Moneys received by him for the Ferme of *London* and *Middlesex,* whilst *Adam de Bentley* was Sheriff and the said *Henry* was *Adam*'s Clerk or Receiver (*i*). The Mayor and Sheriffs of *London* were committed to the Custody of the Marshall, for the Areres of an Aid towards the King's Voyage into *Gascoigne* (*k*). The Sheriffs of *London* were committed to the Custody of the Marshall for Queens-gold due from the Citizens (*l*): And again in the 39th Year (*m*): They had Day as Prisoners to appear before the Barons, and found Sureties for their Appearance (*n*). *John de la Lee,* late Sheriff of *Essex* and *Hertfordshire,* being indebted

(*h*) Memorandum quod, præsente hic in Curia Nicholao de Tykehull nuper Custode Victualium Regis in Castro Dovorriæ, modo xxij die Julij hoc Termino, idem Nicholaus eodem die commissus fuit prisonæ de Flete, custodiendus quousq; invenerit sufficientem manucaptionem de compoto Regi reddendo de victualibus prædictis. *Trin. Commun.* 15. *E.* 2. *Rot.* 27. *b.*

(*i*) Londonia. Henricus Persona de Greneford liberatus est Marescallo pro denarijs quos recepit de firma Com. Londoniæ & Middelsexiæ, tempore quo Adam de Benetlega fuit Vicecomes & idem Henricus clericus & receptor ipsius, sicut idem H. recognovit coram Baronibus quod receptor ejus fuit. *Trin. Communia* 31. *H.* 3. *Rot.* 7. *a.*

(*k*) Johannes de Tolesan Major Londoniæ, Et Ricardus Picard & Johannes de Norhamton Vicecomites Londoniæ, liberantur Marescallo pro CCC marcis, quas Regi debent de Auxilio ad Passagium Domini Regis in Wasconiam. *Memor.* 37. *incipien.* 38. *H.* 3. *Rot.* 4. *b.*

(*l*) Johannes de Norhampton & Ricardus Pikard Vicecomites Londoniæ liberantur Marescallo pro Auro Reginæ. Et quia Major & Cives non permiserunt prædictos Vicecomites distringere pro Auro Reginæ sicut eis fuit præceptum, capta fuit Libertas Civitatis in manu Domini Regis. *Memor.* 38. *H.* 3. *Rot.* 17. *b.*

(*m*) Præceptum fuit Vicecomitibus Londoniæ, quod distringerent Cives Londoniæ pro Auro Reginæ, ita quod haberent denarios coram Baronibus die Lunæ proximo ante festum S. Barnabæ Apostoli. Quo die dicti Vicecomites venerunt coram dictis Baronibus ; & cum requisitum esset ab eis si dictos denarios haberent, Dixerunt quod non ; sed quod Vadia dictorum Civium ceperunt & penes se habuerunt, set non invenerunt qui ipsa emerent. Postea injunctum fuit eis, quod dicta Vadia afferrent coram Baronibus die Martis sequenti. Quo die venerunt, & dixerunt quod fere Mille homines de Civitate restiterunt eis, & non permiserunt dicta Vadia asportare ; Et cum quæreretur ab eisdem Vicecomitibus, Qui essent illi Impeditores, Dixerunt quod plures Draperij, Aurifabri, Speciarij, Cordewanarij, & alij Ministeriales de Civitate ; set nullum nomen exprimere voluerunt: Et ideo liberati fuerunt dicti Vicecomites Marescallo. Postea habent dies ut Prisones usq; ad diem Martis proximum ante festum S. Johannis Baptistæ. *Memor.* 39. *H.* 3. *Rot.* 14. *a.*

(*n*) Vicecomites Londoniæ detenti in prisona pro Auro Reginæ habent diem ut Prisones, usq; ad diem Jovis proximum post festum S. Barnabæ ; Et Michaël Tony, Robertus Hardell, Thomas Adrian, & Simon de Cobham, pro Communitate totius Civitatis manuceperunt &c habere eos coram dictis Baronibus ad dictum diem. *Ib. Rot.* 14. *b.*

Chap. XXIII.   *and* ACCOUNTANTS.

to the Crown upon his Account in a hundred fourscore and seven Pounds and odd, was committed to the Custody of the Marshall; and the next Day to the Fleet Prison. And all his Lands were ordered to be extended, &c (*o*). The late Sheriff of *Surrey* and *Sussex* was committed to the Marshall for several Sums of Money, wherewith he stood charged upon his Account (*p*). The Keeper of the King's Mints of *London* and *Canterbury* was committed to the Marshall, for Money due to the King upon his Account (*q*). When an Accountant was committed to the Marshall, he often used to make Oath to the Marshall not to go out of Town till he had finished his Account, or till he had paid his Areres. Such an Oath was made by *Walter de Verdun* (*r*), *Stephen Sibri* (*s*), *Adam de Montalt* (*t*), *John*

(*o*) —— Ideo ipse Johannes die Martis prædicto committitur Marescallo. Postea die Mercurij in crastino committitur prisonæ de Flete &c. Postea die Veneris proxima post festum S. Barnabæ, videlicet xij die Junij, prædictus Johannes solvit xx l per unam Talliam ——. *It was ordered, That all his Lands be extended; and that he pay yearly the Moiety of the Extent, till all his* debet *be paid off. Certain Persons became Manucaptours, to have him forth-coming* ad faciendum & recipiendum &c. *By that Manucaption he was for the present delivered out of Prison. However the Sheriff of the County was commanded to extend and apprize his Lands and Tenements. Afterwards an Attermination was granted to him, for him and his Heirs, at xl s a-year, by Writ of the Great Seal.* Trin. Recorda 2. E. 2. Rot. 88. b.

(*p*) Robert de Glammorgan, *late Sheriff of Surrey and Sussex, was charged with several Sums of Money upon his Account.* Postea xx die Octobris anno sexto, præfatus Robertus liberatur Marescallo; Et dictum est ei per Barones, quod habeat hic coram Baronibus de die in diem corpus præfati Roberti, ad satisfaciendum Regi de debitis prædictis. Postea xxj die octoctris deliberatur a custodia Marescalli, & affidavit iterato Marescallo pro debitis prædictis. Trin. Commun. 5. E. 2. Rot. 66. a.

(*q*) Londonia. Audito compoto Johann's de Lincolnia Custodis Cambiorum Regis Londoniæ & Cantuariæ; Debet *so much.* *Several Sums of which Total were respited;* Et debet Cxix l vij s vij d; Pro quibus liberatur Marescallo xx die Februarij. Postea die crastino dictus Johannes deliberatur a custodia.. Marescalli, per manucaptionem Willelmi Servat & Willelmi de Hedersete. Hil. Status & Visus 9. E. 2. Rot. 139. b.

(*r*) Walterus de Verdun affidavit, quod fideliter computavit, & quod non recedet nisi facta pace de arreragijs. Memor. 2 & 3. H. 3. Rot. 3. b.

(*s*) Linc. Stephanus Sibri affidavit Marescallo, quod non recederet a Civitate per unam leucam, donec satisfecerit Regi de Cxl marcis in quibus Regi tenetur de diversis debitis sicut recognovit coram Baronibus de Scaccario. Memor. 52. H. 3. Rot. 1. b.

The like Affidavit, quod non recederet a Civitate Londonia per unam leucam, donec habuerit allocationes suas & brevia. Ib. juxt. Norhamton.

(*t*) Herefordia. Adam de Monte alto affidavit Marescallo, quod non recedet a Civitate quousq; reddiderit compotum suum de tempore quo fuit Vicecomes Lancastriæ. Postea habet diem ad reddendum prædictum compotum a die Paschæ in tres septimanas, & non venit primo die, nec secundo, nec tertio; Ideo amerciatur ad xv l pro defectu trium dierum &c. Mich. Communia 52, incip. 53. H. 3. Rot. 5. b.

de Caunvill (*u*), *Peter de Nevill* (*w*), and *Henry de Notingham* (*x*). But sometimes the Accountant, after making Oath to the Marshall, as above is said, had Leave given him by the Barons to go into his County upon Parole, *ut Priso* as a Prisoner (*y*). As in the Case of *Warner de Hamstaple*, of *Thomas Fitz-Hugh* (*z*), the Citizens of *Hereford* (*a*), and the Sheriff of *Yorkshire*'s Deputy or Clerk (*b*). If a Debtor, so committed to the Marshall, withdrew from his Custody without Leave, he was to be arrested, and brought forth at a prefixed Day, to answer for that Trespass (*c*).

If

(*u*) Johannes de Caunvill affidavit Marescallo, quod non recedat a Civitate quousq; reddiderit compotum suum de tempore quo fuit Vicecomes Essexiæ & Hertfordiæ. *Memor.* 55. *H.* 3. *Rot.* 2. *a.*

(*w*) ... pro Rege. Quia Petrus de Nevill qui tenetur Regi in diversis debitis, & pro eisdem affidavit Marescallo coram Baronibus de Scaccario, & clauso Scaccario, secundum consuetudinem ejusdem, liberatus fuit in prisona Regis, & postea per bonam manucapcionem liberatus ab eadem venit die Sabbati proximo ante festum S. Jacobi Apostoli proximo præteritum coram eisdem Baronibus, satisfacturus Regi de eisdem debitis, & tunc tanquam Priso admisit diem usq; ad diem Lunæ proximo sequentem dictum diem Sabbati ad idem faciendum. Ad quem diem Lunæ non venit, set sine licentia prædictorum Baronum sine die recessit, in contemptum Regis & Curiæ suæ. Et Rex præcepit sicut alias præcepit, quod assumpto secum sufficiente posse Comitatus sui, & si necesse fuerit requisito auxilio Vicecomitum Norhamtoniæ Warrewici & Leycestriæ, quibus Rex scribit, capiat corpus prædicti Petri & salvo custodiat, ita quod eum habeat coram præfatis Baronibus apud Westmonasterium in crastino Animarum, ad satisfaciendum Regi de prædictis debitis, & ad respondendum Regi de contemptu prædicto. Rex præcipit etiam eidem Vicecomiti quod —scire faciat. Postea remittitur amerciamentum xl; quia non potuit exequi præceptum Regis, eo quod idem Petrus non habuit certum domicilium in balliva sua. *Ex Memor.* 1 & 2. *E.* 1. *Rot.* 3. *a.*

(*x*) Leyc. Henricus de Notingham affidavit Marescallo pro vj l xvj s viij d, quos Regi debet de Remanenti Vicesimæ de tempore quo fuit unus Assessorum & Collectorum ejusdem Vicesimæ in Comitatu prædicto. Postea solvit idem Henricus pro se & Ada de Wletheslesberwe xiij l & j marcam de vicesima prædicta. Et sic absolutus est a Fide. *Memor.* 1 & 2. *E.* 1. *Rot.* 4. *a.*

(*y*) War. Leyc. Concessum est Warnero de Hamstaple Senescallo Davidis de Lymesye, quod recedat ut Priso pro debitis ejusdem Davidis usq; ad festum S. Michaelis; ita quod tunc habeat dicta debita vel redeat Priso. *Memor.* 22. *H.* 3. *Rot.* 11. *b.*

(*z*) Et concessum est per Barones Thomæ filio Hugonis qui affidavit pro debitis dicti Burgi [viz. de Wic], quod eat ad Patriam suam ut Priso, & in crastino S. Michaelis veniat Priso. *Ib. Rot.* 11. *b.*

(*a*) Heref. Cives Herfordiæ recesserunt de Scaccario die Jovis proximo post Purificationem ut prisones de die in diem. Revertantur ad mediam Quadragesimam ut prisones, donec solverint albam firmam, qua soluta recedent ut prisones de die in diem usq; ad clausam Paschæ, ut tunc reveniant ut prisones donec solverint finem suum, quo soluto habebunt respectum de tallagio donec Dominus Rex aliud inde præceperit. T. ut supra [i. e. T. J. septimo die Februarij anno regni nostri xiiij°.] *Ex Memor.* 14. *H.* 3. *Rot.* 10. *a.*

(*b*) Clericus Vicecomitis Eboraci affidavit Marescallo pro DCCC xl marcis. Postea habet diem ut Priso usq; ad diem qua cantatur *Lætare Jerusalem. Memor.* 35. *H.* 3. *Rot.* 9. *a.*

(*c*) Londonia. Johannes Silbeling liberatus fuit Marescallo pro Lx s quos Regi debuit; & quia recessit a custodia Marescalli

If Accountants departed from the Exchequer, before their Accounts were speeded, or without Leave of the Barons, they were (if Commoners) to be attached by their Bodies. As in the Case of *William de Lucy* (d), *Warner Engayne* (e), *Adam de Weston* (f), and others. Sometimes Accountants found Sureties, not to depart from *London* without Leave of the Treasurer and Barons. *John*, Priour of *Newburg*, *Roger de la Leye*, Master *R. de Gosebec*, Marshal of the Exchequer, and *Richard de Hereford*, became Sureties before the Barons, that *Gilbert de Geyles*, Sheriff of *Lincolnshire*, should not depart from *London* without Leave of the Treasurer and Barons (g). *Thomas Corbet* being under Arrest for the Areres of his Account, the King by Writ commands the Barons to set him at Liberty, upon his giving Security to pay the said Areres at *Michaelmass* (h). And *Guy Fitz-Robert* having

scalli sine licentia, Mandatum fuit Vicecomitibus Londoniæ, quod ad certum diem eis præfixum haberent corpus ipsius Johannis coram Baronibus, ad respondendum de prædicta transgressione. Et prædicti Vicecomites posuerunt ipsum per Plegium unius qui ipsum Johannem ad diem ei præfixum non habuerunt: Ideo mandatum fuit Vicecomitibus prædictis, quod venirent coram Baronibus, audituri Judicium suum eo quod mandatum Domini Regis per Barones eis factum non fuerunt exsecuti. Qui venerunt & dixerunt quod nullam fecerunt transgressionem, quia liberaverunt prædictum Johannem per plegium, sicut in hujusmodi casibus semper facere consueverunt & debent secundum usum & consuetudinem Civitatis. Dicunt etiam quod eorum consuetudo est ponere per plegium omnes tales quos alij Vicecomites Forinseci committunt in baillium pro quibuscumq; transgressionibus. Et si aliqua fuit transgressio quod prædictus Johannes non venit, Plegius ipsius illam facit transgressionem & non Vicecomites. *Ex Memor.* 38. *H.* 3. *Rot.* 5. *b.*

(d) War. & Leic. Mandatum est Vicecomiti, quod habeat coram Baronibus &c, in octabis S. Martini, corpus Willelmi de Lucy, ad reddendum Regi debita quæ ei debet, & ad audiendum Judicium suum de hoc quod recessit ab eodem Scaccario sine licentia Baronum &c, desicut idem W. fuit priso Regis ad idem Scaccarium —. *Ex Memor.* 25. *H.* 3. *Rot.* 2. *a.*

(e) Wychardo de Sabaudia. Rex eidem; Quia Warnerus Engayne, qui remansit Priso ad Scaccarium pro Dxvij l xvj s ij d, quos nobis debet pro arreragijs Compoti sui, de tempore quo idem W. habuit custodiam Maneriorum nostrorum, recessit de eodem Scaccario sine licentia Baronum Scaccarij, in Contemptum nostrum: Tibi præcipimus, quod habeas coram Baronibus de Scaccario nostro, a die S. Johannis Baptistæ in xv dies, corpus prædicti Warneri, ad respondendum nobis de prædicto debito, & de contemptu suo nobis & Baronibus facto. Et habeat tunc breve. T. ut supra [i. e. T. A. Thesaurario S. Pauli Londoniæ decimo quarto die Junij]. *Trin. Commun.* 29. *H.* 3. *Rot.* 9. *b.*

(f) Norhamtonia. De Ada de Weston judicato prisonæ Turris Londoniæ. *Hil. Communia* 23 & 24. *E.* 1. *Rot.* 19. *b.*

(g) Johannes Prior de Novo Burgo, R. de la Leye, Magister R. de Gosebee Marescallus Scaccarij, & Ricardus de Hereford, manuceperunt coram Baronibus, quod Gilbertus de Geyles Vicecomes Lincolniæ non recedet a Civitate Londoniæ, sine licentia Thesaurarij & Baronum de Scaccario. *Memor.* 39. *H.* 3. *Rot.* 9. *b.*

(h) Rex Baronibus; Mandamus quod accepta securitate a Thoma Corbet, qui pro arreragijs compoti sui coram vobis est arrestatus, de eidem arreragijs nobis in festo S. Michaelis reddendis, facta securitate prædicta ipsum Thomam libere abire permittatis quo voluerit. *Ex Mem.* 35. *H.* 3. *Rot.* 15. *b.*

found

found Security for paying at the King's Wardrobe certain Arerages of his Account, as Sheriff of the Counties of *Oxford* and *Berk*; the King by Writ commands the Barons to releafe him from the Prifon wherein he was held for the faid Arrerages (*i*). *William de Bicok*, Clerk of *Simon de Bradenham*, late Sheriff of the Counties of *Bedford* and *Bukingham*, was committed to Prifon for giving *fictas & falfas refponfiones*, when he was oppofed concerning divers Debts which went out in Summonce againft *Roger Leftrange* (*k*). The King by his Writ commanded the Barons, that as to the Imprifoning of fuch Sheriffs as were in Arere, or did not duly account, or the committing of them to the Marfhall, they fhould do as the Barons were formerly wont to do in like Cafes (*l*).

Lords and others, who claimed to have Franchifes within their Seigneurie or Liberty, were to come yearly to the King's Exchequer, when the Sheriff of their County was paffing his Account; and then they were to render an Account there of the Iffues of their Franchife: and upon fuch Account rendered, they were allowed to their own Ufe fo much of the Iffues of their Franchife, as they were rightfully intituled unto by Charters from the Crown. But if the faid Lords and others failed to appear by their Bailiff or Attorney upon the Sheriff's Account, or did not make due Execution and Retorn of the King's Summonces fent forth to them, or made Default in paying their Ferms or other Debts payable at the Exchequer; in thefe Cafes it was ufual for the King to feize their Franchife into his own Hands. The Town of *Walingford* was feized into the King's Hand, becaufe they did not appear at the Exchequer upon the Sheriff's View of his Account (*m*); and the Liberty of St. *Edmund* for the fame Caufe (*n*).

The

(*i*) Rex Baronibus; Quia Gwydo filius Roberti invenit nobis fufficientem fecuritatem de Lxvij l xv s iiij d ob., de arreragijs compoti fui de tempore quo habuit cuftodiam Comitatuum noftrorum Oxoniæ [&] Berk., nobis in Garderoba folvendis —, ipfum Gwydonem a prifona qua detinetur pro arreragijs prædictis, deliberari faciatis. *Ex Memor.* 35. *H.* 3. *Rot.* 7. *a.*

(*k*) Buk. De Clerico Vicecomitis adjudicato prifonæ. *Hil. Recorda* 25 & 26. *E.* 1. *Rot.* 48. *b.*

(*l*) Rex mandat Baronibus firmiter injungens, quod de Vicecomitibus qui in arreragijs aliquibus fuerint ad Scaccarium Regis vel ibidem non refponderint ut deberent, quo ad retentionem corporum eorundem ac liberationem eorundem Marefcallo Scaccarij prædicti, faciant prout hactenus fieri confuevit; Et hoc nullatenus omittant. T. Rege apud Ebor. iiij° die Junij Anno quinto. Per ipfum Regem. *Trin. Brevia* 5. *E.* 2. *Rot.* 53. *a.*

(*m*) Berkfire. Mandatum eft Vicecomiti, quod reddat Hominibus de Walingford Villam fuam quæ capta fuit in manum Domini Regis, quia non fuerunt fuper Vifum Vicecomitis. *Memor.* 11. *H.* 3. *Rot.* 3. *a.*

(*n*) Præceptum eft per Jufticiarium, quod Libertas S. Edmundi capiatur in manum Domini Regis; Quia Bailivus S. Edmundi non venit fuper Vifum Vicecomitis; Ita quod

Chap. XXIII. *and* ACCOUNTANTS.

The Town of *Huntendon* was taken into the King's Hand, for that the Townsmen did not come to the Exchequer upon the Sheriff's Account, nor paid their Ferm (*o*). The Abbot of *Fischamp*'s Liberty in *Gloucestershire* was seized into the King's Hand, for not appearing upon the Sheriff's Account (*p*). The Liberty of the City of *York* (*q*), and likewise the Liberties and Towns hereafter-mentioned, were seized for the same or like Cause; namely, the several Liberties of the Canons of St. *Peter* of *York*, and of the Citizens of that Town, were ordered to be seized into the King's Hands, for not answering the King's Debts which came out in Summonce (*r*), the Town of *Winchester* for not accounting (*s*), the Liberty of St. *Edmund* for the like Cause (*t*), the Town of *Bedford* (*u*), the City of *Norwich* (*w*), the City of *Canterbury* (*x*), the Liberty of the City of Oxford,

quod non obstante Libertate prædicta, vel Libertatibus de Norwyz, Dunewiz, Gipewiz, & Gernemue, respondeat de debitis in prædictis Libertatibus contentis super arreragia sua. *Ib. Rot.* 7. *a. Norfuk. Suffok. Visus.*

(*o*) Præceptum est Vicecomiti, quod capiat Villam de Huntedon in manum Regis, & salvo custodiat donec &c ; quia homines ejusdem Villæ non venerunt super compotum Vicecomitis nec solverunt firmam suam. *Memor.* 29. *H.* 3. *Rot.* 13. *b.*

(*p*) *Ex Memor.* 35. *H.* 3. *Rot.* 19. *a. Glouc.*

(*q*) Præceptum est Vicecomiti, quod capiat in manum Regis Libertatem hominum de Eboraco, & salvo custodiat, Ita quod ipse respondeat de omnibus debitis quæ veniunt in summonitione Regis infra eandem Libertatem, Quia baillivi ejusdem Villæ non respondent super compotum Vicecomitis sicut debuerunt. *Memor.* 38. *H.* 3. *Rot.* 13. *a.*

(*r*) Quod nullus venit &c super compotum Vicecomitis Eboracisciræ pro Canonicis S. Petri, nec pro Civibus Eboraco, ad respondendum de debitis quæ veniunt in Summonitione Scaccarij. Et ideo consideratum est, quod prædictæ Libertates capiantur in manum Regis. *Memor.* 40. *H.* 3. *Rot.* 19. *a.*

(*s*) Memorandum quod die Veneris proxima post festum S. Dunstani, præceptum fuit Vicecomiti Suthamptoniæ per Thesaurarium & Barones, quod caperet in manum Regis Villam de Wyntonia, & eam salvo custodiret, ita quod de exitibus inde provenientibus possit Regi respondere ; eo quod homines ejusdem Villæ non fuerunt ad Scaccarium Regis super compotum Vicecomitis, ad respondendum Regi de debitis quæ Regi debentur in Villa prædicta, *Pas. Commun.* 56. *H.* 3. *Rot.* 6. *b.*

(*t*) Præceptum est Vicecomiti [Suff.], quod capiat in manum Regis Libertatem S. Edmundi, quia nullus fuit pro Abbate ejusdem Loci super compotum Vicecomitis ad calumpniandum Libertates suas. *Memor.* 1. *E.* 1. *Rot.* 7. *b.*

(*u*) Bed. De Fine. Burgenses Bedfordiæ dant Regi v marcas pro Villa sua rehabenda, quæ capta fuit in manum Regis, pro eo quod non fuerunt super compotum Vicecomitis redditum ad Scaccarium in Octabis S. Martini, ad respondendum de diversis debitis quæ veniunt in summonitione infra Villam prædictam. Et mandatum est Vicecomiti, quod eandem Villam una cum exitibus medio tempore inde perceptis Burgensibus ejusdem Villæ restituat. *Mich. Commun.* 14. *E.* 1. *Rot.* 5. *a. in bund.* 13 & 14. *E.* 1.

(*w*) *Pas. Memor.* 18. *E.* 1. *Rot.* —. *a.*

(*x*) *Kancia.* Cives Cantuariæ finem fecerunt cum Rege per C s, quos solverunt ad Scaccarium pro Villa sua rehabenda, quæ capta fuit in manum Regis, pro eo quod non fuerunt super Compotum Willelmi de Chelefeud quondam Vicecomitis Kanciæ, redditum ad Scaccarium in crastino S. Trinitatis,

Oxford (y), the City of *Canterbury* (z), the Town of *Portsmouth*, the Liberty of the Prioress of *Ambresbury*, and others (a). The Town of *Walingford* was ordered to be taken into the King's Hand for their Ferm, &c (b). The Town of *Yarmouth* was taken into the King's Hand for the Debts they owed to the King (c); and the Town of *Kingston* in *Surrey* for the like (d). The Town of *Wiche* was taken into the King's Hands for the Areres of their Ferm (e); the Town of *Rochester* for not paying their Ferm (f); the City of *London* for the Debts they owed the King (g); the Town of *Grimesby* for their Ferm (h). The Town of *Kingston* was ordered to be taken into the King's Hand, unless they paid such a Debt due to the King by such a Time (i). The City of
London

ad respondendum de diversis debltis quæ Regi debentur infra Villam prædictam. Et mandatum est Vicecomiti, quod restituat illis Villam prædictam; Salvis Regi exitibus ejusdem medio tempore perceptis. *Trin. Memor.* 18. *E.* 1. *Rot.* —. *a.*

(y) *Mich. Fines* 9. *E.* 2. *Rot.* 110. *b.*

(z) *Hil. Fines* 9. *E.* 2. *Rot.* 112. *a.*

(a) Suhamton. *It was ordered that the Town of* Portsmouth *be not permitted to have Return of Writs and Summonces, for that they did not come nor send upon the Sheriff's last Account, to answer to the King for the leviable Debts within their Liberty. One of their Bailiffs came and prayed to be admitted to fine; and he was admitted.* Et fecit finem cum Domino Rege per dimidiam marcam, pro Libertate prædicta rehabenda. *Hil Communia* 15. *E.* 2. *Rot.* 30. *a.*

Suhamton. *The Prioures of* Aumbresbury *was in the same Case, for the same Cause. Her Bailiff* Robert de Savaray *came and made Fine* in di. marca *in like Manner, to have again the Liberty, and had it. Trin. Commun.* 15. *E.* 2. *Rot.* 32. *a. inter Fines &c.*

And the Abbot of Evesham *was in the like Case. Ib. Trin. Commun. Rot.* 32. *b.*

(b) Præceptum est Vicecomiti, quod capiat in manum Domini Regis villam de Walengeford, pro firma villæ suæ, & quia non fuerunt super Visum Vicecomitis. *Ex Memor.* 11. *H.* 3. *Rot.* 5. *b. Berk.*

(c) Norfuk. Villa de Gernemua quæ capta fuit in manum Domini Regis reddita est hominibus de Gernemua, hoc pacto quod super compotum Vicecomitis satisfaciant de omnibus debitis suis, alioquin amittent Villam suam. Habent Breve. *Mich. Commun.* 11. *H.* 3. *Rot.* 1. *a.*

(d) Surr. Præceptum est quod Villa de Kingestone capiatur in manum Domini Regis, propter debita quæ debent Domino Regi. *Ib. Rot.* 1. *b.*

(e) *Memor.* 22. *H.* 3. *Rot.* 11. *b.*

(f) Kancia. Mandatum est Vicecomiti, quod replegiari faciat usq; a die S. Michaëlis in unum mensem, hominibus de Roffa, villam suam; quæ capta fuit in manum Regis, eo quod non reddiderunt firmam. *Ex Memor.* 28. *H.* 3. *Rot.* 12. *b.*

(g) Simon filius Mariæ & Laurentius de Frowyk Vicecomites Londoniæ & Middelsexæ liberati sunt Marescallo xx die Februarij, pro debitis quæ Regi debent; Et Civitas Londoniæ capta est in manum Domini Regis, quia non solverunt Regi debita quæ ei debent de tallagio & de alijs, & quia contempnunt adimplere mandata Domini Regis. Et inhibitum est Majori & Vicecomitibus & Aldermannis, ne ipsi in aliquo se intromittant, vel aliquis pro eis, quousq; Dominus Rex aliud præceperit. Postea in respectum usq; in Crastinum per Edwardum de Westminstre. *Hil. Communia* 31. *H.* 3. *Rot.* 5. *a.*

(h) Homines de Grimesby debent Cxj l de firma. Præceptum est Vicecomiti quod capiat Villam de Grimesby in manum Regis, quia non reddiderunt firmam; & salvo custodiat, ita quod possit respondere de omnibus exitibus. *Memor.* 32. *H.* 3. *Rot.* 14. *b.*

(i) Præceptum est Ballivis de Kingestun, quod solvant ad Scaccarium in die Cinerum x marcas,

Chap. XXIII.   *and* ACCOUNTANTS.   247

London was taken into the King's Hand for Non-payment of the Queen's Gold (*k*), the Town of *Lincoln* for their Ferm (*l*), the Town of *Northampton* for their Ferm (*m*), the Town of *Bedford* for Non-payment of their Profer (*n*), the City of *Norwich* for the Areres of their Ferm (*o*), the Town of *Walingford* for the Areres of their Ferm (*p*). The Citizens of *Canterbury* were indebted to the King in xx Marks for a Fine to have their City restored to them. And because *John Paiable*, Bailiff of the City, had not paid in the said Fine as he was enjoined, a Writ was awarded to the Sheriff of *Kent*, to take the City into the King's Hands, and to attach *John*. Afterwards the Citizens paid the xx Marks by Tally. And thereupon the Treasurer restored to them their City, with the Issues thereof (*q*). The Town of *Appleby* was taken into the King's Hands for the Areres of their Ferm (*r*); and was thereupon committed to the Custody of *Alexander de Berewyz*, during the King's Pleasure (*s*).

There were several other Causes for which the King used to take Towns or Liberties of Lords into his Hands; as for Trespasses committed by the Men of a Town, or by the Lord of a Liberty, or his Men and Tenants, for Contempts, Defaults, or false Claims made by their Bailiffs, and the like. The City of *Norwich* was seized for a

x marcas, de quibus Nicholaus de Wauncy oneratur pro eis. Et consideratum est per Barones, quod nisi dicti denarij eo die persolvantur, quod villa de Kingestun capiatur in manum Regis. *Ex Memor.* 35. *H.* 3. *Rot.* 8. *b.* Nicolas de Wauncy *was Sheriff of* Surrey *and* Sussex; *Ib. juxt.*

(*k*) Rex mandat Baronibus, quod ad instanciam Reginæ replegiavit Majori & Communitati Londoniæ usq; ad — proximo futuro. Civitatem Londoniæ quam capi fecerat in manum suam pro Auro Reginæ, quod a prædictis Majore & Communitate exigitur, Ita quidem quod nisi interim satisfaciant eidem Reginæ pro Auro suo, Civitas illa esset in manu sua in statu quo tunc fuit. *Ex Memor.* 40. *H.* 3. *Rot.* 4. *a.*

(*l*) Quia Cives Lincolniæ non responderunt ad Scaccarium de firma Villæ suæ in crastino Clausi Paschæ, præceptum est Vicecomiti, quod capiat prædictam Villam in manum Regis, & ingrediatur & levari faciat prædictam firmam, ita quod inde respondeat per manum suam. *Pas. Memor.* 41. *H.* 3. *Rot.* 11. *b.*

(*m*) *Memor.* 52. *H.* 3. *Rot.* 25. *b.*

(*n*) Homines Bedfordiæ dant Regi xx s pro Villa sua rehabenda, quæ capta fuit in manum Regis, pro eo quod non solverunt xx l de Profro suo in crastino Clausi Paschæ, sicut continetur in Rotulo Brevium. *Trin. Commun.* 18. *E.* 1. *Rot.* — *b.*

(*o*) De Civitate Norwici capta in manum Regis. *Pas. Commun.* 18. *E.* 1. *Rot.* 10. *b.* De Civitate Norwici restituta Civibus ejusdem. *It was seized into the King's Hands for the Areres of their Ferm. Trin. Commun.* 18. *E.* 1. *Rot.* 21. *b.*

(*p*) Robertus de Meleburn Major Burgi Walingfordiæ fecit finem hic cum Rege, pro se & cæteris Burgensibus Burgi prædicti, per xl s, pro Burgo prædicto, quod super compotum Vicecomitis Berk. captum fuit in manum Regis pro quater xx l Blancis, quæ Regi aretro fuerunt de firma ejusdem Burgi, rehabendo. *Trin. Commun.* 35. *E.* 1. *Rot.* 65. *a.*

(*q*) *Pas. Recorda* 34. *E.* 1. *Rot.* 31. *a.*
(*r*) *Pas. Commun.* 5. *E.* 2. *Rot.* 44. *b.*
(*s*) *Hil. Commissiones & Lit. Pat.* 5. *E.* 2. *Rot.* 4. *b.*

Contempt done by their Bailiffs in departing from the Court without Licence (*t*). The Liberty of the Hundred of *Rochford* was taken into the King's Hands, because *John de Burgh* and his Bailiffs did not execute the King's Writs within that Liberty, nor suffer the Sheriff of *Essex* to execute them (*u*). The City of *London* was taken into the King's Hand for a Trespass of the Assize: and the Custody of it was delivered to *John de Gizors* (*w*). *Kenebalton* and other Liberties of *Humfrey de Bohun*, Earl of *Essex* and *Hertford*, were seized into the King's Hand for a Default which the Earl had made in the Exchequer (*x*). The several Liberties of *Robert de Champeyne*, *William de Goldingham* (*y*), and *Hugh de Cancellis* (*z*) were seized for Defaults. The Liberty of the Bishop of *Worcester* was seized into the King's Hands, for a false Claim made by the Bishop's Attorney. But it appearing that the Claim was made through Ignorance, the Liberty was restored (*a*). *Thomas de Pirie* came to the Exchequer to account there as Bailiff of the Town of *Oxford*, and took the usual Oath of an Accountant. Upon Examination, *Thomas* acknowledged that he was not Bailiff of the said Town, but a Clerk of the Bailiffs of the Town. For this Deception, he was committed Prisoner to the Fleet. And

---

(*t*) Memor. 52. H. 3. Rot. 1. b.

(*u*) Essex. De Hundredo de Rocheford capto in manum Regis. Quia Johannes de Burgo senior & Ballivi sui Hundredi de Rocheford, postquam per Vicecomitem receperint returna brevium Regis, non exequntur præcepta Regis infra Libertatem prædicti Hundredi, nec permittunt quod Vicecomes ea exequatur in eadem, sicut retornavit. Rex attendens quod per hoc perit Justicia, dignitas Coronæ læditur, & executio juris impeditur, Mandat Vicecomiti, quod eandem Libertatem capiat in manum Regis, & eam salvo custodiat, ita quod de exitibus Regi respondeat ad Scaccarium. T. &c. x die Octobris. *Mich. Communia* 52 & 53. *H.* 3. *Rot.* 1. *b.*

(*w*) Rex mandavit Philippo Lovel & Edwardo de Westminstre, quod sine dilatione capiant in manum suam Civitatem Londoniæ pro transgressione Assissarum, et eam salvo custodiant, ita quod de exitibus ejusdem respondeant donec &c. Breve est in f. M. Teste R. Comite Cornubiæ &c. xxviij die Octobris &c. Et tradita est custodia ejusdem Civitatis per eosdem P. & E. Johanni de Gizors. *Memor.* 39. *H.* 3. *Rot.* 4. *a.*

(*x*) *Mich. Commun.* 17. *incipien.* 18. *E.* 1. *Rot.* — *a.*

(*y*) Norhamton. Robertus de Champeyne venit eodem die [in octabis S. Michaelis], et petijt Libertatem suam in Dodington, quæ capta fuit in manum Regis pro defalta, per plevinam. Et concessum est ei usq; eundem diem. Et hoc mandatum est Vicecomiti. *Mich. Commun. ib. Rot.* — *a.* William de Goldingham *had his Liberty in Rischeton by Plevin the same Day. Ib. juxt. Norhamton.*

(*z*) Norhamton. Hugo de Cancellis de Upton venit coram Baronibus in octabis S. Michaelis, & petijt Libertatem suam Visus Franci plegij in Upton, quæ nuper capta fuit in manum Regis pro defalta, de placito de Quo Waranto, per plevinam. Et concessum est ei usq; ad quindenam S. Edwardi Regis. Et hoc mandatum est Vicecomiti. *Ib. Rot.* — *a.*

(*a*) Glouc. De Libertate Episcopi Wygorniensis capta in manum Regis & postmodum deliberata. *Pas. Communia* 9. *E.* 2. *Rot.* 99. *b.*

because

because the Bailiff of the Town did not appear to account, and to do what appertained to him, the Liberty of the Town was seized into the King's Hands (*b*). The Abbot of *Peterburgh*'s Liberty was seized, for a false Claim made by his Bailiff at the Exchequer (*c*).

XXIII. If the King's Debtor was a Clergyman, and had no Lay-fee whereby he might be distreined, Writs were wont to issue to the Bishop of the Diocese, commanding him to distrein such Debtor by his Ecclesiastical Benefices. Many of these Writs had in them a Clause, importing, that if the Bishop failed to make due Execution, the King would cause the Debt to be levied on the Bishop's Barony (*d*). Sometimes these Writs of *Distringas* were directed to the Bishop's Official. The Official of *Norwich* was commanded to distrein *Michael de Polstede* by his Ecclesiastical Benefices, to render to the King xxvj *l* ix *s* viij *d* (*e*). The Bishop of *Exeter* was commanded to distrein *John Wake* by his Ecclesiastical Benefice, to render to the King a Debt of xl *l*: or in Default of executing the *Distringas*, the King would betake himself to the Bishop's Barony (*f*). A *Pluries Distringas* issued. The Bishop failed in executing it. Whereupon the Sheriff was commanded by Writ to levy the xl *l* on the Bishop's Chatels, and to have the Money at the Exchequer on such a Day: because, saith the Writ, by the Assize of our Exchequer and Custom of our Realm, we may betake us to the Bishop's Barony, when upon our Command, he doth not distrein the Clerks of his Diocese to pay the Debts which they owe to us (*ff*). The Bishop of *Saresbury* was commanded by Writ, to distrein

---

(*b*) Mich. Præcepta 9. E. 2. Rot. 148. a.
(*c*) Hil. Communia 25 & 26. E. 1. Rot. 48. a.
(*d*) Vide infr. in the Case of John Wak and Oliver de Tracy.
(*e*) Mandatum est Officiali Norwici, quod distringat Michaelem de Postede per beneficia sua Ecclesiastica, ad reddendum Domino Regi xxvj l ix s viij d, & quod habeat debitum illud ad Scaccarium per aliquem suorum in crastino S. Martini. Cancellarius S. Pauli cepit in manum quod tunc satisfaciet pro eo; et mandatum est Officiali quod interim pacem habeat. Mich. Memor. 11. H. 3. Rot. 1. a.
(*f*) Episcopo Exoniensi. Rex eidem; Quia Johannes Wak non habet laicum feodum per quod possit distringi — : Vobis mandamus, sicut pluries, quod distringatis ipsum per Ecclesiasticum beneficium, ad reddendum nobis prædictum debitum — : Alioquin sciatis quod præceperimus Vicecomiti Devoniæ, quod illud capiat de Baronia vestra. Teste &c. Ex Memor. 28. H. 3. Rot. 7. a.

(*ff*) Devon. Rex Vicecomiti; Pluries mandavimus per Litteras, W. Exoniensi Episcopo, quod distringeret Johannem Wak per Ecclesiasticum beneficium, ad reddendum nobis xi l quas nobis debet pro habenda gratia, eo quod dictus Johannes non habet laicum feodum per quod possit ad hoc distringi. Et quia dictus Episcopus mandatum nostrum non est executus, Tibi præcipimus, quod de catallis prædicti Episcopi in balliva tua facias prædictas xl l, ita quod eas habeas ad

distrein the Executors of the Testament of Bishop *William* his Predecessor by their Ecclesiastical Benefices, to render unto the King C *l*, which the said Bishop *William* owed; and to return the Money to the Exchequer by such a Day; or else the King would cause it to be levied on the present Bishop's Barony (*g*). At another Time, the Bishop of *Exeter* was commanded by several Writs, to distrein *Oliver de Tracy* by his Ecclesiastick Benefice. The Bishop had failed to execute those Writs. The Sheriff of *Devonshire* was ordered to levy the Money due to the King from *Oliver* on the Goods of the Bishop's Barony (*h*). The Distress in these Cases was (as I take it) by way of Sequestration. And when by sequestring the Issues of the Benefice, or by other Means, the King's Debt was secured, then the Sequestration was released. So it was in the Case of *John Wak*. He was indebted to the King in Lx Marks. The King by his Writ commanded the Bishop of *Exeter* to distrein him by his Ecclesiastical Benefices. The Bishop distreined him in seven several Benefices, and received out of the Profits thereof the Sum of Lviij Marks and xl *d*; and *John* found Security for the Residue of his Debt; whereupon the King ordered the Sequestration to be released (*i*). Or if a Man was in general entituled

ad Scaccarium nostrum in crastino —— per aliquem de tuis; Quia per assisam Scaccarij nostri & consuetudinem regni nostri possumus nos capere ad Baroniam suam, cum ad mandatum nostrum non distringit Clericos Episcopatus sui ad debita in quibus nobis tenentur nobis reddenda: Et distringas prædictum Episcopum quod venire facias coram prædictis Baronibus ad eundem diem aliquem de suis, qui nobis possit respondere de carucagio terrarum suarum, quod nobis debet sicut nobis constat per rotulos Scaccarij nostri; Et habeas &c. *Memor*. 28. *H*. 3. *Rot*. 10. *b*.

(*g*) Episcopo Sar. pro Rege. Mandatum est eidem Episcopo, quod distringat executores testamenti Willelmi prædecessoris sui per ecclesiastica beneficia sua, ad reddendum Regi C l quas idem W. Regi debuit; ita quod habeat denarios per aliquem de suis ad Scaccarium, die Lunæ proxima post Dominicam qua cantatur *Lætare Jerusalem*; Alioquin Rex levari faciet dictos denarios de Baronia ipsius Episcopi. *Ex Memor*. 42. *H*. 3. *Rot*. 12. *b*.

(*h*) Vicecomiti Devoniæ pro Rege. Rex meminit se pluries mandasse W. Episcopo Exoniensi, quod quia Oliverus de Tracy Clericus non habuit laicum feodum per quod potuit distringi, ipsum per Beneficium suum Ecclesiasticum quod habuit in Episcopatu suo distringeret —: Et quia idem Episcopus mandatum Regis non est executus, Mandatum est Vicecomiti, quod sicut seipsum & omnia sua diligit, dictos denarios de bonis Baron[iæ] ejusdem Episcopi in balliva sua inventis levari faciat, ita quod eos habeat ad idem Scaccarium &c. *Memor*. 1. *E*. 1. *Rot*. 1. *a*.

(*i*) Episcopo Exoniensi. Rex [eidem]; Ostendit nobis Johannes Wak Clericus, quod cum dedissemus vobis in mandatis, quod ipsum per Ecclesiastica beneficia sua distringeretis, ad reddendum nobis Lx marcas quas nobis debuit, vos de beneficijs suis recepistis usq; ad summam Lviij marcarum et xl d, videlicet de Ecclesia de Hellesfton ix marcas, de Ecclesia Sancti Budoci v marcas, de Ecclesia Sancti Mawen. v marcas, de Ecclesia de Worlegyan iiij marcas, de Ecclesia de Sancto Claro xx marcas, de Ecclesia de Alverinton L s, de Ecclesia de Bikbir.

tituled to the Privilege of the Church, and had no Lay-fee, he was to be diftreined by the Ordinary. *Robert de Witney* had no Lay-fee, but lived on a Corrody in the Abbey of *Eynſham:* the Ordinary was commanded to diftrein him by his Corrody (*k*).

XXIV. The Accountants, at the Time of Paffing their Accounts, did, as it ſeems, fometimes fit upon a Bench or Benches in the Court of Exchequer. In the firſt Year of K. *Edward* I, it was adjudged at the Exchequer, that the Biſhop of *Norwich* ought not to anſwer for the King's Debts *per manum ſuam*. And thereupon *John de Roynges*, the Biſhop's Attorney, was ordered to go-off from the Bench of Accountants (*l*). *Simon de Bradenham*, Sheriff of *Eſſex* and *Hertford*, fat at the Exchequer in rendering his Account. And after he had been fworn to charge himfelf duly with the King's Debts, he was appoſed by the Barons upon the Summonce of the Pipe (*m*). *Richard de Welleford* and *Simon de Mereworth*, Sheriffs of *London* and *Middleſex*, fat at the Exchequer to make the View of their Account. And the Mayor and Aldermen of the City were called to make their Claim touching certain Ferms and other Debts running in Demand upon the Citizens, to the King's Uſe (*n*).

XXV. It was obſerved in another Place (*o*), that although the King's Money was moſt generally paid-in at his Exchequer, yet it was alſo fometimes paid to the King himſelf in his Palace, *in Camera Regis*. So it may be obſerved here, that although Accounts were properly to be rendered at the Exchequer, yet they were alſo fometimes rendered, either wholly or in Part, to the King, or his Officers

---

Bikbir. dimidiam marcam. Et ideo vobis mandamus, quod dictos denarios habeatis ad Scaccarium in Craſtino Animarum per aliquem de veſtris, alioquin præcepimus Vicecomiti noſtro Devoniæ quod ad ſolutionem prædictorum denariorum vos per catalla veſtra diſtringat. Et quia Idem Johannes fecit nos ſecuros de reddendo nobis reſiduo prædicti debiti, Vobis mandamus quod ſequeſtrum prædictorum beneficiorum ſuorum in manus veſtras factum pro prædicto debito ei relaxetis. T. A. Theſaurario S. Pauli Londoniæ primo die Octobris. *Mich. Commun.* 29. *H.* 3. *Rot.* 1. *a.*

(*k*) Quia Robertus de Witteneye, qui manet in Abbatia de Eyneſham, non habet laicum feodum per quod &c; mandatum eſt Epiſcopo Lincolnienſi, quod diſtringat ipſum per Liberationem ſuam quam habet in eadem Abbatia, quod ſit coram &c. *Memor.* 42. *H.* 3. *Rot.* 5. *b.*

(*l*) Conſideratio contra Epiſcopum Norwycenſem. Johannes de Roynges Attornatus Epiſcopi Norwycenſis amotus fuit a Banco in Scaccario; quia idem Epiſcopus non debet reſpondere de debitis Regis per manum ſuam. *Memor.* 1. *E.* 1. *Rot.* 7. *a.*

(*m*) *Mich. Communia* 26 & 27. *E.* 1. *Rot.* 5. *b.*

(*n*) *Trin. Communia* 5. *E.* 2. *Rot.* 58. *b.*

(*o*) *Vol.* 1. *Chap.* 8. *Sect.* 2.

in Camera Regis. In the 9th Year of K. *Henry* II, *Maurice de Tiretai* rendered his Account to the King himself, for the Ferm of the Counties of *Essex* and *Hertford* (*p*). *Richard de Luci*, for the Ferm of *Colchester* (*q*), and *William de Chaisney*, for the Ferm of *Norfolk* (*r*). In the 15th Year of K. *Henry* II, *Ralf Briton* accounted to the King himself for the Honours of *Henry de Essex* and Earl *Eustace* (*s*): and again in the 18th (*t*) and 19th Year (*u*). In the 26th Year of K. *Henry* II, *Walter de Constantijs* rendered an Account for the Abbies of *Wilton* and *Ramsey, in Camera Regis* (*w*). And *Robert de Gloucester* rendered an Account *in Camera Regis*, for the Bishoprick of *Chichester* (*x*). And when an Accountant had rendered his Account to the King himself, the same was wont to be signified to the Barons of the Exchequer by the King's Writ; and thereupon the Accountant was discharged at the Exchequer; as it appears by the Instances above cited. But I am to treat only of the Accounts that were rendered at the Exchequer.

(*p*) Mauricius de Tiretai reddit compotum de xvij l & iij s & xj d Bl. de Veteri firma de Essexa & de Hurtfordscira, In thesauro liberavit; Et est Compotus redditus Regi; Et Quietus est. *Mag. Rot.* 9. *H.* 2. *Rot.* 2. *b.*

(*q*) Ricardus de Luci r c de veteri firma Colecestriæ; In thesauro liberavit; Et Compotus inde redditus est Regi, Et Q. e. *Ib. Rot.* 2. *b.*

(*r*) Willelmus de Chaisneio r c de Veteri firma de Norfolch, In thesauro xxix l & vij s & vj d Bl. & xl l numero, De quibus compotus redditus est Regi, Et xxvij l & xix s & vj d Bl. & xx s & vj d numero pro Combustione, De quibus Compotus debet reddi Regi, Et Q. e. *Mag. Rot.* 9. *H.* 2. *Rot.* 3. *a.*

(*s*) Radulfus Brito non reddit compotum de Terra Henrici de Essexa de Militibus ejus, neq; de terra Comitis Eustachij nec de Militibus suis de hoc anno nec de annis præteritis, quia Rex prohibet per breve suum; Quia reddidit ei Compotum inde, Et Quietus est per Breve Regis. Idem debet C s de Lillecherche & de Lagæfara de eodem Auxilio; sed non reddet de eis Compotum, neq; de exitu eorundem Maneriorum donec Rex præcipiat. *Mag. Rot.* 15. *H.* 2. *Rot.* 9. *a. Tit.* Honor Boloniæ.

(*t*) Honor Boloniæ: Radulfus Brito r c de C s de Haukesberga &c. Ab eodem non debet exigi compotus de Terra Comitis Eustachij nec de Militibus ejus, nec de Terra quæ fuit Henrici de Essexa nec de Militibus ejus de hoc anno, per breve Regis; Quia inde compotum reddidit Regi, Et Q. e. *Mag. Rot.* 18. *H.* 2. *Rot.* 4. *a. Essexa & Hurtf.*

(*u*) Ab eodem [Radulfo Britone] non debet exigi compotus de terra Comitis Eustachij nec de Militibus ejus, nec de terra quæ fuit Henrici de Essexa nec de Militibus ejus de hoc anno; quia inde reddidit compotum ipsi Regi, per breve Regis; Et Quietus est. *Mag. Rot.* 19. *H.* 2. *Rot.* 3. *a.*

(*w*) A Magistro Waltero de Constantijs non est exigendus compotus de Abbatia de Wiltona, vel de reditu vel de perquisitis, vel de exitu ejusdem Abbatiæ, de tempore quo Abbatia fuit in manu Regis, & in custodia jamdicti Walteri, quia reddidit idem in Camera Regis, per breve Regis. *Mag. Rot.* 26. *H.* 2. *Rot.* 9. *a. & Ib. Rot.* 3. *a.*

(*x*) Compotus Episcopatus Cicestrensis non redditur hic de anno præterito & de hoc anno, Quia per præceptum Regis redditus fuit in Camera per Magistrum Robertum de Gloecestria, coram Ricardo de Marisco & Roberto de Braibroc. *Mag. Rot.* 11. *J. Rot.* 1. *a. Sudsexia.* There is the like Entry in totidem verbis, *touching the Bishoprick of* Lincoln; *Ib. Rot.* 7. *b.*

Chap. XXIII. *and* ACCOUNTANTS.

XXVI. There were in ancient Time many Ways of putting Debts in Charge *pro Rege*. For Example: Debts were put in Charge, First, By virtue of the King's Writ (*y*): Secondly, By the Writ or personal Testimony of the Chief Justicier, or some other Justicier or Baron of the Exchequer (*z*): Thirdly, By Judgment or Award of the Justicier or Treasurer and Barons of the Exchequer in Court (*a*): Fourthly, By the Rolls or Estreats of the Justiciers (*b*): Fifthly, By the Acknowledgment (*c*) of the Parties: Sixthly, From the Original of the Chancery (*d*); and by other Ways.

XXVII.

(*y*) Ricardus de Luci debet C & xx marcas & j palefridum, pro Custo quod Willelmus Briewerre posuit in terra quæ fuit Hugonis de Morevilla, antequam idem Ricardus finiret pro terra illa. Quod debitum intravit in Rotulum per breve Regis. *Mag. Rot.* 6. *Joh. Rot.* 11. *b. Cumb.*

Ante, vol. 1. *cap.* 10. *sect.* 4. *ad ann.* 6. *Joh.* H. Cantuariensis.

(*z*) Debita Regis de eodem Honore [Lancastræ] a tempore Galfridi de Valonijs, per Breve Johannis Malduit & Willelmi filij Martini, & Rescriptum Willelmi de Vesci. *Mag. Rot.* 16. *H.* 2. *Rot.* 3. *b. Lancastra.*

Robertus Malduit [debet] x marcas & j palefridum, pro claudendo Bosco suo de Benleia ad Parcum faciendum; Ita quod possit includere de terra arabili de Dominico suo quantum voluerit. Qui Finis intravit in Rotulum per Os G. filij Petri & H. de Nevill coram H. Cantuariensi Archiepiscopo. *Mag. Rot.* 4. *J. Rot.* 2. *b. Buk. & Bedef.*

Radulfus Abbas de Westmonasterio debet xl marcas, Ut habeat nemora sua de Persore quieta, ita ut nullus Forestarius intromittat se de nemoribus illis nec ea ingrediatur. Qui Finis intravit in Rotulum per Os Hugonis de Nevill; De quibus ipse H. debet respondere, qui recognovit quod eas recepit, nec debet Abbas amplius inde summoneri. *Mag. Rot.* 4. *J. Rot.* 2. *a. Wirecestr.*

Baldewinus Wac r c de xx marcis de eodem [viz. de Finibus & scutagijs Militum de quarto Scutagio]: Qui finis intravit per os Justiciarij. *Mag. Rot.* 5. *J. Rot.* 9. *a. Linc.*

(*a*) *Vid. hanc Hist. passim.*

(*b*) De Placitis Forestæ per H. de Nevill & B. de Insula: Stephanus de Seagrave r c de xx l & ix d, de Misericordijs hominum quorum nominibus præponitur Litera T. in una Summonicione quam Vicecomes tulit ad Scaccarium sub sigillo Justiciarij, & alia Summonicione quam idem tulit in qua sigillum Vicecomitis Wigorniæ pendebat similiter de eodem Itinere in Wigornia. *Mag. Rot.* 13. *H.* 3. *Warewyk & Leicestr.*

Amerciamenta per Thomam de Multon, Robertum de Laxinton, & Socios suos: Idem Vicecomes r c de C & Lxxviij l & xxij d, de Misericordijs Hominum, Hundredorum, Villarum, & Borgarum, quorum nominibus præponitur Litera T. in Rotulo quem prædicti Justiciarij liberaverunt in Thesauro: In th. l, Et Q. e. *Mag. Rot.* 14. *H.* 3. *Sudsex.*

De Amerciamentis per S. de Segrave: Idem Vicecomes [Henricus de Aldithelega] r c de iiij l v s & iiij d, de Misericordijs hominum quorum nominibus præponitur Litera T, in Summonicione quam Vicecomes tulit ad Scaccarium signatam sigillo Justiciar.; In th. l, Et Q. e. *Mag. Rot.* 14. *H.* 3. *Salopeschir.*

(*c*) De Oblatis Curiæ: Idem Vicecomes debet j marcam, quam habuit de Hominibus de Mienestoch, per Recognitionem suam ad Scaccarium. *Mag. Rot.* 28. *H.* 2. *Rot.* 11. *a. Sudhantescira.* Galfridus filius Azonis, *Sheriff*

Stephanus de Turncham [debet] D l, quas recognovit super Scaccarium quod eas recepit de fine G. Wintoniensis Episcopi. *Mag. Rot.* 2. *J. Rot.* 14. *a. Sudhant. m.* 2.

Margareta quæ fuit uxor Johannis de Baketon debet xl marcas —.. Sed non debet inde summoneri; quia Walterus de Grai Cancellarius debet inde respondere, sicut recognovit & manucepit coram Rege. *Mag. Rot.* 14. *Joh. Rot.* 17. *a. Cumb.*

(*d*) *Instances of this, and of the other Particulars*

XXVII. It hath been shewn above (*e*), that in the most ancient Times, the Chancery was usually holden at the Exchequer: or, if you please, many or most of the Chancery Writs were then dispatched and sealed at the Exchequer; at which Place the Great Seal was commonly kept. When therefore the Chancery was separated from the Exchequer, and the Charters, Writs, and Precepts of the Great Seal came to be entered by themselves in the *Rotuli Cancellariæ* (such as the Charter-Rolls, Patent-Rolls, &c.) at or about the Beginning of K. *John*'s Reign; then, as it seems, commenced the Method (which has been continued ever since) of sending Estreats from the Chancery into the Exchequer. But this I propose as a Conjecture. In Fact, from the Beginning of the Reign of K. *John*, they wrote every Year the said *Rotuli Cancellariæ*, and afterwards made Estreats thereof; which Estreats were transmitted into the Exchequer, and were called *Originale* or *Originalia*, the *Originals*, and *Extractæ Cancellariæ*, the Estreats of the Chancery. They were written out of the Fine Rolls, Patent-Rolls, and other Rolls of the Chancery. And out of them, Fines, Ferms, &c. were taken, and put in Charge at the Exchequer for the King's Profit. In some of the ancient Chancery-Rolls extant in the Tower of *London*, we find Breaks in the Rolls, with these or such-like Words: *Mittendum*, or *Hinc mittendum est ad Scaccarium*, intimating, that what followed there in the Roll was not yet estreated. This Kind of Note was made in the Chancery-Rolls of the 2d Year of K. *John* (*f*), the 18th Year of K. *Henry* III. (*g*), and in the Rolls of many other Years. These Notes made upon the Rolls were for a *Memorandum* to the Clerk or Officer in Chancery, of what had been estreated from thence into the Exchequer, and what not; that he might be sure he did not fail in his Duty of estreating. When this Record was actually brought into the Exchequer, it was there immediately called *Originale*, the *Original*; which Name is probably as ancient as the Usage of estreating. Mention is made of the *Original* of the 9th Year of K. *John* (*h*), of the 12th

---

ticulars just above-mentioned, may be seen in divers Places in this History.

(*e*) *Vol.* 1. *Cap.* 4. *sect.* 10.

(*f*) Hinc mittendum est ad Scaccarium. *Oblata* 2. *J. m.* 5.

Mittendum est ad Scaccarium. *Ib. m.* 8. *in marg.*

(*g*) Hinc mittendum est ad Scaccarium. *Fin.* 18. *H.* 3. *m.* 6.

Hinc mittendum est ad Scaccarium. *Ib. m.* 2.

Hinc mittendum est ad Saccarium; *which Words are cancelled; and 'tis added*, quia postea missum. *Ib. m.* 6.

(*h*) Galfridus de Sachevill & Radulfus de Marci r c de M marcis, pro habenda benevolentia Regis, & ut quieti sint de retto forestæ Regis unde retati fuerunt, & pro habendis Terris suis unde occasione illa fuerunt dissaisiti, Per Plegios annotatos in Originali. *Mag. Rot.* 9. *Joh. Rot.* 9. *b. tit.* Essexa & Hurtfordscira.

Year

Chap. XXIII.   *and* ACCOUNTANTS.

Year (*i*), and of the 14th Year of K. *John* (*k*). And frequently in the Reign of K. *Henry* III: for Inftance, in the 11th Year (*l*), the 13th Year (*m*), the 18th Year (*n*), the 22d Year (*o*), the 25th Year (*p*), the 26th Year (*q*), and many other Years of K. *Henry* III. But I need not infift on this, becaufe there remains in the Exchequer to this Day (to wit, in the Lord Treafurer's Remembrancer's Office) a Series of thefe *Originals*, from the Reign of K. *Henry* III inclufive, to the prefent Times. Next, as to the Manner of eftreating or delivering in thefe *Originals*. In the 22d Year of K. *Henry* III, the Original was fent to *H. de Patefhull*, Treafurer, under the Seal of the King's Chancellour, on the Eve of St. *John Baptift* (*r*). In the 18th Year of K. *Edward* I, it was delivered to *J*. Bifhop of *Ely*, Treafurer, by the Hand of *R*. Bifhop of *Bath* and *Wells*, Chancellour (*s*). In the 27th Year of the fame King, it was delivered to the Bifhop of *Coventry* and *Lichfeld*, Treafurer, by the Hand of *John de Langeton*, Chancellour (*t*). In the 34th Year of the fame King, it was delivered

to

(*i*) Hugo de Nevill r c de Mille marcis de fine quem fecit cum Rege J, eo quod permifit P. Wintonienfem Epifcopum claudere Parcum de Tamton fine waranto, ficut continetur in Originali anni xij Regis J; qui finis non inrotulatur in Rotulis præcedentibus. *Mag. Rot.* 12. *H.* 3. *tit. Effex & Hurtford.*

(*k*) Sumerf. & Dorf. Reginaldus de Moun habet refpectum ufq; —, de xl s de præftito, ficut continetur in Originali de præftito in anno regni Regis J. xiiij°. *Ex Memor.* 28. *H.* 3. *Rot.* 4. *a.*

(*l*) Gilebertus de Aquila reddit compotum de D marcis, pro habenda faifina de terris fuis quæ captæ fuerunt in manum Regis, Reddendis ad terminos contentos in Originali de Cancellaria; Ita quod in ultimo termino, fcilicet ad Natalem Domini Anni xij allocentur ei ea quæ capta funt de terris prædictis tempore quo exiterunt in manu Regis. *Mag. Rot.* 11. *H.* 3. *Sudfex.*

(*m*) Originalia debitorum fubfcriptorum, de Amerciamentis Jufticiariorum miflorum ad Affifas capiendas in hoc Comitatu, nondum tradita funt Thefaurario. *This is a Title in Mag. Rot.* 13. *H.* 3. *Lincoll. b.*

(*n*) —— ficut continetur in Originali. *Mag. Rot.* 18. *H.* 3. *tit.* Refiduum Cumbriæ.

Per plegios annotatos in Originali Anni xviij. *Ib. Tit.* Sudfexia ; *in dorfo.*

(*o*) Sicut continetur in Originali. *Mag. Rot.* 22. *a. H.* 3. *Lond. & Midd.*

(*p*) Sicut continetur in Originali anni xxiiij. *Mag. Rot.* 25. *H.* 3. *Oxon.*

(*q*) Drogo de Barentin r c de CCCL marcis de firma Infularum de Gerefey & Gernefey, quas Rex conceffit ei tenendas per talem firmam quamdiu Regi placuerit, ficut continetur in Originali. *Mag. Rot.* 26. *H.* 3. *Oxon.*

(*r*) Hunc rotulum recepit H. de Patefhull Thefaurarius, fub figillo Cancellarij, vigilia S. Johannis Baptiftæ, anno regni Regis Henrici filij Regis Johannis xxij. *Orig.* 22. *H.* 3. *m.* 1. *in dorfo.*

(*s*) Extractæ Cancellariæ de anno xvij. Hunc Rotulum recepit J. Elienfis Epifcopus Thefaurarius, vj° die Decembris anno regni Regis Edwardi xvij, per manum R. Bathonienfis & Wellenfis Epifcopi Cancellarij. *Orig.* 17. *E.* 1. *m.* 1. *in dorfo.*

(*t*) Hunc Rotulum recepit Venerabilis pater W. Coventrenfis & Lichefeldenfis Epifcopus Thefaurarius apud Eboracum, xxv die Novembris anno regni Regis Edwardi vicefimo octavo, per manus Domini Johannis de Langeton Cancellarij. Et fummonitus eft Rotulus ifte xv die Decembris

anno

to *John de Droknesford*, the Treasurer's Lieutenant, by the Hand of *W. de Hamelton*, Chancellour of *England* (*u*). In the tenth Year of K. *Edward* II, the Original was, it seems, delivered in to the Exchequer by *William de Ayreminne*, Keeper of the Rolls of the Chancery; as the first Membrane of the Bundle for that Year witnesseth; and the Debts contained therein were straitway sent out in Summonce for the King's Use (*w*). The same *William* delivered into the Exchequer a Cedule (Part of the *Original* of that Year) in the Room of a Roll or Membrane contained in that Bundle, which had been amended in the Chancery, after the Original was estreated. The Cedule is titled, *De arentatione & excultura Vastorum forestæ de Wyndesore*; and is endorsed in the Words hereunder written (*x*).

Estreats were also wont to be made of Fines, Amercements, and such like, from the Court holden *coram Rege*, and from the *Common Bench*, and from the *Iters*, &c. All these were, I think, called the foreign Estreats; and were sent out in another Summonce than that which was awarded for the Debts contained in the *Originals*. If these Estreats, or others which ought of Right to be delivered in, were not brought-in in due Time, a Writ or Writs were wont to issue to the Justices or Persons before whom they lay, to bring them in. In the 30th Year of K. *Henry* III, Amerciaments were estreated into the Exchequer from the Common Bench (*y*); and in the 18th Year of K. *Edward* I (*z*). In the 42d Year of K. *Henry* III, the Barons of

---

anno prædicto; ita quod Vicecomites inde respondeant in crastino Purificationis, sub testimonio Johannis de Cobeham, propter absenciam Thesaurarij. *Orig.* 27. *E.* 1. *m.* 1. *in dorso.*

(*u*) Hunc Rotulum recepit J. de Droknesford Tenens locum Thesaurarij, per manus W. de Hamelton Cancellarij Angliæ, xxij die Novembris anno R. R. E. filij Regis H. tricesimo quarto incipiente. Et summonitus est in singulis Comitatibus contentis in eodem; ita quod Vicecomites de denarijs inde Regi respondeant in crastino S. Hillarij. Teste prædicto Tenente locum Thesaurarij, ij die Decembris anno prædicto. *Orig.* 34. *E.* 1. *m.* 1. *in dorso.*

(*w*) Hunc Rotulum liberavit ad Scaccarium Willelmus de Ayreminne Custos Rotulorum Cancellariæ, xxiij die Januarij anno Regni R. E. filij Regis E. Decimo. Et summonitus fuit xxx die Januarij dicto anno decimo, sub testimonio W. de Norwyco Thesaurarij, ita quod Vicecomites habeant denarios hic in crastino clausi Paschæ. *Orig.* 10. *E.* 2. *m.* 1. *in dorso.*

(*x*) Hanc Cedulam liberavit hic Willelmus de Airemynne Custos Rotulorum Cancellariæ, xxiiij die Novembris anno R. R. E. filij Regis E. undecimo; eo quod post liberationem extractarum fuerunt emendatæ in Cancellaria. *Orig.* 10. *E.* 2. *Ced. ad m.* 2.

(*y*) Idem Vicecomes r c de viij l & dimidia marca, de misericordijs hominum quorum nominibus præponitur Littera T. in Rotulo extractarum de Banco. *Mag. Rot.* 30. *H.* 3. *Sudsex. m.* 1. *b.*

(*z*) Memorandum quod secundo die Maij anno xviij°, Margeria quæ fuit uxor Thomæ de Weylond liberavit ad Scaccarium, per manus Thomæ de Grey Valleti ejusdem Margeriæ, quendam forulum cum Rotulis de Extractis, Amerciamentorum de Banco de diversis annis in diversis Comitatibus. *Pas. Commun.* 18. *E.* 1. *Rot.*—*a.*

the

the Exchequer were commanded [by Writ] to enquire diligently, in whose Hands were the Rolls and Cirographs made as well before the Justices in Eire, as in the Court *coram Rege,* and in the *Bank,* since the King's first Coronation at *Gloucester,* which still remained abroad, and to cause them to be brought to the Exchequer, to be laid up in the King's Treasury; and to enjoin all the Justices, to deliver in to the Barons for the future their Rolls and *Chirographa,* relating to the King, that the same might be kept in the Treasury (*a*). In the same Year, several Writs were awarded to several Persons, ordering them to bring in the Rolls of the Justices remaining in sundry Places. The Abbot of *Leicester* was ordered to bring in all the Rolls left in his Abbey, of the Pleas had before *Stephen de Segrave,* as well in the *Bank* as in *Iters;* and likewise the Priour of *Kenilworth.* The like Writs were sent to *Henry de Bratton* touching the Rolls of *Martin de Pateshell* and *William de Radley* (*b*). In the 14th Year of K. *Edward* I, *Salomon de Rochester* and his Conjustices were commanded by Writ to send into the Exchequer with all Speed, the Estreats of Amercements set in their *Iter* in the County of *Essex,* that the same might be in Readiness for the King's Service and might be laid up in the Treasury. And these Estreats were afterwards brought in by the Hand of *Hugh de Kendale* (*c*).

(*a*) Mandatum est Baronibus, quod diligenter inquirant ad quorum manus devenerunt Rotuli & Cyrographa tam de Itinere Justiciariorum, quam coram Rege, & in Banco facta post primam Coronationem Regis apud Glouceftriam, quæ penes Justiciarios remanserunt; & Rotulos illos & Cyrographa venire faciant ad Scaccarium reponenda & reservanda in Thesaur[aria] Regis; Et quod injungant omnibus Justiciarijs, ut Rotulos suos & Cyrographa ad Regem spectantia de cætero Baronibus liberent, custodienda in Thesaur[aria]. *Ex Memor.* 42. *H.* 3. *Rot.* 8. *a.*

(*b*) Pro Rege, de Rotulis Justiciariorum suorum per diversa loca. Mandatum est Abbati de Leyceftre, quod omnibus dilationibus & occasionibus postpositis, habeat coram &c in crastino Clausi Paschæ, omnes Rotulos in Abbatia sua residentes, de placitis quæ fuerunt coram Stephano de Seggrave quondam Justic. &c, tam in Banco quam in Itinere per diversos Comitatus &c, Et habeat breve. Eodem modo mandatum est Priori de Kenilworth. Et eodem modo mandatum est Henrico de Bratton de Rotulis Martini de Pateshell & Willelmi de Radleye. *Ex Memor.* 42. *H.* 3. *Rot.* 12. *b.*

(*c*) Salomoni de Roffa & focijs suis Justiciarijs Itinerantibus in Comitatu Norfolciæ. Quia Extractis Amerciamentorum de Itinere prædicti S. & sociorum suorum in Comitatu Essexiæ, pro quibusdam negocijs Regem super instantem compotum Vicecomitis Essexiæ ad Scaccarium contingentibus, ac eciam pro alijs, plurimum Rex indiget; mandatum est Salomoni de Roffa & Socijs suis, quod extractas prædictas cum omni celeritate ad Scaccarium prædictum mittant, in Thesauraria Regis ibidem liberandas; Ne pro defectu sui negocia prædicta remaneant infecta. T. &c xvij die Januarij. Postea liberatæ sunt prædictæ extractæ ad Scaccarium per manum Hugonis de Kendale Clerici de Cancellaria. *Hil. Brevia pro Rege* 14. *E.* 1. *Rot.* 25. *a.*

XXVIII. Tallies

XXVIII. Tallies were of great and constant Use in the Exchequer. The Use of them was very ancient; coeval, for ought that I know, with the Exchequer itself in *England*. The Word, Tallie, is originally *French*. It signifies *Cutting*; as every Body knows. These Tallies were Pieces of Wood cut in a peculiar Manner of Correspondency. For Example: A Stick or Rod of Hazel (or perhaps of some other Wood) well dried and seasoned, was cut square and uniform at each End and in the Shaft. The Sum of Money which it bore was cut in Notches in the Wood by the *Cutter* of the Tallies, and likewise written upon two Sides of it by the *Writer* of the Tallies. The Tally was cleft in the Middle, by the Deputy Chamberlains, with a Knife and Mallet, through the Shaft and the Notches; whereby it made two Halves, each Half having a Superscription and a Half Part of the Notch or Notches. A Notch of such a Largeness signified M *l*; a Notch of another Largeness, C *l*; of another Size, xx *l*; of another, xx *s*; of another, j *s*, &c. It being thus divided or cleft, one Part of it was called a Tally, the other a Countertally; or a Tally and a Foil, *Folium*. One of the Parts was also sometimes called *Scachia*, and the other *Contratallia* (*d*); and sometimes one was called *Contratallia*, and the other *Stipes* (*e*), and *Chacia* (*f*). However these were in Effect one Tally, or two Parts of one entire Thing. And when these two Parts came afterwards to be joined, if they were genuine, they fitted so exactly that they appeared evidently to be Parts the one of the other. Concerning Tallies, the Reader may also please to consult the Dialogue *de Scaccario* (*g*). The Use of them (like as the Design or Use of indenting of Charters) was to prevent Fraud.

(*d*) Et C s, de quibus oneratur pro Willelmo de Breuse, & de quibus contratallia invenitur ad Scaccarium, & scachia amittitur. *Memor.* 13 & 14. *E.* 1. *Rot.* 31. *a*. *Præcepta facta super compot. Ric. de Peverss[el] Vic. Surr. & Sussexiæ.*

(*e*) Bukingham. *In the Case of* William Bykot, *upon View of the Rolls of the* Receipt *of Exchequer, the Barons ordered a Countertally which contained less by* iiij d *than the* Stipes, *to be mended and made to agree with the* Stipes. *Hil. Commun.* 25 & 26. *E.* 1. *Rot.* 65. *b.*

(*f*) Kancia. De Nicholao de Kiriel attachiato. Memorandum quod cum Willelmus Trussel Vicecomes Kanciæ federet super compotum suum ad Scaccarium die Jovis in festo Sanctæ Luciæ virginis anno xxv, & inter cæteras tallias de Scaccario quas protulit ibidem allocandas super compotum prædictum inventa fuit una falsa tallia sub nomine Nicholai de Kiriol, eo quod in chacia sive stipite ejusdem talliæ continebatur una marca quam solvisse debuit ibidem de quodam fine pro licentia concordandi, & in contratallia ejusdem quæ residebat ad Scaccarium in custodia Camerariorum ibidem non continebantur nisi x solidi tantum. *This Falsity was enquired into, and divers Persons examined touching the same. Mich. Commun.* 25. *E.* 1. *Rot.* G. *in dorso.*

(*g*) *Dial. L.* 1. *cap.* 5. Immo quia de taleis.

Tallies,

Tallies, as well those that were made out at the Exchequer, as those which were used *in pais,* were wont to have a Superscripture, importing of what Nature they were, and for what Purpose given. *Robert de Fulham* gave a Tally of Acquittance. It was superscribed to be for Money which he had received in *Lincolnshire,* and that he was to acquit the Payer *de tanto* at the King's Exchequer. This was a Tally made in the Countrey (*h*). The Tallies of the Exchequer were frequently allowed at the Upper Exchequer, by Award of the Justicier or of the Treasurer and Barons; as in the Case of the Earl *de Ferrers* (*i*), the Earl of *Essex* (*k*), the Town of *Wilton* (*l*), and others. In the 49th Year of K. *Henry* III, *Philipp de Keylmers* came before the Barons, and produced a Tally of Acquittance given to him by *William de Lisle.* It had been broken by Mischance, and was left in the Custody of the Remembrancer (*m*). In the 13th and 14th Year of K. *Edward* I, Master *Henry Sampson* brought before the Barons of the Exchequer [the Pieces of] a whole Tally for iiij *l,* levied by the Sheriff of *Rutlandshire;* which Tally was by Mischance

(*h*) Et super hoc quia in prædicto brevi continetur quod prædictus Simon protulit talliam contra prædictum Robertum [de Fulham] de prædictis denarijs, quæsitum est ab eadem Ermetruda, si eandem talliam penes se habeat &c; Quæ dicit quod sic; & eam coram Baronibus instanter protulit & liberavit &c; Cujus quidem Talliæ superscriptio talis est: " Contra Robertum " de Fulham de denarijs quos recepit in " Com. Lincolniæ, de arreragijs W. de " Leyrton, unde debet acquietare Exe- " cutores dicti W. ad Scaccarium Domini " Regis.—&c. *Trin. Commun.* 1. *E.* 2. *Rot.* 73. *b. Notingham.*

(*i*) Comes de Ferrarijs r c de xl l Bl. & de xx l numero de Firma de Werkeworde de dimidio anno xvij°: In thesauro xxxviij l & xvj s & viij d Bl., & xx l numero, per ij taleas ante guerram, allocatas per H. de Burgo Justiciarium, coram R. Sar., J. Bathon., R. Cyceftr. Episcopis, & alijs Baronibus de Scaccario; Et debet xxiij s & iiij d Bl.: Idem r c de eodem debito; In thesauro liberavit, Et Q. e. *Mag. Rot.* 8. *H.* 3. *Rot.* 16. *b. Not. & Dereb.*

(*k*) W. de Mandevill Comes Essexiæ r c de ——; Summa, MMMM & CCCC & Lxv l & iijs & xj d: In thesauro CCC & Lij l per ij taleas ante guerram, allocatas per H. de Burgo Justiciarium, coram R. Cycestr. Episcopo Domini Regis Cancellario, H. Linc. J. Bathon. B. Roffensi, W. Carleol. Episcopis; Et in tercio denario Comitatus Essexiæ de viij annis, quos percepisse debuerat & non percepit, CCC & xxiiij l & dim. marc., scilicet quolibet anno xl l & x s & x d, per breve Regis —. *Mag. Rot.* 9. *H.* 3. *Rot.* 8. *b.*

(*l*) Villata de Wilton debent xxxiiij l xxij d ob. de veteri tallagio facto pro relaxatione Interdicti. Præceptum est per Justiciarium quod tallia illa allocetur. *Memor.* 11. *H.* 3. *Rot.* 11. *a. parte* 1.

(*m*) Tallia Philippi de Keylmers irrotulata. Idem Philippus venit coram Baronibus, & protulit quandam talliam factam contra Willelmum [de] Insula, de duabus marcis quas ab eo recepit pro transgressione tempore quo fuit Vicecomes Regis in Comitatu Norhamtoniæ; & dicta Tallia ignoranter fracta remanet in custodia Rememoratoris. *Pas. Commun.* 49. *H.* 3. *Rot.* 8. *a.*

broken

broken in the Presence of the said *Henry* and his Servants (*n*). K. *Edward* I (*Anno Regni* 14) made a Provision or Order, to be observed in the Exchequer, concerning Tallies that happened to be lost, *viz.* that such Tallies should be innovated, and the Countertallies thereof quashed; with some other Particulars to be practised upon that Occasion. This Provision is set forth in *Ryley*'s Appendix (*o*). A Countertally, containing less than the *Stipes* by iiij *d*, was, upon View of the Rolls of the Receipt, ordered by the Barons to be mended, and made to agree with the *Stipes*; in the Case of *William Bykot* (*p*). A Tally was to be innovated for *John de Escudemor*. He was ordered by the Barons to sue to the Treasurer to get it innovated; without whose Presence at the Exchequer it could not be done (*q*). The Mayor, Aldermen, and Community of *London* fined to K. *Edward* I, in MM*l*, for the Vintisme of the Cities, Burghs, and Demeanes, granted to the King in Aid *pur faire Fitz Chivaler*. Part of this Fine, to wit, one thousand Marks, payable by the Mayor and Citizens on the Morrow of *All Souls*, was assigned by the Treasurer and Barons to *William Trente*, the King's Butler, towards the Payments and Purveyances to be made by *William* in his Office. And a Tally was made at the Exchequer under the Name of the said Citizens, and delivered to *William*, who was to deliver it to the Citizens when they paid him the said Sum. And a Writ of the Exchequer was issued to the said Mayor, Alder-

---

(*n*) De quadam tallia per infortunium fracta. Memorandum quod Magister Henricus Sampson tulit coram Baronibus de Scaccario quandam talliam integram de quatuor libris cujus scriptura est hæc, Contra P. de Asserug Vicecomitem Rotelandæ de denarijs ei liberatis de Summonicione Scaccarij anno xliiij^{to} de execucia G. de Rokingham; quæ postea in præsencia eorundem inter ipsum Magistrum Henricum & servientem suum incaute fracta fuit. *Mich. Commun.* 13 & 14. *E.* 1. *Rot.* 1. *b.*

(*o*) *Plac. Parl. p.* 450.

(*p*) *Hil. Commun.* 25 & 26. *E.* 1. *Rot.* 65. *b.*

(*q*) Berk. De Willelmo de Boxhore adjudicato prisonæ. William *had received of* John de Escudemor *Lx s, which he was to pay at the Exchequer for* John, *and with it a Tally upon which* John *had before paid in v* marks. William *converts to his own Use the Lx s; and writes it upon the Tally as paid in. This Falsity was discovered. And for the Trespass,* William (*who was an* Attornatus coram Justiciarijs in Banco) *was committed.* Consideratum est, quod idem Willelmus adeat prisonam, ibidem moraturus per unum annum & unum diem, videlicet a die. Sancti Edmundi Confessoris anno xxv^o finiente, & exinde redimendus and voluntatem Regis. Et quia prædicta tallia quo ad quinque marcas prius Solutas per eandem allocari non potest, prædictos Lx s falso super eandem appositos absq; inovatione illius Talliæ; quæ fieri non potest sine præsencia Thesaurarij, qui ad præsens stat cum Rege in partibus transmarinis, Ideo dictum est prædicto Johanni quod sequatur Innovationem illius Talliæ in adventu Thesaurarij &c. *Mich. Communia* 25 & 26. *E.* 1. *Rot.* 22. *a.*

men, and Community, to pay the said thousand Marks to *William*, and then take up the said Tally (*r*).

XXIX. Counters were sometimes used at the Exchequer in the Way of Computation. In which Case, the Counters were laid in Rows upon the several Distinctures of the chequered Cloth; *viz.* one Row or Place for Pounds, another for Shillings, &c (*s*). In the seventeenth Year of K. *John*, ten Shillings of *Venetian* Money, and likewise two Besants, were used at the Exchequer for Counters. The ten *Venetian* Shillings were valued at xv *s*, and the two Besants at iij *s* vj *d* (*t*). In the 33d Year of K. *Henry* III, a certain Thief was apprehended in *Rochester*. Several Counters belonging to the King's Exchequer were found about him. Some of the Men of that Town were imprisoned upon that Occasion. The King ordered the Counters to be returned to the Exchequer from whence they were taken (*u*). In the twelfth Year of K. *Edward* II, *Rogiero Ardyngelli*, a *Florentine* Merchant, came before the Treasurer and Barons, and brought with him xx Shillings of the new Money of *Venice*, which exceeded Sterling Money in Weight and Value. They were delivered to the Bishop of

---

(*a*) Londonia. Memorandum quod de illis MM l, per quas major Aldermanni et communitas civitatis Londoniæ nuper finem fecerunt hic cum Rege, pro vicesima Domino Regi concessa a Civibus Burgensibus et tenentibus Dominicorum Regis, in auxilium ad Primogenitum filium Regis militem faciendum sicut continetur alibi in hijs memorandis inter recorda de termino Sancti *Michaelis*, Thesaurarius & Barones assignarunt Willelmo Trente Pincernæ Regis mille marcas, illas videlicet quas ijdem cives soluturi sunt Regi de fine illo in crastino Animarum proximo futuro percipiendas et habendas per manus civium prædictorum pro solucionibus & providentijs officium ejusdem Willelmi tangentibus faciendis. Et tallia fit ad Scaccarium sub nomine dictorum civium, et liberatur prædicto Willelmo, prædictis civibus liberanda cum dictas mille marcas receperit. Et mandatum est Majori Aldermannis & communitati civitatis prædictæ vj°. die Julij, sub testimonio Thesaurarij, quod dictas mille marcas præfato Willelmo liberent &c, Recipiendo inde &c. talliam supradictam. *Trin. Com*munia 35. *Edw.* 1. *Rot.* 56. *b.* Pars. 1. 34 & 35. *E.* 1.

(*s*) *Dial. de Scacc. L.* 1. *cap.* 5. Hujus autem hæc.

(*t*) Et pro x solidis de Venecia, ad computandum ad Scaccarium, xv s, Et pro ij Bisancijs ad idem officium, iij s & vj d. *Mag. Rot.* 17. *Joh. Rot.* 6. *b. in compoto Cambij Londoniæ.*

(*u*) Rex Baronibus; Mandamus vobis quod homines nostros de Roffa detentos in prisona nostra de Flete, pro quodam Fure invento & capto in prædicta Villa cum Computar. Scaccarij nostri, statim liberetis ab ipsa Prisona; Ita tamen quod Libertates ejusdem Villæ capiatis in manum nostram, & quod unusquisq; eorum sit plegius alterius, ad respondendum nobis a die S. Michaelis in xv dies ubicumq; tunc fuerimus in Anglia, super Transgressione facta apud Roffam; Et xiij l xijs xj d inventos in manibus ipsorum retineatis ad opus nostrum; Et dictos Computatores ponatis ad Scaccarium nostrum ubi fuerunt. Breve est in f. M. *Memor.* 33. *H.* 3. *Rot.* 9. *a.*

Winchester,

Winchester, the Treasurer; who assigned the same (except two Pence only) to the Use of the Exchequer, to remain there and in the Receipt, for Counters. And Part thereof, *viz.* xiij *s.* iiij *d.* were delivered to *Ambrose de Nuburg*, the Marshall for his Office, and other Part, *viz.* vj *s.* vj *d.* to *John Devery*, one of the Chamberlains of the Exchequer, for the Receipt, to remain at the Exchequer and be used for Counters (*w*).

(*w*) De Compotar[ijs] argenteis de Moneta Venis. datis per Thesaurarium, moraturis in Scaccario. Memorandum quod Rogerus Ardyngelli Mercator de Societate Bardorum de Florencia, die Jovis proxima post festum S. Michaelis hoc anno xij, venit coram Thesaurario & Baronibus de Scaccario, & tulit viginti solidos de Nova moneta de Venisis, qui excedunt ster[lingos] in pondere & valore, & eos dederunt Venerabili Patri J. Wyntoniensi Episcopo tunc Thesaurario, qui dictos xx solidos, præter duos denarios tantum, dedit & assignavit Curiæ isti, moraturos in Scaccario & in Recepta pro compotar[ijs.] Et de eisdem liberati fuerunt eodem die Ambrosio de Novo Burgo tunc Marescallo de Scaccario, pro officio suo, xiij s iiij d, Et Johanni Devery uni Camerar[iorum] de Scaccario pro Recepta vj s vj den. moraturi ibidem pro compotar[ijs] &c. *Hil. Commun.* 12 *E.* 2.

CHAP.

CHAP. XXIV.

Of the Officers *or* Ministers *of the* Exchequer.

I. *Introduction.*
II. *Of the two Remembrancers.*
III. *Of the Ingroffer of the Great Roll, and of the Comptroller.*
IV. *Of the Ufher.*
V. *Of the Conftable.*
VI. *Of the Marfhall.*
VII. *Of the Auditours.*
VIII. *Of the Clerks of Eftreats.*
IX. *Of the* Clericus Brevium.
X. *Of the Chamberlains.*
XI. *Of the Treafurer's Clerks.*
XII. *Of the Tellers.*
XIII. *Of the Pefour.*
XIV. *Of the Fufour.*

I. LET me now fpeak concerning the Officers or Minifters of the Exchequer. I fhall be very brief in what I fay concerning them, becaufe I intend to purfue the fame Method in this Cafe, which I have obferved in the foregoing Parts of this Hiftory; that is, I fhall fet down only fuch Things as I find in Records: In Truth, one is able to give but an imperfect Account of feveral Officers or of their Functions, efpecially during the firft Period and for fome time after. For in thofe Times they are (if I obferve right) commonly fpoken of in indefinite Terms, and not diftinguifhed from one another by a particular Name, or by a Character of their proper Office. The Clerks of the Great Exchequer or moft of them were then ufually comprehended under the general Name, of *Clericus Scaccarij*: And in like Manner the Clerks employed at the *Receipt*, or moft of them, under the general Style of *Clerici Thefaurarij & Camerariorum*, or *Clerici de Recepta*. I fpeak now of thofe Clerkfhips or Offices which were not Serjeanties. For the Serjeanties were eafily diftinguifhable from the reft. The Perfons following are refpectively

styled

styled *Clericus de Scaccario*; viz. *Richard de Staunford* (*a*), *Nicolas de Castello* (*b*), *Elias de Hereford* (*c*), *Hugh de Oyldebof* and *Laurence de London* (*d*), *Adam de Stratton* (*e*), *William de Rowell* (*f*), and *William Flore* (*g*). *Elias de Hereford* was a Remembrancer of the Exchequer before and at this Time (*h*); and so was *Nicolas de Castello*. The like Way of speaking was used in former Times concerning the Officers or Clerks of the King's Chancery. Then the Clerks of the Chancery, as well of higher as lower Rank, whose Offices have since been discriminated from one another by distinct and proper Names, were commonly called by the general Name of *Clerici Cancellariæ*; as sufficiently appeareth to them that are conversant in Records. Again, sometimes the Officers of the Exchequer are called *Ministri Regis de Scaccario* (*i*). For the Reasons mentioned here above, I shall discourse of the Officers of the Exchequer, under both Periods together. The principal Officers of the Great or Superiour Exchequer were, the two Remembrancers, the Ingrosser of the Great Roll, the Usher, the Constable, the Marshal, the Auditours, the Clerk of Estreats.

II. Of the Clerk or Officer called *Remembrancer, Memorator,* and *Rememorator*. There were anciently at the Exchequer two Remembrancers. As other Clerks of the Exchequer were sometimes called in general Terms, the King's Clerks [and other Ministers there, the King's Ministers of his Exchequer]: So the Remembrancers were, as it seems, sometimes called *Rememoratores Regis*. In the 38th Year of K. *Henry* III, the Sheriff of *Oxfordshire* was commanded to distrein the Bailiffs of *Richard* Earl of *Cornwall*, the Abbot of *Westminster*, and other Noblemen, to answer to the King, wherefore they do not distrein for the King's Debts within their Liberties, nor will permit the King's Bailiffs or the Sheriff to enter and distrein for the said Debts. A Roll containing the Names of those Noblemen was laid up in the Chest of the King's Remembrancer at the Ex-

(*a*) *Mich Recognitiones* 56. *H*.3. *Rot*. 8. *a*.
(*b*) *Ib. Rot*. 8. *a*.
(*c*) *Ib. Rot*. 8. *a*.
(*d*) *Ib. Rot*. 8. *b*.
(*e*) *Ib. Rot*. 8. *b*.
(*f*) *Hil. Recogn*. 56. *H*. 3. *Rot*. 9. *a*.
(*g*) *Pas. Recogn. ib. Rot*. 10. *a*.
(*h*) Recognitio Henrici de Boclaunde. Idem venit coram Baronibus, & recognovit se teneri Elyæ de Hereford Rememoratori de Scaccario Regis in xx solidis, solvendis eidem in crastino Animarum ———. *Mich. Recognit*. 56. *H*. 3. *Rot*. 8. *a*. *In this Roll*, paulo infra, Elias de Hereford *is styled* Clericus de Scaccario. *He is called* Elyas de Hertford Rememorator Scaccarij; *Hil. Recognit. ib. Rot*. 9. *a*.
(*i*) *Ryl. Plac. Parl. p*. 256. 33. *E*. 1.

chequer.

chequer (*k*). Or perhaps this *Memorator Regis* might be the particular Officer who has been since called the King's Remembrancer. Again, one of them was called *Unus Rememoratorum*, and the other *Alter Rememoratorum*. *Nicolas de Castle* was the *Unus*, and Master *Odo de Westminstre* was the *Alter* (*l*).

In the 19th of K. *Edward* I, an Entry was made in the Roll of one of the Remembrancers. About seven Years after the Matter of this Entry came to be questioned. The Chancellour of the Exchequer and three of the Barons, who were Chancellour and Barons in the said 19th Year, declared expresly that they knew nothing of it; but did believe it was written by *John de Kyrkeby*, the Remembrancer (for it was in his Hand) by Order of the Bishop of *Bath* and *Wells*, who was then Treasurer. And *John de Kyrkeby* declared, that he wrote it by the Order of the said Treasurer (*m*). Here *John de Kyrkeby* is styled a Remembrancer; but it doth not appear which of the two he was.

In Process of Time, one of them came to be called the *King's Remembrancer*, the other the *Treasurer's Remembrancer*. And their Offices were distinct. As doth sufficiently appear by the distinct Remembrances or Bundles of *Memoranda*, which have been made up in their respective Offices, and remain there from very antient Time to this Day. On the 26th Day of *February*, in the 27th Year of K. *Edward* I, *Walter* Bishop of *Coventry* and *Lichfeld*, the Treasurer, delivered to *Robert de Balliol*, Sheriff of *Northumberland*, the Transcript of an Ordinance and Extent of the Town of *Berwick upon Tweed*, in five Rolls, under the Seal of *John de Kyrkeby*, the King's

(*k*) Oxon. Mandatum est Vicecomiti, quod venire faciat in crastino Animarum, Ballivos R. Comitis Cornubiæ, Abbatis Westmonasterij in Istlep, & aliorum Magnatum quorum nomina continentur in rotulo quod est in cista Memoratoris Regis ad Scaccarium, ad respondendum Regi de hoc quod non distringunt pro debitis Regis infra Libertates suas, nec permittunt Ballivos Regis nec Vicecomitem ingredi ad distringendum pro prædictis debitis. Et habeat breve. *Memor.* 38. *H.* 3. *Rot.* 1. *b.*

(*l*)—Nicholao de Castello uni Rememoratorum Scaccarij nostri —— & Magistro Odoni de Westminstre alteri Rememoratorum ejusdem Scaccarij nostri ——. *Lib.* 14. *E.* 1. *m.* 3.

(*m*) Et eo comperto & per Thesaurarium & Barones inspecto, Philippus de Wyllughby Cancellarius de Scaccario, Johannes de Cobeham, Willelmus de Carleton, & Petrus de Leycestre Barones de eodem Scaccario, qui fuerunt Barones prædicto anno xix° & extunc deinceps, præcise dicunt & recordati sunt, quod nunquam sciebant de Concessione prædicta quousque facta & inserta fuit in Rotulis prædictis, ex manu Johannis de Kyrkeby Rememoratoris, qui eam scripsit, ut pro certo intendunt, ex præcepto W. Bathoniensis & Wellensis Episcopi; Et idem Johannes super hoc allocutus, dicit quod scripsit Concessionem prædictam ex præcepto dicti Thesaurarij —. *Pas. Commun. in bund.* 26 & 27. *E.* 1. *Rot.* 23. *a.*

Remembrancer of the Exchequer (*n*). At this Time there was also an Officer called Treasurer's Remembrancer, *Rememorator Thesaurarij*. *John le Boteler*, an Attorney of the *Common Bench*, delivered into the Exchequer, by Command of the Treasurer and Barons, a Charter made to *Robert Burnel*, late Bishop of *Bath* and *Wells*, of the Homage and Service of *Roger de Owelton*. And that Charter was left in the Custody of the Treasurer's Remembrancer (*o*). K. *Henry* III (*anno regni* 35) granted to *Roger de la Leye* the yearly Fee of xx *l*. payable at the two Exchequers of *Michaelmass* and *Easter*, so long as he continued in the Office of a Remembrancer at the Exchequer, until the King provided better for him [in some Ecclesiastical Benefice] (*p*).

In *Trinity* Term, in the 18th Year of K. *Edward* I. *Richard de Luda* was a Remembrancer (*q*): and in the same Term *Nicolas de Castello* was a Remembrancer (*r*). On St. *Martin*'s Day, in the 21st Year of K. *Edward* I. *John de Kyrkeby* was admitted to the Office of Remembrancer in the Exchequer; and was sworn before the Treasurer and Barons (*s*). *John de Kyrkeby* had been a Remembrancer of the Exchequer for several Years in the Reign of K. *Edward* I. And K.

(*n*) Memorandum quod xxvj die Februarij anno xxvj°, liberata fuerunt per manus W. Coventrensis & Lichfeldensis Episcopi Thesaurarij, Roberto de Balliolo Vicecomiti Norhumbriæ, transcriptum Ordinationis & Extentæ Villæ Berewici super Twedam, in quinque Rotulis, sub sigillo Johannis de Kirkeby Rememoratoris Regis de Scaccario sigillata, ad deferendum Waltero de Agmondesham Cancellario Regis de partibus Scociæ. *Hil. Communia* 26 & 27. *E*. 1. *Rot*. 13. *a*.

(*o*) Bedfordia. — Et est carta prædicta in quadam pixide in custodia Rememoratoris Thesaurarij. *Hil. Commun*. 26 & 27. *E*. 1. *Rot*. 14. *b*.

(*p*) Rex omnibus &c, salutem; Sciatis quod commisimus dilecto Clerico nostro Rogero de la Leye xx libras, annuatim percipiendas ad Scaccarium nostrum ad duos terminos, videlicet medietatem ad Scaccarium Sancti Michaelis, & Medietatem ad Scaccarium Paschæ, quamdiu moratus fuerit in Officio Rememoratoris ad idem Scaccarium nostrum, donec eidem Rogero uberius providerimus. In cujus &c; Teste Rege apud Westm. xj° die Maij. *Pat*. 35. *H*. 3. *m*. 11.

(*q*) Luda. xxxj die Maij. Hic venit Ricardus de Luda loco Remembrancar[ij]. *This is written in a large Hand in the Middle of the Roll, in two Places in the Bundle here cited, viz. Trinit. Commun*. 18. *E*. 1. *Rot*. — *b*. *and Trin. Recognit. ib. Rot*. — *b*. Idem [Johannes de Ingeham Miles] venit coram Baronibus, & recognovit se teneri Ricardo de Luda Rememoratori de Scaccario in xl s, solvendis &c. *Trin. Recogn*. 18. *E*. 1. *Rot*. — *b*.

(*r*) Ricardus de Arras venit coram Baronibus, & recognovit se teneri Nicholao de Castello Rememoratori de Scaccario & Magistro Petro de Guldeford in xiij s x d, solvendis — &c. *Trin. Recognit*. 18. *E*. 1. *Rot*. — *a*. Peter de Guldeford *is styled* Clericus de Scaccario. *Ib. eod. Rot*. *b*.

(*s*) De Officio Rememoratoris commisso. Memorandum quod die Sancti Martini Episcopi, anno Regni Regis Edwardi vicesimo finiente, incipiente vicesimo primo, admissus fuit Johannes de Kirkeby ad Officium Rememoratoris in Scaccario Domini Regis; & eodem die præstitit Sacramentum ad Scaccarium coram Thesaurario & Baronibus, quod bene & fideliter se habebit in Officio prædicto. *Mich. Communia* 21. *E*. 1. *Rot*. 6. *b*

Edward

Edward II. continued him in that Office during his Pleasure by the Writ hereunder recited (*t*). On the first Day of *March*, in the first Year of K. *Edward* II. *Walter de Bedewynde*, Clerk, was admitted to the Office of a Remembrancer of the Exchequer, in the Room of *John de Kyrkeby* deceased; and the same Day *Walter* was sworn before the Treasurer, Barons, and King's Council at the Exchequer (*u*). On *Monday* the 11th Day of *October*, in the 5th Year of K. *Edward* II. *William de Everdon* was admitted to the Office of Treasurer's Remembrancer in the Exchequer; and the same Day was sworn to behave himself well therein (*w*). In the same 5th Year, the King by his Writ of the Great Seal commanded the Treasurer and Barons to deliver to *Adam de Lymbergh*, Clerk, the Office of Remembrancer in the Exchequer, which *John de Cokermuth* lately held, to hold to *Adam* during the King's Pleasure. And on *Monday* next, after the Octaves of St. *Michael*, *Adam* came before the Treasurer and Barons, and by virtue of the said Writ was admitted and sworn into the said Office (*x*). K. *Edward* II. in the 15th Year of his Reign, sent to the Exchequer a Patent Writ of the Great Seal, whereby he committed to *Robert de Notingham* the Office of a Remembrancer of his Exchequer, which *Adam de Lymbergh* lately held; to hold during his Pleasure, with the

(*t*) Johanni de Kyrkebi Clerico per Regem. Quia Rex wlt quod idem Johannes officio Rememoratoris intendat quamdiu Regi placuerit, sicut tempore celebris memoriæ Domini E. quondam Regis Angliæ patris Regis intendit: Mandat eidem Johanni, quod omnibus alijs prætermissis, ad dictum Scaccarium apud Westmonasterium ad cicius quod poterit accedat, ad faciendum officium prædictum. T. Rege apud Clipston xx die Septembris anno primo. Per breve de Magno Sigillo. *Mich. Commun.* 1. *E.* 2. *Rot.* 16. *a.*

(*u*) Die Veneris primo die Marcij hoc anno primo, Walterus de Bedewynde Clericus admissus fuit ad officium Rememoratoris Regis in Scaccario loco Johannis de Kyrkeby nuper defuncti, qui fuerat unus Rememoratorum in Scaccario prædicto. Et eodem die præfatus Walterus, coram Thesaurario & Baronibus & alijs de Consilio Regis in eodem Scaccario præsentibus, præstitit Sacramentum de bene & fideliter se habendo in officio antedicto. *Hil. Commun.* 1. *E.* 2. *Rot.* 40. *a.*

(*w*) Memorandum quod modo die Lunæ proximo post octabas S. Michaelis videlicet xj die octobris, Willelmus de Everdon admissus fuit ad officium Rememoratoris Thesaurarij in Scaccario. Et eodem die præstitit sacramentum de bene & fideliter se habendo in officio prædicto. *Mich. Commun.* 5. *E.* 2. *Rot.* 23. *a.*

(*x*) De officio Rememoratoris commisso. Memorandum quod Dominus Rex mandavit Thesaurario & Baronibus breve suum de Magno Sigillo datum apud Londoniam viij die octobris hoc anno quinto, quod est inter Communia de hoc anno, quod ipsi Thesaurarius & Barones liberent Adæ de Lymbergh Clerico officium Remembranciæ cum pertinentijs in Scaccario, quod Johannes de Kokermuth habuit, & quod Rex concessit eidem Adæ, Habendum quamdiu Regi placuerit &c. Prædictus Adam modo die Lunæ proxima post octabas S. Michaelis venit coram præfatis Thesaurario & Baronibus, & prætextu brevis prædicti idem Adam admissus est ad officium prædictum, & præstitit sacramentum de bene & fideliter se habendo &c. *Mich. Commun.* 5. *E.* 2. *Rot.* 18. *a.*

accustomed

accustomed Fee of that Office. He also sent a Close Writ of the Great Seal, whereby he commanded the Treasurer and Barons to admit *Robert* into that Office, and to deliver to him the Rolls and *Memoranda* belonging to it. Accordingly *Robert*, being present in Court, was sworn; and had the said Rolls and *Memoranda* delivered to him (*y*). *John de Kyrkeby*, one of the Remembrancers of the Exchequer, was sent into *Gloucestershire* to survey, hasten, and ascertain the Debts due to the King in that County (*z*). K. *Edward* I. in the 13th Year of his Reign, by Writ of *Liberate* assigned to *Nicolas de Castello*, one of his Remembrancers of his Exchequer, ten Marks, for the Charges and Expences which *Nicolas* and his Clerks had been at in making-out the Summonces of the Exchequer (*a*); and in the 15th Year of his Reign, ten Pounds more for the like Service (*b*). K. *Edward* II. in the 10th Year of his Reign, in respect of the good Service done by *William de Everdon* in the Office of a Remembrancer of the Exchequer, granted him xx *l.* a-Year *de Dono*, besides the Fee belonging to his Office, until the King should provide him an Eccle-

(*y*) Dominus Rex mandavit hic breve suum de Magno Sigillo suo patens in hæc verba: Rex omnibus ad quos &c salutem; Sciatis quod commisimus dilecto Clerico nostro Roberto de Notingham, officium Rememoratoris Scaccarij nostri quod dilectus clericus noster Adam de Lymbergh nuper habuit; habendum quamdiu nobis placuerit; percipiendo in eodem officio feodum consuetum. In c r th L n f f P; T. me ipso apud Thorpe Episcopi, xxj die Junij anno Regni quintodecimo. Per ipsum Regem nunciante Thesaurario: Et similiter breve suum clausum sub eodem Sigillo, per quod mandat Thesaurario & Baronibus, quod ipsum Robertum ad officium illud admittant, & Rotulos & memoranda prædictum officium tangencia ei habere faciant &c. Et idem Robertus præsens hic in Curia, modo xxij die Junij, præstitit Sacramentum de bene & fideliter se habendo &c. Et eodem die ei liberantur Rotuli & omnia alia Memoranda dictum officium tangencia &c. *Trin. Communia* 15. *E.* 2. *Rot.* 25. *a. Et vid. Trin. Brevia* 15. *E.* 2. *Rot.* 60. *b.*

(*z*) Et super hoc, Johannes de Kirkeby unus Rememoratorum de eodem Scaccario præsens hic in Curia testatur, quod quando ipse ultimo extitit in Comitatu prædicto [Gloucestriæ], pro debitis Regis quibuscunq; supervidendis festinandis & discutiendis, compertum & discussum fuit coram eo, quod prædictæ xxij l non conprehendebantur in atterminatione prædicta, & quod ipse injunxit eidem Vicecomiti quod debitum prædictum ad opus Regis celeriter levari faceret —. *Pas. Memor.* 34. *E.* 1. *Rot.* 31. *a. in bund.* 33 & 34. *E.* 1. *parte* 1.

(*a*) Rex Thesaurario & Camerarijs suis salutem. Liberate de thesauro nostro, dilecto Clerico nostro Nicholao de Castello, uni rememoratorum nostrorum Scaccarij nostri, decem marcas, quas ei concessimus pro expensis & misis, quas ipse & Clerici sui nuper fecerunt circa summonitiones prædicti Scaccarij faciendas. T. R. apud Bristoll xxvij die Decembris. *Lib.* 13. *E.* 1. *m.* 8.

(*b*) Rex Thes. & Camer. suis salutem. Liberate de thesauro nostro Nicholao de Castello uni rememoratorum Scaccarij nostri, decem libras, quas ei concessimus pro misis & expensis, quas ipse & clerici sui nuper fecerunt, circa Summonitiones Scaccarij nostri faciendas. T. Edmundo Comite Cornubiæ Consanguineo nostro apud Westm. xxiiij die Octobris. Per Thesaurarium. *Lib.* 15. *E.* 1. *m.* 1.

siastical

Chap. XXIV. *of the* Exchequer.

fiastical Benefice suitable to his Degree (c). In the 6th Year of K. *Edward* II. *Adam de Limbergh*, one of the Remembrancers, had xx *l.* yearly Stipend allowed to him by the Crown, for executing his Office (d); and *William de Everdon*, the other Remembrancer, xl Marks yearly Stipend for himself and his Clerks (e).

III. The Engrosser of the *Great Roll* was a most ancient and a considerable Officer in the Exchequer. His Office is, for ought that appears, as ancient as the Exchequer itself; that is, when the Exchequer was first instituted in *England*, then some Person or Persons was or were employed to write the *Great Rolls*. Insomuch, that one can hardly form a distinct Notion of an Exchequer, without two Things, to wit, a *Chequered Board*, and a *Great Roll*; which two Things have been steadily retained through the Course of several Ages, wherein the Exchequer hath undergone some Alterations in other Particulars. It is true, the Stile or Name of *Engrosser* of the *Great Roll* doth not, for ought that I know, occur in the most ancient Times next after the Conquest. However, the coeval Antiquity of his Office is, I suppose, sufficiently evinced by the coeval *Great Rolls* which still remain.

In the third Year of K. *Edward* I. *Richard de Staunford* and *Robert de Walmesford* were *Writers* of the *Great Roll (f)*. In the 4th Year of K. *Edward* I. the Barons enjoined the said *Richard de Staunford*, a Clerk of the Exchequer, to go and take the Nomination of an Attorney of *Philipp de Paunton*, in a Plea of Debt depending between him and the Men of *Graham* (g). K. *Edward* I. in the 30th Year

(c) *Pat.* 10. *E.* 2. *par.* 2. *m.* 22.

(d) Liberate de thesauro nostro dilecto Clerico nostro Adæ de Limbergh, uni rememoratorum Scaccarij nostri decem libras, de termino S. Michaelis proximo præterito, de annuo feodo suo viginti librarum quod ei concessimus percipiendum in officio supradicto. T. Rege apud Wyndesore viij° die Novembris. *Liberate* 6. *Edw.* 2. *m.* 3. & *Ib. m.* 2.

(e) Liberate de thesauro nostro Willelmo de Everdon, uni rememoratorum Scaccarij nostri viginti marcas, de termino S. Michaelis proximo præterito, de annuo feodo suo quadraginta marcarum, quod ei concessimus ad sustentationem suam & clericorum secum in officio illo existentium. T. Rege apud Wyndesore xxviij die Novembris. *Ib. m.* 3. & *Ib. m.* 2.

(f) Peter de Montfort *made a Deed of Quit-claimance to K.* Edward I. *It ends*,— præsenti scripto sigillum meum apposui in præsencia Fratris J. de Kauncy tunc dicti Domini Regis Thesaurarij, Johannis de Sancto Walerico & Rogeri de Nortwode Baron[um], Rogeri de la Leye, Magistri Odonis, Nicholai de Castello Rem[emoratorum], Ricardi de Staunford & Roberti de Walmesford Scriptorum Magni Rotuli, & aliorum. Datum in Scaccario in festo S. Edmundi Martiris anno regni Regis tercio. *Mich. Commun.* 4. *E.* 1. *Rot.* 5. *a.*

(g) Injunctum est Ricardo de Staunford Clerico de Scaccario, quod capiat attornatum Philippi de Paunton versus Homines de Graham & alios, de placito debiti. *Trin. Commun.* 4. *E.* 1. *Rot.* 10. *a.*

of

of his Year, by Letter Patent, committed to *Nicolas de Balscote* the Office of the *Grossaria* [or Engrossership] which *William le Deveneys* lately had in the Exchequer of *Dublin,* to hold during his Pleasure: and by a Close Writ commanded the Treasurer and Barons of the said Exchequer to give him Possession of that Office (*h*). K. Edward II. in the first Year of his Reign, sent a Writ of the Great Seal to *Hugh de Notingham,* Clerk; reciting, that the King willed that the said *Hugh* should execute the Office of Keepership of the Great Rolls of the Exchequer during the King's Pleasure, in like Manner as he had done in the Reign of K. *Edward* I; and commanding *Hugh* forthwith to repair to the Exchequer at *Westminster* to execute the said Office (*i*). In the 52d Year of K. *Henry* III. *Robert de Verun,* late Sheriff of *Wiltshire,* was amerced before the Barons of the Exchequer at C *s.* for a Contempt. This Sum was by the Treasurer and Barons assigned to *William de Rowell,* Clerk, for writing the *Great Roll* of the first Year of K. *Edward* I. And a Writ of *Fieri facias* issued to the Sheriff to enable him to levy it upon the Goods and Chatells of the said *Robert* (*k*). In the 19th Year of K. *Edward* II. an Order was made for increasing the Stipends of the Engrosser of the Exchequer and of the Remembrancer. It seems, in *Trinity* Term, in the 16th Year of the King, by virtue of a Writ directed to the Treasurer and Barons in that Behalf, a Provision was made at *York* for regulating certain Things in the Exchequer. The Articles of that Provision were entered in the *Red-Book* remaining in the Custody of the King's

(*h*) Rex omnibus ad quos &c salutem. Sciatis quod commisimus dilecto nobis Nicholao de Balscote Clerico, Officium grossariæ quod Willelmus le Deveneys habuit in Scaccario nostro Dublini: Habendum cum omnibus ad officium illud spectantibus & custodiendum quamdiu nobis placuerit. In c &c; T. R. apud Grenewyz xxv die Maij. Per breve de Privato Sigillo.

Et mandatum est Thesaurario & Baronibus de Scaccario Dublini, quod eidem Nicholao officium illud liberent: Habendum & custodiendum in forma prædicta; T. ut supra. *Pat.* 30. *E.* 1. *m.* 22.

(*i*) Hugoni de Notingham Clerico per Regem. Quia Rex wlt quod idem H. Officio Custodiæ Magnorum Rotulorum de Scaccario intendat quamdiu Regi placuerit, sicut tempore celebris memoriæ Domini E. quondam Regis Angliæ Patris Regis intendit: Mandat eidem Hugoni quod omnibus alijs prætermissis, ad dictum Scaccarium apud Westmon. ad cicius quod poterit accedat, ad faciendum Officium supradictum. T. Rege apud Clipston xx die Septembris anno primo. Per Breve de Magno Sigillo. *Mich. Commun.* 1. *E.* 2. *Rot.* 16. *a. inter Brevia.*

(*k*) Memorandum quod Centum solidi ad quos Robertus de Verun quondam Vicecomes Wyltesiræ amerciatus fuit coram Baronibus de Scaccario anno regni Regis H. Lij° pro contemptu, assignantur Willelmo de Rowell Clerico per Thesaurarium & Barones, pro Magno Rotulo Regis Edwardi scribendo in æstate anno isto. Et præceptum est Vicecomiti Wiltesiræ, quod de bonis & catallis ejusdem Roberti fieri faciat prædictos denarios. *Memor.* 1. *E.* 1. *Rot.* 7. *b.*

Remembrancer. Part of thofe Articles relates to the Engroffer's Office. And therein it is fet-forth, that the Great Roll of one Year was now larger than it was wont to be in three or four Years in the Time of the King's Anceftours; that there were feveral Accounts for former Years ftill in Arere; and that the Bufinefs in the faid Exchequer daily increafed. And therefore it was ordained, that two Clerks, who were to be at the King's Wages, fhould be employed to engrofs the foreign Accounts in Aid of the faid Engroffer, until the Affairs of the Exchequer could be put into a better Method of Difpatch. Other Part of the Articles relates to the Treafurer's Remembrancer's Office. Therein it is fet-forth, that the Bufinefs of the faid Office was very much increafed in the prefent King's Reign, and did daily increafe; that therefore it was as laborious to write the Rolls and Writs of that Office for one Year, as for five or fix Years in the Time of the King's Progenitours; and that the faid Remembrancer's Fee for executing his Office, was no more than what was accuftomed in the Time of the faid Progenitours. And therefore it was ordered that the faid Remembrancer, befides the ufual Fee, fhould have and receive of the King yearly, by Advifement with the Treafurer and Barons for the Time being, a competent Sum for reteining of two more Clerks, befides thofe which he hath already, to difpatch the Bufinefs of the faid Office; and that this Order fhould be obferved till further Meafures could be taken. But in regard it was not exprefsly mentioned in the faid Articles, how much the faid Engroffer and Remembrancer fhould receive for the Maintenance of the faid two Clerks; now, in this prefent *Trinity* Term, in the 19th Year of the King, the Archbifhop of *York*, Treafurer, and the Barons of the Exchequer, upon Confideration of the Cafe, unanimoufly agreed and ordered, that the faid Engroffer and Remembrancer, befides the accuftomed Salary for their refpective Offices, fhould each of them, in Relief of their Expences, receive for the Maintenance of two Clerks twelve Marks yearly, from the Time of the faid Ordinances; and fo from henceforward till further Directions fhould be given therein (*l*).

IV. The Office of *Ufher* of the Exchequer was a very ancient and an hereditary Office. K. *Henry* II. by his Charter granted to *Roger de Warenguefort* the Miniftry of the Chief Ufhery of his Exchequer, with the Appurtenances; to hold to *Roger* and his Heirs, as amply as

(*l*) *Trin. Communia* 19, *E.* 2. *Rot.* 6. *b.*

any other held it in the Time of K. *Henry* I (*m*). This Office was vested in the said *Roger* and his Heirs; and was holden of the King and his Heirs by Serjeanty, as will appear hereafter in this Section. The Chief or Hereditary Usher had several Persons that acted under him in the Great Exchequer, in the Exchequer of the *Jews*, and in the Common Bank. In the 37th Year of K. *Henry* III. *Roger del Escheker* was seised of this Office. He committed a great Trespass against the King. And for that Cause, the King, by a Writ of the Great Seal, commanded the Barons of the Exchequer to seize the said *Roger*'s Bailywick or Office into the King's Hand, and to remove all his Under-ushers: and by another Writ of the Great Seal the King commanded the Justices of the Common Bench to seize into his Hand the Bailywick which the said *Roger* had in the Common Bench: and all the Lands belonging to the said Serjeanty were likewise taken into the King's Hand (*n*). Many curious and uncommon Memoires relating to this Office do occur in Records. I shall set down a few of them; taking Notice of the Succession of Ushers, which is, I suppose, deducible from *Roger de Walingford* abovenamed. In the second Year of K. *Henry* II. the Sheriffs of *London*, by virtue of the King's Writ in that Behalf, paid to *Roger* the *Ostiarius de Thesauro* xxviij s. v d. for his Livery or Corrody (*o*): and in the same Year, the Sheriff of *Kent* paid to the said *Roger* a Mark of Silver, by Order of the Bishop of *Ely*, a Justicier or Baron of the Exchequer (*p*). In the 7th Year of K. *Henry* II. the same *Roger* was Usher of the Exchequer (*q*): and

(*m*) H. Rex Anglsiæ] &c. Sciatis quod ego dedi Rogero de Warenguefort servienti meo ministerium de Hostieria de Scaccario meo, pro servicio suo, cum omnibus pertinentijs eidem ministerio. Quare volo & firmiter præcipio, quod idem Rogerus & hæredes sui, habeant & teneant prædictum ministerium de Magistratu Hostieriæ de Scaccario meo, bene & in pace, & honorifice, & libere & quiete, sicut aliquis illud melius habuit tempore H. Regis avi mei, quod nullus de eodem ministerio se intromittat nisi per eum. T. Warino filio Geroldi, Man. Biset, Willelmo filio Hamonis, Mag. Alueredo, apud Pontem Aldomari. *Chart. Antiq.* J. *in dorso nu.* 25. *tit.* Carta Rogeri de Walingeford.

(*n*) De Balliva Rogeri de Scaccario capta in manum Regis. Mandatum est Baronibus de Scaccario, quod Ballivam quam Rogerus de Lescheker habet ad Scaccarium Regis, capiant in manum Regis pro transgressione quam idem Rogerus Regi fecit, & ipsum & omnes servientes suos amoveant a balliva illa. T. Rege apud Portesmuth xxj die Julij. Eodem modo mandatum est Justiciarijs de Banco, de Balliva quam habet in Banco; T. ut supra. Et omnes terras ad eandem Serjantiam spectantes capiant in manum Domini Regis, & salvo custodiant donec &c. T. ut supra. *Cl.* 37. *H.* 3. *m.* 5.

(*o*) Et in liberatione Rogeri Ostiarij de Thesauro, xxviij s & v d, per breve Regis. *Mag. Rot.* 2. *Hen.* 2. *Rot.* 1. *a.* Lundonia.

(*p*) Et Rogero Ostiario j marca argenti, præcepto Episcopi Eliensis. *Ib. Rot.* 12. *b.* Chent.

(*q*) Et Rogero Ostiario de Thesauro, iij s & iiij d. *Mag. Rot.* 7. *H.* 2. *Rot.* 7. *a.* Cant. & Hunt.

Chap. XXIV. *of the* EXCHEQUER.

in the 12th Year of the fame King (*r*). In the 13th, 14th, and 15th Year of that King, *Elias* was Ufher of the Exchequer, and had the Care of conveying the Summonces that iffued for levying the King's Debts throughout *England* (*s*). Peradventure the Ufhery (it being held of the King *in Capite* by Serjeanty) was now in the King's Hand by the Death of *Roger* the Ufher, whofe Children were under Age, and his Widow in the King's Donation. For in the 16th Year of that King, *Elias* the Ufher fined in xx Marks, that he might have the Widow of *Roger* the Ufher and his Office, until *Roger*'s Children fhould come to full Age (*t*). In the 21ft Year, the Sheriffs of *London* paid to *Elias* the Ufher one Mark, towards his Charges in tranfmitting the Summonces for *Danegeld* through *England* (*u*). In the 22d Year of that King, *Elias* the Ufher paid all that was behind of his Fine of xx Marks, for the Wife and Office of *Roger* the Ufher (*w*). In the 29th Year, *Elias* the Ufher was allowed xij *d*. for Wax to feal the Writs of Summonces, and a Mark for tranfmitting the Summonces through *England* (*x*). In the 31ft Year, *Elias* the Ufher had a Mark paid to him for conveying the Summonces through *England*, which were retornable in *Eafter* and *Michaelmafs* Term (*y*). In the fecond

---

(*r*) Et Rogero Oftiario xiij s & iiij d, ad portandas Summonitiones, & xij d pro Cera ad Summonitiones. — Et Rogero Oftiario j marcam, ad portandas alias Summonitiones; Et Aluredo ij s ad portandas Summonitiones ad Hantonam. *Mag. Rot.* 12. *H.* 2. *Rot.* 10. *b.* Lundonia & Midd.

(*s*) Et Helyæ Hoftiario j marca, pro portandis Summonitionibus per Angliam. *Mag. Rot.* 13. *H.* 2. *Rot.* 1. *a. Lundonia & Middelfexa.*

Et Helyæ Oftario j marcam, ad brevia Summonitionum portanda. *Mag. Rot.* 14. *H.* 2. *Rot.* 13. *b. tit.* Berrochefcira.

Et Helyæ Oftiario j marca, ad portandas Summonitiones per Angliam, per breve Regis. *Mag. Rot.* 15. *H.* 2. *Rot.* 12. *Lundonia & Midd.*

(*t*) Helyas Oftiarius debet xx marcas, pro habenda uxore Rogeri Oftiarij & pro Minifterio fuo quoufq; pueri Rogeri ætatem habeant. *Mag. Rot.* 16. *H.* 2. *Rot.* 2. *b. Buk. & Bed.*

(*u*) Et Heliæ Oftiario j marcam, ad portandas Summonitiones de Danegeldo per Angliam, per breve Regis. *Mag. Rot.* 21.

H. 2. *Rot.* 3. *a. Londonia & Middilfexa.*

(*w*) Helyas Oftiarius reddit compotum de ij marcis, pro habenda uxore Rogeri Oftiarij, et pro Minifterio fuo quoufq; pueri Rogeri ætatem habeant ; In Thefauro liberavit, Et Quietus eft. *Mag. Rot.* 22. *H.* 2. *Rot.* 2. *a. Bukingehamfcira & Bedef.*

(*x*) Et Helyæ Oftiario xij d, ad emendam Ceram ad Summonitiones figillandas, per breve Regis ; Et eidem j marcam ad eafdem Summonitiones deferendas per Angliam, per idem breve in Termin. S. Michaelis ; Et eidem Helyæ j marcam ad deferendas Summonitiones per Angliam, per breve Regis, in Termin. Pafchæ. *Mag. Rot.* 29. *H.* 2. *Rot.* 13. *b. Londonia & Midd.*

(*y*) Et Elyæ Oftiario j marcam, ad deferendas Summonitiones per Angliam contra terminum Pafchæ, per breve Regis ; Et eidem xij d ad ceram ad eafdem Summonitiones figillandas, per idem breve ; Et item eidem Elyæ j marcam ad deferendas Summonitiones contra feftum S. Michaelis, per breve Regis. *Mag. Rot.* 31. *H.* 2. *Rot.* 14. *b. Londonia & Midd.*

Year of K. *Richard* I. two Marks were paid to *Elias* the Usher for transmitting the Summonces twice in that Year (*z*). In the 3d Year of K. *Richard* I. *Laurence* was Usher of the Exchequer; and had three Marks for conveying the Summonces over *England* three Times, and two Shillings for Wax to seal them (*a*). In the 4th Year of that King, *Laurence* the Usher was paid Lxvj *s* xj *d* for the like Service (*b*). In the 5th Year, *Laurence* the Usher had one Mark paid to him, for sending the Writs of Summonce to the Sheriffs of *England*, for geting-in the King's Money that was to be paid for the Ransom of his Person (*c*). In the same 5th Year, there was paid to *Laurence* the Usher xx *s*. for conveying over *England* the King's Summonces for calling a Council to meet at *Oxford*; to *Thomas* the Writer of *Hugh Peverell*, two Marks and a half, for a Horse to carry to *Gloucester* the Rolls and Summonces which *Hugh* and he had written; and to the *Spigurnell* iij *s* iiij *d*, for Wax to seal the Summonces, which were sent to the Barons all over *England*, for the Army of *Gloucester* (*d*). In the 6th Year, *Laurence* the Usher received a Mark, for transmitting the King's Summonces to the King's Barons, whereby they were enjoined to come before the King at *Southwell* (*e*). In the 8th Year of the same King, *John de Wika* was Usher of the Exchequer. There was paid to him one Mark, for conveying the King's Summonces for Aids, Hidages, and Tallages over *England*; and xij *d* for Wax to seal those Summonces; and to *Thomas*, *Hugh Peverell*'s Clerk, ij *s* vj *d*,

---

(*z*) Et Elyæ Ostiario ij marcas, pro Summonitionibus portandis ij vicibus, per breve Regis. *Mag. Rot.* 2. *Ric.* 1. *Rot.* 12. *b*. *Londonia & Midd*.

(*a*) Et Laurentio Ostiario de Scaccario iij marcas, ad deferendas Summonitiones per Angliam tribus vicibus; Per iij Brevia Regis; Et pro Cera ad prædictas Summonitiones sigillandas ij s, Per prædicta Brevia. *Mag. Rot.* 3. *R.* 1. *Rot.* 11. *a*. *Londonia & Middelsexa*.

(*b*) Et Laurentio Ostiario Lxvj s & xj d, ad deferendas Summonitiones Regis de Scaccario per totam Angliam per diversos terminos, Et pro Cera ad easdem Summonitiones sigillandas, Per brevia Regis. *Mag. Rot.* 4. *R.* 1. *Rot.* 11. *b*. *Londonia & Midd*.

(*c*) Et item Laurentio Ostiario j marca, ad deferendas Summonitiones per Angliam de Pecunia Regis congreganda ad deliberationem Regis, per breve Regis. *Mag. Rot.* 5. *R.* 1. *Rot.* 12. *b*. *Londonia & Middelsexa*.

(*d*) Et Laurentio Ostiario xx s ad deferendas Summonitiones Regis per Angliam pro Concilio convocando apud Oxinefordiam, Per breve Regis; Et Tomæ Scriptori Hugonis Peverelli ij marcas & dimidiam, pro j Equo ad deferendos Rotulos & Summonitiones factas per eosdem, apud Gloecestriam, Per breve Regis; Et Spigurnello iij s & vj d, pro Cera quam invenit ad sigillandas Summonitiones, quæ missæ fuerunt ad Barones per Angliam propter Exercitum de Gloecestria, Per breve Regis. *Ibid. Rot.* 12. *b*. *Londonia & Midd*.

(*e*) Et Laurentio Ostiario j marcam, ad deferendas Summonitiones Regis Baronibus Regis, veniendi coram Rege apud Sudwell; Per breve Regis. *Mag. Rot.* 6. *R.* 1. *Rot.* 12. *b. Tit*. *Londonia & Middelsexa*.

for his Corrody for six Days whilst he wrote the said Summonces *(f)*. In the 6th Year of K. *John, Laurence* Son of *Alienor* fined to the King in Lx Marks and one Palfrey, that he might have his Inheritance, the Ushery of the Exchequer at *Westminster*, with the Appurtenances *(g)*. In the 2d Year of K. *Henry* III. *William Druell* fined in C Marks and a Palfrey, to have the Office late of *Laurence* the Usher of the Exchequer, and to have the Wardship of the Land and Heirs of the said *Laurence*, with the Marriage of them and of the said *Laurence*'s Widow *(h)*. In the 27th Year, a Writ issued to the *Custos* of the Honour of *Walingford*, commanding him to respite, till his next Account, the Demand which he made on *Roger*, the Usher of the Exchequer, of military Service for his Land of *Eston*, and to shew Cause before the Barons at that Day, why he demanded such Service, in regard *Roger* did not hold the said Land of the Honour of *Walingford*, but by the Serjeanty of Ushery of the Exchequer, as it was found by Inquisition *(i)*. *Roger* was Usher in the next Year (*viz.* the 28th of K. *Henry* III) *(k)*. In the 33d Year, in regard *Matthew de Wikes*, Usher of the King's Exchequer, was attending at the said Exchequer on *Friday* next after the Feast of St. *Matthew* the Apostle, so that he could not appear at the Court of *Hese* to do Suit there, the King by Writ commanded the Bailiffs of *Hese* not to put him in Default for his Absence on that Day, because the King warranted him for that Day. Perhaps *Matthew de Wikes* might be an Under-usher *(l)*. On *Monday* next after the Octaves of the *H. Trinity*, in the 40th Year of K. *Henry* III. *Roger del Exchequer* came before the Barons, and presented *Nicholas de Winton*, to execute in his Stead the Office of Ushery during the Life of *Nicholas*, provided he behaved himself well and truly in the said Office. *Nicholas* was sworn and admitted

---

(f) Et Johanni de Wika j marcam ad deferendas Summonitiones Regis de Auxilijs, & Hidagijs, & Tallagijs, per Angliam; Per Breve Regis. Et eidem xij d propter Ceram quam invenit ad præfatas Summonitiones sigillandas; Per idem breve. Et Tomæ Clerico Hugonis Peverelli ij s & vj d, de Liberatione sua vj dierum, quibus scripsit prædictas Summonitiones; Per idem breve. *Mag. Rot.* 8. *R.* 1. *Rot.* 23. *b. Tit. Londonia & Middelsexa.*

(g) Laurentius filius Alienoræ r c de Lx marcis & j Palefrido, Pro habenda hæreditate sua de Ostio Scaccarij de Westmonasterio cum pertinentijs suis. *Mag. Rot.* 6. *Joh.* *Rot.* 8. *a. Londonia & Middelsexa.*

(h) Willelmus Druellus [debet] C marcas & j palefridum, pro habendo officio quod fuit Laurencij Hostiarij de Scaccario, & pro habenda custodia Terræ & hæredum ipsius Laurencij cum maritagio eorum & uxoris quæ fuit ejusdem Laurencij. *Mag. Rot.* 2. *H.* 3. *Rot.* 6. *b. Buk. & Bedef.*

(i) Mich. Communia 27. *H.* 3. *Rot.* 4. *b.*

(k) Cyrographum inter Johannem Malherbe & Rogerum Hostiarium de Scaccario. *The Chirograph is recorded at large. Ex Memorand.* 28. *H.* 3. *Rot.* 2. *a.*

(l) Memoranda 33. *H.* 3. *Rot.* 4. *b.*

the same Day in Form aforesaid (*m*). In the 52d Year of the same King, *Roger del Eschequer* was Chief Usher, and *Nicholas de Winton* and *Simon de Creton* were his Deputy-ushers. *Roger* came before the Barons, and presented *Simon de Creton* to the Office of an Usher, in the Room of *Taylefer* the Usher deceased. At this Time, a Writ issued to the Sheriff of *Oxfordshire*, reciting, that it appeared by Inquisition, that *Roger del Exchequer* and his Ancestours held their Land of *Eston* in the County of *Oxford*, of the King and his Ancestours, Kings of *England*, by the Service of keeping the Door of the King's Exchequer, and not by Knight's Service of the Honour of *Wallingford*; and therefore the King commanded the Sheriff by that Writ, to surcease the Demand which the Bailiffs of that Honour made on *Roger* for the *Aid* to the Ransom of the King of *Alemaigne*, payable out of the said Land (*n*). In the next Year, *Roger de Scaccario* granted for himself and his Heirs to *Richard de Hederſete* the Office of Usher of the Exchequer during his Life, so that *Roger* or his Heirs might not put him out of the said Office (*o*); and *Roger* presented him before the Barons, and he was sworn into the said Office (*p*). *Richard de Hederſete* was amerced for not coming to take Knighthood. K. *Edward* I. pardoned his Amercement (*q*). In the first Year of K. *Edward* I. *Laurence del Eschequer* granted for himself and his Heirs to *Richard de Mendesham*, that he would give *Richard* the first Bailywick in his Gift that should become void, either in the Common Bench, or in the Exchequer of the *Jews*; that in the mean time, till he could provide for *Richard* in that Manner, he would give him two Marks Sterling *per Annum de Camera sua*; that when he provided for him as aforesaid, he would make to him a Letter Patent of the Office for his the said *Richard*'s Life; that if he should grant to *Richard* an Office or Serjeanty at the Common Bench, *Richard* should pay him for it yearly half a Mark; if an Office or Serjeanty at the Exchequer of

---

(*m*) [Præsentatio] Rogeri de Scaccario. Idem venit coram Baronibus die Lunæ post octabas Trinitatis, & præsentavit Nicholaum de Wintonia, ad intendendum loco suo Officio Hostiariæ in Scaccario tota vita ipsius Nicholai; dum tamen bene & fideliter se habuerit in Officio prædicto. Qui eodem die sacramentum præstitit, & admissus fuit in forma prædicta. *Ex Memor.* 40. *H.* 3. *Rot.* 17. *a. in imo.*

(*n*) *Memor.* 52. *H.* 3. *Rot.* 1. *a. Ib. Rot.* 6. *b. & Rot.* 9. *b.*

(*o*) Idem Rogerus [de Scaccario] concessit pro se & hæredibus suis Ricardo de Hederſete Officium Hostiarij de Scaccario ad totam vitam suam; Ita quod prædictus Ricardus de prædicto officio per ipsum Rogerum aut hæredes suos non posset removeri. *Trin. Commun.* 52 *& 53. H.* 3. *Rot.* 14. *b.*

(*p*) Idem [Rogerus de Scaccario] venit coram Baronibus, & præsentavit Ricardum filium Simonis de Hederſete ad officium Ostiarij de Scaccario. Et præstitit sacramentum de fideliter serviendo in officio prædicto. *Ib. Rot.* 14. *b.*

(*q*) *Mich. Memor.* 7. *E.* 1. *Rot.* 2. *b.*

the *Jews*, *Richard* should pay or render to him for it as much as other of his the said *Laurence*'s Serjeants or Substitutes used to render in like Case. And for Performance of this Contract, *Laurence* subjected himself to the Coercion of the Barons of the Exchequer (*r*). In the 32d Year of K. *Edward* I. a Writ was sent to the Barons, commanding them to certify to the King under the Exchequer-Seal, whether it would be to the Damage of the King, or of any other Persons, if he should grant Leave to *Maud de Dagworth*, one of the Sisters and Heiresses of *Simon del Exchequer*, to alien her Purpart of the Office of Ushery of the Exchequer, and to *William Peyforer*, and *Lora* his Wife, another of the Sisters and Heiresses of *Simon*, to alien her the said *Lora*'s Purpart of the said Office to *Reginald Herlizoun*, and *Hawise*, Daughter of the said *Maud*; to hold to *Reginald* and *Hawise* of the King and his Heirs: And if it was to the Damage of the King, or of any others, to whose Damage it was, and how much, and in what Manner; and how much the said Purparts were worth by the Year. Hereupon the Barons certified, that they conceived it would not be to the Damage of the King, or of any others, if such a Grant was made as the Writ mentioned; because the Serjeanty is now divided amongst three Parceners, and by the Grant two Parts would be united: they could not certify the Value, because much of the Profits of the Office arose in the *Iters* of Justices (*s*). In the second Year of K. *Edward* II. *Maud de Daggeworth* held, for the Term of her Life, the third Part of the Bailywick of the Ushery of the Exchequer, granted to her by *John de Daggeworth*, by Fine levied thereof, with the King's Licence. In the Reign of K. *Edward* I. *Maud* died. K. *Edward* II.

(*r*) Recognitio Laurentij de Scaccario. Idem venit coram Baronibus, & recognovit quod concessit pro se & hæredibus suis Ricardo de Mendesham, quod faciet ei habere primam Ballivam vacantem in Banco, vel ad Scaccarium Judæorum, ad ipsum pertinentem. Et quod dabit ei interim singulis annis de camera sua duas marcas Sterlingorum, ad duos anni terminos, videlicet unam Medietatem ad fæstum Sancti Michaelis, & aliam medietatem ad Pascha Et sic de anno in annum ad eosdem terminos, donec eidem Ricardo de officio prædicto, sicut prædictum est, provideatur. Et cum sibi super hoc provisum fuerit, faciet ei Litteram suam patentem de retinendo dictum officium ad terminum vitæ suæ. Et tunc cessabit solutio dictarum duarum marcarum. Et sciendum est, quod si prædictus Laurentius faciet eidem Ricardo habere Serjàntiam ad Bancum; idem Ricardus ex tunc solvit eidem Laurentio dimidiam marcam singulis annis pro eadem Serjantia. Et si ei habere faciet Serjantiam ad Scaccarium Judæorum, reddet ei pro eadem sicut alij servientes eidem Laurencio prius reddere consueverunt. Et nisi fecerit, concessit pro se & hæredibus suis & executoribus suis, quod Barones de Scaccario præmissa omnia faciant ipsam observare; Et quod prædictas duas marcas de terris tenementis bonis & catallis suis fieri faciant ad opus ejusdem Ricardi. *Rec.* I. *E.* I. *Rot.* 13. *a.*
(*s*) *Hil. Brevia* 32. *E.* I. *Rot.* 25. *b.*

received of *John de Daggeworth* his Homage for the said third Part, and rendered the same to him; and then by his Writ commanded the Barons of the Exchequer to give the said *John* full Seisin thereof; saving to every Man his Right. Upon this, *John* came before the Barons, and took the Oath to demeane himself well and truly in his said Office (*t*).

It was the Usher's Duty, to keep the Exchequer safely, and to take Care of the Doors and Avenues to it, so that the King's Records, which were laid up there, might be in Safety (*u*). It was also his Duty, to transmit the Writs of Summonces which issued out of the Exchequer for the King's Debts; that is, to cause them to be delivered to the respective Sheriffs to whom they were directed. This doth appear by the Precedents cited above in this Section, and by two or three more here subjoined. The Sheriff of *Hereford* retorned *Tarde* upon a Writ of *Distringas*. *James de Eggemere*, Usher of the Exchequer, who (saith the Record) ought to convey the Writs issuing *pro Rege* to the respective Sheriffs, being examined by the Court touching the Delivery of the said *Distringas*, one *Walter de Ellesfeld*, Clerk to the Sheriff of *Hereford*, was found faulty and committed to Prison (*w*). On the 22d Day of *December*, in the 27th Year of K. *Edward* I,

(*t*) *Pas. Brevia* 1. *E.* 2. *Rot.* 50. *a.*

(*u*) De secure custodiendo Palacium Regis. Septimodecimo die Februarij, post Scaccarium Clausum pro hoc Termino, W. de Norwyco Tenens locum Thesaurarij, vocato coram ipso in eodem Scaccario, præsentibus ibidem & assidentibus Johanne de Merkyngfeld Cancellario, Magistris Ricardo de Abyndon & Johanne de Everdone Baronibus de eodem Scaccario & alijs de Consilio Regis, Ricardo Abbot locum tenenti Johannis Shenche Custodis Palacij Regis Westmonasterij & Johanne Dymmok & Johanne de Eggemere Hostiarijs de eodem Scaccario, injunxit eisdem ex parte Regis, sub forisfactura omnium quæ ipsi Regi forisfacere poterunt, Quod videlicet dictus Ricardus omnes portas & alios introitus & exitus dicti Palacij quoscumque ita custodiat, quod quolibet die ad occasum Solis ferantur & firmiter opturentur, nec aperiantur ante ortum Solis die crastino, & aliunde ita vigilanter diligenter & solicite circa custodiam ejusdem Palacij intendat, quod dampnum aliquod non eveniat Domino Regi aut eidem Palacio pro defectu bonæ custodiæ ejusdem: Et quod dicti Ostiarij habeant suos pro quibus voluerint respondere qualibet nocte cubantes in Scaccario usque Crastinum Clausi Paschæ proximo futurum, quousque videlicet Curia redierit, nec deferant in Palacium ignem in candela vel aliquo alio modo infra idem tempus vel deferri permittant quantum in ipsis fuerit, set diligencius quo poterint intendant circa custodiam dicti Scaccarij & Memorandorum Regis ibidem. Et nichilominus ijdem Ricardus Abbot & Ostiarij eodem die præstiterunt sacramentum de solicite & diligenter observando præmissa. Et super hoc prædictus Johannes Dymmok posuit loco suo Johannem Doget, & dictus Johannes de Eggemere Rogerum servientem suum. *Hil. Communia* 5. *E.* 2. *Rot.* 32. *b. in imo.*

(*w*) De Clerico Vicecomitis Herefordiæ liberato prisonæ. —— Ob quod Jacobus de Eggemere Hostiarius de Scaccario qui brevia pro Rege exequenda singulis Vicecomitibus debet deferre, positus inde ad rationem, dixit

ward I, the Estreats of Fines, Amercements, and Issues set and lost before *W. de Beauchamp*, Steward of the King's Houshold, in the 24th and 25th Years of the King, were sent out in Summonce into the several Counties of *England*, except *Cumberland* and *Devonshire*. The said Summonces were sealed with the Exchequer Seal, under the Testimony of *Walter* Bishop of *Coventry*, Treasurer, and delivered to *John Dymmok*, Usher of the Exchequer, that he might send them with Speed to the Sheriffs of the said Counties (*x*). In the second Year of K. *Edward* II, a Writ issued to the Sheriff of *Norfolk* and *Suffolk*, ordering him to seize into the King's Hands all the Lands and Tenements of *Walter de Langeton*, late Bishop of *Coventry* and of the *Templars*. The like Writs issued into several other Counties. And all the said Writs were delivered at the Exchequer to *John de Eggemere*, Usher of the Exchequer, to be sent with all Speed to the Sheriffs of the several Counties. And to prevent Delay in conveying the Writs, the Treasurer's Lieutenant delivered to the said Usher as much Money as was needful for the Stipends of the several Messengers who were to carry them (*y*). The same King by his Writ commanded the Abbot of *Peterburgh*, to be in Person before the King's Council at *Westminster* such a Day, and to have with him there Frere *William de la More*, who, as the King had heard, resided in the Abbey of *Peterburgh*, and other Templars, if any of them were in the Abbot's Power. This Writ was delivered at the *Receipt* of Exchequer to *John Doget*, Servant to *John Dymmock*, an Usher of the Exchequer, to be conveyed to the said Abbot (*z*). In the 5th Year of K. *Edward* II, on the third Day of *December* at one a-Clock, several close Writs of the Great Seal were delivered to *John de Eggemere*, Usher of the Exchequer. They were

dixit quod qualitercumque breve prædictum sit retornatum, illud tamen prædicto xv die Novembris quo sigillatum fuit tradidit in pleno Scaccario Waltero de Ellesfeld Clerico prædicti Vicecomitis Domino suo Vicecomiti deferendum—. *Mich. Commun.* 21. *E.* 1. *Rot.* 13. *a. in bund.* 20 & 21. *E.* 1.

(*x*) *Mich. Communia* 26 & 27. *E.* 1. *Rot.* 7. *b.*

(*y*) Norf. Suff. *The Writ is* Teste J. de Sandale Tenente locum Thesaurarij apud Westmon. xxv die Junij anno secundo.

Et memorandum quod omnia brevia prædicta consignata fuerunt xxv die supradicto, & incontinenti liberata Johanni de Eggemere Hostiario Scaccarij, mittenda Vicecomitibus Comitatuum prædictorum cum festinatione qua &c. Et ne super hoc aliqua fieret dilatio, J. de Sandale Tenens locum Thesaurarij liberavit dicto Hostiario tantam pecuniam, quantam ipsum habere oportuit pro stipendijs Nunciorum brevia prædicta deferencium. *Trin. Commissiones* 2. *E.* 2. *Rot.* 21. *b.*

(*z*) Abbati de Burgo S. Petri. *The Writ is*, Teste W. Wygornensi Episcopo Thesaurario xxx die Decembris anno secundo.

Et memorandum quod eodem die hora tercia idem breve tradebatur Johani Doget servienti Johannis Dymmok unius Hostiar. Scaccarij, in Recepta ejusdem Scaccarij, ad mittendum prædicto .. Abbati &c. *Mich. Brevia Retornabilia* 2. *E.* 2. *Rot.* 117. *b.*

titled

titled at the Tails of them, *De terris capiendis* &c; and were to be transmitted by the Usher to the respective Sheriffs (*a*). In the 12th Year of K. *Edward* II, Writs were awarded to the several Sheriffs of *England*, for summoning the Taxours of the King's *Eighteenth* and *Twelfth* to appear before the King's Council at *Westminster* [to receive their Formule or Articles of Instruction]. To some of the Sheriffs or their Clerks, who were then present at the Exchequer, the Writs for their respective Counties were delivered in the Presence of the Treasurer and Barons; and other Writs were delivered to *John de Eggemere*, Usher of the Exchequer, to be by him sent to the respective Sheriffs of the other Counties (*b*). In the 15th Year of K. *Edward* II, certain Writs relating to Master *Jordan Moraunt*, late Constable of *Bourdeaux*, were sealed, and then delivered to *John de Stokesby*, one of the Ushers of the Exchequer, who was to deliver them to certain Messengers, to be by them conveyed with all Speed to the Bishops and Sheriffs to whom they were directed (*c*). There were some other Things pertaining to the Usher's Office or Duty. For Example: In the 52d Year of K. *Henry* III, *Nicolas de Wynton*, Usher of the Exchequer, was commanded by the Barons to go unto *John de Aubernun*, late Sheriff of *Surrey* and *Sussex*, now accounting, and to take the said *John*'s Appointment of an Attorney to make his *Sum* for him, and to charge and discharge him upon his Account (*d*). In the 4th Year of K. *Edward* I,

(*a*) Anglia. De brevibus Regis ad diversos Vicecomites deferendis. Memorandum quod modo tercio die Decembris hora prima, liberata fuerunt Johanni de Eggemere Hostiario de Scaccario brevia de Magno Sigillo clausa, titulata in caudis, De Terris capiendis in manum Regis, in Comitatibus videlicet Devoniæ, Notinghamiæ, Wiltesiæ, Londoniæ, Essexiæ, Oxoniæ, Berk., Ebor., Cornubiæ, Surreiæ. *Mich. Commun.* 5. *E.* 2. *Rot.* 22. *a.*

(*b*) De quibusdam brevibus Regis liberatis ad mittendum. Memorandum quod brevia de venire faciendo illos qui assignati sunt ad taxandum Decimamoctavam & duodecimam Regi apud Eboracum concessas coram Consilio Regis apud Westmonasterium in quindena S. Johannis Baptistæ, liberantur subscriptis in præsencia Thesaurarij & Baronum xvj die Junij; videlicet, Johanni Sefoul Vicecomiti Norfolciæ & Suffolciæ duo brevia; Augustino Bik de Notingham, Clerico Vicecomitis Notinghamiæ & Derbiæ duo brevia; Willelmo de Haywode Clerico Vicecomitis Somersetæ & Dorsetæ duo brevia; Willelmo de Crowerst Clerico Vicecomitis Devoniæ j breve; & Johanni de Eggemere Hostiario Scaccarij xxxvj brevia mittenda Vicecomitibus subscriptis, videlicet Vicecomitibus Essexiæ Hertfordiæ, Warwici Leycestriæ, Oxoniæ Berksiræ, Surreiæ Sussexiæ, Bedfordiæ Bukinghamiæ, Salopiæ Staffordiæ, Cantabrigiæ Huntendoniæ, cuilibet eorum duo brevia; & Vicecomitibus subscriptis, Norhamtoniæ, Rotelandiæ, Kanciæ, Cornubiæ, Wyltesiræ, Suhamtoniæ, Lincolniæ, Middlesexiæ, Wygorniæ, Herefordiæ, Glouceftriæ, cuilibet eorum unum breve. *Trin. Communia* 12. *E.* 2. *Rot.* 30. *b.*

(*c*) *Hil. Brevia* 15. *E.* 2. *Rot.* 86. *a.*

(*d*) De attornato Johannis de Aubernum capiendo per Nicholaum de Wynton Ostiarium. Præceptum est Nicholao de Wynton Ostiario Scaccarij, quod accedat ad Johannem de Aubernum, & capiat attornatum

ipsius

Chap. XXIV. *of the* EXCHEQUER.

K. *Edward* I, the Goods and Chatells which *Luke de Batencurt* had in *London* at the Time of his Death were, by Order of the Treasurer and Barons, appraised by the Sheriffs of *London* and *Richard de Hederfete*, Usher of the Exchequer (*e*). The Sheriff of *Cornwall* was attached by *James de Eggemere*, Usher of the Exchequer, to appear before the Barons, and to answer a Plaintif for a Trespass (*f*).

V. The Constable of the Exchequer was Deputy to the Constable of *England*, and was nominated by him in this Manner: The Constable of *England* (usually, in Person) presented either to the King himself, or to the Treasurer and Barons, some fit Person to act for him as Constable at the Exchequer; and thereupon the Person presented was wont to be sworn and admitted before the Treasurer and Barons. This may be seen in the following Instances. The Earl of *Hereford* nominated to the King Master *Roger* (his Clerk) to execute the Office of Constable at the Exchequer; and thereupon the King commanded the Treasurer and Barons to admit him to that Office (*g*). The Earl of *Hereford* presented to the Barons *Robert de Fulham* to execute for him the Office of Constable of the Exchequer, during his Pleasure; and he was sworn and admitted (*h*). The Earl of *Essex*

and

---

ipsius Johannis ad faciendam summam pro eo de tempore quo fuit Vicecomes Surreiæ & Sussexiæ, & ad ipsum plene onerandum & exonerandum &c. *Ex Memorand.* 52. *H.* 3. *Rot.* 15. *a.*

(*e*) Memorandum quod die Veneris in festo S. Luciæ Virginis appreciata fuerunt bona & catalla quæ Lucas de Batencurt habuit in Civitate Londoniæ die quo obijt, per Vicecomites Londoniæ & Ricardum de Hederfete Hostiarium de Scaccario, de præcepto Thesaurarij & Baronum, ad xvj l xj s iiij d, præter utensilia quæ fuerunt ipsius Lucæ precij xv s, quæ liberata fuerunt Matildæ le Blund quæ fuit uxor ejusdem Lucæ, per eosdem Thesaurarium & Barones. *Mich. Commun.* 4. *E.* 1. *Rot.* 4. *b.*

(*f*) Vicecomes Cornubiæ attachiatus est per Jacob[um] † Hostiarium de Scaccario, ad respondendum Johanni Julio de Sancto Thoh', de dimidia marca, quam de eo cepit injuste. Et datus est ei dies quod sit coram Baronibus in quindena S. Micaelis, ad respondendum de prædicta transgressione per manucapcionem Rogeri de Dreyton & Rogeri de Bikerwyk; nisi interim emendetur per Comitem Cornubiæ. Et liberatur eidem districtio per prædictum Jacob[um]. *Trin. Commun.* 18. *E.* 1. *Rot.*—. *a.*

† Recognitio Jacobi de Eggemere Hostiarij de Scaccario. Idem venit coram Baronibus, & recognovit se teneri Gregorio de Rokesle Civi Londoniæ in C s, solvendis—&c. *Hil. Recognit.* 18. *E.* 1. *Rot.* — *a.*

(*g*) De Officio Constabularij ad Scaccarium. Mandatum est E. Thesaurario, & Baronibus de Scaccario, quod loco H. Comitis Herefordiæ Constabularij Regis de Scaccario, recipiant Magistrum Rogerum Clericum ipsius Comitis ad Officium Constabularij exequendum ad Scaccarium. T. Rege apud Muntgomery xxj die Septembris. *Cl.* 12. *H.* 3. *m.* 2.

(*h*) De Clerico Constabularij. Humfridus Comes Herefordiæ Constabularius præsentavit ad Scaccarium coram Baronibus, Robertum . . . . ad Scaccarium, & faciendum officium Constabularij

and *Hereford* presented to the Barons *John Peverel*, to execute the Office of Constable of the Exchequer in the Absence of *Robert de Foleham* (*i*); whom the King had lately made Remembrancer of the Exchequer (*k*). H. *de Bohun*, Earl of *Hereford*, presented to the Barons *John Peverel* to execute in his room the Office of Constable in the Exchequer till the next Christmass (*l*). And soon afterwards, he presented *Nicholas de Blaby*, to execute the said Office of Constable under *Robert de Foleham*, as often as *Robert* should happen to be absent (*m*). *Humfrey*, Earl of *Hereford*, presented before the Treasurer and Barons *Ralph de Brochion*, his Clerk, to execute for him his Office of Constable at the Exchequer; and *Ralph* was sworn and admitted (*n*). *Humfrey de Bohun*, Constable of *England*, presented before the King *Richard de Ketsteven* to act for him at the Exchequer; and the King by his Privy Seal commanded the Treasurer and Barons to receive him in that Behalf, and to excuse the Earl for his Absence at this Time: Whereupon *Richard* was admitted and sworn (*o*).

Humfrey

stabularij pro eo quamdiu ei placuerit; Qui præstito sacramento . . . . *Mich. Commun.* 32. H. 3. *Rot.* 2. b. Robert de Fuleham *was about this Time Constable of the Exchequer*; *Memor.* 32. H. 3. *Rot.* 3. b.

(*i*) Præsentatio Comitis Essexiæ & Herefordiæ. Idem Comes venit coram Baronibus, & præsentavit Johannem Peverel, ad intendendum Officio Constabulariæ Scaccarij, quamdiu Robertus de Foleham eidem officio intendere non potest. *Mich. Commun.* 49. H. 3. *Rot.* 1. a.

(*k*) Roberto de Foleham. Rex mandat eidem, quod, quia de Consilio suo provisum est, quod officio Rememoratoris Scaccarij Regis intendat, firmiter injungens quod officio illi intendat. Et hoc nullatenus omittat. T. &c. *Mich. Commun.* 49. H. 3. *Rot.* 1. a. *Sensus in ipsa membrana imperfectus est.*

(*l*) Præsentatio H. de Bohun Comitis Herefordiæ: Idem venit coram Baronibus in crastino Animarum, & præsentavit Johannem Peverel ad intendendum, loco suo, Officio Constabularij in Scaccario usque at Natale Domini. *Mich. Commun.* 52, *incip.* 53. H. 3. *Rot.* 3. b.

(*m*) Præsentatio Comitis Herefordiæ. Idem Comes præsentavit coram Baronibus in crastino S. Hillarij, Nicholaum de Blaby ad intendendum Officio Constabularij sub Roberto de Foleham, quociens eundem Robertum abesse contigerit. Et idem Robertus debet exibere prædictum Nicholaum, quam diu steterit pro eo in Officio prædicto. *Mich. Commun.* 52, *incip.* 53. H. 3. *Rot.* 5. b.

(*n*) Memorandum quod in crastino S. Hilarij anno regni Regis E vicesimo, venit Humfridus de Booun Comes Herefordiæ & Constabularius Angliæ, & præsentavit coram Thesaurario & Baronibus Radulphum de Brochion clericum suum ad Officium Constabular. pro eodem Comite in eodem Scaccario faciendum, & locum suum in omnibus ibidem tenendum &c; Et idem Radulphus eodem die præstitit sacramentum, quod bene & fideliter se habebit in Officio prædicto &c. *Hil. Communia* 20. E. 1. *Rot.* 10. a.

(*o*) De Constabulario præsentato in Scaccario. Rex mandavit Breve suum Thesaurario & Baronibus in hæc verba. Edward par la grace de Dieu Rei Dengleterre &c, Au Treforier & as Barons del Eschequier, salutz. Sachiez qe nostre feal & loial Humphrey de Boun Counte de Hereford,

Chap. XXIV. *of the* EXCHEQUER. 283

Humfrey de Bohun granted and surrendered to K. *Edward* I. all his Castles, Manours, Lands, and Tenements, in *England* and *Wales*, which he held in Fee, and all his Right, Honour, and Lordship *Nomine Comitis* in the Counties of *Hereford* and *Essex*, and his Constableship of *England*, to hold to the King and his Heirs in Fee; and K. *Edward* I. afterwards, *viz.* 26 *Novemb. Anno Regni* 31°, by his Charter, gave and granted to *Humfrey de Bohun* and *Elizabeth* Countess of *Holland* his Wife, the King's Sister, all the said Castles, Manours, Lands, Tenements, Right, Honour, Lordship, and Constableship of *England*, &c. to hold to the said *Humfrey* and *Elizabeth*, and the Heirs of the Body of the said *Humfrey* begotten, of the King and other chief Lord and Lords of the Fees (*p*). And afterwards K. *Edward* I, by his Writ, commanded the Barons to deliver unto *Humfrey de Bohun* and *Elizabeth* his Wife, the Office of Constableship in the Exchequer, and other Things mentioned in the Writ, according to the Tenour of the King's Charter made in that Behalf (*q*). K. *Edward* II. (*Anno Regni* 17°) by Writ of the Great Seal committed to *Richard de Luda* the Office of Constable of his Exchequer (being then for certain Causes seized into his Hands) to hold during Pleasure: And the Treasurer and Barons were commanded to admit *Richard* to the said Office (*r*). I can say but little concerning the Powers or Duty of this Officer; save that he seemeth to have had in some Cases a concurrent or like Power with the Marshall. In the 39th Year of K. *Henry* III, *Robert de Fulham* (then Constable of the Exchequer) was commanded

---

ford & Dessex & Conestable Dengletere, ad presente par devaunt Nous, Richard de Ketsteven son Clerk portur de ces Lettres, pur estre al Eschequier en son lieu, sicome avaunt ces houres ad este vse en temps de ses aunceftres. E pur ceo qe nous entendoms, qe le Counte ad fait envers nous en celes parties ce qe a lui appent, & nous ne les pooms desporter quant a ore: Vous maundoms, que le dit Richard receivez, a demorier a nostre dit Escheqier en le lieu de devauntdit Conte, ausi avant come si le Counte meismes y feust present; Issint qe le Conte se soit achesonez pur sabsence a ceste foiz. Donez souz nostre Prive Seal a Estebbenheth, le vij jour de Maij, lan de nostre regne vint & septisme. Prætextu cujus brevis, prædictus Ricardus de Kestan admissus est ad Officium Constabularij in Scaccario; & præstitit sacramentum coram Thesaurario & Baronibus, de fideliter se habendo in eodem Officio. *Pas. Præsentationes* 26 & 27. *E.* 1. *Rot.* 60. *a.*

(*p*) Baronibus, pro Humfrido de Bohun. '*Tis a Writ, reciting all the said Matter, as above.* Trin. Brevia 2. *E.* 2. *Rot.* 79. *b.*

(*q*) Hil. Brevia 35. *E.* 1. *Rot.* 30. *a.*

(*r*) Rex commisit dilecto Clerico suo Ricardo de Luda Officium Constabularij Scaccarij Regis, in manu Regis quibusdam de causis existens, habendum quamdiu Regi placuerit. In cujus &c. Teste Rege apud Faxflete x° die Julij. Per ipsum Regem.

Et mandatum est Thesaurario & Baronibus de Scaccario, quod ipsum Ricardum ad Officium prædictum admittant, habendum in forma prædicta. Teste Rege ut supra. Per ipsum Regem, *Pat.* 17. *E.* 2. *p.* 1. *m.* 22.

by

by the King's Writ to go to *Lincoln*, and arrest the Sheriff of *Lincolnshire*, and bring him up before the Barons of the Exchequer *ad audiendum & faciendum* (*s*). In the same Year the King sent *Robert de Fuleham* to the Coroners of *Lincoln*, to levy and collect all Arerages or Debts due to *Gilbert de Cheyles*, Sheriff of *Lincoln*, by View and Testimony of the said Coroners: And in regard *Gilbert* owed to the King CCxliij Marks *de claro*, the King commanded *Robert* to levy the same on the Goods and Chatells of *Gilbert*, and to have the Money at the Exchequer (*t*). In ancient Time there was also a Constable in the Court of Common Bench, who enrolled Essoignes, and did other ministerial Acts there (*u*).

VI. The Office of Marshall of the Exchequer is very ancient: There is Mention made of him in the Reign of K. *Richard* I. He was sometimes called Marshall of the Exchequer (*w*); sometimes Clerk of the Marshalsey of the Exchequer. Master *G.* is styled *Clerk of the Marshalsey* (*x*). *Roger de Gosebec*, *Clerk of the Marshalsey* of the Exchequer (*y*), *John de Nevill*, *Clerk of the Marshalsey* (*z*). He was wont to be appointed to his Office by the Marshall of *England* for the Time being; that is to say, the Marshall of *England* used to present to the King, or to the Barons of the Exchequer, a Clerk to execute for him the Office of Marshall in the Court of Exchequer; which Clerk was thereupon admitted and sworn in the Exchequer. But

---

(*s*) Rex mandavit Roberto de Fuleham, quod quamcitius posset adiret Civitatem Lincolniæ, & caperet corpus Vicecomitis Lincolniæ, & secum duceret coram Baronibus de Scaccario, ad audiendum & faciendum præceptum Domini Regis. *Memor*. 39. H. 3. *Rot*. 7. *a*.

(*t*) *Ib*. *Rot*. 9. *b*.

(*u*) *Bract. de Leg*. L. 5. *tract*. 2. *cap*. 13. *sect*. 4.

(*w*) Et Ricardo Britoni & socijs suis Lx marcas, in ij Taleis factis ab ipsis quæ sunt in forulo Marescalli; Et Quietus est. *Mag. Rot*. 7. R. 1. *Rot*. 7. *a*.

Robertus filius Pagani debet xxx l de debitis Aaron; De quibus attulit cartam prædicti Aaron de quietantia de xv l, quæ est in forulo Marescalli; Et debet xv l. *Mag. Rot*. 10. R. 1. *Rot*. 4. *b*. *Linc*.

(*x*) Et Magistro G. Marescallo Clerico Maresc., xx s de prædicta firma [presturarum], per breve G. filij Petri. *Mag. Rot*. 3. *J. Rot*. 19. *b*.

(*y*) *Suff*. Mandatum est Vicecomiti, quod habeat &c in crastino clausi Paschæ corpus Henrici Personæ de Eys, ad respondendum Magistro Rogero Gosebec Clerico de Marescalcia de Scaccario, de hoc quod ipsi ceperunt averia sua, & ea contra vad. &c, ut idem Magister dicit. Et habeat breve. *Memor*. 39. H. 3. *Rot*. 9. *a*. He is called Clericus de Marescalcia Scaccarij; *Ib*. *Rot*. 12. *b*. *Essex*.

(*z*) Mandatum est Vicecomiti, quod venire faciat in crastino S. Michaelis Willelmum Kake *and two others*, ad respondendum Johanni de Nevill Clerico de Marescalcia, de hoc quod Willelmum de Tarente hominem suum verberaverunt, wlneraverunt, & ipsum de denarijs suis spoliaverunt, contra pacem, ut dicitur. Et habeat breve. *Trin. Commun*. 32. H. 3. *Rot*. 10. *b*.

when

Chap. XXIV.   *of the* Exchequer.

when the Office of Marshall of *England* hath happened to be in the King's Hand, then the Marshall of the Exchequer was appointed, either by the King himself, or by the Person to whom the King committed the Office of Marshall of *England*. I will give some Instances of these Things. K. *Henry* III. signified by his Writ to the Barons of the Exchequer, that at the Presentation of *G. Mareschall* Earl of *Pembroke* he had admitted Matter *Richard de Swindon*, the Earl's Clerk, to reside at the Exchequer as Marshall in the Earl's Stead, until the King should come again to the Exchequer: And therefore by this Writ he commanded them to admit *Richard* to the said Office, and to certify him at his next Coming, whether *Richard* was fit for it (*a*). About the 31st Year of K. *Henry* III, *Maud* Countess of *Warenne* and *Norfolk* had the Esnece of the Inheritance of *Walter Mareschall* late Earl of *Pembrok*; for which Reason the King committed to her the Staff of the Mareschalsey; and she, with the King's Licence, committed the said Staff to *Roger le Bigod* Earl of *Norfolk*, her Son and Heir, who did Homage to the King for the same: The King thereupon by his Writ commands the Barons, to let the said Earl have what pertained to the said Staff or Office, and to admit such Person (being fit) as he should appoint to act for him at the Exchequer (*b*). And soon after, the said Earl presented to the Treasurer and Barons *John de Nevill*, Clerk, to execute for him the Office of Marshall at the Exchequer, during his Pleasure; who was sworn and admitted to that Office (*c*). *Anno* 49° *Hen*. III, there being no Marshall resident at the Exchequer,

---

(*a*) Baronibus, pro G. Marescallo Comite Penbrokiæ. Rex Baronibus; Sciatis quod ad præsentationem dilecti &c, admisimus Magistrum Ricardum de Swindon Clericum suum, ad residenciam faciendam ad Scaccarium nostrum tanquam Marescallum ejusdem Scaccarij loco ipsius Comitis, quousque illuc venerimus: Et ideo vobis mandamus, quod ipsum Magistrum Ricardum ad hoc admittatis sicut prædictum est: Et cum illuc venerimus, nobis scire faciatis, si ad hoc idoneus fuerit. *Ex Memorandis* 22. *H*. 3. *Rot*. 2. *a. in imo*.

(*b*) Baronibus, pro Rogero le Bigod. Rex eisdem; Cum Matill. Comitissa Warennæ & Norfolciæ, quæ [habet] Esnetiam hæreditatis Walteri Mar. quondam Comitis Penbrok, cui ea ratione commiseramus virgam Marescalciæ, eandem virgam Marescalsciæ commiserit de licencia nostra dilecto & fideli nostro Rogero le Bigod Comiti Norfolciæ filio & hæredi suo, & Homagium ipsius Comitis inde ceperimus: Vobis mandamus, quod id quod ad prædictam virgam pertinet de cætero eidem Comiti habere faciatis, & ipsum quem loco suo assignare voluerit ad sedendum pro eo ad Scaccarium nostrum, dum modo Idoneus sit ad Officium illud, sine difficultate ad hoc admittatis. *Mich. Communia* 31. *H*. 3. *Rot*. 2. *a*.

(*c*) De Marescalcia commissa J. de Nevill. Rogerus le Bygod Comes Norfolciæ Marescallus, præsentavit ad Scaccarium Thesaurario & Baronibus quarto die Februarii, Johannem de Nevill Clericum, ad faciendum pro eo Officium Mar. ad Scaccarium, quamdiu ei placuerit: Qui facto sacramento sicut moris est, ad idem per eosdem Thesaurarium & Barones est admissus. *Hil. Commun*. 31. *H*. 3. *Rot*. 4. *b*.

the

the King by his Writ commanded *Roger le Bigod,* Earl-Marshall, to appoint some Person to act for him as Marshall at the Exchequer (*d*). In the 10th Year of K. *Edward* I, the Earl-Marshall presented before the Barons *John de la More,* to the Office of Marshall of the Exchequer; who was admitted and sworn (*e*). In the 34th Year finient of K. *Edward* I, it being reported that *Roger le Bygot,* Earl of *Norfolk* and Mareschall of *England,* was dead, the Office of Marshall in the Exchequer (belonging to the said Earl) was taken into the King's Hands. And immediately the said Office was, on the King's Behalf, committed to *William de Spanneby,* Clerk, for him to hold it till further Order was taken therein. And *William* was sworn (*f*). K. *Edward* II, in the first Year of his Reign, committed to *Nicolas de Segrave* the Office of Marshall of *England* during Pleasure; and thereupon commanded the Treasurer and Barons to admit such Person as *Nicolas* should present to them, to act for him in the Exchequer: And *Nicolas* presented *Elias Puger* to act for him at the Exchequer; who was admitted and sworn (*g*). The same King, in the 5th Year of his Reign, granted the Office of Marshall of the Exchequer to *Arnald de Tylye* during Pleasure; and *Arnald* was sworn accordingly (*h*). And

(*d*) Rogero le Bigod pro Rege. Quia in apertione Scaccarij in festo S. Michaelis proximo præterito, nullus fuit pro Rogero le Bigod Comite Marscallo, ad intendendum officio suo ibidem: Mandatum fuit eidem Rogero, quod aliquem tempestive mitteret ibidem qui officio prædicto intenderet; ne pro defectu ipsius negocia Regis ad idem Scaccarium expedienda retardarentur. *Mich. Commun.* 49. *H.* 3. *Rot.* 1. *a.*

(*e*) Memorandum quod in vigilia Apostolorum Simonis & Judæ, Comes Marescallus venit coram Baronibus, & præsentavit Johannem de la More, ad intendendum Officio Mareschalciæ, Brevia custodienda, & alia facienda quæ ad officium Mareschalciæ pertinent; Qui admissus fuit, & sacramentum præstitit de fideliter se habendo in eodem Officio. *Mich. Commun.* 9 & 10 *E.* 1. *Rot.* 1. *b.*

(*f*) Memorandum quod modo x° die Decembris, audito rumore de morte Rogeri le Bygot Comitis Norfolciæ & Marescalli Angliæ, Officium Marescalli in Scaccario quod ad ipsum Comitem pertinuit, captum est in manum Regis. Et statim idem officium committitur ex parte Regis Willelmo Spanneby Clerico, custodiendum donec Rex aliud &c. Et idem Willelmus super hoc præstitit sacramentum de bene & fideliter se habendo &c. *Mich. Commun.* 34 & 35 *E.* 1. *Rot.* 19. *a. Parte* I.

(*g*) Rex per breve suum de Magno Sigillo Patens, datum apud Westmon. xij° die Marcij anno primo, quod Nicholaus de Segrave modo xvij die Maij profert hic, mandat Thesaurario & Baronibus hic, quod cum ipse Rex commiserit eidem Nicholao Officium Marescalciæ Angliæ, Habendum & tenendum, cum omnibus ad officium illud spectantibus, quamdiu &c, ijdem Thesaurarius & Barones ipsum quem præfatus Nicholaus loco suo deputaverit ad faciendum ea quæ ad Officium illud pertinent in Scaccario loco ipsius Nicholai, recipiant. Et idem Nicholaus modo super hoc præsentat coram Thesaurario & Baronibus Elyam Puger, ad faciendum loco suo ea quæ ad Officium Marescalli &c. hic in Scaccario &c. Et idem Elyas ad hoc admissus est &c, & præstitit sacramentum de bene & fideliter se habendo &c. *Pas. Commun.* 1. *E.* 2. *Rot.* 55. *a.*

(*h*) *Mich. Commun.* 5. *E.* 2. *Rot.* 21. *a.*

quickly

quickly afterwards, the King commanded the Treasurer and Barons to admit such Person to the Office of Marshall of the Exchequer, as *Nicholas de Segrave* (to whom the King had granted the Marshalsey of *England*) should depute in that Behalf; he deputed *Joceline de Brantescombe*, who was admitted and sworn (*i*). *Roger le Bygod*, Earl of *Norfolk* and Mareshall of *England*, granted and remised to K. *Edward* I. the Mareschalsey of *England*, with all Things pertaining thereunto. K. *Edward* II, by his Charter, granted the said Mareschalsey to his Brother, *Thomas de Brotherton*, Earl of *Norfolk*, to hold to him and the Heirs Males of his Body, of the King and his Heirs; and to do unto the King and his Heirs the Services which were wont to be done to the King's Progenitours, the ancient Kings of *England*, for the same; and sent a Writ of the Great Seal to the Treasurer and Barons of the Exchequer, commanding them to admit such Person to the Office of Marshalsey in the Exchequer as the King's said Brother should nominate, or by his Letters Patent depute thereunto. Afterwards, in the Octaves of *Easter*, the Earl of *Norfolk* came into the Exchequer before the Treasurer and Barons, and nominated *Ambrose de Newburgh* to execute the Office of Marshall in the Exchequer, in the Name and Stead of the said Earl; praying the said *Ambrose* might be admitted thereto. And by virtue of the said Mandate *Ambrose* was admitted, and sworn to his good Demeaner (*k*).

I will here set down some Things relating to the Duty or Business of this Officer. Whilst an Account pended, he had the keeping of several Sorts of Writs and Vouchers produced to the Court by Debtors or Accountants. These he used to keep in Forules or Binns, or in Filets or Files, or in a Burse or Bag. The Forules were, it seems, digested by Counties. In the Exchequer-Records frequent Mention is made of the *Forulus Marescalli*, and sometimes of the *Forulus Marescalli* of such or such a County. For Example: There was the Marshall's Forulus of *Lincolnshire* (*l*); his *Ligula* or Filet (*m*); and

(*i*) *Hil. Commun.* 5. *E.* 2. *Rot.* 36. *a.*

(*k*) *Pas. Communia* 9. *E.* 2. *Rot.* 99. *a.*

(*l*) Thomas filius Godwini debet xl marcas super terram suam in atrio S. Petri & alia vadia quæ supra annotantur; Et Lxxiij s per Cartam suam. Quia attulit Cartam ipsius Aaron de quietantia prædictorum debitorum, quæ est in forulo Marescalli in Lincollscira, consideratum est per Barones quod ulterius de illis debitis non summoneatur, Et sic Quietus est. *Mag. Rot.* 10. *Ric.* 1. *Rot.* 4. *b. Linc. Tit.* De debitis Aaron.

(*m*) Ebor. Johannes de Crepping — venit & petit exonerari de compoto prædicto, unde habet Breve de Magno Sigillo in Ligula Marescalli de anno xxiij°, ad ipsum inde exonerandum. *Trin. Dies dati* 26 & 27. *E.* 1. *Rot.* 61. *b.*

—— solom la forme qe meisme celuy Roi Edward manda al Efchiqiere per son Bref, qe est en filetz de Mareschal lan trentisme ——. *Trin. Commun.* 5. *E.* 2. *Rot.* 62. *a.*

his Burſe or Bag (*n*). He performed ſeveral Acts relating to Accountants in the Exchequer. For Inſtance: When an Accountant, having been ſworn to account, did not proſecute his Account *bona fide*, but made Default at any Day prefixed to him, or did not duly anſwer the Arerages of his Account; in ſuch Caſes he was committed in Cuſtody to the Marſhall, to remain his Priſoner till the Court made a Receſs. *Ralf Baſſet* was delivered to the Marſhall, for the Arrerages of his Account. He had Day given him as a Priſoner upon his Parole, for ſo long as the King was in Town, and the Exchequer was ſitting (*o*). Upon making-up the *Sum* of *Thomas de Pyn*, Sheriff of *Devonſhire*, for the ſecond Year of K. *Edward* I. *Thomas* owed the King xv *l* xv *s* vj *d*; for which he was committed to the Marſhall's Cuſtody (*p*). When the Court finiſhed their Seſſion, the Marſhall delivered up his Priſoner, who was thereupon committed to the Fleet, or ſome other Priſon (*q*). If an Accountant at the Exchequer was arreſted, the Marſhall claimed to have the Cuſtody of him. In or about the 38th Year of K. *Henry* III. *Roger* Earl of *Norfolk*, and Marſhall of *England*, complained to the King, that whereas by the ancient Cuſtom of the Exchequer, if a Sheriff or other Perſon, being upon his Account at the Exchequer, was arreſted, he ought to be committed to the Cuſtody of the Marſhall; ſuch Accountants had then of late been frequently committed to the *Flete* Priſon: whereupon, the King by his Writ commanded the Barons, that if it were ſo, they ſhould ſee Right done to the Marſhall in that Caſe (*r*). And at another Time, Complaint was made on Behalf of *Roger* Earl of *Norfolk*, Marſhall of *England*, before the Juſticier, the Treaſurer and Barons, and other great Men of the King's Council in full Exchequer, that whereas *Licoricia* the *Jeweſs* was committed to the Cuſtody of *R. de Goſebec*, the Earl's

(*n*) —— quia Litera prædicta de acquietantia debet remanere in burſa Mareſcalli cum brevi de Allocate. *Mich. Memor.* 26 & 27. *E.* 1. *Rot.* 4. *b.*

Et ſuper hoc oſtendit diverſas Literas eorundem Mercatorum illud idem teſtificantes, quæ ſunt in burſa Mareſcalli de hoc compoto. *Trin. Commun.* 1. *E.* 2. *Rot.* 71. *a. ad imum.*

(*o*) Linc. Radulphus Baſſet liberatus eſt Mareſcallo pro arreragijs compoti ſui; Set habet diem ut Priſo, quamdiu Rex fuerit in Civitate & Scaccarium ſederit. *Hil. Commun.* 31. *H.* 3. *Rot.* 5. *a.*

(*p*) Devonia. Facta ſumma Thomæ de Pyn Vicecom. Devoniæ de anno ſecundo, debet xv l xv s vj d; pro quibus liberatur Mareſcallo. *Mich. Commun.* 4. *E.* 1. *Rot.* 1. *a.*

(*q*) Memorandum quod in vigilia S. Thomæ Apoſtoli, Johannes de Stafford Mareſcallus Scaccarii liberavit hic Johannem de la Wade, qui fuerat in cuſtodia ſua uſq; nunc pro diverſis debitis quæ Regi debet, tam de tempore quo ſuit Vicecomes Lincolniæ, quam aliunde; Et in continenti idem Johannes de la Wade committitur priſonæ de Flete. *Mich. Commun.* 25 & 26. *E.* 1. *Rot.* 23. *b.*

(*r*) *Memor.* 38. *H.* 3. *Rot.* 14. *a.*

Deputy-

Deputy-Marshall, for certain clear Debts which she owed to the King; she was wrongfully removed from his Custody, and committed to the Constable of the Tower of *London*; but it being found, upon due Examination, and Search of Precedents, that both *Jews* and *Christians*, who owed to the King any clear Debts enrolled at the Great Exchequer, ought to be committed to the Marshall for the same; it was adjudged, that *Licoricia* should be redelivered to the Marshall (*s*). Again; it was usual for Accountants (being in the Marshall's Custody) to make Oath to him, before the Barons of the Exchequer, that they would not depart from the Court without Licence, or would not go above such a Distance from the Cout without Licence, or that they would answer the Arerages of their Account. Of these Matters I have already given some Instances in another Place (*t*). Accountants assigned before him their Attornies, whom they deputed to act for them in their Accounts. *Hugh de Kynardele*, Sheriff of *Herefordshire*, was sick in *London*. The Treasurer and Barons sent *John de Nevill*, Marshall of the Exchequer, to *Hugh*, to receive his Nomination of an Attorney. And *Hugh*, in the Marshall's Presence, appointed *Robert de Trillet* and *Reginald de la Rode*, to render his Account, and to make his *Sum* for him (*u*). It seems he had the Fee of half a Mark by the Day from Persons committed to his Custody: *John Sampson* came and acknowledged before the Barons, that he owed *Roger de Gosebec*, the Marshall, two Marks and a half for five Days Commitment (*w*). And *Richard le Escot*, who had been arrested at the Exchequer, made the like Acknowledgment before the Barons, for two Marks and a half, Fees due to the Marshall for five Days Custody (*x*). *Simon de London*, Attorney of *Thomas Corbet*, acknowledged before the Barons, that he owed to the same *Roger* Lx *s* Commitment-Fees (*y*); upon which Acknowledgment, *Roger* had afterwards a Writ of *Fieri facias*, to levy the Lx *s* upon the said *Thomas Corbet* (*z*). K. *Edward* II. in the first Year of his Reign,

(*s*) Memorandum quod in præsentia H. le Bigot Justiciarij Angliæ, Episcoporum Wygorn. & Sarr. Thesaurarij & Baronum de Scaccario, & aliorum magnatum de Consilio Domini Regis in pleno Scaccario, cum ostensum esset pro Domino R. le Bigot Comite Norfolciæ & Marescallo Angliæ, quod Licoricia Judæa Wintoniæ quæ &c. *Hil. Memor.* 44. *H.* 3. *Rot.* 7. *a*.

(*t*) *Cap.* 23. *sect.* 22.

(*u*) Hugo de Kynardele Vicecomes (viz. of Heref.) ægrotavit in Civitate; & J. de Nevill Marescallus Scaccarij per præceptum Thesaurarij & Baronum missus fuit ad eum ad recipiendum Attornatum suum; coram quo idem H. posuit loco suo Robertum de Trillet Clericum & Reginaldum de la Rode, ad reddendum compotum suum, & summam faciendam pro eo. *Ex Memor.* 35. *H.* 3. *Rot.* 17. *b*.

(*w*) *Memor.* 52. *H.* 3. *Rot.* 13. *a*.

(*x*) *Hil. Recognit.* 52 & 53. *H.* 3. *Rot.* 16. *a*.

(*y*) *Memor.* 38. *H.* 3. *Rot.* 18. *a*.

(*z*) *Memor.* 39. *H.* 3. *Rot.* 14. *a*.

being willing to know what Rights, Fees, and Devoirs did belong to the Mareschall of *England* by reason of the Office of the King's Mareschalsey; by his Writ of Privy-Seal commanded the Barons of the Exchequer to certify him distinctly and plainly by their Patent Letters, concerning the said Rights, Fees, and Services, with all commodious Speed (a). I have not found the Certificate which the Barons made to the King upon this Mandate. But the same King, in the second Year of his Reign, sent a Writ of the Great Seal to the Barons of the Exchequer; signifying, that he willed that the Mareschalls of the Exchequer should receive and enjoy all and singular the Fees which rightfully belonged to them on account of the said Office of Mareschalsey, in like Manner as former Mareschalls, in the Time of the King's Father, used to receive and enjoy the same; and therefore commanding the Barons to suffer the said Mareschalls to have and enjoy the said Fees which belonged to them by means of the said Marshalsey, as it had been accustomed in the Time of the King's Father. This Writ issued at the Relation of *W. de Melton* (b). In fine, the Word Marshall seems to have been sometimes used with Latitude. The Persons that were wont to be employed at the Exchequer, in arresting Accountants or other Delinquents, were sometimes called by that Name (c).

VII. In Process of Time there were Officers at the Exchequer, who were called *Auditores Compotorum Scaccarij*. In the Reign of K. *Edward* II. certain Clerks were appointed to audite the foreign Accounts in the Exchequer, who seem to have been settled Officers; because upon the Death or Removal of one of them, another was put into his Place: But then it is said, that those Clerks were *nuper deputati*, lately assigned to that Employment; which leads one to think they were Officers then newly introduced. Thus in the 9th Year of K. *Edward* II, *Richard de Luda* was admitted to be *unus Clericorum nuper deputatorum ad compotos forinsecos audiendos hic in Scaccario*, in the Room of *Edmund de Dynington*; and took an Oath for his good

---

(a) Baronibus, pro Rege, De Officio Marescalciæ. Quia Rex super juribus feodis & deverijs Marescallo Angliæ ratione Officij Marescalciæ Regis quoquo modo spectantibus, quibusdam certis de causis vult certiorari, Mandat Baronibus quod scrutatis Rotulis & libris Scaccarij, Regem de juribus feodis & servicijs prædictis per Literas suas distincte & aperte reddant quamcicius commode poterunt certiorem. Datum sub Privato Sigillo apud Langele xj die Junij anno primo. *Trin. Brevia* 1. *E.* 2. *Rot.* 64. *a.*

(b) *Trin. Brevia* 2. *E.* 2. *Rot.* 80. *a.*

(c) — per Marescallos Scaccarij arrestari feceritis. *Pas. Commun.* 53. *H.* 3. *Rot.* 11. *a. in Cedula.*

Abearance

Abearance in that Office (*d*). In the preceding Times (for ought that I have observed) Accounts of some Part of the Revenue were usually audited, either by some of the Justices or Barons, or by Clerks or Persons assigned *hac vice* for that Purpose, by the King, or the Treasurer and Barons. For Example: In the tenth Year of K. *Henry* III, *Stephen*, Archbishop of *Canterbury*, accounted for CC Marks Imprest-money; and for Dxxxij *l* xviij *s* xi *d*, the Quinzime of his Demeane, and of his Men, and of the Men of his Knights; and for CLxj*l* x *s*, the Quinzime of the *Religious* of his Diocese in *Kent*, and of their Men; except the Abbat of St. *Austin*, and the Priour of the *Trinity* of *Canterbury*, and their Men; for the Abbat and Priour were to answer for themselves. The Account for this Quinzime, rendered by the Archbishop's Bailiffs, was audited by the Bishops of *Bathe* and *Saresbery*, and their Companions (*e*). K. *Henry* III, in the tenth Year of his Reign, by Writ of his Great Seal, commanded R. Bishop of *London*, one of his Council, to appoint Master *Michael Belet* and *William del Castel* to hear or audite the Account of the Justices or Commissioners of the King's Quinzime, who were to yield their Account at a Day prefixed to them in *Hilary* Term then next following (*f*). In the 20th Year of K. *Edward* I, *Thomas de Bellehus, W. de Carleton,* and *H. de Cressingham*, were appointed to audite and purify all Manner of Debts, and to sum up and report before the King the Sums of all the Debts of K. *Henry* III. But probably this was in Parliament (*g*).

(*d*) Anglia. De Ricardo de Luda admisso ad Compotos audiendos. Memorandum, quod vicesimo tertio die Aprilis hoc Termino, Ricardus de Luda Clericus admissus fuit unus Clericorum nuper deputatorum ad compotos forinsecos audiendos hic in Scaccario, loco Edmundi de Dynington nuper deputati ad auditionem hujusmodi Compotorum. Et idem Ricardus præstitit Sacramentum de bene & fideliter se habendo &c. *Pas. Communia* 9. *E.* 2. *Rot.* 98. *a.*

(*e*) S. Archiepiscopus Cantuariæ r c de CC marcis de præstito ei facto de Thesauro Regis anno Regis vij° — , Et de D & xxxij l xviij s & xj d de quintadecima Dominici sui & hominum suorum & hominum Militum suorum, Et de C & Lxj l & x s de Quintadecima virorum Relligiosorum parochiæ suæ in Kantia & hominum eorundem, Exceptis Abbate S. Augustini & Priore S. Trinitatis Cantuariæ hominibus ipsorum, unde dicti Abbas & Prior debent pro se respondere; De qua Quintadecima Episcopi Bathoniæ & Saresberiæ & Socij eorum audierunt compotum a Ballivis prædicti Archiepiscopi. *Mag. Rot.* 10. *H.* 3. *tit. Surreia.*

(*f*) Mandatum est R. Londoniensi Episcopo, quod assignet Magistrum Michaelem Belet & Willelmum de Castello, ad audiendum compotum Justiciariorum quintædecimæ Domini Regis; qui summoniti sunt ad reddendum inde compotum suum a die S. Hyllarij in xv dies, in eadem forma quam Dominus Rex alias eis assignavit de hijs qui compotum suum reddere debeant in octabis S. Hyllarij. *Rot. Liberat.* 10. *H.* 3. *m.* 2.

(*g*) Ad audienda [&] purificanda omnimoda debita, & ad summanda & summas reportandum coram Domino Rege, de debitis H. Regis Patris Domini Regis nunc, assignentur Thomas de Bellehus, W. de Carleton, & H. de Cressingham. *Ryl. Plac. P. p.* 104. *These and others were (it seems) Auditours and Receivers of Petitions. Ib. p.* 105.

In

In the 35th Year of K. *Edward* I, the Merchants *Friscobalds* were to account at the Exchequer for the King's Customs. The King, by his Letters Patents, assigned certain Persons to audite their Account. But in regard two of those Persons could not attend to act therein, one by reason of other Affairs, the other by reason of Sickness; thereupon the King's Council at the Exchequer appointed two others to join with the Persons before assigned by the King, in auditing the said Account (*h*). In or about the same 35th Year, *John del Isle* and others were appointed to be Auditours of the Accounts of the Disme imposed by the Pope on the Clergy (*i*). In the 12th Year of K. *Edward* II, *John de Foxle*, Master *John de Everdon*, *John de Ocham*, and *Robert de Wodehous*, Barons of the Exchequer, and *Adam de Lymbergh*, a Remembrancer of the Exchequer, were assigned to audite the Account of *John* Bishop of *Bathe* and *Wells*, for the Time that he was Keeper of the Wardrobe of K. *Edward* I; so that they jointly and severally, or at least two of them together, should dispatch that Affair (*k*). *Walter de Gatelyn*, Custos of the Manour of *Clarendon*, expended several Sums of Money in Works and Repairs about the Manour. Rolls of the Particulars thereof, and likewise Counter-rolls of the King's Viewers of those Works, were delivered in at the Exchequer; which were examined by *Robert de Thorpe*, a Clerk, assigned by the Barons for that Purpose (*l*). *Richard Squier*, *Custos* of the Manour of *Fekenham*, delivered in a Cedule of Particulars of the Works done about that Manour; and it was examined by *J. de Okham*, a Baron of the Exchequer (*m*). In the 15th Year of K. *Edward* II,
Mention

(*h*) *Trin. Commun.* 35. *E.* 1. *Rot.* 59. *a.*

(*i*) Recognitio Abbatis de Langale. He *came and acknowledged before the Barons, that he owed the King* D iij *l* xvj *s* iij *d q.* de arreragijs compoti sui coram Johanne de Insula & socijs suis Auditoribus compotorum nuper apud Westmon. redditorum, de Decima Cleri per Bonifacium Papam octavum Ecclesiæ Anglicanæ imposita per tres annos —. *Pas. Recognit.* 35. *E.* 1. *Rot.* 74. *a.*

(*k*) Memorandum quod Johannes de Foxle Magister J. de Everdon Johannes de Ocham & Robertus de Wodehous Barones de Scaccario, & Adam de Lymbergh Rememorator de Scaccario, assignantur ad audiendum compotum Venerabilis patris J. Bathonienfis & Wellensis Episcopi de tempore quo fuit Custos garderobæ Domini E. Regis Angliæ Patris Regis nunc. Ita quod ipsi ad compotum illum audiendum conjunctim & divisim intendant, ad minus duo eorum simul, si omnes vel plures quam duo interesse non possint &c. *Hil. Commun.* 12. *E.* 2.

(*l*) Wyltes. Visores. — De quibus quidem operationibus Willelmus de Waleton Attornatus prædicti Walteri [de Gatelyn] liberavit hic Rotulos de particulis, & prædicti Philippus [de la Beche] & Willelmus de Rude (*the Viewers*) liberarunt hic Contrarotulos, qui concordant cum Rotulis de particulis dictarum operationum in particulis & summa totali; & qui examinati fuerunt per Robertum de Thorpe Clericum assignatum ad hoc per Barones. *Mich. Fines &c.* 12. *E.* 2. *Rot.* 43. *a.*

(*m*) Wygorn. *Two Viewers came and made*

Chap. XXIV. *of the* EXCHEQUER. 293

Mention is made of Auditours of the Accounts of Bailiffs and Miniſters (*n*). K. *Edward* II, *Anno Regni* 16, appointed *Henry de Leiceſter* and *William de Oterhampton*, jointly and ſeverally, Auditours of the Accounts of the *Cuſtodes* of the Goods and Chatells, and of the Bailiffs and *Cuſtodes* of the Lands and Tenements of *Thomas* late Earl of *Lancaſter*, and of others of the King's Enemies and Rebells in *Norfolk*, *Suffolk*, and other Counties. The Commiſſion is *Teſte W. Exonienſi Epiſcopo Theſaurario vij die Octobris* (*o*).

VIII. Little occurs within the Cycle of my preſent Hiſtory, concerning the Clerk of the Eſtreats and foreign Summonces. On the twelfth Day of *November*, in the eighteenth Year of K. *Edward* II, all the Eſtreats as well of Fines and Iſſues forfeited, as alſo of Amercements before Juſtices of either Bench, Barons of the Exchequer, Juſtices in Eire, and other Juſtices aſſigned, ariſing in the Reign of K. *Edward* I, and of the preſent King, and likewiſe all other Eſtreats of Green-wax, which were in the Cuſtody of the Treaſurer's Remembrancer, were by Command of the Treaſurer and Barons delivered to *John de Chiſenhale*, Clerk of the Summonces, to keep (*p*). In *Michaelmaſs* Term, in the 19th Year of K. *Edward* II, *William de Bereford*, Chief Juſtice of the Common Bench, delivered into the Court of Exchequer ſeveral Files of Rolls, containing the Eſtreats of divers Fines, Iſſues, and Amerciaments; which Rolls were delivered to *Nicolas de Lye*, to be by him ſent out in Summonce (*q*). In the ſame

---

made Oath to the Expenſes about the Works of the ſaid Manour — De quibus operacionibus prædictus Ricardus liberavit hic quandam Cedulam de particulis earundem operationum, quæ examinata fuit per J. de Okham Baronem hujus Scaccarij. *Paſ. Commun.* 12. E. 2. Rot. 46. a.

(*n*) Rex Theſaurario & Baronibus ſuis de Scaccario ſalutem. Cum manſiverimus Cuſtodibus terrarum & tenementorum quæ fuerunt inimicorum & rebellium noſtrorum —, ac Auditoribus Compotorum Ballivorum, Miniſtrorum, & aliorum Receptorum in terris & tenementis illis, quod — —. *Trin. Brevia* 15. E. 2. Rot. 63. a.

(*o*) *Mich. Commiſſiones* 16. E. 2. Rot. 2. a.

(*p*) Anglia. De extractis liberatis Johanni de Chiſenhale. Memorandum quod xij die Novembris hoc anno, omnes extractæ tam de finibus & exitibus forisfactis quam de amerciamentis coram Juſticiarijs de utroq; Banco, Baronibus de Scaccario, Juſticiarijs Itinerantibus, & alijs Juſticiariis aſſignatis quibuſcumq; tam de tempore Regis nunc, quam de tempore Regis E. patris, & etiam omnes aliæ extractæ de Viridi cera quæ fuerunt in cuſtodia Rememoratoris Theſaurarij, liberantur de præcepto Theſaurarij & Baronum, Johanni de Chiſenhale Clerico Summonitionum cuſtodiendæ &c. *Mich. Communia* 18. E. 2. Rot. 4. parte 2.

(*q*) Memorandum quod W de Berfod Capitalis Juſticiarius de Banco liberavit hic xiij die Novembris hoc anno, unum ligamen rotulorum de finibus & exitibus forisfactis coram Juſticiarijs de Banco, de terminis S. Michaelis & Hiilarij de anno Regis nunc xviij; quod quidem ligamen continet lxij Rotulos;

same Year, on the third Day of *February*, the Estreats were, by the Command of the Treasurer and Barons, delivered to *Hugh de Colewyk*, Clerk. And *Hugh*, being then present before the Treasurer and Barons, took an Oath that he would well and truly keep the said Estreats, and all other Estreats hereafter delivered to him; and that he would well and truly send out in Summonce, with all the Haste and Dispatch he conveniently could, as well the Estreats which were not yet summoned, as also all such as should thenafter be delivered to him (*r*).

IX. There was also a *Clericus Brevium de Scaccario*. In the 5th Year of K. *Edward* I, *Laurence de Lincoln* was in that Office (*s*). It belonged to the Office of Chancellour of the Exchequer. In the 6th Year of K. *Edward* I, *Laurence de Lincoln* was *Clericus Brevium*, and had one *Adam* for his Companion or Fellow-Clerk. In that Year the King impowered the Treasurer to reward such Officers of the

Rotulos; & aliud ligamen Rotulorum de finibus & exitibus de Banco de terminis Paschæ & S. Trinitatis eodem anno, continens Liij Rotulos; & quoddam aliud ligamen de amerciamentis de Banco, de diversis terminis & diversis annis in diversis Comitatibus, continens v^{xx} & j & unam cedulam, de amerciamentis Vicecomitum in Banco de diversis terminis & de diversis annis, qui quidem Rotuli liberantur Nicholao de Lye xiiij die Novembris proximo sequenti ad summonendum. *Mich. Commun.* 19. *E.* 2. *Rot.* 2. *a.*

(*r*) De extractis Scaccarij liberatis Hugoni de Colewyk. Memorandum quod tertio die Februarij hoc anno, omnes extractæ tam de finibus & exitibus forisfactis quam de Amerciamentis, coram Justiciarijs de utroq; Banco, Baronibus de Scaccario, Justiciarijs Itinerantibus, & alijs Justiciarijs assignatis quibuscumq;, tam de tempore Regis nunc, quam de tempore Regis E. patris, & eciam omnes aliæ extractæ de Viridi cera, quæ fuerunt in custodia Johannis de Chisenhale, sicut continetur in Memorandis anni præcedentis inter Recorda de termino S. Michaelis, liberantur Hugoni de Colewyk Clerico de præcepto Thesaurarij & Baronum. Et prædictus Hugo præsens coram prædictis Thesaurario & Baronibus eodem die, præstitit sacramentum de custodiendo bene & fideliter extractas prædictas, & eciam alias extractas imposterum ei liberandas, & quod extractas quæ adhuc restant summonendæ, & eciam alias quæ ei imposterum liberabuntur, bene & fideliter summoniri faciet cum omni festinatione & expeditione quibus poterit bono modo. *Hil. Commun.* 19. *E.* 2. *Rot.* 4. *a.*

(*s*) Memorandum quod de Finibus & amerciamentis coram Baronibus anno Regni Domini Regis quarto, conceduntur & assignantur per Thesaurarium & Barones Laurencio de Lincolnia Clerico Brevium de Scaccario pro Laboribus suis Domino Regi impensis xl solidi, percipiendi & habendi de particulis subscriptis, scilicet De Johanne de Insula xx s quos Regi debet pro licentia concordandi, de Priore de Ponte fracto, unam marcam, quam Regi debet pro eodem; De Ricardo le Graunt de Dunmawe dimidia marca, quam Regi debet pro falso clamore. Postea recepit dictus Laurentius inde dimidiam marcam de Ricardo le Graunt per manus Germani Clerici Vicecomitis Essexiæ. Item recepit xx s de Johanne de Insula, per manus Willelmi Favelore Clerici Vicecomitis Dorsetæ. Item postea recepit unam marcam de Priore, per manus Vicecomitis Eboraciscira. *Pas. Communia* 5. *E.* 1 *Rot.* 5. *a.*

Exchequer as had not due Recompence for their Attendance and Labour about the King's Business. Whereupon the Treasurer, considering the great Labour and small Profit of the said *Laurence* and *Adam*, did, with the Consent of the Chancellour and Barons, grant to the said *Laurence* and *Adam*, that for the future they should receive to their own Use the Monies arising from the Issues of divers Lands, which were levied and answered by divers Sheriffs; so as that when such Issues were sent by the Sheriffs to the Exchequer, the same were to be delivered to *Laurence* and *Adam*; provided, that when Persons who had forfeited their Issues came at their Days and healed their former Defaults, then the Issues should be restored to such Persons; and instead of the Issues *Laurence* and *Adam* should receive the Money paid for healing the said Defaults (*t*).

X. Amongst the Officers of the Exchequer during the second Period, we may reckon the Chamberlains. In the first Period, or great Part of it, the Chamberlains in Fee, who were great Officers in the King's Court, sometimes sat and acted in Person in the King's Exchequer; and are numbered amongst the Barons there (*u*). But afterwards the Chamberlains in Fee usually deputed others to execute their Offices for them, both in the Great Exchequer and at the Receipt. The Persons so deputed were at first wont to be Knights. But others were sometimes deputed, who were not Knights. K. *Henry* III. gave *William Mauduit* Time till the Feast of the *H. Trinity*, to provide himself a Knight to serve for him in the Office of Chamberlain (*w*). The same King commanded the Barons to admit such Person as *Margaret de Riparijs* should present to them, to reside in her Room at the Exchequer, though he were not a Knight, in case they thought him fit in other Respects (*x*). When the Chamberlain in Fee deputed one to execute his Office for him, he was regularly to come in Person, and present his Deputy to the Treasurer and Barons at the Exchequer; and thereupon the Deputy used to be sworn and admitted. But sometimes he presented his Deputy to the Barons by his Steward, or other

(*t*) *Trin. Commun.* 6. *E.* 1. *Rot.* 7. *b.*
(*u*) *Hic*, cap. 25.
(*w*) Rex dedit respectum Willelmo Mauduit usq; ad festum S. Trinitatis, ad providendum sibi in Officio Camerariæ de quodam Milite qui Officium illud loco sui competenter gerere possit. *Pas. Commun.* 32. *Hen.* 3. *Rot.* 7. *a.*

(*x*) Baronibus, pro Margareta de Riparijs. Rex eisdem; Quod si Marger. de Riparijs præsentaverit eis virum idoneum ad residendum in Scaccario Regis loco suo, non omittant quin eum ad hoc recipiant, quamvis Miles non fuerit, dum tamen de persona ipsius in alijs rebus fuerint pacati. *Ex Memor.* 25. *Hen.* 3. *Rot.* 4. *b.*

Attorney

Attorney appointed for that Purpose; and sometimes by his Letters Patent directed to the Treasurer or Barons. Sometimes also he presented his Deputy to the King himself; and then, upon the King's Writ sent to the Barons of the Exchequer certifying the same, such Deputy was admitted. Of these several Presentments I shall set down some Instances according to the Order of Time. In the 29th Year of K. *Henry* III, *Margaret de Riparijs* presented to the King, *Thomas Esperun*, to act for her [as Chamberlain] in the Exchequer (*y*). In the 49th Year of the same King, *William Mauduit*, Earl of *Warwick*, by his Letters Patent presented *David* his Chamberlain to the Office of Usher of the *Receipt*; who was admitted and sworn (*z*). In the same 49th Year *Isabell* Countess of *Albemarle*, by her Attorneys, presented *Ralph de Stratton* to act for her in the Office of Chamberlain of the Exchequer during her Pleasure (*a*). In the 51st Year of K. *Henry* III, *William Mauduyt*, Earl of *Warwick*, deputed before the King, *Richard le Chamberleng*, to execute for him before the Barons his Office of Chamberlain of the Exchequer during his Pleasure; and the King commanded the Barons to admit *Richard* to the said Office (*b*). In the 52d Year *William de Beauchamp*, Heir of *William Mauduit*, late Earl of *Warwick*, came to the Exchequer, and presented *David de la More* to the Office of Usher of the *Receipt*, during his Pleasure; who was sworn and admitted (*c*). In the same 52d Year, *Isabell* Countess of *Albemarle* came in Person before the Barons of the Exchequer, and presented *Ralf de Bray* (her Deputy) to the Office of

(*y*) Rex eisdem [Baronibus]; Sciatis quod Marger. de Riparijs venit ad nos & præsentavit nobis Thomam Esperun, ad residendum loco suo in Officio suo ad Scaccarium. Et ideo &c. Breve est in forulo Marescalli. *Pas. Commun.* 29. *H.* 3. *Rot.* 8. *b.*

(*z*) Warr. Willelmus Maudut Comes Warwici præsentavit per Literas suas Patentes Davit Camerarium suum ad officium Ostiarij de Recepta; qui admissus ad hoc, juramentum præstitit. *Pas. Commun.* 49. *H.* 3. *Rot.* 10. *a.*

(*a*) Præsentatio Ysabellæ Comitissæ Albemarliæ. Hervicus de Borham & Adam de Stratton venerunt coram Baronibus de Scaccario pro eadem Comitissa, & præsentaverunt nomine suo, Radulphum de Stratton Clericum suum, ad residendum in eodem Scaccario loco ipsius Comitissæ, in Officio Camerarij, quamdiu dictæ Comitissæ placuerit. *Mich. Commun.* 49. *H.* 3. *Rot.* 1. *a.*

(*b*) Baronibus, pro Willelmo Mauduyt Comite Warr. Idem Willelmus attornavit coram Rege loco suo Ricardum le Chamberleng, ad exercendum coram Baronibus officium suum Camerarij, quod habet in Scaccario, quamdiu ei placuerit; Et ideo Rex mandat, quod prædictum Ricardum loco ipsius Willelmi ad hoc recipiant. *Ex Memor.* 51. *H.* 3. *Rot.* 4. *a.*

(*c*) Willelmus de Bello Campo hæres Willelmi Maudut quondam Comitis Warr. venit ad Scaccarium die Veneris proxima post Inventionem Sanctæ Crucis, & præsentavit Davidem de la More, ad officium Hostiarij Scaccarij de Recepta, Custodiendum quamdiu eidem Willelmo placuerit. Qui eodem die Sacramentum præstitit, & admissus fuit ad idem officium in forma prædicta. *Memor.* 52. *H.* 3. *Rot.* 9. *b.*

Chamberlain (*d*). In like Manner, *W. de Beauchamp*, Earl of *Warwick*, presented to the Treasurer and Barons *John Peverel*, to act for him in the Office of Chamberlain in the Exchequer till the *Michaelmass* then next following (*e*). About this Time also, *James* Earl of *Albemarle* was a Chamberlain in Fee of the Exchequer (*f*). In the Reign of K. *Edward* I, *Isabell* Countess of *Albemarle*, by *John de la Ware* her Steward, and by her Letter Patent and the King's Writ, presented *William de Cotton* to the Office of Chamberlainship of the Exchequer, to execute that Office until *Michaelmass* next (*g*). This was in the first Year of K. *Edward* I. In the same or the next Year, *William de Beauchamp* Earl of *Warwick* presented *William de Bradecote* (*h*); and *William* Earl of *Worcester* presented *William Golafre* (*i*). Soon after, *Isabell* Countess of *Albemarle* presented to the Barons *William de Cotton*, to act for her in the Great Exchequer during her Pleasure; and *Adam de Stratton* to act for her in the Exchequer of Receipt (*k*). In the 4th Year of K. *Edward* I, *Isabella de Fortibus*, Countess of *Albemarle*, Chamberlain in Fee of the Exchequer, granted

(*d*) Memorandum de quodam Camerario præsentato per Isabellam de Fortibus Comitissam Albermalliæ. Eadem venit coram Baronibus die Lunæ proximo ante festum S. Lucæ Ewangelistæ, & præsentavit ibidem Radulfum de Bray ad officium Camerariæ; qui eodem die admissus fuit ad idem Officium, & Sacramentum præstitit de fideliter se habendo &c. *Memor.* 52. *H.* 3. *Rot.* 2. *a.*

(*e*) Præsentatio W. de Bello Campo Comitis War. Memorandum quod xxvij die Maij, præsentavit dictus Willelmus per Literas suas Patentes directas Thesaurario & Baronibus, Johannem Peverel, ad intendendum Officio Camerarij in Scaccario loco ejusdem Comitis, usq; ad festum S. Michaelis proximo futurum. *Trin. Communia* [52 &] 53. *H.* 3. *Rot.* 12. *a.*

(*f*) *Ante*, cap. 20. sect. 7. ad ann. 52 & 53. *H.* 3. Ebor. Mandatum est.

(*g*) Præsentatio Isabellæ de Fortibus Comitissæ Albæmarliæ. Memorandum quod eadem Comitissa die Lunæ proximo ante festum Nativitatis S. Johannis Baptistæ, per Johannem de la Ware Seneschallum suum præsentavit Willelmum de Cotton ad Officium Camerariæ de Scaccario quod pertinet eidem Comitissæ, per Literam præfatæ Comitissæ Patentem & Breve Domini Regis, quod idem Willelmus stabit in Officio prædicto usq; ad festum S. Michaelis proximo futurum. *Ex Mem.* 1. *E.* 1. *Rot.* 7. *b.*

(*h*) Præsentacio Willelmi de Bello Campo Comitis Warwici. Idem venit coram Baronibus die Martis proximo post festum S. Agnetis, & præsentavit Willelmum de Bradecote, ad faciendum pro eo officium Camerar. in Scaccario: Qui eodem die admissus fuit per Thesaurarium & Barones, & præstitit Sacramentum de fideliter se habendo in Officio prædicto. *Ex Memor.* 1 & 2. *Edw.* 1. *Rot.* 4. *b.*

(*i*) Præsentatio Willelmi de Bello Campo Comitis Wygorniæ. Idem venit coram Baronibus die Lunæ in crastino clausi Paschæ, & præsentavit Willelmum Golafre ad attendendum ad officium Camerar. in Magno Scaccario. *Ex Memor.* 1 & 2. *E.* 1. *Rot.* 6. *b.*

(*k*) Præsentatio Isabellæ Comitissæ Albæmarliæ. Eadem venit in propria persona sua die Mercurij proximo ante festum S. Elphegi Martiris, & præsentavit Willelmum de Cotton ad Officium suum in Magno Scaccario pro ea faciendum quamdiu eidem Comitissæ placuerit, Et Adam de Stratton Clericum ad Officium suum ad Scaccarium de Recepta faciendum. *Ib. Rot.* 7. *b.*

by her Charter to *Adam de Stratton*, a Clerk of the Exchequer, the Manour of *Senehampton*, with the Hamlets of *Worth, Stratton,* and *Crikelad*, and with the Chamberlainship and Office thereof which she had in the Exchequer, with all its Appurtenances, to hold of the King and his Heirs, to *Adam* and his Heirs, doing the Office of Chamberlain of the Exchequer, in the same Manner as she and her Ancestours were wont to do the same. And the King received the Homage of *Adam* thereupon, and confirmed the said Charter of *Isabell*; and commanded the Treasurer and Barons to admit to the said Office *Adam* and his Heirs, or their Attorneys, in like Manner as had been used in the Time of *Isabell* and her Ancestours (*l*). *William* Earl of *Warwick* presented *William de la Porte* (*m*). At another Time, *William* Earl of *Warwick* presented *Philipp de Dounesley* by his Letter Patent directed to the Treasurer. *Philipp* was for this Time admitted out of the Treasurer's special Grace, till such Time as the Earl could come in Person before the Treasurer and Barons (as he ought by the Custom of the Exchequer) to make his Presentation (*n*). In another Year, *William* Earl of *Warwick* sent his Letter to the Treasurer's Lieutenant and Barons of the Exchequer, praying them to suffer such Person as *William de Pershore* should present to them, to supply the Earl's Place at the Exchequer (in the Room of *John de*

(*l*) *Mich. Communia* 4 & 5. *E*. 1. *Rot.* 2. *a.*

(*m*) Memorandum quod x° die Maij anno regni Regis E. xviij°, Willelmus de Bello Campo Comes Warrewici venit coram Baronibus & præsentavit Willelmum de la Porte ad Officium Camerariæ. Et idem Willelmus præstitit sacramentum coram eisdem, quod bene & fideliter se habebit in Officio prædicto. *Pas. Commun*. 18. *E*. 1. *Rot.* — *a*.

(*n*) De Camerario loco Comitis Warr. admisso ad Officium Camerarij in Seaccario. Memorandum quod die Martis videlicet proximo post Clausum Paschæ anno xxij°, Willelmus de Bello Campo Comes Warrwici direxit Litteras suas Patentes quæ sunt in custodia Rememoratoris, Willelmo Bathoniensi & Wellensi Episcopo Domini Regis Thesaurario in hæc verba, A sun treshonurable Pere en Dieu, Sire Willame par la grace de Deu Esvek de Baa e de Welles, Tresorer noster Seignur le Rey, Willame de Beauchamp Counte de Warrewyk saluz en noster Seignur; Por coe, Sire, ke Sire Wauter de Chastel ke aad garde le office ke a nus apent devaunt ws al Escheker, ne peut mes a cel office entendre, nus enveyoms a vus Sire Phelippe de Dounesley noster Clerk, e ws prioms, Cher Sire, sil ws plest, le memes cely Phelippe al avaundit office garder e sere volyet receure. En temonye de coe ws enveyoms ceste noster Lettre Patente; Done a Hampslape la veyle de Pask, lan del Regne noster Seignur le Rey vintyme secounde. Per quod dictus Thesaurarius de gratia sua speciali admisit hac vice prædictum Philippum ad officium prædictum faciendum, quousque prædictus Comes in propria persona sua coram eisdem Thesaurario & Baronibus venerit, & ipsum Philippum præsentaverit, prout de jure & secundum consuetudinem Scaccarij fuerit faciendum. *Pas. Communia* 22. *E*. 1. *Rot.* 1. *a.*

London)

London) till he could provide some other to do it (*o*). A while after, *Guy* Earl of *Warwick*, being then in the King's Service in the Marches of *Scottand*, by his Letters Patent, directed to the Treasurer and Barons, presented *Adam de Herwynton* to be his Deputy Chamberlain at the Exchequer during his Pleasure; who was by the Favour of the Court admitted and sworn (*p*). And afterwards the said Earl came in Person, and was himself sworn as Chamberlain; and then he nominated *William de Pershore* and the said *Adam de Herwynton* his Deputy Chamberlains, and likewise *Adam de Ramesey* Usher of the Receipt, who were admitted by the Court (*q*). In or about the 30th Year of K. *Edward* I, the Moiety of the Ushery of the Receipt was forfeited to the King by the Felony of *Adam de Stratton* (*r*). In the second Year of K. *Edward* II, the Earl of *Warwick*, one of the Chamberlains of the Exchequer in Fee, by his Letter presented *Peter le Blound* to act for him in that Office at the Exchequer; who was by the Favour of the Court admitted for this Time, provided that the Earl do come hereafter in Person to present his Chamberlain (*s*). When a Chamberlain in Fee was in Wardship, the Guardian nominated a Deputy. The Queen, having the Custody of *Baldwin del Isle*, appointed *Thomas Esperon* to be Deputy Chamberlain (*t*). Or, if the Office of the Chamberlain in Fee was seized into the King's Hands, or became devolved to him, then the King assigned one or more Per-

---

(*o*) Baronibus, pro Comite Warrewici. A ses treschiers amis Sire Philippe de Willughby Tenaunt le lieu Sire Wauter de Langeton, Treforer nostre Seignour le Roy al Escheker, e as autres Barons del Escheker, Willame de Beauchamp Counte Warrewik, si leur plest, salutz de e chieres amistes. Por ce que Johan de Loundres nostre Clerk qui tient nostre lieu devant vous al Escheker, ne poet nent plus illoeqs demorer: Vous prioms, si vous plest, que vous voillez suffrir de celuy, qe Sire Willame de Porshore vous presentera, pusse nostre lieu tenir tant come nous nous pussoms porver de un autre qe pusse nostre lieu tenir: E si rien voillez ver nous qe fere pussoms, le nous voiliez mander, come a celui qe voluntiers freit chofe qe bone vous fust. Adieu, qe touz jours vous gard. *Mich. Memorand.* 25 *E.* 1. *Rot.* —. *in bund.* 24 & 25 *E.* 1.

(*p*) *Mich. Præsentat.* 26 & 27 *E.* 1. *Rot.* 56. *b.*

(*q*) *Mich. Communia* 26 & 27 *E.* 1. *Rot.* 4. *b. tit* Brevia.

(*r*) Breve tangens Medietatem Hostiæ Receptæ forisfactam per Feloniam Adæ de Stratton. *Mich. Commun.* 30 & 31 *E.* 1. *Rot.* 4. *a. ex parte Remem. Thes.* The same is also entered in *Memor.* 30 & 31 *E.* 1. *Rot.* 9. *a. ex parte Remem. Reg.*

(*s*) *Pas. Præsent.* 2. *E.* 2. *Rot.* 76. *a.*

(*t*) Rex mandavit Baronibus [quod] liberari faciant Roberto de Chaure Clerico Dominæ Reginæ Officium Camerar. quod Thomas Esperon tenet in Scaccario, & quod ad ipsam Reginam pertinet ratione Custodiæ Baldewini de Insula quam ipsa Regina habet, & quod ipsi assignent eidem Thomæ officium Contrarotuli Receptæ de prædicto Scaccario. Breve est in f M. Et Regina mandavit prædictis Baronibus per breve suum, quod ipsi admittant prædictum Robertum. Clericum suum ad prædictum officium, sicut Rex mandavit eis. *Memor.* 39. *H.* 3. *Rot.* 8. *a.*

sons to execute the Office. K. *Edward* I, in the 6th Year of his Reign (the Office of Chamberlain of the Exchequer being then seized into his Hands) committed the same Office to *Ralph de Besages* during Pleasure (*u*). In the 7th Year of the same King, the Office of Chamberlain of the Exchequer was, by the King's Command, restored to *William de Beauchamp* Earl of *Warwick*; who, being present in Court, appointed two Persons to act for him in that Office, one at the Great Exchequer, the other at the *Receipt*; and they were admitted accordingly (*w*). In the 18th Year of K. *Edward* I, *Adam de Stratton* was removed from the Office of Chamberlain. Upon his Removal, an Account was taken of the Money then remaining in the Treasury. *William de Estden* was put in his Place (*x*). In the 26th Year of the same King, it being reported that *William de Beauchamp* Earl of *Warwick*, Chamberlain in Fee of the Exchequer, was dead; the Lieutenant of the Treasurer, the Barons and Justices at the Exchequer, took into the King's Hands the Office of the said Chamberlainship, and put out the several Persons who had acted in that Office under the Earl. Nevertheless, in regard the said several Persons so put out had well behaved themselves in their respective Places, the Lieutenant of the Treasurer, the Barons, and Justices appointed them to continue in their Places, and to act now under the King (in like Manner as they had lately done under the Earl) until the King should

(*u*) *Pas. Communia* 6. *E.* 1. *Rot.* 5. *b.*

(*w*) De Præcepto facto Baronibus de Scaccario pro Willelmo de Bello Campo Comite Warwici. Memorandum quod die Martis proximo ante festum S. Martini, venit Nicholaus de Stapleton ad Scaccarium, & injunxit Thesaurario. & Baronibus ex parte Domini Regis, quod rehabere facerent Willelmo de Bello Campo Comiti Warr. Ballivam suam de Cameraria tam ad Magnum Scaccarium quam ad Scaccarium de Recepta. Et idem Comes præsens in Scaccario admisit Ballivam suam prædictam & posuit loco suo ad Magnum Scaccarium prædictum, Radulphum Basset ad Officium suum ad idem Scaccarium pro eo faciendum, & Petrum de Leycestre Clericum, ad Scaccarium de Recepta, ad Officium suum pro eo faciendum ibidem; qui præsentes fuerunt coram eisdem Baronibus, & præstiterunt Sacramentum de fideliter se habendo in Officijs prædictis. *Mich. Commun.* 7° *incip. E.* 1. *Rot.* 2. *a.*

(*x*) Memorandum quod die Martis xvij die Januarij, anno regni Regis E. xviij, amotus fuit Adam de Stratton ab officio Camerarij in Scaccario Domini Regis. Quo die remanserunt in Thesauro Domini Regis *such a Sum of Money*. Et postea eodem die Martis receperunt Thesaurarius & alius Camerarius *such a Sum*; & die Jovis proximo sequente *such a Sum*: Summa duorum dierum cum billa rem. *so much*. De quibus dictus Thesaurarius & unus Camerarius solverunt Alianoræ Reginæ Angliæ Consorti Regis C l per breve Regis de Liberate. Et sic remanent *so much*. Et postea cessavit Scaccarium de Recepta quod nichil in eo Receptum fuit aut liberatum usq; diem Veneris xxvij diem Januarij, illo die computato. Et die Sabbati in crastino recepit Willelmus de Estden Officium Camerariæ supradictæ. *Ex Hilar. Commun.* 18. *E.* 1. *Rot.*—*a.*

further

further declare his Pleasure therein; and the said Officers were sworn and admitted accordingly (*y*). In the 26th Year of K. *Edward* I, *William de Brykhull* was commanded by the King's Writ (which is entered *inter Hil. Brevia* 26 *Edw.* 1. *Rot.* 116. *a.*) to appear in Person at the Exchequer such a Day, to hear and do what the Barons there should enjoin him. He came accordingly, and was admitted by the Treasurer and Barons to the Office of Chamberlain of the Exchequer, in the Room of *Richard de Luda*; and was sworn into that Office. And on the Day following he appointed one to be his Deputy Chamberlain, as to the Custody of Countertallies; which Deputy was sworn and admitted (*z*). K. *Edward* II. constituted *Henry de Lutegereshale* Chamberlain of the Exchequer, during Pleasure, in the Room of *William de Brikhull* (*a*); who afterwards made humble Suit to the King to be discharged from that Office, and was discharged accordingly by Writ of Privy Seal (*b*). K. *Edward* II, *Anno Regni* 9°, by his Letters Patent constituted Master *William de Maldon* Chamberlain in the Receipt of the Exchequer (in the Room of Master *John de Golafre*, deceased, who had lately executed that Office for *Guy de Beauchamp* late Earl of *Warwick*, Chamberlain in Fee) and commanded the Treasurer and Chamberlains to admit him to the said Office. Accordingly he was admitted and sworn before the Treasurer, Barons, and Chamberlains. And *John de Aston*, Clerk to the said Master *John* [*de Golafre*] surrendered to the Court two great Keys and three-and-twenty lesser Keys (being Keys to the Doors of the Treasury and

---

(*y*) *Trin. Commun.* 26. *E.* 1. *Rot.* 84. *a.*

(*z*) *Pas. Commun.* 26. *E.* 1. *Rot.* 68. *a.*

(*a*) Cum Rex per Litteras suas Patentes, loco Willelmi de Brikhull nuper unius Camerarij de Scaccario, constituerit Henricum de Lutegereshale Camerarium ibidem quamdiu Regi placuerit, prout in Litteris Regis prædictis plenius continetur: Mandat Thesaurario [& Baronibus], quod ipsum Henricum ad Officium illud admittant, & ea quæ ad Officium illud pertinent liberent, prout alias fieri consuevit. Teste Rege apud Comenok, xxiij die Augusti anno primo. Per breve de Magno Sigillo. *Mich. Commun.* 1. *Edw.* 2. *Rot.* 16. *a.*

(*b*) Baronibus, pro Henrico de Lutegarshale. Edward par la grace de Dieu &c, Au Tresorier & as Barons de nostre Eschekier salutz. Nous vous fesoms savoir, qe noster cher Clerc Henri de Lutegarshale, qi ad este un de nous Chaumberleyns de nostre dit Escheqiere, & qi bien & loiaument nous ad servien cele office, & en autres, tant come il fuist en nostre Houstel, Nous ad fait requerre, qe com il soit greve de une forte maladie, par quei il ne puet mes suffire a nous servir en le deit office: Nous luy voloms asoudre de meisme loffice, & lui en tenir pur excusez & nous endonantz foi a lexcusacion avaunt dite, tout soit ceo qe nous voudriens volunters avoir le servise du dit Henri, come de celui qe nous tenoms bon & loial: Nepurquant pur lesement de lui, & a sa requesté, nous lui tenoms a deschargeez de ci enavant del Office avantdit. Don soutz nostre Privee seal a Everwyk, le xxviij jour de Feverir, lan de nostre regne quint. *Pas. Brevia* 5. *E.* 2. *Rot.* 39. *a.*

to the Coffers there) which were the same Day delivered to the said Master *William* (*c*). At the same time, the Office of Keeper of the Tallies in the Exchequer, which *Robert de la Feld* lately held under the Earl of *Warwick*, was, on behalf of the King, committed by the Treasurer and Barons to *John de Vyene*, Clerk; who was sworn into that Office: And the said *Robert* having surrendered in Court before the Treasurer and Barons six Keys belonging to the Coffers of Tallies, the same were delivered to the said *John* (*d*). And at the same time likewise, *Hugh de Bray* was appointed by the Treasurer and Barons, on behalf of the King, to be Usher of the Receipt, in the Room of *Adam de Rameseye* (who had lately been one of the Ushers of the Receipt under the said Earl) and he was sworn accordingly (*e*). In the 16th Year of K. *Edward* II, *Richard de Luda*, one of the Chamberlains for Tallies, being at present hindered from executing his said Office personally, sent to the Exchequer by his Clerk, *Walter Skyp*, eight Keys belonging to his said Office. Whereupon, the Barons of the Exchequer ordered, that *Richard de Ty* should have the Custody of the said Keys, and should execute the said Office [of Keepership of the Tallies] in the mean time. And *Richard de Ty* was sworn to behave himself well therein (*f*). K. *Edward* II. committed the Office of Chamberlain to *Richard de Crumbwell*; and *Richard* came before the Barons, and deputed *Geoffrey de la Thorne* to act for him as Keeper of the Tallies; who was admitted and sworn (*g*). In the Room of *Richard de Crumbwell*, the same King constituted his Kinsman, Master *James Despaigne*, one of the Chamberlains of the Receipt of Exchequer, during his Pleasure, with the accustomed Salary (*h*). In the

(*c*) *Mich. Communia* 9. *E.* 2. *Rot.* 89. *a.*
(*d*) *Ib. juxt.*
(*e*) *Ibid.*
(*f*) De Ricardo de Ty admisso ad custodiam Talliarum in Scaccario. Ricardus de Luda unus Camerar [iorum] tall. hujus Scaccarij, qui quibusdam de causis impeditus est ad præsens quominus deservire potest in officio suo prædicto, misit hic modo xx die Januarij per Walterum Skyp Clericum suum octo claves de officio suo prædicto. Et concordatum est per Barones, quod Ricardus de Ty habeat Custodiam dictorum clavorum, & quod intendat dicto officio quousq; &c. Et præstitit sacramentum de bene &c. *Hil. Commun.* 16. *E.* 2. *Rot.*—*a.*

(*g*) Memorandum quod Ricardus de Crumbwell, cui Dominus Rex commisit Officium Camerariæ quod Henricus de Lutegarshale nuper habuit in Recepta Scaccarij, venit hic coram Baronibus modo die Martis proximo post Crastinum Clausi Paschæ, & ponit loco suo Galfridum de la Thorne Clericum, ad custodiendas Tallias hic in Scaccario &c. Et idem Galfridus ad hoc admissus per eosdem Barones præstitit Sacramentum de bene & fideliter se habendo &c. *Pas. Commun.* 5. *E.* 2. *Rot.* 50. *a. inter Præsentationes.*

(*h*) De Camerario constituto. Rex omnibus ad quos &c, salutem. Sciatis quod loco Ricardi de Crombwell nuper unius Camerariorum Scaccarij nostri de Recepta, constituimus

the Reign of K. *Edward* I, *Richard de Lue*, a Chamberlain of the Exchequer, for speaking rash and outrageous Words in Court to *John de Cobham*, a Baron of the Exchequer, was put out of his Office of Chamberlainship. *John de Cobham*, in his Life-time, and *Henry de Cobham*, his Heir and Executour, after *John*'s Death, forgave *Richard* that Trespass. Hereupon the King, by his Writ of Privy Seal, commanded the Treasurer and Barons to restore him to his said Chamberlainship, or else to put him into some other proper Office at the Exchequer. And Prince *Edward*, by his Writ of Privy Seal, recommends *Richard de Lue* to the Treasurer for the same Purpose (*i*).

XI. The Treasurer and Chamberlains had under them certain Clerks attending on the King's Business at the Exchequer. These Clerks, during the Time of their Attendance there, were at Livery or Allowance from the King. So it was (for Example) in the First Year of K. *Richard* I, whilst they staid at *Westminster* to attend the Sealing of the King's Summonces (*k*); and whilst they (together with Ten *Tellers*) were at *Saresbury*, receiving the King's Money arising by the Dismes (*l*). The Clerks employed under the Treasurer and Chamberlains at the *Receipt* of Exchequer were usually called, during the First Period, *Clerici Thesaurarij & Camerariorum*, and *Clerici de Thesauro* or *de Recepta*, without distinguishing them from one another by particular Names of Office. Hence hath risen some Obscurity. It seemeth (but I speak only upon Conjecture) that under the Terms *Clerici Thesaurarij*, were comprehended the Officers who in Process of Time were called, Clerk of the Pells, Writer of the Tallies, &c. and indeed all the Officers of the *Receipt*, except those whose Offices were Serjeanties, and those who served under the Chamberlains in such Acts of Clerkship as related immediately to the Chamberlain's Office. In the Upper Exchequer there are but few Memorials concerning the Officers or Clerks of the *Receipt*. The Names of some of them do casually occur; and little or nothing more is said. *John de*

---

constituimus dilectum Consanguineum nostrum Magistrum Jacobum de Ispania, ad dictum officium ibidem exercendum, quamdiu nobis placuerit; percipiendo in eodem officio feodum consuetum. In cujus &c; T. Rege apud Crokeham xxx die Januarij. Per breve de Privato Sigillo. *Pat.* 10. *Edw.* 2. *m.* 30.

(*i*) *Trin. Brevia* 33 & 34. *E.* 1. *parte* 1. *Rot.* 41. *a.*

(*k*) Et in liberationibus Clericorum Thesaurarij & Camerariorum, qui moram fecerunt apud Westmon. ad Summonitiones sigillandas, xij s & vj d. *Mag. Rot.* 1. *R.* 1. *Rot.* 13. *a. Lond. & Midd.*

(*l*) Et in liberationibus clericorum Thesaurarij & Camerariorum & x Computatorum qui receperunt denarios Decimarum apud Sar., Cs: Et Quietus est. *Ib. Rot.* 10. *a. Wilt.*

Lincoln,

Lincoln, *John Dunden*, and *Richard de Ceftreford*, are ftyled Clerks of the *Receipt* (*m*). And others are mentioned after the like Manner. In the 31ft Year of K. *Edward* I, *Nicolas de Okham*, the Treafurer's Clerk, who made or wrote the Tallies at the *Receipt* of Exchequer, being unable to attend at the faid *Receipt*; whereby the Bufinefs there was put to a Stop: The Chancellour of the Exchequer (who was alfo the Treafurer's Lieutenant) and the Barons, unanimoufly agreed, that till fuch Time as *Nicolas* returned and acted at the faid Receipt, or fome other Perfon was deputed to execute that Office, *John de Brantingham*, the faid Chancellour's Clerk, fhould execute the faid Office. And *John* was accordingly fworn to behave himfelf well therein (*n*). In *Hilary* Term in the 34th Year of K. *Edward* I, *Nicolas de Ocham*, a Clerk in the Receipt of Exchequer, to whom it belonged to write the Tallies of Acquittance for Perfons who paid Money into the King's Exchequer, was fo fick, that he could not write the Tallies, nor do other Things pertaining to his faid Office; by means whereof, feveral Perfons who had paid Monies at the Receipt of Exchequer, had not yet received their Tallies (as regularly they ought) but only Bills tefti-

(*m*) Recognitio Alexandri de Suffolk. Idem venit & recognovit fe teneri Johanni de Lincolnia Clerico de Recepta in ix marcis ——. *Hil. Recognit.* 52 & 53. *H.* 3. *Rot.* 16. *b.*

Eadem [Matilda quondam uxor Henrici de la Pomereye] venit coram Baronibus, & recognovit fe debere Johanni Dunden Clerico de Scaccario de Recepta pro quodam equo xl s —. *Paf. Recognit.* 52 & 53. *H.* 3. *Rot.* 16. *b.*

Idem [Mathæus de Ceftria] venit coram Baronibus, & recognovit fe teneri Ricardo de Ceftreford Clerico de Recepta in quindecim folidis. *Paf. Recogn. ib. Rot.* 16. *b.*

(*n*) De Johanne de Brantingham Clerico deputato ad Tallias fcribendas. Die Mercurij in craftino Sancti Vincencij, videlicet xxiij° die Menfis Januarij nunc, Philippus de Wylugby Cancellarius de Scaccario & tenens locum Venerabilis Patris W. Coventrenfis & Lichefedenfis Epifcopi Thefaurarij Regis Scaccarij prædicti, Willelmus de Carletone, Petrus de Leyceftria, Johannes de Infula, Rogerus de Hegham, & Magifter Ricardus de Abyndon Barones de Scaccario prædicto, unanimiter concordarunt, quod quia plures qui denarios ad Scaccarium ad opus Regis folvere debent, ut fertur, Solutiones fuas differunt & differre proponunt, quoufq; Nicholaus de Okham Clericus Thefaurarij prædicti ad Tallias debita folventibus ad Receptam Scaccarij prædicti faciendas deputatus, qui jam moratur extra Curiam, præfens exiftat ad Receptam prædictam, ad faciendas tallias omnibus & fingulis pecuniam ibidem folventibus, de fuis folutionibus &c, vel quod alius loco ipfius Nicholai ad hoc deputetur; ac de die in diem neceffario nofcitur, oportere pecuniam ad partes Scotiæ de Thefauro Regis ad fuorum negociorum expeditionem ibidem multipliciter emittere, quod nullo fenfu fieri valeret, nifi qui folutiones fuas ad dictum Scaccarium funt facturi, eas ibidem faciant, & celerius quo poterunt; Johannes de Brantingham Clericus dicti Cancellarij intendat loco dicti Nicholai, ad Tallias faciendas omnibus & fingulis pecuniam folventibus ad opus Regis ad Receptam prædictam, ufq; ad adventum ejufdem Nicholai, & idem ad hoc intendere valeat. Et prædictus Johannes præftitit Sacramentum de fideliter fe habendo &c. *Hilar. Communia* 31. *E.* 1. *Rot.* 28. *a. in bundello anni* 30 & 31. *E.* 1. *ex parte Remem. Thef.*

fying

Chap. XXIV.   *of the* EXCHEQUER.   305

fying the Receipt of the Money; upon which Bills a final Allowance could not be made to them at the Exchequer: Whereupon, this present seventh Day of *February*, it was ordered by *John de Drokenesford*, the Treasurer's Lieutenant, and the Barons, that some Clerk be appointed to write the said Tallies, and to execute the said Office *par interim*. And instantly the said Lieutenant and Barons appointed *John Deverey* Clerk thereunto; namely, to write as well the Tallies for the Time past, for Payments upon which Bills had been made, as the Tallies for the Time to come upon Payments hereafter to be made, until the Treasurer's Return; that the said Treasurer, when he came, might dispose of the said Office as he thought meet; unless the said *Nicolas* should in the mean time recover his Health and be able to execute the Office himself. And the said *John* was sworn (*o*). *Nicolas de Ocham* died of his said Sickness. Afterwards, on *Monday* the Morrow of the Close of *Easter*, to wit, the 12th Day of *April*, the Bishop of *Coventry* and *Lichfeld*, the Treasurer, presented here in the Exchequer before the Barons and Chamberlains of the Exchequer, *William de Eston* his Clerk, to execute in the Exchequer of *Receipt*, in the said Treasurer's Room, the Office which *Nicolas de Ocham*, lately the Treasurer's Clerk there, now deceased, did in his Life-time execute; that is, to keep the Keys of the King's Treasury, which do belong to the said Treasurer, in his stead, and to enroll the Receipts and Issues made in the Exchequer of *Receipt*, &c, and to write the Tallies of the Exchequer, and to do other Things pertaining to that Office. And the said *William* was admitted; and immediately was sworn, that he should behave himself well and truly, and that he

(*o*) De Clerico deputato ad scribendas tallias in Scaccario. Memorandum quod cum Nicholaus de Ocham Clericus de Recepta Scaccarij, ad quem spectat scribere tallias de acquietancia solvencium denarios ad Scaccarium Regis dum officio illi intendit, tali infirmitate ad præsens detineatur, quod hujusmodi tallias scribere non possit, nec aliunde eidem officio intendere &c; per quos [*rectius*, quod] plures solventes denarios ad ipsam receptam Scaccarij, nondum habent tallias quas inde habere deceret, set tantummodo billas testificantes receptionem &c, per quas finalem allocationem hic ad Scaccarium habere non possunt: Concordatum est nunc vij⁰ die Februarij, per J. de Drokenesford tenentem locum Thesaurarij & Barones, quod aliquis Clericus assignetur ad tallias hujusmodi scribendas, & ad intendendum officio illi &c quousq; &c. Et instanter idem . . tenens locum Thesaurarij & Barones assignarunt ad hoc Johannem Deverey Clericum, ut videlicet scribat tam tallias de tempore præterito de solutionibus &c de quibus fiunt billæ &c, quam de tempore futuro de solutionibus faciendis &c, usq; ad adventum Thesaurarij, ut idem Thesaurarius inde in adventu suo disponat quod inde &c, nisi dictus Nicholaus interim convalescat &c, per quod ipse met scribere & intendere valeat &c. Et dictus Johannes præstitit sacramentum de bene & fideliter se habendo &c. *Hil. Communia* 34. *E.* 1. *Rot.* 20. *b. parte* 1.

would

would not, by Pretext of any Precept from the Treasurer, or from his Lieutenant in his Absence, or from any other, deliver any Money out of the King's Treasury, to any Person without the King's Writ, or procure or consent to have the same delivered, &c. (*p*).

The Clerkship of the *Pells* is probably an ancient Clerkship. There remaineth in the Treasury at the *Receipt* of Exchequer, a *Pell* (or it may be a *Counter-pell*) of the ninth Year of K. *Henry* III; which is the most ancient of any that I have yet seen. I have quoted some Things out of it at the Conclusion of this Chapter. In the 35th Year of K. *Henry* III, we find the Pell or Pell-roll is called *Magnus Rotulus de Recepta* (*q*); in the 5th (*r*), and the 9th (*s*) Year of K. *Edward* II, *Pellis Memorandorum de Recepta Scaccarij*.

(*p*) De Willelmo de Efton admiffo ad officium in Scaccario. Memorandum quod modo die Lunæ in craftino claufi Paschæ, videlicet xij° die menfis Aprilis, Venerabilis pater Walterus Coventrenfis & Lichfeldenfis Epifcopus Thefaurarius præfentavit hic in Scaccario coram Baronibus & Camerarijs de Scaccario, Willelmum de Efton Clericum fuum, ad officium illud in Scaccario Receptæ loco ipfius Thefaurarij exercendum, quod Nicholaus de Ocham nuper Clericus ejufdem Thefaurarij ibidem, jam defunctus, dum vixerat excercebat &c, videlicet, ad claves Thefaurariæ Regis ad ipfum Thefaurarium pertinentes loco fuo cuftodiendas, & recept[as] & liberationes in Scaccario Receptæ faciendas irrotulandas &c, & tallias Scaccarij fcribendas, & ad alia facienda quæ officio illi incumbunt &c. Et idem Willelmus ad hoc admiffus eft &c; & inftanter præftitit facramentum, de bene & fideliter fe habendo &c, & quod prætextu præcepti ipfius Thefaurarij vel . . tenentis locum ejus in abfencia ipfius, vel alicujus alterius, ei faciendi, nullam pecuniam de Thef[auro] Regis alicui liberabit fine brevi Domini Regis, feu liberari procurabit vel confenciet &c. *Paf. Commun.* 34. *E.* 1. *Rot.* 31. *a. parte* 1.

(*q*) Et de MMM, DC & xxiiij l xix s iiij d ob., de exitibus diverforum Comitatuum, & placitis Juftic. Itinerantium tam de Forefta quam ad alia placita, & Tallagijs plurium villarum per manus diverforum Vicecomitum & Ballivorum, quorum particulæ continentur in quodam Rotulo extracto de Magnis Rotulis de Recepta de prædicto tempore; Et de DCCCC Lxxviij l x s ob. de Vinis venditis per manus diverforum, quorum particulæ continentur in quodam Rotulo extracto de Magnis Rotulis de Recepta de prædicto tempore; Et de CLv l xiij s v d de Pannagio Foreftæ & Hayarum Wiltefyræ, Suthamtoniæ, Norhamtoniæ, & Notingehamiæ, ficut continetur in Rotulo de particulis extracto de Magnis Rotulis de Recepta; Et de MDC Lxvj l xv s iij d de Donis diverforum, quorum particulæ continentur in quodam Rotulo exftracto de Magnis Rotulis de Recepta; Et de D & xx l xvj s & viij d, de Finibus pro Cartis de Warenna, mercatis, foris, nundinis, & pro brevibus habendis, ficut continetur in rotulo de particulis extracto de Magnis Rotulis de Recepta. *Mag. Rot.* 35. *H.* 3. *Rot. Compotor. in Compo. de Garderoba. m.* 1. *a.*

(*r*) Londonia. Memorandum quod cum in Pelle Memorandorum de Recepta Scaccarij, de Termino S Michaelis anno Regis nunc tercio, oftenfa hic coram . . tenente locum Thefaurarij & Baronibus, modo in craftino S. Martini contineatur, quod——. *Mich. Commun.* 5. *E.* 2. *Rot.* 21. *a.*

(*s*) —irrotulandum in Memorandis Scaccarij hic, & in Pelle Memorandorum de Recepta Scaccarij. *Paf. Commun.* 9. *E.* 2. *Rot.* 99. *a. citat. hic Cap.* 20, *fect.* 7. Memorandum quod.

Chap. XXIV. *of the* EXCHEQUER.

XII. In the 28th Year of K. *Henry* III, *Simon de Westminstre* was chosen one of the Tellers of the Exchequer by the Treasurer, and was sworn before the Barons to behave himself truly in that Office (*t*). In the next Year *Ralf Sumer* was put into the Office of a Teller by the Treasurer, and was sworn before the Barons (*u*). *Anno* 52 of the same King, *James de Langedone* was made one of the four Tellers of the Exchequer by the Treasurer, and was sworn before the Barons (*uu*). In the 26th Year of K. *Edward* I, *Thomas de Helles* came into the Exchequer, and surrendered his Office of Teller to the Treasurer, who thereupon the same Day gave that Office to another, who was then admitted, and sworn before the Treasurer and Barons (*w*).

XIII. At the *Receipt* of Exchequer there were also some Serjeanties or Hereditary Offices; namely, a *Pesour* and a *Fusour*. First of the former of these two, *viz.* the *Pesour, Ponderator,* or *Weigher*. This, I suppose, was the Serjeanty which in the 4th Year of K. *John* was vested in *Thomas de Windesore* (*x*), and remained in that Family for some Time afterwards. About the 22d Year of K. *Henry* III, it was vested in *John de Wyndesore*, and from him descended to his Son *Thomas* (*y*). About the 35th Year of K. *Henry* III, it was vested in *John,*

Son

(*t*) Die Lunæ in festo S. Priscæ Virginis venit Simon de Westm. electus ut esset unus de Numeratoribus ad Scaccarium de Recepta; appositus est ad Officium illud per Dominum Willelmum de Haverhull Thesaurarium; & fecit sacramentum fidelitatis coram Baronibus. *Ex Memor.* 28. *H.* 3. *Rot.* 5. *b. ad imum.*

(*u*) Memorandum de Numeratoribus faciendis. Die Veneris proxima post festum S. Andreæ, venit Radulfus Sumer, electus ut esset unus de Numeratoribus ad Scaccarium de Recepta; appositus est ad Officium illud per Dominum Willelmum de Haverhull Thesaurarium; & fecit sacramentum fidelitatis coram Baronibus. *Mich. Commun.* 29. *H.* 3. *Rot.* 4. *a.*

(*uu*) Jacobus de Langedone, cui Magister Thomas de Wymundeham Thesaurarius dedit officium unius de quatuor Numeratoribus, fecit sacramentum coram Baronibus, quod fideliter serviet Regi in officio prædicto. *Memor.* 52. *H.* 3. *Rot.* 1. *a.*

(*w*) Memorandum quod Thomas de Helles, qui habuit Officium unius Numeratoris ad Receptam Scaccarij, ex dono Fratris Josep quondam Prioris S. Johannis Jerusalem in Anglia Thesaurarij Domini Regis, & quod Officium ad donationem Thesaurarij qui pro tempore fuerit pertinet ab antiquo, Venit ad Scaccarium ij° die Maij anno xxvj°, & reddidit W. Coventrensi & Lich. Episcopo Officium prædictum. Et idem Episcopus Thesaurarius, eodem die dedit Officium illud   de Helles Fratri dicti Thomæ, qui eodem die admissus est ad idem Officium; qui coram eodem Thesaurario & Baronibus hic præstitit sacramentum, quod bene & fideliter se habebit in Officio supradicto. *Pas. Commun.* 26. *E.* 1. *Rot.* 77. *a.*

(*x*) Tomas de Windlesores r c de v marcis pro Serjanteria sua: In thesauro nichil, Et in Perdonis ipsi Tomæ v marcas, Quia residens est ad Scaccarium Regis, per breve Regis, Et Q. e. *Mag. Rot.* 4. *J. Rot.* 7. *b. Dorsete & Sumersete.*

(*y*) Rex eisdem [Baronibus;] Sciatis quod cepimus Homagium Thomæ de Wyndesore filij Johannis de Wyndesore, de terris quas prædictus

Son and Heir of *Thomas de Windesor* (*z*). In the 41ft and 42d Years of that King, it was vefted in *John de Windesor* (*a*). In the 48th Year of that King, it was vefted in Sir *John de Windesor*, who conveyed it in Fee to *Adam de Stratton* by Feoffment; which Feoffment was infpected and confirmed by the King (*b*). It was conveyed to *Adam de Stratton* in Mortgage; and *Adam* was to reconvey it to Sir *John*, whenever Sir *John* or his Heirs enfeoffed *Adam* or his Heirs of twelve Librates in Land or yearly Rent, quit-free, payable out of one entire Eftate of one Tenure, according to a good and large Valuation, fuch as fhould be to the Content of *Adam* or his Heirs; as appeareth by the Deeds of the faid Parties acknowledged and enrolled in the Excheqner (*c*). In the 18th Year of K. *Edward* I, *William de Stratton* was *Weigher* at the *Receipt*. He came then before the Barons, and attorned *Henry del Palace* to execute for him the Office of *Weigher*; and *Henry* was fworn before the [Treafurer and] Chamberlains to behave himfelf well (*d*). The fame K. *Edward* I, by his Letters of the Privy Seal, fignified to the Treafurer and Barons of his Exchequer, that he had granted to *John le Convers* the Office of *Pefour* of Silver at the *Receipt*, in the Room of *William de Stratton*, with the ufual Fee; and commanded them to caufe Letters Patent of the Exchequer to be made to him of the faid Office for his Life, and to put him in

prædictus J. de nobis tenuit in Capite, & quæ ipfum Thomam hæreditarie contingunt, & ei feifinam fieri præcepimus de omnibus terris prædictis cum pertinentijs fuis: Et ideo vobis mandamus, quod eundem Thomam ad Officium quod prædictus Johannes habuit ad Scaccarium noftrum, & quod præfatum Thomam hæreditarie contingit, recipiatis, & ei inde plenam faifinam habere faciatis. *Memor*. 22. *Hen*. 3. *Rot*. 8. *a*.

(*z*) Rex Baronibus. Sciatis quod cepimus homagium Johannis filij & hæredis Thomæ de Windlefore, de omnibus terris & tenementis quæ idem Thomas tenuit de nobis in Capite. Et ideo vobis mandamus, quod de officio quod idem Thomas habuit in Scaccario noftro, de quo fuit feifitus tamquam pertinente ad tenementum fuum quod de nobis tenuit die quo obijt, eidem Johanni plenam feifinam habere faciatis. *Memor*. 35. *H*. 3. *Rot*. 1. *a*.

(*a*) Mandatum eft Vicecomiti Sumerfetæ & Dorfetæ, quod habeat coram &c in craftino S. Johannis Baptiftæ corpus Aluredi de Nicole, ad refpondendum Johanni de Wyndefor Ponderatori Regis de Scaccario, de xxx s, ficut rationabiliter &c; Et habeat breve. *Paf. Commun*. 41. *H*. 3. *Rot*. 15. *a*.

Mandatum eft Vicecomiti Suhamtoniæ, quod diftringat Adam Gurdun per terras & catalla ———, ad refpondendum Johanni de Windlefore Ponderatori de Scaccario, de hoc quod pratum fuum falcavit ———. *Memor*. 42. *H*. 3. *Rot*. 5. *a*.

(*b*) *Mag. Rot*. 49. *Hen*. 3. *Rot*. 9. *a*. Item Wylt.

(*c*) *Mich. Recognit*. 49. *H*. 3. *Rot*. 13. *a*.

(*d*) De Attornato Willelmi de Stratton. Memorandum quod viij die Junij anno xviij°, Willelmus de Stratton venit coram Baronibus, & ponit loco fuo Henricum de Pallacio, ad faciendum pro eo ad Receptam Scaccarij officium Ponderar[iæ]. Et idem Henricus præftitit facramentum coram Camerar[ijs] †, quod bene & fideliter fe habebit in officio prædicto. Per Thefaurarium. *Trin. Commun*. 18. *Edw*. 1. *Rot*.— *a*. † *pro* Camerarijs, *forfan legendum* Baronibus.

Poffeffion

Possession thereof in due Manner (*e*); and Letters Patent were made to him accordingly (*f*). It appeareth by the Roll of Serjeanties (which is without Date) that *Thomas de Windesore*'s Serjeanty of *Weigher* at the Exchequer was alienated in Part. The Lands alienated were valued at xiij *l* vij *s* viij *d*. And thereupon *Thomas de Windesore* made Fine to the King, for the Tenants of those Lands, and with their Consent, at iiij *l* ix *s per Annum*; and each of the Tenants was to answer to *Thomas* for the third Part of the yearly Value of his Tenement; and *Thomas* was to do the Service of the said Serjeanty for his Part, which was not alienated (*g*).

XIV. Another Serjeanty at the *Receipt* of Exchequer was the *Fuforie*. By *Fusor*, I suppose, we are to understand *Melter*. One *William* was *Fusor* in the Reign of K. *Henry* II and *Richard* I. And after *William*'s Death, *Joia* his Widow profered to the King x Marks, to have the Lands and Chatells of her Husband, and to have Right for the Debts due to her Husband, and to have her Husband's Office at the Exchequer for the Benefit of his Children; but she not having Money wherewith to pay the Fine so profered, *Andrew del Eschequer* paid it: And thereupon the Custody of the Heir of *William*, with his Land and Debts (saving to *Joia* her Dower) was granted to *Andrew* by the Chief Justicier and his Companions (*h*). In the 24th Year of K. *Henry*

(*e*) Edward par la grace de Dieu &c, Au Tresorier & as Barons del Escheqier salutz. Come nous eoms grantez a nostre chier & amez Serjaunt Johan le Convers, qil soit Pesour del argent a nostre Receite, en lieu de Willam de Stratton; l'arnaunt pur lossiz autiel feodz come le dit Willame prist: Vous maundoms, qe sur ceo facez aver au dit Johan Lettres overtes de nostre Eschequier a durer a tute sa vie, e le mettez en possession e en estat du dit office en due manere. Done souz nostre Prive Seal a Steynwigges le xxiiij jour de Septembre, lan de nostre Regne xxvj. *Mich. Commun.* 26 & 27. *Edw.* 1. *Rot.* 1. *a.*

(*f*) Rex omnibus ad quos p L p. Sciatis quod concessimus dilecto Servienti nostro Johanni le Convers, Officium Ponderariæ Receptæ nostræ, quod Willelmus de Stratton tenuit, Habendum ad totam vitam ipsius Johannis, Percipiendo pro officio prædicto tantum quantum prædictus Willelmus pro eodem officio ad Receptam prædictam percipere consuevit. In cujus r t &c; T. W. Coventrensi & Lich. Episcopo Thesaurario &c, xxij die Octobris anno xxvj°. Per breve de Privato Sigillo. *Mich. Commun.* 26 & 27. *Edw.* 1. *Rot.* 46. *a.*

(*g*) Windesore. Serjantia Thomæ de Windesore in Windesore, pro qua debuit esse Ponderator denariorum ad Scaccarium Domini Regis, alienata est in parte. *Then several small Parcels of Land are recited.* Et est summa dictæ alienationis xiij l vij s viij d. Et dictus Thomas de Windesore fecit inde finem pro dictis tenentibus de consensu eorundem, videlicet per annum iiij l ix s; Ita quod quilibet dictorum tenencium respondeat eidem Thomæ de tercia parte valoris tenementi sui per annum, Et ipse Thomas faciat servicium prædictæ Serjantiæ pro parte sua quæ non est alienata. *Rot. de Serjantijs Angliæ Rot.* 13.

(*h*) Joia quæ fuit uxor Willelmi Fusoris debet

K. *Henry* III, *Odo*, Son of *John* the *Fusor*, by his Charter granted, confirmed, and quitclaimed, for himself and his Heirs, to *Edward* [*de Westminster*] Son of *Odo* the Goldsmith, all the Right he had in the Office of *Fusor* of the King's Exchequer, to hold to the said *Edward*, and his Heirs and Assignes; doing for the same what belonged to the Office of *Fusorie* of the said Exchequer: For which Grant and Quitclaimer, *Edward* gave to *Odo* twelve Marks of Silver towards his Voyage into the Holy Land. This Grant was made in the Presence of K. *Henry* III, who in the Presence of *Odo*, and at his Instance, received *Edward*'s Homage for the said Office; and K. *Henry* III, by his Charter, confirmed the whole Transaction (*i*). In the Reign of the same K. *Henry* III, this Office being vested in *Odo de Westminstre*, that King (*Anno* 51°) gave Leave to *Odo* to depute one to execute his Office for two Years, whilst he should be engaged in his Studies; and thereupon *Odo* deputed *Hamon de Wroxhull* (*k*). And soon after, *Odo* (by virtue of the King's Writ in that Behalf) appointed *Gerand. de Ely* to present for him to the Barons an Attorney to execute his said Office, and likewise to pursue another Business depending between him and *William Fitz-Richard* (*l*). Afterwards Master *Odo de Westminstre*, for himself and his Heirs, surrendered and quitclaimed the said Office of *Fusorie* to K. *Edward* I (*m*).

Concerning the Usher of the *Receipt* I find nothing memorable within this Period.

debet x marcas, pro habendis terris & catallis Viri sui ad opus puerorum suorum, & pro habendo Recto de debitis Viri sui, & pro habendo Officio Viri sui ad Scaccarium ad opus puerorum suorum. Set requirendæ sunt ab Andrea de Scaccario, cui concessum est a Justiciario, quod habeat prædictam Conventionem cum hærede ipsius Willelmi, Salva Dote prænominatæ Joiæ. Et quia ipsa nichil Regi reddere potuit pro paupertate.

Andreas de Scaccario reddit compotum de x marcis, pro habenda Custodia hæredis Willelmi Fusoris donec ætatem habeat, cum terra sua & debitis suis; Salva Dote Joiæ uxoris suæ. *Mag. Rot.* 4. *Ric.* 1. *Rot.* 11. *a. Tit.* Sudhantescira; De Novis Oblatis per Archiepiscopum Rothomagensem & alios Justiciarios.

(*i*) *Cart. Antiq.* L. *n.* 12. *tit.* Carta Edwardi filij Odonis de Westmonesterio.

(*k*) Baronibus, pro Odone de Westminstre. Rex concessit eidem, quod per biennium dum studio vacet, ponat loco suo ad officium Fusoriæ quod habet in Scaccario, aliquem idoneum & fidelem pro quo velit respondere, interim explendum. Postea idem Odo posuit loco suo ad idem Officium explendum, ut prædictum est, Hamonem de Wroxhull. *Memor.* 51. *Hen.* 3. *Rot.* 1. *a.*

(*l*) *Hil. Communia* 52 & 53. *H.* 3. *Rot.* 7. *a.*

(*m*) Rex Thesaurario & Camerarijs suis salutem. Liberate de thesauro nostro, dilecto Clerico nostro Magistro Odoni de Westmon. quinquaginta marcas, pro officio Fusoriæ quod idem Odo habuit in Scaccario nostro, & quod in manus nostras reddidit, quietum de se & hæredibus suis imperpetuum. Et facta ei liberatione pecuniæ prædictæ, recipiatis ab eodem Odone literas suas patentes de redditione & quieta clamancia officij prædicti. T. R. apud Westm. primo die Julij. *Lib.* 13. *E.* 1. *m.* 3.

An

Chap. XXIV. *of the* EXCHEQUER.

An Allowance was wont to be made to several Ministers of the *Receipt* of Exchequer for their Liveries or Corrodies, and for divers Necessaries. In the ninth Year of K. *Henry* III, the Allowance was in this Manner: " The Liveries of the Ministers of the Exchequer,
" of the Term of St. *Michael*, in the ninth Year of K. *Henry* III,
" for fourscore Days, to wit, from the Feast of St. *Michael*, until
" the *Monday* next after the Feast of St. *Lucia*, including both those
" Days: To three Scribes C *s*; to the two Knights of the Chamber-
" lains viij Marks; to *John de Windresor* iiij *l*; to *John* the *Fusour*
" ij Marks and a half; to *Simon Druel* ij Marks and a half; to the
" four Tellers iiij *l*; to the *Vigil* and for Light x *s*; for a Hutch to
" lay up the *Memoranda* of the Great Exchequer vij *d*; for Rodds
" for the Tallies v *s*; for Parchment for the Use of the Chamberlains
" and the [Chief] Justicier's Clerk iiij *s*; for Ink during the whole
" Year iij *s*; for Litter for the Chamber of the Barons and the House
" of the *Receipt* xij *d*; for Necessaries for the said Chambers xx *d*;
" for ten Dozen of Hutches xx *s*; for Wax ij *s*; for Leather for the
" Tallies ix *d*; for a Hutch to lay the Inquisitions in ij *d*; for the
" Mareschall's Hutch xij *d*; for a great Sack to put the allowed Tallies
" in xiiij *d*; for carrying and recarrying the Hutches v *s*; for a Tonell
" to put in the D Marks that were sent to the King at *Oxford* by *R.*
" Bishop of *Chichester* xij *d*; for Locks, Girts, and other small Ex-
" pences iiij *s*; Total xxiiij *l* xiij *s* viij *d*: Item, to the Treasurer's
" Clerk and to the Chamberlain's two Knights, whilst they staid at
" *Westminster* by Command of the [Chief] Justicier, from the *Monday*
" next after the Feast of St. *Lucia* unto the Day of St. *Hilary*, to
" wit, for xxx Days Lx *s*; to the four Tellers for six Days vj *s*;
" for carrying the Hutches vj *d*. Again, the Liveries of the Mi-
' nisters of the Exchequer, of the Term of St. *Hilary*, for forty
" Days, to wit, from the Day of St. *Hilary* unto St. *Peter in Cathe-*
" *dra*, both the Days included: To the three Scribes L *s*; to the two
" Knights of the Chamberlains iiij Marks; to *John de Windresor* xl *s*;
" to *John* the *Fusor* xvj *s* viij *d*; to *Simon Druel* xvj *s* viij *d*; to the
" four Tellers xl *s*; to the *Vigil* and for Light v *s*; for Leather for
" the Tallies iij *d*; for Wax v *d* ob.; for twenty Furells xl *d*; for
" Wood and Coal xij *d*; for Litter for the Chamber of the Barons x *d*;
" for Carriage and Recarriage of Hutches (*n*)."

(*n*) *Ex Pelle (sive Contrapelle) Receptæ de anno* 9. *Hen.* 3. *Rot. ult. in dorso, penes Thes. & Camer.*

CHAP.

CHAP. XXV.

Barones Scaccarij Regij.

I. *Regnante R. Willelmo* I.
ODO Episcopus Baiocensis, Justiciarius Regis (*a*).
Willelmus filius Osberni (*b*).
Goisfridus Episcopus Constantiensis (*c*).

II. *Dominante R. Willelmo* II.
Odo Episcopus Baiocensis (*d*).
Ranulfus Episcopus Dunelmensis (*e*).

III. *Imperante R. Henrico* I.
Ranulfus Dunelmensis Episcopus *(f)*.
Rogerus Episcopus Saresberiæ (*g*).
Galfridus de Clynton Thesaurarius & Camerarius (*h*).

IV. *Sceptrum tenente R. Stephano.*
Gaufridus de Clintona (*i*),
Radulfus Basset (*k*),
Ricardus Basset, & Willelmus de Albini Brito (*l*), Justiciarij.
Comes Gloëcestræ, & Brientius filius Comitis (*m*).
Gaufridus Cancellarius (*n*).
Willelmus Maledoctus Camerarius (*o*).

V. *Anno* I, II, & III. *Henrici* II. *Regis.*
Willelmus Thesaurarius (*p*).
Episcopus Lincoliæ,
Johannes Thesaurarius (*q*).

(*a*) *Hunt. L.* 6. *p.* 371. *n.* 40. *Chron. Sax. p.* 190. *Angl. Sacr. T.* 1. *p.* 339.
Admonendus est Lector, me in Baronibus Scaccarij de tempore priorum post Conquestum Regum Angliæ *hic recensendis, hoc modo procedere, viz. Si qui fuerunt tunc temporis Magni Justiciarij Regis, eos pro more istius seculi ad Scaccarium residisse præsumo, idcoque pro Baronibus hic repono.*
(*b*) *Hoved. P.* 1. *p.* 450. *n.* 20.
(*c*) *Angl. Sacr. T.* 1. *p.* 335.
(*d*) *Hunt. L.* 7. *p.* 372. *n.* 20.
(*e*) *Hoved. P.* 1. *p.* 468. *n.* 20. *citat. Vol.* 1. *Cap.* 1. *sect.* 2.
(*f*) *Hoved. P.* 1. *p.* 477. *n.* 50. *Angl. Sac. T.* 1. *p.* 705.
(*g*) *Chron. Sax. p.* 225. *n.* 5. & *p.* 226. *n.* 30.
(*h*) *Cart. Antiq. N. N. nu.* 47.

(*i*) *Mag. Rot.* 5. *Ste. Rot.* 1. *b. Not.* & *Dereb.*
(*k*) *Ib. Rot.* 2. *a. Wilt. ad imum.*
(*l*) *Ib. Rot.* 6. *b.* & *Ib. Rot.* 12. *a. Linc.*
(*m*) *Ib. Rot.* 13. *b.*
(*n*) *Ib. Rot.* 14. *b.*
(*o*) *Ib. Rot.* 14. *a. Et vid. ante, Vol.* 1. *Cap.* 2. *sect.* 8.
(*p*) Et Johanni Marescallo v s, Et Willelmo Thesaurario v s; *and the like to others.* Et Q. e. *Mag. Rot.* 2. *H.* 2. *Rot.* 10. *a. Devenesc.*
(*q*) Everwichscira. Bertram de Bulemer r c de Nova firma. In thesauro CC & xvj l Bl. Et in Restauratione Maneriorum Comitatus Lxvij l v s & viij d, per Episcopum Lincoliæ & Johannem Thesaurarium. Et in Terris datis &c. *Mag. Rot.* 2. *H.* 2. *Rot.* 5. *a.*

Anno

Anno incerto Henrici II.
Ricardus de Luci, & alij Barones (r).

Anno incerto R. Henrici II.
Nigellus Episcopus Eliensis,
Willelmus Cumin,
Johannes Marescallus (s).

Anno XI. *Regis Henrici* II.
Nigellus Episcopus Heliensis,
Galfridus Archidiaconus Cantuariæ,
Ricardus Archidiaconus Pictaviæ,
Ricardus Thesaurarius Regis,
Wido Decanus de Waltham,
Robertus Comes Legreceſtriæ,
Ricardus de Luci,
Henricus filius Geroldi,
Willelmus Malduit,
Simon filius Petri,
Alanus de Novilla,
Gaufridus Monachus,
Willelmus filius Andel.,
Philippus de Davenceſtria (t).

Anno circiter XVI. *Henrici* II.
Ricardus de Luci,
Ricardus Archidiaconus Pictaviæ,
Reginaldus de Warenna,
Henricus filius Geroldi Camerarius,
Wido Decanus de Waltham,
Ricardus Thesaurarius,
Willelmus Basset,
Alanus de Novill,
Willelmus Malduit,

Adam de Gernemue (u).

Anno XXVI. *Henrici* II.
Ricardus Wintoniensis,
Gaufridus Eliensis,
Johannes Norwicensis, Episcopi,
Ranulfus de Glanvilla,
Ricardus Thesaurarius,
Willelmus Basset,
Alanus de Furnellis,
Robertus Mantell, & alij Barones (w).

Anno XXIX. *Henrici* II.
R. Wintoniensis,
G. Eliensis,
J. Norwicensis, Episcopi,
Godefridus de Lucy,
Ricardus Thesaurarius,
Rogerus filius Remfridi,
Willelmus Basset,
Ranulfus de Geddyng,
Robertus de Wytefeld,
Michael Belet, & alij Barones (x).

Anno XXX. *Henrici* II.
Rannulfus de Glanvilla,
Robertus Marmiun,
Radulfus filius Stephani Camerarius,
Hugo de Morewic,
Hugo Bardolf Dapifer,
Robertus de Whitefeld,
Rannulfus de Geddinges,
Gilebertus filius Reinfridi (y).
Gaufridus Elyensis,
Johannes Norwicensis, Episcopi,

(r) *Cap.* 6. *sect.* 3. Hæc est Conventio.
(s) *Ante, cap.* 6. *sect.* 2. Nigellus Eliensis.
(t) *Form. Anglic. in Differt. p.* 19.
(u) *Form. Anglic. nu.* CCXCI.
(w) *Dugd. Orig. Jurid. p.* 50. *col.* 2.
(x) *Cap.* 6. *Sect.* 2. Hæc est Finalis.
(y) *Form. Anglic. nu.* CCCLVII.

Ricardus Decanus Lincolnensis Regis Thesaurarius,
Willelmus Anglicus frater Thesaurarij,
Hubertus Walteri,
Hugo Murdac,
Radulfus Murdac,
Radulfus de Wirecestria,
Willelmus Malduit Camerarius,
Rogerus de Glanvilla (*z*).

Anno XXXI. *Henrici* II.
J. Norwicensis Episcopus,
Rannulfus de Glanvilla,
Ricardus Thesaurarius,
Godefridus de Luci,
Hubertus Walteri,
Willelmus Basset,
Nigellus filius Alexandri (*a*).

VI. *Anno* I. *Ricardi* I.
Ricardus Thesaurarius (*b*),
Warinus filius Henrici Camerarius (*c*).

Anno IV. *Ricardi* I.
Walterus Rothomagensis Archiepiscopus,

R. Londoniensis,
H. Coventrensis, Episcopi,
Galfridus filius Petri,
Rogerus filius Renfredi (*d*).

Anno V. *Ricardi* I.
Rogerus filius Reinfredi (*e*).

Anno VI. & VII. *Ricardi* I.
H. Archiepiscopus Cantuariensis,
Willelmus Briewerre (*f*).
W. Rothomagensis Archiepiscopus,
Ricardus Londoniensis Episcopus,
Galfridus filius Petri (*g*).
Hugo Bardolf (*h*),
G. Roffensis Episcopus,
Rogerus Comes de Norfolcia (*i*).

Anno VIII. & IX. *Ricardi* I.
H. Cantuariensis Archiepiscopus,
Hugo Bardolf,
Willelmus Briewerre (*k*).

Anno IX. & X. *Ricardi* I.
H. Cantuariensis Archiepiscopus (*l*).

(*z*) *Cap.* 6. *Sect.* 3. Anno ab incarnatione.
(*a*) *Formul. Anglic. nu.* CCCLVIII.
(*b*) *Mag. Rot.* 1. R. 1. Rot. 2. *a. Essex & Hurtf.*
(*c*) *Ib. Rot.* 10. *b. Wilt.*
(*d*) Ysaac Judæus & Fluria uxor ejus r c de xij libris, super domum suam in Schortenestreta in Wintonia: In Perdonis per breve Regis ipsi Ysaac & Floriæ uxori ejus xij l; Quia recognitum est apud Westmonasterium ad Scaccarium, coram Waltero Rothomagensi Archiepiscopo, & R. Londoniensi Episcopo, & cæteris Justiciarijs Domini Regis, per H. Coventrensem Episcopum, & Galfridum filium Petri, & Rogerum filium Renfredi, quod inde quieti sunt per ix marcas & vj s & viij d, quos liberaverunt in thesauro; Et sic Quieti sunt. *Mag. Rot.* 4. R. 1. Rot. 11. *b. Sudhantescira.*
(*e*) *Ante*, *cap.* 20. *Sect.* 7.
(*f*) *Mag. Rot.* 6. R. 1. Rot. 9. *a.* Cumb.
(*g*) *Ib. Rot.* 11. *b. Everwichsc.*
(*h*) *Mag. Rot.* 7. R. 1. Rot. 9. *a. Cantebrugg. & Huntend.*
(*i*) *Mag. Rot.* 7. R. 1. Rot. 16. *b. Sudhamtescira.*
(*k*) *Mag. Rot.* 8. R. 1. Rot. 16. *a. Dorseta & Sumerf.* Et vid. *Dugd. Orig. Jurid p.* 50. *col.* 2.
(*l*) *Mag. Rot.* 10. R. 1. Rot. 3. *b. Everwichsc.*

Galfridus

Galfridus filius Petri Jufticiarius Regis (*m*),
Philippus Dunelmenfis Epifcopus (*n*),
Epifcopus Londonienfis (*o*),
Simon de Patefhull,
Henricus de Wichenton,
Benedictus Judæus de Talemunt,
Jofeph Aaron, Jufticiarij Judæorum (*p*).

VII. *Anno* I. & II. *Regis Johannis.*
H. Cantuarienfis Archiepifcopus,
G. Filius Petri (*q*),
J. Norwicenfis Epifcopus,
G. de Bocland (*r*),
Willelmus Briewerre (*s*),
Willelmus Thefaurarius (*t*),
Benedictus de Talemunt, Cuftos Judæorum (*u*).

Anno III. *R. Johannis.*
Galfridus filius Petri Jufticiarius,
Willelmus Briewerre,
H. de Burgo Camerarius,
Galfridus de Bocland,
Magifter Willelmus de Neketon,
Robertus Malduit (*w*).

Willelmus de Ely Domini Regis Thefaurarius (*x*).

Anno IV. *R. Johannis.*
H. Cantuarienfis Archiepifcopus,
G. filius Petri,
H. de Nevill (*y*).

Anno IV & V. *R. Johannis.*
Willelmus Thefaurarius Regis (*z*),
G. filius Petri,
Simon de Patefhull (*a*),
Alexander de Luci (*b*),
Ricardus de Heriet,
Magifter Godefridus de Infula,
Euftachius de Faukenberge,
Walterus de Crepping (*c*).

Anno V. & VI. *R. Johannis.*
H. Cantuarienfis Archiepifcopus,
G. filius Petri Jufticiarius Domini Regis (*d*).
Willelmus de Warenna,
Galfridus de Norwiz,
Tomas de Nevill, Jufticiarij Judæorum (*e*).

Anno VII. *R. Johannis.*
G. filius Petri Jufticiarius;

(*m*) *Form. Anglic. nu.* CXLII. *Et Mag. Rot.* 10. *R.* 1. *Rot.* 11. *b. Cant. & Hunt.*
(*n*) *Form. Anglic. nu.* CXLII.
(*o*) *Mag. Rot.* 10. *Ric.* 1. *Rot.* 12. *a.*
(*p*) *Mag. Rot.* 10. *R.* 1. *Rot.* 8. *b. Rotelanda. Form. Anglic. nu.* CXLII.
(*q*) *Mag. Rot.* 1. *J. Rot.* 18. *a. War. & Leirceftr.*
(*r*) *Mag. Rot.* 2. *J. Rot.* 11. *b. Wilt.*
(*s*) *Mag. Rot.* 1. *J. Rot.* 13. *b. Wilt.*
(*t*) *Liberate* 2. *J. m.* 1.
(*u*) *Mag. Rot.* 1. *J. Rot.* 19. *a. Norfolch & Sudf.*
(*w*) *Form. Anglic. nu.* VI.

(*x*) *Mag. Rot.* 3. *J. Rot.* 19. *a. Londonia & Midd.*
(*y*) *Mag. Rot.* 4. *J. Rot.* 2. *b. Buk. & Bedef.*
(*z*) *Mag. Rot.* 4. *J. Rot.* 10. *b. Sudfexia.*
(*a*) *Ib. Rot.* 19. *b. Effex & Hurtf.*
(*b*) *Ib. Rot.* 18. *b. Cumb.*
(*c*) *Mag. Rot.* 5. *J. Rot.* 1. *b. Londonia & Midd.*
(*d*) *Mag. Rot.* 5. *J. Rot.* 5. *a. Gloec.*
(*e*) *Mag. Rot.* 6. *J. Rot.* 8. *b. Poft Surreiam.*

Willelmus

Willelmus de Warenna,
Tomas de Nevill,
Galfridus de Norwiz, Custodes Judæorum.
Willelmus Marescallus,
R. Comes Cestriæ,
W. Comes Saresbiriæ,
W. Comes Arundelliæ,
W. Thesaurarius, Et alij Barones (*f*).

Anno VIII. *R. Johannis.*
J. Norwicensis Episcopus,
G. filius Petri Justiciarius,
Robertus filius Rogeri,
Simon de Pateshull (*g*).

Anno X. *R. Johannis.*
W. Thesaurarius,
Willelmus Archidiaconus Huntedonensis,
Gerardus de Canvill,
Willelmus de Boveneia, Et alij Barones (*h*).
Cancellarius (*i*).

Anno XIII. *R. Johannis.*
S. Comes Wintoniæ,
Willelmus Domini Regis Thesaurarius,
R. de Marisco,
W. Archidiaconus Huntedonensis,
Et alij Barones (*k*).
W. Briwere,
Et alij Barones (*l*).

Anno XIV. *R. Johannis.*
G. filius Petri Justiciarius Regis,
Saherus Comes Wintoniæ,
W. Briwar,
Magister Ricardus de Mariscis (*m*);
P. Wintoniensis Episcopus (*n*).

VIII. *Anno* I. & II. *H.* III.
W. Mariscallus Comes de Pembroc, Rector Regis & Regni,
P. Wintoniensis Episcopus,
H. de Burgo Justiciarius,
Et Consilium Regis (*o*).
Eustachius de Faukenberg Thesaurarius (*p*).

Anno III. *Henrici* III.
Walo Legatus,
Justiciarius,
Episcopus Wintoniensis,
Falco [de Breaute] (*q*);
Eustacius de Faucumberg, Thesaurarius (*r*).

Anno VI. *Hen.* III.
Falcasius de Breaute Camerarius Scaccarij (*s*).

(*f*) *Mag. Rot.* 7. *J. Rot.* 1. *b. Londoria & Midd.*
(*g*) *Mag. Rot.* 8. *J. Rot.* 18. *b. Wilt. & Ib. Rot.* 13. *a.*
(*h*) *Mag. Rot.* 10. *J. Rot.* 14. *a. Lincollscira.*
(*i*) *Mag. Rot.* 10. *J. Rot.* 11. *a. Dorsete & Sumer.*
(*k*) *Mag. Rot.* 13. *J. Rot.* 1. *b.*
(*l*) *Ib. Rot.* 7. *b. Post Dorf. & Sumerf.*

(*m*) *Dugd. Orig. Jur.* p. 50. col. 2.
(*n*) *Mag. Rot.* 14. *J. Rot.* 16. *a. Wilt.* Willelmus Comes Saresberiæ.
(*o*) *Mag. Rot.* 2. *Hen.* 3. *Rot.* 4. *b.*
(*p*) *Clauf.* 2. *H.* 3. *m.* 3. *Pat.* 2. *H.* 3. *m.* 3.
(*q*) *Ante, cap.* 23. *sect.* 2.
(*r*) *Ante, cap.* 21. *sect.* 2. Hæc est Finalis.
(*s*) *Memor.* 6. *H.* 3. *Rot.* 3. *a.*

Chap. XXV.   *of the* Exchequer.   317

Anno VII. & VIII. *Henrici* III.
H. de Burgo Jufticiarius;
R. Sarefberienfis,
J. Bathonienfis,
R. Cyceftrenfis, Epifcopi;
Et alij Barones (*t*).

Anno IX. & X. *Henrici* III.
H. de Burgo Jufticiarius;
R. Cyceftrenfis Epifcopus Domini Regis Cancellarius,
H. Lincolnienfis,
J. Bathonienfis,
B. Roffenfis,
W. Carleolenfis, Epifcopi (*u*).
R. Sarefbirienfis Epifcopus,
Et alij Barones (*w*).

Anno XI. H. III.
H. de Burgo Jufticiarius (*x*).

Anno XIII. H. III.
H. de Burgo Jufticiarius (*y*).
W. Thefaurarius (*z*).

Anno XIV. *Henrici* III.
J. Bathonienfis,
R. Dunelmenfis, Epifcopi (*a*);
W. Thefaurarius,
S. de Segrave (*b*);
W. Carliolenfis Epifcopus (*c*).

Anno XV. *Henrici* III.
Simon de Patteſhull & Socij fui, Jufticiarij Judæorum (*d*).

Anno XX. & XXI. *Henrici* III.
Willelmus Brito,
Philippus de Afcell.
Elyas de Sunning, Cuftodes Judæorum (*e*).

Anno XXI. & XXII. *Henrici* III.
W. de Bello Campo,
A. Archidiaconus Salopiæ, idemq; Thefaurarius S. Pauli Londoniæ,
H. de Pateſhull Thefaurarius,
Magifter M. Belet,
J. filius Roberti (*f*).

Anno

(*t*) *Mag. Rot.* 8. *H.* 3. *Rot.* 16. *b. Not. & Dereb.*
(*u*) *Mag. Rot.* 9. *H.* 3. *Rot.* 8. *b. Citat. cap.* 23. *fect.* 28.
(*w*) *Mag. Rot.* 9. *H.* 3. *Rot.* 9. *b.*
(*x*) *Mag. Rot.* 11. *H.* 3. *in Wiltefire.*
(*y*) *Mag. Rot.* 13. *H.* 3. *in dorfo. Effex & Hertf.*
(*z*) *Mag. Rot.* 13. *H.* 3. *in dorfo. War. & Leic.*
(*a*) Rex Domino Luc. Electo Dublinenfi. Mandamus vobis rogantes, quatinus venire faciatis coram Venerabilibus Patribus, J. Bathon. & R. Dunelm. Epifcopis, apud Weftmon. a die S. Hylarij in xv dies, Willelmum de Caudefton quondam Officialem veftrum in Archidiaconatu Norwicenfi, ad reddendum compotum coram eifdem Epifcopis, de Sexta-decima ejufdem Archidiaconatus, & ad refpondendum de arreragijs prædictæ Sextæ-decimæ. T. J. xix. die Novembris anno r n xiiij. *Mich. Commun.* 14. *H.* 3. *Rot.* 2. *b.*
(*b*) Adam de Pedleia & Ricardus de Neketon Monetarij Lundoniæ fecerunt Sacramentum de fidel[itate] ad Scaccarium Judæorum, coram W. Thefaurario & S. de Segrave. *Paf. Commun.* 14. *H.* 3. *Rot.* 6. *b.*
(*c*) T. W. Karl. Epifcopo, xij die Novembris anno r n xiiij. *Mich. Commun.* 14. *H.* 3. *Rot.* 2. *a.*
(*d*) *Memor.* 25. *H.* 3. *Rot.* 4. *b.*
(*e*) Debita de Judaifmo liberata in Scaccario anno xx, per Willelmum Britonem, Philippum de Afcell. & Elyam de Sunning tunc Cuftodes Judæorum. *Mag. Rot.* 21. *H.* 3. *Rot.* 1. *a. Kancia.*
(*f*) Tefte A. Archidiacono Salopiæ xvj die

Anno XXIV. & XXV. *Henrici* III.
Willelmus de Haverſhull Domini Regis Theſaurarius,
Petrus Grimbald,
Radulphus de Ely (*g*).
Archiepiſcopus Eboracenſis & Conſiliarij Regis (*h*).

Anno XXVII. & XXVIII. *Henrici* III.
Willelmus de Haverſhull Theſaurarius (*i*);
R. Abbas de Weſtmonaſterio (*k*);
A. Theſaurarius S. Pauli Londoniæ (*l*);
J. Francigena (*m*);
Radulphus de Ely (*n*).

Anno XXXII. *Henrici* III.
Willelmus de Haverſhull, Theſaurarius Domini Regis (*o*),
Radulfus de Leyceſtre Cancellarius de Scaccario [officium ſuum Regi ſurſum reddit] (*p*),
Edwardus de Weſtminſtre [fit Cancellarius Scaccarij] (*q*),
J. Francigena (*r*).

Anno XXXV. *Henrici* III.
Abbas de Weſtmonaſterio,
W. de Haverſhull Theſaurarius,
E. de Weſtminſtre (*s*).
Philippus Luvel & J de Wyvile Juſticiarij Judæorum (*t*).

Anno XXXIV. *Henrici* III.
Philippus Lovel Theſaurarius Regis (*u*),
Petrus Chaceporc Theſaurarius Regis (*w*).

---

die Octobris anno xxj°. *Memor.* 22. H. 3. *Rot.* 2. *a.*

Teſte W. de Bello Campo &c. ij die Octobris anno xxj. *Memor.* 22. H. 3. *Rot.* 2. *b.*

Teſte Magiſtro M. Belet, xxiiij die Novembris anno xxij. *Ib. Rot.* 3. *b.*

Teſte A. Archidiacono Salopiæ xxvj die Novembris anno xxij. *Ib. Rot.* 3. *b.*

Teſte H. de Pateſhull &c. xxvj die Aprilis. *Ib. Rot.* 7. *b.*

Inter Hugonem de Pateſhull Theſaurarium noſtrum, & Ricardum de Argentum—. *Ib. Rot.* 9. *b.*

Teſte J. filio Roberti &c. xvj die Junij. *Ib. Rot.* 9. *a.*

Teſte A. Theſaurario Londoniæ apud Weſtmonaſterium, xxj die Julij anno r n xxij. *Ib. Rot.* 11. *b.*

(*g*) *Mag. Rot.* 24. H. 3. *Rot.* 1. *Cumbria.* Johannes Francigena [debet] dimidiam marcam.

Teſte P. Grimbald] v. die Octobris. *Memor.* 25. H. 3. *Rot.* 1. *a.*

(*h*) Et modo per Archiepiſcopum Eboracenſem & Conſiliarios Regis conſideratum eſt, quod hæres prædictus reſpondebit. *Mag. Rot.* 25. H. 3. *Ebor.* Hæres Petri de Malo lacu.

(*i*) *Memor.* 28. H. 3. *Rot.* 8. *a.*
(*k*) *Paſ. Memor.* 28. H. 3.
(*l*) Teſte A. Theſaurario S. Pauli Londoniæ. *Ex eiſd. Memor. ib.*
— ad reſpondendum Magiſtro A. de Swareford Baroni de Scaccario —. *Memor.* 27. H. 3. *Rot.* 3. *a.*
(*m*) *Paſ. Commun.* 27. H. 3. *Rot.* 10. *b.*
(*n*) *Ante,* cap. 20. ſect. 7.
(*o*) *Memor.* 32. H. 3. *Rot.* 7. *a.*
(*p*) *Ib. Rot.* 8. *b.*
(*q*) *Ib. Rot.* 8. *b.*
(*r*) *Ib. Rot.* 9. *a.*
(*s*) *Memor.* 35. H. 3. *Rot.* 12. *b.*
(*t*) *Cap.* 22. Sect. 9.
(*u*) *Pat.* 36. H. 3. *m.* 3.
(*w*) *Pat.* 36. H. 3. *m.* 9.

Anno XL. & XLI. *Henrici* III.
Philippus Lovel Thesaurarius Regis (*x*).
Philippus Baffet,
Philippus Luvell,
Henricus de Bathonia,
Simon Paffel,
    Justiciarij ad Custodiam Judæorum assignati (*y*).

Anno XLII. *Henrici* III.
R. Abbas Westmonasterij (*z*),
Magister Thomas de Wymundeham (*a*),
E. Abbas de Persore (*b*),
Johannes Renger (*c*),
P. de Rivalle (*d*),
Radulfus de Norwyc (*e*),
Johannes de Launfare (*f*).
Adam de Greynvile, Justiciarius Judæorum (*g*).

Anno XLV. *Hen.* III.
Johannes Abbas de Burgo Thesaurarius (*h*).
Henricus de Tracy.

Anno XLVIII. *Henrici* III.
Magister Nicholaus de Ely Thesaurarius,
Magister Johannes de Chishull Cancellarius Scaccarij,
Edwardus de Westminstre,
Arnaldus de Berkel[e], Barones (*k*).

Anno XLIX. *Henrici* III.
Henricus Prior Sanctæ Radegundæ Thesaurarius Regis (*l*),
Rogerus de la Leye, Baro (*m*);
Nicholaus de Crioll, Baro (*n*).
Adam de Wyntonia [amotus],
Robertus de Crepping,
Willelmus de Haselbech, Justiciarij Judæorum (*o*).

Anno LI. *Henrici* III.
Magister Thomas de Wymundeham Thesaurarius Regis (*p*);
Magister Godefridus Giffard Cancellarius de Scaccario (*q*).

Anno LII. *Henrici* III.
Magister Thomas de Wymundeham Thesaurarius (*r*);

(*x*) *Ante, cap.* 20. *sect.* 7.
(*y*) *Pat.* 41. *H.* 3. *m.* 4. *n.* 6.
(*z*) *Memor.* 42. *H.* 3.
(*a*) *Memor.* 42. *H.* 3. *Rot.* 16. *b.*
(*b*) *Ib. Rot.* 2. *a.*
(*c*) *Ib. Rot.* 7. *a.*
(*d*) *Ib. Rot.* 11. *b.*
(*e*) *Ib. Rot.* 15. *a.*
(*f*) *Ib. Rot.* 1. *a.*
(*g*) *Ib. Rot.* 10. *a.*
(*h*) Norhamton. *Rot. Placitor. Hil.* 45. *Hen.* 3. *Rot.* 6. *a. ex parte Remem. Thes.*
(*i*) Berk. *Ib. Rot.* 7. *b.*
(*k*) *In Charta Johannis de Windlesore Militis facta Adæ de Stratton, de Officio Ponderiæ ad Scaccarium de Recepta:* Testibus Magistro Nicholao de Ely tunc Domini Regis Thesaurario, Magistro Johanne de Chishull tunc Cancellario ad Scaccarium, Edwardo de Westm[instre], Arnaldo de Berkel[e] tunc Baronibus de Scaccario. Datum apud Westmonasterium, die Mercurij in vigilia Omnium Sanctorum, anno r R H filij R. J. quadragesimo octavo. *Mag. Rot.* 49. *H.* 3. *Rot.* 9. *a. m.* 2. *in imo.*
(*l*) *Pas. Recognit.* 49. *H.* 3. *Rot.* 14. *a.*
(*m*) *Trin. Commun.* 49. *H.* 3. *Rot.* 12. *a.*
(*n*) *Hil. Commun.* 49. *H.* 3. *Rot.* 7. *a.*
(*o*) *Trin. Commun.* 49. *H.* 3. *Rot.* 11. *b. Mich. Recogn. ib. Rot.* 13. *a.*
(*p*) *Mich. Memor.* 51. *H.* 3. *Rot.* 2. *b.*
(*q*) *Ib. Rot.* 2. *b.*
(*r*) *Memor.* 52. *H.* 3. *Rot.* 4. *b. Trin. Recognit.* 53. *H.* 3. *Rot.* 17. *a.*

Rogerus

Rogerus de le Leye Cancellarius Scaccarij (*s*);
Willelmus de Grauncurt (*t*),
Simon Passelewe (*u*).

Anno LV & LVI. *Henrici* III.
Philippus de Eya Thesaurarius (*w*);
Magister J. de Chishull Thesaurarius (*x*),
Rogerus de la Leye Cancellarius Scaccarij (*y*),
Magister Willelmus de Clifford Cancellarius Scaccarij (*z*);
Willelmus de Watford,
Willelmus de Thurlaeston,
Robertus de Fulham, Justiciarij Judæorum (*a*).

IX. *Anno* I & II. *Edwardi* I.
Philippus de Eye, Thesaurarius,
Frater Josep [de Cauncy] Prior Hospitalis S. Johannis Jerusalem in Anglia, Thesaurarius (*b*).
Hervicus de Borham,
Rogerus de la Leye, Barones (*c*).
W[alterus] de Hopton, Baro (*d*).

Anno III & IV. *Edw*. I.
Frater J. de Kauncy Thesaurarius,
Johannes de S. Walerico,
Rogerus de Nortwode, Barones (*e*).
Rogerus de la Ley Cancellarius Scaccarij (*f*).

Anno IV & V. *Edw*. I.
Frater Joseph de Kauncy, Thesaurarius (*g*).
Magister Ricardus de Stanes, Cancellarius de Scaccario (*h*).

(*s*) *Memor.* 52. *H*. 3. *Rot*. 7. *b*.
(*t*) *Ib. Rot.* 14. *a*.
(*u*) *Ib. Rot.* 15. *b. Trin. Recognit*. 53. *H*. 3. *Rot.* 17. *a*.
(*w*) *Hil. Memor.* 56. *H*. 3. *Rot*. 4. *a*.
(*x*) *Memor.* 55. *H*. 3. *Rot*. 12. *b*.
(*y*) *Memor.* 55. *H*. 3. *Rot*. 6. *a*.
(*z*) *Paf. Recogn.* 56. *H*. 3. *Rot*. 10. *a*.
(*a*) *Trin. Memor.* 56. *H*. 3. *Rot*. 7. *a*.
(*b*) Mandatum est Philippo de Eye, quod clavem Thesaurariæ Regis Westm. una cum omnibus in eadem existentibus, liberet Fratri Josep Priori Hospitalis S. Johannis Jerusalem in Anglia Thesaurario Regis, custodiend. quamdiu Regi placuerit, prout ad officium Thesaurarij pertinet. Datum per manum W. de Merton Cancellarij nostri apud Westm. ij die Octobris. *Clauf.* 1. *E*. 1. *p*. 1. *m*. 3. *Memor*. 1 & 2. *E*. 1. *Rot*. 12. *a*.
(*c*) *Memor.* 1. *E*. 1. *Rot*. 6. *b*.
(*d*) *Lib.* 2. *E*. 1. *m*. 6. *dat*. apud Westm. xxiiij die Aprilis. *Et ib. m.* 7. He was *one of the Justices* ad Placita coram Rege, *in the 3d of E*. 1; *Lib.* 3. *E*. 1. *m*. 3; *and in the 4th of E*. 1; *Lib.* 4. *E*. 1. *m*. 6.

(*e*) Quieta clamantia Petri de Monte Forti facta Domini Regi. Universis —— &c; In præsentia Fratris J. de Kauncy tunc dicti Domini Regis Thesaurarij, Johannis de Sancto Walerico & Rogeri de Nortwode Baronum, Rogeri de la Leye, Magistri Odonis, Nicholai de Castello Rememorator. , Ricardi de Staunford & Roberti de Walmesford Scriptorum Magni Rotuli, & aliorum. Datum in Scaccario, in festo S. Edmundi Martiris anno Regni Regis tercio. *Mich. Commun.* 3 & 4. *E*. 1. *Rot*. 5. *a*.
Liberate de thesauro nostro di & fi nostro Rogero de Norwod uni Baronum nostrorum de Scaccario decem libras in subventionem expensarum suarum, de dono nostro. Teste 25 Julij. *Liberate* 4. *E*. 1. *m*. 5.
(*f*) *In the same* 4*th Year*, Rogerus de la Leye Archidiaconus Essexiæ *is styled* nuper Cancellarius Scaccarij nostri; *Lib*. 4. *E*. 1. *m*. 7.
(*g*) *Mich. Recognit.* 4 & 5. *E*. 1. *Rot*. 8. *a*.
(*h*) *Ib. Rot*. 7. *a*.

Rogerus

Chap. XXV.   *of the* EXCHEQUER.

Rogerus de Northwode, Baro (*i*).
Philippus de Wileby, Baro (*k*).
Johannes de Cobbeham, Baro (*l*).

Anno V & VI. *Edw.* I.
Galfridus de Neubaud Cancellarius Scaccarij (*m*).
Philippus de Wilegheby, Baro (*n*).

Anno VII. *Edw.* I.
Frater Josep de Chauncy [Prior Hospitalis S. Johannis Jerusalem in Anglia] Thesaurarius (*o*).
Galfridus de Neubaud Cancellarius Scaccarij;
Rogerus de Northwode,
Johannes de Cobeham,
Philippus de Wyleghby, Barones (*p*).
Hamo Hauteyn,
Robertus de Ludham, Justic. Judæor. (*q*).

Anno VIII. *Edw.* I.
Galfridus de Neubaud Cancellarius Scaccarij;

Rogerus de Norwood,
Johannes de Cobeham,
Philippus de Wyleby, Barones (*r*).
Hamo Hauteyn,
Robertus de Ludham, Justiciarij ad custodiam Judæorum assignati (*s*).

Anno IX. *Edw.* I.
Abbas Westmonasterij Thesaurarius (*t*).
Galfridus de Neubaud Cancellarius Scaccarij,
Rogerus de Northewod,
Johannes de Cobeham,
Philippus de Wileby, Barones (*u*).
Hamo Hauteyn,
Robertus de Ludham, Justiciarij ad custodiam Judæorum assignati (*w*).

Anno X. *Edw.* I.
Frater R. Abbas Westmonasterij, Thesaurarius de Scaccario (*x*).

(*i*) *Ib. Rot.* 7. *a.*
(*k*) *Ib. Rot.* 7. *b.*
(*l*) *Hil. Recognit. Rot.* 8. *b.*
(*m*) *Lib.* 8. *E.* 1. *m.* 6.
(*n*) *Lib.* 6. *E.* 1. *m.* 4.
(*o*) *Mich. Recognit.* 7. *E.* 1. *Rot.* 8. *b. & Rot.* 11. *a.*
(*p*) *Each of them at* xl *Marks annual Fee*; *Lib.* 7. *E.* 1. *m.* 1. *& m.* 3. Philip de Wyleghby *was Keeper of one of the four Keys of the Treasury*; Rex Thes. & Camer. suis salutem; Liberate de thesauro nostro dilecto Clerico nostro Philippo de Wylegheby custodi quartæ clavis Thes. nostri centum solidos de termino S. Michaelis proximo præterito de annuo feodo suo decem librarum quod de nobis percipit pro custodia Clavis prædictæ. T. R. apud Westm. xv die Nov. *Lib.* 7. *E.* 1. *m.* 1.
(*q*) *Ib. m.* 1.
(*r*) *Lib.* 8. *E.* 1. *m.* 3. *& m.* 6.
(*s*) *Lib.* 8. *E.* 1. *m.* 2.
(*t*) Rex Thes. & Camer. suis salutem. Liberate de thesauro nostro, dilecto nobis in Christo Abbati Westmonasterij Thesaurario nostro quinquaginta marcas de termino Paschæ proximo præterito de annuo feodo suo quod ei concessimus percipiendum in Officio prædicto. *Lib.* 9. *E.* 1. *m.* 8.
(*u*) *Lib.* 9. *E.* 1. *m.* 4. *& m.* 8.
(*w*) *Lib.* 9. *E.* 1. *m.* 4.
(*x*) Recognitio Fratris R. Abbatis Westmonasterij, Thesaurarij de Scaccario. *Trin. Recognit.* 10. *E.* 1. *Rot.* 14. *a.*

Johannes

Johannes de Cobeham, Baro (*y*).
Philippus de Wileby, Baro (*z*).

Anno XI. *Edw.* I.
Johannes de Cobeham, Baro (*a*).

Anno XII. *Edw.* I.
Johannes de Kyrkeby Thesaurarius (*b*).
Philippus de Wylheby Cancellarius Scaccarij;
Rogerus de Norwod,
Johannes de Cobeham, &
Petrus de Cestria Præpositus Beverlaci, Barones (*c*).
Hamo Hauteyn, &
Robertus de Ludham, Justic. ad custodiam Judæorum assignati (*d*).

Anno XIII. *Edw.* I.
Johannes de Kirkeby Thesaurarius;
Philippus de Wylegheby Cancellarius Scaccarij;
Rogerus de Northwod,
Johannes de Cobeham, &
Petrus de Cestria Præpositus Beverlaci, Barones (*e*),
Hamo Hauteyn, &
Robertus de Ludham, Justiciarij ad custodiam assignati (*f*).

Anno XIV. *Edw.* I.
Johannes de Kirkeby, Thesaurarius (*g*).
Philippus de Wyleghby Cancellarius Scaccarij,
Johannes de Cobeham,
Petrus de Cestria Præpositus Beverlaci,
Willelmus de Middelton, Barones (*h*).
Hamo Hauteyn, &
Robertus de Ludham, Justiciarij ad custodiam Judæorum assignati (*i*).

Anno XX. *Edw.* I.
J. Eliensis Episcopus Thesaurarius (*k*).
Philippus de Wylegheby Cancellarius Scaccarij,
Johannes de Cobeham,
Petrus de Cestria Præpositus Beverlaci,
Willelmus de Middilton, Barones (*l*).
Willelmus de Karleton unus Justic. ad custodiam Judæorum assignatus (*m*).

Anno XVII & XVIII. *Edw.* I.
Johannes Elyensis Episcopus, Thesaurarius;

(*y*) *Ib. Rot.* 14. *b.*
(*z*) *Ib. Rot.* 13. *a.*
(*a*) *Lib.* 11. *E.* 1. *m.* 1.
(*b*) *Lib.* 12. *E.* 1. *m.* 4. *in ced. annexa.*
(*c*) *Ib. m.* 4.
(*d*) *Ib. m.* 4.
(*e*) *Lib.* 13. *E.* 1. *m.* 1.
(*f*) *Ib. m.* 2.
(*g*) *Mich. Commun. in bund.* 13 & 14. *E.* 1.

Rot. 4. *b.* At C Marks yearly Fee; *Liberat.* 14. *E.* 1. *m.* 3.
(*h*) *Liberat.* 14. *E.* 1. *m.* 3.
(*i*) *Ib. m.* 2.
(*k*) *At the yearly Fee of* C *Marks.* *Lib.* 15. *E.* 1. *m.* 1. & *m.* 3.
(*l*) *Ib. m.* 2.
(*m*) *Ib. m.* 3.

Philippus

Chap. XXV. *of the* EXCHEQUER. 323

Philippus de Willeby, Cancellarius Scaccarij;
Petrus de Ceftria,
Johannes de Cobeham,
Willelmus de Middelton, Barones (n).
Magifter Willelmus de Marchia Thefaurarius Regis (o).
Willelmus de Carleton, &
Petrus de Leyceftre Jufticiarij ad cuftodiam Judæorum affignati (p).

Anno XVIII. & XIX. *Edw.* I.
Magifter Willelmus de Marchia, Domini Regis Thefaurarius (q).
Idem Magifter Willelmus, Thefaurarius Scaccarij (r).
Philippus de Wilegby, Cancellarius de Scaccario (s).
Petrus de Ceftria, Baro (t).
Johannes de Cobeham, Baro (u).
Willelmus de Middelton, Baro (w).
Willelmus de Carleton,
Petrus de Leyceftre, Barones (x).

Anno XX. & XXI. *Edw.* I.
Magifter Willelmus de Marchia Thefaurarius (y).
W. de Langeton, Thefaurarius (z).
Philippus de Wilgheby Cancellarius Scaccarij,
Johannes de Cobeham,
Willelmus de Carleton,
Petrus de Leyceftre, Barones (a).

Anno XXII. & XXIII. *Edw.* I.
Willelmus Bathonienfis & Wellenfis Epifcopus, Thefaurarius (b).
Philippus de Wylgheby Cancellarius Scaccarij;
Johannes de Cobeham,
Willelmus de Carleton,
Petrus de Leyceftre, Barones (c).

Anno XXIII. *Edw.* I.
Walterus de Langeton Thefaurarius Regis (d).
Philippus de Wilughby Cancellarius Scaccarij,
Johannes de Cobeham,

(n) *Mich. Memor.* 17. *fin.* & 18. *incipiend.* E. 1. *Rot.* 1. a. *Parte* 1.
(o) *Trin. Commun.* 18. E. 1, *Rot.* — a.
(p) *Lib.* 19. E. 1. m. 3.
(q) *Lib.* 19. E. 1. m. 4. *at* C *Marks* per Annum *Stipend.*
He had been before Clerk of the King's Wardrobe. *Lib.* 13. E. 1. m. 4.
(r) *Paf. Memor.* 18. E. 1. *Rot.* — a.
(s) *Trin. Recognit.* 18. E. 1. *Rot.* — b.
(t) *Mich. Recogn.* 18. E. 1. *Rot.* — a.
(u) *Paf. Recogn.* 18. E. 1. *Rot.* — a.
(w) *Mich. Recogn.* 18. E. 1. *Rot.* — b.
(x) *Paf. Memor.* 26 & 27. E. 1. *Rot.* 23. a.
(y) *Lib.* 20. E. 1. m. 4. *at* C *Marks* per Ann.

(z) *Mich. Commun.* 25. E. 1. *inter Manucapt.*
(a) *Lib.* 20. E. 1. m. 3.
(b) *Paf. Commun.* 22. E. 1. *Rot.* 1. a.
(c) *At* 40 *Marks* per Annum, *each;* Lib. 22. E. 1. m. 2.
(d) Liberate de thefauro noftro Roberto de Colbrok — —. T. R. apud Wycoumbe xxx die Junij. Per ipfum Regem, nunciante Waltero de Langeton Cuftode Garderobæ Regis. *Lib.* 23. E. 1. m. 1. *in Ced.* Liberate de thefauro noftro Iterio de Ingolifma — T. R. apud Cantuar. 1º die Octobris. Per ipfum Regem nunciante W. de Langeton Thefaurario Regis. *Ib. juxt.*

Willelmus

Willelmus de Carleton,
Petrus de Leyceftre, Barones (*e*).

Anno XXIV. & XXV. *Edw.* I.
W. de Langeton Coventrenfis & Lich. Electus, Thefaurarius (*f*).
P. de Wylughby, Tenens locum Thefaurarij, & Cancellarius Scaccarij (*g*).
J. de Drokenesford Tenens locum Thefaurarij (*h*).
Johannes de Infula, Baro (*i*);
Johannes de Cobeham,
Willelmus de Carleton,
Petrus de Leyceftre, Barones (*k*).

Anno XXVI. *Edwardi* I.
W. Coventrenfis & Lich. Epifcopus Thefaurarius (*l*).
P. de Wylughby [Decanus Linc. Paf. Commun. 26. & 27. E. 1. Rot. 24. b.], Cancellarius Scaccarij (*m*).
Johannes de Cobeham,
Willelmus de Carleton,
Petrus de Leyceftria,
Johannes de Infula, Barones (*n*).
Johannes de Infula, Baro (*o*).

Anno XXVII. *Edw.* I.
W. Coventrenfis & Lychfeldenfis Epifcopus Thefaurarius Regis (*p*);
Philippus de Wylgheby Cancellarius Scaccarij;
Johannes de Cobeham,
Willelmus de Carleton, & Petrus de Leyceftre, Barones (*q*).

Anno XXXI. *Edw.* I.
W. Coventrenfis & Lichfeldenfis Epifcopus Thefaurarius (*r*).
Philippus de Wylgheby Cancellarius Scaccarij;
Willelmus de Carleton,
Petrus de Leyceftre, Barones (*s*).
Willelmus de Carleton, & Petrus de Leyceftre, Jufticiarij ad cuftodiam Judæorum affignati (*t*).

Anno XXXI. *Edw.* I.
W. Coventrenfis & Lich. Epifcopus Thefaurarius,
Philippus de Wylugby Cancellarius de Scaccario, & Tenens locum Thefaurarij;
Willelmus de Carletone,

(*e*) *Cap.* 25. *ad Ann.* 27. E. 1.
(*f*) *Mich. Memor.* 25. E. 1. *Rot. notato.* R, *in dorfo.*
(*g*) *Trin. Commun.* 24. E. 1. *Rot.* 38. *a. Mich. Recorda* 25. E. 1.
(*h*) Tefte J de Drokenesford Tenente locum Thefaurarij xxiiij die Octobris anno xxv *Mich. Commun.* 25 & 26 E. 1. *Rot.* 39. *b.*
(*i*) Literæ Patentes factæ Johanni de Infula, de Octavo in Londonia affidenda; Tefte 8 Dec. anno 25. *Mich. Record.* 25. E. 1.
(*k*) *Cap.* 25. *ad ann.* 27. E. 1.

(*l*) *Hil. Commun.* 26 & 27 E. 1. *Rot.* 15. *a.*
(*m*) *Hil. Commun. ib.*
(*n*) *Hil. Commun. ib.*
(*o*) *Hil. Commun.* 27. E. 1. *Rot.* 15. *a.*
(*p*) *Lib.* 27. E. 1. *m.* 3.
(*q*) *A Liberate for the Areres of their yearly Fee due to them* de annis regni noftri vicefimo tercio, vicefimo quarto, vicefimo quinto, vicefimo fexto, & vicefimo feptimo, *Ib. juxt.*
(*r*) *Lib.* 31. E. 1. *m.* 2.
(*s*) *Ib.*
(*t*) *Ib.*

Petrus

Petrus de Leyceſtria,
Johannes de Inſula,
Rogerus de Hegham,
Magiſter Ricardus de Abyndon,
Barones (*u*).

Anno XXXII. *Edwardi* I.
Philippus de Wylgheby Cancellarius Scaccarij (*w*).
Rogerus de Hegham, Baro (*x*)

Anno XXXIV. & XXXV. *Edw.* I.
Walterus Coventrenſis & Lich. Epiſcopus, Theſaurarius (*y*).
W. de Carleton, Tenens locum Theſaurarij (*z*).
Willelmus de Carleton,
Magiſter Ricardus de Abyndon; Barones (*a*).
Rogerus de Hegham, Baro (*b*).
Johannes de Benſtede Cancellarius Scaccarij (*c*).
Humfridus de Waleden, Baro (*d*).

Anno I. *Edw.* II.
W. Wygornenſis Electus, Theſaurarius,
J. de Drokenesford Cancellarius Scaccarij (*e*).
Johannes de Sandale Cancellarius Scaccarij,
Willelmus de Carleton,
Rogerus de Hegham,
Magiſter Ricardus de Abyndon,
Magiſter Johannes de Everdon; Barones (*f*).
[Die 14°. Martij, Aſſidebat Amadeus Comes Sabaudiæ] (*g*).
[Die Maij 27, Aſſidebant,
J. Ciceſtrenſis Epiſcopus Cancellarius Angliæ,
Rogerus de Brabanzon Juſticiarius de Banco Regis,
Radulphus de Hengham Juſticiarius de altero Banco,
Johannes de Benſtede Cuſtos Garderobæ Regis,
Et alij de Conſilio Regis] (*h*).
[Die Sabbati in Supervigilia Nativitatis S. Johannis Baptiſtæ, adfuerunt
J. de Langeton Epiſcopus Ciceſtrenſis Cancellarius Angliæ,
W. Wygornenſis Electus Theſaurarius,
R. le Brabanzoun Juſticiarius de Banco Regis,
J. de Drokenesford Cancellarius Scaccarij,
J. de Benſtede Cuſtos Garderobæ Regis,
Willelmus de Carleton,
Rogerus de Hegham,
Magiſter R. de Abendon,
Magiſter J. de Everdon, Barones,
Willelmus de Bereford Juſticiarius de Banco] (*i*).

(*u*) *Hil. Commun.* 31. *E.* 1. *Rot.* 28. *a.*
(*w*) *Lib.* 32. *E.* 1. *m.* 1.
(*x*) *Ib.*
(*y*) *Trin. Commun.* 35. *E.* 1. *Rot.*—*a.*
(*z*) *Hil. Commun.* 35. *E.* 1. *Parte* 2. *Rot.* 31.
(*a*) *Hil. Commun.* 34. *E.* 1. *Rot.* 20. *a.*
(*b*) *Trin. Commun.* 35. *E.* 1. *Rot.*—*a.*
(*c*) *Trin. Commun.* 35. *E.* 1. *Rot.* 59. *a.*
(*d*) *Trin. Commun. Ib. Rot.* 59. *b.*
(*e*) *Trin. Brevia* 1. *E.* 2. *Rot.* 68. *b.*
(*f*) *Hil. Commun.* 1. *E.* 2. *Rot.* 40. *b.*
(*g*) *Ib. Rot.* 40. *b.*
(*h*) *Paſ. Record.* 1. *E.* 2. *Rot.* 56. *a.*
(*i*) *Trin. Commun.* 1. *E.* 2. *Rot.* 69. *a* & *b.*

Anno.

Anno II. *Edw.* II.
W. Wygorn. Episcopus, Thesaurarius.
W. de Carleton, Baro (*k*).
J. de Sandale Tenens locum Thesaurarij,
J. de Foxle, Baro (*l*).

Anno V. *Edw.* II.
W. de Norwyco Tenens locum Thesaurarij & Baro.
J. de Merkyngfeld Cancellarius Scaccarij.
J. de Foxle,
Magister Ricardus de Abindon,
Mag. Johannes de Everdon; Barones (*m*).
Johannes Abel, Baro (*n*).

Anno VI. *Edw.* II.
Johannes de Merkyngfeld Cancellarius Scaccarij (*o*).

Waltero de Norwyco Tenens locum Thesaurarij (*p*) & Baro Johannes de Foxle (*q*).
Magister Johannes de Everdon
Magister Ricardus de Abyndon (*r*).
Johannes Abel (*s*).
[Assidebant W. Wygornensis Episcopus,
Adomarus de Valencia Comes de Pembrok,
H. le Despenser,
J. de Sandale Tenens locum Thesaurarij,
Et alij de Consilio] (*t*).

Anno VIII. *Edw.* II.
W. de Norwyco Thesaurarius (*u*).
Hervicus de Staunton (*w*).

Anno IX. *Edw.* II.
Walterus de Norwico Thesaurarius (*x*).

(*k*) *Mich. Brev. Retornab.* 2 *E.* 2. *Rot.* 114. *a.*
(*l*) *Trin. Commun.* 2. *E.* 2. *Rot.* 89. *a.*
(*m*) *Hil. Commun.* 5. *E.* 2. *Rot.* 31. *b.*
(*n*) *Ante, cap.* 21.
(*o*) Rex tenenti locum Thesaurarij & suis Camerarijs salutem. Liberate de thesauro nostro dilecto Clerico nostro Johanni de Merkyngfeld Cancellario Scaccarij nostri viginti marcas de termino Paschæ proximo præterito de annuo feodo suo quadraginta marcarum quod ei concessimus percipiendum in Officio supradicto. T. R. apud Westm. xv die Julij. *Liberate* 6. *Edw.* 2. *m.* 4. & *Ib. m.* 3.
(*p*) Rex tenenti locum Thes. & Camerarijs suis salutem. Liberate de thesauro nostro dilecto & fideli nostro Waltero de Norwyco tenenti locum Thes. prædicti, quinquaginta libras quas ei concessimus de dono nostro in subventionem expensarum & misarum quas hactenus fecit in obsequio nostro in Officio supradicto. T. Rege apud Westm. xxij die Julij. Per ipsum Regem, nunciante Comite Pembrochiæ. *Ibid.*
(*q*) R. eisdem salutem. Liberate de thesauro nostro dilecto & fideli nostro Johanni de Foxle uni Baronum nostrorum de Scaccario nostro, viginti marcas de termino S. Michaelis proximo præterito, de annuo feodo suo quadraginta marcarum quod ei concessimus in Officio supradicto. T. R. apud Wyndesore ix die Octobris. *Ibid.*
(*r*) *Sub stipe xl marcarum per annum. Ibid.*
(*s*) *Habuit xl marcas per annum. Ib. m.* 3.
(*t*) *Hil. Commun.* 1. *E.* 2. *Rot.* 40. *b.*
(*u*) Anglia. De W. de Norwyco admisso ad Officium Thesaurarij. *Mich. Commun.* 8. *E.* 2. *Rot.* 1. *a.*
(*w*) *Mich. Commun.* 8. *E.* 2. *Rot.* 1. *a.*
(*x*) *Hil. Recogn.* 9. *E.* 2. *Rot.* 73. *a.*

Johannes

Johannes de Hothum Cancellarius Scaccarij (*y*).

Anno XII. *Edw*. II.

Johannes Walewyn Thesaurarius (*z*).
H. de Stanton (*a*).
Magister Johannes de Everdon (*b*).
W. de Norwyco (*c*).
J. de Foxle (*d*).

J. Wintoniensis Episcopus, Thesaurarius (*e*).
J. de Okham (*f*).
Robertus de Wodehouse (*g*).
J. Abel (*h*).

Anno XX. *Edw*. II.

Robertus Ayleston Cancellarius Scaccarij (*i*).
Johannes Reedswell Baro (*k*).

(*y*) *Pas. Recogn.* 9. *E.* 2. *Rot.* 75. *b.*
(*z*) Edward par la grace de Dieu &c, Au nostre cher Clerc Mestre Johan Walewyn nostre Tresorer, saluz.—. Don 29. Sept. an. 12. *Mich. Brevia* 12. *Edw.* 2. *Rot.* 62. *a.*
(*a*) *Hil. Commun.* 12. *Edw.* 2. *Rot.* 54. *a.*
(*b*) *Ib.*
(*c*) *Ib. Rot.* 54. *b.*
(*d*) *Pas. Commun. ib. Rot.* 56. *a.*

(*e*) Edward par la grace de Dieu &c, Al. honourable Pier en Dieu J. par la meisme grace Evesq; de Wyncestre nostre Tresorer. salutz—. Don 28. Novemb. an. 12. *Mich. Brevia* 12. *Edw.* 2. *Rot.* 71. *b.*
(*f*) *Ib. juxt.*
(*g*) *Ib. Rot.* 56. *b.*
(*h*) *Trin. Commun. ib. Rot.* 57. *a.*
(*i*) *Pat.* 20. *E.* 2. *m.* 27.
(*k*) *Ib. m.* 19.

The END *of the* HISTORY *of the* EXCHEQUER.

ANTIQUUS DIALOGUS

De Scaccario;

Gervasio de Tilbury vulgo adscriptus:

E duobus vetustis Codd. MSS.

Nigro & Rubro,

In Scaccario Regio asservatis.

Dialogum recensuit, & primùm edidit, Lectiones variantes, Notasque adjecit, ac Dissertationem Epistolarem præmisit,

Thomas Madox.

DISSERTATIO EPISTOLARIS.

Ampliſſimo & Nobiliſſimo Baroni,

CAROLO Domino HALIFAX,

Pari MAGNÆ BRITANNIÆ,

Thomas Madox S. P.

TRACTATUS ſive *Dialogus* ſequens, Baro Nobiliſſime, Hiſtoricis atque Antiquarijs noſtræ gentis jampridem in pretio fuit; etiam dum in codicibus MSS delituit. Quin & mihi videbatur aptiſſime coincidere argumento Hiſtoriæ quam de Scaccario in præcedentibus ſchedis concinnavi. Propterea huic volumini inſerendum duxi. Nunquam antehac totus integerque editus, jam tandem Tuis auſpicijs in lucem prodit. Tuis inquam auſpicijs. Quum enim conſilium inibam edendi ad calcem meæ Hiſtoriæ accuratum *Dialogi* exemplar juxta Codicem MS qui *Liber Niger Receptæ* dicitur; ſimulatque honorem conſecutus eram id mei conſilij Tibi exponendi, copiam mihi pro Tua humanitate feciſti quatenus in Te erat, non illius tantum Codicis MS, ſed & aliarum membranarum veterum authenticarum, quotquot reconduntur in Scaccarij Regij Theſauraria, quæ tribus obſerari ſolet clavibus, quarum unam

ut

ut *Auditor* quem vocant *Receptæ* geris. Complufcula fane hujus *Dialogi* exemplaria MSS, moderno charactere exarata, in Bibliothecis tum publicis tum privatis reperiuntur. Honos mihi obtigit mutuo accipiendi exemplaria ejus duo, quæ quidem præ alijs quæ mihi forte obvenerant legibilia & emendata funt, extantia nimirum in inftructiffima Bibliotheca Doctiffimi Baronis *Johannis* Domini *Somers*. Horum dum exemplarium ope tranfcriptum integri *Dialogi* fieri juffi. Deinde illud tranfcriptum ipfemet quam potui diligentiffime cum *Libro Nigro* MS fupra memorato, atque etiam cum *Libro Rubro* MS in Scaccario Regio affervato contuli; ficut mox fufius exponam. Et quoniam exemplarium examinatio nonnifi a duobus, altero prælegente altero codicem infpiciente, fit; in hoc tranfcripto ad fidem utriufque illorum Librorum MSS examinando, opem operamque petij & obtinui a Viro ftrenuo mihique amiciffimo *Georgio Holmes*, vicemgerente Viri Clariffimi *Ricardi Topham*, facrarum membranarum in archivis Turris *Londonienfis* repofitarum Cuftodis Regij, Amici mei humaniffimi. Adeoque hæc editio jufta & caftigata jure cenfenda. Jamque adfum, Baro Ornatiffime, ut quem mihi Tractatum in *Nigro Libro* defcriptum fuppeditafti, eum typis expreffum Tibi præfentem. Præfentoque quanta maxima poffum cum obfervantia, pro eo ac Tua Dignitas Virtufque expofcunt. Sunt autem aliæ rationes, ob quas exoptavi hanc editionem Tuo nomine præfixo ornari. Per orbem *Britannicum* inclaruifti literatorum Patronus: uti & ipfe literis ingenioque præcellis. Ita ferio doctrinæ provehendæ operam dedifti, ut folidam ifto pacto exiftimationem comparafti & ad feros nepotes duraturam. Speciatim vero, hoc potiffimum nomine a me celebrandus es, quod nempe Hiftoricen Scientiamque Antiquariam promovere curafti. Baro *Somers* ac Tuipfe, pro ea qua apud Dominos *Wilhelmum* & *Mariam* pridem Regem & Reginam *Angliæ* felicis memoriæ valuiftis gratia, auctores fuiftis ut juffu Regio inchoaretur præclarum illud opus Colligendi & in lucem emittendi Fœdera, Conventa, & Acta Publica, quotquot ufpiam in Archivis reperiri poterant, quæ inter *Anglorum* Reges & Exteros Reges atque Refpublicas per aliquot præterita fecula intercefferunt. Quod quidem opus gratia Sereniffimæ Reginæ ANNÆ etiamnum utcunque pergit. Præterea, juftum rectumque eft maximas ab Antiquarijs noftræ *Britanniæ* gratias referri, perquam Honorabilibus & perquam Reverendis Proceribus ac Prælatis felecti cœtus, a Camera Procerum in Parlamento confidentium (Te ibi coram & palam proponente) delegatis, ad perluftranda fingula *Recordorum* (a) Repofitoria

---

(a) *Vocabulo noftratium forenfi utor.*

quæ

quæ *Londoniæ* sunt (*b*), & Tibi in specie, Baro eruditissime, Quod vos omnes Proceres Delegati negotium illud tam solerti cura peregistis: Quod *Recordorum* repositoria ipsimet adijstis; Quod recorda quo essent in statu sagaciter perspexistis; Quod providistis ea a tempestate alijsque damnosis casibus illæsa servari, quin & in methodum redigi, indicibusque si qui defuerant adjectis publico usui aptos reddi; In summa, quod a Regia Thesauraria amplas impetrastis pecuniæ summas (quæ pro innata Reginæ Optimæ munificentia facile concessæ) ad ædes camerasque in quibus recorda asservantur instaurandas & reficiendas. Hoc sane sicut est suapte natura opus summis laudibus efferendum; ita non potest non esse apprime gratum acceptumque ijs omnibus, quibus veneranda Antiquitatis monumenta in pretio sunt.

Indultus est mihi honor vos Proceres Delegatos comitandi: Semel videlicet, quum Archivum Regium Turris *Londoniensis* visum ibatis; quo tempore ibi aderant perquam Honorabiles Domini, *Thomas* Comes de *Stamford*, *Radulphus* Baro *Grey* de *Werk*, *Johannes* Baro *Poulet* de *Hinton St. George* nunc Comes *Poulet*, *Johannes* Baro *Somers*, *Carolus* Baro *Halifax* (Amplitudinem Tuam innuo), ac plurimum Reverendi *Johannes Cicestrensis* & *Wilhelmus Carliolensis* Episcopi: Itemque alia vice quando perlustrastis Domum Capitularem *Westmonasterij*, aliud Recordorum Regiorum Repositorium; quo die ibi adfuerunt Perillustres Domini *Thomas* Comes de *Stamford*, *Carolus* Comes de *Sunderland*, *Johannes* Comes de *Anglesey*, *Laurentius* Comes de *Rochester*, *Carolus* Vicecomes *Towneshend*, *Johannes* Baro *Poulet*, jam Comes *Poulet*, *Johannes* Baro *Somers*, & Tuipse Baro Amplissime, ac admodum Reverendus *Wilhelmus* Episcopus *Carliolensis* (*c*), associato ipsis *Christophoro Wren* Equite Aurato, Architecto Regio: Iterumque alia vice, quum Repositoria Turris *Londoniensis* denuo inviseretis; quo tempore ibi præsentes erant perquam Honorabiles Domini *Thomas* Comes de *Stamford*, *Johannes* Baro *Somers*, & Tuipse, ac plurimum Reverendus *Gilbertus* Episcopus *Saresberiensis*. Permitte autem si placet ut hic profitear, maximo me oblectamento perfusum fuisse, videntem atque notantem quam solicite omnes Proceres Delegati prospexistis, ut Regia Recorda tuta & sarta tecta serventur. Neque vero heic loci a me reticendum est propositum aliud laudatissimum (cujus

(*b*) *Vernacule appellamus*, The Lords Committees to consider the Method of keeping Records in Offices.

(*c*) *Neminem e Proceribus qui in Domo Capitulari tunc aderant prudens scienfque omisi. Si quis forte omissus, is mihi benignus ignoscat & memoriæ lapsui tribuat oro atque obtestor. Omissi sunt autem complures alij Proceres ac quantum scio Prælati, qui pro Delegatis nominabantur, sed alijs negotijs impediti vel casu abfuerunt.*

Tu

Tu vel auctor vel adjutor), providendi nimirum pulcram & magnificam Bibliothecam ad Codices MSS Musei *Cottoniani* quod *Westmonasterij* est (Thesaurum certe quantivis pretij) condendos promendos. Quod quidem propositum gratia & munificentia ANNÆ Reginæ pientissimæ aliquando adimpletum iri sperare licet.

Proximo loco nonnihil dicendum erit, Baro Illustrissime, de Tractatu sive Dialogo quem hic Tibi in manus do. Duo illius vetusta exemplaria MSS hodie supersunt. Unum descriptum in *Nigro Libro* qui est in *Recepta* Scaccarij Regij, in custodia Thesaurarij & Camerariorum; Alterum in *Libro Rubro* qui custoditur a Rememoratore Reginæ in Scaccario Baronum : utrumque antiqua exaratum manu. Exemplar quod in *Libro Nigro* extat charactere minusculo & densiusculo scribitur : Et scriptum fuit, ut conjicio, tempore circiter *Edwardi* I. Regis *Angliæ*. Transcriptor, quisquis is fuit, aliquoties vacua in textu spatia reliquit; siquando scilicet exemplar quo usus est non potuit perfecte legi : Eaque vacua spatia (nonnunquam ad instar trium aut quatuor linearum) supplentur ab alterius cujusdam penna, & diversa quidem a reliquo textu scriptura; at simili illi quæ sub *Edwardo* I. Rege vulgo usurpata fuit; sicut, inter examinandum, attentius intuentes conjectabamur. Hujus exemplaris textus integer est. Sed nulli habentur tituli seu lemmata capitum. Ubi ea inseri debuerant, passim relinquuntur spatia vacua; sicut per linearum fracturas quæ sunt ad initium quamplurium e capitibus conjicere licet; quæ spatia (ut fit) Transcriptor postea non adimplevit. Indicium autem, ex quo liquere possit quisnam vel Dialogum composuerit vel istius exemplaris scriptor fuerit, in *Libro Nigro* nullum reperio.

Exemplar alterum quod est in *Libro Rubro*, scribitur charactere admodum parvo & compresso; & scribi potuit (conjectando loquor) circa *Henrici* III. Regis tempora anteriora, vel forsan *Johanne* regnante. Nullum habet Titulum generalem, neque auctoris nomen præfixum. Nam folio 31. a. sic infit, *Ordinatis a Deo potestatibus* &c; Et in dorso ejusdem folij sic orditur, *Anno xxiij regni Regis* Henrici *secundi, cum sederem ad fenestram speculæ* &c. Deinde sequitur Dialogus columnatim scriptus. Iste *Liber Ruber* quondam fuit *Alexandri* Archidiaconi *Salopiæ*. Id quod ipse disertis verbis testatur in charta sive scripto cujus tenorem in margine apposui, de quadam Concordia facta coram Rege & compluribus Magnatibus, inter Episcopum *Herefordiæ* & illius Urbis Cives (*d*). Hæc Concordia in *Libro Rubeo* sequitur continuo

post

(*d*) Anno Domini Mccxxvij°, Regni Regis H. filij Regis J. xj, vigilia S. Margaretæ fuit Rex Londoniæ apud Westmonasterium in capella S. Johannis cum Magnatibus

post finem Tractatus de cujus auctore disquirimus; scripta scilicet eadem pagina seu dorso folij in quo Tractatus definit, & quidem charactere ni fallor coævo illi in quo Tractatus scribitur. Hanc Concordiam scribebat ipse Alexander; ipsomet testante *se interfuisse & hoc scripsisse.*

Iste *Alexander* Archidiaconus *Salopiæ,* fuit *Alexander de Swereford,* vir præstantissimus, cujus memoria fausta est, & apud Antiquarios hodiernum viret floretque. Scaccarij primum Clericus, dein Baro. Cognominatus *de Swereford,* a villa sive parochia ejus nominis in Comitatu *Oxoniensi.* Cujus parochiæ fuit primum Vicarius, deinde Rector (*Personam* vocarunt), ab Abbate & Conventu *Oseneiæ* præsentatus (*e*). Anno Regis *Johannis* 17°, fuit Clericus familiaris Episcopi *Coventrensis*; & Regis permissu obviam Episcopo suo trans mare profectus est. Occurrit *Salopiæ* Archidiaconus, & testis chartæ *Roberti de Watford* Decani ac Capituli *Londoniensis* 5 *Kal. Dec.* 3. *H.* 3. (*f*). Concessit ei *Henricus* III. Rex, tunc Archidiacono *Salopiæ* & Clerico Regis, xx marcas per annum, ad se sustentandum (*g*). Anno 18 *H.* III. die 6 Julii, in Scaccario Regis recedit tanquam Baro (*h*). Anno 123½, die 15 Jan. memoratur Thesaurarius S. *Pauli Londoniæ* (*i*). Item A. D. 1241, ut Thesaurarius S. *Pauli Londoniæ* attestabatur chartæ qua *Adam Scotus* donavit Ecclesiæ *Paulinæ* reditum annuum duodecim solidorum (*k*). Obijt 14 Kal. Novemb.

natibus quibusdam. Et venit ibi H. Foliot Herefordensis Episcopus, qui Cives Herefordiæ xl nominatim excommunicaverat, eo quod in communi tallagio Regis in Civitate homines suos concives & inhabitantes Civitatem, & homines Canonicorum talliaverant, & namia pro tallagio ceperant. Civitatem etiam totam interdicto suposuerat. Hijs igitur coram Rege propositis, sub tali forma quievit negocium in eadem Capella eadem die: videlicet quod Episcopus absolveret excommunicatos omnes in forma ecclesiæ, & interdictionem relaxaret, restitutis namijs captis Hominibus Episcopi & Canonicorum; & Archiepiscopi & Episcopi dijudicarent postmodum de emenda & satisfactione [Ecclesiasticorum jurium]. Hijs interfuerunt & consenserunt, Ipse Rex H, Et H. de Burgo Justiciarius, Episcopi Eustachius Londoniensis, Ricardus Sarresburiensis, Radulfus Cicestrensis Regis Cancellarius, Jocelinus Bathoniensis, Walterus Karleolensis; Justiciarij de Banco, Thomas de Muleton, Robertus de Lessinton, Thomas de Haidon, Henricus de Braibroc; Baronibus & Militibus alijs, Radulfo filio Nicholai, Godefrido de Craucumbe, Nicholao de Molis, Theobaldo Hautein, Reimundo de Burgo, Guillelmo filio Garen., Philippo de Obeigny, Henrico filio Acherij, Henrico de Capella; Clericis, Radulfo de Norwiz Justic. Judæorum, Ranulfo Britone Consiliar. Justiciarij, Magistro Henrico de Bissopesbirie, Henrico de Cornhull Cancellario Londoniæ, & Alexandro Archidiacono Salopiæ Clerico tunc Domini Regis, qui interfuit, & hoc scripsit; Cujus liber iste fuit. *Lib. Rub. Scacc. fol. numerato xlvj, b. col.* 2.

(*e*) *Bib. Cott. Vitell. E.* 15. *fol.* 204. *col.* 1.
(*f*) *Ib. Tiber. C.* 5. *fol.* 156.
(*g*) *Pat.* 12. *H.* 3.
(*h*) *Cl.* 18. *H.* 3. *dorf. m.* 16.
(*i*) *Pat.* 16. *H.* 3. *m.* 9.
(*k*) Testibus, Petro Londoniensi Archidiacono, Henrico Cancellario, Alexandro Thesaurario, Rogero Præcentore, Willelmo de Sanctæ Mariæ Ecclesia, Godefrido de Wesham, Ricardo de Wendovere, Ricardo Foliot, Ricardo de Stanford, Hugone de Sancto

vemb. anno 1246 (*l*); fepultus in ecclefia S. *Pauli,* ad altare S. *Ceddæ*; ubi quandam cantariam fundavit. Hæc memoranda de infigniffimo *Salopiæ* Archidiacono nuperrime mecum communicavit Rev. & Cl. Vir, idemque in me amiciffimus, *Matthæus Hutton* de *Aynho* S. T. P. Et funt alia aliquammulta, ut memini, hoc genus, de vita moribufque *Alexandri* Archidiaconi, quæ non eft hic recenfendi locus. Progredior.

Quanquam *Alexander* fortean vel collegerit vel fcribi fecerit in *Libro Rubeo* exemplar illud Dialogi quod in eodem Libro extat; verifimile tamen eft, Dialogum ipfum ante *Alexandri* tempora compofitum; fcilicet ante tempora R. *Henrici* III, aut etiam *Johannis*. Hoc exemplar proculdubio ex aliquo alio exemplari aut libro fuit exfcriptum. Nam exfcriptor nonnunquam alba fpatiola repofuit pro verbis quæ vel legere non potuit vel non fatis intellexit: Et alibi nonnulla verba per errorem fcripfit loco aliorum, quæ ijs, juxta modum fcripturæ & abbreviationis illis temporibus ufitatum, fimilia erant; ficut & D. *Georgius Holmefius* & egomet, *Librum Rubrum* oculis infpicientes, conjectati fumus. Porro, *Alexander* qui Regi in Scaccario fuo jam inde a diebus *Willelmi de Ely* fervierat (*Willelmi,* inquam, *de Ely,* qui in initio imperij R. *Johannis* Thefaurarius Regis fuit) fedulam operam impenderat colligendis quas potuit rebus memorabilibus, ad Scaccarium, Regiumque Proventum, & Tenuras pertinentibus. Hoc fane confilio in *Librum Rubrum* (quo ufus videtur pro Collectaneorum penu) multa e Rotulis Annalibus (quos hodie *Magnos Rotulos Pipæ* vocamus) de Servitijs Militaribus excerpta retulit. Et inter alia quæ in Libro illo congeffit, integrum confervare fategit noftrum hunc de Scaccario Dialogum. Sed Dialogum fuperius innui, Baro Ampliffime, Alexandri Archidiaconi ævo antiquiorem effe. Idque ex intrinfecis quibufdam notis five indicijs vero fimile videtur. Exempli gratia. Dialogi auctor eo ipfo modo de *Curia Regis* loquitur, quo loqui folitum eft ante Curiarum juridicarum partitionem (*m*). Pleraque Brevia ab ipfo citata ftylum Regalem fingularis numeri præ fe ferunt (*n*); ubi R. *Henricus* II, annis imperij fui pofterioribus, & poft eum omnes *Angliæ* Reges, numero plurali fcripferunt, *Nos* & *Noftrum* &c. Ufitatæ funt apud ipfum phrafes five dictiones quædam antiquitatem primævam

---

Sancto Edmundo, & Willelmo de Welleburn, Canonicis Sancti Pauli; Radulfo Efwi tunc Majore Lond[oniæ], Roberto filio Johannis Aldermanno, Simone filio Mariæ tunc Vicecomite Midelfexiæ ———.

Actum Londoniæ 1241———. *E pixide,* P, *in archivo Decani & Cap. Londoniæ.*
(*l*) *Bibl. Cott. Vitell.* E. 15. *f.* 198.
(*m*) L. 1. *cap.* 6.
(*n*) L. 1. *c.* 6. Thefaurarius &.

fpirantes.

spirantes. Legem seu Statutum, *Assisam* vocat (*o*), Judices itinerantes, *errantes* (*p*), Auxilia Civitatum & Burgorum Regi præstita, *Dona* (*q*), Navem Regis qua mari iter facere solitus est, *Esneccam* (*r*). Adde, si placet, ea quæ auctor dicit de *Danegeldo* (*s*), *Ordalio* (*t*), catallis Usurariorum (*u*), & in similibus. Revera, e Tractatu ipso apparet, ævo Henrici II. Regis compositum. Nam illi Regi inscribitur; & ipse in eo sæpius memoratur tanquam tunc vivus ac superstes (*w*). Conjecerim auctorem annis jam dicti Regis prioribus, & post aliquandiu, vixisse. Norat sane vel viderat *Robertum Leicestriæ* Comitem, qui Capitalis Justiciarij munere temporius sub *Henrico* II functus est (*x*), vitaque excessit A. D. 1168, [14. *H*. 2.] referente *Houedeno* (*y*). Colloquium habuerat cum *Henrico* [*de Blois*] *Wintoniensi* Episcopo (*z*); qui A. D. 1171, obijsse dicitur (*a*). Magnis elogijs cumulat *Nigellum Eliensem* Episcopum, ut qui ipsum probe norat (*b*); & expressim dicit, se *Nigelli*, cum Thesaurarius esset, locum in Scaccario absentis supplesse (*c*). Enimvero creditur *Nigelli* filius (*d*). *Nigellus* Episcopus obijt A. D. 1169, (15 *H*. 2.), ut habetur in Annalibus *Wintoniæ* & Historia *Eliensi* (*e*). Manifeste, mortuus erat anno circiter R. *Henrici* II. 15° (*f*). In summa, Tractatus iste videtur vel partim scriptus vel forsan perfectus statim post annum R. *Henrici* II. quartum & vigesimum. Testatur auctor se scribere incepisse anno Regis illius vigesimo tertio (*g*). Loquiturque de Brevi Regio emanante sub Termino S. *Michaelis* anni vigesimi quarti (*h*), tanquam de re tunc recens facta. Et ad hoc fere temporis spatium refertur alia clausula Dialogi. ———
" A *Ricardo* (inquit auctor) *Pictavensi* Archidiacono, nunc *Winto-*

(*o*) *L*. 2. *c*. 10. Sic est, sed de.
(*p*) *L*. 2. *c*. 10. Fit interdum.
(*q*) *L*. 2. *c*. 13. Quid assisa communis.
(*r*) *L*. 1. *c*. 6. Ad hanc, sicut ad.
(*s*) *L*. 1. *c*. 8. Sic est, sed prosequamur. *L*. 1. *c*. 11. Quid Danegildum. *L*. 2. *c*. 12. Placita autem dicimus.
(*t*) *L*. 2. *c*. 7. Adverte autem.
(*u*) *L*. 2. *c*. 10. Sic est, sed de.
(*w*) *L*. 1. *c*. 11. Insula nostra suis. *Ib*. *L*. 2. *c*. 2. Licet hæc ad opus. *Ib*. *L*. 2. *c*. ult.
(*x*) *L*. 1. *c*. 11. Insula nostra suis.
(*y*) *P*. 2. *p*. 512. *n*. 50.
(*z*) Hujus institutionis causam ab Henrico quondam Wintoniensi Episcopo sic accepi. *Dialogi L*. 1. *c*. 15.
(*a*) *Annal. Ecclef. Wint. ap. Angl. Sacr.* *T*. 1. *p*. 301.

(*b*) *Dialog. L*. 1. *c*. 8. Movet te? nec.
(*c*) *L*. 1. *c*. 11. Insula nostra suis.
(*d*) *Angl. Sacr*. *P*. 1. *p*. 304.
(*e*) *Annal. Ecclef. Wint. ap. Angl. Sac.* *T*. 1. *p*. 301. *Hist. Elien. ibid. p.* 629.
(*f*) Nigellus Elyensis Episcopus r c de L marcis, de Promissione sua ad maritandam filiam Regis: In Thesauro xxx marcas, Et debet xx marcas. Sed mortuus est; & requiescat in pace. *Mag. Rot.* 15. *H.* 2. *Rot.* 10. *b*. *Cantebr. & Hunt*.
Nigellus Elyensis Episcopus debet xx marcas. Sed mortuus est; & requiescat in pace. *Mag. Rot.* 16. *H.* 2. *Rot.* 6. *b*. *Cant. & Hunt*.
(*g*) Anno xxiij regni Regis Henrici secundi, cum sederem ad fenestram &c. *Dial. in procem*.
(*h*) *L*. 1. *cap*. 8. Movet te? nec.

" *niensi*

"*nienfi* Episcopo (*i*)." Ille autem *Ricardus* Archidiaconus electus dicitur Episcopus *Wintoniensis* Kal. Maij A. D. 1173, (Anno 19°, ineunte 20° R. *Henrici* II); obijtque A. D. 1188, (viz. anno ultimo R. *Henrici* II) (*k*).

Jam, si Tuæ Amplitudini placeat, inquirendum venit, Utrum *Gervasius Tilburiensis* istius Tractatus auctor fuerit, an quis alius. Per aliquammultos annos elapsos *Gervasio* quasi communi hominum antiquariorum sententia adscriptus innotuit: atqui ob quam rationem adscriptus, augurari nequeo. Ea res mihi videtur adeo in obscuro posita, ut profecto si quæratur, Quisnam *Gervasius Tilleberiensis* fuerit, lubens fateor me inter antiquas membranas nihil de eo reperisse. A scriptoribus modernis traditur materno genere ab *Henrico* II. *Anglorum* Rege ortum duxisse. Literarum scientem fuisse. Et complura scripsisse; speciatim historiolam de Regibus *Angliæ* & *Franciæ*, quam *Othoni* IV. Imperatori *Alemanniæ*, filio *Henrici* Ducis *Saxoniæ* & *Matildæ* filiæ *Henrici* II. Regis *Anglorum* inscripsit (*l*). Historiola illa a *Chesnio* edita est inter Scriptores *Francicos*. Gerit ibi titulum hic in margine inferius memoratum (*m*); continetque quasdam Regum *Angliæ* & *Franciæ* res gestas breviter perstrictas. *Gervasius* magna apud *Othonem* Imperatorem gratia fuisse (*n*), & ab ipso Marescallus Regni *Arelatensis* designatus, fertur (*o*). Floruit (inquit *Balæus* loco supra citato) tempore R. *Johannis*. Et quidem circa illud idem tempus floruit *Otho*; nimirum, regnantibus R. R. *Ricardo* I, & *Johanne*; sicut e memorandis quæ mox citaturus sum liquere poterit. Tuæ Amplitudinis favore & patientia fretus, paulisper ab argumento meo digrediens, nonnulla hic de *Othone Gervasij* Patrono enarrabo. Recolligendum est, *Othonem* (qui suo seculo eousque emicuit, ut *Germaniæ* Imperator

(*i*) L. 2. cap. 2. Cum sicut commemoras.

(*k*) *Angl. Sac.* T. 1. p. 301.

(*l*) Gervasius Tilberiensis, Henrici II. Anglorum Regis nepos———. Quæ recte didicerat homo candidus, posteritati editis libellis consecravit; maxime Othoni quarto Imperatori, Joannis Regis ex matre nepoti, domino suo incomparabili. Qua apud eum authoritate & gratia fuerit hinc apparet, quod Arelatensis ditionis Marescallus designatus sit. Causa ejus transmigrationis fuit, quod Otho maternum genus ab Anglica muliere Mathilde, Henrici Anglorum Regis filia, duxerit.——— Claruit anno incarnati Messiæ 1210. sub Rege Joanne. *Balæi Scriptor. Brit. Centur.* 3. p. 250. Ex eodem Rege Henrico prodijt hinc Ducissa Saxoniæ, cujus Flos tu, Serenissime Princeps, ut bonæ arboris dulcissimum beneficium processisti. *Gerv. Tilleber. Fragment. ad Otton. IV. Imp. edit. a Duchesnio inter Hist. Franc. scriptor.* T. 3. p. 373. b.

(*m*) Fragmentum de Regibus Francorum & Anglorum, ex Libro de Memorabilibus mundi, qui alias Solatium Imperatoris seu Otia Imperialia nominatur. Auctore Gervasio Tilleberiensi Marescallo Regni Arelatensis. Ad Ottonem IV. Imperatorem. *Ibid. apud Duchesn. Hist. Franc. Script.* T. 3. p. 373. a. b.

(*n*) *Bal. ubi sup.*

(*o*) *Duchesn. ubi sup.*

eligeretur,

eligeretur, seu electus renunciaretur) Regia stirpe *Angliæ* prognatum. Mater ei fuit Domina *Matilda,* filia primogenita *Henrici* II. Regis *Angliæ,* principis potentissimi & magnificentissimi (*p*) : Pater, *Henricus* Dux *Saxoniæ.* Illius Conjugij soboles mascula fuerunt *Henricus, Otho,* & *Willelmus* cognomento *Anglicus. Willelmo Anglico* procreati sunt Duces *Brunswici* & *Luneburgi.* Sicque fundamentum positum est antiquæ inter Regalem *Angliæ* stirpem, ac Illustrissimas *Brunswici* & *Hannoveræ* familias, consanguinitatis; Quæ sane temporibus modernis in persona Dominæ *Elisabethæ,* matris Serenissimæ Principis *Sophiæ* nunc Electricis Dotissæ de *Hannovera,* feliciter renovata fuit & confirmata. Ea de causa æquum bonumque judicavi, ab interitu conservare, quin & perpetuæ quantum in me est memoriæ tradere, aliqua ex ijs quæ notabilia in antiquis membranis occurrunt de illustrissima illa Familia, quam gens *Anglorum* altissima ut par est veneratione prosequitur.

Annales *Waverleienses* tradunt *Othonem* A. D. 1198 [10 Ric. I.] electum fuisse Imperatorem (*q*) ; & A. D. 1209, a Papa *Innocentio* III. *Romæ* coronatum (*r*). Frequens in antiquis *Anglicæ* gentis membranis tum de *Othone* tum etiam de *Willelmo Anglico* mentio fit (mitto enim de reliquis e Serenissima illa stirpe loqui ad præsens). Instantiæ gratia: Anno circiter *Henrici* II. trigesimo secundo, *Willelmus Anglicus* hic in *Anglia* degebat, sub cura ac tutela avi sui jam dicti Regis *Henrici* II. (*s*); & postea, regnante *Ricardo* I. avunculo suo, sub illius cura positus (*t*). *Otho* utique sub id tempus in *Anglia* vitam egit, habuitque præcep-

(*p*) Que el Rey de Ingalaterra su suegro era el mas estimado Rey que avia en la Christiandad, y fue Senor de muy grandes estados en Francia : y assi por su respeto, a quien llamava invictissimo y siempre triumfador. [*Innuendo,* R. Henricum II. Angliæ *fuisse* Christianorum *principum suo ævo æstimatissimum, salutatumque Invictissimum & semper Triumphatorem.*] Annales de Aragon T. 1. L. 2. *f.* 77. *a.* ad *A. D.* 1170.

(*q*) Mcxcviii, Anno x⁰ Regis Ricardi; Oto minor filius Henrici Ducis Saxoniæ, nepos Ricardi Regis Anglorum, electus est in Imperatorem Alemanniæ. *Annal. Waverl. p.* 166.

(*r*) Mccix, Oto filius Ducis Saxoniæ, nepos Regis Johannis, proxima Dominica post festum S. Michaelis diademate Imperiali coronatus est Romæ a Domino Papa Innocente III. Et cito inter Imperium & Summum Pontificem orta est discordia. *Ib. ad ann. ill.*

(*s*) Et pro acquietandis pannis Willelmi Anglici, filij Ducis Saxoniæ, & Nutricum suarum, & Lotricis suæ, & Magistri sui, viij l & xviij s & viij d, per breve Rannulfi de Glanvilla. *Mag. Rot.* 32. *Hen.* 2. *Rot.* 4. *a. Londonia & Middelsexa. Et vid. ante, Hist. Scacc. Vol.* 1. *cap.* 10. *Sect.* 12. *ad ann.* 1. *Ric.* 1. Henricus de Cornhill &.

(*t*) Et in procurationibus Willelmi filij Ducis Saxoniæ, & filiæ Comitis Galfridi Britanniæ, a festo S. Hylarij usque viij diem post Cineres, Lxix s & viij d. per breve Regis, & per visum Willelmi Talliatoris. *Mag. Rot.* 2. *Ric.* 1. *Rot.* 11. *tit.* Civitas Wintoniæ.

torem *Morbodonem* quendam (*u*). Rex *Ricardus* I, anno imperij sui 3º, dedit *Othoni* palefridum (*w*); & cuidam Equiti suo, *Jordano*, xx marcas (*x*). Idem Rex (anno suo quinto & sexto) vestimenta quædam emi & provideri jussit, in usum Regis *Othonis* & sodalium suorum quum ab *Anglia* in *Germaniam* proficiscerentur (*y*). Sub idem fere tempus Rex *Othoni* dedit tres penulas panni de *Lindesia* & duas robas panni de *Stanfordia* tincti (*z*). Rex idem *Ricardus* I. (anno suo decimo) misit Domino *Othoni* in *Germaniam* magnam pecuniæ vim; cujus illuc vehendæ expensa ad xx marcas attigit (*a*). Deinceps, regnante Rege *Johanne*, *Otho* sæpius occurrit memoratus nomine Regis *Othonis*, Regis *Romanorum* seu *Alemanniæ*, ac Imperatoris. Rex *Johannes*, anno suo primo, misit ei in *Germaniam*, grandem pecuniæ summam, per manum quorundam Comitum & aliorum (*b*); & solvi jussit *Constantino de Colonia* xlv l, in exonerationem æris alieni *Othonis* Regis Romanorum (*c*). Anno R. *Johannis* quarto quidam Camerarius Regis *Othonis* in *Anglia* fuerat; item quidam *Gerardus de Rodes* & *Radulfus de Ardenna* ad Regem *Othonem* ab *Anglia* missi; itemque duo Nuncij ac duo Tubicinæ ab Rege *Othone* missi ad Avunculum suum R. *Johannem* in *Anglia* (*d*). Proxi-

(*u*) Et Morbodoni Magistro Otonis filij Ducis Saxonum, x l, ad eundem ad Regem in negocijs suis; per breve Cancellarij. *Mag. Rot.* 2. *R.* 1. *Rot.* 12. *a. Chent.*

(*w*) Et Otoni filio Ducis Saxoniæ xl s, ad emendum 1 palefridum; per breve Cancellarij. *Mag. Rot.* 3. *R.* 1. *Rot.* 9. *b. Cantebrugescira & Huntedonescira.*

(*x*) Et Jordani Militi Othonis nepotis Domini Regis, filij Ducis Saxonum, xx marcas, per breve Cancellarij. *Mag. Rot.* 3. *R.* 1. *Rot.* 11. *a. Londonia & Midd.*

(*y*) Et pro Robis emptis ad opus Regis Otonis filij Ducis Saxoniæ & Sociorum suorum quando perrexerunt in Alemanniam, xviij l & viij d; per Breve Regis. *Mag. Rot.* 5. *R.* 1. *Rot.* 12. *Londonia & Midd.*

(*z*) Et Otoni filio Ducis Saxonum L s, pro tribus penulis de Lindesia & duabus robis de Stanford tinctis per breve Regis. *Mag. Rot.* 6. *R.* 1. *Rot.* 15. *b. Surreya.*

(*a*) Et Roberto de Wanci & Ricardo de Heriet xx marcas ad Thesaurum Regis conducendum ad Dominum Otonem in Alemannia, & ad alia necessaria eis invenienda. *Mag. Rot.* 10. *R.* 1. *Rot.* 14. *a. Kent.*

(*b*) Reginaldus de Cornhull r c de CCCC & xij l & vij s & vj d. ob., Et de C & Lxv l & xiij s & iiij d Numero de firma de Kent ———; Et in custamento Passagij cum thesauro quem Rex misit Otoni Regi Romanorum, per Comites & alios transfretantes, vij l & dimidia marca, per Breve Regis. *Mag. Rot.* 1. *Joh. Rot.* 5. *a. Kent.*

(*c*) Et Constantino de Colonia xlv l, in solutione debiti Otonis Regis Romanorum quod Rex pro eis solvit. *Mag. Rot.* 1. *J. Rot.* 9. *b. Londonia & Middelsexa.*

(*d*) Et pro Passagio Camerarij Regis Otonis Alemanniæ & Sociorum suorum xvij marcæ, per Breve Galfridi filij Petri. Et pro Passagio Gerardi de Rodes & Radulfi de Ardenna ad Regem Ottonem, v marcæ, per idem Breve. Et Rogero Balistario iiij marcæ pro opere Balistarij, per idem Breve. Et Nuntijs Regis Ottonis euntibus ad Regem, x l & iij marcæ & j palefridus de Dono Regis, per Breve Galfridi filij Petri ———. Et in Passagio duorum Trumpatorum Regis Alemanniæ & duorum Nuntiorum ejusdem, xl s, per Breve ejusdem. *Mag. Rot.* 4. *J. Rot.* 15. *b. Kent.*

DISSERTATIO EPISTOLARIS. 341

mo anno R. *Johannes* dono dedit Regi *Othoni* palefridum (*e*). Anno Regis *Johannis* octavo, *Lambertus* Senefcallus Regis *Othonis* in *Angliam* miffus fuit (*f*) ; Itidemque *Conradus* R. *Othonis* Senefcallus (*g*). Anno R. *Johannis* nono, in *Anglia* moram trahebant quidam Nuncij Regis *Othonis* (*h*) ; itemque *Johannes* Camerarius ejus ac *Lambertus de Colonia* [rerum fuarum in *Anglia*, uti videtur, procuratores] (*i*). Anno R. *Johannis* decimo, Rex *Alemanniæ* habuit quofdam Nuncios fuos in *Anglia* morantes (*k*). Anno R. *Johannis* undecimo, triginta fex libræ & una marca, jubente *Galfrido filio Petri*, folutæ *Conrado* Senefcallo [*Othonis*] Imperatoris, ad pretiofam fuam fupellectilem & alia *Coloniæ* invadiata redimenda (*l*). Anno R. *Johannis* decimo tertio, mille marcæ juffu Regis folutæ *Conrado de Wilre* Imperatoris [*Othonis*] in *Anglia* Nuntio (*m*). Eodem anno, Rex dono dedit Duci *Saxoniæ* quatuor pateras deauratas, & unam deauratam Ducis Nuntio (*n*). Anno ejufdem Regis quartodecimo, *Henricus* filius Ducis [*Saxoniæ*] ab *Anglia* in *Germaniam* reverfus eft. Quo etiam tempore quidam Nuntij *Othonis* Imperatoris in *Anglia* morabantur (*o*).

(*e*) Et Normanno de Camera eunti in Alemanniam iiij libras, ad unum palefridum emendum ad opus Regis Ottonis; per Breve G. filij Petri. *Mag. Rot.* 5. *J. Rot.* 1. *a. Londonia & Midd.*

(*f*) Et in paffagio Lamberti Senefcalli Regis Otonis & fociorum fuorum xxij s, per Breve Galfridi filij Petri. *Mag. Rot.* 8. *J. Rot.* 5. *a. Kent.*

(*g*) Et Conrado Senefcallo Regis Otonis xiij l & x s, ad expenfas fuas, per idem Breve [i. e. Galfridi filij Petri]. *Mag. Rot.* 8. *J. Rot.* 6. *a. Londonia & Middelfexa.*

(*h*) Et Nuncijs Regis Otonis v marcas, per breve Galfridi filij Petri. *Mag. Rot.* 9. *J. Rot.* 4. *a. Kent.*

(*i*) Robertus de Infula reddit compotum de x l & ij s & v d, ficut fupra continetur; In Thefauro nichil; Et Johanni Camerario Regis Alemanniæ & Lamberto de Colonia, x l & ij s & v d, per Breve G. filij Petri; Et Quietus eft. *Mag. Rot.* 9. *J. Rot.* 10. *a. Cantebrig. & Huntend.*

(*k*) Et in paffagio Archidiaconi Staffordiæ & Nuntiorum Regis Alemanniæ, xx s, per Breve Regis. *Mag. Rot.* 10. *J. Rot.* 1. *a. Kent.*

(*l*) Galfridus filius Petri reddit compotum de CCCC marcis quas recepit de Reginaldo de Cornhill — De quibus debet refpondere. Abbati fcilicet de Binnendon xl marcas; Et Conrado Senefcallo Imperatoris xxxvj l & j marcam, ad vadia fua & jocalia acquietanda apud Coloniam. *Mag. Rot.* 11. *J. Rot.* 6. *b. poft Wireceftrefciram.*

(*m*) Fratres Militiæ Templi reddunt compotum de x millibus marcarum quas receperunt de pecunia Regis: In Thefauro nichil: Et Conrado de Wilre Nuntio Imperatoris mille marcas, per breve Regis; Et debent ix mille marcas. *Mag. Rot.* 13. *J. Rot.* 9. *b. Londonia & Middelfexa.* Ac *Mag. Rot.* 15. *J. Rot.* 11. *b. Londonia & Midd.*

(*n*) *Computatum fuit ad Scaccarium* Johanni filio Hugonis *Firmario de* Cocham *&* Bray — viz. Pro iiij Cupis deauratis datis Duci Saxoniæ xxv l, per idem Breve [Regis]; Et pro una Cupa deaurata data cuidam Nuntio Ducis Saxoniæ **C** s, per idem Breve. *Mag. Rot.* 13. *Joh. Rot.* 22. *a. Oxenef.*

(*o*) Et in expenfis Henrici filij Ducis, & in warnillura Navis fuæ quando receffit, xxv l & iij s & iiij d, per breve Regis; Et Willelmo de Cantilupo ad expenfas Nuntiorum Imperatoris, iiij l & x s & viij d, per idem breve. *Mag. Rot.* 14. *J. Rot.* 18. *a. Norfolch & Sudfolch.*

Ad

Ad summam, *Otho* mortem obijsse fertur in *Saxonia* A. D. 1218 (*p*).

Persuasum habeo, Vir Illustrissime, Te mihi condonaturum hanc etsi praelongam digressionem; praesertim cum ea subjectam materiam introducit nostrum utrique acceptissimam. Familiam Serenissimam *Hannoverae* singulari veneratione colis. Id quod ore proprio testandi opportunitatem habuisti. Quando nimirum non ita pridem (*q*), ANNÆ Reginae potentissimae jussu *Hannoveram* profectus eras; a Curia *Hannoverana* magna gratia & benevolentia exceptus.

Ad Tractatum de quo disquiritur redeo. Manifestum sane est, ejus Tractatus auctorem fuisse in rebus Fiscalibus versatissimum; quin & in Scaccario Regio plurimis annis deservijsse, munusque insigne obijsse. Exadverso, e nullo quod quidem sciam Recordo seu scripto authentico enotescit, *Gervasium Tilburiensem* aliquas in Scaccario Regis tanquam Baronem aut aliud genus Ministrum partes egisse. Fuit sane sub initium imperij R. *Henrici* II, quidam *Gervasius* qui fuisse videtur Clericus sive Officiarius in *Recepta* Scaccarij; quia *Gervasius de Thesauro* (quasi dixerit, *Gervasius de Thesauraria* seu *Recepta*) nuncupatur. Iste *Gervasius* in *Magno* Rotulo anni secundi Regis *Henrici* II, immunitatem habuit Danegeldi (*Quietantiam* vocabant a *Danegeldo*) in Comitatu *Suthamtoniae*, virtute rescripti Regij (*r*). In *Magno Rotulo* anni quarti ejusdem Regis, *Gervasius de Thesauro*, virtute Brevis Regii de *Perdono*, quietantiam habuit in Comitatu *Suthamtoniae* de summa ei imposita nomine *Doni Comitatus* (*s*). Anno ejusdem Regis decimoquinto, quietantiam assecutus est *Gervasius de Thesauro* per Breve Regis, de Communi assisa sive amerciamento propter *murdrum* Hundredo de *Netham* irrogato (*t*). Atqui non constat, hic vocatum *Gervasium de Thesauro*, fuisse *Gervasium Tilleberiensem*. Multo verisimilius, fuisse quempiam alium. Etenim si *Gervasius Tilleberiensis* materno sanguine ab Rege *Henrico* II, ortum duxerit; hic *Gervasius de Thesauro* non potuit per aetatem, ut opinor, idem esse qui *Gervasius*

(*p*) *Catal. Honor.* p. 342.
(*q*) A. D. 1706.
(*r*) *Hist. Scacc. Vol.* 1. *Cap.* 17. *sect.* 1. *tit. De Danegeldo.*
(*s*) Et idem Vicecomes [Turstinus] r c de C marcis argenti de Dono Comitatus; In Thesauro xxxv l & vij s & ij d; Et in Perdonis per Brevia Regis, Episcopo Wintoniae xxij l & xij s & iiij d, Et Johanni Marescallo xix s & ij d, Et Willelmo Maled[octo] x s & vj d, Et Gervasio de Thesauro ij s & iiij d, Et Gaiolarijs Regis xviij d; &c. *Mag. Rot.* 4. *H.* 2. *Rot.* 8. *a. Hantescira.*

(*t*) Et idem Vicecomes r c de Lxvj s & ij d, de Netham hundredo pro j murdro. In Thesauro xxviij s; Et in Perdonis, per brevia Regis, Abbati de Bello ij s & x d. Et Willelmo Malduit Camerario iiij s & iiij d, Et Gervasio de Thesauro viij d: Et debet xxxj s & iiij d. *Mag. Rot.* 15. *H.* 2. *Rot.* 11. *a. Hantescira.*

de

DISSERTATIO EPISTOLARIS. 343

de Tilleberia. Siquidem *Gervafius de Thefauro* anno fecundo Regis *Henrici* II, quippe qui tunc Clericus in *Recepta* meruit, matura faltem ætate fuit. Verum Rex ipfe *Henricus* II, anno imperij fui fecundo, annis duntaxat viginti tribus aut eo circiter natus erat.

Præter hæc, probabiliter inferri poteft *Gervafium de Tilleberia* virum Laicum fuiffe, ex eo quod Regni *Arelatenfis* Marefcallus nominatus fuit. Ex altera parte, hujus auctorem Dialogi virum Ecclefiafticum fuiffe prægnantibus quibufdam ab ipfo Dialogo defumptis indicijs evincitur. Forfan objecerit quis Marefcalli non fuiffe ufque adeo Laicum officium, quin eo interdum Clerici fungerentur. Sic in Scaccarij Curia factum eft. Is qui ibi vices Marefcalli *Angliæ* gerere folebat, quandoque Clericus fuit, denominatufque *Clericus Marefcalciæ*. Hujufce rei complures inftantias fuppeditat præcedens Hiftoria (*u*) : Pariliter, Conftabularij, quod perinde ac Marefcalli officium Laicum videatur, non raro a Clericis adminiftrabatur. Qui enim in Scaccario vice Conftabularij *Angliæ* fervire folebant, utplurimum Clerici erant, nuncupati utique *Clerici de Conftabularia* (*w*). Quinetiam, regnante *Henrico* III, *Eboracenfis* Archiepifcopus Turris *Londonienfis* Conftabularius fuit (*x*) : & regnante *Edwardo* I, vir ecclefiafticus *Antonius Bek* Conftabularius fuit Turris *Londonienfis* per annos bene multos, tum antequam Epifcopus *Dunelmenfis* factus effet, tum etiam poft (*y*). Veruntamen, vel ifta quam pofui objectio, vel quæ ad eam fulciendam adduci poffint argumenta, nihil, ut mihi perfuadeo, impedient, quin Marefcalli officium proprie Laicum fuiffe arbitremur. Notandum eft, quod Marefcalli & Conftabularij de Scaccario officia actis præcipue Clericalibus confiftebant. Id quod etiam, opinor, fupponendum de officio Conftabulatus Turris *Londoniæ*, quatenus illud executus eft *Antonius de Bek*. Non enim probabile eft, ipfummet *Antonium* in fuo Conftabularij officio ejufmodi acta peregiffe, quæ proprie erant *Militum Servientum*, & *Hominum ad arma* (*z*), at potius ea quæ ordini Clericali erant confentanea. Quocirca Marefcallatum *Arelatenfem* fuiffe proprie Laicum munus, ad præfens aufim Tua venia

---

(*u*) *Hift. Scacc. cap.* 24. *fect.* 6.
(*w*) *Hift. Scacc. cap.* 24. *fect.* 5.
(*x*) Liberate——, W. Archiepifcopo Eboracenfi Conftabulario Turris Londoniæ——. *Lib.* 57. *H.* 3. *m. unica.*
(*y*) Liberate de thefauro noftro, dilecto Clerico noftro Antonio Bek Conftabulario noftro Turris noftræ Londoniæ, quinquaginta libras——. *Lib.* 3. *E.* 1. *m.* 3.
Antony Bek *had* C l per annum, pro Cuftodia Turris Londoniæ. *Lib.* 8. *E.* 1. *m.* 5. *Lib.* 9. *E.* 1.
Liberate——A Dunelmenfi electo, Conftabulario Turris noftræ Londoniæ——. *Lib.* 11. *E.* 1. *m.* 3.
Liberate——Venerabili patri A Dunelmenfi Epifcopo Conftabulario Turris noftræ Londoniæ——. *Lib.* 12. *E.* 1. *m.* 1.
(*z*) *Anglice vocabantur*, Knights, Sergeants, and Men at Arms ; *Anglonormannice*, Chivalers, Sergeanz, & Gentz d'armes.

pro

pro admisso sumere. E contrario, satis liquet hujus Tractatus auctorem virum fuisse Ecclesiasticum. Ejus rei testimonia aliqua ex ipso Tractatu hauriri possint. Auctor passim tali stylo modoque scribendi utitur, qualis illo seculo viris ecclesiasticis fere usitatus fuit. Possessiones prædiales vocat, *Temporalia* (a); vocabulo tunc temporis & etiam usque hodie Prælatorum reditus annuos denotante. Scribit ut peritior Textuarius quam pro virorum sui ævi Laicorum modulo. Abundat enim allusionibus ad S. Scripturæ dictiones; sicut in locis infra citatis (b) & alibi videre est; imo ipsum quem de Scaccario sermonem habuit ad sensum spiritualem seu sacramentalem convertit (c). Sed non est verbis opus. Auctor ipse palam fatetur se virum Ecclesiasticum. " In " sponte oblatis (inquit) apud omnes lex una servatur, ut sive Cleri- " cus sit sive Laicus, qui solvendo non fuerit, donec satisfecerit careat " impetrato. Observatur etiam idem in omnibus alijs quæ quovis " pacto Regi debentur a Clericis, cum scilicet suæ dignitatis & liberæ " possessionis privilegium allegare neglexerint. De allegantibus autem " quid fieri debeat, a discretis & Deum timentibus Laicis, si placet " rescito; hijs enim ad præsens ex industria supersedeo, ne dicar " meæ conditionis hominibus ultroneas leges & mitiora jura " dictasse (d)." His quæ dixi pensatis, verisimile videatur *Gervasium de Tilleberia* Dialogum hunc non composuisse. Succrescit ergo heic loci, Magnifice Baro, alter nodus. Nimirum, si modo *Gervasius de Tilleberia* non esset Dialogi auctor, quærendum quis demum fuerit. Profecto Dialogi auctor is idem fuit qui librum seu tractatum contexuit inscriptum, *Tricolumnus*. Expresse testatur se juvenem scripsisse librum illum; redditque rationem cur eo nomine, *Tricolumni*, vocaverit (e). Hoc quidem evincit, eundem fuisse Dialogi auctorem qui *Tricolumni*; sed quisnam is fuerit non edocet. In summa; hujusce nodi solutio facilis erit, si fides in hoc casu danda sit (& jure merito, ni fallor, danda est) *Alexandro de Swereford*, viro insignissimo, cujus ante sæpius meminimus. Is in procemio collectaneorum quæ de Feudis Militum coëgerat, in hunc modum profatur. Hic *Alexandri* sensum in arctum redigam; ipsa ejus verba statim in margine descripturus. Anno (innuit) R. *Henrici* III. decimoquinto, ego *Alexander* Archidiaconus *Salopesbiriæ*, *Westmonasterij* in Regis Scaccario

(a) *L.* 1. *c.* 5. Sic fit ut quivis.
(b) *Procem. incipien.* Ordinatis a Deo. *L.* 2. *cap.* 2, Licet hæc ad opus. *L.* 2. *cap.* 18, Satis audisti. *L.* 2. *c.* 25, Item fit interdum.
(c) *L.* 1. *cap.* 5. Noscis quod sermo.
(d) *L.* 2. *cap.* 26. In sponte oblatis.
(e) *L.* 1. *cap.* 5. Libellus quidem est.

residens,

residens, antiquos Rotulos Annales diligenter evolvi; omnique opera enitebar ad Militaria servitia quæ Regi per totam *Angliam* præstari debuerunt pernoscenda: Et in id eo magis solicite animum intendi, quod neque *Nigellus* quondam *Eliensis* Episcopus Regis *Henrici* I. Thesaurarius, rerum Scaccarij peritissimus, neque *Ricardus Londoniensis* Episcopus (qui *Nigello* in Thesaurariatu successit) tametsi in suo Tractatu sive libello superius conscripto satis copiose de his quæ ad Scaccarium spectant disseruit, neque vero *Willelmus de Ely* (*f*), vir utique rerum Fiscalium admodum peritus, sub quo, imperante R. *Johanne*, ego in Scaccario servire solebam; quod, inquam, horum trium nullus vel ea plene exquisierit, vel exquisita commendaverit literis. Hic sane *Alexander* Archidiaconus luculenter enarrat, quis composuit Tractatum de Scaccario *Gervasio Tilburiensi* vulgo addictum; *Ricardum* scilicet *filium Nigelli* Episcopum *Londoniensem*, illum ipsum fuisse. Iste *Ricardus filius Nigelli* olim Clericus fuerat R. *Henrici* II; cui etiam Thesaurarij munere fungens aliquam-multis annis in Scaccario servierat (*g*); a R. *Ricardo* I. ineunte imperio suo factus *Londoniensis* Episcopus. Hoc proinde notandum. Proœmium *Alexandri* Archidiaconi incipit in *Libri Rubri* folio 47°. Et Tractatus de Scaccario *Gervasio de Tilleberia* attributus, in eodem *Libro Rubro* (sicut in principio hujus epistolæ innuebam) describitur in folijs proximo & immediate isti 47° præeuntibus. Nam Tractatus a folio 31° incipit, & 46° definit. Neque ullus præter hunc Tractatus sive Libellus de rebus Scaccarij in præcedentibus *Libri Rubri* folijs reperitur. Adeoque ex ijs quæ *Alexander* Archidiaconus de *Ricardo Londoniensi* Episcopo, suoque de Rebus Scaccarij Tractatu in præcedentibus *Libri Rubri* folijs scripto dicit, liquido constat ni fallor, *Alexandrum* credidisse *Ricardum* illum *Londoniensem* Episcopum fuisse Tractatus hujusce auctorem. Verba ipsa Proœmij *Alexandri* quod jam in testimonium voco, hic infra in margine sunt apposita (*h*). Ad eundem fere modum,

in

(*f*) *Non* Willelmus de Longocampo *Episcopi* Eliensis; *sicut* V. Cl. Johannes Selden, *in Libro suo inscripto*, Titles of Honour, *viz.* p. 572, *errore leviculo abreptus posuit.*

(*g*) *Hist. Scacc. Vol.* 1. *cap.* 2. *sect.* 10.

(*h*) Anno Domini MCCxxx, Anno videlicet xv° Regni Regis Henrici filij Regis Johannis qui fuit frater Insuperabilis imperij Regis Ricardi, qui fuit filius Regis Henrici, Cujus mater Matildis imperatrix, Cujus mater Matildis Regina Anglorum, Cujus mater Margareta Regina Scotorum, Cujus pater Eadwardus, Cujus pater Eadmundus ferreum latus, Cujus pater Ædelred, Cujus pater Eadgarus pacificus, Cujus pater Eadmundus, Cujus pater Eadwardus senior, Cujus pater nobilis Aluredus, qui fuit filius Eadwlfi Regis, Qui fuit filius Egbrichti, Cujus pater Alcmundus, Cujus pater Effa, cujus pater Eppa, Cujus pater Ingels, Cujus frater fuit famosissimus Rex Ine nomine, quorum pater Ceonred,

qui

in alio *Libri Rubri* loco, præclarus ille vir *Alexander* Archidiaconus Dialogum nostrum memorat per verba *Libro superiori*. " Quid (inquit ibi) sit Danegeldum, & propter quod assisum, Libro superiori est expressum (*i*);" plane ad Dialogi Librum Primum & caput undecimum referendo. Quem igitur *Alexander* Archidiaconus, *Londoniensi* Episcopo *Ricardo filio Nigelli* pene coætaneus, hujus Tractatus auctorem credidit, quidni nos etiam credamus.

Jam videmur, Amplissime Baro, Dialogi auctorem comperisse. Hoc comperto, illum effuse laudare non est necesse. Sufficiat dicere, Dialogum scriptum esse a viro rerum Fiscalium scientissimo, & ut suum

qui fuit filius Cedwald, qui fuit Cutha, qui fuit Cuthwin, qui fuit Chelulin, qui fuit Chenric, qui fuit Creoda, qui fuit Ceordic, qui fuit Elesa, qui fuit Ecla, qui fuit Genuis ;. Iste fuit capud gentis suæ, a quo & tota illa gens nomen accepit. Hujus pater fuit Wig, Cujus pater fuit Frewine, Cujus pater fuit Freodegar, Cujus pater Brand, cujus pater Bealdaes, cujus pater Woden, qui fuit Fredewald, qui fuit Freolof, qui fuit Fredewlf, qui fuit Fringoldwlf, qui fuit Geta, qui fuit Geatwa, qui fuit Beu, qui fuit Sceldwa, qui fuit Heremod, qui fuit Itermod, qui fuit Bathka, qui fuit Wala, qui fuit Beadwid, qui fuit Sem, cujus pater Noe, qui fuit Lamech, qui fuit Mathussale, qui fuit Enoch, qui fuit Jareth, fuit qui Malaleel, qui fuit Cainan, qui fuit Enos, qui fuit Seth, qui fuit Adam, filij Dei vivi : sub Huberto de Burgo Comite Kanciæ Angliæ Justiciario, Thesaurario Scaccarij Waltero Kaerleon. Episcopo, Regis prædicti Cancellario Radulfo Cicestrensi Episcopo, Residens ego Alexander Archidiaconus Salopesbiriæ apud Westmonasterium in Regis Scaccario, antiquorum Regum Angliæ rotulos revolvens annales, ad hoc sollicitus animum direxi, ut per regna Angliæ debita Regi servicia militaria quatenus potui plenissime percunctarer. Cum neque Nigellus quondam Elyensis Episcopus Regis Henrici primi Thesaurarius vir quidem in scientia Scaccarij plenius instructus, nec ejusdem successor officij Ricardus Londoniensis Episcopus licet in sui libelli tractatu superius multa de negocijs Scaccarij degereret, nec vir valde peritus in eisdem Willelmus Elyensis, sub cujus regimine temporibus Regis J. multociens ibidem militavi, super hijs certum aliquid diffinirent. Illud commune verbum in ore singulorum tunc temporis divulgatum fatuum reputans & mirabile, Quod in regni conquisitione Dux Normannorum Rex Willelmus servicia triginta duo mille militum infeodavit. Cum nec super hoc posteris suis Regibus Anglorum rotulos reliquerit, Nec annalia sua temporibus meis a quibusquam visa sint ; Rotulo quidem Wintoniæ sive Domusdey vel Libro Hidarum excepto ; quo quidem Hidas tocius Angliæ earundemque tenentes anno regni sui xxiiij° per tocius regni Comitatus recensens satis compendiose conclusit, Ignorasse quidem hæc servitia militaria Regis ejusdem postmodum successores subsequentium argumento non immerito potuit dubitare. Quia cum Rex Henricus filius Imperatricis Duci Saxoniæ filiam suam Matildem nuptui traderet, a quolibet sui regni Milite marcam unam in subsidium nuptiarum exegit, puplico præcipiens edicto quod quilibet Prælatus & Baro quot Milites de eo tenerent in Capite pupplicis suis instrumentis significarent ; quæ quidem instrumenta per singulos Comitatus distincta sub præfato Willelmo Elyensi in unum recollegi volumen. Nomina quidem Cartas suas mittentium, numerum etiam feodorum, & pecuniam pretaxatam solutam reperies inferius, In Rotulo Regni Regis ejusdem xiiij, sub illo tytulo, De Auxilio ad maritandam Primogenitam filiam Regis. *Lib. Rub. fol. notato xlvij a.*

(*i*) *Lib. Rub. fol.* 186. *a citat. in Hist. Scacc. Vol.* I. *cap.* 17. *sect.* 1.

erat

erat feculum eruditiffimo. Si quis autem Dialogum diligenter perlegere velit, una mecum, confido, judicabit, tum quod nullis meis laudibus indiget, tum etiam quod pretio & dignitate longe fuperat quafcunque attulero. Nec tamen meæ folius opinioni innitor. Ad alios provoco. Jampridem a literatis plerifque citari confuevit tanquam Tractatus magnæ famæ & fidei, etiam quantæ haud temere alius ejus generis. Equidem Vir Cl. *Jacobus Tyrellus* (qui in Hiftoria *Anglicana* defudavit) in quadam fua Introductione (k), parum honorifice de eo loqui videtur. Dicit, " multum dubitatum effe a quibufdam e " noftris Antiquarijs, utrum Tractatus ifte a *Gervafio Tilburienfi* fcriptus " fuerit necne: Nam Equites Aurati *Willelmus Dugdale* & *Simonds* " *Dewes* credebant ab eo non fcriptum; ficut liquebat a quibufdam " Notis quæ in manufcriptis ipforum hodie vifuntur: Nefciebat fane " quibufnam rationibus adducti in hanc opinionem ibant; fed veri- " fimile videbatur ipfos fatis validis rationibus fuiffe perfuafos, Tracta- " tum illum (fc. Dialogum) *Spurium* effe; alioqui notas in eam fen- " tentiam poft fe non reliquiffent." In hunc modum Eruditus *Tyrellus*. Veruntamen, quum apud eum de hac re pridem differerem, is mihi ultro faffus eft, quin & confenfit ut hic publice proteftarer fuo nomine, Se per vocem, *Spurium*, hoc innuiffe, nimirum quod Dialogus auctori non vero fuit vulgo adfcriptus, five quod *Gervafius Tilburienfis* non fuit, fua quidem opinione, illius auctor. Quod ad me attinet, dicam quemadmodum fentio. Stabilior fane ac confirmatior mihi videtur Dialogi exiftimatio ac fides, quam ut cujufvis privati fcriptoris judicio labefactari vel etiam infirmari queat.

Hanc igitur editionem in lucem emiffurus id egi potiffime, ut lectori proftituatur genuinus quoad fieri poffit Dialogi textus. Eo fine, defcripfi textum perpetuum prout in *Nigro Libro* Scaccarij fe habet; & lectiones quæ in *Rubro* Variantes reperiuntur, in margine cujufvis paginæ repofui. Attamen neceffe habui quandoque verba e *Rubro* fumpta in textum adfcire; ut fcilicet textum, ubi vitiofus erat aut mutilatus, utriufque codicis ope reftituerim & integriorem ponerem. Annotationes etiam aliquot, quas quidem in præfenti licuit, fparfim adjeci; plures fortaffe additurus, nifi res meæ domefticæ & valetudo vetuiffent. Nec tamen, ut fpero, annotationes aut explicationes multum defiderabuntur: quum eas ex præcedenti hiftoria diligens lector de facili utplurimum fupplere poterit. De Dialogo plura hic dicere omitto. Vale Baro Illuftriffime. Dabam e *Medio Templo* Jurifconfultorum quod *Londoniæ* eft, A. D. 1708.

(k) *Tyr. Hift. Angliæ*, Vol. 2. Introd. p. 47, 48. *Ubi etiam funt quædam alia de Gervafio; quæ vellem non dicta.*

DIALOGUS de SCACCARIO, &c.

LIBER PRIMUS.

ORDINATIS a Deo poteſtatibus in omni timore ſubici ſimiliter (*a*) & obſequi neceſſe eſt. Omnis enim poteſtas a Domino Deo eſt. Non ergo videtur abſurdum vel a viris Eccleſiaſticis alienum, Regibus quaſi præcellentibus & cæteris poteſtatibus ſerviendo, ſua jura ſervare; præſertim in hijs quæ veritati vel honeſtati non obviant. Oportet autem hijs (*b*) ſervire, non in conſervandis tantum dignitatibus, per quas gloria Regiæ poteſtatis elucet, verum in mundanarum facultatum copijs, quæ eos ſui ſtatus ratione contingunt: illa enim illuſtrant, hæ ſubveniunt. Porro nobilium copia vel defectus, Principum poteſtates humiliat vel exaltat. Quibus enim hæc deſunt, hoſtibus præda erunt: quibus autem hæc ſuppetunt, hijs hoſtes in prædam cedunt (*c*). Sane licet hæc Regibus

---

Erudito Lectori placeat quæ ſequuntur paucula notare in anteceſſum. Dialogi hujus textus currens a Nigro Libro Scaccarij maxima ex parte deſumptus eſt; niſi ſiquando Liber Ruber habet textum plane integriorem ac emendatiorem; & tunc verba Libri Rubri in textum aſſumuntur, & verba Nigri in margine ponuntur. Nonnunquam res arbitraria mihi videbatur, quaſdam voces ex Libro Rubro an ex Nigro depromere; veluti his an hijs, indemnis an indempnis, & in ſimilibus: & ibi unum vel alterum poſui, caſu magis quam conſilio. Quoniam autem Capitum omnium Numeri & Lemmata in Nigro Libro deſunt; ea ex Rubro, in quo omnia deſcripta minio habentur, deſumpta poſui. Accedunt lectiones Libri Rubri a Nigri textu variantes, in quavis Dialogi impreſſi pagina in margine truſæ. Mihi autem non debet vitio verti, quod nonnullis in Locis, textu codicum MSS vitiato vel non ſatis integro, ſenſus Cl. auctoris in ſuſpenſo eſt. Literæ L. R. Librum Rubrum denotant, L. N. Librum Nigrum.

Hæc Præfatio incipiens Ordinatis habetur in Libro Nigro, folio 18. a; in Libro Rubro, folio 3. a. columna 1.

(*a*) L. R. ſimul &.
(*b*) L. R. his.
(*c*) L. R. Quibus enim hæc ſuppetunt his hoſtes in prædicta cedunt.

plerunque

plerunque jure non prorfus examinato, fed patrijs quandoq; legibus, quandoque cordium fuorum confilijs occultis, vel folius interdum fuæ voluntatis arbitrio provenire contingat, eorum tamen facta ab inferioribus difcutienda vel condempnanda non funt. Quorum enim corda & motus cordium in manu Dei funt, & quibus ab ipfo Deo fingulariter eft credita cura fubditorum eorum, caufa divino tantum non humano judicio ftat aut cadit. Nemo tamen quantumlibet dives, fi fecus egerit, de impunitate fibi blandiatur, cum de hujufmodi fcriptum fit, potentes potenter tormenta patientur. Igitur qualifcunq; fit vel videatur acquirendi (*d*) caufa vel modus, ijs qui ad eorum cuftodiam ex officio deputantur, cura remiffior effe non debet. Sed in eifdem congregandis, confervandis, vel diftribuendis, follicitam decet effe diligentiam quafi rationem reddituris de Regni ftatu, qui per hos incolumis perfeverat. Novimus quidem prudentia, fortitudine, temperantia, five juftitia, cæterifq; virtutibus principaliter regna regi (*e*); unde & hijs mundi rectoribus totis eft viribus infiftendum. Sed fit interdum ut quod fano confilio vel excellenti mente concipitur, per hanc quafi per quandam negotiorum methodum facilem confequatur (*f*) effectum. Non folum autem hoftilitatis, fed & pacis tempore neceffaria videtur: illo enim in municipijs firmandis, in ftipendijs miniftrandis (*g*), & in alijs plerifque locis pro qualitate perfonarum ad confervandum Regni ftatum effunditur: hoc vero licet arma quiefcant, a devotis principibus conftruuntur bafilicæ, Chriftus alitur & veftitur in paupere, & cæteris operibus mifericordiæ infiftendo, in mifericordia diftribuitur: in utriufq; vero temporis ftrenuis actibus gloria (*h*) principum eft; fed excellit in hijs ubi pro temporalibus impenfis fælici mercimonio manfura fuccedunt. Ea propter, Rex illuftris, mundanorum principum maxime, quia fæpe te vidimus utroque tempore gloriofum, non parcentem quidem pecuniæ thefauris, fed pro loco, pro tempore, pro perfonis, legitimis fumptibus infiftentem, modicum opus excellentiæ tuæ devovimus, non de rebus quidem magnis vel luculento fermone compofitum, fed agrefti ftylo de Scaccarij tui neceffarijs obfervantijs. Porro fuper hijs te vidimus quandoque folicitum (*i*), adeo ut miffis (*k*) a latere tuo viris difcretis, de eodem Dominum tunc Elienfem conveneris. Nec fuit abfurdum tam excellentis ingenij virum, tam fingularis potentiæ principem inter cætera majora hæc etiam curaffe. Sane Scaccarium fuis legibus non

(*d*) L. R. acquirenda.
(*e*) L. R. regna regi juraq; fubfiftere.
(*f*) L. R. confequitur.
(*g*) L. R. *defunt* in ftipendijs miniftrandis.
(*h*) L. R. gratia prin.
(*i*) L. R. foliciti.
(*k*) L. R. *defunt* ut miffis.

temere,

temere, sed Magnorum consideratione subsistit; cujus ratio si servetur in omnibus, poterunt singulis sua jura servari, & tibi provenient quæ fisco debentur; quæ possit opportune nobilissimæ mentis tuæ Ministra manus effundere.

Incipiunt Capitula Libri primi.

I. *Quid sit Scaccarium, & quæ (l) ratio hujus nominis.*
II. *Quod aliud est Inferius atq; aliud superius, una tamen origo utriusque.*
III. *Quæ sit ratio, vel institutio Inferioris per singula officia.*
IV. *Quæ sit auctoritas Superioris, & unde sumpsit originem.*
V. *Quod sit Officium Præsidentis in illo & quæ sint singulorum sibi assidentium officia.*
VI. *Quis sit tenor brevium Regis factorum ad Scaccarium, sive de exitu thesauri, sive de computandis, sive de perdonandis.*
VII. *A quibus & ad quid instituta fuit argenti examinatio; sed hoc incidenter.*
VIII. *Quæ sint jura & dignitates residentium ad Scaccarium vel ex officio, vel ex solo Regis mandato; & quædam incidencia necessaria.*
IX. *Quid Scutagium, & quare sic dicatur.*
X. *Quid Murdrum, & quare sic dictum.*
XI. *Quid Danegildum, & quare sic nominatum vel institutum.*
XII. *Quid foresta Regis, & quæ ratio appellationis.*
XIII. *Quid Essartum, vel quid vastum, & quæ rationes horum nominum.*
XIV. *Quod (m) Thesaurus dicitur interdum (n) locus in quo servatur interdum ipsa pecunia.*
XV. *Qui sit usus Sigilli Regij, quod est in Thesauro.*
XVI. *Quid Liber Indiciarius, & ad quid compositus.*
XVII. *Quid Hyda, quid Centuriata, quid Comitatus, secundum Vulgarem de hijs Opinionem.*
XVIII. *Quid Rotulus Exactorius.*

ANNO xxiij Regni Regis Henrici Secundi, cum federem ad fenestram speculæ quæ est juxta fluvium Tamensem, factum est verbum hominis in impetu loquentis ad me, dicens, Magister, non legisti, quod in scientia vel thesauro abscondito nulla sit utilitas?

Hæc Capitula habentur in L. N, fol. 18. b. sed sine Numeris: in L. R, fol. 31. a. col. 2. habentur prout hic.
(*l*) L. N. quid.
(*m*) L. R. Quid.
(*n*) L. R. interd. ipsa pecunia, interd. l. in quo serv.

Cui

Cui cum respondissem, legi; statim intulit, Cur ergo Scientiam de Scaccario quæ penes te plurima esse dicitur alios non doces, & ne tibi commoriatur scripto commendas? Tum ego; Ecce, frater, ad Scaccarium iam per multa tempora resedisti, & nihil te latet (*a*), cum scrupulosus sis; sic & de cæteris qui assident probabile est. At ille, sicut qui in tenebris ambulant & manibus palpant, frequenter offendunt: Sic illic multi resident, qui videntes non vident, & audientes non intelligunt. Tum ego; irreverenter loqueris; nec enim scientia tanta est vel de tantis; sed forte sunt illis qui magna occupantur corda, ut pedes aquilæ, qui parva non retinent, & quos magna non effugiunt. Et ille, esto: Sed licet Aquilæ celsius (*b*) volant, tamen in humilibus quiescunt & reficiuntur; & ob hoc humilia vobis (*c*) exponi petimus ipsis Aquilis profutura. Tum ego; veritus sum de hijs rebus opus contexere, quia corporeis sensibus subjecta sunt, & cotidianis usibus vilescunt; nec est vel esse potest in eis subtilium rerum descriptio, vel jocunda novitatis inventio. Et ille; qui novitatibus gaudent, qui subtilium rerum fugam appetunt, habent Aristotelem & libros Platonicos, audiant illos. Tu scribe non subtilia, sed utilia. Tum ego; de hijs rebus quas petis impossibile est, nisi rusticano sermone & communibus loqui Verbis. At ille, velut succensus in iram, desideranti enim animo nihil satis festinatur, ait: Artium scriptores ne multa parum scisse viderentur, & ut ars difficilior cognita fieret, multa conquisierunt, & verbis incognitis palliarunt: Tu vero scribendam artem non suscipis, sed quasdam consuetudines & jura Scaccarij; quæ quia Communia debent esse, communibus necessario utendum est verbis; ut sint cognati (*d*) sermones rebus de quibus loquimur. Præterea, quamvis plerunq; nova liceat nomina fingere, rogo tamen, si placet, ut usitatis rerum ipsarum vocabulis, quæ ad placitum sunt uti non pudeat, nec nova difficultas ex insolitis verbis oborta amplius perturbet. Tum ego; sensi te iratum; sed animo æquior esto; faciam quod hortaris. Surgens ergo se e ex adverso; & de hijs (*e*) quæ te offendunt interroga. Quod si quid inauditum proposueris, non erubesco dicere, nescio. Sed conveniamus ambo discretiores. Et ille; ad vota respondes. Licet autem turpis & ridicula res sit elementarius senex, ab ipsis tamen elementis incipiam.

In Libro Rubro, *Dialogus incipit fol.* 31.
b. col. 1.
(*a*) L. R. latet te.
(*b*) L. R. celerius.
(*c*) L. R. nobis.
(*d*) L. N. congrati.
(*e*) L. R. his.

I. *Quid sit Scaccarium, & quæ ratio hujus nominis.*

Discipulus. Quid est Scaccarium?

Magister. Scaccarium tabula est quadrangula (*f*) quæ longitudinis quasi decem pedum, latitudinis quinque, ad modum mensæ circumsedentibus apposita undiq; habet limbum altitudinis quasi quatuor digitorum, ne quid appositum excidat. Superponitur autem Scaccario Superiori pannus in Termino Paschæ emptus, non quilibet, sed niger virgis distinctus, distantibus a se virgis vel pedis vel palmæ extentæ spacio. In spacijs autem Calculi sunt juxta ordines suos de quibus alias dicetur. Licet autem tabula talis Scaccarium dicatur, transmutatur tamen hoc nomen ut ipsa quoque Curia qua consedente Scaccario est Scaccarium dicatur; adeo ut si quandoq; (*g*) per Sententiam aliquid de communi consilio fuerit constitutum (*h*), dicatur factum ad Scaccarium illius vel illius anni. Quod autem hodie dicitur ad Scaccarium, olim dicebatur ad Taleas.

D. Quæ est ratio hujus nominis?

M. Nulla mihi verior ad presens occurrit, quam quod Scaccarij lusilis similem habet formam.

D. Nunquid antiquorum (*i*) prudentia pro sola forma sic nominavit, cum & simili ratione possit Tabularium appellari?

M. Merito te Scrupulosum dixi. Est & alia, sed occultior. Sicut enim in Scaccario lusili quidam ordines sunt pugnatorum, & certis legibus vel limitibus procedunt vel subsistunt, præsidentibus alijs & alijs præcedentibus (*k*): Sic in hoc quidem præsident, quidam assident ex officio; Et non est cuiquam (*l*) liberum leges constitutas excedere; quod erit ex consequentibus manifestum. Item sicut in lusili, pugna committitur inter Reges: Sic in hoc inter duos principaliter conflictus est & pugna committitur, Thesaurarium scilicet & Vicecomitem qui assidet (*m*) ad compotum; residentibus alijs tanquam Judicibus ut videant & judicent (*n*).

D. Nunquid a Thesaurario Compotus suscipitur, cum illic multi sunt qui ratione potestatis Majores videantur?

M. Quod Thesaurarius a Vicecomite compotum suscipiat, hinc manifestum est (*o*), quod idem ab eo cum Regi placuerit requiritur:

(*f*) L. R. tab. quad. est.
(*g*) L. N. si quis per sent.
(*h*) L. N. institutum.
(*i*) L. N. anticorum.
(*k*) L. R. præsidentibus alijs præced.
(*l*) L. N. cuique.
(*m*) L. N. Vic. q. assident.
(*n*) L. R. *desunt* & judicent.
(*o*) L. N. est manif.

Nec enim (*p*) ab ipso requireretur quod non suscepisset. Sunt tamen qui dicunt Thesaurarium & Camerarios obnoxios tantum hijs quæ scribuntur in rotulis in Thesauro, ut de hijs (*q*) Compotus ab eis exigatur. Sed verius creditur ut de tota Scriptura rotuli respondeant; quod ex consequentibus constare poterit.

II. *Quod aliud est inferius, aliud superius ; Una tamen origo utriusque.*

D. Nunquid solum illud (*r*) Scaccarium est in quo est talis conflictus (*s*) ?
M. Non. Est enim inferius Scaccarium, quod & Recepta dicitur, ubi pecunia numeranda traditur, & scriptis & tallijs committitur, ut de eisdem (*t*) postmodum in superiori compotus reddatur (*u*) ; una tamen est utriusq; origo (*w*) ; quia quicquid solvendum esse in majori deprehenditur, hic solvitur ; & quod hic solutum fuerit, ibi computatur.

III. *Quæ sit ratio vel institutio inferioris per singula officia.*

D. Quæ est ratio vel institutio inferioris Scaccarij?
M. Ut video nullius horum ignorantiam sustines. Noveris autem quod inferius illud Scaccarium suas habet personas, ratione quidem officiorum a se distinctas, sed in regis utilitatem, salva tamen æquitate, pari intentione devotas ; omnes quidem dominorum suorum nominibus non proprijs militantes exceptis duobus militibus duntaxat (*x*) qui præsunt (*y*) examinibus, & fusore. Horum officia de Regis nostri pendent arbitrio ; unde magis ad superius quam ad inferius pertinere videntur, sicut infra dicetur. Illic est Clericus Thesaurarij (*z*) cum sigillo ejus. Sunt & duo milites Camerariorum. Est & Miles quidam (*a*) qui Argentarius dici potest ; quia ex officio argento examinando præest. Est & Fusor qui argentum examinat. Sunt & quatuor Computatores ad numerandam pecuniam. Est & Hostiarius Thesauri, & vigil. Horum autem hæc sunt officia. Clericus Thesaurarij, cum fuerit numerata pecunia, & in forulos missa

(*p*) L. R. *deest* enim.
(*q*) L. R. his.
(*r*) L. N. *deest* illud.
(*s*) L. R. conflictus est.
(*t*) L. R. ijsdem.
(*u*) L. R. compotus fiat.
(*w*) L. R. origo est.
(*x*) L. R. *deest* duntaxat.
(*y*) L. R. scilicet qui præest.
(*z*) L. R. Thesauri.
(*a*) L. R. *deest* quidam.

per Centenas libras, apponit figillum, & deputat fcripto, quantum, vel a quo, vel ob quam Caufam recepit; Taleas quoque de eadem Recepta a Camerarijs factas inbreviat; non folum autem pecuniæ faccis fed & archis & fingulis forulis in quibus Rotuli vel Talliæ collocantur fi libet aponit figillum (*b*); & ad omnia fubjecta officia diligenter profpicit, & nihil eum latet. Militum, qui & Camerarij dicuntur quod pro Camerarijs miniftrant, hoc eft officium: Hi claves archarum bajulant; archæ enim cuilibet duæ feræ funt diverfi generis, hoc eft cujus neutri clavis alterius poffit aptari; & hij claves earum deferunt; circumcingitur autem quælibet arca corrigia quadam immobili, in qua defuper firmatis feris Thefaurarij figillum apponitur; ut nulli eorum nifi de communi affenfu acceffus pateat. Item officium horum eft, numeratam pecuniam & in vafis ligneis per centenos folidos compofitam ponderare ne fit error in numero, tunc demum in forulos mittere per Centenas ut dictum eft libras. Quod fi vas aliquod inventum eft minus habens, non quidem per æftimationem quod deeffe putatur, apponitur, fed ftatim de quo dubitatur in acervum numerandorum prohifcitur. Et nota quofdam Comitatus a tempore Regis Henrici primi & in tempore regis Henrici fecundi licite potuiffe cujufcunq; monetæ denarios folutioni offerre, dummodo argentei effent & ponderi legitimo non obftarent. Quia fcilicet monetarios (*c*) ex antiqua inftitutione non habentes, undecunq; fibi denarios perquirebant; quales funt Norhumberland & Cumberland; fic autem fufcepti denarij licet de firma effent feorfum tamen ab alijs cum quibufdam fignis appofitis mittebant (*d*). Reliqui vero Comitatus, folos ufuales & inftantis monetæ legitimos denarios tam de firmis quam de placitis afferrebant. At poftquam Rex illuftris, cujus laus eft in rebus magnis excellentior, fub Monarchia fua per univerfum regnum unum pondus & unam monetam inftituit, omnis Comitatus una legis neceffitate teneri & generalis Commercij (*e*) folutione cœpit obligari. Omnes itaq; idem monetæ genus quomodocunq; teneant (*f*) folvunt. Sed tamen examinationis (*g*) quæ de combuftione provenit jacturam omnes non fuftineant. Item hij taleas faciunt de receptis, & commune eft eis cum Clerico Thefaurarij, ut per brevia Regis vel præcepto Baronum, Thefaurum fufceptum expendant; non tamen inconfultis Dominis fuis. Hij tres fimul omnes

(*b*) L. R. figillum fi libet.
(*c*) L. N. Quod fol. monetarios.
(*d*) L. R. *pro* mittebant[ur] *habet vacuum fpatium.*

(*e*) L. R. *pro* comercij *habet album fpatium.*
(*f*) L. R. teneantur.
(*g*) L. N. exactionis.

vel

vel viciffim cum thefauro mittuntur cum oportuerit. His (*h*) tribus præcipua cura eft in omnibus his quæ in inferiori Scaccario fiunt (*i*).

D. Ergo, ut video licet his per breve Regis, vel præcepto eorum qui præfident thefaurum fufceptum confultis tamen Dominis fuis expendere.

M. Licet, inquam, hoc modo de Liberationibus fervientum inferioris Scaccarij, & de minutis neceffarijs Scaccarij emendis, qualia funt vafa illa lignea, & alia, de quibus infra dicetur, eorum fidei committitur; alias autem non. Qui vero breve regis vel cartam detulerit pro pecunia, præcipientibus Dominis fuis, hac ei lege folvatur id quod expreffe nominatur (*k*) in brevi, ut antequam exeat, fufceptam pecuniam numeret; quod fi quid defuerit, redeat ad Scaccarium is qui fufcepit et fidei religionem præftet fub hac forma: quod quantum fufcepit reportavit, non appofito, fecundum confcientiam fuam, ut fit in alijs; & hoc facto, folvatur ei quod reftat; numerata prius eadem coram omnibus ab conftitutis Computatoribus. Si vero lege fibi propofita oftium Thefauri egreffus fuerit; quæcunque fuerit perfona, vel quantacunq; jactura, non ei refpondeatur. Militis argentarij & Fuforis officia fibi videntur annexa, & ad Superius Scaccarium magis pertinentia; & ob hoc ibidem cum cæteris officijs explananda. Quatuor (*l*) Computatorum officium hoc (*m*) eft. Cum in Scaccarium numeranda pecunia mittitur, unus eorum diligenter totam commifcet, ut non feorfum meliores & feorfum deteriores fint, fed mixti, ut ponderi refpondeant; quo facto, Camerarius ad libram Scaccarij ponderat quantum oportet in trutina. Quod fi numerus xx Sol. plus quam vj nummis excreverit refpectu libræ, integra (*n*) recipi dicitur: Si vero vel ad vj vel infra fe cohibet, Sufcipitur; & a computatoribus diligenter per centenos folidos, ut prædictum eft, numeratur. Si vero de firma funt denarij & fint examinandi, facta commixtione XLiiij folidorum de acervo in loculum feorfum mittuntur, & huic Vicecomes fignum apponit; ut ex hijs poftmodum Examen, quod vulgo Effayum dicitur, fiat, ficut ex confequentibus (*o*) liquebit. Erit autem curæ eorum qui præfunt receptæ gratia dominorum fuorum, hoc eft, Clerici Thefaurarij & Camerariorum, ut recepta pecunia feorfum mittant examinati argenti pondera & Denarios de firma, appofitis quibufdam fignis faccis eorum, ut fi Rex vafa ar-

(*h*) L. N. hijs.
(*i*) L. R. fuerit.
(*k*) L. R. *defunt* id quod expreffe nominatur.
(*l*) L. N. *deeft* Quatuor.
(*m*) L. N. *deeft* hoc.
(*n*) L. R. indigna recipi.
(*o*) L. N. ex confeq. ficut liquebit.

gentea

gentea ad cultum domus Dei, vel ad Domus propriæ obsequium, vel forte monetas transmarinas fieri voluerit ex hijs fiant.

D. Est aliquid in prædictis quod me pulsat.

M. Dic ergo.

D. Dixisti, si bene memini quod ad Scaccarium quandoq; differtur (*p*) solvenda pecunia, quæ judicatur indigna recipi si scilicet pensata cum libra ponderis de Scaccario, inventa est minus habens ultra vj. Cum ergo quælibet Moneta regni hujus impressam habere debeat Regis imaginem, & ad idem pondus omnes monetarij teneantur operari, qualiter fieri poterit (*q*) ut non omne eorum opus ejusdem ponderis sit?

M. Magnum est quod quæris, & alterius egens inquisitionis, attamen fieri potest per falsarios & nummorum decuratores vel detonsores. Noveris autem monetam Angliæ in tribus falsam deprehendi, in falso scilicet pondere, in falsa lege, in falsa imagine (*r*). His (*s*) tamen falsitatibus par pœna non debetur. Sed de hijs alias.

D. Si placet, prosequere de officijs, ut cœpisti.

M. Ad Hostiarij curam spectat, ut exciudat vel admittat quod oportet, & diligens sit in custodia omnium quæ ostio concluduntur; unde & ratione ostij de singulis brevibus exitus duos habet denarios. Hic ministrat forulos ad pecuniam reponendam & rotulos, & taleas, & cætera necessaria per annum, & pro singulis forulis (*t*) duos habet denarios. Hic in omnem Receptam ligna opportuna ministrat ad taleas Receptæ, & compotorum, & semel hoc est, in termino Sancti Michaelis v Solidos pro lignis talearum percipit. Hic vascula lignea, Cnipulos, loculos, & corrigias, & cætera minuta necessaria de fisco invenit. In termino eodem pro incausto totius anni ad utrumq; Scaccarium ij solidi debentur, quos sibi de antiquo jure vendicat sacrista majoris Ecclesiæ Westmonasterij (*u*). Vigilis officium idem est ibi quod alibi; diligentissima scilicet de nocte custodia, thesauri principaliter, & omnium eorum quæ in domo thesauri reponuntur. Sic habes omnium officia distincta, qui inferius ministrant. Sunt & hijs liberationes constitutæ dum Scaccarium est, hoc (*w*) est a die qua convocantur, usq; ad diem quæ generalis est secessio. Clericus Thesaurarij qui infra est, quinque denarios habet in die. Scriptor ejusdem Thesaurarij in superiori Scaccario similiter v. Scriptor Cancellarij v. Duo milites bajuli clavium, quisque in die viij, ratione militiæ.

(*p*) L. N. solv. differtur.
(*q*) L. R. potest.
(*r*) L. N. *habet clausulam incipientem* Angliæ *& desinentem* imagine, *quindecim vocalis constantem, charactere moderniori scriptam.*
(*s*) L. R. Hijs.
(*t*) L. R. per singulos forulos.
(*u*) L. N. Westmonasterium.
(*w*) L. N. hic.

Asserunt

Asserunt enim, quod equis necessarijs & armis instructi fore teneantur, ut cum thesauro missi, quod sui officij fuerit aportunius (*x*) sic exequantur. Miles argentarius xij denarios (*y*) in die. Fusor v. Hostiarius majoris Scaccarij v. Quatuor Computatores, quisq; iij den. (*z*) si Londoniæ fuerint (*a*) si Wintoniæ, quia inde (*aa*) solent assumi, duos quisq; habet. Vigil unum denarium. Ad Lumen cujusq; noctis circa Thesaurum ob.

D. Hostiarius

(*x*) L. R. *deest* aportunius.
(*y*) L. R. *deest* denarios.
(*z*) L. R. *deest* den.
(*a*) L. R. sunt.
(*aa*) *Memoriæ proditum est, Regis Thesaurarium primævis seculis fuisse* Wintoniæ *perinde ac* Westmonasterij. Se cyng fenda to Winceaftne &c. Rex [Willelmus II.] *proficiscebatur* Wintoniam, & *aperuit illud ærarium, ac thesauros quos pater collegerat auri & argenti &c ; referente Chronico Sax. p.* 192. *n.* 20. Ob hanc *forte causam,* Liber Domesday *qui (teste Cl. auctore hujus Dialogi) in* Thesauraria *Regis continuo asservari solebat,* Liber Wintoniæ *vocatus est. Ita vocatum reperimus in supervisu Feudi* Roberti de Bruis, *adjecto ad calcem dicti Libri, scriptura etsi non eadem tamen non longe diversa :* Hic est feudum Rotberti de Bruis, quod fuit datum postquam liber de Wintonia scriptus fuit. videlicet, In Oustredinc. In Bortona & in soca ejus tenet hic Rotbertus xliiij carrucatas terræ —. *Lib. Domesd. fol.* 333. *b. col.* 1. *post Euruicscire. Hinc etiam frequens mentio Thesauri Regij* Wintoniam *perducti, illic repositi, & inde abducti. Temporibus R.* Henrici II. *ac postea, computabantur Vicecomitibus* Hantesciræ, *Firmarijs Civitatis* Wintoniæ, *alijsq; complures summæ ab ipsis erogatæ in reficienda domo Thesaurariæ* Wintoniæ, *in forulis, & alijs necessarijs, in pecunijs ibidem numerandis, ac adducendis & abducendis, & in similibus. Verbi gratia. Anno* 18º R. Henrici II, *hujusmodi expensæ computabantur* Hugoni de Gundevill *Vicecomiti* Hantesciræ *& firmario Civitatis* Wintoniæ : Idem Vicecomes [Hugo de Gundevill] r c de firma Civitatis Wintoniæ ; In thesauro nichil ; Et in elemosina constituta Militibus de Templo j marca ; Et in Conductu thesauri per totum annum, & pro thesauro onerando & exonerando, & in alijs minutis negocijs thesauri per Odonem de Falesia & Walerannum da Crickelada & alios servientes Thesauri, xlviij s & vj d ; Et Servientibus Willelmi de Lanvalei xxx l, ad operiendam domum Thesauri, & ad Gaiolam faciendam, per breve Regis. *Mag. Rot.* 18. H. 2. *Rot.* 6. *b. Hantesc.* Anno 20º *H. II, Vicecomitibus* Londoniæ : Et pro ducendo Thesauro tribus vicibus, semel ad Windresore, bis ad Wintoniam, xvj s & vj d ; *Mag. Rot.* 20. H. 2. *Rot.* 2. *a. Londonia & Middlesexa : Anno* 21º *&* 24. *H. II, Vicecomitibus* Londoniæ *qui tunc erant :* Et pro locandis carretis ad portandum thesaurum de Termino S. Michaelis ad Wintoniam, xj s ; *Mag. Rot.* 21. H. 2. *Rot.* 3. *a. Lond. & Midd. :* Et pro ducendo Thesauro tribus vicibus a Londonia ad Wintoniam, Lxxvij s & vj d, per Odonem de Falesia, & Ricardum de Windresore, & Andræam Clericum ; *Mag. Rot.* 24. H. 2. *Rot.* 9. *b. Lond. & Midd. : Eodem anno* 24º, Hugoni de Gundevill *firmario* Wintoniæ : Et pro ij Magnis Hugijs, & Ostio Thesauri Wintoniæ reficiendo, & pro ducendo thesauro pluribus vicibus, per Andream & Ricardum Clericos & alios servientes Thesauri, xxv s & ij d ; *Mag. Rot.* 24. H. 2. *Rot.* 8. *a. Civitas Wintoniæ : Anno* 33º *H. II,* Galfrido filio Azonis *Vicecomiti* Hantesciræ : Et in custamento numerandi & ponderandi thesaurum apud Wintoniam post Natale, & pro Forulis novis ad reponendum eundum thesaurum, & pro alijs minutis negotijs ad prædictum opus, per Archidiaconum Cantuariæ, & Hugonem Bardulf, & Radulfum filium Stephani, vj l & xix s & viij d ; Et pro carriando thesauro a Wintonia ad Saresberiam, & ad Oxinefordiam, & ad Geldeford, & ad plura loca per Angliam, iiij l & viij s & iij d ; *Mag. Rot.* 33. H. 2. *Rot.* 14. *a. Sudhantesc.* Galfridus filius Azonis *Vicecomes : Anno decimo* R. Johannis, *firmario Civitatis* Wintoniæ : Et in Liberationibus

Lib. I.   Dialogus de Scaccario.   359

D. Hoftiarius Thefauri, qua ratione liberationem folus non percipit?

M. Non fatis novi. Sed tamen quia videtur aliquid percipere ratione Oftij, & pro forulorum & talearum minifterio, liberationem forte non recepit; vel forte quia non Regi, fed magis Thefaurario & Camerarijs fervire videtur in cuftodia Oftij Domus eorum. Hac lege minoris Scaccarij vel Receptæ ratio fubfiftit.

D. Sic mihi fatisfactum eft in hac parte ut nihil deeffe videatur. Nunc ergo, fi placet, profequere de majore.

    IV. *Quæ fit authoritas Superioris, & unde fumpfit originem?*

M. Licet eorum qui ad Scaccarium majus refident, officia quibufdam videantur proprietatibus effe diftincta: Unum tamen omnium (*b*) officium eft & intentio; ut Regis utilitati profpiciant; falva tamen æquitate fecundum conftitutas leges Scaccarij. Ejus autem ratio vel inftitutio cum ipfa temporis antiquitate, cum Magnorum qui affident auctoritate roborata fubfiftit. Ab ipfa namque regni Conquifitione per Regem Willelmum facta cœpiffe dicitur, fumpta tamen ipfius ratione a Scaccario tranfmarino: Verum in plurimis & pene majoribus diffident. Sunt etiam (*c*) qui credunt ufum ejus fub regibus Anglicis extitiffe; hinc fumentes rei hujus argumentum, quod coloni & jam decrepiti fenes fundorum illorum qui coronæ annominantur, quorum in hijs cana (*d*) memoria eft, optime noverint a patribus fuis edocti, quantum de Albo firmæ pro fingulis libris folvere teneantur. Sed hæc ratio cognitionis eft de firmæ folutione, non de Scaccarij feffione. Videtur autem eis obviare, qui dicunt Album firmæ a temporibus Anglicorum cœpiffe, quod in Libro Judiciario in quo totius regni defcriptio diligens continetur, & tam de tempore Regis Edwardi, quam de tempore (*e*) Regis Willelmi fub quo factus eft, fingulorum fundorum valentia exprimitur, nulla prorfus de Albo firmæ fit mentio: unde probabile videtur, quod facta illa defcriptione tempore jamdicti Regis de Albo firmarum fuerit a ftudiofis ejus conftitutum propter caufas,

---

tionibus Thefaurarij & Camerariorum, qui moram fecerunt apud Wintoniam, ad numeranda xl Millia marcarum ibidem; & pro faccis emptis, & plumbis, afferibus furratis & feris & cordis emptis, & alijs neceffarijs, ix l & j marca, per breve Regis; Et pro uno Scuto & una Targia ad opus Regis xxx s, per breve ejufdem: Et item Servientibus Thefaurarij & Camerariorum ad expenfas factas apud Wintoniam, xx s, per breve ejufdem. *Mag. Rot.* 10. *Joh. Rot.* 6. *b. tit.* Civitas Wintonia: *aliifq; fimili modo.*

(*b*) L. N. *deeft* omnium.
(*c*) L. R. & qui.
(*d*) L. R. fana.
(*e*) L. N. *defunt hic de tempore.*

quæ inferius annotantur. Quocunq; vero tempore cœperit ufus ejus, certum eft quod Magnorum auctoritate roboratur; adeo ut nulli liceat ftatuta Scaccarij infringere, vel eis quavis temeritate refiftere. Habet enim hoc commune cum ipfa Domini Regis Curia, in qua ipfe in propria perfona jura decernit *(f)*, quod nec recordationi, nec fententiæ in eo *(g)* latæ licet alicui contradicere. Huic autem Curiæ tam infignis auctoritas eft, tum propter Regiæ imaginis excellentiam quæ in figillo ejus de thefauro individua lege fervatur; tum propter eos qui affident, ut dictum eft, quorum folertia totius regni ftatus indemnis *(h)* fervatur. Illic enim refidet Capitalis Domini Regis Jufticia, primus poft Regem in Regno ratione fori, & Majores quiq; de regno, qui familiarius Regijs fecretis affiftunt; ut quod fuerit fub tantorum præfentia conftitutum vel terminatum, inviolabili jure fubfiftat. Verum quidam ex officio, quidam *(i)* ex fola juffione principis refident. Ex officio principaliter refidet imo & præfidet primus in regno, Capitalis fcilicet Jufticia. Huic autem affident *(k)* ex fola juffione Principis, momentanea fcilicet & mobili actoritate quidam, qui majores & difcretiores videntur in regno, five de Clero fint five de Curia. Affident inquam ad difcernenda jura & dubia determinanda quæ frequenter ex incidentibus quæftionibus oriuntur. Non enim in ratiocinijs fed in multiplicibus judicijs excellens Scaccarij fcientia confiftit *(l)*. Facile enim eft propofita fumma quæ exigitur, & fuppofitis ad collationem ejus hijs quæ foluta *(m)* funt per fubtractionem difcernere, fi fatisfactum eft, vel fi quid reftat. At cum cœperit multiplex inquifitio fieri de hijs rebus, quæ variæ fifco proveniunt & diverfis modis requiruntur, & a Vicecomitibus non eodem modo perquiruntur, difcernere fi fecus egerint, quibufdam grave eft, & ob hoc circa hæc fcientia Scaccarij major effe dicitur. Dubiorum vero vel dubitalium judicia, quæ frequenter emergunt fub una tractatus ferie comprehendi non valent; quia necdum omnia *(n)* dubiorum genera in lucem prodierunt. Quædam tamen ex hijs *(o)* quæ propofita vel determinata cognovimus, fuis locis inferius annotabimus.

(f) Vid. ante in *Hiftor. Scacc. Vol.* 1. *Cap.* 3. *Sect.* 5 & 6.
(g) L. R. *pro* in eo *habet* ejus.
(h) L. N. indemnis ftatus.
(i) L. R. *defunt* ex officio, quidam.
(k) L. R. affident autem.
(l) L. R. confulit.
(m) L. R. qui foluti.
(n) L. N. omnium.
(o) L. R. his.

V. *Quid*

V. *Quid sit officium Præsidentis, & omnium illic ex officio residentium; & quæ dispositio sedium.*

D. Quid est hujus tam excellentis Sessoris officium?

M. Aliud verius attribui sibi non valet, nisi quod omnibus quæ inferiore vel superiore Scaccario fuerint (*p*), hic prospicit & ad nutum ipsius quælibet officia subjecta disponuntur. Sic tamen ut ad Domini Regis utilitatem juste proveniant. Hoc tamen inter cætera videtur excellens, quod potest hic sub testimonio suo breve Domini Regis facere fieri, ut de Thesauro quælibet summa liberetur, vel ut computetur alicui quod sibi ex Domini Regis mandato prænoverit computandum; vel si maluerit, breve suum faciet sub aliorum testimonio de his (*q*) rebus.

D. Magnus est hic, cujus fidei totius regni cura, immo & cor Regis committitur. Scriptum quippe est; ubi est thesaurus tuus, ibi est & cor tuum. Sed jam si placet prosequere de cæteris.

M. Vis prosequar de ipsis secundum gradus dignitatum an secundum dispositionem Sedium?

D. Secundum quod quisq; ratione officij sui sedem adeptus est. Facile enim erit ut credo ex officijs perpendere dignitates.

M. Ut noveris quo ordine disponantur, scias ad quatuor Scaccarij latera quatuor poni sedilia vel Scanna. Ad caput vero Scaccarij, hoc est unde latitudo discernitur, in medio non sedilis sed Scaccarij, locus est illius Principalis de quo supra diximus. In læva ejus primo loco residet Cancellarius ratione officij, si adesse eum contingat: post hunc miles gregarius quem Constabularium dicimus: post hunc duo Camerarij, prior autem, qui intuitu provectioris ætatis venerabilior esse videbitur: post hos miles qui vulgo dicitur Marescallus: inseruntur tamen quandoq; alij his absentibus, vel forte eis præsentibus, si tanta scilicet fuerit auctoritas eorum qui a Rege destinantur, ut eis cedere debeant. Et hæc est dispositio primi sedilis. In secundo vero quod est ad latus longitudinis Scaccarij, in primo capite residet Clericus vel alius serviens Camerariorum cum recautis, hoc est, cum contratalcis de Recepta. Post hunc interpositis quibusdam (*r*) qui non ex officio resident sed sunt a Rege missi locus est quasi in medio lateris Scaccarij illi qui compotos (*s*) positione ponit calculorum. Post hunc aliqui non ex officio,

(*p*) L. N. fuerit.
(*q*) L. N. hijs.
(*r*) L. N. quibus qui.
(*s*) L. R. compoto.

necessarij

necessarij tamen. In fine sedilis illius residet Clericus qui Scriptorio præest; & hic ex officio. Sic habes secundi Scanni dispositionem. Verum ad Dextram præsidentis Justiciarij residet primo loco nunc Wintoniensis Episcopus quondam Pictaviæ Archidiaconus, non ex officio quidem sed ex novella constitutione; ut scil. proximus sit Thesaurario, & scripturæ Rotuli diligenter intendat. Post hunc residet Thesaurarius in Capite Secundæ sedis in dextra, cui diligentissima cura est per singula quæ illic geruntur, quasi rationem de hijs omnibus si oportuerit reddituro. Post hunc residet Clericus ejus Scriptor Rotuli de Thesauro: post hunc alius Scriptor Rotuli de Cancellaria: post hunc Clericus Cancellarij, qui occulta fide semper prospicit, ut Rotulus suus alij per singula respondeat, ut nec Iota unum desit, nec alius sit ordo scribendi: post hunc quasi in fine sedilis illius residet Clericus Constabularij, magnus quidem & officiosus in Domini Regis Curia, & hic quidem habens officium quod per seipsum vel per Clericum discretum, si Regi visus fuerit alias magis necessarius, administrat. Et hæc est descriptio tertiæ sedis. In quarto scanno, quod est oppositum Justiciario (*t*) in Capite residet Magister Thomas cognomine (*u*) Brunus, cum Rotulo tertio qui ex novella constitutione, hoc est a Domino Rege nostro additus est; Quia scriptum est, funiculus triplex difficile solvitur. Post hunc Vicecomites & clerici sui, qui assident ad compotum cum taleis & alijs necessarijs. Et hæc est dispositio quartæ sedis.

D. Scriptor Magistri Thomæ nunquid sedem habet cum alijs scriptoribus sed super alios (*w*)?

M. Sedem quidem habet non cum alijs sed super alios (*x*).

D. Quare sic?

M. Cum enim sic dispositæ essent sedes ab initio, ut scriptor Thesaurarij ad latus suum resideret, ne quid scriberetur, quod oculum ejus effugeret; & item scriptor Cancellariæ ad latus scriptoris Thesaurarij, ut fideliter exciperet quod ille præscribebat; & item Clericus Cancellarij necessario proximus esset illi scriptori, ne posset errare; non superfuit locus in quo scriptor ille resideret in serie scanni, sed datus est ei locus in eminenti, ut prospiciat & immineat scriptori Thesaurarij qui primus scribit, & ab ipso quod oportet excipiat.

D. Huic oculi Lyncei necessarij essent, ne erraret; periculosus enim in hijs error dicitur.

(*t*) L. R. Justiciarijs.
(*u*) L. R. cognomento.
(*w*) L. R. *desunt* scriptoribus sed super alios.
(*x*) L. R. *desunt* M. sedem quidem h. n. c. a. s. s. alios.

M. Licet

M. Licet erret interdum in excipiendo, quia remotus est; tamen dum Rotuli corriguntur (*y*) facta omnium trium collatione, facile erit errata corrigere.

D. Satis hactenus dictum est de ordine sedentium. Nunc de eorum officijs si placet exequere, incipiens a læva Presidentis.

Quid ad Cancellarium.

M. Cancellarius in ordine illo primus est; & sicut in Curia sic ad Scaccarium magnus est: adeo ut sine ipsius consensu vel consilio nil magnum fiat, vel fieri debeat. Verum hoc habet officium dum residet ad Scaccarium, ad ipsum pertinet custodia Sigilli Regij, quod est in Thesauro, sed inde non recedit nisi cum præcepto Justitiæ ab inferiore ad superius Scaccarium a Thesaurario vel Camerario defertur, ad explenda solum negotia Scaccarij. Quibus (*z*) peractis in Loculum mittitur, & Loculus a Cancellario consignatur, & sic Thesaurario traditur custodiendus. Item, cum necesse fuerit, signatus sub omnium oculis Cancellario offertur; nunquam ab ipso, vel ab alio alias offerendus. Item ad ipsum pertinet Rotuli qui est de Cancellaria, custodia per suppositam personam; & sicut viris magnis visum est de omni scriptura Rotuli Cancellarius æque tenetur ut Thesaurarius, excepto duntaxat de hoc, quod scribitur in thesauro receptum: licet enim non præscribat ut Thesaurarius conscribit (*a*) tamen etsi ille erraverit, licet ipsi (*b*) vel Clerico ejus Thesaurarium cum modestia corripere, & quid debeat suggerere. Quod si Thesaurarius perseveraverit, & mutare noluerit, poterit eum si de parte sua confidit tantum coram Baronibus arguere, ut ab eis quid fieri debeat judicetur.

D. Verisimile etiam videtur custodem tertij Rotuli eadem scripturæ lege constringi.

M. Non est verisimile tantum sed verum: par enim est auctoritas illis (*c*) duobus Rotulis ratione scripturæ; quia sic placuit ejus auctori.

Quid ad Constabularium.

Constabularij officium est ad Scaccarium, ut in brevibus Regis de exitu thesauri, vel de aliquibus computandis his (*d*) qui compotum faciunt, simul cum Præsidente testis existat. In omnibus enim hujus-

(*y*) L. R. corriguntur Rotuli.
(*z*) L. N. Quilibet peractis.
(*a*) L. R. scribit.
(*b*) L. R. illi.
(*c*) L. N. illius.
(*d*) L. R. hijs.

modi brevibus ex antiqua inftitutione duos oportet confcribi teftes. Item ejus officium eft cum ad Scaccarium ftipendiarij Regis venerint pro ftipendijs fuis, five fint refidentes in caftris Regis five non, affumpto *(e)* fecum Clerico Conftabulariæ, cujus eft terminos eorum noffe, & Marefcallo Scaccarij, computet eorum liberationes, & de retractis fidem fufcipiat, & refiduum folvi faciat. Omnis enim liberatio quorumcunq;, five Accipitrariorum five Falconariorum, five Bernariorum ad officium ejus *(f)* fpectat, fi præfens fuerit; nifi forte Dominus Rex ad idem aliquem prius affignaverit: quia Conftabularius a Rege non facile poteft avelli, propter majora & magis urgentia. Notandum vero quod Marefcallus Scaccarij de liberationibus refidentium militum percipit, quod ad eum pertinet ratione officij fui; de commeantibus autem non. Item huic cum alijs magnis commune eft, ut nihil magnum eo inconfulto fieri debeat.

Quid ad Camerarios.

Camerariorum officium annexum eft officio Thefaurarij, quia uno & eodem prætextn honoris vel difpendij militare nofcuntur; & eft eis idem velle ad honorem Regis, adeo ut quod ab uno factum fuerit, a nullo eorum dicatur infectum. Thefaurarius enim pro fe & pro eis fufcipit compotos, & fecundum qualitates exactorum verba miniftrat in Scripturam Rotuli, in quibus omnibus pari jure Societatis obligantur, & fic de alijs quæ vel ab hoc, vel ab hijs, falva fide Domini Regis, fiunt, five in fcriptis, five in receptis, five in taleis, five in expenfis.

Quid ad Marefcallum.

Marefcalli cura eft taleas debitorum quas *(g)* Vicecomes reddiderit, quæ tamen *(h)* annotantur in Rotulo, mittere feorfum in forulo fuo: Brevia quoq; regia de computandis, vel perdonandis, vel dandis, his *(i)* quæ exiguntur a Vicecomite per fummonitionem. Illi vero forulo fuperfcriptio Comitatus, cujus hæc funt apponitur, & fingulis Comitatibus fingulos oportet forulos, a Vicecomite qui computat, Marefcallo miniftrari.

D. Eft hic aliquid quod me movet.
M. Satis præfenfi. Suftine tamen modicum. Plana enim erunt

(*e*) L. N. afcito fecum.
(*f*) L. R. ejus officium.
(*g*) L. R. quos.
(*h*) L. R. *defunt* quæ tamen.
(*i*) L. R. hijs.

omnia

omnia ex confequentibus. Item fi quis debitor non fatisfaciens de fummonitione meruerit comprehendi, huic traditur fervandus, & (k) foluto Scaccario illius diei, fi voluerit, mittet (l) eum in carcerem cuftodiæ publicæ, non tamen vinculabitur, vel in ima (m) trudetur, fed feorfum vel fupra carcerem, licet enim folvendo non fit, tamen ob hoc non meruit fceleratis (n) deputari; ita tamen fi miles non fuerit; de militibus namq; pro pecunia retentis, illuftris Regis conftitutio eft, quæ infra annotabitur in agendis Vicecomitis. Item ad hunc fpectat, ut peracto compoto Vicecomitis, vel cuftodis, vel cujufcunq; perfonæ qui ad compotum refidet, fidem ab ipfo fufcipiat, in publico, quod legitimum compotum fecundum confcientiam fuam fecerit. Si vero Vicecomes, vel qui computavit, aliquo debito tenetur, addet quod a Scaccario, hoc eft, a leugata Villæ, in qua eft, non difcedet, nifi ipfa die rediturus, fine licentia Baronum. Item hic factas Summonitiones contra terminum alterius Scaccarij a latere figilli Regij fignatas fub numero fufcipiet, & Oftiario fuperioris Scaccarij per manum fuam diftribuet, per Angliam deferendas. Sic habes eorum, qui in primo Scanno refident, officia diftincta.

Quid ad Factorem Talearum.

In capite vero fecundæ fedis primus eft ferviens Camerariorum, Clericus feu Laicus, cujus officium paucis expediri poteft, verbo tamen non opere. Hic taleas de thefauro contra Vicecomitem, vel eum qui computat, miniftrat, & cum oportuerit fecundum quod ratio computationis exegerit, mutat, vel minuit, vel addit in talea, appofita eidem contratalea (o) Vicecomitis. Quo facto in termino Pafchæ longiorem Vicecomiti reddit iterum in termino Sancti Michaelis afferendam. In termino vero Sancti Michaelis, cum in Rotulo fumma ejus fcripto fuerit deputata, tradit eandem longiorem Marefcallo, in forulo fuo reponendam.

D. Miror, quod dixifti taleam femel compoto ablatam (p) iterum (q) alij compoto offerendam.

M. Noli mirari; quoniam quicunq; (r) exacta, vel foluta fuerint (s) a Vicecomite in termino Pafchæ, neceffe eft iterato fummoneri;

(k) L. N. & etiam.
(l) L. N. mittetur.
(m) L. N. in arma trudetur. *Corrigitur autem textus manu recentiori; & pro* arma *ponitur* ima.
(n) L. R. cum fceleratis.
(o) L. R. contratallea.
(p) L. N. ablatam receptæ.
(q) L. N. *deeft* iterum.
(r) L. N. *pro* quoniam quicunq; *habet vacuum fpatium.*
(s) L. N. fuerit.

non tamen ut secundo solvatur quod jam solutum fuerit, sed ut offerant se compoto, & oblata talea solutionis jamdudum (*t*) factæ redigatur in scripturam Rotuli; & sic absolvatur a debito. Dum enim taleam penes se habuerit, liberatus non erit, sed semper summonendus.

D. Et hæc necessaria visa sunt; sed prosequere, si placet, de officijs.

M. Immo quia de taleis mentionem fecimus, quo ordine taliandi ratio consistat, paucis adverte. Talearum igitur alia est, quæ simpliciter Talea dicitur; alia, quam numerandam nuncupamus. Legitimæ vero Taleæ longitudo a summitate indicis usq; ad summitatem extenti pollicis est: illic terebro modico perforatur. Memoranda vero quæ de firma Bl[anca] semper fieri solet, paulo brevior est; quia facto Essayo, per quod firma dealbatur, prima illa confringitur, & apposita sibi talea combustionis taleæ longitudinem tunc primo meretur. Hac autem ratione fit incisio. In summo ponunt M libr.; sic ut incisio ejus spissitudinis palmæ capax sit; C l ut pollicis; xx l ut auricularis; libræ unius incisio quasi grapi Ordei tumentis; solidi vero minus; sic tamen ut ex concisionibus loco vacuato modicus ibi sulcus fiat; denarius (*u*) facta incisione nullo dempto signatur. Ex qua vero parte millenarius inciditur, alium non pones numerum; nisi forte mediam ejus partem; sic ut mediam similiter incisionis ejus partem demas, & infra constituas. Sic si C l incisurus est, & non sit tibi Millenarius, facies sic; & de xx l. sic; & de xx Sol. quos libram dicimus. Quod si multi Millenarij, vel centenarij, vel vigenæ librarum incidendæ sunt, lex eadem servetur, ut ex patentiore parte ejusdem taleæ, hoc est, quæ directe tibi (*w*) proponitur facta annotatione major numerus, ex altera vero minor incidatur; ex patentiore (*x*) vero parte semper est (*y*) major numerus in summo, ex minus patente semper minor, hoc est denarij. Marcæ argenti ad Scaccarium incisio sola significativa non est; sed per solidos designatur. Marcam autem auri in medio taleæ, sicut libram unam incidas. Aureum vero unum non prorsus ut argenteum, sed ducto directe incidentis cultello per medium taleæ, non obliquando sicut fit in argenteo. Sic igitur ipsa locorum dispositio & incisionis differentia, quid aureum vel quid sit argenteum, utrumq; determinat. Cæterum oportunius hæc omnia Visu quam verbo cognosces.

D. Quod de his restat oculata fide constabit. Nunc si placet de officijs prosequere.

M. Post hunc ut supra diximus interpositis viris aliquibus discretis a rege missis, residet (*a*) is qui ex præcepto Regis computationes facit

(*t*) L. R. jam dictum *si recte cerno*.
(*u*) L. R. denarius vero.
(*w*) L. N. tibi.
(*x*) L. N. potentiore.
(*y*) L. N. *deest* est.
(*a*) L. R. & residet.

positione

Lib. I.   Dialogus de Scaccario.   367

positione numerorum pro calculis. Officium quidem satis perplexum est & laboriosum; & sine eo vix vel nunquam Scaccarij ratio possit expediri; sed nulli illic residenti convenit ex officio, nisi (*b*) cui Rex vel Justicia mandaverit exequendum. Laboriosum inquam; quia caetera officia lingua vel manu; haec hijs duobus explentur; sed in hoc, lingua, manus, oculi, mens indefessa laborant.

Quid ad Calculatorem.

Hujus autem haec est ratio. Secundum consuetum cursum Scaccarij non legibus Arismeticis. Memoriter, ut credo, dixisse me retines, Scaccario superponi pannum virgis distinctum, in cujus interstitijs numerales acervi collocantur. Porro Calculator in medio lateris residet, ut pateat omnibus, & ut liberum habeat ministra (*c*) manus excursum. Statuit autem ad dextram in spacio inferiore acervum nummorum (*d*) ab xj & infra; in secundo solidorum a xix & infra; in tertio vero librarum. Et hic quidem ipsi recta fronte debet (*e*) opponi quia medius est in consuetis compotis Vicecomitis; in quarto acervus est vigenarum; in quinto centenarum; in sexto Millenarum; in septimo, sed raro, decem mille librarum; raro inquam, hoc est, cum a Rege vel mandato ejus, a Magnis Regni (*f*) compotus a Thesaurario & Camerarijs Regni totius recepte suscipitur. Licet autem Calculatori pro decem solidis argenteum (*g*) pro decem vero libris obolum aureum apponere ut compotus expeditius (*h*) fiat. Cavendum vero est, ne manus praeambula linguam praeveniat, vel e converso; sed simul qui computat, & calculum mittat & numerum designet, ne sit error in numero. Deposita igitur per acervos summa quae a Vicecomite requiritur, disponuntur infra similiter per acervos, quae soluta fuerint, vel in Thesauro vel alias. Quod si fuerit firma numero quae ab ipso requiritur, vel quodlibet aliud debitum cui solo possit numero satisfieri, simplex fiet detractio inferioris a superiore summa, & de residuo tenebitur; secus autem fiet si firmam Bl. sit soluturus, quod in agendis Vicecomitis plenius ostenditur (*i*).

D. Parce parumper currenti Calamo ut liceat paucis uti.
M. Ad aleam resides, nec sunt tibi verba neganda.

(*b*) L. R. *deest* nisi.
(*c*) L. R. ministrat.
(*d*) L. R. *vel* nummorum *vel* numerorum.
(*e*) L. R. det.
(*f*) L. N. *desunt* compotus a Thesaurario & Camerarijs Regni.

(*g*) L. R. *desunt* pro decem solidis argenteum.
(*h*) L. R. *deest* expeditius.
(*i*) L. R. ostendetur.

D. Videre

D. Videre mihi videor fieri posse ratione calculandi, ut idem denarius pro calculo missus, nunc unum, nunc solidum, nunc libram, nunc centum, nunc (*k*) mille significet.

M. Sic est quibusdam tamen appositis; itemq; fieri potest eisdem demptis si Calculatori placeat, ut qui mille significat gradatim descendens unum significet.

D. Sic fit ut quivis de plebe, cum homo sit & aliud esse non possit, temporalibus appositis voluntate Præsidentis ab imo conscendat in summum (*l*), ac deinceps fortunæ lege servata retrudatur in imum (*m*), manens quod fuerat, licet videatur ratione dignitatis & status (*n*) a se sibi mutatus.

M. Noscis, quod sermo tuus non capit in omnibus; verum quicquid alijs videatur, mihi satis placet, quod ex hijs alia conicis (*o*); in mundanorum vero tribulis mistici (*p*) intellectus flores quærere laudabile est. Nec in hijs tantum quæ (*q*) commemoras, sed in tota Scaccarij descriptione Sacramentorum quædam latibula sunt. Officiariorum (*r*) namq; diversitas, judiciariæ potestatis auctoritas; Regiæ imaginis impressio, citationum emissio; Rotulorum conscriptio, Villicationum ratio, debitorum exactio, reorum condempnatio vel absolutio, districti examinis figura sunt, quod revelabitur cum omnium libri aperti erunt & janua clausa. Sed de his hactenus. Nunc prosequamur de officijs; Post hunc qui Calculis inservit, primus residet ex officio Clericus qui præest Regis Scriptorio.

Quid ad Clericum qui præest Scriptorio.

Ad hunc (*s*) pertinet scriptores idoneos ad Rotulum Cancellariæ, & ad brevia Regis quæ in Scaccario fiunt, nec non ad Summonitiones conscribendas, invenire, & ut bene fiant prospicere; quæ quidem officia, licet paucis exprimatur verbis, infinitis tamen vix expleri possunt laboribus; quod norunt hij, qui hæc ipsa rerum experientia didicerunt. Sic habes officia dispositorum in secundo sedili.

(*k*) L. R. *pro* nunc, *habet* nec *quinquies in hac clausula repetitum.*
(*l*) L. N. summa.
(*m*) L. N. ima.
(*n*) L. N. & factus.
(*o*) *pro* conjicis.
(*p*) L. R. misti.
(*q*) L. N. qui.
(*r*) L. R. offerrorum, *mendose pro* officiorum *vel* officiariorum.
(*s*) L. N. Ad huc.

Lib. I.   Dialogus de Scaccario.

Quid ad Pictavenfem Archidiaconum nunc Wintonienfem Epifcopum.

D. Si bene memini primus ad dextram Prefidentis refidet Wintonienfis Epifcopus, cujus (*t*) officium in Scaccario vellem protinus expediri. Magnus enim eft & nifi magnis occupari non debeat.

M. Magnus eft proculdubio; & magnis intentus in multa diftrahitur, ficut in Tricolumni (*u*) plenius eft oftenfum. Hic autem tempora (*w*) promotionis (*x*) dum paulo inferior in Regis Curia militaret, vifus eft fide & induftria Regis negotijs neceffarius, & in computationibus atq; in Rotulorum & Brevium fcripturis fatis alacer (*y*) & officiofus. Unde datus eft ei locus ad latus Thefaurarij, ut fcilicet fcripturæ Rotulorum, & hijs omnibus cum ipfo intenderet. Thefaurarius quidem tot & tantis curis & follicitudinibus per omnia diftrahitur, ut fas fit interdum tanto operi fubrepere fomnum. In humanis autem actionibus vix aliquid eft ufquequaq; perfectum.

D. Quid eft quod dicis? nec enim novi quid fit Tricolumnis (*z*).

M. Libellus quidem eft a nobis utcunq; tempore Juventutis editus de tripartita Regni Angliæ hiftoria, fub illuftri Anglorum Rege Henrico fecundo; quem quia per tres Columnas per univerfum digefimus, diximus Tricolumnum (*a*). In prima quidem de Ecclefiæ Anglicanæ negotijs plurimis, & de nonnullis refcriptis fedis Apoftolicæ. In fecunda vero de infignibus prædicti Regis geftis, quæ fidem humanam excedunt. In tertia vero de pluribus negotijs tam publicis (*b*) quam familiaribus, necnon Curiæ & Judicijs (*c*) agitur. Hic fi forte in manus tuas inciderit, cave ne te effugiat; utilis enim poterit (*d*) futuris effe (*e*) temporibus & jocundus his, qui de Regni ftatu fub prædicto principe folliciti fuerint. Hic enim Rex licet atavis Regibus æditus fuerit, & per longa Terrarum fpatia triumphali victoria fuum dilataverit Imperium; majus tamen eft, quod prodigum in fe famæ titulum ftrenuis actibus fuperavit. Sed de his (*f*) actenus. Nunc cœpta negotia profequamur.

D. Efto, fi (*g*) fic placet. Salva fit igitur reverentia Thefaurarij:

(*t*) L. R. *pro* cujus *habet album fpatiolum.*
(*u*) L. N. Tricolumpni.
(*w*) *forfan legendum* ante tempora.
(*x*) L. N. procurationis.
(*y*) L. N. alloc.
(*z*) L. N. Tricolumpnis.
(*a*) L. N. Tricolumpnum.
(*b*) L. R. in publicis.
(*c*) L. R. in Curiæ [ ].
(*d*) L. R. poteft.
(*e*) L N. effe vero.
(*f*) L. N. hijs.
(*g*) L. R. quia fic.

hic

hic videtur ejus dignitati derogatum, quia non est soli fidei ipsius per omnia creditum.

M. Absit; imo magis sic ejus laboribus parcitur & indemnitati providetur; non enim quod vel ipsi vel alij non creditur, tot & tanti resident ad Scaccarium: sed quia rebus magnis & Regni negotijs sub tanto principe decet magnos ac multos deputari, non tamen ut utilitati (*h*) prospiciant, sed excellentiæ & honori Regis (*i*) deserviant.

D. Prosequere, si placet, de officijs.

Quid ad Thesaurarium.

M. Officium Thesaurarij, vel cura vel sollicitudo ipsius vix explicari posset verbis, etiamsi esset mihi Calamus (*k*) velociter scribentis. In omnibus enim & per omnia, quæ vel in inferiori Scaccario vel in superiori geruntur, ipsius sollicita diligentia necessaria est. Ex prædictis tamen magna ex (*l*) parte constare potest, in quibus amplior sit ejus cura, adeo ut ab hijs avelli non possit manente Scaccario; in recipiendis scilicet compotis Vicecomitum, & in scriptura Rotuli. Ipse namq; ministrat verba secundum qualitatem negotiorum in scripturam Rotuli sui, a quo postmodum illud idem excipitur ab alijs Rotulis; sicut supra dictum est; & cavendum est ipsi, vel in numero, vel in causa, vel in persona sit error; ne absolvatur qui quietus non est, vel rursus conveniatur qui meruit absolvi. Tanta namque Rotuli ejus auctoritas est, ut nulli liceat ei contradicere vel mutare; nisi forte tam manifestus error fuerit, ut omnibus pateat: neque tunc nisi de communi consilio omnium Baronum mutari debet, & ipsis præsentibus cum ad huc scilicet Scaccarium illius diei (*m*) perseverat: Scripturam vero Rotuli præterito anno factam, vel etiam hujus anni extantis post solutum Scaccarium nulli mutare licet nisi (*n*) Regi, cui semper his (*o*) licent quæcunq; (*p*) libent. Item ad eum spectat, ut ad omnia magna negotia cum Superioribus assumatur, & nil (*q*) eum lateat.

Quid ad scriptorem Thesaurarij.

Scriptoris qui proximus ut Thesaurario (*r*) officium est præparare Rotulos ad Scripturam ex pellibus Ovinis non sine causa. Longitudo

(*h*) L. N. *pro ac multos deputari non tamen ut utilitati habet vacuum spatium.*
(*i*) L. R. honori Regio.
(*k*) L. R. Calamus scribæ.
(*l*) L. N. pro parte.
(*m*) L. N. *deest diei.*
(*n*) L. R. *deest* nisi.
(*o*) L. N. hijs.
(*p*) L. R. quicunq;
(*q*) L. N. nichil.
(*r*) L. R. Thesaurio.

autem

autem (*s*) eorum est quanta surgit ex duabus membranis; non tamen quibuslibet, sed magnis, ad hoc opus ex industria procuratis: Latitudo vero paulo plus una expansa & semis. Regulatis igitur Rotulis a summo pene usque deorsum, & ex utraq; parte, lineis a se decenter distantibus praenotantur (*t*) in summo Rotuli Comitatus & Bailliae, de quibus infra compotus redditur: facto vero modico intervallo quasi trium vel quatuor (*u*) digitorum, praescribitur in medio lineae nomen Comitatus de quo primo loco agendum est. Deinde in Capite sequentis lineae nomen Vicecomitis depingitur, subsequente hoc tenore verborum. Ille vel ille Vicecomes reddit compotum de firma illius vel illius Comitatus. Deinde paulo post in (*w*) eadem linea scribitur; In Thesauro, nec apponitur aliud nisi consummato compoto, propter urgentem causam, quae in agendis Vicecomitum manifesta est. Deinde in capite sequentis lineae, quid in Elemosina & Decimis constitutis, quid etiam in liberatione, de firma Comitatus expendatur, exprimitur. Post haec (*x*) in capite lineae inferioris in Terris datis annotantur ea quae Regum munificentia contulit Ecclesijs, vel his quae eis militarunt, in fundis suis quae Coronae annominantur, quibusdam Bl., quibusdam numero.

D. Movet me quod dicis quosdam fundos dari Bl[ancos], quosdam numero.

M. Prosequamur ad praesens de Scriptoris officio; & in agendis Vicecomitis super hoc, si libet, interroga. Post Terras datas, facto intervallo unius lineae ut videantur etiam ipsa sui ratione sejuncta, annotantur ea quae jussa sunt de firma expendi per Brevia Regis; quia haec constituta non sunt, sed casualia; quaedam etiam, quae sine brevibus computantur per consuetudinem Scaccarij, de quibus infra dicetur: & sic terminatur compotus de Corpore Comitatus. Post hoc facto intervallo quasi sex vel septem linearum, fit compotus de Purpresturis & Escaetis (*y*) sub his (*z*) verbis. Idem Vicecomes reddit compotum de firma Purpresturarum & Escaetarum (*a*); sed & de omnibus firmis Maneriorum & de censu Nemorum, quae annuatim debentur & solvuntur. Post haec (*b*) suo ordine compoti collocantur, exceptis quibusdam Civitatibus & Villis & Baillijs, quorum majores compoti sunt; quia constitutas habent Elemosinas vel liberationes, & terras datas; & ad Custodes earum terrarum (*c*) propriae summonitio-

---

(*s*) L. N. *deest* autem.
(*t*) L. N. numerantur in.
(*u*) L. N. quaesitum digitorum.
(*w*) L. R. *deest* in.
(*x*) L. R. hoc.

(*y*) L. N Excaetis.
(*z*) L. R. hijs.
(*a*) L. N. Excaetarum.
(*b*) L. R. hoc.
(*c*) L. R. *deest* terrarum.

nes de debitis Regis (*d*) diriguntur. De his (*e*) autem compoti fiunt post consummatum omnino compotum de Comitatibus in quibus sunt. Qualia sunt Lincolnia, Wintonia, Mienes, Berchamstede, Colecestria, pleraq; alia.

D. Miror dixisse te quosdam reditus constitutos dici firmas, quosdam vero census.

M. Firmæ Maneriorum sunt, census autem nemorum tantum. Quæ enim ex manerijs proveniunt, quia per agriculturam quolibet anno renovantur & redeunt ; & præter hæc (*f*) in ipsis certi sunt constituti redditus consuetudinum jure perpetuo, merito firma (*g*) & immutabilia nominantur. Quæ vero ex nemoribus quæ quotidie (*h*) succiduntur & pereunt annua lege debentur, quorum non est tam firmus vel immobilis quæstus, sed est in eis ascensus & descensus, licet non annuus frequens tamen, Census dicuntur : & sic per Aphæresim (*i*) redditus hos censeri (*k*) dicunt. Sunt tamen qui credunt, censum dici quæ a singulis hominibus solvuntur ; firma vero quæ ex his (*l*) surgit ; ut sit firma nomen collectivum, sicut turba : ob hoc igitur sicut creditur sic censetur, ut annuum indicet, & firmum non esse designet. Post hæc constituta, facto iterum intervallo fit compotus de debitis, super quibus summonitus est Vicecomes ; prætitulatis tamen nominibus illorum Judicum quorum hæc sunt. Ultimo vero de Catallis Fugitivorum, vel mutilatorum pro excessibus suis. Et his (*m*) expletis, compotus illius Vicecomitatus terminatur. Cavendum autem est scriptori, ne aliquid motu animi sui scribat in Rotulo, nisi quod Thesaurario dictante, didicerit. Quod si forte per negligentiam vel alium quemlibet casum, contigerit eum errare in scriptura Rotuli, vel in nomine, vel in numero, vel in causa, in quibus vis major scripturæ consistit ; non præsumat abradere, sed linea subtili subducta cancellet, & scribat in serie quod oportet : habet enim Rotuli sciptura hoc commune (*n*) cum chartis (*o*) & alijs scriptis patentibus, quod abradi non debet (*p*) : & ob hoc cautum est ut de pellibus Ovinis fiant ; quia non facile nisi manifesto vitio rasuræ cedunt.

D. Scriptor iste de proprio an de fisco Rotulos invenit ?

(*d*) L. R. Regijs.
(*e*) L. R. hijs.
(*f*) L. R. hoc.
(*g*) Perperam, me judice, Cl. Auctor innuit Firmam dici a firmitate.
(*h*) L. N. cotidie.
(*i*) L. N. Afferesim.

(*k*) L. N. censiri.
(*l*) L. R. hijs.
(*m*) L. N. hijs.
(*n*) L. N. idem cum.
(*o*) L. N. cartis.
(*p*) L. N. debent.

M. In

M. In termino iste (*q*) Sancti Michaelis v solidos de fisco recipit, & scriptor Cancellariæ alios nihilominus v ; ex quibus ad utrumq; Rotulum, & ad summonitiones & receptas inferioris Scaccarij membranas inveniunt.

Quid ad Scriptorem Cancellariæ.

Cura labor studium reliqui scriptoris ad ejus latus residentis in his maxime consistit, ut scilicet excipiat de Rotulo altero verbum e verbo, eodem ut prædiximus ordine servato. Item ad hunc pertinet Brevia Regis de exitu Thesauri (*r*) scribere, de his (*s*) tantum rebus quæ consideratione Baronum, considente Scaccario, a Thesaurario & Camerarijs liberari debent: nihilominus hic Brevia Regis scribit de computandis vel perdonandis his, quæ Barones ad Scaccarium computanda vel perdonanda decreverint (*t*). Ad hunc (*u*) etiam spectat, ut peractis compotis Vicecomitum, & taxatis debitis Regis de quibus Summonitiones fiunt, easdem per totum Regnum dirigendas diligenti simul & laboriosa discretione conscribat: ex quibus, & in (*w*) quorum gratia sequentis termini Scaccarium convocatur.

VI. *Quis sit tenor Brevium Regis factorum ad Scaccarium, sive de exitu Thesauri, sive de computandis, sive perdonandis.*

D. Brevia Regis de exitu Thesauri sub quo tenore verborum fiunt (*x*) ?

M. Thesaurarius & Camerarij nisi Regis expresso mandato vel præsidentis Justiciarij, susceptam pecuniam non expendunt : oportet enim ut habeant auctoritatem rescripti Regis de distributa pecunia, cum ab eis compotus generalis exigetur ; est autem hic tenor ; H. Rex &c ; N. Thesaurario & illi & illi Camerarijs salutem. Liberate de Thesauro meo (*y*) illi vel illi, hanc vel hanc summam. Testibus (*z*) his apud N, ad Scaccarium. Additur autem ad Scaccarium, ut sic fiat discretio Brevium quæ in Curia Regis fiunt. Oportet etiam ut facto brevi de exitu thesauri, ut diximus, faciat idem scriptor rescriptum ejus, quod (*a*) vulgo dicitur contrabreve ; & illud penes se reservabit

(*q*) L. R. isto.
(*r*) L. R. Thesaurarij.
(*s*) L. N. hijs.
(*t*) L. R. decreverunt.
(*u*) L. N. ad huc.
(*w*) L. N. *deest* in.
(*x*) L. N. tenore fiuntur.
(*y*) L. N. nostro.
(*z*) L. N. Teste his.
(*a*) L. R. ejusq; vulgo.

Clericus.

Clericus Cancellarij in testimonium liberatæ factæ per breve Regis originale, quod **Thesaurarius** & Camerarij habent. Brevia quoq; de computandis vel perdonandis his, quæ Barones decreverint (*b*) computanda vel perdonanda, præcognita Domini Regis voluntate, sub hoc tenore verborum fiunt. H. Dei gratia &c, Baronibus de Scaccario salutem. Computate illi vel illi (*c*) hanc vel hanc summam, quam liberavit ad hoc vel ad illud negotium meum. Testibus hijs ibi ad Scaccarium. Item; Rex Baronibus de Scaccario (*d*) salutem. Perdono illi, vel clamo quietum hunc vel illum de hoc vel de illo (*e*). Testibus hijs ibi ad Scaccarium. Horum autem omnium brevium rescripta penes jamdictum Clericum residebunt, in testimonium factorum Brevium. Originalia enim computatorum vel perdonatorum Brevia forulis Marescalli factis Vicecomitum compotis includuntur; de cætero, nisi contentio de eis oriatur, non exponenda. Quod autem de brevibus Regis dicimus, intelligendum est similiter be brevibus Præsidentis Justiciarij (*ee*), tantum cum Rex absens est; & cum sigilli ejus impressione jura regni statuuntur, & causæ citantur ut condemnentur (*f*) vel absolvantur qui vocantur ad Curiam. Cæterum dum Rex in Regno Angliæ fuerit; Brevia Scaccarij nomine Regio fient, sub ejusdem Præsidentis & alicujus alterius magni testimonio. Quis autem sit tenor Brevium illorum quæ Sommonitiones dicuntur, plenius infra dicetur in titulo de Summonitionibus.

Quid ad Clericum Cancellarij.

Clericus Cancellarij qui huic proximus est, licet non proprio sed alieno nomine militet, magnis tamen occupatur, & in multa distrahitur: adeo ut ab ipso initio compotorum usq; ad finem inde avelli non possit; nisi forte dum sibi propitius est (*g*); substituto sibi interim discreto vicario. Huic tantum prima cura est post Thesaurarium in hijs omnibus quæ illic geruntur; maxime tamen circa Rotulorum ac Brevium scripturam; in hijs (*h*) enim præcipue versatur; nam ne

---

(*b*) L. R. decreverunt.
(*c*) L. N. illis.
(*d*) L. R. ad Scaccarium.
(*e*) L. R. vel illo.
(*ee*) *Rege agente ultra mare, fiebant sæpenumero brevia nomine summi Justiciarij. Exempli causa:* Paganus de Mundublel debet xviij l & xiij s & iiij d de Militibus. Sed debent requiri, per breve Comitis Legercestriæ [*Capitalis Justiciarij*] per breve Regis de Ultra mare, a Comite Patricio & Gaufrido de Ver, qui eosdem Milites habent. *Mag. Rot.* 13. *Hen.* 2. *Rot.* 2. *a. tit.* Berrochescira. *Cujus etiam rei exempla alia in præeunte historia notantur.*
(*f*) L. N. condempnentur.
(*g*) L. N. *pro* propitius est *habet album spatiolum.*
(*h*) L. R. his.

forte

forte sui calamus scriptoris aberret prospicit hic, alium sequitur dum passibus æquis. Item hic intuetur diligenter alterius anni Rotulum sibi propositum, donec a Vicecomite satisfactum fuerit de debitis hijs (*i*) quæ illic annotantur, & de quibus summonetur. Item residente Vicomite ad compotum, computatis & scripto deputatis his quæ constituta sunt in Comitatu, Breve summonitionis, cui Regis sigillum appensum est, suscipit a Vicecomite, & de his (*k*) debitis quæ illic scripta sunt urget Vicecomitem, pronuncians in publicum & dicens, Redde de hoc tantum, & de illo tantum. Debita vero quæ solvuntur in integrum, & de quibus satisfit, cancellet idem Clericus linea ducta per medium; ut sit distintio per hoc etiam inter soluta & solvenda. Hic etiam custodit contrabrevia factorum ad Scaccarium. Hic etiam summonitiones factas ut prædictum est corrigit, & sigillat; & est ei labor infinitus, atq; post Thesaurarium maximus.

D. Utilis hic esset magis Argus, quam Polyphemus.

Quid ad Clericum Constabulariæ.

M. Clericus Constabulariæ magnus & officiosus in Regis Curia, ad Scaccarium etiam ad majora quæq; cum Magnis ascitur, & assensu ejus Regia fiunt negotia. Destinatur autem a Rege ad Scaccarium cum contrabrevibus ad terminos Scaccarij, de hijs tantum quæ ad Curiam fiunt. Hic etiam cum (*l*) Constabulario liberationibus Militum vel quorumlibet eorum intendit, ut prædictum est; & est interdum laboriosum satis officium ejus (*m*), licet paucis exprimatur. Explet tamen illud frequentius per suppositam personam sicut Cancellarius; quapropter Majores (*n*) non facile possunt a Regis præsentia longius ire. Sic habes dispositorum in secundo sedili ad dextram Præsidentis utcunq; distributa officia.

Quid ad Brunum.

Porro in (*o*) capite quarti sedilis quod opponitur Justiciarijs, residet Magister Thomas cognomento Brunus (*oo*). Hujus ad Scaccarium non

(*i*) L. R. ijs.
(*k*) L. N. hijs.
(*l*) L. R. cura *pro* cum.
(*m*) L. N. ejus officium.
(*n*) L. N. Majora.
(*o*) L. R. *deest* in.
(*oo*) *Magister* Thomas Brunus *semel atq*;

iterum *in* Magnis Rotulis R. Henrici II. memoratur: *Anno quinto illius Regis, quidam* Radulfus *nepos* Magistri Thomæ *annuam pensionem a Rege accepit*: Et in liberatione constituta Radulfo nepoti Thomæ Bruni, vj l & xx d; *Mag. Rot.* 5. *H.* 2. *Rot.* 7. *b. Herefordscira: Anno decimoquarto*

non vilis est auctoritas. Magnum enim (*p*) & validum fidei ejus & discretionis est argumentum, quod a tam excellentis ingenij Principe electus est, ut præter antiquam consuetudinem tertium habeat Rotulum, in quo Regni jura Regisq; secreta conscribat, & eundem penes se reservans quocunq; voluerit deferat. Habet etiam Clericum suum in inferiore (*q*) Scaccario, qui juxta Clericum Thesaurarij residens, liberam habet facultatem scribendi, quæ recipiuntur & expenduntur in Thesauro.

D. Nunquid Principi cognita est eo usq; fides ejus atq; discretio, quod ad hoc opus merito non æstimetur alius ad illum?

M. Magnus hic erat in magni Regis Siculi curia, consilijs providus, & in Regis secretis pene præcipuus. Surrexit interea Rex novus qui ignorabat illum, qui prava habens latera patrem persequebatur in suis. Compulsus est igitur vir iste, mutatis rebus prosperis, vitæ suæ consulere, & licet pateret ei cum summo honore accessus ad Regna plurima; tamen frequenter vocatus ab illustri Rege Anglorum Henrico, cum fama veritate ipsa minor (*r*) est, præelegit ad natale solum & successorium ac singularem dominum suum accedere. Susceptus igitur ab ipso sicut utrumque decuit, quia apud (*s*) Siculum magnis intenderat, hic etiam ad magna deputatur negotia Scaccarij. Sic igitur & locum & dignitatis officium adeptus est; ad quælibet etiam Scaccarij magna negotia cum Magnis assumitur. Sic habes omnium qui ad majus Scaccarium ex officio resident jura distincta. Consequens autem est, ni fallor, ut quæ sint eorum dignitates ratione sessionis ad Scaccarium prosequamur.

D. Imo, si placet, de officio Militis quem Argentarium dicis, nec non de Fusoris officio dicendum est; quia cum sibi videantur annexa, & ad majus Scaccarium pertinentia, hucusq; dilata sunt.

---

ac vicesimosecundo, ipse Magister Thomas *fruebatur pensione annua a Rege concessa:* Johannes Constabularius Cestriæ r c de DC l pro terra Matris suæ; In thesauro xlvij l & xiij s & iiij d; Et in soltis, per breve Regis, Magistro Thomæ le Brum ix l, de Liberatione sua de quarta parte anni, Et Waltero Vitulo x l, de liberatione Esneccæ &c; *Mag. Rot.* 14. *H.* 2. *Rot.* 6. *b. Tit. Tichebilla :* Et Magistro Thomæ Bruno lxxvj s & ob. de dimidio anno, *Mag. Rot.* 22. *H.* 2. *Rot.* 3. *b. Herefordscira in Walia: Anno decimoquinto, idem Magister* Thomas *fuit Eleemosynarius Regis :* Et Magistro Thomæ Brun Elem[osinario] Regis, vij l & xij s & j d; *Mag. Rot.* 15. *H.* 2. *Rot.* 10. *a. Herefordscira in Walijs. Cl. Dialogi auctor hic testatur, Magistrum* Thomam *insigni functum officio ad Scaccarium. Quodnam illud fuerit, non est satis compertum. Fortasse idem, ac quod temporis progressu vocabatur* Cancellariatus Scaccarij. *Conjectando loquor.*

(*p*) L. R. *deest* enim.
(*q*) L. R. inferiori.
(*r*) L. N. mino.
(*s*) L. N. aput.

M. Cerno quod te promissorum memoria non præterit, ex quo spes certa concipitur, quod te jam dictis non fraudabit oblivio. Credebam sane de officijs tibi fuisse (*t*) satisfactum, quia de residentibus ad Scaccarium neminem prætermiseram. Sed hij de quibus commemoras certas non habent sibi deputatas sedes, immo pro imperio Præsidentis vel Thesaurarij suum explent officium.

Quid ad Militem Argentarium.

Porro Miles Argentarius ab inferiori Scaccario ad superius defert loculum examinandi argenti, cujus supra meminimus; quem cum intulerit signatum sigillo Vicecomitis, sub omnium oculis effundit in Scaccario quadraginta quatuor solidos, quos de acervo sumptos prius signaverat, factaq; commixione eorundem, ut ponderi respondeant, mittit (*u*) in unum Vasculum trutinæ libram ponderis, in alterum vero de denarijs quod oportuerit, quo facto numerat eosdem, ut ex numero constare possit, si legitimi ponderis sint; cujuscunq; vero ponderis inventi fuerint, seorsum mittit in Ciffum libram unam, hoc est xx Sol. (*w*) ex quibus examen fiat; reliquos vero xxiiij Sol. (*x*) mittit in loculum. Item duo denarij præter libram examinandam dantur Fusori, non de fisco sed de parte Vicecomitis, quasi in præmium sui laboris. Tunc eliguntur a Præsidente, vel a Thesaurario si ille absens fuerit, alij duo Vicecomites, ut simul cum Argentario nec non & Vicecomite cujus examen faciendum est, procedant ad ignem; ubi Fusor ante Præmonitus præparatis necessarijs eorum præstolatur adventum: ibi (*y*) iterum præsente Fusore & hijs (*z*) qui a Baronibus missi sunt, diligenter computantur, & fusori traduntur.

Quid ad Fusorem.

Quos ille suscipiens manu propria numerat, & sic disponit eos in Vasculum ignitorum cinerum quod in fornace est. Tunc igitur artis fusoriæ lege servata redigit eos in massam, conflans & emundans argentum. Cæterum cavendum est ei, ne citra perfectum subsistat, vel importunis (*a*) æstuationibus vexet illud atq; consumat; Illud propter Regis, hoc propter Vicecomitis jacturam; sed modis omnibus pro-

---

(*t*) L. R. fuisse tibi.
(*u*) L. R. mittat.
(*w*) L. R. viginti solidos.
(*x*) L. R. viginti quatuor solidos.
(*y*) L. R. *deest* ibi.
(*z*) L. R. his.
(*a*) L. N. inportunis.

videat (*b*) & procuret quanta poterit (*c*) induſtria, ut non vexetur, ſed ad parum tantum excoquatur: hoc autem ipſum (*d*) providere debent (*e*) hij, qui ad idem miſſi ſunt a Majoribus. Facto igitur examine, defert illud Argentarius ad Barones comitantibus illis, & tunc in omnium oculis ponderat illud cum libra prædicta ponderis: Supplet autem mox, quod ignis conſumpſit appoſitis denarijs ejuſdem loculi, donec æquilibriter ſe habeat examen cum pondere; tunc inſcribitur idem examen deſuper ducta creta his verbis, Everwicſcira. Libra arſit tot, vel tot denarijs; & tunc illud Eſſaium dicitur non enim inſcribitur niſi præconceſſo (*f*) quod ſic ſtare debeat. Quod ſi Vicecomes cujus eſt, calumpniatus fuerit illud quaſi plus juſto conſumptum fuerit, ignis ſcilicet ex æſtuatione, vel plumbi infuſione; vel etiam fuſor ipſe qualibet occaſione defeciſſe fateatur examen, iterum numerentur, viginti Solidi, qui reſidui ſunt in Loculo prædicto, coram Baronibus ſicut dictum eſt, ut eadem Ratione ſervata fiat Examen. Hinc tibi conſtare poteſt, qua conſideratione de acervo magno præpoſitæ pecuniæ quadraginta quatuor ſolidi ſeorſum ab initio mittantur in loculum appoſito Vicecomitis ſigillo. Notandum vero eſt, quod Fuſor duos percipit denarios pro examine, ſicut diximus. Quod ſi quovis caſu aliud faceret, etiam ſi tertio examinaverit, non percipiet quicquam, ſed contentus erit ſemel ſuſceptis duobus.

D. Miror a tantis tantam adhiberi diligentiam (*g*) in unius libræ examinatione, cum nec magnus ex eo quæſtus nec multa jactura perveniat.

M. Non propter hanc tantum fiunt hæc, ſed propter Omnes illas quæ ab eodem Vicecomite ſub eodem nomine firmæ ſimul cum hac perſolvuntur. Quantum enim ab hac libra per ignem purgatorium decidit, tantundem ex ſingulis alijs libris noverit Vicecomiti de ſumma ſua ſubtrahendum: ut ſi centum libras numeratas ſolverit, & libra examinis xij denar. exciderit, non computentur ei niſi nonaginta quinque.

D. Nunc videre videor, quæſtum ex hijs provenire poſſe non modicum, ſed cui cedere debeat ignoro.

M. Semel dictum eſt & ſemper intelligatur, ſoli Regiæ utilitati in his omnibus ſerviri. Licet autem a talea Vicecomitis combuſtio detrahatur mittitur tamen ſeorſum in taleam alteram breviorem, ut de ſumma ejus Theſaurarius & Camerarij reſpondeant. Sciendum vero quod per hanc taleam combuſtionis dealbatur firma Vicecomitis; unde in teſtimonium hujus rei ſemper majori taleæ appenſa (*h*) cohæret.

(*b*) L. R. procuret.
(*c*) L. N. & quanta procuret induſtria.
(*d*) L. R. ipſum autem.
(*e*) L. N. dicunt hij.
(*f*) L. N. præconceſſio.
(*g*) L. R. diligentiam adhiberi.
(*h*) L. R. *deeſt* appenſa.

D. Pulſat

D. Pulsat adhuc me quæstio non dissimilis illi, quam in agendis inferioris Scaccarij proposuisse me memini; quare videlicet libra una plus altera decidat, cum par debeat esse conditio omnium operantium in moneta.

M. Ad hanc sicut ad illam quæstionem sufficit respondere, fieri posse hoc per falsarios & nummorum detonsores. Fuerunt autem, qui crederent (*i*), quibus nec ego dissentio, non esse legitimam hujus regni monetam, si examinata libra (*k*) decidat (*l*) plusquam VI. a pondere, quam (*m*) numerata respondet; & etiam delatam ad Scaccarium hujusmodi pecuniam fisco debere cedere, nisi forte novi sint (*n*) &·non usuales denarij, quorum etiam superscriptio suum prodat (*o*) auctorem; tunc enim idem monetarius super opere suo districte convenietur, & legibus constitutis sine jactura Vicecomitis condemnabitur vel absolvetur. Quod si per examinationem probatis & reprobatis denarijs monetarius condemnatus & punitus fuerit, denarij a Fusore Scaccarij præsentibus alijs hujus artis peritis redigentur (*p*) in massam, & pondus ejus Vicecomiti computabitur. Verum totum hoc pene nunc abolitum est & multum relinquitur, quoniam in moneta generaliter peccatur ab omnibus (*q*). Cum autem ad debitum & lege determinatum modum moneta pervenerit, primitivæ constitutionis legem observari necesse erit (*r*). Contra, si quis Vicecomes nummos attulisset, quorum libra combusta a v vel iiij vel (*s*) infra se cohiberet, & viderentur de novo facti, non usuales vel cursorij, simili modo non legitimi dicebantur, quasi excedentes legem communem; unde & infiscari poterant sicut & alij. Item sunt ad Scaccarium liberationes constitutæ (*t*) quæ statutis terminis sine Brevi Regis solvuntur: qualis est liberatio Nauclerī, Custodis scilicet navis Regiæ quam Esneccam (*tt*) dicimus,

(*i*) L. N. crediderent.
(*k*) L. R. *deest* libra.
(*l*) L. R. subdecidat.
(*m*) L. N. qua.
(*n*) L. R. sunt.
(*o*) L. N. probat.
(*p*) L. N. redigetur.
(*q*) L. R. *deest hic clausula incipiens* Vicecomiti computabitur *& desinens* ab omnibus.
(*r*) L. R. *habet hic* Verum totum hoc pene nunc abolitum est & multum relinquitur, quoniam in moneta generaliter peccatur ab omnibus.
(*s*) L. R. combusta ad vj l iiij l infra.

(*t*) L. N. constitæ.
(*tt*) *Exempli gratia:* Anno duodecimo Regis Henrici II, *Firmarius villæ* Hantonæ, *in composito ad Scaccarium reddito, habuit de firma sua subductas expensas quæ sequuntur; similiq; modo, anno vigesimosecundo ejusdem Regis, firmarius illius villæ qui isto anno compotum reddidit:* In Liberatione Esneccæ, quando Rex transfretavit in quadragesima, vij l & x s; Et in passagio Regis Scotiæ, vij l & x s, per Breve Regis: Et in passagio Domini Gaufridi filij Regis, Esneccæ & duabus alijs Navibus, x l. *Mag. Rot.* 12. *Hen.* 2. *Rot.* 8. *b. tit.* Hantona: Et item in liberatione Esneccæ, quando filia Regis transfretavit itura

dicimus, qui xij percipit quaq; die; de qua & (*u*) confimilibus taleæ fiunt a Camerarijs, quia de hijs brevia non habent. Miles autem Argentarius horum recauta habet, i. e. contrataleas. Hic fimul & fufor rogati a (*w*) Camerarijs cum necefse fuerit, & plurima delata pecunia opprimit Computatores, juvant eos in computatione: voluntarium tamen eft eis, non necefsarium. Sic habes militis Argentarij & (*x*) Fuforis officia.

D. Quæ fint figna facti vel infecti examinis.

M. Non fatis novi; quia nec follicitus fuper hijs fui. Verum quamdiu fuper jam liquidum argentum nigra quædam nubecula circumferri confpicitur, infectum dicitur. At cum quædam quafi grana minuta ab imo deducuntur ad fummum, & illic difsolvuntur, fignum eft examinati.

VII. *A quibus vel ad quid inftituta fuit argenti examinatio.*

D. A quibus vel ob quam rem inftituta fuit examinatio hæc vel combuftio?

M. Ut de his (*y*) tibi conftare pofsit, paulo altius oriendum eft. Sicut traditum habemus a patribus, in primitivo regni ftatu poft Conquifitionem, Regibus de fundis fuis non auri vel argenti pondera fed fola victualia folvebantur; ex quibus in ufus cotidianos domus Regiæ necefsaria miniftrabantur. Et noverant, qui ad hæc deputati fuerant, quantum de fingulis fundis proveniebat. Cæterum ad ftipendia vel donativa Militum & (*z*) alia necefsaria, de placitis Regni vel conventionibus, & ex civitatibus vel caftellis a quibus agricultura non exercebatur, pecunia numerata fuccrefcebat. Toto igitur Regis Willelmi primi tempore perfeveravit hæc inftitutio, ufq; tempora Regis Henrici filij ejus; adeo ut viderim ego ipfe quofdam, qui victualia ftatutis temporibus de fundis Regijs ad Curiam deferri viderint: certumq; habebant (*a*) officiales domus Regiæ a (*b*) quibus Comitatibus triticum, a quibus diverfæ fpecies carnium vel equorum pabula, vel quæ necefsaria, debebantur. Hijs vero folutis

itura in Siciliam, vij l & x s, per breve Regis. Et in liberatione feptem navium quæ cum ea transfretaverunt, x l & xij s per breve Regis. *Mag. Rot.* 2². *Hen.* 2. *Rot.* 13. *b. tit. Hantona. Quin & Navis Epifcopi* Elienfis *vocabatur* Efnecca *ejus*: Et in reparatione Efneccæ Epifcopi [*fc.* Elienfis] xxvij s, per idem breve. *Mag. Rot.* 19. *Hen.* 2. *Rot.*

4. *b. in compoto de Epifcopatu de* Ely *vacante.*
(*u*) l. N. *deeft &.*
(*w*) L. R. *rogatia.*
(*x*) L. R. *fimul &.*
(*y*) L. N. *hijs.*
(*z*) L. R. *ad alia.*
(*a*) L. N. *habebat.*
(*b*) L. R. *deeft* a.

secundum constitutum modum cujusq; rei, Regij officiales computabant Vicecomiti redigentes in summam denariorum. Pro mensura scilicet tritici ad panem C hominum, Solidum unum ; pro corpore bovis pascualis solidum unum ; pro Ariete vel Ove iiij d ; pro præbenda xx equorum similiter iiij d. Succedente vero tempore, cum idem Rex in transmarinis & remotis partibus, sedandis tumultibus bellicis operam daret, contigit ut fieret sibi summa necessaria ad hæc explenda (*c*) numerata pecunia. Confluebat interea ad Regis Curiam querula multitudo colonorum, vel quod gravius sibi videbatur prætereunti frequenter occursabat, oblatis Vomeribus in signum deficientis agriculturæ; innumeris enim molestijs premebantur occasione victualium, quæ per plurimas Regni partes a (*d*) sedibus proprijs deferebant. Horum igitur querelis inclinatus Rex diffinito Magnorum consilio destinavit per Regnum quos ad id prudentiores & discretiores cognoverat (*e*), qui circueuntes & oculata fide fundos singulos perlustrantes, habita æstimatione victualium, quæ de hijs (*f*) solvebantur, redegerunt in summam denariorum. De summa vero summarum quæ ex omnibus fundis surgebat in uno Comitatu, constituerunt Vicecomitem illius Comitatus ad Scaccarium teneri ; addentes, ut ad scalam solveret, hoc est propter quamlibet numeratam libram vj d. Rati sunt enim tractu temporis de facile posse fieri, ut moneta tunc fortis a suo statu decideret. Hæc eos fefellit opinio ; unde coacti sunt constituere ut firma maneriorum non solum ad scalam, sed ad pensum solveretur ; quod perfici non poterat nisi longe pluribus oppositis. Servabatur per plures annos ad Scaccarium lex hujus solutionis : unde frequenter in veteribus (*g*) Annalibus Rotulis Regis illius invenies scriptum, in thesauro C libras ad scalam ; vel, in thesauro C libras ad pensum. Surrexit interea vir prudens, consilijs providus, sermone discretus, & ad maxima quæque negotia per Dei gratiam repente præcipuus, dicens, in eo completum quod scriptum est ; nescit tarda molimina Spiritus sancti gratia. Hic ab eodem Rege ad Curiam vocatus, licet ignotus non tamen ignobilis suo perdocuit exemplo

Paupertas tenuis quam sit fœcunda virorum !

Hic igitur, succrescenti in eum principis ac cleri, populiq; favore, Sarisburiensis Episcopus factus, maximis in Regno fungebatur hono-

(*c*) L. N. hæc exempla.
(*d*) L. R. de sedibus.
(*e*) L. N. connoverat.
(*f*) L. R. his.
(*g*) L. N. veteris.

ribus, & de Scaccario plurimam habuit scientiam; adeo ut non sit ambiguum sed ex ipsis Rotulis manifestum, plurimum sub eo floruisse; de cujus stillicidijs nos quoque modicum id quod habemus per traditionem accepimus. Super hoc ad præsens multa loqui supersedeo; quia pro qualitate sui status nobilissimæ mentis indicem superstitem sibi memoriam dereliquit (*h*). Hic postmodum ex mandato principis (*i*) accessit ad Scaccarium; ubi cum per aliquot annos persedisset, comperit hoc solutionis genere non plene fisco satisfieri: licet enim in numero & pondere videretur satisfactum non tamen in materia: consequens enim non erat, ut si pro libra una numeratos xx Sol. etiam libræ ponderis respondentes solvisset, consequenter libram solvisset argenteam: poterat enim cupro vel quovis ære mixtam solvisse, cum non fieret examinatio (*ii*). Ut igitur Regiæ simul & publicæ provideretur utilitati, habito super hoc ipso Regis consilio, constitutum est ut fieret ordine prædicto firmæ combustio vel examinatio (*k*).

D. Quomodo publice?

M. Sentiens enim Vicecomes se prægravari (*l*) per combustionem deterioris monetæ, cum firmam est soluturus solicitam adhibet diligentiam ut monetarij sub eo constituti (*ll*) legis constitutæ fines non excedant;

(*h*) L. N. dereliquid.
(*i*) L. N. precipis access—
(*ii*) *Cl. auctor videtur hic innuere, Combustionem a* Rogero Saresberiæ *Episcopo, Capitali Justiciario & Scaccarij Præside, vel inventam vel in usum inductam. Sed constat ante* Rogeri *ævum in usu fuisse, ex indubiæ fidei monumento* Libro Domesday; *in quo de libra arsa & arsura semel atque iterum mentio fit. Exempli gratia:* Burgum Hertforde: Hoc suburbium reddit xx libras arsas & pensatas; & iij molini reddunt x libras ad numerum. Quando Petrus Vicecomes recepit, xv libras ad numerum reddebat; T. R. E. vij libras & x solidos ad numerum. *Lib. Domesd. fol.* 132. *tit.* Herfordscire. Terra Judhel de Totenais: Judhel tenet de Rege Totenais burgum, quod Rex Eduuardus in dominio tenebat. Ibi sunt intra burgum C burgenses v minus, & xv extra burgum terram laborantes. Inter omnes reddunt viij libras ad numerum. Olim reddebant iij libras ad pensum & arsuram. *Lib. Domesd. tit.* Devenescire, *fol.* 108. *b.* *col.* 1. [Sulfretone] Reddit xl libras ad pondus & arsuram. [Teintone] Reddit xiiij libras ad pensum & x solidos ad numerum. [Alseminstre] Reddit xxvj libras ad pensum & arsuram. *Ib. fol.* 100. *a col.* 2. *tit.* Devenescire. [Wachetone] reddit iij libras ad pondus [Sudtone] reddit xx solidos ad pensum. [Ermentone] reddit xiij libras & x solidos ad pensum & arsuram. *Ib. fol.* 100. *b. col.* 1. *eod. tit.* [Blachepole] valet xx solidos ad pensam & arsuram. [Mortone] redit xij libras ad pensam & arsuram. *Ib. fol.* 101. *a. col.* 1. *eod. tit. Et vid.* Spelm. *Glossar. ad vocem* Libra, *p.* 366. *col.* 2. *Sed videamus annon hoc dubium submoveri poterit; hoc modo. Fortasse* Rogerus *Episcopus vel invenerit vel introduxerit* Combustionem Nominalem (*de qua locutus sum in præeunte historia Vol.* 1. *cap.* 9. *sect.* 2.); *puta solutionem pecuniæ auctariæ vice Combustionis.*

(*k*) L. R. *desunt vel* examinatio.
(*l*) L. R. pergravari.
(*ll*) *Exempli gratia:* Robertus de Vallibus [Vicecomes Cumbriæ] debet C marcas, pro pluribus

excedant; quos cum deprehenderit, sic puniuntur, ut eorum exemplo cæteri terreantur.

D. Nunquid de omnibus Comitatibus firma Bl[anca] solvi debet, vel ex omnibus Comitatibus (*m*) examinatio fieri?

M. Non; sed qui de antiquo (*n*) jure Coronæ Regiæ annominantur sic solvunt. Qui vero per incidentes aliquos casus infiscantur, solo numero satisfaciunt; quales sunt Salop (*o*), Sudsex, Northumberland (*p*) & Cumberland. Liberum est etiam (*q*) Vicecomiti ut pro firma Bl[anca] solvat examinati argenti pondera; & sic effugiat jacturam combustionis; Sic tamen ut Fusor Regis eadem suscipienda discernat. Habes igitur quod petisti, a quibus scilicet & ob quam causam instituta fuerit examinatio.

D. Video (*r*) per hanc ad literam impletum quod scriptum est: quale fuerit cujusq; opus ignis probabit. Sed jam nunc placeat cœptis insistere.

M. Fiat. Consequens est ut credo secundum dispositæ rationis ordinem, ut quæ sunt dignitates residentium ad Scaccarium ex officio, vel ex Regis mandato prosequamur.

D. Miror satis qua consideratione cum de officijs ageretur, de Ostiario majoris Scaccarij & ejus officio vel ex industria suppressisti, vel oblivionis injuria resistente præteriisti.

M. Gratulor te memorem prædictorum; in proficiente quippe discipulo gloria Doctoris est. Nosti jam dictam Ostiarium liberationem percipere cum alijs officialibus, & ideo merito requiris, quid sit ejus officium. Est autem hujusmodi.

Quid ad Ostiarium Superioris Scaccarij.

Ostium domus illius in qua Scaccarium residet, Ostiarius ille solus sine consorte custodit; nisi cum de domo propria servientes assumit in onus officij sui. Nihilominus (*s*) custodit idem ostium thalami secretarum, qui collocatus est juxta domum ubi Scaccarium est. Ad hunc accedunt Barones, cum proponitur eis verbum ambiguum ad Scaccarium, de quo malunt seorsum tractare quam in auribus omnium;

pluribus diffaisinis: & quia cognovit prisones evasisse de custodia sua; & quia cum esset Vicecomes sustinuit cursum veteris monetæ post generalem prohibitionem. *Mag. Rot.* 1. *l. ic.* 1. *Rot.* 8. *a. tit.* Cumberland.

(*m*) L. R. *desunt hic* ex omnibus Comitatibus.

(*n*) L. N. antico.
(*o*) L. N. Salopscir.
(*p*) L. R. Norhumberland.
(*q*) L. N. etiam est.
(*r*) L. R. Vide.
(*s*) L. N. Nichilhominus.

maxime

maxime autem propter hoc in partem secedunt, ne compoti qui ad Scaccarium fiunt impediantur; quibus moram facientibus in consilijs, consuetus cursus compotorum agitur. Si quid vero natum fuerit quæstionis, referetur ad eos. Liberum etiam est Ostiario, ut quibuslibet magnæ auctoritatis viris ad hoc opus non necessarijs impune præcludat aditum cum voluerit. Solis vero hijs qui ad Scaccarium ex officio vel ex Regis mandato resident, voluntarius patet ingressus in utrumq; thalamum. Quod si auctenticæ sint personæ, quas singulariter incedere non est idoneum, unum vel duos introducere poterunt in exteriorem domum Scaccarij, sed in thalamum secretorum soli Majores introeunt, cæteris exclusis; nisi cum ad quælibet Regia negotia explenda a Dominis suis vocantur. Item Ostiarius factas Summonitiones & signatas a Marescallo suscipit; soluto Scaccario illius termini, in propria persona vel per fidelem nuncium per Angliam, sicut supra dictum est, easdem defert. Hic etiam ex mandato Præsidentis convocat in præsentiam (t) ejus Vicecomites qui extra domum ubicunq; dispersi sunt, cum indiguerit illis. Item ad hunc pertinet, ut sollicitus sit circa minuta quælibet necessaria quæ in domo Scaccarij sunt velut (u) ad sternenda & præparanda sedilia circa Scaccarium, & hujusmodi. Ex prædictis, ut credimus, de officijs omnium qui ad Scaccarium resident tibi constare potest. Nunc quæ sunt eorum jura vel dignitates ratione sessionis ad Scaccarium ostendemus.

VIII. *Quæ sunt jura & dignitates residentium ad Scaccarium ratione sessionis.*

Oportet autem de cætero nobis amplius parcat lingua detractoris, & dens æmulus ne laniet insultando; vix enim ad notitiam tuam aliquid horum pertingeret, si non usitatis rerum vocabulis, sed exquisito verborum scemate vel confectis (w) nominibus duxerimus insistendum.

D. Solam verborum novitatem a principio vitare præmonui, & circa communia communibus & usitatis uti verbis obtinui, ne disciplinalia rudimenta novitas insueta turbaret. Sic igitur, ut cœpisti, cœptum libeat iterum explere. Quod si te sic gradientem detractoris æmula mens vel lingua repererit (x) illud obtineas ab eo, ut qui in scriptis suis sine peccato est, primus in te lapidem mittat.

M. Sponte pareo, dumodo lex ista servetur. Dignitas residentium ad Scaccarium in pluribus consistit. Sive enim de Clero sint sive de Regis Curia qui assident ex mandato, ab ea die qua convenient usq;

(t) L. R. præsentia.
(u) L. N. velud.
(w) L. R. conflictis.
(x) L. N. repperit.

ad

ad generalem Seſſionem, ad alias quaſlibet cauſas ſub quibuſcunq; judicibus non evocantur; & ſi forte vocati fuerint, ratione publicæ poteſtatis excuſantur. Quod ſi ſint actores & non rei qui aſſident, & alias habent lites, in eorum erit arbitrio vel experiri per procuratorem, vel abſq; omni detrimento ſui juris diem prorogare. Si vero judex ſub quo litigant, ſive ſit Eccleſiaſticus ſive Forenſis, legis hujus ignarus, ab jam dicta die convocationis ad Scaccarium citaverit quemlibet eorum, & abſentem forte per ſententiam poſſeſſione ſua vel quovis jure ſpoliaverit, auctoritate Principis & ratione ſeſſionis revocabitur in eum ſtatum cauſa (*y*) ipſius, in quo erat, ante citationem: Sed judex propter hoc puniri non meruit; quod enim ſui officij eſt, eſt exequutus; licet pro publica poteſtate non conſequatur effectum. Quod ſi ſic citatus fuerit, ut fatalis dies lege determinatus ſibi conſtitutus, diem convocationis ad Scaccarium præveniat, non poterit ſe per illud excuſare, vel Judicis ſententiam declinare (*z*), vel in ſe latam irritam facere, etiamſi alter alteri ſic proximus ſit, ut iterum cogatur arripere. Procuret itaque ſibi procuratorem vel reſponſalem, & ipſe Regijs addictus (*a*) negotijs ad Curiam ſine ſimulatione feſtinet. Præterea Barones qui ad Scaccarium reſident, de victualibus ſuæ domus in urbibus & Caſtellis & Maritimis emptis, nomine conſuetudinis nihil ſolvunt. Quod ſi miniſter Vectigalium de hijs quicquam ſolvere compulerit, dummodo præſens ſit ſerviens ejus qui in ſuis uſibus empta fuiſſe oblata fide probare voluerit, Baroni quidem exacta pecunia reſtituetur in integrum, & improbus exactor pro qualitate perſonæ pecuniariam pœnam luet. Item ſi quilibet etiam Magnus in regno inconſulto calore animi quemlibet ad Scaccarium reſidentem probris vel convicijs laceſſierit (*b*), ſi preſidens ille præſens eſt, exceſſus hujuſmodi ultricem pœnam pecuniariam ſtatim excipiet. Abſente vero præſidente, illatam injuriam ſi conſtanter ille negaverit, & acclamaverint confedentes dixiſſe eum quod ſibi obicitur, nihilominus (*c*) Regi cui militatur in pecuniam reus ſtatim judicabitur, niſi feſtinaverit poſtulando miſericordiam prævenire judicium. Quod ſi ſe invicem hij qui ad Scaccarium reſident, contumelioſa qualibet objectione moleſtaverint, Mediantibus alijs ſui ordinis miniſtris in pacem redeant; ut ſatisfiat ab ipſo qui innocentem læſit, ad eorum æſtimationem. Si vero acquieſcere noluerit, ſet magis in ſua teme-

---

(*y*) L. R. caſa.
(*z*) L. R. declarare.
(*a*) L. N. additus.

(*b*) L. N. proprijs vel convifcijs laſceſcierit.
(*c*) L. N. nichilhominus.

ritate

ritate perseveraverit (*d*), proponatur verbum Præsidenti, & ab eo postmodum quod justum fuerit uterque suscipiat. Cæterum si per incentorem malorum diabolum, qui fraternæ pacis jocundam lætitiam non æquis aspicit oculis, fieri contigerit, ut inter ipsos Majores dissentionis oriatur occasio, deinde quod absit succrescant conviciorum jurgia, & addente stimulos Sathana, per alios collegas operis ejus pax reformari non possit; horum omnium cognitio ipsi Principi reservabitur; qui secundum quod cordi suo Deus, in cujus manu ipse est, inspiraverit, excessum puniet; ne qui præsunt alijs ferre videantur impune quod decernunt in alijs puniendum.

D. Ex his manifestum est, quod Salomon ait, mors & vita in manibus linguæ; Et item Jacobus; lingua modicum membrum est, & magna exaltat.

M. Sic est (*e*); sed prosequamur de dignitatibus. Fiunt interdum per Comitatus communes Assisæ, a Justitijs *(f)* itinerantibus quos nos deambulatorios vel perlustrantes Judices nominamus; quæ ideo dicuntur Communes, quia cognita summa quæ de Comitatu requiritur communiter ab his qui in Comitatu (*g*) fundos habent, per hydas distribuitur, ut nihil desit de illa cum ventum fuerit ad Scaccarium solutionis. Ab hijs omnibus omnes hij qui ad Scaccarium ex Principis mandato resident liberrimi sunt; adeo ut non solum a dominiis sed etiam ab omnibus feodis suis nihil horum exigatur (*gg*). Si vero qui residet ibi fundum habeat (*h*) vel ad firmam, vel in custodiam, vel etiam in pignus pro pecunia, liber non erit, sed magis de hijs legibus publicis obnoxius fiet. Amplius autem præter has liber erit ad Scaccarium a Murdris, Scutagijs, & a Danegeldis (*i*) (*ii*). Quod autem ad

---

(*d*) L. R. *desunt* set magis in sua temeritate perseveraverit.

(*e*) L. R. *desunt* sic est.

(*f*) L. N. *Justitijs*.

(*g*) L. R. *desunt* requiritur communiter ab his qui in Comitatu.

(*gg*) *Barones & Residentes Scaccarij Regij, residentiæ suæ privilegio consueverunt esse immunes amerciamentorum nomine murdri, & communium assisarum impositarum Comitatibus, hundredis, & villis, ob defaltas, transgressiones, & delicta ejusmodi. De hac re consulatur* Historia Scaccarij, *cap.* 20. *Sect.* 7.

(*h*) L. R. *habet.*

(*i*) L. R. Danegildis.

(*ii*) *Instantiæ causa. Anno secundo R.* Henrici II, *Comes* Albericus, *Episcopus* Lincoliensis, *Comes* Leicestriæ, *Episcopus* Eliensis, *ac* Thesaurarius, *absoluti scribebantur a summis in terras ipsorum irrogatis in* Cantebrugescira *nomine* Danegeldi; *idq; si recte judico, per residentiæ suæ privilegium.* Idem Vicecomes [Paganus] r c de Danegildo; In thesauro xxxviij l & iij s; Et in Perdonis per brevia Regis, Comiti Alberico xviij s, Et Episcopo Lincoliæ xxxvj s & vj d, Et Comiti Legrecestriæ xiiij s, Et Episcopo de Eli xxix l & vj d, Et Thesaurario xiiij s, itemq; alijs; *Mag. Rot. H.* 2. *Rot.* 2. *b.* Cantebr. *Eodemq; anno, Episcopus* Eliensis, Thesaurarius, *Comes* Leicestriæ, *&* Warinus filius Geroldi, *utiq; absoluti scripti sunt a summis in ipsos impositis in* Cantebrugescira *nomine* Doni. Et idem Vicecomes r c de

ad ipsum pertinet a summa constituta decidet, & Vicecomiti computabitur per hæc verba; in perdonis per Breve Regis, illi vel illi hoc vel illud; cum tamen nullum super hoc Breve Regis habuerit. Caveat autem cui dimittitur aliquid a Principe, ne postea sibi dimissum requirat a subditis, sed magis memor sit verbi illius; dimittite & dimittemini; quia cum hoc fuerit deprehensum, Princeps Evangelicæ æmulator doctrinæ nec dimittet eum nec debitum dimittet ei, sed forsitan in centuplum puniet; quia impensa sibi gratia videtur abuti, cum ab alijs irreverenter exigit quod gratis sibi dimissum est.

D. Dictum est, si bene memini, quod quicunque Regis præcepto residet ad Scaccarium quibusdam a lege determinatis ratione sessionis liber est. Additum est etiam, si bene recolo, considere Scaccarium in termino Paschæ, non tamen quæ (*k*) illic fiunt omnino terminari, sed eorum consummationem termino Sancti Michaelis reservari. Cum igitur possibile sit, imo & frequenter contingat, aliquem ex Regis mandato in Termino Paschæ ad hoc assumi, qui in termino Sancti Michaelis vel fati debita solvit, vel ad alia Regni negotia mandato Regis transfertur (*l*), vel quod fortius quibusdam visum est, medio tempore Principi factus exosus, tam excellentibus negotijs indignus judicatur: Quæro si qui Termino Paschæ quietus est quo pauca terminantur, sed omnia per iteratam summonitionem innovantur, hic talis in termino Sancti Michaelis absolvi mereatur, cum etiam & Scaccarij sessionem & ipsam principis gratiam demeruerit.

M. Ad hujus quæstionis partem utramq; construendam copiosa forsitan est rationum inventio, sed noveris Regiæ munificentiæ libertatem, post semel (*m*) indultam absolutionis gratiam etiam cum pecuniæ dispendio in partem meliorem semper esse proniorem: quippe similis est donorum & perdonorum Regis ratio, ut sicut dona ejus revocari vel repeti non debent; sic nec Regis dismissa quæ vulgo perdonata dicuntur, nequeunt in irritum devocari. Liber igitur & absolutus est in termino consummationis, qui quocunque modo in præcedenti meruit absolvi.

D. Movent me quædam, quæ prædicta sunt. Primo quod dicis aliquid alicui dimitti sub hoc tenore verborum; In perdonis per Breve Regis, illi vel illi hoc vel illud, cum tamen nullum Breve Regis di-

---

l.iij l & vj s & viij d de Dono Comitatus: In Soltis Willelmo Cade xx l; Et in Perdonis per brevia Regis, Episcopo de Eli xxiij l & viij s, Et Thesaurario ix s & iiij d. Et Comiti Legrecestriæ xiij s & iiij d, Et Warino filio Geroldi xvj s, & alijs. *Ib. juxt. Cantebrig.*

(*k*) L. R. qui.
(*l*) L. R. transferatur.
(*m*) L. R. primo semel.

missionis obtinuerit. Quomodo enim fieri potest, ut sic falsa non deprehendatur Scriptura Rotuli, non video.

M. Movet te? Nec immerito; quod me diu movit; atq; (ut credo) nondum patuit omnibus hæc Scripturæ ratio : unde licet non sit magnum quod petis, attamen est insolitum, & videtur absurdum, ut per Breve Regis dicatur dimissum quod sine Brevi semper est dimittendum. Ea propter de hac ipsa sollicitus fui circa Dominum Eliensem virum itaq; hujus officij peritissimum, cujus memoria in benedictione sit in æternum. Hic illustris illius Anglorum Regis Henrici primi Thesaurarius, & nepos Sarisburiensis cujus supra meminimus, incomparabilem suis temporibus habuit Scaccarij scientiam : Maximus etiam existens in hijs (*n*) quæ ad sui status dignitatem pertinebant, celebrem sui nominis famam fecit, adeo ut pene solus in regno sic vixerit & sic decesserit ut gloriam ejus invida lingua denigrare non audeat. Hic etiam ab illustri Rege Henrico secundo frequenter rogatus, Scaccarij Scientiam continuata per multos annos bellica tempestate pene prorsus abolitam reformavit, & totius descriptionis ejus formam, velut alter Esdras bibliothecæ sedulus reparator, renovavit. Credidit sane vir prudens satius esse, constitutas ab antiquis leges posteris innotescere, quam sua taciturnitate ut novæ conderentur efficere; vix enim modernitas in quæstu pecuniæ mitiora prioribus jura dictavit. Ab hoc igitur super hoc hujusmodi responsum accepi; frater, qui aures audiendi avidas habet, facile detractoris linguam invenit; etiam is qui non habet non facile eandem effugiet. Accessit itaq; ad Regem Henricum primum vir aliquis habens sibila Serpentis, dicens ei; Barones vestri qui ad Scaccarium resident ut quid quæ de terris eorum exurgunt non solvunt? Cum quidam constitutas habeant ad Scaccarium liberationes pro sessione sua; quidam etiam pro officio suo fundos habent & fructus eorum; hinc ergo gravis jactura fisco provenit. Cum igitur ille Principis emolumentum allegans frequenter instaret, mentem ejus vix tandem verbum istud eo usque possedit, ut omnia constituta ab omnibus solvi præciperet, nec aliquid alicui dimitti, nisi quis super hoc expressum ejus obtinuisset mandatum : factumq; est ita. Succedente vero tempore, cum recordaretur Princeps consilij Achitophel (*o*) pœnituit eum acquievisse. Decrevit autem omnibus illic Ministrantibus omnia prædicta computari, nihil ducens jacturam modici æris respectu magni honoris. Destinavit itaq; breve suum ad Scaccarium, ut assidentes illic ab his liberi essent jure perpetuo. Ab hoc igitur Brevi ex tunc & modo dicitur, In perdonis per breve Regis; sicq; factum est, ut

(*n*) L. N. his.   (*o*) L. N. Architophel.

quod

quod indultum eft patribus (*p*) etiam nunc perfeveret in Pofteris. Simile autem huic aliquid temporibus modernis nos vidiffe meminimus, quod tractu temporis fub confimili verborum tenore hijs (*q*) qui abfolvi meruerint computabitur. Præcepit namque Domirus Rex Henricus fecundus in termino Sancti Michaelis xxiiij anni Regni fui, ut milites Templi, & fratres Hofpitalis & Monachi Ciftercienfis ordinis, quibus per chartæ fuæ libertatem longe ante quietantiam indulferat omnium qui ad denarios pertinent, excepta jufticia mortis & membrorum a modo quieti effent de hijs omnibus quæ (*r*) ad Denarios per fingulos Comitatus pertinerent, adeo ut de cætero chartas fuas ad Scaccarium deferre non cogerentur. Hoc enim regiæ pietatis decrevit auctoritas, ut fic femel Baronum confideratione de hijs omnibus expedirentur; ne qui ad frugem vitæ melioris tranfierunt, & orationibus potius vacare tenentur, ad Scaccarium propter hoc cum chartis fuis inutilem & tediofam moram facere compellantur. Confilio igitur & confideratione Baronum qui interfuerunt factum eft Breve Domini Regis (*s*) fub hoc tenore; Clamo quietos milites templi de quinque Marcis, quæ exiguntur ab hominibus (*t*) eorum pro defectu; & prohibeo ne a modo ab ipfis vel hominibus eorum vel terris aliquid exigatur vel capiatur, quod ad denarios pertineat.

Teftibus his (*u*) ibi. Sic & fratribus hofpitalis, & monachis prædictis. Hujus autem (*w*) auctoritate mandati, a modo per fingulos Comitatus de omnibus quæ ad denarios pertinent quieti erunt: Sic ut dicatur in Annali, In perdonis per breve Regis illud, fcilicet cujus fupra meminimus.

D. Satis intellexi quod dictum eft. Nunc fi placet, quid fit Scutagium (*x*) Murdrum vel Danegeldum (*y*) aperire non differas. Barbara quidem effe videntur; fed eo magis me follicitant, quod ab hijs (*z*) dicis liberos effe Scaccarij miniftros.

IX. *Quid Scutagium, & quare fic dictum eft.*

M. Fit interdum, ut imminente vel infurgente in Regnum hoftium machinatione (*a*) decernat (*b*) Rex de fingulis feodis Militum fummam aliquam folvi, marcam fcilicet vel libram unam; unde militibus fti-

(*p*) L. R. Prioribus.
(*q*) L. R. his.
(*r*) L. R. qui.
(*s*) L. R. breve Regis.
(*t*) L. N. omnibus.
(*u*) L. R. hijs.
(*w*) L. R. *deeft* autem.
(*x*) L. R. Scutagium aperire.
(*y*) L. R. Danegildum.
(*z*) L. R. his.
(*a*) L. R. machinatione vel infurgente.
(*b*) L. R. *deeft* decernat.

pendia

pendia vel donativa succedant. Mavult enim princeps stipendiarios, quam domesticos bellicis apponere casibus. Hæc itaq; summa, quia nomine Scutorum solvitur, Scutagium nuncupatur. Ab hoc (*c*) autem quieti (*cc*) sunt ad Scaccarium residentes.

X. *Quid Murdrum, & quare sic dictum.*

Porro Murdrum proprie dicatur mors alicujus occulta, cujus interfector ignoratur. Murdrum enim idem est quod absconditum vel occultum. In primitivo itaq; Regni statu post Conquisitionem, qui relicti fuerant de Anglicis subjectis in suspectam & exosam sibi Normannorum gentem latenter ponebant insidias, & passim ipsos in nemoribus & locis remotis, nacta opportunitate, clanculo jugulabant: in quorum ultione cum Reges & eorum ministri per aliquot annos exquisitis tormentorum generibus in Anglicos desævirent, nec tamen

---

(*c*) L. N. hac.

(*cc*) *Mihi non est usquequaq; compertum, Barones & Justiciarios ad Scaccarium residentes a Scutagio immunes fuisse residentiæ privilegio. Hujuscemodi immunitatis exempla nusquam vidi, quantum scio. Utcunq; memorabo hic instantiam ab argumento non penitus alienam; quæ extat in magno Rotulo anni secundi R. Ricardi* I. *Ibi* Galfridus filius Petri, *tunc temporis residens ad Scaccarium, scribitur Regi obæratus in* xlix l iij s iiij d *de Scutagio* Walliæ: Galfridus filius Petri debet xlix l & iij s & iiij d, de eodem Scutagio [sc. exercitus Waliæ]. In Perdonis, per Libertatem sedendi ad Scaccarium xlix l & iij s & iiij d, Et Quietus est; *Mag. Rot.* 2. Ric. I. *Rot.* 9. *a. Essex & Hurtf. Sed ista verba,* In Perdonis & *quæ sequuntur, cancellantur in* Magno Rotulo; *nempe linea sub iis ducta, ut erat illius seculi mos. Eademq; summa a* Galfrido filio Petri *exigitur in quolibet Magno Rotulo sequentium annorum Regis* Ricardi I, *usq; ad annum primum* R. Johannis. *In* Rotulo *anni primi* R. Johannis, Galfridus *illa absolvitur; non per* Libertatem sedendi ad Scaccarium; *sed quia terra pro qua summa illa exigebatur, fuit in manu Regis, non* Galfridi, *tempore quo Scutagium* Walliæ *erat irrogatum:* Galfridus filius Petri debet xlix l & iij s & iiij d, de eodem [sc. Scutagio Waliæ]. Sed consideratum est per Barones, quod non debet inde summoneri, Quia Terra fuit in manu Regis quando Scutagium illud assisum fuit; *Mag. Rot.* 1. *Joh. Rot.* 7 *a. Essexa & Hurtf. Et quidem* Galfridus filius Petri *anno primo* R. Johannis *fuit Capitalis* Angliæ *Justiciarius ac Scaccarij Præsidens; ideoq;* Scaccarij *privilegiorum compos ut qui maxime. Simili modo* Henricus filius Geroldi Camerarius *in Magno Rotulo anni secundi* R. Ricardi I. *memoratur Regi debuisse* xxvj l ix s v d *de antedicto Scutagio* Walliæ: Henricus filius Geroldi Camerarius debet xxvj l & ix s & v d de eodem Scutagio; In Perdonis per Libertatem Scaccarij, eidem Henrico xxvj l & ix s & v d, Et Q. e.; *Mag. Rot.* 2. R. 1. *Rot.* 9. *a. Essex & Hurtf.: Et verba illa,* In perdonis &c. *hic etiam annullantur linea subtus ducta: Quin & ista summa nomini* Henrici *continuo imponitur in sequentibus* Magnis Rotulis R. Ricardi I: *Tandemq;* Warinus filius Geroldi *hæres* Henrici *anno primo* R. Johannis *a compluribus debitis tam suis quam matris suæ, interq; reliqua ab hoc* Scutagio Walliæ *absolutus renuntiatur virtute Brevis Regij:* Warinus filius Geroldi r c de summis illis, speciatim de hoc scutagio Walliæ; In thesauro nichil; Et in Perdonis ipsi Warino CC & vij marcas & dimidia, per breve Regis, Et debet *summam illam; Mag. Rot.* 1. *Joh. Rot.* 16. *b.* Oxenefordscira. *Et vid. Hist.* Scacc. *Cap.* 20. *Sect.* 7. *ad finem;* Kancia. De servicio Rogeri de Northwod.

sic

sic omnino desisterent, in hoc tandem devolutum est consilium, ut Centuriata quam Hundredum dicunt, in qua sic interfectus Normannus inveniebatur, quia quod (*d*) mortis ejus minister non extabat, nec per fugam, quis esset, patebat, in summam grandem argenti examinati, fisco condemnaretur, quædam scilicet in xxxvj, quædam in xliiij l (*e*), secundum locorum diversitatem & interfectionis frequentiam; quod ideo factum dicunt, ut scilicet pœna generaliter inflicta prætereuntium indemnitatem *(f)* procuraret, & festinaret quisque tantum punire delictum, vel offerre judicio per quem tam enormis jactura totam lædebat viciniam. Ab horum, ut prædiximus, solutione sedentes ad Tabulam liberos noveras.

D. Nunquid pro murdro debet imputari clandestina mors Anglici sicut Normanni?

M. A prima institutione non debet, sicut audisti: sed jam cohabitantibus Anglicis & Normannis, & alterutrum uxores ducentibus vel nubentibus, sic permixtæ sunt nationes, ut vix discerni possit hodie, de liberis loquor, quis Anglicus quis Normannus sit genere; exceptis duntaxat adscriptitijs qui Villani dicuntur, quibus non est liberum obstantibus dominis suis a sui status conditione discedere. Ea propter pene quicunque sic hodie (*g*) occisus reperitur, ut Murdrum punitur exceptis his (*h*) quibus certa sunt ut diximus servilis conditionis indicia.

D. Miror singularis excellentiæ Principem & (*i*) acerrimæ virtutis hominem, in subactam & sibi suspectam Anglorum gentem hac usum misericordia, ut non solum Colonos per quos agricultura posset exerceri indempnes (*k*) servaret; verum ipsis Regni majoribus fundos suos & amplas possessiones relinqueret.

M. Licet hæc ad suscepta negotia (*l*) quibus debitor factus sum non attinent, tamen quæ super hijs ab ipsis indigenis accepi, gratis exponam. Post Regni conquisitionem, post justam Rebellium subversionem, cum Rex ipse Regisq; proceres loca nova perlustrarent, facta est inquisitio diligens, qui fuerunt qui contra Regem in bello dimicantes per fugam se salvaverint. His (*m*) omnibus & item hæredibus eorum qui in bello occubuerunt, spes omnis terrarum & fundorum atq; redituum quos ante possederant, præclusa est: magnum namq; reputabant frui vitæ beneficio sub inimicis. Verum qui vocati

(*d*) L. R. *deest* quod.
(*e*) L. R. xxiiij l.
(*f*) L. N. indempnitatem.
(*g*) L. R. odie.
(*h*) L. N. hijs.
(*i*) L. R. ac.
(*k*) L. R. indemnes.
(*l*) L. R. *deest* negotia.
(*m*) L. R. hijs.

ad bellum nec dum convenerant, vel familiaribus vel (*n*) quibuslibet necessarijs occupati negotijs non interfuerant, cum tractu temporis devotis obsequijs gratiam dominorum possedissent sine spe successionis filij (*o*) tantum pro voluptate tamen dominorum possidere cœperunt. Succedente vero tempore cum Dominis suis odiosi passim a possessionibus pellerentur, nec esset (*p*) qui ablata restitueret, communis Indigenarum ad Regem pervenit querimonia, quasi sic omnibus exosi & rebus spoliati ad alienigenas transire cogerentur. Communicato tandem super his (*q*) consilio, decretum est, ut (*r*) quod a dominis suis exigentibus meritis interveniente pactione legitima poterant obtinere, illis inviolabili jure concederentur: cæterum autem nomine successionis a (*s*) temporibus subactæ gentis nihil sibi vendicarent. Quod quidem quam discreta consideratione cautum sit, manifestum est, præsertim cum sic modis omnibus ut sibi consulerent, de cætero studere tenerentur devotis obsequijs Dominorum suorum gratiam emercari. Sic igitur quisquis de gente subacta fundos vel aliquid hujusmodi possidet, non quod ratione successionis deberi sibi videbatur, adeptus est; sed quod solummodo meritis suis exigentibus, vel aliqua pactione interveniente, obtinuit.

D. Quid sit Centuriata vel Hundredum non satis novi.

M. Sustine modicum; scies postea loco suo, hoc est in titulo de Libro judiciario. Nunc prosequamur de Danegeldo (*t*) & ut ratio nominis tibi constet, paulisper adverte.

XI. *Quid Danegildum, & quare sic dictum.*

Insula nostra suis contenta bonis peregrinis non eget. Hanc igitur merito dixere priores, divitijsq; sinum (*u*) delicijsq; (*w*) Larem. Propter hæc innumeras ab exteris injurias passa est; quia scriptum est; furem preciosa signata sollicitant. Circumjacentium enim insularum prædones irruptione facta maritima depopulantes, aurum argentum & quæque pretiosa tollebant. Verum cum Rex & Indigenæ bellicis apparatibus instructi in suæ gentis defensionem instarent, illi fugas aggrediebantur æquoreas. Inter hos itaq; pene præcipua & semper pronior ad nocendum erat bellicosa illa & populosa gens Dacorum; qui præter communem raptorum avaritiam acrius instabant, quia aliquid

(*n*) L. N. seu quibusl.
(*o*) L. R. sibi tantum.
(*p*) L. R. essent.
(*q*) L. R. hijs.
(*r*) L. R. *deest* ut.
(*s*) L. R. *deest a*.
(*t*) L. R. Danegildo.
(*u*) L. R. Divitijsq; suum.
(*w*) L. N. dilicijsq;

de antiquo jure in ejufdem regni dominatione vendicabant, ficut Britonum plenius narrat Hiftoria. Ad hos igitur arcendos a Regibus Anglicis ftatutum eft, ut de fingulis hidis regni jure quodam perpetuo duo folidi argenti folverentur in ufus virorum fortium, qui perluftrantes & jugiter excubantes maritima impetum hoftium reprimerent. Quia igitur principaliter pro Dacis inftitutus eft hic redditus, Danegildum vel Danegildus (*x*) dicitur. Hic igitur annua Lege, ficut dictum eft, fub Indigenis Regibus folvebatur, ufque ad tempora Regis Willelmi primi de gente & genere Normannorum. Ipfo namque regnante, tam Daci quam cæteri terræ marifq; prædones hoftiles cohibebant incurfus; fcientes verum effe quod fcriptum eft; cum fortis armatus cuftodit atrium fuum, in pace funt ea quæ poffidet. Noverant autem etiam (*y*) quod acerrimæ virtutis homines impunitas non ferunt injurias. Cum ergo diu folviffet terra fub ejufdem Regis Imperio, noluit hoc ut annuum folvi, quod fuerat urgente neceffitate bellicæ tempeftatis exactum, nec tamen omnino propter inopinatos cafus dimitti. Raro igitur temporibus illius vel fuccefforum ipfius folutus eft: hoc eft cum ab exteris gentibus bella vel opiniones bellorum infurgebant. Verum quocunque tempore folvatur ab ipfo liberi funt qui affident ad Scaccarium ficut dictum eft. Vicecomites quoq; licet inter Barones Scaccarij non computantur, ab hoc quieti funt de dominijs fuis, propter laboriofam ejufdem cenfus collectam (*z*). Noveris autem dominica cujuflibet hæc dici, quæ proprijs fumptibus vel laboribus excoluntur; & item quæ ab afcriptitijs fuis fuo nomine poffidentur. Quia enim afcriptitij de Regni jure non folum ab hijs quæ modo poffident, ad alia loca a dominis fuis transferri poffunt: verum etiam ipfi quoq; licite venduntur vel quomodo libet diftrahuntur; merito tam ipfi quam terræ, quas excolunt ut dominis fuis ferviant, Dominia reputantur. Item fertur ab his quibus antiqua Scaccarij dignitas oculata fide pernotuit, quod Barones ejus ab Effartis Foreftarum liberi funt de Dominijs fuis. Quibus & nos confentire videmur; adjecta determinatione, ut de hijs Effartis dicantur quieti, qui fuerant ante diem qua Rex illuftris Henricus primus rebus humanis exemptus eft. Si enim de omnibus quocunq; tempore factis vel faciendis quieti effent, liberum videretur Baronibus propter impunitatem nemora fua in quibus Regia forefta confiftit, pro fui arbitrij voluntate fuccidere; quod nequaquam impune poffunt, nifi præcedente Regis confenfu vel principalis Foreftarij. Porro in neceffarios etiam ufus fuæ domus de proprijs

(*x*) L. N. Danegeldum vel Danegeldus.   (*z*) L. R. collatam.
(*y*) L. R. *deeft* etiam.

nemoribus non assumant hij, qui in foresta sua habent Domicilia, nisi per visum eorum qui ad forestæ custodiam deputantur. Verum sunt plures qui suis velint argumentis astruere, quod de Essartis hijs nullus liber sit ratione Sessionis ad Scaccarium. Si quis omnium illic residentium erga Principem quovis delinqueret infortunio, unde pecuniariter puniri mereretur, a pœna illa liber non esset nisi speciali Principis mandato. Cum ergo Essartum factum excessus sit in forestam Regis, non debet, ut dicunt, is (*a*) qui sic delinquit & propter hoc punitur, nisi Regis expresso mandato liberari. Hæc itaque ratio licet subtilis sit, & videatur aliquibus pene sufficiens, obviat tamen illi quod pœna pro Essartis constituta sit & communis in illos, qui sic delinquunt; Ut scilicet pro Essarto jugeris unius triticei solidus unus solvatur; pro jugere vero quo seritur avena, vj d (*b*) jure perpetuo. Ex hijs autem particulis coacta summa quædam exurget, de qua Vicecomes ad Scaccarium respondere tenetur; sicut ex constitutis duobus solidis vel uno per singulas hidas Comitatus summa una quæ communis assisa nuncupatur, excrescit. Quia igitur in hijs (*c*) expressam habet similitudinem Essartum cum Assisa communi, sicut dictum est, videri potuit non immerito similiter quietos habendos illos ab Essartis ut ab alijs communibus Assisis. Item obviat eis consuetudinis ususq; longævi non vilis auctoritas. Sic enim retroactis temporibus fuisse commemorant quibus cana (*d*) memoria est. Vidi ego (*e*) ipse qui loquor tecum temporibus modernis Legrecestriæ comitem Robertum, virum discretum, literis eruditum & in negotijs forensibus exercitatum. Hic ingenitam habens animi virtutem, paternæ quoque prudentiæ æmulator effectus est: cujus industria pluribus examinata est penes *(f)* Principem nostrum Henricum secundum, quem nec palliata prudentia nec dissimulata fallit ineptia; ut (*g*) ex mandato ipsius non solum ad Scaccarium, verum etiam (*h*) per universum regnum Præsidentis dignitatem obtinuerit. Hic semel imminente visitatione nemorum quam Reguardam vulgo dicunt, quæ tertio anno fit, Breve Regis obtinuit, ut quietus esset ab hijs quæ de terra ipsius pro Essartis exigebantur, apposito numero (*i*) qui de his exurgebat: quo delato & lecto ad Scaccarium in publico (*k*) stupebant omnes & mirabantur, dicentes; nonne Comes iste libertatem nostram infirmat? Contuentibus igitur se in-

(*a*) L. R. his.
(*b*) L. R. v d.
(*c*) L. R. *desunt* in hijs.
(*d*) L. R. sana.
(*e*) L. R. ergo ipse.
(*f*) L. N. plene est.
(*g*) L. R. Atq; adeo convaluit penes ejus, ut ex.
(*h*) L. R. *deest* etiam.
(*i*) L. R. apposito non qui.
(*k*) L. N. puplico.

Lib. I.   Dialogus de Scaccario.   395

vicem qui affidebant, exorfus eft fælicis memoriæ Nigellus tunc (*l*) Elienfis Epifcopus, fic inquiens cum modeftia: Domine Comes, irritam feciffe videris per hoc Breve Scaccarij dignitatem, qui mandatum Regis de hijs Rebus impetrafti, a quibus liber es per Seffionem Scaccarij: ac fi confequenter amodo (*m*) per locum a majori debeat inferri; Qui de Effartis Breve Regis non obtinet, folutioni mox obnoxius fiat; fed falva reverentia, pernitiofus eft propter exemplum hic abfolutionis modus. Cum igitur, ut fit in dubijs, quidam fic quidam aliter fentirent, allatus eft in hujus rei validum argumentum, Rotulus annalis de tempore Regis (*n*) illius Magni cujus fupra meminimus, fub quo plurimum floruiffe dicitur dignitas, & fcientia Scaccarij; & (*o*) inventum eft aliquid, quod (*p*) Epifcopo de dignitate refidentium alleganti confonum videbatur: quibus auditis, paulifper deliberans fecum (*q*) Comes, fic ait; Fateor me (*r*) fuper hijs rebus Breve Regis impetraffe; non ut jus veftrum infirmarem, fed ut fic fine moleftia declinarem importunam nimis Regi tamen incognitam alaniorum (*s*) exactionem. Abdicans ergo Breve fuum, per libertatem feffionis præelegit abfolvi. Succedente tempore cum prædictus Epifcopus infirmitate detentus adeffe non poffet, me ipfo fupplente ad Scaccarium vices (*t*) ipfius in quibus poteram, contigit Effarta folvi; cum ergo de dominio ejus exacta folverentur, queftus fum in publicum allegans jus abfolutionis. De communi ergo omnium confilio, & confideratione quæ jam foluta fuerat, mihi reftituta eft fumma, refervans autem, quæ de Dominio fuo provenerant, afcriptitijs ejus quod de quolibet exactum fuerat cum integritate reftitui, ut hujus rei teftis effet fuperftes memoria.

D. Salva Reverentia, non exemplis fed rationibus in hijs utendum eft.

M. Ita eft; fed fit interdum, ut caufæ rerum dictorumq; rationes occultæ fint, & tunc fufficit de his (*u*) exempla (*w*) fubicere, præfertim de viris prudentibus fumpta, quorum opera circumfpecta funt & fine ratione non fiunt. Verum quicquid fuper his (*x*) dixerimus allegantes pro hac libertate vel contra eam, certum habeas quod nihil in hac parte certum dicimus, nifi quod principis auctoritas decreverit obfervandum. Sane Foreftarum ratio, pœna quoq; vel abfolutio de-

(*l*) L. R. *deeft* tunc.
(*m*) L. R. *deeft* amodo.
(*n*) L. R. *defunt* validum argumentum Rotulus annalis de tempore Regis.
(*o*) L. R. *deeft* &.
(*p*) L. R. *deeft* quod.
(*q*) L. R. fecum deliberans.

(*r*) L. R. *deeft* me.
(*s*) *Forfan errore fcribæ, pro* aliquorum *aut fimili vocula.*
(*t*) L. R. *deeft* vices.
(*u*) L. R. hijs.
(*w*) L. N. emfempla.
(*x*) L. R. hijs.

linquen-

linquentium in eas five pecuniaria fuerit five corporalis, feorfum ab alijs Regni judicijs fecernitur, & folius Regis arbitrio vel cujuflibet familiaris ad hoc fpecialiter deputati fubicitur. Legibus quidem proprijs fubfiftit; quas non communi Regni jure, fed voluntaria principum inftitutione fubnixas dicunt; adeo ut quod per legem ejus factum fuerit, non juftum abfolute, fed juftum fecundum legem Foreftæ dicatur. In foreftis etiam penetralia Regum funt, & eorum maximæ deliciæ; ad has enim Venandi caufa curis quandoq; depofitis accedunt, ut modica quiete recreentur (*y*). Illic ferijs fimul, & innatis Curiæ tumultibus omiffis, in naturalis libertatis gratiam pauliſper refpirant; unde fit, ut delinquentes in eam foli Regiæ fubjaceant animadverfioni.

D. Ab ungue primo didici, quod prave prudentis eft ignorantiam pati malle, quam dictorum caufas inquirere; ut ergo de prædictis plenius conftet, aperire non differas quid Forefta fit, & quid Effartum.

XII. *Quid Regis Forefta, & quæ ratio hujus nominis.*

M. Forefta Regis eft tuta ferarum manfio; non quarumlibet fed filveftrium; non quibuflibet in locis fed certis & ad hoc idoneis; unde forefta dicitur, *e* mutata in *o*, quafi Ferefta, hoc eft ferarum ftatio.

D. Nunquid in fingulis Comitatibus Forefta Regis eft?

M. Non; Sed in nemorofis, ubi & ferarum latibula fint & uberrima pafcua: nec intereft cujus fint nemora, five fint Regis, five regni procerum, liberos tamen & indempnes (*z*) habent feræ circumquaque difcurfus

XIII. *Quid Effartum, & quare fic dictum.*

Effarta vero vulgo dicuntur, quæ apud Ifidorum (*a*) occationes (*b*) nominantur; quando fcilicet foreftæ nemora vel dumeta quælibet pafcuis & latibulis opportuna (*c*) fucciduntur; quibus fuccifis, & radicibus avulfis terra fubvertitur & excolitur. Quod fi nemora fic excifa fint, ut fubfiftens quis in vix extante fuccifæ quercus vel alterius arboris ftipite, circumfpiciens V fuccifas viderit, Vaftum reputant, hoc eft, vaftatum per Syncopen fic dictum. Exceffus autem talis etiam in proprijs cujufq; nemoribus factus, adeo gravis dicitur, ut nunquam

(*y*) L. N. recentur.
(*z*) L. R. indemnes.
(*a*) L. N. Yfidorum.
(*b*) L. N. occafiones.
(*c*) L. N. oportuna.

Lib. I. DIALOGUS de SCACCARIO.

inde per feſſionem Scaccarij liberari debeat; ſed magis juxta ſui ſtatus poſſibilitatem pecuniariter puniri. Hactenus de dignitatibus reſidentium ad Scaccarium, quod brevitas ſuccincta permiſit, & menti meæ repente ſe obtulit, utcunq; figuraliter expoſui. Cæterum Regum munificentiæ terminum in hijs quem non tranſgrediatur non conſtituti; proni etiam ſunt omnes propter gratiam ſibi creditam in ſuæ dignitatis gloriam promovenda, qui recte (d) ſapiunt: at ille maxime mundanorum Principum maximus illuſtris Anglorum Rex Henricus ſecundus in augendis dignitatibus ſibi militantium ſemper aſpirat; ſciens pro certo, quod indulta ſuis beneficia nominis ſui gloriam immortalis famæ titulis emercantur. Nunc igitur ad alia currentem calamum convertamus.

D. Conſequens eſt, ni fallor; ſicut ex prædictis videor comperiſſe, ut de Regis ſigillo, & (e) Libro Judiciario proſequaris, quorum primum ſi bene memini in theſauro ſervatur (f) & inde non recedit.

M. Imo & utrumque, ſed & pleraque alia.

XIV. *Quod Theſaurus interdum ipſa pecunia, interdum locus in quo ſervatur.*

Noveris autem Theſaurum quandoq; dici pecuniam ipſam numeratam; vaſa diverſi generis aurea vel argentea, ac veſtimentorum mutatoria. Secundum hanc acceptionem dicitur, Ubi eſt theſaurus tuus, ibi eſt cor tuum. Dicitur enim Theſaurus locus in quo reponitur, unde Theſaurus auri Theſis id eſt (g) poſitio nominatur (h); ut nunc incongrue reſpondeatur quærenti de quolibet ubi ſit, in Theſauro eſt, hoc eſt, ubi Theſaurus reponitur. Numerata quidem pecunia vel alia prædicta ſemel in tuto loco repoſita non efferuntur, niſi cum ex Regis mandato in neceſſarios uſus diſtribuenda ſibi mittantur. Verum plura ſunt in repoſitorijs archis theſauri, quæ circumferuntur, & includuntur & cuſtodiuntur a Theſaurario & Camerarijs, ſicut ſupra plenius oſtenſum eſt: qualia ſunt Sigillum Regis de quo quæris, liber Judicarius, Rotulus qui exactorius dicitur, quem quidem nominant Breve de firmis. Item magni annales, compotorum Rotuli, privilegiorum (i) numeroſa multitudo, receptarum recauta ac Rotuli receptarum, ac Brevia Regis de exitu theſauri, & pleraq; alia quæ conſedente Scaccario cotidianis uſibus neceſſaria ſunt.

(d) L. R. hij præſertim qui recte.
(e) L. R. *deeſt* &.
(f) L. R. ſervabatur.
(g) L. R. *deſunt* id eſt.

(h) *Danda eſt Auctori venia fingenti* Theſaurum *dici quaſi* Theſin auri.
(i) L. N. previlegiorum.

XV. *Qui sit usus Sigilli Regij quod est in Thesauro.*

Usus Sigilli Regij qualis esse debeat ex præmissis constare potest: hoc enim factæ summonitiones & alia pertinentia duntaxat ad Scaccarium Regis mandata signantur; nec effertur alias; sed sicut supra dictum est, a Cancellario custoditur per Vicarium. Expressam autem habet imaginem & inscriptionem cum deambulatorio Curiæ sigillo, ut par cognoscatur utrobiq; jubentis auctoritas, & reus similiter judicetur pro hoc & pro illo, qui secus egerit. Porro liber ille de quo quæris sigilli Regij comes est individuus in Thesauro. Hujus institutionis causam ab Henrico quondam Wintoniensi Episcopo sic accepi.

XVI. *Quid Liber Judiciarius, & ad quid compositus.*

Cum insignis ille subactor Angliæ Rex Willelmus ejusdem Pontificis sanguine propinquus, ulteriores Insulæ fines suo subjugasset imperio, & rebellium mentes terribilium perdomuisset exemplis; ne libera de cætero daretur erroris facultas, decrevit subjectum sibi populum juri scripto Legibusq; subicere. Propositis igitur (*k*) Legibus Anglicanis secundum tripartitam (*l*) earum distinctionem, hoc est Merchenelage (*m*), Denelage (*n*), Westsaxenelage, quasdam reprobavit, quasdam autem approbans, illis transmarinas Neutriæ (*o*) leges, quæ ad Regni pacem tuendam efficacissime videbantur, adjecit. Demum ne quid deesse videretur (*p*) ad omnem totius providentiæ summam communicato consilio, discretissimos a latere suo destinavit viros per Regnum in circuitu. Ab hijs (*q*) itaq; totius terræ descriptio diligens facta est, tam in nemoribus, quam pascuis & pratis, nec non & agriculturis, & verbis communibus annotata in librum redacta est; ut videlicet quilibet jure suo contentus, alienum non usurpet impune. Fit autem descriptio per Comitatus, per Centuriatas, & per Hidas (*r*), prænotato in ipso capite Regis nomine, ac deinde seriatim aliorum procerum nominibus appositis secundum status sui dignitatem, qui videlicet de Rege tenent in Capite. Apponuntur autem singulis numeri secundum ordinem sic dispositis, per quos inferius in ipsa libri serie, quæ ad eos pertinent, facilius occurrunt (*s*). Hic liber ab indigenis Domesdei (*t*) nuncu-

(*k*) L. R. *deest* igitur.
(*l*) L. N. tripertitam.
(*m*) L. N. Merchenlage.
(*n*) L. R. *deest* Denelage.
(*o*) *Legendum* Neustriæ.

(*p*) L. N. videtur.
(*q*) L. R. his.
(*r*) L. N. & Hidas.
(*s*) L. R. occurrant.
(*t*) L. R. Domesdai.

patur,

patur, id est, dies judicij per Metaphoram (*u*); Sicut enim districti & terribilis examinis illius novissimi sententia nulla tergiversationis arte valet eludi: Sic (*w*) cum orta fuerit in regno contentio de his (*x*) rebus quæ (*y*) illic annotantur; cum ventum fuerit ad Librum, sententia ejus infatuari non potest vel impune declinari. Ob hoc nos eundem librum Judiciarium nominavimus; non (*z*) quod in eo de propositis aliquibus dubijs feratur sententia; sed quod ab eo sicut a prædicto judicio non licet ulla ratione discedere.

D. Quid Comitatus, quid Centuriata, vel quid sit Hida, si placet edissere; alioquin plana non erunt quæ præmissa sunt.

XVII. *Quid Hida, quid Centuriata, quid Comitatus, secundum Vulgarem Opinionem.*

M. Ruricolæ melius hoc norunt; verum (*a*) sicut ab ipsis accepimus, Hida a primitiva institutione ex centum acris constat: Hundredus vero ex Hydarum aliquot centenarijs, sed non determinatis; quidam enim ex pluribus, quidam (*b*) ex paucioribus Hidis constat. Hinc hundredum in veteribus Regum Anglorum privilegijs centuriatam nominari frequenter invenies. Comitatus autem eadem lege ex hundredis constant (*c*), hoc est quidam ex pluribus quidam ex paucioribus, secundum quod divisa est Terra per viros discretos. Comitatus igitur a Comite dicitur, vel Comes a Comitatu. Comes autem est qui tertiam portionem eorum quæ de placitis proveniunt in quolibet Comitatu (*d*) percipit. Summa namq; illa quæ nomine firmæ requiritur a Vicecomite, tota non exurgit (*e*) ex fundorum redditibus, sed ex magna parte de placitis provenit; & horum tertiam partem Comes percipit; qui ideo sic dici dicitur, quia fisco socius est & comes in percipiendis. Porro Vicecomes dicitur (*ee*), quia vicem Comitis suppleat

(*u*) L. N. Methaforam.
(*w*) L. R. *deest* Sic.
(*x*) L. R. hijs.
(*y*) L. R. *deest* quæ.
(*z*) L. R. *deest* non.
(*a*) L. R. veruntamen sicut.
(*b*) L. N. quædam.
(*c*) L. R. constat.
(*d*) L. N. Comitatu quolibet.
(*e*) L. R. exivit.
(*ee*) Vicecomes *dicebatur, eo quod vices* Comitis *gerebat. Quo autem sensu sive respectu gerebat, id quidem dubium est. Eruditus Dialogi auctor hic dicit,* Vicecomitem Comitis vices supplere in placitis illis in quibus Comes ratione dignitatis suæ [cum Rege] *participat; & inde* Vicecomitis *nomen sumpsisse innuit. Illum e recentioribus pleriq; secuti sunt. Sed fas est rem denuo perpendere. Profecto verum est,* Vicecomitem placita Comitatus cujus erat Vicecomes tenere solitum. *Tenuitne autem illa placita vice vel loco* Comitis? *Proculdubio vice Regis; utpote habens* Comitatus curam & custodiam sibi, a Rege ipso commissam. *Etenim in* Anglia Vicecomes *minister erat Regis, nequaquam Comitis. Verum utiq; est,*

suppleat in placitis illis, quibus Comes ex suæ dignitatis ratione participat.

D. Nun-

est, Tertium denarium *placitorum Comitatus, Comiti tum cum crearetur Comes, a Rege concedi solitum; Qui* Tertius denarius *a modernis usitato vocatus est Anglice* Creation-money. *Participatne autem Comes ratione dignitatis suæ in placitis Comitatus cum Rege, ut Cl. auctor hic innuit?* Dubito. *Una duntaxat instantia mihi in veteribus membranis, quantum memini, occurrit, in qua* Tertius denarius *Comitis dicitur* pars sua Comitatus. *Ea instantia est in persona Comitis* Patricij; *& sic se habet:* Wiltescira. Comes Patricius r c de xxxviij l & ix s & iij d Bl. de veteri firma: Comiti Patricio xxij l & xvj s & vij d de parte sua Comitatus, numero: Et in respectu per Regem hoc anno, per Warinum filium Geroldi, xviij l Bl. Et habet de superplus xxiiij s & vij d Bl. Et idem Vicecomes r c de Nova firma: In thesauro &c. Et in tertio denario Comitatus Comiti Patricio, xxij l & xvj s & vij d per breve Regis —. *Mag. Rot.* 3. *Hen.* 2. *Rot.* 3. *a. Quid hinc sequitur? Comes sane eatenus cum Rege participare dicatur, quatenus is partem unam placitorum Comitatus nempe* Tertiam *habet,* & Rex aliam, *scilicet duas* Tertias; *participat, inquam; sed forsan non ratione Dignitatis suæ. Plane enim largitione Regia* Tertius denarius *Comiti obtigit: ideoq; interdum appellatur* Annuum feodum Comitatus; *tanquam si esset donarium ex gratia Regis. De hoc vide, si placet, Historiam Scacc. cap.* 23. *Sect.* 2. *ad annum* 13. *E.* 1, Et Isabellæ sorori; *ac ibid. ad ann.* 26. *E.* 1, Petitio Hugonis de Courteney. *Et quidem ex eo quod* Tertius denarius *Vicecomitis manu Comiti solutus fuit, non est quod illum hujus substitutum credamus. Quinetiam meminisse oportet, aliquoties eundem fuisse, si Regi visum,* Comitatus & Comitem & Vicecomitem. *Verbi gratia.* Anno 2º R. Henrici II, Ricardus Comes Devoniæ *fuit ejusdem Comitatus Vicecomes Regis:* Ricardus Comes r c de firma de Devenescira. *Mag. Rot.* 2. *H.* 2. *Rot.* 10. *a.* Anno 4º ac etiam 5º R. Henrici II, Patricius Comes Saresberiæ *sive* Wiltescire *fuit* Vicecomes *seu* Regis Firmarius Wiltescire: Comes Patricius reddit compotum de firma de Wiltescira. — Et in tertio denario Comitatus Comiti Patricio, xxij l & xvj s & vij d; *Mag. Rot.* 4. *H.* 2. *Rot.* 2. *a.* Comes Patricius r c de firma de Wiltescira. — Et in tertio denario Comitatus Comiti Patricio, xxij l & xvj s & vij d; *Mag. Rot.* 5. *H.* 2. *Rot.* 6. *a.* Anno quarto & quinto R. Ricardi I, Galfridus filius Petri Comes Essexiæ *fuit* Vicecomes Essexiæ & Hurtfordscire, *priorisq; duorum Comitatuum Tertio denario potitus est:* Galfridus filius Petri, Ricardus de Heriet pro eo, reddit compotum de xlv l & ij s & vj d Bl. de Veteri firma de Essexa & de Hurtfordscira: In thesauro liberavit, Et Quietus est: Et idem de Nova firma: In thesauro *summam illam;* — Et Galfrido filio Petri xl l & x s & x d numero, in tertio denario Comitatus; Et ipsi Vicecomiti xviij l & xj s & xj d in Villa de Hurtford, pro custodia Castelli de Hurtford; &c. *Mag. Rot.* 4. *R.* 1. *Rot.* 1. *a. Mag. Rot.* 5. *R.* 1. *Rot.* 1. *a. m.* 1. *tit.* Essexa & Hurtfordscira *in totidem verbis.* Anno octavo R. Ricardi I, Willelmus Comes Saresberiæ *fuit* Vicecomes Regius Wiltescire: Willelmus Comes Sar[esberiæ], Tomas filius Willelmi pro eo, reddit compotum de firma de Wiltescira: In thesauro *summam illam* &c. *Mag. Rot.* 8. *R.* 1. *Rot.* 2. *a.* Anno nono R. Henrici III, Willelmus de Warenna Comes Surreiæ *fuit illius Comitatus Vicecomes:* Willelmus de Warenna Comes Surreiæ, Willelmus de Mara ut Custos pro eo, reddit compotum de C & Lxxiiij l & v.j s Bl. de firma Comitatus; *Mag. Rot.* 9. *H.* 3. *Rot.* 3. *a. m.* 1. Surreia: *Idemq; anno decimo:* Willelmus de Warenna Comes Surreiæ, Willelmus de Mara ut Custos pro eo, reddit compotum de C & Lxxiiij l & vij s Bl. de firma Comitatus; *Mag. Rot.* 10. *H.* 3. *Rot.* — *m.* 1. *a.* Surreia. *Anno undecimo (aliisq; annis)* R. Henrici III, Hubertus de Burgo Comes Kantiæ *fuit illius Comitatus Vicecomes:* Hubertus de Burgo, Willelmus Brito ut Custos pro eo, reddit compotum de *summa illa,* de firma Comitatis: — Et H. de Burgo Comiti Kantiæ L l, de Tertio denario Comitatus, per breve Regis; *Mag. Rot.* 11. *H.* 3.

D. Nunquid ex singulis Comitatibus Comites ista percipiunt?

M. (f)

H. 3. Rot. — a. m. 1. *tit.* Kantia. *Anno* 52° *&* 53° *R.* Henrici III, Edwardus *filius Regis primogenitus (paucis post annis Rex* Angliæ*) fuit Vicecomes Comitatuum* Buckinghamiæ *&* Bedefordiæ. Edwardus *filius* Regis Primogenitus, Bartholomæus le Joevene *subvicecomes suus pro eo, reddit compotum de CCC* Lxxix l xix s xj d B!, *& de* Cviij l *numero de firma Comitatuum:* Et *de [eisdem summis] de eadem, de anno præterito; Mag. Rot.* 53. *H.* 3. *Buk. & Bedef. m.* 1. *b.* Non est autem, opinor, quod credamus Dominum Edwardum hæredem Coronæ Angliæ *(ut vocamus) apparentem cujusvis Comitis substitutum fuisse. Huc etiam referri possunt Vicecomites in feodo sive Hæreditarij. Quorum singulis non est immorandum. Ex his similibusq; instantijs credibile videatur, Vicecomitem fuisse Regis, non Comitis, Vicarium. Mitto autem de Comite ulterius loqui. Ad Vicecomitem redeo; de ejus nomine & officio pauca dicturus.*

Quas vocabuli, Vicecomes, *explicationes afferunt Glossaristæ omitto hic recensere. Ipsos Lector si placuerit per otium consulat. Libet hic de ea re conjecturam subjungere, quam nostratium nemo hactenus quod sciam proposuit; Lectoris tamen judicio permittendam. Dicitur igitur* Vicecomes, *eo quod vice fungitur* Comitis, *id est* Principis. *Notandum inprimis est, quod nonnullarum regionum supremi Rectores antiquitus erant* Comites, *sicut* Angliæ *antiquitus hodieq;* Reges: Normanniæ *enim compluriumq; aliarum regionum* Principes, Comitum *subinde ac* Ducum *subinde titulo insigniti erant; uti in illarum regionum historia veteri videre est. Ab illis Comitibus, ad quasdam regionis suæ provincias tuendas regundasque, ab antiquo instituti officiarij magna potestate donati; qui quoniam* Comitem *id est* Principem *suum in sua quisq; provincia repræsentabant, ejusq; vices gerebant,* Vicecomites *dicti. Hanc explicationem quasi disertis verbis supportant Annalium* Flandrensium *scriptores. Illi testantur* Flandriæ *Principes antiquos instituisse nonnulla officia hæreditaria, feudisq; annexisse; Quædam scilicet ad peragenda servitia hic inferius memorata; & quædam ad justitiam subditis ministrandam; Quod genus erat* Vicecomitum; *qui ita dicti eo quod illis* Comites *[sive* Principes*] in Burgis arcibusq; moderandis vices suas permiserant, alijs insuper privilegijs ac potestatibus, quales erant* Castellanorum *&c. additis. Verba ipsa ex* Annalibus Belgicis *hic reponam:* Curiæ Feudales Comitis [Flandriæ]. Vetus Burgum Gandense, Burgum Brugense &c, Castellum Duacense, Curtracense &c. Pierron sive Puteal Alostanum &c. Domus Teneramundana &c. Sala Yprensis, Insulana. Territorium Wasium. Curia Harlebecana, Tiletana, Balliolana. —— Burgum sive πύργον *turrim instructam* Græci *vocant.* —— *Enimvero feudis annexa officia ut ad hæredes transferrentur olim* Flandriæ Principes *(antequam in* Burgundiæ Austriæq; *nomen concessere) instituerunt: Quædam ad jus cuiq; suum reddendum designata. Hic inter alios comprehenduntur* Vicecomites: *hoc est, quibus* Comites *in burgorum arciumve moderamine vices suas additis privilegijs atq; commodis permittebant. Unde etiam* Castellani *dicebantur. Alia ad rationes reditu q; principis domesticos* ——. *Quædam ad servitia domestica* ——. *Alia ad rem militarem. Huc pertinet* Conestablius. *Ad præcedentia reducitur* Hamyrallus ἡ Θαλασσίαρχ⊙ — *atq;* Marescalcus *&c.* Adriani Barlandi *& aliorum* De rebus Belgij memorabil. *p.* 77. *Neq; vero in* Flandria *solum, sed in alijs etiam regionibus, puta in* Normannia *&c. eodem fere modo se res habuit: quod scilicet* Vicecomes Comitis *seu* Principis *vices gessit. Adde, quod* Vicecomitis *quam supra ex* Barlando *posui descriptio ad amussim convenit antiquo apud* Anglos Vicecomitis *officio, quale post* Conquestum Normannicum *fuit: nam* Vicecomiti Anglico, *ex antiquo more non* Comitatus *tantum custodia, sed & juris dicundi & capella Regia tutandi cura a* Rege *committi solita; sicut in præcedenti historia mea compluribus exemplis monstratum est. Similis etiam fuit in* Normannia *mos. Ibi quidam Judices erant qui* Vicecomites

M. (*f*) Nequaquam : sed hij tantum ista percipiunt, quibus Regum munificentia obsequij præstiti, vel eximiæ probitatis intuitu Comites sibi creat, & ratione dignitatis illius hæc conferenda decernit, quibusdam hæreditarie quibusdam personaliter.

XVIII. *Quid Rotulus Exactorius?*

Rotulus exactorius ille est, in quo distincte satis & diligenter annotantur firmæ Regis, quæ ex singulis Comitatibus exurgunt, cujus summa minui quidem non potest, sed per operosam Justiciarij (*g*) diligentiam frequenter augetur. Reliquorum (*h*) ratio, scilicet Anna-

mites *dicebantur, testante* Duareno : — quem [*scil.* Judicem] etiam vocat Comitem; quod nomen est Officij: Hinc Vicecomitis nomen; & in Normandia quidam Judices adhuc Vicecomites dicuntur; Duaren. *in Consuetudd. Feud. c.* 20. *Sect.* 3. *Quod ad* Anglos; *Vicecomitis officium (quale nimirum post* Conquestum *fuit) a* Normannis *in* Angliam *invectum arbitror: nomine* Vicecomitis *una cum ipso officio a* Comitum *dominijs ad* Regum *facile translato. Temporibus sane* Anglosaxonicis *ea regionis apud* Anglos *divisio dicta erat* Scipe *seu* Scira, *quæ postmodum* Anglonormannis, Comitatus. *Fuitq; apud* Anglosaxones *officialis* Scipe-ʒepeɼa *dictus seu* Sciræ *præfectus aut præfectus* Regius; *cui scilicet Rex Sciræ custodiam vel præfecturam commisit. Isti quodammodo successit post* Conquestum Vicecomes; *at potestate, ni fallor, & officij genere longe diverso; sicut ex utriusq; officij comparatione liquere poterit. Mutato tamen officio, remansit antiquum nomen* Shireve, *simulq; locum obtinuit* Normannicum *nomen* Vicecomes.

Juvabit hic paucula profari de modo Vicecomitis constituendi; eoq; potius propterea, quod quidam auctores minus recte de ea re scripserunt. Post Conquestum Normannicum *Vicecomites Comitatuum a Rege pro suo arbitrio constituti: Quidam ad quartam anni partem, quidam ad semiannum; alij (idque usitatissime) ad annum unum, alij de anno in annum ad annos simul complusculos, quin & alij nonnulli (si Regi placuerit) jure hæreditario. Item alijs com-*

missi sunt Comitatus tanquam Firmarijs, *alijs tanquam* Custodibus *sive (ut vocabant)* Appruatoribus. *Singuli autem Regi immediate subjecti ac respondentes erant. Nec mirum; nam Regiorum proventuum principales Collectores, Justiciarij Regis Itinerantes ad placita terminanda, tallagia assidenda &c, simulq; Castrorum Regis Custodes, & Maneriorum ejus Curatores, fere consueverunt esse in suis quiq; Comitatibus. Quare falsus mihi videtur doctissimus* H. Spelmanus, *inquiens* (in Glossario, *ad vocem,* Vicecomes, *p.* 555, col. 1.) *Vicecomites antiquitus eligi solitos a Liberis hominibus in Curia Comitatus, haud secus ac hodie solent Milites Parliamentarij. Nam plane res longe aliter comparata fuit post* Conquestum Normannicum. *A quo tempore, Vicecomites Comitatuum universos a Rege solo constitutos agnovimus; nisi si quibus Regia gratia indultum fuit, ut suos ipsi Vicecomites eligerent sicut in* Londonia *fiebat. Hoc fere modo constituebantur Vicecomites Comitatuum, donec statutis quibusdam (puta, statuto* Lincolniæ *anni noni R.* Edwardi II, *ac statutis anni* 14 *R.* Edwardi III, *cap.* 7, *& anni* 12 *R.* Ricardi II, *cap.* 2.) *decerneretur eos a Consiliarijs Regis nominatos fore ad Scaccarium in* Craftino Animarum *quovis anno; a Rege ipso postmodum eligendos ac constituendos. Qui mos hodieq; permanet.*

(*f*) L. N. *deest* M.
(*g*) L. R. Justiciariorum.
(*h*) L. N. Relicorum.

lium

lium Rotulorum, & aliorum quorum supra meminimus, quæ in Thesauro sunt & inde non recedunt, ex prædictis satis liquet. Restat igitur ut ad majores & magis necessarias institutiones Scaccarij convertamur, in quibus ut prædictum est excellentior est & utilior & a pluribus remotior Scaccarij scientia.

Explicit liber Primus.

Incipiunt

Incipiunt Capitula Secundi Libri.

I. *Ex quibus & qualiter & ad quid fiunt Summonitiones.*
II. *Quæ sit differentia Summonitionum utriusq; Termini.*
III. *De agendis Vicecomitis multipliciter.*
IV. *Quibus de causis absentia Vicecomitis valeat excusari.*
V. *Quid sit quosdam fundos dari Bl[ancos] quosdam numero.*
VI. *Quæ sunt (i) Vicecomiti computanda. Elemosinæ (k) scilicet, Decimæ, Liberationes utriusq; generis, & Terræ datæ.*
VII. *Quæ sunt (l) per solam consuetudinem Scaccarij Vicecomiti computanda, hoc est sine brevi.*
VIII. *Quo ordine computanda sunt Vicecomiti quæ in operibus missa sunt per breve Regis numero non determinans.*
IX. *Quod non absolvitur quis (m) per breve Regis numerum non habens (n), etiamsi causam determinet.*
X. *De excidentibus & occupatis, quæ (o) usitatius dicimus de Purpresturis & Escaetis.*
XI. *De censu nemorum, qualiter de his compoti fieri debeant.*
XII. *De Placitis & Conventionibus quo ordine de hijs (p) compoti fiant cum exacta solvuntur.*
XIII. *De distinctione (q) personarum quæ solvendo non sunt; de quibus autem Vicecomitis fides (r) offertur, & sub quo tenore Verborum detur.*
XIV. *Quæ Catella debitorum vendenda sint (s) cum ipsi non solvunt, & quis in vendendis ordo sit observandus.*
XV. *Quod Vicecomes a Debitoribus debitoris illius qui Regis non solvit debita, Regis summam prius suscipiat.*
XVI. *Quod Vicecomes a fundis ejus, qui non solvit, quod requiritur percipiet, etiamsi eosdem, ex quo Regi teneri cœpit quomodolibet alienaverit (t).*
XVII. *Quod non licet Vicecomiti debitam sibi pecuniam a non solventibus suscipere, & quid sit agendum si forte susceperit.*

(i) L. N. sit.
(k) L. R. *deest* Elemosinæ.
(l) L. N. sit.
(m) L. N. quis autem debet.
(n) L. N. habente.
(o) L. N. quod.
(p) L. R. his.
(q) L. R. destinatione.
(r) L. R. de quibus a Vicecomite fides.
(s) L. R. sunt.
(t) L. R. alienavit.

XVIII.	*Qualiter vir pro uxore, vel uxor pro viro convenienaa, cum ille vel illa solvendo non est.*
XIX.	*Quod non sit idem modus coertionis Baronum Regis (u) & aliorum in pœnis pecuniarijs.*
XX.	*Quid faciendum, cum Oeconomus (w), qui fidem dedit de satisfaciendo, non comparet.*
XXI.	*Quid cum veniens non satisfacit, si Miles est, & quid si non Miles.*
XXII.	*Qualiter ipse Dominus puniendus est qui sponte Militem exposuit ut possit (x) interim liberari.*
XXIII.	*Quid de sponte offerentibus faciendum, cum & ipsi non solvunt.*
XXIV.	*Quid de Relevijs (y) sponte non solutis (z).*
XXV.	*Quid de avibus ablatis faciendum, & quo tempore summonendæ.*
XXVI.	*De auro Reginæ.*
XXVII.	*Quod aliter de firmis, aliter de custodijs respondendum, & sub alio tenore fides danda.*
XXVIII.	*Quod fides Vicecomitis semel data (a) de legitimo compoto sufficiat per universum.*

Incipit Liber Secundus.

AUDI me, frater, & auribus audiendi percipe quæ loquor tibi. Non pœnitebit te modicum tempus ereptum otijs impendere velle negotijs. Sunt enim nonnulli, qui non (b) erubescunt dicere in cordibus suis, qui apponit scientiam, apponit & dolorem Hijs onerosa (c) est doctrina & jocundum decipere. Propter hoc ab hijs longe facta est veritas, qui metuentes jocundum disciplinæ laborem incident in errorem. Fiunt igitur cæci corde, viarumq; pericula non videntes pronis gressibus in præcipitium ruunt. Verum te, frater, nullus dies otiosum inveniat; ne (d) te forte vacantem (e) pessimis quibusq; subjiciat (f) pronior in malum infirmitatis humanæ conditio. Quod si forte tibi nulla sunt (g) honesta tamen finge negotia; ut semper exercitatus animus expeditior sit ad doctrinam. Hijs igitur

(u) L. R. Regis Baronum.
(w) L. N. Economus.
(x) L. R. *desunt* ut possit.
(y) L. N. Relevio.
(z) L. N. soluto.
(a) L. R. data est.

(b) L. N. *deest* non.
(c) L. N. honerosa.
(d) L. N. nec te.
(e) L. N. vocantem.
(f) L. N. subiciat.
(g) L. R. sint.

negotijs

negotijs in quæ nos impegisti paulisper attende; non ut ex eis magnos (*h*) laboris metas fructus, sed tantum ne [sis] otiosus.

D. Vereor ne instantis noctis crepusculum præcipitem imponat finem negotijs, & omissis pluribus necessarijs acceleres, ut careas importutitate quærentis.

M. Imo ego magis veritus sum, ne te post longa silentia, propter agrestem stilum, diu suppressus cachinnus succuteret, vel forte tacitus tecum pertractasses, qualiter sine nostra molestia ab his (*i*) avelli posses, ad quæ nos coegisti. Ob hoc fateor me finem intempestivum pene posuisse dicendis: sed tamen cum docilis sis & in te nondum tepuerit attentionis industria (*k*) cœpto ferar itinere. Ut igitur dispositæ rationis ordini satisfiat, de summonitionibus primo loco dicendum est: ex quibus scilicet & qualiter, & ad quid fiant. Atq; ut de his tibi plenius constet, sit trium præmonstrandorum, primo, prius, ultimum, hoc est, ad quid fiant.

Fiunt autem summonitiones, ut Scaccarium fiat.

Præcedente namque brevi summonitionis, quod Regiæ auctoritatis (*l*) signatur imagine, convocantur ad locum nominatum qui necessarij sunt; nec enim necesse habent accedere, nisi summonitione præmissa. Accedent autem quidam ut sedeant & judicent (*m*), quidam ut solvant & judicentur. Sedent & judicant ex officio vel ex principis mandato Barones quorum supra meminimus. Solvunt autem & judicantur Vicecomites & alij plures in regno, quorum quidam voluntarijs oblationibus quidam necessarijs solutionibus obnoxij sunt, de quibus infra plenius dicemus in agendis Vicecomitis. Horum itaq; cum per omnes Comitatus numerosa sit multitudo, oportet in ipsa citatione emissa de singulis seriatim exprimi, quantum in instanti termino solvi debeat, adjecta etiam causa; ut si (*n*) dicatur, de illo habeas hanc vel illam summam (*o*), propter hanc vel hanc causam. Quod si autem residente ad compotum Vicecomite, requiratur aliquid de quovis debitore qui sit in Comitatu suo, de quo tamen in summonitione nulla fuit (*p*) mentio, non tenebitur respondere; sed magis excusabitur; quia non præcessit hujus rei summonitio. Ad

(*h*) L. N. magni.
(*i*) L. R. hijs.
(*k*) L. N. attentionis materia.
(*l*) L. N. auctoritas.
(*m*) L. R. ut sed judicent.
(*n*) L. N. ut sit.
(*o*) L. N. *deest* summam.
(*p*) L. N. nullam fiat.

hoc ergo summonitiones fiunt (*q*), ut firmæ Regis & debita multiplici ratione requirenda fisco proveniant. Verum sunt aliqua, quæ per manum Vicecomitis provenire necesse est, etiamsi nulla de his (*r*) summonitio fiat; sed (*s*) hæc magis casualia sunt quam constituta vel certa, sicut ex consequentibus liquebit.

Qualiter Summonitiones fiant.

Qualiter autem vel quo ordine fiant, primo dicendum est, ac demum ex quibus. Noveris autem (*t*) quod soluto Scaccario termini illius quo fiunt summonitiones, excipiuntur a clericis Thesaurarij debita Regis per singulos Comitatus a Magno Rotulo illius anni, & in brevioribus annotantur, simul (*u*) cum causis, quo facto secedunt (*w*) hij in partem quos majores diximus, præposito Comitatu quolibet, & de singulis debitoribus illius decernunt quantum summoneri (*x*) debeat, habita consideratione secundum qualitatem personæ, & secundum qualitatem negotij & causæ pro qua Regi tenetur. Auctenticus (*y*) etiam Annalis Rotulus a quo debita excepta sunt, tenetur a (*z*) Thesaurario vel ejus clerico, ne forte fuerit in excipiendo quomodolibet erratum (*a*). Est etiam alius Clericus, qui quod illi taxaverint in exceptis annotat studiose; de quibus Summonitio fit per hæc verba. H. (*b*) Rex Anglorum, illi vel illi Vicecomiti salutem. Vide sicut te-ipsum & omnia tua diligis, quod sis ad Scaccarium ibi vel ibi, in crastino Sancti Michaelis, vel in crastino clausi Paschæ, & habeas ibi tecum, quicquid debes de (*c*) veteri firma vel nova, & nominatim hæc debita subscripta; de illo x marcas pro hac causa, & sic deinceps. Annotatis autem omnibus debitis illic seriatim cum causis, quæ in majori Annali Rotulo continentur, proferuntur minores quiq; Perambulantium Judicum (*d*) Rotuli, ex quibus excipiuntur quæ in singulis Comitatibus domino Regi debentur, labore & industria ipsorum (*e*); & hijs taxatis a Majoribus, in Summonitionibus annotantur; quibus ordine (*f*) digestis, terminatur summonitio per hæc verba: Et hæc omnia tecum habeas in (*g*) denarijs taleis & brevibus & quietantijs,

(*q*) L. N. fuerit.
(*r*) L. R. de hijs nulla.
(*s*) L. N. fet.
(*t*) L. R. *deest* autem.
(*u*) L. R. similiter cum.
(*w*) L. N. secederit.
(*x*) L. R. Summonitioni debeat.
(*y*) L. N. Autenticus.
(*z*) L. N. tenetur autem Thes.
(*a*) L. N. erratam.
(*b*) L. N. N. Rex.
(*c*) L. N. *deest* de.
(*d*) L. N. Judicij.
(*e*) L. R. ipsarum.
(*f*) L. R. per ordinem.
(*g*) L. R. & denarijs.

vel capientur de firma tua ; Teste illo vel illo, ibi ad Scaccarium. Fuerunt tamen qui crederent dicendum in denarijs vel taleis vel brevibus vel quietancijs; non intelligentes *vel* quandoq; subdisjunctive poni. Superflua tamen est hujusmodi de verbis contentio, cum de eorum intellectu constiterit : sive enim dixeris in denarijs vel brevibus vel quietancijs, vel in denarijs & brevibus & quietancijs, idem est intellectus; ut scilicet in hijs omnibus vel eorum aliquibus, satisfiat de his (*h*) quæ in Summonitione continentur. Præterea, quia novis morbis per nova remedia decet subveniri (*i*), additum fuit in Summonitionibus hoc subscriptum, ex novella constitutione, hoc est post (*k*) tempora Regis Henrici primi : Quod si forte de alicujus debito sommonitus es, qui terram vel catalla non habet (*l*) in baillia (*m*) tua, & noveris in cujus baillia (*n*) vel Comitatu habuerit ; tu ipse Vicecomiti illi vel ballivo per breve tuum hoc ipsum significes, deferente illud aliquo a te misso, qui ei breve tuum in Comitatu, si potest, vel coram pluribus liberet. Hæc quæ prædiximus (*o*) apponere, ridiculosa satis & dispendiosa quorundam subterfugia compulerunt. Cognito enim quibus determinatis Summonitiones emittebantur, antequam pervenisset ad Comitatum summonitorio de debito suo, vacuatis horreis & pecunijs suis quocunq; sibi distractis (*p*) vel ad loca tuta translatis, vacuus in domo sua residens, Vicecomitis & cæterorum officialium securus expectabat adventum ; & hac arte plurimis annis Regiæ Summonitionis auctoritas non sine dispendio videbatur eludi. Ille enim, ad quem cum facultatibus suis metus hujus causa transierat cum inde mandatum non haberet in res suas manum mittere non præsumebat. Hac ergo consideratione per aliquot annos in Summonitionibus appositum fuit verbum quod præmissum est ; nec postea alicui patuit locus subterfugij, quin satisfaciat omnis debitor per omnem modum, nisi quem sola suprema excusat inopia. Cum autem jam omnibus Vicecomitibus & debitoribus constituisset quia sic sophisticæ poterant importunitates determinari, non oportuit amplius illud verbum apponi, nec apponitur : modus tamen ille qui dictus est coercionis debitorum quacumq; se transtulerint, perseverat apud Vicecomites, & quasi quodam jure perpetuo constitutus servatur (*q*).

(*h*) L. R. ut scilicet unde in his quæ in Summon.
(*i*) L. R. subvenire.
(*k*) L. N. per tempora.
(*l*) L. N. habent.
(*m*) L. R. ballia.
(*n*) L. R. ballia.
(*o*) L. N. prædicimus.
(*p*) L. N. districtis.
(*q*) L. R. conservatur.

D. Audivi

D. Audivi jamdudum referentibus multis, quod bis (*r*) in anno Scaccarium convocetur, hic est in termino Paschæ & in termino S^{ti} Michaelis. Dixisti etiam si bene memini, nisi præmisis summonitionibus Scaccarium (*s*) non teneri. Cum ergo Summonitiones ad utrumq; terminum fiant, rogo te, si placet, aperias, si in utrisq; Summonitionibus lex una servetur, vel, si in (*t*) verborum tenore dissonantia est, quæ sit, & quare sic (*u*).

II. *Quæ sit differentia summonitionum utriusq; termini.*

M. Magnum tuæ provectionis est argumentum quod super hijs jam (*w*) nosti dubitare. Porro certo certius est, quod bis (*x*) Scaccarium in anno convocatur & tenetur; Præcedentibus tamen, ut prædictum est, summonitionibus. Terminorum utriusq; sessionis satis bene meministi. Sed (*y*) attende, quod in termino Paschæ a Vicecomitibus non compoti sed quidam visus compotorum fiunt; unde pene nihil eorum quæ illic tunc geruntur scripturæ commendatur; sed totum reservatur alij termino; tunc diligenter in Magno annali Rotulo singula per ordinem annotentur; tamen quædam Memoranda quæ frequenter incidunt (*z*) a clerico Thesaurarij seorsum conscribuntur; ut soluto Scaccario illius termini de hijs discernant Majores; quæ quidem non facile propter numerosam sui multitudinem, nisi scripto commendarentur (*a*), occurrerent. Insuper quid Vicecomes in Thesauro solverit de firmis; ac deinde si satisfacit (*b*), in eadem linea scribitur, & quietus est: si non, debitum ejus in inferiori linea distincte ponitur, ut sciatur, quantum de summa illius termini desit; & statim satisfaciat ad arbitrium Præsidentium. Quilibet enim Vicecomes medietatem firmæ illius quæ de suo Comitatu per annum exurgit, in termino illo soluturus est. Noveris autem, quod in hijs summonitionibus tenor verborum non mutatur nisi quod ad terminum pertinet vel locum (*c*); si scilicet decreverint Majores alias tenendum Scaccarium Paschæ, & alias Scaccarium Sancti Michaelis; sed eadem virtute verborum in utrisq; Summonitionibus servata. Dissimilis est debitorum exceptorum annotatio. In summonitione namq; contra

(*r*) L. N. vis in anno.
(*s*) L. N. Scaccarij.
(*t*) L. R. *deest* in.
(*u*) L. R. *deest* sic.
(*w*) L. N. hijs omnia nosti.
(*x*) L. N. vis.

(*y*) L. N. set.
(*z*) L. N. incident.
(*a*) L. N. commendaretur.
(*b*) L. R. satisfiet.
(*c*) L. R. vel ad locum.

terminum Paschæ facta, quod tunc annus ille dicitur initiari, simpliciter dicetur de illo, habeas x; & de hac summonitione non nisi solvendo tunc vel satisfaciendo de x absolvetur. Ac cum facienda est Summonitio de termino S^ti Michaelis in quo clauditur & terminatur idem annus, & fit annalis Rotulus, addetur prædictis x aliæ (*d*) x, vel plura, sicut Præsidentibus (*e*) visum fuerit, & dicetur; de illo habeas xx (*f*) qui tamen termino Paschæ de hac ipsa summa x (*g*) solverat (*h*) sed solvens x in denarijs nunc, & proferens taleam de x jamdudum (*i*) solutis, absolvi merebitur a summonitione: dictum est enim in Summonitione, Hæc omnia (*k*) habeas in denarijs & brevibus & taleis. Noveris præterea, quod facta summonitione, si dum corrigitur inventus fuerit error, non debet subducta linea cancellari, sed nec abradi, quia patens (*l*) scriptura est: imo potius, in quo erratum fuerit, debet penitus obliterari, ut quid scriptum fuerat (*m*) nulli pateat; cujus rei causa, si tecum super hijs (*n*) actitaveris, facile tibi valet occurrere.

D. Cum sicut commemoras patens (*o*) sit illud scriptum, & sic Vicecomiti destinetur, & per longa tempora penes ipsum suosq; resideat, soli fidei ejus summonitionis indemnitas (*p*) committitur (*q*). Posset enim, quod vellet impune delere mutare vel minuere (*r*), cum non extet (*s*) aliquod penes Barones ejus rescriptum.

M. Posset fortasse, si vellet; sed foret hoc (*t*) insani capitis argumentum, si tantis se periculis sponte (*u*) opponeret; præsertim cum non auferre sic Regis debita posset, sed vix differre (*w*). Omnia namque debita de quibus Summonitiones fiunt, alias diligenter annotata servantur; unde non posset quis a debito suo etiam procurante Vicecomite hac arte liberari. Verum ad majorem hujus rei cautelam vidimus a Pictavense Archidiacono nunc Wintoniense Episcopo omnium Summonitionum rescripta fieri, nec aliquatenus originales emitti, nisi factis & diligenter correctis earum rescriptis. Cum autem sedente Vicecomite ad compotum legeretur Summonitio (*x*) a clerico Cancellarij, inspiciens Clericus Archidiaconi rescriptum, observabat eum ne exorbitaret. Procedente vero tempore cum numerus debitorum

(*d*) L. N. alia x l. vel.
(*e*) L. R. Præsidentibus taxantibus.
(*f*) L. R. ix.
(*g*) L. R. *deest* x.
(*h*) L. N. solvatur.
(*i*) L. N. jam ducturus.
(*k*) L. R. Hæc etiam habeas.
(*l*) L. N. pacteris.
(*m*) L. R. fuerit.
(*n*) L. R. his.

(*o*) L. N. pactercis.
(*p*) L. N. idempnitas.
(*q*) L. R. committatur.
(*r*) L. R. *desunt* vel minuere.
(*s*) L. R. exstet.
(*t*) L. R. sed foret sed insani.
(*u*) L. R. se sponte periculis.
(*w*) L. R. deferre.
(*x*) L. R. legentur summam.

cresceret

crefceret in immenfum (*y*), adeo ut uni Summonitioni (*z*) unius membranæ longitudo fufficeret, ceffum eft multitudini & laboriofo operi, & fola originali Summonitione, ficut antiquitus contempti funt. Sic habes, ut credo, quantum brevitas permifit, qualiter & ad quid fummonitiones fiant. Nunc ex quibus fieri debeant libet intueri ; licet ex præmiffis hoc ipfum magna pro parte jam conftet.

Ex quibus Summonitiones fiant.

Illuftris Anglorum Rex Henricus hoc nomine participiantium Regum fecundus dictus eft, fed nulli modernorum fuiffe creditur in rebus componendis animi virtute fecundus : ab ipfo enim (*a*) fuæ dominationis exordio totum in hoc direxit animum, ut Paci rebellantes & difcolos (*b*) multiplici fubverfione conteret (*c*), & pacis ac fidei bonum in cordibus hominum modis omnibus confignaret. Hujus igitur infignia cum jam in omnes gentes celeberrima fama vulgaverit, adeo ut his exponendis infiftere fupervacuum videatur : unum tamen eft, quod cum filentio præterire non valeo, ex quo folo fingularis ejus probitas & pietas inaudita firmatur. Non tamen hoc hominis fuit immo Dei miferentis, Quod fibi quod toti cum (*d*) paucis reftitit orbi.

D. Qualiter fibi refiftere dici poffit opus infigne, nifi planum feceris non video.

M. Licet hæc ad opus cœptum vel propofitum non adpertineant (*e*), memor tamen Regis illius magnanimi, cum pace meæ mentis hijs fuperfedere non valui. Videas ergo quam miraculofe (*f*) vir ille fibi reftitit, in fuos filios quidem fuæ carnis, immo & animæ fuæ fpem poft Deum unicam & gloriam fingularem ; dum parvuli effent, & ratione ætatis cerei fupra modum & in omnem animi motum proni, vulpeculæ pertinaces confilijs pravis demolitæ funt, & tandem in patrem tanquam in hoftem fua vifcera converterunt ; facti funt etiam inimici homines domeftici ejus, & qui cuftodiebant latus ejus, confilium inierunt adverfus eum ; dicentes filijs & hoftibus perfequemini (*g*) contra eum, quia non eft qui eripiat (*h*) ; diceres in hijs (*i*)

(*y*) L. R. *pro* in immenfum *habet album fpatiolum.*
(*z*) L. N. Summonitione.
(*a*) L. R. *deeft* enim.
(*b*) L. R. difcoles.
(*c*) *rectius* contereret.
(*d*) L. N. quod paucis cum toti.

(*e*) L. N. non animi pertineant.
(*f*) L. N. miraculo fe.
(*g*) L. R. perfequamini.
(*h*) L. N. perfequamini & 9 e. q. n. e. q. e.
(*i*) L. N. dicens in his.

verbum

verbum completum Prophetæ; filios enutrivi (*k*) & ecce ipsi spreverunt me (*l*). Cum igitur uxor in virum, filij in patrem suum, domestici sine causa desævirent (*m*) in dominum; nonne satis optime sibi rebellantem virum diceres? Verum contra numerosam hostium multitudinem solius Divinæ gratiæ magnitudo subvenit, & quasi pugnante pro se Domino, sic in brevi pene rebelles omnes obtinuit, ut longe fortius quam prius ex eo quo infirmari debuit confirmaretur in Regno.

Norunt enim per hoc potissimum (*n*) qui conspiraverant (*o*) adversus eum in omni virtute sua clavam a manu Herculis nisi vix extorqueri non posse. Comprehensis insuper hostibus tam enormis seculi incentoribus inaudita (*p*) pepercit misericordia; ut eorum pauci rerum suarum, nulli vero status sui vel corporum dispendia sustinerent (*q*). Si legeres ultionem quam exercuit David in subversores Absolonis filij sui, diceres hunc illo longe mitiorem extitisse (*r*): cum tamen de illo scriptum sit; inveni virum secundum cor meum. Licet autem Rex (*s*) insignis pluribus abundaret exemplis, & posset in eos (*t*) vel vilissimam exercere vindictam; maluit tamen expugnatis parcere quam eos punire, ut ejus regnum crescere videant vel inviti. Vivat igitur in longo tempore Rex ille gloriosus & fælix, & (*u*) pro inpensa (*w*) gratia gratiam mereatur ab alto. Vivat & proles ejus ingenua, patri suo subjecta nec ei dissimilis: & quia nati sunt populis imperare, paterno simul & proprio discant exemplo, quam gloriosum sit parcere subjectis & debellare rebelles. Nos autem suscepta negotia prosequamur. Quod si de hijs & alijs strenuis ejus actibus libet plenius instrui, libellum cujus supra meminimus, si placet, inspicito. Igitur post naufragum Regni statum pace reformata, studuit iterum (*x*) Rex avita tempora renovare; & eligens discretos viros secuit Regnum in vj partes, & eas electi Judices quos Errantes vocamus perlustrarent, & jura destituta restituerent. Facientes ergo sui copiam in singulis Comitatibus, & hijs qui se læsos putabant Justiciæ plenitudinem exhibentes, pauperum laboribus & sumptibus pepercerunt. Contigit autem in hijs excessus varios (*y*)

(*k*) L. R. enutrivit.
(*l*) L. N. & ex ipsi autem sp. me.
(*m*) L. R. discurenti dominum.
(*n*) L. N. potissimi.
(*o*) L. N. conspiraverat.
(*p*) L. N. tam enormis seculis inscentoribus inaudita.
(*q*) L. R. sustineret.

(*r*) L. N. exisse.
(*s*) L. N. Licet enim res insignis.
(*t*) L. R. eis.
(*u*) L. R. *desunt* felix, &.
(*w*) L. R. impensa.
(*x*) L. R. iterum studuit.
(*y*) L. R. varios excessus.

plerumq;

Lib. II.   DIALOGUS de SCACCARIO.   413

plerumq; varijs modis pro negotiorum qualitate puniri, ut quidam corporalem, quidam pecuniariam pœnam luant (z). Porro pecuniariæ delinquentium pœnæ in Rotulis Errantium diligenter annotantur; & confedente Scaccario coram omnibus Thesauro traduntur. Caveant autem Judices, ut correctos & per ordinem depositos (a) Rotulos Thesaurario liberent; non enim fas erit (b) ipsis etiam Judicibus facta traditione iota unum mutare etiam in quod omnes Judices consenserint.

D. In hoc mirabile est, quod cum scriptorum suorum auctores sint, & non nisi de ipsorum industria vel labore proveniat (c) etiam in unum aliquid consentientes scriptum proprium mutare non possunt.

M. Cum indulta sint correctionis tempora, & legem noverunt (d) constitutam (e), sibi imputent; oblatorum enim summa vel ab ipsis debitoribus si in hanc condempnati sunt, vel ab ipsis Judicibus requiretur. Ut si in Rotulo condempnatum aliquem in solutione xx descripserint, & tradita jam cautione Thesaurario recordati fuerint, quod non teneatur ille nisi in x; ipsi Judices de residuo satisfacient; quia scriptum suum cum deliberatione factum & correctum, post traditionem revocare non possunt. Susceptorum vero Rotulorum debita Thesaurarius in Magno annali Rotulo diligenter & distinate per singulos Comitatus annotari facit, simul cum causis; prænotatis, ut jam dictum est, nominibus Judicum; ut per hoc exactorum fiat discretio. Ex his (f) igitur summonitiones fiant sic; De placitis illorum N de illo illud; secundum quod Præsidentes prius debita taxaverint. Habes ex prædictis, ut credimus, quantum necesse est, ex quibus & qualiter & ad quid summonitiones fiant: nunc ad agenda Vicecomitis transeamus. Decet autem te dicendis sollicitam adhibere diligentiam, quia in hijs excellentior Scaccarij scientia consistit, sicut dictum est ab initio.

III. *De agendis Vicecomitum multipliciter.*

Omnes igitur Vicecomites & Ballivi, ad quos Summonitiones diriguntur, eadem necessitate legis constringuntur; hoc est, auctoritate Regij mandati; ut scilicet die nominato designatoque loco conveniant, & de debitis satisfaciant; quod ut manifestius fiat ipsius Summoniti-

(z) L. N. luatur.
(a) L. R. desunt & per ordinem depositos.
(b) L. N. factis erit.
(c) L. R. proveniant.
(d) L. N. noverit.
(e) L. R. constituta.
(f) L. R hijs.

onis tenorem diligentius intuere ; ait enim : Vide sicut teipsum &
omnia tua diligis, ut sis ad Scaccarium ibi tunc ; & habeas tecum
quicquid debes de veteri firma & nova, & hæc debita subscripta.
Attende igitur, quia duo dicuntur, quæ duobus sequentibus coaptantur:
hoc enim, Vide sicut teipsum diligis, refertur ad sis ibi tunc ; illud
vero, & sicut omnia tua diligis, referri videtur ad hoc, & habeas tecum (*g*) hæc debita subscripta : ac si aperte dicatur ; Absentia tua,
tu quicunq; suscipis summonitionem, nisi necessarijs & lege definitis
causis possit excusari ; in capitis tui periculum redundabit ; videris
enim sic Regium sprevisse mandatum, & in contemptum Regiæ majestatis irreverenter egisse. Si citatus super Regis quibus addictus (*h*)
es negotijs nec veneris, nec excusatorem miseris   Verum si per te (*i*)
steterit, quo minus debita subscripta solvantur, tunc de firma quam
soluturus es, aliena debita de quibus summonitus es capientur : Firma
vero de catallis & fundorum tuorum redditibus perficietur (*k*) ; te interim, si Barones decreverint, in loco tuto sub libera custodia collo-
cato. Cum ergo præmissa fuerint (*l*) a Vicecomite suscepta summonitio, ipsa die nominata veniat & ostendat se Præsidenti, si adesse eum
contigerit, vel Thesaurario, si Præsidens ille præsens non fuerit. Deinde salutatis Majoribus, ipsa die sibi vacet, & in (*m*) crastino & deinceps die qualibet ad Scaccarium rediturus.   Quod si forte nec venerit
nec justam præmiserit excusationem, prima die Regi condempna-
bitur in C solidis argenti de quolibet Comitatu, sequenti vero (*n*) in x
libris argenti, similiter in C, tertia, sicut ab his (*o*) accepimus, qui
nos præcesserunt, in beneplacito Regis erunt quæcunque mobilia
possidet ; quarto vero quia jam ex hoc contemptus Regiæ majestatis
convincitur, non solum in rebus suis, sed in propria persona soli
Regiæ misericordiæ subjacebit.   Sunt tamen qui credant ad omnem
summam solam pœnam pecuniariam sufficere ; ut scilicet prima die in
C solidis ; secunda similiter in C sol. (*p*) ; & ita deinceps per singulos dies in singulis centenis puniantur absentes. His ego non dissentio ; si tamen his cui delinquitur, & in (*q*) hoc ipsum consenserint (*r*) ;
hunc autem pœnæ modum velle Regem admittere satis probabile est,
cum ejus gratia singularis ad pœnam pigra sit, & hæc ad præmia velox.

(*g*) L. R. habeas ibi.
(*h*) L. R. additus.
(*i*) L. N. si parte steterit.
(*k*) L. R. proficietur.
(*l*) L. R. fuerit & a.
(*m*) L. R. *deest* in.

(*n*) L. N. sequenti ut in.
(*o*) L. R. hijs.
(*p*) L. R. centum solidis.
(*q*) L. R. *deest* & : L. N. *deest* in.
(*r*) L. R. consenserit.

D. Impru-

D. Imprudentis pariter & impudentis eſt auditoris currentem calamum ante proviſum dicendorum finem præoccupare; ideoque ſuſtinui volvens (*s*) in animo quod ex parte me turbat: dixiſti enim, ſi per Vicecomitem ſteterit quo minus debita ſubſcripta ſolvantur, tunc de firma quam ſoluturus eſt capientur. Si ergo Vicecomes per brevia Regis, vel in operationes vel alias univerſa diſtribuerit, quæ hic fuerat ſoluturus; quid fiet

M. Cum ex Regis mandato vel in Camera Curiæ, vel in operationibus, vel in quibuſlibet alijs, firmam Comitatus expenderit, ſi in debitis ſolvendis minus egiſſe deprehenditur (*t*), per fidem ſuam ubi Majores decreverint detinebitur, donec de hijs ſatisfaciat ſicut de firma ſatisfacturus fuerat.

D. Cum citatum Vicecomitem & non venientem vel excuſantem, tum rerum mobilium tum immobilium cum & (*u*) proprij (*w*) corporis gravis jactura ſequatur, niſi ſuam non voluntariam ſed neceſſariam abſentiam excuſaverit. Rogo te, ſi placet, ut quas (*x*) citatus prætendere poſſit abſentiæ ſuæ ſufficientes cauſas aperire non differas.

IV. *Quibus de cauſis abſentia Vicecomitum ſervatur indempnis.*

M. Plures ſunt excuſationem modi, quibus Vicecomitis abſentia ſervatur indemnis, ſic tamen ut occaſione vel excuſatione poſtpoſita die nominata per legitimos viros pecuniam Regis ante collectam præmittat; qui porrigentes Præſidenti literas excuſationis, & abſentiæ Domini ſui cauſas neceſſarias allegantes, etiam ſacramento corporaliter præſtito, ſi Præſidenti placuerit, eaſdem confirment. Quod ſi Vicecomes, vel alius ſerviens citatus, infirmitate detentus adeſſe non poterit; addat in literis excuſationis, quæ ad Scaccarium diriguntur: Et quia venire non poſſum; mitto vobis hos ſervientes meos N. & N, ut loco meo ſint, & quod ad me pertinet faciant, ratum habiturus quod ipſi fecerint.

Provideat autem qui excuſat, ut alter vel uterque miſſorum Miles ſit, vel laicus alius ratione ſanguinis vel aliter ſibi conjunctus, hoc eſt cujus fidei vel diſcretioni ſe & ſua committere non diffidat: ſolos enim Clericos ad hoc ſuſcipi non oportet; quia ſi ſecus egerint, non decet eos pro pecunia vel ratiocinijs comprehendi. Si vero citatum Vicecomitem abeſſe contigerit, non infirmitate quidem ſed qualibet alia

(*s*) L. N. volumine.
(*t*) L. R. comprehenditur.
(*u*) L. R. *deſunt* tum immobilium cum &.
(*w*) L. R. tunc in proprij.
(*x*) L. N. quis.

cauſa

causa præpeditum, sic forsitan a pœna constituta poterit liberari: Verum ad explendum compotum suum nullus pro eo suscipietur, nisi primogenitus filius ; nec generalis ejus procurator, etiamsi breve suum direxerit, se ratum habiturum, quod ille vel ille pro se fecerit; solius vero mandati Regij vel etiam Præsidentis auctoritate, si Rex absens fuerit, ad compotum suum explendum alium (*y*) poterit substituere: si tamen aliud a Domino Rege negotium sibi gerat assignatum ipse ad Scaccarium (*z*) in propria persona præsentem nominet, qui juxta quod supra dictum est, possit & debeat Vicecomitis absentis negotia procurare. Illud autem Breve Regis vel Præsidentis, vel Vicecomitis excusantis in forulo Marescalli, cujus supra meminimus, in testimonium hujus rei reservabitur. Quod si Vicecomes alias Regi necessarius ab ipso vocatus fuerit extra regnum, vel accepta licentia pro familiaribus negotijs exire disposuerit, prius Præsidentem adeat (*a*), & viva voce vices suas ad Scaccarium deleget cui voluerit viro legitimo ; quo facto, cum absens fuerit, nec breve mittere, nec absentiam suam excusare cogetur. Excusante vero se Vicecomite causa infirmitatis, cum necesse (*b*) fuerit ad scribendum ejus compotum in Annali Rotulo, dicetur, Willelmus Vicecomes de Lundonijs, Robertus filius ejus pro eo, reddit compotum de firma de Lundonijs (*c*). At si per Regis mandatum alius sibi substituitur, vel ipse viva voce, sicut prædictum est, aliquem pro se designaverit Præsidenti, sic per omnia dicendum est ac si ipse in propria persona ad compotum resideret.

D. Nunquid infirmitas sola sufficiens est excusatio, per quam citatus absens servetur indempnis ?

M. Absit: sunt enim plures ad Scaccarium ; sed hæc tam in litibus quam in alijs negotijs Ecclesiasticis & Forensibus est usitatior. Porro decet te memorem esse prædictorum, ut intelligas (*d*) nullam excusationem hoc efficere, ut Regis pecunia de Comitatu collecta penes eum detineatur impune, vel ad Scaccarium die nominata non mittatur. Præmissa ergo pecunia, poterit excusari per infirmitatem, sicut dictum est. Item si filius ejus primogenitus, quem declaravit hæredem post se futurum, morti proximus adjudicetur, excusabitur. Item si uxor ejus dolore partus periclitari cœperit, vel quavis alia de causa morti proxima decubuerit, quia portio suæ carnis est, excusari poterit. Item si Dominus ejus, qui vulgo Ligius dicitur, hoc est, cui soli ratione

(*y*) L. R. *desunt* explendum alium.
(*z*) L. N. ipse adjectum.
(*a*) L. N. adheat.
(*b*) L. R. cum ventum.
(*c*) L. N. London.
(*d*) L. N. Ecclesiasticus prædictorum ut intelligas.

Dominij

Dominij fic (*e*) tenetur, ut contra ipfum nichil (*f*) alij debeat Rege duntaxat excepto, vocaverit ipfum, ut adfit fibi tracto in jus de toto feudo fuo (*g*) vel ejus maxima parte, vel fuper alia caufa quæ in ftatus vel corporis fui detrimentum redundare videatur, excufari poterit; fic tamen fi Dominus ille nec amplius excufare nec aliter litem (*h*) declinare valuerit. Quod fi idem Dominus alium fuper hujufmodi follicitaverit, & liberum fit ei abfque enormi damno diem prorogare (*i*), fi vocaverit Domini Regis Vicecomitem hominem quidem fuum, venire non tenebitur; quia nec (*k*) fic ad Scaccarium poffet excufari. Item fi idem Dominus (*l*) infirmitatis pondere preffus, teftamentum coram fuis condere voluerit, & ad hoc cum alijs fidelibus fuis ipfum evocaverit, excufabitur. Item fi Dominus ejus, vel uxor, vel filius debita carnis folverit, & hic debita funeris obfequia procuraverit, excufari merebitur. Sunt & aliæ plures excufationes abfentiæ Vicecomitis neceffariæ quidem & legibus determinatæ quas non abdicamus vel excludimus, immo cum fufficientes vifæ fuerint a Majoribus libenter fufcepimus; fed has quæ menti meæ fe ad præfens obtulerunt, quafi frequentiores exempli caufa fubjecimus.

D. Videor ex prædictis perpendere, quod Miles, vel quilibet alius difcretus poffit a Rege Vicecomes vel alius Ballivus creari, etiamfi nil ab ipfo poffideat, fed folum ab alijs.

M. Debetur hæc Prærogativa dignitatis publicæ (*m*) poteftati, ut cujufcunque fit, cuicunque vir aliquis in Regno militet vel miniftret, fi regi neceffarius vifus fuerit, libere poffit affumi, & Regijs obfequijs deputari.

D. Ex hoc etiam cerno verum effe quod dicitur,

An nefcis longas Regibus effe manus?

Sed jam nunc, fi placet, ad agenda Vicecomitis manum mittere non differas; ad hæc (*n*) enim, te monente, totam attentionis (*o*) induftriam jam collegi; fciens ex his (*p*) excellentem Scaccarij fcientiam, ficut prædictum eft, debere requiri.

M. Gratulor te memorem præmifforum; unde fateor languenti pene calamo te ftimulos addidiffe. Noveris autem quod Vicecomes, nifi

(*e*) L. R. *deeſt* fic.
(*f*) L. R. nihil.
(*g*) L. R. ut adfit fibi tractaturus de toto feodo suo.
(*h*) L. N. poterit; fic tamen fi Dominus ille nec aliter litem.
(*i*) L. R. dampno dicit prorogare.
(*k*) L. R. noc fic.
(*l*) L. R. Dominus ejus.
(*m*) L. N. puplicæ.
(*n*) L. R. hoc.
(*o*) L. R. intentionis.
(*p*) L. R. hijs.

facto prius examine debitisque de quibus summonitus est solutis, residere non debet ad compotum : cum autem accesserit & jam resederit alij Vicecomites excludantur ; & resideat solus cum suis, ad interrogata responsurus. Provideat autem ut ipsa die vel præcedente, debitoribus sui Comitatus innotuerit qua die sit ad compoum sessurus ; vel etiam circa domum Scaccarij vel vicum vel villam voce præconia ipsis denunciet se tunc vel tunc sessurum. Tunc sedentibus & audientibus omnibus, Thesaurarius, qui sicut (*q*) dictum est, ratione officij sui sibi videtur adversari, quærat, si paratus est reddere compotum ; quo respondente præsto sum, inferat Thesaurarius, Dic igitur imprimis si Elemosinæ, si decimæ, si liberationes constitutæ, si Terræ datæ sic se habent hoc anno sicut in præterito. Quod si similiter se habere responderet ; tunc scriptor Thesaurarij præteritum Annalem Rotulum diligenter in hijs constitutis scribendis sequatur, contuente (*r*) simul Thesaurario, ne forte manus scriptoris aberret. Et quia satis in titulo de officio Scriptoris Thesaurarij de ordine scripturæ dixisse me memini hijs (*s*) ad præsens supersedeo.

D. Dic ergo, si placet, de hijs quæ (*t*) jamdudum usque ad agenda Vicecomitum distulisti (*u*) quid (*w*) scilicet sit, quasdam terras a Rege dari Bl[ancas] quasdam numero ; hoc enim me sollicitavit ab initio.

M. Satis (ut credo) tibi constat ex prædictis, quid sit quasdam firmas solvi Bl. quasdam numero. Firma quidem Bl. solvitur, cum ipsa facto examine dealbatur.

V. *Quid sit quosdam fundos dari Bl. quosdam numero.*

Quis insuper fuerit (*x*) hujus institutionis auctor, & quæ instituendi ratio, satis innotuit. Porro firmam numero solvi diximus, cum tantum numerando non examinando de ipsa satisfit. Cum ergo Rex fundum aliquem alicui contulerit simul cum Hundredo vel placitis (*y*) quæ ex hoc proveniunt, dicunt fundum illum illi Bl. collatum : ac (*z*) cum retento sibi Hundredo per quod firma dealbari dicitur, simpliciter fundum dederit, non determinans cum Hundredo vel Bl. , numero datus dicitur. Oportet autem ut de fundo collato Breve Regis, vel

(*q*) L. N. qui si cum dictum.
(*r*) L. N. continente.
(*s*) L. N. me inicium his ad.
(*t*) L.R. placet qui jamdudum.
(*u*) L. N. distilisti.
(*w*) L. N. quod.
(*x*) L. R. fuit.
(*y*) L. N. placito.
(*z*) L. R. at.

cartam

cartam ejus in termino S^{ti} Michaelis cui collatus eft ad Scaccarium deferat (*a*) ut Vicecomiti computetur; alioquin in Magno Annali Rotulo non fcribetur, nec Vicecomiti computabitur; fcribetur autem fic: Poft Elemofinas & decimas & liberationes utriufque generis conftitutas, in capite lineæ, In terris datis illi N. xx 1 Bl. ibi, & illi N. xx 1 numero ibi. Adverte etiam, quod fi forte inter Terras datas inveneris, illi vel illi x 1 Bl. vel numero ibi de præftito Regis; cum is qui commodati vel præftiti beneficio gavifus eft fati debita folverit, nifi per gratiam Regis non uxori non liberis non alicui nomine ejus propter præftitum reclamandi locus relinquitur; fimiliter fi dictum fuerit, illi X quamdiu Regi placuerit.

VI. *Quæ fint conftituta Vicecomiti computanda, Elemofinæ fcilicet & decimæ liberationes utriufque generis & terræ datæ.*

D. Quid eft, quod dixifti liberationes utriufque generis?

M. Liberationum quædam funt indigentium; cum ex folo charitatis intuitu ad victum & veftitum alicui a Rege denarius diurnus vel duo vel plures conftituuntur. Quædam vero funt fervientium, ut has pro ftipendijs fufcipiant; quales funt (*b*) cuftodes domorum ædituì Regij Tibicines luporum comprehenfores (*bb*) & hujufmodi. Heæ funt igitur diverfi generis liberationes quæ diverfis ex caufis folvuntur, inter conftituta tamen computantur. Et nota quod licet liberum fit Regi quibuflibet indigentibus has liberationes conferre; ex antiqua tamen inftitutione folent his affignari, qui in Curia miniftrantes, cum redditus non habeant, in corporum fuorum invaletudinem decidant, & laboribus inutiles fiunt. His omnibus per ordinem annotatis, quærit Thefaurarius a Vicecomite, fi quid expenderit de firma Comitatus per Brevia Regis præter conftituta; tunc feriatim miffa fibi Regis Brevia tradit clerico Cancellarij, qui lecta in publicum eadem liberat Thefaurario, ut ipfe fecundum formam in brevibus conceptam in fcrip-

(*a*) L. N. differat.
(*b*) L. N. funt 1. cuftodes.
(*bb*) *Prifcis temporibus luporum venator in* Wireceftrefcira *confuevit effe ad ftipem Regis; ut in exemplis fubnexis patet: Nimirum, anno* 13. *R.* Henrici II: Et Venatori qui capit Lupos in forefta, iij s; *Mag. Rot.* 13. *H.* 2. *Rot.* 5. *a. Wireceftrefcira: Anno* 17° *ejufdem Regis:* Et Venatori qui Lupos capit, iij s; *Mag. Rot.* 17. *H.* 2. *Rot.* 6. *b. Wireceftrefcira: Anno* 27° *ejufdem:* Et Venatori qui capit Lupos iij s; *Mag. Rot.* 27. *H.* 2. *Rot.* 2. *a. Wireceftrefcira: Annoque* 5° *R.* Johannis: Et Venatori qui capit Lupos, iij s; *Mag. Rot.* 5. *J. Rot.* 4. *b. Wireceftrefcira: Tempore R.* Henrici III. *& poftea, hujus Venatoris mentio vel non omnino vel raro (quantum memini) in Rotulis fit.*

turam

turam Rotuli sui opportuna verba miniftret. Ipfe namque ficut dictum eft præfcribit, & alij confcribentes ab eodem accipiunt; hoc facto oftendit Vicecomes fi quid expenderit, non per brevia fed per conftitutam Scaccarij legem fibi computandum ; qualia funt liberationes probatorum Regis, & item ea quæ mittuntur in Jufticijs & Judicijs explendis

VII. *Quæ fint per folam confuetudinem Scaccarij computanda, hoc eft fine brevi.*

Adverte autem, Jufticias hic ufualiter nuncupari prolati in aliquos viros juris (c) executiones: Judicia vero, leges Candentis ferri vel aquæ. Liberationes igitur probatorum hac ratione fiunt. Propter innumeras regni hujus divitias, & item propter innatam Indigenis crapulam, quam femper comes libido fequitur, contingit in ipfo frequenter (d) furta fieri manifefta vel occulta, nec non & homicidia & diverforum generum fcelera, addentibus ftimulos mœchis, ut nichil (e) non audeant vel non attentent (f) qui fuis fe confilijs fubjecerunt. Cum autem a Regijs miniftris regni pacem excubantibus, reus horum famofus aliquis conprehenditur (g), propter numerofam fceleratorum multitudinem, ut vel fic (h) perverfis terra purgetur, confentiunt & in (i) hoc interdum Judices, quod fi quis hujufmodi de fe crimen confitens, fceleris ejufdem confortes provocare voluerit, & objectum alij vel alijs crimen commiffo duello (k) probare valuerit, mortem, quam meruit effugiat, & cum impunitate fui corporis, exiens tamen totius Regni fines demereatur (l) & abjuret ingreffum. Quidam autem conventione cum Judicibus prius facta, licet objecta probaverint, non tamen immunes abfcedunt, fed effugientes fufpendium vel aliud turpe genus mortis quam de fe confeffi meruerint, mutilatione tamen membrorum puniti miferabile fpectaculum fiunt in populo, & temerarios aufus confimilium terribilibus compefcunt exemplis. Quod (m) igitur objecto & probato ejufdem criminis (n) reatu vitam fibi falvare poteft, & item quia ad Regis utilitatem proculdubio fit quicquid ad regni pacem videtur accedere, Regis Probator dicitur. A die vero qua ad probationem fufcipitur, ufque ad ex-

(c) L. R. *deeft* juris.
(d) L. R. frequencius.
(e) L. R. nihil.
(f) L. N. attempnent.
(g) L. R. deprehenditur.
(h) L. R. vel fi.
(i) L. R. *deeft* in.
(k) L. R. duello commiffo.
(l) L. N. Regni tamen totius demereatur.
(m) L. R. Quum igitur.
(n) L. R. criminis ejufdem.

pletum

pletum promissum, vel usque quo defecerit, ad victualia de fisco percipit quaque die denarium unum, qui Vicecomiti per solam consuetudinem Scaccarij computatur. Quod si probator ille jussus (*o*) fuerit ad alia loca transferri, ut convenientibus illic Judicibus opportunius promissum expleat, vel forte deficiens scelerum suorum pœnam condignam excipiat, solum id quod in vehiculis illuc conducendis, & Victualibus illi ministrandis (*p*) invenit, Vicecomiti computabitur per consuetudinem; cætera vero non nisi per breve Regis. Sunt præterea in quibusdam Comitatibus plures, qui ratione fundorum suorum in condempnatos ultrices manus mittunt; ut alios suspendio, alios membrorum detruncatione, vel alijs modis juxta quantitatem perpetrati sceleris puniant. Sunt & quidam Comitatus, in quibus sic condempnandi, non nisi numerata de fisco pecunia, puniuntur. Quicquid igitur ad hæc Judicia vel Justitias effectui mancipandas detestabilis avaritiæ hominibus, qui hæc pro sanguinis effusione suscipiunt, a Vicecomite numeratur, per consuetudinem Scaccarij sibi computatur; hoc est, non per Breve Regis. Est & aliud quod per consuetudinem solum Vicecomiti debeat computari: cum Regis thesaurus de loco in locum Majorum consideratione deferendus, vehiculis & hujusmodi minoribus indiguerit: præcipiente (*q*) Thesaurario vel Camerarijs, vel servientibus eorum ad hæc (*r*) missis, Vicecomes de firma sua quod oportuerit invenit, & hoc ipsum Vicecomiti sine brevi computatur; perhibente tamen super hoc testimonium coram Majoribus ipso Thesaurario vel quolibet prædictorum qui hæc fieri mandaverit; & tunc dicetur in Rotulo, In hijs vel illis necessarijs Thesauri, hoc vel illud, per hunc vel illum. Item si piscis Regius, Rumbus vel Cetus vel alius hujusmodi comprehenditur, quod in his saliendis & alijs necessarijs ministrandis a Vicecomite mittitur, sine Brevi computatur. Item quod in excolendis Dominicis vineis Regis, & hijs vindemiandis, vel vasis & alijs necessarijs ministrandis expenditur, sine brevi per fidem Vicecomitis computatur; de qua fide si semel aut sæpius, qualiter fiat, infra dicetur. Hæc sunt igitur quæ ad præsens nobis occurrunt, Vicecomiti, per solam consuetudinem computanda. Nunc de cæteris quæ ad compotum de Corpore Comitatus pertinent prosequamur.

(*o*) L. R. missus.
(*p*) L. R. ministrandis per denarium diurnum invenit.
(*q*) L. R. præcipiente & Thes.
(*r*) L. R. hoc.

VIII. *Quo ordine computanda sunt Vicecomiti quæ in operibus missa sunt per breve Regis numero non determinans.*

Fit interdum ut præcipiat Rex Vicecomiti per breve suum, quod in (*s*) Castris firmandis vel in ædificijs & hujusmodi instruendis de firma sua necessaria ministret, per visum duorum vel trium virorum quorum nomina in ipso brevi exprimuntur; & addat in fine verbum breve sed computantibus necessarium; & computabitur tibi ad Scaccarium. Cum igitur ventum fuerit ad compotum Vicecomitis, veniunt simul qui electi sunt Custodes operum, & fide in publica ab ipsis præstita, quod secundum conscientiam suam ad Regis utilitatem in ipso opere nominata summa pervenerit (*t*), fiat inde breve Regis ad Scaccarium sub testimonio Præsidentis & (*u*) alterius quem præceperit, in quo (*w*) summa illa de qua testati sunt, & item nomina Custodum exprimantur; & tunc demum Vicecomiti (*x*) computabitur. Quod si per hæc missa (*y*) consummatum Regis opus fuerit, primum illud breve de necessarijs ministrandis quod Vicecomiti directum est, & hoc ultimum quod ad Scaccarium fit, in forulo Marescalli de compotis factis recluduntur. Si quid autem restat de ipso opere faciendum, Vicecomes quod sibi directum est Breve usque ad idem opus completum penes se reservabit; ut hinc sit ei auctoritas operi perficiendo necessaria ministrare; reliquum vero in forulo de quo dictum est recludetur. Cum enim scribatur in annali: In operatione illa centum libras; oportet consequenter apponi per breve Regis, & per visum horum N; quod si non (*z*) extaret Breve Regis numerum ipsum & nomina custodum continens, falsa videri posset scriptura Rotuli dicentis per Breve Regis.

D. In hoc verbo sic mihi (*a*) satisfactum est, ut hijs ad quæ requirenda jam ora laxaveram, sponte supersedeam. Cum enim Vicecomiti delatum sit Breve Regis de necessarijs ad hoc vel illud opus inveniendis, & sit adjectum; & computabitur tibi ad Scaccarium; vel hoc, Inveni de firma tua; quod ejusdem pene est auctoritatis, superfluum videbatur, ut super alio Brevi sollicitus esset; nec enim intelligebam, quod in ipso brevi numerus esset exprimendus, ut sic eodem verborum tenore auctentico (*b*) respondeat Annali.

(*s*) L. R. *deest* in.
(*t*) L. N. provenerit.
(*u*) L. N. *deest* &.
(*w*) L. N. qua.
(*x*) L. R. *deest* Vicecomiti.
(*y*) L. R. *deest* missa.
(*z*) L. N. *deest* non.
(*a*) L. N. michi.
(*b*) L. R. attentico.

IX. *Quod*

IX. *Quod non absolvitur quis a debito per breve Regis numerum non exprimens, etiamsi causam determinet.*

M. Intellige (c) similiter quod in Scaccarij negotijs secus est quam in alijs: dicitur enim in plerisque, quod expressa nocent, non expressa non nocent (e): verum hic expressa juvant & non expressa fatigant: verbi gratia; si tenetur quis Regi in centum; & breve ejus deferat ad Scaccarium: ut quietus sit de debito quod ei debet, addat etiam toto, & causam simul exprimat set (e) non numerum; non propter hoc absolvetur, sed magis per hoc (f) dilationem usque ad aliam summonitionem promerebitur. Oporteret enim scribi in Rotulo, In perdonis per breve Rgis illi N, C; sed quia non videtur omnino dimissum quod (g) nondum est in brevi expressum, cogetur is multo labore quærere per quod mereatur absolvi: ergo in hijs non expressa fatigant.

D. Salva sit reverentia Præsidentis & assidentium, hic non videtur per omnia Regis mandato satisfactum; nec enim quietus est quem quietum esse mandavit, addens etiam causam pro qua sibi tenebatur.

M. Immo salva sit in hijs Scrupulosæ mentis tuæ subtilitas. Nosse quidem debueras, quod ei qui lege plurimum indiget, ejus ignorantia non subvenit. Is ergo qui Regi tenetur qualiter ab hoc absolvi plene possit, hoc est secundum legem de hijs (h) constitutam diligenter inquirat; quod si non fecerit, non Præsidenti sed sibi imputet; nec enim licet Præsidenti ab eo quod detulit in Brevi iota mutare: cum ergo per hoc quietus non sit, festinet quod expedit impetrare.

D. Cerno quod hæc maxime propter hoc observantur, ut Scripturæ Rotuli non obloquantur. Sed jam nunc prosequere de cæteris.

M. Cum igitur omnia fuerint annotata, quæ vel constituta sunt, vel per brevia Regis, vel per consuetudinem Scaccarij computanda, sic compotus velut infectus relinquitur, & ad alia convertuntur; nec enim & quietus est vel & debet in Annali scribetur, per quæ scilicet compotus consummatus dicitur, donec de omnibus quæ in Summonitione continentur satisfecerit; cujus rei causa satis ex consequentibus liquere poterit; post compotum de Corpore Comitatus hoc est de principali firma, qui sicut prædictum est usque in finem infectus relinquitur; post modum interstitium ponitur compotus de Veteri firma Comitatus, hoc est quæ casu aliquo de anno præterito remanserat, ita tamen si

(c) L. R. Intelligite.
(d) L. R. expressa juvant non expressa fatigant. Verbi gratia.
(e) L. R. sed.
(f) L. R. pro hac.
(g) L. R. quia nondum.
(h) L. R.

Vicecomes qui tunc miniſtravit mutatus fuerit; quod ſi idem perſeverat etiam hoc anno (*i*), de veteri firma ante inchoatum compotum de nova ſatisfaciet; & diligenter & diſtincte ſcribetur de veteri in principio, & conſequenter de nova. Ad hæc noveris mutatum Vicecomitem de firma veteri ſummonendum, ſicut quemlibet aliorum debitorum; non de parte ejus ſed de univerſo; quia firma eſt cujus ſolutio differri non debet; ſed debitum firmæ veteris, quo tenetur is qui ad huc miniſtrat, ſufficit ſub hoc prætextu verborum ſummonuiſſe, Quicquid debes de veteri firma & nova. De quo ſatis ſupra dictum eſt in titulo de Summonitionibus.

X. *De excidentibus & occupatis quæ uſitatius dicimus de Purpreſturis & Eſcaetis.*

Poſt hæc autem, facto intervallo, quaſi ſex linearum, ſequitur compotus de excidentibus & occupatis quæ (*k*) nos uſitatius dicimus de purpreſturis & eſcaetis. In medio quidem lineæ ſit prænotatio literis capitalibus, De Purpreſturis & Eſcaetis; in capite vero inferioris ſic ſcribitur; Idem Vicecomes reddit compotum de firma Purpreſturarum & Eſcaetarum, ſcilicet de x l de hoc & de xx l de illo, & ita deinceps, ſicut ex Rotulo perluſtrantium Judicum ante conceptum eſt in annali ſumma C l. Dehinc in fine ejuſdem lineæ ubi ſumma eſt, ſcribitur, In Theſauro xx l in tot taleis & debet quantum xx l; vel, In theſauro liberavit, & quietus eſt. Horum autem ſcribendorum ordinem magis oculata fide quam verborum quantalibet argumentoſa deſcriptione cognoſces.

D. Quæ ſint hæc excidentia, vel occupata, & qua ratione fiſco proveniunt, niſi plenius aperueris, non video.

M. Fit interdum per negligentiam Vicecomitis vel ejus miniſtrorum, vel etiam per continuatam in longa tempora bellicam tempeſtatem, ut habitantes prope fundos qui Coronæ annominantur, aliquam (*l*) eorum portionem ſibi uſurpent & ſuis poſſeſſionibus aſcribant. Cum autem perluſtrantes Judices per ſacramentum legitimorum virorum hæc deprehenderint, ſeorſum a firma Comitatus appreciantur (*m*) & Vicecomitibus traduntur ut de eiſdem ſeorſum reſpondeant; & hæc dicimus purpreſturas vel occupata; quæ quidem cum deprehenduntur, a poſſeſſoribus ſicut prædictum eſt tolluntur & ab hinc fiſco cedunt.

(*i*) L. R. perſeverat in hoc anno.
(*k*) L. N. quod nos.
(*l*) L. N. aliqua.

(*m*) L. R. a firma comitantur & Vicecom.

Verum

Verum si is a quo tollitur occupatum auctor est facti, simul etiam nisi Rex ei pepercit pecuniariter gravissime punietur; quod si non auctor sed hæres auctoris fuerit, ad pœnam sufficit fundi ejusdem sola revocatio. Ex quo sane, sicut ex alijs pluribus, Regis misericordia comprobatur; dum patris tam enormis excessus non punitur in filio, qui usque ad factam inquisitionem publicæ potestatis jactura ditabatur. Porro Escaetæ vulgo dicuntur (*mm*) quæ decedentibus his (*n*) qui de Rege tenent in Capite, cum non extet ratione sanguinis hæres, ad fiscum relabuntur. De his autem simul cum purpresturis (*o*) compoti fiunt sub una scripturæ serie (*p*); sic tamen ut singulorum nomina per ordinem exprimantur. At cum paterfamilias Miles vel serviens de Rege tenens in Capite fati debita solverit, relictis tamen liberis, quorum primogenitus minor est annis, redditus quidem ejus ad fiscum redeant; sed hujusmodi non simpliciter Escaeta dicitur, sed Escaeta cum hærede; unde nec hæres ab (*q*) hæreditate, nec ab ipso hæreditas tollitur; set (*r*) simul cum hæreditate sub Regis custodia constitutus tempore pupillaris ætatis de ipsa hæreditate per Regis officiales, tam ipse quam cæteri liberi necessaria percipiunt. Cætera vero quæ de ipsa proveniunt, Regijs usibus cedunt. De his autem seorsum compoti fiunt; quia non perpetuo, sed quodam temporali jure fisco debentur. Cum enim hæres nunc minor legitimæ ætatis adeptus beneficia, sibi (*s*) suisque disponere noverit, quod jure sibi paterno debetur, a Regia munificentia suscipiet, quidam gratis per solam scilicet gratiam Principis, quidam promissa summa aliqua; de qua cum compotus fiet, dicetur in Annali; Ille vel ille reddit compotum de C l de Relevio terræ patris sui; in Thesauro hoc, & debet hoc: de hoc autem ultra in Annali compotus non fiet; cum ad fiscum post hoc (*t*) non redeat. Verum dum in manu Regis est, de hoc sic scribetur in Annali; Ille Vicecomes reddit compotum de firma illius Honoris, si Baronia (*u*) est; In Thesauro hoc; & in procuratione liberorum illius hoc, per Breve Regis; quod ibi ad Scaccarium per consuetudinem fiet; & debet hoc, vel & quietus est. Quod si minor est possessio hæc, ut sit fundus unus vel duo vel tres, sic dicetur; Ille Vicecomes vel

(*mm*) Excaetæ *seu* Escaetæ *dicuntur ea quæ in manum Domini, puta Regis, excidunt. Exempli gratia :* Idem Rogerus [de Stutevill, *Vicecomes*] reddit compotum de xl s, de duabus domibus de Baenburg venditis, quæ exciderant in manu Regis. *Mag. Rot.* 31. Hen. 2. *Rot.* 10. *b. Nordhumberland.*
(*n*) L. N. is.
(*o*) L. N. propresturis.
(*p*) L. R. *deest* serie.
(*q*) L. R. Escaeta cum ab hæreditate nec.
(*r*) L. R. *deest* set.
(*s*) L. N. & sibi.
(*t*) L. R. fiscum prius hoc.
(*u*) L. N. scilicet Baronia.

ille N cui forte Rex ejusdem rei custodiam deputavit reddit compotum de firma terræ illius N. quæ fuit illius N, quam rex habet in manu sua, vel quæ est in manu Regis cum hærede; In Thesauro hoc; & debet hoc; vel & quietus est. Attende præterea, quod Honor ille vel fundus dum in manu Regis cum hærede fuerit, omnes Elemosinæ & liberationes indigentium a prioribus Dominis solo charitatis intuitu constitutæ, his quibus debentur cum integritate solvuntur, & (*w*) ad Scaccarium Custodi computantur: liberationes vero Servientum, qui Dominis suis ad explenda quælibet obsequia necessarij nisi sint, & ob hoc constituuntur, dum Rex possidet, voluntariam habent solutionem. Cum autem in manu hæredis devoluta fuerit hæreditas, oportet eum patris inhærere vestigijs; ut scilicet quoad usque vixerint hij quibus hæc a patre suo constituta sunt vita comite percipienda illis satisfaciat, & post hæc (*x*) si voluerit, eorum utatur vel non utatur (*y*) obsequijs.

D. Dixisti si bene memini quod si quilibet de Rege tenens in Capite decedens minorem annis hæredem reliquerit; tandem idem relictus post legitimæ ætatis tempora, quidam gratis quidam promissa pecunia, quod sibi debetur a Rege suscipit. Quod autem sic solvitur, Relevium dicis. Dic ergo si cujuslibet fundi qui de Rege est in Capite, Relevium sub consimili summa debeat exigi; vel si sub dissimili, quare sic?

M. In propriam te videor armasse perniciem. Ex prædictis enim alia conjiciens armatis me vexas quæstionibus. Noveris autem quod Releviorum quæ Regi debentur, secundum dissimiles possidentium status dissimilis summa consurgit: quidam enim de Rege tenent in Capite quæ ad Coronam pertinent; Baronias scilicet majores seu minores; si ergo pater possessor hujusmodi mortuus fuerit, relicto hærede, qui jam adultus sit, non secundum constitutam de his summam Regi satisfaciet, sed secundum quod a Rege poterit obtinere. Quod si minor ætate fuerit hæres, in custodia constitutus legitimam ætatem præstolabitur; tunc autem vel gratis sicut dictum est vel secundum beneplacitum Regis sicut adultus hæreditatem paternam nanciscetur: Si vero decesserit quis tenens tunc de Rege feodum Militis, non quidem ratione Coronæ Regiæ, sed potius ratione Baroniæ cujuslibet quæ quovis casu in Manum Regis delapsa est (*z*); sicut est Episcopatus vacante sede; hæres jam defuncti si adultus est pro feodo Militis C. sol. numerabit, pro duobus x l, & ita deinceps juxta numerum Militum quos

---

(*w*) L. R. *deest* &.
(*x*) L. R. hoc.
(*y*) L. N. *desunt* vel non utatur.
(*z*) L. N. *deest* est.

Domino

Domino debuerat antequam ad fiscum devoluta foret (*a*) hæreditas. Quod si minor annis hæres relictus fuerit, quæ de hæreditate ejus perveniunt ratione Custodiæ tempore pupillaris ætatis fisco provenient sicut dictum est: relictus (*b*) a patre jam adultus pro singulis feodis militum C solvet, vel etiam infra, hoc est L sol. si (*c*) dimidium Militis feodum possederit, & sic deinceps. Nec te lateat quod ejus quem in custodia per aliquot annos habueris & possessionis ejus fructum, cum ad ætatem legitimam pervenerit Relevium repetere non valebis.

D. In hac parte pro pupillis lex judicat, quod pijs mentibus bene sedet decernit.

M. Sic est; sed de propositis prosequamur. Item est & tertium (*d*) genus Excidentium vel Escaetarum, quod fisco provenit jure perpetuo. Cum aliquis de Rege tenens in Capite perpetrati sceleris sibi conscius sive sit ei objectum sive non (*e*) relictis tamen omnibus per fugam vitæ consulit: vel si super eodem objecto convictus vel confessus, terra simul & vita judicatur indignus; omnia quæ sui juris fuerant mox infiscantur, & redditus omnes annuo immo & perpetuo jure ad Scaccarium a Vicecomite persolvuntur, & quod ex mobilibus eorum venditis provenit Regi cedit (*f*). Similiter si cujuscunque conditionis vir vel cujuscunque (*g*) Domini servus aut liber, metu arctioris Assisæ quam Rex propter sceleratos constituit, a sede sua fugerit, & per constitutos ac lege definitos terminos (*h*) juri se non obtulerit vel excusaverit, vel etiam si acclamante in ipsum vicinia suspectus & postmodum comprehensus, per legem Assisæ constitutam reus sceleris convictus fuerit; omnia ejus mobilia fisco cedunt, immobilia vero Dominis suis. Mobilium vero precia per manum Vicecomitis ad Scaccarium deferuntur, & in Annali sic annotantur; Idem Vicecomes reddit compotum de catallis fugitivorum vel mutilatorum per Assisam de loco illo (*i*); scilicet de hoc v, de illo x, & sic deinceps per singula capita, expressis eorum nominibus & summis quæ de Catallis singulorum exurgunt; fiet autem in fine summa omnium; & circa finem ejusdem lineæ in qua summa est, scribetur, In Thesauro xl l in tot vel tot taleis, & debet x l, vel & quietus est. Hæc sunt frater, (*k*) quorum supra meminimus, quæ ad Scaccarium a Vicecomite deferenda sunt, etiamsi

---

(*a*) L. N. fuerit.
(*b*) L. N. devoluta fuerit, quæ de hæreditate ejus proveniunt ratione Custodiæ tempore pupillaris ætatis fisco provenient, sicut dictum est: relictus autem a patre.
(*c*) L. N. set dimidium.
(*d*) L. R. est interdum genus.

(*e*) L. R. *deest* non.
(*f*) L. N. *desunt* Regi cedit.
(*g*) L. R. *desunt* conditionis vir vel cujuscunque.
(*h*) L. R. *deest* terminos.
(*i*) L. R. loco N.
(*k*) L. R. sunt super quorum.

Summonitio nulla præcesserit. Sic & Thesaurus effossa tellure vel aliter inventus. Item cum quis Laicum fundum habens, vel quis (*l*) etiam publicis inservit usuris; si hic intestatus decesserit, vel etiam his (*m*) quos defraudavit non satisfaciens, testamentum de prave acquisitis visus est condidisse, sed (*n*) eadem non distribuit, imo penes se reservavit; quia sic perquisitis incumbens animum possidendi deseruisse non creditur, pecunia ejus & omnia mobilia mox infiscantur; & non summonita per officiales ad Scaccarium deferuntur; hæres autem jam defuncti fundo paterno & ejus immobilibus sibi vix relictis gaudeat.

D. Ex præmissis, quæ de Foeneratoribus dicta sunt quæstio gravis animum pulsat, quam vellem, si placet, plenius expediri; dixisti enim, cum quis Laicum fundum habens, vel etiam civis publicis inservit usuris &c; ex quibus verbis personarum quædam distinctio (*o*) inter sic delinquentes fieri posse videtur; & alia sit Clericorum, alia Laicorum conditio, cum pares sint in delicto. Item ex eo quod additur, publicis (*p*) inservit usuris, credi potest esse quasdam non publicas (*q*), quibus si quis adhæserit, an legi publicarum subjaceat prorsus ignoro.

M. Frustra credidi brevibus & communibus tibi satisfaciendum; cum ex hujusmodi questionem elicias cujus absolutio peritorum quosdam huc usque latuit. Verum quod dicis, ex verbis tuis, Clericorum & Laicorum sic delinquentium videtur esse dispar (*r*) conditio, cum pares sint in delicto, non approbro (*s*): sicut enim in (*t*) gradibus sic & in culpis diffident; juxta verbum illud; quanto gradus altior, tanto casus gravior; in bonis etiam & meritorijs operibus ut quibusdam visum est dispares sunt: Laici enim, qui voti necessitati minus tenentur, ampliorem gratiam promereri videntur; sicut in perversis actibus, hij qui voto religionis inserviunt, gravius offendunt. Sed de his actenus. Habes autem ex præcedentibus unde tuæ quæstionis pars prima valeat absolvi. Ex eo enim quod Clericus usuris inserviens dignitatis suæ privilegium demeretur, parem Laico sic delinquenti pœnam sibi mereatur, ut ipso videlicet de medio sublato omnia ejus mobilia fisco debeantur. Cæterum sic a prudentibus accepimus. In (*u*) sic delinquentem Clericum vel Laicum Christianum Regia potestas actionem non habet, dum vita comes fuerit: superest enim pœnitentiæ tempus; sed magis Ecclesiastico judicio reservatur, pro sui status

(*l*) *forsan legendum* civis.
(*m*) L. R. is.
(*n*) L. N. set.
(*o*) L. R. quæ inter.
(*p*) L. N. puplicis.
(*q*) L. N. publicas.
(*r*) L. R. *deest* dispar.
(*s*) L. R. opprobrio.
(*t*) L. R. sicut enim & gradibus.
(*u*) L. R. *deest* In.

qualitate

qualitate condempnandus : cum autem fati munus expleverit, sua omnia, Ecclesia non reclamante, Regi cedunt : nisi, sicut dictum est, vita comite digne pœnituerit, & testamento condito quæ legare decreverit, a se prorsus alienaverit. Restat itaque, ut quas puplicas (w) dicamus usuras & quas non publicas (x) expediamus ; deinde si pari lege teneantur, qui in utrisque delinquunt. Puplicas (y) igitur & (z) usitatas usuras dicimus, quando more Judæorum in eadem specie ex conventione quis amplius percepturus est quam commodavit; sicut libram pro marca, vel pro libra argenti duos denarios in septimana de lucro præter sortem : non (a) puplicas autem sed tamen damnabiles, cum quis fundum aliquem vel Ecclesiam pro commodato suscipit, & manente sortis integritate, fructus ejus, donec sors ipsa soluta fuerit, sibi percipit. Hoc genus propter laborem & sumptum qui in agriculturis solent impendi, licentius visum est; sed proculdubio Sordidum est & inter usuras computandum merito (b). Quod si creditor avarus & in ruinam animæ suæ pronus in scripto sic exprimi dignum duxerit, ut dicatur ; Notum sit omnibus, quod ego N debeo N centum marcas argenti ; & pro his centum marcis invadiavi ei terram illam pro xl; quousque ego vel hæres meus solvam ipsi vel hæredi suo prædictas centum marcas. Cum post mortem creditoris ad Regis vel Principalis Justiciarij notitiam hujus famosæ cartæ tenor pervenerit : imprimis fœdus fœnoris quæstus condemnabitur, & creditor scripto suo deprehensus fœnerator, mobilibus suis indignus judicabitur (c). Quod si is cujus fundus est a Rege quomodolibet obtinuerit, ut sic distractus sibi restituatur, in sorte (d) tota Domino Regi tenebitur, etiamsi creditor per biennium vel amplius possederit, Regis tamen munificentia de summa sortis illius taxare consuevit, maxime propter (e) singularis gratiæ munus, in quo fidelibus suis debito prælationis tenetur, & tunc (f) quia creditoris sed fœneratoris qui sui fidelis (g) enormi jactura ditatus fuerat, ratione publicæ potestatis bona omnia percepturus est. Sunt & pleraque alia quæ singulariter ad fiscum pertinent, quæ non facile sub una Scripturæ serie redigi possunt ; quia non constituta sed casualia sunt. De hijs (h) tamen excidentibus hujus tertij generis, non supra post firmas, sed infra post omnia placita compoti fiant ante catalla fugitivorum ; ut ipsa quoque locorum posi-

(w) L. R. publicas.
(x) L. R. *deest* publicas.
(y) L. R. Publicas.
(z) L. R. *deest* &.
(a) L. N. sortem : nunc puplicas.
(b) L. R. *deest* merito.
(c) L. R. *deest* judicabitur.
(d) L. R. *pro* in sorte *habet* & forte.
(e) L. N. maxime singularis propter.
(f) L. N. & item quia.
(g) L. N. fideli.
(h) L. R. his.

tione

tione videantur pro enormibus culpis delinquentium ad fiscum pertinentia.

D. Miror super his quæ dixisti; non (*i*) enim cum prioribus stare posse videntur. Cum enim Ascriptitiorum Dominis liberum sit, non solum illos transferre, verum etiam quibuscunque modis distrahere, sicut supra dictum est; & non tantum Catallorum sed & corporum merito Domini reputentur (*k*); mirandum est cum Dominus rerum & hominis rei nil delinquat in legem, quare possessione sua privetur: videri enim justum posset, ut Regis constitutio in personam delinquentis puniret excessum, mobilia vero cum ipsis fundis in usus Dominorum cederent.

M. Movet te quod me movet; verum in his longam fieri moram superfluum credo, cum ab inceptis negotijs aliena sint. Ut tibi satisfiat; propter solam Regis Assisam sic esse cognoscas; nec enim est qui Regiæ constitutioni, quæ pro bono pacis fit, obviare præsumat. Quod si Dominis Catalla suorum per Assisam condempnatorum provenirent, forte quia cupiditatis humanæ fervida sitis in medio posita est, propter modicum quæstum quidam in necem suorum etiam innocentium grassarentur: ea propter Rex ipse, cui generalis est & a Deo credita cura subditorum hoc ita decrevit ut sic rei legi satisfacientes corpore puniantur, & retentis sibi ipsi mobilibus, domesticis hostibus hoc est Dominis suis non exponantur (*l*): verum sicut jam diximus, sola Regis institutio urgente necessitate pro bono pacis facta, hujus quæstionis principalis solutio est.

D. Video quod non sine causa sit. Nunc, si placet, prosequere. Verum restat in præcedentibus quiddam, quod vellem altius (*m*) si placet, expediri. Dixisti enim, quod fugitivorum & mutilatorum per Assisam mobilia summonita ad Scaccarium deferuntur, & in Annali suo loco scribuntur: Quid autem de prædonum vel furum Catallis fieri debet non dixisti; si scilicet ad Regem pertineant, vel cui de jure cedere debeant.

M. Prædonum, qui & fures manifesti dicuntur, & latenter furantium conditio (*n*) dissimilis est; Porro tam horum quam illorum duo sunt genera, ex quorum singulis Catalla diversis diverso modo proveniunt. Prædonum quidem sicut & (*o*) furum quidam exleges sunt, quos usitatius Utlagatos (*p*) dicimus, quidam non: Utlagati (*q*) vero

(*i*) L. N. nec enim.
(*k*) L. R. reputantur.
(*l*) L. R. exponuntur.
(*m*) L. N. alcius.
(*n*) L. R. *pro* latenter furantium *habet album spatium.*
(*o*) L. R. *desunt* sicut &.
(*p*) L. N. uthlagatos.
(*q*) L. N. Uthlagati.

vel exleges fiunt (r) quando legitime citati non comparent, & per legitimos & conſtitutos terminos expectantur & etiam requiruntur, nec juri ſe offerunt. Horum itaque catalla ſicut & vita in manibus comprehendentium ipſos eſſe noſcuntur, nec ad Regem pertinere qualibet ratione poſſunt: Prædonum autem bona qui nondum in hanc miſeriæ ſummam delapſi ſunt, ſi comprehendantur ad fiſcum proveniunt: furum autem ad Vicecomitem ſub quo deprehenſi & puniti ſunt. Quod ſi Vicecomes furis cauſam ad Curiam (s) deduci dignam duxerit, ut ibi judicetur (t), nihil ipſis ſed totum Regi debetur, quod fur ille poſſedit (u). Si vero furem proprium quis inſecutus fuerit, & in Curia prima Domini Regis, vel etiam in Comitatu ipſum comprehenderit (w), & reum furti adjudicata lege probaverit; de catallis furis ſi ad id ſuffecerit ablata vero (x) primum læſo reſtituantur (y), præſidente ſi placet Domini Regis Juſticiario de ſumma ablatorum fide ejus qui petit vel Sacramento: poſt modum autem ex provida ſtudioſorum pacis inſtitutione, idem de bonis furis tantundem accepturus & (z) in laboris & ſumptus ſui ſolacium, quantum prius dolo furis amiſerat. Hæc autem duplex & prudenter procurata ſolutio ab antiquis Solta (zz) & Perſolta vel Proſolta non immerito dicta eſt: primo enim quod ablatum fuerat & ſolvitur, & ob hoc Solta dicitur: deinceps pro laboris & ſumptus impendio quod adicitur Pro vel Perſolta nuncupatur. His in hunc modum expletis, quod fuerat in bonis Rei reſiduum fiſco proveniet.

D. Et hæc neceſſaria viſa ſunt; ſed nunc juxta promiſſum, de cenſu nemorum, ſi placet, proſequere.

M. Gratulor quod te tam dictuum (a) virtutem (b) quam dicendorum ordinem memoriter tenuiſſe conſpicio. Supereſt igitur ut votis tuis ſatisfacere pro viribus non omittam.

(r) L. R. eleges ſunt.
(s) L. R. pro Curiam habet vacuum ſpatiolum.
(t) L. N. videatur.
(u) L. N. poſſiderit.
(w) L. R. Si vero furem Domini Regis vel etiam in Comitatu ipſum ut ibi comprehendunt, & reum.
(x) L. R. deeſt vero.
(y) L. N. reſtituerentur.
(z) rectius eſt.
(zz) Exempli gratia: —— Et in Soltis Regis, Willelmo Cumin & Johanni Mariſcallo, vj l & xiij s & iiij d; Mag. Rot. 2. H. 2. Rot. 1. a. Nortfolc.

In Soltis Reginæ xl l, per breve Regis, Willelmo Cumin & Willelmo de Haia & Roberto Fot; Ib. Rot. 1. b. Sudfolc.

Willelmo Cade xxx l in Soltis Regis per taleam, Et Willelmo Cumin & Johanni Maricallo C s in Soltis Regis; Ib. Rot. 1. b. Sudf.

In Soltis, per breve Regis, Aaron Judæo, xxx l; Mag. Rot. 12. H. 2. Rot. 6. a.
(a) L. R. dictuum; fortaſſe pro dictorum.
(b) L. N. tam ductum virtutem quam.

XI. *De Censu nemorum.*

Post compotum Purpræsturarum & Escaetarum sequitur compotus de Censu (*bb*) nemorum, brevis satis & expeditus, sub hoc tenore verborum: Idem Vicecomes vel ille alius N. reddit compotum de xx l, de Censu illius nemoris vel forestæ de Norhamtescira (*c*); In Thesauro liberavit, & quietus est. Sunt tamen quædam Forestæ de quibus decimæ constitutorum censuum Ecclesijs majoribus solvuntur; sicut de Wiltescira, & de Hamptescira Ecclesiæ Sarisburiensi, de Norhamtescira vero Ecclesiæ (*d*) Lincolniensi: cujus solutionis causam sic accepi; quod enim de forestis solvitur pene totum vel ejus maxima pars (*e*) ex placitis & exactionibus provenit; sic igitur per datas decimas illiciti quæstus utcumq; *(f)* redimi posse visi sunt. De his (*g*) autem sic compoti fiunt: Ille vel ille reddit compotum de xx l, de Censu forestæ illius; in thesauro xviij l; & in capite proximæ lineæ inferioris sic; & in decimis constitutis illi Ecclesiæ xl s; deinde in fine ejusdem lineæ paulo seorsum ab alia scriptura sic, & quietus est. Intellige etiam semel tibi dictum, quod omnia debita & item ea quæ in Thesauro soluta fuerint seorsum ab alia scriptura collocanda (*h*) sunt (*i*); ut juvanti animo & discurrenti oculo facilius occurrant; quoniam ex solvendis Summonitiones, & ex (*k*) jam solutis Absolutiones fiunt. Post diligentem firmæ principalis Veteris sive Novæ compotum, & item post compotum Purpræsturarum & Escaetarum, & Census nemorum, quæ omnia sicut dictum est annuo jure solvuntur, sequitur Compotus de placitis [&] conventionibus; in quo primum post modicum intervallum in medio lineæ prænotatio fit quorum scilicet Judicum hic sint.

(*bb*) *Proventus annuus Forestarum usitato vocabatur* Censu. *Exempli causa,* Rogerus de Powis [debet] L l, de censu forestæ de Dena de v annis quibus tenuit forestam. *Mag. Rot.* 26. *Hen.* 2. *Rot.* 1. *b. Salopescira.* Idem Vicecomes reddit compotum de xxx s, de censu forestæ de Graveling. *Ib. Rot.* 9. *a. Wiltescira.* Walterus Walranus reddit compotum de xxv l, de censu Novæ forestæ. *Ib. Rot.* 10. *a. Sudhantescira.* Radulfus filius Stephani debet xx l, de censu forestæ de Scirwude. *Ib. Rot.* 10.

b. *Not. & Derbiscira.*
(*c*) L. R. Norhamtesir.
(*d*) L. R. *desunt* & de Hamptescir. Ecclesiæ Sarisburiensi de Norhamtescira vero Ecclesiæ.
(*e*) L. N. paris.
(*f*) L. R. ubicunque.
(*g*) L. R. hijs.
(*h*) L. R. collocata.
(*i*) L. R. *deest* sunt.
(*k*) L. R. *deest* ex.

XII. De

XII. *De Placitis & Conventionibus quo ordine de his compoti fiant cum exacta solvuntur.*

Placita autem dicimus pœnas pecuniarias in quas incidunt delinquentes: Conventiones vero Oblata (*kk*) spontanea. Cum ergo de hijs (*l*) instat exactio, tunc primum Clerico Cancellarij traditur Summonitio; qui seriatim de singulis urget Vicecomitem, dicens; Redde de illo X, pro hac causa; quod si in Thesauro solvitur (*m*) quod requiritur, sic scribetur (*n*) in Annali; N reddit compotum de x l pro hac causa, et ex ordine tota redigatur in scriptum, In Thesauro liberavit, & quietus est: Si vero per breve Regis quietus est, ut (*o*) diximus numerus exprimatur in Brevi, dicetur; N reddit compotum de x l, & addat causam; Deinde paulo inferius in ipsa linea, per breve Regis ipsi N x l, & quietus est; quod si de C summonitus sit, cum tamen summa debiti sint in Annali x l & C solverit in denarijs, vel de C Breve Regis impetraverit, dicetur; N reddit compotum de x l in Thesauro Centum Solidos, & debet C Solidos, vel in perdonis per breve Regis ipsi N C Solidos, & debet C Solidos. Et nota, quod in omnibus compotis de placitis & conventionibus singuli per se respondebunt, ut scilicet onus debiti, si non satisfecerit, vel absolutionem si universum solverit, suo nomine suscipiant exceptis Communibus assisis & Danegeldis & Murdris; de his enim Vicecomes compotum reddit, & super his ipse vel quietus in Annali scribitur vel in debito. Quod si mutatus fuerit (*p*) Vicecomes, nihilominus is qui succedit ei de eisdem respondebit & de eis (*q*) summonebitur; & nisi satisfecerit, per firmam quam soluturus est coercendus est. Quisquis enim in onus ejusdem officij mutato succedit Vicecomite, ab ipso suscipit rescripta debitorum Regis in ipso Comitatu; ut per hoc nosse valeat a quibus quæ debeant requiri, cum Summonitionem ad se delatam susceperit. Ad Vicecomitem ergo spectat compotus Communium, ad quem solum pertinet coercio singulorum; & qui Vicecomes fuerit, dum compotus fit, vel quietus vel in debito hac ratione scribetur.

(*kk*) *Exempli gratia:* Ricardus de Lifewis debet v marcas, pro habenda Magna assisa versus Galfridum Talebot de terra de Streta. Et hoc venit de Oblato Ricardi. *Mag. Rot.* 1. *R.* 1. *Rot.* 9. *a. Dorf. & Sumerf. tit.* De Oblatis Curiæ.

(*l*) L. R. his.
(*m*) L. R. solverit.
(*n*) L. R. scribet.
(*o*) L. R. ut sicut diximus.
(*p*) L. R. fuerat.
(*q*) L. R. his.

D. Teneo

D. Teneo memoriter quod fieri debeat cum quis super aliquo debito summonitus Breve Regis detulerit, quod numerum qui requiritur exprimat. Quod si Regis cartam de quietancia rerum ejusdem generis ad Scaccarium deferat; ut sic dicatur; Volo igitur ut hæc omnia teneat libere & quiete de placitis & murdris, & his & his, & hujusmodi; nunquid in perdonis erit?

M. Erit revera; sed non dicetur, In perdonis per cartam Regis, vel per libertatem cartæ, hoc vel illud; immo per breve Regis (*qq*): Quod si carta quidem non specificans sic contineat, libere & quiete ab omni exactione & seculari servitio prædicta possideat; non tamen ab his quæ (*r*) requiruntur, per hoc quietus est vel in perdonis scribetur: nolunt enim qui assident, speciali debito per generalem absolutionem derogari

D. Pernitiosa satis est ista subtilitas: qui enim a generibus singulorum liber est, & a singulis generum meretur absolvi.

M. Verum est quod dicis; neque nos dissentimus; sed tamen quid fiat dicimus, non quid forte fieri debeat. Igitur cum de omnibus hijs (*s*) quæ in Summonitione continentur, vel per numeratam pecuniam vel per Brevia Regis satisfactum fuerit, hac lege scripturæ quæ supra dicta est semper utendum est: verum cum non solverit aliquis universum quod ab ipso requiritur, sed partem ejus vel forte nihil, causa statim a Vicecomite requirenda est cur is solvendo non fuerit. Quod si responderit Vicecomes, quæsisse se diligenter ejus de quo agitur nec catalla invenire potuisse; Inferet Thesaurarius, Cave tibi; nam hujus rei fidem, scilicet quæsisse te nec invenire potuisse per quod satisfieri posset, fide corporaliter præstita confirmabis; Quo respondente, præsto sum; in consummatum compotum fidei susceptio differetur; ubi (*t*) super multis consimilibus semel data sufficiat. De hac tamen fide jam circa initia plura dicta sunt, & restant aliqua suo loco dicenda.

(*qq*) *Antiquitus in Magno Rotulo scribi solitum est*, In Donis *seu* In Perdonis *huic vel illi. Exempli causa:* — Et Cadawadladro vij l de præstito Regis. Et in Donis per breve Regis, Maddoch viij l & x s, Et Gernetto xl s, et Hoelo filio Joaf xl s. *Mag. Rot.* 3. *Hen.* 2. *Rot.* 5. *a. Salopescira.* Walterus de Lindesia r c de x marcis: In Perdonis, per breve Ricardi de Luci, ipsi Waltero x marcæ; quia debent requiri de Comite Willelmo, Per idem breve; Et Quietus est. *Mag. Rot.* 13. *Hen.* 2. *Rot.* 11. *a. Cantebr. & Hunt. Cujus etiam rei plurima exempla in præcedenti historia mea sunt.*

(*r*) L. N. hijs qui.
(*s*) L. R. his.
(*t*) L. N. ut super.

XIII. De

XIII. *De distinctione personarum quæ solvendo non sunt; de quibus a Vicecomite fides offertur, & sub quo tenore Verborum fides detur.*

Porro hic primum distinguendum est circa debitores & debita; ut in quibus fides oblata locum habeat, & quibus non, tibi constet: si enim Miles, vel Liber alius, vel ascriptitius, vel quælibet hujusmodi cujuscunque conditionis aut Sexus persona, Regi tenetur in quovis debito, quod quidem pœna sit pro excessu, non oblatum spontaneum, fide illa Vicecomitis oblata & in fine suscipienda contentus erit Thesaurarius; & iterato scribetur debitor in hoc Annali, sicut in præterito, vir vel mulier cujus actio per inopiam inanis facta est; verum secus est si debitor ille de quo quæritur Civis est vel Burgensis, si scilicet genere civis sit, vel facta sibi necessitate commorantium civium legibus sponte se subjecerit; non enim sufficit Vicecomiti, quod horum si qui de requisita summa non satisfaciunt mobilia tamen solvat, vel quæsisse se nec invenisse fidem offerat, ut sic ad Scaccarium liberetur, nisi eorum & domos & fundos & quoslibet urbium redditus infiscet, & penes alios collocer, ut vel sic debita Regi pecunia proveniat; quod si non inveniantur qui suscipiant, parcentibus sibi invicem ejusdem conditionis hominibus, domos eorum seris obstruat, & fundos diligenter excoli faciat. Si vero interim hij solverint quæ requiruntur, ad proprietarios ipsos per manum Vicecomitis sine molestia quæ sui juris sunt reddent.

D. Mirari satis non possum, ubi culpa dispar non est, cur genus hoc hominum gravius lex nostra coercet.

M. Maxima pars possessionis eorum qui fundos habent & per agriculturam sustentantur, in pecudibus in animalibus & in frugibus est, & item in hijs quæ non facile cohabitantium notitiam possunt effugere: at hijs (*u*) qui mercimonijs inserviunt, & qui parcentes sumptibus, multiplicandis possessionibus totis viribus & modis omnibus insistunt, in numeratam pecuniam sollicitior cura consistit. Per hæc enim, commercia facilius exercentur; & possunt hæc in locis tutis & ignotis facile reponi: unde fit ut sæpe qui dives est, non patentibus his quæ latent, pauper reputetur: propter hæc (*w*) igitur in hos gravius lex illa decernit; quia superabundans (*x*) pecuniarum puteus non de facile videtur exhaustus.

(*u*) L. R. his.
(*w*) L. R. hoc.

(*x*) L. N. superhabundans.

D. Quid

D. Quid Affifa communis, & quis vel quo ordine de ipfa refpondeat, ex prædictis magna ex (*y*) parte jam conftat. Nunc fi placet de Auxilijs, vel Donis Civitatum feu Burgorum; qualiter ex hijs compoti fiant, & qui principaliter conveniendi vel coercendi fuper his fuerint (*z*) ediffere; modus enim coercionis ex prædictis jam patet.

M. Gaudeo te memorem prædictorum; & hinc, fateor, me magis animafti. Noveris itaque quod plurimum intereft, fi Donum vel Auxilium Civitatis per fingula Capita commorantium in ea a Jufticijs conftituatur: vel fi Cives fummam aliquam quæ Principe digna videatur Jufticiarijs offerant & ab eis fufcipiatur (*a*): difpar enim in his duobus modus eft coercionis; fi enim per fingulos a Judicibus conftitutum eft Donum, & quilibet eorum folvendo non fuerit, lex prædicta de Civibus non folventibus fervatur; ut fcilicet domibus & redditibus ufque ad folutionem privetur. At fi dictum eft (*b*) a Civibus, dabimus Regi mille; & hæc fumma digna fufcipi judicetur; ut ftatutis terminis eadem exurgat ipfi provideant. Quod fi forte excufare cœperint, allegantes quorundam inopiam (*c*) qui in aliqua parte fummæ hujufmodi tenebantur; tunc diligentur hoc eft per fidem Vicecomitis inquirendum eft, fi a tempore conftituti per eofdem Cives Doni vel Auxilij hij tales extiterint ut folvere non valerent; quod fi inventum fuerit, provideant (*d*) alios ex quibus fumma prior exurgat, vel per Commune (*e*) diftribuatur quod reftat; verum fi tempore conftitutionis habundabant, fed lege fortunæ natura mobilis nunc egeant (*f*), fuftinendum eft de hijs (*g*) quoufque per Dei gratiam ditentur.

D. Cerno quod in omnibus modum fervantes femper Regijs commodis inhæretis.

M. Memoriter tenes quid de Civibus vel Burgenfibus non folventibus fit agendum. Quod fi forte Miles aliquis vel Liber alius (*h*) a fui ftatus dignitate quod abfit degenerans, multiplicandis denarijs per publica mercimonia, vel per turpiffimum genus quæftus hoc (*i*) eft per fœnus inftiterit, & exacta fponte non folverit, non per fidem tantum de (*k*) non inventis Vicecomes abfolvetur, verum cum hæc (*l*)

(*y*) L. N. pro parte.
(*z*) L. N. hijs fuerit.
(*a*) L. R. fufcipiat.
(*b*) L. R. *deeſt* eft.
(*c*) L. R. eorundem inopiam.
(*d*) L. R. provideat.
(*e*) L. N. Communem.

(*f*) L. N. *defunt* fed lege fortunæ natura mobilis nunc egeant.
(*g*) L. R. his.
(*h*) L. R. vel liberalis a.
(*i*) L. R. *deeſt* hoc.
(*k*) L. N. *deeſt* de.
(*l*) L. R. hoc.

Præsidenti suggesserit, districtum ab ipso mandatum suscipiet ut de summa quæ ab illo requiritur statutis terminis solvenda fidejussores inveniat; quod si noluerit, omnes ejus redditus infiscentur; ut in hac parte merito fiat hijs (*m*) similis qui multiplicant quocunque modo rem.

D. Dignum revera est, ut a statu suo pro turpi quæstu recedens degener Miles vel Liber alius, præter communem Liberorum legem puniatur. Sed jam nunc si placet edissere, quæ sunt quæ pro catallis ejus qui Regi tenetur debeat imputari, & utrum ab omnibus omnia tollenda sunt a Vicecomite, quousque summa quæ requiritur exurgat, quando scilicet principalis debitor exacta sponte non solvit.

XIV. *Quæ Catalla debitorum vendenda non sunt cum ipsi sponte non solvunt, & quis in vendendis ordo sit observandus.*

M. In pelagus me quæstionum impellis, nescio, Deus scit, qua emersurum. Noveris itaque, quod sic iterum personarum distinctio necessaria est, sicut ex consequentibus liquebit; vellem tamen in hac parte mihi parceres, ne pluribus displicitura proferre compellas.

D. Dum a legis constitutæ tramite non exorbitaveris, justam prudentis offensam non mereberis: quod si cui grave videbitur quod lex statuit, ei qui condidit irascatur non tibi.

M. Ab initio debitor tibi factus sum ex promisso. Hinc est, quod volens (*n*) teneor parere vel volenti (*o*) petenti. Debitorum igitur qui exacta sponte non solvunt Catalla quæ licite venduntur, sunt eorum mobilia ac sese moventia; qualia sunt aurum, argentum & ex hijs (*p*) vasa composita, lapides quoque preciosi, & mutatoria vestimentorum, & hijs similia; item equorum utrumque genus, usuales scilicet & indomiti, armenta quoque boum & greges ovium, & cætera hujusmodi; frugum etiam & quorundam victualium mobilis est natura; ut scilicet libere vendi possint, deductis necessarijs sumptibus debitoris ad sola victualia, hoc est ut necessitati non superfluitati, & item ut naturæ satisfiat non crapulæ; nec soli debitori, sed uxori ejus ac filijs ac familiæ quam prius exhibuerat dum sibi viveret, huic necessaria ministrantur.

D. Quare dicis quorundam?

M. Victualia quæ ab eis cotidianis usibus præparantur & quæ sine

(*m*) L. R. *his.*
(*n*) L. R. *nolens.*
(*o*) L. R. *desunt* vel *volenti.*
(*p*) L. R. *deest* hijs.

sui mutatione esibus (*q*) accommodantur, qualia sunt panis & potus, nulla ratione vendi possunt; victualium igitur ea duntaxat, quæ præter usus necessarios ab ipsis dominis reservanda fuerant ut venalia fierent, licite venduntur, qualia sunt carnes sale conditæ, casei, mella, vina, & his similia. Et nota, quod si debitor ille qui solvendo non est, Militiæ cingulum semel obtinuerit, venditis cæteris, equus tamen ei, non quilibet sed unus (*r*) usualium reservabitur; ne qui dignitate factus est eques, pedes cogatur incedere. Quod si Miles ejusmodi fuerit, quem juvat armorum decor & juvat usus eorum, & qui meritis exigentibus debeat inter strenuos computari, tota sui corporis armatura cum equis ad id necessarijs a venditoribus erit liberrima; ut, cum oportuerit, ad Regis & regni negotia armis & equis instructus possit assumi. Si tamen hic idem cui lex in parte pepercit, audita necessitate Regis vel Regni, delitescens se absentaverit, vel ad hoc vocatus non venerit, sic tamen ut (*s*) non proprijs, sed Regijs stipendijs militet, & evidenter absentiam suam non excusaverit, nec ab his venditores temperabunt; sed solo contentus equo propter dignitatem Militiæ sibi relicto juri communi vivat obnoctius. Caveat autem Vicecomes & venditores suos præmonuerit in vendendis hunc ordinem observare; mobilia cujusque primo vendantur, bobus autem arantibus per quos agricultura solet exerceri quantum poterint parcant; ne ipsa deficiente debitor amplius in futurum egere cogatur. Quod si nec sic quidem summa quæ requiritur exurgat; nec arantibus parcendum est. Cum igitur omnia, quæ ad ipsum specialiter pertinent venalia venundata sunt; si nondum satisfactum est, ascriptitiorum ejus fundos adeant, & eorum catalla licite vendant, ordinem simul & legem prædictam observantes; hæc enim ad Dominum pertinere noscuntur, sicut supra dictum est: quo facto, sive sic de requisita summa satisfactum sit sive non, venditores jubet Lex nostra quiescere (*t*); nisi forte Scutagium sit quod a Domino requiritur; pro Scutagio namque si non solverit qui Regi tenetur Dominus principalis, non tantum propria sed & Militum suorum & ascriptitiorum catalla passim venduntur; ratio namque Scutagiorum Milites suos magna pro parte respicit; qui non nisi de Militibus & ratione Militiæ regi debentur. Vidi tamen ego ipse cui nondum cana memoria est (*u*), pro singulis debitis eorum qui non satisfaciebant, non solum propria sed etiam Militum (*w*) suorum & ascriptitiorum Catalla licite vendi. Sed illustris Regis constitutio in

(*q*) L. R. usibus.
(*r*) L. N. sed usus.
(*s*) L. R. *deest* ut.
(*t*) L. N. *desunt* Lex nostra quiescere.
(*u*) L. N. *deest* est.
(*w*) L. N. sed & multum suorum.

Scutagijs

Scutagijs tantum hoc obfervari decrevit, ordine fervato ut prius propria dehinc aliena vendantur. Quod fi Milites ea quæ de feodis fuis proveniunt Domino folverint, & hoc oblata cautione probare voluerint, pro hijs quæ a Dominis requiruntur catalla fua venundari lex prohibet.

XV. *Quod Vicecomes a Debitoribus debitoris illius qui Regi non folvit debitam Regis fummam fufcipiat.*

Item admonendus eft Vicecomes ut diligenter & follicite quantum poterit inveftiget (x) fi quis in Comitatu fuo debitori illi in folutionem fibi præftitæ vel penes eum depofitæ pecuniæ teneatur: quod fi inventum fuerit, a debitore illo fumma illa quæ ab ejus creditore qui Regi tenetur requiritur, exigatur, & ne ei fuper eodem refpondeat auctoritate publicæ poteftatis inhibeatur.

XVI. *Quod Vicecomes a fundis ejus, qui non folvit, quod requiritur percipiat, etiamfi eofdem, ex quo Regi teneri cœpit quomodolibet alienaverit.*

Item, fi debitor a tempore quo Regi teneri cœpit, fundum fuum vel redditum alij locaverit, vel pignus pro pecunia dederit, vel etiam quod abfurdum tibi forte videbitur dominium ejus per venditionem a fe tranftulerit; fi alias inventa non funt per quæ Regi fatisfiat, quæcunque perfona fuerit, quocunque titulo poffeffionem nactus fuerit, nihilominus ex eodem (y) quod ad Regem pertinet accipietur; falva proprietate domino (z) qui jufto eam titulo cœperit poffidere; nifi forte debitor ille fundi venditi pretium ab initio fponte Regi folverit; tunc enim tuta erit penes emptorem poffeffio. Hujus autem rei caufam, licet diftorta modicum & Regiæ nimis utilitati ferviens videtur, evidentem tamen & fatis juftam fecundum patrias leges comprobabis. Quifquis enim in Regiam Majeftatem deliquiffe (a) deprehenditur, uno (b) trium modorum juxta qualitatem delicti fui Regi condempnatur: aut enim in univerfo mobili fuo reus judicatur, pro minoribus culpis; aut in omnibus immobilibus, fundis fcilicet & redditibus, ut eis exhæredetur, quod fi

(x) L. N. inveftigiet.
(y) L. N. nichilhominus ex eadem.
(z) L. N. domino proprietate.

(a) L. R. delinquiffe.
(b) L. R. *deeft* uno.

pro majoribus culpis, aut pro (c) maximis quibuscunque vel enormibus delictis, in vitam suam vel membra. Cum igitur aliquis de mobilibus in (d) beneplacito Regis judicatur, lata in eum a Judicibus sententia per hæc verba, Iste est in misericordia Regis de pecunia sua; Idem est ac si de tota dixissent. Laicorum enim (dd) indefinitæ, non his pro quibus tutius est eas accipi, hoc est particularibus, sed semper universalibus æquipollent. Cum igitur fundi illius catalla quæ (e) debitor prius distraxit (ee) in beneplacito Principis adjudicata fuissent, & ipse de requisita summa non satisfecerit, videri potest injustum ut rem non suam in fisci jacturam alienaverit.

XVII. *Quod non licet Vicecomiti debitam sibi pecuniam a non solventibus suscipere; & quid sit agendum si forte susceperit.*

Item admonendus est Vicecomes propter fidei Religionem quæ ab ipso de non solventibus exigitur, immo quam ipse sponte visus est obtulisse, ut sic a Summonitione sibi facta liberari valeat, ne a debitore quolibet qui Regi non solvit, interim aliqua quæ sibi juste debebantur suscipiat. Non enim verisimile est, non posse Vicecomitem de Catallis ejus invenisse, per quæ Regi debita summa solvatur, qui (f) ipsi Vicecomiti sponte vel invitus quod requiritur exsolvit. Si tamen ante datam fidem per se vel per alium recordatus fuerit Vicecomes de his aliqua se suscepisse, vel etiam post datam, nondum tamen soluto Scaccario diei illius, hoc est dum compotus ejus recens est, & veniens in publicum querula voce se suscepti tunc immemorem (g) estitisse fide de his oblata (h) confirmare voluerit, susceptam summam nomine debitoris persolvens liberabitur. Si vero quod absit post fidem datam, post solutum Scaccarium per alium hoc innotuerit, non jam suscepta tantum solvens absolvetur: Sed pro excessu suo in Regis beneplacito judicandus pecuniariter punietur. Postremo Vicecomitem commonuisse sufficiat, ut post susceptam Summonitionem diligenter inquirat per viciniam, si vir qui solvendo non est, uxorem ducens vel mulier ditiori nubens, vel quovis alio modo ditescat, quatenus de requisitis satisfacere valeat: quod si inventum fuerit, propter fidem Vicecom. solvere compellatur: quod si nihil horum inventum fuerit;

(c) L. N. *deest* pro.
(d) L. R. & in.
(dd) *Subintelligi videtur* sententiæ.
(e) L. N. quem.
(ee) L. N. post distrixit.
(f) L. R. quæ.
(g) L. N. inmemorem.
(h) L. N. fide de his oblata fide.

poterit tunc purgata confcientia de hijs rebus fidem dare, & imminentem rerum fuarum jacturam declinare.

XVIII. *Qualiter vir pro uxore, vel uxor pro viro convenienda eſt, cum ille vel illa folvendo non eſt.*

D. Nunquid vir pro uxore, quæ Regi tenebatur, & fati debita jam folvit, vel pro viro fuo mulier ei fuperſtes conveniri debet?

M. Satis audiſti, quod qui adhæret mulieri unum corpus efficitur; fic tamen ut Caput ejus fit. Merito ergo pro ea conveniendus eſt; quia mulier fui poteſtatem non habet fet vir (*i*). Quod fi vir ex ea prolem fufceperit, cui ratione uxoris debeatur hæreditas, & mortua jam uxore nondum foluta Regi debita pecunia fuerit; vir ille nomine hæredis conveniendus & coercendus eſt; alias autem non. Porro mulier viro fuo fuperſtes prolem habens, & in viduitate cum ipfa permanens; ratione prolis, cui debetur hæreditas, convenienda & coercenda (*k*) eſt; fic tamen ut doti ejus parcatur, quia præmium pudoris eſt. Quod fi relictis liberis alij viro mulier adhæferit; legitimus hæres pro debito patris conveniendus eſt: verum fi mulier quæ deliquit & regi tenetur, priore viro fine liberis mortuo, ad alium fe cum fua hæreditate tranſtulerit, debitum ejus a viro (*l*) requirendum eſt. Hoc eſt igitur quod petiſti. Et fic vir caufa uxoris, & uxor caufa viri convenienda eſt. Certum autem habeas, quod femper legitimus hæres qui debitori fuccedit, pro illo conveniendus eſt: ut ficut in emolumentum fic in onus fubeat. Solus autem afcriptitius & is, qui fine hæreditate decedit, venditis Catallis per extremam mortis aleam a debito liberantur; non tamen ab Annali in quo debita hæc annotantur nifi per Breve Regis auferentur, (*m*) cum fcilicet de hijs (*n*) a Thefaurario Regi fuggeſtum fuerit quod inutiliter in Rotulo fcribantur, cum nullo pacto fieri (*o*) poffit ut ab hijs (*p*) debita pecunia proveniat.

(*i*) L. R. non habet poteſtatem fui fed vir.
(*k*) L. R. convenienda eſt & coercenda.
(*l*) L. N. *defunt* a viro.
(*m*) L. R. offerentur.
(*n*) L. R. *defunt* de hijs.
(*o*) L. N. *deeſt* fieri.
(*p*) L. R. his

XIX. *Quod non sit idem modus cohertionis Baronum Regis & aliorum in pœnis pecuniarijs.*

Ad hæc nosse te convenit, quod in debitis Regis requirendis & debitoribus cohercendis, Baronum Regis (*pp*) & cæterorum qui passim pro suis excessibus pecuniariter Regi puniuntur, par conditio non est. Porro de hijs qui de Rege nihil (*q*) habent in Capite, lex prædicta servatur. At si de Rege tenens Baroniam, audita Summonitione fidem in propria persona, vel manu generalis Oeconomi (*r*) quem vulgo Senescallum dicunt, in manum Vicecomitis dederit sub hac tenore verborum; quod de hac summa & de hac Summonitione grantum (*s*) Baronum Scaccarij die compoti sui faciet (*t*); sic Vicecomes contentus sit.

XX. *Quid faciendum cum Oeconomus, qui fidem dedit de satisfaciendo, non comparet.*

Si vero die compoti voce præconia requisitus non venerit, nec per se nec per alium satisfecerit Vicecomes quod ad ipsum pertinuit fecisse judicabitur, causa vero hæc seorsum in Memorandis Scaccarij præ-

(*pp*) *Verisimile videtur,* Barones *sic appellatos propterea, quod* Homines Regis *fuerint,* (*sive summi ac præcipui Regis* Tenentes); *ut qui Regi hominium vel homagium juraverint; sicut Vir Doctissimus D.* Georgius Hickesius *in amplo & immortali opere suo notavit; viz. in* Thesauro Lingg. Septentr. de Gramm. Anglosax. *p.* 146; *& sicut res ipsa loquitur. Hos* Barones *seu* Magnates *noster Cl. Auctor hic vocat* Barones Regis; *nec immerito: nam priscis temporibus omnes* Magnates Angliæ (*proprie sic dicti*) *fuerunt* Homines *sive* Barones Regis; *quippe qui* (*sicut hic supra innui, & ante in mea Historia viz. Vol.* 1. *Capp.* 15, 16, 17, *fusius exposui*) Baronias suas *immediate sive in* Capite *tenuerunt de* Rege. *Profecto vir apud Antiquarios* Angliæ *dum viveret satis clarus, parum recte ut opinor de hac re scripsit. Nomini ejus parcendum duxi, tum quia jam Vita functus est, tum quia mihi pridem vel amicus vel sodalis fuit. Is in quodam libro suo typis excuso dicit, fuisse olim* Barones Regni *differentes a* Baronibus Regis; *itemque* Milites ac libere tenentes in Capite de Regno, *alios quam* Milites ac libere tenentes in Capite Rege. *Per quam quidem distinctionem quid sibi voluit, mihi non est exploratum. Fuerunt olim, nec dubium,* Barones *improprio sive minus principali sensu sic dicti; qui nempe erant capitales* Tenentes *seu vassalli* Comitum *aliorumque* Baronum Regis. *Fuerunt etiam alij his multo inferiores* Barones, *magisque improprie sic dicti; quales erant* Barones *id est* Homines Quinque Portuum *aliarumque* Villarum. *Sed nec illi nec isti, quantum scio,* Barones Angliæ *seu* Regni *fere vocari, aut* Baronagij *nomine comprehendi solebant. Si autem voluit nuperus ille auctor fuisse* Barones *aliquos* (*proprie sic dictos*) *qui* Baronias *suas tenuerunt non de* Rege *sed de* Regno *ipso; et fuisse* Milites ac libere Tenentes *quia* Feoda *sua per* Militiam *tenuerunt de* Regno: *is mihi videtur lectoribus incautis struere insidias, rem plane chimæricam proponendo.*

(*q*) L. N. nichil.
(*r*) L. N. vel per manum Economi.
(*s*) L. N. graantum.
(*t*) L. R. fiet.

cepto

cepto Thesaurarij diligenter annotata in finem Scaccarij reservabitur; ut tunc communicato consilio, gravius qui sic deliquit (*u*) puniatur. Quod si post consummatum compotum Vicecomitis sui venerit & satisfecerit; de affidentium gratia, & de legis indulgentia poterat absolvi; verum necesse est ut Vicecomes fidem ejus in Comitatu sub omnium oculis suscipiat : quia si forte qui dederit volens malignari, datam inficiari voluerit, adversus eum ad omnem probationis summam recordatio Comitatus sufficiet. Quod si alias sibi datam Vicecomes confessus fuerit, nihil egisse judicabitur ; unde mox de firma sua requisita summa capietur, ut Summonitioni satisfaciat in hac parte dicenti, vel capientur de firma tua.

XXI. *Quid cum veniens non satisfaciat, si Miles est ? Quid si non Miles ?*

Si vero qui fidem se dedisse non diffitetur die nominata venerit nec satisfecerit, si Dominus est, ad Scaccarium quamdiu sederit detinebitur, fide data in manu Marescalli, sicut supra diximus, quod a leugata villæ nisi Baronum licentia non recedet : soluto vero Scaccario illius termini, si nondum satisfecerit, in loco tuto sub libera custodia collocabitur (*w*), quousque Rex ipse si præsens fuerit, vel Præsidens cum alijs affidentibus, quid de ipso agendum fuerit decernat, qui fidem se dedisse de satisfaciendo confessus, nullo modo satisfecit ; quod si miles vel alius ejus Oeconomus (*x*) venerit, nec satisfecerit, pro fide læsa (*y*) comprehendetur, & Marescallo custodiendus tradetur, post (*z*) solutum Scaccarium licite vinculandus, & in carcerem mittendus, sive Miles fuerit sive non. Miles vero super debito proprio non satisfaciens, cum tamen de satisfaciendo fidem dederit, post solutum Scaccarium non in carcere sed infra septa domus carceralis libere custodietur, fide corporaliter præstita quod inde sine (*a*) Regis vel Præsidentis licentia non recedet. Decrevit enim memorandæ nobilitatis Rex illustris, ut quisquis Militiæ dignitate præfulget, pro debito proprio, cum pauper a Vicecomite simul & a vicinia reputetur, in carcerem non mittatur (*b*), sed seorsum infra septa domus carceralis libere custodiatur : verum quisquis mandato Domini fidem dederit sicut prædictum est Vicecomiti, & veniens non solvit; hunc comprehendi, & in car-

(*u*) L. N. deliquid.
(*w*) L. R. collocatur.
(*x*) L. N. Economus.
(*y*) L. R. pro læsa fide.

(*z*) L. N. primo solutum, & *deest* post.
(*a*) L. R. & L. N. *deest* sine.
(*b*) L. N. mutatur.

cerem foluto Scaccario mitti, five Miles fit five non, lex ftatuit: & quoniam liberum eft cuilibet Baroni, pro debito, quod ab ipfo requiritur fidem officialis opponere, ut fic (*c*) interim Vicecomes (*d*) importunitate careat, & de rebus fuis opportunius ipfe difponat; ne fic [in] immenfum Regij mandati videatur auctoritas eludi, decretum eft, ut comprehenfo illo qui læfæ fidei reum fe non fatisfaciens judicavit (*e*), ftatim a Vicecomite fervientes dirigantur, qui fundos principalis Domini perluftrantes, venditis quocunque modo Catallis fummam requifitam ad Scaccarium ejufdem termini deferant; & tandem ille comprehenfus pro læfa fide juxta poffibilitatem fuam pecuniariam pœnam luat, & amplius fuper eodem debito, etiamfi Dominus præceperit, ad fidem dandam non admittatur.

XXII. *Qualiter Dominus puniendus eft, qui fponte Militem expofuit, ut poffit interim liberari.*

Principalis etiam Dominus ne hæc inpune præfumpfiffe videatur, non per fidem fuppofitæ perfonæ fed folum per propriam (*f*) dilationis beneficium promerebitur, fi forte fuper eodem debito (*g*) ipfum iterato fummonitioni (*h*) contigerit. Sunt tamen qui credant ut de cætero fuper eodem debito nec etiam per fidem propriam ufque ad Scaccarium a Vicecomite dilationem (*i*) obtineat; quod quidem beneficium dilationis magnum dicunt qui fifco tenentur; poffunt enim interim de rebus fuis mitius difponere & dilatæ per aliquot tempus folutioni neceffaria præparare; quin potius dicunt quod fufcepta Summonitione liceat Vicecomiti juxta communem aliorum legem ftatim in catalla ipfius manum mittere. Hijs ego, fateor, prorfus non diffentio; fed tamen multis judicijs (*k*) & teftimonijs verifimile videatur procuraffe Dominum, ut Miles fuus his (*l*) cafibus exponeretur, quatenus poffet ipfe vel fic interim liberari; hujus autem rei validiffimum eft contra Dominum argumentum, fi copiofus, fi rebus habundus, fi folutioni fufficiens a Vicecomite fimul & a vicinia judicetur.

D. Dignum (*m*) revera eft ut is (*n*) indultam fibi gratiam demereatur, qui in datoris ejus perniciem eadem abufus eft.

(*c*) L. R. *pro* ut fic, nifi fic.
(*d*) *Mallem* Viceconitis.
(*e*) *Malim* indicavit.
(*f*) L. R. proprium.
(*g*) L. N. *deeft* debito.
(*h*) *elegerim* fummoneri.
(*i*) L. N. dilatione.
(*k*) *forfan* indicijs.
(*l*) L. R. *deeft* his.
(*m*) L. N. *deeft* Dignum.
(*n*) L. N. ut his.

M. Habes

M. Habes ex præcedentibus utcunque (*o*) diſtinctum, quæ catalla vendi debeant & quæ non, & etiam in quibus perſonarum diſcretio tenenda eſt & in quibus non; tunc ſcilicet cum debitores, qui in pecuniarijs pœnis Regi tenentur, ſolvendo non fuerint : reſtat, ut quid de oblatis ſpontaneis fieri debeat, cum item non ſoverint, oſtendamus.

XXIII. *Quid de ſponte offerentibus faciendum, cum & ipſi non ſolvunt.*

Noveris igitur, quod oblatorum Regi quædam in rem quædam in ſpem offerentur (*p*). In rem quidem offerri dicimus, cum oblatum a Rege ſuſcipitur, & offerens conſequenter pro quo obtulit (*q*) a Rege ſuſcipit ; ut ſi quis pro libertate aliqua, pro fundo, vel pro firma, vel pro cuſtodia cujuſque qui minor eſt annis uſque ad annos legitimos habenda, vel pro quovis alio quod ad ſuam utilitatem vel honorem accedere videatur ſponte Regi C l vel C m. offerat, & aſſentiente Rege ſtatim poſt oblatum ſuſcipiat optatum. De hijs igitur qui ſponte ſe obligant, & qui Conventione cum Principe facta poſſidere jam cœperint lex noſtra decernit, ut quam diu ſolvendo fuerint indultis ſibi beneficijs gaudeant & utantur. Quod ſi de Regis debito ſummoniti ſolvere deſierint, ſtatim careant impetratis; ſic tamen ut ſi manente Scaccario ſuper eodem ſatisfecerint, ablata (*r*) omnia ſine moleſtia ſibi reſtituantur. Et nota, quod qualiſcunque perſona, cujuſcunque etiam conditionis aut ſexus fuerit, huic obſervantiæ de ſponte oblatis ſemper erit obnoxia, ut ſcilicet Summonitioni ſatisfaciat vel impetrato careat, niſi Rex ipſe obſequij præſtiti vel paupertatis intuitu aliquid ſibi præter communem legem indulgeat; velut (*s*) ſi de oblatore grandis ſumma, ad quodlibet Scaccarium modicum quid ab ipſo ſolvi conſtituat ; & hoc per breve ſuum Baronibus innoteſcat. In ſpem vero dicuntur offerri, cum quis exhibendæ ſibi juſtitiæ cauſa, ſuper fundo vel redditu aliquo Regi ſummam aliquam offert ; non tamen ut fiat, ne in nos excandeſcas, & venalem penes eum juſticiam dicas, immo ut ſine dilatione fiat. Noveris tamen non quæcunque ſic offeruntur a Principe ſuſcipi, etiamſi modum videatur excedere : gratis enim quibuſdam juſticiæ plenitudinem exhibet, obſequij præſtiti vel ſolo charitatis intuitu. Quibus (*t*) autem lege conditionis humanæ nec prece

(*o*) L. R. utrum diſtinctum.
(*p*) L. R. *deeſt* offerentur *ſeu potius* offeruntur.
(*q*) L. N. optulit.
(*r*) L. N. oblata.
(*s*) L. N. velud.
(*t*) L. R. Quibuſdam autem.

nec pretio vult acquiefcere, obftantibus interdum eorum meritis qui poffidere nofcuntur; vel forte proprijs poftulantium meritis nequaquam hoc exigentibus qui vel in Regnum vel in Regem ipfum aliquid deliquiffe culpantur: de hijs (*u*) autem fic conftituit Rex infignis, ut antequam Rectum habuerint, hoc eft (*w*) antequam per fententiam obtinuerint, vel re fibi penitus abjudicata (*x*) ab omni fpe ceciderint, de oblatis nichil (*y*) folvant, fed fufficiat de hujufmodi Vicecomiti refpondere, Rectum nondum habuerunt. Provideat tamen (*z*) Vicecomes ne per ipfum debitorem ftet, quo minus caufa ejus executioni mandetur, fi fcilicet juri fe nolit offerre, ut hac arte promiffa fibi pecunia Rex fraudetur. Cum enim hoc compertum fuerit, dolus ei non fubveniet, fed per omnia fic coercebitur (*a*) ac fi per fententiam obtinuiffet. Hujus autem fpontaneæ dilationis eft fignum (*b*) cum Breve Regis penes fe detinens, eo non utitur. Solet tamen cum his miferente Principe mitius agi, qui poft promiffam pecuniam a caufa cadunt, ne fpe fua fruftrati, rebus etiam fine emolumento fpoliati, duplici contritione conterantur.

XXIV. *Quid de Relevijs fponte non folutis.*

Sunt item (*c*) tertij generis Obventiones, quæ non videntur prorfus inter oblata computandæ, fe magis Fines ad Scaccarium dicuntur; cum fcilicet de Rege tenens in Capite Baroniam relicto hærede deceffcrit, & idem hæres cum Rege in quam poteft fummam componit, ut paterni juris mereatur ingreffum; quem finem Relevium vulgo dicimus. Quod fi Baronia eft, in Regis eft beneplacito quæ debeat effe fumma Relevij; fi vero de Efcaeta fuerit, quæ in manu Regis deficiente hærede vel aliter inciderit, pro feodo Militis unius hoc tantum Regi nomine Relevij folvet, quod effet fuo Domino foluturus, hoc eft centum folidos. Sunt autem qui credant eos qui in Relevijs Regi tenentur nec fummoniti folvunt, fpontaneorum oblatorum legibus obnoxios; ut cum folvendo non fuerint, careant impetratis: at verius dici poteft, ut ficut de pecuniarijs pœnis fit fic fiat (*d*) de Relevijs; debita namque filijs ratione fucceffionis hæreditas a lege fponte oblatorum videtur excludere.

(*u*) L. R. his.
(*w*) L. N. *deeft* eft.
(*x*) L. R. adjudicata.
(*y*) L. R. dum oblatis nihil.
(*z*) L. R. *pro* tamen *habet* inde.

(*a*) L. N. cohercebitur.
(*b*) L. R. *deeft* fignum.
(*c*) L. R. funt etiam.
(*d*) L. N. fit ut fiat.

XXV. *Quid*

XXV. *Quid de avibus oblatis faciendum, & quo tempore summonendæ.*

Item fit interdum ut Aves Regiæ Regi qualibet ex causa promittantur; Accipitres scilicet vel Falcones. Quod si promittens determinans dixerit, Accipitrem instantis anni vel Mutatum; vel locum etiam exprimat, dicens Hibernensem (*e*) Hispanensem, Norrensem dabo; sic satisfaciat. Si vero nec qui promittit nec cui promittitur determinaverit; in arbitrio promittentis erit, si Mutatum vel non sit soluturus. Sed si integer & sanus a Regis Asturcarijs judicetur, quacunque exclusus fuerit, suscipitur. Porro si summonitus dignum suscipi ad Scaccarium detulerit, nec sic *(f)* tum qui suscipiat; etiamsi post hoc in annum vel biennium vel amplius differatur summonitio, nisi quem maluerit, Mutatum scilicet vel ornum solvere non cogetur. Quod si summonitus solutionem quomodolibet differri (*g*) procuraverit, juxta numerum annorum quibus indulta sibi est dilatio, biennium scilicet (*h*) vel triennium vel deinceps, mutatum solvet. De hijs (*i*) autem contra terminum Paschæ Summonitio non fit; quia earum æstivo tempore rarus est usus; tunc enim Cavearum antris inclusæ diligenter custodiuntur, ut redeat deposita vetustate pennarum decor, & eorum ut Aquilæ juventus renovetur: verum contra terminum Sti Michaelis quæ Regi debentur summonentur, ut instante tunc hyeme Regijs aptentur obsequijs. In cohercendis autem his qui sic se sponte obligant nec solvunt, lex prædicta de sponte oblatis servatur.

XXVI. *De auro Reginæ.*

Ad hæc noverint hij qui in pecunia numerata Regi sponte se (*k*) obligant, quod Reginæ similiter tenentur, licet expressum non fuerit. Quamvis autem non sit expressum, est tamen promisso compromissum; ut cum Regi C vel ducentas marcas promiserit, Reginæ pariter teneatur pro centum marcis argenti Regi promissis, in una Marca auri; pro ducentis in duabus marcis auri; & sic deinceps. In his (*l*) autem perquirendis eadem lege Vicecomes per omnia utetur, qua in Regijs usus est, non tamen (*m*) ante sed post. Cum ergo de Regijs debitis Summonitiones fiunt, adest Clericus Reginæ ad hoc constitutus, &

(*e*) L. R. Hibernicum.
(*f*) *Malim* sit.
(*g*) L. N. solutione differri quomodolibet.
(*h*) scilicet biennium.
(*i*) L. N. his.
(*k*) L. N. *deest* se.
(*l*) L. N. hijs.
(*m*) L. R. non tam.

addit

addit in Summonitione, De illo habeas (*n*) centum Marcas pro causa illa, & ad opus Reginæ unam marcam auri. Summonita autem ad Scaccarium ab ejus Officialibus ad hoc (*o*) constitutis seorsum suscipiuntur. Noveris etiam quod licet Rex de promissa sibi pecunia (*p*) mediam partem dimiserit vel universam, vel etiam summonere distulerit, de hijs tamen (*q*) quæ ad Reginam pertinent, secundum quod sibi visum fuerit per omnia fiet; ut ea nolente neque dimittantur neque differantur quæ sibi debentur (*r*); sed summonita solvantur, & non solventes prædicto modo coerceantur (*s*).

D. Nunquid de Promissis Regi citra centum marcas aliquid Reginæ debetur?

M. Quibusdam sic videtur, ut usque ad x marcas teneatur; ut scilicet is qui x Regi promiserit (*t*), in una uncia auri Reginæ teneatur; alijs non nisi de C & supra ab initio promissis. De his (*u*) igitur ad præsens cum modestia sustine: quia re nondum terminata, suspensa resolutio est. Litigat sane de his (*w*) Pars Reginæ cum debitoribus; & adhuc sub Judice lis est. De Misericordia autem Judæorum & de Redemptione Monetariorum, sicut de sponte oblatis dictum est, sua portio secundum formam prædictam Reginæ debetur.

D. Nunquid in pecuniarijs & sponte oblatis, Clericos & Laicos sine differentia Lex una cohercet (*x*)?

M. In sponte oblatis apud omnes lex una servatur; ut sive Clericus sit sive Laicus qui solvendo non fuerit, donec satisfecerit careat impetrato. Observatur etiam idem in omnibus alijs quæ quovis pacto Regi debentur (*y*) a Clericis; cum scilicet suæ dignitatis & liberæ possessionis privilegium allegare neglexerint: de allegantibus autem quid fieri debeat, a discretis & Deum timentibus Laicis, si placet, rescito; hijs enim ad præsens ex industria supersedeo, ne dicar meæ conditionis hominibus ultroneas leges & mitiora jura dictasse.

D. Dixisti, si bene memini, frequenter in manum Regis Baronias vel fundos incidere; vellem igitur si placet explicares quo ordine redditus Escaetarum ad fiscum proveniant; si uno modo vel dissimiliter.

(*n*) L. R. *illo has centum.*
(*o*) L. N. *hæc.*
(*p*) L. N. *sibi summa.*
(*q*) L. R. *hijs autem quæ.*
(*r*) L. R. *desunt* quæ sibi debentur.
(*s*) L. N. *coherceantur.*
(*t*) L. R. *qui Regi promiserit x.*
(*u*) L. N. *hijs.*
(*w*) L. N. *hijs.*
(*x*) L. R. *Clerici & Laici sine differentia coercentur.*
(*y*) L. R. *desunt* quæ quovis pacto Regi debentur.

XXVII. *Quod*

XXVII. *Quod aliter de firmis atque aliter de Custodijs respondendum, & sub alio tenore fides danda.*

M. Cum in manum Regis Baronia vel magnum aliquid excidit, mandato ejus vel Præsidentis ad hoc discreti utriusque Ordinis viri diriguntur, qui (*z*) singula perlustrantes redditus eorundem in summam redigunt, & de hac (*a*) in Scaccario teneri Vicecomitem vel quemlibet alium constituunt: satisfaciens igitur de hac summa is qui ad hoc constitutus est, in denarijs vel brevibus vel taleis, subsequente fide de legitimo compoto, meretur absolvi; & de ea (*b*) sic scribetur in Annali: Ille vel ille reddit compotum de firma Honoris illius; in Thesauro hoc; & (*c*) quietus est; vel & debet. Verum cum Rex Escaetæ suæ custodiam fidei alicujus commiserit, ut videlicet quod inde provenerit, ad Scaccarium solvat post factum compotum fides illa sub prædicto verborum tenore non dabitur: immo quod quantum inde vel in denarijs vel alijs quibuscunque rebus susceptis (*d*) tantum secundum conscientiam suam ad Scaccarium solvit; exceptis his (*e*) duntaxat victualibus, quæ ipso nomine xeniorum non procurante, sibi collata sunt.

D. Nunquid custos ille de his redditibus victui necessaria percipit?

M. Licet scriptum sit non alligabis os bovi trituranti; tamen nisi expresso Regis mandato de his nihil (*f*) percipiet; proprijs enim stipendijs, quisquis ille fuerit, in his Regi militabit: de hujusmodi autem sic in Annali scribetur: Ille vel ille reddit compotum de exitu illius Honoris per veredictum suum. Cum igitur de omnibus prædictis constitutis vel casualibus satisfactum fuerit, & fuerint singula per ordinem autentice Rotuli scripturæ deputata, convocatis omnibus assidentibus ad principalis firmæ compotum consummandum, qui in summo Rotuli annotatus est redditur, & hoc ordine perficitur; soluta hoc Termino a Vicecomite firma de qua examen factum est, In primis a Calculatore per numerales acervos in distantium virgarum spatijs distribuetur; deinde facta detractione per combustionem, sicut supra dictum est, eadem dealbatur, & appensa sibi taleola combustionis, quæ tamen Vicecomiti non computatur, summa quæ relinquitur in taleam

(*z*) L. N. quæ.
(*a*) L. R. hoc.
(*b*) L. R. eo.
(*c*) L. R. *deest* &.
(*d*) L. N. rebus suscepit.
(*e*) L. N. hijs.
(*f*) L. N. hijs nichil.

redigitur.

redigitur. Similiter & quod solutum fuerat in Termino Paschæ, & dealbatum in eadem talea sic (*g*). Et combustio de eodem termino cum combustione finalis termini mittitur; ut una sit utriusque solutionis talea, & similiter una combustionis: quo facto Thesaurarius Rotulum exactorium cujus supra meminimus proferens, summam quæ de Comitatu illo per acervos supra & seriatim (*h*) disponi facit; ab hac igitur imprimis quod solutum est in Thesauro & dealbatum detrahitur; deinde quod Rex de firma Comitatus contulit aliquibus Bl[ancum]; Post hæc iterum, quæ alias soluta sunt per brevia Regis vel aliter, per acervos disponuntur, & hæc per subtractionem xij denariorum (*i*) e singulis libris dealbantur, sicut quæ in Thesauro solvuntur dealbata per combustionem. Tunc ergo fit inferioris expensæ a superiore summa detractio; & si penitus absolvi meruerit, in fine compoti ejusdem literis patentibus scribitur, & quietus est; vel infra in capite lineæ inferioris, & debet; & tunc demum consummato compoto numerus solutorum in Thesauro apponitur ei quod jamdudum diximus scriptum in Thesauro, & quod fuerat huc usque sic ex (*k*) industria relactum (*l*), ne forte cogatur abradere qui scribit; quod maxime circa numeros & nomina & causas jamdudum vitandum diximus (*ll*).

XXVIII. *Quod fides de legitimo compoto semel data sufficiat per universum.*

Consummato vero sicut dictum est de Corpore Comitatus compoto, a Marescallo fides Vicecomitis sub forma prædicta semel suscipitur, & sic absolutus dimittitur. Fuerunt tamen qui crederent, de singulis per fidem firmandis sigillatim fidem a Vicecomite dandam; ut (*m*) quotiens diceret sic esse aliquid quod sola posset fide confirmari, totiens fidem daret: Sed a prudentibus & legis Divinæ peritis perniciosa satis visa est subtilitas; cum semel fidem dederit se legitimum per omnia compotum salva Conscientia fecisse. Ea propter hæc sententia post

(*g*) L. R. talea sit.
(*h*) L. N. desunt & seriatim.
(*i*) L. R. xij d.
(*k*) L. N. deest ex.
(*l*) forsan pro relictum.
(*ll*) Hæc est, ni fallor, auctoris mens. Quum referebatur compotus in Rotulum Annalem, & scribendum erat, In Thesauro summa illa; *relinqui solebat in Rotulo Annali vacuum spatium; in quo spatio summa illa inferebatur, finito demum compoto; nec ante; ne qua forte postmodum causa esset mutandi summam aut verba quævis emphatica, per Rotuli rasuram.*

(*m*) L. R. & quotiens.

modicum

Lib. II. Dialogus de Scaccario. 451

modicum meruit cum suo auctore (n) contempni; & una fide, hoc est semel data, contenti sunt; quia in unius fidei confessione unum sunt (nn).

D. Sentio, jam languente stylo, quod dicendorum finis adesse festinat; verum licet instantis noctis crepusculum & productioris operis labor prolixior ad alia (o) nos evocent, & paululum respirare compellant; vellem tamen, si fieri posset, ut suspensam & hactenus fluctuantem in verbo tuo discipuli tui mentem (p) confirmares, ostendens quid sit, quod ab initio dixisse te recolo, totam scilicet Scaccarij descriptionem, quædam esse Sacramentorum latibula, quæ revelanda sunt cum omnium libri aperti erunt & janua clausa.

M. Magnum est quod quæris & alterius egens inquisitionis; nec his (q) exponendis ex promisso debitor tibi (r) factus sum. His (s) igitur ad præsens supersedeo, in alterius diei disputationem eadem reservans; vereor quidem ne si pluribus onerato novam sarcinam imponerem, sub pondere deficeres; item si jam dictis, & memoriæ commendandis novarum rerum studia consuerem, utraque te fastidire compellerem. Contentus ergo jam dictis esto, ad quæ me coegisti; habes enim in his (t) quantum madidæ se potuit offerre memoriæ quæcunque circa Scaccarij scientiam potiora tibi visa sunt, initialiter utcunque distincta. Ceterum ad singula, quæ tractu temporis videri poterunt necessaria, ungue tenus explananda, nec virtus hominis nec vita forte sufficeret; ex varijs enim & insolitis casibus vel nulla fiet vel adhuc incognita disciplina. Unde fit ut detractorijs linguis hinc potius exponar, dum succedente tempore pleraque dubia nec dum audita proponi continget; de quibus, aut consimilibus cum hic nihil (u) invenerint, incipiant illudere, dicentes, hic homo cœpit ædificare, & non potuit vel non novit consummare. His ego non dissentio; pessimum namque Magistrum meipsum secutus sum; feci tamen, te cogente, quod potui, duce carens & exemplari; de intacta namque rudique silva Regijs ædificijs missa securi ligna (w) secui, prudentioris Architecti dolabro complananda. Cum igitur ex hijs Regiæ domus struc-

(n) L. R. amore.
(nn) Hujuscemodi argutijs fere sibi placebant quo seculo Cl. auctor floruit.
(o) L. R. ad illa.
(p) L. R. desunt in verbo tuo discipuli tui mentem.
(q) L. N. hijs.
(r) L. R. tibi debitor.
(s) L. N. Hijs.
(t) L. N. hijs.
(u) L. N. nichil.
(w) L. R. lingua secui.

tura surrexerit, is qui dedit initia, primam licet non præcipuam gratiam mereatur. Valeat Rex illustris.

Explicit Liber Secundus (*x*).

(*x*) L. N. *desunt* Explicit Liber secundus.

Nos quorum nomina infra visuntur, qua licuit diligentia ac fide, exemplar hoc impressum Dialogi contulimus cum MS Libro Rubro Scaccarij, mense Junij A. D. 1707, necnon cum MS Libro Nigro Scaccarij de Recepta, mense Augusti eodem anno; altero nostrûm Librum prælegente, altero simul exemplar inspiciente.

THO. MADOX.   GEO. HOLMES.

DISCEPTATIO

EPISTOLARIS

DE

Magno Rotulo Scaccarij

omnium id genus qui hodie extant antiquiſſimo,

ROTULO

Anni Quinti Regis Stephani utplurimum appellato.

DISCEPTATIO EPISTOLARIS.

Ampliffimo & Nobiliffimo Baroni,

JOHANNI Domino SOMERS,

Pari Magnæ Britanniæ,

Thomas Madox S. P.

BONI hiftorici eft, Ampliffime Baro, id agere imprimis, ut lectori conftet eorum quæ tradit veritas ac certitudo. Ideo maximi momenti eft, ut notitijs & monumentis indubiæ fidei ubique fi fieri poffit utatur. Illa autem indubiæ fidei monumenta dicantur; quæ nempe fcripta erant, Primo, quo tempore geftæ funt res in ijs contentæ; Secundo, publica auctoritate; Tertio, ab his qui norunt proprie exprimere (pro more feculi) ea quæ defcripturi erant;

erant; Quarto, bona fide, five nullo fucandi aut fallendi studio. Hæc quatuor optime quadrant *Recordis* publicis. Siquando forte incertum sit, cui demum seculo aut Regis imperio *Recordum* aliquod quod data careat, rectissime assignari debeat; tunc necesse erit, summa ope niti ad illam incertitudinem tollendam, & rei veritatem in aprico ponendam; præsertim si Recordum illud sæpe citandum veniat, & magnæ sit fidei ac dignitatis. Sane inest in Recordo de quo sum locuturus hujusmodi dignitas; inest etiam hujusmodi temporis incertitudo in ea instantia quam Tibi, Nobilissime Baro, jam submisse propositurus sum. Submisse, inquam: immo diffidenter. Ut enim es judicio acutissimo, vereor ne, qui claritati & certitudini es adsuetus, disceptationem hanc meam, umbratilem, imbecillem, & conjecturis repletam, dedigneris. Est tamen quod mihi animos addit. In Te agnosco singularem benignitatem atque candorem. Facile igitur perspicies id quod res est; nec in subjecto quod sua natura est obscurum discutiendo, certitudinem a me exspectabis.

Quocirca Tuo candore fretus ad quæstionem progrediar. Sciendum quod in Scaccario, jam inde a tempore quo illud primo apud *Anglos* institutum fuit, solenne erat quolibet anno *Magnum Rotulum* componere: qui Regiorum redituum ac proventuum compotos sive rationes, per singulos *Angliæ* Comitatus distinctus, complectebatur; antiquitus vel absolute *Rotulus*, vel *Rotulus Annalis*, postea est usque hodie *Magnus Rotulus* Scaccarij seu *Pipæ*, appellatus. Quamplures hujusmodi Magni Rotuli, annis plerisque Regum *Henrici* II, *Ricardi* I, & *Johannis* scripti, in Thesauraria sive Officio *Pipæ Westmonasterij* conservantur; Recorda, omnium quæ in archivis Regijs usquam vidisse me memini, splendidissima; post Rotulum Censualem quem *Librum Domesday* vocant; quin ei æquiparanda. Inter illos reconditur etiam ibidem *Magnus* quidam *Rotulus* reliquorum vetustissimus, *Quintus* R. *Stephani* vulgo dictus. Præclarum & magnificum antiquitatis monumentum; sive scripturam spectemus sive res contentas. Hic *Magnus Rotulus* (seu ut vocamus *Bundellum*) consistit Rotulis peramplis sedecim; ex utraque parte conscriptis; & filo pergamenaceo in capite sive summo consutis. Singuli Rotuli totius fasciculi non sunt vel longitudine vel latitudine ad amussim æquales. Sed permistim longi sunt sive alti (nempe a summo ad imum) quatuor pedes circiter, & lati pedem plus minus unum. Quilibet Rotulus duabus prælargis membranis constat; nisi si qua forte avulsa perijt; sicut in *bundelli* Rotulo Quarto fit; cujus una membrana (id est, Rotuli pars dimidia) perijt, altera superest. Facies loci in quo *Magni Rotuli* antedicti asservantur, æri incisa in fronte hujus Dissertationis & in hac pagina visitur. Ob

oculos

DISCEPTATIO EPISTOLARIS. 457

oculos hominum pofui venerabundus. Sane delineatu dignam cenfuit monuitque me V C *Johannes Talman* Junior, architecturæ & graphices peritiffimus, fummaque mihi neceffitudine conjunctus. Illius

monitis facile obtemperans, delineari atque æri incidi curavi: ut pofteris aliquatenus innotefcant facrorum Rotulorum forma ac fitus. Hæc autem eft figuræ illius æneæ mens: Capfa infcripta numero I continet ordines five abacos decem; in quibus conduntur *Magni Rotuli* qui hodie extant vetuftiffimi: hac nimirum ferie: abacus primus, five a folo altiffimus, continet *Magnum Rotulum* illum de anno Quinto R. *Stephani* vulgo dictum, aliofque feptendecim; nam fingo Quintum *Stephani* eum effe qui in menfa expanfus jacet: abacus ejufdem capfæ fecundus continet *Magnos Rotulos* quindecim, fcilicet reliquos quotquot hodie fuperfunt R. *Henrici* II; nam *Magnus Rotulus* illius Regis Primus itemque Octavus defiderantur: abacus tertius habet *Magnos Rotulos* decem R. *Ricardi* I, duofque primos R. *Johannis*: quartus reliquos R. *Johannis*: quintus priores *Magnos Rotulos* R. *Henrici* III: fextus alijque habent alios ejufdem Regis ac R. *Edwardi* I. In fumma, capfa II, III, & IV, complectuntur *Magnos Rotulos* Regum ordine fuccedentium. Redeo ad rem. Hic de quo loquimur *Magnus Rotulus* omnium vetuftiffimus (quæ eft infelicitas) data caret; imo nullum quantum reperio temporis veftigium præ fe fert. Incertum ergo eft,

non

non folum ad quem annum, fed etiam ad cujus Regis imperium, an ad *Henrici* I, aut *Stephani*, aut *Henrici* II, referendus fit. Hinc ab auctorum alijs (*a*) citatus fuit ut Rotulus anni primi R. *Henrici* II; ab alijs (*b*) ut Rotulus anni quinti R. *Stephani*; ab alijs (*c*) ad annum aliquem R. *Henrici* I. relatus. Ego, tametfi illum plus femel nec indiligenter evolvi, cui anno aut tempori affignarem dubius hæfi. Quare ad præfens operæ pretium duxi nonnulla in unum cogere & æqua lance librare, quæ huic quæftioni lumen aliquod immiffura arbitrarer.

Imprimis quæratur, utrum fit *Magnus Rotulus* anni primi R. *Henrici* II. Si qui effe crediderunt, his rationibus fuffulti videntur. *Magni Rotuli* tam anni Secundi quam aliorum ferme omnium annorum R. *Henrici* II, continua ferie extant; fimul videlicet in armario Pipæ eodemque pluteo affervati. Sed nullus reperitur *Magnus Rotulus* anni Primi illius Regis; nifi hic is fit. Hunc autem eum effe ideo conjectabantur, quod juxta & proximo ante *Magnum Rotulum* anni Secundi reponi confuevit. Accedit etiam cujufdam antiqui Clerici de Scaccario in eandem fententiam opinio. Verbi gratia: In dorfo Rotuli Sexti hujus Bundelli, membrana fecunda, duæ notæ vifuntur. Una charactere minufculo hujus tenoris, De tempore Regis Henrici fecundi: altera charactere majufculo ita, Annus primus Regis H. fecundi. Has notas non uno tempore nec ab uno fcriptas conjecerim. Utrarumque autem fcriptura fimilis eft illi, quæ temporibus R. R. *Henrici* III, aut *Edwardi* I, circiter ufurpata fuit. Hæc fi Tuæ Amplitudini placet perpendantur. Si quidem *Magnus Rotulus* anni Primi R. *Henrici* II, revera interijt, fruftra ejus jacturam figmentis fupplere conabimur; vel Bundellum impar in archivo *Pipæ* juxta pofitum, vel confuetum plutei ordinem in opem vocando. Atqui forfan momentofior habebitur antiqui illius Clerici annotatio quam fuperius memoravi, annum primum *Henrici* II defignans. Libere dicam. Adeo non femper accuratæ funt veterum Clericorum notæ ejufcemodi, ut interdum falfæ deprehendantur, fpeciatim de rebus diu ante tempora quibus vixerunt geftis. Inftantiæ caufa: Bundellum five Magnus Rotulus anni trigefimi quarti R. *Henrici* II; in Rotulo de *Berrochfcira* membrana fecunda in dorfo, infcribitur charactere qualis in ufu erat circa tempora R. *Edwardi*, vel Primi, vel Secundi, vel Tertij ineuntis, his verbis, Annus Secundus Regis H. Secundi; & juxta fcriptura recentiori qualis tempore Henrici VI, aut Edwardi IV, ufitata fuit, Annus

---

(*a*) Spelm. *in Gloffario ad verbum*, Achata.
(*b*) Dugd. *de Baronagio paffim*; &c.
(*c*) Prynn. *de Auro Reginæ, in append.* p. 5.

fecundus

secundus Hen. Secundi. Quæ quidem notæ tam futiles funt, ut etiam omni probabilitatis fpecie careant; ficut cuiquam infpicienti facile patebit.

Potiora ego fi poffum Tuæ Amplitudini proferam. Satis, opinor, certi fumus, quis fit *Magnus Rotulus* anni Secundi R. *Henrici* II. Illum vir præftantiffimus *Alexander de Swereford*, primus auctor five poffeffor *Libri Rubri* qui in Scaccario eft, nobis digito commonftravit, & ex illo complufcula in *Libro Rubro* citavit de primo Scutagio R. *Henrici* II, & de *Danegeldo* (*d*); id quod etiam in Hiftoria mea fuperius oftenfum eft (*e*). Sic autem quoad veteres *Magnos Rotulos* fe res habet. Sequens *Magnus Rotulus* præcedenti in compluribus correfpondere folet. Adeo ut cognito Rotulo cujufvis anni, diligens lector facile perviderit alterum alterius fequacem effe; nimirum comparando nomina Computantium, fuorumque debitorum fummas, ficut in Rotulo unius atque alterius anni fcripta cernuntur. Nam Rotulus anni fequentis ita compotum excipere folet, prout in Rotulo præeunte definebat. Hoc modo: *Ille* Vicecomes fe ad Scaccarium fiftens, anno puta R. *Henrici* II primo, *reddit compotum* (vocibus utar Scaccarialibus) de CCCC l firma Comitatus *illius*: folvit ad *Receptam* five ut vocant *in Thefauro*, C l. Et factis fibi legitimis allocationibus, id eft, fubtractis pecunijs a Vicecomite erogatis juffu Regio, alijsque jure fubtrahendis, ad CC l: Debet [Regi] C l. In *Magno Rotulo* proximi nempe fecundi anni *Henrici* II, inveniemus regeftum ad hunc modum: *Ille* Vicecomes *reddit compotum de C l de Veteri firma* Comitatus *illius*, five *de firma anni præteriti*; fi folvat partem, puta dimidiam, dicetur, *In Thefauro L l, Et debet L l:* Si totum perfolvat, *Ille* Vicecomes *reddit compotum de C l de Veteri firma*, five *de firma anni præteriti*; *In Thefauro liberavit, Et quietus eft:* Si nullam partem folvat, *Ille* Vicecomes *debet C l de Veteri firma*. Et fic de alijs Computantibus perinde ac de Vicecomite, mutatis fcilicet mutandis. Pariliter, ex *Magno Rotulo* anni fequentis invenerit quis *Magnum Rotulum* præcedentis, comparatione reflexa. Præcedens fequentis index, fequens præcedentis. Quandoquidem igitur, Baro eruditiffime, compertum habemus Rotulum anni Secundi R. *Henrici* II; reftat, ut illum cum hoc vetuftiffimo Rotulo conferendo, videamus an hic fit Rotulus anni Primi Regis *Henrici* II, ficut ille eft anni Secundi. Contuli ego jamdiu eft. Sed fruftra tentavi concordantiam inter duos iftos Rotulos invenire. Nihil difpexi quod fidem faciat conjunctorum annorum

---

(*d*) *Lib. Rub. Scacc. fol.* 47. *b. col.* 1. *Ib. fol.* 186. *a.*

(*e*) *Hift. Scacc. Vol.* 1. *Cap.* 17. *Sect.* 1. Kent. Radulfus Picot. & *Cap.* 16. *Sect.* 1.

Rotulos esse. Quinimo alter ab altero toto cœlo differt. Longe diversa sunt nomina Computantium & Debitorum quæ in horum duorum Rotulorum uno ac quæ in alio continentur, diversæque itidem summæ. Præterea, *Libri Rubri* auctor nomina eorum sigillatim descripsit qui anno Primo R. *Henrici* II, Comitatuum *Angliæ* Vicecomites fuerant. Quorum nomina, ut pronum est credere, ex Rotulo Annali anni Primi ejusdem Regis (antequam perierat Rotulus iste) desumpsit. Ea autem Vicecomitum nomina quæ in Vetustissimo hoc Rotulo memorantur, non eadem sunt ac quæ auctor *Libri Rubri* ex Rotulo anni Primi *Henrici* II. excerpsit; imo sunt prorsus aliena. Istud comparatio facta indicabit. Hic annotabo quosdam e Vicecomitibus Comitatuum prout in Veteri illo Rotulo habentur; deinde Vicecomites eorundem Comitatuum de anno Primo R. *Henrici* II, ex fide *Libri Rubei:* Ejusmodi collatio nominum Vicecomitum monstrabit discordantiam quæ est eatenus inter Veterem illum Rotulum, & Vicecomites anni illius Primi in *Libro Rubro* recensitos. Subjiciam, si placet, in margine nonnullos etiam Vicecomites anni Secundi R. *Henrici* II, prout in *Magno Rotulo* anni illius Secundi memorantur: Et collatio anni Secundi cum anno Primo ostendet congruentiam quæ est inter duos annorum illorum Vicecomites: sed hoc obiter. Exempli gratia: Vetus hic *Magnus Rotulus* habet Vicecomites *Essexæ*, *Ricardum Basset* & *Albericum de Ver*; *Liber Ruber*, *Ricardum de Luci*; *Magnus Rotulus* anni secundi R. *Henrici* II, *Ricardum de Luci (f)*. Vetus Rotulus ponit Vicecomites *Huntedonescirę Ricardum Basset* & *Albericum de Ver*; *Liber Ruber Paganum* cognomento *Vicecomitem*; *Rotulus* anni Secundi *Henrici* II, eundem *Paganum (g)*. In Veteri Rotulo comperimus Vicecomitem *Kanciæ Rualonum*; In *Libro Rubro Radulfum Pichot*; In *Magno Rotulo* prædicti Anni Secundi *Radulfum Picot (h)*. In Veteri Rotulo legitur Vicecomes *Staffordscirę Milo de Gloceestra*; In *Libro Rubro Robertus de Stafford*; In *Magno Rotulo*

(f) Ricardus Basset & Albericus de Ver r c de firma de Essexa & Heortfordscira. *Mag. Rot.* 5. *Ste. Rot.* 6. *a.*

Ricardus de Lucy r c de firma Essexæ; In thesauro quater xx xiiij l xij s ij d numero. *Lib. Rub. Scacc. fol.* 184. *b.*

Ricardus de Luci r c de firma Essexæ. *Mag. Rot* 2. *H.* 2. *Rot.* 3. *a*

(g) Ricardus Basset & Albericus de Ver r c de firma de Sudreia, & de Grentebrugescira. & de Huntedonescira. *Mag. Rot.* 5. *Steph. Rot.* 5. *a.*

Huntingdonesire. Paganus Vicecomes r c de quater xx l xxxv s vij d Bl. de dimidio anno. *Lib. Rub. Scacc. fol.* 185. *a.*

Huntendunescira. Paganus Vicecomes r c de Veteri firma; Et idem Vicecomes de Nova firma. *Mag. Rot.* 2. *H.* 2. *Rot.* 2. *a.*

(h) Rualonus Vicecomes r c de firma de Chent. *Mag. Rot.* 5. *Ste. Rot.* 7. *a.*

Radulfus Pichot r c de iij partibus anni. *Lib. Rub. fol.* 184. *b*

Chent. Radulfus Picot r c de viij l & xiiij s & ij d Bl. de Veteri firma. Et idem Vicecomes r c de Nova firma. *Mag. Rot.* 2. *H.* 2. *Rot.* 12. *b.*

anni

anni illius Secundi *Robertus de Stafford* (*i*). Vetus Rotulus memorat *Gaufridum de Furnell*. Vicecomitem *Devenesciræ*; *Liber Rubeus Ricardum de Riveres*; *Magnus Rotulus* anni illius Secundi Comitem *Ricardum* [*de Redvers*] (*k*). Vetus Rotulus exhibet Vicecomitem *Gloecestrescira Milonem de Gloecestra*; *Liber Ruber Osbertum de Westbery*; *Rotulus* anni secundi *Walterum de Hereford* (*l*). Quid multa? Ex jam adductis exemplis elucet, multum inter se dissidere Veterem hunc Rotulum, & *Librum Rubrum* qui continet excerpta e *Magno Rotulo* anni Primi R. *Henrici* II; elucet etiam, concordiam esse inter *Librum Rubrum* & *Magnum Rotulum* anni Secundi ejusdem Regis. Quid hinc sequitur? Plane hoc; nempe Veterem hunc Rotulum non esse anni Primi R. *Henrici* II: tum quia Vicecomites in Veteri hoc Rotulo memorati, non sunt ijdem ac quos *Liber Ruber* dicit Comitatus tenuisse anno illo Primo; tum etiam quia nomina Vicecomitum de anno hujus Veteris Rotuli, non concordant cum ijs quæ *Magnus Rotulus* indubius anni Secundi illius Regis posuit pro Vicecomitibus ejusdem anni Secundi. Quod ad Veterem illum Rotulum; unicum aliud addam. Nonnihil sane differentiæ mihi videre videor inter characterem sive scripturam illius Rotuli, & Rotulorum tam anni Secundi quam aliorum sequentium annorum R. *Henrici* II. Rotulus ille comparatus cum singulis Rotulis priorum annorum R. *Henrici* II, scripturæ forma magis ab istis, ni fallor, differt, quam Rotuli isti inter se comparati differunt alij ab alijs. Adeo ut, quantum ex scripturæ facie conjectari licet, illum his antiquiorem censerem. Pensatis igitur quæ superius dixi, verisimile videatur, Veterem illum non esse Rotulum de anno Primo R. *Henrici* II. Neque profecto comperire possum, quod ad ullum alium annum ejusdem Regis jure referri debeat.

Proximo, considerandum est, Domine Illustrissime, utrum Rotulus ille de quo disquirimus (Veterem voco) rite attribui possit anno

---

(*i*) Milo de Gloecestra r c de ―― de Veteri firma Statfordscira, Et idem de Nova firma. *Mag. Rot.* 5. *Ste. Rot.* 8. *a.*

Staffordshire. Robertus de Stafford r c de firma Staffordscira; In Thesauro xviij l iiij s Bl. &c. *Lib. Rub. fol.* 185. *a.*

Robertus de Stafford r c de firma de Staffortscira. *Mag. Rot.* 2. *H.* 2. *Rot.* 6. *a.*

(*k*) Gaufridus de Furnell. r c de ―― de Veteri firma Devenescira; Et idem de Nova firma. *Mag. Rot.* 5. *Ste. Rot.* 16. *a.*

Devenesire. Ricardus de Riveres r c de quater xx xviij l x s ij d de firma Comitatus.

Lib. Rub. fol. 185.

Ricardus Comes r c de firma de Devenescira. *Mag. Rot.* 2. *H.* 2. *Rot.* 10. *a.*

(*l*) Milo de Gloecestra r c de firma de Gloecestrescira [Veteri & Nova]. *Mag. Rot.* 5. *Ste. Rot* 8. *a.*

Gloucestr. Osbertus de Westbery Vicecomes r c de CCxlix l x s ij d Bl. de tribus partibus anni. *Lib. Rub. fol.* 184. *b.*

Walterus de Hereford r c de viij l & xj s & v d Bl. de Veteri firma de Gloecestrescira. In th. l, Et Q. e. Et idem r c de Nova firma. *Mag. Rot.* 2. *H.* 2. *Rot.* 10. *a.*

Quinto R. *Stephani.* Nescio qui factum est ut a modernis Quinto illi anno attribueretur; nisi forte ansam præbuit adnotamentum quoddam parvula pergamena scriptum & hujus Bundelli sive Veteris Rotuli tegumento annexum. Pervulgatum est, Equitem Auratum *Simonds Dewes*, non infimi subsellij Antiquarium, illud jamdudum annexisse vel annecti jussisse. Ita audierat Vir strenuus *Willelmus Prynn* (m), & hodierni etiam fando audivimus. Istius adnotamenti verba sequuntur: *Rotulus Magnus* Pipæ *de anno* 5° *Regis* Stephani. *Qui Rotulus per aliquos centenos annos elapsos, errore Librarij in Rotulo* 6°, *m.* 2, *in tergo annotatus & signatus fuit quasi Rotulus Magnus* Pipæ *fuisset anno primo* H. II. *Quod falsissimum esse ex indubio Rotulo Magno* Pipæ *de anno secundo Regis ejusdem facillime evinci possit; cum nulla inibi ratiocinia istis in hoc Rotulo expressis, uti in cæteris omnibus observatum est, respondeant; & nomina Vicecomitum anni Primi dicti Regis in Libro Rubro* Scaccarij *designata fol.* 184. *b, ab eis in hoc Rotulo exhibitis omnino differunt; Et postremo, quod hic Rotulus sit de anno* 5° *Regis* Stephani, *& non de tempore* H. I, *evidentissime colligi possit ex Rotulo* 14° *m.* 2, *& Rotulo* 5° *m.* 1, *& Rotulo* 12° *m.* 1, *invicem collatis in hoc Rotulo Magno.* Hactenus Cl. *Dewesius.* Isque pro certo & evidenti sumpsit, illum de quo loquimur esse Rotulum anni Quinti R. *Stephani.* Probare conatur hoc modo: Dicit, evidenter liquere posse, si quis Rotulum 14um, 5um, & 12um (particulares Rotulos hujus Fasciculi sive Bundelli) invicem conferre & librare velit. Sed quia instantias quas in mente habuit, speciatim non proposuit, difficile est discernere rectene judicaverit an secus. Circumspexi igitur quam potui oculatissime, ut ipse invenirem, vel instantias quas innuit, vel forsan valentiores in eam quam posuit sententiam. Sequentes acu tetigi: In Rotulo 14°, *Brientius filius Comitis* computat de veteri Auxilio Burgi de *Warengeford* pro Tertio anno, deinde de Auxilio præteriti anni, & postremo de Novo Auxilio, id est de Auxilio anni hujus Magni Rotuli (n). Ecce annus Regis Tertius expresse designatus, & annus Quartus sub nomine anni præteriti; deinde sequitur annus novissimus qui est Quintus. Hinc (ex mente *Dewesij*) constat, Veterem hunc esse *Magnum Rotu-*

(m) Prynn. *append. ad* Aurum Reginæ, *p.* 5.

(n) Et idem [Brientius filius Comitis] reddit compotum de Veteri Auxilio burgi [de Warengeford] tercij anni: In Perdonis, per breve Regis, Burgensibus de Warengeford, xv l pro paupertate eorum; Et Quietus est.

Et idem r c de xv l de Auxilio burgi præteriti anni: In Perdonis, per breve Regis, Burgensibus de Warengeford xv l, pro paupertate eorum, Et Q. e.

Et idem r c de xv l de Novo Auxilio burgi; In Perdonis, per breve Regis, Burgensibus de Warengeford xv l, pro paupertate eorum; Et Q. e. *Mag. Rot.* 5. Steph. *Rot.* 14. b.

lum

lum anni Quinti alicujus Regis: Cujufnam vero? Non R. *Henrici* I; id plus jufto tempus anticipat: Non R. *Henrici* II; *Magnus Rotulus* anni Quinti R. *Henrici* II indubius in archivo *Pipæ* extat: Ideo R. *Stephani*. Præterea, in fupra citato Rotulo 14° hujus bundelli, m. 2, inftantia alia occurrit. Reperio *Hamonem de Sancto Claro* reddentem compotum de Auxilio Civitatis *Coleceftræ* pro tribus nuper exactis annis, his fere verbis, viz. *de Veteri Auxilio Civitatis Tercij anni, de Auxilio Civitatis præteriti anni, ac de Auxilio Civitatis*; *Tercij anni* (ut forte *Dewefius* voluit) fignificante annum Tertium R. *Stephani, præteriti anni* Quartum, & *de Auxilio* (fubaudi, *hujus anni*) Quintum illius Regis (*o*). In Rotulo 5° m. 1. b. hoc folum invenio *Dewefij* opinioni confentaneum, quod fcilicet *Johannes Belet* Vicecomes *Surreiæ* reddit ibi rationem de præterito *Danegeldo* quarti anni (*p*); puta anni qui præceffit annum hujus bundelli, nempe Quintum R. *Stephani*. In Rotulo 4° hujus bundelli, Vicecomes *Hamtefciræ* reddit compotum de Auxilio Civitatis *Wintoniæ* anni Tertij, ac de præterito Auxilio nempe Quarti, ac de Auxilio [noviffimo] nempe Quinti (*q*).

Hæc dixi ad mentem Cl. *Dewefij*. Sed fieri poteft ut is a fcopo erraverit. Si ita; certe in errorem incidit, quem *Magnos Rotulos* paulo attentius legendo, notandoque ufitatum computandi modum, facile caviffet. Nam plane, in fupra adductis inftantijs, *annus Tertius* non denotat annum Regis Tertium, fed annum illum præteritum qui eft Tertius a præfenti. In hoc cafu tunc temporis numerabant retrorfum. Ad hunc modum: Si forte in compoto reddendo defcendebant, dixerunt, Ille *reddit compotum de firma Tertij anni*; *Idem reddit compotum de firma anni præteriti*; *Et idem reddit compotum de firma hujus*

(*o*) Hamo de Sancto Claro reddit compotum de firma Civitatis Coleceftræ; In thefauro xxxviij l & xvj s & ij d; Et debet xxiij s & x d Bl[ancos].

Et idem Hamo reddit compotum de j marca argenti, de Veteri Auxilio Civitatis Tercij anni; In thefauro liberavit, Et Quietus eft.

Et idem Hamo reddit compotum de xx l, de Auxilio Civitatis præteriti anni; In thefauro xiij l & ij s & iiij d. ———.

Et idem Hamo reddit compotum de Auxilio Civitatis Coleceftræ; In thefauro x l & x s & x d; Et in Perdonis, per breve Regis, Omnibus Burgenfibus de Coleceftra [*fummam illam*]: Summa, ix l & viij s & vj d, Et Quietus eft. *Mag. Rot.* 5. *Ste. Rot.* 14. *a. m.* 2.

(*p*) Et idem Vicecomes [Sudreiæ, fcil. Johannes Belet] reddit compotum de C s de præterito Danegeldo iiij anni: In Thefauro liberavit, Et quietus eft. *Mag. Rot.* 5. *Ste. Rot.* 5. *b. Sudreia. m.* 1. *b.*

(*q*) Et idem Vicecomes reddit compotum de C & xiiij s, de præterito auxilio Civitatis tercij anni: In thefauro liberavit, Et Quietus eft.

Et idem Vicecomes r c de xvij l & xx d, de præterito auxilio Civitatis, In Perdonis &c, Et Q. e.

Et idem Vicecomes r c de quater xx l, de auxilio Civitatis: In thefauro xx l & xiij s: Et in Perdonis &c; Et debet xxxj s. *Mag. Rot.* 5. *Ste. Rot.* 4. *b. Hamtefcira.*

anni; seu mutatis mutandis. Sin compotum formando ascendebant, dixerunt, Ille *reddit compotum de firma* [seu de *Nova firma*]; *Idem de firma anni præteriti*; *Idem de firma anni Tertij*; & sic mutatis mutandis, si casu exigente procederetur ad annum Quartum aut Quintum. Ita enim se res habuit. Describenda erant firmarum ac debitorum arreragia, perinde ac firmæ anni præsentis. Idque fere factum est modo superius memorato. Adeoque verba *reddit compotum de firma* [seu *de firma hujus anni*] designant annum præsentem sive annum *Magni Rotuli*; *de firma anni præteriti*, annum proximo præcedentem; *d firma anni Tertij*, annum præteritum qui est Tertius inclusive a præsenti; & sic de anno Quarto ac deinceps. Recte ergo judicemus, has & istiusmodi phrases pure a modo computandi, seu compotos in Magnis Rotulis discribendi, illis temporibus usitato, resilire. Harum similiumque formularum seu phrasium exempla in *Magnis Rotulis* vetustissimis abundant. Recapitulemus, si placet. In supra posita instantia *Brientij filij Comitis*, is revera reddit rationem de Auxilio Burgi *Warengefordæ* hoc modo: Descendendo computatur; Incipitur ab anno præterito remotiore; Computat de Auxilio anni Tertij, Secundi, ac Novissimi qui est annus hujus *Magni Rotuli*. In instantia *Hamonis de Sancto Claro* firmarij *Colcestræ*, is compotum reddit de Auxilio *Colecestræ* trium annorum, incipiendo ab anno Tertio præterito, & dein progrediendo ad annum Secundum, ac Novissimum. Quin & in instantia Vicecomitis *Hamtescire*, is rationem reddit de Auxilio *Wintoniæ* eodem prorsus modo. His exemplis addam quædam alia. Anno secundo R. *Henrici* II, Comes *Patricius* computavit de Lxxij s iij d Blancis, firma *Wiltescire* pro *anno Tertio*: Solvit in Thesauraria Regis, Lxxvj s pro illis Lxxij s iij d blancis; & absolutus recessit (*r*). Heic *tertij anni* denotat, non annum imperij illius Regis Tertium, is enim nondum advenerat; sed annum præteritum, Tertium a præsenti, nempe ultimum R. *Stephani*. Anno quarto ejusdem Regis compotus redditur de firma *Lundoniæ*. Incipitur ab anno Tertio, dein pergitur ad Secundum, & Novissimum. *Gervasius* & *Johannes filius Radulfi* computant de anno Tertio ac Secundo; Quinque alij, infra in margine memorati, Vicecomitum officio functi, de anno Novissimo, nempe anno istius *Magni Rotuli* (*s*). Incipitur, inquiebam,

ab

(*r*) Wiltescira. Comes Patricius r c de firma de Wiltescira tercij anni, de Lxxij s & iij d Bl. In Thesauro Lxxvj s pro Lxxij s & iij d Bl.; Et Quietus est. *Mag. Rot.* 2. *H.* 2. *Rot.* 11. *b.*

(*s*) Gervasius & Johannes filius Radulfi reddunt compotum de Lxxj l & xxij d Bl. de Veteri firma Lundoniæ de tertio anno.

Et idem reddunt compotum de firma anni præteriti.

Vicecomites Lundoniæ. Reinerus, filius Berengarij, & Gaufridus Bursarius, & Josce Vinitarius,

ab anno Tertio. Quisnam autem fuit iste annus Tertius? Non annus hujusce Regis Tertius regnandi; sed annus præteritus Tertius a præsenti; qui annus Tertius a præsenti erat annus Regis Secundus regnandi. Quodque revera ita sit, hinc apparet. Anno illo Secundo, *Gervasius* & *Johannes* supra memorati fuerant Vicecomites *Lundoniæ* (*t*). Nec id solum. Enotescit ex summa. Anno secundo in fine compoti debebant Regi Lxxj l & xxij d Blancos: Et in hoc Magno Rotulo anni quarti (nam in Rotulo anni Tertij, quem consului, nullus redditur compotus de illis areragijs) respondent de eisdem Lxxj l & xxij d Blancis de Veteri firma. Anno Sexto ejusdem Regis, Vicecomitissa *Rothomagi* scribitur computatura de firma villæ *Hantonæ* Tertij anni, & *de Veteri firma*, & *de Nova* (*u*): Manifeste, de firma anni Quarti imperij hujus Regis, ac Quinti, & Sexti. In *Magno Rotulo* anni vicesimi primi R. *Henrici* II, *Gervasius de Cornhill* reddidit compotum de Veteri firma *Kantij* pro Tertio anno; Idemque de firma ejusdem Comitatus pro anno præterito; Ac *Robertus filius Bernardi* de firma ejus Comitatus pro anno præsenti, sive anno hujus Magni Rotuli (*w*). Hic per verba *anni tercij* intelligendus est, non annus *Henrici* II tertius regnandi, sed annus ejus decimus nonus, videlicet tertius retrorsum numerando ab anno istius Rotuli; per verba *anni præteriti*, annus dicti Regis vicesimus; per verba *hoc anno*, vicesimus primus. Porro, Anno primo R. *Ricardi* I, *Galfridus filius Petri* computavit ad Scaccarium de Veteri firma tertij anni de *Norhantescira*; & idem de firma anni præteriti (*x*). Hic certe, *Tertij anni* non denotat annum Tertium imperij R. *Ricardi* I; is nondum advenerat; sed annum Tertium a præsenti, nempe tricesimumtertium sive penultimum R. *Henrici* II, parique modo *anni præteriti* designat tricesimum-

Vinitarius, & Ricardus Vetulus, & Brihtmer de Haverhell, reddunt compotum de firma Lundoniæ. *Mag. Rot.* 4. *H.* 2. *Rot.* 1. *a.*

(*t*) Lundonia. Gervasius & Johannes r c de firma Lundoniæ de tribus partibus anni. — *in fine Compoti:* Et debent Lxxj l & xxij d Bl. *Mag. Rot.* 2. *H.* 2. *Rot.* 1. *a.*

(*u*) Vicecomitissa Roth[omagi] debet CC & xxxvij l & iiij s Bl[ancos] de firma Tercij anni de Hantona; Et eadem debet CC & xxxviij l & v s & v d Bl[ancos] de Veteri firma; Et eadem reddit compotum de Nova firma; In elemosina noviter constituta Militibus de Templo j marca; Et in decimis constitutis Monachis de Lira & de Corme-lijs xviij l numero. *Mag. Rot.* 6. *H.* 2 *Rot.* 3. *b. tit.* Hantona.

(*w*) Gervasius de Cornhill reddit compotum de C & xix l & vj s & ij d Bl[ancis], de Veteri firma tercij anni. *Mag. Rot.* 21. *Hen.* 2. *Rot.* 13. *a.* Chent, *m.* 1.

Gervasius de Cornhill reddit compotum de firma anni præteriti —. *Ib. m.* 1.

Robertus filius Bernardi reddit compotum de firma de Chent de hoc anno. *Ib m.* 2.

(*x*) Galfridus filius Petri reddit compotum de xiiij l & v s Bl[ancis] de Veteri firma tertij anni de Norhantescira; Et de xiiij l & v s Bl[ancis] de firma anni præteriti; In thesauro liberavit, Et Quietus est. *Mag. Rot.* 1. *Ric.* 1. *Rot. t. a.*

quartum

quartum five ultimum R. *Henrici* II. Neque vero ex conjectura tantum hoc dico. Res ipsa loquitur. Nam *Galfridus filius Petri* anno illo penultimo ac ultimo Vicecomes fuerat *Norhantescirae* (*y*). Et quidem anno penultimo, in fine compoti sui debebat Regi xiiij l v s Blancos, itemque anno ultimo alios xiiij l v s Blancos: de quibus duabus summis in *Magno Rotulo* anni primi R. *Ricardi* I, sub nomine Veteris firmae Regi plenarie respondit, & absolutus recessit; sicut infra in margine videre est. Eodem anno primo R. *Ricardi* I, Burgenses *Cantabrigiae* scribuntur Regiae Majestati obaerati pro firma Burgi sui his verbis, viz. *de hoc anno, de quatuor annis praeteritis, & de dimidio quinti* (*z*). Haec verba, *de hoc anno*, haud dubie significant annum primum R. *Ricardi* I, & verba, *de quatuor annis praeteritis & de dimidio quinti*, ultimos quinque annos (semianno dempto) R. *Henrici* II. Hactenus de modo, in compotis describendis, annos retrorsum numerandi. Quin regnante *Ricardo* I, ac postea, modus iste paulatim desuevit. Et exinde per seriem annorum imperij cujusvis Regis fere numerabant. Ex his quae dixi, satis ni fallor liquet. Cl. *Dewesij* opinionem cujus superius memini, nullo fundamento innixam. Id aliunde etiam evincitur. Exempli gratia: In hoc *Magno Rotulo* nuncupato Quinto R. *Stephani*, *Paganus Trencardus* scribitur computaturus de praeteritis *Danegeldis* Insulae de *Wicht*, pro quinque annis, de tempore *Hugonis Gern*[*un*]: Sic fiunt Quinque anni. Idem *Paganus* computat de Novo *Danegeldo* Insulae: Sicque fit annus Sextus (*a*). Juxta *Dewesij* opinionem consequeretur, hunc esse *Magnum Rotulum* anni Sexti R. *Stephani*. At juxta interpetationem quam supra posui, nihil difficile suboritur. Haec enim est rei summa, quod scilicet hic describitur compotus seu potius notamentum de *Danegeldo* sex praeteritorum annorum. Praeterea,

(*y*) Galfridus filius Petri reddit compotum de xiiij l & v s Bl., de veteri firma de Norhantescira; In th. l, Et Q. e. Et idem de Nova firma; In thesauro *summam illam*; Et in Elemosina constituta —, Et in Terris datis, *summam illam*; Et debet xiiij l & v s Bl[ancos]. *Mag. Rot.* 33. *Hen.* 2. *Rot.* 8. *a.*

Galfridus filius Petri debet xiiij l & v s Bl[ancos] de veteri firma de Nordhantescira. Et idem [reddit compotum] de Nova firma; In thesauro *summam illam*; Et in Elemosina constituta —, Et in Terris datis, *summam illam*; Et debet xiiij l & v s Bl[ancos]. *Mag. Rot.* 34. *Hen.* 2. *Rot.* — *a. m.* 1.

(*z*) Burgenses de Cantebrigia debent Lx l Bl., de firma Burgi de Cantebrigia de hoc anno; Et C & quater xx Bl. de iiij annis praeteritis; Et xxx l Bl. de dimidio anno de firma Quinti anni. *Mag. Rot.* 1. *R.* 1. *Rot.* 11. *a.*

(*a*) Insula de Wicht. Paganus Trencardus debet iiij l de praeteritis danegeldis Insulae v annorum de tempore Hugonis Gern.

Et idem Paganus reddit compotum de Novo Danegeldo Insulae: In thesauro xj l & viiij s: Et in Perdonis, per breve Regis, Willelmo de Vernun xxxij s, Radulfo de Belingeturt xij d, Et Quietus est. *Mag. Rot.* 5. *Ste. Rot.* 4. *b. Hantesc.*

Robertus

Robertus de Stanlega in hoc Rotulo memoratur Comitatum *Gloeceſtriæ* tenuiſſe annis quinque elapſis. Pro eorum uno, nempe quarto, debebat Regi Liij l xix s Blancos, ac pro alio nempe tertio Lxxviij l xij s ij d Blancos: Quas duas ſummas *Milo de Gloeceſtria* vice *Roberti* (ſcilicet ut plegius ejus) ſolvit Regi ad Scaccarium. Simul prædictus *Milo* ut Vicecomes, ſuo ipſius nomine Regi reſpondet pro duobus alijs annis, per verba, *de Veteri firma*, & *de Nova* (*b*). Sicque reſponſum eſt in toto pro annis Septem. Inde autem certe non conſequetur, hunc eſſe *Magnum Rotulum* anni Septimi alicujus Regis. Quin hic utique non alio modo quam regula quam ſuperius poſui, res explicanda eſt. Super hac quæſtione hæc dicta ſunto.

Reſtat ut inquiram, Utrum Vetus hic Rotulus ſit de aliquo anno R. *Henrici* I. Ad præſens, Amplitudinis Tuæ venia, negativam quæſtionis partem tentaminis cauſa tueri libet. Propono, non eſſe Rotulum alicujus anni R. *Henrici* I. Primo, quia in eo nomen R. *Henrici* I, ne quidem ſemel occurrit. Secundo, quia hic Rotulus commodiſſime referendus videtur ad annum aliquem paulo poſt *Matildæ Imperatricis* adventum in *Angliam*; eaque in *Angliam* venit ſub initium regni R. *Stephani* (*c*), Coronæ Regiæ quam ille occupaverat adipiſcendæ cauſa; & in hoc Veteri Rotulo de *Imperatricis* in *Angliam* adventu ut de re non ita pridem geſta mentio fit (*d*). Jam ex altera quæſtionis parte proponam. Priori iſti argumento ad hunc modum ſatisfit. In hoc Rotulo non ſolum R. *Henrici* I nomen non occurrit, ſed neque *Stephani*, *Henrici* II, aut alterius Regis. Sunt etiam Rotuli complurium annorum *Henrici* II, in quibus nulla de ipſius Regis nomine fit mentio; de quorum tamen Rotulorum tempore lis nulla eſt; quoniam id aliunde enoteſcit. Iſtud ergo ſilentium, ſi quid cerno, in hoc negotio nec prodeſt nec obeſt. Secundo argumento obviam itur in hunc modum. Fatendum *Imperatricem* in *Angliam* veniſſe, ad jus ſuum contra R. *Stephanum* adſtruendum. Sed illa in

---

(*b*) Milo de Gloeceſtra reddit compotum de Lxxviij l & xij s & x d Bl. de Veteri firma Statfordſciræ: In theſauro liberavit, Et Quietus eſt. Et idem de Nova firma.

Et idem Vicecomes r c de Liij l & xix s Bl. pro plegio Roberti de Stanlega, de veteri firma quarti anni; Et de Lxxviij l & xij s & ij d Bl. de veteri firma tercij anni, pro plegio ejuſdem Roberti: In theſauro xxix l & xj s Bl. Et debet C l & Lx s Bl.

Robertus de Stanlega debet xx marcas argenti, pro Comitatu habendo uſque ad v annos: Et ipſe tantum tenuit. *Mag. Rot.* 5. *Ste. Rot.* 8. *a.*

(*c*) Ðen eꞃꞇen com &c. Poſtea Regis Henrici filia, quæ fuerat Imperatrix in Alamannia, tunc autem erat Comitiſſa in Angeou, venit Londoniam. *Chron. Sax.* p. 241. n. 45. *ad A. D.* 1140.

(*d*) —— de præſtitis Regis, quas Rex ei præſtitit quando Imperatrix venit in Angliam. *Mag. Rot.* 5. *Ste. Rot.* 16. *a. Nomen perſonæ hic compotum reddentis deeſt; particula membranæ lacerata.*

Angliam

Angliam venit etiam ante illud tempus; nempe poft *Imperatoris* mariti fui obitum, regnante R. *Henrico* I: ficut *H. Huntendonienfis, Chronicon Saxonicum,* alijque (ut memini) teftantur (*e*). Et quidem *Imperatricis* in *Angliam* adventum cujus in Veteri noftro Rotulo mentio fit, de primo illo adventu potius intelligendum putem. Eruditi Lectores dijudicent.

Jam vero, Nobiliffime Baro, Tua pace pro affirmativa quæftionis parte experiri velim. Propono igitur, hunc effe Rotulum alicujus anni R. *Henrici* I. Idque probare conabor quibufdam argumentis ac indicijs ex ipfo Rotuli gremio petitis. Dubitandum non eft quin *Magni Rotuli* tempore R. *Henrici* I, & antiquius componi confueverint. *Ricardus* Thefaurarius Regis meminit (*f*) Rotulorum Annalium R. *Henrici* I; eorumque paucos fe vidiffe teftatur *Alexander de Swereford* (*g*); quinetiam is pro admiffo fumit, Rotulos Annales fub Rege *Willelmo* I fuiffe compofitos, etfi neminem fuo feculo novit qui eos viderat (*h*). Quod autem ad Rotulos Annales R. R. R. *Willelmi* I, *Willelmi* II, & *Henrici* I; minime mirum eft, fi poft rabiem bellorum quæ regnante *Stephano* miferrimam hac gentem lacerabant, eorum plerique, feu tantum non omnes, vel perierint, vel *Alexandri,* qui multis poft annis vixit, confpectum effugerint; mirandum potius, ullum aliquem ad fuum ufque feculum fuperfuiffe. Ad probationem fupra propofitam feftino.

In hoc Rotulo, *Turftinus Eboracenfis* Archiepifcopus folvit Regi debitum decem librarum, quas Rex ei in *Normannia* accommodavit (*i*). Dubitatur, utrum *Turftinus* habuit in *Normannia* alloquium R. *Henrici* I, an vero *Stephani*. Super ea re difquirendum. *Turftinus* ad fedem *Eboracenfem* promotus A. D. 1114, [R. *Henrici* I anno 15°] (*k*), ancipitemque fortunam expertus, poftquam federat annis plus minus

---

(*e*) Vigefimo fexto anno regni fui rex Henricus — adduxit fecum filiam Imperatricem tanto viro (ut prædictum eft) viduatam. *Hunt. L.* 7. *p.* 383. *n.* 1, 10.

Anno Mcxxvi. ꝼall þiꞃ ᵹean &c. Annum hunc egit Heanricus Rex in Normannia ultra autumnum: poftea autem venit in hanc terram, atque illum comitabatur fua uxor, fua item filia, quam olim dederat Heanrico Imperatori de Loherenge in uxorem. *Chron. Sax. p.* 230.

(*f*) *Dialog. de Scac. L.* 1. *c.* 7. A quibus vel ob.

(*g*) — licet ejufdem [Henrici I,] paucos infpexerim Annales. *Lib. Rub. fol.* 47. *a. col.* 2.

(*h*) Nec Annalia fua [R. Willelmi I,] temporibus meis a quibufquam vifa fint. *Lib. Rub. f.* 47. *a.*

(*i*) Turftinus Archiepifcopus de Everwic reddit compotum de x l, quas Rex ei præftitit in Normannia: In Donis, per breve Regis, eidem Archiepifcopo x l; Et quietus eft. *Mag. Rot.* 5. *Ste. Rot.* 3. *a. Everwicfcira.*

(*k*) Turftinus Regis Capellanus ad Eboracenfem

minus viginti quinque aut sex (expulsionis suæ tempore incluso), tandem vita decessit mense *Februarij* A. D. 1140, [R. *Stephani* sexto]; ut Cl. *Godwinus* alijque retulerunt (*l*). Quanquam autem *Turstini* vita imperium utriusque illorum Principum ingrediebatur; attamen multum ut opinor interest, utram in partem de hac quæstione statuamus. Præponderant enim, ni fallor, argumenta quæ ex una parte sunt. *Turstinus* sub R. *Stephano* vixit annis quinque duntaxat & quod excurrit, idque prope vitæ suæ finem: sub R. *Henrico* I, multo pluribus; nempe in præsulatus sui priori parte, antequam ætas ingravesceret. Constat etiam *Turstinum* in *Normannia* fuisse (id quod mox ostendam) tempore R. *Henrici* I; sed ibi fuisse tempore R. *Stephani*, nulla quantum scio memoria est. Sane Regem *Stephanum* semel omnino *Normanniam* adeuntem comperi. *Chronicon Saxonicum* refert illuc transfretasse A. D. 1137 (*m*). Atqui *Turstinum* ibi etiam tunc fuisse aut colloquium cum illo habuisse, mihi nondum compertum est. Quin reipsa parum credibile arbitror, *Thurstinum Normanniam* adijsse vel ibi moratum fuisse anno illo 1137°, qui tribus tantum annis distat a 1140°; quo tempore is senio ærumnisque fractus in *Anglia* morti occubuit. Forsitan hic objicietur, *Thurstinum* etiam anno proximo scilicet 1138° adeo corpore valuisse, ut de facili in *Normanniam* iter capessere potuit; nam anno illo exercitum coegit duxitque, ad repellendum *Davidem* Regem *Scotorum*, *Angliæ* fines hostiliter invadentem; de quo, ut aiunt, victoriam reportavit. Respondeo. inter Historicos non convenit, *Turstinum* istius exercitus profectioni prælioque commisso personaliter interfuisse. Etenim *Rogerus de Houedene*, homo *Eboracensis*, rerumque borealium tum sui temporis tum etiam antecedentis præ alijs sciens, tradit *Turstinum* tunc morbo detentum (*n*). Præterea, R. *Henricus* I, sæpe diuque in *Normannia* agere consuevit. Immo *Turstinus* alloquium ejus ibidem habuit plus semel. A. D. 1116, *Turstinus* R. *Henricum* I, ad *Normanniam* mari iter facientem comitabatur (*o*). Eum etiam sub idem tempus, in *Normannia* Regis

racensem Archiepiscopatum die assumptionis S. Mariæ eligitur Wintoniæ. *Hoved. Annal.* P. 1. p. 473. *n.* 10.

(*l*) *Godwin. de Præsul. provinc. Ebor.* p. 31.

(*m*) Anno Mcxxxvii. Ðis gære for þe king Stephne ofer sæ to Normandi. *Chron. Sax.* p. 238.

(*n*) Cum autem morbi causa non posset Archiepiscopus Eboracensis interesse pugnæ, misit loco sui Radulfum episcopum Orcadum. *Houed.* P. 1. p. 483. *n.* 20.

(*o*) Eodem tempore Rex Anglorum Henricus mare transijt, comitante secum Turstino Eboracensi electo. *Houed. ib.* p. 474. *n.* 10. *ad A. D.* 1116.

præ-

præsentiam adijsse, memorat *Eadmerus*; si mentem ejus assequor (*p*). Et anno decimo octavo R. *Henrici* I, *Turstinus* iterum *Normanniam* petijt, Regemque invenit *Rothomagi* (*q*). Ex his autem quæ de *Turstino* Archiepiscopo superius dixi, probabile videtur, Regem *Henricum* I, non *Stephanum*, decem illas libras in Veteri nostro Rotulo memoratas ei in *Normannia* mutuo præstitisse.

Hic *Magnus Rotulus* meminit *Stephani* Comitis *Britanniæ*. Perdonavit ei Rex sex marcas argenti (*r*). Comes *Stephanus* videtur gratia Regis potitus. Prece Comitis Rex remisit *Godrico di Belesbi* xx s (*s*). Quidni Comes ille *Stephanus* fuerit Tertius ejus nominis, qui decessit A. D. 1138, si fides *Augustino du Paz* (*t*). Hic autem aliquid incerti subest. Comes *Stephanus* vitam egit tam R. *Stephano* quam R. *Henrico* I regnante. Annus mortis Comitis *Stephani* incidit in annum tertium R. *Stephani*. Fateor. Sed quoniam Comes *Stephanus* vixit multo pluribus annis regnante R. *Henrico* I. quam regnante R. *Stephano*; tanto probabilius videtur, ea quæ citavi esse potius intelligenda de R. *Henrico* I, quam de R. *Stephano*, quanto Comes diutius tempore illius Regis quam hujus vixit.

Pridem antequam hic *Magnus Rotulus* vetustissimus conficeretur, Episcopatus *Dunelmi* vacavit, fuitque in manu Regis. Quin & ipso anno hujus Rotuli, episcopatu nondum cuiquam collato, census seu reditus præsentis anni, atque annorum præeuntium arreragia Regi

(*p*) Restitutus ad Pontificatum Thurstanus venit Angliam circa Februarium mensem, anno scilicet secundo quo ipse in Normanniam ad Regem venerat. *Eadm. Hist. Nov. L.* 5. *p.* 121. *n.* 20.

(*q*) Quæ ubi Thurstano Eboracensi innotuerunt, relicta Anglia, mare transijt, & Rotomagum venit. Ubi a Rege, quod se inconsulto, transfretaverit, redargutus, ultra procedere inhibitus est. *Eadm. Hist. Nov. L.* 5. *p.* 123. *n.* 1. *Eadmerus hic non expresse posuit A. D.* 1118; *sed Turstini iter recenset paulo post obitum Matildæ Reginæ, quam circa illud tempus obijsse concordant Historici.*

(*r*) Et idem Vicecomes [Rainer de Bada] reddit compotum de Lxxiiij marcis argenti & dimidia, de placitis Ricardi Basset de Minutis hominibus; In Thesauro xvij l; Et in Perdonis per breve Regis, Alano de Moncellis xl s, Regi Scotiæ v marcas argenti, Comiti Stephano Brit[anniæ] vj marcas argenti, Pagano Peur. xl s &c. *Mag. Rot.* 5. *Ste. Rot.* 12. *b. m.* 1. *Linc.*

(*s*) Godricus de Belesbi reddit compotum de v marcis argenti, de eisdem placitis [sc. Ricardi Basset & W. de Albini]: In Perdonis per breve Regis, Eidem Godrico xx s, pro amore Com[itis] Brittan[niæ]: Et debet xlvj s & viij d. *Mag. Rot.* 5. *Ste. Rot.* 12. *b. m.* 1. *Linc.*

(*t*) Estienne 3. du nom fils d'Eudon premier Comte de Donnonee ou Pentheure, & d'Onguen de Cornoüaille, jouit de sa part du dit Comté avec ses freres Geffroy, Alain, Robert, Derien, & Briend, qui tous se nommoient Comtes de Bretagne, auoient partagé la succession paternelle & maternelle esgalement. — *Histoire Geneal. de Bretagne p.* 9. — L'an mil cent trente & huict deceda le dit Estienne, qui se nommoit Comte de Bretagne, & fut son corps inhumé en l'Eglise Cathedrale de sainct Brieuc, prés le Duc Eudon son pere. *Ib. p.* 10.

penduntur.

penduntur. *Gaufridus Efcollandus* refpondet ad Scaccarium Regium de Veteri firma Epifcapatus & de Nova, ac de alijs proventibus, forma qua inferius in margine videre eft (*u*). Eodem tempore *Anfchetillus de Wireceftria* reddidit Regi compotum de Veteri firma & de Nova Maneriorum Epifcopatus, in alijs (ut conjicio) extra *Dunelmenfem* Comitatibus jacentium (*w*). Notatu autem dignum eft, quod vacatio epifcopatus *Dunelmenfis*, qua durante reditus ejufdem annui Regi in hoc *Magno Rotulo* penduntur, eft eadem vacatio quæ accidebat antequam *Gaufridus* Cancellarius ad Sedem *Dunelmenfem* promoveretur. Id elucet ex hoc *Magno Rotulo* ac Hiftoria *Dunelmenfi* una comparatis. Quid *magnus* hic *Rotulus* declarat jam modo recenfui. Hiftoria *Dunelmenfis* teftatur Epifcopatum eo tempore aliquantifper commiffum *Gaufrido* illi quem *Efcorlandum* vocat & cuidam *Hugoni de Anundavilla* (*x*). Item *Magnus* hic *Rotulus* prodit, *Gaufridum* Cancellarium Regis ha-

(*u*) Gaufridus Efcollandus reddit compotum de quater xx l & Lviij s & vj d, de remanente firmæ Epifcopatus de tempore Epifcopi. Sed de iftis habuit Willelmus de Pontearc[a] xxx l. De quibus reddidit compotum quando Comes Gloeceftræ & Brient[ius] audierunt compotum de Thefauro apud Wintoniam.

Et idem Gaufridus reddit compotum de Nova firma Epifcopatus: In Thefauro CCC & xxxvj l & x s & xiiij d; Et in Liberationibus conftitutis viij l & xiiij s & j d; Et in Corredio Regis Scotiæ redeundo de Curia xxxiij s; Et in Corredio Archiepifcopi Eborac[enfis] veniendo ad Epifcopatum & redeundo xviij s & vij d; Et in Liberationibus Walteri Efpec & Euftacij filij Johannis dum fuerunt ad neceffaria Regis facienda in Epifcopatu xxij s & ix d; Et in præterito anno quando Comes Gloec[eftræ] & Brientius filius Comitis audierunt compotum de thefauro, iiij l & iiij s fine tal[ea] ad perficiendum plenum numerum; Et in Donis, per breve Regis, Priori de Sancto Ofwaldo, xiij l & vj s & viij d; Et in Liberatione Willelmi de Pontearc[a] quando venit de Normannia & perrexit ad Epifcopatum Dunelm[enfem] recipiendum, xv l & xv s de Lxiij diebus; Et in Perdonis, per breve Regis, tribus Clericis de Epifcopatu C s de ij Ecclefijs quæ ad firmam pertinebant: Et debet xLj l & xiij s & viij d.

Et idem Gaufridus reddit compotum de C & x l & v s & v d de Cornagio animalium Epifcopatus: In Thefauro quater xx l & xxxvj s & iij d: Et debet xxviij l & ix s & ij d.

Et idem Gaufridus reddit compotum de Lviij l & vj s & viij d de Don[o] Militum Epifcopatus: In Thefauro xlv l & xvj s & viij d cum Militibus de Lindefia: Et debet xij l & x s.

Et idem Gaufridus reddit compotum de xlvj l & v s & iiij de Tainis & Dreinnis & Smalemannis inter Tinam & Teodam: In Thefauro xxxvj l: Et debet x l & v s & iiij d. *Mag. Rot.* 5. *Ste. Rot.* 13. *b. in compoto de Epifcopatu Dunelmi.*

(*w*) Anfchetillus de Wirec[eftria] reddit compotum de x l, de Veteri firma Maneriorum Epifcopatus Dunelmi: In Thefauro liberavit, Et quietus eft.

Et idem de Nova firma: In Thefauro CC & ix l & x s: Et in Corredio Regis Scotiæ, Lxx s & viij d; Et in Donis, per breve Regis, Bernardo Clerico xx s in quadam Ecclefia: Et in Domibus de Houendena reparandis, Lxx s; Et in ij Navibus emendis, xl s: Et debet ix s & iiij d. *Mag. Rot.* 5. *Ste. Rot.* 13. *b.*

(*x*) Eo [fc. Ranulfo Flambardo] autem defuncto, committitur Epifcopatus duobus Baronibus, viz. Hugoni de Anundavilla & Gaufrido feniori Efcorland ad opus Regis cenfum colligentibus: vacavitque Epifcopatus per quinquennium excepto uno menfe *Hift. Dunelm. ap. Angl. Sac. T.* 1. *p.* 709.

buiffe

buisse tunc temporis custodiam, Regis nomine, episcopatuum *Coventriæ* & *Herefordiæ* (*y*); nondum (ut fas est credere) evectum ad episcopatum *Dunelmi*; quia simpliciter Cancellarius Regis dicitur anno hujus *Magni Rotuli*; quo etiam anno episcopatus *Dunelmi*, ut ante monstravi, actu vacavit. Et sane Historia *Dunelmensis* refert *Gaufridum* Cancellarium electum in Episcopum dictæ sedis A. D. 1133, R. *Henrici* I 33 (*z*). Anno igitur quo hic *Magnus Rotulus* scriptus erat, nondum donabatur *Gaufrido* Cancellario Episcopatus *Dunelmi*; necdum annus R. *Henrici* I trigesimus tertius advenerat. His quidem omnibus *Henrico* I regnante gestis.

Anno hujus Rotuli computatæ sunt Vicecomitibus *Londoniæ* quædam nummorum summæ, quas ipsi eodem anno eregarant in pannis alijsque necessarijs providendis ad opus [*Roberti*] Comitis *Normanniæ* (*a*). Hic æquum est quædam in antecessum notare. Nemo ignorat principes *Normannorum* antiquos, Comites perinde ac *Duces* sive *Marchisos* aut *Marchiones* passim appellatos; ipsumque adeo, de quo hic res est, *Robertum* fratrem R. *Henrici* a coævis historicis *Comitem* fere vocatum (*b*). Non est autem celandum, verba quæ posui producte [*Comitis Normanniæ*], in rotulo a me juxta ante citato breviate scribi [*Com. Norman.*]; quæ forsan nunnullis videbuntur aliquousque dubia sive incerta. Verum tamen, non est, me judice, quod in hac re hæreamus. Ego saltem nullam aliam ea quam posui aptiorem lectionem invenire possum. Præterhac meminisse oportet, apud veteres

---

(*y*) *Hist. Scacc. Cap.* 5. *Sect.* 4.

(*z*) Anno Incarnationis Dominicæ Mcxxxiii in Episcopum Dunelmensem eligitur Gaufridus Regis Henrici Cancellarius, qui Rufus dicebatur; consecratusq; est Eboraci a Turstino Eboracensi Archiepiscopo. Cujus anno tertio Rex Henricus moritur anno Dominicæ Incarnationis MCXXXV. *Hist. Dun. Angl. S. T.* 1. *p.* 709.

Anno Domini 1133, *juxta Matthæum Parisiensem: Anno* 1134° *juxta Rogerum de Houedena, in Hist. P.* 1. 480. *n.* 20.

(*a*) Quattuor Vicecomites Londoniæ reddunt compotum de firma Londoniæ: In Thesauro xvjl & xiiijs & ixd Bl.: Et in liberatione Archiepiscopi Rothomag., & in Pannis Com. Norman. xxiij l & x s numero. *Mag. Rot.* 5. *Ste. Rot.* 15. *a*.

Et in Soltis, per breve Regis, Fulcheredo filio Walteri, xij l, pro Estruct. Com. Norman. *Ibid. Sane quid hæc vox* Estruct. *significat, penitus ignoro*.

(*b*) Adventus Comitis Roberti fratris Regis in Angliam totam Regalem Curiam commovit. *Eadm. hist. Nov. p.* 48. *nu.* 50.

Ferebatur rumor Rodbertum Normanniæ Comitem ex Apulia adventantem jam jamque affore. *Malm. hist. Hen.* 1. *p.* 156. *nu.* 10.

Robertus Normanniam veniens Comitatum suum obsistente nullo recepit. *Malm. ib. p.* 156. *nu.* 20.

A Sigeberto in anno Mvi Richardus Comes Northmannorum dicitur. In anno Llxvj Guillermus Comes Northmannorum, Rotbertus item in anno Mxcvi Comes Normanniæ, quem & Anselmus Abbas Gemblacensis Rotbertum Comitem Northmanniæ appellat, Fulcherius Carnotensis Robertum Normanniæ Comitem. *Valesij Notit. Gall. p.* 380. *col.* 1.

DISCEPTATIO EPISTOLARIS. 473

moris fuisse, quas Vicecomes anno officij sui in obsequio Regis pecunias expenderat, eas ipsi in ratiocinio suo pro anno illo ad Sccaccarium reddito computari. Id quod factum est a Vicecomitibus *Londoniæ* in instantia supra allata. His præmissis, revocanda est in memoriam sors luctuosa *Roberti* Comitis *Normanniæ* in hoc Veteri Rotulo memorati. Is filius erat *Willelmi Victoris* natu maximus. Ab R. *Henrico* I fratre ejus juniore in prælio victus in *Normannia*, ductus erat in *Angliam* captivus. Ibi quum libertate ipsisque (ut aiunt) oculis privatus, annis compluribus degisset, tandem mense Februarij A. D. 1134, imperij R. *Henrici* I penultimo, castro *Carduili* inclusus fato concessit (c).

In *Magno Rotulo* anni noni R. *Ricardi* I memoriæ proditum est, Manerium de *Danecastria* in agro *Eboracensi* situm, invadiatum fuisse R. *Henrico* I pro marcis monetæ quingentis (d). Istius autem Manerij invadiatio in hoc Veteri nostro Rotulo memoratur disertis verbis, sicut hic in margine patet (e). Manerium illud Regi traditum erat in vadio ad debitum prædictum securum præstandum. Et quidem tempore procedente, debitum ipsum sive Finis in *Magnis Rotulis* annuatim scribi desijt; postmodumque Regi continuo responsum est in *Magnis Rotulis* R. *Henrici* II de exitibus sive fructibus *Danecastriæ*, tanquam si Rex tenuisset in dominio (f). Sic ergo se res habuit. *Robertus Fossard finem fecit* (uti vocarunt) cum R. *Henrico* I, in quingentis marcis argenteis, pro saisina terrarum suarum habenda. Et summæ illius cavendæ gratia, tradidit Regi Manerium *Danecastriam*; redi-

(c) Anno ab incarnatione Domini Mcxxxiiii indictione xij, Rodbertus II Dux Normannorum, xviij anno ex quo apud Tenerchebraicum captus est & in Carcere fratris sui detentus est mense Februario Carduili Britanniæ obijt, & in Cœnobio Monachorum S. Petri Apostoli Gloucestriæ tumulatus quiescit. *Order. Vit.* f. 893. D.

(d) Robertus de Turneham reddit compotum de D marcis, Pro quietantia Manerij de Danecastria, quod est de hæreditate Johannæ uxoris suæ, quod Manerium fuit invadiatum Regi H. primo pro D marcis. *Mag. Rot.* 9. *Ric.* 1. *Rot.* 4. *a. Everwicsira.* citat. in *Hist. Scacc. Vol.* 1. *Cap.* 13. *sect.* 8.

(e) Robertus Fossardus r c de xlij s & viij d, pro recuperanda terra sua primitus; In thesauro xx s, Et debet xxj s & viij d.

Et idem debet D marcas argenti, Ut iterum rehabeat terram suam, excepta Donecastra, quam concessit Regi tenere in manu sua usque ad xx annos: Et si tunc reddiderit D marcas argenti insimul, rehabebit Donecastrum. *Mag. Rot.* 5. *Ste. Rot.* 3. *a. Everwicscira.*

(f) Danecastra. Eudo Præpositus reddit compotum de Lxvj l & xiij s & iiij d numero de firma de Danecastra: In th. l, Et Q. e. *Mag. Rot.* 17. *H.* 2. *Rot.* 5. *a. Everwicscira.*

Radulfus Clericus de Danecastra r c de Lxvj l & xiij s & iiij d numero, de firma de Danecastra; In th. l, Et Q. e. *Mag. Rot.* 27. *H.* 2. *Rot.* 3. *b. Everwicsc.*

Radulfus Clericus & Adam de Everwich & Willelmus Prat r c de Lxvj l & xiij s & iiij d numero de firma de Danecastra; In th. l, Et Q. s. *Mag. Rot.* 28. *H.* 2. *Rot.* 4. *b. Everwichsc.*

mendum

mendum scilicet, simulatque *Robertus* pecuniam illam una integraque summa solverit. Pensatis autem Recordi citati verbis, fas est credere, conventionem hanc inter Regem & *Robertum Fossard* tunc recenter fuisse initam. *Robertus* finem fecit pro nova & recenti saisina terræ suæ [*pro recuperanda terra sua primitus*]. Deinde, concessit *Danecastriam* Regi : id est, Regi jamtum regnanti. Si enim ista conventio continuaretur adusque tempora R. *Stephani*, & in ejus *Magnis Rotulis* inventa esset, probabiliter dictum fuisset, non *Regi* simpliciter, sed Regi *Henrico* I ; ut fit in *Magno Rotulo* supra laudato R. *Ricardi* I. Quocirca, rebus collatis, minime dubitemus, quin Rex in hac conventione memoratus, fuerit *Henricus* I.

In hoc Rotulo describitur primus *Eliensis* Episcopus *Herveius*, varia cum Rege negotia peragens. Computat Regi de septem marcis aureis & dimidia, pro officio *Willelmi* nepotis sui : partem summæ solvit, de residuo scribitur obæratus. Pacificatur cum Rege pro immunitate Militum Episcopatus sui atque Abbatiæ de *Cateriz*. Denique, rationem init cum Rege de summa Mille librarum, ut Rex jubeat Milites Episcopatus *Eliensis* excubias agere in insula de *Ely*, quemadmodum consuetum est in Castro *Norwici:* illius summæ partem, nempe trescentas sexaginta quatuor libras solvit in Thesauraria Regia, & de reliqua summa Regi obstrictus scribitur (*g*). Certe anno hujus Rotuli *Herveius* in vivis fuit : nam memoratur hic ut compotum reddens & pecuniam in Scaccario solvens ; quæ sunt acta viventis. Obijtque, secundum quosdam, anno Domini 1131, [R. *Henrici* I anno circiter 32], secundum alios A. D. 1133 [ejusdem Regis anno 34 ineunte] (*h*).

Præterea, in Veteri nostro Rotulo, Vicecomitibus *Londoniæ* rationem officij sui in Scaccario Regio reddentibus, computati erant (inter plu-

---

(*g*) Herveius Episcopus de Ely reddit compotum de vij marcis auri & dimidia, pro Ministerio Willelmi nepotis sui. In Thesauro xviij l pro iij marcis auri. Et debet iiij marcas auri & dimidiam. Et quater xx & xij l & x s.

Et idem Episcopus debet C marcas argenti, pro quadam veteri Conventione quæ facta fuit inter eum & Regem in Normannia.

Et idem Episcopus debet C l, pro placito quod fuit inter eum & Abbatem S. Edmundi & Abbatem de Ramesia.

Et idem Episcopus debet CC & xl l, ut Rex clamet eum quietum de superplus Militum Episcopatus, & ut Abbatia de Cateriz sit quieta de Warpenna.

Et idem Episcopus reddit compotum de M l, ut Milites Episcopatus de Ely faciant Wardam suam in Insula de Ely, sicut faciebant in Castello de Norwic : In Thesauro CCCLxiiij l ; Et debet DC & xxxvj l. *Mag. Rot.* 5. *Ste. Rot.* 5. *a. tit.* Grentebrugescira.

(*h*) Herveus (episcopus Eliensis) obijt A. D. 1131, 30 Augusti, ex fide Annalium Winchelcumbæ, Continuatoris Florentij, & obituarij Eliensis vetustioris ; *Angl. Sac.* T. 1. *p.* 615 ; sed A. D. 1133, ex Ricardi Continuatione Hist. Elien. ; *Ib. p.* 618.

rima

DISCEPTATIO EPISTOLARIS.

rima alia) sumptus quos posuerunt, in parandis tam oleo lampadum juxta sepulchrum Reginæ ardentium, quam pannis eidem sepulcro imponendis (*i*). Hinc inferendum est, Reginam nuperrime, atque adeo intra limites Comitatuum (*Ballivam* vocamus) Vicecomitum *Londoniæ*, quin & ipso circiter anno de quo Vicecomites rationem hic reddunt, obijsse. Per *Reginam* intelligo Reginam *Consortem*, sive quæ hora mortis *Consors* fuit. Sciscitamur autem, ecquænam Regina. Regisne *Henrici* I una vel altera, an vero Regis *Stephani*. Non *Matilda* R. *Stephani*; si recte judico. Illa enim mortem obijt tertio die Maij A. D. 1151, anno currente R. *Stephani* decimosexto (*k*); adeo ut illius mors intra nostrum præsentem temporis cyclum non cadat, nec illam hic intelligendam verisimile sit. Non *Adeliza*, sive *Alicia* secunda uxor R. *Henrici* I. Illa enim ei nupta fuit paulo ante diem Purificationis S. *Mariæ*, A. D. 1121, R. *Henrici* I anno vicesimo secundo gyrante (*l*); eique supervivens postmodum nupta erat *Willelmo de Albini*. Quocum vixit, ut fertur, multis annis. Cyclo nostro utique non comprehensa. Quam igitur Reginam sciscitamur, ea, ni male auguror, est *Matilda* uxor prima R. *Henrici* I. Quæ *Westmonasterij* animam efflavit, Aprilis die 29ª aut 30ª, anno Domini N. J. C. 1118, imperij R. *Henrici* I decimo octavo volvente; in Abbatia *Westmonasteriensi*, intra ballivam sive districtum Vicecomitum *Londoniæ* & *Middlesexæ*, sepulta; sicut *Chronicon Saxonicum*, *Eadmerus*, & *Rogerus de Houdene*, testantur (*m*). Sane *Wilhelmus Prynn* Antiquarius diligentissimus, intuitu eorum que de Regina tunc nuper demortua, necnon de *Herveio* Præsule *Eliensi*, in Veteri nostro Rotulo continentur, non dubitavit pronunciare, illum esse Rotulum de tempore R. *Henrici* I, immo de anno decimo octavo ejusdem Regis (*n*). Ego in hoc negotio vereor adseverare seu fidenter sententiam ferre.

(*i*) Et in oleo ad ardendum ante sepulchrum Reginæ, xv s & ij d & obolus. *Mag. Rot.* 5. *Ste. Rot.* 15. *a. Londonia.*

Et in panno emendo ad ponendum super sepulchrum Reginæ, iijs Numero. *Ib. juxt.*

(*k*) *Sandfordi Geneal. Hist. p.* 40.

(*l*) Anꝺ ꞇoꞃopan Ꝺanƿel-mæꞃꞃan &c. Et ante festum Candellarum, in Windlesora ei in uxorem data est Athelis, quæ postea in Reginam fuit sacrata. Eratque illa filia Ducis de Luvain. *Chron. Sax. p.* 222. *ad A. D.* 1121.

(*m*) Anꝺ ꞃeo ꞇƿon Mahalꝺ ꝼoꞃꝺ-ꝼeꞃꝺe on Weꞃꞇmynꞃꞇꞃe ꝼæꞃ ꝺæꝩeꞃ kl. Mai.] þæn ꝼæꞃ bebyꞃꝥeꝺ. Et Regina Mahald obijt Westmonasterij Calendis Maij; ibique sepulta fuit. *Chron. Sax. p.* 221. *ad A. D.* 1118.

His diebus gravi damno Anglia percussa est, in morte Reginæ. Defuncta siquidem est apud Westmonasterium Kl. Maij, & in ipso Monasterio decenter sepulta. *Eadm. Hist. Nov. L.* 5. *p.* 122. *lin.* 37.

Anno 1118 —, Matildis Regina Anglorum pridie kal. Maij apud Westmonasterium obijt, & in ipso Monasterio decenter est sepulta. *Houed.* 1. *p.* 474. *n.* 20, 30.

(*n*) *Prynn. de Auro Reginæ. in append p.* 5.

Hactenus,

Hactenus, Amplissime Baro, tanquam in lance libravi subjectam materiam in tres queftiones divifam; Primam, Utrum Vetus hic Rotulus fit Regis *Henrici* II; Secundam, An R. *Stephani*; Tertiam, An R. *Henrici* I. Libramenti iftius hic eft effectus: Majus rationis pondus in Tertiam quæftionem recidit: nempe Rotulum illum ad R. *Henrici* I tempora oportere referri: Utrum autem ad annum decimumoctavum, an alium quempiam annum dominationis illius Regis, periti judicent. Utcunque; ego adeo caute ac diffidenter egi, ut in tota præeunte Hiftoria, quoties Veterem hunc Rotulum citare opus fuit, eum, pro more hucufque fueto, *Magnum Rotulum* anni Quinti R. *Stephani* appellare malui, quam mea privata opinione fretus, a communi ufu difcedere, novamque Rotulo illi denominationem indere. Idque profecto confultiffimum duxi. Non enim meum effe puto, & caufam dicere & fimul judicium ferre. Nihilominus, penes Antiquarios erit (nec repugnabo) fi quidem ex ijs quæ fuperius dixi, aut quæ ipfi melius norunt, caufam effe viderint, ftylum in hoc cafu in pofterum mutare, ac Rotulum iftum a R. *Henrici* I imperio denominare.

Jamque huic Difceptationi finem imponere cupio: Maximas Tibi gratias habiturus, quod meis ftudijs favere dignaris. Sed quid dico? Tua etiam funt. Amplitudinem Tuam in partes noftras trahere molior. Neque id temere. Nam artem hiftoricam amas ut qui maxime. Ejus excolendæ, ornandæ, & illuftrandæ caufa, variam fupellectilem antiquariam collegifti. Nec intra Patriæ fines cohibetur illud Tuum difciplinæ ftudium. Hiftoriæ & Antiquitatum *Græciæ, Italiæ*, aliarumque politarum *Europæ* nationum fcientiffimus es. Quocirca, non eft quod dubitem, rogata prius venia, Te Antiquarium falutare. Immo ut Talem Te hucufque adloquutus fum. Poftpofui enim aliquoties *Romanam* puritatem; vocibus fub medio feculo introductis utens. Idque feci ex induftria, ut tulit occafio; malens barbarice loqui, quam obfcure aut incerte. Equidem vir Cl. *Henricus Meibomius* antiquitatis monumentum a viris doctis in pretio habendum cenfuit, propterea folum quod pervetuftum erat: *propter antiquitatem* (inquit) *quæ apud litteratos omnes in pretio eft* (o). Nec fane immerito. Sed mihi non licet effe tam animofo: nam e noftratibus pauci in *Meibomij* fententiam eunt. Quid autem? Hic conjungitur cum antiquitate utilitas. Difcepto jam nunc de *Magno Rotulo* non folum antiquo, fed etiam utili & momentofo.

(o) *Meib. notæ ad Chron. Corbeienfe, p.* 134, *n.* 10.

Utcunque autem hæc sint, Baro eruditissime, floreat doctrina Antiquaria Historica & Philologica, virorum præstantissimorum ac præsertim Regiæ Majestatis auspicijs. Floreat, inquam, in alma nostra patria, Antiquitatum scientia, justa, candida, fidelis, ingenua. Floreat Historia *Britannica*. Recordis authenticisque expromatur. Scribatur lente, mature, ordinate, sincere, dilucide; sine partium studio, sine pravo consilio, sine omni vili affectu viris literatis indigno. Ad summam; tota disciplina encyclia, quæ dudum (ut aiunt) marcescere visa est, reflorescat: Omnesque laudandæ Artes vigeant & augeantur quandiu terrarum orbis consistet. Faxit autem Deus Ter Optimus Maximusque ut quæ hic supplex voveo, felicem aliquando sortiantur effectum. Quod reliquum est, Perillustris Baro, ad Tuam benignitatem recurro. Speroque hanc meam qualemqualem Disquisitionem Tibi non inacceptam fore, propterea saltem quod procedat a viro Tuarum virtutum cultore humillimo atque observantissimo. Dabam *Londoniæ* Kalendis Maijs Anno D. N. J. C. 1708.

INDEX.

ADVERTISEMENT

TO THE

INDEX.

THE Judicious Author of the History of the Exchequer *was pleased, towards the Close of his Life, to distinguish the Compiler of this* Index *with frequent and familiar Conversation; and, among other Instances of Regard, did consult with him, and ask his Care in the Publication of* Firma Burgi.

That Labour, under the Author's own Inspection, being satisfactorily performed, He sundry Times mentioned, with great Regret, the Want of an Index *to the* History of the Exchequer; *and was so explicit as to insist, that on Subjects of this Nature, the* Index *should contain Chronological References, and likewise supply the Place of a Glossary.*

⁎⁎⁎ *The*

ADVERTISEMENT.

The Dates of the Kings Reigns therefore, in which particular Persons lived, or filled such a Station, or enjoyed such an Estate, or performed such an Action, are at First View One obvious Reason of running out this Index *to so great a Length.*

A Glossary to explain uncommon Words cannot be without its Use; especially to Persons not intimately acquainted with these Subjects: And it is hoped there is not a single Instance through the Whole, where the Author's Explication of any Word is omitted, much less if it is explained by any original Instrument.

It is conceived the Antiquaries will on many Accounts be indebted to this Index, *in having these noble Materials, which in some respects lay buried and concealed out of Sight, digested and brought into open Light.*

The Antiquity of Families and of our Laws in numerous Instances may be reduced to a short Inquiry from hence.

Here likewise many Articles towards a Chronicon Preciosum *may be gathered.*

The Heralds may be rescued from the Uncertainties arising from Change of Names, or from Estates and Titles descending to Heirs general, by Esnecy *or otherwise.*

The

ADVERTISEMENT.

The Original of the Names of Places may frequently be ascertained, by observing the ancient and different Orthography, which has constantly been attended to.

I am persuaded there is no History of any County in England, which will not receive some Ornaments and Improvements from the Assemblage of Persons, Places, and Facts here made; the Earldoms and Baronies with their Knights Fees; the Sherifs of Counties and Proprietors of Manors; the Sergeanties annexed to Offices; the several Sorts of Tenure, particularly of Ecclesiasticks; the Estates and Indowments of Bishopricks and Religious Houses, being some of the many Curiosities crowded into this Treasure.

INDEX.

INDEX.

N. B. The Reader is desired to consider the Direction in this Index pointing to c. 1. 2. as referring to the First or Second Column of Notes.

Aron the Jew of Lincoln, his forfeited estate 3 Richard i. I. 192. whence Aaronis scaccarium or receipt, 190.

Aatiham, I. 439. c. 1. g.

Abadam, John, summoned to the expedition against Scotland among the barons of Glocestershire, 26 Edw. i. I. 655. c. 1.

Abbat of Westminster and Saint Alban, 11 Henry ii. I. 44. Many parliamentary Abbats enumerated, 3 Hen. iii. I. 67. c. 2. x. The order of their signing, ibid. Before the temporal lords, ibid. Abbat de Valle Dei, I. 430. c. 1. y. Richard Abbot has the custody of the palace of Westminster, 9 Edward ii. II. 85. Abbats swore to the king, 12 Edward ii. II. 149.

Abbeton, Saffrid chaplein of, 10 Hen. iii. I. 239. c. 1. x.

Abbetot, John de, 2 Henry iii. I. 475. c. 2. n. Alexander's tenure according to B. de Frivils plea, 38 Henry iii. I. 597. c. 1. z. Geoffrey de Abbetost custos of the honor of Wilekin de Beauchamp, 11 John, I. 644. c. 2. p.

Abbey of Fontanelle, I. 49. c. 1. d. Of Saint John of Colchester when founded, I. 49. c. 2. i. Of Ousche and Fontanelle in Normandy, not to be impleaded but before the king, I. 92. Many abbeys enumerated, 26 Edward i. II. 123. c. 1. u.

Abdodesbirie, that Abbey accompted for, 14 John, I. 312. c. 2. a. Its fine, 13 Henry iii. I. 661. c. 1. i. Abbotsbury accompts for one fee, 5 Henry iii. I. 667. c. 1. m.

Abbreviations both of christian and sirnames frequent in old membranes, Pref. I. xi.

Abel, John, assess'd the tillage in Surry and Sussex, 6 Edward ii. I. 744. c. 1. w, c. 2. x. Was baron of the Exchequer, 5 Edward ii. II 26. c. 2. d. II. 59. c. 1. d. Richard Abel goldsmith cut the dyes of the moneyours, 27 Henry iii. II. 88. c. 1. c.

Abendon, Robert de, his interest in the village of Bocklande, 13 John, I. 218. c. 2. w. Thomas de Hesseborn accompts for the honor of Abendon, 31 Henry ii. I. 309. c. 2. s. Abbat of Abendon has the hundred

INDEX.

dred of Hornemere, Berkshire, 13 Henry iii. I. 416. c. 2. *a*. Abendon cloth temp. Henry iii. I. 550. That abbats scutage for the Irish expedition, 18 Henry ii. I. 629. c. 2. *a*. See Abyngdon. and II. 278. c. 1. *u*.

Abernum, Ingelram de, his knights fees in Cambridgeshire, 41 Henry iii, I. 47. c. 1. *w*. Jordan de Abernun one of the heirs of Henry de Secchevil, 10 Richard i. I. 514. c. 2. *c. e*. V. Daubernum.

Abjurers of counties, &c. I. 471. c. 2.

Abrancis, William de, one of the inquisitors upon the sherifs, 16 Henry ii. I. 140. Robert de Abrincis fines for his fury, 5 Stephen, 473. c. 1. *l*. William de Abrincis his knights fees in Kent, temp. Henry ii. l. 579. c. 1. *i*. Simon de Abrincis his escuage, 6 Ricardi i. p. 590. c. 2. *l*. Richard de Abrincis fines for his lands in the bishoprick, 8 Richard i. I. 715. c. 2. The scutages of William de Abrincis, 9 Henry iii. II. 27. c. 2. *e*. Turgis de Abrincis attests a charter of king Stephen, II. 139. c. 1. *e*. Bishop of Exeter has the ward of the land and heir of William de Abrincis, 18 Henry iii. II. 198. c. 2. *u*.

Abyndon, Mr. Richard de, baron of the Exchequer, 1 Edward ii. I. 75. c. 1. *t*. again 2 Edward ii. II. 8. c. 2. *m*. II. 46. c. 2. *u*. replaced baron of the Exchequer, 1 Edward ii. II. 57. c. 2. *y*. Is superannuated, 10 Edward ii. II. c. 2. *f*. Baron of the Exchequer, 34 Edward i. II. 66. c. 1. *g*. Assign'd one of the surveyors of the king's castles and manors, 1 Edward ii. II. 67. c. 2. *q*. Occurs again baron of the Exchequer, 34 Edward i. II. 71. c. 2. *l*. Shephen de Abyndon sherif of London, 8 Edward ii. II. 161. c. 2. *q*. Abbat of Abyndon collector of disme, 9 Edward ii. II. 181. c. 2.

Accha fil. Ernebrand, 5 Stephen, I. 147. c. 1. *r*.

Accley prior has two knights fees in Herefordshire, 29 Henry iii. I. 596. c. 1. *s*. Reginald de Acle to seize the sherifalty of Glocestershire, 1 Edward i. II. 68. c. 2. *y*. Mentioned as late sherif of Gloucester, 56 Henry iii. II. p. 180.

Accompts, with the manner of accompting at the Exchequer, II. 127, &c. The difference between the accompting of commoners, and lords, II. 242, 243.

Aca, Benet, accompts for the king's wines, 30 Henry iii. I. 768.

Achard de Sproxton, 4 John, I. 217. c. 1. *l*. Achard the king's moneyour, his aid for marrying the king's daughter, 14 Henry ii. I. 568. c. 2. *i*. William Achard's fees in Berkshire, 18 Henry ii. I. 648. c. 1. *a*. Which were granted to William's grandfather temp. Henry i. ibid. A tallager of Berkshire, 8 Richard i. I. 705. c. 1. *t*. Robert Achard had the manors of Aldermanston and Spersholt before 26 Edward i. II. 8. c. 1. *l*.

Achatum or purchase, I. 425. c. 1. *c*.

Achley belonged to the king of Scots, 13 Henry ii. I. 539. c. 1. *w*.

Aclet, Mr. Ernald de, his fine of an hundred and forty palfreys with accoutrements, 14 John, I. 273. c. 2. *i*.

Acre, Derekin del, 9 Richard i. II. 198. c. 1. *r*.

Adam,

INDEX.

Adam, or Fitz-Adams, William son of, his pardon, an. 1184. I. 168. c. 2. Robert son of Adam of Westmoreland, 3 John, I. 206. c. 1. *o.* William's interest in Northumberland, 3 John, I. 404. c. 1. *a.* His land in Baenburg, ibid. Odard and Adam Fitz-Adam, their tenure by cornage, 3 John, I. 658. c. 2. *n.* Robert Fitz-Adam his estate in Carlisle, 3 John, I. 659. c. 2. *b.*

Adelakeston, a town of the king of Scots, 14 Henry ii. I. 540. c. 1. *y.*

Adeling, Edward, 26 Henry ii. I. 549. c. 2. *g.*

Adeliza, queen of Henry i. I. 58. c. 1. *a.*

Adeliza the wife of Roger Bigot had the honour of Belveder from her father, I. 315. c. 2. *q.*

Adelpald and Adonald, Pref. xxvii. c. 2.

Adintone in Surrey, lands held there in serjeanty to find a cook at the coronation, I. 651. c. 2. *r.*

Adnebec, Philip de, 4 John, I. 763. c. 1. *b.*

Adretiare, what, I. 140. c. 2. *w.*

Adrian, John, one of the fermers of the city of London, 52 Henry iii. I. 779. c. 1. *e.* John Adrien mayor of London, 55 Henry iii. II. 93. c. 1. *k.* One of the bailifs of London, 51 Henry iii. II. 95. c. 2. *t.* Custos of London, 53 and 54 Henry iii. II. 202. c. 2. *a.* His allocatio in that station, ibid. The chatels of John Adrien late sherif of London seiz'd, 52 Henry iii. II. 237. c. 2. *q.* Thomas Adrian one of the manucaptors for the community of the city of London, 39 Henry iii. II. 240.

Adventus, or the Advents of the accomptants to the Exchequer, II. 114.

Advouson belong'd to the lord of the fee, I. 435. c. 1. *n.*

Ædmond, provost of Lincoln, fermer there, 26 Henry ii. I. 331. c. 2. *p.*

Ægelric, bishop of Chichester in the Conqueror's time, I. 32. c. 2. *e.* his skill in our laws, ibid.

Æmilius Paulus, his account of the chancellors of France, I. 62.

Æthelic, wife of the emperor of Sexlande and daughter of Henry i. I. 13. c. 1. *q.* All the archbishops, bishops, earls, theins, swear to her succession at Windsor, an. 1127. ibid.

Aencurt, Walter de, fines for a concord with Maurice de Creun, 5 Henry ii. I. 511. c. 2. *m.* Walter de Ajencurt's knights fees in Lincolnshire, 14 Henry ii. I. 584. c. 2. *p.* Oliver's fees paid scutage, 33 Henry ii. I. 713. c. 2. *d.*

Affeered or admeasured, when the misericordia was reduced to a certain sum, I. 577. Barons of the Exchequer affeered amerciaments temp. Edward i. II. 65. So did other Justices and commissioners, II. 66.

Afton, Richard de, sherif of Hampshire, 22 Edward i. II. 173. c. 2. *q.*

Agbrig wapentake has a commission of array sent to it, 16 Edward ii. II. 112. c. 1.

Agerney, Thomas de, fined a Besant, &c. an. 1184. I. 166. c. 1. *i.*

Agmondesham, Walter de, kings chancellor for the parts of Scotland, 27 Edward i. II. 266. c. 1. *n.* See Amundesham.

Aguilon, William, of Surrey, married the heiress of Bartholomew de Cheney
before

INDEX.

before 18 Henry iii. I. 651. c. 1. r. With whom he had lands in Kery, Elveyn, and Adintone, ibid. In ferjeanty, to find a cook at the coronation, ibid. Robert de Aguillun cuftos of the wardrobe, 57 Hen. iii. I. 778. c. 1. b. William Aguillum fines for law againft Manfel and Richard Aguillun, 7 Richard i. I. 789. c. 2. g. And demands of them a knight's fee in Nordborne, ibid. Robert Aguillon one of the king's council, 53 Henry iii. II. 171. c. 1. h.

Ahford manor belonged to Griffin fon of Wenunwen, 29 Henry iii. II. 222.

Aids, three notable ones, I. 570. c. 1. a. In Burgundy, thofe who had feigneury could impofe four forts of aid, I. 571. See on to 618. Aid to marry the king's daughter, 14 Henry ii. I. 572, &c. For the ranfom of Richard i. I. 589. c. 2. i. For the marriage of the king's fifter and daughter, I. 594. c. 1. g. For making the king's eldeft fon a knight, at forty fhillings a fee, I. 596. c. 2. x. Other aids, I. 600. Aids impofed on particular counties and places, I. 612. Lords had aids of their tenants conform to thofe of the crown, I. 614.—See II. 276.

Aillefbiri tallaged, 1 John, I. 747. c. 2. l. A tallage levied on the men Aillefbiri for the ufe of John Fitz-Geoffrey, 14 Henry iii. I. 752. c. 1. f.

Ailred, Thomas, keeper of the ordinance for money at Ipfwich, 32 Edward i. I. 294. c. 1. g.

Ailric, William, Hafcuil and Geoffrey his fons, 23 Henry ii. I. 210. c. 1. f. Ailric the carpenter of Devonfhire, 14 Henry ii. I. 588. c. 1. b.

Ailfi, William, fon of one of the fermours of Lincoln, 14 Henry ii. I. 585. c. 1. s.

Ailward the chamberlain, 18 Henry ii. I. 336. c. 2. f. King's ferjeant, 14 Henry ii. I. 565. c. 1. g. Ailward, fon of Seric, his aid and fees in Cornwal, 23 Henry ii. I. 604. c. 2. m.

Ailwin, Merciarius, fines for a concord with the city of Glocefte, 12 Henry ii. I. 511. c. 2. o. His tallage, 19 Henry ii. I. 701. c. 2. c.

Ailword, archdeacon [of Colchefter] 1142. I. 198. c. 1. e.

Ailworth, land of, I. 213. c. 2. r.

Aimovefdal, Robert de, 14 John, I. 117. c. 2. n. His writ of protection, 2 John, I. 478. c. 1. n.

Ainesford, William de, 14 John, I. 444. c. 1. q. See Einesford. William de Ainesford his gerfom to be fherif of Effex and Hertfordfhire, 5 Stephen, I. 458. c. 1. z. His fine for accord with Hugh de Beauchamp, 14 John, I. 472. c. 2. f.

Ainefmere, Hugh fon of William de, his land in Gucefton, 13 John, I. 218. c. 2. t.

Aiftan, Robert de, married the fifter of Hugh de Flammavil before 7 Richard i. I. 323. c. 2. a.

Aivilla, Robert de, 24 Henry ii. I. 103. c. 2. k.

Aketon, terra de, in Norf. belong'd to Ralf de Heldebovil's heir, 7 Richard i. I. 323. c. 1. z. In cuftody of Geoffrey de Cramavil, ibid.

Akfted, Roland de, 22 Henry iii. I. 648. c. 1. c.

Alan

INDEX.

Alan Fitz Odo, his tenure from the fee of Norwich, 5 Stephen, I. 112. c. 2. o. Frere Alan, preceptor of the new temple, 52 Henry ii. I. 270. c. 2. e. Alan difpenfator, deputy of Ralf Fitz-Stephen, 1 Richard i. I. 289. c. 1. r. The honor of William Fitz Alan in cuftody of Guy Leftrange fherif of Shropfhire, 19 Henry ii. I. 297. c. 2. n. Roald, fon of Alan, 13 John, I. 411. c. 1. r. Alan, fon of Roland, fines for lands in Teineford, 7 Richard i. p. 484. c. 1. t. John Fitz-William, fon of Alan, fines in ten thoufand marks, 5 Henry iii. I. 492. c. 1. p.

Alard, William fon of, and Wiard, held of the bifhop of Chichefter temp. Henry ii. I. 576. c. 1. y.

Alban S. that monaftery confecrated an. 1116. I. 12. c. 1. l. Henry de S Albano, 9 Henry iii. I. 389. c. 1. g. See S Alban, and I. 762.

Albaneftou hundred, ibid.

Albemarle, William earl of, one of the jufticiers on the entrance of king Richard i. I. 34. William earl of, 3 Henry iii. I. 67. c. 2. x. William earl of Albamara, 23 Henry iii. I. 302. c. 2. b. William de Alba-mara, 5 Stephen, I. 449. c. 1. u. His dapifer fines to be difcharged, 5 Stephen, I. 457. c. 1. o. Hawife countefs of Albemarle fines to marry at her difcretion, 13 John, I. 465. c. 2. u. William de Alba-Mara, 5 Stephen, I. 481. c. 2. x. A girdle to be given to the countefs of Albermarle, 11 John, I. 507. c. 1. c. Baldwin earl of Albemarle, 4 John, I. 537. c. 1. His number of fees in Yorkfhire, 14 Henry ii. I. 580. c. 2. r. William de Albemarle, 7 Richard i. I. 591. c. 2. t. Countefs has aid of her tenants, 26 Edward i. I. 614. c. 2. w. Earls fcutage, 18 Henry ii. I. 629. c. 2. z. The fcutage of that honor for the Welch war, 3 Richard i. I. 637. c. 2. f. James earl of Albemarle, chamberlain of the Exchequer, has the caftle of Schipton, 52 Henry ii. II. 15. c. 1. t. And Ifabella de Fortibus his wife, II. 15. c. 1. u, w. William earl of Albemarle fat in the Exchequer, 14 Henry iii. II. 27. c. 2. g. That honor in the king's hand, 14 Edward i. II. p. 100. c. h. William earl of Albemarle, temp. Stephen, II. 138. c. 2. e. William de Forz earl of Albemarle, 5 Richard i. II. 189. c. d.

Albernum, Gilbert and Ingelram de, their tenure of four knights fees from the earl of Glocefter in Surrey, 19 Henry iii. I. 320. c. 1. k. John de Albernun fheriff of Surrey and Suffex, 51 Henry iii. II. 180. c. 1. b. V. Daubernoon.

Albini Brito, William de, temp. Henry i. I. 56. c. 2. o. William de Albineio, 3 Henry iii. I. 68. c. 2. x. His grant to the monks of Sabrictfwurth, I. 120. c. 2. h. William de Albeneio pincerna, 14 Henry ii. I. 142. c. 2. f. Held pleas, 5 Stephen, I. 148. c. 1. n. William de Albini Brito cuftos of the honor of Otuer Fitz Count, 5 Stephen, I. 297. c. 1. b. William de Albineo earl of Arundel, his relief, 6 Henry iii. I. 317. c. 2. r. Robert de Albeniaco his barony before 21 Henry iii. I. 317. c. 2. t. Divided among his daughters, ibid. William Albini Brito fermer of Rutland, temp. Stephen,

INDEX.

Stephen, I. 328. c. 1. *f.* Robert de Albineio, 26 Henry ii. I. 431. c. 1. *i.* Son of Nigellus de Albini, 5 Stephen, I. 449. c. 2. *t.* Malgerus de S. Albino, 14 Henry ii. I. 558. c. 2. *y.* William de Albineio Brito, 14 Henry ii. I. 574. c. 2. *o.* William de Albeneio, 7 Richard i. I. 591. c. 2. *t.* William de Albini pincerna, 2 Richard i. I. 664. c. 1. *z.* William de Albenni, one of the wardens of the sea-ports in Lincolnshire, 15 John, I. 773. William de Albenni Britto attests a charter of king Stephen, I. 139. c. 1. *e.* Henry de Albiniaco, late earl of Arundel, 38 Henry iii. I. 190. c. 1. *i.* Hugh de, 18 Henry iii. I. 198. c. 2. *t.* William de Albenni custos of Warwick and Leicestershire, 7, 8, 9 Richard i. I. 226. c. 2. *y.*

Albric the chamberlain, Robert son of, 14 Henry ii. I. 574. c. 1. *n.*

Album Firmæ under the Anglo-Saxons, I. 177. Album or combustion money, I. 280. Alba firma, II. 242. c. 2. *a.*

Alcmundebir and Bramton, the fees of earl David in Cambridge and Huntingdonshire, 13 John, I. 666. c. 2. *i.*

Aldebery, Essex, its aid, 14 Henry ii. I. 587. c. 1. *x.*

Aldefeld, Alan de, his lands, 26 Edward i. II. 46. c. 1. *t.*

Aldelega, Adam de, sheriff of Warwick and Leicestershire, 26 Henry ii. I. 139. c. 1. *i.*

Alden barony in the bishoprick, 8 Richard i. I. 716.

Alderman-Buri, Gilbert de, his charter temp. Richard i. I. 540. Aldermen of London gilds, I. 562. The Aldermen of London, 14 Henry iii. I. 709. c. 1. *t.* Again, 2 Edward ii. II. 235.

Aldermannesbiria, Gervase de, chamberlain of London, 10 Richard i. I. 766. Again, 767.

Aldermannus, Tomas, sherif of London, 11 John, I. 194. c. 1. *n.*

Aldermanston manor, Berks, had belong'd to Robert Achard, II. 8. And passes to Robert son of Elias de Coleshulle, 26 Edward i. II. 8. c. 1. *l.*

Aldid, William son of, fines to continue in Essex after he had abjur'd it, 31 Henry ii. I. 471. c. 2. *w.*

Aldithlega, or Audley, Sir William de, and Luke, fine for their release, 13 John, I. 495. c. 1. *c.* Henry, I. 734. c. 2. *d.* Henry de Aldithlega sherif of Shropshire, 14 Henry iii. II. 253. c. 2. *b.* See Audeley.

Aldredeshul, William de, claims from Tomas de Seleby in Lincolnshire, 2 John, I. 434. c. 2. *l.*

Aldredesley, Liulf de, in Staffordshire, amerc'd for the death of Gamel, 10 John, I. 543. c. 2. *c.*

Aldrete, Bernard, of the Castilian tongue or romance, Pref. xi. c. 1. *k.*

Ale made of wheat, barley, and honey, 31 Henry ii. I. 368. c. 2. *w.*

Alechester escheated to the crown, 24 Henry ii. I. 300. c. 1. *r.*

Alemannia, Henry de, one of the king's council, 53 Henry iii. II. 171. c. 1. *b.* An aid to ransom the king of Alemaign, 52 Henry iii. II. 276.

Alençon, John de, archdeacon of Lisieux, vice-chancellor of Normandy, temp. Richard i. I. 77. Claims to be patron of Hoton, Linc. 3 John, I. 447. c. 2. *c.*

Alexander

INDEX.

Alexander and Niel his son, custodes of the abbey of Bardeney, 31 Henry ii. I. 309. c. 2. *u.* Alexander, king of Scots, his travelling expences, 35 Henry iii. II. 202. c. 1. *w.*

Alfonso, king of Castile, an. 1254. I. 5. c. 1. Has the vassalage of the kings of Granada, Murcia, and Stebula, his vassals, ibid.

Algar and Sprackling fined for coining or uttering false money, 5 Stephen, I. 277. c. 2. *g.*

Algeis, Martin, steward of Gascony, 5 John, I. 53. c. 2. *u.*

Alice, daughter of Ostelin of Kent, 6 Henry iii. I. 454. c. 2. *i.* Alice Bertram amerc'd for not obeying her summonce for marriage, 1 John, I. 565. c. 2. *q.*

Alienor, wife of William de Bohun, descended from the Marescals earls of Pembroc, I. 47. c. 1. *w.*

Alienor, wife of Henry iii. made joint regent with Richard earl of Cornwal, 37 Henry iii. I. 68. c. 2. *b.* What bishopricks and abbies she could dispose of, ibid. Has the custody of the great seal, I. 69. c. 2. *c.* Sits in the court and hears pleas vice regis, I. 102. c. 2. *g.* Has her gold when dowager, I. 351. c. 1. *b.*

Alienor, queen consort of Edward i. I. 230. c. 2. *k.* Her queen's gold, 1 Edward i. I. 350. c. 2. *q.* Her grant of the hundred of Gattre, &c. 13 Edward i. I. 361. c. 1. *t.* Her grant from Henry iii. upon the men of Sumerton, I. 362. c. 1. *b.* Alienor, consort of prince Edward, has the hundred of Sumerton, 52 Henry iii. II. 167. c. 1. *u.* Alienor, the queen mother and consort, support Edmund Spigurnel, 1 and 4 Edward i. II. 233. c. 1. *k, l.*

Alienor, the king's cozen, wife of Alexander de Balliol, 5 Edward i. and widow, 7 Edward i. I. 682. c. 2. *t.*

Alif, Alexander son of Alif and Beatrice his daughter, of Cumberland, attach'd for murder, 6 Henry iii. I. 496. c. 1. *m.*

Alina la Mareschal, her scutage of Gannoc, 38 Henry iii. I. 678. c. 1. *f.*

Allemannebiry, in Yorkshire, its tallage, 30 Henry iii. I. 710. c. 1. *w.* The forinseci tallaged here, ibid. and p.

Allodium, what, p. 186. c. 1. *m.*

Almodintona, Robert de, holds of the bishop of Chichester, temp. Henry ii. I. 576. c. 1. *y.*

Almoner of the king, I. 348.

Alnage, or assise of cloth, I. 785.

Alneto, John de, claims the patronage of Steinton, Linc. 30 Henry ii. I. 407. c. 1. *l.* Robert de Alneto, 5 Henry iii. I. 453. c. 1. *q.* Robert fines, 6 Henry iii. I. 492. c. 1. *s.* William de, occurs, 9 John, I. 791. c. 2. *t.*

Alnodus ingeniator, 9 Henry ii. Pref. xiv. c. 2. *d.*

Alnou, Hugh de, 7 Richard i. I. 216. c. 1. *e.*

Alreford burgh, the bishop of Winchester's, I. 719. c. 2. *r.*

Alrewas manor, in Staffordshire or Shropshire, held in Fee-ferm by Roger de Somervil, 27 Henry iii. I. 678. c. 2. *i.*

Alshiesholt, forest of, I. 45. c. 2. *n.* William de Venuiz forester of it, 4 Richard i. I. 497. c. 2. *s.*

Alstanesfeld, Staffordshire, by whom claimed,

INDEX

claimed, 2 Henry iii. I. 793. c. 1. *d.*

Alſtineſwich, terra de, I. 105. c. 2. *q.*

Alſwick, Richard, one of the keepers of the king's palace at Weſtminſter, 41 Henry iii. II. 23. c. 2. *n.*

Alta Ripa, William Painel de, an.1184. I. 168. c. 2. *l.* William de Alta Ripa, 7 John, I. 448. c. 1. *g.* Richard de Alta Ripa eſcapes from the cuſtody of Hugh Nevil before 14 John, I. 475. c. 1. *k.* William Painel de Alta Ripa, his ſcutage for his Yorſhire lands, 18 Henry ii. I. 629. c. 2. *z.* The ſcutage for his terra in the king's hands, 33 Henry ii. I. 635. c. 1. *r.*

Altar of the Chancery waſh'd with wine, I. 195. c. 2. *a.*

Altebarge, that town fined for taking and concealing a large fiſh, 16 Henry ii. I. 558. c. 2. *x.*

Alto Boſco, Peter de, fines to be ſteward of Hulm-abbey, &c. 12 John, I. 462. c. 1. *m.*

Alverinton, one of John Wak's ſeven churches in the dioceſe of Exeter, 29 Henry iii. II. 250. c. 1. *i.*

Alvertona, Jukel de, 21 Henry ii. I. 546. c. 1. *o.* Soke of, I. 557. c. 2. *h.* See its array, II. 112. c. 2.

Alviva, of Bramton, I. 588. c. 1. *b.*

Alured, ſon of Ralf, 28 Henry ii. I. 104. c. 2. *n.* Alured de Lincoln, 12 John, I. 507. c. 1. *d.* Alured de Keteleſtan periſhed by the judgment of water, 18 Henry ii. I. 345. c. 1. *t.* II. 131.

Alwardebi, Cicely de, ſiſter of Geoffrey Martel's wife, 5 Richard i. I. 483. c. 2. *o.*

Alwineſſune, Otho, one of the ſureties of Hugh Cordele, 5 Stephen, II. 197. c. 2. *q.*

Amadeo, earl of Savoy, 30 Edward i. I. 73. Has the iſſues of vacant biſhopricks, 32 Edward i. I. 313. Sits at the Exchequer, 1 Edward ii. II. 29.

Amadour, Tecla, merchant of Florence, 5 Edward i. II. 77. c. 1. *k.*

Amalm, Peter, canon of Bourdeaux, adminiſtrator of the ſee of Canterbury, 35 Edward i. II. 224.

Amandus the parſon, amerc'd for hunting in the king's foreſt without licence, 10 John, I. 566. c. 2. *z.*

Ambarii of Corbey and Neel, duties ariſing from them, I. 779. c. 2.

Ambaſia, George, cardinal of, I. 111.

Ambaſſadors, II. 218.

Ambreſbury prioreſs has the manor of Melkeſham, 9 Edward ii. I. 753. c. 2. *n.* Fines by her bailif Robert de Savary, 15 Edward ii. II. 246. c. 1. *a.*

Ambreſley foreſt in Worceſterſhire deafforeſted, 14 Henry iii. I. 418. c. 2. *k.* Richard de Ambreſley juſticier about 6 Richard i. I. 592. c. 2. *y.*

Amelberge hundred, amerc'd for a murder, 10 Henry iii. I. 528. c. 2. *k.*

Amerciaments ſet on people by the chancellor, I. 61. Amerciaments in the king's iters, I. 150. 168. Amerciaments for miſdemeanours, I. 221. Difference between Amerciaments and Miſericordia, I. 526. Amerced as a baron, I. 527—535. Amerciaments for the faults of others, I. 537, & ſeq. When they fell on the king's demeans were diſcharged. And on the king of Scot's lands. Or on the lands or tenants of barons of the Exchequer. Amer-

INDEX.

Amerciaments pro foresta, I. 541. For serving the enemy, I. 546. c. 1. *n.* For disseising, I. 549. For recreancy and duels, ibid. Amerciaments for defaults, I. 552. For decisions concerning lay fees in ecclesiastical courts, I. 561. c. 2. *q.* Accrued to the chief lord only by charter, II. 10. c. 1. *v.* How and by whom affeered, II. 66. Amerciaments, distress, and seisure of land for want of due payment at the Exchequer, II. 234.

Ammirata, I. 40. c. 1. *c.* I. 55. 60.

Amortizing lands, a fine for it, II. 63.

Amundesham, Walter de, 14 Edward i. I. 254. c. 2. *c.* Adam de Agmondesham, baron of the Exchequer, assigned to survey the king's castles and manors, 1 Edward ii. II. 67. c. 2. *q.*

Amundevill, Walter de, sherif of Lincolnshire, 5 Henry ii. I. 222. c. 1. *a.* Agnes de Amundevill of Lincolnshire, 17 Henry ii. I. 427. c. 1. *c.* Helyas de, 17 Henry ii. I. 429. c. 2. *r.* Joslan de Amundevill, steward of the land and houshold of the bishop of Lincoln by descent, I. 440. c. 1. *n.* Again, I. 458. c. 2. *e.* John de Amundevill claims the land of Hocton and Hastley, 5 Stephen, I. 482. c. 1. *y.* Niel de Aumundevil, his interest in the shires of Cambridge and Huntingdon, 31 Henry iii. I. 594. c. 2. *k.* Elyas de, marries a sister and coheiress to the barony of Niel de Luvetot before 6 Henry iii. I. 640. c. 1. *r.* Barony of Robert de Amundevil in the bishopric, 8 Richard i. I. 716. c. 2. *h.*

Andebury, was Alexander de Swereford's, 29 Henry iii. II. 13. c. 2. *k.*

Andeford, William de, his father killed, 9 John, I. 441. c. 2. *x.*

Andeliaci insula, I. 766. c. 2. *o.*

Andeura or Andover fines for the same liberties to their gild as Wilton and Saresbery have, 22 Henry ii. I. 398. c. 1. *r.* Its assise, 22 Henry ii. I. 703. c. 1. *i.* Its tallage, 30 Henry iii. I. 711. c. 1. *x.* I. 736. c. 1. *q.*

Andreu, John, alderman of Redingate, Canterbury, 32 Edward i. I. 741. c. 1. *g.* Andrew, prior of S. Swithun, and bishop elect of Winchester, 43 Henry iii. II. 3. c. 2. *l.* Has two thousand marks annually while his election is debated, ibid.

Anegous, earl of, one of the king's courtiers, 26 Edward i. I. 655. c. 2.

Anesia, William de, fines for the rectum of the land which William de Colevil holds, 22 Henry ii. I. 427. c. 1. *e.* The land and heir of Richard Anesy in the ward of Walter de Avenbury, 35 Henry iii. II. 190. c. 2. *n.*

Anesti wapentac in Yorkshire fines to quiet of the forest, 5 Richard i. I. 399. c. 1. *c.* Fine again to be quiet of forestagium, 10 John, I. 409. c. 2. *d.* The donum of Anesti wapentak, 9 Richard i. I. 699. c. 2. *r.* See Aynsty.

Anevil, Alured de, slain in William Torel's town of Yle, 31 Henry ii. I. 556. c. 2. *s.*

Anger, the dean, amerced for hunting in the king's forest, 10 John, I. 566. c. 2. *z.* Ralf de Aungers, sherif of Wilts before 51 Henry iii. II. 68. c. 2. *x.* and before 49 Henry iii. II. 158. c. 2. *b.*

Angervil, William and Robert de, contend for the patronage of the church of that name, 2 John, I. 538.

INDEX.

518. c. 2. *u.* was a fief del haubert, ibid.

Anglicus, Willelmus, brother of Richard Fitz-Niel the treasurer, and baron of the Exchequer, 30 Henry ii. I. 216. c. 1. *d.*

Angria, that honour accounted for by Robert Peverel, 14 John, I. 291. c. 1. *e.*

Anjou, Geoffrey earl of, his grant from Robert king of France of the majoratus domus regiæ, I. 53 c. 2. *y.* There ftiled Gaufridus Grifogonella, ibid.

Anne, William de, has a commiffion of array for Tykhil wapentak, 16 Edward ii. II. 112. c. 1. *c.*

Anfelm, held a fynod an. 1102. I. 9. c. 1. *x.*

Anfelm, vifcount of Roan, fines to the bifhop of Winton, 5 Stephen, I. 500. c. 2. *h.* I. 622. c. 1. *c.*

Anfketil, Herbert fon of, amerced, 31 Henry ii. I. 552. c. 2. *s.* Anfketil, prefbyter of Burgh, fined ten marks for faying what he could not prove, 5 Stephen, I. 557. c. 1. *z.* Anketil held of the bifhop of Chichefter, temp. Henry ii. I. 576. c. 1. *y.* Mr. Anketil fubcuftos of the fee of Durham, temp. Richard i. I. 714. c. 1. *g.* the donum of Anketil the prefbyter was thirty-two marks, 8 Richard i. I. 715. c. 2. *g.* Anfchetil, nephew of Roger, a furety of Hugh Cordele, 5 Stephen, II. 197. c. 2. *q.*

Antiquities, the ufe and improvement of ftudying them, Pref. i. ii. vii.

Apotecarius regis, or treafurer, I. 79. c. 2. *u.*

Appelthweit, William de, of Cumberland, flain, 6 Henry iii. I. 496. c. 1. *m.*

Appleby, Richard, fon of Gerard de, fherif of Weftmoreland, temp. Stephen, I. 328. c. 1. *i.* The town taken into the king's hand, and committed to Alexander de Barewyz, 5 Edward ii. II. 247.

Appleton, priorefs, her liberties, 9 John, I. 408. c. 1. *p.* Appleton, Berkfhire, its donum, 33 Henry ii. I. 713. c. 2. *e.*

Appofals of fherifs, II. 170.

Apprizer of goods taken by the fherifs of counties on diftrefs, II. 196. That office, how claimed as hereditary, and abufed, II. 196. c. 1. *o.*

Aquila, Richer de, his knights fees, 14 Henry ii. I. 577. c. 2. *a.* Small fees of that honor, I. 649. Gilbert de Aquila in Suffex charged for fmall fees, as Moreton and earl Reginald were, 6 Richard i. I. 649. c. 1. *e.* and 33 Henry ii. ibid. c. 2. *i.* Earl Warenne has cuftody of thirty-five fees of this honor, 13 John, I. 666. c. 2. *k.* Gilbert de Aquila has reftitution of his lands, 11 Henry iii. II. 255. c. 1. *l.*

Ar, to whom that land belonged, 9 Richard i. I. 790. c. 1. *i.*

Aragon has its jufticier, I. 38. That kingdom has its Mayordomo's, I. 54. c. 2. *f.*

Arald or Herald, archdeacon of Bath, I. 110, 111. c. 2.

Aram in Wiltfhire, its donum, 33 Henry ii. I. 631. c. 1. *q.*

Araz, Robert de, fherif of London, 5 Edward i. II. 96. c. 2. *y.*

Arcaldus, S. Romano de, keeper of the wardrobe, 40 Henry iii. I. 268. c. 2. *r*

Archdeacon, the ftile of mafter affigned him, I. 85. Archdeacon of Berks occurs jufticier and fermer of the tallage, 9 Richard i. I. 705. c. 1. *t.* Archdeacon of Weftminfter, treafurer

INDEX.

furer of a private exchequer there, 30 Henry iii. II. 3. c. 2. *k*. For the receipt of 2591 *l*. granted to the fabric of that church by Henry iii. ibid.

Arches, Henry de, 27 Henry ii. I. 96. c. 2. *q*. Robert de Archis pays Queens-gold, 12 John, I. 351. c. 1. *x*.

Arches of London bridge, two cost twenty-five pound, 5 Stephen, I. 364. c. 2. *n*.

Arden, William de, his interest in Gorcote and Witteshage, 31 Henry ii. I. 97. c. 2. *y*. Robert, son of William, 1 Richard i. I. 98. c. 1. *g*. Ralf de Arden, sherif of Herefordshire, amerced for not keeping time of payment, 1 Richard i. II. 235. c. 2. *x*.

Ardern, Thomas de, 10 John, I. 103. c. 2. *w*.

Ardre, Robert de, justicier, settles the tallage in Lincolnshire, 5 Richard i. I. 486. Seems to be the same with Robert de Hardre, I. 79.

Ardyngelli, Roger, merchant of Florence, 12 Edward ii. II. 262. c. 1.*w*. Delivered Venetian shillings at the Exchequer exceeding the sterling, ibid.

Argenteim, Richard de, seneschal, 11 Henry iii. I. 63. c. 2. *l*. Occurs 16 Henry iii. I. 64. c. 1. *m*. Giles de, 49 Henry iii. I. 70. Reginald de Argentoem, 5 Richard i. I. 142. c. 1. *b*. Richard one of the justices in Normandy, 2 John, I. 156. c. 2.*i*. Herbert de, an. 1184. I. 168. c. 2. *l*. Reginald, sub-sherif for Cambridge and Huntingdonsh. 5 John, I. 206. c. 2. *q*. Reginald de Argenteim claims the land of Guy, son of Tierce, 4 Richard i. I. 451. c. 1. *x*. Again, I. 483. c. 1. *m*. Reginald de Argentem holds pleas at Dunmawe, 5 Richard i. II. 20. c. 2. *a*.

Arlansa, monastery of St. Peter of, Pref. xi.

Armenters, Geoffrey de, 12 Henry iii. I. 416. c. 1. *x*. Robert, executor of John de Armenters, late alderman of Langebourn ward, 2 Edward ii. II. 235. c. 1. *t*.

Arnulph, emperor, an. 888. 897. I. 25.

Arras, Richard de, 18 Edward i. II. 266. c. 2. *r*.

Array, commissions of, for raising all the men from sixteen to sixty, 16 Edward ii. II. 111.

Arsic, Alexander, his escuage for the king's ransom, 6 Richard i. I. 591. c. 1. *p*. His capital barony in Oxfordshire, ibid.

Artemidorus, I. 158. 160.

Arundel, baron Rodbert, 1 Stephen, I. 14. c. 2. William earl of, 1 John, I. 57. c. 1. *r*. William earl of, 3 Henry iii. I. 67. c. 2. *x*. Robert Arundel held pleas of the forest in Dorsetshire, 5 Stephen, I. 148. c. 1. *k*, and c. 2. *q*. The honor of Arundel fermed by Walter de Constanciis, 26 Henry ii. I. 201. c. 1. *n*.— Earl of Arundel had the manor of Rowel, 1 Richard i. I. 229. c. 1. *e*. William earl of Arundel, 4 John, I. 250. c. 1. *n*. William earl of Arundel, 4 Henry iii. I. 274. c. 2. *n*. The honor of Arundel in the king's hands, 31 Henry ii. I. 298. c. 1. *h*. Arundel, Mr Roger, one of the fermers of the manors of the fee of York about 31 Henry ii. I. 309. c. 1. *r*. Again, 1 Richard ii. I. 311. c. 2. *b*. Again, 33 Henry ii. I. 625. c. 1. *r*. John de Arundel

INDEX.

del had the custody of the nunnery of Werewel about 9 Edward i. I. 313. c. 1. *f.* William earl of Arundel, 4 Henry iii. I. 500. c. 1. *d.* William earl of Arundel, 6 Richard i. I. 484. c. 2. *w.* The burgh of Arundel free from common amerciaments, 7 Richard i. I. 540. c. 2. *d.* Earl of Arundel's knights fees, 14 Henry ii. I. 571. c. 2. *a.* His escuage towards the king's ransom, 6 Richard i. I. 591. c. 1. *l.* Heirs of the earl of, their number of forty odd fees in Norfolk, 31 Henry iii. I. 594. c. 2. *i.* Earl of Arundel accompts for the fees of the earl de Auco, 18 Henry ii. I. 632. c. 2. *n.* Richard earl of Arundel summoned on the Scotch expedition, 26 Edward i. I. 655. c. 1. *a.* Had lands in Staffordshire or Shropshire, ibid. Earl quit of his scutage in Essex, 1 John, I. 665. c. 1. *d.* Quit of scutage for his fourscore and four fees, 13 John, I. 666. c. 2. *k, l.* Edmund de Arundel, son and heir of Richard Fitz Alan earl of Arundel, 2 Edward ii. II. 82. The pleas of Robert Arundel, 5 Stephen, II. 220. c. 1. *l.*

Arwrthel, in Cornwal, its tallage, 1 John, I. 733. c. 2. *t.*

Aseeles a Scot, John called earl of, hanged, beheaded, and burnt, 35 Edward i. I. 375. c. 2. *u.*

Ash, see de Fraxino.

Asheby canons, prior of, held in Frankalmoign, temp. Edward i. I. 671. c. 2. *g.*

Askebi and Tinton in Lincolnshire, I. 428. c. 2. *c.*

Askebi and Teinton belonged to Henry de Nevil, 1 John, I. 486. c. 1. *i.*

Aslagby, John de, to arrest ships carrying uncustomed goods, 36 Edward i. I. 785.

Assaium, the tryal of money by the fire, I. 281. Assayers to attend, 9 Edward i. I. 291. c. 1. *a.* Pixides of Assay at London and Canterbury, ibid. Assaiatores monetæ were sworn, 6 Henry iii. II. 87. c. 2. *a.*

Asseley, Philip de, sherif of Yorkshire before 22 Henry iii. II. 195.

Assherugge, collegiate church in Oxfordshire, held in Frankalmoigne, 34 Edward i. I. 671. c. 1. *g.* P. de Asserug, sherif of Rutland, 14 Edward i. II. 260. c. 1. *n.*

Assisa, how far the same with donum, I. 694. Assise or tallage of the king's domaines and burghs, 19 Henry ii. I. 700, &c. The tryal by grand assise first established here by Henry ii. I. 801. City of London seized for trespass of an assise, 39 Henry iii. II. 248. c. 1. *w.*

Aston, Adam de, tallager of the see of Coventry, 37 Henry iii. I. 718. c. 2. *o.* Richard de Aston protected for being in the Irish service, 5 Edward i. II. 219. c. 1. *b.*

Asturcarius, William, opposed by the men of Derbi, 9 Henry ii. I. 336. c. 1. *d.*

Aswi, Ralf, 12 John, I. 263. c. 2. *q.* — de Assewy draper, sherif of London, 40 Henry iii. II. 95. c. 2. *s.* See Eswy.

Attachment against commoners not accounting, II. 243.

Atte-Berwe, John, committed, II. 238.

Atte-Boure, Havering, seems to be one of the king's palaces, 19 Edward ii. II. 51. c. 2. *q.*

Attemersh, John, dismissed from being attorney to William de Ripariis, 30 Edward i. II. 180. c. 1. *y.*

Atter-

INDEX.

Attermination, granting of terms or days for payment of debts, II. 208. The barons Attermination made void, 5 Edward ii. II. 213. c. 1. *l*. If the king's debtors neglected the days of their Attermination, they forfeited their former payments, II. 235.

Avalagium Thamisiæ, what, I. 771, &c.

Aubeala, John de, 2 John, I. 521. c. 1. *b*.

Aubeny, Walter de, collector of the queen's gold, 1 Edward i. I. 351. c. 2. *b*. William de, 5 Henry iii. I. 640. c. 1. *s*.

Aubrey, or Alberic earl of Oxford, see Ver. Fines for the tertius denarius, 6 John I. 407. c. 1. *z*. The knights fees of earl Alberic, 14 Henry ii. I. 573. c. 2. *m*. Earl Alberic's knights fees, 13 John, I. 579. c. 2. *l*.

Aucerra, wine of, I. 409. c. 1. *a*.

Aucher, Thomas, son of, has respite for payment of queen's gold, 22 Henry iii. I. 352. c. 1. *h*. Richard, son of Aucher, 49 Henry iii. I. 492. c. 2. *a*.

Auco, earl de, his knights fees accompted for by the earl of Arundel, 18 Henry ii. I. 632. c. 2. *n*. His scutage, 6 Richard i. I. 649. c. 1. *e*. Quit of scutage for his lands in Essex, 1 John, I. 665. c. 1. *d*.

Audeley, James de, 52 Henry iii. I. 101. c. 1. *d*. Audidele, Nicholas de, 26 Edward i. I. 655. c. 1. Henry de Aldithlega or Audeley, I. 734. c. 2. *d*. Sherif of Staffordshire, 13 Henry iii. II. 169. c. 2. *f*. James de Audithele has the manor of Echemendon, Shropshire, 2 Edward i. II. 101. c. 2. *y*.

Audenard, Giles de, late clerk of the wardrobe, &c. 1 Edward i. I. 610. c. 1. *i*. Clerk of the treasury, 4 Edward i. II. 60. c. 2. *k*.

Audham, Thomas de, 40 Henry iii. I. 466. c. 1. *y*.

Auditors of the accompts of the Exchequer were in process of time, II. 290, 291. Anciently the accompts were audited by the barons, I. 730.

Avelent, Arnold de, 16 John, II. 211. c. 2. *b*.

Avenebury, Walter de, has the wardship of the land and heir of Richard de Aneseye, 35 Henry iii. II. 190. c. 2. *n*.

Avenel, Nicolas, accompts for the ferm of Gloucestershire, 1 John, I. 329. c. 1. *s*. Ralf Avenel fines to have Soke and Sake in his terra, 5 Stephen, I. 397. c. 2. *l*. Roaut Avenal of Normandy, 2 John, I. 521. c. 1. *h*.

Avener, Richard le, 2 John, II. 179. c. 2. *x*.

Averium de pondere, or Averdupoise, I. 786. c. 2. *b*. See Scale, Tronage, Wool.

Aversa, John bishop of, his law suit with Walter Abbat of St. Laurence there, an. 1144. I. 184. c. 1. *s*.

Augi, earl of, 4 John, I. 453. c. 1. *s*. See Ou. The rapp of Hastings belonged to this honor, 9 John, I. 790. c. 2. *m*. Earl of Augi has the honor of Tikehul, 6 Henry iii. II. 68. c. 1. *t*. Alice, countess of, 22 Henry iii. II. 122. c. 1. *l*.

Aula, Thomas de, fines for the land of Bridlesford, accruing by the felony of William de Bridlesford, 6 John, I. 448. c. 1. *y*.

Aulcagium at Sandwich, where they bought wines, I. 768. c. 2. *u*.

Aulton in Hantshire, John Oter, John Swele, and Adam de Gurdon, bailifs

INDEX.

lifs of it before 16 Henry iii. I. 334. c. 2. *y.* Peter de Aulton, clerk, 25 Edward i. I. 379. c. 1. *p.* Its tallage, 30 Henry iii. I. 711. c. *x.*

Aumeri, Richard de, precentor of Lincoln, and fermer of that fee, 16 Henry ii. I. 307. c. 2. *z.* Again, 18 Henry ii. I. 346. c. 1. *i.* Mr. Richard D'aumary, sherif D'oxenford and de Berkshire, 1 Edward ii. I. 380. c. 2. *u.* Robert, under sherif, 9 John, II. 168. c. 1. *y.*

Aumfreton in Essex, II. 84.

Auney, Richard del, 5 Edward i. II. 81. c. 1. *b.*

Aungers, see Anger.

Aunteseye, Maud, wife of Roger de, 13 Henry iii. II. 206. c. 1. *b.* And heiress of William de Mandevil earl of Essex, ibid.

Avon, Ralf and Richard de, of Normandy, 2 John, I. 519. c. 1. *y.*

Aura, Walter de, 5 John, I. 118. c. 2. *w.* William de Aura's mother fines, 10 Richard i. I. 658. c. 2. *q.* Aura in Glocestershire tallaged, 7 Richard i. I. 704. c. 1. *n.* Philip de Aura, Glouc. 12 Henry iii. II. 27. c. 2. *f.*

Aurenches, Simon de, his visus, 2 Richard i. I. 388. c. 1. *z.*

Austin. Cant. See abbat of St. Augustin, his donum, 5 Henry ii. I. 627. c. 2. *t.* The tallage of the abbat's moveables, made at la Bretton in Burgate, I. 740. c. 1. *e.* Called la Berton, I. 741. c. 1. *g.* See Bertona.

Auvers, terra Ruelent de, 33 Henry ii. I. 4. c. 1. The heir of Rueland de Auvers in the wardship of Jordan and Robert de Valeines, 8 Richard i. I. 324. c. 1. *c.*

Awelton, men of, in Hampshire, 14 Henry iii. II. 28. c. 1. *i.*

Axebridge, the men of, and Geoffrey de, 14 Henry ii. I. 588. c. 2. *c.*

Axminster, its aid, 14 Henry ii. I. 588. c. 1. *b.* See Exminster. Its tallage or assise, 19 Henry ii. I. 701. c. 2. *b.*

Aydenn, Thomas de, has a gift of the land of Constantia, daughter of Robert Furre, 5 John, I. 488. c. 2. *f.*

Aylesford, Sir Gilbert de, of Herefordshire, 9 Edward ii. II. 41. c. 2. *a.*

Aylesham and Westhal, Norf. I. 594. c. 2. *i.*

Ayleston, Robert de, created chancellor of the Exchequer, 19 Edward ii. II. 54. c. 1. *f.*

Aynsty wapentake has a commission of array, 16 Edward ii. II. 112. c. 1. *c.* See Anesti.

Ayremayne, William de, keeper of the rolls, and of the house of converts, temp. Edward ii. I. 259. c. 2. *n.* Again, 10 Edward ii. II. 256. c. 1. *w.* c. 2. *x.*

Ayvil of Yorkshire, Robert de, his executors to accompt for the ferm of the mill of Eslingwald, 28 Henry iii. II. 184. c. 2. *g.*

Aze, Benet, 28 Henry iii. II. 190. c. 1. *g.*

Azon, Geoffrey, son of, sherif of Hantshire, 31 Henry ii. I. 568. c. 2. *w.* Again, 28 Henry ii. II. 253. c. 2. *c.*

B.

Baalon, John son of John de, of Herefordshire in Wales, 19 Henry iii. I. 320. c. 2. *m.* See Balun.

Babington, Hugh de, has the counties of Cambridge and Huntendon with Cambridge castle, 18 Edward i. II. 143. Committee of William archbishop of York for the counties of Nottingham

INDEX.

Nottingham and Derby, 55 Henry iii. II. 153. c. 1. *a*.

Bachard, Waleram, 6 John, I. 441. c. 1. *r*.

Bacon, Alexander, cuſtos of Hange, Halikeld and Gillinge wapentacks belonging to the honour of Richmond, 19 Henry iii. I. 335. c. 1. *z*. Edmund Bacoun cuſtos of the honor of Walingford, 12 Edward ii. I. 354. c. 2. *r*.

Bacſcete in Surrey, the land of Robert de Londonia, temp. John, I. 491. c. 1. *e*.

Bada or Bath, Walter de, ſherif of Devonſhire, 30 Henry iii. I. 281. c. 1. *e*. Rainer de Beda ſherif of Lincolnſhire, temp. Stephen, I. 327. c. 2. *d*. viz. 5 Stephen, I. 340. c. 2. *h*. See Bath.

Badebery, Wiltſhire, its donum, 33 Henry ii. I. 634. c. 2. *q*.

Badeford, Robert de, of Eſſex, 35 Henry iii. II. 192. c. 1. *t*.

Badeleſmar, Giles de, fines for the king's goodwill, 4 John, I. 473. c. 2. *x*. Bartholomew de, 35 Edward i. II. 216. *e*.

Badvent, Walter de, the ſcutage for his ſergeanty in Lincolnſhire, 5 John, I. 650. c. 2. *n*.

Baenburgh in Northumberland, the terra of William ſon of Adam, 3 John, I. 404. c. 1. *a*. That land in the anceſtors of the Odo's at the Conqueſt, I. 487. c. 1. *q*. Simon, ſon of Philip de Kyme wages duel for it, 5 Richard i. I. 503. c. 1. *p*. William, ſon of Waldef, amerc'd for not helping the works of the caſtle, 16 Henry ii. I. 559. c. 1. *h*, *i*. A burgeſs here amerc'd for buying a horſe without pledge, 16 Henry ii. I. 560. c. 1. *t*. See Bamburc.

Baentona in Devonſhire, Robert de, his contention with Raif de Morſel, 5 Stephen, I. 425. c. 2. *d*.

Bag or purſe, of the marſchal of the Exchequer, II. 288.

Baggard, Robert de, his writ of Mordanceſter, 3 John, I. 213. c. 2. *x*.

Baggod, James and Walter, 3 John, I. 436. c. 1. *r*. The contention between them repeated, I. 796.

Baggodeby, in Yorkſhire, ſeems to belong to the family of Baggod, I. 436.

Bagot, Hervey and Miliſent his wife, 6 John, I. 99. c. 2. *u*. Summons the Jews to take their debts, 2 John, I. 250. c. 1. *l*. Hervey and Miliſent charged with intruſion into Lutiwude, 6 John, I. 794. c. 1. *h*. Hervey Bagot's ſcutage in the time of Richard i. II. 207. c. 1. *d*.

Bajazet in the hands of Temyr, I. 161. c. 1. *g*.

Bail for murder, 4 John, I. 493. c. *k*. A proclamation againſt Bail for murder without the king's ſpecial command, 9 John, I. 494. c. 2. *u*.

Baillol, Euſtace de, his lands ſeiſed before 9 Richard i. I. 39. c. 2. *z*. John ſon of Hugh de Bailiol, 13 Henry iii. I. 319. c. 1. *d*. His relief for his thirty knights fees in Eſſex and Hertfordſhire, ibid. Hugh de Balleol mortgages his lands in Northumberland to king John, I. 388. c. 2. *e*. Hugh de Bailloel is ſurety, 10 John, I. 480. c. 2. *n*. Gilbert de Bailloet fined for carrying a bow in the foreſt of Lancaſhire, 9 John, I. 499. c. 2. *y*. Bernard de Baillol has the town of Niwebigging, 16 Henry ii. I. 554. c. 1. *n*. The fees of Bernard de Baillol in Northumberland, 14 Henry ii. I. 581. c. 1. *u*. John de Baillol

INDEX.

Baillol has thirty knights fees in Northumberland, 30 Henry iii. I. 595. c. 2. o. Alexander de Baillol in the king's court, and summoned by writ to the war against Scotland, 26 Edward i. I. 655. c. 2. a. Gocelin de Bailol, temp. John, I. 673. c. 1. m. Alexander de Baillol, husband of Alienor the king's cousen, 5 Edward i. I. 682. c. 2. t. Eustace de, 8 Richard i. I. 714. c. 2. John de Balliol's tallage granted to John de Britannia before 34 Edward i. I. 752. c. 1. i. John de Bayliol, 52 Henry iii. II. 80. c. 1. z. John de Baillol, late sherif of Cumberland, 40 Henry iii. II. 193. c. 2. d. Robert de Balliol, sherif of Northumberland, 27 Edward i. II. 266. c. 1. n.

Bainard, Gosfrei, challenges the earl of Ou for treason against William Rufus, I. 8. c. 2. p. Fulk Bainard claims a ward, 8 John, I. 441. c. 1. u. Roger de Baygnard, 34 Edward i. II. 74. c. 2. w.

Bakehouse or ovens, a settled tax on them, 11 Edward i. I. 720. c. 1. t.

Bakemore, Ralf de, in misericordia, 23 Henry ii. I. 201. c. 1. o. Again, 23 Henry ii. I. 211. c. 1. h.

Bakepus, Robert de, 4 John, I. 453. c. 2. t.

Baketon, in Norfolk, answers for a wreck, 7 Richard I. 343. c. 2. k. Margaret, widow of John de Baketon, Cumberland, 14 John, II. 253. c. 2. c.

Baldedone in Oxfordshire was the land of the prior of Noyon, 1 John, I. 216. c. 2. g.

Baldock, Ralf de, bishop of London and chancellor, 35 Edward i. I. 74. c. 2. Reimund de Baldac fined for an appeal, 14 Henry ii. I. 429. c. 2. p. R. de Baldoc, chancellor, 19 Edward ii. II. 54. c. 1. f.

Baldric, William son of, 3 Richard i. I. 54. c. 2. q. Alexander Baldric, 12 John and 5 Henry iii. I. 453. c. 2. y. & 454. c. 1. d.

Baldus, what, I. 273. c. 2. h.

Baldwin, emperor of Constantinople, a gift to him, 31 Henry iii. I. 391. c. 1. s.

Baldwin, archbishop of Canterbury, crowns Richard i. an. 1189. I. 21. c. 2. s.

Baldwin earl of Flanders, commonly called Securis, an. 1111. I. 92. c. 2. s. See Flandrensis.

Baldwin, constabulary of the honor of Bolonge, 2 Henry iii. I. 491. c. 2. m. Baldwin, son of William, 5 Stephen, I. 501. c. 1. o. William son of Baldwin, his fees held for the honor of Glocester, 15 John, I. 639. c. 1. o.

Baldwin the tanner of Lincoln's tallage, 4 John, I. 738. c. 1. w.

Balistarius, Geoffrey, had land in Hamelton, Lancashire, which was William Colmose's in the time of king John, 13 Henry iii. I. 416. c. 2. z. Balistarii of king John, I. 564. c. 2. c.

Balscote, Nicolas, ingroffer of the Exchequer of Dublin, 30 Edward i. II. 270. c. 1. h.

Balun, John de, of Herefordshire, his knight's fee, 38 Henry iii. I. 596. c. 2. x. Philip Balun's tenure in London from a charter of Roger le Bygod, 2 Edward ii. II. 83. See Baalon.

Baluzius, his capitulars, Pref. x. c. 1, 2. b, i. xiii. c. 1. r. xvi, xvii, &c.

Bamburc castle in Northumberland, I. 593. c. 2. e. See Baenburg.

Banastre,

INDEX.

Banaftre, Alard, juftice errant, 20 Henry ii. I. 124. c. 1. *x*. And fherif of Oxfordfhire, ibid.

Banham, in Norfolk, its affife, 22 Henry ii. II. 703. c. 1. *k*.

Bank, or court of common bench, when erected, I. 787. Jufticiarii de Banco, 17 John, ibid. Common bench removed to Shrewfbury, 13 Edward i. II. 7. c. 2. *i*.

Banleuca, or Banlieue, I. 524. c. 2. *x, z*.

Banftede in Surrey tallaged, 6 Edward ii. I. 744. c. 1. *w*.

Bantefcnappe of Devonfhire, Bernard de, amerc'd for recreancy, 1 Richard i. I. 550. c. 1. *u*.

Banton honor, accompted for by Fulk Paniel, 3 John, I. 205. c. 2. *n*.

Baquelle, Cicely, widow of John de, of London, her quinzime remitted, 2 Edward ii. II. 230. c. 2. *y*.

Barat, Adam, amerc'd, 6 Henry iii. I. 564. c. 1. *s*.

Barbara, Robert cum, feems to inherit part of the land of Ofbert Martel, 18 Henry ii. I. 580. c. 2. *q*.

Barbeflet, provoft of, commanded to find paffage for the king's men and horfes, 2 John, I. 172. c. 1. *c*. & c. 2. *d*.

Barber, Renald le, collector of the king's duty on wines, 25 Edward i. I. 770. c. 2. *b*.

Barde, merchants favoured, 12 Edward ii. II. 123. Peter Bard has a writ of refpite, 15 Edward ii. II. 216.

Bardelby, Robert, how he has the great feal, 30 Edward i. I. 74. c. 1. *r*. & c. 2. *s*.

Bardenei abbey in cuftody, 31 Henry ii. I. 309. c. 2. *u*. Abbat of Bardenay quit of tallage, 9 Edward ii. I. 745. c. 2. *a*.

Bardolf, Hugh, diffeifed of the fherivalty of Yorkfhire, caftle of York, &c. temp. Richard i. I. 23. Again, 34. & 35. Held the office of Dapifer, 30 Henry ii. I. 51. c. 1. *y*. And was the king's fenefchal, 30 Henry ii. I. 51. c. 2. *g*. One of the jufticiers, 9 Richard i. I. 113. Receives the king's corrodies, an. 1184. I. 168. c. 2. Occurs, for refpite, 15 Henry ii. I. 189. c. 1. *x*. Hugh Bardolf, fherif of Wiltfhire, 1 Richard i. I. 289. c. 1. *r*. Many of the fmall efcheats committed to him, temp. Richard i. I. 300. c. 1. *p*. Hugh Bardolf accompts for the ferm of Lincoln during 4 Richard i. I. c. 1. *y*. Has the honor of Peverel in Nottinghamfhire in cuftody, 5 John, I. 405. c. 1. *p*. And fines that the fherif may not interfere in the manors of that honor, ibid. Ralf Bardolf, his fingular fine, 11 John, I. 472. c. 1. *e*. Thomas, fon of Hugh Bardolf, amerced for a falfe plaint, 11 Edward ii. I. 530. c. 1. *q*. The pleas of Hugh Bardul, 2 Richard i. I. 556. c. 1. *k*. Hugh Bardulf, fherif of Northumberland, 1 John, I. 565. c. 2. *q*. Hugh, fherif of Yorkfhire, 7 Richard i. I. 643. c. 2. *b*. Hugh Bardulf fummon'd among the barons, 26 Edward i. I. 655. Tallager of Yorkfhire, 9 Richard i. I. 699. c. 1. *r*. and Glocefterfhire, 7 Richard i. I. 707. c. 1. *n*. and Worcefterfhire, 8 Richard i. ibid. c. 2. *q*. Peter Bardulf's tenure in the foke of Pikering, 30 Henry iii. I. 710. c. *w*. Hugh Bardolf in his iter fets the tallage of Shropfhire, 9 Richard i. I. 733. c. 1. *q*. & c. 1. *r*. and Lincoln. 10 Richard i. c. 1. *r*. and Glocefterfhire, 1 John, I. 734. c. 1. *w*. Hugh Bardul,

INDEX.

Bardul, 34 Henry ii. I. 736. c. 2. *p*. Thomas Bardolf has the queen's writ for respiting his debts, 34 Edward i. II. 125. c. 1. *k*. Hugh Bardul, seneschal of the king, fermer of the honor of Glocester, 30 Henry ii. II. 206. c. 1. *x*. Occurs, 10 Richard i. ibid. *z*. Dodo Bardorlf married Beatrice daughter and heiress of William de Warenne about the reign of Richard i. II. 214. c. 1. *r*. Hugh Bardolf, baron of the Exchequer, 7 Richard i. II. 228. c. 2. *k*.

Bardul, Hugh, sherif of Notingham and Derbyshire, 16 Henry ii. I. 209. c. 2. *d*. Hugh Bardolf, sherif of Notingham and Derbyshire, 3 John, I. 369. c. 2. *c*. Doun Bardulf married Beatrice, heiress of William de Warrene, before 11 John, I. 490. c. 1. *s*. Hugh Bardulf, king's dapifer and tallager, 33 Henry ii. I. 634. c. 1. *q*. See Bardolf.

Bardun, John, of Norfolk, 7 Edward i. II. 86. c. 2. *u*.

Barentin, Alexander de, fermer of the see of Rochester, about 31 Henry ii. I. 311. c. 2. *e*. Was the king's butler, 22 Henry ii. I. 368. c. 1. *r*. Robert de Barentin, 31 Henry iii. I. 476. c. 1. *t*. Barenton, Cambr. tallaged, I. 748. c. 2. *t*. Drogo, fermer of Geresey and Gernesey islands, 26 Henry iii. II. 255. c. 2. *q*.

Bareswurd, Richard de, 10 John, I. 151. c. 1. *w*. Amerc'd as pledge, &c. ibid.

Barinton, John de, 31 Henry ii. I. 558. c. 1. *l*. Unfrid de Barenton, under-sherif of Essex, 9 Richard i. II. 164. c. 2. *g*. See Barenton.

Barkeston, Oto de, fined for marrying the king's ward without leave, 3 Richard i. I. 105. c. 2. *q*. That wapentake has a commission of array sent to it, 16 Edward ii. II. 112. c. 1. *c*.

Barlinges, abbat in Lincolnshire, to pray for the soul of king John, 11 Henry iii. II. 227. c. 2. *c*.

Barnage, Ralf, 5 Stephen, I. 448. c. 2. *o*. Fines that he may not plead, ibid.

Barnebi, land of, whose, I. 431. c. 1. *k*.

Barneby, Alured de, married Juliana, daughter and coheir of Philip de Ulecot, before 5 Henry iii. I. 463. c. 1. *r*.

Barnevile, frere John de, abbat elect of Muchelny, 36 Henry iii. I. 923. c. 2. *h*.

Baronies and honors held immediately of the king, I. 107. Barons had officers of their house conform to those of the king, ibid. Sometimes hereditary, I. 108. The extent of the title Barones, I. 141. Baro, its significations, I. 197. When a Barony paid only a hundred marks for relief, I. 321. Baronies different in quantity and value, ibid. When several were united in one person they did not consolidate, I. 322. A large list of barons, 26 Edward i. I. 653, 654. Barons turbulent, 50 Henry iii. II. 174. c. 2. *r*. Not accompting were punish'd by seisure of their seignuries, II. 244. See Exchequer.

Barons amerce the men of Cambridge by William de Windsor, 12 John, I. 528. c. 2. *i*. Amerc'd as a baron, I. 529, & seq.

Barr, Richard, justicier, 7 Richard i. I. 502. c. 1. *x*. Ralf Barre, 31 Henry ii. I. 549. c. 1. *e*. Amerc'd for a disseisin, ibid. Ralf de Barre, alderman

INDEX.

alderman of the guild of S. Lazarus, 26 Henry ii. I. 562. c. 1. z.

Barſham, Maurice de, fined and why, 31 Henry ii. I. 513. c. 1. y.

Bartholomew London, hoſpital of S, 26 Edward i. II. 47. c. 2. y.

Barton, Yorkſhire, the tenants of Euſtace de Stotevil, tallaged, 14 Henry iii. I. 708. c. 2. p.

Barton, Ærnald de, ſherif of Warwick and Leiceſterſhire, 26 Henry ii. I. 139. c. 1. i. The quinzime of the port of Barton, 6 John, I. 772. c. 2. i. William de Barton ſeems to be meſſinger of the treaſury, 26 Edward i. I. 783. c. 2. s. John de Barthon, official of the biſhop of Worceſter, 1 Edward i. II. 19. c. 1. r.

Baſchiervill, Walter de, his privilege for his lands in Gloceſterſhire, 12 12 Henry ii. I. 117. c. 1. g. Ralf de Baſkervil fines for the concord of a duel, 31 Henry ii. I. 471. c. 1. r. Walter Baſkervil married Emme de S. Leodegario, I. 513. c. 2. b. Robert's fees in Herefordſhire, 7 Henry ii. I. 628. Walter fines to ſtay in England, 8 Richard i. I. 658. c. 1. m.

Baſenvil, William de, has ſhare of the lands of Oſbert Martel, 18 Henry ii. I. 580. c. 2. q.

Baſing, Hugh de, juſtice of the Jews, 51 Henry iii. I. 236. c. 1. i.

Baſinges, Robert de, mercer, 12 Henry iii. I. 708. c. 1. n. Hugh de Baſinges of London, his tallage, 14 Henry iii. I. 709. c. 1. s. Hugh and Peter de Baſinges of London, tallaged, 19 Henry iii. I. 738. c. 1. y. Euſtace de Baſingham, deputy of the ſea-ports, 15 John, I. 774. c. 1. l. Thomas de Baſing, cuſtos of London, 55 Henry iii. II. 169. c. 1. d. His allocatio forth at office, II. 202. a.

Baſingſtok, change their market by charter from Sunday to Monday, 5 John, I. 505. c. 1. o. Their tallage, 30 Henry iii. I. 711. c. 1. x. King's caſtle near Baſingwerc, 5 Edward i. II. 53. c. 1. a.

Baſſet, Ralph, with the king's theins, held a council of the proceres at Hundehoge in Leiceſterſhire, when the king was in Normandy, I. 12. c. 2. p. anno 1124. Richard, chief juſticier to Henry i. I. 33. c. 1. n. Richard, temp. Henry i. I. 56. c. 2. o. Gilbert, atteſts a charter, 16 Henry iii. I. 64. c. 1. m. William Baſſet, one of the barons of the Exchequer, 29 Henry ii. I. 82. c. 1. b. Thomas and William Baſſet held pleas for the king, 21 Henry ii. I. 94. c. 1. b. Philip Baſſet, juſticiary of England, 47 Henry iii. I. 100. c. 1. c. William Baſſet, one of the juſticiaries, 22 Henry ii. I. 103. c. 1. b. Reginald Baſſet accompts, 24 Henry ii. I. 103. c. 1. k. Robert Baſſet's inheritance before 10 Richard i. I. 114. c. 2. t. William and Thomas Baſſet, juſtices, 20 Henry ii. I. 125. c. 1. i. & c. 2. k. William, ſherif of Lincolnſhire, 25 Henry ii. I. 136. c. 1. x. William, ſherif of Warwick and Leiceſterſhire, fined, 20 Henry ii. I. 141. c. 1. x, y. I. 220. Richard Baſſet holds pleas, 5 Stephen, I. 148, 149. Was ſherif of Eſſex and Hertfordſhire, 5 Stephen, I. 164. William Baſſet, one of the barons of the Exchequer, 29 Henry ii. I. 213. c. 1. p. and 215. c. 1. a. Thomas Baſſet accompts for the ferm of Benſenton, 10 John, I. 280. c. 2. b. Richard Baſſet, joint ſherif with Aubrey

INDEX.

Aubrey de Ver of eleven counties, about 5 Stephen, I. 327. c. 1. *t, u, w, x, y.* William Baſſet, fermer of Lincolnſhire, 30 Henry ii. I. 328. c. 1. *o.* Richard Baſſet occurs ſherif again, 5 Stephen, I. 364. c. 1. *l.* Bartholomew Baſſet of Heminton, 6 Henry iii. I. 445. c. 1. *y.* Ralf Baſſet, 2 Henry iii. I. 454. c. 1. *a.* Richard Baſſet, ſherif of Grentebr. and Huntendonſhire, 5 Stephen, I. 541. c. 2. *b.* Ralf Baſſet holds pleas in Surrey, ibid. c. 2. *i.* William Baſſet, 7 Richard i. I. 555. c. 2. *d.* Thomas Baſſet ſeems to be ſherif of Berkſhire, 18 Henry ii. I. 580. c. 1. *o.* William Baſſet, juſtice itinerant, 14 Henry ii. I. 587. c. 1. *x.* Gilbert Baſſet, 7 Richard i. I. 591. c. 2. *t.* and Richard, ibid. Faulk Baſſet, provoſt of Beverley, 18 Henry iii. I. 617. c. 2. *b.* Richard, temp. Richard i. I. 625. c. 2. *m.* Richard Baſſet's ſcutage for his knights in Northamptonſhire, 3 Richard i. I. 636. c. 2. *w.* Ralf Baſſet ſummon'd to the Scotch war among the Shropſhire barons, 26 Edward i. I. 655. c. 1. *a.* Turſtan de Baſſet fines for his ſix fees held of the honor of Walingford, 2 John, I. 659. c. 1. *u.* Warin Baſſet married the daughter and heireſs of John de Montacute before 14 Henry iii. I. 661. c. 1. *i.* Gilbert, Thomas, and Alan Baſſet, their fees in Oxfordſhire, 4 John, I. 666. c. 1. *h.* William aſſiſes the king's demeans in Notinghamſhire before 21 Henry ii. I. 702. c. 2. *g.* Simon ſets the tallage of Nottinghamſhire, 9 Richard i. I. 733 c. 1. *p.* Alan Baſſet held Wicumbe, 1 John, I. 745. c. 2. *b.* Thomas Baſſet, 2 Henry iii. I. 793. c. 1. *d.* And his wife Philippa, ibid. Reginald Baſſet, 2 Henry iii. II. 26. c. 2. *a.* Gilbert Baſſet, archdeacon of Totneſs and prebendary of Exeter, 8 John, II. 43. c. 1. *i.* Richard Baſſet, that great lord, one of the ſherifs of Eſſex and Hertfordſhire, 5 Stephen, II. 145. c. 2. *s.* Thomas Baſſet, his dividend from the manor of Hedindon, 11 Henry iii. II. 166. c. 1. *o.* Thomas Baſſet, ſherif of Oxfordſhire, 6 John, ii. II. 168. c. 1. *y.* Philip Baſſet, one of the king's council, 53 Henry iii. II. 171. c. 1. *h.* William Baſſet has reſpite in Staffordſhire for his debts to the king, 1 John, II. 217. c. 1. *q.* Pleas held before Ralf Baſſet, 5 II. 224. c. 2. *o.* Ralf Baſſet deliver'd to the mareſchal of the Exchequer, 31 Henry iii. II. 228. c. 1. *o.* Made chamberlain of the Exchequer, 7 Edward i. II. 300. c.1.*w.*

Baſſingeburne, Wimar de, 7 Richard i. I. 106. c. 1. *t.* Warin de, one of the ſherifs of Cambridge and Huntingdonſhire, 23 Henry ii. I. 132. c. 1. *g.* Again, 22 Henry ii. I. 702. c. 2. *h.* Humfrey de Baſſingburn, ſherif of Northamptonſhire, 15 Edward ii. II. 159. c. 2. *g.* Warin de Baſſingburn, 51 Henry iii. II. 178. Nicholas de Baſſingburn, taxor and collector of the trentiſme, Cambr. II. 230. c. 1. *t.* Was plunder'd at Coſteſheye, 14 Edward i. ibid. c. 1. *t.*

Baſſuſhagward, in London, its tallage, 14 Henry iii. I. 709. c. 2. *t.* Baſſieſaye ward, 19 Henry iii. I. 739. c. 1. *z.*

Baſtard, if one dyed without lawful heirs his eſtate went to the duke, in Burgundy, I. 185. One could not ſucceed

INDEX.

succeed to his father or mother intestate, ibid.

Baſtard, William, juſtice errant, 20 Henry ii. I. 125. William Baſtard and Bencia his wife, 4 John, I. 453. c. 2. w.

Baſtonthwait, Alexander de, ſherif of Cumberland, 1 Edward ii. II. 156. c. 2. p.

Bat, Peter, a viewer of merchandice for the king, 10 Richard i. I. 776. c. 2. r. Nicolas, mayor of London, 38 Henry iii. II. 92. c. 1. h.

Batail, of Northumberland, Henry, fines not to be impleaded out of that county, 6 John, I. 406. c. 2. w.

Batayle. See Battle.

Batencurt, Luke de, one of the fermers of the city of London, 52 Henry iii. I. 779. c. 1. e. One of the bailifs, 51 Henry iii. II. 69. c. 1. t. His chatels ſeiz'd as late ſherif of London, 52 Henry iii. II. 237. c. 2. q. His chatels ſeiz'd after his death, 4 Edward i. II. 281. c. 1. e.

Bath, the exemption granted to the monks of, by Henry i. I. 3. c. 1. b. Joſceline, biſhop of, 11 Henry iii. I. 63. Biſhop of Bath was chancellor, 11 Edward i. I. 71. c. 2. l. John, biſhop of Bath, his method of keeping his court, an. 1121. I. 100. Lord prior of Bath, I. 112. Lord biſhop of Bath in the time of king Stephen, I. 112. c. 1. m. Joſcelyn, biſhop of, obtains to his fee from William Briwerre the advouſon of Melverton, 10 Henry iii. I. 115. c. 2. w. Robert, biſhop of Bath and Wells, chancellor, 5 and 6 Edward i. I. 254. c. 1. b. That fee in the king's hands, 16 Henry ii. I. 306. c. 2. t. Again, 14 John, I. 312. c. 2. s. Prior of Bath had the ferm there, 9 Henry iii. I. 334. c. 1. t. William [de Marchia] biſhop of Bath and Wells, treaſurer, 22 Edward i. I. 387. c. 1. w. Some account of the biſhop's lands, 14 Henry iii. I. 414. c. h. Biſhop of Bath fines for the ſame liberties as the fee of Lincoln enjoy'd, 15 Henry iii. I. 419. c. 1. p. The biſhop's grant to the family of Burne, I. 541. c. 1. f. Its aid, 14 Henry ii. I. 589. c. 2. g. Paid double the ſum that Saliſbury did, ibid. Its ſcutage while in the king's hand, 14 Henry ii. I. 642. c. 2. a. Fines for not paſſing the ſea, I. 661. c. 2. k. Had quittance of the ſcutage of Biham, 5 Henry iii. I. 667. c. 1. m. And for the abbey of Glaſton, ibid. The donum of the biſhop of Bath and his knights, 5 Henry ii. I. 697. c. 2. d. Its tallage, 14 Henry iii. I. 708. c. 1. o. Robert, Bath and Wells, chancellor, 17 Edward i. II. 255. Robert Burnel, late biſhop of Bath, 27 Edward i. II. 256. John biſhop of Bath, keeper of the wardrobe to Edw. i. II. 291. c. 2. e.

Bath, Hugh de, juſtice of the Jews, 18 Henry iii. I. 234. c. 1. a. Reginald de Bathonia, 5 John, I. 494. c. 1. o. Henry de Bathonia ſeems to belong to the king's treaſury, 39 Henry iii. I. 712. c. 1. a. Henry de Bathonia appears juſticier, 42 Henry iii. II. 68. c. 1. n. Walter de Bath, ſherif of Devonſhire, diſcharged from his impriſonment for ſuffering bad money, 32 Henry iii. II. 223. c. 1. b.

Battle, Robert abbot of, 3 Henry iii. I. 67. c. 2. x. This abby impleaded by Robertſbridg about the marſh of Primhill, 4 John, I. 107. c. 2. b. In the king's hands, 19 Henry

INDEX.

ii. I. 308. c. 1. *d.* In cuftody of Peter de Bello and Hugh de Begge, 18 Henry ii. I. 346. c. 2. *k.* Fine to have the cuftody of their houfe on the demife of an abbat, 13 John, I. 411. c. 1. *s.* The abbat's claim, 22 Henry ii. I. 560. c. 2. *d.* Frier William de Batayle, folicitor for the Minours of Northampton, 52 Henry iii. I. 749. c. 2. *y.*

Batvent, Roger de, under fherif of the archbifhop of York, temp. Richard i. I. 35. Eudo de Batvent, his affignment upon Hornchefter, 30 Henry ii. I. 328. c. 2. *o.* See Bavent.

Baud, Robert le, knight, 18 Edward i. I. 199. c. 1. *f.*

Baudritor, Ralf de, fines for a fair at the chapel of S. Michael de Stublelond, 2 John, I. 518. c. 2. *s.*

Bavent, Sir Thomas de, his land of Efton on the coaft of Suffolk, 2 Edward ii. I. 343. c. 2. *l.* His conteft with the king about a wreck between Benacre and Snodefpyk, ibid. Walter de Bavent of Lincolnfhire fines for not paffing the feas, 7 John, I. 660. c. 1. *a.* Sir Thomas de Bavent convicted and fined for promoting a falfe profecution, 33 Edward i. II. 65.

Bauton, Simon de, juftice itinerant in Bucks, 39 Henry iii. II. 22. c. 2. *r.*

Bayliwick and county equivalent, II. 140. Bailifs and Bayliwicks of the king, how regulated, 42 Henry iii. II. 147, 148.

Bealchamp, Ralf de, about the time of Henry ii. I. 3. c. 2. See Bello Campo. William de Beauchamp received the king's fcutage in Worcefterfhire, 15 Henry ii. I. 190. c. 2. *i.* William de Beauchamp, fherif of Worcefterfhire, 4 Henry ii. I. 365. c. 1. *s.* Walter de Beauchamp has the cuftody of Worcefterfhire, 14 Henry iii. I. 463. c. 2. *s.* William de Beauchamp, 14 Henry ii. I. 581. c. 2. *y.* Sherif of Herefordfhire, 14 Henry ii. I. 584. c. 1. *o.* William, his tenure from the bifhop of Worcefter, 38 Henry iii. I. 597. c. 1. *z.* Again, I. 622. c. 2. *f.* Robert de Beauchamp held of the king in capite by barony, temp. Henry iii. I. 622. c. 1. *h.* Had the manors of Stok, Merfton, Schepton & Hacche, ibid. William de, fherif of Worcefterfhire, 5 Henry ii. I. 628. c. 1. *u.* The barony of Robert de Beauchamp of Hacche, 20 Henry iii. I. 632. William's knights fees, 5 Richard i. I. 643. c. 2. *k.* Honor of Wilekin, late fon of William de Beauchamp, 11 John, I. 644. c. 2. *p.* Robert de Beauchamp, one of the cuftodes of Wilekin's honor, ibid. John de Beauchamp, one of the barons fummoned by writ againft the Scots, 26 Edward i. I. 655. c. 2. Walter de Beauchamp, one of the barons in the king's court, 26 Edward i. ibid. Guy de Beauchamp earl of Warwick, 35 Edward i. I. 657. c. 1. *g.* Walter's fees in Worcefterfhire, 14 Henry iii. I. 660. c. 2. *g.* Simon's honor in Buckingham and Bedfordfhire before 2 Henry ii. I. 688. c. 1. *m.* William de, fherif of Herefordfhire, 9 Henry ii. I. 661. c. 1. *y.* Thomas de Beauchamp, earl of Warwick, created earl Marefchal during pleafure, 18 Edward iii. I. 798. c. 2. William de Beauchamp made baron of the Exchequer, 18 Henry iii. II. 54. c. 2. *i.* Walter de Beauchamp, fherif of Worcefterfh. with his fureties,

INDEX.

ties, 1 Henry iii. II. 150. c. 1. *n.* William de, sherif of Worcestershire, 12 Edward ii. II. 156. and 42 Henry iii. II. 168. c. 1. *z.* Maud de Beauchamp distreined by dower for her late husband's debt to the king, but relieved 22 Henry iii. II. 191. c. 2. *q.* Had Roger de Beauchamp for her first husband, and Robert de Turvil for her second, ibid. Ralf de Beauchamp was pledge, 9 John, II. 198. c. 2. *s.* Stephen de Beauchamp in wardship to Bertram de Verdun, 1 and 7 Richard i. II. 228. c. 2. *k.* Walter de Beauchamp, sherif of Worcestershire, 13 Henry iii. II. 234. c. 1. *p.* William de Beauchamp, heir of William de Maudut earl of Warwick, makes David de la More usher of the Receipt of the Exchequer, 52 Henry iii. II. 296. c. 2. *c.* Nominates John Peverel chamberlain, II. 297. c. 1. *e.* William de Beauchamp, earl of Warwic, made William de Bradecote chamberlain of the Exchequer, 1 Edward i. II. 297. c. 2. *h.* Was likewise earl of Worcester by presenting William Golafre, ibid. c. 2. *i.* Was earl of Warwic, 25 Edward i. II. 299. c. 1. *o.* His death, 26 Edward i. II. 300. See Guy, Warwick, Belchamp, and Bello Campo.

Beans at two shillings and eleven pence the quarter, 14 Henry iii. II. 152. c. 2. *z.*

Bear, a white one from Norway, used to catch fish in the Thames, 37 Henry iii. I. 376. c. 2. *b.*

Bearn, Gaston, viscount of, does homage to the king of Aragon, an. 1187. I. 5. c. 1.

Beatrice, wife of Geoffred earl of Moreton, I. 108. c. 1. *h.* Whose daughter she was, ibid. Beatrix de Faierford, 11 John, I. 794. c. 2. *i.*

Beauclare or Beuclare, John de, has the castle of Herdelagh, 13 Edward i. II. 4. c. 2. *s.*

Beaulieu or Bello Loco, prior of, 9 John, I. 273. c. 2. *g.* Abbat of, 2 John, I. 458. c. 1. *r.* A cell of St. Albans, 10 Richard i. I. 760. c. 2. Occurs, I. 765. c. 2. *t.*

Beaumes, Sir Walter de, 2 Henry iii. I. 319. c. 2. *e.*

Beaumont, Robert earl of Leicester, justicier, an. 1162. I. 34. c. 1. *u.* Walter de Bello Monte, 4 Henry iii. I. 495. c. 2. *f.* The lands of Thomas de Beaumont in Normandy, 2 John, I. 518. c. 1. *t.* Robert de Beaumont has a commission of array for the wapentak of Agbrig, 16 Edward ii. II. 112. c. 1. William de Beaumont, pledge, 40 Henry iii. II. 150. c. 2. *p.*

Beaurepeyr, Hugh de, 15 Edward ii. II. 40. c. 2. *x.*

Beautie in Yorkshire, its tallage, 30 Henry iii. I. 710. c. 2. *w.*

Bec monastery has lands in England, 4 John, I. 203. c. 1. *d.* Have the manor of Suinecumb with a fair, 5 John, I. 396. c. 2. *c.* Their Danegeld remitted, 2 Henry ii. I. 686. c. 1. *f.* In several counties, I. 168. Antony Bek from archdeacon made bishop of Durham, 4 Sept. 11 Edward i. I. 720. c. 1. *t.* John Bek, 14 Edward i. II. 103. c. 2. *d.*

Bech, Ebrard de, one of the sherifs of Huntingdon and Cambridgeshire, 23 Henry ii. I. 132. c. 1. *g.* Hugh del Bech, 22 Henry ii. I. 561. c. 1. *i.* Data per manum Th. Beck, 7 Edward i. I. 662. c. 1. *o.* See Beche.

Becham, in Kent, the abbat of Westminster's

INDEX.

minster's land there, 14 Henry ii. I. 558. c. 2. *t*.

Beche, terra de, belonging to Bath, I. 112. c. 2 *n*. Geoffrey Beche, 5 Richard i. I. 564. c. 2. *f*. Ebrard de Beche, joint sherif of Cambridge and Huntedonshire with Warin de Bassingeburne, 22 Henry ii. I. 702. c. 2. *h*. Philip de la Becke, viewer of the king's works at Clarendon, 12 Edward ii. II. 292. c. 2. *l*. See Bech.

Becket, archbishop, some account of his differences with Henry ii. I. 15. Louis king of France visits his tomb out of devotion, an. 1179. I. 27. Accused for doing wrong to the king's Mareschal, I. 46. The same charge repeated, I. 112. The first native Englishman, who was archbishop from the conquest, I. 182. Opposed the statutes of Clarendon as prejudicial to the old laws and English nation, ibid. Had been acquitted by law of what he was accused, I. 191. c. 2. *s*.

Bedefont, village of, to whom it appertained, 1 John, I. 216. c. 1. *f*. Turold de Bedefont, ibid. c. 2. *f*.

Bedeford, Lambert de, his grant, temp. Henry ii. I. 722. c. 1. *z*. See Bedford.

Bedellus, Alsfi, 24 Henry ii. I. 103. c. 2. *k*. Accompts for a defalt, ibid.

Bedewind in Wiltshire, its aid, 14 Henry ii. I. 589. And again, I. 604. c. 1. *l*. Its donum, 33 Henry ii. I. 634. c. 1. *q*. Its assise, 19 Henry ii. I. 702. c. 1. *d*. Walter de Bedewynde, baron of the Exchequer, surveyed the king's manors and castles in Yorkshire, 1 Edward ii. II. 67. c. 2. *q*. Walter de Bedewynde succeeds John de Kirkeby as remembrancer, 1 Edward ii. II. 267.

Bedford, Burgenses de, 5 Richard i. I. 332. c. 2. *d*. Again, 13 Henry ii. I. 398. c. 1. *o*. Simon de Bedford taxed for the death of G. de Spondon, 3 John, I. 504. c. 1. *z*. An army here, I. 509. c. 1. *s*. Citizens amerced for being in the castle against the king, 2 Henry ii. I. 557. c. 2. *g*. Knights of the county of Bedford all in actual service, 8 Henry iii. I. 669. c. 2. *b*. The aid of Bedford, 2 Henry ii. I. 688. c. *m*. Its donum, 5 Henry ii. I. 697. c. 1. *x*. See I. 740. c. 1. *d*. II. 245. c. 2. *u*.

Bedingho or Bovingho, those lands belonged to the prior of Bermondsey, 6 John, I. 439. c. 2. *l*.

Bedintun, Peter de, pays 160 pounds from the abbey of Evesham before 40 Henry iii. I. 271. c. 2. *h*.

Bedley, Adam de, moneyour of London, 14 Henry iii. II. 317. c. 2. *h*.

Beer, Ralf, fines for Wurle mill, 3 Henry iii. I. 492. c. 1. *o*.

Begford, its assise or tallage, 19 Henry ii. I. 701. c. 1. *z*.

Begge, Hugh de, fermer of Battle Abbey, 19 Henry ii. I. 308. c. 1. *d*.

Beiford and Essenden, an assignment out of them to the treasurer Fitzneal, 4 Richard i. II. 41. c. 2 *b*. and 42. c. 1. *c*.

Bekebroch, who claimed that land, 1 Richard i. I. 155. Claimed by Richard, son of Meine and William de Salcey, 1 Richard i. I. 213. c. 2. *u*.

Bekingham, Elias de, keeper of the rolls and writs of the common bench, 13 Edward i. II. 7. c. 2. *i*.

Bel, Hugh le, of the Exchequer, I. 62. c. 1. *e*. John le Bel, fermer of Chichester, 52 Henry iii. I. 718. c. 2. *p*. Robert le Bel seems sherif of

INDEX.

of London, 10 Richard i. II. 21. c. 1. *b*.

Belchamp, Richard de, I. 277. c. 2. *d*. Roger de Belchamp, 6 Henry iii. I. 454. c. 1. *e*. Simon de Belchamp, sherif of Buckingham and Bedfordshire, 6 Richard i. I. 459. c. 1. *o*. William de, amerced, 1 Richard i. I. 555. c. 1. *z*. Hugh de Belchamp, his wrong plevine, 2 John, I. 564. c. 2. *b*. William de, 14 Henry ii. I. 574. c. 2. *o*. See Bealchamp and Bello Campo.

Beler, Roger, vice-treasurer, 19 Edward ii. II. 51. c. 1. *q*. Made baron, 15 Edward ii. II. 60. c. 2. *i*. Sherif of Lincolnshire, 40 Henry iii. II. 142.

Belesham, Hugh and Norman de, 5 Stephen, I. 557. c. 1. *b*.

Belesme, Robert earl of, condemned in the king's court, an. 1113. I. 93. Robert de Belesme gives judgment in his court in Normandy on Sunday, I. 108. His terra in Shropshire descended to William Pantol, I. 318. c. 2. *b*.

Belestan, Baldwin de, 14 John, I. 554. c. 1. *l*. Amerced, ibid.

Belet, Michael, baron of the Exchequer, 29 Henry ii. I. 82. c. 2. *b*. and 28 Henry ii. I. 113. c. 2. *r*. Justice errant, 23 Henry ii. I. 130. Sheriff of Worcestersh. ibid. c. 2. *s*. Occurs again, I. 213. c. 1. *p*. Robert Belet, 1 John, I. 460. c. 2. *y*. Michael Belet fines for the office of pincerna, 14 John, I. 462. c. 2. *o*. Pays for the goodwill of the king, 13 John I. 474. c. 2. *h*. I. 556. c. 2. *x*. Robert Belet fines for non-passage, scutage, and that he may not be knighted, 14 Henry iii. I. 661. c. 1. *i*. Michael Belet, one of the justiciers who settled the tallage in Norfolk, 9 Richard i. I. 705. c. 1. *u*. Michael and Robert settled the tallage in Cornwal, 1 John, I. 733. c. 2. *u*. Michael tallaged Kent, 33 Henry ii. I. 736. c. 1. *o*. Michael audites the accompts of the quinzime, 10 Henry iii. II. 291. c. 2. *f*.

Belfago, Agnes de, fines for her son's joining the earl of Flanders, 5 Stephen, I. 501. c. 1. *m*.

Belfo, Emma de, 12 John, I. 453. c. 2. *y*. Ralf de Belfo, his lands, 5 Stephen, I. 487. c. 1. *s*.

Belhus, Richard de, I. 280. c. 1. *z*.

Belkthorp, John de, 16 Edward ii. II. 112. c. 1. *z*. To raise all the defensible men in the wapentake of Buckros, ibid.

Bellard, Thomas, messenger of the Exchequer, 26 Edward i. I. 655. c. 2. *z*.

Bellehus, Thomas de, auditor, &c. 20 Edward i. II. 291. c. 2. *g*.

Bello Campo, William de, 3 Henry iii. I. 68. c. 1. *x*. Simon de, 9 Richard i. I. 85. c. 1. *q*. Stephen de, 29 Henry ii. I. 105. c. 1. *p*. Andrew de Belchamp, his interest in Robert Basset's inheritance, 10 Richard i. I. 114. c. 2. *t*. Robert de Bello Campo, sherif of Dorset and Summersetshire, 23 Henry ii. I. 129. c. 2. *l*. Hugh de, I. 215. c. 2. *a*. Richard de Belchamp, I. 277. c. 2. *d*. Geoffrey de Bello Campo, his relief for the third part of a barony, I. 317. c. 2. *t*. William, bishop of Ely, has the wardship of Stephen de Bello Campo, 5 Richard i. I. 323. c. 1. *x*. Hugh de Bello Campo, 14 John, I. 472. c. 2. *f*. See Bealchamp, Belchamp.

Bello Vario, Richard de, 10 John, I. 218. c. 1. *p*. Fines for the great roll, ibid.

Belmeis,

INDEX.

Belmeis, Richard de, archdeacon [of Middlesex] an. 1142. I. 198. c. 2. e. William de, his scutage, 7 Richard i. I. 591. c. 2. t.

Belnei, Jordan de, attached for murder, 9 John, I. 441. c. 2. x.

Belveeir, honor of, I. 309. c. 1. p. and I. 315. c. 2. q. Belveher priory, a cell of St. Alban's, 10 Richard i. I. 760. c. 2. Robert de Belvero, treasurer of the Exchequer of Kaernarvan, 14 Edward i. II. 5. c. 1. t. Robert de Beuver losing the publick rolls of his accompts, has a reasonable fine imposed on him, 27 Edward i. II. 230.

Bendinges or Bendeng, William de, one of the justiciers, 25 Henry ii. I. 94. c. 1. a. Again, 26 Henry ii. I. 138. c. 2. a. William de, sherif of Dorset and Somersetshire, 29 Henry ii. I. 285. c. 1. u.

Benedicite of Norwich, Robert, 34 Edward i. II. 75. c. 1. w.

Benefacta, Richard de, when chief justicier, an. 1073. I. 32. c. 2. f. Son of earl Gilbert, ibid.

Beneit, the Jew of Canterbury, amerced twenty marks for demanding a debt which had been paid, I. 212. c. 2. o.

Benet, Mr. when he had the custody of the king's seal, I. 77. c. 1. c. William son of Benet, alderman of London, de warda fori, his tallage, 14 Henry iii. I. 709. c. 1. t. Again, 19 Henry iii. I. 738. c. 2. z. I. 739. c. 1. a. and I. 740. c. 1. c.

Benflet, that town released to the church of Westminster, 1 Richard i. I. 155.

Benigwurd, Linc. the fee of the archbishop of York, 33 Henry iii. I. 713. c. 1. d

Benley park, inclosed by Robert Malduit, 4 John, II. 253. c. 1. z.

Bensenton, in Oxfordshire, the ferm of it, 10 John, I. 280. c. 2. b. Assigned to Robert de Harecurt, 9 John, II. 168. c. 1. y. Was Godfrey de Craucumbe's, 16 Henry iii. II. 222. c. 1. x.

Benstede, John de, king's clerk, 26 Edward i. I. 72. c. 1. n. Keeper of the wardrobe, 1 Edward ii. I. 269. c. 2. z. John de Benstede justicier, 5 Edward ii. II. 7. c. 1. e. See II. 29. Justice of the bank, II. 31. Chancellor, 35 Edward i. II. 46. c. 1. u. and II. 49. c. 2. m.

Bentley, Richard de, assayer of the money at St. Edmunds, 5 Edward i. II. 90. Adam de Bentelega, sherif, II. 240.

Bentum, in Oxfordshire, the earl of Flanders's, 2 Henry ii. II. 163. c. 2. y.

Bera, Richard and William de, have the terra de Burbec, Hampshire, 5 Stephen, I. 448. c. 2. p. The tallage of Bera, 14 Henry iii. I. 708. c. 1. o. Castle of Bere in custody of Walter de Huntercombe, 12 Edward i. II. 4. c. 2. r.

Berchamsted amerced, I. 568. c. 2. t. The honor of, I. 587. c. 1. Its aid, 14 Henry ii. ibid. The assise of the soke of Berchamsted, 19 Henry ii. I. 701. c. 1. z. John de Berchamsted fined for attempting to carry a filet into Flanders, 10 Richard i. I. 776. c. 2. r. Gilbert de Berkhamsted, 18 Edward i. II. 179. c. 1. t.

Berdestaple, Roger, archdeacon of, 31 Henry ii. I. 310. c. 2. a. Hundred of, I. 543. c. 1. y. Belonged to Robert de Fuleham, 39 Henry iii. II. 22. c. 1. r. The hundred claimed by William Giffard against William de Munchenesy, 56 Henry iii. II. 80. c. 2. a.

Bereford,

INDEX.

Bereford, Alice de, her Gavelkind, 1 John, I. 434. c. 1. *i.* William de Bereford justicier, 11 Edward ii. I. 529, 530. c. 2. *w.* William de Berford, justicier of the common pleas, 26 Edward i. II. 29. See II. 47. Chief justice of the bank, 12 Edward ii. II 67. c. 1. *o.* Osbert, sherif of Warwick and Leicestershire, 13 Edward i. II. 155. c. 2. *k.* William de Berfod or Barefoot, chief justice de banco, 19 Edward ii. II. 293. c. 2. *q.*

Beregefeld, deputy sherif of Surrey, 15 John, I. 490. c. 2. *w.*

Berengaria, Reiner, son of, sherif of London, 11 Henry ii. I. 284. c. 1. *r.* Again, 2 Henry ii. I. 688. c. 1. *k.*

Berenger, John, his wife, 47 Henry iii. I. 100. c. 2. *c.* Reiner, son of, 19 Henry ii. I. 582. c. 2. *g.*

Berewik, Richard, son and heir of Hugh de, his tenure from the fee of Canterbury, I. 320. c. 1. *h.* John de Berwick, keeper of the queen's gold, 14 Edward i. I. 361. c. 2. *t.* That town in Yorkshire tallaged, 30 Henry iii. I. 710. c. 1. *w.* Its Exchequer, II. 4. John's executors, II. 7. c. 1. *e.*

Berkele, Roger de, his land in Derelega, Stanlega and Dodinton, 9 John, I. 251. c. 1. *q.* William de Berchelai, custos of the honor of Berchelai, 5 Stephen, I. 297. c. 1. *aa.* Thomas de Berkeley among the Glocestershire barons to go against the Scots, 26 Edward i. I. 655. c. 1. *a.* William de, his fee in Worcestershire, 3 John, I. 655. c. 2. *f.* Berkelai in Glocestershire without the town of Bristou, 1 John, I. 734. c. 1. *w.* The executors of Thomas de Berkele before 28 Henry iii. II. 184. c. 2. *i.* Arnald de Berkele, baron of the Exchequer, 48 Henry iii. II. 319. c. 2. *k.*

Berking, Walter de, relieved as surety, the principal being responsible, 35 Henry iii. II. 192. c. 1. *t.*

Berkley, Eustace and Alice de, their oblatum, 29 Henry ii. I. 105. c. 1. *p.*

Bermingeham, William de, clerk of the treasury of the tower, 14 Edward i. I. 270. c. 1. *b.*

Bermondsey priory, I. 439. c. 2. *l.*

Bernard the scribe, 5 Stephen, I. c. 1. *b.* Adam, 5 Edward ii. II. 7. c. 1. *e.* and II. 31. c. 1. *m.*

Bernay, abbat of, answers for his donum, I. 167. Receives the duke of Saxony, I. 169. c. 1. *n.*

Berners, Ralf de, 15 Edward i. I. 240. c. 1. *e.* Seems to be sherif of Oxfordshire, 19 Edward i. I. 271. c. 1. *g.*

Berneval, Hugh de, II. 43. c. 2. *m.*

Bernevel prior, II. 119. c. 1. *q.*

Bernham, Walter de, fined, 33 Edward i. II. 64.

Berrochscira, Hugh de S. Germano sheriff there, 23 Henry ii. I. 130. c. 1. *o.*

Bertona Bristolli, balliage, I. 334. c. 1. *s.* Bertona Radulfi de Cahanniis, I. 553. c. 1. *y.* in Glocestershire, I. 703.

Bertram, Alice, I. 464. Again, 11 Edward i. I. 466. c. 1. *a.* Roger, 14 John, I. 481. *r.*

Besages, Ralf de, his office in the Exchequer of Berwick, 6 Edward i. II. 5. c. 1. *x.* and I. 300.

Beston, Ralf de, amerced for the recreancy of Papeillon, 18 Henry ii. I. 549. c. 2. *n.*

Beston, Adam de, I. 442. c. 1. *e.*

Betoygne, Sir David de, 15 Edward ii. II. 102. c. 2. *b.* Has the king's dogs, ibid.

Betun,

INDEX.

Betun, Robert de, a benefactor to Feversham abbey before 18 Henry iii. I. 413. c. 2. *k*. Advocate of Artois, ibid.

Beverley, its charter of liberties, 2 John, I. 401. c. 2. *f*. Simon, provost, 5 John, I. 406. c. 1. *u*. Who had a claim in Beverly, 7 Richard i. I. 432. c. 2. *z*. Robert, provost of Beverly, 5 Stephen, I. 477. c. 1. *e*. Wapentak of Beverly under a commission of array, 16 Edward ii. II. 112. c. 2. Robert de Beverly, 49 Henry iii. II. 218.

Beurel, Richard de, an. 1184. I. 168. c. 2.

Beuveys, Thomas de, citizen of Canterbury, 36 Edward i. I. 421. c. 1. *w*.

Bezil, Matthew, 39 Henry iii. II. 150. c. 2. *o*. Becomes pledge, ibid.

Bicok, William de, clerk of Simon de Bradenham, 26 Edward i. II. 244.

Bidford, Adam de, 5 Henry iii. I. 793. c. 1. *e*.

Bidun, John de, seems to be sherif of Buckingham and Bedfordshire, 2 Henry ii. II. 220. c. 1. *n*.

Bigot, earl Roger, temp. Richard i. I. 35. Roger le Bigod earl mareschal, 27 Edward i. I. 41. On the determination of the male line of the Mareschals that office was vested in the Bigots, I. 45. Roger Bigod earl of Norfolk mareschal, 7 Edward i. I. 47. Roger and Ralf, 2 Edward ii. I. 48. c. 2. *y*. William, dapifer, I. 49. c. 2. *m*. Hugh the king's seneschal, an. 1136. I. 49. c. 2. *n*. William Bigod, I. 53. c. 1. *p*. Hugh, temp. Henry i. I. 56. c. 1. *o*. Roger le Bigot one of the justiciers, 9 Richard i. I. 113. His fine and sureties, 15 John, I. 190. c. 1. *f*. Roger Bigot has the land of Belveder with his wife Adeliz, 5 Stephen, I. 315. c. 2. *q*. Hugh Bigod, earl of Norfolk, his land and heirs in the wardship of Alexander king of Scots, 10 Henry iii. I. 325. c. 2. *k*. Hugh Bigot has the manor of Seham, Norfolk, 5 Stephen, I. 482. c. 1. *c*. Roger le Bigod's knights fees in Norfolk and Suffolk, 31 Henry iii. I. 594. c. 2. *i*. Roger le Bigot's scutage for Wales, 2 Richard i. I. 664. c. 1. *z*. Earl Roger has an hundred five and thirty fees, 5 Henry iii. I. 666. c. 2. *l*. Earl Roger Bigot fines in two thousand marks, and finds five pledges for his fealty, 13 John, I. 667. c. 1. *o*. Bartholomew de Bygod, 46 Henry iii. I. 668. c. 2. *y*. Earl Roger le Bigot, his pleas in Norfolk, 7 Richard i. II. 21. c. 1. *e*, *f*. Roger le Bygod, his tenure near Brokenwharf, London, before 2 Edward ii. II. 83. His death before that date, ibid. Roger le Bigot earl of Norfolk, 5 Edward i. II. 165. c. 1. *i*. Roger le Bigod mareschal of England in right of his mother Maud, heiress of Walter Mareschal, 31 Henry iii. II. 285. c. 1. *b*. and II. 286. c. 1. *c*. Again, 49 Henry iii. ibid. Had omitted to have any person resident in the Exchequer, ibid. Roger le Bygot said to be dead, Dec. 10. 34 Edward i. II. 286. c. 1. *f*. Claims the custody of the prisoners of the Exchequer, 38 Henry iii. II. 287. Hugh le Bigot justicier of England, 44 Henry iii. II. 289. c. 1. *s*.

Biham, scutage of, 5 Henry iii. I. 639. c. 2. *q*. I. 642. c. 1. and I. 666. c. 2. *l*. Ten shillings de scuto raised for that army, I. 677. c. 1. *a*.

Bihamel, Maud de, charged with felony by Simon de Lindon, 12 John, I.

152.

INDEX.

152. c. 1. a. Charged again with felony by the name of Mary, I. 443. c. 1. i.

Bik of Notingham, Auguſtin, clerk of the ſherif of Notingham and Derbyſhire, 12 Edward ii. II. 280. c. 1. b.

Bikbir, one of John Wak's ſeven churches in Exeter diocefe, 39 Henry iii. II. 250. c. 2. i.

Bikele, Richard de, 5 Edward i. II. 80. William de Bickele ſherif of Devonſhire, 52 Henry iii. II. 180. c. 1. z.

Bikerwik, Roger de, manucaptor, &c. 18 Edward i. II. 281. c. 2. f.

Billeſdon in Bucks, 4 John, I. 437. c. 2. z.

Billingley, Lincolnſhire, archbiſhop of York, has cuſtody of its heir, 33 Henry ii. I. 713. c. 2. d. Tallaged, ibid. William de, 1 Edward ii. II. 83.

Billingſgate duties, I. 775. Alberic de, charged with the duties of Billingeſgate, Botulfeſgate, and Gerſcherche, 3 Richard i. I. 788. c. 2. c. Which balliage he held from William de Haverell, 7 Richard i. II. 175. c. 2. x.

Binham abbey, a cell of St. Albans, 10 Richard i. I. 760. c. 2.

Binteworth in Hampſhire, I. 302. c. 1. z.

Birkin, John, his relief for the lands of Maud de Kauz, 8 Henry iii. I. 264. c. 1. s. And for the cuſtody of Notingham and Derby foreſts, ibid. Fines to plead for lands in Yorkſhire againſt Robert de Budliers, 3 John, I. 790. c. 2. l.

Birſtaſbrum in Lancaſhire, I. 397. c. 1. g.

Birton in Lincolnſhire had been the fee of Ralph de Waltervil, 33 Henry ii. I. 713. c. 2. d.

Bifantia, I. 106. c. 2. y. Again, I. 166. c. 2. i. Beſant was of the value of two ſhillings, I. 278. The value of one and twenty pence, 17 John, II. 261. c. 2. t.

Bifech, Gilbert de, claims Thorp, 7 Henry iii. I. 445. c. 2. e.

Bifet, Manſer, dapifer, temp. Henry ii. I. 50. c. 2. s. Henry Bifet, 4 John, I. 217. c. 1. l. Henry fines to de-afforeſt the boſch of Borleſc and the manor of Kedeminiſtre, 11 John, I. 410. c. 1. h. Iſolda Biſet deſired for Richard de Nevil by the king's petition, 12 John, I. 481. c. 1. o.

Biſhops chuſe William de Curboil archbiſhop, an. 1123. againſt the monks, earls and theins, I. 12. c. 2. o. The manner of their ancient court-keeping exemplified in the biſhop of Bath, I. 109. The reaſons why the crown ſeized vacant biſhopricks, I. 302, &c. Biſhop of Lincoln vacant eighteen years together, I. 308. The ſtyle of one by Edward ii. Al honourable pere en Dieu, I. 380. c. 1. t. Biſhop of Lincoln fines for ſelf and ſucceſſors to have his moveables and the product of lands ſown at his death, 15 Henry iii. I. 419. c. 1. o. Biſhops had dapifers hereditary, I. 457. c. 1. i. And ſeneſchals, I. 440. c. 1. n. I. 458. c. 2. e. Caution of the biſhops in granting aid or ſcutage, 13 Henry iii. I. 607. c. 1. z. Number of their fees often doubtful, ibid. Their grant of aid voluntary and ſpontaneous, 20 Henry iii. I. 401. ibid. Biſhoprick called an honor, 33 Henry ii. I. 634. c. 1. q. The king could take to their barony if they did not diſtrain clergymen who had no lay fees, II. 249.

Biſſa

INDEX.

Biffa or Doe, I. 560. c. 2. d.

Bitebroc, Sir Richard de, recovers his land of Bitebroc, 9 John, I. 235. c. 1. e.

Bitterle, John de, bailif of Havering, imprisoned for not paying his arrears, 27 Edward i. II. 155.

Bixla, the bishop of Chichester's four fees there, temp. Henry ii. I. 557. c. 1. y.

Bixtrop, Matthew de, fines for being a follower of Falkes de Breaut, the king's enemy, 8 Henry iii. I. 475. c. 2. q.

Blaby, Nicolas de, made constable of the Exchequer under Robert de Foleham, 52 Henry iii. II. 282. c. 2. m.

Blachampton, Hamo de, 11 Henry iii. II. 27. c. 1. f. Fines for his father's trespass, ibid.

Blachehadfeld hundred, I. 543. c. 2. h. I. 544. c. 2. q.

Blachetoritan hundred, amerc'd, 14 Henry ii. I. 556. c. 1. h.

Blackoker, the man of Robert de Burun, 10 John, I. 495. c. 2. a.

Blafeld hundred, in custody of Nicolas Castle, 9 Edward i. II. c. 2. f.

Blakeham, Bennet de, 8 John, I. 441. c. 2. z.

Blakeney, lady of, I. 504. c. 1. x.

Blakethorn, John de, one of the curators of St. Edward's shrine, 53 Henry iii. II. 91.

Blaneford, the terra of Brian de Lisle, how it descended, 19 Henry iii. I. 492. c. 2. z.

Blank, blanched or de-albated, when payments were made by combustion, I. 257.

Blankbully, John, to have the great ship Queen for life, 19 Henry iii. I. 509. c. 2. u.

Blebury, Mr. John de, 9 Edward ii. II. 75.

Blecchesdon, that terra in Oxfordshire tallaged, I. 721. c. 2. y.

Blez, William des, fines for a recognition of novel disseisin, 7 Richard i. I. 789. c. 1. d.

Blida, the king's lordship, I. 383. c. 2. g.

Blochesham, Oxfordshire, Richard de Luci's interest in it, 2 Henry ii. See Bloxeham.

Blockele, William de, justice itinerant for assise, the aid of the bishopric, 13 Henry iii. I. 716. c. 1. m.

Bloet, Roeland, one of the custodes of the sea-ports in Kent and Sussex, 15 John, I. 773. c. 2. l.

Bloio, Alan de, and Henry de, his son, had seven knights fees in Cornwal, 6 John, I. 317. c. 1. n. Henry Bloio pays queen's gold, 12 John, I. 351. c. 1. z. Robert de Bloy, 5 Henry iii. I. 452. c. 2. l.

Bloifton in Cornwal, its aid, 23 Henry ii. I. 604. c. 2. m. Bleifton its tallage, 1 John, I. 733. c. 2. t.

Blome, Walter, one of the king's enemies, 10 Richard i. I. 776.

Blossevil, Jordan de, sherif of Lincolnshire, 3 Henry ii. I. 207. c. 1. w.

Blount, Stephen le, keeper of the stores in the tower, 15 Edward ii. I. 382. c. 2. g. John le Blount, alderman of the ward of Flori, 2 Edward ii. II. 235. c. 1. t.

Bloweberme, Walter de, vanquishes Hamun le Stare in combat, temp. Henry iii. I. 550.

Bloxeham, Robert de, accompts for a wreck in Lincolnshire, 5 Stephen, I. 343. c. 2. h. John de Bloxham of London refused to be tallaged with the

INDEX.

the citizens, 2 Edward ii. I. 727. c. 2. *n.*

Blund, Geoffry de, his privilege of protection, 25 Henry ii. I. 117. c. 2. *k.* Again, I. 263. c. 1. *h.*

Blundel, Ralph, 6 Henry iii. I. 454. c. 2. *i.* Gilbert, one of the king's taxors, 22 Edward i. II. 119.

Blundi, Reginald, son of Roger, 29 Henry ii. I. 212. c. 2. *o.* Roger Blundus accompts for the old ferm of London, 20 Henry ii. I. 284. c. 2. *s.* Was one of the four sherifs of London, 19 Henry ii. I. 363. c. 1. *e.* Edward Blundus, the king's robemaker, 19 Henry ii. ibid. Adam Blundus de Bomine, 6 Henry iii. I. 445. c. 1. *c.* Fines for a duel, ibid. William Blund's merchandice with the men of Brich and Estrop, 7 John, I. 469. c. 2. *f.* The heir of Robert Blundi of London, 2 Henry iii. I. 491. c. 2. *l.* Robert Blundus of Stanh. 24 Henry iii. I. 496. c. 2. *q.* William Blundus, 10 John, I. 499. c. 2. *z. e.* Robert Blund amerc'd for recreancy, 26 Henry ii. I. 550. c. 1. *s.* Edward Blund, 16 Henry ii. I. c. 2. John Blund, 7 John, ibid. c. 1. *o.* Robert Blundus of Dedham, his aid, 14 Henry ii. I. 586. c. 2. What the fee of William Blundus paid for the king's ransom, 6 Richard i. I. 590. c. 2. *l.* John le Blound, mayor of London, 34 Edward i. I. 614. c. 2. Roger Blundus, alderman, the tallage for his ward, 14 Henry iii. I. c. 2. *t.* And the tallage for his ward, 14 Henry iii. I. 709. c. 2. *t.* And the tallage of alderman James's, ibid. The tallage of the wards of alderman James and Roger Blundus, 19 Henry iii. I. 739. c. 1. *z.* & c. 2. *a.* Robert Blund, 14 Henry ii. I. 747. c. 1. *g.* Stephen le Blund, fermer of tronage and the sextarius, 3 and 9 Richard i. 2 and 4 John, I. 779. c. 2. *f, g, h.* William, fermer of Queenhith, 23 Henry ii. I. 781. c. 1. *l.* Robert, son of Bartholomew Blund of London, 9 Richard i. I. 789. c. 2. *b.* His concord with Roger Ginges, ibid. Peter le Blund, one of the chamberlains of the Exchequer, 5 Edward ii. II. 6. c. 2. *d.* Adam Blundus, one of the custodes cuneorum, 6 Henry iii. II. 87. c. 2. *a.* Ralf le Blund, cutter of the dyes of London, 53 Henry iii. II. 89. c. 2. *q.* John le Blund, mayor of London, 1 Edward ii. II. 97. c. 1. *b.* William Blundus, sherif of London, temp. John, II. 215. c. 1. *u.* Maud le Blund, widow of Luke de Batencurt, 4 Edward i. II. 281. c. 1. *e.* Peter le Blound chamberlain of the Exchequer, 2 Edward ii. II. 299.

Bluntesden, Henry de, king's almoner, 30 Edward i. I. 73. c. 1. *q.*

Bocheiorum gilda, William Lafeite, alderman of it, 26 Henry ii. I. 562. c. 1. *z.*

Bocland, William de, accompts for Cornwal, 9 Richard i. I. 85. c. 2. *r.* Fined 30 pounds for a default of six days in his accompt, ibid. Frere Adam de Bocland, treasurer of the hospital of Clerkenewel, king's lieutenant, 1 Edward i. I. 610. c. 1. *i.* Hugh de Bocland's scutage for his Berkshire fees towards the Irish expedition, 18 Henry ii. I. 629. c. 2. *a.* Hugh de Bockland, justice of assise in Devonshire, 19 Henry ii. I. 701. c. 2. *b.* William de

INDEX

de Bocland, one of the sureties of Hugh Cordele, 9 Richard i. II. 198. c. 1. *r.* Sherif of Cornwal amerced, 1 Richard i. II. 236. c. 1. *a.*

Boclande, belonged to Alice de Hepworth and Robert de Abendon, 13 John, I. 218. c. 2. *w.* Nuns of Bockland, 20 Henry iii. I. 350. c. 1. *p.*

Bocton hundred amerc'd, 7 Richard i. I. 565. c. 1. *i.*

Bodeham, Margaret de, amerc'd, 12 John, I. 554. c. 1. *h.*

Bodmin, accompts for a gild without warrant, 26 Henry ii. I. 563. c. 1. *d.*

Boebi, Hugh de, justice itinerant, settled the tallage in Lincolnshire, 8 Richard i. I. 704. c. 1. *p.* Again, 4 John, I. 717. c. 1. *h.*

Bohun, Mat. de, wife of Walter Fitz-Robert, I. 45. c. 1, 2. *i.*

Bohun, Humfrey de, constable, 23 Henry ii. I. 41. Has that office by marriage, ibid. Reginald and Franco de, I. 46. c. 2. *a.* How that family was intitled to the mareschalsy, ibid. Humphrey fines to be the king's dapifer, 5 Stephen, I. 50. c. 2. *r.* Humphrey de Bohun, temp. Henry i. I. 56. c. 2. *o.* Henry de Bohun, earl of Hereford, attests the Jews charter, 2 John, I. 256. c. 2. Humfrey de Bohun, earl of Hereford, 5 Edward ii. I. 267. c. 2. *o.* Humfrey de Bohun, earl of Hereford and Essex, 12 Edward ii. I. 292. c. 2. *c.* Humfrey de Bohun fined for a relief, 5 Stephen, I. 315. Margaret de Bohun, 14 Henry ii. I. 554. c. 1. *o.* Humfrey de Bohun, earl of Hereford, 18 Edward i. I. 599. c. 1. *e.* Margaret de Bohun has the honor of Humfrey de Bohun, 33 Henry ii. I. 634. c. 1. *q.* Humfrey de Boune summon'd by writ to the Scotch war, 26 Edward i. I. 655. c. 1. Humfrey de Bohun, his scutage in Wiltshire for the Welch army, 2 Richard i. I. 664. c. 1. *a.* Humfrey de Bohun, his donum in Wiltshire, 5 Henry ii. I. 698. c. 1. *h.* Humfrey de Bohun, earl of Essex and Hereford, had Kenebalton, 18 Edward i. II. 248. Humfrey de Bohun, earl of Essex and Hereford, was constable of the Exchequer as constable of England, 12, 32, 49, 53 Henry iii. II. 281. *g, h, i, k, l, m.* and 20, 26, 27, 35 Edward i. and 2 Edward ii. II. 282. *n, o, p, q.* Humfrey de Bohun married Elizabeth, sister of Edward i. II. 283. And surrendered all his claims to make her a settlement, ibid.

Boiton, that chapel granted to the prior of Leeds, 10 John, I. 217. c. 2. *n.*

Bolbec, Walter de, dyed before 10 John, I. 480. c. 2. *n.* The knights fees of Walter de Bolebec, 14 Henry ii. I. 583. c. 2. *l.* Ysabel de Bolebec fines that she might not be distrein'd to marry, 9 John, I. 616. c. 2. *b.* And that she might have aid of her free tenants to pay the fine, ibid. Hugh de Bolebec's iter through Durham, 13 Henry iii. I. 717. c. 2. *l.*

Boleby, Lincolnshire, lands held there in Frankalmoign by the priory of Semplingham, I. 672. c. 1. *k.* Granted by Nigel Fitz Alexander, ibid.

Bolengarii, or Bakers of London, what they paid the crown for their gild, I. 338. c. 1. *m, n, o,* &c.

Bolesoure castle, in custody of Richard de

INDEX.

de Pec, 3 Richard i. II. 220. c. 2. *q*.

Bologne, honor of, 17 Henry ii. I. 263. c. 1. *f*. William of Bolonge, I. 776. To whom that honor belonged, 17 Henry ii. II. 200. c. 1. *c*. Honor of the earl of Bologne in custody of Ralf Brito before 29 Henry ii. II. 229. c. 1. *m*.

Bologne, Warenne, and Moreton, William earl of, temp. John, I. 57. c. 1. *r*. The honor of Boloigne in custody of Ralf Briton, 29 Henry ii. I. 297. c. 1. *h*. William earl of Boloign, Warenne, and Moreton, was a benefactor to Feversham abbey before Henry iii. I. 413. c. 2. *k*. The manor of Erefwel, Suffolk, parcel of that honor, I. 623. That honor in Ralf Briton's hand, 15 and 18 Henry ii. II. 252. c. 1. *s*, *t*.

Bolton, Thomas de, has the wapentake of Rydale in his commission of array, 16 Edward ii. I. 112. c. 2.

Bomine and Bodmin, I. 445. c. 1. *c*.

Bonawik, Loter, merchant of Florence, 5 Edward i. II. 77. c. 1. *k*.

Bonaventure, Richard, presented to be assayer, 32 Henry iii. II. 88. c. 2. *e*. Kept the key of the house of St. Edward's shrine, 53 Henry iii. II. 91.

Bondi in the bishopric, I. 710. c. 2. Bund of Derlinton, I. 714. c. 2. Tallage of the bonds of Stoketon, I. 720. c. 2. *u*.

Bonele, Aline de, 1 Edward ii. II. 123. c. 2. *x*. Has a writ of favour, ibid.

Bonet, John, deputy sherif of Wiltshire, 10 John, I. 285. c. 2. *z*.

Bonevil, Roger de, amerc'd for abusing the king's officers, 17 Henry ii. II. 559. c. 2. *n*.

Boniface VIII. pope, imposed a disme on the clergy for three years, which expir'd on or before 35 Edward i. II. 292. c. 2. *i*.

Boots for the king, ten pair cost fifteen shillings, 18 Henry ii. I. 367. c. 2. *g*.

Bordesley, monks of, taken into the king's protection by Henry ii. I. 117. Occur in claim of their manor of Cumbe, temp. Henry ii. I. 209. c. 1. *b*.

Borham, Hervey de, Baron of the Exchequer, 1 Edward i. II. 28. Attorney of Isabella [de Fortibus] countess of Albermarle, 49 Henry iii. II. 296. c. 1. *a*.

Borlesc in Worcestershire, the bosch of, I. 410. c. 1. *b*.

Borscombe lordship in Wiltshire, holds of Estegreenwich, Kent, I. 621. c. 2.

Boschet, Walter, justiced, 6 Henry iii. I. 454. c. 1. *g*.

Bosco, Hugh de, sherif of Northfolk and Suffolk, 7 Henry ii. I. 207. c. 2. *z*. Geoffrey de Bosco, his forfeiture in Kent, 8 John, I. 428. c. 2. *e*. William de Bosco, 4 Henry iii. I. 454. c. 1. *b*. Robert de Bosco, alderman of the gild de Ponte, 26 Henry ii. I. 562. c. 1. *z*. John de Bosco, his tenure from the church of Chichester, temp. Henry ii. I. 577. c. 1. Ralf and Robert de Bosco, 29 Henry iii. II. 17. c. 1. *d*. Hugh de Bosco, sherif of Hampshire, accompts for the price of cattle at exceeding low rates, 9 Richard i. II. 152. c. 2. *x*. Laurence de Bosco, of Waltham abbey, 9 Edward ii. II. 177. c. 1. *d*.

Boseham manor in Sussex, tallaged, 6 Edward ii. I. 744. c. 2. *x*. Belonged to Thomas de Brotherton

earl

INDEX.

earl of Norfolk, 9 Edward ii. I. 752. c. 2. *l.*

Bofel of Lincoln, John, fon of Theobald de, 28 Henry iii. II. 8. c. 1. *w.*

Bofevil, William de, his claim on Robert Baffet's inheritance, 10 Richard i. I. 114. c. 2. *t.* Ralf de Buefevil had Springfeld, Effex, before 1 Richard i. I. 703. c. 1. *l.*

Bofiet, belonging to the king of Scots, 13 Henry ii. I. 579. c. 1. *w.* How much in Bofeyate, Northamptonshire, has held by hidage and by chivalry, 15 Edward ii. I. 592. c. 1. *w.*

Boteler, Alexander le, one of the juftices itinerant, 20 Henry ii. I. 123. See Botiller. John de Boteler, attorney of the common bench, 27 Edward i. II. 266.

Botell, John de, an. 1184. I. 168. c. 2. Provoft of Dieppe, ibid.

Boterelles, William, fon of William de, fines for his father's lands, 6 Henry iii. I. 492. c. 1. *q.* William de Boterels, fherif of Cornwal, 5 John, II. 139. c. 2. *h.* William de Boterellis, fherif of Devonfhire, 5 Henry ii. II. 164. c. 1. *b.* William de Boterell has his debt refpited, 15 Henry ii. II. 213. c. 2. *p.* William des Boterels, fherif of Cornwal, 6 John, II. 232. c. 1. *e.*

Botetourt, fir John de, one of thofe who infulted Walter Langton, openly forbidding him to act as treafurer, 5 Edward ii. I. 267. c. 1. *o.* Has five hundred pound prefent for the good fervice done at fea near Scotland, 9 Edward ii. I. 392. c. 2. *c.* John de Botetourt, conftable in the Scotch army to the earl of Warrenne, 35 Edward i. I. 657. c. 2.

Again, 34 Edward i. II. 49. c. 1. *b.*

Botiller, Mr. Thomas le, fon and heir of Adam le Botiller, accompts for the abbey of Evefham, 10 Edward i. I. 720. c. 1. *s.* John le Butiler, valet of the Exchequer, 52 Henry iii. II. 17. c. 2. *g.* Efmon Butiller has a commiffion of array for the wapentakes of Ofgotecros and Stayncros, 16 Edward ii. II. 112. c. 1. Walter de Butiller to accompt for Alan la Zuche, fherif of Northamptonfhire, 52 Henry iii. II. 180. c. 2. *c.*

Botreaux, William de, his tenants in Cornwal, 9 Edward ii. I. 650. c. 1. *k.*

Botte, Robert, 28 Henry iii. I. 567. c. 2. *o.* The counties of Notingham and Derby fined for refufing to give judgment on him, ibid.

Botulvefbrug, the land of William de Gimeges, 2 Henry iii. I. 319. c. 2. *e.* Men of Bofton or St. Botulph's in Hoiland, belong'd to the honor of Richmond, I. 406. c. 1. *u.* Under a bailif of their own choice, 5 John, ibid. St. Botulph's in the king's hand fo far as it belong'd to the earl of Britainy, 30 Henry ii. I. 450. c. 2. *t.* The quinzime of this port almoft as high as that of London, 6 John, I. 772. c. 2.

Bough of a tree, feifin of land given by it, I. 621.

Boughton, Ifold, one of the coheireffes of Stephen de, fined to marry as fhe pleafed, 18 Edward i. I. 466. c. 1. *b.*

Bovinton, Walter de, under-fherif of Yorkfhire, 3 John, I. 361. c. 1. *a.*

Boaland, Yorkfhire, feveral towns in it tallaged, 30 Henry iii. I. 710. c. 1. *w.*

Boum,

INDEX.

Boum, Roheife, widow of Franco de, 7 Richard i. I. 170. c. 1. *r.* See Bohun.

Bourdeaux, William archbifhop of, 16 John, II. 43. c. 1. *m.*

Bouvil, William de, his diftreffes refcued, 22 Henry ii. I. 561. c. 1. *h.* Thomas de Boyvil, 26 Edward i. II. 188. c. 1. *c.* His writ, ibid.

Bow, Gilbert de Bailloel fined for carrying one in the foreft, 6 John, I. 499. c. 2. *y.*

Bowic and Engelingham, by whom claim'd, I. 435. c. 2. *q.* Called Bewick and Egelingham, ibid.

Box, William, who amerc'd, 26 Henry ii. I. 554. c. 2. *w.* Walter Box pays the vintifm of London in the clofe of Henry iii. I. 610. c. 2.

Boxgrave priory, its lands in nine towns, Suffex, I. 599. c. 2. *g.* Held in Socage and Frankalmoign, ibid.

Boxhore, William de, 26 Edward i. II. 280. c. 1. *g.* Imprifon'd for falfifying a tally, ibid.

Boxtede, Robert de, his wife had the land of Otrepol in dower, 4 Richard i. I. 564. c. 2. *d.*

Bozal, William de, late fherif of Yorkfhire, 5 Henry iii. II. 236. c. 2. *h.*

Brabant, Margaret, daughter of Edward i. married the duke of, before 26 Edward i. II. 785. c. 2. *a.*

Brabazon, Roger le, jufticiary ad placita coram rege, 35 Edward i. I. 74. c. 2.

Brabanzon, Roger le, chief juftice, 26 Edward i. II. 25. c. 1. & 29.

Braburne in Kent, its aid, 14 Henry ii. I. 489. c. 1.

Bracebridg, John de, fines for juftice againft Thomas Ardern, 10 John, I. 151. c. 1. *w.*

Braci, William de, I. 542. c. 2. *q.* In mifericordia for the foreft, ibid.

Bracket, what, I. 273. c. 2. *h.*

Bracton, I. 528. c. 2. *n.* See Laws, Briton.

Bracy, Robert and William, their tenure from William de Beauchamp, 38 Henry iii. I. 598. c. 1. *c.* and I. 597, 598. c. 1. *c.*

Bracyngton manor in Derbyfhire, parcel of the honor or Tuttebury held by Thomas de Furnival, 14 Edward ii. I. 534. c. 1.

Brada, John de, temp. Henry ii. I. 577. c. 1. Held of Chichefter, ibid.

Bradecote, William de, chamberlain of the Exchequer, 1 Edward i. II. 297. c. 2. *h.*

Bradeham, Alexander de, 49 Henry iii. II. 130. c. 1. *e.* Controller, ibid. and 57 Henry iii. II. 158. c. 2. *e.*

Bradelega, Ralf de, his tenure in focage and fergeanty before 15 Henry iii. I. 326. c. 1. *l.* Edilda de Bradele, 6 Henry iii. I. 454. c. 1. *g.* The patronage of that church, 3 John, I. 498. c. 2. *n.* Of Lincolnfhire tallaged, 10 Richard i. I. 733. c. 1. *r.* Walter de, keeper of the wardrobe, 33 Henry iii. II. 129. c. 1. *a, b.* Henry de Bradele, fherif of Hereford, 35 Henry iii. II. 158. c. 1. *z.*

Bradenham, Simon de, late fherif of Bedford and Buckinghamfhire, 26 Edward i. II. 244. See 251.

Bradeftede in Kent, its tallage, 34 Henry ii. I. 736. c. 1. *p.*

Bradeftock, prior of, 9 John, I. 273. c. 2. *g.*

Bradewell, how that cell was releas'd from the claims of the prior of Luffeld. I. 3. c. 2.

Bradford in Bonland, Yorkfhire, its tallage, 30 Henry iii. I. 710. c. 1. *w.* Another, ibid.

Bradfot, Reginald, anfwers for his father's

INDEX.

ther's amercement, 3 Richard i. I. 116. c. 2. c.

Bradfot, Wulmarus and Gerbodo, amerced for a meslet with the men of the canons of Carlisle, 18 Henry ii. I. 560. c. 1. s.

Braeby, the court of St. Peter de, Yorkshire, 5 Richard i. I. 98. c. 1. l.

Bragefeld, Northamptonshire, belong'd to the king of Scots, 13 Henry ii. I. 539. c. 1. w.

Braham, Eustace de, amerc'd for ill keeping a duel, 14 Henry ii. I. 545. c. 1. y.

Brai, Roger de, has the terra de Maldon in the beginning of Henry ii. I. 215. c. 1. a. Henry de Bray, his station in the treasury of the Exchequer, 10 Edward i. I. 232. c. 2. s. Escheator and custos of the see of Ely, 14 Edward i. I. 313. c. 2. i. Escheator on this side Trent, I. 389. c. 2. r. Silvester de Brai has the pledge of Sivelisho, 21 Henry ii. I. 430. c. 1. a.

Braibroc, Robert de, has the land of Horsindon, 12 John, I. 218. Accompts for the ferm of Bitebroc, Rutlandshire, 9 Richard i. II. 235. c. 1. e. Accompted for Northamptonshire as custos, 12 John, I. 384. c. 1. l.

Brailleford, Henry and Hugh de, 1 John, I. 555. c. 1. a. Henry amerc'd for Hugh's burgary, ibid.

Bramble honour in the king's hand, 11 John, I. 410. c. 1. i.

Bramham, Nicholas de, 22 Henry ii. I. 560. c. 2. d. Amerc'd for a false report, ibid.

Bramton, Huntingdonshire, the fee of earl David, 13 John, I. 666. c. 1. i. Had been in the family of Hastynges from king John's time, 9 Edward ii. I. 755. c. 1. q.

Brampton, a mile from Huntendon, I. 13. c. 1. r. Pleas of the forest held there, ibid.

Brand, Hamon, 4 Henry iii. I. 454. c. 1. b. c. 2. l. Yvo and Alan, sons of Brand, tallaged in Lincolnshire, 4 John, I. 737. c. 2. w.

Brandon, Richard de, 53 Henry iii. I. 752. c. 1. k. Not to contribute to the tallage of Hengham, ibid.

Brantescumbe, Richard de, clerk of Gilbert de Knovil, 26 Edward i. II. 156. Joscelin de Brantescumbe sworn mareschal of the Exchequer, 5 Edward ii. II. 287.

Brantingham, John de, chancellor's clerk, 31 Edward i. II. 304. c. 1. n.

Branton in Devonshire, fine against Robert de Sechevil, 13 John, I. 411. c. 1. u. Repeated, I. 507. c. 2. f. The men of Bramton in Devonshire, their aid, 14 Henry ii. I. 588. c. 1. b.

Brascur, Azo le, seems to be sherif of Surrey, 14 Henry ii. I. 587. c. 2.

Braunceftre, Bartholomew de, assayer of the coin in London, 2 Edward i. II. 90. c. 1. r.

Bray, William de, 2 Henry iii. I. 454. c. 1. a. William de Brai fines for his release, 1 Richard i. I. 493. c. 1. f. Roger de Brai amerc'd, 22 Henry ii. I. 560. c. 2. c. Ralf de Bray, his aid, 29 Henry iii. I. 594. c. 1. g. Osbert de Brai fined for refusing Danegeld in Berkshire, 20 Henry ii. I. 692. c. 1. i. Fermer of Windresore, 19 Henry ii. I. 774. c. 2. n. See II. 146. c. 1. x. Ralf de Brai, chamberlain of the Exchequer, 52 Henry iii. II. 297. c. 1. d.

Braybeof,

INDEX.

Braybeof, William de, one of the commissioners for the forfeited estates of the Jews, temp. Edward i. I. 231. c. 1. *m.* Joan, his widow, ibid.

Braybrok, Henry de, 6 Henry iii. I. 676. c. 2. *z.* Where his lands lay, ibid. Occurs again, 6 Henry iii. II. 27. c. 1. *c.* Robert de, whether baron, 11 John, II. 252. c. 2. *x.* See Braibroc.

Breach of peace severely amerc'd, I. 557. c. 1, 2. passim.

Breaut, Falk. de, teste, 3 Henry iii. I. 67. c. 2. William de Braiosa, sherif of Herefordshire, 20 Henry ii. I. 124. c. 2. *d.* The honor of Braiose in Normandy, I. 150. The privileges granted to William there, ibid. c. 1. *t.* An instrument with a teste William de Breosa, 4 John, I. 173. c. 1. *b.* William de Braiosa's grant to Oliver de Traci, 7 Richard i. I. 266. His fine how paid in cattle, &c. I. 273. c. 2. *g.* Falkesius de Breaute, sherif of Cambridge and Huntedonshire, 6 Henry iii. I. 286. c. 2. *g.* Falkes de Breaut, 9 John, I. 442. c. 1. *b.* William de Braiosa junior, 5 John, I. 446. c. 1. *f.* Falkes de Breaute, 7 Henry iii. ibid. c. 2. *n.* Falkes de Breaut, the king's enemy, 8 Henry iii. I. 475. c. 2. *q.* William de Braiosa, sherif of Herefordshire, 9 John, I. 480. c. 2. *l.* Has the honor of Limerick, 2 John, I. 486. c. 1. *l.* William de Brewose amerc'd for defalts, 10 Edward ii. I. 530. c. 1. William de Breouse pleads that his ancestors came to the inheritance under age, 35 Edward i. I. 536. c. 1. Had Brembre castle in Sussex, and the manor of Guher in Wales, ibid. Summon'd by writ as a baron in Surrey or Sussex to the Scotch war, 26 Edward i. I. 655. c. 2. Fulk Breautee has ninety fees of the honor of Eye, 5 Henry iii. I. 666. c. 2. *l.* William de Breose, justicier, 5 John, I. 771. c. 2. Fulk de Breaute, chamberlain of the Exchequer, 6 Henry iii. II. 21. c. 2. *m.* The fee of his office in Suffolk, ibid. William de Braiosa's lands in Herefordshire, temp. Stephen, II. 138. c. 2. *e.* William, sherif of Herefordshire, seiz'd, 4 Richard i. II. 176. c. 2. *b.* Mary, widow of William, 20 Edward i. II. 187. See 14 Edward i. II. 258. c. 1. *d.*

Brecham, Ralf de, 1 Richard i. I. 477. c. 2. *k.* Fines for protection, ibid.

Brecknock, that honor in Miles de Glocester, temp. Henry i. and king Stephen, I. 199. c. 2. *i.*

Breideshal, Robert de, of Yorkshire, 14 Henry ii. I. 512. c. 1. *q.* Fines for the concord of a duell, ibid.

Brembre honor in Sussex. See Breaut.

Bremensis ecclesia, a grant to it, I. 159. c. 1.

Bremesgrave, Richard de, king's clerk, 25 Edward i. I. 378. c. 2. *p.*

Bret, Simon le, 22 Henry ii. I. 103. Miles le Bret had letters patents of privilege for his lands in Ireland, 9 John, I. 119. c. 1. *b.* Simon and William le Bret, 4 John, I. 438. c. 1. *a.*

Bretefchia, I. 141. c. 1. *x.* Bretesche regis, I. 331. c. 1. *g.*

Brettevil, Nicolas, son of Richard de, his homage, 5 John, I. 488. c. 1. *x.*

Brichtwius Presbyter, seems sherif of Leicestershire, 5 Stephen, I. 147. c. 2. *b.*

Briddehal,

INDEX.

Briddehal, Yorkshire, its tallage, 30 Henry iii. I. 710. c. 1. *w.*

Briddingehurst, Robert de, 15 Henry ii. I. 545. c. 2. *c.* Amerced for disturbing jurors, &c. ibid.

Brideport, Mr. John de, fines, 5 John, I. 118. c. 2. *w.* Bridport occurs, II. 166.

Bridlesford, forfeited by Thomas de, for felony, before 6 John, I. 488. c. 1. *y*

Bridlington priory, Yorkshire, II. 79.

Bridport fines to be a free burgh, and for their ferm, 38 Henry iii. I. 421. c. 1. *u.* Was tallaged, 14 Henry iii. I. 708. c. 1. *o.* Again, 19 Henry iii. I. 735. c. 1. *i.*

Brien, Richard son of, in misericordia, 23 Henry ii. I. 201. c. 1. *o.* Again, I. 211. c. 1. *h.* Robert son of, 23 Henry ii. I. 497. c. 2. *e.*

Brikehull, William de, clerk, has custody of the see of Worcester, 1 Edward ii. I. 314. c. 1. *l.*

Brikevil, Fryar Richard de, attorney for Joan de Braybeof, &c. I. 231. c. 1. *m.*

Brirelai, Yorkshire, tallaged, 9 Richard i. I. 699. c. 1. *r.*

Bristou, the citisens fined for Sturmis the usurer, 23 Henry ii. I. 211. c. 1. *i.* Its ferm, temp. John and Henry iii. I. 333. c. 2. *n. s.* Not to be impleaded out of the walls of their villa till the king's return, 30 Henry ii. I. 398. c. 2. *y.* Fined for not meeting the justiciers, I. 503. c. 2. *s.* Bristou castle besieged, temp. Richard i. I. 564. c. 1. *w.* Abbat of St. Austin's Bristol, his five knights fees, 29 Henry iii. I. 596. c. 1. A treasury here, 12 John, I. 606. c. 2. *x.* Tallages for its burgh and fair, 7 Richard i. I. 703. c. 2. *n.* and I. 735. c. 2. *l.* Complaint against them for their customs, I. 784. c. 1. *u.*

Britain, John de, of the king's council, 30 Edward i. I. 73. Has the manor of John Balliol's, 34 Edward i. I. 752. c. 1. *i.*

Britannia, John de, taken by the Scots, his ransom, 17 Edward ii. I. 615. c. 2. *z.* See Richmond.

Briton, Walter de, how his inheritance descended, I. 115. c. 1. Ralf Briton justice errant, 23 Henry ii. I. 131. Roger Briton his knights, 7 Henry ii. I. 207. c. 2. *y.* William Briton justice of the Jews, 18 Henry iii. I. 234. c. 1. *a.* Richard Briton, 3 John, I. 237. c. 2. *p.* Ralf, 17 Henry ii. I. 263. c. 1. *f.* Ralf Briton has custody of the honor of Boloigne, 19 Henry ii. I. 297. c. 1. *h.* Richard [Briton] archdeacon of Covintre, 31 Henry ii. I. 309. c. 2. *w.* Custos of the see of Lincoln, ibid. and of London, 1 Richard i. I. 311. c. 2. *i.* Walter Briton pays for the relief of his lands in Dorsetshire, 20 Henry ii. I. 316. c. 1. *z.* Tomas Brito fines, 10 Richard i. I. 428. c. 1. *x.* Humfrey Brito, his fee, 31 Henry ii. I. 431. c. 2. *q.* William Briton has the manor of Chigewel, 2 John, I. 434. Thomas Briton, and Alice his wife, one of the heirs of Brian de Lisle, 19 Henry iii. I. 492. c. 2. *z.* Ralf Briton fines to be quit of the profits of the land of Henry de Essexa, and of the honor of the earl of Bologn, 31 Henry ii. I. 498. c. 1. *i.* He had the land of Lageford and Chigwel, temp. Henry ii. I. 703. c. 1. *l.* John le Bretun custos of London, 25 Edward i. II. 96. c. 2. *a.* Ralf Briton, 25 Henry iii. II. 189. c. 2. *f.* and II. 200. c. 1. *c.* Custos of the land of

INDEX.

of Henry de Effexa and the honor of Bologne, 29 Henry ii. II. 229. c. 1. *m.* Again, 15 Henry ii. II. 252. c. 1. *s, t.* Richard feems jufticier, 7 Richard i. II. 284. c. 1. *w.* William, juftice of the Jews, 21 Henry iii. II. 317. c. 2. *e.*

Brochion, Ralf de, made conftable of the Exchequer, 20 Edward i. II. 282. c. 2. *n.*

Brocton, Gerard de, pays his fine to have a duel in the king's court, 31 Henry ii. I. 97. c. 2. *b.* One of the knights deciding between Robert de Mandevil and Henry de Tilli on the barony of Merfwude, 10 John, I. 489. c. 2. *q.*

Brodehamme, Gregory de, had the ferm of Surry and Suffex, 27 Henry iii. II. 141. c. 1. *r.*

Brodercrofs and Galho hundred in Norfolk, I. 502. c. 1. *z.*

Brok, Simon del, king's attorney, 47 Henry iii. I. 100. c. 1. *c.* Ralf de Broc fermer of the fee of Canterbury, 14 Henry ii. I. 584. c. 2. *q.* The barony of Henry del Broch in the bifhopric, 8 Richard i. I. 715. c. 2. John de Brok one of the deputy marefcals, 18 Edward iii. I. 798. c. 2. Thomas del Brock committee of the manor of Selvefton, 56 Henry iii. II. 67. c. 2. *s.*

Brokedyfh, Reynald de, tenant of Gilbert Peche, 25 Edward i. II. 75. c. 1.

Broken-wharf, London, its vifnue, 2 Edward ii. II. 83.

Brokefwor or Brokfeffe hundred in Herefordfhire, II. 122. c. 1. *m.*

Bromceftre, John de, archdeacon of Worcefter, had the feal after the death of Hubert, 7 John, I. 67. c. 1. *s.*

Bromford, Hubert de, married a fifter and one of the coheireffes of Niel de Luvetot before 6 Henry iii. I. 640. c. 1. *r.*

Bromley, William de, cuftos of Staffordfhire for Henry de Aldithelega fherif, 13 Henry iii. II. 169. c. 2. *f.*

Brotherton, Thomas de, earl of Norfolk, tallages his manor of Bofeham, Suffex, 9 Edward ii. I. 752. c. 2. *l.* Was brother of Edward ii. II. 287. Marefchal of England and the king's brother, 9 Edward ii. ibid.

Brouli, Henry de, of Oxfordfhire, manucaptor, 14 Edward i. I. 254. c. 2.

Brudeford wapentak under the commiffion of array, 16 Edward ii. II. 112. c. 1.

Bruere, William, one of king Richard's regency in the beginning of his reign, I. 35. Sent by Hubert to determine the controverfy between the archbifhop of York and the canons, I. ibid. William Briwer, 3 Henry iii. I. 67. c. 1. *x.* Was one of the jufticiers, 9 Richard i. I. 113. His fine for the moiety of Walter Briton's land, 4 John, I. 114. Some account of his lands and his fon Richard's, ibid. William was fherif of Devonfhire, 26 Henry ii. I. 139. c. 1. *g.* Jufticier, 3 John, I. 205. c. 2. *n.* William de Brueria the archdeacon, 9 John, I. 217. c. 1. *m.* Roger, Reinfrid, and Ralf de Brueria his brothers, ibid. William Briwer, 2 John, I. 256. c. 2. Sherif of Devonfhire, 30 Henry ii. I. 276. c. 2. *u, x.* William fherif of Wiltfhire, 10 John, I. 285. c. 2. *z.* John de Briewerre, 1 John, I. 401. c. 1. *a.* William Briwer, 5 John, I. 406. c. 2. William Briwere's proportion for de-afforefting Cornwal, 11 Henry iii. I. 414. c. 1. *n.* William de Briwerre has the cuftody of the drengage of Gilbert de Calverley,

INDEX.

verley, 3 John, I. 487. c. 1. p. William Briewerre, 4 John, I. 505. c. 2. p. William Briewerre had oppressed the counties of Dorset and Somerset, 12 John, I. 508. c. 1. k. William de Briwerre, king's tallager in Wiltshire, 33 Henry ii. I. 634. c. 1. q. William de, baron of the Exchequer, 5 Henry iii. I. 675. c. 1. q. Richard Briewerre custos of the see of Durham, temp. Richard i. I. 714. c. 1. g. William Briwerre settles the tallage of Notinghamshire, 9 Richard i. I. 733. c. 1. p. William Briwer sherif of Hampshire, 9 John, II. 139. c. 2. i. And of Somerset and Dorsetshire, ibid. c. 2. k. William Briewerre accompts for Robert del Estre, 6 John, II. 200. c. 2. i. And for the land, late Roger de Planes's, 10 Richard i. II. 226. c. 1. w. William de Briwerre baron of the Exchequer, 7 Richard i. II. 228. c. 2. k. Had a surplusage in his accompt for Cornwal, 6 John, II. 232. c. 1. e.

Bruges or Bridgnorth, in Shropshire, its ferm, 8 John, I. 333. c. 1. h. Their fine to have their ferm, 16 Henry ii. I. 398. c. 1. q. Their charter of liberties, 7 Henry iii. I. 412. c. 2. d. The tallage of Bruges, 1 John, I. 705. c. 2. y. and 8 John, I. 734. c. 1. z. and II. 6. c. 1. a. Had a castle, 40 Henry iii. II. 141. c. 2. u.

Brumeshage, Wiltshire, I. 634. c. 2.

Brumeshel village, Staffordshire, amerced, 7 Richard i. I. 546. c. 1. m. Amerced, I. 565. c. 1. l.

Brumesgrave, Worcestershire, its tallage, 8 Richard i. I. 704. c. 2. q. Again, Bremmegrave tallaged, 14 Henry iii. I. 708. c. 2. r.

Brumley manor in Shropshire belonged to Cicely de Hadley, 6 John, I. 188. c. 1. a.

Brummore, Ralf de, wounded, 18 Henry ii. I. 503. c. 1. i. See I. 767. c. 2. t.

Brumton of William de Vescy, tallaged, 14 Henry iii. I. 708. c. 2. p.

Brun, Hugh le, 8 Richard i. I. 29. c. 2. q. Roger Brune dapifer [to the bishop of London probably] an. 1142. I. 198. c. 1. e. William le Brun and Isolde his wife, 18 Edward i. I. 243. c. 1. m. Aschil Brun, his money, 13 Henry ii. I. 263. c. 1. d. The honor of Brun belonging to Maud de Doura, to whom it descended, 31 Henry ii. I. 512. c. 2. u. Robert Brun of Cuningestrete, York, 21 Henry iii. I. 546. c. 2. p. Bartholomew le Brun of London, his tallage, 14 Henry iii. I. 709. c. 1. s. William Brunus fermer of Queenhith, 23 and 28 Henry ii. I. 781. c. 1. l, m. Hugh, II. 78. c. 1. q. Walter le Brun mareschal of the Strand or farrier, 19 Henry iii. II. 100. c. 2. n.

Brunden, Henry de, 10 Richard i. I. 433. c. 1. d. Fines for a writ of Mortdancestre for the gaol of Winchester, ibid.

Brus, Peter de, has the village of Danebi, 4 John, I. 191. c. 1. o. Peter, son of Peter de Brus, his relief for his barony, 6 Henry iii. I. 317. c. 2. q. Peter de Brus, his ferm of the wapentak of Langeberge, Yorkshire, 9 John, 31 and 52 Henry iii. I. 336. c. 1. e. c. 2. f, g. Adam de Brus, 22 Henry ii. I. 541. c. 2. k. Adam de Bruis held of the earl of Chester, 14 Henry ii. I. 580. c. 2. r. Robert Brus the king's enemy, 34 Edward i. I. 613. c. 2. t.

Robert

INDEX.

Robert and Adam de Brus, their scutage for their fees in Yorkshire, 18 Henry ii. I. 629. c. 2.

Brweys, Robert de, his tenure in Runham, Norfolk, 56 Henry iii. II. 101. c. 1. *t*.

Brykhull, William de, made chamberlain of the Exchequer, 26 Edward i. II. 301. c. 1. *y*. Removed or dead, 1 Edward ii. II. 301. c. 1. *a*.

Buba, Henry, accompts, 18 Henry ii. I. 559. c. 2. *p*. Secreted the effects of the abbat of Hide, and afterwards owned it, ibid.

Bucca, Fegga, in misericordia, 12 Henry ii. I. 541. c. 1. *g*

Bucca uncta, or Buccuinte, Andrew de, 5 Stephen, I. 482. c. 1. *d*.

Buccuinte, Laurence, of St. Paul's, an. 1142. I. 198. c. 1. *e*. John Bucuint accompts for the ferm of London before 20 Henry ii. I. 284. c. 2. Sherif of London, 19 Henry ii. I. 363. c. 1. *e*. Humfrey his claim of the land of Eggefwer, 17 Henry ii. I. 429. c. 2. *s*. John, sherif of London, &c. by ferm, 3 Richard i. II. 169. c. 1. *b*.

Buccunden, Turgis de, his recreancy, 26 Henry ii. I. 550.

Bucel, Ernald, 26 Henry ii. I. 458. c. 1. *c*. Ralf his promissio for the citizens of London, 19 Henry ii. I. 582. c. 2. *g*.

Buchard, treasurer of York, his tallage, 8 Richard i. I. 715. c. 1.

Buche, Roger, his interest in the terra de Walton, 8 Richard i. I. 106.

Buckros wapentake, Yorkshire, a commission of array directed to it, 16 Edward ii. II. 111.

Bucttan, Ailric, amerced, 16 Henry ii. I. 559. c. 2. *k*.

Buddele, William de, sherif of London, 9 Edward ii. II. 97.

Budicumbe, Alexander de, I. 621.

Budiford, I. 634. c. 2. Adam de Budeford, vicesherif of Herefordshire, 52 Henry iii. II. 180. c. 1. *a*.

Bueles, Hugh de, plegius of Hugh de Dacovere, 40 Henry iii. II. 150. c. 2. *q*.

Buelt castle, II. 208.

Buffle, Walter le, of London, his tallage, 14 Henry iii. I. 709. c. 1. *s*.

Buggerden, paid Peter-pence, and had a winepress, &c. when in the king's hands, 31 Henry ii. I. 310. c. 1.

Buggethorp, Hamelin de, married Margaret, coheir of Philip de Ulecot before 5 Henry iii. I. 463.

Buhurt, William de, whether rightly appealed, 5 John, I. 439. c. 1. *g*.

Buinebroc, terra de, I. 447. c. 2. *a*.

Buissei, Bartholomew de, 24 Henry ii. I. 211. c. 2. *b*. See Wach. William de Buissei fines for a partition of Walter Espec's land, 6 Henry ii. I. 501. c. 1. *p*. Again, 4 Henry ii. I. 511. c. 2. *n*.

Buistard, Robert son of, his privilege in Yorkshire, 31 Henry ii. I. 117. c. 2. *l*. Again, Robert son of Bustard's fine, 26 Henry ii. I. 398. c. 1. *s*.

Bukerel, Beatrix, 26 Henry ii. I. 104. c. 1. *b*. Thomas Bukerel sheriff of London, 2 Henry iii. I. 193. c. 1. *f*. Matthew seems to be a descendent of Geoffrey Fitz Peter, 25 Henry iii. I. 235. c. 2. *g*. Stephen Bukerel sherif of London, 13 Henry iii. I. 283. c. 1. *o*. Geoffrey fines to be quit of the sherifwick of London, 5 Stephen, I. 457. c. 2. *t*. Fines that an exchange between him and Adeluif the Fleming may be superseded, 5 Stephen, I. 511. c. 1. *k*. Citisens of London amerced for harbouring Walter Bukerel, 30 Henry

INDEX.

Henry iii. I. 568. c. 1. *p.* Andrew, 11 Henry iii. I. 707. c. 2. *m.* Andrew alderman of London, his tallage, 14 Henry iii. I. 709. c. 1. *t.* and 19 Henry iii. I. 730. c. 2. *z.* I. 739. c. 1. *a.* Andrew fermer of Queenhith, 11 and 14 Henry iii. I. 781. c. 1. *o.* c. 2. *q.* Mayor, 18 Henry iii. II. 35. Sherif, 8 Henry iii. II. 95. c. 1. *q.* William and Thomas fon of Odo, 5 Stephen, II. 197. c. 2. Andrew bailif of Ripa Reginæ, 8 and 9 Henry iii. II. 228. c. 1. *f.*

Buketot, William de, a pledge, 2 John, I. 521. c. 1.

Bukingham, John de, clerk of the chamberlain, 1 Edward ii. I. 75. c. 2. Mr. William de, one of the barons of the Exchequer, 1 John, I. 190. c. 2. *k.*

Bulehufe, John de la, of Hampfhire, 28 Henry iii. II. 190. c. 1. *g.*

Bullialdus, I. 161. c. 1.

Bulls counterfeit made ufe of by Walter de Maidefton, 26 Edward i. II. 82.

Bulmer, Bertram de, fherif of Yorkfhire, 5 Stephen, I. 327. c. 1. *q.* Again, I. 364. c. 1. *m.* Again fherif, 3 Henry ii. I. 365. c. 1. *r.* Occurs again, 5 Stephen, I. 456. c. 1. *d.* Bertram de Bulemer fherif of Yorkfhire accompts for the donum of the city and county, 4 Henry ii. I. 696. c. 1. *i.* Bulmer wapentake under a commiffion of array, 16 Edward ii. II. 112. c. 1. Bertram de Bulemer fherif of Yorfhire, 2 Henry ii. II. 312. c. 2. *q.*

Bumfted, in Effex, its affife or tallage, 19 Henry ii. I. 701. c. 1. *z.* Little Bumfted tallaged, 1 Richard i. I. 703. c. 1. *l.* c. 2. *m.*

Bunch, Roger, of Hereford, difcharged of tallage, 7 Richard i. I. 767. c. 1. *k.*

Bundles made up by the two remembrancers of the Exchequer, II. 114.

Bur or Burre, Robert, of Canterbury, relieved of his unequal affeffment, 51 Henry iii. I. 742. c. 2. *b.*

Burbeche, Ralf de, died by the trial of water about 18 Henry ii. I. 344. c. 2. *t.* Who has the land of Burbec, 5 Stephen, I. 448. c. 2. *p.* See II. 131. c. 2.

Burc, in Langelande, Norfolk, its aid, 14 Henry ii. I. 589. c. 2. *f.* Thomas de Burc fenefchal of the countefs of Britain, 6 Richard i. I. 591. c. 2. *u.* Accompts for the counteffes knights, 1 John, I. 638. c. 1. *i.*

Burcote, William de, impleaded for debt, 49 Henry iii. II. 17. c. 2. *f.*

Burdegala, Oliver de, cuftos of the caftle of Guldeford, 15 Edward ii. I. 383. c. 2.

Burdun, William and John, refpited, 15 Henry ii. I. 189. c. 1. *x.* John, 16 Henry ii. I. 209. c. 2. *d.* Peter Burdun has the land of Penros, 3 John, I. 406. c. 2. *n.* Nicolas Burdun, manucaptor, 39 Henry iii. II. 150. c. 2. *o.*

Burels of London, temp. Henry iii. I. 550.

Burewel, the tallage of the men of, 7 Henry iii. I. 729. c. 1. *q.*

Burford in Oxfordfhire, tallaged, 3 John, I. 721. c. 2. *y.*

Burga, widow of William de Vaux, 9 Edward ii. II. 117. c. 2. *e.*

Burgary, feems to be robbing in a burgh, I. 555. c. 1. *a.*

Burgate ward in Canterbury, tallaged at la Bretton, and belonged to St. Auftin's abbey, 33 Edward i. I. 740. c. 1. *e.*

Burge, Serlo de, cuftos of the archbifhoprick

INDEX.

bishoprick of York, about 5 Stephen, I. 306. c. 1. *m*. Occurs again, 5 Stephen, I. 456. c. 2. *e*. Fines for his son Osbert's office, ibid.

Burgenses & homines burgorum & villarum, I. 333. The aid of Burghs, I. 600, 601.

Burges, John, his share of the lordship of Borscombe, Wiltshire, 42 Elizabeth, I. 621. c. 2. Walter de Burges, custos of Winchester, 52 Henry iii. I. 719. c. 1. *r*. and II. 4. c. 1.

Burgh, Sarah de, fined to king John about her marriage, I. 3. c. 2. John de Burgh, son and heir of Hawisia de Launvaley, 1. 320. c. 2. *o*. Columbus de Burgo had custody of the castle of Cusac in Gascoigne, before 39 Henry iii. I. 391. c. 2. *w*. Sara, widow of Tomas de, 3 John, I. 465. c. 1. *n*. Margaret, wife of John de Burgo, 29 Henry iii. I. 511. c. 1. *h*. John de Burgh held the manors of Causton and Sutherton, 36 Henry iii. I. 752. c. 1. *g*. John's debts to the crown, 27 Henry iii. II. 5. c. 2. *y*. Walter de Burgh has custody of many of the king's manors, 28 Henry iii. II. 176. c. 1. *a*. Raimund de Burgh, 14 Henry iii. II. vol. 217. c. 2. John de Burgh has Rocheford hundred in Essex, 53 Henry iii. II. 248. c. 1. *u*.

Burgh, Hubert de, made justicier, temp. Henry iii. I. 37. His assignment as justicier, ibid. Earl of Kent and justicier, 11 Henry iii. I. 63. c. 1. *b*. Justiciary of England, 3 Henry iii. I. 67. c. 1. *x*. Signs before the bishops, ibid. Sherif of Norfolk and Suffolk, 4 Henry iii. I. 226. Justiciary, 6 Henry iii. I. 236. c. 1. *h*. Again, 9 Henry iii. I. 252. c. 1. *t*. Sherif of Norfolk and Suffolk, 5 Henry iii. I. 286. Sherif of Kent, 7 Henry iii. I. 329. c. 2. *x*. Accompts for the ferm of Kent, 4 Henry iii. I. 372. c. 1. *n*. Justicier, 6 Henry iii. I. 668. c. 1. *w*. Justicier, 5 Henry iii. I. 675. c. 1. *q*. Justicier, 2 Henry iii. II. 26. c. 1. *a*. Sherif of Norfolk and Suffolk, II. 140. c. 1. *n*. Occurs in several instances, 3 and 4 Henry iii. II. 146. c. 2. *e*, *f*. Indebted to the crown at his death, 35 Henry iii. II. 193. c. 1. *b*. Occurs, 13 Henry iii. II. 206. c. 2. *b*. One of the pledges of Peter de Maillai, 16 John, II. 211. c. 1. *b*. Married Beatrice, widow of Dodo Bardulf, and heiress of William de Warenne, temp. John, II. 214. c. 1. *r*.

Burgh-Abbey, their oblatum for the ransome of king Richard, I. 400. c. 2. *u*. Men of Burgh fine in twenty marks for a market every Sunday, 3 John, I. 403. c. 2. *u*. Renew their charters, 10 John, I. 409. c. 2. *g*. Fine to have the custody of their house on a vacancy, 13 John, I. 411. c. 1. *t*. See Nassum Burgi. Acknowledge sixty knights fees, 14 Henry ii. I. 574. c. 1. *n*. Its escuage for the king's ransom, 6 Richard i. I. 591. c. 1. *m*. The abbat has an aid from his tenants to pay the king's fine, 7 John, I. 616. c. 1. *a*. Its scutage for the Welch expedition, 3 Richard i. I. 636. c. 2. *w*.

Burghershe, Robert de, warden of the cinque ports, 33 Edward i. I. 421. c. 2. *x*.

Burghul, Roger de, discharged from being custos of the county and castle of Hereford, 15 Edward i. II. 143. c. 1. *e*.

Burghunte, Richard de, sherif of the counties of Dorset and Somerset,

and

INDEX.

and custos of the castle of Shyreburne, 18 Edward i. II. 143. c. 2. *f.*

Burghis, Richard, custos of Gloucestershire for Engelard de Ciconiaco, 12 John, II. 146. c. 2. *c.*

Burguignon, John le, fines, 26 Henry ii. I. 104. c. 1. *l.* Ralf de, amerced, 14 Henry iii. I. 544. c. 1. *i.*

Burial in religious houses a great favour, and granted to benefactors, I. 204. c. 2. *k.*

Burne, John de, one of the custodes of St Augustin's Canterbury, 11 Edward i. I. 313. c. 1. *g.* Geoffrey de, fines to be released, 5 Stephen, I. 493. c. 1. *c.* William and Thomas de Burne, 14 Henry iii. I. 441. c. 1. *f.*

Burnel, Robert, seems to be head of the king's council, 1 Edward i. II. 207. c. 2. *g, gg.* King's agent in Ireland, 49 Henry iii. II. 218.

Burnewel, William, 26 Henry ii. I. 555. c. 1. *x.* Robert Burnel one of the receivers of the last vintism of Henry iii. I. 610. c. 1. *i.*

Burnham, Thomas de, king's tallager, 33 Edward i. I. 741. c. 2. *i.* and 34 Edward i. I. 752. c. 1. *i.* That hundred Geoffry Fitz Peter's, 2 Richard i. II. 20. c. 1. *y.* Thomas de Burnham, sherif of Lincolnshire, 34 Edward i. II. 174.

Burserius, Roger, of London, his tallage, 14 Henry iii. I. 709. c. 1. *s.* The tallage of Roger Bursarius, alderman of London, 19 Henry iii. I. 738. c. 2. *z.*

Burstow, John de, collector of the disme and sisme in Surrey, temp. Edward i. II. 233.

Burton belonged to the barony of Guischart Ledet in Northamptonshire, I. 48?. c. 1. *z.*

Burton, to whom it in part belonged, 24 Henry ii. I. 103. c. 2. *k.* Abbat of Burton upon Trent obtains a market at their manor of Bromley, 5 Henry iii. I. 415. c. 1. *rr.* Walter and Nicolas de Burton, 15 Henry ii. I. 429. c. 2. *q.* Samuel de, has the terra de Burton, 2 Henry iii. I. 491. c. 2. *k.* Abbat of Buerton in Staffordshire accompts for his knights fees, 14 Henry ii. I. 582. c. 1. *e.* Master of the hospital of Burton Lazars, I. 671. Burton in Glocestershire the abbat of Westminster's, 19 Henry ii. I. 701. c. 2. *c.* Burton in Hampshire, I. 744. c. 2. *y.*

Burun, Roger de, his reliefs for his lands in Notingham and Derbyshire, 3 and 4 Henry ii. I. 315. c. 2. *w.* Geoffrey de Burun, 30 Henry ii. I. 431. c. 1. *g.* Robert de Burun, 10 John, I. 499. c. 2. *a.* Roger's escuage for the king's ransom, 6 Richard i. I. 591. c. 1. *o.* Roger's scutage, 1 John, I. 638. c. 2. *k.*

Burwardescot, to whom that manor belonged, 5 Stephen, I. 511. c. 1. *l.*

Busca, or firewood, perhaps beech, II. 48. c. 1. *b.* c. 2. *d.*

Bussel, Robert, fines, 3 John, I. 397. c. 1. *f.* Hugh de Bussel intitled to the honor of Pelwrdam, 4 John, I. 487. c. 2. *u.* William Buscel of Yorkshire, 7 Henry iii. I. 492. c. 1. *u.* Richard de Bussel arrested, 4 Henry iii. I. 495. c. 2. *f.*

Butlership of England held by William Martel, temp. Henry i. I. 50. Perquisites and offices of the king's butler, 1 John, I. 459. c. 2. *t.*

Buttesthorn, Walter de, 5 Edward ii. II. 7. c. 1. *e.* One of the executors of John de Berewyk, II. 31. c. 1. *m.*

Buzun, Simon, 10 John, I. 489. c. 2. *q.*

Byflet, Richard de, accompts for John de

INDEX.

de Montague, sherif of Somerset and Derbyshire, 34 Edward i. II. 180. c. 2. *k*.

ykot, William, his countertally, 26 Edward i. II. 258. c. 1. *e*. Again, II. 260.

Byriden in the bishopric tallaged, 11 Edward i. I. 720. c. 2. *u*.

Byrking, to whom it belonged, 5 Richard i. I. 432. c. 1. *w*.

Byrlande in Devonshire, a silver mine there, 24 Edward i. I. 291. The warden and controller of it, 2 Edward ii. II. 8. c. 2. *m*.

Byrlay, William de, has the great seal under his custody, 30 Edward i. I. 73. c. 2. *r*.

Byroun, John, sherif of Yorkshire, 27 Edward i. II. 106. John Byrun, sherif of Yorkshire, 26 Edward i. II. 234. c. 2. *s*.

C.

C, William de, 11 Henry iii. II. 177. c. 2. *g*.

Cabuis, John, fines for a plea, 1 Richard i. I. 432. c. 1. *t*.

Cacegai, Walter, had the land of Pacey, an. 1184. I. 168. c. 2.

Cade, William, seems to belong to the treasury, 7 Henry ii. I. 602. c. 2. *d*. Receives the king's mony by writ, 2 Henry ii. I. 688. c. 1. *m*. 693. c. 2. *r*. and 695. c. 1. *w*.

Cadiol, Turchil, 14 Henry ii. I. 553. c. 2. *c*. Amerc'd for not appearing before the justiciers, ibid.

Cadurcis, Patrick de, his terra in Berkshire, temp. Stephen, I. 148. c. 1. *h*. Robert de Caorces, an. 1184. I. 196. c. 1. *n*. See Chaworth, Chaurz. Thomas de Cadurcis, his tenure in Derbyshire, 2 Edward ii. I. 646. William de Chaurcis held of Alice countess of Ou, 22 Henry iii. II. 122. c. 1. *l*.

Caen, John de, the great seal under his care, 30 Edward i. I. 73. Richard de, claims Crokeston, 30 Henry ii. I. 97. c. 1. *t*. Mr. John de Cadomo, chancellor's lieutenant, 27 Edward i. I. 423. c. 1. Abbess of Caen, I. 476. c. 1. *t*. A communa granted to Caen, 5 John, I. 525. c. 1. *a*. Again, 7 Henry iii. I. 738. c. 1. *x*. Nuns of Caen had an interest in Dunmawe hundred, 5 Richard i. II. 20. c. 2. *a*.

Caernarvan or Kaernarvan, the exchequer there, 12 Edward i. II. 4. c. 2. *r, s.* 5. c. 1. *t*. Sherif of Caernarvan under the chief justice of Chester, II. 235.

Cahaignes, Richard and William de, fine for a partition of lands, 23 Henry ii. I. 103. c. 2. *i*. William de Cahaignes fines for confirmation of charters, 24 Henry ii. I. 473. c. 1. *u*. Ralf de, 15 Henry ii. I. 502. c. 2. *e*. Bertona belongs to Ralf de Cahaignes, 14 Henry ii. I. 553. c. 1. *y*. William's nine fees, 33 Henry ii. I. 649. c. 2. *h*.

Cahul, Urvey de, 1 Richard i. I. 493. c. 1. *f*. Fined to be under plevine, ib.

Cail, Oliver de, amerc'd for the slaughter of the sons of Tochi, 5 Stephen, I. 543. c. 2. *e*.

Caisn, Bartholomew de, his scutage, 7 Henry ii. I. 628. c. 2. *x*.

Caisnedoit, Simon, his terra in custody of Geoffrey the Chancellor, 5 Stephen, I. 297. c. 1. *f*.

Caisne, William de, sherif of Norfolk and Suffolk, 4 Henry ii. I. 278. c. 2. *m* The same, 7 Henry ii. I. 501. c. 2. *s*. William de Caisney or Chainey attended the king's daughter into Saxony, 13 Henry ii.

II.

INDEX.

II. 217. c. 1. *p.* See Cheney, Cheyny. Roger de Cheigny, sherif of Shropshire and Staffordshire, 9 Edward ii. II. 238.

Calcatraps or heel traps, persons fined for setting them in their lands, I. 499. c. 2. *w, x.*

Caldecot, Hugh de, passes with lands, 28 Henry ii. I. 113. c. 2.

Calehul, William de, his grant of a lease of the manor of Sokele from the bishop of Bath, 8 Edward i. I. 729. c. 2. *t.* See Cahul.

Caleston in Wiltshire, Roger de Caleston of, held that land in capite by socage, 32 Henry iii. I. 622. c. 2. *g.*

Calna, William de. See Osmund Croc. The aid of the men of Calne in Wiltshire, 14 Henry ii. I. 588. Again, 23 Henry ii. I. 604. c. 1. *l.* Its donum, 5 Henry ii. I. 697. c. 1. *r. w.* Its tallage, 10 Richard i. I. 700. c. 1. *s.* Its assise, 19 Henry ii. I. 702. c. 1. *d.* Its tallage, 1 John, I. 705. c. 2. *z.*

Calne, Ruald de, 1 Richard i. I. 98. c. 1. *i.* His livery by order of the chancellor, 5 Henry ii. I. 207. c. 1. *x.*

Calniz, William de, an. 1184. I. 168. c. 2. Seems to belong to the treasury of Caen, ibid.

Calverd, Henry de, of York, 5 Edward ii. II. 74. c. 2. *u.*

Calverley, the drengage in Northumberland of Gilbert de, 3 John, I. 487. c. 1. *p.*

Calvo Monte, Gacius de, mayor of York, 41 Henry iii. II. 154. c. 2.

Calz. See Cauz.

Camarun army, 7 Richard i. I. 663. c. 1. *r.*

Cambho, John de, 27 Edward i. II. 219.

Cambium or mint of London, I. 283. Cambia of London and Canterbury, I. 292. c. 1. *c.* Again, Cambium or mint, I. 568. c. 2. *t.* See II. 132, 133.

Cambridge, fines for the ferm of their town, and for exemption from the sherif of the county, 31 Henry ii. I. 399. c. 1. *z.* Have their ferm and a confirmation of liberties, 1 John, I. 401. c. 1. *b.* Again, 7 Henry iii. I. 414. c. 2. *p.* Men of Cambridge amerced three hundred and fifty marks by the barons, 12 John, I. 528. c. 1. *i.* Cambridge and Huntingdonshire amerced, 31 Henry iii. I. 567. c. 2. *l.* Some barons and knights here, I. 594. c. 2. *k.* Its aid, 37 Henry iii. I. 609. c. 2. *g.* The assise or tallage of Cambridge, 22 Henry ii. I. 702. c. 2. *h.* Cambridge and Huntedon have two sherifs jointly, ibid. Cambridge tallages, 14 Henry ii. I. 708. c. 2. *q.* Sir Thomas de Cantebrug, baron of the Exchequer, 2 Edward ii. II. 8. c. 2. *m.* Thomas de Cantebrugg, baron of the Exchequer, 1 Edward ii. II. 57. c. 2. *x.* and 2 Edward ii. ibid.

Cambrun, Wale de, I. 673. c. 1. *m.*

Camei, terra de, I. 205. c. 1. Ralf de Cameis seems to be sherif of Surrey and Sussex, 31 Henry iii. I. 609. c. 2. *f.* See Camoys and Kameis.

Cameis, Stephen de, his terra, 10 Richard i. I. 324. c. 1. *d.*

Camel, its tallage, 14 Henry iii. I. 708. c. 1. *o.* Was one of the king's manors, 14 Henry iii. II. 152. c. 2. *z.*

Camera regis used for his treasury, I. 157. c. 2. 158. c. 1. Again, Camera curiæ, 5 Stephen, I. 263. c. 1. The

INDEX.

The several senses of that word, I. 264. Accompts sometimes passed in Camera regis, II. 251.

Camera, Turpin de, the king's chamberlain, I. 263. c. 2. i. 264.

Camoys, Ralf de, constabulary of Windsor-castle, 15 Edward ii. I. 383. c. 1. Margaret, widow of John de Camoys, 26 Edward i. I. 466. c. 2. d. Margaret, widow of John de Cameys, 26 Edward i. II. 100. Ralf de Comeys, sherif of Surrey and Suffex, 27 Henry iii. II. 141. c. 1. r.

Camp Ernulf, Henry de, 2 John, I. 522. c. 1. o. Fines for a partition of his father's land, ibid.

Campanea, Warner de, his duel with William Fitz-Robert for the terra de Saxebi, 18 Henry ii. I. 512. c. 1. r. Richard de Campanea has share of the lands of Osbert Martel. 18 Henry ii. I. 580. c. 2. q.

Campio or pugil, I. 765. c. 1. m.

Campis, Simon de, merchant of Duay, no prise to be taken of his cloth, &c. 30 Henry iii. I. 765.

Camville, Gerard de, to be replaced in his sheriffwick of Lincolnshire, temp. Richard i. I. 22. c. 2. x. Disseised by king Richard i. I. 22. Impleaded for harbouring of robbers and adhering to earl John, I. 23. See Canvil and Chanvill.

Cancelles, Hugh de, 35 Henry iii. II. 119. c. 2. r. Had Upton in Northamptonshire, 18 Edward i. II. 248. c. 2. z.

Canci, Simon de, fines, 27 Henry ii. I. 427. c. 1. g. Walter de Canceio fines to marry whom he pleases, 5 Stephen, I. 464. c. 1. u. Robert de Cancy has the land of Scirpenbec, Yorkshire, 30 Henry iii. I. 710. c. 1. w.

Candida Casa, Christian bishop of, present at a council of Henry ii. an. 1177. I. 19.

Candle lighted not to be in the Exchequer while shut, II. 278. c. 1. u.

Candos, Roger de, 24 Henry ii. I. 211. c. 2. b. Ralf de Candos betroth'd the daughter of Richard de Flet, Norfolk, 5 Richard i. I. 503. c. 1. o. Robert de Candos, his knights in Herefordshire, 7 Henry ii. I. 628. c. 2. y. Roger de Chaundos attermin'd for his debts to the crown, 2 Edward ii. II. 209. c. 2. s.

Canevaz, for the king's chamber, I. 367. c. 2. p.

Cansi, Geoffrey de, claim'd Muleford against William de Callou, 10 John, I. 451. c. 2. c.

Cantelu, William de, 12 John, I. 481. c. 1. o. Pledge for Richard de Nevil, ibid. See Cantilupe.

Canterbury city fines for liberties, &c. 27 Edward i. I. 421. Its aid, 14 Henry ii. I. 588. c. 2. d. Its aid, 2 Henry ii. I. 693. c. 2. r. John de Cantuaria, 26 Edward i. I. 782. c. 2. John de Cantuaria, late alderman of Tower ward, Lond. 2 Edward ii. II. 235. c. 1. t. Why seiz'd into the king's hand, 18 Edward i. II. 245. c. 2. x.

Canterbury, the precedence of its primates debated at Winchester, anno 1072. I. 6. c. 1. b. That see in the king's hands before 19 Henry ii. 309. c. 1. o. Again, I. 312. c. 1. b. Its reliefs paid to the crown when the see was in the king's hands, 14 Henry ii. I. 584. c. 2. q. Its tallage, 8 John, I. 717. c. 1. i. and 34 Henry ii. I. 736. c. 1. p. and 8 Rich. i. I. 737. c. 1. s. Six aldermen of Canterbury, I. 740. Their wards enumerated, I. 741. c. 1. g. The arch-

INDEX.

archbishop had three eights out of the profits of the mint here, 29 Henry iii. II. 134. c. 1. s. Liberties of the archbishop in Rochester, II. 201. c. 1. p. The see kept void for the use of the pope, 35 Edward i. II. 224. Archbishop Steven's quinzime, 10 Henry iii. II. 291. c. 1. e.

Cantilupo, William de, one of the king's council, 3 Henry iii. I. 67. c. 1. x. Thomas de, chancellor, 49 Henry iii. I. 70. c. 2. i. 71. c. 1. k. & 234. c. 1. c. Has the grant of 500 marks a year, I. 76. c. 1. u. Robert de Cantilupo, 6 John, I. 99. c. 2. t. Walter de, an. 1184. I. 168. c. 2. Fulk de Cantelu accompts for the lands of the countess of Perch, 14 John, I. 298. c. 2. c. William de, sherif of Warwick and Leicestershire, 4 John, I. 606. c. 1. w. William and John de Cauntelou, two of the king's barons in his court, 26 Edward i. I. 655. c. 2. William de, 16 Henry iii. II. 34. c. 1. ibid. 118. c. 2. h. William de Cantilupe, sherif of Worcestershire, 10 John, II. 152. c. 2. y. Had licence to make his will before, 39 Henry iii. II. 185. c. 1. l. William, son of William de Cantilupe, 22 Henry iii. II. 222. c. 2. y.

Cantok, Roger, burgess of Bristol, 5 Edward i. II. 81. c. 1. c.

Cantorp, Siward de, 5 Stephen, I. 147. c. 2. g. Accomps for the pleas of Geoffrey de Clinton, ibid.

Canvil, Gerard de, sherif of Lincolnshire, 5 Richard i. I. 458. c. 2. k. See Chanvil. His share of the marsh between the waters of Spalding and Tid hundreds, 7 John, I. 506. c. 1. w. Cherleton was the town of Gerard de Camvil, 31 Henry ii. I. 547. c. 2. i. Geffrey de Caunvil, a baron, 26 Edward ii. I. 655. c. 2. Gerard de Canvil's fees in Oxfordshire, 4 John, I. 666. c. 1. h. Gerard, sherif of Lincolnshire, 5 John, II. 139. c. 1. g.

Capel, Robert, accompts for the scutage of the knights of the earl of Leicester, 18 Henry ii. I. 630. c. 2. e. William, deputy for the sea-ports to Brian de Lisle, 15 John, I. 774. c. 1. Robert Capel accompts for the scutage of the knights of the earl of Leicester, 19 Henry iii. II. 183. c. 1. z.

Capite, tenure in, how misunderstood, I. 620. c. 1. b. Tenure in Capite is holding immediately of the crown, and not a distinct tenure of itself, I. 621. c. 2. Holding in Capite ut de corona, required personal service more strictly than holding of an honor, I. 652.

Capoun, Robert, commissioner of the array for the wapentak of Langebrug, 16 Edward ii. II. 112. c. 2.

Carbonel, Richard, 2 John, I. 520. c. 2. h. Gilbert Carbunel had the balliage of the tower of London from earl William de Mandevil before 8 Richard i. II. 176. c. 1. y.

Carburra, William de, his lands in Cornwal discharg'd from scutage as fee-ferm, 9 Edward ii. I. 673.

Cardigan, Robert de, his nepos, before Henry iii. II. 27. c. 1. d.

Cardinal Legate, viz. Walter titulo S. Martini, signs before the archbishop of Canterbury, 3 Henry iii. I. 67. c. 1. x. Cardinal Hugh de S. Caro. 35 Henry iii. II. 202.

Cardinan, Robert de, fines in ten marks for a market in Loftwetel, Cornwal, 6 Richard i I. 399. c. 1. e.

Cardvil,

INDEX.

Cardvil, or Carlifle, Robert fon of Adam de, whofe fteward, 6 John, I. 465. c. 1. p. William de Stutevil has the ferm of Cardvil, 3 John, I. 516. c. 1. l. Adam de Cardvil, cuftomer of Newcaftle, 25 Edward i. I. 782. c. 2.

Carenton in Cornwal, its tallage, 1 John, I. 733. c. 2. t.

Carledecotes, II. 122. c. 2. p.

Carleton, William de, baron of the Exchequer, 35 Edward i. I. 74. c. 1. s. Juftice of the Jews, 18 Edward i. I. 236. And fuch had a falary of forty marks a year, ibid. Baron of the Exchequer, 26 Edward i. I. 467. c. 1. The manor of Carleton in Lindric, 30 Henry iii. I. 707. c. 2. b. Sir William de, baron of the Exchequer, 2 Edward ii. II. 8. c. 2. m. and 35 Edward i. II. 30. Again, II. 46. c. 1. u. Again, 1 Edward ii. II. 57. c. 1. x. Has a difpenfation to attend at the Exchequer when his health and affairs would permit, 2 Edward ii. II. 57. Baron, 31 Edward i. II. 63. c. 2. p. 34 Edward i. II. 65. c. 2. g. II. 71. c. 2. l. Holds pleas at Colchefter, 2 Edward ii. II. 84. Occurs, 26 Edward i. II. 100. c. 2. m. Baron, 19 and 27 Edward i. II. 265. c. 1. m. William de Carleton, auditor, 20 Edward i. II. 291. c. 2. g. Baron, 31 Edward i. II. 304. c. 1. n.

Carlifle, Walter bifhop of, was treafurer before 40 Henry iii. I. 271. c. 1. h. Canons of, 16 Henry ii. I. 560. c. 1. s. Walter, bifhop, accompts for the tallage of Walter le Buffle of London, 14 Henry iii. I. 709. c. 1. t. Bifhop, Walter Mauclerc, treafurer of the Exchequer for life, 16 Henry iii. II. 33. But depos'd, 17 Henry iii. II. 34. c. 2. y. The mine of Carlifle, 19 Henry ii. II. 205.

Carlifle has a confirmation of liberties, 5 Richard i. I. 399. c. 1. d. See 420. c. 2. s. To have coroners in the city among themfelves, ibid.

Carminou, John de, 9 Edward ii. I. 650. c. 1. k. Has a writ of difcharge for his fmall fees of Moreton, Cornwal, ibid.

Carneton in Cornwal, its aid, 23 Henry ii. I. 604. c. 2. m.

Carrou, William de, fines in forty ounces of gold for the land of Muleford, 10 John, I. 451. c. 2. c. Nicolas de Carro, 52 Henry iii. II. 80. c. 1. z.

Carter, Reimun le, has the commiffion of array for the wapentak of Scardeburgh, 16 Edward ii. II. 112. c. 2.

Cartmel, or Kertmel, prior, fines to have his charter of privileges mended, 7 Henry iii. I. 412. c. 2. e.

Carton, Walter de, one of Richard Malebiffe's knights in the flaughter of the Jews at York, before 4 Richard i. I. 483. c. 1.

Carucat, Richard i. demands two fhillings from every one, I. 24. c. 1. y. Carucage of the honor of Lancafte for the king's ranfom, 6 Richard i. I. 593. c. 1. a. Two fhillings for each carue, 5 Henry iii. I. 706. c. 2. f. For land held by bafe tenure, l. 729.

Carun, Ralf de, accompts for the pleas of Geoffrey de Clinton in Norfolk, 5 Stephen, I. 147. c. 2. c. Wichard de Charun, fherif of Northumberland, amerc'd for not making his profer, 1 Edward i. II. 155. c. 1. h.

Carwinton

INDEX.

Carwinton in Cornwal, its aid, 23 Henry ii. I. 604. c. 2. *m.*

Cary, William de, fines for the manor of Mideford, Berkshire, and for the land of Reimund Grossus, his uncle, 15 John, I. 491. c. 1. *f.*

Casamentum, marriage, Pref. xxvi.

Cassel, Henry de, the liber hospes of the knights Templars, 16 Henry ii. I. 746. c. 2. *f.*

Casteillun, Henry de, accompts for the chamberlainship of London, 8 Richard i. I. 775.

Castello, Walter de, clerk and keeper of the queen-mother's gold, 9 and 10 Edward i. I. 351. c. 2. *e.* Nicolas de, 4 Edward i. I. 391. c. 2. *y.* Bartholomew de Castello employ'd in the payments of London to the king, 1 Edward i. I. 610. c. 2. *i.* Nicolas de, has the hundreds of Humilierd, Blafeld, Taverham, and Walsham, 9 Edward i. II.2.c.2. *f.* Bartholomew de Castello, keeper of the London mint, 2 Edward i. II. 90. c. 1. *r.* Nicolas de Castello, clerk of the Exchequer, 4 Edward i. II. 2. c. 2. *f.* Bartholomew de Castello, keeper of the London mint, 2 Edward i. II. 90. c. 1. *r.* Nicolas de Castello, clerk of the Exchequer, 4 Edward i. II. 112. c. 2. *f.* Bartholomew de Castello accompts for the mint of London, 7 Edward i. II. 135. c. 1. *t.* Nicolas, ibid. The executors of Bartholomew Castle, 25 Edward i. II. 187. Bartholomew occurs, 1 Edward i. II. 207. c. 2. *gg.* Nicolas, clerk of the Exchequer, 56 Henry iii. II. 264. First Remembrancer, 14 Edward i. ibid. 265. c. 1. *l.* Allowed charges and expences in making out the summonces, 13 Edward i. II. 268. c. 2. *a.* William de, audites the accompts, 10 Henry iii. II. 291. c. 2. *f.* Sir Walter de Castel, chamberlain of the Exchequer, before 22 Edward i. II. 298. c. 1. *n.* Nicolas de, remembrancer, 3 Edward i. II. 320. c. 2. *e.*

Castile, the mayordomo's in that kingdom, I. 55.

Castles, an enumeration of many of them in England, 15 Edward ii. I. 383. An enumeration of the barons of the Exchequer assign'd to survey the king's Castles and manors, 1 Edward ii. II. 67. c. 1. *q.*

Castre in Lincolnshire, its tallage, 10 Richard i. I. 705. c. 1. *w.* Again, 33 Henry ii. I. 713. c. 1. *d.*

Castro-Radulphi, Domina de, daughter to the earl of Glocester, 1 Richard i. I. 369. c. 1. *x.*

Catalunna, earls of, I. 54.

Catell, called Averia, I. 438. c. 1. *c.*

Cathangre, that land given to William de Wroteham by Richard i. I. 477. c. 2. *m.*

Catmera, Adam de, sherif of Berkshire, 13 Henry ii. II. 205. c. 2. *q.*

Cattun and Hamelinton, two challenges about the right of them, between Dammartin and Hacun, 6 Henry iii. I. 445. c. 2. *d.* Catton in Yorkshire tallaged, 30 Henry iii. I. 710. c. 1. *w.*

Caturca, John de, had the coinage of London and Canterbury, 14 Edward i. II. 90.

Caudebec, Alexander de, in Cumberland, 8 John, I. 428. c. 2. *d.* How a moiety of that village belong'd to Robert de Curtenai, ibid

Caudeston,

INDEX.

Caudeſton, William de, official of the archdeacon of Norwich, 14 Henry iii. II. 317. c. 1. a.

Cavelin in Normandy, the terra of Richard de, before 2 John, I. 521. c. 2. l.

Caugi, terra Ralf de, 33 Henry ii. I. 4. c. 4. The honor or barony of Ralf de Caugi, in the king's hand, 31 Henry ii. I. 297. c. 2. r.

Caune in Wiltſhire, its donum, 33 Henry ii. I. 634. c. 1. q. See Calne.

Caunvil, John de, late ſherif of Eſſex and Hertfordſhire, 55 Henry iii. II. 242. c. 1. u. See Canvil.

Cauſton, that town's aids for marrying the king's daughter, 14 Henry ii. I. 589. c. 2. f. Its tallage in Norfolk, 9 Richard i. I. 705. c. 1. u. The manor of John de Burgh, 36 Henry iii. I. 752. c. 1. g.

Cauz, Geoffrey de, witneſs to a charter, 16 Henry iii. I. 64. c. 1. m. Maud de Calz or Cauz, her land of Leiſſington in the king's hands, 8 John, I. 298. c. 2. b. Roger de Chalz, 29 Henry ii. I. 427. c. 1. k. Maud fines in a thouſand and fifty marks, 6 Henry iii. I. 492. c. 1. s. Geoffry de Cauz, 16 Henry iii. II. 34. c. 1.

Caworſini & Ultramontani, II. 70. Thoſe ſocieties to raiſe money, ibid.

Cayly, Oſbert de, 2 Edward ii. I. 47. c. 1. y. Witneſs to a charter of Maud mareſchalleſs of England, ibid.

Ceccano, John de, his grant to the abbey of S. Maria del Fiume, an. 1209. I. 571. c. 1. f.

Ceddre manor, the biſhop of Bath's, 14 Henry iii. I. 418. c. 1. h. Ceddra or Cheddre, its aid, 14 Henry ii. I. 588. c. 2. c.

Celeſtia, wife of Richard, ſon of Colbern of Chent, 32 Henry ii. I. 323. c. 1. w. Fines to the king, that ſhe might have the wardſhip of her own children, and not marry againſt her will, ibid.

Cendaz, I. 426. c. 1. b.

Cerne, Ralf de, cuſtos of Devonſhire, 14 Henry iii. I. 277. c. 1. y. The abbat's fine and ſcutage, 14 Henry iii. I. 661. c. 1. i. Abbat de Cerne in Dorſetſhire has a plea about land with the prior of St Swithun, 27 Henry iii. II. 78. c. 1. q. William de Cerne, ibid. Philip de Cerne, ſherif of Somerſetſhire, 45 Henry iii. II. 79. c. 1. y.

Certificates of knights fees, I. 575. and I. 632.

Ceſtreford, the town of Maud, who is ſtyled mareſcalla, I. 47. How granted to St Mary and St George, Thefford, ibid. c. 1. y. Richard de Ceſtreford, clerk of the receipt of the Exchequer, 52 Henry iii. II. 18. c. 2. q. Again, II. 304. c. 1. m.

Ceſtrehunt, its tallage, 19 Henry ii. I. 701. c. 1. z. Pleas held here, 38 Henry iii. I. 761. c. 1.

Ceſtreton by Cambridge, I. 447. c. 2. e. Who claimed land there, 5 John, I. 517. c. 1. p. Cheſterton hundred, I. 543. c. 1. x. Its aſſiſe or tallage, 22 Henry ii. I. 702. c. 2. b. Belonged to the priory of Bernewel, 25 Henry iii. II. 119. c. 1. q.

Chaceporc, Peter, keeper of the wardrobe, 37 Henry iii. I. 609. c. 2. h. Again, 30 Henry iii. I. 709. c. 2. u. Peter de Chacepork, keeper of the wardrobe, accompts for more money than he had received, 29 Henry iii. II. 116. c. 2. y. II. 117. c. 1. z. Accompts for the receipts in the wardrobe,

INDEX.

wardrobe, 36 Henry iii. II. 129. c. 2. d. Occurs, 35 Henry iii. II. 202. c. 1. w.

Chacia, in the Exchequer, ibid. II. 258.

Chadelefwurthe, the land of Robert, fon of Ralf de Chadelefwurthe, I. 673. c. 1. m. Held in focage of Thomas de St Valery, ibid.

Chainefbery, that land belonged to Jordan Tolebu, 24 Henry ii. I. 211. c. 2. b.

Chaifneduit, Ralf, his aid for marrying Maud the king's daughter, 14 Henry ii. I. 474. c. 2. o.

Chaifnet in Berkfhire, Ralf de, his fine, 29 Henry ii. I. 430. c. 1. z. Nicolas de Chaifneto imprifoned for the foreft, &c. 5 Richard i. I. 493. c. 1. h. Walter de Chaifnet, 16 Henry ii. I. 544. c. 1. k. Fines for the efcape of his fervant, who had been guilty of manflaughter, ibid.

Chaifney, William de, accompts for the ferm of Norfolk, 9 Henry ii. II. 252. c. 1. r.

Chaldefy, belonged to William de Montague, 1 John, I. 485. c. 2. f.

Chalveduna, Algarus, prefbyter of, 14 Henry ii. I. 586. c. 2.

Chalvely, Gilbert de, one of the theins of Northumberland, 1 Richard i. I. 698. c. 2. o. See Calverly.

Chamberlain of the king, I. 55. From ancient time hereditary, I. 58. Anciently acted in the king's court and Exchequer, I. 59. Chamberlain [of the Exchequer] in fee, I. 75. and II. 14. In the firft period fat among the barons, II. 295. Afterwards deputed ones were knights, ibid. c. 1. w. The feveral ways of prefenting them, ibid. Richard le Chamberleng of the Exchequer nominated by William Malduyt earl of Warwic, 51 Henry iii. II. 296. c. 2. b. Chamberlains of the Exchequer in fee, II. 299. Chamberlains of the Exchequer had an allowance of two knights, 9 Henry iii. II. 311.

Chamberlain, Gilbert, fines for an appeal, 3 Henry iii. I. 445. c. 1. x. Martin la Chamberleng belonged to H. de Ver, 31 Henry iii. I. 593. c. 2. f. Richard Chamberlain clerk of the Exchequer, 35 Henry iii. II. 18. c. 1. m.

Chamberlain of London, what duties he received for the king's ufe, I. 775. &c. Chamberlain of the king's wines, or Cameraria Londoniæ, I. 765. &c. Two chamberlains of London, 5 Edward i. I. 770. c. 1. y, z. William de Betoyne chamberlain of London, 26 Edward i. I. 783. c. 1. s.

Champel, William de, of Devonfhire, 5 John, I. 438. c. 1. c. Fines to have Oliver de Traci fummoned, ibid.

Champeynes, Robert de, fon of Juliana, daughter of Fulk de Neweham, 29 Henry ii. I. 82. c. 1. b. His final concord with the prior and monks of Rochefter, I. 155. and I. 213. c. 1. p. Roger le Champenois, 14 Henry iii. II. 78. c. 1. o. Robert de Champeynes had Dodington in Northamptonfhire, 18 Edward i. II. 248. c. 2. y.

Chancel, Guy de, accompts for three hundred twenty-feven fees of the honor of Gloucefre, 15 John, I. 639. c. 1. o. Guy de Chancels accompts for the barony of William de Beauchamp, 15 John, I. 717. c. 1. k.

Chancellor ordinarily fat at the Exchequer among the barons, Pref. v. c. 2. b.

INDEX.

2. *b.* Was a churchman in Sicily, France, and Germany, I. 60. In England was the king's chief chaplain, ibid. Had the care of the king's chancery and chapel, ibid. His power advanced upon the decline of the high justicier, I. 52. During life, I. 63. Chancellor and lieutenant of the Exchequer the same person, I. 75. c. 1. *t.* Chancellor of England his allowance, I. 76, c. 1. *u.* Again, 52 Henry iii. I. 76. c. 2. *w.* The chancellor's allowance according to the red book, I. 194. Sat in the Exchequer, temp. Stephen, I. 206. Chancellor of the Exchequer was the treasurer's lieutenant, I. 291. c. 2. *b.* and I. 303. Seem to be two chancellors at one time, data per manus S. Wellensis and J. de Gray, 1 John, I. 401. c. 1. *a.* Peter Fitz Adam amerced an hundred pound for not coming at the chancellor's summonce, 3 Richard i. I. 564. c. 1. *a.* Chancellor appoints a sherif of Devonshire, 8 Edward ii. I. 31. c. 2. *q.* And declares a counsellor, ibid. Chancellor of the Exchequer seems to have been appointed as a check on the treasurer, I. 113.

Chancery and Exchequer, its antiquity, I. 178. c. 1. *z.* The originals of the Chancery, II. 115. Chancery in ancient times usually held at the Exchequer, II. 254. What estreats or extracts of the Chancery were, ibid. Ancient rolls of Chancery in the tower of London, ibid. Clerks in Chancery and Exchequer not formerly well distinguished, II. 263.

Chandeler, John le, of London, not tallaged with the citizens, I. 728. c. 1. *o.*

Chaning, a manor of the bishop of Sarum, its tallage, 33 Henry ii. I. 634. c. 2.

Chanvil, Gerard de, sherif of Lincolnshire, 5 Richard i. I. 332. c. 1. *y.* See Canvil. Richard de Chanvil sherif of Berkshire, 2 Henry ii. II. 166. c. 1. *r.*

Chapels of St John and Stephen, Westminster, have five chaplains appropriated, 29 Henry iii. I. 394. c. 1. *h.* John de la Chapel, parson of the chapel of St Thomas the Martyr on Lincoln bridge, 9 Edward ii. I. 745. c. 1. *a.* Chapel of St Cross of Haliwel belonged to the scholars of Merton, 9 Edward ii. ibid.

Chaplein, Walter, prebendary of Sarum about 31 Henry ii. I. 311. c. 1. *d.*

Chapmanneshal, in the city of Winchester, the ferm of it, I. 341. c. 2. *o.* &c.

Chappel, Wimar, sherif of Norfolk and Suffolk, 23 Henry ii. I. 131. c. 2. *b.* Again, 25 Henry ii. I. 212. c. 1. *m.* H. de Capella, 16 Henry iii. II. 34. c. 1. Attests the king's charter, ibid.

Charkason, Maurice de, 26 Henry ii. I. 289. c. 2. *t.* Had livery as the king's cambitor, ibid.

Charles, emperor, an. 883. I. 25. c. 2. *g.* Adjudged causes in his own person, I. 91.

Charne, Guichard or Givehard de, accompts for the fee of Durham, 11 Edward i. I. 720. c. 1. *t.* John Chern occurs, 14 John, I. 792. c. 1. *y.* Fined for an unjust detention, ibid.

Charta, its several significations, Pref. xv. xvi. Charters of confirmation of liberties under Henry ii. and king John, I. 396, &c. Magna Charta explained, I. 455. The great charter

INDEX X.

ter of king John, Henry iii. and Edward i. I. 528. c. 2. *m*. Certificates of the knights fees in the Exchequer called Cartæ baronum, 14 Henry ii. I. 575. 577. c. 1. Farther discussed, I. 578. A passage in Magna Charta against granting leave to the great lords to demand aid of their tenants, except in certain cases, temp. John, I. 618. c. 1. *i*.

Chaschia Brullii de Keinesham, belonging to Bristol, I. 333. c. 2. *s*.

Chascur, I. 118. c. 1. *q*. Chascurs or dogs for game, I. 272.

Chastellione, Guy de, earl of St Pauls, his relief for the lands left him by the countess Isabella, made Guy her heir, 4 Henry iii. I. 319. c. 2. *f*.

Chattels of felons, fugitives, and outlaws belonged to the crown, I. 342. And of usurers, recreants, intestates, felo's de se, and executed persons, I. 342, 343.

Chauches of Normandy, Ralf de, 2 John, I. 520. c. 2. *b*. One of the pledges of Roger de Planes, ibid.

Chaucumbe, Hugh de, justicier of Normandy, 2 John, I. 171. Again, 3 John, I. 171. c. 2. *x*. Has his debt to the king respited so long as he shall be in his service, I. 175. His relief for six knights fees, 14 Henry ii. I. 316. c. 1. *y*. Sherif of Staffordshire, 7 and 8 Richard i. I. 459. c. 2. *p*. Hugh de Chaucumb, 30 Henry ii. I. 497. c. 2. *g*. Robert's debts to the crown to be first paid by his executors, 22 Henry iii. II. 183. c. 2. *d*.

Chaumberlein, Peter le, marries Isabel, one of the heiresses of Adam de Faintre, before 15 Edward i. I. 321. c. 1. *q*.

Chauncy, Frere Joseph de, assessor of the Jews tallage, 3 Edward i. I. 243, 244. Treasurer of the Exchequer, 6 Edward i. II. 5. c. 1. *x*. William de Chauncy de Monketon, 26 Edward i. II. 45. c. 2. *t*. See Josep, Kauncy.

Chaurea, Roger de, amerced for putting one to the tryal of water without warrant, 31 Henry ii. I. 547. c. 1. *a*. Robert de Chaury of the Exchequer, 33 Henry iii. II. 129. c. 1. *c*. Made chamberlain by the queen's presentation, 39 Henry iii. II. 299. c. 2. *t*.

Chaurz, Patrick de, an. 1171. witness to a charter and judgment of the bishop of Bath, I. 111. Is pardoned for his queen's gold by the queen, 28 Henry iii. I. 352. c. 1. *g*. Patrick de Chaurcis his scutage and fees under the honor of Striguil, 33 Henry ii. I. 636. c. 2. *y*.

Chauvant, Peter de, one of the barons in the king's court, 26 Edward i. I. 655. c. 2.

Chaworth or Cadurcis, Pain de, assessor of the tallage on the Jews, 3 Edward i. I. 244. ibid. c. 1. *r*. Thomas de Chaworth has the manor of Middleton, Derbyshire, in fee, 14 Edward ii. I. 534. c. 1. See de Cadurcis.

Chederington, William de, custos of the honor of Wilekin de Beauchamp, 11 John, I. 644. c. 2. *p*.

Chedny, John de, sherif of Bedford and Bukinghamshire, 10 Edward i. II. 178. c. 1. *o*.

Chelardeston, II. 200. c. 2. *h*.

Chelefeud, William de, late sherif of Kent, 18 Edward i. II. 245. c. 2. *x*.

Chelesford, Petronil de, her action against the priory of Sudwerck, 3 Richard i. I. 106. c. 1. *s*.

Chelfeld, Simon de, 29 Henry ii. I. 212. Simon de Chelefeld, 10 Edward i. I. 266. c. 2. *k*.

Chel-

INDEX.

Chelmarford, II. 22. c. 1. r. See Northchelmelesford.

Chelmodefton tallaged, I. 725. c. 2. g.

Chelton in Hampſhire, its aſſiſe, 22 Henry ii. I. 702. c. 2. i.

Chelvedun, its aſſiſe or tallage, 19 Henry ii. I. 701. c. 1. z.

Chent, or Kent, I. 132. c. 2. l. I. 137. c. 1. o. I. 129. c. 1. f. and I. 145. c. 2. t. paſſim. Its donum, I. 695. c. 1. u.

Cheny, Edmund de, married Johan, widow of John Shench, 9 Edward ii. II. 85.

Cheppman, Robert le, and Simon the merchant, amerced for the defect of their cloth, 13 Henry iii. I. 567. c. 1. e.

Cheriton manor, in Wilts, belonged to the knights Templars, I. 265. c. 1. d.

Cherleton, Berks, terra de, to whom it belonged, 3 John, I. 106. c. 2. z. Cherleton the town of Gerard de Canvil, 31 Henry ii. I. 547. c. 2. i. Thomas de Cherlinton held in ſocage, 9 Edward ii. I. 673. c. 2. n. Cherleton in Gloceſterſhire, the land of Walter de Eſſelega before 31 Henry iii. I. 755. c. 2. r. Deſcended to Mabel Revel, or Rivel, ibid. Cherton, Glouc. how far it belonged to a knight of Walter de Eſſeley, 14 Henry iii. II. 116. c. 1. u. Alan de Cherleton his caſe, 12 Edward ii. II. 191.

Chert, Winod de, his land, temp. Henry ii. I. 205. c. 1.

Chertſey abbey, 5 Stephen, 1. 206. c. 2. s. In cuſtody of Geoffrey the chancellor, 5 Stephen, I. 306. c. 1. q. Has the manors of Eggeham and Thorp, 15 John, I. 490. c. 2. w. Pays for its knights fees, 7 Henry ii. I. 628. c. 2. x. Again, 2 Henry ii. I. 642. c. 2. z. Its carucage, I. 730. c. 1. x.

Cheſter, that biſhoprick in the king's hands, 31 Henry ii. I. 310. c. 2. y. Roger conſtable of Cheſter his redemption, 5 John, I. 388. c. 1. b. Lucia counteſs of Cheſter fined not to marry, 5 Stephen, I. 464. c. 1. x. Earl of Cheſter's claim on the honor of Croyl and Scye, 2 John, I. 518. c. 2. x. Earl of Cheſter, 7 Richard i. I. 591. c. 2. t. Roger conſtable of Cheſter has an aid from his tenants for his ranſom, 5 John, I. 615. c. 1. y. William conſtable of Cheſter, temp. Henry i. I. 625. c. 1. m. Hugh earl of, ibid. c. 2. Roger earl of, 14 Henry iii. II. 27. c. 2. g. Ranulf earl of, 16 John, II. 43. c. 1. m. Ranulf earl, whoſe plegius, 16 John, II. 211. c. 1. b. Sherif of Carnarvan diſtrained by the chief juſtice of Cheſter, II. 235.

Cheſtrefeld, William de, 12 Edward ii. II. 66. c. 2. o. Affeered the king's amerciaments, ibid.

Chevage of Judaiſm, I. 254.

Cheverel, Wiltſhire, I. 634. c. 2.

Cheveringwrth, William de, 9 John, I. 480. c. 1. k. Fined for the king's letter, ibid.

Cheverons, I. 500. c. 1. b.

Chevil, William de, the perquiſites and duties attending his butlerſhip, 1 John, I. 459. c. 2. t.

Chevifance, II. 72.

Cheyles, Gilbert, ſherif of Lincoln, amerced, 40 Henry iii. II. 236. c. 2. f. and II. 284.

Cheyny, Roger de, accompts for the ſherif of Herefordſhire, 56 Henry iii. II. 181. c. 1. l. See Caiſnei.

Chiche, Thomas, of Canterbury, 53 Henry iii. I. 727. c. 1. m. Collector

INDEX.

of the tallage there, 32 Edward i. I. 740. c. 2. *f.* Alderman of Burgate ward, 32 Edward i. I. 741. c. 1. *g.*

Chichester, Ralf, bishop of, had the king's chancery during life, 11 Henry iii. I. 63. John Langeton, bishop of Chichester, chancellor of England, 1 Edward ii. I. 75. c. 1. *t.* Henry, archdeacon of Chichester, fermer of the bishoprick, 16 Henry ii. I. 307. c. 1. *y.* Some accompt of its ferm, 15 Henry iii. I. 334. c. 2. *x.* Canons of Chichester fine for their liberties, 14 John, I. 411. c. 2. *x.* The bishop amerced for hunting without licence in the king's escheats, 33 Henry ii. I. 562. c. 1. *y.* Bishop Hilary's certificate of the knights fees of his see, temp. Henry ii. I. 576. His scutage, I. 578. c. 1. *c, d.* The donum of Chichester, 5 Henry ii. I. 697. c. 2. *y.* Stephen de Berksted elect of, 56 Henry iii. I. 718. c. 2. *p.* See I. 744. c. 2. *x.* The quinzime of this port, 6 John, I. 772. c. 2. Ralf bishop of, 15 Henry iii. II. 2. In the king's hand, 11 John, II. 252. c. 1. *x.*

Chicsand, prior of, his convention, 9 John, I. 480. c. 2. *m.*

Chienewe, William, fines for William Whitewey's office, &c. 5 Stephen, I. 457. c. 1. *k.*

Chigewel, to whom it belonged, 2 John, I. 434. c. 2. *m.* Aubrey de Chigewel, uncle of Geoffrey Malduit, ibid. Hamon de, mayor of London, 15 Edward ii. II. 98. Sherif of London, 8 Edward ii. II. 161. c. 2. *q.*

Childecnol, that land granted to the abbat of Stanley near Chipeham, Wiltshire, 3 John, I. 217. c. 1. *i.* By Michael Cnoel, ibid.

Childon, amerced, I. 556. c. 2. *t.*

Chileham castle, the property of Fulbert de Doura, 1 John, I. 485. c. 2. *e.* Richard de Chileham amerced for taking a whale, Kent, 30 Henry iii. I. 548. c. 2. *y.*

Chiltham, Glocestershire, its aid, 23 Henry ii. I. 604. c. 1. *k.* Its tallage, 7 Richard i. I. 703. c. 2. *n.*

Chimil, William, custos of St Mary, York, 10 Richard i. I, 714. c. 1. *f.*

Chinun, the provost of, 2 John, I. 174. c. 2. *k.* Employed about the king's engines, ibid.

Chippeham, in Wiltshire, 14 Henry ii. I. 217. c. 1. *i.* and I. 589. Its aid, 23 Henry ii. I. 604. c. 1. *l.* The donum of Chepeham, 33 Henry ii. I. 634. c. 1. *q.*

Chirographa and Chirographers, I. 237, &c. Chirographa to be brought into the treasury, II. 257.

Chirographum, to be duly signed and attested, an. 1211. I. 110.

Chisenhale, John de, clerk of the summonces, 18 Edward ii. II. 293. c. 1. *p.*

Chishul, John de, archdeacon of London, and king's chancellor, 49 Henry iii. I. 70. c. 2. *i.* and II. 55. c. 2. *m.* Dean of St Paul's, &c. 53 Henry iii. II. 170. c. 1. *h.* Mr John de Chishul, baron of the Exchequer, 48 Henry iii. II. 318. c. 2. *k.*

Chivill, Hugh, I. 457. c. 2. *w.* The wardship of his office and wife, ibid.

Christ's Church, Canterbury, that priory had the town of Sutchirch, 9 Richard i. I. 113. Some accompt of their lands, I. 204. c. 2. *k.* What they got by the expulsion of the Jews, 19 Edward i. I. 261. c. 2. *s.* Have a grant to receive the French king's hundred modii of wine annually

INDEX.

ally cuſtom free, temp. John, I. 766. c. 1. *o.*

Church, Jeremy of London fined 100 pounds for refuſing to come out of ſanctuary, 26 Henry ii. I. 404. c. 1. *b.*

Cigoinie, Engelarde de, receives ten thouſand marks for the king, 11 John, I. 384. c. 1. *l.* Seems to be the king's treaſurer at Briſtou, 12 John, I. 606. c. 2. *x.* Sherif of Glouceſterſhire and juſticier, 12 John, II. 146. c. 2. *c.* Engelarde de Ciconia, 11 Henry iii. II. 214. c. 2. *s.*

Cinnoc, Sir William de, 10 John, I. 489. c. 2. *q.* One of the jury in Robert de Mandevil's caſe, ibid.

Circuits, who were appointed to go them, 16 Henry ii. I. 140.

Ciriton, William de, I. 428. c. 2. *e.* Fines for the land of Geoffrey de Boſco, ibid.

Ciſſor, Hugh, cuſtos of the ulnage, before 25 Edward i. I. 785. c. 2. *a.*

Clahale, Hugh de, his fiſhery of Staundon, 42 Henry iii. II. 18. c. 2. *n.*

Clapham, Yorkſhire, Alexander, parſon of, his donum, 9 Richard i. I. 699. c. 1. *r.*

Clare and Hertford, Richard and Gilbert, earls of, towards the cloſe of Henry iii. I. 101. c. 2. *e.* Some accompt of their eſtate, ibid. Earl of, 3 Richard i. I. 105. c. 2. *r.* Earl of Clare, 16 Henry ii. I. 140. Earl of Clare has the tertius denarius of Hertfordſhire, 3 Henry ii. I. 281. c. 2. *g.* Richard earl of Clare married to Maud, eldeſt daughter of John earl of Lincoln, I. 326. c. 2. *n.* G. earl of Clare, 3 Henry iii. I. 529. c. 1. *o.* Earl of Clare had more than 140 knights fees, 14 Henry ii. I. 572. c. 1. *l.* His eſcuage towards the king's ranſom, 6 Richard i. I. 590. c. 2. *l.* Occurs again, viz. earl Richard, 31 Henry iii. I. 594. c. 2. *i.* G. de Clare earl of Gloceſter, 18 Edward i. I. 598. c. 2. *e.* See I. 660. c. 1. *d.* I. 664. c. 1. *z.* I. 666. c. 1. *h.* ibid. c. 2. *l.* Richard de Clare, earl of Gloceſter and Hertford, of the king's council, 39 Henry iii. I. 712. c. 1. *a.* Gilbert de Clare earl of Gloceſter and Hertford, 2 Edward ii. I. 728. Earl of Clare has the tertius denarius of Hertfordſhire, 6 Henry ii. II. 164. c. 1. *c.*

Clarel, William, has a commiſſion of array for the wapentake of Strafford, 16 Edward ii. II. 112. c. 1.

Clarendon, ſtatutes of, why prejudicial to England, I. 182. In Wiltſhire, its aid, 23 Henry ii. I. 604. c. 1. *l.* King's houſes there, ibid. Walter de Gatelyn cuſtos of that manor, 12 Edward ii. II. 292.

Clarho wapentak in Yorkſhire tallaged, 9 Richard i. I. 699. c. 1. *r.*

Clavering, John de, a baron in the Scotch war, 26 Edward i. I. 655. c. 1. The liberty of the hundred of Clavering, 5 Edward i. II. 178. c. 2. *p.*

Claverlai in Shropſhire tallaged, 1 John, I. 705. c. 2. *y.*

Clayhangre, Tocgieve, wife of Oſbert Wreng de, her fate, 7 John, I. 498. c. 2. *p.* Alyne Lovel of Clayhangre, 1 Edward ii. II. 122. c. 2. *r.*

Cleeriis, Hugh de, a knight of Fulk earl of Anjou, I. 53. His accompt of the ſeneſchalcy of France, I. 53. c. 2. *a.*

Clements Dane, London, that pariſh, 10 John, I. 218. c. 1. *p.*

Clemeſton in Cornwal, its aid, 23 Henry ii. I. 604. c. 2. *m.*

Clendon,

INDEX.

Clendon, Richard and William de, 10 John, I. 151. c. 1. w. Fined for an accord, ibid.

Clerc, Nicolas le, sherif of Essex and Hertfordshire, 15 Henry ii. II. 164. c. 1. d. Clerks in Chancery and Exchequer not formerly well distinguished, II. 263. Twelve yearly marks for the maintenance of two clerks, 19 Edward ii. II. 271. Treasurer's clerks, II. 303.

Clere hundred in Hampshire, I. 543. c. 1. w. Nicolas de Clere king's treasurer in Ireland, temp. Edward i. II. 136. Again, 20 Edward i. II. 237. c. 2. o.

Clerenbold abbat, a benefactor to the abbey of Feversham before Henry iii. I. 413. c. 2. k.

Clerfai was with the king's enemies at Leicester before 20 Henry ii. I. 344. c. 2. b.

Clergy and Religious, their lands exempt from common amerciaments, 35 Henry iii. I. 540. c. 1. c. No prises on the clergy, I. 765. Used to be punished by the bishop, II. 249.

Clerkenwel, prioress of, 9 Edward ii. I. 745. c. 1. a.

Clermund, Pain de, his fees in Middlesex, 27 Henry iii. I. 682. c. 1. r.

Cliffe in Yorkeshire, its tallage, 30 Henry iii. I. 710. c. 1. w.

Clifford, Agnes, late wife of Walter de, fines for the manor of Witham in Kent, 10 John, I. 409. c. 1. y. Walter de Clifford, 10 John, I. 474. c. 1. d. Walter de Clifford fines that Gilbert de Mortemer might be bailed, 6 Henry iii. I. 496. c. 1. k. Walter de Clifford his scutage for Wiltshire, 33 Henry ii. I. 634. c. 1. q. Robert de Clifford, 26 Edward i. I. 654. c. 1. a. Robert de Clifford commander of the king's garrison against the Scots, 27 Edward i. II. 106. Walter de Clifford surety of Walter de Beauchamp, 1 Henry iii. II. 149. Robert de Clifford, sherif in fee of Westmoreland, 27 Edward i. II. 180. See Clyfford.

Clifton, Cicely, daughter of Gervase de, 3 John, I. 428. c. 1. z. Walter de Clifton held a fee and half of the church of Chichester, temp. Henry ii. I. 476. c. 1. y. Gervase de Clifton sherif of Notinghamshire and Derbyshire, 12 Edward i. II. 173. c. 2. o.

Clinton, Geoffrey de, chamberlain, temp. Henry ii. I. 59. Founded the church of S. Mary de Kenilleworda, I. 58. c. 1. a. Henry de Clinton, 24 Henry ii. I. 103. c. 2. k. Geoffrey was justicier, 5 Stephen, I. 146. c. 2. p. Fined 310 marks for the ministry of the treasury of Winton, 5 Stephen, I. 193. c. 2. i. Ralf de Clinton, 29 Henry ii. I. 232. c. 2. t. Geoffrey de Clinton, temp. Henry i. I. 276. c. 1. r. Geoffrey de Clinton custos of the abbey of Evesham, about 5 Stephen, I. 306. c. 1. o. Geoffrey de Clinton his pleas, 5 Stephen, I. 315. c. 2. s. William de Clinton has seisure of the land of Eston as a serjeanty belonging to the king's lardry, 5 Richard i. I. 484. c. 2. u. Henry de Clinton, 5 John, I. 505. c. 2. n. Geoffrey de Clinton holds pleas of the forest, 5 Stephen, I. 541. c. 2. h.

Clipston, I. 751. c. 1. d. Robert de Clipston lieutenant in the mareschalcy to Thomas de Beauchamp, 18 Edward iii. I. 798. c. 2. Mel Haiarum de Clipston, II. 131. c. 1. g. See Clypeston and Kyngesclypston.

Clive

INDEX.

Clive manor, the prior of Worcester's, I. 408. c. 2. *w.*

Clivedon, Matthew de, fines for not attending the king into Ireland, about 12 John, I. 491. c. 1. *b.*

Cliveland, Galfrid, archdeacon of, 8 Richard I. I. 737. c. 1. *s.*

Cloth for the Exchequer, at one and six pence an ell, 22 Henry ii. I. 192. c. 1. *u.*

Clotherom, William de, has a commission of array for the wapentake of Ripoun, 16 Edward ii. II. 112. c. 1.

Clyfford, Walter de, holds by knight service and not barony, 9 Henry iii. I. 318. c. 2. *a.* See Clifford. Richard de Clifford, king's escheator on this side Trent, before 5 Edward i. II. 219. c. 1. *b.*

Clypeston, the king's house there, 29 Henry ii. I. 535. c. 1. See Clipston and Kyngesclypston.

Cnaveherst in Surrey, terra de, 3 Richard i. I. 105. c. 2. *r.* Belong'd to Elyas de Uttelwurd, ibid.

Cnoel, Michael, son of Reginald, and Everard de, their grant to the abbey of Stanley, 3 John, I. 217. c. 1. *i.*

Cnot, Walter, 14 Henry ii. I. 273. c. 1. *f.* Renders his rent in three hawks and three girfalcons, ibid.

Cobham, John de, baron of the Exchequer, 23 Edward i. I. 291. c. 2. *b.* and 15 Edward i. I. 357. c. 2. *f.* Henry de Cobham, custos of Rochester castle, 15 Edward ii. I. 382. c. 2. *h.* Henry de Cobbeham fines for the king's good-will, 4 John, I. 473. c. 2. *x.* John de Cobeham, baron of the Exchequer, discharged on that account from service in the Welch war, 5 Edward i. II. 20. c. 1. *x.* Was baron, 26 Edward i. II. 29. c. 1. *s.* Baron of the Exchequer, 4 Edward i. II. 56. c. 2. *s.* and 8 Edward i. II. 62. c. 1. *o.* Affeered amerciaments, 26 Edward i. II. 66. and 55 Henry iii. II. 223. c. 1. *d.* Simon de Cobham, one of the manucaptors for the community of the city of London, 39 Henry iii. II. 240. c. 2. *n.* John de Cobeham subscribes in absence of the treasurer, 27 Edward i. II. 255. c. 2. *t.* John de Cobeham, baron of the Exchequer, 19 and 27 Edward i. II. 265. c. 1. *m.* Henry, heir and executor of John de Cobeham, forgave the offence of Richard de Lue, II. 303.

Cocham, its ferm, 2 Henry ii. II. 146. c. 1. *x.*

Cockfeld, Walter de, 9 Edward ii. I. 600. c. 2. *i.* Discharged from the aid for marrying the king's eldest daughter, ibid.

Cocus, Adam, his land given to the prior of St. John of Jerusalem, before 3 John, I. 404. c. 1. *b.* Ralf Cocus amerced an hundred pound for the chatels of the abbat of Hide, 18 Henry ii. I. 559. c. 2. *p.* Thomas Cocus, alderman of the gild de Ponte, 26 Henry ii. I. 652. c. 1. *z.* Wascio Cocus, of Glocester, his tallage, 19 Henry ii. I. 701. c. 2. *c.* Alisaundre Cock, commissioner of the array for the wapentake of Ravenesere, 16 Edward ii. II. 112. c. 2.

Cofho, belonged to the ferm of Lancaster and earl John, 1 Richard i. I. 205. c. 2. *l.*

Coggeshal manor, the abbat of that place fines to make a park there, &c. 6 John, I. 406. c. 2. *y.*

Coining, or uttering false denarii, fined, 5 Stephen,

INDEX.

5 Stephen, I. 277. c. 2. g. New coinage, 22 Henry ii. I. 278. Coinage clipt and counterfeited prohibited by proclamation, 22 Edward i. I. 293. c. 2. f. A counterfeitor of the king's coin hanged, 21 Henry ii. I. 345. c. 2. c. Coinage of tinn in Cornwal, I. 386. c. 1. s. Old Coin prohibited, 5 Richard i. I. 503. c. 2. q. Officers of the Coinage fwore, 6 Henry iii. II. 87. c. 2. a.

Coifneres, Roger de, amerc'd for a falfe charge, 23 Henry ii. I. 553. c. 1. b. His payments in the bithoprick, 8 Richard i. I. 714. c. 1. g. 715. c. 1.

Coke, lord chief juftice, miftaken in calling efcuage a tenure, I. 620. c. 1. a. Miftakes tenancy in capite, ibid. c. 2.

Cokefeld, John de, 34 Edward i. II. 704. c. 2. u. A plea againft him in the Exchequer tranfmitted to the juftices of the common bench, ibid.

Cokerel, Elias, fines to be releafed out of prifon, 6 Henry iii. I. 495. c. 2. b. Alice Cokerel of Suwerk, 51 Henry iii. II. 19. c. 1. s.

Coket, called a part of the king's feal, I. 783. c. 1. s.

Cokinton, Henry de, has a venire facias, 52 Henry iii. II. 18. c. 2. p.

Colbern, amerc'd for a gild fans warant, 26 Henry ii. I. 562. c. 2. c.

Colchefter, granted by Rufus to Eudo Dapifer, I. 49. c. 1. b. Abbat of St. John's, ibid. c. 2. i. Its ferm, 19 Henry ii. I. 331. c. 1. i. Its burgeffes, 5 Richard i. I. 332. c. 1. x. Several perfons amerc'd here for efcapes, 29 Henry ii. I. 556. c. 2. x. Its aid for the marriage of the king's daughter, 14 Henry ii. I. 587. c. 1. Its aid, 5 Stephen, I. 602. c. 1. w. Its fcutage or donum, 5 Henry ii. I. 626. c. 2. q. John de Coleceftra accompts for the aid of that burgh, 2 Henry ii. I. 687. c. 2. k. Its donum, 5 Henry ii. I. 696. c. 2. p. Tallaged, 1 Richard i. I. 703. c. 2. m. Its tallage, 2 Henry iii. I. 706. c. 1. b. The tallage of Adam de Colchefter in Lincoln, 4 John, I. 737. c. 2. w. Accompts for its tallage, 14 Henry iii. I. 743. c. 1. n. The quinzime for the merchandife of this port, 6 John, I. 772. c. 1. i. Men of Colchefter plead poverty, 14 Henry iii. II. 214. c. 2. t. Ferm'd by Richard de Luci, 9 Henry ii. II. 252. c. 1. q.

Coldmoreton, the fridborg of it, I. 554. c. 2. t, u. Belong'd to Richard Fitz William, 22 Henry ii. ibid.

Cole, Robert, of London, his tallage, 14 Henry iii. I. 709. c. 1. s.

Colebroke, Adam de, 1 Richard i. I. 227. c. 2. n. Robert de Colbrook has a writ of Liberate de Thefauro, &c. 23 Edward i. II. 323. c. 2. d.

Colemer in Hampfhire, about 31 Henry ii. belong'd to Henry de Kernet, I. 431. John de Colemer belong'd to the receipt, 29 Henry iii. II. 117. c. 2. a.

Colefhull, Richard de, taken to the affiftance of the fherif of Oxfordfhire, 15 Edward i. I. 240. c. 1. e. Robert, fon of Elias de Colefhul fines for the manors of Aldermanfton and Sperfholt, Berkfhire, 26 Edward i. II. 8. c. 1. b.

Colevil, Thomas de, has the wardfhip of the children and land of Roger Torpel, 22 Henry ii. I. 322. c. 1. t. William de Colevil, 22 Henry ii. I. 427.

INDEX.

I. 427. c. 1. e. Henry de Colevil, justice itinerant, 18 Henry iii. I. 735. c. 1. f. Thomas de Colevil summon'd on the king's council, 31 Edward i. II. 107. c. 2. n. Robert de Colvil has the wapentak of Langebrug under a commission of array, 16 Edward ii. II. 112. c. 2. Henry de Colevil, sherif of Cambridge and Huntingdonshire, II. 196. c. 1. c. Roger de Colevill, sherif of Norfolk and Suffolk, 56 Henry iii. II. 204. c. 1. b. See Colvil.

Colewerda, Gervase de, tenant of the bishop of Chichester, temp. Henry ii. I. 576. c. 1. y.

Colewyk, Hugh de, make clerk of the summonces by the treasurer and barons of the Exchequer, 19 Edward ii. II. 294. c. 1. r.

Colingeburne manor, in Wiltshire, had been the earl of Leicester's, 19 Henry ii. I. 713 c. 1. c. Lately burnt, ibid.

Colingeham and Compton, the lands of Henry de Puteaco, temp. Henry ii. I. 483. c. 2. q.

Coliton, Devonshire, its aid, 23 Henry ii. I. 603. c. 2. i. Colinton, its assise or tallage, 19 Henry ii. I. 701. c. 1. b.

Collectors of tallages, dismes, &c. I. 355. The form of taxing and levying them, with the oath of the collectors, &c. I. 730, 731. Of the customs upon wines, I. 771.

Colmose, William, had land in Hamelton of the bailment of king John, I. 416. c. 2. z.

Colne, Henry de, to accompt for his county, 35 Henry iii. II. 10. c. 2. y. Was a sherif, 28 Henry iii. II. 177.

Cologne city has a guildhal in London, 4 Henry ii. I. 414. c. 1. l.

Colvil, Richard de, one of the judges, 10 John, I. 100. c. 1. b. G. de Colevill, one of the judges, 28 Henry ii. I. 113. c. 1. r. William de Colevil fined twenty marks for a retraxit, 23 Henry ii. I. 211. c. 1. k. Robert de Colevil, serjeant at law, 52 Henry iii. I. 236. The form of his submission for assaulting a judge, I. 236. c. 2. k. William de Coleville occurs, 3 John, I. 237. c. 2. p. See Colevil.

Columbiers, Gilbert de, justice errant, in Wiltshire, 23 Henry ii. I. 131. c. 1. y. Matthew de, married one of the heiresses of Eudo de Morevil, I. 246. c. 1. a. Thomas de Columbiers, 12 John, I. 528. c. 1. b. Baron Philip de Columbiere, 3 John, I. 665. c. 2. g. Occurs, 41 and 46 Henry iii. I. 668. c. 2. y. Quit of scutage for being in the Welch army, ibid.

Combat, sentence about it adjourned, I. 119. See Duell.

Comberton manor in Cambridgeshire, Philip de Hastang's by the service of keeping the king's falcons, 9 Edward ii. I. 642. c. 1. t. Was in wasto, 2 Henry ii. I. 693. c. 1. l.

Combustion, what, I. 275—283.

Comes, its Latin sense alter'd, Pr. xxiii.

Commissioners of divers kinds styled justiciarii, I. 140, 141, & 231.

Commoigne, or Co-monk, I. 530.

Communa granted to several towns of Normandy, 4 John, I. 525. Communia, the common business of the Exchequer, II. 114.

Conan, son of Hellis, 12 Henry ii. I. 450. c. 1. i. Fines not to plead before he is of age, ibid.

Conan,

INDEX.

Conan, the honor of earl, in custody of Ralf de Glanvil, 19 Henry ii. I. 297. c. 1. g. Again, I. 309. c. 1. p. and 21 Henry ii. I. 370. c. 2. g. Again, 22 Henry ii. I. 430. c. 1. b. The fees of earl Conan in Yorkshire, 14 Henry ii. I. 580. c. 2. r. His honor escheated, 18 Henry ii. I. 631. c. 2. l.

Concords final, I. 112. & 212. Several Concords, I. 511. c. 2. m. o. 512. c. 1. p, q. One described, temp. Henry ii. I. 500.

Consilium procerum, several of them, temp. Henry i. I. 12. c. 1. o. c. 2. p.

Constable of England, formerly hereditary, I. 39. Several acceptations of that word, ibid. His fees and allowance, I. 41. His power and jurisdiction, 13 Richard ii. I. 42. Constable of the Exchequer, II. 13. c. 2. m. 14. c. 1. n. Robert le Conestable has a commission of array for the wapentake of Herthill, II. 112. c. 2. Constable of the Exchequer, how nominated deputy by and to the constable of England, II. 282. Seems to have a concurrent power with the mareschal of the Exchequer, II. 283.

Constabulary, that honor in the king's hands, 31 Henry ii. I. 297. c. 2. y. and 30 Henry ii. I. 368. c. 1. u. and likewise 1 Richard i. I. 298. c. 2. q. and 14 John, I. 299. c. 1. d. Again, 19 Henry ii. I. 309. c. 1. p. What belong'd to the Constabulary of Bristol, 8 Henry iii. I. 333. c. 2. s. Constabulary of England, II. 281.

Constantia, countess of Britain, pays scutage for an hundred and forty knights fees for the king's ransom, 6 Edward i. I. 591. c. 2. u.

Constantiis, Walter de, vicechancellor to Henry ii. about an. 1177, I. 77. Fermed the honor of Arundel, 26 Henry ii. I. 201. c. 1. n. John de Constantiis, Walter's nephew, had been prebendary of Lincoln, I. 309. c. 2. w. Walter was archdeacon of Oxford, 22 Henry ii. I. 367. c. 2. p. Custos of the abbeys of Wilton and Ramsey, 26 Henry ii. II. 252. c. 2. w.

Constantius, son of Alulf, seems to be sherif of London, 10 Richard i. II. 21. c. 1. h.

Consuetudo, its original and modern meaning, Pref. xxiii. Signified not only regal dues and payments, I. 764. But ecclesiastical and many other sorts, ibid.

Contrataliator, John, 2 Henry ii. I. 331. c. 1. f. Contratallia, in the Exchequer, II. 258. Counters sometime used in computation, II. 261.

Convers, Alexander le, king's clerk, 25 Edward i. I. 378. c. 2. p. John le Convers made pesour of the Exchequer, 26 Edward i. II. 309. c. 1. e.

Converts, house of, I. 259. See Rolls, and I. 745. c. 1. a.

Cook, by whom land was held in Surrey, to find one at a coronation, I. 651.

Cophin, Hugh de, accompts for the abbey of Tavistock, 31 Henry ii. I. 311. c. 1. c.

Copland, county of, I. 116. c. 2. c. Countess of, Henry son of Arthur, has a recognition against her, 33 Henry ii. I. 432. c. 1. s. Copland in Cumberland belong'd to Richard de Luci, 5 John, I. 493. c. 1. i. Knights of the court of the countess of

INDEX.

of Coupland, 31 Henry ii. I. 548. c. 1. *m*. One knight's fee of it belong'd to Thomas, son of Lambert de Muleton, 38 Henry iii. I. 596. c. 2. *w*. Seems to belong to Alexander de Lucy, 4 John, II. 21. c. 1. *i*. How it pass'd from the family of Lucy to that of Muleton by marriage, before 29 Henry iii. II. 182. c. 2. *x*.

Corbet, Nicolas, of Shropshire, before 10 Edward i. I. 466. c. 1. *z*. Who married Margery his widow, ibid. Robert Corbet amerc'd before 23 Henry ii. I. 542. c. 1. *m*. Peter Corbet summon'd to the Scotch war among the Shropshire barons, 26 Edward i. I. 655. c. 1. Thomas Corbet to accompt for his county, 35 Henry iii. II. 10. c. 2. *y*. Was arrested, 35 Henry iii. II. 243. c. 2. *h*. His attorney committed, 38 Henry iii. II. 289.

Corboil, archbishop of Canterbury, temp. Henry i. William, his contest with Alexander bishop of Lincoln, I. 87.

Cordele, Hugh, fines for his lands and release out of prison, 5 Stephen, II. 197. c. 1. *q*.

Cordubanarius of the queen, 2 Henry ii. I. 602. c. 1. *y*. Walterus Cordewanarius of Glocester, his tallage or assise, 19 Henry ii. I. 701. c. 2. *c*.

Coreby, the bosch of, II. 27. c. 1. *c*. Seems to belong to Hugh de Nevill and Henry de Braybrock, ibid.

Corf Castle, John le Latimer constabulary of it, 15 Edward ii. I. 383. c. 1. The tallage of Corf, 14 Henry iii. c. 1. *o*.

Cormeilles, abbat of, I. 167. Its donum, I. 168. c. 1. *l*. Richard de, his knights fees in Herefordshire, 14 Henry ii. I. 575. c. 1. *q*. Walter Cormeilles of Herefordshire fines to stay in England, 8 Richard i. I. 658. c. 1. *m*. John de Cormailles, sherif of Somerset and Dorsetshire, 9 Edward i. II. 178. c. 1. *n*. John de Cormayles has attermination for his debts, because he was with the king in Flanders, 27 Edward i. II. 210. c. 1. *x*.

Corn, not to be exported without licence, 23 Henry ii. I. 548. c. 1. *r* Again, 12 and 24 Henry ii. I. 557, 558. Amerciaments for corn exported to the king's enemies, 10 Richard i. I. 565. c. 2. *p*. Knights in Cumberland holding by Cornage, 3 John, I. 658. c. 2. *n*. Cornagium of the animals of the bishoprick, 5 Stephen, I. 694. c. 1. *s*. Bread Corn at four shillings a quarter, 14 Henry iii. II. 152. c. 2. *z*.

Corneburc, William de, of Yorkshire, dies imprisoned by king John I. 474. c. 2. *g*. His heir discharged from paying the fine promised for his release, 11 Henry iii. II. 229. c. 1. *n*.

Cornford in the bishoprick, Elfi de, 8 Richard i. I. 715. c. 1.

Cornherde, John de, pledge of Ralf de Gernemu, 8 Richard i. I. 202. c. 1. *w*. Repeated, 323. c. 2. *b*. King's bailif for the honor of Boloign, I. 648. c. 1. *c*.

Cornhill, Gervase de, one of the judges, 28 Henry ii. I. 113. c. 1. *r*. and 20 Henry ii. I. 123. and 23 Henry ii. I. 132. and 15 Henry ii. I. 143. c. 2. *x*. One of the sherifs of London, 6 Henry ii. I. 204.

Cornhul, Henry de, chancellor of St. Paul's, London, 11 Henry iii. I.

INDEX.

63. c. 1. *l.* Son of Gervase de Cornhul, and had the old ferm of Chent, 32 Henry ii. I. 220. c. 1. *a.* c. 2. *b.* Concern'd in fitting out the navy, ibid. Henry's daughter and heirefs married to Hugh de Nevill, 4 John, I. 237. c. 2. *q.* David de Cornhill accompts for the old ferm of London, 20 Henry ii. I. 284. c. 1. *s.* Gervase de Cornhill, sherif of Kent, accompts for the ferm of that county, 21 Henry ii. ibid. c. 2. *t.* Reginald de Cornhull, sherif of Kent, 4 John, I. 285. c. 2. *y.* Henry de Cornhil seizes several lands in his bailywick into the king's hands, 1 Richard i. I. 298. c. 1. *o.* Reginald de Cornhill accompts for deodands in Kent, 4 Henry iii. I. 346. c. 2. *m.* Sherif of Kent, 2 John, I. 348. c. 1. *a.* David de Cornhill, one of the four sherifs of London, 19 Henry ii. I. 363. c. 1. *e.* Henry de Cornhil, fermer of the honor of the conftabulary, 30 Henry ii. I. 368. c. 1. *u.* Sherif of London, 1 Richard i. I. 369. c. 1. *x.* And of Surrey, 1 Richard i. ibid. c. 2. *a.* Reginald de Cornhul, sherif of Kent, 10 John, ibid. c. 2. *d.* Henry occurs again, I. 370, c. 2. *i.* Reginald de Cornhul, sherif of Kent, 6 and 11 John, I. 372. c. 2. *q.* Reginald and William de Cornhul, 7 John, I. 388. c. 2. *c.* Henry de Cornhul, I. 453. c. 1. *s.* Ralf and Reginald, brothers of Henry de Cornhil, 5 Richard i. I. 459. c. 1. *l.* Reginald de Cornhil, 8 Richard i. I. 473. c. 2. *u.* Ralf de Cornhel accompts for the debts of Henry son of Henry ii. 7 Richard i. I. 503. c. 2. *t.* The relict of Ralf de Cornhil fines to be at her own difposal, 2 John, I. 515. c. 1. *h.* Reginald de Cornhil amerc'd pro impressione sigilli, 5 Henry iii. I. 549. c. 1. *c.* Gervase, sherif of London, 7 Henry ii. I. 602. c. 2. *d.* and 12 Henry ii. I. 603. c. 1. *f.* R. de Cornhul accompts for the tallage of the fee of Canterbury, 8 John, I. 717. c. 1. *i.* Gervase de Cornhil, sherif of Surry, 22 Henry ii. I. 732. c. 2. *l.* Reginald accompts for the quinzime and merchandife, 6 John, I. 772. c. 1. *i.* Henry de Cornhil has the mint of England, 3 Richard i. II. 133. c. 1. *n.* And so has Reginald, 3 and 5 John, II. 133. c. 1. *n.* c. 2. *p.* Reginald de Cornhul, sherif of Kent, 4 John, II. 167. c. 1. *t.* Robert de Cornhul, custos of London, 54 Henry iii. II. 196. c. 1. *d.* Henry de, had average of of the cambium of England, 5 Richard i. II. 189. c. 1. *d.* Juliana, widow of John de Cornhull, 22 Edward i. II. 191. c. 2. *r.* Ralf de Cornhul has twenty of the first quality or station his fureties, 9 Richard i. II. 198. c. 1. *r.* Robert de Cornhul, one of the custodes of London, 53 and 54 Henry iii. II. 202. c. 2. *a.* Reginald de Cornhul has a second attermination, 41 Henry iii. II. 212. c. 1. *g.* Reginald de Cornhill, sherif of Kent, 8 Richard i. II. 225. c. 1. *s.* Henry de Cornhil, fermer of the land of the late Henry de Essex, has a surplufage, 1 Richard i. II. 231. c. 2. *d.*

Cornubia, Sampson de, 5 Henry iii. I. 454. c. 1. *c.* Fines for justicing Roger, son of Waldeth, ibid.

Cornwal, Reginald earl of, about an. 1165. I. 16. Earl Reginald has two hundred and fifteen knights fees, 14 Henry ii. I. 575. c. 1. *s.*

INDEX.

s. Occurs, I. 604. c. 1. *l.* See Reginald.

Cornwal, Richard earl of, made joint regent with queen Alienor, 37 Henry iii. I. 68. Lent his brother 500 marks, 39 Henry iii. I. 230. c. 1. *i.* Had Chichester in his hands many years, I. 334. c. 2. *x.* King of Alemain, 55 Henry iii. I. 384. c. 2. *n.* County of Cornwal deafforested with a charter of privileges, 6 John, I. 405. c. 2. *t.* Fine to have a sherif from among themselves, 10 John, I. 410. c. 1. *l.* De-afforested, 11 Henry iii. I. 414. c. 1. *n.* Its aid, 23 Henry ii. I. 604. c. 2. *m.* Richard earl of Cornwal, 39 Henry iii. I. 712. c. 2. Margaret, widow of Edmund earl of Cornwal, 2 Edward ii. I. 754. c. 1. *o.* Has the manor of Fordington, Dorsetshire, in dower, ibid. Richard earl of Cornwal sat in the Exchequer, 14 Henry iii. II. 27. c. 2. *g.* The particular circumstance of some manors in Cornwal, II. 162. Edmund earl of Cornwal, 27 Edward i. II. 180. Was the king's lieutenant in England, 26 and 27 Edward i. II. 204. c. 1. *i.* Earl Richard seems to have his residence at Queenhith, 14 Henry ii. II. 228. c. 1. *f.* His bailifs distrain'd, 38 Henry iii. II. 264. Edmund earl of Cornwal, the king's cozen, 15 Edward i. II. 268. c. 2. *b.* An aid to ransom the king of Alemaign, 52 Henry iii. II. 275.

Coronation of William Rufus by Lanfranc, I. 8. c. 1. *m.* Of Stephen, I. 13. c. 1. *r.* Of Henry ii. on Sunday, I. 15. c. 1. *w.* Of Henry, his son, in the life of his father, an. 1170. I. 17. c. 1. *d.* And that on Sunday, ibid. Of Richard i. on Sunday, 3 non. Sept. an. 1189. I. 21. The order of it as perform'd by Baldwin, ibid. c. 2. *s.* Coronation of Richard i. I. 161. c. 1. *b.* Preparations for the coronation of Richard i. I. 369. And of Edward ii. I. 380.

Corouner, John le, alderman, assesses his ward of Vintry, 32 Edward i. I. 741. c. 1. *b.* John le Coroner, alderman of Vinetry ward, distrained, 2 Edward ii. II. 235. c. 1. *t.* Coroners attach the sherits, II. 238. c. 2. *y.*

Corpus comitatus, what, II. 163, 164. What it consisted of, II. 165. Accompt of it in each county to be writ in a separate roll, II. 173.

Corrodies, I. 168. c. 1. *b.* Corrodie or expence of the duke of Saxony, I. 169. For the king of Scots, 3 Henry ii. II. 207. c. 1. *w.* For the king of Scots, 5 Stephen, I. 364.

Corton, Geoffrey de, justicier in Normandy, 2 John, I. 156. c. 2. *i.* Again, 3 John, I. 171. c. 2. *x.*

Corvesarii of Oxford, what they paid the crown annually for their gild, 12 Henry ii. I. 238. c. 2. *t, u,* &c. Paid five marks of gold for gersom, 5 Stephen, I. 467. c. 1. *f.*

Cosham, Richard and Peter de, Berks, 30 Henry ii. I. 213. c. 2. *s.* Peter fines for a plaint in the Exchequer against Richard, ibid.

Cosin, Peter, remov'd from being sherif of London for a transgression, 2 Edward i. II. 96. c. 2. *x.* William Cosyn, 12 Edward ii. II. 234. c. 1. *o.*

Costein, Henry, his tallage, 4 John, I. 203. c. 1. *c.* Fines for the king's

INDEX

protection as to merchandife, 9 John, I. 477. c. 1. *f.* How charged with tallage for the fee of Lincoln, 4 John, I. 717. c. 1. *b.*

Coftentin, Geoffrey de, fherif of Lincoln, 16 and 17 Henry ii. I. 345. c. 2. *a.*

Cotele, Elias, one of the king's varlets, 26 Edward i. II. 223. c. 2. *b.*

Coterellorum arma, II. 201. c. 2. *r.* William Coterel, 1 Richard i. I. 427. c. 2. *o.*

Cotes, William de, has the toll and mills of Grimefbi, 6 John, I. 468. c. 1. *o.*

Coteflaw hundred amerc'd, 4 Henry iii. I. 563. c. 2. *q.* Had twelve knights, ibid.

Cothun, Lincolnfhire, tallaged, 10 Richard i. I. 733. c. 1. *r.* The quinzime for the merchandife of the port of Cotun, 6 John, I. 772. c. 1.*i.*

Cotton, William de, chamberlain of the Exchequer from Ifabel de Forz, 1 Edward i. II. 297. c. 1. *g.* c. 2. *k.*

Coventry and Lichfield, Walter Langton, bifhop of, the king's treafurer, 30 Edward i. I. 72. c. 2. *p.* Again, 1 Edward ii. I. 74. c. 1. *s.* Infulted fitting in his office, 5 Edward ii. I. 267. c. 1. *o.* Treafurer, 25 Edward i. I. 378. c. 2. *p.* The bifhop ftyled Ceftrenfis on the aid to the king's daughter, 14 Henry ii. I. 582. c. 1. *c.* Hugh [de Nunant] cuftos of the priory of Covintre attended the king in his Welch army, 4 Richard i. I. 637. c. 1. *d.* This See accompts for fifteen fees, 8 Richard i. I. 638. c. 1. *h.* As to its fees, fee I. 658. c. 2. *p.* Tallaged by Adam de Afton, 37 Henry iii. I. 718. c. 2. *o.* Walter treafurer, 26 Edward i. I. 782, 783. and 35 Edward i. II. 29. The falary of Walter Langton as treafurer, 27 and 31 Edward i. II. 42. c. 1. *f, g.* A heavy charge againft him as treafurer, 1 Edward ii. II. 47. c. 2. *z.* Makes William de Carleton his lieutenant, 35 Edward i. II. 49. c. 2. *m.* Walter treafurer, 27 Edward i. II. 255. c. 2. *t.*

Coventry, the prior not to be impleaded for his lands but before the king, I. 117. c. 1. *f.* The men of, have a confirmation of liberties, 28 Henry ii. I. 398. c. 2. *u.* Hugh de Nonant, bifhop, what he accompted for, 2 Richard i. I. 458. c. 2. *f.* The town amerced for adjudging a Withernam when the thing was in plea, I. 548. c. 1. *p.* Knights fees of the priory, 14 Henry ii. I. 574. c. 2. *o.* Again, I. 579. c. 2. *m.* The prior's efcuage for the king's ranfom, 7 Richard i. I. 591. c. 2. *t.* Priory of Coventry accompts for ten fees, 30 Henry iii. I. 595. c. 1. *n.* and 38 Henry iii. I. 597. c. 1. *y.* The prior's fcutage for the Irifh expedition, 18 Henry ii. I. 630. c. 2. *e.* Accompts for 10 fees for the Galwey army, 33 Henry ii. I. 636. c. 2. *z.* In the king's hand, 4 Richard i. I. 637. c. 1. *d.* and 8 Richard i. I. 638. c. 1. *g.* The odious cafe of the prior, I. 640. c. 2. *y.* Henry de Coventre, fherif of London, 2 Edward i. II. 96. c. 2. *x.*

Coumbemartyn, William de, alderman, had the Tower ward, London, 32 Edward i. I. 741. c. 1. *h.*

Counfeller of the king declared by the chancellor, 5 Edward ii. II. 32. c. 1. *r.* The oath of one of the king's council,

INDEX.

council, temp. Edward ii. II. 32. c. 2. w.

Countertallies, or the receipt, II. 301.

Coupen manor, the bishop of Ely's, 18 Edward i. I. 618. c. 1. k.

Court of the king, his palace or royal residence, I. 2. The person who sat and acted in the king's court, temp. Henry ii. I. 93. What pleas were reserved to the king's court, I. 95. Lay fees not to be decided by ecclesiastical court, I. 561. c. 2. r. Division of the king's courts, I. 787.

Courteney, Hugh de, one of the barons summoned to the Scotch war, 26 Edward i. I. 655. c. 2. Hawisa de, holds eighteen fees of the king in capite, in Devonshire, 2 John, I. 659. c. 1. w. Hugh son of Hugh de Courteney inherits the earldom of Devonshire from Isabella [f. Lisle] 26 Edward i. II. 165. c. 2. n.

Coustumier of Normandy, I. 162, 163. passim.

Cows, at six and eight pence, 14 Henry iii. II. 152. c. 2. z.

Crachale, John de, archdeacon of Bedford, 43 Henry iii. II. 36. c. 1. e. Was king's treasurer, ibid.

Craeseregus castle, I. 475. c. 1. k.

Craft, John, 27 Henry iii. I. 622. Bailif or receiver of Almaric de S. Amand, late sherif of Herefordshire, 27 Henry iii. II. 176. c. 1. z.

Crammavilla, Geoffrey de, 6 John, I. 99. c. 2. t. Ralf de, pays a hundred pound for his donum in Yorkshire, 29 Henry ii. I. 272. c. 2. p. Geoffrey has the wardship of the heir of Ralf de Heldebovil, 7 Richard i. I. 323. c. 1. z. Constance, widow of Ralf de Crammavilla, fines not to marry against her will, 10 Richard i. I. 464. c. 2. h. Henry de Crammavilla fines, 6 Henry iii. I. 492. c. 1. t. Henry de Crammavilla occurs, 33 Henry ii. I. 636 c. 1. s. Roger de Crammavil disseised of his land for not attending the king in his Irish war, temp. John, I. 663. c. 2. x.

Crassus, Stephen, alderman of London, tallaged, 19 and 20 Henry iii. I. 739. c. 1. z, a. Occurs, 10 Richard i. I. 776. c. 1. r.

Craucumb, Geoffrey de, seneschal, 11 Henry iii. I. 63. c. 1. b. Occurs, 16 Henry iii. I. 64. c. 1. m. Godfrey de Craucumb, 17 Henry iii. I. 65. c. 2. Not to be impleaded but before the chief justice, 15 Henry iii. I. 119. c. 1. d. Godfrey assesses the tallage of Norfolk, 14 Henry iii. I. 725. c. 2. g. Godfrey de Craucumbe, 16 Henry iii. II. 33. c. 2. x. Godfrey sherif of the county of Oxford, 16 Henry iii. II. 141. c. 1. q. And of the castle, ibid. Godfrey de Craucumb sherif of Oxfordshire has the manor of Bensintone, 16 Henry iii. II. 222. c. 1. x.

Crauley, Michael de Punninges fines for a market there, 4 John, I. 104. c. 2. i.

Crech, Bartholomew de, his relation to Sudfeld, 27 Henry ii. I. 104. c. 1. m. Again, his right to Sudflet, 1 Richard i. I. 427. c. 2. p. Arthur de Crec, 18 Henry ii. II. 132. c. 1. William, ibid.

Crede, Alexander, 4 John, I. 453. c. 2. t. Fined to have right, ibid.

Crediho, Philip de, 2 Henry iii. I. 793. c. 1. c. Fines for his plaint, ibid.

Creistok, John, baron of, 26 Edward i. I. 654. c. 1. a.

Crek and Burnham in Norfolk, the interest of Ralf de Belfo in them, 5 John, I. 487. c. 1. s.

Crecn, Maurice and Guy de, 26 Henry ii.

INDEX X.

ry ii. I. 96. c. 2. *p.* Alan de Creon of Lincolnshire, 5 Stephen, I. 147. c. 2. *g.* Maurice de Creon, 2 Henry ii. I. 273. c. 1. *d.* Maurice de Creon amerced for a false judgment in his court, Lincolnshire, 15 Henry ii. I. 556. c. 1. *g.*

Crepping, Walter de, justicier, 49 Henry iii. I. 76. c. 1. *u.* Robert de Crepping was justice of the Jews, 49 Henry iii. I. 234. c. 1. *c.* Alan de Crepping fines for hastening his plea, 7 Henry iii. I. 448. c. 2. *m.* Walter Creppinges king's tallager, 8 Richard i. I. 704. c. 1. *o.* John de Crepping has the county with the castle of York, 1 Edward ii. II. 144. c. 1. *l.*

Cressi, Hugh de, one of the king's justiciers, 23 Henry ii. I. 44. and 21 Henry ii. I. 125. c. 1. *h.* and I. 126. 23 Henry ii. I. 130, 131. Hugh de Cressy occurs, an. 1184. I. 168. c. 2. William de Cressi, 3 John, I. 428. c. 1. *z.* Roger de Cressi, 9 John, I. 489. c. 1. *o.* Roger de Creissy has a moiety of Hubert de Rya's fees, 5 Henry iii. I. 666.

Cressingham, Hugh de, auditor of the accompts, 20 Edward i. II. 291. c. 2. *g.*

Cressoniere, Gilbert de, fined seventy pounds for being present at the wedding of Robert de Sakenvill, I. 167. c. 2.

Creton in Devonshire, Agnes, wife of Nicolas de Creton of Heyen, 5 Edward i. II. 88. c. 2. *b.* Simon deputy usher of the Exchequer, 52 Henry iii. II. 276.

Crevequoer, Robert de, 9 Richard i. II. 198. c. 1. *r.* Hamon de, 27 and 41 Henry iii. II. 228. c. 1. *g.*

Creun, Maurice de, fines for a concord with Walter de Aencourt, 5 Henry ii. I. 511. c. 2. *m.* See Creon.

Crikelade, Andrew de, 1 John, I. 493. c. 1. *g.* Again, 1 John, I. 498. c. 1. *m.* That hamlet belonged to the chamberlainship of the Exchequer, II. 298.

Criol, Bertram de, 30 Henry iii. I. 568. c. 1. *r.* Custos of the fee of Canterbury, 32 Henry ii. I. 595. c. 2. *p.* Again, 13 Henry iii. I. 718. c. 1. *n.* Nicolas baron of the Exchequer, 49 Henry iii. II. 13. c. 2. *l.*

Crispus, Baldwinus, accompts for the old ferm of London, I. 284. c. 1. *s.* One of the four fermers or sherifs of London, 19 Henry ii. I. 363. c. 1. *e.*

Cristemereford, Wiltshire, its donum, 33 Henry ii. I. 634. c. 1. *q.*

Criticks of several kinds, Pref. xiv.

Croc, William, fines for delaying his plea, 5 Stephen, I. 448. c. 2. *s.* Osmund de Croc fines to have his land again, which was pledged to William de Calna, Hampshire, 5 Stephen, I. 482. c. 1. *a.* Thomas Croc fined for compounding the appeal for his father's death, 9 John, I. 499. c. 2. *t.* Walter Croc in misericordia, 5 Stephen, I. 544. c. 2. *u.* William Croc fines for his lands in Wiltshire, 1 John, I. 664. c. 2. *c.* Stephen Croc's debts to the crown to be first discharged, 22 Henry iii. II. 183. c. 2. *d.*

Crocards, a species of coin, temp. Edward i. and Edward ii. I. 294.

Croce, Walter de la, justice of the Jews, 55 Henry iii. I. 240. c. 1. *d.*

Croere, Geoffrey Mandevil of, I. 489. c. 2. *q.* Several successions of that family, ibid.

Croft, Philip de, sherif of Surry and Sussex,

INDEX.

Suffex, before 27 Henry iii. II. 141. c. 1. r. Was deputy fherif under John de Gatefden, 22 Henry iii. II. 177. c. 1. c.

Crofton, Richard de, clerk of the fherif of Norfolk and Suffolk, 9 Edward ii. I. 381. c. 1. x.

Croi, John de, traded with the king's enemies in the beginning of king John, I. 776. c. 1. r.

Croin, Seifil, amerced for recreancy before 7 Richard i. I. 550. c. 1. x.

Croinden in Surrey, belonging to the archbifhop of Canterbury, amerced, 31 Henry ii. I. 552. c. 2. r.

Crokedak, Mr Adam de, 18 Edward i. I. 242. Late guardian of Roger fon of Sir Robert de Hereford, I. 242. c. 1. l.

Crokel, Richard de, his tenure, I. 650. c. 2. o.

Crokefle, John de, accompts for the manor of Skipton, 22 Edward i. I. 721. c. 1. w, x.

Crokefton, terra de, to whom it belonged, 30 Henry ii. I. 97. c. 1. t. See Croxton.

Crombwel, Richard de, chamberlain of the Exchequer, 5 Edward ii. II. 6. c. 2. d. John de Crombwell conftable of the tower of London, 5 Edward ii. II. 239. See Crumwella.

Cropeftoft, terra de, I. 448. c. 1. i.

Cropton in Yorkfhire, belonging to William de Stotevil, tallaged, 14 Henry iii. I. 708. c. 2. p.

Crofs, Geoffrey de, has cuftody of the lands and heirs of Sampfon de Mules, 19 Henry iii. I. 326. c. 2. m. John de Cruce, 6 Henry iii. I. 454. c. 2. i. Geoffrey de Cruce fherif of Surrey and Suffex amerced for Default, 40 Henry iii. II. 236. c. 1. e.

Crowerft, William de, clerk of the fherif of Devonfhire, 12 Edward ii. II. 280. c. 1. b.

Croxton abbey, has an affignment to pray for the foul of king John, I 393. c. 2. g.

Croyl and Scye honor in Normandy, claimed by the earl of Chefter againft Peter de Sabloil, 2 John, I. 518. c. 2. x.

Croyland, abbat of, 5 John, I. 118. Has a confirmation of liberties, 4 John, I. 405. c. 1. k. Abbat of Croyland amerced for feizing the advowfon of Wygetoft, 8 Edward ii. I. 530. c. 2. Amerced as a baron, ibid. Again, I. 531. c. 1. r.

Cruket, Sir Ralf de, 10 John, I. 489. c. 2. q. Peter de Cruket and Joan his wife, their interest in Stanebrugge, 35 Henry iii. II. 78. c. 2. r.

Crul in Lincolnfhire, belonged to the abbat of Selebi, 33 Henry ii. I. 492. c. 2. d.

Crumwella, Ralf de, his claim of Widmerepol, 30 Henry ii. I. 447. c. 2. x. Richard de Crumbwell, chamberlain, made Geoffrey de la Thorne keeper of the tallies, 5 Edward ii. II. 308. c. 2. g.

Crufade, publifhed at Geldeford by Henry ii. I. 222. c. 2. f. A payment towards it, 19 Edward i. I. 271. c. 1. g. Cruce fignati quit of tallage, I. 749. c. 1. u.

Cryol, Bertram de, the Jews fine to have his verdict, 30 Henry iii. I. 228. c. 2. y. See Criol.

Cudinton, William de, 9 John, I. 749. c. 1. u. His tallage as citizen of London, ibid.

Culerne and Cumbe, Wiltfhire, had been the fees of earl Reginald, 33 Henry ii. I. 634. c. 1. q.

Culinton

INDEX.

Culinton in Devonshire, 24 Henry ii. I. 605. c. 1. *o*. Its aid charged on earl Richard, ibid.

Culumb, Master, of Yorkshire, fines for stealing cheverons out of the forest, 12 John, I. 499, 500. c. 1. *b*.

Cumbe in Glocestershire, that manor vested in the monks of Bordesly, I. 209. c. 1. *b*. Mazelina de Cumba in Sussex, 6 John, I. 440. c. 2. *o*. Richard de Cumb fines, by his brother Humfrey de Scovil, for going over to William de Braiosa in Ireland, 12 John, I. 490. c. 2. *a*. Cumb in Surrey, its aid, 14 Henry ii. I. 583. c. 1. *y*. Cumbe in Wiltshire, earl Reginald's, its aid, 23 Henry ii. I. 604. c. 1. *l*. West Cumbe in this county, its aid, ibid. Its donum, 33 Henry ii. I. 634. c. 1. *q*. Again, ibid. c. 2. Its assise, 19 Henry ii. I. 702. c. 1. *d*. The tallage of Cumb, 1 John, I. 705. c. 2. *z*. John de Cumbes, 7 Richard i. I. 789. c. 1. *e*, *f*.

Cumberland fines for trespasses of the forest, I. 500. c. 2. *e*. Its hidage for the king's ransom, 6 Richard i. I. 592. c. 2. *z*. Cumberland and Carlisle, their donum, 4 Henry ii. I. 695. c. 2. *d*.

Cumin, John, one of the justices, 31 Henry ii. upon dividing England into Iters, I. 93. Again, 20 Henry ii. I. 123. Again, I. 124. Again, 26 Henry ii. I. 139. c. 2. *l*. William Cumin one of the king's receivers, 4 John, I. 176. c. 1. *s*. Attests the king's writ, temp. Henry ii. I. 209. c. 1. *b*. John Cumin passes sherifs accompts, 26 Henry ii. I. 289. c. 1. *s*. John Cumin has the custody of the fees of Hereford and Bath, I. 306. c. 2. *s*, *t*. And of Hereford, 14 Henry ii. I. 504. c. 1. *o*. William Cumin of Hemelhamstede, Essex, his aid, 14 Henry ii. I. 587. c. 1. William Cumin seems to be fermer of London, 2 Henry ii. I. 602. c. 1. *y*. And the king's receiver, 2 Henry ii. I. 695 c. 2. *b*. John, justice of the assise, 19 Henry ii. I. 701. c. 2. *c*. and 20 Henry ii. I. 767. c. 1. *h*. William Cumin accompts for the ferm of Hurtfordshire under Richard de Luci, 2 Henry ii. II. 151. c. 2. *s*.

Cumton, exchanged for Aynho, I. 144. See Colingham. I. 483. c. 2. *q*. Geoffrey Cumpton challenged for the murder of Osbert, son of Hilary de Estwud, 10 John, I. 495. c. 1. *w*. Teding of Cumpton in the West, I. 547. c. 1. *x*.

Cundet, Robert de, 5 Stephen, I. 477. c. 1. *d*. Fines for a concord with the bishop of Lincoln, ibid.

Cunedore in Shropshire, tallaged, 1 John, I. 705. c. 2. *y*. Again, 8 John, I. 734. c. 1. *z*.

Cuneus parvus and major, sherifs accompted for the profits of them, 30 Henry iii. I. 281. c. 1. *e*. Summonce to the custodes Cuneorum, 9 John, I. 290. c. 2. *zz*. The custodes Cunei upon oath, 6 Henry iii. II. 87. c. 2. *a*.

Curboil, William de, chosen archbishop by the bishops, an. 1123. against the monks, earls, and theins, I. 12. c. 1. *o*. The oath then taken about Maud's succession, an. 1136. I. 49. c. 2. *n*.

Curcy, William de, dapifer, temp. Henry ii. I. 51. William le Puher and Hugh Pincerna have the ferm of the honor of William de Curci, 19 Henry ii. I. 297. c. 1. *i*. That honor in the king's hand, 1 Richard i. I. 298. c. 1. *m*. John de Curci his going into Ireland, temp. John, I. 489. c. 1. *m*. William de Curci's knights

INDEX.

knights fees, 14 Henry ii. I. 575. c. 2. *t.* Accompts for the knights of the barony of William Meschin, ibid. The honor and knights of the heir of William de Curci dapifer, 33 Henry ii. I. 636. c. 1. *s.*

Curia Christianitatis, I. 105. c. 1. *q.*

Curia and Curtis equivalent, I. 4. c. 2.

Curia regis, the principal acceptations of that phrase, I. 81, &c. Courts of several denominations, I. 82.

Curlevach, Simon, has licence to export goods, temp. John, I. 2. c. 2. *b.* Pays twenty shillings per last for transporting hides to S. Valery, 10 John, I. 469. c. 2. *h.*

Curtays, Roger le, attorney of William de Ripariis for his Irish affairs, 30 Edward i. II. 180. c. 1. *y.*

Curtenai, Robert de, his claim of a moiety of Caudebec, 8 John, I. 428. c. 2. *d.* William de, 3 Henry iii. I. 492. c. 1. *o.* The widow of Reginald de, 2 John, I. 523. c. 1. *r.* Reginald de, accompts for the knights of Walter de Bolebec, 14 Henry ii. I. 583. c. 2. *l.* Robert's executor was the abbat of Forde, 28 Henry iii. II. 184. c. 1. *e.* Robert de, 9 Richard i. II. 198. c. 1. *r.*

Curton, William de, challenged by Julian de Swadefeld for land in Elingeham, 9 John, I. 507. c. 1. *a.* Richard de Curton valett, 39 Henry iii. II. 17. c. 1. *e.* William de Curtun had the ferm of Lincolnshire before 35 Henry iii. II. 141. c. 2. *s.* Was sherif of Lincolnshire, 33 Henry iii. II. 215. c. 1. *y.* And tallager of the king's demeans, ibid.

Curumba, Simon de, 17 Henry ii. I. 331. c. 1. *g.* Has money ad bretefchas regi faciendas, ibid.

Cusac castle in Gascoigne, I. 391. c. 2. *w.*

Cusances, William de, clerk of the wardrobe, 15 Edward ii. I. 393. c. 1. *d.*

Cuserugge, Baldwin de, one of the justiciers to settle the tallage of Berkshire, 9 Richard i. I. 705. c. 1. *t.*

Cusin, Robert, claims the land of Maleswurd, 1 Richard i. I. 227. c. 2. *o.* Gilbert custos of the escheats of the honor of Lancaster, 3 Henry iii. I. 308. c. 2. *w.* William custos of the custom of wool, 2 Edward ii. I. 780. c. 1. *i.* Roger 12 John, I. 795. c. 1. *m.* Fined for an escape, ibid.

Custom to the king, in what sense used, I. 764, &c.

Customers, I. 355.

Customs feudal, I. 4. c. 1. *d.* Custom of three pence in the pound collected at Yarmouth, I. 385. c. 1. *q.* Custom of two shillings upon every dolium of wine, 25 Edward i. I. 770. c. 2. *b.* When called Custuma, I. 781. Concealment of customs, I. 784.

Custos, where appointed, I. 305. Custos of a bishoprick, was frequently elect, and succeeded to the see, I. 308. c. 2. *g, m.* Custos seems to accompt for particulars, and fermer for a fixed sum, I. 327. c. 1. *p.* The custody of Yorkshire, &c. 3 John, I. 461. c. 1. *a.* Custodes of several sorts, II. 128. Difference between the custos and fermer of a county, II. 168. The allowance yearly to the five custodes of London, 55 Henry iii. II. 220. c. 2. *a.*

Custumier, the grand, compiled by William le Rouillé, licentiate of laws, I. 180. c. 2. Was in great measure transcribed by Glanvil in his system, I. 183.

Cuteler, Solomon le, sherif of London, 17 Ed-

INDEX.

17 Edward i. II. 96. c. 2. z. William le Cutiller of Hoyland, merchant of Oxford, discharged of tallage, 35 Henry iii. II. 223. c. 1. c.

Cuthbrichill, Walter de, amerced for recreancy, 16 Henry ii. I. 550. c. 1. p.

Cuverill, Maud de, I. 166. c. 2. Fines for a recognition, ibid.

Cybecay, Robert de, 31 Henry ii. I. 452. c. 1. e. Fines in half the principal, ibid.

Cygoini, or Ciaconia, Engelard de, accompts for the ferm of Bristo, 12 John, I. 333. c. 2. n. And for the king's wines, I. 766. c. 1. n. See Cigoinie. Accompts for the manor of Odiham, 26 and 27 Henry iii. II. 201. c. 2. s. His executors quit of all accounts for his good services done the king, 29 Henry iii. II. 229.

Cyrai, William de, his claims in Burton, 24 Henry ii. I. 103. c. 2. k.

Cyrencester fermed by the abbat of that name, 5 Richard i. I. 332. c. 2. c. The abbey has twenty knights fees, 29 Henry iii. I. 595. c. 2. q. The aid of that town, 23 Henry ii. I. 603. c. 1. k. The assise or tallage of Cirencester, 19 Henry ii. I. 701. c. 2. c. The abbat of Cyrncestre, 40 Henry iii. I. 746. c. 1. c. Thomas de, one of the custodes of Queenhith, 14 Henry iii. I. 781. c. 2. q. Sherif of Dorset and Somersetshire, 14 Henry iii. II. 152. Abbat of Cyrencester, one of Almaric de S. Amand's executors, 28 Henry iii. II. 190. c. 1. k. Thomas de Cyrencester's impleading for Queenhith, 14 Henry ii. II. 228. c. 1. f.

Cyrinton, Mr. Odo, son of William de Cyrinton, has the custody of that church, 13 John, I. 508. c. 1. l.

D.

D, the import of that letter in the great roll, II. 170, 171. c. 1, 2.

D'Abetot, Osbert, in misericordia, 26 Henry ii. I. 554. c. 1. n.

Dacenvill, Robert de, fined twenty pounds for disobeying the summonce of the justiciers, I. 167. c. 1. k.

Dacovere, Hugh de, sherif of Stafford and Shropshire, 40 Henry iii. II. 150. c. 2. q.

Dacre, Ralf de, constable of the tower before 14 Edward i. I. 270. c. 1. b. Robert de Dacre seems to be sherif of Cumberland, 39 Henry iii. II. 117. c. 2. d.

Dacus, William, fines for a dissaisin, 6 John, I. 441. c. 1. t. William the Dane fines to have the custody of Pereton park, 1 John, I. 460. c. 1. x. Nicolas the Dane his merchandise, 6 John, I. 469. c. 2. e. William the Dane, 12 John, I. 794. c. 2. l.

Dagworth, Maud de, one of the sisters and heiresses of Simon de Leschequer, II. 277. Held the third part of the ushery of the Exchequer, 32 Edward i. ibid. Which share devolves to John de Dagwurth, 1 Edward ii. II. 278.

Daivil, Eudo de, had the tallage of the bishopric, 8 Richard i. I. 714. c. 2.

Dalee, William de, has the land of Hebinton, Kent, 29 Henry ii. I. 212. c. 2. o.

Dallyng, John de, sherif of London, 12 Edward ii. II. 98. c. 2. d. Has leave from the treasurer to go out of his sherifalty, 12 Edward ii. II. 181. c. 2. r.

Dalton, Ralf de, to arrest ships carrying

INDEX.

ing uncuftomed goods, 26 Edward i. I. 785.

Damianus the clerk, fined, 8 Richard i. II. 210. c. 2. *y*.

Dammartin, Manefier de, 16 Henry ii. I. 140. Odo de Dammartin diffeifes Reginald de Luci, 25 Henry ii. I. 212. c. 1. *n*. Stephen de Dammartin, 2 Henry ii. I. 273. Odo de Dammartin has wardfhip of the fon and land of Hugh Pincerna, 28 Henry ii. I. 322. c. 1. *u*. Odo de Dammartin has two duels againft Richard Hacun of Norfolk for land in Hamelinton and Cattun, 6 Henry iii. I. 445. c. 2. *d*. Graleng de Damartin amerc'd for being prefent at the concord of a plea of the crown, 32 Henry ii. I. 549. c. 1. *a*. The one knight's fee of Odo de Dammartin, 14 Henry ii. I. 573. c. 1. William de Dammartin's fcutage towards the king's ranfom, 6 Richard i. I. 590. c. 2. *l*. William and Albric de Dammartin, their fcutage, 2 Richard i. I. 664. c. 1. *z*. Odo de Dammartin quit of fcutage by the king's writ, I. 666. c. 2. *l*.

Danebi, the village of Peter de Brus, 4 John, I. 191. c. 1. *o*. Its tallage in Yorkfhire, 9 Richard i. I. 699. c. 1. *r*.

Danecaftre, or Doncafter, ferm of, I. 331. c. 2. *s*. Fine for the ferm of their town and foke, I. 400. c. 1. *n*. The manor pafs'd to Robert de Turneham with Joan [daughter of William Foffard] 9 Richard i. I. 484. c. 2. *z*. Niel de Doncaftre, 5 Stephen, I. 443. c. 2. *f*. Men of Danecaftre occur, 17 Henry ii. I. 559. c. 2. *m*. The men and Hugh Ferling of Danecaftre, their donum, 9 Richard i. I. 699. c. 2. Tallaged, 30 Henry iii. I. 710. c. 2. Villa and Reginald de, 8 Richard i. I. 737. c. 1. *s*. Has a fair of three days, II. 28. c. 1. *k*.

Danegeld continued after the Conqueft, I. 685. Remitted to feveral, for fuperhidage, &c. I. 686. c. 2. *f*. What it is, I. 689. c. 1. *p*. A fettled revenue, render'd as the yearly ferms of counties, I. 690. A kind of hidage or revenue from lands divided into hides, I. 694. When the county paid Danegeld the city render'd a donum, I. 693. c. 1. *p*. c. 2. *q, r*. Danegeld collected, 21 Henry ii. II. 273. c. 1. *u*.

Danfront in Normandy, a grant to the good men of, 4 John, I. 524. c. 2. *z*.

Daniel, John, knight of the bifhop of Hereford, 10 Edward i. I. 669. c. 1. *a*.

Dapifer, whether any difference anciently, or what, between that and the fenefchallus in England, I. 49. Where two occur at the fame time, one of England and the other of Normandy, ibid. Dapifers in the reign of Henry ii. I. 51. Dapifer the fame with major domus regiæ, ibid. William Dapifer, an. 1121. c. 1. *l*. Jordan Dapifer of the earl of Glocefter, 23 Henry ii. I. 211. c. 1. *i*. Bifhops had hereditary Dapifers, 5 Stephen, I. 457. c. 1. *i*. Oger Dapifer, 14 Henry ii. I. 573. c. 2. Dapifers of the nobility permitted to anfwer for their barons per verum dictum, II. 182, 183. But upon detection abridg'd of that privilege, II. 183.

Danyel, John, father of Richard, had the grant of Tydefwel manor in Derby-

INDEX.

Derbyshire from king John, I. 723. c. 1. d.

Darcy, or de Areci, Robert, fines for a concord, 5 Stephen, 471. c. 1. p. Philip Darcy summon'd with the barons in Lincolnshire to the Scotch war, 26 Edward i. I. 654. c. 2. William de Areci accompts for the remainder of Lincolnshire, 10 Richard i. II. 183. c. 1. b.

Darel, William, has a commission of array for the wapentake of Alverton, 16 Edward ii. II. 112. c.1. Ralf Dayrel, his wages, 27 Henry iii. II. 120.

Darrein presentment, or pleas de ultima præsentatione, II. 218. c. 1. a.

Daubernoon, John, a collector of the disme and sisme in Surry, 33 Edward i. II. 233. John de Aubernum, late sherif of Surrey and Sussex, 52 Henry iii. II. 280. c. 2. d.

Daubigny, William de, holds the manor of Oskinton, Com. Notingham, by knight service, 6 Henry iii. I. 281. c. 1. c. Elias Daubeny, one of the barons, summon'd by writ to the Scots war, 26 Edward i. I. 655. c. 2.

Daventre John, son of Philip de, holds of the king in Thirneby of the fee of Martein, 34 Edward i. I. 670. c. 2. f. See Dauntry.

Daughter, aid to marry the eldest, I. 569, &c.

David, archdeacon and sherif of Buckinghamshire, 18 Henry ii. I. 315. c. 1. m. Has custody of Peter Morel's land, ibid.

David king of Scots present at Windsor when the nobles swore to the succession of Æthelic, daughter of Henry i. an. 1127. I. 13. c. 1. q. Earl David, 1 John, I. 57. c. 1. r.

Earl David, 3 Richard i. I. 58. c. 2. c. Earl David has the wardship of Stephen de Cameis, 10 Richard i. I. 324. c. 1. d. Earl David, 4 John, I. 404. c. 2. i. Earl David fines for his son's release, 13 John, I. 495. c. 1. b. Earl David, 7 Richard i. I. 591. c. 2. t. Quit of his scutage, 10 John, I. 666. c. 1. i. Has Bramton and Alcmundebir, ib. Occurs, 9 Richard i. II. 198. c.1. r.

David, son of Oën, had married the sister of the king, 20 Henry ii. I. 367. c. 1. k.

Davidvilla, Richard de, 5 Stephen, I. 449. c. 2. b. Fines not to plead for the land of Weston, ibid.

Daulling, Robert de, 4 Henry iii. I. 119. c. 1. f. On the tryal about the presentation to the church of Briseley, Norfolk, ibid.

Dauntry, Philip de, sherif of Cambridgeshire and Huntingdonshire, 13 Henry ii. I. 540. c. 1. x. Walter de Davintre, collector of the scutage, 34 Edward i. I. 646. c. 2.

Dean Anger, 10 John, I. 566. c. 2. z. Nicolas decanus, sherif of Essex and Hertfordshire, 14 Henry ii. I. 574. c. 1. Dean and chapter of Chichester, collectors of the disme, 9 Edward ii. II. 181. c. 2. o.

Dearces, William, a baron in the Conqueror's time, I. 32. See Darcy.

Dabenham, Luke de, his scutage for lands in Suffolk, 20 Henry ii. I. 630. c. 1. c.

Debt, the demanding one which had been paid punish'd, I. 212. c. 1. o. Frequently the third part of a Debt paid as fine for the recovery of the rest, I. 453. Persons in Debt to the king to obtain his licence to make a will, 38 and 39 Henry iii. II.

INDEX.

II. 184, 185. Heir of the king's debtor not to be diftrein'd if the chattels of the deceafed would anfwer, II. 190. Pledges for Debtors in London, 38 Henry iii. II. 242. c. 2. c. All who owed the king any clear Debts inrolled in the Exchequer were committed to the marefchal there, II. 288.

Deerftealing in the time of king Stephen and Henry ii. I. 150. c. 1. s.

Defaults, and amerciaments fet upon them, I. 552. Making Defalt at the Exchequer forfeited former payments, II. 235.

Deforz, Helyas de, of Normandy, has the cuftody of the land and heirs of Peter de Ortis, 2 John, I. 523. c. 2. s. See Albemarle, Ifabella de Fortibus, and Desforz.

Deirel Roger, grandfon of, 5 Stephen, II. 197. c. 1. q. Accompts, ibid. See Darel.

Delamare, Thomas de, one of the efquires of the bifhop of Hereford, 10 Edward i. I. 669. c. 1. a. See Mara.

Delce in Kent, the terra de, I. 428. c. 2. e. Forfeited by Geoffrey de Bofco, ibid.

Deldrevill, Geoffrey, I. 166. Fines for expediting his plaint, an. 1184. I. 166. c. 1. i.

Delegates or judges, 9 Richard i. I. 485. c. 1. c.

Delveday, Peter, affayer of Winchefter, 33 Henry iii. II. 89. c. 1. i.

Demeans of the crown ancient, I. 295. &c.

Demetrius Poliorcetes, king of Macedon, heard caufes in perfon, I. 88.

Denarius tertius comitatus, means the third part of the profits arifing from the pleas, I. 210. paffim.

Dene, Ralf de, the articles he was to inquire about, 16 Henry ii. I. 140. Geoffrey de Dene, 1 John, I. 504. c. 1. w. Ralf de, holds of the fee of Chichefter, temp. Henry ii. I. 576. c. 2. Who Sibylla and Robert de were, 11 Henry iii. II. 78. c. 1. n.

Deodands, I. 346. c. 2. m, n.

Derby, William de, officiated in the Judaifm, 3 Edward i. I. 243, 244. c. 1. r. That town has confirmation of its liberties, 3 John, I. 404. c. 1. f. and 6 John, I. 407. c. 1. c. Ifold, widow of Philip de Derebi, 1 John, I. 473. c. 2. w. William de Ferrers earl of Derby, 38 Henry iii. II. 185. c. 2. m. Dyed in or before 40 Henry iii. ibid. n.

Dercet, that land in the Giffard's family, 21 Henry ii. I. 450. c. 2. p.

Derewold, William fon of, of Thetford, king's moneyour, 14 Henry ii. I. 590. c. 1. k.

Derham, Ralf abbat of, has the terra de Walton, 8 Richard i. I. 106. c. 1. u.

Derherft in Gloeceftrefc. prior of, 31 Henry ii. I. 97. c. 1. w. II. 119. c. 1. p.

Derlavefton or Darlfton, Staffordfhire, Orm de, I. 457. c. 1. c. Amerc'd for breaking the peace, ibid.

Derley abbat has a confirmation of liberties, 13 Henry iii. I. 417. c. 2. c. Geoffrey de Derley, 10 Richard i. I. 433. c. 1. e. Abbat of Derlega, I. 473. c. 2. w.

Derlinton, in the bifhopric, the bund of, I. 714. c. 2. That burgh tallaged, ibid. Bund de, ibid. That manor was not de corpore comitatus, 11 Henry iii. II. 167. c. 2. w.

Derneford, Richard de, one of the jufticiers who fettled the Wiltfhire tallage, 20 Henry iii. I. 707. c. 1. k. Roger de Derneford, 12 John, I.

795.

INDEX.

795. c. 1. *m.* Fines as not producing the person he was manucaptor for, ibid.

Dersingham, Godwin de, amerc'd for lading ships, 12 Henry ii. I. 558. c. 1. *n.*

Derteford belonged to the earl of Albemarle, before 23 Henry ii. I. 302. c. 2. *b.* Was the manor of the earl of St. Paul's, ibid. Dertford or Tarenteford, its aid, 14 Henry ii. I. 588. c. 2. *d.* William de, one of the curators of St. Edward's shrine, 53 Henry iii. II. 167. c. 2. *x.*

Dertemue, the quinzime for the merchandise of this port, 6 John, I. 772. c. 2.

Dertinton honor in Devonshire seiz'd, because Alice de Nonant married without leave, 33 Henry ii. I. 637. c. 1. *a, b,*

Dervorgulla, daughter and heiress of John de Burgo, married to Robert Fitz-walter before 14 Edward i. I. 320. c. 2. *o.* Has a Moiety of the barony of Hawis de Launvalley, ib.

Dery, John son of, 5 Edward i. II. 219. c. 1. *c.* Not to be served with a writ, being in the king's service in Wales, ibid.

Descrupes, Richard, 6 John, I. 250. c. 2. *p.* His scutage for his three fees in Worcestershire, 3 John, I. 660. c. 1. *f.*

Desforz or de Fortibus, William, accompts for the scutage of the honors of Scipton and Albemarl, 3 Richard i. I. 637. ibid. c. 1. *f.*

Despaigne, Mr. James, his privilege, 1 Edward ii. II. 76. c. 2. *d.* Garsias de Hispania, king's equerry, 21 Edward i. II. 81. James Despaigne, the king's kinsman, made chamberlain, 10 Edward ii. II. 302. c. 2. *h.*

Despenser, Hugh le, justicier of England, 49 Henry iii. I. 70. Hugh le Despenser, 1 Edward ii. I. 75. See Dispenser.

Deveneis, John le, accompts for Robert de Haya as sherif of Bedford and Bucks, 25 Henry iii. II. 177. c. 2. *f.* William de Deveneys, late ingrosser of the Exchequer at Dublin, 30 Edward i. II. 270. c. 1. *h.*

Deverel, Ralf de, holds of the church of Chichester, temp. Henry ii. I. 576. c. 1. *y.* The tallage of that town, 33 Henry ii. I. 634. c. 1. *q.*

Devery, John, chamberlain of the Exchequer, 12 Edward ii. II. 262. c. 2. Appointed clerk for writing the tallies, 34 Edward i. II. 305. c. 2. *o.*

Devises have a confirmation of liberties, 2 John, I. 402. c. 2. *i.* Their aid, 23 Henry ii. I. 604. c. 1. *l.* Devises in Wiltshire, its donum, 33 Henry ii. I. 634. c. 1. *q.* Its tallage, 10 Richard i. I. 700. c. 1. *s.* The assise or tallage of the Devises, 19 Henry ii. I. 702. c. 1. *d.* Tallaged again, 1 John, I. 705. c. 2. *z.* And again, 30 Henry iii. I. 711. c. 1. *y.* Tallaged, 20 Henry iii. I. 743. c. 2. *r.* Castle of Devises kept by John Mareschal before 11 Henry iii. I. 765. c. 1. *i.* Knights of Wiltshire owned ward to the castle of Devises, II. 117.

Devonshire had two sherifs, 23 Henry ii. I. 133. c. 1. *n.* De-afforested, 6 John, I. 406. c. 2. *x.* Fine for a sherif from among themselves, 14 Henry iii. I. 417. c. 2. *g.* William earl of, before 9 Henry iii. I. 445. c. 2. *f.* Fine to be kindly treated, 7 Richard i. I. 502. c. 1. *x.* The aid of this county, 23 Henry ii. I. 603. c. 2. *i.* Richard earl of Devonshire,

INDEX.

vonshire, his aid from Plomton, Plumland, Tiverton, Huneton, &c. 24 Henry ii. I. 604. c. 2. n. 605. c. 1. o. H. Devoniensis, justicier, 13 Henry iii. I. 718. c. 1. m. Margaret, countess of Devonshire, 45 Henry iii. II. 15. c. 1. u. Amicia countess, 56 Henry iii. ibid. c. 1. w. Geoffrey and William de Mandevill, earls of Devonshire, 6, 15, and 31 Henry ii. II. 164. c. 1. c, d, c. 2. e. William de Vernun, earl of Devon, 5 John, II. 165. c. 1. b. Baldewyn de Lisle, late earl of Devon, 13 Edward i. II. 165. c. 1. k. Hugh, son of Hugh de Courteney earl of Devon, inherits the title from Isabella [f. Lisle] 26 Edward i. II. 165. c. 2. n.

Dewias, Robert, had the right of homage for five fees for Godfrey de Scudemor, 14 Henry ii. I. 583. c. 1. b. Robert Dewias, his scutage in Herefordshire, 8 Richard i. I. 664. c. 2. b.

Dexlesalt the Jew, his fine, I. 166.

Deyvil, John, discharg'd from scutage, 12 Edward ii. I. 673. c. 2. n. Roger Deyvil, commissioner of the array for the wapentake of Hovenden, 16 Edward ii. II. 112. c. 2.

Dichford, Geoffrey de, sherif of Glocestershire, 4 Henry iii. I. 495. c. 2. f.

Dicton, Ralf de, bailif of earl Richard at Queenhith, 14 Henry iii. II. 228. c. 1. f.

Dieppe, the scaccarium of, I. 164. c. 2. d. The provost of Dieppe, I. 168. c. 2.

Diganeswel, to whom that land belonged about an. 1162. I. 34. c. 1. u.

Digneneton, Hugh de, clerk, accompted for the chevage of the Jews, 5 and 6 Edward i. I. 254. c. 1. h.

Dimmebac, Richard, 5 John, I. 471. c. 2. z. His appeal against Walter de Trailli for a breach of peace, ibid.

Dimmoc and Menstrewrda manors, I. 192. c. 1. t. Dimmoch in Glocestershire, its tallage, 19 Henry ii. I. 701. c. 2. c. Again, 7 Richard i. I. 703. c. 2. n. John Dimmok sued for the king, 21 Edward i. II. 81. See Dymmok.

Dinan, Rolland de, has the fee of Wepham, 14 Henry ii. I. 583. c. 1. k. Oliver de Dinan has Nutwel, Devonshire, 14 Henry ii. I. 588. c. 2. b. Rolland de, 18 Henry ii. I. 632. c. 2. n. Gotso de Dinan's lands in Herefordshire, temp. Stephen, II. 138. c. 2. e.

Dionysa, daughter of Roland, 53 Henry iii. I. 253. c. 2. a. Her complaint to the king that the judges acted contra legem terræ, ibid.

Dionysia, daughter of Robert de Traci, fines for a recognition of land, which her father was seiz'd of when he went to Jerusalem, I. 431. c. 2. p.

Dionysius or Denys, canons of St. their land from Richard i. I. 409. c. 1. a. Were probably in Southampton, ibid.

Discharges and pardons, II. 220.

Disme in aid of the Holy Land, 34 Henry ii. I. 20. The refractory opposers imprison'd, 34 Henry ii, ibid. Disme or decima, I. 730. passim.

Dismembring, I. 8. c. 2. p. & I. 12. c. 2. p. By cutting off the foot and fist, 3 Henry iii. I. 347. c. 1. w.

Dispenser, Hugh, teste, 11 Henry iii. I. 63. c. 2. l. Geoffrey teste, 17 Henry iii. I. 56. c. 2. n. Hugh Despencer, justiciary of England, I. 76. c. 1. u. William Dispensator, 18 Henry ii. I. 559. c. 2. p. Hugh le

INDEX.

le Despenser, one of the king's barons and courtiers, 26 Edward i. I. 655. c. 2. Hugh le Dispenser, 5 Edward ii. II. 7. c. 1. e. Geoffrey le Despenser of Glocestershire distrain'd, 35 Henry iii. II. 17. c. 2. i. Hugh le Despenser sat in the Exchequer, 2 Edward ii. II. 30. c. 2. g. and in 5 Edward ii. II. 37. c. 1. m. Geoffrey Dispenser, 16 Henry iii. II. 33. c. 2. x. Hugh le Dispenser, justicier, 49 Henry iii. II. 36. c. 2. f. Hugh occurs again in the Exchequer, 2 Edw. ii. II. 90.

Disseisins, amerciaments for them, I. 549. passim.

Distreining of clerks, II. 248.

Ditton seems to be a palace royal, 9 Edward ii. I. 599. c. 2. g. passim.

Diva, Maud de, loses some lands in Lincolnshire, 10 John, I. 107. c. 2. c. Maud de Diva fines that she may not be compel'd to marry, 10 Richard i. I. 464. c. 2. k. Gamel Fitz Hugh de Dive slain, 14 John, I. 495. c. 2. d. Ralf Dives of Lidford amerc'd for a gild without warant, 26 Henry ii. I. 562. c. 2. c. Guy de Diva quit of escuage for the king's ransom, 7 Richard i. I. 591. c. 2. t.

Division of the king's courts, I. 788. 800.

Doai, Roger de, 12 John, I. 794. c. 2. k. His house, gardens, and lands in Ketelberge, carried off, burnt, &c. ibid.

Dodinton wood, the interest of the prior of St. Thomas's hospital, Stamford, there, II. 48. c. 2. d. The men of Doddington to pay their debts to the crown, salvo contenemento, 14 Edward i. II. 209. c. 1. o. The liberty of Robert de Champeyne, 18 Edward i. II. 248. c. 2. y. In Northamptonshire, ibid.

Doge, Hamon, of Canterbury, not tallaged, because he exercised no merchandize, 53 Henry iii. I. 727. c. 1. m.

Doget, John, servant of John Dymmok, usher of the Exchequer, 2 Edward ii. II. 279. c. 2. z.

Dolfin, Richard, 9 Richard i. I. 789. c. 2. h. His tenure from Roger de Ginges, ibid.

Dolium of wine at two marks, 29 Henry iii. I. 768. c. 1. n.

Domerham, Wiltshire, its donum, 33 Henry ii. I. 634. c. 2.

Domesday book, an exact description of the lands of the whole realm, I. 177. Attended upon the king's seal, I. 194. c. 1. r. Dated at the end in a coeval hand, an. 1086. I. 296. a.

Domisellæ or damsels of the queen, 10 John, I. 369. c. 2. d.

Domus Dei Dovor, hospital of, I. 73. c. 1. q. The master and brothers hold in Frankalmoign, temp. Edward i. I. 670.

Donum to the crown styled auxilium, I. 602, 603. Donum prælatorum, 5 John, I. 605. Why scutage titled de Dono, I. 625, 626. Donum, a general word used with great latitude, I. 695. But in later times chiefly signified tallagium, ibid. The same with Assisa, I. 696.

Dorchestre, Mr. Osbert de, fermer of the abbey of Middelton, 31 Henry ii. I. 310. c. 2. b. Dorchester in Dorsetshire, its aid, 5 Stephen, I. 600. c. 2. b. Its tallage, 19 Henry iii. I. 735. c. 1. i.

Dorescuilz, Richard, amerc'd for being at the siege of Bristou castle, 7 Richard i. I. 564. c. 1. w.

Dorsete, Alexander de, his mint, 9 Henry iii. I. 389. c. 1. g. How far the counties of Dorset and Somerset

INDEX.

merſet were de-afforeſted, 3 Henry iii. I. 412. c. 2. *g*. Dorſet and Somerſetſhire fine for a ſherif from among themſelves, William Briewerre excepted, 12 John, I. 508. c. 1. *k*. Alexander de Dorſete ſettles the tallage of Lancaſhire, 11 Henry iii. I. 707. c. 1. *h*. Delivers the dies of the mint, 13 Henry iii. II. 134. c. 1. *r*.

Douketon in Hampſhire, tallaged, 6 Edward ii. I. 744. c. 2. *y*.

Douneſley, ſire Phelippe de, chamberlain of the Exchequer, 22 Edward i. I. 298. c. 2. *n*.

Doura or Dovor, John de, his claim on Gorcote and Witteſhage, 31 Henry ii. I. 97. c. 2. *y*. Again, 1 Richard i. I. 38. c. 1. *g*. A monk and attorney for Chriſtchurch, Canterbury, 9 Richard i. I. 114. c. 1. *s*. One of the chief juſtices errant, 20 Henry ii. I. 125. c. 1. *f*. Caſtle of, I. 212. c. 1. *o*. Prior of St. Martin's of Dovor, 29 Henry iii. I. 238. c. 1. *r*. Fulbert, ſon of John de Doura, 10 Richard i. I. 252. c. 1. *s*. Sherif lays out 13 *l*. 6 *s*. 8 *d*. at the knighting of William de Doura, 2 Henry ii. I. 372. c. 1. *o*. Roheis de Doura fines for the moiety of the lands of Richard de Luci, her grandfather, 7 Richard i. I. 464. c. 2. *e*. Fulbertus de Doura fines for the caſtle of Chilham, 1 John, I. 485. c. 2. *e*. Maud de Doura, to whom her honor of Brun deſcended, I. 512. c. 2. *u*. Stephen de Peneceſtre, conſtable of Dovor, 1 Edward i. I. 610. c. 2. John de Doura's ſcutage for his fees in Chent, 18 Henry ii. I. 630. c. 1. *d*. The honor of Piperel of Doura, ibid. The quinzime for the merchandiſe of this port, 6 John, I. 772. c. 1. *i*. Huiam, parcel of the barony of Dovor, in whoſe hands at and before 10 Richard i. II. 226. c. 1. *w*. Nicolas de Tykehul, late keeper of the king's victuals in the caſtle of Dovor, 15 Edw. ii. II. 226. c. 1. *h*.

Dower, not to be diſtrein'd for debts of the deceas'd, II. 191.

Drahton belonged to the king of Scots, 13 Henry ii. I. 539. c. 1. *w*.

Drayton, Suſſex, the priory of Boxgrave had lands there, 9 Edward ii. I. 599. c. 2. *g*.

Dravet, Lambin, of Canterbury, cuſtos cunei there, 22 Henry iii. II. 88. c. 1.

Draxe, Yorkſhire, the burgh of Hugh Paynel, tallaged, 30 Henry iii. I. 710. c. 2.

Drengs and Theins, 23 Henry ii. I. 130. c. 2. *u*. See Theins. The drengage of Uctred de Stanhol in Lancaſhire, 3 John, I. 333. c. 1. *i*. Drengage of Gilbert de Calveley in Northumberland, 3 John, I. 487. c. 1. *p*. Service of Drengs belonging to earl Conan's honor, 18 Henry ii. I. 631. c. 2. *l*. Eighteen Drengs of Weſtmerland, 2 John, I. 659. c. 1. *x*. ibid. c. 2. *z*. Drengs and fermours of the biſhopric, 8 Richard i. I. 714. c. 2. Drengs, theins, and villani of the biſhopric, 13 Henry iii. I. 717. c. 2. *l*. Their tallage, ibid.

Dreyton, Roger de, 18 Edward i. II. 281. c. 1. *f*. A manucaptor, ibid.

Driffeld, the men of, I. 329. c. 1. *w*. Their donum, 3 Richard i. I. 698. c. 2. *p*.

Drincourt, its tallage, I. 167.

Droeis, Hugh le, one of the juſticiers ſettling the Wiltſhire tallage, 20 Henry iii. I. 707. c. 1. *k*.

Drogo,

INDEX.

Drogo, Ralf son of, 2 Henry iii. I. 273. c. 1. d. Richard, son of Drue, 7 John, I. 791. c. 1. o. Ralf, son of Drogo, had the ferm of Grimesbi, 14 Henry ii. II. 220. c. 2. p. Which is answer'd by his sons Walter and Drogo, ibid.

Drokenesford, John de, keeper of the wardrobe, has the custody of the king's seal, 30 Edward i. I. 72. The barons of the Exchequer to do as he should direct them, 26 Edward i. I. 380. c. 1. s. Sir John de Drokensford has the writs to send to the barons at court, 26 Edward i. I. 655. c. 2. Was chancellor of the Exchequer, 1 Edward ii. II. 30. Again, II. 53. c. 1. c. Keeper of the wardrobe, 24 Edward i. II. 71. c. 1. k. and 34 Edward i. ibid. c. 2. l. John de Drokenesford, lieutenant of the treasury, 25 and 26 Edward i. II. 165. c. 2. m. John de Drokenesford, treasurer's lieutenant, 34 Edward i. II. 256. c. 1. u. Again, 34 Edward i. II. 305. c. 1. o.

Dru, Walter, vicesherif of John de Albernum for Surrey and Sussex, 51 Henry iii. II. 180. c. 1. b.

Druel, John, commissioner of the array for the wapentake of Pykering, 16 Edward ii. II. 112. c. 2. Simon Druel, an officer of the Exchequer, 9 Henry iii. II. 311.

Drumar, Reynald de, 49 Henry iii. I. 769. c. 2. Has an hogshead of wine assign'd him by the king, ibid.

Drury, Nigel, sherif of London, 1 Edward ii. II. 97. c. 1. b.

Dryby, Simon, son of Robert de, his lands in Little Askeby held by Beatrice, widow of Robert de Kirkeby, in Hoyland, 9 Edward ii. I. 646. c. 1. x. Simon de Dryby appears to be chief commander at sea, 12 Edward ii. II. 110. c. 1. z.

Duarenus, Pref. xxiii. c. 1. s.

Dublin, Laurence, archbishop of, an. 1175. I. 18. c. 1. f. John archbishop of, an. 1189. I. 22. Bishop of Dublin sat in the Exchequer, 26 Edward i. II. 29. Luke, elect of Dublin from the archdeaconry of Norwich, 14 Henry iii. II. 317. c. 1. a.

Duc, Peter le, sherif or fermer of London, 11 John, I. 193. c. 2. n.

Duchesne, I. 92. c. 2. t. 93. c. 1. u.

Dudavill, Robert de, his relief, 24 Henry ii. I. 316. c. 2. d. Seems to be father of De Odavil, I. 316. c. 2. e.

Duddeleg honor in Worcestershire belong'd to Roger de Sumery, 17 Henry iii. I. 510. c. 2. e.

Duel, a fine owing to have one in the king's court, 30 Henry ii. I. 97. c. 1. u. Again, 31 Henry ii. I. 97. c. 2. b. A fine for one, 28 Henry ii. I. 104. c. 2. n. One executed who was vanquish'd in a duel, 2 Henry ii. I. 372. c. 2. s. Recovery of land by duel, I. 426. c. 2. s. Mabel Pancefot fined, that a duel between her and Robert her brother might be hindred, 31 Henry ii. I. 451. c. 1. w. Other fines for concords of duels, I. 470. c. 2. o. I. 471. c. 1. r, s.

Dufresne's Latin glossary, Pref. xviii. c. 2. xix. c. 1. i.

Dugdale, sir William, I. 45. His collections, I. 56. Corrected about the meaning of the word justiciarius, I. 142. c. 2. i.

Duket, Nicolas, executed the office of chamberlain of London in the close of Richard i. I. 776. c. 1. r.

Dulzan, Ernald, 22 Henry ii. I. 561. c. 1. g. In misericordia for demanding

INDEX.

manding land which he had before quitclaimed, ibid.

Dumar, Engelram de, his fine, 21 Henry ii. I. 450. c. 2. *q*. Ralf de Dumere, I. 649. c. 1. *f*. His fees of Moreton where three make two, ibid.

Dumbarr, Patrick de, one of the king's barons and courtiers, 26 Edward i. I. 655. c. 2.

Dun, Roger, plegius of Walter de Clyfford, 9 Henry iii. I. 318. c. 2. *a*. William de la Duna, his aid, 14 Henry ii. I. 586. c. 2. *x*. Aldrede de Duna of Devonshire, I. 588. c. 1. *b*. The assise or tallage of de la Duna [f. Dunchurch] 19 Henry ii. I. 701. c. 1. *z*.

Dunden, John, clerk of the receipt of the Exchequer, 53 Henry iii. II. 304. c. 1. *m*.

Duneslie in Essex escheated, and not the terra of William Pollard, 11 Henry iii. II. 118. c. 2. *i*.

Dunestanvilla, Adeliza de, 5 Stephen, I. 425. c. 1. *b*. Walter de Dunstanvill accompts for the fees of the earl of Arundel, 14 Henry ii. I. 583. c. 1. *k*.

Dunestaple, Henry i. kept his Christmass there, and received an embassy from the earl of Anjou, an. 1123. I. 12. c. 1. *o*. Final concord made there, I. 215. c. 1. *a*. William and Robert de Dunestapele, temp. Edward i. and Edward ii. II. 102. c. 1. *z*. Held the lands of William de Taillour in Winchester, ibid.

Dungion, Laurence de, 4 John, I. 176. c. 2. *t*. The king's debt to him, ibid.

Dunham Soke, its liberties from Henry i. confirm'd, 29 Henry ii. I. 398. c. 2. *x*.

Dunmowe, St. Mary, a grant to that church, I. 45. c. 1. *i*. The hundred of Dunmawe, I. 321. c. 2. *r*. That hundred fines for a murder, 5 Richard i. II. 20. c. 2. *a*. The interest of the nuns of Caen in Dunmawe, ibid.

Dunolmo, William de, bailif of London, accompts as one of the custodes, 52 Henry iii. I. 779. c. 1. *e*. A præcipe to him, 52 Henry ii. II. 237. c. 2. *q*. See Durham.

Dunstor, Richard, provost of, amerc'd for exporting corn, 29 Henry ii. I. 558. c. 1. *p*. William de St. Leodegario holds of the honor of Dunestor, Dorsetshire, 2 John, I. 659. c. 1. *w*.

Dunwich, their charter of privileges at large, 1 John, I. 401. c. 2. *g*. Their large tallage, 2 Henry iii. I. 706. c. 2. *e*. Tallaged, 14 Henry iii. I. 725. c. 2. *g*. The quinzime for the merchandise of the port of Dunwiz, 6 John, I. 772. c. 1. *i*. Seiz'd into the king's hand, 11 Henry iii. II. 244. c. 2. *n*.

Durandus, the depriv'd prior of Montacute, 10 John, I. 479. c. 1. *x*. Walter, son of Durand, one of the Westmorland Drengs, 2 John, I. 659. c. 1. *x*. John Duraunt, 14 Edward i. II. 103. To treat of the affairs of the merchants of England and Flanders, ibid.

Dureford, abbat of, holds in frankalmoigne, 9 Edward ii. I. 600. c. 1. *g*.

Durham, Hugh bishop of, sent by Henry ii. into Scotland to collect the disme for the crusade, I. 21. Geoffrey bishop of, chancellor, tem. Henry i. I. 56. c. 1. *o*. The executors of Philip bishop of Durham, 10 John, I. 263. c. 2. *n*. That fee in the king's hands, 5 Stephen, I. 303. c. 1. *g*. and 306. c. 1. *p*. Philip inrich'd his fee, 1 John, I.

400.

INDEX.

400. c. 2. *z.* And obtains several liberties for it, 9 John, I. 408. c. 2. *u.* The prior of Durham has the bosch of Heiwurd, I. 409. c. 2. *b.* The tenants of this fee in Lincolnshire, 12 John, I. 410. c. 2. *n.* Richard [Poor] bishop of Durham fines to disforest all the land between Ouse and Derwent, 19 Henry iii. I. 420. c. 1. *q.* Philip occurs bishop, 4 John, I. 517. c. 1. *o.* Daniel de Duralme amerc'd, 12 Henry ii. I. 552. c. 2. *n.* Its aid to the marriage of the daughter of Henry ii. I. 581. c. 2. *x.* And an accompt of its knights fees, ibid. Its scutage for its Yorkshire lands towards the Irish expedition, 18 Henry ii. I. 629. c. 1. *z.* The scutage for its Yorkshire land, 1 John, I. 638. c. 1. *i.* Accompt of the profits of the fee during several years vacancy, 13 John, I. 644. c. 1. *o.* Intitled to fines for marriage, ibid. In the king's hands, temp. Richard i. I. 714. c. 1. *g.* The bishop's great ship, ibid. Issues and titles of its baronies, I. 715. c. 2. See I. 717. 720. 733. Bishop Philip, 10 Richard i. II. 220. c. 1. *s.*

Durvile, Eustace de, held of the king in capite, I. 622. Hang'd for felony, 6 Edward i. ibid.

Duston, Thomas de, chancellor's purveyour or rather puletarius, 10 Edward ii. I. 76. c. 2. *x.*

Duties upon the exportation of hides, salt, cheese, &c. temp. John, I. 470. c. 1, 2.

Dyed cloth, fines paid for licence to sell it, 6 John, I. 468. c. 1. *o.*

Dykryng wapentake, has a commission of array directed to it, 16 Edward ii. II. 111. c. 1. *c.*

Dymmok, John, ostiary of the Exchequer, 26 Edward i. I. 360. c. 1. *q.* Styled usher, 26 Edward i. II. 9. John Dymmok, usher of the Exchequer, has custody of the Flete prison, 9 Edward ii. II. 85. John Dymmok, usher of the Exchequer, 5 Edward ii. II. 278. c. 1. *u.* II. 279.

Dynington, Edmund de, late auditor of the accompts of the Exchequer, 9 Edward ii. II. 291. c. 1. *d.* & pass.

Dytton, the king's court held there, 36 Henry iii. II. 36. c. 1. *d.*

Dyve Hugh, his barony, how it descended in part, I. 321. John, son and heir of William Dyve, held of the honor of Albemarle, 14 Edward i. II. 100. c. 1. *h.*

Dyvelyn, Robert, usher of the Exchequer, 25 Edward i. II. 104.

E.

Eadmer, a writer coeval with the Conquest, I. 180. And compiler of the dialogue de Scaccario, ibid.

Earls and barons not to be amerced but before their peers, I. 528.

Eat, John son of Henry fined in four marks for leave to eat, 7 Henry iii. I. 509. c. 1. *r.*

Eboraco, William de, amerces the citizens in the tower of London, 30 Henry iii. I. 568. c. 1. *p.* Adam de, late customer of the port of Newcastle, 25 Edward i. I. 782. c. 1. *r.* See York.

Ebrardus dapifer, 5 Stephen, I. 277. c. 2. *c.* Ebrard, the goldsmith, 20 Henry ii. I. 284. c. 1. *s.* Ralf, son of Ebrard, 5 Stephen, I. 426. c. 1. *f.* Ebrard, dapifer of William de Albamara, fines to be quit of

his

INDEX.

his office, 5 Stephen, I. 457. c. 1. *o.* John and Robert, sons of Ralf son of Ebrard, 5 Stephen, I. 482. c. 1. *d.* Ralf, son of Ebrard, custos of the see of Sarum, 31 Henry ii. I. 311. c. 1. *d.* and 33 Henry ii. I. 634. c. 1. *q.* John, son of Ralf son of Ebrard, accompts for the old ferm of London, 5 Stephen, I. 686. c. 2. *d.*

Ebrois, Reginald, son of Robert de, of Cornwal, 5 Stephen, I. 426. c. 1. *o.* Fines pro recto of his father's lands, ibid.

Ecchingham, Simon de, contends for the seneschalcy of the rapp of Hastinges, 9 John, I. 790. c. 2. *m.*

Ecclesclive in Durham, Roger de, his relief, 8 Richard i. I. 714. c. 1. *g.* The church of Egglesclive charged, I. 714.

Ecclesfield, the land of the archbishop of York, 3 John, I. 436. c. 2. *t.* The parson and bosch, ibid.

Ecclesiastical censure, to force women to marry to particular persons, 6 John, I. 465. c. 1. *p.*

Echemendon manor in Shropshire, belonged to James de Audithle, 2 Edward i. II. 101. c. 2. *y.* See Egmendon.

Echingeham, Margery de, her executors, 42 Henry iii. II. 185. c. 1. *k.*

Edburg in Warwickshire, 3 John, whose, I. 436. c. 2. *u.*

Edburgheton, that land bequeathed by Ralf Pevrel, to find lights for the church of St Paul's, London, I. 198. c. 1. *e.*

Edelmeton hundred, I. 544. c. 1. *p.* William de Edelmeton or Edmonton, of London, his tallage, 14 Henry iii. I. 709. c. 1. *s.* Pieres de Edelmeton, alnager of cloth, 26 Edward i. I. 785. c. 1. z. c. 2. *a.*

Edgar earl, uncle of earl Waltheof, the father of earl Patric in Northumberland, 2 John, I. 435. c. 1. *p.* Edgar was son of Gospatric, I. 440. c. 1. *m.* Some account of his lands, ibid.

Edingrave, the land of Peter Morel, 18 Henry ii. I. 315. c. 1. *m.*

Edinton manor in Yorkshire, the claimants, 12 John, I. 448. c. 2. *l.*

Edmund, the king's son, has the grant of all the forfeitures of Simon Montfort earl of Leicester, 49 Henry iii. I. 52. Has an assignment from his brother, 18 Edward i. I. 231. c. 1. *l.* Some farther accompt of the assignment to Edmund earl of Cornwal, 26 Edward i. I. 466. Edmund, brother of Henry iii. I. 476. c. 2. *w.* Edmund the king's brother, 18 Edward i. I. 598. c. 2. *e.* Edmund, son of Edward i. 35 Edward i. II. 125. c. 1. *l.* Edmund earl of Cornwal, 26 and 27 Edward i. II. 180.

Edmund St, his shrine, 42 Henry iii. I. 378. c. 1. *m.* Henry, prior of St Edmund, and Richard the sacrist, fine for the custody of their abbey, 13 Henry iii. I. 416. c. 1. *y*

Edmund late archbishop of Canterbury, II. 190. His legacy to William Talebot, 28 Henry iii. ibid.

Edric, son of Godric, his tedering, 26 Henry ii. I. 555. c. 1. *y.*

Edulf, William, son of, 10 Richard i. I. 452. c. 1. *i.* Fines to deraign the burgesses of Uctred, ibid.

Edward, while prince, adheres to the rebellious, 49 Henry iii. I. 234. c. 1. *c.* Banishes the Jews, 18 Edward i. I. 261. See Alienor queen. Had a queen Margaret, I. 361. c. 2. *x.* Well served in his law-courts, I. 536. Forty shillings out of each knight's fee to marry the king's eldest daughter, 18 Edward i. I. 600.

INDEX.

His laſt expedition againſt Wales, 18 Edward i. I. 611. c. 1. k. A large liſt of his barons ſummoned to attend the war againſt Scotland, 26 Edward i. I. 653, 654. A liſt of his courtiers, I. 655. c. 2. Had the manor of Tikehil, 37 Henry iii. I. 752. c. 1. b. Seiſes goods and money for his neceſſary ſervice, which he requires to be repaid, 35 Edward i. II. 46. c. 1. u. Edward, while prince, had an eldeſt ſon John, 55 Henry iii. II. 93. c. 2. k. Had two ſons, prince Thomas and Edmond, 35 Edward i. II. 125. c. 1. l. Paid nine or ten thouſand marks annually to the pope, nomine cenſus, 9 Edward i. II. 137. c. 1. a. Was of the king's council, 54 Henry iii. II. 170. c. 1. b. Died on the day of the tranſlation of Thomas a Becket, 35 Edward i. II. 174. His aid to make his ſon a knight, II. 261. c. 1. r. Had a ſiſter Elizabeth married to Humfrey de Bohun, II. 283.

Edward ii. how abuſed by his judges, I. 536. A vintiſm to make him a knight while prince, I. 618. c. 2. t. His titles of prince of Wales, earl of Cheſter, Pountyf, and Monſtroil, 35 Edward i. I. 657. c. 2. Changes his treaſurers of the Exchequer, II. 38, 39. Removes all the ſherifs in England, 8 Edward ii. II. 69. A proſecution for irreverent words againſt him, 9 Edward ii. II. 84. c. 1. p. Another, ibid. 85. c. 1. r. His judges ſuffer it to be debated at the Exchequer, whether the ſherifs of London ſhould ſwear there, 9 Edward ii. II. 97. c. 2. c. His commiſſion of array againſt the Scots, II. 110, 111. Remits the arrears of taxes to thoſe who had ſerved his father againſt the French in Aquitain, 12 Edward ii. II. 231. c. 1. n. Had a brother, viz. Thomas de Brotherton, II. 287.

Edward, alderman of the gild of pepperers, 26 Henry ii. I. 562. c. 1. z.

Egeneſham abbey, or Eynſham, I. 582. c. 1. d.

Eggeham and Thorp manors belonged to the abbat of Chertſey, 15 John, I. 490. c. 2. w.

Eggemere, John de, oſtiary of the Exchequer, 9 Edward ii. I. 381. c. 1. x. II. 101. Adam de Eggeſmare, 12 John, I. 453. c. 2. y. James de Eggemere, uſher of the Exchequer, 14 Edward i. II. 238. John de, uſher of the Exchequer, 5 Edward ii. II. 278. c. 1. u. 279. c. 1. y. James de Eggemere, uſher of the Exchequer, 20 Edward i. II. 278. c. 2. w. John de, II. 279. James de, 18 Edward i. II. 281. c. 1. f. Being uſher of the Exchequer, he attaches the ſherif of Cornwal, ibid.

Eggeſwer, terra de, I. 429. c. 2. s.

Eggeton in Yorkſhire, its tallage, 30 Henry iii. I. 710. c. 1. w.

Eggleſhey, Matthew de, ſherif of Devonſhire, 5 Edward i. II. 142. c. 2. b.

Eggulf, amerced for a gild ſans warant, 26 Henry ii. I. 562. c. 2. c.

Egidius, biſhop of Hereford, 7 John, I. 407. c. 2. g. Obtains a charter of liberties, ibid.

Egilton, Rutlandſhire, how tallaged, I. 724.

Eginedon in Shropſhire tallaged, 1 John, I. 705. c. 2. y.

Eglesfeld, Adam de, baron of the Exchequer, aſſigned to ſurvey the king's caſtles and manors, 1 Edward ii. II. 67. c. 1. q.

Egmendon in Shropſhire, its tallage, 8 John, I. 734. c. 1. z.

Egremunt,

INDEX.

Egremunt, William de, suspected for the death of Walter Belle, Cumberland, 10 John, I. 495. c. 1. *y.*

Eightpence, Osbert, surety for Hugh Cordele, 5 Stephen, II. 197.

Eilesham, prior of, 7 John, I. 448. c. 1. *g.*

Eimeric, archdeacon of Durham, had received the crown revenues, 11 John, I. 384. c. 1. *l.* One of the executors of bishop Philip, and pays large sums for the king's goodwill, 10 John, I. 477. c. 1, 2. *h.* That bishop's nephew was custos of Durham, 13 John, I. 644. c. 1. *o.*

Einesford, William de, his release to the church of Westminster, 1 Richard i. I. 155. See Ainesford.

Eir, Roger de, amerced for not answering in the court of the dean of Waltham, 14 Henry ii. I. 559. c. 1. *c.*

Eland, John de, has a commission of array for the wapentak of Morley, 16 Edward ii. II. 112. c. 1.

Elcoft, Stephen de, of Yorkshire, 52 Henry iii. II. 15. c. 1. *t.* His trespass, ibid.

Eleford, Robert de, fines for non-passage, &c. 26 Henry iii. I. 660. c. 1. *e.*

Elemosinarius, William, his dane-geld, 5 Stephen, I. 686. c. 1. *b.*

Elephant in the tower, 39 Henry iii. I. 377. c. 1. *c.*

Elefwurth, Simon de, dead, 25 Edward i. II. 44. c. 2. *q.*

Elfeifcote, Oxfordshire, tallaged, 3 John, I. 721. c. 2. *y.*

Elingeham, a duel depending between Julian de Swadefeld and William de Curton for that land, 9 John, I. 507. c. 1. *a.*

Elinant, Rad. sherif of London, 2 Henry iii. I. 193. c. 1. *f.*

Elleford, William de, an outlaw, a reward for bringing his head to Westminster, 7 Richard i. I. 201. c. 2. *t.*

Ellesfeld, Walter de, clerk of the sherif of Hereford, 21 Edward i. II. 278. c. 2. *w.*

Ellestede, Robert de, fines in six vulperets or fox dogs, 16 John, I. 274. c. 1. *k.* The same repeated, I. 444. c. 1. *r.*

Ellethorn hundred, I. 544. c. 1. *o.*

Elmeham, its liberties, II. 21. c. 1. *e.*

Elmifhal in Yorkshire, its tallage, 30 Henry iii. I. 710. c. 1. *w.*

Elnefted, Sussex, I. 599. c. 2. *g.*

Elnod and Norman brethren, 5 Stephen, I. 557. c. 1. *d.* Amerced for breach of peace, ibid.

Elvefton, the land of Robert de Joy, 22 Henry ii. I. 300. c. 1. *q.*

Elveyn in Surrey, land held there, to find a cook at the coronation, I. 651. c. 1. *r.*

Ely, William de, king's treasurer, 3 John, I. 80. c. 1. *b.* Peter de Ely conveies the king's money arising from the carucage, 2 John, I. 173. c. 1. *c.* William de Ely treasurer, 2 John, I. 175. c. 2. *p.* John de Ely servant in the Exchequer, 42 Henry iii. II. 18. c. 2. *o.* Geoffrey de Ely accompts for John Howard, sherif of Norfolk and Suffolk, 12 Edward ii. II. 181. c. 2. *q.* Emme, widow of John de Ely, 32 Henry iii. II. 229. c. 2. *q.* Gerand. de Ely attorney of Odo de Westminster, 53 Henry iii. II. 310. Nicolas de Ely king's treasurer, 48 Henry iii. II. 319. c. 1. *k.*

Ely, William Longchamp, bishop of, justicier, chancellor, pope's legate, and one of the regency, temp. Richard i. I. 35. Is deposed, ibid. Nigellus bishop of, temp. Henry i. I. 56. c. 1. *o.* I. 78, 79. Monks of Ely,

INDEX.

Ely, 14 Henry ii. I. 82. That fee in cuftody of Geoffrey Ridel, 16 Henry ii. I. 307. c. 1. *x*. and 19 Henry ii. I. 308. c. 2. *g*. Its efcuage for the king's ranfom, 6 Richard i. I. 590. c. 2. *l*. Some accompt of the tenants of this fee, I. 618. Scutage of Gannoc for that fee, 30 Henry iii. I. 667. c. 1. *n*. Monks indeavour to replevy their priory, 27 Edward i. II. 178. The inclufa de S. Maria here, II. 207, c. 1. *c*. Quæ folebat habere difcum epifcopi, ibid. William bifhop of Ely, 7 Richard i. II. 228. c. 2. *k*. John bifhop of Ely treafurer, 17 Edward i. II. 225. c. 2. *s*.

Ely, Richard, archdeacon of, 9 Richard i. one of the jufticiers, I. 113. Stephen de Ely, 13 Henry ii. I. 201. c. 2. *s*. Ifle of Ely in cuftody of William de Marifco, 7 Richard i. I. 459 c. 2. *q*. William [de Laventona] archdeacon, 2 Henry ii. I. 687. c. 1. *i*.

Elyas, ufher of the Exchequer, 13 Henry ii. 2 Richard i. II. 273. c. 1, 2, &c. Marries the widow of Roger de Walingford, and has the wardfhip of his children before 16 Henry ii. II. 273. c. 1. *t*.

Elyas the dean, fines for his miftrefs and children, 3 John, I. 493. c. 2. *i*. William, fon of Elyas, fines for a falfe oath or verdict, 9 John, I. 507. c. 1. *b*. Simon, fon of Elyas, has fhare of Ofbert Martel's land, 18 Henry ii. I. 580. c. 2. *q*. Ingeniator, 10 Richard i. II. 206. c. 2. *a*.

Emma de S. Leodegario, wife of Walter de Bafkervil, and mother of Geoffrey Longcamp, I. 513. c. 2. *b*. Henry, fon of Emma, his tallage, 12 Henry iii. I. 708. c. 1. *n*.

Emprefs Maud, her grant to Geoffrey earl of Effex, II. 138. c. 1. *d*.

Enewurd in Chent, the land of William Fulkelin there, 17 Henry ii. I. 429. c. 2. *u*.

Engaine, Richard, accompts for Cambridge and Huntingdonfhire, 15 John, I. 274. c. 1. *l*. Warner Engayne, cuftos of the honor of Richmond before 19 Henry iii. I. 335. c. 1. *z*. Richard Engaine, fherif of Northamptonfhire, 3 Richard i. I. 458. c. 2. *h*. Vitalis Engayne, 22 Henry iii. I. 648. c. 1. *c*. John fummoned with the barons againft the Scots, 26 Edward i. I. 655. c. 1. Warner Engayne, late keeper of the king's manors, attached, 29 Henry iii. II. 243. c. 1. *e*.

Engelby, William de, fherif of Lincolnfhire before 52 Henry iii. II. 202. c. 2. *z*.

Engelfeud, William de, fherif of Devonfhire, 39 Henry iii. I. 597. c. 2. *a*. II. 193. c. 1. *d*.

Engelram, Randulf, fon of, fherif of Notingham and Derbyfhire, 9 Henry ii. I. 336. c. 1. *d*.

Englefchery, what, I. 565. c. 1. *g, h*.

Eoda, earl of Campania, Rufus's fon-in-law, I. 8. Deprived of his lands for treafon, ibid.

Erardus, Mr. of Yorkfhire, 8 Richard i. I. 737. c. 1. *s*. Tallaged for his lands in Yorkfhire, and the king's favour, ibid.

Erchembald, Stephen, fon of, fines for homicide, 5 Stephen, I. 497. c. 1. *z*. Again, I. 543. c. 2. *d*.

Erclave, John de, protected as in the Welch expedition, 5 Edward i. II. 219. c. 1. *c*.

Erenbald, William, fon of, fermer of the mine of Carlifle, 19 Henry ii. II. 205.

Erefwell

INDEX.

Erefwell manor in Suffolk, held by Robert de Tudenham and Eve his wife, temp. Henry iii. I. 623. c. 1. *i.* But came to Eve by enfeoffment, and was parcel of the honor of Boloigne, I. 623. After a pretty long fuccession through the hands of Ralf fenior, William, Peter, Henry, and Ralf de Rouceftre, I. 623. c. 1. *i.* Held by the fervice of two knights fees, ibid.

Erghum, the heirs of William de, of Yorkfhire, tallaged, 14 Henry iii. I. 708. c. 2. *p.*

Erham, Richard de, held of the church of Chichefter, temp. Henry ii. I. 576. c. 1. *y.*

Erleia, John de, his record, 3 John, I. 106. c. 2. *y.* Styled de Derleia, ibid. John de Erlega, 9 Henry iii. I. 492. c. 2. *y.* Plegius of Richard de Wroteham, ibid.

Erlham, Rofamund de, of Hamfhire, her proffrum, 56 Henry iii. II. 87. c. 2. *y.*

Erlinton, Ralf de, of Northumberland, 10 John, I. 489. c. 2. *p.* Has feifin of the bofch of Langele called Wiveteley, and holds of the king of Scots, ibid.

Ermentruill, an award on a horfe's killing a woman at the market there, I. 163. c. 2. *x.*

Ermina, William de Sancta, 55 Henry iii. II. 203. c. 1. *b.*

Ernald, man of the bifhop of Carlifle, 10 Henry iii. I. 793. c. 2. *f.* Sampfon Ernald, his cafe, I. 793. c. 2. *g.*

Ernald, fon of Fromond, 5 Stephen, I. 204. c. 1. *f.* Ernald, fon of Enifand, his homicides in Staffordfhire, 5 Stephen, I. 497. c. 2. *d.* Prefbyter, 1 Richard i. I. 563. c. 2. *n.*

Ernifa, clerk of the earl of Glocefter, 31 Henry ii. I. 549. c. 2. *f.*

Ernuceon, Robert, fon of, 5 Stephen, I. 426. c. 1. *g. l.* Pines for his father's debts, ibid.

Ernulf, abbat of Burgh, compelled to take the fee of Rochefter, an. 1114. I. 11. c. 2. *k.*

Efberga, Bucks, a knight's fee there, by whom claimed, 29 Henry ii. I. 105. c. 1. *p.*

Efcheats of honours, baronies, and vacant bifhopricks, I. 295. By devolution, forfeiture, or feifure, I. 296. The king had the relief, wardfhip, and marriage of them, I. 299. Began about the clofe of Henry ii. ibid. See 306.

Efcheats and wardfhips rendered aid, 14 Henry ii. I. 299, 300. Efcuage rendered by efcheats, I. 641.

Efcheatours brought in the king's money, I. 355. And that anciently, II. 128. Henry de Bray, efcheatour on this fide Trent, amerced for not bringing in his payment, 18 Edward i. II. 155. c. 2. *i.* Sherifs to be efcheators in their counties, 5 Edward i. II. 175. c. 2. *u, w,* &c. Henry de Brai, efcheator on this fide Trent, 27 Edward i. II. 204.

Efchelling, John, his claim on the land of Aileworth againft Avizia, 30 Henry ii. I. 213. c. 1. *r.* His claim in Normandy, 2 John, I. 435. c. 1. *o.* Alice, wife of John de Efchellinges, fines that her hufband may not crofs the seas, 1 John, I. 477. c. 2. *l.*

Efcollandus, Geoffrey, 5 Stephen, I. 79. c. 1. *n.* Cuftos of the fee of Durham, 5 Stephen, I. 306. c. 1. *p.* I. 694. c. 1. *s.* Jordan, 8 Richard i. I. 715. c. 1.

Efcorcevielle, his efcuage towards the king's ranfom, 6 Richard i. I. 590. c. 2. *l.*

Efcorchebou,

INDEX.

Escorchebou, Sell. de, justice in Normandy, 2 John, I. 156. c. 2. *i.*

Escot, Henry le, 26 Edward i. I. 782. c. 1. *r.* Customer of Newcastle upon Tyne, ibid. Richard le Escot pays half a mark a day commitment fees, 53 Henry iii. II. 289.

Escientona, the land belonging to the prior of Bath in the time of bishop Rodbert, I. 112. c. 2. *n.*

Escuage, the revenue arising from it, and whence, I. 619. Was servitium scuti, and rendered according to the knights fees, ibid. Escuage and donum the same, I. 625, 626. Escuage for Ireland, 18 Henry ii. I. 629. and 33 Henry ii. I. 633. And for Wales, 3 Richard i. I. 637. From what tenures this service arose, I. 641. 650, 651. Escuage money in lieu of personal service, I. 652. Some serjeanties paid it, I. 650. How barons or knights holding in capite were acquitted, I. 653. Not chargeable on lands in frankalmoign or socage, I. 670. How escuage was collected, I. 679.

Escuris, Matthew de, justice errant, 20 Henry ii. I. 125.

Esenden, its tallage, 19 Henry ii. I. 701. c. 1. *z.* An assignment to the king's treasurer out of Essenden and Belford, II. 41. c. 2. *b.* II. 42. c. 1. *c.*

Esingwald, Yorkshire, its donum for the Irish expedition, 33 Henry ii. I. 635. c. 2. The tallage of Esingwald and Hoby, 30 Henry iii. I. 710. c. 2.

Esnecca and Snecca, I. 365. c. 2. *t, u, z.*

Esnecy, II. 285. c. 1. *b.*

Espec, Walter, his pleas, 5 Stephen, I. 146. c. 2. *r.* I. 147. c. 1. *s.* Walter Espec, 5 Stephen, I. 303. c. 1. *g.* Fines to be quit of holding pleas in Yorkshire, I. 457. c. 2. *u.* Walter Espec, 6 Henry ii. I. 501. c. 1. *p.* 4 Henry ii. I. 511. c. 2. *n.*

Especer, Nicolas le, belonged to the abbat of St Alban, 38 Henry iii. I. 760, 761. John le, Yorkshire, 52 Henry iii. II. 15. c. 1. *t.*

Espee, Richard le, sworn moneyour of Canterbury, 52 Henry iii. II. 89.

Esperun, John le, attorney for the abbat of Evesham, 56 Henry iii. I. 181. c. 1. *l.* Thomas Esperun, chamberlain of the Exchequer, from Margaret de Ripariis, 29 Henry iii. I. 296. c. 1. *y.* Made controller of the receipt, 39 Henry iii. I. 299. c. 2. *t.*

Espigornel, Nicolas le, custos of Essex and Hertfordshire, 49 Henry iii. I. 287. c. 1. *o.* See Spigurnel.

Espreton, Johel de, of Devonshire, 25 Henry ii. I. 135. c. 1. *q.* Seems to be sherif of Devonshire, 24 Henry ii. I. 732. c. 2. *m.*

Essart, Robert de, 8 Richard i. I. 433. c. 1. *c.* Fines for an inquiry, ibid.

Esse, the quinzime of the merchandise of that port, 6 John, I. 772. c. 2.

Essebi, William de, his fine, 5 Henry ii. I. 449. c. 2. *f.*

Essebiri, Berkshire, I. 705. c. 1. *t.*

Esseburn, amerced for selling stretched cloth, I. 566.

Esseburn hundred, Sussex, II. 20. c. 2. *c.*

Esselega, Walter de, his lands, I. 755. c. 2. *r.* Occurs, 14 Henry iii. II. 116. c. 1. *u.*

Esserefton, Edwi de, of Devonshire, 31 Henry ii. I. 550. c. 1. *t.*

Essewel, Gervase de, amerced for a trespass of the mint, 49 Henry iii. I. 568. c. 2. *t.*

Essewy, William, sherif of London, about 42 Henry iii. I. 253. c. 1. *z.*

Essex county de-afforested from Colchester to Storteford, 6 John, I. 405. c. 2.

INDEX.

c. 2. *r.* Its donum, 4 Henry ii. I. 696. c. 1. *g.*

Effexa, terra Henrici de, 33 Henry ii. I. 4. c. 1. Henry was conftabulary, 2 Henry ii. I. 41. Again the king's conftable, I. 42. See II. 200. c. 1. *c.* and II. 252. c. 2. *s, t.* See Effex.

Effex, Geoffrey earl of, his grant from Maud of the office and lands of Eudo Dapifer in Normandy, I. 49. William earl of, 3 Henry iii. I. 67. c. 1. *x.* Geoffrey orders reftitution to the canons of St Martin, temp. Henry i. I. 108. c. 2. *k.* William de Mandevil earl of Effex, 28 Henry ii. I. 113. c. 1. *r.* Henry de Effex's court, 30 Henry ii. I. 116. c. 1. *a.* Geoffrey Fitz-Peter, earl of Effex, jufticier, 2 John, I. 256. c. 2. Geoffrey had the tertius denarius, 3 Henry ii. I. 281. c. 2. *f.* The honor of Henry de Effexa in the king's hands, 31 Henry ii. I. 298. c. 1. *a.* And likewife, 1 Richard i. I. 298. c. 2. *r.* Henry de Effex, conftabulary and fermer of Buckingham and Bedfordfhire, 2 Henry ii. I. 328. c. 1. *m.* Geoffrey Fitz-Peter, 4 and 5 John, I. 390. c. 1. *o, p.* Henry de Effex, conftable and fherif of Buckingham and Bedfordfhire, 2 Henry ii. I. 688. Settles the affife of Effex, 2 Henry ii. I. 732. c. 1. *k.* Geoffrey's vaft privileges from Maud the emprefs, II. 138. c. 1. *d.* His father William and grandfather Geoffrey, ibid. Geoffrey Fitz-Peter has the land of earl William de Mandevil, 8 Richard i. II. 176. c. 1. *y.* Henry de Effexa's land in cuftody of Ralf Brito, 29 Henry ii. II. 229. c. 2. *m.*

Effingwald in Yorkfhire, the ferm of that mill, II. 184. c. 2. *g.* See Efingwald.

Effington in the bifhopric, the parfons of, 8 Richard i. I. 715. c. 1. Tallaged, 11 Edward i. I. 720. c. 1, *t.*

Effoignes, I. 253. and II. 78.

Effulf, John, fon of, claimed the land of Beldun, 31 Henry ii. I. 431. c. 1. *l.* See Leelay.

Eftbrig hofpital in Canterbury, I. 740. c. 2. *f.*

Eftcoat, Gundwin de, 2 Richard i. I. 564. c. 1. *x.* Difturbed jurors, ibid.

Eftdene, W. de, king's treafurer of Ireland, 22 Edward i. II. 136. c. 1. *x.* William de fucceeded Adam de Stratton as chamberlain, II. 300. c. 2. *x.*

Eftebenhithe feems one of the king's palaces, 26 Edward i. II. 223. c. 2. *l.* Eftebenheth again, II. 283. c. 1.

Eftgreenewich in Kent, manor of, I. 621. c. 2.

Eftland, Richard de, fines for his outlawry or abjuration, 4 John, I. 505. c. 1. *g.*

Eftley, Andrew de, one of the barons fummoned to the Scotch war, 26 Edward i. I. 655. c. 1.

Eftmerden, Suffex, the prior of Boxgrave had lands in it, I. 599. c. 2. *g.*

Eftmerefey in Effex, II. 84.

Efton in Northamptonfhire belonged to Alan, fon of Rolland, 7 Richard i. I. 484. c. 1. *t.* Matthew de Efton his tenure, 11 Henry iii. II. 21. c. 2. *n.* Efton belonged to Alan de Lindon, 14 Henry iii. II. 116. c. 2. *w.* Efton a ferjeanty of the ufhers of the Exchequer, II 275. William de, clerk of the Exchequer, 34 Edward i. II. 306. c. 1. *p.*

Eftorp and Brich, the men of, 7 John, I. 469. c. 2. *f.*

Eftovaria, I. 114. c. 2. *s.*

Eftourneau, a bird, I. 264. c. 2. *y.*

Eftre, Richard del, his three knightsfees from the honor of Moreton, 10 Rich-

INDEX.

10 Richard i. I. 316. The homage and services of Robert del, 6 John, II. 200. c. 2. *i.*

Estreats to be delivered in at the Exchequer by writ of privy seal, II. 7. c. 1. *f.* Estreats or Extractæ Cancellariæ, II. 254. From other courts than the Chancery were called foreign, II. 256. Clerk of the Estreats and foreign summonces, II. 293.

Estreche, Richard, 29 Henry ii. I. 563. c. 2. *l.* Amerced pro falso dicto de Rappo, ibid.

Estrepi, Alard de, 4 John, I. 390. c. 1. *o.* Made the king's man with a fee, ibid.

Esturmit, Richard, who, I. 147. c. 2. *d.* Adam Esturmy, 15 Henry iii. I. 326. c. 1. *l.* Henry Esturmi, sherif of Wiltshire, 2 Henry ii. I. 348. c. 2. *e.* Henry Esturmit, 5 Stephen, I. 456. c. 1. *b.* Henry Esturmi fines for the bailywick of the forest of Savernak, &c. 1 John, I. 460. c. 1. *w.* John Esturmit, his lands, Wilts, 5 Stephen, I. 500. c. 2. *g.*

Estwud, Osbert, son of Hilary de, 10 John, I. 495. c. 1. *w.* Killed in Glocestershire, ibid.

Eswald, Simon de, of Shropshire, 3 John, I. 99. c. 1. *s.* Fines for a plaint, ibid.

Eswy, William, sherif of London, 39 Henry iii. II. 95. c. 1. *r.* See Aswi. Mayor of London, an. 1241. Dissert. Epist. II. 335. c. 2. *k.*

Ethelred in Norfolk, five hundreds and a half of Saint, I. 502. c. 1. *y.*

Eton, William de, 23 Henry ii. I. 210. c. 1. *f.* Fines for an unjust disseisin, ibid. The fair and prior of Eton, 28 Henry iii. II. 19. c. 2. *w.*

Etton in Berkshire, that manor belonged to John Fitz-Walter, 5 Stephen, I. 500. c. 2. *i.*

Eva, Alexander, son of, fines for a disseisin, 10 John, I. 151. c. 2. *x.*

Eve, niece of Hamon Pecche, and wife of Ralf de Roucestre, conveyed the manor of Ereswel to her second husband Robert de Tudenham, I. 623. c. 2. *i.* Simon and Gerard, sons of Eva, 8 Richard i. I. 714. c. 1. *g.* William, son of Eve, a fugitive, 18 Henry ii. I. 344. c. 2. *t.* and II. 131. c. 1. *g.*

Eudo dapifer occurs, 13 John, I. 579. c. 2. *l.*

Eudo, bishop of the Camertes, an. 944. Pref. xxii. c. 2. *r.* Eudo, dapifer of the Conqueror, I. 49. c. 1. *d.* Dapifer in the reign of William Rufus, c. 1. *b.* The honor of Eudo, dapifer, in custody of Hamond de St Clare, 5 Stephen, I. 297. c. 1. *e.* William, son of Eudo, 5 Stephen, I. 476. c. 2. *a.* The fees of Eudo, dapifer, 14 Henry ii. l. 573. c. 2. *m.*

Everard, clerk of Peter de Rival, baron of the Exchequer, 42 Henry iii. II. 17. c. 2. *h.*

Everdon, Alan de, his chattels escheated, 31 Henry ii. I. 345. c. 2. *d.* John de, baron of the Exchequer, 1 Edward ii. I. 75. c. 1. *t.* and 5 Edward ii. II. 6. c. 2. *d.* Again, 1 Edward ii. II. 30. Assigned to survey the king's castles and manors, 1 Edward ii. II. 67. c. 1. *q.* R. de Everdon, baron, 15 Edward ii. II. 182. c. 1. *t.* William, remembrancer, 5 Edward ii. II. 267. II. 269. c. 1. *e.* John de Everdone, baron of the Exchequer, 5 Edward ii. II. 278. c. 1. *u.* Baron of the Exchequer and auditor, &c. 12 Edward ii. II. 292. c. 1. *k.*

Everlai, Wiltshire, the earl of Leicester's

INDEX.

cester's before 19 Henry ii. I. 713. c. 1. *c.*

Everton, Alured de, committed for burning of houses, 12 John, I. 495. c. 1. *z.*

Everwic. See York. The king's works there, 5 Stephen, 146. I. c. 2. *r.* Burgenses de, ibid. Thomas de Everwic, son of Ulivet, fines for alderman, 5 Stephen, I. 397. c. 2. *m.* viz. Of the merchants gild there, ibid.

Evesham abbey, I. 271. c. 1. *b.* In custody about 5 Stephen, I. 306. c. 1. *o.* Accompt of its knights fees, 14 Henry ii. I. 582. c. 1. *b.* The scutage or donum of that abbat, 5 Henry ii. I. 628. c. 1. *u.* The abbat's fees, 14 Henry iii. I. 660. c. 2. *g.* The donum of the abbat and his knights, 5 Henry ii. I. 698. c. 1. *g.* Accompted for, 10 Edward i. I. 720. c. 1. *s.*

Evreux in Normandy, William earl of, an. 1074. I. 49. c. 1. *d.* The abbess of, I. 164. c. 1. *z.* The church of St Taurus, I. 167. Precentor of, I. 311. c. 1. *e.*

Eustachius, earl, his honor in the king's hand, 31 Henry ii. I. 298. c. 1. *b.* and 1 Richard i. I. 298 c. 2. *s.* and 17 Henry ii. II. 200. c. 1. *c.* II. 229. c. 1. *m.* II. 252. c. 1. *s, t.*

Eustachius, elect of Ely, officiates as chancellor, 8 Richard i. I. 29. c. 2. *q.* Was the king's vice-chancellor, 8 Richard i. I. 77. c. 2. *h.*

Ewel, William de, executor of Walter de Merton, 17 Edward i. I. 47. c. 1. *x.* Richard de Ewel, sherif of London, about 42 Henry iii. I. 253. c. 1. *z.* Its aid, 14 Henry ii. I. 587. c. 1. *y.* Richard, 40 Henry iii. II. 18. Sherif of London, 40 Henry iii. II. 95. c. 1. *s.*

Ewiun, Ralf de, 5 Richard i. I. 432. c. 1. *x.* Fines for a record, ibid.

Ewurth barony in the bishopric, 8 Richard i. I. 715. c. 2.

Examen, or tryal by combustion or assay, viz. of the king's money, I. 281, &c.

Exchequer, erected and contrived with great wisdom, Pref. xii. Exchequer of the king a member of his court, I. 1. When it began to be called curia regis, I. 81. Was the king's chamber of accompts, I. 154. Its relation to the king's court, I. 155. A similitude between the Exchequer of Normandy and England, I. 162. Intended to correct false judgments and defects, I. 163. Exchequer of Normandy was a juridical court, I. 164. The first institution of the Exchequer in England, I. 177. Author of the dialogue concerning it, I. 178. Enquiry about the antiquity of the English and Norman Exchequer, I. 187. The terms or emphatical words used in it of Norman extraction, I. 188. Easter and Michaelmass the principal times of payment there, I. 189. King present there, 6 John, I. 192. c. 1. *t.* And acted when he pleased, ibid. The persons who presided in the Exchequer, I. 197. The chief justicier, chancellor, and all the great officers of the court formerly sat in the Exchequer, I. 200. The business of the Exchequer, I. 208. When common pleas were forbid to be held in the Exchequer, I. 214. Thalamus secretorum in the Exchequer, I. 219. The upper Exchequer, I. 254. c. 1. *c.* Signifies the place where it was managed as well as paid, I. 262. A neglect in the Exchequer, I. 354. c. 1. *q.* Ancient ways of bringing in the king's money by summonce of the Exchequer,

INDEX.

chequer, I. 355. Memoranda of the Exchequer, I. 531. Barons of the Exchequer had exemption from common amerciaments for their lands and tenants, I. 540. Baron of the Exchequer has precedence of the constable of the tower, 16 Edward ii. I. 611. c. 2. *m*. Division of the Exchequer from the other courts, I. 796. Fell from its ancient grandeur in the end of Henry iii. II. 2. Inferior Exchequers, with the motto of that at Woodstock, 25 Henry iii. II. 3. c. 1. *i*. A new or private Exchequer at Westminster, 30 Henry iii. II. 3. c. 2. *k*. An Exchequer of London, Durham, Chester, Carlisle, Berwick, and Kaernarvan, II. 4. The principal times of session at the Exchequer, II. 5. The Exchequer not always held at Westminster, II. 7. Exchequer remov'd to the Hustings, London, 18 Edward i. I. 9. c. 2. *n*. Privileges enjoyed by those employed in the service of the Exchequer, II. 11. &c. Constable of the Exchequer, II. 13. c. 2. *m*. II. 14. c. 1. *n*. No toll paid by the residents of the Exchequer for things they used, II. 19. John and Thomas de Windlesore were ponderatores of the Exchequer, 6 and 25 Henry iii. II. 21. c. 2. *b*. Conservator of the prerogative, II. 23. Its acts not to be examined or controuled in any other court, II. 24. A repository for records, II. 25, 26. Four bishops barons at one time, 9 Henry iii. II. 27. c. 1. *e*. King's council frequently sat in the Exchequer, II. 28, 29, &c. Treasurers of the Exchequer, and king's treasurer the same, in the reigns of Henry iii. Edward i. and Edward ii. II. 41. Salary of forty marks to a baron of the Exchequer, 18 Henry iii. II. 54. c. 2. *i*. The chancellor's oath, II. 54. c. 2. *h*. The desolation of the Exchequer, 48 Henry iii. II. 55, 56. The accustom'd fee of a baron of the Exchequer, 2 Edward ii. II. 58. c. 2. *b*. Enquiry whether the barons of the Exchequer were not too numerous, 12 Edward ii. II. 61. Keys of the Exchequer, II. 34. c. 2. *q*. &c. II. 62. c. 1. *o*. Common pleas how remov'd from the Exchequer, II. 73. Barons of the Exchequer had a discretional power to remove sherifs, 35 Edward i. II. 109. c. 1. *w*. The several rolls of the Exchequer, II. 112. Chancellor of the Exchequer seems to be appointed as a check on the treasurer, II. 113, 114. Wrong entries there, II. 116. Style of their awards, II. 118. When judgment was given against the king, it was entered into salvo jure regis, II. 121. Three sorts of writs or messages sent hither, II. 122, 123. Our kings reserved the supreme direction, II. 126. Ireland and Gascony obliged to accompt at the Exchequer of England, 21 Edward i. II. 135. The barons often made sherifs, II. 142. Tallies of acquittance, and touching dividends here, 12 Edward i. II. 172. Accomptants at the Exchequer sometimes answered on their verum dictum, II. 182. Exchequer at York, 27 Edward i. II. 196. c. 1. *n*. Atterminations of the barons made void, 5 Edward II. 208. c. 2. *l*. In ancient times the chancery held at the Exchequer, II. 254. Robb'd, 33 Henry iii. II. 261. c. 2. *u*. Rank of the officers of the Exchequer, II. 263. Roger del Exche-

INDEX.

Exchequer, usher of the Exchequer, appoints his deputy, 40 Henry iii. II. 276. The ushers to appoint persons for whom they will be responsible to lodge in the Exchequer, II. 278. c. 1. *u.* The constable's office, II. 281. And mareschal's, II. 284. Auditor's, II. 290. Chamberlain's, II. 295. Their number of keys, II. 301. Clerks, II. 303. Tellers, II. 307. Pesours, ibid. Fusors, ibid. An entire list of the barons, II. 312.

Executed persons, their chattels accrued to the king, I. 342. 344, 345. Several Executions, 2 Henry ii. I. 372.

Executors, John de Burstowe grants for him, his heirs, and executors, 9 Edward ii. II. 233.

Exemue, the quinzime of the merchandise of that port, 6 John, I. 772. c. 1. *i.*

Exeter, an assignment out of that ferm to the prior of Trinity, London, I. 276. c. 1. *r, s.* That bishopric in the king's hands, about 31 Henry ii. I. 310. c. 2. *a.* And accompted for by Henry archdeacon of Exeter, 14 John, I. 312. c. 1. *r.* Burgesses have their charter triplicate, 3 John, I. 403. c. 1. *r.* Men of Exeter to have equal liberties with the men of Lideford, 9 John, I. 408. c. 2. *t.* Bishop of Exeter de-afforests Cornwal, 11 Henry iii. I. 414. c. 1. *n.* Its aid, 5 Stephen, I. 601. c. 2. *t.* Its aid, 23 Henry ii. I. 603. c. 2. *i.* The bishop's fine, 22 Henry iii. I. 661. c. 2. *m.* The donum of Exeter, 5 Henry ii. I. 697. c. 2. *b.* Its tallage or assise, 19 Henry ii. I. 701. c. 1. *b.* The king gives them one hundred marks for walling their town, 2 Henry iii. I. 706. c. 1. *c.* Their tallage, ibid. Walter Stapledon, bishop of Exeter, chancellor of the Exchequer, 13 Edward ii. II. 39. c. 2. *s.*

Exminster or Axminster, its aid charg'd on earl Richard in Devonshire, 24 Henry ii. I. 605. c. 1. *o.*

Exton, Robert de, of Leicestershire, 28 Henry iii. II. 14. c. 1. *o.* A venire facias against him for an assault, ibid.

Eye, honor of, I. 201. c. 2. *s.* The castle of Oreford belonging to it, ibid. Was not accompted for, 19 Henry ii. I. 309. c. 1. *p.* Oger dapifer has part of the honor of Eye, 14 Henry ii. I. 573. c. 2. *b.* The aid of the honor and town of Eye, 14 Henry ii. I. 589. c. 2. *f.* Fulk Breaut has ninety fees of this honor, 5 Henry iii. I. 666. c. 2. *l.* See I. 667. c. 2. *q.* William of Eys, Henry person of Eys, and Adam sergeant of the person of Eys, 38 Henry iii. II. 12. c. 1. *f.* Philip de Eye treasurer, 1 Edward i. II. 28. Advowson of Stradebroc belong'd to the honor of Heya, 9 John, II. 43. c. 1. *k.* Philip de Eye treasurer, 1 Edward i. II. 233. c. 1. *k.* Henry parson of Eye, 39 Henry iii. II. 284. c. 2. *y.* Philip de Eye delivers the key of the treasury to frere Joseph, &c. 1. Edward i. II. 320. c. 1. *b.*

Eyes put out, a punishment of thieves, I. 12. c. 2. *p.*

Eylesbury, Walter de, executor of Edmund earl of Cornwal, 26 Edward i. I. 467. c. 1.

Eynesford, William de, whether he was seneschal, 11 Henry iii. I. 63. c. 1. *l.* See Ainesford and Einesford.

Eynsham abbey in Oxfordshire, its aid, 14 Henry ii. I. 582. c. 1. *d.*

Styled

INDEX.

Styled Egenesham, ibid. Had near three knights fees in Glocestershire, 29 Henry iii. I. 595. c. 2. *q*.

Eyom manor in Derbyshire, part of the honor of Peverel, held of the king by Thomas de Furnival, 19 Edward ii. I. 534. c. 1, &c.

Eystan, in Dunmawe hundred, Essex, was a serjeanty of the king's lardinary, 26 Edward i. I. 321. c. 2. *r*.

Eyvill, John de, 52 Henry iii. I. 207. c. 2. *e*. The principal of the barons who supported prince Edward against his father, 50 Henry iii. II. 174. c. 1. *r*.

F.

Faber or Smith de Odiham, Robert, fined for setting calcatraps, 9 John, I. 499. c. 2. *x*. A venire facias against Symon and John Faber of Northampton, 42 Henry iii. II. 16. c. 2. *z*. Ralf Faber, sherif of London, 5 Edward i. II. 96. c. 2. *y*. Peter Fabre of Montpelier, keeper of the king's lion in the Tower, 9 Edward ii. II. 161. c. 2. *q*.

Faburn, John de, has Ouse and Derewent wapentakes under a commission of array, 16 Edward ii. II. 112. c. 2.

Faierford, Beatrice de, her dower there, 11 John, I. 794. c. 2. *i*.

Faintre in Shropshire, Adam de, his land there before 15 Edward i. I. 321. c. 1. *q*. Marries one of his daughters and heirs to Peter le Chaumberlein, ibid. Had the serjeanty of the ushery in the king's army, ibid.

Fairemanneby in the soke of Pikering, Yorkshire, 30 Henry iii. I. 710. c. 1. *w*.

Fairs tallaged, I. 703: c. 2. *n*.

Falais, the concord between the king of England there, and his liege the king of Scots, an. 1175. I. 17. c. 2. *e*. That balliage belonged to the honor of Braiole in Normandy, I. 150. c. 1. *t*. Ernise, son of Andrew de Falais, 2 John, I. 520. c. 1. *d*. A grant to the men of Faleise, 4 John, I. 524. c. 1. *x*.

Falc, Walter, of Somersetshire, 45 Henry iii. II. 79. c. 1. *y*. Attach'd for opposing the sherif, ibid.

Falconer, William, fined, 10 John, I. 151. c. 1. *w*. Opposed by the men of Derby, 9 Henry ii. I. 336. c. 1. *d*. Henry Falconarius quit of his escuage, 7 Richard i. I. 591. c. 2. *t*. See Fauconer. Robert Falconer and Maud his wife, &c. 7 Richard i. I. 789. c. 1. *f*.

Falcons, Comberton manor in Cambridgeshire appropriated to keep the king's, 9 Edward ii. I. 652.

Falesly hundred in Hampshire, amerc'd, I. 543. c. 1. *w*.

False claims how punish'd, II. 247.

Falterel, William, holds of the see of Chichester, temp. Henry ii. I. 576. c. 2.

Faramusi destructio, an article occasioning the wastum of Saham, 2 Henry ii. I. 693. c. 1. *l*.

Farenham, Nicolas de, mayor of London, 17 Edward ii. II. 99. c. 1. *f*. Thomas de Farendon, sherif of Warwick and Leicestershire, before 18 Edward i. II. 155. c. 2. *k*. Nicolas de Farndon, alderman of Farndon ward, London, 2 Edward ii. II. 235. c. 1. *t*.

Farnham, Pentecost de, the king's porter, 49 Henry iii. I. 349. c. 2. *o*.

Farrier,

INDEX.

Farrier, styled mareschal, II. 100. c. 2. *n.*

Favarc, Geoffrey de, his widow and son, how and to whom dispos'd of, 5 Stephen, I. 501. c. 1. *l.*

Faucillon, Helto and William, brothers, 7 Henry iii. I. 492. c. 1. *t.* Helto fines for seisin, ibid.

Fauconer, John le, accompts for the profits of the great seal, 55 Henry iii. I. 60. Commissioner for the forfeited estates of the Jews before 13 Edward i. I. 231. c. 2. Geoffrey de Faukener of Hurst in Kent, his serjeanty with knight service annex'd, 34 Henry iii. I. 651. c. 1. *p.* See Falconer. Robert le Faukener held of the king in capite by the serjeanty of keeping a falcon, 15 Edward ii. II. 210.

Faucomberge, Walter, of Yorkshire, his summonce, 26 Edward i. I. 654. c. 2. Eustace de Foukenberg justicier, 4 and 5 John, I. 737. c. 2. *u, w.* King's treasurer, 3 Henry iii. II. 43. c. 2. *n.*

Favelore, William de, deputy sherif of John de Cormayles, 9 Edward i. II. 178. c. 1. *n.* Clerk of the sherif of Dorsetshire, 5 Edward i. II. 294. c. 2. *s.*

Faversham, an enumeration of the principal benefactors to that abbey, 3 Henry iii. I. 413. c. 2. *k.* See Feversham.

Fawi port, the quinzime of its merchandise, 6 John, I. 772. c. 1. *i.*

Fay, Ralf de, in ward, 41 Henry iii. I. 597. c. 2. *b.* Ralf de Faia has his danegeld remitted in Surrey, 2 Henry ii. I. 687. c. 1. *g.*

Fealty done at the Exchequer, II. 102.

Fecham, men of, II. 2.

Fees. See Knighthood.

Fefment, the baronies and knights fees of the old, more in value and quantity than the new, I. 321. Old fefments before the death of Henry i. I. 578. The difference of fees of the old and new with regard to scutage, I. 680, 681.

Fekeham in Worcestershire, its tallage, 8 Richard i. I. 704. c. 2. *q.* Again, 14 Henry iii. I. 708. c. 2. *r.* The king's fish ponds at Fekingham, 27 Edward i. II. 64. c. 2. *c.* Fekeham village, II. 152. c. 2. *y.* Fekenham manor in custody of Richard Squier, 12 Edward ii. II. 292.

Feld, Robert de la, late keeper of the tallies under the earl of Warwick, 9 Edward ii. II. 302.

Felmingham, Maud de, fines to marry as she will, 10 Richard i. I. 464. c. 2. *g.*

Feltrarins, Richard Thedr. alderman of a gild, 26 Henry ii. I. 562. c. 1. *z.*

Fencote, Geoffrey de, to be admitted proxy to the constable of Bristow-castle, 14 Edward i. II. 178.

Feodal profits arising from reliefs, wardships, and marriages, I. 295.

Fered, baron Rodbert de, 1 Stephen, I. 14. c. 2.

Fergus, Gilbert son of, pays 1000 *l.* for the king's good-will, 25 Henry ii. I. 263. Again fines in Cumberland, 26 Henry ii. I. 473. c. 1. *o.*

Fering, Anfrid de, his tenure, temp. Henry ii. I. 576. c. 2.

Ferling, Hugh de Danecastre, his donum, 9 Richard i. I. 699. c. 2. *r.*

Ferlington in Yorkshire, Simon de, 4 John, I. 478. c. 1. *r.* Seems to be parson of Hoveden, ibid. The king's receiver from the monks of Durham, I. 517. c. 1. *o.*

Fermailes or Clasps, I. 279.

Fermald,

INDEX.

Fermald, burgess of Bayonne, and Bernard his partner in merchandise, 4 John, I. 470. c. 2. *n*.

Ferms of counties, or the issues of the profits of them, a great branch of the crown revenues, I. 326. The difference between fermer and custos, I. 327. c. 1. *p*. The original of Fee-ferms, I. 335. The king had fermers of divers sorts, I. 355. Ferms for years past how distinguish'd, I. 685. Farther accompt of the difference between the fermer and custos of a county, II. 168.

Ferne and Rokesley, the dowry of Juliana de Kilpec, 7 John, I. 488. c. 2. *g*.

Fernhil, John de, champion of Roger de Haselden, 12 John, I. 795. c. 1. *m*.

Ferrandus, son of the king of Navarr, was pledge in Germany for king Richard i. I. 280. c. 1. *z*.

Ferrieres, Waukelin de, his charter from Richard i. I. 77. c. 1. *d*. Ralf de Ferrariis, 14 Henry ii. I. 150. c. 1. *s*. Walchelin fined a hundred pound for a duel's being ill kept in his court, I. 167. c. 1. *k*. Ralf de Ferrariis impleads Richard Smith for stag-stealing, 14 Henry ii. I. 447. c. 1. *r*. Earl of Fereres has sixty eight knights fees, 14 Henry ii. I. 575. c. 2. *u*. Earl de Ferrariis quit of his escuage for the king's ransom, 7 Richard i. I. 591. c. 2. *t*. William de Feriers among the barons summon'd against Scotland, 26 Edward i. I. 655. c. 1. John de Feriers summon'd with the Northamptonshire barons against the Scots, ibid. Earl de Farrariis, his scutage, 1 John, I. 665. c. 1. *d*. Hugh de Ferrariis has the king's writ to be discharged of his scutage for his fees in Worcestershire, 3 John, I. 665. c. 1. *f*. Richard de Ferrariis his lands in Oxfordshire, 4 John, I. 666. c. 1. *h*. William earl de Ferrariis, 16 John, II. 43. c. 1. *m*. William de Ferrers earl of Derby has licence to make a will, though indebted to the king, 38 Henry iii. II. 185. c. 2. *m, n*. William earl de Ferrariis, 16 John, II. 211. c. 1. *b*. Earl of Derby, 28 Henry, II. 211. c. 2. *c*. Earl Ferrers has the ferm of Werkeworde, 8 Henry iii. II. 259. c. 1. *i*.

Ferun, Face le, amerc'd for burying a man drown'd in a ditch, 31 Henry ii. I. 347. c. 2. *e*.

Ferura equorum, or shooing of horses, II. 130. c. 1. *e*.

Fesnes, William de, holds six fees of the honor of Boloign by service of one knight, 22 Henry iii. I. 648. c. 1. *c*.

Feudum, from fidelitas, Pref. xxiii. c. 1. *s*.

Feversham hundred, I. 543. c. 1. *a*. See Faveresham.

Fevre, William le, of Somersetshire, why attach'd, 45 Henry iii. II. 79. c. 1. *y*.

Fichet, Ralf, held of the church of Chichester, temp. Henry ii. I. 576. c. 1. *y*.

Fidelis, how its Romanick sense varied from the original, Pref. xxii.

Fides, or verumdictum, how or whether it differ'd from an oath, II. 182.

Fief del haubert, what, I. 518.

Fifhyde in Essex, attainted, I. 442. c. 2. *f*.

Fige, Henry de, of London, tallaged, 19 Henry iii. I. 738. c. 1. *y*.

Figeriis,

INDEX.

Filgeriis, Robert de, 1 John, I. 434. c. 1. *i.* A great affise againſt him, ibid.

Filiol, Tierric, ſon of Roger, 5 Stephen, I. 425. c. 1. *b.* Fines pro recto of his inheritance, ibid.

Fin, Ralf, of York, his donum, 9 Richard i. I. 699. c. 2. *r.*

Finch, Ailwin, king's moneyour, 14 Henry ii. I. 589. c. 2. *i.*

Finemere, ſir Gilbert, his intereſt in the manor of Tingwic, 10 John, I. 218. c. 1. *q.*

Fines to be treated of more largely, I. 88. Fines in law proceedings, I. 207. Fines and oblata for liberties, I. 395. The payment of the Fine preceded the charter, I. 396. Fines for right, tryal, diſpatch, delay, &c. I. 425. Robert Fitz-Gerard fines that he might recover his land by duel, I. 426. c. 2. *s.* For expedition, I. 447. Fines for offices, to hold or quit them, I. 456. Fines paid by widows for leave to marry, &c. I. 463, 464. A Fine of 20000 marks to marry, 2 Henry iii. I. 465. c. 2. *uu.* Fines for releaſe out of priſon, I. 493, 494, &c. Concurrent and counterfines, I. 511. Difference between Fines and amerciaments, I. 526. Fines pro paſſagio, I. 652. 660. Impoſ'd at the Exchequer, 27 Edward i. II. 63. c. 1. *b.*

Finke, Ailwin, alderman of the gild de Ponte, 26 Henry ii. I. 562. c. 1. *z.*

Finkenden, half hundred in Hampſhire, I. 548. c. 1. *o.*

Fire and water, a fine for judgment of them, 2 John, I. 403. c. 1. *p.* No fire, not ſo much as of a candle, to be carried into the Exchequer, II. 278. c. 2. *u.*

Fiſchamp, Hugh de, dapifer of the biſhop of Winton, I. 457. c. 1. *i.* Abbat of Fiſcamp, 11 John, I. 470. c. 1. *k.* Albric de Fiſcamp, collector at the port of London, 26 Edward i. I. 782. c. 2. Abbat of, II. 28. c. 1. *k.* Albric commanded to do the duty of chancellor of the Exchequer, 49 Henry iii. II. 52. c. 1. *u.* That abbot's liberty ſeiz'd into the king's hand, II. 244.

Fiſcus, its import, I. 158, 159.

Fiſh, a licence granted for ſalting it in Devonſhire, 6 Henry iii. I. 472. c. 2. *b.* Amercements for taking and concealing large Fiſh, I. 548. c. 2. *w, x, y.* John Fiſh of Shafton, 49 Henry iii. I. 742. c. 1. *k.* Cauſe heard by the king of a royal Fiſh, 35 Henry iii. II. 11. c. 1. *a.* King's Fiſhponds at Fekingham, 27 Edward i. II. 64. c. 2. *c.*

Fitz-Ace, Ralf, amerc'd, 12 Henry ii. I. 557. c. 2. *m.* Ace le Mairener, alderman of a ward in London, 14 Henry iii. I. 709. c. 1. *t.*

Fitz-Adam, William, acquitted, 23 Henry ii. I. 553. c. 1. *b.* See Adam. Peter Fitz-Adam amerc'd an hundred pound for diſobeying the chancellor's ſummonce, 3 Richard i. I. 564. c. 1. *a.* William Fitz-Adam, of London, his tallage, 14 Henry iii. I. 709. c. 1. *s.* Again, 9 John, I. 749. c. 1. *u.* John, ſon of Adam the Mareſchal, 45 Henry iii. II. 79. c. 1. *y.*

Fitz-Alan, William, his honor in cuſtody of Guy Leſtrange, ſherif of Shropſhire, 19 Henry ii. I. 297. c. 2. *n.* Roald Fitz-Alan his charter of liberties, 6 John, I. 407. c. 1. *d.* William Fitz-Alan ſherif of Shropſhire, 5 Richard i. I. 459. c. 1. *m.* Roald Fitz-Alan fines for the

INDEX.

the castle of Richemunt, 9 John, I. 499. c. 1. r. Peter Fitz-Alan alderman of the gild de Ponte, 26 Henry ii. I. 562. c. 1. z. Brian Fitz-Alan, one of the Yorkshire barons, summon'd to the Scotch war, 26 Edward i. I. 654. c. 2. a. Richard Fitz-Alan late earl of Arundel, 2 Edward ii. II. 82. Brian Fitz-Alan, 31 Edward i. II. 107. c. 2. n. Was of the king's council, and to meet at York, ibid.

Fitz-Aldelin, William, mareschal, 14 Henry ii. I. 44. Was dapifer, 23 Henry ii. I. 50. c. 2. w. Again, 6 Henry ii. I. 204. c. 1. h. William's fees in Hampshire, 2 Richard i. I. 667. c. 2. p. William Fitz-Aldelin settles the tallage in Cumberland, 8 Richard i. I. 704. c. 2. s. Was sherif then, II. 157. c. 2. w. Again, 1 Richard i. II. 236. c. 1. b.

Fitz-Alexander, Nigel, gave lands in Boleby to the prior of Semplingham, before 29 Henry iii. I. 672. c. 1. k.

Fitz-Alured, Pincerna, sat on the king's pleas with Ralf Basset, 5 Stephen, I. 62. c. 2. i. and I. 457. c. 2. r. Adam Fitz-Alured, 12 Henry ii. I. 447. c. 1. q.

Fitz-Bernard, Robert, justice, 22 Henry ii. I. 128, 129. Robert sherif of Devonshire, 15 Henry ii. I. 276. His barony in the king's hand, 31 Henry ii. I. 297. c. 2. z. John, 30 Henry iii. I. 389. c. 2. k. and I. 547. Robert Fitz-Bernard had the ferm of Dovor, II. 199. c. 2. x. His heirs in Devonshire, 9 Richard i. ibid.

Fitz-Berners, Helyas, 5 Richard i. I. 98. c. 2. m.

Fitz-Count, Brient, temp. Henry i. I. 56. c. 1. o. H. Fitz-Count, 3 Henry iii. I. 67. c. 1. x. Brient was treasurer, 5 Stephen, I. 79. Audited the accompts, I. 193. The terra of Otuer Fitz-Count in custody of William de Albini Briton, 5 Stephen, I. 297. c. 1. b. Brient accompts for Warengford, I. 330. c. 1. c. Fines for that land, I. 557. c. 2. s. See I. 685. c. 2. b. Henry Fitz-Count, 16 John, II. 43. c. 1. m.

Fitz-Ernise, Philip, justice Itinerant, 20 Henry ii. I. 123. Robert fines, 18 Henry ii. I. 210. c. 1. e.

Fitz-Eustace, steward of England in the time of the Conqueror, I. 49.

Fitz-Galfrid, sir William, 10 John, I. 489. c. 2. q. John fermer of Ailesbury, 14 Henry iii. I. 751. c. 2. f.

Fitz-Gerold, Henry, chamberlain, 11, 12, 13, 14 Henry ii. I. 59. and I. 543. c. 2. b. Had the ferm of Wicumb, I. 59. c. 1. g. Warin Fitz-Gerold, chamberlain in the same reign, I. 59. Maurice Fitz-Gerold, justicier of Ireland, 18 Henry iii. I. 66. Henry chamberlain and justicier, 16 Henry ii. I. 145. c. 2. t. Henry justicier, temp. Henry ii. I. 205. c. 1. Henry, I. 215. c. 1. a. Warin one of the chamberlains, 2 Henry ii. I. 263. 390. c. 2. q. Robert, I. 426. c. 2. s. Warin, I. 448. c. 2. n. William, 5 Stephen, I. 449. c. 2. e. Henry, 9 John, I. 451. c. 1. a. Henry's knights fees, I. 573. Warin's knight's fees, 13 John, I. 579. c. 2. l. Warin, 6 Richard i. I. 590. c. 2. l. and I. 602. c. 1. y. Warin occurs, 37 Henry iii. I. 609. c. 2. g. Warin Fitz-Gerold's fees in Oxfordshire, 4 John, I. 660. c. 2. h. Warin's donum in Essex remitted, 2 Henry iii. I. 687. c. 2. k. Henry, I. 791. c. 2. t. and 7 Richard i. II. 20. c. 2. b.

Fitz-

INDEX.

Fitz-Godfrey, Ralf, chamberlain, temp. Richard i. I. 59.

Fitz-Harding, Robert, 6 Richard i. I. 323. c. 1. *y.* The heir of Robert Juvenis, son of Robert son of Harding, ibid.

Fitz-Henry, Thomas, 1 John, I. 664. c. 2. *c.* His fine for lands in Glocestershire, ibid.

Fitz-Herbert, Peter, I. 67. c. 1. *x.* The barony of Herbert Fitzherbert in the king's hands, 31 Henry ii. I. 298. c. 1. *i.* Peter, 7 Henry iii. I. 329. c. 1. *w.* William Fitz-Herbert of S. Valery, 5 Stephen, I. 556. c. 1. *c.* Henry Fitz-Herbert forestarius, I. 565. c. 2. *f.* Henry's donum, Wiltshire, 5 Henry ii. I. 698. c. 1. *h.* Peter, 2 Henry iii. II. 116. c. 1. *r.*

Fitz-Hervey, Osbert, one of the judges, 28 Henry ii. I. 113. One of the judges, 9 Richard i. ibid. William Fitz-Hervey disclaims the town of Wutton, 6 Richard i. I. 200. c. 1. *k.* Henry Fitz-Hervey married his daughter to Walter Bolbec, I. 480. c. 2. *n.* Osbert one of the judges, 8 Richard i. I. 544. c. 2. *q.* Settles the tallage, I. 704. c. 2. *r.* Henry, I. 704. c. 2. *s, t.* William, 1 Richard i. II. 235. c. 2. *z.*

Fitz-Hugh, Richard, 16 Henry iii. I. 64. c. 1. *m.* William Fitz-Hubert, 29 Henry ii. I. 212. c. 1. *o.* John Fitz-Hugh tallager of the Jews, 13 John, I. 223. John Fitz-Hugh sherif of Surrey, 15 John, I. 498. c. 2. *w.* Robert Fitz-Hugh, 12 Henry ii. I. 541. c. 1. *g.* Osbert's fees in Herefordshire, 7 Henry ii. I. 628. c. 1. *y.* II. 138. c. 2. *e.* John, 15 John, I. 774. c. 2. *m.* Richard, 16 Henry iii. II. 34. c. 1. and II. 74. c. 2. *u.*

Fitz-John, William, seneschal of Normandy, 10 John, I. 53. c. 2. *x.* Simon claims the terra de Witlingham, 10 John, I. 100. c. 1. *a.* Eustace holds pleas, 5 Stephen, I. 146. c. 2. *r.* I. 147. c. 1. *s.* Eustace Fitz-John fines to be no longer judge in Yorkshire, 5 Stephen, I. 457. c. 2. *u.* William Fitz-John seneschal of Normandy, and father of Henry de Tylli, I. 489. c. 2. *q.* William Fitz-John justicier, 14 Henry ii. I. 527. c. 1. *c.* William Fitz-John holds of the bishop of Chichester, temp. Henry ii. I. 576. William Fitz-John held seven fees of Moreton, I. 649. c. 2. *g.* Robert Fitz-John alderman of London, the tallage for his ward, 14 Henry iii. I. 709. c. 1. *t.* and 19 Henry iii. I. 739. c. 1. *z, a.* William Fitz-John fined for the absenting of John de Fernhil champion of Roger de Haselden, 12 John, I. 795. c. 1. *m.* The pleas of William Fitz-John, 9 Henry ii. II. 213. c. 2. *m.*

Fitz-Martin, William, one of the commissioners against the sheriffs, 16 Henry ii. I. 140.

Fitz Mary, Simon, sherif of London, committed, 31 Henry iii. II. 246. c. 2. *g.*

Fitz-Matthew, Herbert, late sherif of Somerset and Dorsetshire, 25 Henry iii. II. 189. c. 1. *e.* Has a second attermination for his debts to the king, 25 Henry iii. II. 212. c. 1. *f.*

Fitz-Nele or Nigel, Richard, justice errant, 20 Henry ii. I. 124. William Fitz-Niel, 16 Henry ii. I. 140. Richard author of the dialogue of the Exchequer, I. 161. William Fitz-Niel holds of the bishop of Chichester, temp. Henry ii. I. 576. c. 2. Richard's capital barony not

INDEX.

in Oxfordshire, 6 Richard i. I. 591. c. 1. *p.*

Fitz-Nicolas, Ralf, 28 Henry iii. I. 451. c. 2. *d.* Daniel Fitz-Nicolas, or Nicholson, married Constance daughter and coheir of Philip de Ulecot before 5 Henry iii. I. 463. c. 1. *r.* Roger Fitz-Nicolas, 14 John, I. 481. c. 1. *r.* Warin Fitz-Nicolas alderman of London accompts for the tallage of his ward, 14 Henry iii. I. 709. c. 1. *t.* Again, 19 and 20 Henry iii. I. 739. c. 1. *z, a.* The debts of Ralf Fitz-Nicolas to the crown attermined, 11 Henry iii. II. 208.

Fitz-Odo, William, 5 Stephen, I. 497. c. 1. *z.* Richard Fitz-Odo held of the bishop of Chichester, temp. Henry ii. I. 576. c. 1. *y.* The claim of Thomas Fitz-Otho from the king sitting in the Exchequer, of the broken dies of the mint of London, 49 Henry iii. II. 11. c. 1. *b.* Teste E. Fitz-Odo, 29 Henry iii. II. 17. c. 1. *d.* Otho Fitz-William keeper in fee of the mint, 27 Henry iii. II. 88. c. 1. *c.* Thomas Fitz-Otho cutter of the king's dyes, 53 Henry iii. II. 89. c. 2. *q.*

Fitz-Oliver, William, his scutage towards the king's ransom, 6 Richard i. I. 590. c. 2. *l.*

Fitz-Osbern, William, custos of England, an. 1067. I. 32. Earl of Hereford, I. 32. c. 1. *b.* Was constable, I. 40. Dapifer of Normandy, I. 49. See I. 78. Benedict Fitz-Osbert provost of Pusinge, 12 John, I. 490. c. 2. *z.*

Fitz-Pain, Robert, sherif of Somerset and Dorsetshire, 14 Henry iii. I. 541. c. 1. *f.* Robert one of the king's barons and courtiers, 26 Edward i. I. 655. c. 2. Robert Fitz-Pain, 10 Richard i. II. 284. c. 1. *w.* His acquittance, ibid.

Fitz-Peter, Geoffrey, one of the regents for Richard i. I. 34. Succeeds archbishop Hubert as justicier, I. 35. Symon, king's mareschal, 14 Henry ii. I. 44. c. 1. *c.* Geoffrey earl of Essex, 2 John, I. 98. c. 2. *o.* Adam Fitz-Peter has the soke of Sneit, 28 Henry ii. I. 104. c. 2. *o.* Geoffrey justicier in the Exchequer, 6 Richard i. I. 200. c. 1. *k.* Geoffrey chief justicier, 3 John, I. 205. c. 2. *n.* and 2 John, I. 228. c. 2. *z.* Simon Fitz-Peter, sherif of Northamptonshire, accompts for thirty hundreds, 14 Henry iii. I. 428. c. 2. *h.* Roger Fitz-Peter, 12 Henry ii. I. 447. c. 1. *s.* Geoffrey Fitz-Peter, 11 John, I. 462. c. 1. *k.* Robert Fitz-Peter, 26 Henry ii. I. 512. c. 1. *s.* Geoffrey Fitz-Peter justicier, 2 John, I. 521. c. 2. *m.* Geoffrey Fitz-Peter, 10 Richard i. I. 527. c. 2. *e.* Simon Fitz-Peter sherif of Northamptonshire, 13 Henry ii. I. 539. c. 1. *w.* Geoffrey amerces the village of Rammesbiri, 31 Henry ii. I. 547. c. 1. *y.* William, 7 Richard i. I. 549. c. 1. *b.* Geoffrey accompts for the fee of William Blundus, 6 Richard i. I. 590. c. 2. *l.* Geoffrey chief justicier, 4 John, I. 606. c. 1. *w.* Geoffrey quit of scutage, 13 John, I. 666. c. 1. *i.* I. 680. c. 2. *n.* Geoffrey occurs, 3 John, I. 706. c. 1. *a.* See I. 733. c. 1. *n.* II. 20. c. 1. *y.* c. 2. *a.* II. 132. II. 164. c. 2. *f, g.*

Fitz-Philip, John, 16 Henry iii. II. 33. c. 2. *x.* and 25 Henry iii. II. 34. c. 2. *l.*

Fitz-Ralf, William, steward of Normandy, 8 Richard i. I. 29. Again, 2 John, I. 156. c. 2. *i.* Again, seneschal

INDEX.

neschal of Normandy, I. 51. c. 1. *a*. Again, I. 53. c. 1. *s*. Justiciary, 26 Henry ii. I. 44. from 21 Henry ii. ibid. Again, 22 Henry ii. I. 103. Justice errant, I. 124, 125. 127, 128, 129, 130, 131. 133, 134, 135. Drogo sherif of Lincolnshire, I. 131. c. 1. *z*. See I. 211. Robert, I. 297. c. 2. *k*. Accompts for the honor of William Piperell, ibid.

Fitz-Ralf, William, seneschal or steward of Normandy, an. 1184. I. 169. Brian Fitz-Ralf his claim on the barony of Pedewurd, 7 Richard i. I. 427. c. 2. *u*. Roger Fitz-Ralf of Winesham, 41 Henry iii. I. 476. c. 1. *t*. Fulk Fitz-Ralf fines to be let out of prison, 5 Stephen, I. 493. c. 2. *b*. William Fitz-Ralf, 23 Henry ii. I. 542. c. 1. *p*. William occurs, temp. Henry ii. I. 576. c. 1. *y*. Ralf Fitz-Ralf exacted thirty shillings to marry his daughter out of each fee, I. 615. c. 1. *x*. Ralf, 31 Edward i. II. 107. c. 2. *n*. William accompts for the paunage of the king's forests, 18 Henry ii. I. 131.

Fitz-Reinfrid, Roger, regent, temp. Richard i. I. 34. Henry Fitz-Gilbert Fitz-Waltheve his transaction with Gilbert Fitz-Reinfred, 1 John, I. 57. c. 1. *r*. Roger one of the barons of the Exchequer, 29 Henry ii. I. 82. c. 1. *b*. Roger occurs again, 25 Henry ii. ibid. Again, I. 94. and 28 Henry ii. I. 113. Again, 22 Henry ii. I. 128, 129. Roger sherif of Suffex, 25 Henry ii. I. 135. c. 2. *u*. Roger baron of the Exchequer, 29 Henry ii. I. 213. c. 1. *p*. His pleas, 23 Henry ii. I. 278. c. 1. *b*. Gilbert fines for liberties, 9 Richard i. I. 400. c. 1. *t*. Roger's pleas, 1 Richard i. I. 544. c. 1. *o*. Gilbert custos of the se of Durham, temp. Richard i. I. 714. c. 1. *g*. Roger settles the tallage of Kent, 33 Henry ii. I. 736. c. 1. *o*. Gilbert warden of the sea-ports in York and Lincolnshire, 15 John, I. 773, 774. c. 1. See 5 Richard i. II. 20. c. 2. *z*. Gilbert's relation to earl John, 4 Richard i. II. 225. c. 1. *q*.

Fitz-Renaud, John, had the third of the fee of the Spigurnels, 22 Edward i. I. 386. Jordan Fitz-Reginald forester, 13 John, I. 481. c. 1. *p*. Robert Fitz-Reginald, 10 John, I. 489. c. 2. *q*. Richard Fitz-Reynaud his scutage in Berkshire, 33 Henry ii. I. 643. c. 1. *g*. John one of the barons summoned to the war in Scotland, 26 Edward i. I. 655. c. 2. And served under Hugh le Despenser, I. 656. c. 2. *f*.

Fitz-Richard, Rodbert, dapifer, 1 Stephen, I. 14. c. 2. William, temp. Richard i. I. 34. Justice errant, 20 Henry ii. I. 124. Sherif of Buckingham and Bedfordshire, I. 132. c. 1. *e*. Roger, temp. Henry ii. I. 193. William of Devonshire, 5 Stephen, I. 425. c. 2. *e*. Robert Fitz-Richard, 1 John, I. 460. c. 2. *y*. William, son of Richard Fitz-Richard, his relief, 6 Henry iii. I. 466. c. 1. *w*. Robert Fitz-Richard de Hac, 10 John, I. 489. c. 2. *q*. Henry's seven fees, 14 Henry iii. I. 661. c. 1. *i*. Thomas, temp. John, I. 673. c. 1. *m*. Robert of Canterbury his tallage, 1 John, I. 737. c. 2. *t*. Thomas mayor of London, 49 Henry iii. II. 11. c. 1. *b*.

Fitz-Robert, Walter, his charter, I. 44. Justiciary, 26 Henry ii. I. 94. c. 2. *h*. Again, 21 Henry ii. I. 126. Edward Fitz-Robert, 25 Henry ii. I. 212.

INDEX.

I. 212. c. 1. *n.* Fitz-Robert of Reydon lord William, 11 Henry iii. I. 239. c. 1. *y.* Philip his wardship, 1 John, I. 324. c. 2. *f.* Nicolas Fitz-Robert, Fitz-Harding, 1 Richard i. II. 447. c. 2. *b.* Nicolas Fitz-Robert, 4 and 5 Richard i. I. 142. c. 1. *b.* I. 451. c. 1. *x.* Claims the land of Guy, son of Tiece, 4 Richard i. I. 483. c. 1. *m.* Richard Fitz-Robert, 10 John, I. 489. c. 2. *q.* William Fitz-Robert challenges the land of Saxeby by duel, 18 Henry ii. I. 512. c. 1. *r.* Walter Fitz-Robert holds pleas, 24 Henry ii. I. 558. c. 1. *o.* Walter's knights fees, 14 Henry ii. I. 573. c. 2. *m.* and I. 637. c. 1. *e.* Discharged of scutage, 14 Henry iii. I. 647. c. 1. *y.* Philip, 10 Richard i. I. 705. c. 1. *w.* Walter, 5 Richard i. II. 20. c. 2. *a.* II. 671. c. 2. *q.* Guy, 35 Henry iii. II. 244. c. 1. *i.*

Fitz-Roger, William, has Hocton and Horthorp, 24 Henry ii. I. 211. c. 2. *l.* Reinfrid fines for attermination of his debts, 5 John, I. 250. c. 1. *m.* Hugh Fitz-Roger, 30 Henry ii. I. 431. c. 1. *g.* Hawise widow of William Fitz-Roger, 11 John, I. 465. c. 2. *t.* Gervase Fitz-Roger his debts, 5 Stephen, I. 482. c. 1. *d.* Richard Fitz-Roger fines for marrying one of his heiresses without licence, and for marrying another, 27 Henry ii. I. 482. c. 2. *h.* William Fitz-Roger married to Agnes de Scoteigni before 6 John, I. 488. c. 1. *c.* Margaret widow of Robert Fitz-Roger of Norfolk, 16 John, I. 491. c. 2. *g.* I. 508. c. 2. *p.* John Fitz-Roger's escape, 7 Richard i. I. 555. c. 2. *d.* Ralf, 15 Henry ii. I. 559. c. 1. *b.* Robert's scutage, 6 Richard i. I. 590. c. 2. *l.* Gervase, 5 Stephen, I. 685. c. 2. *b.* Robert, I. 705. c. 1. *u.* Peter, 19 Henry iii. I. 738. c. 2. *z.* Robert accompts, 15 John I. 774. c. 1. II. 178.

Fitz-Ruald, Alan, has the custody of the castle and constabulary of Richmond, 5 Richard i. I. 459. c. 1. *n.*

Fitz-Simon, Turstin, justice errant, 22 Henry ii. I. 127. c. 1. *k.* I. 128. c. 1. *u.* I. 129, 130. Holds pleas, 23 Henry ii. I. 211. c. 1. *i.* Accompts for the profits of the see of Canterbury, 19 Henry ii. I. 309. c. 1. *o.* Thomas Fitz-Simon, 8 Richard i. I. 323. c. 2. *b.* Ralf Fitz-Simon fines, 12 Henry ii. I. 447. c. 1. *m.* Silvester Fitz-Simon amerced for putting Warin Fitz-Baldwin to the tryal of water without warrant, 31 Henry ii. I. 547. c. 1. *b.* Turstin Fitz-Simon justicier in Devonshire, 23 Henry ii. I. 603. c. 2. *i.* Turstin Fitz-Simon committee of the see of Canterbury, 18 Henry ii. I. 631. c. 2. *h.* Simon Fitz-Simon his barony and fees, 33 Henry ii. I. 636. c. 1. *s.* In Dorset or Somersetshire, ibid. Henry Fitz-Symon, I. 673. c. 1. *m.* Turstin Fitz-Simon justice of the assise in Glocestershire, 19 Henry ii. I. 701. c. 2. *c.* And in Devonshire, 24 Henry ii. I. 732. c. 2. *m.*

Fitz-Siward, William, holds of the church of Chichester, temp. Henry ii. I. 576. c. 2.

Fitz-Stephen chamberlain, temp. Henry ii. I. 59. Ralf and William justices errant, 25 Henry ii. I. 83. c. 1. *e.* Again, I. 123. And again, I. 127, 128, 129, 130. Eustace inquisitor against the sherifs, 19 Henry ii. I. 141. c. 1. *y.* William Fitz-Stephen holds pleas, 23 Henry ii.

INDEX.

ii. I. 211. c. 1. *i.* Ralf, I. 308. c. 2. *i.* Has custody of St Botulf's, 30 Henry ii. I. 450. c. 2. *t.* Is justicier in Devonshire, 23 Henry ii. I. 603. c. 2. *i.* I. 604. c. 1. *k.* Eustace Fitz-Stephen sherif of Cornwal, 23 Henry ii. I. 604. c. 2. *m.* Ralf has the custody of Glaston abbey, 33 Henry ii. I. 636. c. 1. *s.* His scutage, 1 John, I. 638. c. 2. *k.* Tallaged Devonshire, 24 Henry ii. I. 732. c. 2. *m.*

Fitz-Turold, 25 Henry ii. I. 79. c. 2. *x.* Nicolas itinerant, 26 Henry ii. I. 139. Peter Fitz-Turold, 18 Henry ii. I. 559. c. 2. *p.* William's pledges, 5 Richard i. I. 564. c. 2. *f.*

Fitz-Uctred, Robert, imprisoned for the death of Walter Belle, 10 John, I. 495. c. 1. *y.*

Fitz-Walter, Randulf, his fine for going out of England, temp. Henry ii. I. 3. c. 1. *b.* Miles made constable of England by Maud the empress, I. 40. Robert, 3 Henry iii. I. 67. c. 1. *x.* Robert marries Devorgulla, daughter and heiress of John de Burgo before 14 Edward i. I. 320. c. 2. *o.* Gilbert Fitz-Walter, 12 Henry ii. I. 447. c. 1. *n.* Simon Fitz-Walter in the barons wars against king John, I. 475. c. 2. *m.* Roger Fitz-Walter fines for the mother of Roger Bertram, 14 John, I. 481. c. 1. *q.* John Fitz Walter has the manor of Etton, Berkshire, 5 Stephen, I. 500. c. 2. *i.* Robert Fitz-Walter amerced, 8 Edward ii. I. 530. c. 1. Robert amerced, 17 Henry ii. I. 554. c. 2. *p.* William, 22 Henry ii. I. 561. c. 1. *h.* Nicolas, 7 Richard i. I. 546. c. 1. *m.* I. 565. c. 1. *l.* Robert, 26 Edward i. I. 655. c. 2. Humfrey has writ of assistance, I. 675. c. 2. *r.*

Fitz-Warin, Alexander, his perdona, 7 Henry ii. I. 207. c. 2. *y.* Fulk Fitz-Warin his plea for the manor of Edinton, 12 John, I. 448. c. 2. *l.* Fulk, 14 Henry ii. I. 574. c. 2. *o.* Fulk Fitz-Warin summoned to the Scotch war among the Shropshire barons, 26 Edward ii. I. 655. c. 1. Geoffrey, 26 Edward i. II. 24. c. 1. *y.* Fulk's sureties, 9 John, II. 198.

Fitz-William, Robert, 31 Henry ii. I. 97. c. 2. *y.* Warin, 6 John, I. 99. c. 2. *t.* Osbert Fitz-William, 25 Henry ii. I. 212. c. 1. *m.* Simon Fitz-William, 5 Henry ii. I. 263. c. 1. *c.* Geoffrey Fitz-William had the custody of the honor of Giffard, 19 Henry ii. I. 297. c. 2. *m.* William Fitz-William his relief, 2 Henry ii. I. 315. c. 1. *t.* Otto Fitz-William his serjeanty, 41 Henry iii. I. 320. c. 2. *n.* Sampson Fitz-William his claim of Cestreton near Cambridge, 5 John, I. 447. c. 2. *e.* I. 517. Gervase Fitz-William, I. 452. c. 2. *k.* Henry Fitz-William, 4 John, I. 453. c. 2. *u.* Otho Fitz-William sherif of Essex and Hertfordshire, 3 Richard i. I. 458. c. 2. *i.* Ralf Fitz-William fines to marry Margery widow of Nicolas Corbet, 10 Edward i. I. 466. c. 1. *z.* Thomas Fitz-William of Saresbiri, 1 John, I. 471. c. 2. *y.* Osbert Fitz-William, 10 John, I. 489. c. 2. *q.* William Fitz-William, 5 John, I. 505. c. 2. *n.* Alan Fitz-William his land in Hoddesdon, 29 Henry ii. I. 512. c. 1. *t.* Richard Fitz-William, 22 Henry ii. I. 554. c. 2. *u.* Walter, 14 Henry ii. I. 581. c. 1. *u.* Richard Fitz-William held ten fees of Moreton, I. 649. c. 1. *f.* Ralf of Yorkshire, 26 Edward i. I. 654. c. 1. *a.* Richard's grant from K. Stephen,

INDEX.

Stephen, I. 764. c. 1. *b*. Pleas before Otho, 5 Richard i. II. 20. c. 2. *a*. Walter nepos of Robert de Cardigan, 8 Henry iii. II. 27. c. 1. *d*. Otho keeper in fee of the king's mint, 27 Henry iii. II. 88. c. 1. *c*. Ralf, 31 Edward i. II. 107. c. 2. *n*. John, 4 Richard i. II. 167. c. 1. *s*. Robert Fitz-William, 25 Henry iii. II. 201. c. 2. *q*.

Flael, Ralf, alderman of the goldsmiths, amerced, 26 Henry ii. I. 562. c. 1. *z*.

Flamavilla, William de, claims the land of Witlingham, 10 John, I. 100. c. 1. *a*. Lohoud de Flamencvill, 2 John, I. 171. c. 1. *w*. Hugh de, fines to be custos of his sister, widow of Robert de Aistan, 7 Richard i. I. 323. c. 2. *a*. Alan de Flammavil of Yorkshire, 16 Henry ii. I. 426. c. 2. *b*. Fines for a rectum, ibid.

Flambard, Ranulp, his station under William Rufus, I. 78. and I. 303. John Flambard, 7 Henry ii. I. 492. c. 1. *w*.

Flanders, earl of, his land in England, 34 Henry ii. I. 165. c. 2. *h*. How he treats Nicolas Morel, 8 Richard i. I. 452. c. 2. *o*. Earl of Flanders, 5 Stephen, I. 501. c. 1. *m*. Amerciaments for conveying corn thither, they being the king's enemies, 10 Richard i. I. 565. c. 2. *p*. Treaty with that earl, II. 103.

Flandrensis, Tomas, 25 Henry ii. I. 212. c. 1. *m*. Adelulf Flandrensis or Fleming, 5 Stephen, I. 511. c. 1. *k*. Ralf's sergeanty in Lincolnshire, 5 John, I. 650. c. 1. *n*. Richard Flandrensis his tallage, 2 Henry iii. I. 706. c. 2. *e*. Richeward Flandrensis of Canterbury his tallage, 1 John, I. 737. c. 2. *t*.

Flaxwel wapentake, I. 303.

Flechamsted, whether that land belonged to the prior of Kenilworth or the Templars, I. 432. c. 1. *u*.

Flechier, Geoffrey le, 11 Henry iii. II. 166. c. 1. *o*.

Fleming, Michael le, his tenure of the abbat of Furneis, 11 Henry iii. I. 415. c. 1. *t*. Flemings clandestinely withdraw their goods, 21 Henry ii. I. 560. c. 1. *w*, *x*, &c. Idesbold Flamang his aid, 14 Henry ii. I. 588. c. 1. *b*. Henry le Fleming's knights fee in Glocestershire, I. 595. c. 1. *m*. Walter le Fleming custos cunei, dyed 31 Henry iii. II. 88. c. 2. *f*. See Flandrensis.

Flet, Richard de, his daughter betrothed to Ralf de Candos, 5 Richard i. I. 503. c. 1. *o*.

Flete, William de, 1 Richard i. I. 97. c. 2. *e*. Richard de Flet fines for release of his daughter, 5 Richard i. I. 503. c. 1. *o*. Gaol of the bridge of Fliete from the Conquest, I. 514. c. 1. *c*. Johan widow of John Shench forfeits the custody of Westminster palace and the Flete, 9 Edward ii. II. 84. On which the two offices were separated, II. 85. And the Flete committed to John Dymmok, ibid.

Flettewyk, David de, why attached, 35 Edward i. II. 121. c. 2. *g*.

Flore, William, clerk of the Exchequer, 56 Henry iii. II. 264.

Flori, John le Blount, alderman of that ward, 2 Edward ii. II. 235. c. 1. *t*.

Flotthorp, Roger de, 52 Henry iii. I. 752. c. 1. *k*. Why discharged from tallage in the manor of Hengham, ibid.

Focagium, I. 168. c. 2.

Foddicorn manor, the bishop of Ely's, 18 Edward i. I. 618. c. 2.

Fodringey

INDEX.

Fodringey belonged to the king of Scots, 13 Henry ii. I. 539. c. 1. w.

Foil, folium or countertally, II. 258.

Foium, Richard, 18 Edward i. I. 389. c. 2. n. Accompts for the efcheator, ibid.

Fokinton, Hugh, and Edelina de, his wife, 5 John, I. 189. c. 1. z. I. 263. c. 2. l.

Folefham, Norfolk, lord of that manor, 21 Henry iii. I. 102. c. 2. f.

Folet, Fulk, 29 Henry ii. I. 212. c. 2. o.

Foliot, Robert, his claim upon Buterlea, I. 98. c. 1. h. Gilbert and Robert, 29 Henry ii. I. 213. c. 1. q. Geoffrey Foliot fines, ne transfretet, 10 Richard i. I. 658. c. 2. q Jordan, II. 45. c. 2. t. Richard, 4 John, II. 46. c. 1. q.

Follutrier, Ralf and Henry, the men of Roger le, 1 John, I. 767. c. 2. l. Quære, if he were mafter of the knights templars?

Fontanelle in Normandy, abbey of, not to be impleaded but before the king, I. 93. 121. A compofition between him and the abbefs of Evreux, I. 164. c. 1. z. Fulk de Fontibus, 5 Stephen, I. 429. c. 1. l. Henry de Fontibus, 10 John, I. 480. c. 2. n. Abbat de, I. 616.

Forde, monks of, 6 John, I. 118. Prior of, I. 273. c. 2. g. William de, I. 479. c. 2. e. Roger de la Forde, fherif of Dorfet, &c. 6 Henry iii. I. 508. c. 2. n. Forde in Shropfhire tallaged, 1 John, I. 705. c. 2. y. William de, I. 714. c. 2. Abbat, II. 184. c. 1. e.

Fordham, Cambridgefhire, its affife and poverty, 22 Henry ii. I. 702. c. 2. h.

Fordington's tallage, 14 Henry iii. I. 708. c. 1. o. The dower of Margreat widow of Edmund earl of Cornwal, 2 Edward ii. I. 754. c. 1. o.

Foreft, pleas of, I. 13. c. 1. r. Forefta, a large grove without water or inclofure, 1. 186. c. 2. u. Forefters anfwered for the crown revenues, I. 355. Foreftagium, I. 409. c. 2. d. Hufbond of the foreft in Hampfhire, I. 456. c. 2. g. Paunage of the king's forefts, II. 131, 132. Foreft of Awy, I. 174. c. 2. y.

Forefter, Walter le, 51 Henry iii. I. 236. c. 1. i. Ralf, 6 Henry iii. I. 555. c. 2. e. Hugh Forefter of Herefordfhire his efcuage, 7 Henry ii. I. 628.

Forgable, I. 204. c. 2. k.

Forisjuration, I. 156. c. 1. h.

Fornival, Gyrard de, 3 John, I. 766. c. 1. o. See Furnival.

Fortibus, Ifabella de, widow of James earl of Albemarle, 56 Henry iii. II. 15. c. 1. w. Has the chamberlainfhip of the Exchequer, ibid. William de Forz earl of Albemarle, 5 Richard i. II. 189. Ifabel de Fortibus chamberlain in fee of the Exchequer, 49 Henry iii. II. 295. II. 296. c. 1. a. II. 297. c. 1. d. g. c. 2. k. II. 298. c. 1. l. Conveys the manor of Senehampton, with the hamlets of Worth, Stratton, and Crikelad, to Adam de Stratton, 5 Edward i. II. 298.

Fortin, Walter, amerced, 8 John, I. 566. c. 1. s.

Forulus Marefchalli, or Marefchal of the Exchequer, II. 284. The Forules or binns digefted according to counties, II. 287. Furels at twopence a-piece, 9 Henry iii. II. 311.

Foffard, William, 9 Richard i. I. 238. c. 1. u. His daughter married to Robert de Turneham, 1. 299. c. 1. d. Robert Foffard, Yorkfhire, 5 Stephen,

INDEX.

Stephen, I. 481. c. 2. *w*. William Foffard of Yorkfhire, 17 Henry ii. I. 546. c. 1. *i*. William Foffard's knights, 14 Henry ii. I. 574. c. 2. *p*. William Foffard difcharged from efcuage in Yorkfhire, 6 Richard i. I. 591. c. 1. *r*. Becaufe he was with the king, ibid. His fcutage for the Irifh expedition, 18 Henry ii. I. 629. c. 1. *z*. The daughter and heirefs of William Foffard married to Robert de Turneham before 10 Richard i. II. 225. c. 2. *u*.

Foftone manor, I. 721. c. 1. *x*. Its tallage accompted for by John de Crokefle, 22 Edward i. ibid

Fotefton in Devonfhire, the land of Henry de Secchevil, how it defcended, 10 Richard i. I. 514. c. 1. *e*.

Fountain, abbat of, tenant of William de Molbrai, 11 John, I. 616. c. 2. *d*.

Fournival, Thomas de, of Yorkfhire, fummoned for the Scotch war, 26 Edward i. I. 654. c. 2.

Foxle, John de, cuftos of the temporalities of the abbey of Weftminfter, 1 Edward ii. I. 314. c. 1. *k*. Seems to be baron of the Exchequer, 15 Edward ii. I. 770. c. 2. *c*. Was baron of the Exchequer, 5 Edward ii. II. 31. and 15 Edward ii. II. 40. c. 2. *w*. Was made baron of the Exchequer in the room of Roger de Hegham, 2 Edward ii. II. 58. His death, 15 Edward ii. II. 60. c. 2. *i*. Affeers the amerciaments fet in other courts, II. 66. Affigned to furvey the king's caftles and manors, 1 Edward ii. II. 67. c. 1. *q*. See II. 101. c. 2. *w*. and II. 181. c. 1. *t*. Occurs, 15 Edward ii. II. 197. c. 1. *p*. John de Foxle, baron of the Exchequer, audites the accompts of the bifhop of Bath, 12 Edward ii. II. 292. c. 1. *k*. Has a writ of liberate for forty annual marks, 6 Edward ii. II. 326. c. 2. *q*.

Fracenham, whether it belonged to the bifhop of Rochefter, I. 32. c. 1. *d*.

Framelingham caftle belonged to the Bigods, I. 325. c. 1. *k*.

Framiton hundred, in Devonfhire, I. 556. c. 1. *h*. Amerced for a falfe judgment of a duel, 14 Henry ii. ibid.

France, its great officers at court refemble ours, I. 28.

Francis I. changes the fcaccarium of Normandy into a parliament, I. 162. c. 2. *r*.

Francis or Francigena, John le, baron of the Exchequer, his mandatum to the fherifs of London, 29 Henry iii. I. 349. c. 1. *n*. His fummonce to the fherif of Northamptonfhire, 32 Henry iii. I. 353. c. 2. *o*. Robert Franceis, fherif of Devonfhire, amerced for hanging a thief unjuftly, 14 Henry ii. I. 558. c. 2. *x*. Johan. Francigena tefte, 31 Henry iii. I. 593. c. 2. *f*. John le Frauncey*s* baron of the Exchequer held of Ralf Fitz-Ralf, 42 Henry iii. I. 615. c. 1. *x*. I. 615. Tefte Johanne Francigena, 27 Henry iii. I. 677. c. 2. *e*. and 29 Henry iii. II. 13. c. 2. *k*. John le Frauncey*s* at his death had effects in fix counties, 52 Henry iii. II. 186. c. 1. *q*. His executors, ibid.

Francifci, Manento, 12 Edward ii. I. 392. c. 2. *b*.

Frankalmoign, I. 45. An advoufon in Frankalmoign conveyed by the delivery of gloves, I. 115. c. 2. *w*. See I. 218. Lands held in Frankalmoign and focage exempt from feveral aids, I. 599. Frankalmoigne exempt from fcutage, I. 671. c. 1. *g*. So long as the donor had

any

INDEX.

any lands in the county on which the scutage could be levied, ibid.

Frankligneus, or Frankline, Serlo, amerc'd, 5 Richard i. I. 564. c. 2. *f*. Robert Frankeleyn, 51 Henry iii. II. 52. c. 1. *w*. A venire facias against him, ibid.

Frank-pledge, I. 564. c. 2. *f*. &c. View of Frank-pledge, sherif's turn, sherif's aid not to be without warant, II. 103.

Frankton, Richard de, customer of St. Botulph's, 15 Edward ii. I. 360. c. 2. *r*.

Fraxino or Ash, Peter de, justicier in Normandy, 2 John, I. 156. c. 1. *i*. Thomas de Fraxino or Ash, 52 Henry iii. I. 496. c. 2. *t*. Robert de Fraxineto, 5 Stephen, I. 552. c. 1. *k*. William de Fraxineto, sherif of Suffolk, 2 Henry ii. I. 700. c. 2. *w*. Agnes de Fraxino, 5 Edward i. II. 74. c. 1. *t*.

Frederick I. and II. emperors, I. 61. c. 2. *a*. Frederic emperor, I. 570.

Freeman, Herbert the smith amerc'd for pretending to be a Freeman when he was only rusticus, 16 Henry ii. I. 545. c. 2. *f*.

Freinbaud, Nicolas, committee of the fee of Ely, 18 Edward i. I. 618. c. 1. *k*.

Frellancourt, Ralf de, accompts, an. 1184. I. 168. c. 2.

Freningham, Geoffrey de, under the earl of Sarefbury, accompts for the customs of the sea-ports, 15 John, I. 773. c. 1. *b*.

Frere, Adam, of Norwich, 35 Edward i. II. 12. Broke the king's attachment, ibid.

Freser, Simon, one of the king's barons and courtiers, 26 Edward i. I. 655. . 2.

Fresingfeld, Richard, deputy sherif to Hubert de Burgh, 5 Henry iii. I. 286. c. 1. *e*.

Freston, Orger de, monk of Croyland, 10 Edward ii. I. 531. c. 1. *r*.

Fresure, Theobald, the king's balistarius, 4 John, I. 763. c. 1. *b*. Married the daughter of Philip de Adnebec, ibid.

Fridborg of Coldmoreton, I. 554. c. 2. *t, u*.

Friers minors of Northampton quit of tallage, 52 Henry iii. I. 749. c. 2. *y*. See Northampton.

Friscobald, the privilege of the merchants of that society, 1 Edward ii. II. 76. c. 1. *c*. A company of them in Ipswich, 5 Edward ii. II. 239. Accompted for the king's customs, 35 Edward i. II. 292.

Frisebois, William de, 5 Henry iii. I. 152. c. 1. *b*. Amerc'd for a false plaint, ibid.

Frisemareis, Algrin de, in Yorkshire, I. 329. c. 1. *w*. Had the terra of Briggham from Henry i. ibid. His son Osbert, and grandson Walter, 7 Henry iii. ibid.

Friskeny, Walter de, baron of the Exchequer, his death and successor, 17 Edward ii. II. 61. c. 1. *m*. Baron of the Exchequer, 15 Edward ii. II. 182. c. 1. *t*.

Friston, William de, a duel compounded in his court for stealing a cow, 17 Henry ii. I. 502. c. 2. *g*. William de Friston of Lincolnshire amerced for adjudging a duel and robbery in his court. 16 Henry ii. I. 545. c. 2. *e*.

Frivil, Baldwin de, his inquest about the conduct of the sherifs of Cambridgeshire, &c. 40 Henry iii. I. 446. c. 1. *k*. Baldwin de Frivil fines for his brother Roger, accus'd

INDEX.

of the death of Walter de Kellintorp, 20 Henry iii. I. 496. c. 2. *p*. Pleads that he holds of Alexander de Abetot, and Alexander of William de Beauchamp, and William of the bishop of Worcester, and the bishop of the king in capite, 38 Henry iii. I. 597. c. 1. *z*.

Froisselake, William de, amerced for exporting corn without licence, 23 Henry ii. I. 548. c. 1. *r*.

Frowe, Geoffrey de, assayer of the coin, 6 Henry iii. II. 87. c. 2. *a*.

Frowik, Laurence de, of London, 32 Henry iii. II. 193. c. 1. *c*. Laurence Frowyk, sherif of London, delivered to the mareschal, 31 Henry iii. II. 246. c. 2. *g*.

Fuelmere, Cambridgeshire, quit of tallage, 9 John, I. 448. c. 2. *t*.

Fugator, I. 58. c. 2. *b*. passim.

Fugheleston, James de, 6 Henry iii. I. 452. c. 1. *f*. Justiced by Theophania de Westland, Kent, ibid.

Fugitives, their chattels belonged to the crown, I. 342. 344. c. 1. *m, n, o*. c. 2. *p*. Again, II. 131. c. 2.

Fulborne, Cambridgeshire, the town of Roger de Molbrai, quit of tallage, 9 John, I. 748. c. 2. *t*.

Fulchered, son of Walter, accompts for the old ferm of London, 5 Stephen, I. 686. c. 2. *d*. Henry, son of Fulcher of Hirton, Notinghamshire, 39 Henry iii. II. 17. c. 1. *e*.

Fulir, Walter le, of Tresl. Staffordshire, a venire facias against him for an assault, 52 Henry iii. II. 17. c. 2. *g*.

Fulk, earl of Anjou, has the majoratus and senschalcey of the king of France, I. 53. c. 2. *a*.

Fulk, son of Theobald, sherif of Cambridgeshire, &c. 12 John, I. 443.
c. 1. *k*. Firmer of Cambridge and Huntingdonshire for seven years, from 8 John, I. 462. c. 1. *i*. Gilbert, son of Fulk, alderman of a ward in London, his tallage, 14 Henry iii. I. 709. c. 1. *t*. and 19 Henry iii. I. 738. c. 2. *z*.

Fulleham, Robert de, justicier of the Jews, 50 Henry iii. I. 234. c. 1. *b*. Has satisfaction for a violence from Robert de Colevill, serjeant at law, 52 Henry iii. I. 236. c. 2. *k*. Occurs, 41 Henry iii. I. 247. c. 2. *g*. Occurs again, 56 Henry iii. I. 253. c. 1. *x, y*. Robert de Fulham's crimes, as justice of the Jews, 13 Edward i. I. 361. c. 1. *u*. Robert de Fuleham, clerk, constable of the Exchequer, 33 Henry iii. II. 13. c. 2. *m*. Robert de Folleham, clerk, constable of the Exchequer, 39 Henry iii. II. 22. c. 1. *r*. Adam de Fulham, sherif of London, 25 Edward i. II. 96. c. 2. *a*. Robert de Fulham, 1 Edward ii. II. 259. c. 1. *b*. Was constable of the Exchequer about 32 Henry iii. II. 281. c. 2. *b*. Robert de Fuleham made constable of the Exchequer by Humfrey de Bohun, constable of England, 32 and 49 Henry iii. II. 282. c. 1. *k*. Required to attend the office of remembrancer, ibid.

Fullones or Fullers, of Winchester, accompt for their gild, 5 Henry ii. I. 341. c. 1. *l, m, n*. Have a charter of confirmation of liberties, 6 Richard i. I. 399. c. 2. *f*. and 9 Richard i. I. 400. c. 2. *w*. Wulfward the fuller the man of the Templars, 20 Henry ii. I. 767. c. 1. *h*. Walter le Fulir of Tresl. Staffordshire, 52 Henry iii. II. 17. c. 2. *g*.

Fun-

INDEX.

Funtaigne, Thomas de la, does the proffer of the sherifs of London, 31 Edward i. II. 156.

Funtenei, Richard de, justicier in Normandy, 2 John, I. 171. c. 2. x.

Furcis, Roger de, 9 Henry iii. I. 318. c. 2. a. Plegius for Walter de Clyfford's relief, ibid.

Furnel, Alan de, justiciary, 25 Henry ii. I. 94. and 26 Henry ii. and I. 96. c. 2. p. Geoffrey de Furnellis, sheriff of Devonshire, 5 Stephen, I. 276. and II. 220. c. 1. b. Henry de Furnel, deputy sherif of Devonshire, 9 Richard i. I. 276. c. 2. w. Geoffrey de Furnel, sherif of Devonshire, temp. Stephen, I. 328. c. 1. k. And of Cornwal, I. 328. c. 1. l. William de Furnel, one of the fermers of the quinzime of merchandise, 4 John, I. 771. c. 2. g. and 6 John, I. 772. c. 1. i. Henry de Furnel's grant from Henry de Pomeraie, 9 Richard i. I. 790. c. 1. i.

Furneux, abbat of, has the great seal under his own in a purse, 1 Edward ii. I. 74. c. 1. s. Furneis abbey in Lancashire founded by Stephen earl of Moreton and Boloign, before 11 Henry iii. I. 415. c. 1. t. Had the grant of the whole forest of Furneis, ibid. Fines for the renewal of his charter, 19 Henry iii. I. 420. c. 2. r. Michael de Furneis, 15 Henry ii. I. 447. c. 1. u. Abbat of Furneis, 8 John, I. 528. c. 1. f.

Furnival, Gerard de, claims the land of Wulwinely, Yorkshire, 3 John, I. 436. c. 2. t. Has the barony of William de Luvetot, 3 John, I. 486. c. 2. m. Thomas de Furnival senior, amerc'd for defaults, 8 Edward ii. I. 530. c. 2. Discharged, I. 533. c. 1. t. I. 534, &c. Occurs, 30 Edward i. II. 107. c. 1. n. and 16 Edward ii. II. 112. c. 1.

Furre, Robert, before 5 John, I. 488. c. 2. f. Constantia, daughter of Robert, gives her land to Thomas de Aydenn, 5 John, ibid.

Fusor, Richard, 15 Henry ii. I. 263. c. 1. e. Gilbert, 26 Henry ii. I. 289. c. 1. s. The fusor had a sergeanty, ibid.

Fusor or melter of the Exchequer, II. 309. Had a serjeanty, ibid. In Hampshire, ibid. The office sold for fifty marks, 13 Edward i. II. 310. c. 2. m.

Fyens's case, William de, 21 Edward i. II. 120.

Fyndon, Thomas de, made abbat of St Augustin's Canterbury, 11 Edward i. I. 313. c. 1. g.

G.

Gaerst or Gaherst, Hugh de, justiciary, 25 Henry ii. I. 93. Again, 26 Henry ii. I. 138. c. 2. c.

Galcho hundred, II. 21. c. 1. e.

Galewey, bishop of, his allowance from the see of York, 31 Henry ii. I. 309. c. 1. r. And from the abbey of Bardney, I. 309. c. 2. u. See Galwey.

Galeys, Henry le, mayor of the city of London, 26 Edward i. I. 783. c. 1. s. The solemnity of his sending the coket, together with the trone or scale to Lenn, ibid.

Gallia Christiana, Pref. xxii. c. 2. xxiv. xxv.

Galwey, Alan de, son of Elena, heiress of Richard de Morevil, 13 John, I. 443. c. 2. n. Claims Wixindene and Bosegate in right of his mother, ibid.

INDEX.

ibid. Escuage for Galwey, 33 Henry ii. I. 402. Again, scutage for the army in Galway, 33 Henry ii. I. 633, &c.

Game, the lands and chatels of Thomas de Haverhul seized by the king, for three hareskins, and a harrier being found in his house, 9 John, I. 489. c. 1. *k*.

Gamel de Everwich, falsly imprison'd, 22 Henry ii. I. 103. c. 1. *h*. Turbert, son of Gamel of Yorkshire, 5 Stephen, I. 481. c. 2. *w*.

Gannoc army, before 30 Henry iii. I. 663. c. 1. *t*. Scutage of Gannoc at forty shillings a fee, 30 Henry iii. I. 667. c. 1. *n*.

Gant, Walter de, one of his knights, 5 Stephen, I. 426. c. 1. *f*. Robert de Gant of Lincolnshire, what lands he held of earl Simon, 4 Richard i. I. 427. c. 2. *t*. Maurice de Gant, 10 John, I. 479. c. 1. *y*. Gilbert de Gant, 12 John, I. 795. c. 1. *p*. Robert de Gant, chancellor of king Stephen, II. 138. c. 2. *e*. Robert de Gant had land given by earl Simon, II. 225. His interest in Yrneham and Liedes, 9 Richard i. II. 225. c. 1. *t*.

Gardinis, Thomas de, late sherif of Glocestershire, 1 Edward ii. II. 83. William had the ward and marriage of the son and heir of Thomas de la Haye, 42 Henry iii. II. 124. c. 2. *i*. Thomas was discharged from his sherifalty of Gloucestershire, 26 Edward i. II. 144. Was sherif of Gloucestershire, 22 Edward ii. II. 173. c. 2. *p*.

Gardman, Robert de, his attendance as one of the court, 3 Henry iii. I. 68. c. 1. *x*. Mr Robert de Gardman makes a purchase in Lincoln, 28 Henry iii. II. 87. c. 1. *w*.

Garin, John, 35 Henry iii. II. 18. c. 1. *m*. Attach'd for an assault, ib.

Garlanda, Anselm de, temp. Lewis vi. I. 54. c. 1. *b*. And William his son, both stewards of France, I. 54. c. 1. *c*. Hamon and John Garland accompt for the fee of Winton, 1 Richard i. I. 311. c. 2. *f*. John de Garland settled the king's tallage, 8 Richard i. I. 704. c. 1. *o*.

Garner, Ralf son of, amerc'd, 12 Henry ii. I. 552. c. 1. *e*.

Garston, John de, his respite, 14 Edward i. II. 215.

Gascony, its accompts to be render'd yearly at the Exchequer of England, 21 Edward i. II. 135.

Gatelyn, Walter de, custos of the manor of Clarendon, 12 Edward ii. II. 292. c. 2. *l*.

Gatesden, John de, held of Stephen de Turnham and his heirs in Brikehul, 27 Henry iii. I. 677. c. 1. *c*. Richard de Gatesden of the Exchequer, 39 Henry iii. II. 22. c. 2. *r*. John de Gatesden, sherif of Sussex, 22 Henry iii. II. 177. c. 1. *c*. Has a surplusage in his accompts, 42 Henry iii. II. 232. c. 1. *g*.

Gatesheved, Lambert de, 8 Richard i. I. 714. c. 1. *g*. Village tallaged, I. 714. c. 2.

Gatestert in Wiltshire, its aid for marriage of the king's daughter, 14 Henry ii. I. 589. The assise or tallage of Gatesterde, 19 Henry ii. I. 702. c. 1. *d*.

Gatton in Surrey, the moiety of that village belong'd to Geoffrey de Bellavalle, 7 Richard i. I. 428. c. 1. *w*.

Gattre hundred in Leicestershire, in the hand of queen Alienor, 14 Edward i. I. 361. c. 1. *t*. Granted her by Henry iii. ibid.

Gavaston,

INDEX.

Gavaston, Peter de, earl of Cornwal, the king's lieutenant, 1 Edward ii. I. 74.

Gavelikende, 1 John, I. 434. c. 1. i.

Gaufre, Robert de, of Herefordshire, whose plegius, 1 John, I. 324. c. 1. e.

Gauge, a custom so called, I. 770. c. 1. y.

Gaunt, community of, I. 389.

Gawce, Thomas de, one of the king's receivers, 11 Henry iii. I. 707. c. 2. l.

Gay, Robert, his acquittance, 6 John, I. 250. c. 2. o.

Gaynz in Berkshire, II. 166.

Gayzi, Andrew le, a knight of Roger de Huntingfeld, about 41 Henry iii. I. 669. c. 1. z.

Geddeley, Richard de, of Devonshire, his aid, 23 Henry ii. I. 603. c. 2. i.

Gedding, Ralf de, baron of the Exchequer, 29 Henry ii. I. 82. c. 1. b. Ralf de, occurs, 28 Henry ii. I. 113. c. 1. r. Again, 29 Henry ii. I. 213. c. 1. p. Fermer of the honour of the constabulary, 30 Henry ii. I. 368. c. 1. u. Ralf de Gedding covenants to marry his daughter to William de Beaumont, 31 Henry ii. I. 513. c. 1. y. Walter de Gedding remov'd from the sherifalty of Surry and Sussex, 2 Edward ii. II. 69. c. 1. a. Was made sherif, 1 Edward ii. II. 144.

Geld or custom, I. 764.

Geldeford or Guldeford, a crusade publish'd there, temp. Henry ii. I. 222. c. 2. f. Robert de Geldeford, predendary of Sarum, about 31 Henry ii. I. 311. c. 1. d. Henry, vicar of St. Mary de Geldeford, 9 Henry iii. I. 415. c. 1. qq. The men of Geldeford find to go from the army of Bedford, 9 Henry iii. I. 509. c. 1. s. Its aid, 14 Henry ii. I. 587. c. 1. y. Again, 2 Henry ii. I. 602. c. 2. b. Again, I. 690. Its donum, 5 Henry ii. I. 697. c. 1. t. See Guldeford. Mr Peter de Gildeford, remembrancer of the Exchequer, 18 Edward i. II. 159. c. 1. e.

Geldewin or Joldewin, son of Savaric, 6 Henry ii. I. 471. c. 1. q. The daughter of Geldwin de Dol, 5 Stephen, I. 473. c. 1. l. Robert de Abrincis fines for her, ibid.

Gelding punish'd at twenty marks, 11 Henry ii. I. 502. c. 1. w.

Gens, its original and Romantick import, Pref. xxii.

Gentil, Nicolas, sherif of Surrey and Sussex, his case, 16 Edward ii. II. 120. c. 1. x.

Geoffrey, sup-prior of Canterbury, his plea that his house held its lands in capite, I. 305. c. 2. l. and I. 760.

Geoffrey, archdeacon of Canterbury, custos of the bishoprick of Ely, 16 Henry ii. I. 307. c. 1. x. Elect of Ely, 19 Henry ii. I. 308. c. 2. g.

Geoffrey, the king's son, 19 Henry ii. I. 308. c. 1. c.

Geoffrey ingeniator, 5 Stephen, I. 364. c. 1. n.

Geoffrey [Mandevill] had the tertius denarius of Essex, 6 Henry ii. II. 164. c. 1. c. See Essex.

Geoffrey, bishop of Durham, chancellor, temp. Henry i. I. 56. c. 1. o. Geoffrey had the king's seal, 5 Stephen, I. 62. Was chancellor and fermer of the bishoprick of Coventre, 5 Stephen, I. 206. c. 2. s. Geoffrey, chancellor, accompts for the manors in

INDEX.

in his custody, I. 297. c. 1. *f.* And for the honor of Symon Caisnedoit, ibid. Has the custody of the fees of Coventre and Hereford, and the abbey of Chertesey, 5 Stephen, I. 306. c. 1. *q.* How much Geoffrey paid for the seal, 5 Stephen, I. 557. c. 2. *q.* Geoffrey Bursarius, 5 Henry ii. I. 696. c. 2. *n.* Frere Geoffrey the almoner, 25 Henry iii. II. 118. c. 2. *l.*

Gepeswic, Edmund de, amerc'd for breach of peace, 5 Stephen, I. 557. c. 1. *d.* Its third peny earl Conan's, I. 631. c. 2. *l.* Its aid, 2 Henry ii. I. 695. c. 1. *b.* Its donum, 5 Henry ii. I. 697. c. 1. *u.* Its assise, 22 Henry ii. I. 703. c. 1. *k.* Its tallage, 2 Henry iii. I. 706. c. 2. *e.* Its quinzime as a port, 6 John I. 772. c. 2. *i.* Ernald, son of Fromond de Gepeswic, 5 Stephen, II. 224. c. 2. *o.* Had a company of Friscobalds, 5 Edward ii. II. 259. c. 2. *e.* See II. 244.

Gerard, provost of Mealdon, amerc'd, 31 Henry ii. I. 547. c. 2. *d.*

Gerardsvil, Matthew de, 14 Henry ii. c. 2. *m.* His aid, ibid.

Gerbert, Robert, justice itinerant in Dorset and Somersetshire, 8 Richard i. II. 146. c. 1. *b.*

German, clerk of the sherif of Essex, 5 Edward i. II. 294. c. 2. *s.*

Gern. Hugh, accompted for the isle of Wicht at the close of Henry i. I. 686. c. 1. *c.*

Gernagan, his donum of three hundred pound, from Yorkshire, 29 Henry ii. I. 278. c. 2. *p.*

Gernemue, Adam de, one of the justices itinerant, 20 Henry ii. I. 124. Ralf de Gernemu fined for the marriage of his ward, I. 202. c. 1. *w.*

The same instrument repeated, I. 323. c. 2. *b.* The town of Gernemu, its liberties, 10 John, I. 409. c. 2. *e.* Adam, justicier, 19 Henry ii. I. 701. c. 1. *z.* Its tallage, 2 Henry iii. I. 706. c. 2. *e.* The tallage of Gernemue or Yarmouth, I. 725. c. 2. *g.* The quinzime of the merchandise of this port, 6 John, I. 772. c. 2. *i.* Seiz'd into the king's hand, 11 Henry iii. II. 244. c. 2. *n.* Releas'd, II. 246. c. 1. *c.*

Gernesi, I. 774. c. 2. See Geresy.

Gernet, Bennet, has the serjeanty of the forests of Lancashire, 1 John, I. 460. c. 1. *u.* Hasculf Gernet, 10 Henry iii. I. 496. c. 1. *o.*

Gernuns, Willielmus, his fine for false imprisonment, 22 Henry ii. I. 103. c. 1. *b.* Richard was nephew or grandson to William Briewerre, I. 114. c. 2. *u.* Ralf Gernun, 1 John, I. 401. c. 1. *a.* Plegius of Gilbert, son of Reinfrid, ibid. Occurs, 3 Henry iii. I. 445. c. 1. *x.* Ralf Gernun, his park, 13 Henry iii. I. 509. c. 1. *t.* William and Ralf Gernon amerc'd, I. 557. c. 1. *b.* For breach of peace, 5 Stephen, ibid.

Gerold Chanoin, fines to hold his seisin, 12 Henry ii. I. 482. c. 2. *e.*

Geroldon, abbey of, I. 473. c. 2. *w.*

Gerscherche in London, the duties arising from it, I. 482. Garscherche, I. 482. c. 1. *d.*

Gersoma pro palleo, I. 330. c. 1. *c.* See I. 458. c. 1. *y, z, a.*

Gervase of Canterbury, his relation how iters begun, I. 140. Gervase, provost of Southampton, accomptant, 31 Henry ii. I. 365. c. 2. *z.* Gervase, son of Stigand of Winchester, amerced for letting Odo the prover

INDEX.

prover be in his feigneury without pledge, 23 Henry ii. I. 546. c. 1. k. Gervafe, fherif of London, 2 Henry ii. I. 686. c. 2. f.

Geffinges, William de, why amerc'd, 26 Henry ii. I. 561. c. 2. q.

Geftling, John de, one of the jufticiers, 9 Richard i. I. 113. His privilege of not being impleaded but before the king, I. 118. c. 1. r.

Geyles, Gilbert de, fherif of Lincolnfhire, his manucaptors, 39 Henry iii. I. 243. c. 2. g.

Geynfborough, frere William de, bifhop of Worcefter, dies, 1 Edward ii. I. 314. c. 1. l. The land of Geynefburg in Berkfhire belong'd to Henry Fitz-Gerold, 9 John, I. 451. c. 1. a.

Ghilgate, Robert de, of Effex, plegius of Robert de Fuleham, 39 Henry iii. II. 22. c. 1. r.

Gibewin, Geoffrey de, jufticier, 3 Henry iii. II. 43. c. 2. n.

Giddelega, Ofbert de, amerc'd for a refcue, 31 Henry ii. I. 548. c. 2. s.

Gidicon, Bonricini de, of Luka, 9 Edward i. II. 137. c. 1. a. Richard Giudichione, 18 Edward i. II. 194. c. 2. k.

Giffard, Godfrey, bifhop of Worcefter, chancellor, 52 Henry iii. I. 76. Richard Giffard, juftice errant in Berkfhire, 22 Henry ii. I. 128. and 23 Henry ii. I. 132. 134. A mediety of earl Giffard's land goes to William Marefchal, 2 Richard i. I. 169. c. 2. q. Ofbert Giffard of Dorfetfhire, 14 Edward i. I. 254. c. 1. c. The honor of earl Giffard in cuftody of Geoffrey Fitz-William, 19 Henry ii. I. 297. c. 2. m. Was in the king's hands, 31 Henry ii. I. 298. c. 1. f. Adeliza, wife of Robert Giffard, 1 Richard i. I. 447. c. 2. b. William Giffard has the terra de Dercet, 21 Henry ii. I. 450. c. 2. p. Godfrey Giffard, chancellor of the Exchequer, 50 Henry iii. I. 476. c. 1. u. Baldewin de Giffard, one of the heirs of Henry de Secchevil, 10 Richard i. I. 514. c. 1. e. William Giffard accompts for the fees of the earl of Warwick, 5 Henry ii. I. 628. c. 1. w. John Giffard de Bromfield fummon'd by the king's writ among the barons of Glocefterfhire to attend the king in his war againft Scotland, 26 Edward i. I. 655. c. 1. Robert Giffard quit of his fcutage, 1 John, I. 664. c. 2. c. Parcel of the honor of Giffard in Oxfordfhire in the hands of William Marefchal, 4 John, I. 666. c. 1. h. Gerard Giffard's donum in Wiltfhire, 5 Henry ii. I. 689. c. 1. b. William Giffard feems to be fherif of Bucks, 39 Henry iii. II. 22. c. 1. r. Godfrey Giffard, chancellor of the Exchequer, 51 Henry iii. II. 52. c. 1. w, x. William and Gundreda de Giffard his wife, 56 Henry iii. II. 80. c. 1. a. John Giffard, keeper of the caftle of Buelt, 26 Edward i. II. 208. Part of Ofbert Giffard's lands went to John de Kyngefton, 35 Edward i. II. 219. c. 1. b.

Gift, new years, 3 John, I. 504. c. 2. a, c.

Gikel of Yorkfhire, Robert fon of, 31 Henry ii. I. 427. c. 2. n. See Jukel.

Gilbert and his fon, marefchals of Henry i. I. 46. Henry, fon of Gilbert, fon of Waltheve, has the ferjeanty of Wapentake, 18 Edward i.

INDEX.

ward i. I. 57. c. 1. *r.* Gilbert, son of Gilbert, 24 Henry ii. I. 561. c. 1. *k.*

Gilds in London, to the number of eighteen with their aldermen, amerc'd, 26 Henry ii. I. 562. c. 1. *z.* Call'd adulterine because set up without warrant, I. 562. c. 2. *a.*

Giles, hospital of St London, 11 Henry iii. I. 781. c. 1. *o.*

Gilling, Gilbert de, his interest in St Clements Dane, 10 John, I. 217. c. 2. *o.*

Gillingham, the king's buildings there, 6 John, I. 612. c. 2. *q.* Its tallage, 14 Henry iii. I. 708. c. 1. *o.*

Gimeges, William son of Sibyl de, his land of Botulvesbrug, 2 Henry iii. I. 319. c. 2. *e.*

Ginant, Elias, disseiz'd by the constabulary of Warengeford, 12 John, I. 491. c. 1. *d.*

Ginges, Roger de, fines for speeding his right, 7 Henry iii. I. 448. c. 2. *m.* His concord with Robert Blund, 9 Richard i. I. 789. c. 2. *h.*

Girbert or Gisbert, archdeacon of Bath, an. 1121. I. 110. William Girbert his share in the manor of Burwardescot, 5 Stephen, I. 511. c. 1. *l.* William son of Gilbert's house at Ry broke open, 10 Henry iii. I. 793. c. 2. *g.*

Girevals, abbat of, 10 Richard i. I. 549. c. 2. *h.*

Girfals or Girfalcons, I. 273. c. 1. *c, d, e.* Instances of the king's receiving of rents in them, ibid.

Gisburn, prior and canons contend for the profits of the church of Skelton in Yorkshire, 4 John, I. 487. c. 1. *r.* The payment of the prior of Kisburne, 8 Richard i. I. 714. c. 1. *g.*

Giservill, Avice de, I. 167. c. 2. Fines for a disseisin, ibid.

Gisors, John, mayor of London, 5 Edward ii. II. 94. c. 1. *n.* See Gysors.

Gisorz, where, I. 168. and II. 194.

Givelton, sir Hugh de, 10 John, I. 489. c. 2. *q.* One of Robert de Mandevil's jury, ibid.

Glamorgan, sir Robert, of Hampshire, 26 Edward i. I. 466. c. 2. *d.* William de Glamorgan, one of the heirs of Brian de Insula, 19 Henry iii. I. 492. c. 2. *z.* Robert de Glamorgan, late sherif of Surrey and Sussex, 27 Edward i. II. 203. c. 1. *d.* Committed for deficiencies, 5 Edward ii. II. 241. c. 1. *p.*

Glanvil, Bartholomew, 13 Henry ii. I. 201. c. 2. *s.* Roger de, baron of the Exchequer, 30 Henry ii. I. 215. c. 2. *d.*

Glanville, Ranulf de, king's justicier, 30 Henry ii. I. 20. Condemns sir Gilbert de Plumtun to be hang'd for a rape, ibid. Was made justicier, 26 Henry ii. an. 1180. I. 34. Was dapifer, 30 Henry ii. I. 51. c. 1. *y.* Occurs, temp. Richard i. I. 77. c. 1. *y.* His book de legibus, &c. I. 87. One of the justiciary under Godfrey de Lucy, 25 Henry ii. I. 93. Justicier, 28 Henry ii. I. 113. His office, 21 Henry ii. II. 125, 126, &c. Sherif of Yorkshire, 23 Henry ii. I. 130. c. 2. *t.* passim. an. 1184. I. 165. c. 1. *g.* His collection of Anglosaxon laws, I. 181. Drew up a compendium of the laws of England fitted for common use, I. 182. See I. 215. Ralf de Glanvil has custody of the honor of earl Conan and the fair of Hoiland, 19 Henry ii. I. 297. c. 1. *g.*

INDEX.

1. *g.* Fermer of Yorkshire, 30 Henry ii. I. 328. c. 2. *p.* Accompts for the honor of earl Conan, 22 Henry ii. I. 430. c. 1. *b.* His accompt of aids, I. 571. See I. 631. c. 2. *b.* What he means by justiciis in banco sedentibus, I. 799. Randulf de Glanvil accompts for Westmoreland three years by Reiner his dapifer, 23 Henry ii. II. 183. c. 1. *y.* Again, 22 Henry ii. II. 200. c. 2. *g.* Roger de Glanvil, sherif of Northumberland, amerc'd for a defalt, 1 Richard i. II. 236. c. 1. *d.*

Glappion, Warin de, steward of Normandy and justicier, 2 John, I. 170, 171. c. 2. *x,* &c. and I. 176. c. 2. *w.* Occurs again, 2 John, I. 518. c. 1. *s.* c. 2. *x.* I. 520. c. 2. *h.* Glappion occurs, 2 John, II. 3. c. 1. *h.*

Glaston abbey, in the custody of the bishop of Chichester, about 5 Stephen, I. 306. c. 1. *n.* Was in custody of William Fitz-John and William de Gundevil, 19 Henry ii. I. 308. c. 2. *i.* William de Glaston fines for his uncle Walchelin's land, 5 Stephen, I. 457. c. 1. *m.* Accompt of the knights fees belonging to that abbey, I. 581. c. 2. *z.* Its escuage, 6 Richard i. I. 591. c. 2. *s.* Its scutage accompted for by the archdeacon of Poictou, 18 Henry ii. I. 631. c. 1. *f.* In custody, 33 Henry ii. I. 636. c. 1. *s.* and 5 Henry iii. I. 667. Glaston, its land belonged to the bishop of Bath, 8 Henry iii. I. 670. c. 1. *e.* John de Glastonia, 19 Edward i. II. 135. c. 1. *u.* Roger abbat of Glaston ambassador to the pope, 42 Henry iii. II. 218. c. 1. *x.*

Glatton, that land belonged to the Dudavils, 24 Henry ii. I. 316. c. 2. *d.*

Glenham, Alured and Gilbert de, his brother, 5 John, I. 494. c. 1. *m.* Committed in Lincolnshire for murder, ibid.

Glocester, Miles de, holds pleas, 5 Stephen, I. 147. c. 1. *z.* c. 2. *a,* &c. Had the honours of Glocestre and Brecknock from the time of Henry i. I. 199. c. 2. *i.* And was justicier of king Stephen, I. 199. The honor of the earl of Glocester in the king's hands, 31 Hen. ii. I. 298. c. 1. *g.* and 8 John, I. 298. c. 2. *y.* Miles, sherif of Staffordshire and Glocestershire, about 5 Stephen, I. 327. c. 2. *b, c.* Again, I. 364. c. 1. *k.* A fine of twenty thousand marks to marry Isabel countess of Glocester, 2 Henry iii. I. 465. c. 2. *uu.* Walter de Glocestre justicier and tallager of Kent, 32 Edward i. I. 740. c. 2. *f.* Appointed to visit the seaports on the concealment of customs, 27 Edward i. I. 784. c. 2. *w.* Walter de Gloucestre late sherif and improver of Somerset and Dorsetshire, 22 Edward i. II. 169. Robert de Gloucestre accompts for the see of Chichester, 11 John, II. 252. c. 2. *x.*

Gloecestre, Robert earl of, temp. Henry i. I. 56. c. 1. *o.* G. earl of, I. 67. c. 1. *x.* Earl of Glocester has above 260 knights, 14 Henry ii. I. 575. c. 2. *w.* Has three hundred twenty seven fees, 15 John, I. 639. c. 1. *o.* Earl of Glocester rebels, 49 Henry iii. I. 654. Earl of Glocester one of the king's courtiers, 26 Edward i. I. 655. c. 2. G. earl of Glocester sat in the Exchequer, 14 Henry iii. II. 27. c. 2. *g.*

Gloucester-

INDEX.

Gloucestershire, its ferm, 9 John, I. 189. c. 2. *e.* Mr. John de Glouceftre to infpect and arreft bad money in payments, 22 Edward i. I. 294. c. 1. William [de Norhal] archdeacon of Gloecefter, cuftos of the fee of Worcefter, 31 Henry ii. I. 310. c. 1. *x.* Mr. Robert de Glocestre accompts for the fee of Chichefter, 14 John, I. 312. c. 2. *t.* Walter de Glouceftre efcheator on this fide Trent, I. 314. c. 2. *l.* Burgeffes of Glocestre, 9 Henry iii. I. 334. c. 1. *w.* William de Gloucestre, 42 Henry iii. I. 384. c. 2. *o.* See I. 407. c. 1. *b.* c. 2. *k.* The intereft of the burgeffes of Glocestre in Ireland, 5 Stephen, I. 426. c. 1. *p.* Glocefter fines to buy and fell in their gildhal, 5 Richard i. I. 467. c. 2. *l.* Burgeffes of, 2 Henry iii. I. 479. c. 1. *b.* Find neceffaries for the prifoners taken at Poictou, 9 John, 507. c. 2. *h.* Glocefter amerc'd, 16 Henry ii. I. 563. c. 1. *e.* Abbat of Glocefter has thirty three knights fees, 29 Henry iii. I. 595. c. 2. *q.* The aid of the burgh of Glocefter, 23 Henry ii. I. 603, 604. c. 1. *k.* Its aid for the king's paffage into Ireland, 12 John, I. 606. c. 2. *x.* A remark that they are wrote burgenfes and not cives, 19 Henry ii. I. 701. c. 2. *c.* Much inferior to Briftol in its tallage, 2 Henry iii. I. 706. c. 2. *d.* John de Glouceftre the king's plaifterer [cæmentarius] quit of tallage and toll for life, 39 Henry iii. I. 749. c. 1. *w.*

Gloves, feifin granted by the delivery of them in frankalmoigne, I. 115. c. 2. *w.*

Godard of Cambridge, the freeman of the Hofpitallers, 20 Henry ii. I. 767. c. 1. *i.*

Godardevill, Walter de, amerc'd for a diffeifin, 30 Henry iii. I. 152. c. 2. *e.* Walter de Godarvil employ'd in Ireland, 25 Henry iii. II. 217. c. 2. *s.*

Godareda, daughter of Gofpatric fon of Adrete, of Yorkfhire, 5 Stephen, I. 426. c. 2. *y.*

Godchepe, Robert, of London, his tallage, 9 John, I. 749. c. 1. *u.* Hamon Godchep fherif of London, 9 Edward ii. II. 98. c. 1.

Godfrey, fermer of Chapmanfhal in Winchester, 2 Henry ii. I. 341. c. 2. *o.*

Godichefter belong'd to the canons of St Martin's, London, I. 108. c. 2. *k.*

Godicheftre, Walter de, 39 Henry iii. II. 22. c. 1. *r.* Plegius of Robert de Fuleham, ibid.

Godman, one of the king's efquires, 21 Henry ii. I. 367. c. 2. *m.* Seems to be mafter of the king's ftables, ibid.

Godmannefton, Robert de, fermer of the abbey of Middelton, 31 Henry ii. I. 310. c. 2. *b.*

Godric, Ralf fon of, fines that he may not plead, 5 Stephen, I. 448. c. 2. *q.* Henry fon of Godric, alderman of Haliwel, amerc'd, 26 Henry ii. I. 562. c. 1. *z.*

Godftow, abbefs of, held in frankalmoign, paying no fcutage, 34 Edward i. I. 671. c. 1. *g.* The intereft of that abbefs in Hedendun, Oxfordfhire, 2 Henry ii. II. 163. c. 2. *y.*

Godwin, Ralf fon of, amerc'd for fending to Leicefter for a coat of mail, 31 Henry ii. I. 563. c. 1. *f.*

Thomas

INDEX.

Thomas son of Godwin of Lincolnshire, 10 Richard i. II. 287. c. 1. *l.*

Goebold, Robert son of, sherif of Rutlandshire, 4 Henry ii. I. 695. c. 2. *a.*

Goisbert, dapifer of Roger de Molbrai, 5 Stephen, I. 147. c. 2. *f.*

Goislin of London, Henry son of, accompts pro 1 bono famicto, 5 Stephen, I. 426. c. 1. *k.*

Golafre, William, chamberlain of the Exchequer, 1 Edward i. II. 297. c. 2. *i.* Dyes possessed of that office, 9 Edward ii II. 301.

Gold, one mark of it equal to nine marks of silver, I. 277.

Goldastus, Pref. xxiii. c. 1. *s.* I. 61. c. 2. *a.*

Golde, Richard, a sea-officer, 12 Edward ii. II. 110. c. 1. *z.*

Golden bull, granted by Frederick II. an. 1213. I. 61. c. 2. *a.*

Goldesburgh, Richard de, king's commissioner to collect the scutage due to Edward i. 10 Edward ii. I. 684. c. 1. *x.*

Goldhose, Robert, attached for an assault, 35 Henry iii. II. 18. c. 1. *m.*

Goldingham, William de, has the liberty of Rischeton in Northamptonshire, 18 Edward i. II. 248. c. 2. *y.*

Goldington, Peter de, fines to turn the wood of Stokes into a park, 16 John, I. 472. c. 2. *g.*

Goldore, that land belonged to William Fitz-Pain, 2 John, I. 216. c. 2. *h.*

Goldsmith, Nicolas the, and Maud his wife, their grant from the house of converts, 56 Henry iii. I. 259. c. 1. *l.* How Goldsmiths were employed at the Exchequer, I. 289, 290. Allowances made them by the crown, ibid. The gild and aldermen of the Goldsmiths amerced, 26 Henry ii. I. 562. c. 1. *z.* Terric of Canterbury the Goldsmith tallaged, 1 John, I. 737. c. 2. *t.* John le Goldsmith of Canterbury, 2 Edward ii. II. 65.

Goldwin, the mercer of Canterbury, tallaged, 1 John I. 737. c. 2. *t.*

Golosa, Michael de, burgess of London, 18 Edward i. I. 198. c. 2. *f.*

Golle in Lincolnshire, the land of Hugh de Nevil, 30 Henry ii. I. 431. c. 1. *g.*

Gomecestre, Huntingdonshire, tallaged, 14 Henry iii. I. 708. c. 2. *q.*

Gomer, Adam, of Scardeburgh, was not beheaded for felony, II. 121. c. 1. *e.* And therefore his brother Simon succeeded to his estate, 26 Edward i. ibid.

Gorge, Hervey, 31 Henry ii. I. 561. c. 1. *l.* Amerced for refusing a writ of assise, ibid.

Gornaco, Hugh de, witness of a charter, 1 John, I. 57. c. 1. *r.* Occurs again, 4 John, I. 537. c. 1. And again, 3 John, I. 766. c. 2. *o.* Again, 16 John, II. 43. c. 1. *m.*

Goscelin, William, son of, imprisoned for the death of Walter Belle, 10 John, I. 495. c. 1. *y.* Alderman Goscelin amerced with his gild, 26 Henry ii. I. 568. c. 1. *z.* Goscelin the queen's brother, his scutage for his Yorkshire fees, 18 Henry ii. I. 269. c. 1. *z.*

Gosebec, Roger de, resident of the mareschal in the Exchequer, 38 Henry iii. II. 12. c. 1. *f.* Was mareschal, 39 Henry iii. II. 243. c. 2. *g.* II. 284. c. 2. *y.* and 52 Henry iii. II. 289.

Gosebertescherche, Ralf de, of Lincolnshire, 5 Richard i. I. 432. c. 1. *x.*

Gosinton, Reginald de, disseised of his land, I. 491. c. 1. *c.*

Gospatric, earl of Northumberland, I. 440.

INDEX.

I. 440. c. 1. *m.* See Edgar, Waltheof. Patric purchased the county of Northumberland from William i. II. 138. c. 1. *c.*

Gotranvill, Thomas de, an. 1184. I. 166. c. 1. *i.* Conveys his right of presentation to the church of Agerny, ibid.

Gotso, dapifer, 5 Stephen, I. 145. c. 2. *z.* I. 146. c. 2. *o.*

Cousle, Giles de, sherif of Yorkshire before 55 Henry iii. I. 76. c. 2. *w.* viz. 52 Henry iii. I. 269. c. 1. *x.*

Graenvil of Glocestershire, 31 Henry ii. I. 447. c. 2. *z.*

Grafton, Wiltshire, its donum, 33 Henry ii. I. 634. c. 1. *p.*

Graham of Graham, 14 Henry ii. I. 544. c. 1. *i.* Burgesses and soke of, their donum, 5 Stephen, I. 695. c. 1. *t.* Sir Patrick de Graham, a Scots knight, sent to the tower, 34 Edward i. II. 108.

Grammaticus, John, impleads his brother William for Middleton, 1 Richard i. I. 98. c. 1. *f.* William occurs, 9 John, I. 442. c. 1. *c.*

Grandison, Oto de, one of the king's council, 30 Edward i. I. 72. c. 2. *p.* William de Grandison baron summoned to the Scotch war, in the king's court, 26 Edward i. I. 655. c. 2.

Grantham, the ville of John, son of John de Warenne earl of Surrey, 33 Edward i. I. 741. c. 2. *i.*

Grantcurt, Walter de, baron of the Exchequer, 53 Henry iii. I. 356. c. 2. *d.* Walter de Grantcurt, 9 John, I. 441. c. 2. *y.*

Graper, Peter, 26 Edward i. I. 782. c. 2. *r.* Customer of Newcastle, ibid.

Gras, Stephen le, alderman of London, accompts for his ward, 14 Henry iii. I. 709. c. 1. *t.*

Grassus, Hervey, 2 John, I. 453. c. 1. *r.*

Gratia, wife of Adam de Nevil, whose daughter, I. 434. c. 2. *l.*

Gratia Dei, or Gracedieu, abbat of, II. 233. c. 2. *n.*

Grava, Mabel de, and her sisters, their interest in the terra de Cherleton, I. 106. c. 2. *z.* Hugh de la Grave servant of the treasurer, 25 Henry iii. II. 16. c. 2. *a.* Sir Walter de la Grave knight of Walter de Esseleye, 14 Henry iii. II. 116. c. 1. *u.* His claim in Cherton, Glocestershire, ibid.

Graunt, Richard le, of Dunmawe, 5 Edward i. II. 294. c. 2. *s.* Amerced for a false plaint, ibid.

Gray, J. de, archdeacon of Glocester, seems to be chancellor jointly with Simon Wellensis, 1 John, I. 401. c. 1. *a.* Walter de Grey king's chancellor and prebendary of Exeter, &c. II. 42. And person of Stradebroc, II. 43. c. 1. *k.* Reginald de Gray treasurer, 26 Edward i. II. 45. Walter de Grai chancellor, 10 John, II. 211. c. 1. *a.* And bishop of Worcester, 16 John, II. 211. c. 1. *b.* Chancellor, 14 John, II. 253. c. 2. *c.* See Grey.

Greenwax estreats, in custody of the treasurer's remembrancer, II. 293.

Gregory, pope, an. 1080. I. 28. c. 2. *i.*

Gregory, Mr. one of the custodes of the see of Lincoln, 31 Henry ii. I. 309. c. 2. *w.*

Gregory, prior of St Canterbury, I. 727. c. 1. *m.*

Greinvil, Adam de, justicier and assessor of the king's hidage, temp. Richard i. I. 492. c. 1. *x.* William de Greinvil his serjeanty in Oxfordshire,

INDEX.

shire, 4 John, I. 650. c. 1. *m.* William de Graenvil his share in the honor of Stafford, 4 Henry iii. I. 680. c. 1. *m.* William de Grenvil sherif of Oxon and Berks, and custos of the castle of Oxon, 18 Edward i. II. 143.

Greinton, sir Hugh de, 10 John, I. 489. c. 2. *q.*

Grely, Robert, 1 John, I. 57. c. 1. *r.* See Gresle.

Grendon, Serlo de, sherif of Notingham and Derbyshire, 26 Henry ii. I. 140. c. 1. *q.* Ralf de Grendon summoned to the Scotch war among the barons of Shropshire and Staffordshire, 26 Edward i. I. 655. c. 1. Robert de Grendon sherif of Stafford and Shropshire before 40 Henry iii. II. 141. c. 2. *u.* II. 150. c. 2. *q.*

Grenefeld, William de, dean of Chichester, made chancellor, 30 Edward i. I. 73. c. 1. *q.*

Greneford, Henry parson of, committed, 31 Henry iii. II. 240. c. 1. *i.* Was receiver to Adam de Bentley late sherif of London, ibid.

Grenewiz, John de, 7 Henry iii. I. 454. c. 2. *l.* Fines in a third part to recover his debt, ibid.

Grenhou, I. 615. c. 2. *z.*

Grensted hundred amerced, 7 Richard i. I. 565. c. 2. *o.* Richard de Greinstede his tenure, temp. Henry ii. I. 579. c. 1. *b.*

Grentebruge, its aid, 5 Stephen, I. 601. c. 1. *o.* See Cambridge. Its town and mill in wasto, 2 Henry ii. I. 692, 693. c. 1. *l.*

Grentemaisnels family, I. 45. Stewards of England and earls of Leicester soon after the Conquest, I. 49. That honor in Petronil countess of Leicester by inheritance, 6 John, I. 488. c. 1. *b.*

Gresle, the honor or barony of Albert, in the king's hand, 31 Henry ii. I. 297. c. 2. *t.*

Greslet, Robert, 5 Stephen, I. 476. c. 2. *x.* Robert Gresle sherif, 6 Richard i. I. 591. c. 2. *u.* Seems to hold twelve knights fees of the honor of Lancaster, 6 Richard i. I. 593. c. 1. *a.*

Gretelington, Wiltshire, its donum, 33 Henry ii. I. 634. c. 2.

Grettone, Robert de, assayer of the coin, 6 Henry iii. II. 87. c. 2. *a.*

Grevesac, Robert, his relation to the manor of Burwardescot, 5 Stephen, I. 511. c. 1. *l.*

Grey, Walter de, fined to have the king's chancery for life, 7 John, I. 63. Reginald and John de Grey summoned among the barons to the Scotch war, 26 Edward i. I. 655. c. 1. John de Grey justicier of Chester and king's tallager there, 30 Henry iii. I. 735. c. 2. *k.* William, father of Richard de Grey, 52 Henry iii. II. 6. c. 1. *a.* Reginald de Grey his station, 31 Edward i. II. 107. c. 2. *n.* John de Grey justice of Chester, his brother William accompts for him, 32 Henry iii. II. 177. c. 2. *k.* John de Grey has respite of his debts, because in the king's service, 12 Edward ii. II. 219.

Griffin or Girfin son of Wenunwen, his lands in Wales, 29 Henry iii. II. 215. c. 1. *w.* Has the manor of Ahford, 29 Henry iii. II. 222.

Grimbald, P. de, baron of the Exchequer, 25 Henry iii. II. 318. c. 1. *g.*

Grimesbi, Walter de, his forfeiture, 23 Henry ii. I. 279. c. 2. *w.* The canons of, 30 Henry ii. I. 328. c. 2. *o.* Men of Grimesbi have a charter of liberties the same with

Nor-

INDEX.

Northampton, 3 John, I. 403. c. 1. *q*. Have the ferm of their town, I. 408. c. 1. *n*. Abbat and canons of Grimeſbi, I. 408. c. 2. *q*. Was a place of good trade, 6 John, I. 468. c. 1. *o*. Men of Grimeſbi, 10 John, I. 479. c. 1. *z*. Abbat of Grimeſbi his hyde lands, 5 John, I. 605. c. 2. *t*. Its tallage for the king's ſerjeants, 10 Richard i. I. 705. c. 1. *w*. Grimeſbi and its ſoke, their donum, 33 Henry ii. I. 713. c. 1. *d*. The quinzime for the merchandiſe of this port, 6 John, I. 772. c. 2. *i*. Ralf ſon of Drogo fermer of Grimeſbi, 14 Henry ii. II. 220. c. 2. *p*. Had a mayor, 1 Edward i. II. 239. c. 2. *f*.

Grimeſho hundred fined for a murder, 7 Richard i. II. 20. c. 2. *d*.

Grimeſton, Roger de, cuſtos for Kent in the room of Hubert de Burgh, 9 Henry iii. I. 329. c. 2. *x*.

Grimeſwroſn hundred in Herefordſhire, II. 122. c. 1. *m*.

Grindlenton, Yorkſhire, its tallage, 30 Henry iii. I. 710. c. 2.

Gringelay, that terra belonged to the honor of William de Luvetot, 30 Henry ii. I. 535. c. 2.

Griſium opus, I. 775.

Griſogonella, the ſirname of the dukes of Anjou, an. 1168. I. 53. c. 2. *z*.

Groſs, W. le, ſeneſchal of Normandy, 5 John, I. 53. c. 2. *w*. Impleaded by Rafe Fitz-Robert, 1 Richard i. I. 97. c. 2. *c*. Hugh Groſſus impleads earl Aubrey, 11 John, I. 443. c. 1. *h*. Reimund Groſſus uncle of William de Cary before 15 John, I. 491. c. 1. *f*. John le Groſs died before 7 Edward i. II. 86. c. 1. *t*. Of Norfolk, II. 86. c. 1. *u*.

Groſſebi, the land of Humfry Machael, 26 Henry ii. I. 512. c. 1. *s*.

Gruzzi, Roger, atteſts the king's writ, 1 Richard i. I. 369. c. 1. *x*.

Gryk, Thomas, not to be impleaded, 2 Edward ii. II. 74. c. 2. *u*.

Gryvel, Hwe, has the commiſſion of array for the wapentake of Bulmer, 16 Edward ii. II. 112. c. 1.

Guafre, Robert de, of Hereford, plegius of Robert de Watervil, I. 324. c. 1. *e*.

Gualtham and Guarenne. See Waltham and Warenne.

Guardians diſtrained to ſurrender their ward, but not to be in cuſtody, 8 John, I. 441. c. 1. *u*.

Gubaud, John, tallager of the king's lordſhips in Lincolnſhire, 33 Henry iii. II. 215. c. 1. *y*.

Gubiun, Richard, grandſon of Hugh, 1 John, I. 485. c. 1. *a*. Hugh diſtrained for tallage by the mayor of Northampton, 39 Henry iii. I. 726. c. 2. *l*.

Guceſton, whoſe land there, I. 218. c. 2. *t*.

Gudeford, Mr Walter de, collector of the queen's gold, 1 and 2 Edward i. I. 351. c. 2. *c*.

Gudmenceſtre in Huntingdonſhire, fine for their ferm, 13 John, I. 411. c. 2. *z*. And for commonage between Hemmingford and Huntingdonbridge, I. 411. c. 2. *z*.

Guerris, Aelard de, provoſt of Geoffrey earl of Eſſex, temp. Henry i. I. 108. Manaſſer de Guerres has the land of Geoffrey de Mannevill, I. 429. c. 1. *k*.

Guhier, Alan, his land, 28 Henry ii. I. 104. c. 2. *o*. Manor of Guher in Wales belonged to William de Breouſe, 35 Edward i. I. 536. c. 1.

Guihalle in Gloceſter, 9 Henry iii. I. 341. c. 2. *w*.

Guiſchardt Laidet, barony of, I. 48. c. 1. *z*.

Gulafre,

INDEX.

Gulafre, Roger, 3 John, I. 447. c. 2. *d*.

Guldeford caftle, in the cuftody of Oliver de Burdegala, 15 Edward ii. I. 383. c. 2. See Geldeford. Its tallage, 6 Edward ii. I. 744. c. 1. *w*. Robert dean of Gudeford, 1 Edward i. II. 19. c. 1. *r*.

Gumbaud, John, one who affized the Yorkfhire tallage, 30 Henry iii. I. 710. c. 1. *w*.

Gummefelva, I. 53. c. 2. *y*. Gumefelve and Potefdon in Surrey, the tenure of Alan Trenchmere, 6 John I. 440. c. 2. *p*. The aid of Gumfelve to the king, 14 Henry ii. I. 587. c. 2. *y*. Some land of Gomefhulve was the abbat of Nutley's, I. 674. c. 2. *p*.

Gundevill, Hugh de, 20 Henry ii. I. 125. Sherif of Devonfhire, 23 Henry ii. I. 132. c. 1. *f*. And feveral other counties at the fame time, I. 131, 132. William de, I. 306. c. 2. *t*. Accompts for the fee of Lincoln, 19 Henry ii. I. 308. c. 1. *c*. Was clerk of Richard elect of Winchefter, I. 308. c. 2. *i*. Hugh de Gundevil fermer of Winchefter, 17 Henry ii. I. 331. c. 2. *m*. Cuftos of the manor of John de Port, Hampfhire, 22 Henry ii. I. 642. c. 2. *c*. Hugh de Gundovil his hundred in Somerfetfhire, 4 Henry ii. I. 695. c. 2. *e*. Sherif of Hampfhire, 22 Henry ii. I. 702. c. 2. *i*.

Gundobad, king, his preface to the Burgundian laws, Pref. xviii. c. 1. *f*.

Gundrede, widow of Geoffrey Hofe, 1 John, I. 202. c. 1. *z*.

Gundrede the countefs fines not to marry againft her will, 10 Richard i. I. 464. c. 2. *g*.

Gunevil, where, I. 174. c. 1. *g*.

Gunneys, Roger, one of the deputy marefchals, 18 Edward iii. I. 798. c. 2.

Gupilerets, I. 274. c. 1. *l*.

Gurdon, Adam de, bailif of Aulton before 16 Henry iii. I. 334. c. 2. *y*. Adam de Gurdon of Hampfhire, a diftringas againft him, 42 Henry iii. II. 308. c. 1. *a*.

Gurnay, Hugh de, his relief, 32 Henry ii. I. 165. c. 1. *g*. Lewis de Gurnay his pardon, an. 1184. I. 168, 169. c. 1. Adam de Gurnai fermer of Northampton, 5 Richard i. I. 332. c. 2. *a*. Hugh de Gurney has the manor of Wandoure, 11 John, I. 490. c. 2. *x*. Hawife de Gurney gives feifin of part of her land by a bough of a tree, I. 621. The men of Hugh de Gurnay, the king's enemy, plundered, 10 Richard i. I. 776.

Guronde, Nicolas de, holds two fees of the honor of Peverel of Dovor, 14 Henry iii. I. 647. c. 2. *z*.

Gut, the bacons and gammons of William le, 10 Richard i. I. 776. c. 2.

Guthleu, the honor or terra de, in the king's hands, 31 Henry iii. I. 297. c. 2. *o*.

Guy or Wido dean of Waltham, one of the juftices, 15 Henry ii. I. 143, &c. and 14 Henry ii. I. 585. c. 1. *s*. I. 587. c. 1. Guy earl of Warwick fherif in fee of Worcefterfhire, 27 Edward i. II. 149. Guy earl of Warwick in the king's fervice in the marches of Scotland, 26 Edward i. ibid. Chamberlain of the Exchequer in fee, ibid. Had two deputies, II. 299. Guy de Beauchamp late earl of Warwick, 9 Edward ii. II. 301.

Gyng-Mountney, whofe, I. 218.

Gyfors, John, mayor of London, 9 Edward

INDEX.

Edward ii. II. 97. c. 2. c. See Gisors. Hugh de Gisorcio, 52 Henry iii. II. 194. c. 1. *f.* John de Gizors has the city of London delivered to him by the king for trespass of an assize, 39 Henry iii. II. 248. c. 1. *w.*

H.

Hacche, the barony of Robert de Beauchamp of, 20 Henry iii. I. 632. Eustace de Hacche one of the king's barons and courtiers, 26 Edward i. I. 655. c. 2.

Hachoure, Roger de, fines, 28 Henry iii. I. 451. c. 2. *d.*

Hack priory in Lincolnshire, its carucats, 5 John, I. 605. c. 2. *t.*

Hacun, Richard, of Norfolk, his interest in Hamelinton and Cattun, 6 Henry iii. I. 445. c. 2. *d.*

Hacunebi, Lincolnshire, escheated, 14 Henry ii. I. 583. c. 2. *n.* and 18 Henry ii. I. 631. c. 2. *k.*

Haddon, Adam de, of Yorkshire, 15 Henry ii. I. 549. c. 2. *m.*

Hadfeld, Walter de, justice errant, 20 Henry ii. I. 124. Hadfeld Regis tallaged, 1 Richard i. I. 703. c. 1. *l.* c. 2. *m.* Walter de Hadfeld had portion of the manor of Writele granted to him, 4 Richard i. II. 167. c. 1. *s.*

Hadham magna, amerced, 49 Henry iii. I. 568. c. 2. *t.*

Hadinton, Mr Walter de, preferred in the bishopric, 8 Richard i. I. 716. Robert de Hadinton his tallage, I. 715. c. 1.

Hadlega in Suffolk, the interest of Robert de Hardre there, 30 Henry ii. I. 116. c. 1. *a.* Cicely de Hadley has the manor of Brumley in Shropshire, and the guardship of her son, 6 John, I. 488. c. 1. *a.* Herebert person of Hadley clerk of the Exchequer, 40 Henry iii. II. 18. c. 1. *k.*

Hage, William de, Linc. fines, 17 Henry ii. I. 502. c. 2. *f.*

Hagenet, that town's aid, 14 Henry ii. I. 589. c. 2. *f.* That honor in Suffolk, I. 652. c. 1. *u.*

Haget, Geoffrey, custos of Yorkshire, temp. Richard i. I. 35.

Haghele, honor of, I. 653. c. 1. *w.*

Haguniere, Maud de, of Sussex, wife of Robert Falconer, 7 Richard i. I. 789. c. 1. *f.* Her fee in Hen and Melchegrave, ibid.

Hai, Roger, of Sussex, the two knights fees in Wepham, which he held of Rollan de Dinan, 14 Henry ii. I. 583. c. 1. *k.*

Hailrun, Alban de, his knights fee, 14 Henry ii. I. 573. c. 2. *m.*

Haimo, dapifer of the Conqueror, I. 49. c. 1. *c.*

Hait, Walter, his relief for his father's lands in Cornwal, 5 Stephen, I. 315. c. 2. *p.* Sherif of Pembroc, temp. Stephen, I. 328. c. 1. *h.*

Hakelut, Walter, of the king's houshold, and sherif of Herefordshire, 1 Edward ii. II. 145.

Hakepetit, Hugh, fines in forty-five marks to enter into religion, 4 John, I. 505. c. 2. *m.*

Hakewrdam, Peter de, 25 Henry ii. I. 96. c. 2. *o.* Impleaded, ibid.

Hakford, William de, 40 Henry iii. I. 268. c. 2. *r.* Nicolas de Halgford, 1 Edward ii. II. 123. c. 2. *z.*

Hakinton chapel robbed, 7 Richard i. I 556. c. 2. *r.*

Hal. Simon de, tallager of Lancashire, 11 Henry iii. I. 707. c. 1. *h.* And Northumberland, 7 Henry iii. I. 734. c. 2. *e.*

Hale, sir Matthew, said to write A short

INDEX.

short treatise touching sherif's accompts, I. 275. c. 1. *o.*

Halecesira, its tenths, I. 714. c. 2.

Hales, Simon de, tallager of the Jews in Canterbury, 11 Henry iii. I. 223.

Halewarfolk knights, I. 644. c. 2. *o.*

Halimots, 4 John, I. 437. c. 2. *z.*

Halla, Ralf and Warin de, of Hampshire, 31 Henry ii. I. 431. c. 2. *o.* Their fees in Sunderland, ibid.

Hallingebery, Essex, tallaged, 1 Richard i. I. 703. c. 1. *l.* By whom held, 29 Henry iii. II. 101. c. 1. *s.*

Halliwel gild, with alderman Henry son of Godric, amerced, 26 Henry ii. I. 562. c. 1. *z.*

Haltebarge, fines for taking and concealing a royal fish, 17 Henry ii. I. 502. c. 2. *h.*

Halton, Ralf de, son of William the constabulary, 2 John, I. 216. c. 2. *h.*

Haluford, Nicolas de, 2 Edward ii. II. 76. His writ of privy seal, ibid.

Hambee in Normandy, abbat of, 2 John, I. 520. c. 1. *c.*

Hamburg castle, II. 11. c. 2. *d.* Whose; 52 Henry iii. ibid.

Hamby, John de, 16 Edward ii. II. 112. c. 1. His commission, ibid.

Hamel, Buisso, 2 John, I. 161. c. 2. *x.*

Hameldon, to whom it appertained, 12 Edward i. I. 278. c. 1. *i.* and 13 Henry iii. I. 416. c. 2. *z.*

Hamelin the dean [f. Lincoln] 28 Henry ii. I. 450. c. 1. *m.*

Hamelton dean of York, William de, chancellor of England, dies, 35 Edward i. I. 74. c. 1. *s.* Was chancellor's deputy, 26 Edward i. II. 48. c. 2. *e.* See II. 256. c. 1. *u.*

Hamenel in Glocestershire, its assise, 19 Henry ii. I. 701. c. 2. *c.* The terra of William Patric, ibid.

Hamesteda, domus Emmæ de, 5 Stephen, I. 330. c. 1. *c.*

Hamma, a member of Chingeston or Kingston, 14 Henry ii. I. 587. c. 1. *y.* Abbat of Hammes, 2 Henry iii. II. 201.

Hamon son of Meinfelin, his grant of tith bread to the prior of Luffield, I. 3. c. 2. Has the cell of Braddewell, about temp. Henry ii. ibid. Robert son of Hamon, 5 Stephen, I. 557. c. 2. *e.* Hamon son of Hamon quit of scutage for the king's ransom, 7 Richard i. I. 591. c. 2. *t.*

Hampslape, Mr Thurstan de, 25 Edward i. I. 379. c. 1. King's purveyour, ibid.

Hamton, Stephen de, I. 667. c. 2. *r.*

Hamtonet, in part the prior of Boxgrave's, I. 599. c. 2. *g.*

Handlou, Nicolas de, custos of the fee of Winton, 43 Henry iii. II. 3. c. 2. *l.*

Haneley in Worcestershire, its tallage, 8 Richard i. I. 704. c. 2. *q*

Hanfeld, Ernald de, I. 576. c. 1. *y.* Holds of the church of Chichester, ibid.

Hanging for theft, an. 1275. I. 261. c. 2. *r.* William Long amerced for taking down a man who was hanged without the king's bailifs, 2 Richard i. I. 564. c. 1. *y.*

Hanton, Gervase de, his share of merchandise falls to Nicolas de Havent, 9 Richard i. I. 468. Geoffrey de Hanton sherif of London and Middlesex, 31 Henry ii. I. 546. c. 2. *s.* William de, deputy of the sea ports for Hugh de Nevil, 15 John, I. 773, 774. c. 1.

Hanum, Richard de, his tenure of the lord prior of Bath, in the time of bishop Rodbert, I. 112. c. 2. *n.*

Harang, Elyas, Wiltshire, fines to be inrolled

INDEX.

inrolled, 27 Henry iii. I. 246. c. 1. *b*. Walkelin Hareng, Berkshire, 29 Henry ii. I. 430. c. 1. *z*. William de Hareng held of the bishop of Chichester, temp. Henry ii. I. 576. c. 1. *y*. Walkelin Hareng of Berkshire accompts for his scutage, 18 Henry ii. I. 580. c. 1. *o*. Walchelin Harenc his tenure in Oxfordshire, 14 Henry ii. I. 581. c. 1. *t*.

Harcla, Walter de, one of the Westmoreland drengs, 2 John, I. 659. c. 1. *x*.

Hardel, William, II. 227. See II. 117. c. 1. *a*. Ralf mayor of London, 39 Henry iii. I. 712. c. 1. *a*. Juliana of London, 55 Henry iii. I. 750. c. 2. *b*. John keeper of the dye of the mint of London, 31 Henry iii. II. 88. c. 2. *g*. Ralf mayor, 40 and 41 Henry iii. II. 92. c. 2. *i*.

Hardicnute, I. 53.

Hardre, Mr Robert de, accompts for the profits of the fee of Lincoln, 31 Henry ii. I. 309. c. 2. *w*. The claim he had upon Hadley in Suffolk, 30 Henry ii. I. 116. c. 1. *a*.

Hardwin, Robert, tallager of Southampton, 2 John, I. 202. c. 2. *b*. Again tallager of Southampton against the provost, 2 John, I. 460. c. 2. *z*. Amerced for ill buying the king's wines, 8 John I. 566. c. 1. *s*.

Harecurt, Robert de, justicier in Normandy, 3 John I. 171. c. 1. *u*. Occurs, 9 Richard i. I. 202. c. 1. *x*. Again, I. 203. c. 1. *c*. William de Harecurt fermer of Scardeburc, 17 John, I. 384. c. 1. *m*. William de, plegius, 12 John, I. 481. c. 1. *o*. Robert de Harewecurt, Leic. 26 Henry ii. I. 497. c. 2. *f*. and 4 John, I. 537. c. 1. Robert, 6 Richard i. I. 491. c. 1. *p*. Robert, and William de Harecurt his son, 9 Richard i. I. 658. c. 1. *i*. William de Harecurt's fees in Oxfordshire, 4 John, I. 666. c. 1. *h*. Robert de Harecourt, 3 John, I. 766. c. 2. *o*.

Hareflet, William de, his tenure, temp. Henry ii. I. 576. c. 2.

Harege, Ralf, seneschal of Thomas de S. Valery, I. 673. c. 1. *m*.

Harengot, Stephen de, 32 Henry iii. I. 274. c. 2. *m*. Walkelin Hareng. 29 Henry ii. I. 430. Nicolas, 11 Henry iii. II. 78. c. 1. *n*. Robert, II. 120, 121. See Harang.

Haringewurd comitissæ, the king of Scots, 13 Henry ii. I. 539. c. 1. *w*.

Harle, Malcolm de, fermer of Durham, 11 Edward i. I. 720. c. 1. *t*. Malcolm de Harleigh escheatour on this side Trent, II. 188. His executor was Richard de Harle, 26 Edward i. II. 189. c. 1. *c*. More than forty-eight pound allowed by the king for his funerals, ibid.

Harpur, Robert le, arrested for using counterfeit bulls, 26 Edward i. II. 82.

Hasculf son of Ridiou, fines, 5 Stephen, I. 449. c. 2. *c*.

Hasebach, William de, put in the place of Adam de Wyntonia, justicier, 49 Henry ii. I. 234. c. 1. *c*.

Hasecumb, Richard de, heir of Walter Briton, 4 John, I. 114. c. 2. *u*.

Haselberg manor, whose, II. 120.

Haselden, Roger de, 12 John, I. 795. c. 1. *m*.

Haseley, Oliver de, and eleven others fined for an oath, 9 John, I. 507. c. 1. *b*. Robert de, I. 767. c. 1.

Hasthorp, John de, has a commission of array sent to him, 16 Edward ii. II. 111. c. 1. *c*.

Hasting, William de, lost his claim of the Marshalsey by default, under king

INDEX.

king John, I. 46. c. 1. *p.* Robert de, 14 Henry ii. I. 209. c. 2. *c.* William de Haſtings charged in the receipt of the Jews, 7 Henry iii. I. 231. William de Haſtinge's relief for the land of his brother Henry, 7 Richard i. I. 316. c. 2. *f.* Ralf de Haſting ſherif of Kent, 5 Henry ii. I. 365. c. 2. *x.* The Rape of Haſtinges to be free from pleas of the foreſt, 8 John, I. 408. c. 1. *m.* Robert de Haſting, 15 Henry ii. I. 450. c. 1. *l.* William de Haſting, reſpited, 6 Henry iii. I. 454. c. 2. *m.* Under the king's diſpleaſure, 6 Richard i. I. 473. c. 1. *r.* Rap of Haſtings was the earl of Ous, temp. Henry ii. I. 577. c. 2. *z.* William de Haſtinges has five knights fees in Gloceſterſhire, 29 Henry iii. I. 595. c. 1. *m.* Three of which were not found, 15 John, I. 639. c. 1. *o.* Philip de Haſtang, 9 Edward ii. I. 652. John de Haſtinges among the barons of Herefordſhire ſummon'd to the Scotch war, 26 Edward i. I. 655. c. 1. Edmond de Haſtings, one of the king's barons and courtiers, I. 655. c. 2. William fines, 7 Richard i. I. 663. c. 1. *s.* John de, of Gloceſterſhire, his ſcutage, 2 John, I. 676. c. 1. *w.* Henry de Haſtyngges had the ſoke of Oſwardkirke from king Henry, I. 724. c. 1. *e.* The anceſtors of John de Haſtynges had long enjoy'd the manor of Brampton, Nottinghamſhire, I. 755. c. 1. *q.* Robert claims the ſtewardſhip of earl Augi, 9 John, I. 790. c. 2. *m.* Nicolas, his writ, 9 Edward ii. II. 74. John's caſe, 23 Edward i. II. 120.

Hathfeld, tallaged, 2 Henry iii. I. 706. c. 1. *b.*

Hatton in Yorkſhire, its donum, 9 Richard i. I. 699. c. 2. *r.*

Haubeni, Robert de, baron of the Exchequer, temp. Henry ii. I. 215. c. 1. *a.*

Haverhul, William de, treaſurer, 28 Henry iii. I. 378. c. 1. *k.* Thomas de Haverul's lands and chatels ſeiz'd by the king, for three hareſkins and a harrier being found on him, 9 John, I. 489. c. 1. *k.* The gild of alderman William de Haverhill, 26 Henry ii. I. 562. c. 1. *z.* William de Haverhul ſettles the tallage of Norfolk, 14 Henry iii. I. 725. c. 2. *g.* William accompts for the chamberlainſhip of London and Sandwich, I. 768. c. 1. *u.* Had the balliage of Billingſgate before 8 Richard i. I. 778. c. 2. *d.* William de Haverſhal treaſurer, 25 Henry iii. II. 16. c. 2. *b.* and 28 Henry iii. II. 16. c. 2. *c.* and 19 Henry iii. II. 129. c. 1. *a.* William de Haverhell had Billingſgate, Botulveſgate, and Garſchierch, before 7 Richard i. II. 175. c. 2. *x.* William de Haverhul treaſurer nominates the tellers of the Exchequer, 28 and 29 Henry iii. II. 307. c. 1. *t, u.*

Havering, the aid of the men of, 14 Henry ii. I. 586. c. 1. *x.* The provoſt of, ibid. Its aſſiſe or tallage, 19 Henry ii. I. 701. c. 1. *z.* Again, 1 Richard i. I. 703. c. 1. *l.* Its tallage, 2 Henry iii. I. 706. c. 1. *b.* See I. 746. Richard de Havering, 26 Edward i. II. 45. c. 1. *s.* Richard de, his ſtation, 27 Edward i. II. 106.

Haukechurch, Philip de, who, 9 Richard i. I. 85. c. 1. *q.*

Haukeſburg, to be accompted for by Ralf

INDEX.

Ralf Briton, 18 Henry ii. II. 252. c. 1. *t*.

Haukyn, Gilbert de, has the office of tronage, 22 Edward ii. I. 780. c. 1. *i*.

Havoc, Ralf, 5 Stephen, I. 497. c. 1. *b*.

Haured, John de, in Berkshire, his tenure of the king in capite, by saying daily one Pater Noster, and one Ave Maria, 14 Edward i. I. 321. c. 1. *p*. Nicholas Hanred, sherif of Berks and Oxon, 42 Henry iii. II. 236. c. 2. *g*.

Hausard, the barony of Giles, in the bishopric, 8 Richard i. I. 715. c. 2. James Hansard, 56 Henry iii. II. 223.

Hauteyne, Hamon de, of Norfolk, justicier of the Jews displaced, &c. 14 Edward i. I. 254. c. 2. *c*. John de Hauteyn made customer in the port of London, 16 Edward ii. II. 91. c. 1. *a*. Hamon Hautein, justicier, 13 Edward i. II. 209. c. 1. *p*.

Hauvil, Adam de, 31 Henry ii. I. 561. c. 2. *t*.

Hawardesho wapentac in Lincolnshire, 502. c. 1. *b*.

Haya, Nicholas de, 6 Henry iii. I. 86. c. 1. *u*. His barony in Lincolnshire descended to William Longespeye, 40 Henry iii. I. 319. c. 1. *c*. William de Haya his inquisition if Emma de Setuans had a son, 27 Henry ii. I. 430. c. 2. *f*. William de Haya, 2 Henry iii. I. 491. c. 2. *m*. William Hay, serjeant of the bishop of Durham, I. 715. c. 2. The son and heir of Thomas de la Hay, 42 Henry iii. II. 124. c. 2. *i*. Robert de Hay, sherif of Bedford and Buckinghamshire, 25 Henry iii. II. 239. c. 2. *f*. William de Hay, sherif of Oxfordshire, 29 Henry iii. II. 239. c. 1. *a*.

Hayles, monks of, their privilege, 46 Henry iii. I. 119.

Hayrun, Robert, seems to be sherif of London in the close of Henry iii. I. 610. c. 1. *i*. William, in Middlesex distrain'd illegally, 27 Henry iii. I. 682. c. 1. *r*. Was pledge of Patric de Holvesby, 40 Henry iii. II. 142.

Heagday, Geoffrey, 31 Henry ii. I. 563. c. 1. *f*. Why amerc'd, ibid.

Heanlega, Gilbert de, amerc'd pro falso dicto, 29 Henry ii. I. 563. c. 2. *l*.

Hebbeden, William de, who, 10 Edward ii. I. 684. c. 1. *x*.

Hebinton, that land belonged to William de Dalee, 29 Henry ii. I. 219. c. 2. *s*.

Hecham in Northamptonshire, its knights fees, 18 Henry ii. I. 588. c. 1. *p*. and I. 583. c. 2. *m*. Escheated, 33 Henry ii. I. 643. c. 1. *e*.

Hedernweta manor, the bishop of Ely's, 18 Edward i. I. 618. c. 1. *k*.

Hedersete, Richard de, pardon'd for not taking knighthood, 7 Edward i. 510. c. 1. *a*. William de Hedersete remov'd from being customer in the port of London, 16 Edward ii. II. 91. c. 1. *a*. Was plegius, II. 241. c. 1. *q*. Richard de Hedersete, usher of the Exchequer for life, 53 Henry iii. II. 276. c. 1. *o*. Son of Simon de Hedersete amerc'd, and pardon'd for not taking knighthood, ibid. c. 2. *p, q*. Usher, 4 Edward i. II. 281. c. 1. *e*.

Hedfunt, William de, imprison'd for the death of Gamel de Dive, 14 John I. 495. c. 2. *d*.

Hedindon in Oxfordshire, how far appropriated to Hugh de Plugenoi, and

INDEX.

and the abbefs of Godeftou, II. 163. c. 1. *y.* and II. 166. c. 1. *o.*

Hedon, Gerard de, diftrain'd for the remanent of his accompt, 55 Henry iii. I. 386. c. 1. *t.* The burgeffes of Hedon, Yorkfhire, fine for their liberties, 3 John, I. 404. c. 2. *g.* The quinzime for the merchandife of this port, 6 John, I. 77 2. c. 1. *i.* Simon de Heddon of Notinghamfhire, one of Brian de Lifle's executors, 42 Henry iii. II. 191. c. 1. *o.*

Heeftorp, Yorkfhire, its tallage, 30 Henry iii. I. 710. c. 1. *w.*

Hegham, Roger de, baron of the Exchequer, 1 Edward ii. I. 75. and 31 Edward i. II. 304. c. 1. *n.* Again baron, 26 Edward i. I. 467. c. 1. *d.* Again, 33 Edward i. I. 740. c. 2. *f.* and 2 Edward ii. II. 8. c. 2. *m.* and 1 Edward ii. II. 29. and 35 Edward i. II. 49. c. 2. *m.* Roger de Hegham dyed, 2 Edward ii. II. 58. See II. 67. c. 1. *q.* II. 235.

Hegftede, Robert de, fined, 29 Henry ii. I. 212. c. 1. *o.*

Hegtredeberie, its aid, 14 Henry ii. I. 589. Hectredefbery burgh in Wiltfhire, its tallage, 1 John, I. 705. c. 2. *z.*

Heiford manor, I. 499. c. 2. *z.*

Heiho, hundred de, I. 544. c. 2. *q.*

Heir of the king's debtor not to be diftrain'd, if the chatels were fufficient, II. 190.

Heiftildefham, prior of, 5 Richard i. 98. c. 1. *l.*

Heiward, Robert le, of Richelinges, amerc'd for an undue tryal by water, 31 Henry ii. I. 547. c. 1. *c.*

Heiwode, William de, clerk of the fherif of Somerfet and Dorfetfhire, 12 Edward ii. II. 280. c. 1. *b.*

Heiwurd, that bofch belong'd to the priory of Durham, 9 John, I. 409. c. 2. *b.*

Heldebovil, Ralf de, his land of Aketon, before 7 Richard i. II. 323. c. 1. *z.*

Heldebrand, Richard fon of, 23 Henry ii. I. 542. c. 2. *r.* Amerc'd, ibid.

Helebek, Ralf de, has the manor of Ronneham, Norfolk, 9 Edward ii. II. 101. c. 2. *w.*

Helgotus, 5 Stephen, I. 425. Fines for his inheritance, I. 425. c. 2. *e.*

Helles, Thomas de, one of the tellers of the Exchequer, 26 Edward i. II. 307. c. 1. *w.* Succeeded by his brother, ibid.

Hellefton in Cornwal, have a charter of liberties, 3 John, I. 403. c. 2. *w.*

Hellefton, Alanus de, feems to be fherif of Cornwal in accompting for the aid of Hellefton and other towns, 23 Henry ii. I. 604. c. 2. *m.* Its tallage, 1 John, I. 733. c. 2. *t.*

Helt, William fon of, 16 Henry ii. I. 140. His fcutage for his fees in Kent, 18 Henry ii. I. 630. c. 1. *d.*

Helte de Brandefton, his outrage, 12 John, I. 794. c. 2. *k.*

Heltefleg, John de, 40 Henry iii. II. 79. c. 1. *t.* Wrongfully imprifon'd, ibid.

Helyon, Hervey de, 25 Henry ii. I. 96. The relief of Robert in Effex, 5 Stephen, I. 315. c. 2. *u.* Henry has the lands and chattels of William de Strete, 13 Henry iii. I. 347. c. 2. *y.* Hervey de Helyon, 30 Henry ii. I. 563. c. 1. *g.* Robert's fifteen fees in Effex, 5 Henry ii. I. 626. c. 2. *q.* Robert de Helyon's fcutage for the Irifh war, 3 Richard i. I. 637. c. 1. *e.*

Hemel-

INDEX.

Hemelhamstede, Essex, its aid, 14 Henry ii. I. 587. c. 1.

Heminton tenement, I. 445. c. 1. *y*.

Hemmegrave, Thomas de, king's tallager, 19 Henry iii. I. 735. c. 1. *f*. Has a second attermination to pay his debts to the crown, 28 Henry iii. II. 212. c. 1. *d*.

Hen and Melchegrave seem to be in Sussex, I. 789. c. 1. *f*. By whom claim'd, ibid.

Hencsterrigg, to whom that manor belonged, 52 Henry iii. I. 101. c. 1. *d*.

Hendon, the manor of Geoffrey le Rus, 50 Henry iii. II. 174. c. 1. *r*.

Hendremot, seems to signify the hundred court, Cumb. I. 672. c. 2. *l*.

Heneton in Cornwal, its tallage with Tamerton, 1 John, I. 733. c. 2. *u*.

Hengham, William de, 2 Edward ii. I. 47. c. 2. *y*. Ralf de Hengham, justiciary de Banco, 35 Edward i. I. 74. c. 2. Has the manor of Geoffrey de Lezinan, 53 Henry iii. I. 752. c. 1. *k*. Justice of the common bench, 1 Edward ii. II. 30.

Henlee, William de, made sherif of Surry, &c. 2 Edward ii. II. 69. c. 1. *a*.

Henry emperor, I. 26.

Henry i. buried at Reading, I. 13. c. 1. *r*. Some particulars of his government in Normandy, I. 28. Had a son William, an. 1121. I. 109. Grants a charter to the canons of Holy Trinity, London, I. 179. A book learn'd prince, I. 181. Compiled a body of laws agreeable to the Anglo-saxon, I. 182. Raises three shillings on every hide of land to marry his daughter, I. 571. To the emperor Henry IV. I. 685. c. 1. *a*.

Henry ii. an. 1188. sends Hugh bishop of Durham to collect the disme in Scotland, I. 21. Was duke of Normandy and justiciary of England in king Stephen's time, I 34. c. 1. *s*. The constitutions of his houshold, I. 41. His division of England into circuits, I. 95. Came to the crown by an undoubted title, and surpassed all his ancestors, I. 181. Sends his daughter into Sicily, I. 367. c. 2. *p*. His aid, I. 571. His escuage for Galwey and Wales, 18 Henry ii. I. 629, &c.

Henry, son of Henry ii. crown'd during his father's life, an. 1170. at Westminster, I. 17. c. 1. *d*. Was made steward of France, I. 54. c. 1. *d*. Styled the king, I. 93. c. 2. *z*. With others, discharges Becket, I. 191. c. 2. *s*. Occurs, I. 215. Styled king son of the king, 19 Henry ii. I. 363. c. 1. *o*. Some account of the furniture for his coronation, and his queen the daughter of France, I. 366. This seems to be a second coronation at Winchester, 18 Henry ii. I. 336. c. 1. *e*. c. 2. *f*. His debts accompted for, 7 Richard i. I. 503. c. 2. *t*. Henry the king's son, 13 Henry ii. II. 205. c. 2. *q*.

Henry iii. founded the Rolls for convert Jews, I. 259. Grants the Jews liberty to chuse an high-priest, I. 260. His brother Geoffrey de Lezinan, 40 Henry iii. I. 466. c. 1. *y*. Quære. the aids granted him, I. 593. Has a scutage of three marks from every fee, 15 Henry iii. I. 606. Earl of Glocester rebels against him, 49 Henry iii. I. 654. c. 1. *z*. Tallaged thro' England, I. 706. c. 2. *f*.

Henry

INDEX.

Henry IV. emperor, made nine hundred knights at the coronation of Maud, an. 1114. I. 685. c. 1. *a*.

Henry VII. emperor, his cenfure againft Robert king of Sicily, an. 1311. I. 157.

Henry provoft of Hertford, his aid, 14 Henry ii. I. 586. c. 1. *x*.

Hens prized at or about three farthings apiece, 1 Richard i. I. 369. c. 1. *z*. See I. 376. c. 1. *y*. The wife of Hugh de Nevil pays two hundred to lye with her hufband, 6 John, I. 471. c. 2. *a*.

Hepwurth, Alice, daughter of Peter de, 13 John, I. 218. c. 2. *w*. Grants her land of Boclande to Robert be Abendon, ibid.

Heraclius, patriarch of Jerufalem, the occafion of his coming into England, 31 Henry ii. 20.

Herald fon of Humfry, 13 John, I. 443. c. 2. *o*. Fines in Lincolnfhire for the judgment of his country, ibid.

Herbert, archdeacon of Canterbury, fermer of the fee of Sarum, about 31 Henry ii. I. 311. c. 1. *d*. And again, 33 Henry ii. I. 634. c. 2. *q*. Herbert Fitz-Herbert holds of Chichefter, I. 576. c. 2. See Fitz-Herbert.

Herdelagh caftle in cuftody of John de Beauclare, 13 Edward i. II. 4. c. 2. *s*.

Herdewich was the king of Scots, 13 Henry ii. I. 539. c. 2. *w*. William de, 8 Richard i. I. 715. Barony of Herdewich in the bifhopric, 8 Richard i. I. 715. c. 2.

Herebeard, John and Emma, their tenure, 34 Henry iii. I. 651. c. 1. *p*.

Hereford, Henry earl of, 3 Henry iii. I. 67. c. 2. *x*. Hereford in Wallia, 9 John, I. 100. c. 1. *y*. Herefordfhire in Wales, 23 Henry ii. I. 130. c. 1. *q*. and I. 135. c. 2. *w*. Citifens fine for their ferm, gild of merchants, hanfe and other liberties, 2 Henry iii. I. 412. c. 1. *a*. Henry earl of Hereford has twenty knights fees in the honor of Huntendon and Rihale, in right of his mother, temp. Richard i. I. 488. c. 2. *d*. Walter de, 5 Henry ii. I. 628. c. 1. *w*. Earl of, conftable of England, 34 Edward i. I. 657. c. 2. Cecilia countefs of, fines, 3 John, I. 676. c. 2. *y*. Henry de, 9 Henry ii. I. 691. c. 1. *y*. Its donum, 5 Henry ii. I. 697. c. 2. *a*. Richard de, 39 Henry iii. II. 243. c. 2. *g*.

Hereford, fir Robert de, I. 242. Roger fon of Robert, 18 Edw. i. I. 243. c. *l*. Galfrid de Hereford who was flain, forfeited chattels, 15 Henry ii. I. 344. c. 2. *q*. Ailmund de Hereford, 31 Henry ii. I. 447. c. 2. *y*. Richard clerk of the Exchequer, 4 Edward i. II. 112. c. 2. *f*. Richard de Hereford remembrancer of the Exchequer, 56 Henry iii. II. 181. c. 1. *l*.

Hereford, that fee in cuftody of John Cumin, 16 Henry ii. I. 306. c. 2. *s*. The ferm of that county, 5 Richard i. I. 332. c. 1. *z*. Matthew de Hereford has the church of Snchenefrith, 6 John, I. 480. c 2. *l*. Inquifition about the fee's number of knights fees, I. 594. c. 1. *g*. viz. eighteen, 38 Henry iii. I. 596. c. 2. *x*. John Cumin cuftos of this fee, 20 Henry ii. I. 642. c. 2. *b*. Its fcutage, I. 664. c. 2. *b*. William [Ver] jufticier of, 7 Richard i. I. 703. c. 2. *n*. 9 Richard i. I. 733. c. 1. *o*. Richard de Hereford clerk of the Exchequer, 56 Henry

INDEX.

iii. II. 232. c. 2. *i.* Remembrancer of the Exchequer, 1 Edward i. II. 233. c. 1. *k.* Again, II. 264.

Heregrave, Frumbald de, his fine, 6 Henry iii. I. 445. c. 1. *z.*

Hergwinton, Adam de, 26 Edward i. I. 655. c. 1. One of the barons summon'd by writ, ibid.

Herierd, Richard de, one of the justiciers, 9 Richard i. I. 113. His claim on the village of Bedefont, 1 John, I. 216. c. 1. *f.*

Heriz, Henry de, his grant, 3 John, I. 217. c. 1. *k.* Robert, 30 Henry ii. I. 447. c. 2. *x.* Alice widow of William de Heriz fines to marry as she will, 26 Henry ii. I. 464. c. 1. *z.*

Herle, one of the commissioners for the marefchalcy, 18 Edward iii. I. 792. c. 1. *w.*

Herleberg, Roger de, 25 Henry ii. II. 212. c. 1. *m.* 21 Henry ii. II. 200. c. 1. *e.*

Herlewin, William son of, 5 Stephen, I. 426. c. 1. *g.* Ralf son of, sherif of Lond. 5 Stephen, I. 457. c. 2. *t.* Geoffrey son of, 5 Stephen, I. 476. c. 2. *b.*

Herlizum, William, 5 Henry iii. I. 452. c. 2. *m.* Reginald Herlizun married Mawise daughter of Maud de Daggeworth, before 32 Edward i. II. 277.

Herman of Hertford, his aid, 14 Henry ii. I. 586. c. 1. *x.*

Hernesium of the king's chapel, I. 331. c. 1. *g.*

Herolcurt, Anschetil de, Leicestershire, I. 449. c. 1. *x.* Fines that he and his heirs may not plead, ibid.

Heroldus published the Burgundian laws, Pref. xviii. c. 1. *f.* xxii. c. 2. *r.* His account of the Franckick kings, I. 159.

Herrings accompted for in the profits of the see of Chichester, I. 307. c. 1. *y.*

Hertburn in the bishopric, its tallage, 11 Edward i. I. 720. c. 2. *u.*

Herteberghe, Giles de, master of the money in the exchanges or mints, 11 and 12 Edward ii. I. 291. His coinage too light with too great allay, I. 292. c. 1. *c.*

Hertford hundred, I. 543. c. 1. *z.* Men of Hertford break down Ware bridge, 3 Richard i. I. 564. c. 1. *z.* Ten burgesses of Hertford by name, their aid, 14 Henry ii. I. 586. c. 1. *x.* The aid of Heortford, 5 Stephen, I. 601. c. 1. *q.* Earl of, 26 Edward i. I. 655. c. 1. Its tallage or assise, 19 Henry ii. I. 701. c. 1. *z.* Its tallage, 2 Henry iii. I. 706. c. 1. *b.* Priory a cell of St Albans, I. 759. c. 1. *x.* Henry earl of, sat in the Exchequer, 14 Henry iii. II. 27. c. 2. *g.* What the county was held at in the time of Maud, II. 138. c. 1. *d.*

Herthil wapentake under a commission of array, 16 Edward ii. II. 112.

Hertiland abbat holds in frankalmoign, temp. Edward i. I. 671. c. 1. *g.*

Hertinton in Surrey, its aid, 14 Henry ii. I. 587. c. 1. *y.*

Hertmere hundred, I. 545. c. 1. *x.*

Hertrepol in Yorkshire fines for the same laws and liberties as Newcastle, 3 John, I. 404. c. 1. *c.*

Hertwelle, Rafe de, fined to have his duel in the king's court, 30 Henry ii. I. 97. c. 1. *u.*

Herun, William, sherif of Northumberland, 40 and 41 Henry iii. II. 158. c. 2. *a.*

Hervey, Walter, bailif of London, accompts as one of the custodes, 52 Henry iii. 779. c. 1. *e.* Again, 53

and

INDEX.

and 54 Henry iii. II. 202. c. 2. *a*. His allocatio for the discharge of that office, II. 237. c. 2. *q*.

Herwynton, Adam de, baron of the Exchequer, assign'd to survey the king's castles and manors, 1 Edward ii. II. 67. c. 1. *q*. Adam de Herwynton deputy chamberlain of the Exchequer, 26 Edward i. II. 299. Presented by Guy earl of Warwick, ibid.

Hese, a moiety of eight knights fees here claim'd by Turstan de Mumford against Nicolas de Stutevil, 10 John, I. 100. c. 1. *z*. Matthew de Wikes excus'd from his attendance on this court as usher of the Exchequer, 33 Henry iii. II. 275.

Hesingewald in Yorkshire, the donum of the men of, 3 Richard i. I. 698. c. 2. *q*. and 9 Richard i. I. 699. c. 1. *r*.

Hesleham priory in Northumberland, has five knights fees, 29 Henry iii. I. 596. c. 1. *r*.

Hesseburn, Thomas de, accompts for the abbey of Abendon, 31 Henry ii. I. 309. c. 2. *s*.

Hethe, Oxfordshire, tallaged, 3 John, I. 721. c. 2. *y*.

Hethfeld, a cell of St Albans, 10 Richard i. I. 759. c. 2. *x*. See Hathfeld.

Heverdon, Philip de, one of the executors of John de Kirkeby bishop of Ely, 18 Edward i. II. 186. c. 2. *r*.

Heyen in Devonshire, Agnes wife of Nicolas de Creton of, II. 80. c. 2. *b*.

Heyghton, William de, 5 Edward ii. II. 7. c. 1. *e*. One of the executors of John de Berewyc, II. 31. c. 1. *m*.

Hickes, Dr. George, commended, Pref. xv, xvi. xxvii. xxix. His observation of the king's chancellor, I. 60. c. 2. *x*. His opinion of the antiquity of the Chancery and Exchequer, I. 178. c. 1. *z*. Commended again, I. 180. c. 2.

Hidage, an aid charged on lands held by socage or inferior tenure, 15 Edward ii. I. 592. c. 1. *w*, &c. Not paid out of lands of military tenure, I. 694.

Hide abbey in custody of John and Herbert Pincerna, 19 Henry ii. I. 308. c. 2. *l*. Accompted for, 8 John, I. 312. c. 1. *k*. Was in custody, 18 Henry ii. I. 367. c. 1. *i*. Abbat of Hide, 5 John, I. 480. c. 1. *g*. Abbat of Hide justicier, 7 Richard i. I. 502. c. 1. *x*. His knights fees, 29 Henry iii. I. 594. c. 2. *l*. Frere Peter chamberlain of Hyde and Reginald de S. Edward pay fifty marks for the king's passage into Gascoigne, 27 Henry iii. I. 609. c. 1. *d*. Abbat of Hyde's scutage, 2 Richard i. I. 667. c. 2. *p*. Thomas de la Hyde sherif and seneschal of Cornwal, 1 Edward ii. II. 145. c. 1. *p*. Amerc'd for not accompting, but releas'd, 5 Edward ii. II. 237. c. 1. *n*.

Hides, a duty upon their transportation into France, 10 John, I. 469. c. 2. *h*. Exported, 776. c. 1. *r*. The duty upon every last of hides, I. 781. 783. Custom on them, II. 137.

Highway, the town of Malsateby amerc'd for plowing it up, 12 Henry ii. I. 557. c. 2. *k*.

Hikeshelle hundred, William Mareschal's interest in it, 2 Richard i. II. 20. c. 1. *y*.

Hilary bishop of Chichester's certificate

INDEX.

cate into the Exchequer concerning the knights fees of that fee, temp. Henry ii. I. 576.

Hildebrand of Cambridge amerc'd for exporting corn without licence, 23 Henry ii. c. 1. r. See Heldebrand.

Hildret sherif of Cumberland, temp. Stephen, I. 328. c. 1. h.

Hiltun, Richard de, of Yorkshire, amerc'd for freighting corn, 12 Henry ii. I. 552. c. 1. f. Baron Robert de Hilton of Northumberland, 26 Edward i. I. 654. c. 1. a. Alexander de Hilton of Northumberland, 19 and 22 Henry iii. II. 212. c. 1. e.

Hintlesdon, Norfolk, its ferm accompted for by William heir of Walter Pippard, 11 Henry iii. II. 6. c. 1. z.

Hirtiland in Devonshire, its aid, 14 Henry ii. I. 588. c. 1. b.

Hirton, William son of Fulcher de, Notinghamshire, a venire facias against him, 39 Henry iii. II. 17. c. 1. e.

History, the writing of it in some sort a religious act, Pref. vii. How it ought to be undertaken, ibid. History of Alexander to be painted in the queen's chamber at Notingham, 36 Henry iii. I. 377. c. 2. i.

Hlotharius emperor, I. 25.

Ho, Roger de, fines to plead for the land of Cropestoft, against Ralf de Tivil, 9 John, I. 448. c. 1. i. Paid a fine for beating the king's serjeants, 9 John, I. 474. c. 1. c. The tallage of Ho, 33 and 34 Henry ii. I. 736. c. 1. o, p. John de Hoo, late sherif of Essex, 8 Edward ii. II. 239. c. 2. g.

Hobrig, William de, married Agnes one of the heiresses of Robert Picot before 5 Henry iii. I. 318. c. 1. u.

Hoby, the canons of Marton had interest in it, 7 Henry iii. I. 329. c. 1. w.

Hoccende, William de, father and son, an. 1142. I. 198. c. 1. e.

Hocton and Horthorp belonged to William Fitz-Roger, 24 Henry ii. I. 211. c. 2. l. Hocton and Hastley claim'd by John de Amundevil, 5 Stephen, I. 482. c. 1. y. William de Hocton fines for the widow and guardship of the heir of Geoffrey de Favarc. 5 Stephen, I. 501. c. 1. l. Joslen de Hocton amerc'd for making an unsupported charge of homicide, 17 Henry ii. 558. c. 1. q.

Hodierna the nurse, her land in Wiltshire tallaged, 20 Henry iii. I. 707. c. 1. k.

Hogeshawe, Walter de, bailif of Ailesbury, 39 Henry iii. II. 19. c. 2. u.

Hogton, Mr. Richard de, accompts for Thomas earl of Lancastre, 28 Edward i. II. 175. c. 1. t.

Hoiland, the profits of the fair of, I. 297. c. 1. g. The men of Ketsteven and Hoiland in Lincolnshire have a confirmation of liberties, 6 Richard i. I. 399. c. 2. l. Again, 2 John, I. 401. c. 2. e.

Holcham, lands in Norfolk, given to Roger de Toeni, 30 Henry ii. I. 328. c. 1. n.

Holcoltram, abbat of, 3 John, I. 478. c. 1. q.

Holderness wapentake has a commission of array sent to it, 16 Edward ii. II. 112. c. 1.

Holebrock, Richard de, 7 Edward i. II. 203. Seems to be sherif, ibid.

Holegate, William de, mayor of Lincoln in the close of Henry iii. I. 610. c. 2. i. The tallage of John de, in York, 3 John, I. 722. c. 2. b.

INDEX.

Holewell, Alice de, contends with the church of Westminster about the advouson of Holewel, 3 Henry iii. II. 43. c. 2. *n*. William de, late sherif of Bukingham and Bedfordshire, 35 Henry iii. II. 192. c. 2. *y*.

Holewude, I. 430. c. 2. *f*. The terra of Maurice de Wadenhal in Kent, 27 Henry ii. ibid.

Holland, that honor in the king's hands, 14 John, I. 299. c. 1. *f*. Elizabeth countess of Holland sister of Edward i. and wife of Humfrey de Bohun, 31 Edward i. II. 283.

Holm, Philip de, and his son John, I. 523. c. 2. *t*. See Hulm.

Holte, John, alderman of Newingate, Canterbury, tallaged, 32 Edward i. I. 741. c. 1. *g*. Robert de Holt's tenure in Melkesham, 40 Henry iii. I. 746. c. 1. *d*.

Holton, barony in the bishopric, 8 Richard i. I. 715. c. 2. See Hilton.

Holvesby, Patric de, committee of the county and castle of Lancaster, 40 Henry iii. II. 142.

Holweia, Richard de, 5 Stephen, I. 448. c. 2. *r*. His claim of land in Devonshire, ibid.

Homage, the form of doing it to a lord, I. 4. c. 1. *c*. To the king, ibid. Homagium and vassalagium equivalent, I. 5. c. 2.

Homet, William de, constable of Normandy, 8 Richard i. I. 29. And likewise, 1 Richard i. I. 77. c. 1. *d*.

Homicide, fines for it, I. 497. See Manslaughter.

Homo, its different import in Latin and Romanick, Pref. xxiii.

Honey used in making cervisia, 31 Henry ii. I. 368. c. 2. *w*.

Honorius fin'd to be archdeacon of Richmunt, 3 John, I. 515. c. 2. *i*.

Honour of St Saviour, late the possession of Roger the viscount, an. 1202. 3 John, I. 170, 171. Honor of Spiney late of Ingelram de Port, I. 170. c. 2. *t*. Many honors and baronies in custody of the crown, I. 296. Honour of Wallingford, I. 354. c. 2. *r*.

Hopton, Walter de, was one of the justices ad placita coram rege, 3 and 4 Edward i. II. 320. c. 1. *d*.

Horbery, William de, 22 Henry ii. I. 503. c. 1. *l*. Fines that his stepmother might have a reasonable dower, ibid.

Horde in the bishoprick, the ferm of the village and waters of, I. 714. c. 2.

Horend, Wolfward de, bail'd William de Tani, 14 Henry ii. I. 554. c. 2. *q*.

Horepol, Peter de, 49 Henry iii. II. 17. c. 2. *f*. A reteinour of William Mareschal baron of the Exchequer, ibid.

Horewel forest in Worcestershire disforested, 14 Henry iii. I. 418. c. 2. *k*.

Horlesh, William de, collector of the aid, for marrying the king's sister, in the Northreding of Yorkshire, 22 Henry iii. II. 192. c. 2. *w*.

Horm son of Thora, of Yorkshire, with Roger his son, 1 Richard i. I. 493. c. 1. *e*.

Horn, Alexander, his trespass, 15 John, I. 774. c. 1. John sherif of London, 1 Edward i. II. 96. c. 1. *w*.

Hornecastra, its aid, 14 Henry ii. I. 585. c. 2. *w*. Martin de.

Hornemere hundred belong'd to the abbat of Abendon, 13 Henry iii. I. 416. c. 2. *a*.

Horse, a decision on a horse's killing a woman,

INDEX.

woman, an. 1281. I. 163. c. 2. *x*. Horse at three marks price, 11 John, I. 410. c. 2. *m*. Some Horses worth an hundred shillings, 55 Henry iii. II. 93. c. 1. *k*. Cart-Horse at eight shillings, 14 Henry iii. II. 152. c. 2. *z*.

Horsey, Philip de, one of the jury of Ralf de Mandevil, 10 John, I. 489. c. 2. *q*. Fined for an unjust detention, 14 John, I. 792. c. 1. *y*.

Horsindon, that land belonging to John de, conveyed to Robert de Braibroc, 12 John, I. 219. Of the fee of John de Monte Acuto, I. 218. c. 1. *r*.

Horsley priory, its aid, 29 Henry iii. I. 595. c. 2. *q*.

Horton, Gervase de, his case, 39 Henry iii. I. 597. c. 2. *a*. Robert de Horton sherif of Devonshire, 9 Edward ii. II. 238.

Hosdeng, Ralf de, pays queen's gold, 10 John, I. 351. c. 1. *n*.

Hose, Henry, surety for the countess Margery, 7 Richard i. I. 106. c. 1. *t*. Hugh de la Hose deraigned, 30 Henry iii. I. 116. c. 1. *a*. Geoffrey Hose one of the justices, 26 Henry ii. I. 138. c. 1. *a*. Gundred late wife of Geoffrey Hose, has the guard of her son Geoffrey, 1 John, I. 202. c. 1. *z*. Walter Hose has the ferm of Trentham in Staffordshire, 15 Henry ii. I. 279. c. 1. *s*. Hubert Hose had the annual fee of an hundred pounds from Andover, 30 Henry iii. I. 287. c. 1. *n*. Hugh de la Hose, 9 Richard i. I. 453. c. 1. *p*. Hubert Hose escapes from the custody of Hugh de Nevil, before 14 John, I. 475. c. 1. *k*. Roscelin Hose fines that his son John may have pledges for his appearance, 4 John, I. 493. c. 2. *k*. John had killed William son of Jordan, ibid. Geoffrey de la Hose his fine and scutage, 3 John, I. 650. c. 1. *l*. Henry Hose's fee in Wiltshire in the hands of William de Warenne, 1 John, I. 664. c. 2. *c*.

Hospes liber was exempt from assises and tallages, I. 746. The knights Templars and Hospitallers had by ancient grant, each one of them in every burgh, ibid.

Hospital, Ralf del, one of the inquisitours against the sherifs, 16 Henry ii. I. 140. Fermer of the abbey of Tavistock, 31 Henry ii. I. 311. c. 1. *c*. Alice del Hospice of Normandy, her claim on the land of Asclovil, 2 John, I. 518. c. 2. *w*. Hospital of poor priests of Estbrig, Canterbury, I. 740. c. 2. *f*. Hospital of St Giles, London, I. 781. c. 1. *o*.

Hospitallers and Templars, the chief of them come into England, 31 Henry ii. I. 20. See Templars.

Hothum, Richard de, accompts for the vintisme, &c. 5 Edward ii. II. 181. c. 2. *n*.

Hotoman de verbis feudalibus, I. 5. c. 2. His distinction between Ærarium and Fiscus, I. 159. c. 1. *x*.

Hoton, William son of Adam de, justiced, 6 Henry iii. I. 454. c. 1. *e*. The tallage of Hoton in Yorkshire, 30 Henry iii. I. 710. c. 1. *w*. See Houton.

Hotoft, John de, 35 Edward i. II. 87. His tender in behalf of Sir Henry de Leyburn, II. 87. c. 2. *z*.

Hou in Kent, its aid, 14 Henry ii. I. 588. c. 2. *d*. See Ho. Walter de Hou of Yorkshire, and Thomas his brother, 8 Richard i. I. 737. c.

INDEX.

r. s. Their writ to the provosts of Beverley, ibid.

Houcton, Simon de, remov'd from the sherifalty of Cambridgeshire, 37 Henry iii. II. 68. c. 2. w.

Hovenden, I. 8. c. 1. Relates the order of the coronation of Richard i. an. 1189. I. 21. See 25. and 59. Roger de, I. 93. His accompt of the iters, I. 122. See 220. c. 2. c.

Hovedene in Yorkshire, the vast profits accruing from that church, 4 John, I. 478. c. 1. r. Wapentak of Hovedene under a commission of array, 16 Edward ii. II. 112. c. 2.

Houk, William de, sherif of Yorkshire, 34 Edward i. II. 65. c. 2. g. Discharged from being sherif, 1 Edward ii. II. 144. c. 1. f.

Housey, Robert de, fined for a recognition of the right of patronage for the church of S. Victor, I. 166. c. 2. i. The tallage of the king's men of Hussey, 2 Henry iii. 706. c. 2. e.

Houton, William de, his relief for the third part of a barony, 21 Henry iii. I. 317. c. 2. t. The tallage of Houton in the bishopric, 11 Edward i. I. 720. c. 2. u. John de Houton one of the commissioners for the mareschalcy, 18 Edward iii. I. 797. c. 1. w.

Howard, William, justice of the common bank, 26 Edward i. II. 91. c. 2. e. John Howard sherif of Norfolk and Suffolk, 11 and 12 Edward ii. II. 181. c. 2. q.

Hoyvil, Philip de, of Fontely, late sherif of Southampton, 35 Edward i. II. 181. c. 1. m. His accompts adjusted by William his son and heir, ibid.

Hubert cum testa, his controversy with the abbat of Tavistock, 5 Stephen, I. 426. c. 1. n.

Hubert, archbishop, made justicier after the king's return, I. 35. Receives the complaint of the canons of York against their metropolitan, &c. ibid. Was the pope's legate, I. 36. Forbid secular administrations by the pope, ibid. Continued chancellor in the reign of king John, I. 46. c. 1. p. Was chancellor at Mans, Sept. 23. 1 John, I. 57. c. 1. r. Retained the chancellorship to his death, I. 67. c. 1. s. His writ De ultra mare, I. 87. Was justicier, 9 Richard i. I. 113. Several acts of Hubert's as justicier, I. 291, &c. Has the wardship of Robert son and heir of William de Stutevil, 6 John, I. 324. c. 2. h. Makes a tallage in Southampton for the subsistence of the king's serjeants, 10 Richard i. I. 705. c. 2. x.

Huceman de Alto Pecco, Richard, committed to the fleet, 25 Edward i. II. 238. c. 1. t.

Huche, John de, attorney of John de Baillol, 52 Henry iii. II. 80. c. 1. z.

Hudleston, John de, one of the king's barons and courtiers, 26 Edward i. I. 655. c. 2.

Hue and Cry, amercements for not making it, I. 556. Called pursuit, ibid.

Huelina, the widow of Ralf de Bradelega of Lincolnshire, 15 Henry iii. I. 326. c. 1. l. Succeeds in her claim of the wardship of her heirs and lands against Adam Esturmy, ibid.

Hugenden, Ralf de, 1 Richard i. I. 432. c. 1. t. The plaint of John Cabuis

INDEX.

Cabuis against him to be before the justices, ibid.

Hugh di San Caro, cardinal, his present from the king, 35 Henry iii. II. 202. c. 1. *u*.

Hugh bishop of Durham made justicier in the beginning of king Richard i. I. 34.

Hugh, earl, his land in the king's hand, 1 Richard i. I. 298. c. 2. *t*. The 120 knights fees of earl Hugh, 14 Henry ii. I. 573. c. 1.

Hugh bishop of Coventry fermer of Warwick and Leicestershire, 2 Richard i. I. 328. c. 2. *r*. See I. 458. c. 2. *f*.

Hugh son of Emma kills Ralf de Whitefeld before 8 John, I. 494. c. 2. *r*.

Hugh son of Agnes imprisoned in Hertford, 6 Henry iii. I. 496. c. 1. *l*. Thomas Fitz-Hugh, 22 Henry iii. II. 242. c. 2. *z*. Permitted on his parole as a prisoner to retire to the burgh of Wic, ibid.

Huiam, parcel of the barony of Dovor, in possession of Roger de Planes, and then of William Briewerre, 10 Richard i. II. 226. c. 1. *w*.

Huilard, Ralf son of, amerced for a disseisin, 14 Henry ii. I. 549. c. 1. *d*.

Hulf, Robert son of, fined for an accord with Ralf de Brummore, whom he had wounded, 18 Henry ii. I. 503. c. 1. *i*.

Hulle, Ralf de la, man of the brothers of St Lazarus of Jerusalem, 6 John, I. 206. c. 2. *r*. The merchant gild of Thomas del Hull amerced, 14 Henry iii. I. 567. c. 1. *f*. The quinzime for the merchandise of this port, I. 772. c. 1. *i*. The usual custom of the port of Hull, II. 137. c. 1. *a*.

Hulm abbey was in custody about 16 Henry ii. I. 306. c. 2. *r*. In custody of Wimar Chaplain, 19 Henry ii. I. 308. c. 2. *k*. James de Hulmo fermer of Lincoln, 30 Henry ii. I. 331. c. 2. *q*. The steward with some account of the lands of Hulm abbey, I. 462. c. 1. *m*. The abbat's convention with William de Nevil, 9 Henry ii. I. 501. c. 2. *r*. William de Hulmo amerced, 9 Richard i. I. 565. Its donum, 5 Henry ii. I. 627. c. 1. *s*. Gilbert de Holm sherif of Bedford and Buckinghamshire, 1 Edward ii. II. 151. c. 1. *r*.

Humez, Richard de, constabulary of Normandy, temp. Henry ii. I. 41. William de Humet his assignment out of Stanford, 30 Henry ii. I. 328. c. 2. *o*. William de Humez gave the land of Wichenden to his daughter Agnes de Wac in marriage before 9 John, I. 451. c. 2. *b*. John de Humez his fine, 2 Henry iii. I. 475. c. 2. *n*. Emma de Humez widow of Geoffrey de Nevil, 5 Richard i. I. 483. c. 2. *n*. William de Humet constabulary of Normandy, 4 John, I. 537. c. 1. William de Humez quit of scutage in Essex, 1 John, I. 665. c. 1. *d*. Richard de Humez has his danegeld remitted in Hampshire, I. 687. c. 1. *h*.

Humilane, Ralf de, alderman of the ward of Bredstret, distrained, 2 Edward ii. II. 235. c. 1. *t*.

Humilierd hundred in custody of Nicolas Castle, 9 Edward i. c. 2. *f*.

Hundehoge in Leicestershire, a council of the proceres here, I. 12. c. 2. *p*. Held under Ralf Basset, an. 1124. when the king was in Normandy, ibid. Forty four thieves hanged there, ibid.

Hundescote,

INDEX.

Hundefcote, William de, has the terra de Mienes granted by the king, 9 Richard i. II. 152. c. 2. *x*.

Hundredour, II. 48, 49.

Hunechild in Kent, its aid, 14 Henry ii. I. 588. c. 2. *d*.

Huneton in Devonfhire, that lordfhip charged to earl Richard, 24 Henry ii. I. 605. c. 1. *o*.

Hunftan, Roger fon of, amerced for lading fhips againft the affife, 12 Henry ii. I. 558. c. 1. *n*.

Huntendon, Nicolas archdeacon of, one of the chief jufticiers, 20 Henry ii. I. 124. c. 2. *y*. The honor of Huntendon and Gant, lately earl Simon's, were in the king's hands, 31 Henry ii. I. 298. c. 1. *c*. Twenty knights fees of this honor adjudged to Henry earl of Hereford in right of his mother, temp. Richard i. I. 488. c. 2. *d*. The heirs of John earl of Huntendon, 31 Henry iii. I. 594. c. 2. *k*. I. 596. c. 1. *t*. Its aid, 5 Stephen, I. 601. c. 1. *p*. The fcutage of Gannoc from the heirs of John earl of Huntendon, 30 Henry iii. I. 667. c. 1. *n*. The town's affife, 22 Henry ii. I. 702. c. 2. *h*. Tallaged, 14 Henry iii. I. 708. c. 2. *q*. H. earl of, fat in the Exchequer, 14 Henry iii. II. 27. c. 2. *g*. John earl of Huntendon not chargeable with earl Simon's debts, 13 Henry iii. II. 227. c. 2. *e*. See II. 245.

Huntercoumbe, Walter de, of Northumberland, 26 Edward i. I. 654. c. 1. *a*. Has the cuftody of the caftle of Bere with two hundred marks yearly out of the Exchequer of Kaernarvan, 12 Edward i. II. 4. c. 2. *r*. Occurs, 27 Edward i. with a fpecial commiffion from the king, II. 106.

Huntingfeld, William de, 3 Henry iii. I. 68. c. 1. *x*. Peter de Huntingfeld of Kent, 14 Edward i. I. 254. c. 2. *c*. Again fherif of Kent, 11 Edward i. I. 313. c. 1. *g*. Roger de, fent his knight Andrew de Gayzi to the war in Gafcoigne before 39 Henry iii. I. 669. c. 1. *z*. William de, warden of the fea ports for Norfolk and Suffolk, 15 John, I. 774. c. 1. Peter de Huntingfeud, 22 Edward i. II. 191. c. 2. *r*.

Huppelanda de Berkamfted, its aid, 14 Henry ii. I. 587. c. 1.

Hurel, Reginald, alderman of Weftgate, Canterbury, 32 Edward i. I. 741. c. 1. *g*.

Hurle priory was only a cell, 1 John, I. 722. c. 2. *a*. Had Geoffrey Fitz Peter for its advocate, ibid.

Hurtefleye, John and Roger, two of the efquires of S. Thomas de Cantilupe bifhop of Hereford, 10 Edward i. I. 669. c. 1. *a*.

Hurtford, Robert de, claims two hides of land in Hoddefdon, 29 Henry ii. I. 512. c. 1. *t*. See Hertford.

Hufe, Henry, collector of the fcutage, 34 Edward i. I. 646. c. 2. John de la Hufe deputy marefchal againft Scotland, 34 Edward i. I. 657. c. 2. Robert le Hus, 33 Henry iii. II. 13. c. 2. *m*. John de la Hufe deputy of John Lovel, II. 49. c. 1. *h*.

Hufk, the caftle and terra of, belonging to the earl of Clare, I. 102. c. 1.

Huffage tallaged, I. 725. c. 2. *g*.

Huffeburn, Mr Thomas de, jufticier, 9 Richard i. I. 113. Cuftos of the bifhoprick of Chefter, 31 Henry ii. I. 310. c. 2. *y*. And of the abbey, ibid. c. 2. *z*. Accompts for the fee of Winchefter, 1 Richard i. I. 311. c. 2. *f*. And the abbey of Scireburn, ibid. Mr Thomas de, holds pleas, 3 Rich-

INDEX.

3 Richard i. I. 544. c. 1. *p.* King's tallager for Wiltshire, 33 Henry ii. I. 634. c. 1. *q.* Richard de Husseburn accompts for William Mareschal sherif of Gloucestershire, 7 John, II. 158. c. 1. *x.*

Hustengs of London, the king's Exchequer moved thither, 18 Edward i. II. 9. c. 1. *n.*

Hutch in the Exchequer, to lay up the certificates of the knights fees, 14 Henry ii. I. 576. c. 1. *x.* Hutch, to lay up the memoranda of the Exchequer cost seven pence, 9 Henry iii. II. 311. Ten dozen of hutches at twenty shillings, ibid.

Hutime, how to be levied, II. 104. Utime, ibid.

Hwe, Geoffrey Fitz, has the commission of array for the wapentake of Kyngeston upon Hull, 16 Edward ii. II. 112. c. 2.

Hywysh, Richard de, sherif and steward of Cornwal, 9 Edward ii. I. 386. c. 1. *s.*

J.

Jakesley market, a mark of gold given for it by the abbot of Thorney, 5 Stephen, I. 277. c. 2. *d.* Robert de Jakeslea accompts to the king for the profits of Thorney abbey, 16 Henry ii. I. 307. c. 1. *w.* Was a clergiman, 19 Henry ii. I. 308. c. 1. *f.*

James earl of Albemarl, was chamberlain in fee of the Exchequer, about 53 Henry iii. II. 297. See Albemarle.

Jarpunvil, Albreda de, has the serjeanty of the Asturcaria, 13 John, I. 462. c. 2. *n.* Fines to have her office supplied by deputies, ibid. G. P. and D. de Jarpenvile of Hertfordshire, 42 Henry iii. II. 14. c. 2. *s.* Thomas de Jarpenvill, 26 Edward i. II. 24. c. 1.

Jarun, Hugh son of Ranulf de, his donum, 9 Richard i. I. 699. c. 1. *r.* The quinzime for the merchandise of the port of Jarum, 6 John, I. 772. c. 2. *i.* Jarum on the river These, I. 785. c. 1. *x.*

Iclesham, Ralf de, had Sibylla de Dene wife of Richard de la Cumbe for his mother, and Robert de Dene his brother, and Sibylla his daughter and heir, the wife of Nicolas Haringot before 11 Henry iii. II. 98. c. 1. *n.*

Idiot, the lands of William Berthaud an idiot extended, 33 Edward i. I. 348. c. 1. *b.*

Jerusalem, the prior and brethren of, had the land of Adam Cocus, and of Totingwich, 3 John, I. 404. c. 1. *b.* Made a voluntary fine of seven hundred marks, 26 Edward i. I. 612. c. 2. *r.* Were on an equality with the knights Templars, 23 Edward i. I. 744. c. 1. *u.* Had a liber hospes in every burgh whom they could exempt from common assises, I. 746, 747. Frere Josep late prior of St John of Jerusalem, and king's treasurer, 26 Edward i. II. 307. c. 1. *w.*

Jesus, the blasphemers of his name to be speedily attached, 34 Henry iii. II. 102.

Jews, pay the disme for the recovery of the holy land, 34 Henry ii. I. 20. Great outrages committed upon them, I. 21. Abraham the Jew of London, 28 Henry ii. I. 113. c. 2. Aaron the Jew of Lincoln, I. 191. Jews their Exchequer, I. 221. How they inriched the crown by tallages, fines, and amerciaments, ibid. By way of tallage pay a fourth of their chattels,

INDEX.

chattels, 33 Henry ii. I. 222. Are plundered of 66,000 marks by king John, an. 1210. I. 223. c. 1. *i.* Fined in 20,000 marks, 28 Henry iii. I. 224. c. 2. *t.* And 60,000 more imposed, ibid. Wives, children, lands, and rents to be seized for want of payment, I. 229. Paid fines for recovery of their debts, I. 230. Might not intermarry without the king's licence, I. 228. c. 1. *s.* Circumcise a Christian child at Norwich before 31 Henry iii. ibid. *u.* Jews of London fined 2000 pounds for a manslaughter, 5 Stephen, I. 229. c. 1. *a.* Their Exchequer and Rolls or Records, I. 231. Justiciers appointed for them, I. 233. Custodes of the Jews in Normandy, 5 John, I. 237. c. 1. *m.* Whether a Jew may take usury of a Jew, 4 Richard i. I. 244. c. 2. *u.* Judæi falsonarii or forgers, ibid. Jews wife intitled to her thirds, I. 247. Many laws made concerning them, I. 248. To have no schools, I. 249. c. 1. *i.* Had a charter of liberties from king Henry i. and king John, I. 255. Expelled out of England about an. 1290. 18 Edward i. I. 261. House for converted Jews, I. 259. I. 745. c. 1. *a.* A bishop of the Jews in England, 24 Henry ii. II. 206. c. 1. *w.* Exchequer of the Jews, II. 276.

Isfeld, John de, assessed the tallage on Surrey and Sussex, 6 Edward ii. I. 744. c. 1. *w.* c. 2. *x.*

Ilesham, Ralf and Hawise de, sell the land of Ilesham to William Briewerre, 26 Heny ii. I. 215.

Ilger the goldsmith, keeper of the coin, 6 Henry iii. II. 87. c. 2. *a.*

Illebone or Dieppe in Normandy, William the Conqueror holds a council there, an. 1080. I. 92.

Images of St Christopher and St Edward the king, to be painted in the queen's chapel at Winchester, 32 Henry iii. I. 377. c. 2. *h.*

Immediate Baillee to render the accompt, II. 175.

Immerara, I. 581. c. 2. *a.*

Impasterat, Picot, 5 Stephen, I. 426. c. 1. *m.* Fines to recover his debts, ibid.

Imprest money or de præstito, issued out of some of the king's treasuries, I. 387, 388. c. 2. *f.* I. 389. c. 1. *g,* &c.

Imprisonment, false, I. 103, passim.

Indictments for homicide, I. 443. False procurers of them punished, II. 64, 65.

Inge, William, of the king's council, 1 Edward ii. II. 30. Reports Richard de Abyndon baron of the Exchequer, 1 Edward ii. II. 57. c. 2. *y.*

Ingeham, John de, one of the barons summoned by writ against Scotland, 26 Edward i. I. 655. c. 1. John and Reginald de Ingeham, their case, 35 Edward i. II. 121. Sir John de Ingeham, 18 Edward i. II. 266. c. 2. *q.*

Ingelram son of William the clerk, 5 Henry iii. I. 152. c. 1. *b.* Father of Randulph sherif of Notingham, 9 Henry ii. I. 336. c. 1. *d.* Ranulph son of Ingelram, 5 Stephen, I. 481. c. 2. *u.*

Ingepenne, Roger de, sherif of Cornwal, 18 Edward i. II. 179. c. 1. *t.*

Ingenlator, II. 206. c. 2. *a.*

Ingenium, unfair device or engin, Pref. xxiv. See I. 174. c. 2. *k.*

Ingenold, widow of Roger nephew of Hubert, 5 Stephen, I. 481. c. 2. *t.*

Inglesham,

INDEX.

Inglesham, Mr Robert de, custos of the bishoprick of Worcester, 31 Henry ii. I. 310. c. 1. *x*.

Inglesthorp, Thomas de, has a moiety of the manors of Reynham and Islington, 12 Edward ii. I. 653. c. 1. *w*. Held of the honor of Haghele, ibid.

Ingolisma, Iterius de, has a writ of Liberate, &c. 23 Edward i. II. 323. c. 2. *d*.

Ingrosser of the great roll, II. 269. Richard de Staunford and Robert de Walmesford writers of the great roll, 3 Edward i. ibid. Stipends of Ingrosser and Remembrancer of the Exchequer increased, 19 Edward ii. II. 270, 271.

Inheritance of the prior of Bath, I. 109, 110. Offices and serjeanties of Inheritance, I. 299. Hereditary or fee simple, I. 683. The county of Hereford granted to Robert earl of Leicester by king Stephen as inheritance, II. 138. c. 2. *e*.

Ink for the Exchequer, during a whole year, cost three shillings, 9 Henry iii. II. 311.

Innerpeffry the Scot, Malcolm de, committed to the Tower, 35 Edward i. II. 109. c. 1. *s*.

Instaurum de Wicha, de Mapelescamp, &c. II. 152. c. 1. *u, w*. Which was stock on the king's manors, ibid.

Insula. See Lisle.

Interdict, the citizens of London tallaged in two thousand marks for the release of one, 6 Henry iii. I. 388. c. 2. *f*. or rather, 16 John, I. 711. Wilton pays for taking off the interdict, 11 Henry iii. II. 259. c. 2. *l*.

Intestates, their chattels forfeited to the king, I. 245, &c.

Invention of the holy cross on the vigil of the Ascension, I. 74. c. 1. *s*.

Investire, to bring into possession, I. 4. c. 2.

Joan, daughter of Henry ii. married to William king of Sicily, an. 1176. I. 18. c. 2. *h*.

Jocalia, jewels or plate, I. 270.

Jocee the goldsmith, keeper of the dye for coinage at St Edmunds, 5 Edward i. II. 90.

Johel, archdeacon of Salesbury, an. 1121. I. 110. Alan son of Johel held pleas, temp. Stephen, I. 147. c. 2. *g*.

John earl of Moreton, his contests with the bishop of Ely, I. 22. Not to entertain any outlaws or enemies of the king, I. 22. Judgment demanded against him by the king, I. 23. When that king raises two marks and a half out of every knight's fee, I. 24. c. 2. *a*. Voted to be disseised of his lands in England by a council, I. 36. His tenure when earl of Moreton, I. 57. c. 1. *r*. Had a queen Isabel, I. 175. c. 2. *p*. When that king sat in his Exchequer in person, I. 191. In the year 1210. raises 66,000 marks on the Jews, I. 223. c. 1. *i*. Left a son by the title of Richard de Warenne, 25 Henry iii. I. 233. c. 2. *y*. Kept the office of pincerna in his hand, 14 John, I. 462. c. 2. *o*. His grant to the monks of Christ-Church, Canterbury, out of reverence to Thomas a Becket's shrine, I. 766. c. 1. *o*. His great charter granted in his seventeenth year, I. 788. John the eldest son of prince Edward, 55 Henry iii. II. 93. c. 1. *k*. See Moriton.

Joia, the widow of William the fusor

INDEX.

or melter, 4 Richard i. II. 309. c. 2. *b*. In the wardship of Andrew del Eschequer, ibid.

Joimer, William, chamberlain of London, 7 Henry iii. I. 777. c. 1. *u*. ibid. c. 2. *w*, &c. His annual fine, ibid.

Joldevin son of Savaric, 6 Henry ii. I. 501. c. 1. *q*. His fine for a convention in Sussex, ibid.

Jordan, dapifer of the earl of Glocester, 23 Henry ii. I. 211. c. 1. *i*. William son of Jordan slain by John Hose, 4 John, I. 493. c. 2. *k*. Jordan dapifer of the earl of Glocester amerced, 31 Henry ii. I. 552. c. 2. *p*. Jordan, dean of Sarum, 33 Henry ii. I. 634. c. 2.

Josceline archdeacon of Chichester accompts for the profits of the manors of the see of Exeter, 31 Henry ii. I. 310. c. 2. *a*. Bishop of Bath and sherif of Somersetshire, 9 Henry iii. I. 329. c. 2. *y*. Archdeacon Josceline justicier, who settled the tallage in Yorkshire, 33 Henry ii. I. 635. c. 2. And Lincolnshire, I. 713. c. 1. *d*.

Joseberd, William, one of the king's taxors, 22 Edward i. II. 119. c. 2. *s*.

Josep, frere, was treasurer, 1 Edward i. II. 207. c. 2. *g*. Mentioned as quondam prior of St John of Jerusalem and treasurer, viz. 8 Edward i. II. 307. c. 1. *w*. See Chauncy, Kauncy. Receives the key of the treasury from Philip de Eye, 1 Edward i. II. 320. c. 1. *b*. See ibid. c. 2. *e*.

Joy, Robert de, his land of Elveston in Warwicksh. seized into the king's hands for the forest, 22 Henry ii. I. 300. c. 1. *q*.

Ippegrave, Thomas de, assessed the tallage upon the Jews, 49 Henry iii. I. 234. c. 1. *c*.

Ipswich, has its ferm, and a confirmation of liberties, 6 Richard i. I. 399. c. 2. *i*. The aid of Gepeswic, 5 Stephen, I. 601. c. 2. *s*. See Gepeswic.

Ireland, its chancellorship in the same person with that of England, I. 66. Some account of the honor of Limerick there, 2 John, I. 486. c. 1. *l*. Irish cloth, temp. Henry iii. I. 550, 551. c. 1. *d*. Scutage for Ireland, 18 Henry ii. I. 577, 578. 580. Its scutage accompted for by the city of London, 26 Henry ii. I. 605. c. 1, 2. Escuage of Ireland, 18 Henry ii. I. 629. and 12 John, I. 658. c. 1. *k*. Its accompts to be rendered yearly at the Exchequer of England, 21 Edward i. II. 135. Account of several of the treasurers of Ireland, ibid. The king had a nuncius or agent in Ireland, 49 Henry iii. II. 218.

Iron hot, Robert son of Brien gave twenty pounds to be quit of the judgment of it, 24 Henry ii. I. 211. c. 2. *l*. Instances of judgment by it, temp. Richard i. I. 484. c. 1. *r*, *s*. Iron to be heated every ordeal, 21 Henry ii. I. 546.

Irton, Stephen de, whose plegius, 40 Henry iii. II. 150. c. 2. *q*.

Isabel, king John's queen, I. 175. c. 2. *p*. Isabel daughter of king John, or sister of Henry iii. I. 593. c. 1. *d*. An aid of two marks on each knight's fee for marrying her to the emperor, ibid.

Isabel, William son of, sherif of London, 11 Henry ii. I. 284. c. 1. *r*. Again, I. 363. c. 1. *d*. Again, 16 Henry ii. I. 746. c. 2. *f*.

Isabel, queen consort of king Edward ii.

INDEX.

ii. her grant, &c. I. 683. c. 1. *u*. Supports one who spoke irreverently of the king, II. 84. c. 1. *p*.

Isabel countess of St Paul before 4 Henry iii. I. 319. c. 2. *f*. Her demise in favour of Guy de Chastellion, ibid.

Isabel, viscountess dowager of John de Hastynges, has the manor of Brampton in Notinghamshire, 9 Edward ii. I. 755. c. 1. *q*.

Isabella, wife of Reginald de Mohun, and one of the heiresses of W. earl Mareschal, 41 Henry iii. I. 48. c. 1. *a*.

Isabella de fortibus, countess of James earl of Albemarle, 52 Henry iii. II. 15. c. 1. *t, u*. Had in her hands the lands of Margaret countess of Devonshire, ibid. c. 1. *u*. Seems to have the chamberlainship of England in fee, 49 Henry iii. II. 296. c. 1. *a*. Whether joint chamberlain with William Malduit earl of Warwick, 52 Henry iii. II. 296. c. 2. *b*. and 1 Edward i. II. 297. c. 1. *g*. c. 2. *k*.

Isabella sister and heir of Baldewyn de Lisle earl of Devon, 13 Edward i. II. 165. c. 1. *k*. Seems to be ancestor of Hugh son of Hugh de Courteney earl of Devon, 26 Edward i. II. 165. c. 2. *n*.

Iselham, Jordan de, holds of the bishop of Chichester, temp. Henry ii. I. 576. c. 2.

Islington manor, I. 653. c. 1. *w*.

Issues and amerciaments, II. 234.

Istlepe, Walter de, treasurer of Ireland, 15 Edward ii. II. 136. To whom Istlep in Oxfordshire belonged, 38 Henry iii. II. 265. c. 1. *k*.

Iters of the justices when they began, I. 123. Before the 16 Henry ii. I. 146. The king judged in itinere, I. 150.

Judicature of the king's court, I. 81. But one supreme ordinary court of justice near the Conquest, ibid. Of the ancient state and original of that Judicature, I. 84. 92. The Judicature where the king resided in person, I. 150. A complaint against the judges for acting contra legem terræ, 53 Henry iii. I. 253. c. 2. *a*. Judges delegates, 9 Richard i. I. 485. c. 1. *c*. False judgments amerced, I. 550.

Ivelchester in Somersetshire, its donum, 5 Henry ii. I. 697. c. 2. *d*.

Ives, S. a market obtained for it by the abbat of Ramsey, 4 John, I. 404. c. 2. *h*. Thomas son of Ivo, 2 Henry iii. I. 491. c. 2. *h*. A loquela about continuing the fair of S. Ives eight days beyond their charter, 3 Henry iii. II. 116. c. 1. *q*.

Juises of robbers, by whom the poles of them found, I. 373. Priests paid for blessing them, 12 Henry ii. I. 373. c. 1. *z*. See I. 547. c. 1. *a, b, c*. Ten shillings paid to two priests for hallowing the pits [fossas] for the Juises, 12 Henry ii. II. 205.

Jukel, John, justice errant, 20 Henry ii. I. 125. Jukel de Alverton seems to be sherif of Yorkshire, 21 Henry ii. I. 546. c. 1. *o*. Roger son of Jukel of Alverton, his payment in the bishoprick, 8 Richard i. I. 714. c. 2.

Jury of twenty knights in the case of Robert de Mandevil and Henry de Tilli, 10 John, I. 489. c. 2. *q*. Juries ought not to consist of rustics, 31 Henry ii. I. 540. c. 2. *s, t*. Amerciaments for speaking with juries, 8 Richard i. I. 565. c. 1. *m*.

Justicia for Justicier, I. 205. c. 1. and passim.

Justices itinerant, eighteen appointed,

an.

INDEX.

an.' 1176. 22 Henry ii. I. 18. c. 1. *g*. Chief Juſtice of England ſtyled viceroy, I. 31. 37. See 191. The office and power of the Juſticier, I. 31. Three hundred pounds annually aſſigned to Hubert as Juſticier, I. 37. The power of the high Juſticier derived on the chancellor, I. 62. Juſticiers precedency, I. 67. c. 1. *x*. The Juſticier's power devolved on the treaſurer, I. 78. When Juſticiers were appointed for each diviſion, I. 93. An enumeration of them, 28 Henry ii. I. 112. An enumeration of them, 9 Richard i. I. 113. Courts of the Juſtices itinerant, I. 122, 123, 124, 125. A long deduction of them, I. 31, 32, 33, 34, 35, 26 Henry ii. I. 137. 140. Juſtitia and Juſticiarius titles given to the king's commiſſioners, I. 141. Juſticier of the Exchequer, I. 200. Juſticiers of the Jews, I. 225. c. 1. *u*. Had a ſalary of forty marks a year, 18 Edward i. I. 237. c. 1. *l*. Juſticiary of the ports, 7 John, I. 461. c. 2. *d*. Juſtices of the thirteenth, 9 John, I. 449. c. 1. *q*. Briſtou fined for not coming to meet the Juſtices, 5 Richard i. I. 503. c. 2. *s*. Juſticiers itinerant uſually aſſeſſed the king's aid, I. 585. Expences of a Juſticier's travelling from London to Durham and back again, 13 Henry iii. I. 718. c. 1. *m*. No ſherif was to be Juſticier in his own county, temp. Richard i. II. 146. c. 1. *a*. Peter de Malolacu juſtice de la Pes, 35 Edward i. II. 203. c. 2. *e*.

Juveigni, Robert de, owes an hundred Biſantia to the king, 3 John, I. 106. c. 2. *y*.

Juvenal, John, keeper of the London mint, 33 Henry iii. II. 89. c. 1. *k*.

K.

Kadeney, Mr Robert de, his purchaſe, 28 Henry iii. II. 87. c. 1. *x*.

Kaerdif, Jordan de, 3 Henry iii. I. 492. c. 1. *o*. William de Kerdiff, 35 Henry iii. II. 17. c. 2. *i*. William ſon and heir of Paulin de Kerdiff has the manor Queenhul, 15 Edward ii. II. 102. c. 2. *b*.

Kaermerdin has a confirmation of liberties, 3 John, I. 403.

Kailli, Ralf de, 5 John, I. 121. c. 2. *k*. Not to be impleaded, ibid.

Kainſal, Yorkſhire, its tallage, 30 Henry iii. I. 710. c. 1. *w*.

Kake, William, 33 Henry iii. II. 284. c. 2. *z*.

Kalne in Wiltſhire tallaged, 20 Henry iii. I. 707. c. 1. *k*. See Calne.

Kameis, Cameis or Camoys, Ralf de, I. 594. c. 2. *k*. Has the half fee of Roger Torpel, ibid.

Kancia, Hugh de, amerced, being conquered in duel, 5 Henry iii. I. 550. c. 2. *y*.

Kari, that barony in Ralf Luvel, about 6 Richard i. I. 592. c. 1. *x*.

Karlton, William de, amerced, 5 Henry iii. I. 152. c. 1. *b*. Karleton in Notinghamſhire, I. 572. c. 2. *i*. Hugh de Karleton, 31 Henry ii. I. 493. c. 1. *d*. In Yorkſhire, its tallage, 30 Henry iii. I. 710. c. 1. *w*. See Carleton.

Karum, John de, I. 564. c. 1. *t*. Amerced for a ſtultiloquium, Bucks, ibid.

Kavenediſſe, William de, his eſcape, 6 Henry iii. I. 555. c. 2. *e*.

Kauncy, frere Joſep de, king's treaſurer, 4 Edward i. II. 269. c. 2. *f*. See Chauncy, Joſep.

Kaunvile in Oxfordſhire, the barony of

INDEX.

of Gerard de, I. 319. c. 1. c. Descended to the Longefpeys, 40 Henry iii. ibid. Richard de Kanvile, 2 Henry iii. I. 491. c. 2. i. His large fine for his father's lands in Berkshire, ibid. See Canvil.

Kauz, Maud de, her lands before 8 Henry iii. I. 264. c. 1. s. See Cauz.

Kaxton, Jeremy de, cuftos of the profits of the fee of Canterbury, 32 Henry iii. I. 595. c. 2. p.

Kaylan, Peter de, 33 Henry iii. I. 386. c. 2. u. His large debt from the king, ibid.

Kechel, John, of Brampton, 32 Henry iii. I. 446. c. 1. i. Fines for a plaint, ibid.

Kedeminiftre manor belong'd to Henry Bifet, 11 John, I. 410. c. 1. h.

Keeper of the wardrobe had frequently the cuftody of the king's feal, I. 70, &c. Keepers of the king's works at the tower of London, II. 124.

Keilmers, Philip de, 49 Henry iii. II. 259. c. 2. m. His tally for a trefpafs when William de Lifle was fherif of Northamptonshire, ibid.

Keinefham abbat, 9 Edward ii. I. 600. c. 1.

Kelfrimefhereng in Lancashire, I. 397. c. 1. g. How far the land of Robert de Stokeport, 3 John, ibid.

Kelk, Walter de, his cafe, 25 Edward i. II. 32. Impleaded, 2 Edward ii. II. 83.

Kellinthorp, Baldwin de, flain by Roger de Frivil, 20 Henry iii. I. 496. c. 2. p.

Kempe, Swetman, 16 Henry ii. I. 552. c. 2. m. Amerc'd for quitting the court without leave, ibid.

Ken, John de, his fummonce, 6 Henry iii. I. 454. c. 2. h. and 14 Henry iii. I. 661. c. 2. k.

Kendale, the terra de, granted by Richard i. to Gilbert Fitz Remfrid, I. 401. c. 1. a. Hugh de Kendale clerk in chancery, 14 Edward i. II. 257. c. 2. c.

Kenebalton, the liberty of Humfrey de Bohun, 18 Edward i. II. 248.

Kenerby town, I. 555.

Kenetebiry, Edric and Ernewin de, amerc'd, 5 Richard i. I. 565. c. 1. h.

Kenewrec fon of the king of Wales, 8 Richard i. I. 775. c. 2. q.

Kenilleworda, church of St Mary de, founded by Geoffrey de Clinton treafurer and chamberlain, temp. Henry i. I. 58. c. 1. a. That priory accompted for, 14 John, I. 312. c. 2. w. The fiege of Kenilworth caftle expenfive to the king, I. 356. c. 2. c. Garrifon'd by ten knights, I. 370. c. 1. f. See I. 432. c. 1. u. I. 553. c. 2. e.

Keninton, the king's manor, 9 Edward ii. II. 67. c. 2. r.

Kenle, Mr. John de, who, 19 Edward i. II. 135. c. 1. u.

Kent, Thomas de, executor of John de Cantuaria, 2 Edward ii. II. 235. c. 1. t.

Kenteis, Richard fon of Richard le, 5 John, I 487. c. 2. w. Fines for his lands, ibid.

Kentewel, Mr. William de, 12 Henry iii. I. 239. c. 1. z. Roger de Kenetewel his knights fees in Suffolk, 3 Richard i. I. 636. c. 2. x.

Kenthing, the land of Lifwin de, temp. Henry ii. I. 204. c. 2. k.

Kenulf king of the Saxons, his donation to the monks of Bath, I. 110.

Kerdefton, Roger de, his fenefchal, before 8 John, I. 441. c. 1. u.

Kernet, Henry de, and Sabel his wife, their title in Colmere, I. 431. c. 2. r.

Kertmel

INDEX.

Kertmel priory in Lancashire, I. 412. c. 2. *e*.

Kery in Surrey, I. 651. c. 1. *r*. Scutage of, I. 670. c. 1. *n*. I. 718. c. 1. *e*.

Kessewel priory in Herefordshire, I. 596. c. 1. *s*.

Kestan, Richard de, II. 66. Affeers estreats, 26 Edward i. ibid. See Ketsteven.

Ketel, Alan son of, 11 John, I. 442. c. 2. *g*.

Ketelberge belong'd to Roger de Doai, 12 John, I. 794. c. 2. *k*.

Ketsteven, See Hoiland. The marsh or forest of Ketsteven, Linc. disforested, 14 Henry iii. I. 418. c. 1. *i*. Richard de Ketsteven constable of the Exchequer, 27 Edward i. II. 282. c. 2. *o*. Called Kestan, ibid.

Keu, Ralf le, collector of Len, 26 Edward i. I. 781.

Kevilli, William de, Essex, 4 John, I. 494. c. 1. *l*. Fines for his wife in prison, ibid.

Keyvil, John de, erroneously amerc'd, 9 Edward i. II. 223.

Kileboe, the wines of Osbert de, 5 John, I. 767. c. 1. *p*.

Kilkenni, W. de, seems to have the great seal, 37 Henry iii. I. 69. c. 1. Has the seal of the Exchequer instead of the king's seal, ibid. Has the style of archdeacon of Coventry, I. 69. c. 2. *d*. Is succeeded by H. de Hengham, I. 69. c. 2. *e*. Mr. William was in the wardrobe, 36 Henry iii. II. 129. c. 2. *d*. II. 202. c. 1. *w*.

Killum, Yorkshire, who had interest in it, 7 Henry iii. I. 329. c. 1. *w*. Killum cum eleemosyna, its tallage, 14 Henry iii. I. 708. c. 2. *p*.

Kilpec, Juliana de, has the dower of Rokesley and Ferne, 7 John, I. 488. c. 2. *g*.

Kimbrig, Miles de, 2 Henry iii. I. 793. c. 1. *c*.

King, Edith the widow of Richard, 6 Henry iii. I. 452. c. 2. *n*. John le King wrongfully indicted, convicts the procurers, 34 Edward i. II. 65.

Kingeshanger manor belong'd to Brian de Lisle, I. 492. c. 2. *z*.

Kingesmed in Bedfordshire, I. 85. c. 1. *q*.

King's court, a view of it, I. 2. The business or acts of it, I. 6, &c. The great officers of it, I. 30, &c. The judicature of the King's court, I. 81, &c. The form of doing homage to the King, I. 4. c. 1. *c*. Where the kings us'd to keep their Christmass, Easter and Whitsontide, I. 7. c. 1. *i*, &c. King of Scotland's concord with his lord the King of England, an. 1170. I. 17. King Henry ii. was made umpire between the Kings of Castile and Navarre, I. 18. What grants could pass the seal in the minority of king Henry iii. I. 67. c. 1. *x*. And what in his 37 year during his absence, I. 69. King Henry iii. manu sua propria plicavit breve, I. 76. c. 1. *u*. Fountain of justice, and life of the law, I. 84. c. 1. *m*. No novel usage for Kings to sit personally in judicature, I. 88. How Kings administred justice to their subjects, I. 90. King of England said to hold his crown of God Almighty, I. 107. Grants privileges that particular persons should not be impleaded but before him or his chief justicier, I. 116, &c. The ordinary judicature where the King resided in person, I. 150.

The

INDEX.

The King's iter, ibid. On what title the King seized the temporalities of vacant bishopricks and abbeys, I. 302. Kings of England paramount advowees or patrons of the holy church, I. 304. The King had annum and vastum of the estates of persons executed, 42 Henry iii. I. 315. c. 1. *n.* Had the disposal of widows in marriage, 32 Henry ii. I. 323. c. 1. *w.* What the Kings casual revenue consisted in, I. 342. The piety of our ancient Kings in tithes and alms, I. 348, 349. King of the Isles, 4 Henry ii. I. 365. c. 1. *s.* King's expence in making knights, I. 372. c. 1. *o, p, q.* King de Man, 7 John, I. 390. c. 2. *r.* Instances how the Kings were imposed on, I. 394, &c. Harbouring offenders or assisting the King's enemies fined, I. 405. c. 1, 2. The names of the several payments made to the King, I. 569. The King styled charissimus by his barons, temp. Henry ii. I. 577, 578. King's aid assessed by the justices itinerant, I. 585. Aid for marrying the daughter of King Henry ii. I. 572, &c. For the ransom of King Richard i. I. 590. For the marriage of the sister and daughter of King Henry iii. I. 593. When the King requir'd personal services most strictly, I. 652. King Henry ii. and his queen seem each of them to have had a brother William, I. 687. c. 2. *k.* I. 695. c. 1. *u.* King had the wardships of his wards, 33 Henry ii. I. 713. c. 1. *d.* Acted in person in his Exchequer, II. 10. All the King's servants had privilege of being sued in the Exchequer, II. 18. Our Kings reserv'd the supreme direction of the Exchequer, II. 126. King's debt to be paid preferably to any other creditors, II. 183. King grants to William de Cantelupe that he might make a will, &c. 39 Henry iii. II. 185. c. 1. *l.* Could not distrein dower for debts of the deceased, II. 191. Makes void the atterminations of the barons, 5 Edward ii. II. 213. c. 1. *k.* Respites an amerciament in parliament, 22 Edward i. II. 216. c. 1. *d.* Might betake himself to one indebted to his debter, II. 189.

Kingston upon Hull petitions to be a free burgh, and to have a fair for thirty days, 26 Edward i. I. 422. Their charter of privileges, I. 423.

Kingston, Surrey, the accompt for their ferm, 5, 6, 7 Henry iii. I. 333. c. 2. *r.* Fine for the ferm of their town, 10 John, I. 409. c. 1. *x.* Its aid, 14 Henry ii. I. 587. c. 1. *y.* Has Hamma as member of Chingeston, ibid. Kingeston in Berkshire which was the villata of Ralf Basset, 9 Richard i. I. 705. c. 1. *t.* Tallaged with others by Henry de Kingeston justicier, ibid. Chingeston, Sumersetshire, tallaged, 19 Henry ii. I. 713. c. 1. *b.* The ferm of the earl of Leicester, ibid. Carucage for Kingston hundred, Surrey, I. 730. c. 1. *x.* Its tallage, 10 Richard i. I. 733. c. 2. *s.* Seiz'd by the king, 11 Henry iii. II. 246. c. 2. *d. i.*

Kinton, Wiltshire, its tallage, 33 Henry ii. I. 634. c. 2. Geoffrey de la Hose held of the honor of Kinton, I. 650. c. 1. *l.*

Kiohher, the king of Scots man in Tindale, amerc'd, 15 Henry ii. I. 553. c. 2. *c, d.*

Kiriol,

INDEX.

Kiriol, Nicolas, question'd about falsifying a tally, 25 Edward i. II. 258.

Kirkebi, to whom it in part belong'd, 24 Henry ii. I. 103. c. 2. k. William de Kirkeby brother and heir of John de Kirkeby bishop of Ely, 18 Edward i. II. 186. c. 2. r.

Kirkeby, John de, has the dispatch of business in the Chancery during the absence of the chancellor, 6 Edward i. I. 71. c. 2. l. And again, I. 71. c. 2. m. Treasurer of the tower of London about 13 Edward i. I. 270. c. 1. b. Treasurer of the Exchequer, 14 Edward i. I. 357. c. 2. f. John de Kirkeby of York receiver of the vintism in the close of Henry iii. I. 610. c. 2. John de Kyrkeby dies bishop of Ely, 14 Edward i. I. 618. c. 1. k. John de Kirkeby remembrancer of the Exchequer, 35 Edward i. I. 657. c. 1. h. Adam de, holds land in cornage, 3 John, I. 658. c. 2. o. John de, 14 Henry iii. I. 708. c. 2. p. The manor of Nicolas de Stutevil, 5 Henry iii. II. 198. c. 2. w.

Kirkested, abbat of, 10 John, I. 107. c. 2. c. Kierkestal in Yorkshire the abbat fined, 10 John, I. 152. c. 1. z. Claims the grange of Mickelweit, 10 Richard i. I. 428. c. 1. y.

Kirkethet, a custom or payment to the crown, I. 764. c. 1. d. Arising from hens, ibid.

Kirketon, Hugh de, amerc'd for absenting himself from duel, 12 Henry ii. I. 550. c. 2. b. Prior of Kirketon in Lincolnshire his hyde-lands, 5 John, I. 605. c. 2. t. Beatrice widow of Adam de Kirketon, her lands in Little Askeby, 9 Edward ii. I. 646. c. 1. x. Held of Simon son of Robert de Dryby, and not of the king, ibid. Alexander de Kirketon sherif and escheator of Yorkshire, 9 Edward i. II. 175. c. 2. w. Alexander de Kirketon, 7 Edward i. II. 219.

Kirkham, Walter de, has the grant of the manor of Newport, 14 Henry iii. I. 418. c. 2. l. Occurs, 9 Henry iii. I. 509. c. 1. s. As belonging to the wardrobe, ibid.

Kivelefwurd, Roger de, 10 John, I. 151. c. 1. w. Plegius for Robert de Luceles, ibid.

Knareburgh manor accompted for by Brian de Lisle, 17 John, I. 389. c. 1. i. Knaresburgh wapentake has a commission of array, 16 Edward ii. II. 112. This castle and honor in the family of the Vaux's, 9 Edward ii. II. 117. c. 2. e.

Knighthood conferr'd by the Conqueror on his son Henry, I. 7. c. 1. i. Every knight's fee pays a hundred shilling relief, 13 Henry iii. I. 319. c. 1. d. Knights fees different in quantity and value, I. 321. Expences of the crown in making knights, I. 372. Knights and theines of the honour of Lancaster, 3 John, I. 404. c. 1. e. Fines for respite of knighthood, I. 509. One hundred shillings paid the crown for the relief of a knight's fee, I. 538. c. 1. Each knight's fee charged with a mark to marry Maud daughter of Henry ii. I. 572. Hutch in the Exchequer for the certificates of the knights fees, 12 Henry ii. I. 576. c. 1. x. Each fee paid twenty shillings for the king's ransom, 6 Richard i. I. 591. c. 2. u. What paid for marrying the king's sister and

INDEX.

and daughter, I. 598. Forty shillings a fee for making the king's eldest son a knight, 38 Henry iii. I. 596. c. 1. *t*, &c. Uncertainty of knights fees among ecclesiasticks, I. 647. Some knights fees remarkably small, I. 649. Knight service sometimes annexed to a serjeanty, I. 650. Forty pound a fee requir'd from those who did not personally attend, 15 Edward ii. I. 665. c. 2. *q*. John le Knyght servant of Gilbert de Clare, 2 Edward ii. I. 728. The allowance to the two knights of the chamberlains of the Exchequer, 9 Henry iii. II. 311.

Knovil, Gilbert de, late sherif of Devon, 2 Edward ii I. 294. Reliev'd from the king's proclamation about the currency and value of coin, ibid. Bagon de Knouvil summon'd to the Scotch war among the barons of Shropshire and Staffordshire, 26 Edward i. I. 655. c. 1. Gilbert de Knouvil sherif of Devon made his profer by one of his clerks, 26 Edward i. II. 156. Bogo de Knovile sherif and escheator of Stafford and Shropshire, 5 Edward i. II. 175. c. 2. *u*. Gilbert de Knovil sherif of Devonshire, being sick, has a privy seal to accompt by another, 26 Edward i. II. 179. Bogo de Knovil late sherif of Shropshire, 18 Edward i. II. 223. c. 1. *h*.

Kokaine, Robert, is pledge for his brother William, 29 Henry iii. I. 496. c. 2. *r*.

Kokefeld, Robert de, sherif of Yorkshire, before 22 Henry iii. II. 195.

Kokerinton, John de, committee of the county of Lancaster, 42 Henry iii. II. 68. c. 1. *u*.

Kokermuth, John de, succeeded by Adam de Lymbergh as remembrancer of the Exchequer, 5 Edward ii. II. 267. c. 2. *x*.

Kukeney, Richard de, knight of Richard Malebiss, concern'd in the slaughter of the Jews at York, before 4 Richard i. I. 483. c. 1. *l*.

Kyghele, sir Henry de, imprison'd in the Tower, 34 Edward i. II. 108.

Kyllum manor in Yorkshire, partly king's demeans, and partly held in frankalmoigne, 27 Henry iii. I. 745. c. 1. *z*. See Killum.

Kyma, Philip de, fines for delaying his plaint, 31 Henry ii. I. 213. c. 2. *t*. Simon son of Philip de Kyme, 5 John, I. 245. c. 1. *x*. Simon de Kyme sherif of Lincolnshire, before 10 Richard i. I. 329. c. 2. *z*. Simon increas'd the old firm of Lincolnshire, before 8 John, I. 461. c. 2. *g*. Simon son of Philip de Kyme fines to wage duel for the terra de Baenburc, 5 Richard i. I. 503. c. 1. *p*. Simon contends about some lands in Merston, whether they belong'd to the honor of Glocestre, 3 John, I. 516. c. 2. *n*. Impleaded by William de Pontearch, 2 John, I. 519. c. 2. *z*. Pleas held before Simon de Kyma, 3 Richard i. I. 544. c. 1. *p*. Philip sherif of Lincolnshire, 14 Henry ii. I. 583. c. 2. *n*. Philip de Kymbe summon'd with the Lincolnshire barons to the war against Scotland, 26 Edward i. I. 654. c. 2. Simon de Kime sherif of Lincolnshire settles the tallage, 8 Richard i. I. 704. Simon and his son Philip de Kime to be attach'd for intrusion in Faierford, 11 John, I. 794. c. 2. *i*.

Kynardele, Hugh de, sherif of Herefordshire, not excus'd from accompting

INDEX.

ing by sickness, 35 Henry iii. II. 289. c. 1. *u.*

Kyneburle, Nicolas de, 53 Henry iii. I. 752. c. 1. *k.* In the manor of Hengham, ibid.

Kyngesclipton, I. 724. c. 2. Kyngesclipston seems to be a palace, 9 Edward ii. I. 750. c. 1. *z.* Called Clipston, I. 751. c. 1. *d.* See II. 57. c. 2. *x.*

Kyngeston, Nicolas de, officiated in the Judaism, 3 Edward i. I. 243. Was viscunt or sherif de Gloucester, 1 Edward ii. I. 380. c. 1. *i, u.* That town tallaged, 6 Edward ii. I. 744. c. 1. *w.* Wapentake of Kyngeston upon Hull under a commission of array, 16 Edward ii. II. 112. c. 2. John de Kyngeston had part of the lands of Osbert Giffard, 35 Edward i. II. 219. c. 1. *h.* In the king's service in Scotland, ibid.

Kyrch, Walter de, 11 Henry iii. I. 63. c. 1. *l.* Attests a charter, ibid.

Kyrkeby, John de, 27 Henry iii. I. 745. c. 1. *z.* Treasurer of the Exchequer by the death of abbat R. de Ware, 6 Jan. 12 Edward i. II. 36. c. 2. *g.* Kyrkeby Malesart, II. 61. *m.* John de, 26 Edward i. II. 99. c. 1. *g.* Late sherif of Northumberland, 27 Edward i. II. 203. c. 1. *d.* Remembrancer of the Exchequer, 19 Edward i. II. 265. Again remembrancer, 27 Edward i. II. 266. c. 1. *n.* Was properly admitted till 21 Edward i. II. 266. c. 2. *s.* Deceas'd, 1 Edward ii. ib. Sent into Gloucestershire to ascertain and hasten the king's debts, 34 Edward i. II. 263. c. 1. *z.*

Kyrkeham, Walter de, tallager of the Jews in Canterbury, 11 Henry iii. I. 223. c. 2. *n.* Keeper of the wardrobe, 20 Henry iii. I. 350. c. 1. *p.* and 19 Henry iii. II. 129. c. 1. *a, b.*

Kyrketon, the fee of the earl of Flanders, 34 Henry ii. I. 165. c. 2. *h.* See Kirketon.

L.

Labbe, Ralf, one of the justicers in Normandy, 2 John, I. 156. c. 2. *i.* Again, 2 John, I. 171. c. 2. *x.*

Laccum, or deficiency of weight upon combustion, I. 283. c. 2. *q.* See I. 288. See Lakum.

Lacell, William de, impleaded in the king's court, 31 Henry ii. I. 97. c. 2. *a.* Roger de Lacellis of Yorkshire under age, 28 Henry ii. I. 104. c. 2. *o.* John and Simon de Lacell of Yorkshire, 5 Richard i. I. 432. c. 1. *w.* Roger de Lacell, Lincolnshire, 5 Stephen, I. 449. c. 2. *d.* Fines not to plead till Robert Marmiun be knighted, ibid. See Lasceles.

Lachebroch, the land of, whose, 28 Henry ii. I. 113. c. 2.

Laci, baron Ilbert de, attests a charter, 1 Stephen, I. 14. c. 2. *s.* Henry de Lacy earl of Lincoln, 30 Edward i. I. 73. c. 1. *r.* Hugh de Lacy's town charged ten marks for harbouring an outlaw, 14 Henry ii. I. 85. Robert de Laci fined forty marks for a tryal in the king's court, 31 Henry ii. I. 97. c. 2. *z.* Because his men had kill'd outlaws, ibid. Henry de Lacy sequitur pro rege, 52 Henry iii. I. 101. c. 1. *d.* Henry de Laci's fees in Yorkshire, 22 Henry ii. I. 427. c. 1. *d.* Robert de Laci, his lands, 31 Henry ii. I. 431. c. 1. *k.* Hugh de Laci's knights fees, 14 Henry

INDEX.

Henry ii. I. 575. c. 1. r. Again, I. 584. c. 1. o. H. de Lacy earl of Lincoln, 18 Edward i. I. 598. c. 2. e. Henry de Laci's scutage of Ireland for his Yorkshire fees, 18 Henry ii. I. 629. c. 1. z. Henry's contention with Guy de Laval, 7 Richard i. I. 643. c. 2. b. H. de Lacy earl of Lincoln sat in the Exchequer, 1 Edward ii. II. 30. c. 1. e. John de Lacy commissioner of array for the wapentak of Barkeston, 16 Edward ii. II. 112. c. 1. Hugh de Laci's lands in Herefordshire, temp. Stephen, II. 138. c. 2. e. Henry de Lacy earl of Lincoln, 26 Edward i. II. 165. c. 2. m.

Lackingehee market belong'd to the monks of Ely, 4 John, I. 437. c. 1. x. Whether to the hurt of St Edmonds, ibid.

La Dale in Cumberland, abbat of, 9 Edward ii. I. 745. c. 1. a.

Lade, John de la, accompts for the assise of woad in the ports of Yorkshire, 15 John, I. 773, 774, c. 1. Richard de la Lade, 22 Henry iii. II. 123. c. 2. c. His accompts to be immediately pass'd, ibid.

Lætare Jerusalem sung on a crusade, I. 222. c. 2. f.

Lafeite, William, alderman of the Bocheiors gild, 26 Henry ii. I. 562. c. 1. z.

Lafte, William de, has a writ of quittance, 2 John, I. 176. c. 2. w.

Lageford, Essex, tallaged, 1 Richard i. I. 703. c. 1. l. Late the land of Ralf Briton, ibid. The aid of Lagætara owing for by Ralf Brito, 15 Henry ii. II. 252. c. 1. s.

Laidet, Wiscardus, 15 John, I. 277. c. 2. c. Of Northamptonshire pays queen's gold, 15 John, I. 351. c. 1. a. Wiscard Leidet occurs, 9 Richard, i. II. 198. c. 1. r. Plegius of Ralf de Cornhull, ibid.

Lakum and Laccat, when the king's money was wanting in weight, &c. I. 288. c. 1. f. I. 281. c. 2. p. alibi.

Lamara, Ralf de, fines in Northamptonshire not to plead against his grand-children, 5 Stephen, I. 449. c. 1. w. Henry de Lamare fined for his father's office, viz. Veltraria, 5 Stephen, I. 456. See Mara.

Lambert, William, bailif of Ailesbury, 39 Henry iii. II. 19. c. 2. u. Thomas Lambert sherif of London, 6 Henry iii. II. 94. c. 2. p.

Lambrokes, John de, held in capite of Eustace de Durvile, before 6 Edward i. I. 622. Roger son and heir of John de Lambrok, I. 623. c. 1. h.

Lamburne, James de, of Essex, who, 2 Edward ii. II. 24.

Lamheda or Lambeth, Osbert presbyter of, amerc'd for a false judgment, 2 Richard i. I. 556. c. 1. k. And the whole Hallimot amerc'd, I. 556. c. 1. l.

Lamvallei, William de, his pleas in Dorsetshire, 21 Henry ii. I. 125. c. 1. i. Again one of the justices, I. 126, &c. passim. See Lanvalai and Launvalei.

Lancaster, prior of, 2 John, I. 118. c. 1. p. Ferm of the honor of Lancaster, 23 Henry ii. I. 131. c. 1. w. Its lands belong'd to earl John, 1 Richard i. I. 205. c. 2. l. Roger de Lancaster sherif of Lancaster, 51 Henry iii. I. 268. The honor, 1 John, I. 401. c. 1. a. I. 402. c. 2. o. Has a confirmation of liberties, I. 402. The county pays an hundred marks to have Richard

INDEX,

Richard Vernun their sherif, 8 John, I. 461. c. 1. *f.* Thomas earl of Lancaster amerc'd for a false plaint, 8 Edward ii. I. 529. c. 2. *q.* Socage lands of the honor of Lancaster, I. 593. c. 1. *a.* William de Lancastre, to accompt for that honor, 31 Henry iii. I. 609. c. 2. *e.* John de Lancastre, 26 Edward i. I. 654. c. 1. *a.* Earl of Lancaster in court, 26 Edward i. I. 655. c. 2. Its tallage, 11 Henry iii. I. 707. c. 1. *b.* Agnes widow of William de Lancaster, 31 Henry iii. II. 100. c. 1. *i.* Edmund earl of Lancaster brother of king Edward i. left a son Thomas, 28 Edward i. II. 175. c. 1. *t.* William de Lancastre, 28 Henry iii. II. 177. Some accompt of the honor, 16 Henry ii. II. 253. c. 1. *z.* Thomas late earl of Lancaster, king's enemy and rebel, 16 Edward ii. II. 293. His goods, chatels, lands, and tenements forfeited, ibid.

Lancaveton market in Cornwal changed from Sunday to Thursday, 7 John, I. 407. c. 2. *f.* Lanzaventon its aid, 23 Henry ii. I. 604. c. 2. *m.* Its tallage, 1 John, I. 733. c. 2. *t.*

Lancelevee, John, wrongfully impleaded in court Christian for a layfee, 1 Richard i. I. 561. c. 2. *w.*

Lancell, Richard de, of Cornwal, his concord, 4 John, I. 453. c. 2. *u.* and convey'd by delivering a bough of a tree, I. 621. Held by serjeanty and knight-service too, 34 Henry iii. I. 650. c. 2. *o.* I. 651. c. 1. *p, q.*

Lanettee, Thomas official of, amerc'd for hunting in the forest, 10 John, I. 566. c. 2. *z.*

Lanfranc crowns William Rufus, I. 8. c. 1. *m.* His contest with Odo bishop of Bayeux the Conqueror's brother, at Pinnenden, I. 32. Lanfranc's measure, I. 204. c. 1. *k.*

Langale abbat, collector of the disme impos'd by the pope, II. 292. c. 1. *i.*

Langebeniton manor, I. 721. c. 1. *x.*

Langeberg wapentak in Yorkshire held by Peter de Brus, 9 John, and 31 Henry iii. I. 336. c. 1. *e.* I. 336 c. 2. *f, g.* A contest about the advowson of Langeberg church in Dorsetshire, I. 435. c. 1. *n.* That wapentake under a commission of array, 16 Edward ii. II. 112. c. 2.

Langeberg, Glouc. amerc'd for not making hue and cry for a priest murder'd in their church, 5 Richard i. I. 556. c. 1. *p.*

Langecestre, Ysold de, temp. Richard i. I. 714. c. 1. *g.* Her allotment out of the bishopric, ibid.

Langedone, James de, one of the four tellers, 52 Henry iii. II. 307. c. 1. *uu.*

Langeford manor in Glocestershire belong'd to William earl Mareschal, 16 John, I. 481. c. 1. *r.*

Langeham in Rutlandshire, how tallaged, I. 724.

Langetint, William de, of Yorkshire, his fine, 21 Henry ii. I. 450. c. 2. *s.* Maud de Langetot and her son Henry, 2 John, I. 521. c. 1. *k.*

Langetre hundred, I. 543. c. 2. *g.*

Langlegh, John de, sherif of Glocestershire, 26 Edward i. II. 144.

Langrin, William de, 4 John, II. 214. c. 1. *q.* Hugh de Malo Alneto had protection against him, ibid.

Langton, Walter de, treasurer. See Coventry. Walter de Langeton keeper of the wardrobe, 22 Edward i. I. 386. Treasurer of the Exchequer,

INDEX.

chequer, 23 Edward i. II. 37. c. 2. *k.* 25 Edward i. II. 44. c. 2. *q.*

Langton, John de, chancellor of England, 26 Edward i. I. 72. c. 1. *n.* Bishop of Chichester and chancellor, 1 Edward ii. I. 75. c. 1. *t.* Manor of Langton a member of the manor of Scrivelby, I. 651. Chancellor, 26 Edward i. II. 29. John Langeton chancellor, 27 Edward i. II. 255. c. 2. *t.*

Languages derived from the Roman, Pref. xvii.

Lanthony, priory of St Mary of, I. 479. c. 1. *a.* The prior amerced because he had not his manupast, 6 Henry iii. I. 555. c. 2. *f.* Has ten knights fees in Glocestershire, 29 Henry iii. I. 595. c. 2. *q.* And two knights fees in Herefordshire, I. 596. c. 1. *s.*

Lanvalai, William de, justice errant, 22 Henry ii. I. 127. c. 1. *l.* I. 128, 129, 130, &c. John de Lanvalei of Lincolnshire, 4 John, I. 438. c. 1. *a.* See Launvaley.

Lapley amerced, I. 557. c. 1. *c.*

Lardener, Simon le, married Joan one of the heiresses of Robert Hardel, before 14 Edward i. II. 209. c. 1. *p.*

Lardinary of the king, I. 321. c. 2. *r.* David Lardinarius, 3 Henry iii. II. 27. c. 1. *b.*

Lareste, cloth of, I. 371. c. 1. *m.*

Lasceles, Robert de, his terra in Lincolnshire, 3 Henry iii. I. 300. c. 2. *w.* William de Lascell of Yorkshire, prisoner for queen's gold which he had not received, 39 Henry iii. I. 352. c. 2. *l.* Gilbert de Lasci of Northumberland, 5 John, I. 438. c. 2. *d.* Walter de Lascy, 7 John, I. 474. c. 1. *z.* Gilbert de Lasci fines to be the king's dominicus clericus, 10 John, I. 477. c. 1. *g.* Duncan de Lasceles disseised of three fees and a half for not being in the king's army, 12 John, I. 663. c. 2. *w.* Walter de Lascy, 1 Henry iii. II. 149. Gilbert de Lasci, 9 Richard i. II. 198. c. 1. *r.*

Laffebergh, William de, sherif of Gloucester, his pledges, 39 Henry iii. II. 150. c. 2. *o.*

Later de la Westwode, Richard le, father and son, in the liberty of S. Alban, 39 Henry iii. II. 14. c. 1. *p.*

Latimer, John le, constabulary of Castle Corf, 15 Edward ii. I. 383. c. 1. 35 Edward i. II. 87. William le Latimer, 21 Henry ii. I. 546. c. 2. *q.* William junior, 26 Edward i. I. 654. c. 2. *a.* Thomas, I. 655. c. 1.

Laton, Walter de, of Buckinghamshire, manucaptor of Robert de Ludham, 14 Edward i. I. 254. c. 1. *c.* Joan widow of Robert de Lathun, 52 Henry iii. II. 186. c. 1. *p.*

Laval, Guy de, his contest, 7 Richard i. I. 643. c. 2. *b.*

Laudomar's fee under the honor of Glocester, 15 John, I. 639. c. 1. *o.*

Lavendene, Bucks, abbat of, II. 77. c. 2. *m.*

Laventon manor the bishop of Sarum's, 33 Henry ii. I. 634. c. 2.

Laverokefeld hundred amerced, 34 Henry iii. I. 567. c. 2. *i.*

Lavington, Wiltshire, its donum, 33 Henry ii. I. 634. c. 2.

Launvaley, Hawisia de, her barony, I. 320. c. 2. *o.* Mother of John de Burgo, ibid. Her summonce of William de Hasting, 6 Henry iii. I. 454. c. 2. *m, n.*

Laurence archdeacon of Bedford and custos of the fee of York, 31 Henry ii. I. 309. c. 1. *r.* and 33 Henry ii. I. 635. c. 1. *r.* Again, 1 Richard i. I. 311.

INDEX.

I. 311. c. 2. *b*. Laurence the prieſt fined twenty marks for gelding a man in Surrey, 11 Henry ii. I. 502. c. 1. *w*. Laurence uſher of the Exchequer, 3 Richard i. II. 274. c. 1. *a, b,* &c. Sends the ſummonces for collecting the money for the king's ranſom, 5 Richard i. ibid. c. 1. *c*. Laurence ſon of Alienor by heirſhip uſher of the Exchequer, 6 John, II. 275. c. 1. *g*. His widow married to William Druel, 2 Henry iii. ibid. c. 2. *b*.

Laweſhel, Robert de, accompts for W. biſhop of Ely, 8 Richard i. II. 157. c. 2. *w*.

Laws, Burgundian, Pref. xviii. c. 1. *f*. I. 5. c. 2. *d*. Of the Longobards, Pref. xxiii. c. 2. *y*. xxiv. c. 2. *d*. Bractons Engliſh Laws, I. 4. c. 1. *c*. Glanvil's Engliſh Laws, I. 5. c. 2. Longobardick Laws, I. 92. Anglo-ſaxon Laws differ in themſelves and in forms, I. 178. Laws of Normandy, England, Sicily or Naples, and Burgundy have a reſemblance, I. 183, &c. Law terms, II. 2.

Lawyer, how repreſented by Matthew Paris, I. 214. c. 1.

Laxinton, Robert de, juſtice itinerant, 14 Henry iii. II. 253. c. 1. *b*.

Lee, Richard de la, 29 Henry iii. I. 722. c. 1. *z*. John de la Lee, late ſherif of Eſſex and Hertfordſhire, his lands extended, &c. 2 Edward ii. II. 240.

Leaded houſe in Northamptonſhire, 1 John, I. 433. c. 2. *g*.

Leather for the tallies, II. 311.

Lecchesham, Richard de, 5 John, I. 439. c. 1. *h*. Whether attached by atia, ibid.

Lech, William de, viceſherif of Notingham and Derbyſhire, 3 John, I. 369. c. 2. *c*. Richard del, I. 430.

John ſon of William de Lech, 3 Henry iii. I. 500. c. 1. *c*. Peter de Leche archdeacon of Worceſter, juſticier for aſſeſſing the hidage for the king's ranſom, about 6 Richard i. I. 592. Nicolas, parſon of Lech, 8 Richard i. I. 714. c. 2.

Lechin, Henry le, 29 Henry iii. II. 13. c. 2. *k*. Arreſted for a treſpaſs, &c. ibid.

Lectona, Robert and Alwold de, 5 Stephen, I. 147. c. 1. *t*. Men of Lechton, Buckinghamſhire, 4 John, I. 437. c. 2. *z*.

Ledecumbe village, Berkſhire, amerced, 33 Henry ii. I. 546. c. 1. *l*.

Ledenham, Euſtace de, juſticier who ſettled the tallage, 8 Richard i. I. 704. c. 1. *p*.

Ledes, prior de, 10 John, I. 217. c. 2. *n*. Holds in frankalmoign, I. 671. c. 1. *g*. That burgh's tallage, 30 Henry iii. I. 710. c. 2. *w*. Leedes in Kent, II. 102. c. 2. *b*. How far Liedes belonged to Robert de Gant, 9 Richard i. II. 225. c. 1. *t*.

Ledreda, Ralph de, of Surrey, his aid, 14 Henry ii. I. 587. c. 1. *y*.

Leegrave, Peter de la, his caſe, 5 Henry iii. I. 793. c. 1. *e*.

Leelay, William de, his intereſt in the land of Beldun, Yorkſhire, 31 Henry ii. I. 431. c. 1. *l*. William ſon of Hugh de Leelay, I. 512. c. 2. *w*. His marriage, ibid.

Lefwin, Euſtace ſon of, fined for land in Kent, 29 Henry ii. I. 212. c. 1. *o*. Hugh ſon of Lefwin has the village of Corneburc, 7 Richard i. I. 484. c. 2. *y*. Gerard and Hugh ſons of Lefwin amerced for harbouring the chatels of Flemings, 21 Henry ii. I. 560. c. 1. *x*. I. 560. c. 2. *z*. Lefwin Beſant the king's moneyour, 14 Henry ii. I. 589. c. 2. *i*. Lefwin

the

INDEX.

the moneyour allaged in Lincoln, 4 John, I. 737. c. 2. *w.*

Lega, Robert de, married Flandrina defcendent of John Malduit, before 12 John, I. 506. c. 1. *u.* William de Liega's concord with Roger de Mueles, 14 Henry ii. I. 512. c. 1. *p.* Edward Leg fherif of Devonfhire, 31 Henry ii. I. 546. c. 2. *t.* Lega in Devonfhire a lordfhip of earl Richard, 24 Henry ii. I. 605. c. 1. *o.* Gilbert de la Lege of the bifhopric, 8 Richard i. I. 714. c. 2. When in the king's fervice in Normandy, I. 715. c. 1. Roger de la Leye baron of the Exchequer, 1 Edward i. II. 28. Has the feal of the Exchequer, 52 Henry iii. II. 52. c. 2. *y.* Is chancellor and treafurer at one time, 48 Henry iii. II. 55. c. 2. *n.* and II. 55. c. 2. *p.* Robert de la Leye chancellor of the Exchequer, 53 Henry iii. II. 91. Roger de la Leye, chancellor of the Exchequer, 4 Edward i. II. 112. c. 2. *f.* R. de la Leye, 39 Henry iii. II. 243. c. 2. *g.* Roger remembrancer, 35 Henry iii. II. 266. c. 1. *p.* See Le.

Legate, Walo, jufticier, 6 Henry iii. II. 68. c. 1. *t.* Delivers the county of Cumberlaunde to Robert de Viepont, ibid.

Legitimacy of Edward ii. how queftioned, II. 85. c. 1. *r.*

Legreceftria, Roger de, 26 Henry ii. I. 137. c. 1. *n.* Ofbert de, 5 Stephen, I. 227. c. 1. *k.* See Leicefter. Legerceftria famous for coat of mail, 31 Henry ii. and 1 Richard i. I. 563. c. 1. *f.*

Leguine, the toll of that village to maintain the lights of St Victor, Marfeilles, I. 159. c. 2. *z.*

Leibnitz's Codex Diplomaticus, Pref. xx. c. 1. *m.*

Leicefter, Richard de, fines for the king's letters patent of protection, 8 John, I. 119. c. 1. *a.* Controller of the town of Southampton, before 2 John, I. 202. c. 2. *b.* Peter de Leycefter juftice of the Jews, 18 Edward i. I. 237. c. 1. *l.* Baron of the Exchequer, 26 Edward i. I. 354. c. 1. *q.* William de, his plaint againft the abbat of Valdey or de Valle Dei, 18 Henry ii. I. 430. c. 1. *y.* Matt. de Leicefter, 30 Henry ii. I. 452. c. 1. *b.* Ofbert de Leicefter obtains pardon for himfelf and Ofbert his clerk, 5 Stephen, I. 473. c. 1. *k.* Ralf de Leyceftre clerk of the Exchequer, 28 Henry iii. II. 19. c. 2. *w.* The aid of the honor of Leicefter, II. 26. c. 1. *a.* Ralf de Leycefter furrenders the office of chancellor of the Exchequer, 32 Henry iii. II. 52. c. 1. *s.* Peter de Leyceftre baron of the Exchequer, 31 Edward i. II. 62. c. 2. *p.* Ralf de Leyceftre clerk, 42 Henry iii. II. 122. c. 2. *t.* Lands of the earl of Leicefter quit of fherif's aid, 4 John, II. 167. c. 1. *t.* Peter de Leyceftre baron of the Exchequer, 19 Edward i. II. 265. c. 1. *m.* Henry de Leiceftre auditor of the accompts of cuftodes, 16 Edward ii. II. 293. Peter de Leiceftre made clerk of the receipt of the Exchequer, 7 Edward i. II. 300. c. 1. *w.* Baron of the Exchequer, 31 Edward i. II. 304. c. 1. *n.*

Leicefter, Robert earl of, about the year 1165, I. 16. Has a grant of the burgh and caftle of Hereford from king Stephen, II. 138. c. 2. *e.* And of the county, ibid. Robert and Simon earls of Leicefter, temp. John, I. 51. Robert earl of, temp. John, I. 57. c. 1. *r.* Earl of Leicefter

INDEX.

cester accompting sherif for that county, 5 Stephen, I. 207. c. 1. *t.* Robert earl of Leicester, some account of his estate, 5 Richard i. I. 233. c. 1. *w.* See I. 237. c. 2. *o.* The honor of the earl of Leicester in custody of the sherif of Somersetshire, 19 Henry ii. I. 297. c. 2. *l.* Again, 31 Henry ii. I. 297. c. 2. *x.* Petronil countess of Leicester to enjoy the honor of Grentemesnil as her inheritance, 6 John, I. 448. c. 1. *b.* Half the fees of the honor of Leicester exceeded sixty, 30 Henry iii. I. 595. c. 1. *n.* Robert earl of Leicester taken at St Edmonds, about 20 Henry ii. I. 606. c. 1. *w.* Scutage of that earl, 18 Henry ii. I. 630. c. 2. *e.* See I. 644. c. 1. *n.* I. 645. c. 1. *q.* Some accompt of his lands in Sumerset and Wiltshire, 19 Henry ii. I. 713. c. 1. *b, c.* Robert earl of, 5 John, II. 771. c. 1. *e.* The earl justicier, II. 205. See Mallore.

Leissebi, Walter de, 6 John, I. 468. c. 1. *o.* Fermer of the toll and mills of Grimesbi, ibid.

Leissington, terra de. See Calz, Maud. Walter de Leyseton late sherif of Lincoln, II. 184. c. 2. *h.* Leaves frere Gilbert de Leyseton executor, before 42 Henry iii. II. 184. c. 2. *h.*

Lemburec, the passage of Waleran de, 15 John, I. 774. c. 2.

Len, belonged to the bishop of Norwich and earl of Arundel, 5 John, I. 407. c. 1. *e.* Alured and Siward de Len amerced for exporting corn without licence, 24 Henry ii. I. 558. c. 1. *o.* How excepted from the other ports of England, 6 John, I. 772. c. 1. *i.* Its fairs, ibid. Merchandise of several species for many counties to be exported solely at Len, 26 Edward i. I. 782. c. 1. *r.* The solemnity of sending the coket or seals thither, with the trone or scale, I. 783. c. 1. *s.*

Lenfant, Robert, custos of the castle of Shrewsbury, 7 Henry iii. II. 201. c. 1. *o.*

Lenham, Nicolas de, of Kent, 35 Henry iii. II. 222. c. 2. *a.*

Lenna, homines de, their pleas, 16 Henry ii. I. 144. c. 1. *z.* John de Lenna amerced for exporting corn without licence, 23 Henry ii. I. 548. c. 1. *r.* See Len.

Lennton priory to whom indebted for the church of Nutehal, I. 436. c. 1. *s.*

Lenton priory and fair in the king's hands, 27 Edward i. II. 109. c. 2. *l.*

Leofwin, Hugh Fitz, married a daughter of William de Tikehil, before 3 Richard i. I. 105. c. 1. *q.* See Lefwin.

Leopard, the king allows six-pence for his beast, and three half-pence a day for his keeper, 12 Edward ii. I. 381.

Leschecker, Roger de, forfeits the office of usher with the serjeanty by his trespass against the king, 37 Henry iii. II. 272. c. 1. *n.* But yet settles deputies, 40 Henry iii. II. 276. c. 1. *m.* And grants it to Richard de Hedersete for life, 53 Henry iii. II. 276. c. 1. *o.* Laurence's grant to Richard de Mendesham, 1 Edward i. II. 277. c. 1. *r.* The lands of Simon inherited by sisters, 32 Edward i. ibid. Andrew de Leschequer has the wardship of Joia the widow and the heir of William the fusor, 4 Richard i. II. 309. c. 2. *b.*

Lestrange, Guy, sherif and justice errant of Shropshire, 20 Henry ii. I. 124. c. 2. *a.* Again, 23 Henry ii. I. 130. c. 1. *p.* Sherif of Shropshire, and

INDEX.

and had the cuftody of the honor of William Fitz-Alan, 19 Henry ii. I. 297. c. 2. *n*. John Leftrange fummoned to the Scotifh expedition with the barons of Shropfhire and Staffordfhire, 26 Edward i. I. 655. c. 1. John Leftrange has refpite for a debt, 35 Henry iii. II. 124. c. 2. *h*. Roger Leftrange, 26 Edward i. II. 224.

Letvaric of Devonfhire, his aid, 14 Henry ii. I. 588. c. 1. *b*.

Leu, John, keeper of the ordinance for money at Ipfwich, 32 Edward i. I. 294.

Leveland, Nathanael, and Robert de, his fon, hereditary keepers from the Conqueft of the king's houfe at Weftminfter, and of the gail of the bridge of Fliete, 9 Richard i. I. 514. c. 1. *c*.

Leverton, William de, his land, 22 Henry ii. I. 430. c. 1. *b*. Grun de Levertona accompts for the affife of Ofwardifbech, Notinghamfhire, 21 Henry ii. I. 702. c. 2. *g*.

Levefque, Henry, fines for his plaint againft the prior of Ely, I. 448. c. 1. *h*.

Leveftan, Robert fon of, accompts for the weavers gild in London, 5 Stephen, I. 467. c. 2. *g*.

Leukenore, Nicolas de, keeper of the wardrobe, 52 Henry iii. I. 269. c. 1. *w*.

Leutorp, Walter de, his danegeld, 3 Henry ii. I. 690. c. 1. *r*.

Lewellin fon of Griffin, the expedition againft him, 5 Edward i. II. 218. c. 1. *a*.

Lewis amerced for concealing a murder, &c. 22 Henry ii. I. 560. c. 2. *e*. Prior of Lewis his aid from his tenants for difcharging his debts, 18 Henry iii. I. 617. c. 2. *g*. Prior held in frankalmoign, 34 Edward i. I. 671. c. 1. *g*. Thomas de Lewes chaplain of the king's chapel at Weftminfter, 51 Henry iii. II. 19. c. 1. *s*.

Lexdene hundred, I. 543. c. 1. *y*.

Lexinton, J. de, jufticier, amerces Yorkfhire, 30 Henry iii. I. 568. c. 2. *s*.

Leybourne, William de, of Kent, fummoned by writ to the war againft Scotland, 26 Edward i. I. 655. c. 2. Henry de, 35 Edward i. II. 87. c. 2. *z*. Idonea fherif of Weftmoreland, II. 180. William's difcharge, 14 Edward i. II. 223. Roger de Leyburn fherif of Kent, 49 Henry iii. II. 113. c. 1. *g*.

Leyne, Thomas de Furnival, commiffioner of array, 10 Edward ii. II. 112. c. 1.

Leyrton, William, of Lincolnfhire, his arrerages, 1 Edward ii. II. 259. c. 1. *h*.

Leyfton abbat held in frankalmoign, I. 671. c. 1. *g*. Quit of tallage, ibid.

Lezinan, Geoffrey de, has the manor of Hengham, 53 Henry iii. I. 752. c. 1. *k*. See Geoffrey.

Liberatio or livery of the king's fon, I. 204. Liberate Rolls in the Tower, II. 203.

Liberties feized into the king's hand, II. 244. Of holy church to be kept and maintained, II. 102. Seizure of Liberties, II. 237. 244.

Lichesfeld, the dean of, 31 Henry ii. II. 310. c. 2. *y*. See Coventry. Styled the bifhop of Chefter on paying efcuage for the king's ranfom, 6 Richard i. I. 597. c. 1. *q*. paffim.

Licorice, widow of David the Oxford Jew,

INDEX.

Jew, 30 Henry iii. II. 3. c. 2. *k*. To pay 2591 *l*. to the fabric of the church of Weſtminſtre, &c. ibid.

Lid in Yorkſhire, the men of, their tallage, 9 Richard i. I. 699. c. 1. *r*.

Lideford, John de, his fine, 10 John, I. 119. and I. 477. c. 2. *i*. Lidford in Devonſhire, its aid to the marriage of the king's daughter, 14 Henry ii. I. 588. c. 1. *b*. Its aid, 23 Henry ii. I. 603. c. 2. *i*.

Lidegreynz, John de, made juſticier in Eire, 18 Edward i. II. 91. c. 2. *d*.

Lidel, the manor of Nicolas de Stutevil, 5 Henry iii. II. 198. c. 2. *w*.

Lifton in Devonſhire, its aid, 14 Henry ii. I. 588. c. 1. *b*. Again, 23 Henry ii. I. 603. c. 2. *i*. Godfrey de, 32 Henry iii. I. 775. c. 1. *p*. Seems to be ſherif, ibid.

Ligula, a filet or file of the mareſchal of the Exchequer, II. 287.

Lileburn in Northumberland, by whom claimed, 2 John, I. 435. c. 2. *q*.

Lillecherche ſeems to belong to Ralf Brito, 15 Henry ii. II. 252. c. 1. *s*.

Lilleſhul in Yorkſhire, abbat of, 1 John, I. 402. c. 2. *n*.

Limerich, the honor of William de Braioſa with limitations, 2 John, I. 486. c. 1. *l*.

Limeſy, Richard de, mareſchal, tranſported into Ireland, 30 Henry ii. I. 44. c. 2. *b*. Goes in the king's ſervice to Conſtantinople, 31 Henry ii. I. 366. c. 1. *d*. David de Lymeſye has his ſeneſchal, 22 Henry iii. II. 242. c. 2. *y*. viz. Warner de Hamſtaple, who was likewiſe his pledge, ibid.

Limingis, earl de, 8 Richard i. I. 775. c. 1. *q*. The king hires him a ſhip for his paſſage to Andwers, ibid.

Lincoln, Alured de, one of the juſtices, 20 Henry ii. I. 123. Hoſpital of S. Sepulchre there, I. 218. c. 1. *s*. John de Lincoln merchant of Hull to inſpect the money in payments, 22 Edward i. I. 294. c. 1. John earl of Lincoln conſtable of Cheſter fined in 3000 marks to have Maud his daughter married to Richard de Clare, 22 Henry iii. I. 326. c. 2. *n*. Men of Lincoln fine for the ſame liberties as Northampton, 6 Richard i. I. 400. c. 1. *o*. and I. 400. c. 2. *x*. Again, 2 Henry iii. I. 412. c. 1. *b*. and I. 413. c. 1. *b*. Thomas de Lincoln, 7 Henry iii. I. 445. c. 2. *e*. Burgeſſes of, 5 Stephen, I. 501. c. 1. *k*. Citizens of Lincoln fine to have Adam their mayor during the king's pleaſure, and Adam's good behaviour, 12 John, I. 507. c. 2. *i*. The concord of the men of Lincoln with the men of Grimeſbi about toll, 7 Richard i. I. 513. c. 1. *z*. Its aid, 2 Henry ii. I. 602. c. 1. *z*. Earl of Lincoln one of the king's courtiers, 26 Edward i. I. 655. c. 2. The citizens aid, 2 Henry ii. I. 693. c. 1. *p*. The county's donum, 4 Henry ii. I. 696. c. 1. *b*. The aſſiſa of Lincoln, 5 Henry ii. I. 697. c. 2. *z*. Its tallage, 10 Richard i. I. 705. c. 1. *w*. The ſcutage and tallage of the city and ſhire, 33 Henry ii. I. 713. c. 1. *d*. Again, 1 Richard i. I. 737. c. 1. *r*. A chapel of St Thomas the martyr on Lincoln bridge, I. 745. c. 1. *a*. Quinzime for the merchandiſe of this port, 6 John, I. 772. c. 1. *i*. H. earl of Lincoln ſeems baron of the Exchequer, 2 Edward ii. II. 90. Robert de Lincoln ſherif of London, 39 Henry iii. II. 95. c. 1. *r*. William de Lincoln has the commiſſion of array for the wapentake of Hoveden, 16 Edward ii. II. 112. c. 2.

William

INDEX.

William earl of Lincoln attests a charter of king Stephen, II. 138. c. 2. e. John de Lincoln keeper of the king's mints of London and Canterbury, 9 Edward ii. II. 241. c. 1. q. Lincoln in the king's hand, 41 Henry iii. II. 247. c. 1. l. Laurence de Lincoln, clerk of the Exchequer writs, 5 Edward i. II. 294. c. 2. s. Had Adam fellow clerk, ibid. John de Lincoln clerk of the receipt, 53 Henry iii. II. 304. c. 1. m.

Lincoln, tallage for that bishoprick, I. 202. The fee in the king's hands, 16 Henry ii. I. 307. c. 2. z. and I. 308. c. 1. c. Robert archdeacon of, ibid. The fee was in the king's hands eighteen years, I. 308. That fee pays Peterpence, tho' in the king's hands, 31 Henry ii. I. 309. c. 1. w. Had seventy four prebendaries, ibid. Galfrid [de Constantiis] elect of Lincoln, 23 Henry iii. I. 342. c. 1. b. A parliament here, 9 Edward ii. I. 361. c. 2. x. Bishop of Lincoln's liberties for himself and successorss, 15 Henry iii. I. 419. c. 1. o. Its knights fees, 14 Henry ii. I. 584. c. 1. o. Its tallage, 4 John, I. 717. c. 1. h. Claims the chatels of his men who were fugitives or hanged, II. 117. Galfrid elect of Lincoln, and John his brother, 24 Henry ii. II. 206. c. 1. u.

Lindebery castle in Herefordshire, in custody of Geoffrey de Ver, 16 Henry ii. I. 306. c. 2. s.

Lindenbroch of the laws of the Longobards, Pref. xxiii. c. 2. y. xxiv. c. 2. d, e. I. 38. c. 1. p.

Lindesia and its knights within the jurisdiction of Durham, 5 Stephen, I. 694. c. 1. s.

Lindon, Simon de, attaches Maud de Bihamel for felony, 12 John, I. 152. c. 1. a. Repeated, I. 443. c. 1. i. Again, temp. Henry iii. I. 496. c. 2. w. Alan de Lindon's interest in Eston, Northamptonshire, 14 Henry iii. II. 116. c. 2. w.

Lindric, contains the manor of Carleton, 30 Henry iii. I. 707. c. 2. l.

Lindrugge manor, the prior of Worcester's, I. 408. c. 2. w.

Lindsey, William de, his claims in Cumberland, 3 Richard i. I. 116. c. 1. b.

Lingedrapier, Walter le, amerced for not assisting to make the king's money, 29 Henry ii. I. 560. c. 1. r.

Lion, Hugh, alderman of a London gild, 26 Henry ii. I. 562. c. 1. z.

Lions, Peter de, justicier in Normandy, 2 John, I. 170. Again, 3 John, I. 171. c. 2. x.

Lisewis, baron Alexander de, holds of the honor of Dunstor, 3 John, I. 665. c. 2. g.

Lisiardus, clerk of Geoffrey Fitz-Peter, accompts for him, 7 Richard i. II. 132. c. 2. i.

Lisieux, archdeacon of, I. 77. The grant of Robert de Lisieux from king John, I. 121. Ralf de Lisieux justicier in Normandy, 2 John, I. 156. c. 2. i. Some account of the endowment of the church of Lisieux, I. 167. Ralf bishop of, I. 168. c. 2. Ralf justicier, 2 John, I. 171. c. 2. x. The grant to Robert de Lisieux, I. 763.

Lisle or Insula, Walter de, one of the inquisitors against the sherifs of England, 19 Henry ii. I. 141. c. 1. y. Baldwin de Lisle heir of Margaret de Ripariis, 42 Henry iii. I. 241. c. 1. g. Simon de Lisle, 56 Henry iii. I. 253. c. 1. x. Pleas before B. de Lisle, 7 Henry iii. I. 329. c. 1.

INDEX.

c. 1. *w*. Brian de Lisle concerned in the receipt of the crown revenue, 11 John, I. 384. c. 1. *l*. His heirs occur, 28 Henry iii. I. 389. c. 1. *i*. John de Lisle baron of the Exchequer, 26 Edward i. I. 392. c. 1. *z*. B. de Insula holds pleas of the forest with H. de Nevil, 13 Henry iii. I. 417. c. 1. *b*. Robert of the Isle of Wight, 5 Stephen, I. 426. c. 2. *a*. Brian de Lisle, 11 John, I. 470. c. 1. *l*. Geoffry de Lisle fines that the king would remit his indignation, 31 Henry iii. I. 475. c. 2. *s*. Walter and the earl de Lisle, 9 John, I. 478. c. 2. *u*. Brian de Insula his heir's estate, 19 Henry iii. I. 492. c. 2. *z*. Brian's donum on the king's return from Poictou, 12 John, I. 504. c. 2. *d*. The honor of Albreda de Lisle in Setrinton, Yorkshire, its scutage, 33 Henry ii. I. 635. c. 1. *r*. B. de Insula, 13 John, I. 644. c. 1. *o*. William de Lisle collector of the scutage, 34 Edward i. I. 646. c. 1. *x*. John de Lisle one of the Hampshire barons summoned to the war in Scotland, 26 Edward i. I. 655. c. 2. The tallage of alderman Walter Lisle for his ward in London, 14 Henry iii. I. 709. c. 1. *t*. Again, 19 and 20 Henry iii. I. 738. c. 2. *z*. I. 739. c. 1. *a*. Brian de Lisle one of the wardens of the sea ports for the counties of York and Lincoln, 15 John, I. 773, 774. c. 1. Baldwin de Lisle chamberlain of the Exchequer, 42 Henry iii. II. 14. c. 2. *q*. Baldwin de Lisle chamberlain of the Exchequer, 41 Henry iii. II. 22. c. 1. *p*. Brien de Lisle, teste, 16 John, II. 43. c. 1. *m*. John de Lisle baron of the Exchequer, 25 Edward i. II. 44. c. 2. *r*. John de Lisle combaron of the Exchequer, 24 Edward i. II. 56. c. 2. *t*. William de Lisle has the custody of the county and castle of Northampton and of the honor of Peverel there, 40 Henry iii. II. 141. c. 2. *t*. Sherif, 31 Henry iii. II. 158. c. 1. *y*. Isabel sister and heir of Baldwyn de Lisle late earl of Devon, 13 Edward i. II. 164. c. 1. *k*. Simon de Heddon one of Brian de Lisle's executors, 42 Henry iii. II. 191. c. 1. *o*. Brian sherif of Yorkshire, before 22 Henry iii. II. 195. Holds pleas of the forest, 13 Henry iii. II. 253. c. 1. *b*. William late sherif of Northamptonshire, 49 Henry iii. II. 259. c. 2. *m*. John de Lisle and his companions auditors of the accompts of the disme, 35 Edward i. II. 292. c. 1. *i*. John de Lisle occurs, 5 Edward i. II. 294. c. 2. *s*. Baldwin de Lisle in the queen's guardianship, 39 Henry iii. II. 299. c. 2. *t*. John de Lisle baron of the Exchequer, 31 Edward i. II. 304. c. 1. *n*. John de Lisle has letters patent to be assessor in London, 25 Edward i. II. 324. c. 1. *i*.

Lisoriis, William de, fines for his forestery in Northamptonshire, 3 Richard i. I. 458. c. 2. *g*. Fulk de Lisoriis has one knight's fee, 14 Henry ii. I. 574. c. 1. *n*. Warner de Lisoriis sherif of Somersetshire, 7 Henry ii. I. 698. c. 1. *k*.

Lissinton, Lincolnshire, in the archbishoprick of York, 33 Henry ii. I. 713. c. 1. *d*. See Leissinton.

Litham in Yorkshire, its tallage, 30 Henry iii. I. 710. c. 1. *w*.

Litleton, Wiltshire, the land of earl Reginald, its aid, 23 Henry ii. I. 604. c. 1. *l*. I. 634. c. 1. *p*.

Litter for the chamber of the barons, II. 311.

Littleton,

INDEX.

Littleton, sir Thomas, his accompt of escuage, I. 620. c. 1. *a.*

Livet, William de, justicier of Normandy, 2 John, I. 171. c. 2. *x.*

Liulf, Nicolas son of, amerc'd pro stulto dicto suo, 1 Richard i. I. 563. c. 2. *m.* Thomas son of Liulf one of the theins of Northumberland, 2 John, I. 659. c. 2. *y.* Thomas son of Liulf his donum, 1 Richard i. I. 698. c. 2. *o.*

Livremere, Simon de, clerk, 12 John, I. 795. c. 1. *n.*

Livrepol burgesses fine for a free burgh and merchants gild, 13 Henry iii. I. 417. c. 2. *e.* The tallage of Liverpul, 11 Henry iii. I. 707. c. 1. *b.*

Locherons, priory of, I. 77.

Locoveris, archbishop of Roan's scaccarium there, I. 164. c. 2. *d.*

Locum tenens what, II. 48.

Lodbroke, John de, of Warwickshire, pardon'd for not taking knighthood, 1 Edward i. 510. c. 1. *b.*

Lodderden in Yorkshire, the donum of Robert son of Odard de, 9 Richard i. I. 699. c. 1. *r.*

Loges, Robert de, 2 John, I. 177. c. 1. *x.*

Loke, William and J. de la, 41 and 45 Henry iii. I. 775. c. 1. *o, p.* Had the ferm of the avalage of the Thames, ibid.

Lokinton, John de, has attermination for his debts to the king, 25 Edward i. II. 210. c. 1. *w.*

London, Eustace bishop of, 11 Henry iii. I. 63. c. 1. *l.*

Londonia, William de, 11 Henry iii. I. 63. c. 1. *l.* Again, 7 Henry ii. I. 97. c. 1. *s.* Jeremy of London fined an hundred pound for refusing to come out of sanctuary, 26 Henry ii. I. 104. c. 1. *l.* Mayor, sherifs, and barons of London, temp. Henry iii. and Edward i. I. 198. Sherifs of London allowed for the king's huntsmen, 4 Henry ii. I. 207. c. 1. *u.* Henry de Lundon, 16 Henry ii. I. 307. c. 1. *y.* Distrain'd for queen's gold, 39 Henry iii. I. 352. Cambium of London how accompted for, 9 John, I. 283. c. 2. *q.* Four sherifs of London, 19 Henry ii. I. 363. c. 1. *e.* Again, 5 Stephen, I. 364. c. 1. *n.* The citizens tallage for the walling of their city, 6 Henry iii. I. 388. c. 2. *f.* Fine in an hundred marks to choose their sherifs, 5 Stephen, I. 397. c. 1. *h.* Fine for the confirmation of liberties, 1 John, I. 400. c. 2. *y.* Fines for confirmation of liberties, and annulling the weavers gild, 4 John, I. 405. c. 1. *m.* Again, 10 John, I. 409. c. 1. *z.* Their donum, 8 Richard i. I. 473. c. 2. *t.* Fines twenty thousand pounds for the king's good-will, 50 Henry iii. I. 476. c. 1. *u.* William de Londonia fines for being in Notingham castle with earl John, 9 Richard i. I. 485. c. 1. *d.* Robert de Londonia disseiz'd of his land in Bacscete, Surrey, 12 John, I. 491. c. 1. *e.* Roger de Londonia, 24 Henry iii. I. 496. c. 2. *q.* The city's new year's gift, 9 John, I. 504. c. 2. *c.* London fines for a record in the city, I. 508, 509. Burels of London, I. 550, 551. c. 1. *d.* Adulterine gilds in London amerc'd, 26 Henry ii. I. 562. A new donum of the citisens, I. 582. The manner of assessing their aid, 14 Henry ii. I. 585. Moneyours of London, 14 Henry

INDEX.

Henry ii. I. 589. c. 2. *i.* Their payment for the ranfom of Richard i. &c. I. 593. c. 1. *b.* Its aid, 2 Henry ii. I. 602. c. 1. *y.* Accompts for the fcutage of Ireland, 26 Henry ii. I. 605. c. 1. *p.* Aids king John with 1000 *l.* for his paffage beyond fea, 9 John, I. 605. c. 2. *u.* John de Londonia, 6 Edward i. I. 623. c. 1. *h.* The four fherifs accompt for its ferm, 5 Stephen, I. 686. c. 2. *d.* Gervafe and John fherifs of London and Middlefex, 2 Henry ii. I. 686. c. 2. *f.* The crown's gift to wall their city, 11 Henry iii. I. 707. c. 2. *m.* London's tallage, with an account of the aldermen and wards, 14 Henry iii. I. 709. c. 1. *s, t.* Its tallage, 30 Henry iii. I. 709. c. 2. *u.* After long debate allow themfelves talliable, 39 Henry iii. I. 711. Inhabitants chatels not to be tallaged with the citizens, 2 Edward ii. I. 727. c. 2. *n.* Tallage affefs'd upon London by poll and by ward, 19 Henry iii. I. 738. c. 1. *y.* I. 738 c. 2. *z.* Its aid for marriage of the king's daughter, 14 Henry ii. I. 747. c. 1. *g.* John le Luter's grant that he fhall not be made mayor, fherif, efcheator, coroner, provoft, alderman, or any other minifter of London, 9 Edward ii. I. 750. c. 1. *z.* Quinzime for the merchandife of this port, I. 772. c. 1. *i.* The cuftom of fifh brought to Londonbridge-ftreet, 52 Henry iii. I. 779. Some accompt of London markets, ibid. Thomas Fitz-Richard mayor of London, 49 Henry iii. II. 11. c. 1. *b.* John de Wengrave mayor of London judicially proceeded againft, 15 Edward ii. II. 85. How they prefented their mayor and fherifs, II. 92. The fubftance of their oath on that occafion, 55 Henry iii. II. 93. c. 1. *k.* Were to keep their gates fhut by night, and guarded with armed men by day, ibid. Have a grant to chufe two bailifs, 51 Henry ii. II. 96. c. 1. *t.* Plead exemption as to their fherifs fwearing at the Exchequer, II. 97, 98. William de London clerk, 25 Henry ii. II. 118. c. 2. *l.* London and Middlefex ferm'd at three hundred pounds in the time of Maud, II. 138. c. 1. *d.* Cuftos for London when the city was in the king's hand, had twenty-nine pound fix and eight pence allotted, 55 Henry iii. II. 202. c. 2. *a.* Mayor and fherifs of London committed, 38 Henry iii. II. 240. c. 1. *k, l.* And the liberty feiz'd into the king's hand, ibid. Again, 31 Henry iii. II. 246. c. 2. *g.* Again for trefpafs of an affize, 39 Henry iii. II. 248. c. 1. *w.* What it pays for the vintifme to make the king's fon a knight, 35 Edward i. II. 261. c. 1. *r.* Laurence de London clerk of the Exchequer, 56 Henry iii. II. 264. County of London, 5 Edward ii. II. 280. c. 1. *a.* Simon de London attorney of Thomas Corbet, his commitment fees, 38 Henry iii. II. 289. John de London chamberlain of the Exchequer, before 25 Edward i. II. 299. c. 1. *o.*

London, Ralf Baldock bifhop of, chancellor of the Exchequer, 35 Edward i. I. 74. c. 2. Richard fon of Nigel of Ely, bifhop of London and king's treafurer, temp. Henry ii. I. 79. c. 2. *t, u.* Richard bifhop of, jufticier, 6 Richard i. I. 200. c. 1. *k.* Richard bifhop of, commanded by Henry i. to
do

INDEX.

do right to the abbat of Westminster, I. 209. Walter son of the bishop of London his fine, 5 Stephen, I. 426. c. 1. *i*. The dean of London opposes the bishop, 5 Stephen, I. 476. c. 2. *y*. and I. 478. c. 1. *o*. The bishop's donum, 5 Henry ii. I. 626. c. 2. *q*. William archdeacon [of London] ibid. R. bishop fines for not sending to the war against R. Mareschal, 18 Henry iii. I. 661. c. 2. *l*. W. bishop of, his scutage for himself and wards, 1 John, I. 665. c. 1. *d*. The pleas of Richard [Niel] bishop of London, 5 Richard i. II. 20. c. 2. *a*.

Long, Gilbert, amerc'd forty marks for disobeying the justiciers, 21 Henry ii. I. 560. c. 1. *u*.

Longchamp, William de, bishop of Ely, justicier, chancellor and pope's legate while Richard i. was in the Holy Land, I. 22. His contests with John earl of Moreton, ibid. Was chancellor while the king was in Sicily, I. 77. Was chancellor to the day of his death, I. 77. c. 2. *g*. Was remov'd from being justicier by the intrigue of John earl of Moreton, I. 196. Mention'd, I. 441. c. 1. *r*.

Longchamp, dapifer, 1 Richard i. I. 51. c. 2. *c*. Henry Longchamp, 9 John, I. 100. c. 1. *y*. William bishop of Ely, has the custody of Stephen de Beauchamp, 5 Richard i. I. 323. c. 1. *x*. Osbert de Longo Campo, 8 Richard i. I. 323. c. 2. *b*. Geoffrey de Longchamp son of Emma de S. Leodegario, I. 513. c. 2. *b*. Osbert, ibid. & I. 514. c. 1. *c*, *d*. William quit of the scutage for the king's ransom, 7 Richard i. I. 591. c. 2. *t*. Henry sherif of Herefordshire a captive, 3 Richard i. I. 176. c. 2. *b*.

Longespey, William son of William, I. 319. c. 1. *c*. Has the baronies of Haye and Kaunvile from Ydonea his mother, 40 Henry iii. ibid. William's licence from the king to make his will, 41 Henry iii. II. 185. c. 2. *n*.

Longobardick laws, I. 92. See Laws.

Loquendum's, what, II. 115.

Loreni, or reins, II. 130. c. 1. *e*.

Lorimer, Henry son of Simon le, 6 Henry iii. I. 454. c. 1. *f*.

Loriol, Ralf Fitz-Math. de, an. 1184. I. 168. c. 2.

Lose, Terrick de, one of the masters of the money in the Exchanges, 11 Edward ii. I. 292. c. 1. *c*.

Lostwetel in Cornwal, a fine for a market there, 6 Richard i. I. 399. c. 1. *e*.

Lovedon wapentake, Lincolnshire, II. 20. c. 2. *z*.

Lovel, Philip, king's treasurer, 39 Henry iii. I. 712. c. 1. *a*. See Luvel. Symon Lovel has the wapentake of Rydale under a commission of array, 16 Edward ii. II. 112. c. 2.

Louis emperor, I. 25.

Louis king of France comes into England, an. 1179. I. 27. When he makes a present to the monks of Holy Trinity, Canterbury, I. 27. c. 1. *c*.

Louis king of France makes a donation to the monks of Canterbury, an. 1235. I. 27. c. 2. *d*.

Lound, Peter de, 26 Edward i. II. 45. c. 2. *t*.

Lozeng, Robert le, his recognition, 28 Henry iii. II. 87. c. 1. *x*.

Luca

INDEX.

Luca merchants, II. 86. II. 135. c. 1. t. II. 137. c. 1. a. See Luke.

Luceles, Robert de, finds pledges for making an unjust disseisin, 10 John, I. 151. c. 1. w. Richard de Lucellis of Normandy, 2 John, I. 519. c. 2. b.

Luci, Richard de, Pref. xxiii. c. 1. t. Godfrey de, made bishop of Winchester, an. 1189. 1 Richard i. I. 22. c. 1. w. Richard de, justiciary of king Stephen, and sherif of Essex, I. 33. c. 2. r. Again, I. 34. Richard de, his writ, 14 Henry ii. I. 85. c. 1. p. Godfrey de Lucy chief justiciary, 25 Henry ii. I. 93. and 28 Henry ii. I. 113. c. 1. r. Reginald de Luci his land in Cumberland, 3 Richard i. I. 116. c. 2. c. Robert de Luci one of the justices, 20 Henry ii. I. 224. Reginald de Luci justicier, 21 Henry ii. I. 125. Godfrey de Lucy one of the justiciers, 26 Henry ii. I. 137. 146. The pleas of Richard de Luci, 17 Henry ii. I. 146. c. 1. b. The fine which Galfrid or Geoffrey paid for marrying Juliana the widow of Peter de Stokes, 9 John, I. 189. c. 1. b. The fine of Philip de Luci, 9 John, I. 189. c. 2. c. Richard de Luci justicier, 9 Henry ii. I. 201. c. 1. q. Richard, justicier, temp. Henry ii. I. 205. c. 1. Reginald de Luci, 25 Henry ii. I. 212. c. 1. n. Godfrey de Luci justicier, 29 Henry ii. I. 213. c. 1. p. Richard de Luci sherif of Essex, 3 Henry ii. I. 281. c. 2. f. And of Hertfordshire at the same time, ibid. c. 1. g. Justicier, 16 Henry ii. I. 307. c. 1. y. Godfrey de Luci had custody of the abbey of York, 31 Henry ii. I. 309. c. 1. q. Herbert de, has twenty pound from Disse in Norfolk, 30 Henry ii. I. 328. c. 1. n. Richard de Luci accompts for the ferm of Colechester, I. 331. c. 1. i. And of Windsor, 14 Henry ii. I. 373. c. 2. d. Richard de Luci obtains a fair and weekly market for his manor of Renglas in Cumberland, 10 John, I. 409. c. 2. f. Richard a benefactor to Feversham abbey before Henry iii. I. 413. c. 2. k. Richard de Luci his lands of Copland in Cumberland, 5 John, I. 439. c. 1. i. and I. 440. c. 2. q. Richard son of Reginald de Luci has the lands of Copland and Camerberg, 2 John, I. 464. c. 2. m. Richard de Luci sherif, 2 Henry ii. I. 539. c. 1. u. Robert de Luci sherif of Worcestershire, 21 Henry ii. I. 546. c. 2. u. Richard de Luci's pleas, 14 Henry ii. I. 558. c. 2. u. Richard de Luci accompts for the aid of Colchester, 14 Henry ii. I. 587. c. 1. Richard's perdona, 2 Henry ii. I. 602. c. 1. y. Godfrey de, justicier, 33 Henry ii. I. 635. c. 2. r. Richard sherif of Essex, his accompt, 2 Henry ii. I. 687. c. 2. k. And Hertford, ibid. Richard assises York city before 21 Henry ii. I. 702. c. 2. f. Reginald, I. 702. c. 2. g. Godfrey, I. 713. c. 1. d. Stephen, 13 Henry iii. I. 717. c. 2. l. Richard sherif of Essex, 2 Henry ii. I. 732. c. 1. k. Godfrey de Lucy tallaged Lincolnshire, 1 Richard i. I. 737. c. 1. r. Alexander de Luci seems to be baron of the Exchequer and proprietor of Copland, 4 John, II. 21. c. 1. t. Richard de Luci chief justicier and sherif of Essex and Hertfordshire, 2 Henry ii. II. 146. c. 1.

x.

INDEX.

x. Godfrey held pleas in Cumberland, 31 Henry ii. II. 146. c. 1. *z*. Richard has the ferm of Hertfordshire, 2 Henry ii. II. 151. c. 2. *s*. Richard de Luci's interest in Blochesham, Oxfordshire, 2 Henry ii. II. 163. c. 1. *y*. Richard de Luci's assignment on Braiand Cocham, Berkshire, 2 Henry ii. II. 166. c. 2. *r*. William de Lucy late sherif of Warwick and Leicestershire, 25 Henry iii. II. 192. c. 2. *x*. Richard de Lucy gave his interest in Copland to Lambert de Muleton with his eldest daughter, before 29 Henry iii. II. 182. c. 2. *x*. Richard de Lucy, 13 Henry ii. II. 200. c. 1. *b*. and II. 205. c. 2. *p*. Richard de Luci's writ, 19 and 21 Henry ii. II. 205. c. 2. *r, s*. II. 206. c. 1. *t, u*. William de Lucy attach'd, 25 Henry iii. II. 243. c. 1. *d*. Richard de Luci accompts for the ferm of Colchester, 9 Henry ii. II. 252. c. 1. *q*. Fines for the land of Hugh de Morevil, 6 John, II. 253. c. 1. *y*.

Lucia countess of Chester fined that she might do right among her vassals, 5 Stephen, I. 397. c. 2. *i*.

Lucius, pope, his message to the king, 31 Henry ii. I. 20.

Luct, Bartholomew de, about temp. Henry ii. I. 3. c. 2.

Luda, William de, elect of Ely, 18 Edward i. I. 598. c. 1. *e*. and II. 186. c. 2. *r*. One of the king's council, ibid. Keeper of the wardrobe, 18 Edward i. I. 611. c. 1. *k*. Dean of St Martins Magnus, I. 618. c. 1. *k*. Richard de Luda or Lue, chamberlain of the Exchequer, 25 Edward i. II. 29. c. 1. *s*. Sentenced to be remov'd for his contempt of John de Cobeham a baron there, 25 Edward i. ibid. But has his fine remitted, ibid. William de Luda accompts for the wardrobe, 11 and 12 Edward i. II. 124. c. 1. *e*. A letter for favour to Richard de Lue, 33 Edward i. II. 125. William keeper of the wardrobe, 13 Edward i. II. 131. c. 1. *f*. Richard de Luda remembrancer, 18 Edward i. II. 266. c. 2. *q*. Richard de Luda made constable of the Exchequer, 17 Edward ii. II. 283. c. 2. *r*. Auditor of the accompts of the Exchequer, 9 Edward ii. II. 291. c. 1. *d*. Dismiss'd from the chamberlainship of the Exchequer, 26 Edward i. II. 301. Was remov'd for speaking rash and outragious words, II. 303.

Ludelawe, Joan widow of Thomas de, held the manor of Langeton a member of Scrivelby, 9 Edward ii. I. 651.

Ludenham, Eustace parson of, 9 John, I. 499. c. 1. *s*.

Ludesdon, Reginald de, amerced pro impressione sigilli, 6 Henry iii. I. 549. c. 1. *c*. Amerc'd for the same, 13 John, 567. c. 1. *c*.

Ludham, Robert de, justice of the Jews, 7 Edward i. I. 242. c. 1. *k*. Commits falsity, is removed and fined 1000 marks, 14 Edward i. II. 254. c. 1. *c*. The form of his submission, ibid.

Ludhigland tallaged, I. 725. c. 2. *g*. The half manor of Ludingland tallaged, I. 752. c. 1. *i*.

Ludovicus Pius, the division of his dominions among his sons, Pref. xviii.

Luffeld,

INDEX.

Luffeld, a grant of tithe-bread to that priory, I. 3. c. 2. And of the church of Torneberg, ibid. The interest of the prior and monks of St Mary de Luffeld in Selveston, 28 Henry ii. I. 113. c. 2. *r*. The poverty of that priory, 25 Edward i. II. 230.

Lugershal, Henry de, chamberlain of the Exchequer, 1 Edward ii. I. 75. The donum of Lutegareshal, Wiltshire, 33 Henry ii. I. 634. c. 1. *q*. See Lutegareshal.

Lugwardin manor in Herefordshire tallaged, 19 Henry iii. I. 735. c. 1. *b*. Again, 7 Richard i. I. 747. c. 1. *k*.

Luiprand king of the Lombards, Pref. xxvii. c. 2.

Luitorp or Leutorp, Walter de, under-sherif of Yorkshire, 3 Henry ii. I. 690. c. 1. *r*. And of Westmariland, 12 Henry ii. I. 692. c. 1. *b*. See Leutorp.

Luke son of Bernard fined not to be forester, 12 John, I. 462. c. 1. *l*. Henry de Luk supplies the king with silks, 37 Henry iii. I. 609. c. 2. *b*. Reimund de Luk, 7 Edward i. I. 662. c. 1. *o*. Luke de Luca, 40 Henry iii. II. 95. c. 1. *s*.

Lullingston and Framingeham in Kent, the land of Jordan de Ros, 2 John, I. 486. c. 1. *k*.

Lund, William de, his perdona, 25 Henry iii. II. 229. c. 2. *o*.

Lundinaria, I. 164. c. 2. *d*.

Lunesdale or Lonesdale wapentak, Yorkshire, tallaged, 9 Richard i. I. 699. c. 1. *r*.

Lung, John le, has the office of tronage, London, 1 Edward ii. I. 780. c. 2. *k*. Quit of accompts, ibid.

Lungueville, Claria de, 2 John, I. 171. c. 2. *x*. Sir Henry de Lungevill, who, 2 Henry iii. I. 319. c. 2. *e*.

Lupescarius, an officer in Normandy, I. 478. c. 2. *t*.

Lupus, Robert, concern'd in the receipt of the Exchequer, 11 John, I. 384. c. 1. *l*. Amerc'd, I. 555. c. 2. *e*.

Lusteshul, Richard de, clericus cameræ regis, 9 Edward ii. I. 265. c. 1. *d*. N. de Lusteshul sherif of Wiltshire, 30 Henry iii. I. 711. c. 1. *y*.

Lutegareshal, its tallage, 1 John, I. 705. c. 2. *z*. Again, 30 Henry iii. I. 711. c. 1. *y*. See Lugreshal. Tallag'd, 20 Henry iii. I. 743. c. 2. *r*. Their church convey'd to Ralf de Nevil by his own sign manual as keeper, 16 John, II. 43. c. 1. *m*. Henry de Lutegareshale made chamberlain of the Exchequer, 1 Edward ii. II. 301. c. 1. *a*. Who requested his discharge, 5 Edward ii. II. 301. c. 1. *b*.

Luter, John le, I. 750. c. 1. *z*.

Luterel, Geoffrey, amerc'd for defaults, 9 Edward ii. I. 530. c. 1. Andrew sherif of Lincolnshire, 35 Henry iii. II. 141. c. 2. *s*.

Lutiwude, Staffordshire, who claim'd that land, 6 John, I. 99. c. 2. *n*. I. 794. c. 1. *b*.

Luton, Thomas son of William de, amerced for not taking knighthood, 1 Edward ii. I. 510. c. 1. *c*.

Lutre, William de, fines to be quit of the sherifwick of London, 5 Stephen, I. 457. c. 2. *t*. Simon Lutron a surety of Hugh Cordele, 5 Stephen, II. 197. c. 1. *q*.

Luveigni, Alexander de, custos of Muchelney abbey, 19 Henry ii. I. 308.

INDEX.

308. c. 2. b. Godfrey de Luvein fines for the widow of Ralf de Cornhull, 2 John, I. 515. c. 1. b. Walter de Luveng deceas'd, late sherif of Somerset and Dorsetshire, 27 Edward i. II. 187. c. 1. w.

Luvel, Philip, treasurer, 38 Henry iii. I. 229. c. 2. g. Henry, H. and R. Luvel, 10 John, I. 251. c. 1. r. Philip justicier of the Jews, 41 Henry iii. I. 260. c. 2. q. Philip seems to be treasurer, 37 Henry iii. I. 270. c. 2. f. Philip Lovel treasurer, 39 Henry iii. I. 391. c. 2. w. Osbert, 27 Henry ii. I. 503. c. 1. m. Osbert, 17 Henry ii. II. 558. c. 1. q. Ilger amerc'd, 27 Henry ii. I. 561. c. 2. p. Ralf baron of Kari, 6 Richard i. I. 592. c. 1. x. William Luvel holds of the earl of Leicester, 4 John, I. 644. c. 2. n. John Lovel summon'd with the barons of Northamptonshire against Scotland, 26 Edward i. I. 655. c. 1. Was lieutenant of the earl Marescal in Scotland, 34 Edward i. I. 657. c. 2. II. 49. c. 1. h. Baron Ralf Luvel's scutage, 3 John, I. 665. c. 2. g. P. Lovel the king's treasurer, 39 Henry iii. II. 17. c. 1. e. The patent for making Philip de Luvel treasurer, 27 Aug. 36 Henry iii. II. 35. c. 2. c. Philip de, 42 Henry iii. II. 68. c. 1. u. Philip was treasurer, 40 Henry iii. II. 95. c. 1. s. Sire Johan Lovel, 25 Edward i. II. 105. c. 1. i. Alyne Lovel of Clahangre, 1 Edward ii. II. 122. c. 2. r. Philip treasurer, 42 Henry iii. II. 208. c. 2. m. Commanded to seize on the city of London for a trespass, 39 Henry iii. II. 248. c. 1. w.

Luvers, Geoffrey de, of Hantshire, 13 John, I. 350. c. 1. r. Might not be summon'd for queen's gold, because he did not hold in capite, ib.

Luvetot, the barony of William de, in the king's hands, 31 Henry ii. I. 298. c. 1. e. Richard de Luvetot of Lincolnshire, 27 Henry ii. I. 427. c. 1. h. Emma de Luvetot fines to marry, 26 Henry ii. I. 464. c. 1. a. William de Luvetot's barony goes to Gerard de Furnival, 3 John, I. 486. c. 2. m. Nigel de Luvetot has the church of Spofford, 7 John, I. 489. c. 1. h. Robert Luvet plegius, 2 John, I. 520. c. 2. b. See I. 535. c. 1, 2. Richard de, 38 Henry iii. I. 596. c. 1. t. and Niel, ibid. Account of the sisters and heiresses of the barony of Niel de Luvetot, 6 Henry iii. I. 640. c. 1. r. Niel de, holds ten fees in capite and five of the honor of Tikehul, 3 John, I. 665. c. 1. e. —Luvetot has the third part of the fees of Niel de Luvetot, 30 Henry iii. I. 667. c. 1. n. The donum of the knights of Nigel de Luvetot in Huntendonshire, 5 Henry ii. I. 698. c. 1. f. The rolls of John de Luvetot, 18 Edward i. II. 25. c. 2. z. Joan de Lovetot, 1 Edward ii. II. 123. c. 2. y.

Lye, Nicolas de, clerk of the summonces, 19 Edward ii. II. 293. c. 2. q.

Lymbury, John de, 35 Edward i. II. 32. Adam de Lymbergh takes the oath of remembrancer of the Exchequer, 5 Edward ii. II. 267. c. 2. x. II. 269. c. 1. d. Remembrancer and auditor of the accompts of the bishop of Bath, 12 Edward ii. II. 292. c. 1. k.

INDEX.

Lyndhurst in Hampshire, the community of its villains tallaged, 6 Edward ii. I. 744. c. 2. *y*.

Lynton, Walter de, his plea, 5 Edward i. II. 80. c. 2. *b*.

Lytegreynes, John de, custos of the fee of York, 26 Edward i. II. 45. c. 2. *t*.

M.

Maban, Anora, claims the moiety of Alstanesfeld, Staffordshire, against Thomas Basset, 2 Henry iii. I. 793. c. 1. *d*.

Mabel, Arnald son of, fines to export corn into Norwey, 27 Henry ii. I. 467. c. 2. *k*.

Mabilia daughter of William de Orgers, I. 215. c. 1. *a*.

Machael, Humfry, holds the land of Grossebi in capite, 26 Henry ii. I. 512. c. 1. *s*.

Madine, Walter le, his licence to carry a hundred pondera of cheese out of the king's dominions, 13 John, I. 470. c. 1. *m*.

Maene, Walter de, his scutage for his fees in Kent, 18 Henry ii. I. 630. c. 1. *d*.

Maenfinin pays a fine to be sherif of Bucks and Bedfordshire, 5 Stephen, I. 458. c. 1. *y*. See Meinfelin.

Magena, Nicolas de, has respite of a debt during the king's pleasure, 10 Henry ii. I. 204. c. 2. *i*. And again, 9 Henry ii. II. 213. c. 2. *m*.

Magnates distinguish'd from Barones, 18 Edward i. I. 598. c. 2. *e*. And placed after them, ibid. Magnates have a grant to tallage their lordships, before 2 Edward ii. I. 754. c. 1. *o*. I. 754. c. 2. *p*. &c.

Magnavilla, baron Gaufrid de, 1 Stephen, I. 13. c. 1. *s*.

Mahurdin, Walter de, his tenure, 6 John, I. 439. c. 2. *k*. Ralf married the eldest daughter of William de Mahurdin, before 6 John, I. 506. c. 1. *t*. Walter's tenure, 6 John, I. 651. c. 1. *q*.

Maidenestan, their aid, 14 Henry ii. I. 584. c. 2. *q*. Walter de Maideston uses counterfeit bulls, 26 Edward i. II. 82.

Mail, several amerc'd for sending to Leicester for coat of Mail, 1 Richard i. I. 563. c. 1. *f*.

Maillai, Peter de, fines in a horse for hurting one of the king's dogs, 4 John, I. 505. c. 2. *p*. Fines in seven thousand marks for marrying Isabel the daughter and heiress of Robert de Turneham, 16 John, II. 211. c. 1. *b*.

Main, Roger son of, his paunage, 14 Henry ii. I. 559. c. 1. *g*.

Mainnesfeld, Notinghamshire, assised, 21 Henry ii. I. 702. c. 2. *g*. Tallaged with its soke, 30 Henry iii. I. 707, 708. c. 2. *p*. Again, 9 Richard i. I. 733. c. 1. *p*.

Majoratus domus regiæ in France, granted to Geoffrey earl of Anjou, I. 53.

Majors presented, II. 92. Major and aldermen of London refuse their sherifs to be sworn at the Exchequer, 9 Edward ii. II. 97. c. 2. *c*. A custos set over London when the king remov'd the mayor for misrule, II. 110.

Mairemum, or timber, I. 568. c. 1. *q*. Called Maerenum, I. 775. c. 1. *p*.

Maisil, Robert de, 12 Henry ii. I. 450. c. 1. *k*. Fines not to plead. ibid.

Maisnil, Gilbert de, paid ten marks to marry

INDEX.

marry, 5 Stephen, I. 463. c. 2. t. Robert del Meisnil married Emma daughter of Richard de Malebisse, before 9 John, I. 465. c. 2. r. Nicolas de Meynil summon'd among the Yorkshire barons to the Scotch war, 26 Edward i. I. 654. c. 2.

Malarteis, Roger, I. 552. Amerc'd for breaking of the king's assise, 12 Henry ii. I. 552. c. 1. b.

Malclerk, Walter, tallages the town and county of Lincoln, 8 John, I. 734. c. 2. b. See Carlisle, Mauclerk.

Maldon in Bedfordshire, sold to Roger de Bray in the beginning of Henry ii. I. 215. c. 1. a. William de Maldon chamberlain of the Exchequer, 9 Edward ii. II. 301. See Mealdon.

Malduit, William, king's chamberlain, 11 Henry ii. I 44. c. 1. c. Again, under the style of Mauduit and Maledoctus, 5 Stephen, and temp. Stephen, I. 58. c. 2. b, c. Robert, temp. Stephen, I 58. c. 2. John settles the assise on the king's domaines, 20 Henry ii. I. 124. c. 1. t. c. 2. z. Chamberlain William sheriff of Roteland, 26 Henry ii. I. 139. c. 1. f. Robert Malduit sherif of Wiltshire, I. 139. c. 2. n. William chamberlain, 30 Henry ii. I. 215. c. 2. d. Again, 5 Stephen, I. 263. c. 1. a. William chamberlain, 26 Henry ii. I. 289. c. 1. s. John Maulduit accompts for the profits of the see of Canterbury, 19 Henry ii. I. 309. c. 1. o. William Malduit prebendary of Sarum, about 31 Henry ii. I. 311. c. 1. d. Chamberlain, temp. Henry ii. I. 390. c. 2. q. Geoffrey claims the land of Chigewel, 2 John, I. 434. c. 2. m. Mary Malduit fines to marry as she will, 31 Henry ii. I. 464. Robert Malduit's share of the lands of Robert Giffard, 10 John, I. 490. c. 1. t. The estate of John Malduit how it descends, 506. c. 1. u. Robert Malduit seems to be sherif of Wiltshire, 23 Henry ii. I. 604. c. 1. l. John Malduit accompts for the scutage of the see of Canterbury for the Irish expedition, 18 Henry ii. I. 631. c. 2. b. William Maledoct has his danegeld remitted, 2 Henry ii. I. 687. c. 1. b. William Mauduit chamberlain of the Exchequer, 42 Henry iii. II. 14. c. 2. r. The writ of John Malduit, 16 Henry ii. II. 253. c. 1. z. Robert Malduit fines to make a park at Benly, 4 John, ibid. William Mauduit to provide a knight to officiate for him in the office of chamberlain, 32 Henry iii. II. 295. c. 1. w. William Mauduit earl of Warwick makes David his chamberlain usher of the receipt, 49 Henry iii. II. 296. c. 1. z. Makes Richard le Camberleng, 51 Henry iii. II. 296. c. 2. b. His heir, 52 Henry iii. II. 296. c. 2. c.

Malebisse, Richard, claims his homage, 9 John, I. 99. c. 2. x. Claims Etton, 28 Henry ii. I. 104. c. 2. o. Hugh de, impleaded, 18 Henry ii. I. 210. c. 1. e. Richard's relief for the honour of Eye, 22 Henry ii. I. 316. c. 1. b. Occurs, 1 John, I. 401. c. 1. a. and 9 John, I. 465. c. 2. r. Fines for his attachment to earl John, 6 Richard i. I. 473. c. 1. s. Richard de Malebisse's lands seiz'd for killing the Jews at York, 4 Richard i. I. 483. c. 1. l. Richard

settles

INDEX.

settles the tallage, 3 John, I. 722. c. 2. *h.* William Malebys one of the commissioners of the array in the wapentake of Aynsty, 16 Edward ii. II. 112. c. 1.

Malebraunch, Thomas, of Northampton, 42 Henry iii. II. 16. c. 2. *z.*

Malemeyns, Henry, 56 Henry iii. I. 253. c. 1. *y.* Gilbert Malesmain's serjeanty in Oxfordshire tallaged, I. 721. c. 2. *y.* Thomas Malemeyns, 55 Henry iii. II. 223. c. 1. *d.*

Malepalu, William de, I. 477. c. 1. *e.* Fines to have the king's protection, ibid.

Malerbe, John, the king's grant to him, 4 John, I. 173. c. 1. *b.* John Malherbe, 10 John, I. 489. c. 2. *q.* See Malherbe.

Maleswurd, terra de, claimed by Robert Cusin, 1 Richard i. I. 227. c. 2. *o.*

Malet, Gilbert, seneschal, 20 Henry ii. I. 50. c. 2. *x.* Robert Malet his tenure of the chamberlainship, I. 56. c. 1. *o.* I. 56. Again, temp. Henry i. I. 58. c. 1. *u.* William, 12 John, I. 481. c. 1. *o.* Dapifer, 14 Henry ii. I. 577. c. 2. *a.* Baron William Malet's scutage for Dorset or Somersetshire, 3 John, I. 665. c. 2. *g.* Robert Malet late sherif of Bedford and Buckinghamshire, 14 Edward i. II. 237.

Maletere, John, amerced, 35 Henry iii. I. 567. c. 1. *b.*

Maleverer or Mauleverer, John, commissioner of the array for the wapentake of Clarhowe, 16 Edward ii. II. 112. c. 1.

Malfeth, Guy, 5 Stephen, I. 426. c. 2. *q.*

Malger the clerk amerced for causing two duels by one man in a day, Yorkshire, 12 Henry ii. I. 545. c. 1. *w.* Malger held of the church of Chichester, temp. Henry ii. I. 576. c. 1. *y.*

Malherbe, Robert, his lands in England and Normandy, 18 Henry ii. I. 447. c. 1. *w.* Oliver Malherbe his land of Neweton, 1 Richard i. I. 427. c. 1. *r.* The chirograph between John Malherbe and Roger Ostiary of the Exchequer, 28 Henry iii. II. 275. c. 2. *k.*

Mallinges, Henry de, and William, 27 Henry ii. I. 430. c. 2. *f.*

Malliun, Savaric de, plegius, 16 John, II. 211. c. 1. *b.*

Malmsbury abbey in the king's hands, about 16 Henry ii. I. 307. c. 1. *u.* Accompted for, 8 John, I. 312. c. 1. *m.* Its aid, 23 Henry ii. I. 604. c. 1. *l.* Its knights fees, I. 634. c. 1. *q.* Bedeneston a member of it, ibid. The donum of that Burgh, 33 Henry ii. ibid. Abbat of Malmsbury one of the justiciers who settled the tallage, 10 Richard i. I. 700. c. 1. *s.* Its assise or tallage, 19 Henry ii. I. 702. c. 1. *d.* Its tallage, 1 John, I. 705. c. 2. *z.*

Malo Alneto, Hugh de, his respite, 4 John, II. 214. c. 1. *q.*

Malore, Peter, his tenure, 33 Edward i. I. 335. ibid. c. 2. *c.* Anschetil Mallore accompts for the scutage of the knights of the earl of Leicester, 18 Henry ii. I. 630. c. 2. *e.* Thomas Malhore, 3 Henry iii. II. 43. c. 2. *n.* Supports Alice de Holewel against the abbat of Westminster, ibid. Ansketill Mallore accompts for the scutage of the fees of the earl of Leicester, 19 Henry iii. II. 183. c. 1. *z.*

Malsateby amerced for plowing the king's highway, 12 Henry ii. I. 557. c. 2. *k.*

Maltolt,

INDEX.

Maltolt, for persons passing through Rochester towards the holy land, 22 Henry iii. II. 201. c. 1. *p.*

Malton, Robert de, defends the king, 9 Edward ii. II. 85. c. 1. *r.*

Malton or Mealton, Yorkshire, its donum to the Irish expedition, 33 Henry ii. I. 635. c. 2. *r.*

Maltravers, John, fines for quittance, 31 Henry ii. I. 557. c. 2. *k.*

Malus Catulus, Roger, vicechancellor of Richard i. I. 77. Drowned near Cyprus, and lost the king's seal, ibid.

Malus Lacus, Peter, of Yorkshire, on the Scotch expedition, 26 Edward i. I. 654. c. 2. Peter's scutage of Gannoc, 40 Henry iii. I. 678. c. 1. *g.* The heir of Peter Maulay, or de Malo Lacu, 25 Henry iii. II. 28. c. 1. *k.* Peter of the king's council, 31 Edward i. II. 107. c. 1. *n.* Justice de la Pes, 35 Edward i. II. 203. c. 2. *e.* Edmund de Malo Lacu messenger to the barons, 5 Edward ii. II. 213. c. 1. *k.* The heir of Peter de Malo Lacu, 25 Henry iii. II. 318. c. 2. *h.*

Malus Vicinus, Hugh, of Staffordshire, 5 Stephen, I. 147. c. 1. *z.* Adam Malveisin, 4 John, I. 428. c. 1. *b.*

Maminot, Walkelin de, his scutage for his Kentish fees, 18 Henry ii. I. 630. c. 1. *d.*

Man, King de, a grant to him, 7 John, I. 390. c. 2. *r.*

Manasser le fosseur, Mary widow of, king's bailif of Kaernarvon, 14 Edward i. II. 5. c. 1. *t.*

Mandatum, how it came to signify a message, Pref. xxiv. Mandare baronibus to send a message to them, I. 662. c. 1. *o.* passim.

Mandevill, William and Robert de, an. 1162. I. 34. c. 1. *u.* Geoffrey de, deforced of his inheritance in England and Normandy by Henry de Tilli, 7 Richard i. I. 98. c. 2. *n.* Claims the honor of Merswde, 3 John, I. 99. c. 1. *r.* Robert is to have justice of Reginald de Warenne, an. 1162. I. 112. William de Mandevill earl of Essex, 28 Henry ii. I. 114. c. 1. *r.* William de Mandevill earl of Albemarle and Essex, I. 161. c. 1. *b.* And custos of the lands of the earl of Flanders here, 34 Henry ii. I. 165. c. 2. *b.* William de Mandevil earl of Essex, 2 Henry iii. I. 317. c. 2. *p.* Geoffrey de Mandevil pays twenty thousand marks to marry the countess of Glocester, 2 Henry iii. I. 465. c. 2. *uu.* Robert de Mandevil's descent, with his claim of the barony of Merswude, made good, 10 John, I. 489. c. 1. *q.* Robert de Mandevil's esnecy of the lands of Robert Giffard, 10 John, I. 489. c. 2. *t.* Geoffrey de Mandevil of Wiltshire fines for not attending the king beyond sea, 1 John, I. 649. c. 1. *t.* Nephew of Elyas his fine for a retraxit, 1 John, I. 733. c. 2. *t.* Geoffrey and William de Mandevil his son, temp. John, II. 10. c. 1. *x.* John son of Geoffrey his contention with the earl of Hereford his heir, 31 Henry iii. ibid. Geoffrey occurs, 8 Richard i. II. 119. c. 1. *o.* Earl William de Mandevill has the tertius denarius of Essex, 15 and 31 Henry ii. II. 164. c. 1. *d.* ibid. c. 2. *e.* Geoffrey Fitz-Peter had the land of earl William de Mandevil, 8 Richard i. II. 176. c. 1. *y.* Maud de Auntesseye heir of William de Mandevil earl of Essex, 3 Henry iii. II. 206. c. 2. *b.* Geoffrey de Mandevil could not have right, 8 John, II. 226.

INDEX.

II. 226. William de Mandevil earl of Essex, 9 Henry iii. II. 259. c. 1. k.

Maneby, frere Robert de, 42 Henry iii. I. 315. c. 1. n.

Manerby, John de, who, I. 170.

Manna, Nicolas de, impleaded, 18 Henry ii. I. 447. c. 1. w.

Mansel, William, 29 Henry ii. I. 105. c. 1. p. His plaint against John de Caverton for the terra de Schenlega, ibid.

Manslaughter and Murders, amerced, I. 543. See Homicide.

Mantel, Robert, one of the justices errant, 25 Henry ii. I. 83. c. 1. e. Again, I. 94. Again, 20 Henry ii. I. 124. Again, ibid. Again, 22 Henry ii. I. 126, 127. Sherif of Essex and Hertfordshire, I. 131. c. 2. d. Was living, 30 Henry ii. I. 215. c. 2. d. Justice of the forest, 17 Henry ii. I. 344. c. 2. t. Custos of Essex and Hertfordshire, 4 Henry iii. I. 462, 463. c. 1. q. Justicier, 19 Henry ii. I. 701. c. 1. z. Settles the assise of Norfolk and Suffolk, 22 Henry ii. I. 703. c. 1. k. Accompts for the pannage of the king's forests, II. 131. c. 1. g.

Mantel, Matthew son and heir apparent of Robert, an. 1184. 30 Henry ii. I. 215. c. 2. d.

Manupastum, I. 555. c. 2. e, f.

Map, Walter, justice of the assise in Glocestershire, 19 Henry ii. I. 701. c. 2. c.

Mapeldoreham in Hampshire, tallaged, 33 Henry ii. I. 736. c. 2. q.

Mapleschamp in Kent, II. 152. c. 1. w.

Mara, Henry de, 9 John, I. 100. c. 1. y. Robert de, 2 John, I. 171. c. 2. x. William de Mara sherif of Surrey accompts for the chattels of several executed persons, 10 Henry iii. I. 346. c. 1. f. Robert de la Mare, 1 John, I. 401. c. 1. a. William and Robert de Mara of Herefordshire, 5 John, I. 438. c. 1. b. Robert de Mara and Felicia his wife, 5 Henry iii. I. 452. c. 2. l. Emma de Mara in Normandy, 2 John, I. 518. c. 2. w. John de Mara baron and courtier, 26 Edward i. I. 655. c. 1. Robert de, 2 Richard i. I. 664. c. 1. a. and c. 2. e. William de, I. 729. c. 2. u. Henry de, held pleas at Cestrehunt, 38 Henry iii. I. 761. c. 1. Robert de Mara, 9 Richard i. II. 198. c. 1. r. Matthew de la Mare executor of Henry, 42 Henry iii. II. 208. c. 2. m.

Marc, Philip, sherif of Notingham and Derbyshire, temp. John, I. 86. Philip his pension, 7 Henry iii. I. 729. c. 1. q. Attached for robbery and breach of peace, 10 Henry iii. I. 793. c. 2. f.

Marcandus, Richard, of Devonshire, 14 Henry ii. I. 588. c. 1. b.

Marchant, Simon, of London, tallaged, 19 Henry iii. I. 738. c. 1. y.

Marche, earl Patrick de la, one of the king's courtiers, 26 Edward i. I. 655. c. 2. William de Marche treasurer of the Exchequer, 18 Edward i. II. 37. c. 1. h. ibid. c. 2. i. At his death was bishop of Bath and Wells, ibid. c. 2. k.

Marchia, William de, treasurer, had been clerk of the king's wardrobe, 13 Edward i. II. 323. c. 1. q.

Marci, William de, his recognition, 1 Richard i. I. 97. c. 2. d. Ralf de de Marci fines for the king's good will, 9 John, II. 254. c. 2. h.

Marculphus's Formulæ, I. 91.

Marescallare to manage horses, and Marescalcia avium regis, &c. I. 43. See I. 775. c. 1. q. Marescalcia & Ferura equorum, II. 130. c. 1. e.

The

INDEX.

The virga Marefcalciæ delivered, 31 Henry iii. II. 285. c. 1. *b*. M. had the keeping of the writs in the Exchequer, 10 Edward i. II. 286. c. 1. *e*. Accompt of that office as to duty and bufinefs, II. 287. Defaulters in accompts in cuftody of the Marefchal of the Exchequer, II. 288. Enquiry what rights, fees, and devoirs belong to the king's Marefchalcy, II. 290.

Marefchal, William earl of Eftrigol, 8 Richard i. I. 29. c. 2. *q*. Was one of the regents in the beginning of that reign, I. 34.

Marefchal, that office of old, and now, hereditary, I. 43. His fees and allowances, I. 42. c. 1. *u*. Formerly more Marefchals than one, being a general name, I. 44. Marefchalcy of the king's birds, I. 43. And of the king's meafures in Ireland, ibid. A Marefchal fuperiour to the reft, I. 45. Is fuppofed to have both an office and an honour, I. 48. His office in the army and the court, ibid. How the office of the king's chief Marefchal was diftinguifhed, I. 56. The office, 4 Richard i. I. 427. c. 2. *s*.

Marefchalli, the family of the, I. 44. William fenior and junior, 3 Henry iii. I. 67. c. 1. *x*. And John, I. 68. c. 1. Signs next the archbifhops, ibid. G. John and William Marefchal, circa 21 Henry iii. I. 101, 102. c. 2. *f*. William Marefchal has a mediety of earl Giffard's land, 2 Richard i. I. 169. c. 2. *q*. William Marefchal fherif of Glocefterfhire, 6 John, I. 192. c. 1. *t*. John Marefchal jufticier, temp. Henry ii. I. 209. c. 1. *b*. William Marefchal earl of Penbroc attefts the Jews charter, 2 John, I. 256. c. 1. *e*.

William earl Marefchal fermer of Glocefterfhire, 1 John, I. 329. c. 1. *s*. William Marefchal earl of Pembroc, 9 Henry iii. I. 389. c. 1. *g*. G. Marefchal, 20 Henry iii. ibid. c. 1. *h*. William earl Marefchal, 16 John, I. 481. c. 1. *r*. John Marefchal, 9 Henry iii. I. 492. c. 2. *y*. William Marefchal earl of Pembroc bears tefte, 3 Henry iii. I. 529. c. 1. *o*. John Marefchal, 14 Henry ii. I. 581. c. 2. *y*. The fees of John Marefchal in Norfolk, 31 Henry iii. I. 594. c. 2. *i*. Richard Marefchal in rebellion, 18 Henry iii. I. 617. c. 1. *e*. John Marefchal refufes homage in Berkfhire, 33 Henry ii. I. 643. c. 1. *g*. John Marefchal, 26 Edward i. I. 655. c. 1. Earl William, 1 John, I. 665. c. 1. *d*. Has the honor of Giffarde in his hands, 4 John, I. 666. c. 1. *b*. John quit of his danegeld in Wiltfhire, 2 Henry ii. I. 687. c. 1. *i*. John keeper of the caftle of Devifes, I. 765. c. 1. *i*. Office of the Marefchal how executed after the divifion of the king's courts, I. 797. Several grants of that office, ibid. c. 1. *w*. In commiffion, 18 Edward iii. ibid. William Marefchal baron of the Exchequer, 49 Henry iii. II. 17. c. 1. *f*. One of that name in the Exchequer, 2 Richard i. II. 20. c. 1. *y*. See Pembroc. William baron of the Exchequer, 4 Henry iii. II. 56. c. 1. *q*. Executors of William earl Marefchal, 14 Henry iii. II. 116. c. 1. *t*. William le Marefchal forfeits Hafelberg for adhering to Simon Montfort, temp. Henry iii. II. 120. John, 2 Henry ii. II. 151. c. 1. *s*. William fherif of Gloucefterfhire, 7 John, II. 158. c. 1. *x*. Marefchal of the Exchequer, II. 284, 285.

Maretop

INDEX.

Maretot and Wandour, the land of Sibylla de Tingerie, 1 John, I. 464. c. 2. *l.*

Margaret, queen mother of Edward ii. I. 361. c. 2. *x.* Was dead in 12 Edward ii. ibid. c. 2. *y.* Widow of Edmund earl of Cornwal, 2 Edward ii. I. 754. c. 1. *o.* Margaret daughter of Edward i. and wife of the duke of Brabant, 26 Edward i. I. 785. c. 2. *a.* Margaret queen, 34 Edward i. II. 124. c. 2. *k.*

Margaret widow of Robert Hereward, 35 Edward i. II. 125. c. 1. *l.*

Margery the countess has seisin of the terra de Rihale, 7 Richard i. I. 106. c. 1. *t.*

Marines, John de, sherif of Cambridgeshire, before 40 Henry iii. I. 446. John de la, who, 9 Edward ii. I. 784. c. 1. *u.*

Marinus archbishop of Naples, an. 1144. I. 184. c. 1. *s.*

Marisco, Richard de, archdeacon of Richmund and Northumberland, delivered the great seal to the king, 15 John, I. 67. Per Ricardum de Marisco, 10 John, I. 263. c. 2. *o.* William de, 6 John, I. 441. c. 1. *s.* William has the custody of the isle of Ely, 7 Richard i. I. 459. c. 2. *p.* Marsh between Spalding and Tid to whom it belonged, 7 John, I. 506. c. 1. *w.* Subsidy to besiege the isle of William de Marisco, 4 John, I. 612. c. 1. *o.* Richard de Marisco, 13 John, I. 644. c. 1. *o.* Richard de Mareis subcustos of Durham, temp. Richard i. I. 714, 715. See II. 252. c. 2. *x.*

Mark of gold equal to nine of silver, I. 277. To ten, 3 John, I. 487. c. 1. *o.* Aid of a mark on each knight's fee, I. 572. Peter Mark, 11 Henry iii. II. 216. c. 2. *m.* Mareschal of the Exchequer had half a Mark a day for each prisoner, II. 289.

Markebi in Lincolnshire, prior of, his carucats, 5 John, I. 605. c. 2. *t.*

Market, a fine of ten marks for the grant of one, 6 Richard i. I. 399. c. 1. *e.* Another, I. 400. c. 1. *q.* Accompt of several Markets in London, I. 779. Without warrant, or to the nusance of their neighbours, to be certified, II. 102, 103.

Marmiun, Robert son of Robert Marmiun has the castle of Tameworde, 2 Henry iii. I. 301. c. 2. *y.* Robert Marmion, 5 Stephen, I. 449. c. 2. *d.* Fines the citizens of Bristou for not meeting him, 5 Richard i. I. 503. c. 2. *s.* His knights fees, 14 Henry ii. I. 574. c. 2. *o.* Quit of scutage for the king's ransom, 7 Richard i. I. 591. c. 2. *t.* Philip Marmiun has eleven knights fees in Warwick and Leicestershire, 30 Henry iii. I. 595. c. 1. *n.* and 38 Henry iii. I. 597. c. 1. *y.* Robert settled the tallage for Staffordshire, 2 Richard i. I. 698. c. 2. *p.* Robert, his case, 2 Henry iii. II. 2. c. 1. *b.*

Marriage of widows vested in the crown, 32 Henry ii. I. 323. c. 1. *w.* Large fines paid for licence to marry and not to marry, I. 463, &c. Licence for Sarah de Burgh to marry unto any one in the king's terra, except in Scotland or Kent, 3 John, I. 465. c. 1. *n.* Fines for Marriages where the parents of both were living, I. 512. c. 2. *w.* I. 513. *x, y.* Aid for the marriage of the king's eldest daughter, I. 572.

Marseilles, king Pepin's liberality to the bishop of, I. 159. c. 2. *c.*

Marsingham, Robert son of Ralf de, his fine, 9 John, I. 409. c. 2. *c.*

Martel,

INDEX.

Martel, William, butler to Henry i. I. 50. Geoffrey had the office of butler, 18 Henry ii. ibid. Holds six knights fees de Monte-acuto, 18 Henry ii. I. 50. c. 1. *q*. Geoffrey Martel unto the barons of London, I. 198. c. 2. *f*. Geoffrey Martel's wife, sister of Cicely de Alwardebi, 5 Richard i. I. 483. c. 2. *o*. The terra of Osbert Martel, before 18 Henry ii. I. 580. c. 2. *q*. Eudo de Martel parson of Stradebroc, 9 John, II. 43. c. 1. *k, l*. William occurs, temp. Stephen, II. 138. c. 2. *e*.

Marte'ey, Worcestershire, its tallage, 8 Richard i. I. 704. c. 2. *q*.

Martin, Elyas, 8 John, I. 441. c. 2. *w*. William Martyn summoned by writ as a baron, 26 Edward i. I. 655. c. 2.

Martiwast, Ralf de, plegius, 10 John, I. 151. c. 1. *w*.

Marton, canons of, their interest in Hoby, I. 329. c. 1. *w*.

Marton, Peter de, against the earl of Warwick, 3 Richard i. I. 105. c. 1. *q*. William de, sherif of Lincoln, 23 Henry ii. I. 342. c. 1. *b*.

Martre, Henry la, fines for being in the king's forest with leveriers, &c. 9 John, I. 499. c. 2. *u*.

Martynesgrove, Sussex, in part the prior of Boxgrave's, I. 599. c. 2. *g*.

Mascherel, Roger, why amerced, 5 Stephen, I. 557. c. 2. *f*.

Masci, the terra of Hamon de, in the king's hand, 1 Richard i. I. 298. c. 2. *w*.

Masci junior, Hamon de, of Lincolnshire, bastardized in court Christian, 1 John, I. 434. c. 1. *k*.

Massingham, Hugh de, receiver of customs of Len, 26 Edward i. I. 782. c. 1. *r*.

Master, that title given to an archdeacon and judge, I. 124.

Matham, John, of the Exchequer, 18 Henry iii. II. 15. c. 2. *x*. Geoffrey Matham senior, 1 Edward ii. II. 74. c. 2. *u*.

Mattesdon, John de, punished for selling his land to a religious house without the king's licence, 31 Henry iii. I. 320. c. 1. *l*.

Matthew Paris's account of an Exchequer-man, I. 214.

Mauchen, Geoffrey, of Normandy, 2 John, I. 520. c. 1. *c*.

Mauclerc, Walter de, bishop of Carlisle, treasurer, 14 Henry iii. I. 376. c. 1. *x*. Of the Exchequer for life, 16 Henry iii. II. 33. c. 2. *x*. See Carlisle.

Maud, Nicolas son of, 7 Richard i. I. 549. c. 1. *b*.

Maud de Calz her barony, or the terra de Leiffington, was in the king's hands, 8 John, I. 298. c. 2. *b*.

Maud countess of Clare, wife of earl Richard and mother of Gilbert, about 51 Henry iii. I. 101. c. 2. *e*. Maud was daughter of John earl of Lincoln and constable of Chester, 22 Henry iii. I. 326. c. 2. *n*.

Maud wife of Roger de Auntefeye, heir of W. de Mandevil earl of Essex, 13 Henry iii. II. 206. c. 2. *b*.

Maud countess of Norfolk and Warenne, I. 47. Her benefaction to the prioress of Thefford, ibid. c. 1. *y*. Styled Marescalla, ibid. Was heiress with the esnecy of Walter Mareschal earl of Penbrok, II. 285. c. 1. *b*. Mother of Roger le Bigod, ibid.

Maud queen of William i. I. 6. c. 1. *h*. Daughter of Henry ii. married to the duke of Saxony, an. 1164. I. 15. c. 1. *x*. Maud the king's daughter, 14 Henry iii. I. 142. c. 2. *f*. Queen of Henry i. her donation to Trinity priory,

INDEX.

prioury, London, I. 276. c. 1. *r.* Maud the king's daughter had three ships from Shoram which convoyed her towards Saxony, 13 Henry ii. I. 366. c. 1. *b.* Was a benefactress to Feversham abbey, I. 413. c. 2. *k.* The aid for her marriage, I. 572. Daughter of Henry i. married to the emperor, I. 685.

Maufe, William and Joan their assignment, 6 Edward i. I. 335. c. 2. *b.*

Mauham, Gerard, 14 Edward i. II. 90.

Maulay, Peter de, 3 Henry iii. I. 67. c. 1. *x.*, See Malus Lacus. Peter de, justicier in Lincolnshire, 34 Edward i. II. 65.

Mauleone, William de, of Normandy, 2 John, I. 524. c. 1. *u.*

Mauneby, Hugh de, I. 550. c. 2. *z.*

Maunsel, John, how long he had the custody of the great seal, about 31 Henry iii. I. 68. Placed in the receipt of the Exchequer, 18 Henry iii. II. 51. c. 2. *r.*

Maurdyn manor, its tallage, 19 Henry iii. I. 735. c. 1. *h.* Again, 7 Richard i. I. 747. c. 1. *k.*

Maurice an Irish bishop, an. 1121. I. 110. Maurice de foresta has part of the land of Osbert Martel, 18 Henry ii. I. 580. c. 2. *q.*

Mauro, Ralf de, 6 John, I. 441. c. 1. *s.* John Maurus alderman of the gild of Pararii, 26 Henry ii. I. 562. c. 1. *z.*

Maximin of Orleans, abbat of St, I. 107.

Mayngham, Yorkshire, its tallage, 30 Henry iii. I. 710. c. 1. *w.*

Mayordomo's, their power, I. 54, 55.

Mazelinarius, Walcher, 8 Richard i. I. 342. c. 2. *d.* Seems to have hid the king's money under ground, ibid.

Mealdon, the church of St Mary de, its relation to the deanery of St Martins, I. 33. c. 2. *r.* The village and provost of Mealdon amerced, 31 Henry ii. I. 547. c. 2. *d.* William son of Brictive of Mealdon his aid, 14 Henry ii. I. 585. Tallaged, 1 Richard i. I. 703. c. 1. *l.* See Maldon.

Mealse in Yorkshire, Alexander abbat of, 9 Richard i. I. 238. c. 1. *u.* Seems to have had the chattels of Aaron the Jew, II. 225. c. 2. *u.*

Measure, false, men of Wilton amerced for it, 5 Richard i. I. 564. c. 2. *e.*

Meburne, William de, chamberlain of the Exchequer, 28 Henry iii. II. 14. c. 1. *o.* Occurs Medburne, ibid.

Medard, Robert de S. clerk in chancery, 14 Henry iii. I. 195.

Medburn, frere William de, treasurer of the New Temple, London, one of the receivers of the vintism, 1 Edward i. I. 610. c. 1. *i.* Robert de Meldeburn sherif of London, 2 Edward i. II. 96. c. 2. *x.* Medburn in Leicestershire the king's lordship, II. 118. c. 2. *h.*

Medelwode, Simon de, amerced for carrying a lay fee before an ecclesiastical judge, 31 Henry ii. I. 561. c. 2. *s.*

Medicus, Ralf, his scutage in Essex, 5 Henry ii. I. 626. c. 2. *q.*

Meduana, Walter de, succeeded to the twenty knights fees of Geoffrey Tallebot, temp. Henry ii. I. 578. c. 2. *g.*

Mein, Richard son of, 1 Richard i. I. 155. 213. c. 2. *u.* His fine for single combat with William de Salcey, ibid. c. 2. *w.* The barony of Ralf de Mein de Foresta in the king's hands, 31 Henry ii. I. 300. c. 1. *s.*

Meinfelin, several of that family, temp.
Henry

INDEX.

Henry ii. I. 3. c. 2. William Fitz-Meinfelin, 29 Henry ii. I. 105. c. 1. *p.*

Meiremer, Afceus le, alderman of London, the tallage for his ward, 19 and 20 Henry iii. I. 738. c. 2. *z.* I. 739. c. 1. *a.*

Mel and cera, of the king's bees, accompted for at the Exchequer, II. 131. c. 1. *g.* Mel haiarum de Clipfton, ibid.

Melchegrave and Hen, in Suffex, a conteft about a knight's fee there, I. 789. c. 1. *f.*

Melchefham in Wiltfhire, its aid, 14 Henry ii. I. 589. Its aid, 23 Henry ii. I. 604. c. 1. *l.* Its donum, 33 Henry ii. I. 634. c. 2. Its affife or tallage, 19 Henry ii. I. 702. c. 1. *d.* Was the firft burgh in Wiltfhire by its tallage, 1 John, I. 705. c. 2. *z.* Melkefham tallaged, 20 Henry iii. I. 707. c. 1. *k.* and 30 Henry iii. I. 711. c. 1. *y.* The tenure of Robert de Holt here, 40 Henry iii. I. 746. c. 1. *d.* The manor of the priorefs of Ambrefbury, 9 Edward ii. I. 753. c. 2. *n.*

Meldred in the bifhopric, the barony of Robert fon of, 8 Richard i. I. 715. c. 2.

Meleburne's tallage, 14 Henry iii. I. 708. c. 1. *o.* and 19 Henry iii. I. 735. c. 1. *i.* Robert, 35 Edward i. II. 247. c. 2. *p.*

Melecumbe in Somerfetfhire, in cuftody of Peter Malore, 33 Edward i. I. 335. c. 2. *c.*

Meleford, Elias fon of William de, 49 Henry iii. I. 349. c. 2. *o.*

Mellent, Galerius earl of, 1 Stephen, I. 13. c. 2. *s.* Robert earl of Mellent feems to be chancellor of Henry i. an. 1113. I. 29. c. 1. *o.* Earl of Mellent, 2 John, I. 520. c. 2. *h.*

Melton, William de, comptroller of the king's wardrobe, 1 Edward ii. I. 74. William de Melton, 2 Edward ii. II. 290.

Melverton, the advoufon of it granted to the fee of Bath by W. Briwerre, I. 115. c. 2. *w.*

Memoranda of the Exchequer, Mr Odo keeper of them, 4 Edward i. II. 112. c. 2. *f.* What entered there, II. 115.

Mendefham, Richard de, II. 277. c. 1. *r.*

Mendham, William de, fines for a writ, 7 John, I. 791. c. 1. *o.*

Menftrewrd manor, I. 192. c. 1. *t.* Tallaged in Glocefterfhire, 7 Richard i. I. 703. c. 2. *n.*

Menftria, the abbat of St Auftins, 10 Richard i. I. 553. c. 2. *f.*

Ments, Arnold archbifhop of, an. 1166. I. 61. c. 2. *a.* Sigefrid archbifhop of, an. 1213. ibid.

Meones, William de, chamberlain of the Exchequer of Ireland, 22 Edward i. II. 136. c. 1. *x.*

Merc, Walter and William fons of John de Merc, 2 Henry iii. I. 494. c. 1. *n.*

Merc, Simon de, held two fees of the honor of Boloigne, 8 Richard i. I. 643. c. 1. *f.*

Mercerus, Adam, of Canterbury, kept the dye for coinage there, 22 Henry iii. II. 88. c. 1. *b.*

Merchandife, how provided for by treaty, 14 Edward i. II. 103.

Merchants of England ufed to pay the king a quinzime for their goods, I. 771. c. 2. *g.* A ftrict inquiry into their number and effects, 34 Edward i. II. 107.

Mercier, Laurence le, 6 Henry iii. I. 454. c. 2. *h.* Ailwin merciarius of Glocefter, 16 Henry ii. I. 563. c. 1. *e.*

Euftace

INDEX.

Euſtace of London his tallage, 14 Henry iii. I. c. 1. s. Again, 19 Henry iii. I. 738. c. 1. y. Herebert of Bedford, 1 John, I. 747. c. 2. l.

Mere in Wiltſhire, its tallage, 20 Henry iii. I. 707. c. 1. k.

Mereflet, Stephen de, amerc'd for a fooliſh anſwer, 17 Henry ii. I. 563. c. 2. k.

Mereſey, Iſabel widow of Ralf de, 9 John, I. 465. c. 2. s.

Merethin in Cornwal, its tallage, 1 John, I. 733. c. 2. t.

Mereworth, Simon de, ſherif of London, 5 Edward ii. II. 251.

Meriet, Nicolas de, juſticier and aſſeſſor of the hidage for the king's ranſom, temp. Richard i. I. 592. c. 1. x. Hugh's fees, 14 Henry iii. I. 661. c. 1. i. The barony of Nicolas de Meriet, 3 John, I. 665. c. 2. g.

Merkyngfeld, John de, chancellor of the Exchequer, 5 Edward ii. II. 31. Again, 5 Edward ii. II. 278. c. 1. u. John de Merkyngfeld had the annual fee of forty marks, 6 Edward ii. II. 326. c. 1. o.

Merlai, William de, of Northumberland, 5 Stephen, I. 426. c. 2. z. William de Merle, 2 John, I. 522. c. 2. p. Amerc'd in two hundred marks, 16 Henry ii. II. 182. c. 2. w. His effects how protected againſt the crown, ibid.

Merle and Meldeburn, a conteſt about thoſe lands, 9 John, I. 448. c. 1. h.

Merleburg, protected againſt the burgeſſes of Briſtow, 8 John, I. 408. c. 1. o. John de Merleberga accompts for a duel, 7 Henry ii. I. 501. c. 2. t. In Wiltſhire its aid, 23 Henry ii. I. 604. c. 1. l. The foreign manor of Merleburg, 33 Henry ii. I. 634. c. 1. q. Its donum, 5 Henry ii. I. 697. c. 1. r. w. Its tallage, 10 Richard i. I. 700. c. 1. s, t. and 19 Henry ii. I. 702. c. 1. d. Its burgh and Bertona tallaged, 1 John, I. 705. c. 2. z. Its tallage, 30 Henry iii. I. 711. c. 1. y.

Merſwde, the honor of, I. 99. c. 1. r. The claim to this barony made good to Robert de Mandevil againſt Henry de Tylli, 10 John, I. 489. c. 2. q.

Merton, Walter, biſhop of Rocheſter, I. 47. c. 1. x. Chancellor of England, 1 Edward i. I. 391. c. 2. x. Merton, Wiltſhire, its donum, 33 Henry ii. I. 634. c. 1. q. Warden of the houſe of the ſcholars of Merton, Oxford, 9 Edward ii. I. 745. c. 1. a.

Merton prior and convent, their intereſt in the village of Tappelawe, 8 Richard i. I. 106. c. 2. w.

Meſchin, William, his barony, 14 Henry ii. I. 575. c. 2. t. Again, 33 Henry ii. I. 636. c. 1. s.

Meſleta or ſcuffle, I. 560. c. 1. s.

Meſſager, Robert le, of Newenton, proſecuted for irreverent ſpeech of the king, 9 Edward ii. II. 84.

Meſſages of the king, queen and prince ſent to the Exchequer, II. 121.

Meſſinden, Roger de, juſtice of the bank, 72 Henry iii. I. 236. Meſſendoun, the taxours retained the money levied there, II. 119.

Metham, John de, collector of the vintiſme for Yorkſhire, 5 Edward i. II. 181. c. 2. n.

Metingham, John de, juſticier of the common bench, 27 Edward i. II.

Meuling,

INDEX.

Meuling, Peter de, hereditary apprizer of Norfolk, &c. 27 Henry iii. II. 196. His abuse in the discharge of his office, II. 196. c. 1. *o.*

Meysey, Robert de, sherif of Herefordshire, about 52 Henry iii. II. 180. c. 1. *a.*

Micheldover, William de, 42 Henry iii. II. 79. c. 1. *w.*

Michelham, prior of, II. 13. c. 2. *m.*

Middelsex county amerc'd, 9 Edward i. I. 568. c. 2. *u.*

Middelton, See Grammaticus. Middelton hundred in Kent, I. 543. c. 1. *a.* The aid of Middeltoll in Kent, 14 Henry iii. 588. c. 2. *d.*

Middelton, William, made custos brevium of the common bench, 5 Edward i. I. 234. c. 2. *d.* Was custos rotulorum and brevium in the Judaism, 3 Edward i. I. 243 c. 2. *q.* Middelton abbey in the custody of Osbert de Dorchestre and Robert de Godmanneston, 31 Henry ii. I. 310. c. 2. *b.* Again in custody, 14 John, I. 312. c. 2, *e.* William de Middelton custos of the see of Ely, 14 Edward i. I. 313. c. 2. *i.* Manor of Middelton in Derbyshire held by Thomas de Furnival of Thomas de Chaworth, 14 Edward ii. I. 534. c. 1. John de Middelton parson in the bishopric, 8 Richard i. I. 716. The three Middeltons held of the king by earl Patric in theinage, 14 Henry iii. I. 440. c. 1. *m.* and I. 743. c. 1. *o.* Peter de Middelton commissioner of array for the wapentake of Clarhow, 16 Edward ii. II. 112. c. 1.

Midwinter village in Berkshire, 33 Henry ii. I. 546. c. 1. *l.*

Mienestoch in Hampshire, 28 Henry ii. II. 253. c. 2. *c.*

Mikelham, Robert de, his plea, 14 Henry iii. II. 78. c. 1. *o.*

Miklefeud, Edmund de, convicted and fined for procuring another person to be indicted, 34 Edward i. II. 65.

Mildehal, Norfolk, assised by Robert Mantel, 22 Henry ii. I. 703. c. 1. *k.*

Miles constabulary of Glocestre, 1 Stephen, I. 14. c. 2. *s.* John Miles of Somersetshire attach'd, 45 Henry iii. II. 79. c. 2. *y.*

Mills of the bishop of Durham, their ferm, 13 Henry iii. I. 717. c. 2. *l.*

Minaria and cambium, their produce in the bishopric, 8 Richard i. I. 715. c. 2.

Miner, Gislebert de, I. 147. c. 2. *a.* Drue the Miner fines to open a mine, 9 Henry ii. I. 471. c. 1. *u.*

Minority of king Henry iii. no perpetuities to be granted by the king's seal during it, I. 67. c. 1. *x.*

Minsterton, Ernewin de, his land in Notinghamshire, 5 Stephen, I. 426. c. 2. *u.*

Mints of the crown in sixteen principal places, 9 John, I. 290. c. 2. *zz.* Mints or exchanges, I. 290, 291. See Cambium. Mint and exchange of London, II. 98. Cambium or Mint of all England accompted for by Henry de Cornhil, 3 Richard i. II. 133. c. 1. *m.* and Hugh Oisel, 3 John, II. 133. c. 1. *n.* Keeper of the king's Mint had two shillings a day, 35 Henry iii. II. 204. c. 2. *m.*

Misdemeanors committed by sherifs and bailifs, &c. I. 140, 141.

Misericordia and amerciament, their difference, I. 526.

Misterton, Thomas son of Gilbert of, 4 John,

INDEX.

4 John, I. 566. c. 1. *x*. How far this manor in Northamptonshire was the priors de Novo Loco, I. 754. c. 2. *p*.

Mithesford hundred in Norfolk, I. 502. c. 1. *a*.

Modbert, his tenure from the bishop of Bath, an. 1121. I. 110. Married the daughter of Grenta de Stoke, ibid.

Modingham in Kent, the interest of the abbat of St John of Derteford in it, II. 165. c. 2. *x*.

Modius of wine cost seven shillings, 22 Henry ii. I. 368. c. 1. *r*. King of France gave annually to Christ's Church, Canterbury, an hundred modii of wine, in reverence of Thomas a Becket the martyr, before 3 John, I. 766. c. 1. *o*.

Moeles, John de, one of the Hampshire barons, 26 Edward i. I. 655. c. 2.

Mohaut, Roger de, Staffordshire, 2 Henry iii. I. 454. c. 1. *a*. Milisent de Mohaut, 27 Edward i. II. 209.

Mohun, the executors of Roger de, 42 Henry iii. II. 185. c. 1. *k*.

Moigne or Monachus, Henry son and Heir of William le, in Essex, his land which he held in capite by the serjeanty of the king's lardinary, 26 Edward i. I. 321. c. 2. *r*. Ralf predecessor of Henry had the same tenure, ibid. John Moigne, 8 Richard i. I. 323. c. 2. *b*. John le Moigne sherif of Cambridgeshire, before 40 Henry iii. I. 446. c. 1. *k*. Ralf Moin, 15 Henry ii. I. 450. c. 1. *l*. Berenger le Moine, 6 Henry iii. I. 554. c. 2. *k*. Geoffrey Moign has his donum remitted in Essex, 2 Henry ii. II. 687. c. 2. *k*.

Moiun, Durand de, in the time of Henry i. I. 112. c. 1. *m*. Ralf Moin, 14 Henry ii. 209. c. 2. *c*. William son and heir of John de Moiun his relief, 6 Henry iii. I. 318. c. 2. *z*. Lucia de Moiun her scutage fees, 3 John, I. 665. c. 2. *e*.

Molbrai, Roger de, his lands and honors in the custody of Robert de Widvil and Henry de Montfort, 5 Stephen, I. 297. c. 1. *d*. William de Molbrai, 3 John, I. 428. c. 1. *a*. Roger Molbrai's knights fees, 14 Henry ii. I. 574. William de Molbrai's escuage in Yorkshire for the king's ransom, 6 Richard i. I. 591. c. 1. *r*. William de, has the abbats of Fountain, Rival, and Byland his tenants, 11 John, I. 616. Nigel de Molbrai his scutage in Yorkshire, 3 Richard i. I. 637. c. 2. *f*. The scutage of William de Molbrai, 1 John, I. 638. c. 1. *i*. In what counties the fees of Nigel de Mubrai lay, 9 Henry iii. I. 679. c. 2. *k*. Roger de Bolbrai quit of tallage for his lands in Cambrigeshire, 9 John, I. 748. c. 2. *t*. See Mubrai.

Moleton, Thomas son of Lambert de, fines for respite of knighthood, 40 Henry iii. I. 509. Margaret his widow, 22 Edward i. II. 100. c. 1. *k*. See Multon.

Molle, John, 24 Henry iii. I. 496. c. 2. *q*. Roger de Moll. of Devonshire fines in an hundred pounds and two hundred marks for homicide, 5 Stephen, I. 497. c. 1. *y*.

Molseby, nuns of, their interest in the soke of Esingwald, Yorkshire, I. 329. c. 1. *w*.

Monastery of St Peter at Arlansa in in Spain, Pref. xix. c. 2.

Moncada,

INDEX.

Moncada, Don Pedro de, I. 54.
Moncellis, Engeran de, an. 1184. I. 166. c. 1. *i*. Fines for speeding of justice, ibid.
Monci, the executors of the late Walter de, 2 Edward ii. II. 187. c. 1. *x*.
Monemuthe, John de, one of the sureties of Walter de Beauchamp, 1 Henry iii. II. 150. c. 1. *n*.
Monetarii of Thetford and Norwich, I. 222. c. 1. *d*. Of fifteen places more, I. 290. William Monetarius of Carlisle, 16 Henry ii. I. 560. c. 1. *s*. Moneyours of London, Thetford, &c. 14 Henry ii. I. 590. c. 1. *k*. Moneyours excus'd, &c. I. 635. c. 1. *r*. Moneyours of Oxford, 5 Henry ii. I. 696. c. 2. *o*. Moneyours or keepers of the exchange to be free from tallage, I. 748. Moneyours, assayers and custodes cunei, II. 87, 88. Adam de Bedley Moneyour of London, 14 Henry iii. II. 317. c. 2. *b*.
Monks of Bath, temp. Henry i. II. 2. c. 2. *b*. Of Holy Trinity, Canterbury, have a benefaction from Louis king of France, I. 27. Of Ely recover the manour of Stoke, 14 Henry ii. I. 82. c. 1. *a*. Of Rochester, 29 Henry ii. I. 82. c. 1. *b*. Monks of Bath had a donation from Kenulf king of the Saxons, I. 109, 110. Of Holy Trinity in Canterbury not to be impleaded but before the king, I. 117. c. 1. *d*. Monks of Bordesley, ibid. Monks of Scardeburgh of the Cistercian order, I. 118. Monks of Stanlega near Chipeham, I. 217. c. 1. *i*. Monks of Holy Trinity on the Mount of Roan, I. 218. c. 1. *q*. Monks of Mealse in Yorkshire, 9 Richard i. I. 238. c. 1. *u*. Some particulars of the allowances of the Monks of York, I. 309. c. 1. *q*. Monks of Tame, Oxfordshire, I. 327. c. 1. *q*. Monks of Tinemue how they belong to St Albans, 5 John, I. 405. c. 1. *n*. Monks of Ely how impleaded by those of St Edmund about a market, 4 John, I. 437. c. 1. *x*.
Monte Acuto, John de, 12 John, I. 218. c. 1. *r*. The terra of John Montague in the king's hands, 14 John, I. 299. c. 1. *i*. His contest about the advouson of Langeberg, 2 John, I. 435. c. 1. *n*. William de Montacute justicier, 10 John, I. 442. c. 2. *e*. William de Monte Acuto, 1 John, I. 460. c. 1. *y*. Priory of Montague, 10 John, I. 479. c. 1. *x*. William de Montague fines for Chaldesey and Peddelton hundred, 1 John, I. 485. c. 2. *f*. William son of Drue de Montague amerced for not taking knighthood, 17 Henry iii. I. 510. c. 2. *e*. The honor of Richard de Mountague, 14 Henry ii. I. 527. c. 1. *c*. Simon de Mountague a baron summon'd to the Scotch war, 26 Edward i. I. 655. c. 2. John de Monte Acuto his ten fees, 14 Henry iii. I. 661. c. 1. *i*. Marries his daughter, Catharine, and heiress, to Warin Basset, ibid. Baron William's scutage, 3 John, I. 665. c. 2. *g*. John de Mountague gives the manor of Torp to the canons of Wroxton, I. 672. c. 1. *i*. William de Mountague, earl of Saresbiry, made mareschal for life, temp. Edward iii. I. 797. c. 1. *w*. Prior of Montacute, 4 Edward i. II. 77. c. 1. *k*. John de Mountague sherif

INDEX.

rif of Somerset and Dorsetshire, 34 Edward i. II. 180. c. 2. *k*.

Monte Alto, John de, one of the barons summon'd against Scotland, 26 Edward i. I. 655. c. 1. Milisent de Monte Alto, 27 Edward i. II. 119. Adam's oath to accompt as sherif of Lancaster, 53 Henry iii. II. 241. c. 2. *t*.

Monte Aureo, Walter de, 15 John, I. 773. Accompts for the assise of woad in Lincolnshire, I. 774. c. 1.

Montebegun, Roger de, temp. John, I. 57. c. 1. *r*. Attests a grant, ibid.

Montecanesi, Hubert de, had possession of Hugh Bigot's manor of Seham, 5 Stephen, I. 482. c. 1. *c*. See Munchensy. William de Monte Canisio, his claim on the manor or hundred of Berdstaple, 56 Henry iii. II. 80. c. 1. *a*.

Monteigny, Nicolas and Isabel de, an. 1208. make a grant in frankalmoigne to the church of Bonport, I. 163.

Mont Ernulf, William de, 2 John, I. 523. c. 1. *t*. Delivers up the wardship of John son of Philip de Holm, ibid.

Montfort, Robert de, accus'd of high treason, an. 1107. by Henry i. I. 29. c. 1. *m*. Hugh de, in the Conqueror's time, I. 32. c. 1. *e*. Robert was hereditary constable, I. 40. c. 2. *g*. Simon Montfort his share of Robert's lands and honors, I. 51. Simon's treason and forfeiture, I. 52. c. 1. *k*. Robert de Monteforti, 5 Stephen, I. 58. c. 2. *b*. Peter de, 49 Henry iii. I. 70. Clementia de Montfort, an. 1184. I. 168. c. 1. *l*. Robert Montfort, 5 Stephen, I. 262. Henry de Montfort join'd with Robert de Widvil as custos of the lands of Roger de Molbrai, 5 Stephen, I. 297. c. 1. *d*. Simon de Montfort fined in ten thousand marks, 31 Henry iii. I. 326. c. 2. *o*. Simon de Montfort earl of Leycester, I. 496. c. 2. *s*. Simon has the moiety of the honor of Leicester, 29 Henry iii. I. 595. c. 1. *n*. Simon, II. 120. Peter de Montfort ambassador into France, 40 Henry iii. II. 218. c. 1. *w*. See II. 269. c. 2. *f*. Robert de Montfort's quit claim, 3 Edward i. II. 320. c. 2. *e*.

Montgomeri, Bartholomew and Robert de, their tenure in Normandy, temp. John, I. 156. c. 1. *g*.

Montibus, Ralf de, 3 John, I. 171. c. 1. *w*. Quits the mill of Canteraiene, which he held of Ralf Taisson, ibid.

Montpincon, Ralf, dapifer of the Conqueror, I. 53.

Mora, Ralf de, vice-sherif, 7 John, I. 276. c. 2. *x*. William de la More master of the knights Templars, 34 Edward i. I. 613. c. 2. *t*. Poncius, 1 Edward i. I. 770. Poncius de Mora accompts for the years he was chamberlain of London, and buyer of the king's wines, 57 Henry iii. I. 778. c. 1. *b*. William de la More master of the Temple in custody, 1 Edward ii. II. 30. c. 1. *f*. Has liberty to take the air, ibid. Poncius de Mora has preference for the recovery of his debts, 7 Edward i. II. 86. c. 1. *t*. Nicolas de Mora of Shropshire, 29 Henry iii. II. 101. c. 1. *r*. Robert de la More one of the commissioners of array for the wapentak of Holderness, 16 Edward ii. II. 112. c. 1. Poncius, 5 Edward i. II. 218. c. 1. *a*. John de

INDEX.

de la More mareschal of the Exchequer, 10 Edward i. II. 286. c. 1. e. David de la More usher of the Receipt, 52 Henry iii. II. 293. c. 2. c.

Morant, William, pays queen's gold, 10 John, I. 350. c. 2. s. Mr Jordan de Morant, late constable of Bourdeaux, 15 Edward ii. II. 280.

Mordone quit of tallage, 9 John I. 748. c. 2. t.

Moreby, Henry, has Ouse and Derwent under array, 16 Edward ii. II. 112. c. 2.

Morel, Nicolas, 8 Richard i. I. 452. c. 2. o. William Morel, 12 Henry ii. I. 557. c. 2. i.

Moresheved, the manor of Nicolas de Stutevil, 5 Henry iii. II. 198. c. 2. w.

Moreston, John de, of Kent, his aid, 14 Henry ii. I. 584. c. 2. q.

Morevill, Hugh de, how his lands descended, 4 John, I. 114. c. 2. u. Had the officium forestæ, I. 114. Eudo de, before 26 Henry iii. I. 246. c. 1. a. Hugh de, 2 John, I. 403. c. 1. p. Hugh de Morevil, 23 Henry ii. II. 200. c. 2. g. His land went to Richard de Luci, 6 John, II. 253. c. 1. y.

Morewic, Hugh de, dapifer, 30 Henry ii. I. 51. c. 1. y. Occurs, an. 1184. I. 168. c. 2. Baron of the Exchequer, I. 215 c. 2. d. Hugh de Morewic, 5 Henry iii. I. 453. c. 1. q. Hugh de, has one knight's fee in Northumberland, 29 Henry iii. I. 596. c. 1. r.

Morgan, Hamon, justice errant, 20 Henry ii. I. 125.

Morin, Peter, deliver'd in the oblata, 3 John, I. 51. c. 1. m. Reynald son of Morin one of the sureties of Hugh Cordele, 5 Stephen, II. 197 c. 1. q.

Moriton, Geoffry earl of, an. 1094. Pref. xxv. c. 1. f. Goiffred earl of Moreton in Normandy convokes his proceres, I. 18. John earl of Moreton remov'd Longchamp from being chief justicier, I. 196. Had the lands of the honor of Lancaster, 1 Richard i. I 205. c. 2. l. The honor of Moreton, 10 Richard i. I. 316. c. 2. i. Small fees of Moreton, 18 Henry ii. I. 630. c. 2. e. and I. 649. Baron Nicolas de Meriet holds of the honor of Moreton, 3 John, I. 665. c. 2. g.

Morlawe, prioress and nuns of, 22 Henry iii. I. 391. c. 1. u. Have their trentisme remitted in Bucks, ibid.

Morley, William de, one of the barons summon'd by the king's writ on the Scotch expedition, 26 Edward i. I. 655. c. 1. Morley wapentak has a commission of array sent to it, 16 Edward ii. II. 112. c. 1.

Morsel, Ralf de, of Devonshire, 5 Stephen, I. 425. c. 2. d. Fines pro recto against Robert de Baenton, ibid.

Mortdancestour, or de morte antecessorum, writ of, I. 36. c. 2. g. A fine for the recognition of it in the king's court, 1 Richard i. I. 98. 105. Again, I. 116. A writ of Mordancestour, I. 213. Pleas of Mortdancestor when reserved to the bank, I. 790.

Mortemer, Robert de, impleaded, 27 Henry ii. I. 97. c. 1. s. Roger de Mortimer justicier of Normandy, 3 John, I. 171. c. 1. u. Robert de Mortemer fines, 23 Henry ii. I. 211. c. 1. k. Ralf de Mortemer of

INDEX.

of Lincolnshire, 1 John, I. 324. c. 1. e. Robert de Mortemer, 26 Henry ii. I. 431. c. 1. b. Hawise widow of William de Mortemer her fine, 25 Edward i. I. 466. c. 2. c. Gilbert de Mortemer, 6 Henry iii. I. 496. c. 1. k. William de Mortemer, 24 Henry iii. I. 496. c. 2. q. William de, plegius, 2 John, I. 520. c. 2. h. Roger de Mortuo mari quit of scutage for the king's ransom, 7 Richard i. I. 591. c. 2. t. Roger de Mortemer one of the receivers of the last vintism of Henry iii. I. 610. c. 1. i. Robert de Mortemer fines for aid from his tenants, 10 John, I. 616. c. 2. c. Roger de Mortemer summon'd to the war against Scotland by the king's letter, 26 Edward i. I. 655. c. 1. viz. in Shropshire or Staffordshire. Edmund de, one of the Herefordshire barons summon'd to the war against Scotland, 26 Edward i. ibid. Hugh de Mortimer summon'd by writ to the same war though in the king's court, 26 Edward i. I. 655. c. 2. Hugh de Mortuomari's lands in Herefordshire, temp. Stephen, II. 138. c. 2. e. Hugh de Mortemer sherif of Stafford and Shropshire, 56 Henry iii. II. 142. c. 1. a. One of the sureties of Walter de Beauchamp, 1 Henry iii. II. 150. c. 1. n. Roger de Mortuomari one of the king's council, 53 Henry iii. II. 171. c. 1.

Mortgage or vadium of the land of Pacey, an. 1184. I. 168. c. 2. William Fossard amerced for taking a mortgage unjustly, 17 Henry ii. I. 546. c. 1. i.

Morton, Elyas de, undersherif of Kent, instead of William Trussel, before 25 Edward i. II. 44. c. 2. r.

Mot, John, a sea officer, 12 Edward ii. II. 110. c. 1. z.

Mota of Warwick, I. 370. c. 1. f.

Moteier in pleas remov'd, 6 John, I. 405. c. 2. t.

Mouncy, Walter de, one of the king's barons and courtiers, 26 Edward i. I. 655. c. 2. See Monci.

Moune, John de, a baron summon'd to the Scotch war, 26 Edward i. I. 655. c. 2. Reginald de Moun has respite in Somerset and Dorsetshire, 28 Henry iii. II. 255. c. 1. k.

Mountjoye, Ralf de, sherif of Lancaster, amerc'd for not keeping his attermination, 27 Edward i. II. 236. c. 2. l.

Moyne, John le, justicier of the Jews, 50 Henry iii. I. 234. c. 1. b. See Moigne. William le Moyne sherif of Cambridge and Huntendonshire, 7 Edward i. II. 160. c. 2. m.

Mubrai his convention with Stutevill touching a barony, temp. Henry ii. I. 115. Roger de Munbray his annual fee, 4 John, I. 175. c. 2. q. Alexander de Moubray constabulary of the castle of Tunbrugg, 15 Edward ii. I. 383. c. 2.

Mucegros, Miles de, one of the justices, 20 Henry ii. I. 124. c. 2. d. Richard de Mucegros his payment for the ferm of Glocestershire, 9 John, I. 189. c. 2. e. The share which Alice de Mucegros had of Hugh Dyve's barony, before 35 Edward i. I. 321. Richard de Mucegros of Worcestershire, 35 Henry iii. II. 78. c. 2. s. Richard de Mucengros sherif of Gloucestershire, 9 John, II. 140. c. 1. m.

Mucheldene, John de, 5 Edward i. II. 74. c. 1. t. Impleads Agnes de Fraxino

INDEX.

Fraxino in the Exchequer contrary to Magna Charta, ibid.

Muchelgate, Aldred de, of Yorkshire, accompts for the chattels of an intestate, who dyed in his house, 16 Henry ii. I. 346. c. 1 *h*.

Muchelney abbey in custody of Alexander de Luveigni, 19 Henry ii. I. 308. c. 2. *h*. The abbat pays three marks of gold or thirty of silver, 3 John, I. 486. Held of the king in capite, 6 Edward i. I. 623. c. 1. *h*. Frere John de Barnevile abbat elect, 36 Henry iii. I. 623. c. 1. *h*. Accompts for one fee, 14 Henry iii. I. 661. c. 1. *i*.

Mudford fair in Northamptonshire lasts eight days, I. 415. c. 1. *s*. Obtain'd by Roger Bertram, 9 Henry iii. ibid. Terric de Mudiford, 10 John, I. 489. c. 2. *q*. One of Robert de Mandevil's Jury, ibid.

Mulcastre, William de, sherif of Cumberland, 27 Edward i. II. 236.

Muleford in Barrocscira, the land of William de Carrou, 10 John, I. 451. c. 2. *c*.

Mules, Sampson de, his tenure in capite by sergeanty, before 19 Henry iii. I. 326. c. 2. *m*. Roger de Mueles, 14 Henry ii. I. 512. c. 1. *p*. Fines for a concord, ibid.

Multon, Bartholomew de, had a wardship of the land, heir and widow of Lambert de Ybetoft, 4 John, I. 324. c. 2. *g*. Multon in Northamptonshire, claims about it, 4 John, I. 437. c. 2. *y*. Thomas de Muleton fermer of Lincolnshire, 8 John, I. 461. c. 2. *g*. Thomas son of Lambert de Muleton his knight's fee in Copland, 38 Henry iii. I. 596. c. 2. *w*. Thomas de Multon to attend the Scotch expedition with the Lincolnshire barons, 26 Edward i. I. 654. c. 2. Thomas de Muleton tallager of Cumberland, 19 Henry iii. I. 735. c. 1. *g*. Thomas de Muleton amerced, 35 Henry iii. I. 795. c. 2. *r*. Lambert de Muleton has the fee of Copland, 29 Henry iii. II. 182. c. 2. *x*. By marriage with the eldest daughter of Richard de Lucy, ib. Thomas de Multon justice itinerant, 14 Henry iii. II. 253. c. 1. *b*. See Moleton.

Mumfort, Turstan de, 10 John, I. 100. c. 2. *z*. Claims Witton, Cave, Cotingham, Butercram, Schreingham, Langeton, and Hese against Eustace and Nicolas de Stutevil, ibid. Robert de Munfort, 25 Henry ii. I. 210. c. 1. *f*. Simon de Muntfort's land in the hands of the king, 14 John, I. 299. c. 1. *k*. See Montefort.

Munbi, Yvo de, in Lincolnshire, his land and heir in the wardship of Philip Fitz-Robert, 1 John, I. 324. c. 2. *f*. Alan de Munbi, 12 John, I. 410. c. 2. *o*. Fines for liberties, ibid.

Muncelyn, Richard, 25 Henry iii. I. 119. Appeal'd for a battery, I. 120. c. 1. *g*.

Munchensy or Mons Canesii in Kent, I. 446. c. 1. *h*. Warin de, 31 Henry iii. ibid. William de, fines for his lands in Essex and Hertfordshire, 3 John, I. 679. c. 1. *x*. See Muntchenesi.

Munctunehampton subject to the abbess of Caen, had four fees, 29 Henry iii. I. 595. c. 2. *q*.

Mundevil, Helyas de, pays a relief for four knights fees, 14 Henry ii. I. 316. c. 1. *y*.

Mundham,

INDEX.

Mundham, in part was the prior of Boxgrave's, I. 599. c. 2. g.

Mune, Glocestershire, its aid, 23 Henry ii. I. 604. c. 1. k.

Munemue, Gilbert de, amerced, 23 Henry ii. I. 542. c. 1. o. Baderun de, his knights fees in Herefordshire, 14 Henry ii. I. 575. c. 1. q. John de Munemue has fifteen fees in Herefordshire, 38 Henry iii. I. 596. c. 2. x.

Mungay, Rafe de, a recognition against him, 28 Henry ii. I. 104. c. 2. o.

Mungumeri, its relation to the prior of Covintre, I. 640. c. 1. w.

Munketon, Henry de, one of the commissioners of array for the wapentake of Aynsty, 16 Edward ii. II. 112. c. 1.

Munpincon, the wife of Fulk de, 12 Henry ii. I. 447. c. 1. q.

Muntchenesi, Roger de, 14 Henry ii. I. 82. c. 1. a. Monks of Ely recover the manor of Stoke from him and his wife, ibid.

Munteburg, Hugh de, his scutage, 7 Henry ii. I. 628. c. 2. x.

Muntesii catti, mountain-cats, I. 367. c. 1. g.

Muntfichet, Alexander de, 5 John, I. 480. c. 1. h. William de Muntfichet's knights fees, 14 Henry ii. I. 573. Gilbert de Muntfichet his aid, 14 Henry ii. I. 586. c. 1. x. Richard de Muntfichet his scutage for his knights fees, 3 Richard i. I. 637. c. 2. e. Gilbert has his donum in Essex remitted, 2 Henry ii. I. 687. c. 2. k. Richard de Muntfichet baron of the Exchequer, 18 Henry iii. II. 45. c. 2. i. Richard was one of the pledges for Ralf de Cornhul, 9 Richard i. II. 198. c. 1. r.

Muntgumery, the scutage of the army of, 9 Henry iii. I. 679. c. 2. k.

Muntviron, John de, renders his relief for the terra of Ralf de Muntviron in Essex, 22 Henry ii. I. 316. c. 1. a.

Murce, Oboli de, not explained by our author, I. 278.

Murdach, Hugh, justice itinerant, 26 Henry ii. I. 138. c. 1. z. Hugh and Ralf barons of the Exchequer, 30 Henry ii. I. 215. c. 2. d. Hugh accompts for the abbey of Selebi, 31 Henry ii. I. 309. c. 2. t. Ralf Murdac fines for the good will of Richard i. I. 474. c. 1. b. Ralf Murdac fines, 7 Richard i. I. 484. c. 1. t. Ralf Murdac accompts for the ferm and profits of the seigneury of William de Luvetot, 29 Henry ii. I. 535. c. 1. Was then sherif of Notingham and Derbyshire, ibid. Richard Mordac holds of the church of Chichester, temp. Henry ii. I. 576. c. 1. y.

Murders and manslaughter amerced, I. 543.

Musard, the terra of Hasculf de, in the king's hand, 1 Richard i. I. 298. c. 2. u. His daughter refused in marriage, 5 Richard i. I. 503. c. 2. r. Ralf Musard of Notingham or Derbyshire, the scutage for his fees, 1 John, I. 638. c. 2. k. Ralf Musard fines to marry where he will, 3 Richard i. II. 224. c. 2. p. Held of the earl of Moreton, Gloucestershire, ibid.

Muscamp, terra Thomæ de, 33 Henry ii. I. 4. c. 1. The barony or honor of Thomas de Muscamp in the king's hands, 31 Henry ii. I. 297. c. 2. u.

Mustrel, the terra of Engelram de, in the king's hands, 1 Richard i. I. 298. c. 2. x. Mentioned again, II. 189. c. 1. d.

Mutere, Grinchetel, accompts for a wreck

INDEX.

wreck in Lincolnshire, 5 Stephen, I. 343. c. 1. *h.*

Mutford, Roger de, of Somersetshire, attached, 45 Henry iii. II. 79. c. 1. *y.*

Mutton, John de, 6 John, I. 99. c. 2. *u.* John son of Nicolas de Mutton, his claim on Lutiwude, 6 John, I. 794. c. 1. *h.*

Mynty, a member of the manor and abbat of Cirencester, 9 Edward ii. I. 753. c. 1. *m.*

N.

Nafferton and Matsen, those lands belonged to the Ulecots, I. 463. c. 1. *r.* Before 5 Henry iii. ibid. Naffreton tallaged, 30 Henry iii. I. 710. c. 1. *w.*

Nammi or rescues amerced, I. 548. c. 1. *s, t, u.* Pleas de vetito namio, II. 168.

Naparius, Oinus, his wife's livery, 5 Stephen, I. 364. c. 1. *n.*

Naperia of the king, 9 John, I. 461. c. 2. *h.* Walter de la Naperye, 52 Henry iii. II. 6. c. 1. *a.*

Napier, Ralf le, of Waltham, his aid, 14 Henry ii. I. 586. c. 1. *x.*

Naples, Roger the first king of, a vassal of the see of Rome, an. 1130. I. 5. c. 1. Master justicier of Naples, I. 37. Great seneschal, I. 55. Gave the title of Magister to its principal officers, I. 58. Had a grand chamberlain, I. 60. Underwent much the same alterations from the Normans as England, I. 183. And had its great officers conformable, ibid.

Narrator de banco, or sergeant at law, I. 236. c. 2. *k.*

Nassum Burgi deafforested, 2 Henry iii. I. 412. c. 1. *c.*

Navineby in the honor of Lancaster belonged to Robert Ruffus, before 3 Henry iii. I. 300. c. 2. *w.*

Navy, king's commanders there styled constabularii, I. 40. c. 1. *b.* Navigii regis justiciarii, I. 142.

Nazareth, the abbat of Ramsey fines to remove that archbishop, 5 John, I. 505. c. 1. *i.*

Necton or Notton, John de, 9 Edward ii. II. 85. c. 1. *r.* Frere Roger de Neketon monk of St Edmund's, 42 Henry iii. II. 89. c. 1. *l.* Richard de Neketon moneyour of London, 14 Henry iii. II. 317. c. 2. *b.*

Neirenuit, the land and heir of Miro, before 13 John, I. 481. c. 1. *p.*

Nenn, Robert de, of Lincoln, his tallage, 4 John, I. 737. c. 2. *w.*

Ness and Grafho wapentakes, I. 473. c. 1. *m.*

Nessewic, Yorkshire, its tallage, 30 Henry iii. I. 710. c. 1. *w.*

Nethford, Emma, concubine of the presbyter of, amerced, 8 Richard i. I. 556. c. 1. *m.*

Neubaud, Geoffrey de, chancellor of the Exchequer, 5 Edward i. II. 52. c. 2. *a.* and 8 Edward i. II. 62. c. 1. *o.*

Neubote canons discharged by charter from all customs of things for their own use, 2 John, I. 771. c. 1. *d.* See Niwebote.

Newbotel in the bishopric tallaged, 11 Edward i. I. 720. c. 2. *u.*

Neuburg, or Novo Burgo, Robert de, dapifer and justicier of Normandy, an. 1158. I. 53. c. 1. *q.* John prior of Newburg manucaptor of Gilbert de Geyles, 39 Henry iii. II. 243. c. 2. *g.* Ambrose de Novo Burgo mareschal of the Exchequer, 12 Edward ii. II. 262. c. 2. Made so by Thomas de Brotherton earl of Norfolk, 9 Edward ii. II. 287.

Nevelun,

INDEX.

Nevelun, Andrew de, his petition to the prior of Chikefand, 9 John, I. 480. c. 2. *m*. Peter fon of Nevelun, 8 Richard i. I. 775. c. 1. *q*. Peter Nevelun fherif of London, 22 Henry iii. II. 215. c. 1. *u*.

Nevill, Ralf de, carries the great feal to the bifhop of Winchefter, 15 John, I. 67. c. 1. *w*. Geoffrey de Neovill, 6 Henry iii. I. 86. c. 1. *u*. Ærnifius de Nevil, 27 Henry ii. I. 97. c. 1. *r*. William de Nevil, ibid. c. 1. *s*. H. de Nevill his inquifition, I. 98. c. 2. *o*. Alan de Nevill juftice of the foreft, 20 Henry ii. I. 125. Alan de Nevill junior, juftice, 24 Henry ii. I. 133. c. 2. *z*. Holds pleas of the foreft, 16 Henry ii. I. 144. c. 2. *b*. Hugh de Nevill, I. 203. c. 1. *d*. Hugh de Nevill married the daughter and heirefs of Henry de Cornhull, 4 John, I. 237. c. 2. *q*. Pays 500 marks, 10 John, I. 263. c. 2. *o*. Ernife Nevil one of the fermers of the abbey of Selebi, 31 Henry ii. I. 309. c. 2. *t*. Tefta de Nevill's roll, 26 Edward i. I. 321. c. 2. *r*. Geoffrey de Neovil fherif of Yorkfhire, 7 Henry iii. I. 329. c. 1. *w*. Henry de Nevil pays queen's gold, 12 John, I. 351. c. 1. *y*. Euftace de Nevil his affignment, 2 John, I. 393. c. 2. *f*. Henry de Nevill, 6 John, I. 428. c. 2. *c*. Hugh de Nevil has the Golfe in Lincolnfhire, 30 Henry ii. I. 431. c. 1. *g*. Grace wife of Adam de Nevill, 1 John, I. 434. c. 2. *l*. Walter de Nevil, 3 John, I. 447. c. 2. *c*. Hugh de Nevil diftrains the earl of Augi, 4 John, I. 453. c. 1. *s*. Adam de Nevil, 1 John, I. 471. c. 2. *y*. The wife of Hugh de Nevil fines to lye with her hufband, 6 John, ibid. c. 2. *a*. Had the foreftaria, anfwers for efcapes, and paffes a long accompt, 14 John, I. 475. c. 1. *k*. Henry de Nevil of Burrede, Yorkfhire, 7 Henry iii. ibid. c. 2. *p*. Richard de Nevil fines to have the king's requeft, that Ifolda Bifet may take him for her hufband, 12 John, I. 481. c. 1. *o*. Geoffrey de Nevil maried Emma de Humez, before 5 Richard i. I. 483. c. 2. *n*. Henry de Nevil has Afkebi and Teinton in Lincolnfhire, 1 John, I. 486. c. 1. *i*. William de Nevil's convention with the abbat of Hulm, 9 Henry ii. I. 501. c. 2. *r*. Hugh de Nevil's new year's gift, 3 John, I. 504. c. 2. *a*. Henry de Nevil, 6 John, I. 506. c. 1. *s*. John de Nevil, 2 John, I. 520. c. 2. *h*. Henry de Nevil, 8 John, I. 528. c. 1. *f*. Pleas of Alan de Nevil, 13 Henry ii. I. 539. c. 1. *w*. Henry de Nevil, 10 Richard i. I. 542. c. c. *u*. Turold de Nevil, 14 Henry ii. I. 545. c. 1. *z*. Tefta de Nevil his accompt of certificates, &c. I. 632. Joflen de Nevil, 33 Henry ii. I. 636. c. 1. *s*. Thomas, 31 Henry ii. I. 645. c. 1. *q*. Henry fon of Geoffrey de Nevil, and Henry fon of Hugh de Nevil, their fcutage, 5 John, I. 650. c. 1. *n*. Herbert de Nevil's tallage for his lands in the foke of Pikering, 30 Henry iii. I. 710. c 1. *w*. Joflan de Nevil tallages Lincolnfhire, 8 John, I. 734. c. 2. *b*. Hugh de Nevil warden of the fea ports in the counties of Devon, Cornwal, Dorfet and Southampton, 15 John, I. 773. Robert de Nevil conftable of the caftle of Hamburg, 52 Henry iii. II. 11. c. 2. *d*. Hugh de Nevil, 6 Henry iii. II. 27. c. 1. *c*. Ralf de Nevil keeper of the feal, has the church of Lutegarefhal and Stratton, by

INDEX.

by his own sign manual, 16 John, II. 43. c. 1. *m.* Robert de Nevil justicier, 3 Henry iii. ibid. c. 2. *n.* Ralf de Nevil's relation to Wichtone, 2 Henry iii. II. 116. c. 1. *r.* Geoffrey de Nevil sherif of Wiltshire, 9 John, II. 140. c. 1. *l.* John de Nevil sherif of Lincolnshire, 12 Edward ii. II. 179. c. 2. *w.* William de Nevil late sherif of Warwick and Leicestershire, 15 Edward ii. II. 103. c. 2. *f.* Henry son of Hugh de Nevil disseised of his land for not paying his fine, 3 John, II. 210. c. 2. *z.* Alan de Nevil to accompt for the forest of Savernak, Wiltshire, 9 Henry ii. II. 220. c. 1. *o.* Hugh de Nevil amerced for the forfeit of John Wac, 12 John, II. 235. c. 2. *w.* Peter de Nevil amerced, &c. 1 Edward i. II. 242. c. 1. *w.* H. de Nevil, 4 John, II. 253. c. 1. *z.* John de Nevil mareschal of the Exchequer, 32 Henry iii. II. 284. c. 2. *z.* and 31 Henry iii. II. 285. c. 2. *c.* Again, 35 Henry iii. II. 289. c. 1. *u.*

Newburne near Newcastle, I. 403. c. 2. *y.*

Newcastle on Tine has a grant that no Jew should live among them, 18 Henry iii. I. 260. Have a confirmation of liberties, 3 John, I. 403. c. 2. *y.* How far it belonged to the Ulecots, I. 463. c. 1. *r.* Fine for the king's welcome, 3 John, I. 504. c. 2. *b.* Amerced for forcing a knight to swear, 14 Henry ii. I. 558. c. 2. *u.* The custody of its castle, 21 Henry iii. I. 593. c. 2. *e.* Newcastel, Staffordshire, its donum, 2 Richard i. I. 698. c. 2. *p.* See I. 716. 772.

Neweham, Juliana daughter of Fulk de, I. 82. Her final concord with the prior and monks of Rochester, 29 Henry ii. I. 155. 213. c. 1. *p.*

Newenham bailifs supply the king with lampreys, 32 Henry iii. I. 376. c. 2. *z.*

Newent priory, I. 595. c. 2. *q.*

Newerk, William de, official of York, 42 Henry iii. II. 184. c. 2. *h.*

Neweton land, I. 427. c. 2. *r.*

Neweton park, I. 492. c. 2. *y.*

Newinton, Cumberland, I. 672. c. 2. *l.*

Newport [Paignel] manor granted to Walter de Kirkham, 14 Henry iii. I. 418.

New Temple at London, one of the king's treasuries, I. 267. 271.

Neyr, Robert le, 45 Henry iii. II. 79. c. 1. *y.*

Nicholescira, I. 143. c. 1. *k.* See Lincoln.

Nichtwac, Stephen, 23 Henry ii. I. 548. c. 1. *r.* Amerced for exporting corn without licence, ibid.

Nicol or Lincoln, Alured de, has Winterburn, 11 John, I. 472. c. 1. *d.* Alured de Nicole to be arrested by the sherif of Somersetshire, 41 Henry iii. II. 308. c. 1. *a.*

Nicolas archdeacon of Ely has the king's seal, 44 Henry iii. I. 70. c. 1. *h.* His commendation, ibid. Nicolas archdeacon of London, 1 Richard i. I. 311. c. 2. *i.* Jeremy of S. Nicolas sherif of London, 21 Henry ii. II. 206. c. 1. *t.*

Niewebote, the daughter of Philip de, 9 Richard i. I. 202. c. 1. *w.* See Niwebote.

Nieweham, Glocestershire, tallaged, 7 Richard i. I. 703. c. 2. *n.* See Newenham.

Niewentone, Thomas and Walter, about 7 Richard i. I. 316. c. 2. *h.* Walter son of Thomas de Niewenton, 7 Richard i. I. 184. c. 2. *x.*

Nigel

INDEX.

Nigel bishop of Ely, I. 79. The provision he made for his son, ibid. Bishop of Ely baron of the Exchequer, and the king's treasurer, temp. Henry ii. I. 209. c. 1. *b.*

Nimelande, Daniel de, 10 John, I. 442. c. 2. *d.* Appealed of manslaughter, ibid.

Niwebald, a village in Yorkshire, I. 547. c. 2. *g.*

Niwebigging village belonged to Bernard de Baillol, 16 Henry ii. I. 554. c. 1. *n.* Its donum, 3 Richard i. I. 698. c. 2. *q.*

Niwebote, Philip de, in whose custody his daughter was, 8 Richard i. I. 202. c. 1. *w.* I. 323. c. 2. *b.*

Niweport, its aid, 14 Henry ii. I. 586. c. 2. Nieweport repaired by Richard de Luci sherif of Essex, 2 Henry ii. I. 687. c. 2. *k.* Its tallage or assise, 19 Henry ii. I. 701. c. 1. *z.* Again, 1 Richard i. I. 703. c. 1. *l.* Its tallage, 2 Henry iii. I. 706. c. 1. *b.*

Niwerch, I. 307. c. 2. *z.* The provosts and hundred of, ibid.

Niwiton, William, clerk of Bayeux fines for this church, 10 John, I. 489. c. 1. *n.*

Niz, Reginald de, 2 John, I. 520. c. 1. *c.* The summ he was condemned in to be levied by lay force, if the ecclesiastics could not compel him, ibid.

Nocton, Afzelin de, 24 Henry ii. I. 211. c. 2. *l.* Accompts as pledge of Jordan de Waltervill, ibid.

Noel, Tomas, a writ of Mortdancestour against him in Shropshire, 3 John, I. 213. Custos of the bishoprick and abbey of Chester, 31 Henry ii. I. 310. c. 2. *y, z.* William Noel sued for trespass, 21 Edward i. II. 81.

Nonant. See Nunant. Henry de Nonant of Devonshire, 23 Henry ii. I. 542. c. 1. *l.* Alice de Nonant's honor of Dertinton, Devonshire, seized for marrying without the king's licence, 33 Henry ii. I. 637. c. 1. *a, b.*

Non-appearances amerc'd, & quia non habuit quem plegiavit, I. 554.

Nonewyc, Roger de, has a commission of array for the wapentake of Rypoun, 16 Edward ii. II. 112. c. 1.

Norcuri in Devonshire, Robert provost of, their aid, 14 Henry ii. I. 588. c. 2. *c.*

Nordley, Shropshire, tallaged, 1 John, I. 705. c. 2. *y.* Again, 8 John, I. 734. c. 1. *z.*

Noreis, Ralf le, amerced for not taking a thief, 14 Henry ii. I. 555. c. 1. *c.*

Norflet in Kent, its aid, 14 Henry ii. I. 584. c. 2. *q.*

Norfolcia, Goddard and Robert de, fine for a concord, 26 Henry ii. I. 104. c. 1. *l.* Gilbert de Norfolch, 1 John, I. 401. c. 1. *a.* Whose pledge, ibid.

Norfolk, that title united with Warenne, 2 Edward ii. I. 47. c. 1. *y.* That county amerced, 31 Henry iii. I. 556. c. 1. *n.* Repeated, I. 567. c. 2. *m.* Its aid for marrying the king's daughter, 14 Henry ii. I. 589. Accompt of its chief barons, 31 Henry iii. I. 594. c. 2. *i.* Norfolk and Suffolk seem to be under different sherifs, 2 Henry ii. I. 700. c. 2. *u, w.* The assise of the two counties settled by Robert Mantel, &c. 22 Henry ii. I. 703. c. 1. *k.* Thomas de Brotherton earl of Norfolk, 9 Edward ii. I. 752. c. 2. *l.* Thomas earl of Norfolk has the mareschalcy granted to him and his male-heirs by Edward i. I. 797. But dies

INDEX.

dies without heirs male, ibid. See Bigot.

Norhala, William de, archdeacon of Gloceſtre, accompts for the ſee of Rocheſter, 31 Henry ii. I. 311. c. 1. e.

Norham caſtle ſupplied from the revenues of the ſee of Durham, 8 Richard i. I. 714. c. 1. g. Salomon de Norham, ibid. c. 2. Caſtle, I. 717. c. 2. l.

Norman, of Yorkſhire, Adam ſon of, fines to marry his daughter to William ſon of William, ſon of Hugh de Leelay, 31 Henry ii. I. 512. c. 2. w. The tallage of John Norman of London, 14 Henry iii. I. 709. c. 1. s.

Normandy, how far its court has preſcribed to England, I. 28. Its great officers, I. 28, 29. Henry duke of, made juſticiary of England after the pacification between him and king Stephen, I. 34. c. 1. s. Conformity between the juſticier of Normandy and England, I. 37, 38. Its Exchequer, I. 156. The Exchequer of Normandy differs from ours, I. 177. The Normans ſettle much the ſame economy in Naples as in England, I. 183. Normans recovered Naples from the Greeks and Saracens, ibid. The like method was uſed in Normandy as here, I. 518. c. 1. s, t, &c.

Normanton, Henry de, underſherif of Yorkſhire, 1 Edward i. II. 207. c. 2. g.

Normanvil, Hugh de, of Northumberland, fines for a writ, 10 John, I. 443. c. 2. l. Robert de Normanvil claims Thorp, 7 Henry iii. I. 445. c. 2. e. Emma de Normanvil with her three ſiſters, Roheiſe, Margaret, and Juliana, fine to marry to whom they will, 7 Richard i. I. 464. c. 1. d.

Norreis, Roger le, 9 John, I. 452. c. 2. k. Deraigned for juſticing of Robert de Ros, ibid. See Noreis.

Northampton, the monks and caſtle of, 5 Stephen, I. 330. c. 2. d. Fine for their ferm and liberties, 3 Richard i. I. 399. c. 1. b. Fine to hold their town in capite, 31 Henry ii. I. 503. c. 1. n. Abbat of St James without Northampton held in frankalmoign, 34 Edward i. I. 671. c. 1. g. Its donum, 2 Henry ii. I. 695. c. 1. z. Friers minours of Northampton quit of tallage, 52 Henry iii. I. 749. c. 2. y. Abbat of St James, I. 756. c. 1. s. St James without Northampton has the mill of Upton, II. 119. c. 2. r. John de Northampton ſherif of London committed, 38 Henry iii. II. 240. c. 1. l.

Northburc, John and Henry ſons of the parſon of, 14 John, I. 495. c. 1. a.

Northchelmelesford hundred, I. 543. c. 1. y.

Northgate ward in Canterbury tallaged, with its alderman Simon Bertelot, 32 Edward i. I. 741. c. 1. g.

Northton, the advowſon of that church awarded to the prior and monks of Rocheſter, 29 Henry ii. I. 82. c. 1. b. and I. 213. c. 1. p.

Northumberland in the hand of the biſhop of Durham, 6 Richard i. I. 643. c. 2. l. Has Robert Fitz-Roger ſherif, 7 John, II. 158. c. 1. x.

Northwode, Roger de, his pleas, 21 Henry (iii.) I. 726. c. 1. k. Baron of the Exchequer, 5 Edward i. II. 20. c. 1. x. and 8 Edward i. II. 62. c. 1. o. His ſalary, ibid. Baron, 4 Edward i. II. 112. c. 2. f. Occurs

INDEX.

curs baron, 4 Edward i. II. 269. c. 2. *f.* Roger de Northwode baron of the Exchequer, 3 Edward i. II. 320. c. 2. *e.*

Norton in Northamptonshire, the lord of that manor, 21 Henry iii. I. 102. c. 2. *f.* Robert de Norton his payment to the earl of Cornwal, 55 Henry iii. I. 384. c. 2. *n.* Norton in the bishopric has several parsons at one time, I. 715. c. 1. Tallaged, 11 Edward i. I. 721. c. 2. *y.* Geoffrey de Norton's appeal against the robbery of William son of John de Harpetre, 5 Henry iii. I. 793. c. 1. *e.* James de Norton sherif of Hampshire, 12 Edward ii. II. 70. c. 1. *e.*

Norwey, archbishop of, his corrody for seventeen weeks, 28 Henry ii. I. 366. c. 1. *c.* A gift to the bishop of Norwegia, 12 Henry ii. I. 341. c. 1. *g.*

Norwi, Alured de, 7 John, I. 498. c. 2. *p.* Has letters patents to discharge him from an appeal for the death of Toegieve, ibid.

Norwich, Thomas bishop of, 11 Henry iii. I. 63. c. 1. *l.* A grant from that see, I. 112. c. 2. *o.* The privilege of the monks of Norwich, 5 John, I. 118. c. 2. *x.* Tallage of the Jews of Norwich and Thetford, 5 Henry ii. I. 223. Freres of the hospital at Norwich, 30 Henry ii. I. 328. c. 1. *n.* Knights fees belonging to this see, 14 Henry ii. I. 573. c. 1. Moneyours of Norwich their aid, 14 Henry ii. I. 590. c. 1. *k.* The bishop's donum, 5 Henry ii. I. 627. c. 1. *s.* Its scutage, 2 Richard i. I. 664. c. 1. *z.* Had forty eight fees and a half, &c. 5 Henry iii. I. 666. c. 2. *l.* Prior has all the privileges as the city, 29 Henry iii. I. 726. c. 1. *h, i.* A royal fish taken on the land of a ward of the bishops, 35 Henry iii. II. 11. c. 1. *a.*

Norwich, Walter de, remembrancer of the Exchequer, 1 Edward ii. I. 75. William de Norwyco clerk of the receipt in the Tower, 13 Edward i. I. 270. c. 1. *b.* W. de Norwyco vice-treasurer, 5 Edward ii. I. 358. c. 2. *l.* Privy seal, 15 Edward ii. I. 359. c. 1. *n.* Treasurer, 9 Edward ii. I. 381. c. 1. *x.* Again, 9 Edward ii. ibid. c. 1. *y.* W. de Norwyco privy seal, 15 Edward ii. I. 382. c. 1. *g.* Norwich fines to have an exchange, liberties, &c. 29 Henry ii. I. 398. c. 2. *w.* Has a confirmation of liberties, &c. 6 Richard i. I. 399. c. 2. *k.* Men of Norwich have their liberties confirmed, 7 Henry iii. I. 414. c. 2. *o.* Again, 13 Henry iii. I. 417. c. 2. *f.* Castle of Norwich belonged to the Fitz-Rogers, 16 John, I. 491. c. 1. *g.* The aid of Norwich, 5 Stephen, I. 601. c. 1. *r.* Walter de Norwich baron of the Exchequer and receiver of the king's subsidy, 16 Edward ii. I. 611. c. 2. *m.* The riches of this city to be collected from its donum, 5 Henry ii. I. 627. c. 1. *s.* Its assise, 22 Henry ii. I. 703. c. 1. *k.* Its tallage, 2 Henry iii. I. 706. c. 2. *e.* Again, 14 Henry iii. I. 725. c. 2. *g.* Fee of the castle of Norwich, I. 726. c. 1. *k.* G. de Norwiz tallager of Bedford, 1 John, I. 747. c. 2. *l.* Monks of Holy Trinity, Norwich, quit of tallage, I. 748. c. 1. *p.* The quinzime of the merchandise of the port of Norwiz, 6 John, I. 772. c. 2. *i.* W. de Norwyco baron of the Exchequer, 5 Edward ii. II. 6. c. 2. *d.* See II. 31. Treasurer of the Exchequer, 8 Edward

INDEX.

ward ii. II. 39. c. 1. *o.* Seems to be guardian of the Exchequer, II. 40. King's treasurer, 9 Edward ii. II. 48. c. 1. *c.* II. 49, 50. Discharged from the treasury, and made chief baron with an encomium, 10 Edward ii. II. 59. c. 2. *g.* Was remembrancer, 2 Edward ii. II. 84. The citizens of Norwich distrained, 14 Edward i. II. 212. c. 2. *b.* Teste W. de Norwico, 5 Edward ii. II. 213. c. 1. *l.* Norwich in the king's hand, 18 Edward i. II. 245. c. 1. *o.* Seized for a contempt offered by their bailifs, 52 Henry iii. II. 247. W. de Norwyco treasurer, 10 Edward ii. II. 256. c. 1. *w.* W. de Norwyco directs how the Exchequer and king's palace should be managed when shut, II. 278. c. 1. *u.* Has a writ of liberate for a gift of fifty pounds, 6 Edward ii. II. 326. c. 1. *p.* Was made treasurer, 8 Edward ii. ibid. c. 2. *u.*

Notingham, a council held there by Henry ii. an. 1176. I. 18. The queen's chamber here painted with the history of Alexander, 36 Henry iii. I. 377. c. 2. *i.* Disforested in part, 13 Henry iii. I. 417. c. 1. *b.* Notingham castle maintained by earl John, I. 485. c. 1. *d.* Robert de Notingham remembrancer of the Exchequer, 19 Edward ii. I. 534. c. 1. Notingham and Derbyshire amerced for refusing to give judgment on Robert Botte, 28 Henry iii. I. 567. c. 2. *o.* Its tallage, 30 Henry iii. I. 707. William de Notingham king's attorney, 5 Edward ii. I. 732. c. 1. *i.* Henry de Notingham collector of the vintisme in Leicestershire, 1 Edward i. II. 242. c. 1. *x.* Robert de Notingham succeeds Adam de Lymbergh as remembrancer of the Exchequer, 15 Edward ii. II. 267, 268. c. 1. *y.* Hugh de Notingham keeper of the great rolls, 1 Edward ii. II. 270. c. 1. *i.*

Notte, Algar le, amerced for exporting corn, 29 Henry ii. I. 558. c. 1. *p.*

Nova placita & novæ conventiones, what, I. 123. Nova placita & novæ conventiones, passim.

Nova villa, William de, sherif of Norfolk, 2 Henry ii. I. 700. c. 2. *u.*

Novel lieu en Shirewode, 9 Edward ii. I. 755. c. 1. *q.* See Novo Loco.

Novo Burgo, Robert de, dean of Roan and prebendary of Sarum, about 31 Henry ii. I. 311. c. 1. *d.* That burgh in Shropshire tallaged, 1 John, I. 705. c. 2. *y.* See Neuburgh.

Novo Castello, Gospatric de, 5 Stephen, I. 497. c. 1. *w.* Fines for the tryal of the hot iron, ibid. See Newcastle.

Novo Loco in Shyrewode, prior de, I. 754. c. 2. *p.* His claim on the manors of Waltringham, Misterton, and Papewyk, ibid. Q. Newstede.

Novo Mercato, Adam de, seems one of the chief justiciers, 49 Henry iii. I. 76. c. 1. *u.* William de Novo Mercato his fine for relief, 10 Richard i. I. 316. c. 2. *k.* James de, his queen's gold, 13 John, I. 351. c. 1. *t.* William de Novo Mercato, in Dorset and Somersetshire, pledge of William de Wroteham, 1 John, I. 460. c. 2. *y.* William de Novo Mercato, his relation to William de Waddon, 5 Stephen, I. 482. c. 1. *z.* Ralf de, holds of the honor of Tikehul, Notinghamshire, 2 John, I. 659. c. 1. *w.*

Novus, Geoffrey, outlawed, 4 John, I. 612. c. 1. *p.*

Noyon, or de Nugione, Oxfordshire, Herbert

INDEX.

Herbert prior of St Martins de, 1 John, I. 216. c. 2. g. Grants his land of Baldedone, ibid.

Numerator, computator or teller of the Exchequer, II. 303. c. 2. l. They were ten in number, ibid. See II. 307.

Nunant, Hugh de, bishop of Coventry, I. 23. For what crimes king Richard i. demanded judgment against him, ibid. Was elect of Chester, 31 Henry ii. I. 310. c. 2. z. Was fermer of Warwick and Leicestershire, 2 Richard i. I. 328. c. 2. r. See I. 458. c. 2. f. Was custos of the priory of Covintre, employed in the king's affairs, and attended his army in Wales, 4 Richard i. I. 637. c. 1. d.

Nuns of Thefford, I. 47. c. 1. y. Nuns of St Clement, York, 31 Henry ii. I. 309. c. 1. r. Nuns of Charho, I. 328. c. 1. n. Nuns of Bocland, 19 Henry iii. I. 350. c. 1. p.

Nurse Hodierna's land tallaged, 20 Henry iii. I. 707. c. 1. k.

Nutehal church assigned to the prior of Lenton, I. 436. c. 1. s.

Nutewel in Devonshire, the men of Oliver de Dinan, 14 Henry ii. I. 588. c. 1. b.

Nutfield, that manor belonged to the abbat of Boloign, I. 300. Seized by Richard i. because that abbat was a subject of the king of France, I. 300, 301.

Nutley abbat claims the land of Wichenden, 9 John, I. 451. c. 2. b. Free from scutage and tallage, temp. Henry iii. I. 674. c. 2. p. Styled Natele from St Edward, ibid. Mentioned, II. 121.

Nuttele, John de, holding in socage, discharged from scutage, 9 Edward ii. I. 673. c. 1. n.

O.

Oath used in conveying titles, 2 John, I. 156. c. 1. h. Oath of one of the king's council, temp. Edward ii. II. 32. c. 2. w. Oath taken by the chancellor of the Exchequer, II. 54. c. 2. h. The Oath of a baron of the Exchequer, II. 61. c. 2. n. Oath taken of widows not to marry without the king's consent, II. 100. c. 1. i. The form of a sherif's Oath, about 42 Henry iii. II. 147. Abbat of Malmsbury's Oath to the crown for his good behaviour, 12 Edward ii. II. 149. How per fidem or verum dictum differed from an oath, II. 182. Accompts to be rendered at the Exchequer on Oath, ibid. Oath of accomptants to the mareschal, II. 241. Oath of a remembrancer of the Exchequer, II. 267. The contents of the oath of an usher of the palace or Exchequer, II. 278. c. 1. u.

Oats at three shillings the quarter, 14 Henry iii. II. 152. c. 2. z.

Oblata's or voluntary fines, I. 115. and passim. Nova Oblata contained all great, or known and clear debts to the crown, 54 Henry iii. II. 170.

Occasion or delay, I. 735. c. 2. n. passim.

Ocham in Kent, the liberties of that church, I. 408. c. 1. l. See Okham.

Odard sherif of Northumberland, 5 Stephen, I. 327. c. 1. r.

Odavil, Robert de, seems to be the same with Dudauvil, I. 316. c. 2. e.

Oddingseles, John de, seems to be sherif of Oxfordshire, 8 Edward ii. II. 233. c. 2. n. Assigns his surplusage to the abbat of Gracedieu, ibid.

Odiham in Hantshire, their fine, 6 John,

INDEX.

John, I. 407. c. 1. *a*. That manor in custody of Engelard de Cygoini, 26 and 27 Henry iii. II. 201. c. 2. *s*.

Odo, Clement, archdeacon of Paris, an. 1208. I. 163. c. 2. *y*.

Odo son of Godric, husbond of the forest in Hampshire, 5 Stephen, I. 456. c. 2. *g*.

Odo bishop of Bayeux and justicier, I. 8. Chief man in England in the time of Rufus, ibid. Chief man on the Conqueror's going into Normandy, an. 1067. I. 31. Managed the king's revenue as well as presided in his court, I. 78.

Odo Walensis, William son of, his land in Baenburc, Northumberland, 3 John, I. 437. c. 1. *w*. Occurs, I. 543. c. 2. *d*.

Odo son of Alsi amerced for the slaughter of the sons of Tochi, 5 Stephen, I. 543. c. 2. *e*.

Odo, Mr, keeper of the memoranda of the Exchequer, 4 Edward i. II. 112. c. 2. *f*. Remembrancer, 4 Edward i. II. 269. c. 2. *f*. Odo de Westminstre has a deputy allowed for two years as fusor of the Exchequer, 51 Henry iii. II. 310. c. 1. *k*. That he may studio vacare, ibid. See Westminstre. Odo remembrancer, 3 Edward i. II. 320. c. 2. *e*.

Odo son of John the fusor transfers his office to go into the holy land, 24 Henry iii. II. 310.

Officers of the king's court, viz. the great ones, I. 31, &c. The title of magister given to the principal officers in Naples, I. 57. c. 2. *t*.

Offices of inheritance, I. 299.

Offinton, John de, chaplain of Roger de la Leye chancellor of the Exchequer, 52 Henry iii. II. 52. c. 2. *z*.

Oger, dapifer, I. 50. c. 2. *u*. Oger Fitz-Oger, 28 Henry ii. I. 113. Oger dapifer was justicier, 16 Henry ii. I. 144. c. 1. *z*. Oger son of Oger sherif of Buckingham and Bedfordshire, 1 Richard i. I. 369. c. 1. *z*. Oger son of Oger justicier, 7 Richard i. I. 502. c. 1. *x*. Oger dapifer has ninety knights fees and an half of the honor of Eye, 14 Henry ii. I. 573. c. 2. *l*.

Oil to burn at the queen's sepulcre, 5 Stephen, I. 364. c. 1. *n*.

Oilley or Doily, in Normandy, the honor de, 2 John, I. 156. c. 1. *g*. Henry de Oilli sherif of Oxfordshire, 5 Henry ii. I. 222. c. 1. *b*. Again, 10 John, I. 263. c. 2. *m*. Nigellus de Oilli part of his land goes to Brient Fitz-Count, 5 Stephen, I. 457. c. 2. *s*. Henry de Oilli sherif of Oxfordshire, 10 Richard i. I. 459. c. 2. *s*. John de Oilli fined for a false oath or verdict, 9 John, I. 507. c. 1. *b*. Alanus Oil de Larrun amerced, 1 Richard i. I. 564. c. 1. *u*. Richard de Oilli has not his principal barony in Oxfordshire, 6 Richard i. I. 591. c. 1. *p*. William de Oilli's lands in Oxfordshire, 4 John, I. 666. c. 1. *b*. Henry de Oilli sherif of Oxfordshire, 5 Henry ii. I. 696. c. 2. *o*. Henry de Oilli sherif of Oxfordshire, 2 Henry ii. II. 163. c. 1. *y*. Henry de Oilli, 10 John, II. 210, 211. c. 1. *a*.

Oisel, Hugh and Adam, their grant from Richard i. I. 2. c. 2. *b*. That grant repeated, 8 Richard i. I. 468. c. 1. *m*. Hugh's merchandise in Flanders, 5 John, I. 479. c. 2. *f*. Hugh fines for the quinzime of merchandise, 5 John, I. 771. c. 2. *g*. Has the ferm of the mint of all England, 3 John, II. 133. c. 1. *n*. See Oysel.

Oisun, Richard, temp. Richard i. I.

INDEX.

714. c. 1. g. His vifus in the bifhopric, ibid.

Okbeare, Richard de, brother and heir of Roger, has fhare in the manor Rillaton in Cornwal, 8 Edward ii. I. 624. c. 1. k.

Oketon, John de, fherif of Yorkfhire, could not levy his fumm by reafon of the civil wars, 52 Henry iii. II. 160. c. 2. l. Late fherif of Yorkfhire, 51 Henry iii. II. 236. c. 2. h.

Okham, Nicolas de, clerk of the treafury of the Tower, 14 Edward i. I. 270. c. 1. b. Ocham in Rutlandfhire how tallaged, 9 Edward ii. I. 724, 725. c. 1. f. John de Okham made baron of the Exchequer in the room of Richard de Abyngdon, 10 Edward ii. II. 59. c. 2. f. Was baron and auditor of the accompts of the bifhop of Bath, 12 Edward ii. II. 292. c. 2. m. Nicolas de Okham treafurer's clerk, who wrote the tallies at the receipt, 31 Edward i. II. 304. c. 1. n. His death, 34 Edward i. II. 306. c. 1. p.

Old Winchelfey, a conteft about the right of fepulture in it, 20 Edward i. II. 81. c. 2. d.

Oldebuf, Hugh de, clerk of the Exchequer, 1 Edward i. II. 19. c. 1. r.

Olney in Northamptonfhire, knights of, 18 Henry ii. I. 580. c. 1. p. Efcheated, I. 583. c. 2. m.

Omero, William de S. late fherif of Herefordfhire, 38 Henry iii. II. 122. c. 1. m. Thomas de S. Omero fherif of Norfolk and Suffolk with the caftle of Norwich, 1 Edward ii. II. 144.

Opton, Walter de, the knights fees he held of Geoffrey de Ver, temp. Henry ii. I. 579. c. 2. k.

Ordinance, the keepers of it explained to be keepers of the money, 32 Edward i. I. 294. c. 2. g.

Ordlavefton, William fon of John de, 13 John, I. 218. c. 2. t. Grants his land in Gucefton, Kent, to Hugh fon of William de Ainefmere, ibid.

Oreford caftle in the cuftody of John de Sturmy, 15 Edward ii. I. 383. c. 2. Affife of this burgh in Suffolk, 22 Henry ii. I. 703. c. 1. k. Its tallage, 9 Richard i. I. 705. c. 1. u. Again, 2 Henry iii. I. 706. c. 2. e. And again, 14 Henry iii. I. 725. c 2. g. The quinzime of the merhandife of the port of Oreford, 6 John, I. 772. c. 2. i. Its caftle and fee-farm granted to the men of the town, before 42 Henry iii. II. 207. c. 1. f.

Orgers, Mabel daughter of William de Orgers, her concord at Dunftaple with Roger de Brai, I. 215. In which fhe grants the terra de Maldone, early temp. Henry ii. ibid. c. 1. a.

Orham, Robert de, holds of the church of Chichefter, temp. Henry ii. I. 576. c. 2.

Oriefcuilz, William, an inquifition about him, whether he was with earl John, 7 Richard i. I. 432. c. 2. b.

Originalia of the Exchequer, II. 254. With other eftreats, ibid.

Ormefbi, its aid, 14 Henry ii. I. 589. c. 2. f.

Orphants, infants, and widows to be protected, and to have fpeedy juftice, 34 Henry iii. II. 102.

Orpinton, Ralf de, monk of Chriftchurch, Canterbury, 9 Richard i. I. 113.

Orri, John, of Somerfetfhire, attached, 45 Henry iii. II. 79. c. 1. y.

Ortis, Peter de, his land and heirs in cuftody

INDEX.

custody of Heylas Deforz, 2 John, I. 523. c. 2. *s.*

Orton, Robert de, his serjeanty, 4 John, I. 650. c. 1. c. 1. *m.* Orton Robert and Overorton, Oxfordshire, tallaged, 4 John, I. 721. c. 2. *y.*

Os justiciarii, 4 John, II. 253. c. 1. *z.*

Osbern dapifer of Normandy about the time of Hardicnute king of England, I. 53.

Osbert clerk of the chamber placed before the king's chamberlains, 18 Henry ii. I. 366. c. 2. *f.* Osbert presbyter of Lamheda amerc'd, 2 Richard i. I. 556. c. 1. *k.* John son of Osbert citizen of Lincoln, 6 Henry iii. II. 23. c. 1. *z.* Osbert son of Hugh's lands in Herefordshire, temp. Stephen, II. 138. c. 2. *e.*

Osgodby, Adam de, keeper of the rolls in chancery, 30 Edward i. I. 72. Has the king's seal, I. 73. Keeper of the king's house of convert Jews, 9 Edward ii. I. 745. c. 1. *a.*

Osgotecros wapentake has a commission of array sent it, 16 Edward ii. II. 112. c. 1.

Oskinton in Notinghamshire, that manor given to William Daubigny in knight service, about 6 Henry iii. I. 281. c. 1. *c.*

Osmundesley, Mr. Nicolas, Elyas and Robert parsons of, 8 Richard i. I. 715. c. 1.

Ospring town amerc'd for not following a hue and cry, 6 Richard i. I. 556. c. 2. *q.* Its aid for marrying the king's daughter, 14 Henry ii. I. 588. c. 2. *d.* Master of that hospital has his tallage remitted, 53 Henry iii. II. 230. c. 1. *s.*

Ostexhel, or Osteshul, how far the land of Adam de Peryton, 30 Henry iii. I. 595. c. 1. *n.* and I. 597. c. 1. *y.*

Ostiarius or usher of the Exchequer, I. 188. Ostiarius Helyas, 33 Henry ii. I. 232. c. 1. *o.* The serjeanty of the Ostiaria in the king's army, I. 321. c. 1. *q.* Ostiarius of the Exchequer, I. 354. c. 1. *q.* Robert Ostiarius son of Giffard, 5 Stephen, I. 457. c. 1. *n.* Elias, 21 Henry ii. I. 692. c. 2. *k.* Taylefer hostiary of the Exchequer, 49 Henry iii. II. 16. c. 1. *y.* Roger hostiary of the Exchequer, 14 Henry iii. II. 22. c. 1. *q.* Ostiary carried summonces thro' England, II. 273. c. 1, 2. II. 274. c. 1, 2. Held the land of Eston by sergeanty and not of the honour of Walingford, II. 275. To take care of the doors and avenues of the Exchequer, II. 278. c. 1. *u.* And to transmit the writs of summonce to the sherifs for the king's money, ibid. To lock and bolt the gates of the palace at sunset, ibid. David chamberlain made Ostiary of the receipt, 49 Henry iii. II. 296. c. 1. *z.* Nothing memorable of the usher of the receipt within the first period, II. 310.

Osturius what, I. 98. c. 2. *o.* Osturus a hawk, I. 330. c. 1. *b.*

Oswald, canons of St, I. 329. c. 1. *w.* Osmund the provost, fermer of Glocester, 16 Henry ii. I. 331. c. 1. *g.* and 19 Henry ii. I. 331. c. 1. *k.*

Oswardisbech, Notinghamshire, its assise, 21 Henry ii. 702. c. 2. *g.* The tallage of Oswardebec, 30 Henry iii. I. 707. c. 2. *l.* Tallage of the soke of Oswardesbech, 9 Richard i. I. 733. c. 1. *p.*

Oswardkirke soke granted by king Henry to Henry de Hastynges, I. 724. c. 1. *e.*

Oterhampton,

INDEX.

Oterhampton, William de, auditor of the accompts of cuftodes, 16 Edward ii. II. 293.

Otefwyche, William de, 2 Edward ii. II. 76. c. 2. *f.* Has a writ to qualify him to fue in the Exchequer for his debts, ibid.

Otheford in Kent, its aid, 14 Henry ii. I. 584. c. 2. *q.*

Oto fon of William fherif of Effex and Hertfordfhire, 1 Richard i. I. 369. c. 1. *y.* William fon of Otho, 5 Stephen, I. 477. c. 1. *c.* Hugh fon of Otho, one of the cuftodes of London, 54 Hen. iii. II. 169. c. 1. *d.*

Otrepol, that land the dower of the wife of Robert de Boxtede, 4 Richard i. I. 564. c. 2. *d.*

Otringeham, William de, impleaded for his land, 30 Henry ii. I. 497. c. 2. *b.* Amerc'd for default, 12 Henry ii. I. 552. c. 1. *l.*

Otto emperor, an. 1002. I. 26. c. 1. *o.* Oto king of Alemaign, 3 John, II. 133. c. 1. *n.*

Ou, William de, Rufus's kinfman, I. 8. c. 2. *i.* Accufed of treafon, and vanquifhed in fingle combat, ibid. His punifhment, ibid. Was the fon of Rufus's aunt, ibid. William de Ou his fteward, an. 1096. I. 51. c. 2. *d.* Geoffrey de Ou, accompts, 5 Stephen, I. 147. c. 1. *u.* William de Ou, 31 Henry ii. I. 427. c. 1. *i.* Walter and Thomas de Ou, their claim in Beverley, 7 Richard i. I. 432. c. 2. *z.* John earl of Augi or Ou, temp. Henry ii. I. 577. c. 2. *z.* His knights in the rap of Haftinges, I. 577. c. 2. *a.* Countefs of, 31 Henry iii. I. 594. c. 1. *h.* Her aid, 18 Henry iii. I. 617. c. 2. *b.* Earl of Augi has the honor of Tikehul, 6 Henry iii. II. 68. c. 1. *t.*

Oüen, monks of St, at Roan, I. 163. and 390. c. 1. *p.* William de, 42 Henry iii. II. 232. c. 1. *f.* fherif of Oxfordfhire.

Overtes lettres, II. 309. c. 1. *e.*

Overton, William de, clerk of the fherif of Hantfhire, 9 Edward ii. I. 381. c. 1. *x.*

Oughtretfate, Joan widow of Bertun de, fwears not to marry without the king's leave, 27 Edward i. II. 100. c. 2. *m.*

Oufche, the charter of that monaftery in Normandy, I. 28. See I. 29. Hath a charter of confirmation, an. 1113. I. 92. and I. 121.

Oufe and Derwent wapentakes under a commiffion of array, 16 Edward ii. II. 112. c. 2.

Outi of Lincoln, 5 Stephen, 273. c. 1. *c.*

Outlaw, Hugh de Lacy fined ten marks for harbouring one, 14 Henry ii. I. 85. c. 1. *p.* See I. 98. c. 2. *z.* An Outlawry, I. 99. c. 1. *q.* A reward for bringing the head of one, 7 Richard i. 201. c. 2. *t.* Their chattels forfeited, I. 345. c. 1. and I. 347. Outlawry or abjuration, I. 505. c. 1. *g.*

Owelton, Roger de, a homager of the bifhop of Bath, 27 Edward i. II. 266.

Ox valued at five fhillings, 30 Henry ii. 535. c. 2. At eight fhillings, 14 Henry iii. II. 152. c. 2. *z.*

Oxeneford, a council held there by king Stephen, an. 1137. I. 14. c. 2. earl Richard of Oxon, 3 Henry iii. I. 67. c. 1. *x.* Conft. de Oxeneford juftice errant, 20 Henry ii. 124. The burgeffes to have the fame liberties as London, 2 John, I. 401. c. 2. *c.* The aid of Oxeneford, 5 Stephen, I. 601. c. 2. *u.* The tallage

INDEX.

lage of the town and county, 19 Henry ii. I. 701. c. 1. *a*. The tallage of Henry de, 14 Henry iii. I. 709. c. 1. *s*. That burgh tallaged, 18 Henry iii. I. 743. c. 1. *p*. John de, sherif of London, 17 Edward ii. II. 99. c. 1. *f*. G. de Craucumb sherif of the county and castle, 16 Henry iii. II. 141. c. 1. *q*. Henry de Oxinefort, 2 Henry ii. II. 163. Ralf de Oxeneford, 5 Stephen, II. 197. c. 1. *q*. How seiz'd into the king's hand, 9 Edward ii. II. 249. c. 1. *b*. A council call'd there, 5 Richard i. II. 274. c. 2. *d*.

Oxhay, Richard de, chamberlain of the Exchequer, 39 and 42 Henry iii. II. 14. c. 1. *p*. c. 2. *s*. II. 21.

Oxonia, Henry de, of London, tallaged, 19 Henry iii. I. 738. c. 1. *y*.

Oyldebof, Hugh de, clerk of the Exchequer, 56 Henry iii. II. 264. See Oldebuf.

Oyri, Fulk de, 9 John, I. 142. c. 1. *e*. Again Fulk de Oyri appeals to the justiciers of the thirteenth, 9 John, I. 499. c. 1. *q*. Fulk de Oyri his share of the marsh between the waters of Spalding and Tid, 7 John, I. 506. c. 1. *w*.

Oysel, Richard, of Yorkshire, 34 Edward i. II. 120. c. 2. *a*. Seems to have been sherif of Yorkshire, being discharg'd from his accompt by judgment of the court, ibid. See Oisel.

Ozum, Gerard de, 1 Edward ii. II. 76. His writ of privy seal for the recovery of his debts, ibid.

P.

P. abbat of Whitby, 2 John, I. 515. c. 1. *g*.

Pabenham, John de, sherif of Bedford and Buckinghamshire, 9 Edward ii. II. 238.

Pacey, land of, I. 168.

Pacheford in Wiltshire, the mills and lands of William Isenbert, hang'd before 42 Henry iii. I. 315. c. 1. *n*.

Page, Robert, 18 Edward i. I. 153. c. 1. *f*. To find manucaptors in Suffolk, ibid.

Paiable, John, bailif of Canterbury arrested, and the city seiz'd for neglect of payment, 34 Edward i. II. 247.

Pain, sherif of Surrey, 9 Henry ii. I. 349. Paganus of Cornwal, 5 Stephen, I. 425. c. 2. *e*. Pain sherif of Surrey, 2 Henry ii. I. 687. c. 1. *g*. Pain sherif of Huntingdon, 2 Henry ii. I. 688. c. 1. *n*. Pain sherif of Surrey his danegeld, 5 Henry ii. I. 690. c. 2. *x*. I. 691. c. 1. *b*. c. 2. *c, d, e*. and 7 Henry ii. I. 697. c. 2. *m*. Pain sherif of Surrey and Huntingdon had a surplusage in his accompts, 2 Henry ii. II. 231. c. 2. *c*.

Painel, terra Willelmi, 33 Henry ii. I. 4. c. 1. His lands seised, 10 Richard i. I. 39. c. 2. *a*. Gervase de Painel, has Waltham, 26 Henry ii. I. 96. c. 2. *p*. William had the land of Pacey mortgaged to him, an. 1184. l. 168. c. 2. Fulk accompts for the honor of Banton, Devonshire, 3 John, I. 205. c. 2. *n*. The barony or honor of William Painel in the king's hands, 31 Henry ii. I. 297. c. 2. *w*. William Painel's relief for his lands in Lincolnshire, 4 Henry ii. I. 316. c. 1. *x*. Adam Painel pays queen's gold, 12 John, I. 351. c. 1. *w*. William Painel, 13 John, I. 481. c. 1. *p*. Adam Painel amerc'd for a disseisin, I. 552.

INDEX.

I. 552. c. 1. e. Gervase Painel's fee and scutage in Staffordshire, 6 Richard i. I. 591. c. 1. q. William Painel's fees in Yorkshire, 18 Henry ii. I. 629. c. 1. z. Thomas, 26 Edward i. II. 123. c. 1. u. Ralf Painel late sherif of Lncoln, 27 Edward i. II. 203. c. 1. d. See Paynel.

Painting incouraged, temp. Henry iii. I. 377. c. 2. h, i. Of the hall at Wudestoke, 25 Henry iii. II. 3. c. 1. i.

Palaces of Henry ii. II. 368. c. 1. r. Henry de Palace weigher of the Exchequer, 18 Edward i. II. 308. c. 1. d.

Palerna, Ralf de, his livery, 18 Henry ii. I. 367. c. 1. g.

Palfreys two good ones valued at ten mark, 2 John, I. 118. c. 1. p. Again, I. 402. c. 2. o.

Palmer, Walter, amerced for the non-appearance of William Walwein, 14 Henry ii. I. 554. c. 2. s. Henry Palmarius holds of the bishop of Chichester, temp. Henry ii. I. 576. c. 2.

Pandulf, elect of Norwich, 4 Henry iii. I. 119. His tryal with William de Stutteville about the patronage of the church of Briselea, Norfolk, ibid.

Panetarius of the king, I. 770. Panetery or Pantry, II. 130.

Panforiere, William, 4 John, I. 473. c. 2. x. Fines in Kent for the king's good-will, ibid.

Pantol, William son of Hugh, his relief and five knights fees, 9 Henry iii. I. 318. c. 2. b. Has the terra of Robert de Belesme in Shropshire, ibid. William Pantolf justicier and tallager in Staffordshire, 7 Henry iii. I. 734. c. 2. d.

Panzevot or Pancefot, Mabel, fines that a duel between her and her brother Robert may be hindred, 31 Henry ii. I. 451. c. 1. w. Richard Pancevot tallager of Herefordshire, Pa 19 Henry iii. I. 735. c. 1. h.

pewyk manor in Notinghamshire, belong'd to the prior de Novo Loco, Pa 34 Edward i. I. c. 2. p.

ppewurd in Cambridgeshire, a contentention about land there, 10 John, I. 517. c. 2. q. Helena and her son Walter de, ibid.

Pararii, John Maure alderman of their gild, 26 Henry ii. I. 562. c. 1. z.

Parcarius, Ralf, of Norfolk, 5 Stephen, I. 148. c. 2. p.

Parcertes, William, held of the bishop of Chichester, temp. Henry ii. I. 576. c. 2.

Parco, Ysapel wife of Simon de, her claim on Multon in Northamptonshire, 4 John, I. 437. c. 2. y.

Parcus a large grove, with water and walls, or pales, I. 186. c. 2. u.

Pardons, I. 168. Again, II. 229.

Parentes in later ages denote kinsfolk, Pref. xxiii.

Paris, Reginald de, 5 John, I. 264. c. 1. r. Again, I. 517. c. 1. p. William de Paris his serjeanty in Ayston and Clinton charged with knight service, 42 Henry iii. I. 650. c. 2. o.

Park, Roger and William del, 55 Henry iii. I. 241. c. 1. h.

Park, Roger de Rannes fined for making one without licence, 5 Stephen, I. 557. c. 1. y.

Parliament in Normandy its original, I. 162, 163. One held at Lincoln, 9 Edward ii. I. 361. c. 2. x. Burgesses of parliament formerly summon'd by the sherif, I. 758. passim.

Parmentarius, John, of Doncaster, 17 Henry

INDEX.

Henry ii. I. 559. c. 2. *m.* Geoffrey, 5 Richard i. I. 564. c. 2. *f.*

Parfons, feveral of one church, 8 Richard i. I. 714. c. 1. *g.*

Particum in Normandy fubject to the earl of Moretun, I. 108. c. 1. *b.* See Perch and Pertico.

Paffagium, or fines laid on tenants by military fervice inftead of their going beyond fea with their knights, I. 652.—662.

Paffeflambard, Ranulf, Rufus's chaplain, bifhop of Durham and chief jufticier, I. 32. His character, I. 33. c. 1. *i.*

Paffelewe, Robert, jufticier, 34 Henry iii. I. 46. c. 2. *q.* Occurs, 17 Henry iii. I. 65. c. 2. Hugh Paffelewe of Northamptonfhire, his liberties, 12 John, I. 410. c. 2. *q.* Roger Paffelewe of Wigenhale, Norfolk, amerc'd for exporting corn without licence, 24 Henry ii. I. 558. c. 1. *o.* Simon Paffeleawe jufticier, 53 Henry iii. I. 727. c. 1. *m.* Robert Paffelewe, who, 17 Henry iii. II. 34. c. 2. *y.* Edmund Paffele fucceeds Walter de Frifkeny baron of the Exchequer, 17 Edward ii. II. 61. c. 1. *m.*

Paffing-bell, charity-money for ringing it for the poor, 19 Henry iii. I. 350. c. 1. *p.*

Pater nofter and Ave Maria, an eftate held of the king in capite by faying one every day, 14 Edward i. I. 321. c. 1. *p.*

Patefhill, Simon de, jufticier, 9 Richard i. I. 114. c. 1. *s.* Jufticier in the time of king John, I. 151. Juftice of the Jews, 10 Richard i. I. 235. c. 1. *e.* c. 2. *g.* Jufticier, 9 John, I. 451. c. 1. *a.* Simon de, 4 John, I. 606. c. 1. *w.* Accompts for the drengs of Weftmoreland, 2 John, I. 659. c. 1. *x.* Settles the tallage, 7 Richard i. I. 703. c. 2. *n.* and 8 John, I. 734. c. 1. *z.* Simon, I. 737. c. 2. *u, w.* See I. 791. Hugh de, treafurer, 18 Henry iii. II. 35. Martin de Patefhul jufticier, 3 Henry iii. II. 43. c. 2. *n.* Treafurer, 18 Henry iii. II. 51. c. 2. *r.* Simon de Patefhil accompts for the ferm of Northamptonfhire, 8 Richard i. II. 157. c. 2. *w.* H. de Patefhul treafurer, 22 Henry iii. II. 255. c. 2. *r.* The rolls of Martin de Patefhel, 42 Henry iii. II. 257. c. 1. *b.*

Patefley, Herbert de, 10 John, I. 471. c. 1. *s.* Fines forty marks to accord a duel, ibid.

Patric earl of Northumberland fon of Waltheof, 2 John, I. 435. c. 1. *p.* In the war between Henry ii. and his fon, ibid. c. 2. *q.* See, I. 440. c. 1. *m.* Patric fon of Edgar, I. 552. c. 1. *q.* I. 553. c. 1. *z.* Earl Patric fherif of Wiltfhire, 2 Henry ii. I. 691. c. 2. *f.* His tenure in Northumberland by theinage, 14 Henry iii. I. 743. c. 1. *o.* Has Wiltfhire, 5 Henry ii. II. 164. c. 1. *a.*

Patric, William, one of the heirs of Niel de Luvetot, 6 Henry iii. I. 640. c. 1. *r.*

Paveilli, Geoffrey de, of Rutinton, 5 John, I. 438. c. 2. *e.* Sir Walter de Pavely of Wiltfhire, 26 Edward i. I. 466. c. 2. *d.*

Paulefhol, Richard de, his debet in Wiltfhire, 2 Henry iii. I. 444. c. 2. *u.*

Paunage or pannage, for the maft of the king's forefts, II. 131.

Paunton, William de, his relief, 35 Edward i. I. 320. c. 1. *i.* Philip de Paunton fherif of Notingham

and

INDEX.

and Derbyshire, 22 Edward i. II. 173. c. 2. *q.* Philip de Paunton, 1 Edward i. II. 194. c. 1. *g.* Seems to be heir of James de Paunton sherif of Lincolnshire, 54 Henry iii. ibid. Philipp de Paunton, a capias against his attorney in favour of the men of Graham, 4 Edward i. II. 269. c. 2. *g.*

Paxton in Norfolk answers for a wreck, 7 Richard i. I. 343. c. 2. *k.* Paxton in Cambridgeshire, a town of the king of Scots, 13 Henry ii. I. 540. c. 1. *x.*

Payments in Thesauro, and elsewhere, I. 262, &c.

Payne, William, has the commission of array for the wapentak of Whiteby, 16 Edward ii. II. 112. c. 2.

Paynel, sir William de, of Sussex, 26 Edward i. I. 466. c. 2. *d.* John Paygnel summon'd by writ to the Scots war, and one of the king's courtiers, 26 Edward i. I. 655. c. 2. See Painel. Hugh Paynel has the burgh of Draxe, Yorkshire, 30 Henry iii. I. 710. c. 1. *w.*

Peacocks crests in use, 14 John, I. 273. c. 2. *i.* Again, I. 371.

Peccatum, Hamon, of Essex, in misericordia, 23 Henry ii. I. 542. c. 2. *s.*

Pecco, Pech, Pek, Richard de, one of the justices, 26 Henry ii. I. 137. Gilbert Pecche his escuage for the king's ransom, 6 Richard i. I. 591. c. 1. *n.* For marriage of the king's daughter, 31 Henry iii. I. 594. c. 2. *k.* His knights fees, 38 Henry iii. I. 596. c. 1. *t.* Gilbert de Pecche among the Lincolnshire barons for the Scotch war, 26 Edward i. I. 654. c. 2. Gilbert Pecche fines, 12 John, I. 658. c. 1. *k.* Teste Bartholomew Pech, 16 Henry iii. II. 34. c. 1. Gilbert and John, their charter, 25 Edward i. II. 75. c. 1. *z.*

Pech, honor of, exempt from the county, 23 Henry ii. I. 140. c. 1. *r.* Richard de Pec custos of the castle of Bolesoure, 3 Richard i. II. 220. c. 2. *q.*

Peckham hundred amerc'd, 7 Richard i. I. 565. c. 1. *k.*

Pecunia for catals at large, I. 502. c. 2. *e.*

Pedewurd barony had fifteen knights fees, 7 Richard i. I. 427. c. 2. *u.* Claim'd by Brian Fitz-Ralf and Henry de Perci, ibid. How far Pedewurd was parcel of the honor of Arundel, 6 Richard i. I. 484. c. 2. *w.* See Petworth.

Pedinton, the king of Scots, 13 Henry ii. I. 539. c. 1. *w.*

Peers or convassals, I. 4.

Peilleve, Simon de, his grant, 2 John, I. 156. c. 2. *i.*

Peiters, William de, the queen's brother, has his donum remitted, 2 Henry ii. I. 695. c. 1. *u.*

Peivre, Paulinus de, late sherif of Buckingham and Bedfordshire, 25 Henry iii. II. 192. c. 2. *x.* Again, II. 201. c. 2. *r.*

Pelham castle amerc'd, I. 568. c. 2. *t.*

Pells, clerks of the, II. 303. One as old as 9 Henry iii. II. 306. Out of the Pells an accompt of the allowances to the officers of the Exchequer, 9 Henry iii. II. 311.

Pelokin bailif of Battle abbey dying intestate, his chattels go to the king, temp. Henry ii. I. 346. c. 2. *k.*

Pelwrdham honor belong'd to Hugh Bussel, 4 John, I. 487. c. 2. *u.*

Pembroc,

INDEX.

Pembroc, William Mareschal earl of, has the office of mareschal granted to him and his heirs, 1 John, I. 46. See I. 48. Was mareschal, 3 Henry iii. I. 67. c. 1. x. Adomar de Valence earl of Pembroc, 1 Edward ii. I. 75. and 15 Edward ii. I. 383. c. 1. Insults Walter de Langton sitting in the Exchequer, 5 Edward ii. I. 267. c. 1. o. A countess of Penbroc, 20 Henry iii. I. 389. c. 1. h. William Mareschal earl of Penbroc, 3 John, I. 766. c. 1. o. A. de Valencia earl of Penebroc, 5 Edward ii. II. 7. c. 1. e. William Mareschal earl of Pembroc guardian of the king and realm, 2 Henry iii. II. 26. c. 1. a. A. de Valencia occurs again, 5 Edward ii. II. 31. c. 1. m. William Mareschal earl of Pembroc rector of the king and kingdom, 2 Henry iii. II. 227. c. 1. a. Henry de Penbroc seems to have been sherif of Gloucestershire, 49 Henry iii. II. 232. c. 2. b. G. Mareschal earl of Penbrok makes Richard de Swindon mareschal of the Exchequer, 22 Henry iii. II. 285. c. 1. a.

Peneceftre, Stephen de, constabulary of Dovor, and receiver of the vintism of the cinque ports in the close of Henry iii. I. 610. c. 2. Constable of Dover castle, and warden of the five ports for the port of Hasting, 33 Edward i. I. 613. c. 1. s.

Penedoc, Thomas parson of, amerc'd, 14 Henry iii. I. 567. c. 1. f.

Penkeston manor in Derbyshire held of Thomas de Cadurcis, by Dionysia Wyne, 2 Edward ii. I. 646. c. 1. u.

Penne, Hugh de la, accompted for the queen's wardrobe, 41 and 49 Henry iii. II. 130. Again, 57 Henry iii. II. 158. c. 2. c.

Pennebiri, Adam de, 2 Henry iii. I. 462. c. 2. p. Has the balliage of Saufordesir, Lanc. ibid.

Penpol, Margaret widow of Warin de, Devonshire, 10 John, I. 151. c. 2. y.

Penreth, Baldwin de, 38 Henry iii. I. 596. c. 2. w. Its tallage in Cumberland, 19 Henry iii. I. 735. c. 1. g.

Penros in Cornwal, that land given by earl Reginald to the father of Peter Burdun, before 3 John, I. 486. c. 2. n.

Pensum, ad, what that payment, I. 274.

Penton, Reginald de, justice itinerant in Dorset and Somersetshire, 8 Richard i. II. 146. c. 1. b.

Pepperers, Edward alderman of the gild of, 26 Henry ii. I. 562. c. 1. z.

Per Fidem or verumdictum at the Exchequer, whether an oath. II. 182.

Perambulations, fines paid to obtain them for ascertaining the bounds of baronies, hundreds, &c. temp. John, I. 506. Perambulation between the king's forest and the men of Devonshire, 11 John, I. 566. c. 2. b. Commissioners for the Perambulation of the forests were sworn, 26 Edward i. II. 91, 92.

Perariis, Peter de, fined to salt fish as Peter Chivalier did, 6 Henry iii. I. 572. c. 2. b. See Pirariis.

Percehale, Walter de, his concord about a duel, 14 Henry ii. I. 512. c. 1. q.

Perch, earl of, his knights fees in Kent, 5 John, I. 41. c. 2. t. Perch or de Pertico, 14 John, I. 298. c. 2. c.

Perdona, or money remitted by the king's writs, I. 686. passim.

Perci, Margaret de, releases Rokesbi

to

INDEX.

to the knights Templars, 4 Richard i. I. 230. c. 2. *k*. Again, I. 241. c. 2. *i*. Elena de Perci abbefs elect of Werewel, 9 Edward i. I. 313. c. 1.*f*. Henry de Perci claims the honor of Pedewurd, 7 Richard i. I. 427. c. 2. *u*. William de Perci fherif of Yorkfhire under William de Stutevil, 3 John, I. 461. c. 1. *a*. William de Perci's knights fees in Yorkfhire, 14 Henry ii. I. 574. c. 2. *p*. The knights fees of Richard and William de Perci, 31 Henry iii. I. 594. c. 1. *h*. The fcutage of Agnes de Perci, 1 John, I. 638. c. 1. *i*. Henry de, baron, and one of the king's court, 26 Edward i. I. 655. c. 2. Richard de Percy's tallage for his lands in the foke of Pikering, 30 Henry iii. I. 710. c. 1. *w*. A conteft between Richard and William de Percy, 18 Henry iii. I. 796. c. 1. *u*.

Peregrinorum gilda, Warner le Turnur alderman of it, 26 Henry ii. I. 562, c. 1. *z*.

Pereton park in cuftody of William the Dane, 1 John, I. 460. c. 1. *x*. The land of Adam de Peryton in Oftexhel, 30 Henry iii. I. 595. c. 1. *n*. Call'd Ofteshul, I. 597. c. 1. *y*. Belonged to the abbat and monks of of Weftminfter, temp. Henry i. I. 625. c. 1. *m*.

Peri, Ralf de, amerc'd for wounding a prieft, 14 Henry ii. I. 558. c. 2. *w*.

Perfhette, Nicolas de, king's bailif, 26 Edward i. I. 614. c. 2. *w*.

Perfolta, I. 167.

Perfon, accompts at the Exchequer to be render'd in, II. 176.

Perfonal fervice, where required moft ftrictly, I. 625.

Perfone, William, judgment againft him, 35 Edward i. II. 120. c. 2. *a*.

Perfore, abbat of, the king's efcheator, 40 Henry iii. I. 319. c. 1. *c*. Fines ten marks for a market at Bradewey, 8 Richard i. I. 400. c. 1. *q*. Occurs, 9 John, I. 480. c. 1. *k*. Hundred of Perfore, Worcefterfhire, I. 544. c. 2. *t*. Eleric abbat of Perfore, capital efcheator on this fide Trent, 36 Henry iii. I. 623. c. 1. *b*. That abbat's fees in Worcefterfhire, 14 Henry iii. I. 660. c. 2. *g*. Abbat fines, 7 Richard i. I. 663. c. 1. *r*. How far Perfore belongs to the abbat of Weftminfter, 4 John, II. 253. c. 1. *z*.

Perth, St John's town of, Edward i. was there in his 31 year, 15 July, I. 392. c. 1. *a*.

Pertico, Stephen de, one of the jufticiers, 2 John, I. 228. c. 2. *z*. See Particum. Fulk de Cantelu's compotus of the lands of the countefs de Pertico, 14 John, I. 298. c. 2. *c*. Earl de Pertico his fcutage in Effex, 1 John, I. 665. c. 1. *d*.

Pefagia in London, I. 779. c. 1. *e*.

Pefemere, Martin fon of Gilbert de, his relief, 6 Henry iii. I. 318. c. 1. *w*. Turold de, his fcutage in Berkfhire, 33 Henry ii. I. 643. c. 1. *g*. c. 2. *i*. Richard lord of the fee, I. 643. c. 2. *i*.

Pefnudus, William, one of the fureties of Hugh Cordele, 5 Stephen, II. 197. c. 1. *q*. See Bereford.

Pefour or weigher of the king's revenue had a ferjeanty, 1 Richard i. I. 289. c. 2. *u*. Again, II. 307. See Ponderator. An hereditary office, II. 308. In the family of John, Thomas, and John de Windefores, 4 John, II. 307, c. 2. *z*, *y*. II.

INDEX.

y. II. 308. c. 1. *z, a.* and 48 Henry iii. II. 21. c. 1. *k.* c. 2. *l.*

Peffaigne, Anthony de, has the cuftoms of St Botulf's, 5 Henry ii. I. 385. c. 1. *p.*

Peftur or Piftor, Nicolas le, of Somerfetfhire, 45 Henry iii. II. 79. c. 1. *y.* Robert, 5 Edward i. II. 81. c. 1. *c.* Jordan fon of Gilbert le Peftour, 1 Edward ii. II. 82.

Peter bifhop of Winchefter, jufticier, 15 John, I. 36.

Peter fon of Alan, a reteinour of earl John, 6 Richard i. I. 346. c. 1. *e.* Jocey fon of Peter alderman of London, the tallage for his ward, 14 Henry iii. I. 709. c. 1. *t.*

Peter chamberlain of the bifhop of Winton, 5 Stephen, I. 493. c. 1. *c.*

Peter pence paid at York, 31 Henry ii. I. 309. c. 1. *r.*

Peteresfeld in Hampfhire tallaged, 33 Henry ii. I. 736. c. 2. *q.* William de Peteresfeld his tenure in Guldeford quit of tallage, 52 Henry iii. I. 749. c. 2. *x.*

Petipas, Richard, attorney of Mr. William de Ripariis in Ireland, 30 Edward i. II. 180. c. 1. *y.*

Petit or Parvus, Odo le, accompts, 8 Richard i. I. 280. c. 1. *z.* Accompts again to the king for the profits of the exchange of London, 9 John, I. 283. c. 2 *q.*

Petraponte, Simon de, held of the church of Chichefter, temp. Henry ii. I. 576. c. 2.

Petworth or Pedewurda honor in the king's hands, 31 Henry ii. I. 298. c. 1. *b.* Again in the king's hands, 1 Richard, I. 298. c. 2. *p.*

Pevenfe Caftle in the cuftody of Robert de Sapy, 15 Edward ii. I. 383. c. 2. Barons of Pevenfel fine for the fame liberties as the cinque ports have, 9 John, I. 408. c. 2. *r.* Have a Sunday's market, ibid. Donum of the knights of Pevenfel, 5 Henry ii. I. 697. c. 2. *y.* Accompts by the fherif of Suffex, ibid. The quinzime of the merchandife for the port of Pevenefel, 6 John, I. 772. c. 1. *i.* Richard de Pevenfel, fherif of Surrey, 14 Edward i. II. 258. c. 1. *d.*

Peurel, baron William, 1 Stephen, I. 14. c. 2. Thomas Peverel of Hampfhire, 50 Henry iii. I. 100. Ralf Pevrel buried in St Paul's London, before an. 1142. I. 198. c. 1. *e.* And bequeathed to it the land of Edburgheton to find lights, ibid. The honor of William de Pevrel of London in the cuftody of William Trefgoz, 5 Stephen, I. 297. c. 1. *c.* The honor of William Pevrel of Notingham in cuftody of Robert Fitz-Ralf, 19 Henry ii. I. 297. c. 2. *k.* The honor of William Peverel in the king's hands, 31 Henry ii. I. 298. c. 1. *d.* The honor of Peverel of Notingham in the king's hands, 8 John, I. 298. c. 2. *a.* Robert Peverel accompts for the honor of Angria, 14 John, I. 299. c. 1. *e.* And for the fee of Exeter, 14 John, I. 312. c. 1. *r.* Honor of William Peverel of Notingham in cuftody of Hugh Bardolf, 5 John, I. 405. c. 1. *p.* Hugh Peverel, 10 John, I. 442. c. 2. *d.* Cecily widow of Hugh Peverel, 22 Henry iii. I. 466. c. 1. *x.* Alice Peverel and her fon Geoffrey contend for their fhare of the honor of Brun which was Maud de Doura's, 31 Henry ii. I. 512. c. 2. *u.* The honor of W. Peverel in the king, 14 Edward ii. I. 535. c. 1.

INDEX.

c. 1. Robert Peverel held of the bishop of Chichester, temp. Henry ii. I. 576. c. 2. Scutage of the honor of Peverel of London, 3 Richard i. I. 637. c. 1. e. Nicolas de Guronde held two fees of the honor of Peverel of Dovor, 14 Henry iii. I. 647. c. 2. z. Hugh Peverel settles the king's tallage in Hertfordshire, 8 Richard i. I. 704. c. 1. o. John Peverel constable of the Exchequer, 51 Henry iii. II. 14. c. 1. n. Impleads several for beating his servant Eudo Haddoc, ibid. Robert Peverel, who, 34 Edward i. II. 74. c. 2. u. Honor of Peverel in Northamptonshire, II. 141. c. 2. t. Honor of Peverel of London accompted for by the sherif of Essex on his verumdictum, 14 Henry ii. II. 182. c. 2. u. Thomas the writer of Hugh Peverel, 5 Richard i. II. 274. c. 2. d. and 8 Richard i. II. 275. c. 1. f. John Peverel made constable of the Exchequer till Robert de Foleham could attend, 49 Henry iii. II. 282. c. 1. i. Again made constable by Humfrey de Bohun earl of Hereford, 52 Henry iii. II. 282. c. 1. l. John Peverel deputy chamberlain of the Exchequer, 53 Henry iii. II. 297. c. 1. e.

Peverelli, Hadfeld, its aid, 14 Henry ii. I. 586. c. 2.

Peyforer, Fulk, 56 Henry iii. I. 253. c. 1. x, y. Fulk Payforer sherif of Kent, 49 Henry iii. II. 202. c. 2. y. Lora wife of William Peyforer sister and one of the heiresses of Simon del Eschequer, 32 Edward i. II. 277. Inherited her share of the ushery, ib.

Peyntur, Alexander le, has the office of tronage in London, 2 Edward ii. I. 780. c. 1. i.

Peytevin, Ralf le, deputy of William de Bickele sherif of Devonshire, 52 Henry iii. II. 180. c. 1. z.

Philip king of France, an. 1188. raises a disme of rents and movables for the crusade, I. 21. His long reign, an. 1221. I. 28. c. 1. f. His grant to the citisens of Roan, an. 1207. I. 763. c. 2. c. Gave to Christ Church of Canterbury an hundred modii of wine out of reverence to Thomas a Becket the martyr, before 3 John, I. 766. c. 1. o.

Philip son of Robert, son of Hugh, his scutage for his knights fees in Lincolnshire, 33 Henry ii. I. 713. c. 1. d.

Philip late mayor of Grimesbi, 1 Edward i. II. 239. c. 2. f.

Philippa widow of Robert Briton, 5 John, I. 438. c. 2. d.

Pichard, Hamon, whether intitled to the land of Wereslea, 15 Henry ii. I. 447. c. 1. t. Richard Picard sherif of London committed, 38 Henry iii. II. 240. c. 1. k, l.

Picheford, Geoffrey de, constable of Windsor castle, 26 Edward i. II. 224. c. 1. m.

Pichot sherif of Cambridgeshire, I. 32. c. 1. d. Ralf Picot, 2 Henry ii. I. 61. c. 2. b. Ralf Pikot's interest in Reines and Ardlega, of the fee of Henry de Essex, 6 Richard i. I. 316. c. 2. g. Robert Picot to whom his two daughters were married, before 5 Henry iii. I. 318. c. 1. u. Ralf Pikot a benefactor to the abbey of Feversham, before temp. Henry iii. I. 413. c. 2. k. Ralf Picot sherif of Kent, 2 Henry ii. I. 689. c. 1. p. Gregory and Ralf Picot their assise, 2 Henry ii. I. 690. c. 1. s. Nicolas Pycot sherif of London, 1 Edward ii. II. 97. c. 1. b.

Piddelton

INDEX.

Piddelton hundred belonged to William de Montague, 1 John, I. 485. c. 2. f. Samuel priest of Pilton in the honor of Richard de Montague, 14 Henry ii. I. 527. c. 1. c.

Pietas, pity or mercy in Romance, Pref. xxiv.

Pigace, John, one of the justices in Normandy, 2 John, I. 156. c. 1. i.

Pikeringlith, I. 506. c. 2. y. The donum of Pikering, Yorkshire, towards the expedition in Galway, 33 Henry ii. I. 635. c. 2. The donum of Pikering, 3 Richard i. I. 698. c. 2. q. Pikering wapentak and town tallaged, 9 Richard i. I. 699. c. 1. r. The tallage of the town and soke, 11 Henry iii. I. 707. c. 1. i. Again, I. 710. c. 1. w. Forest of Pikering, II. 132. c. 1. h.

Pikenot, Robert, justice itinerant, 22 Henry ii. I. 128.

Piledon, Simon de, Dorsetshire, 6 Henry iii. I. 445. c. 1. a. Fines to have mention in his writ of grand assise, of the time of Richard i. ibid.

Pilevel, Mirabel daughter of John de, 10 John, I. 218. c. 1. p. Her quit claim, ibid.

Pin, Thomas de, sherif of Devonshire, before 18 Edward i. II. 159. c. 1. e. Hawise his widow, ibid. Thomas del Pyn sherif of Devonshire, 10 Edward i. II. 162. c. 2. w. See Pyn.

Pincerna, Fitz-Alured, 5 Stephen, I. 67. c. 2. i.

Pincerna, William de Albino, 1 Stephen, I. 14. c. 2. s. His knights, 14 Henry ii. I. 142. c. 2. f. Hugh Pincerna fermer of the honor of William de Curci, 19 Henry ii. I. 297. c. 1. i. Master John and Herbert Pincerna have the custody of Hide abbey, 19 Henry ii. I. 308.

c. 2. l. Richard Pincerna married Alice one of the heiresses of Robert Picot, before 5 Henry iii. I. 318. c. 1. u. The son and land of Hugh Pincerna in Surrey in the wardship of Odo de Dammartin, 28 Henry ii. I. 322. c. 1. u. Richard Fitz-Alured Pincerna, 5 Stephen, I. 457. c. 2. r. Ernald Pincerna held of the bishop of Chichester, temp. Henry ii. I. 576. c. 1. y. Pincerna accompted for the king's wines, temp. Henry iii. I. 766. Henry de Say Pincerna and king's attorney, 1 Edward ii. II. 82. William Trente the king's Pincerna, 35 Edward i. II. 261. c. 1. r.

Pincernaria. See Butlership, Martel.

Pincun, Robert, his land in Edburg, Warwickshire, 3 John, I. 436. c. 2. u.

Pine, William, of Somersetshire, attached, 45 Henry iii. II. 79. c. 1. y.

Pinkenni, Robert de, 10 Richard i. I. 39. c. 2. a. Gilbert de Pinkeni, 16 Henry ii. I. 140. c. 1. w. Henry de Pynkeny a baron summoned by writ to the Scotch war, 26 Edward i. I. 655. c. 2. And one of the king's court, ibid.

Pipard, Gilbert, justice errant in Devonshire, 22 Henry ii. I. 128, &c. Sherif of Lancashire, 1 Richard i. I. 205. c. 2. l. Justicier at Lincoln, 27 Henry ii. I. 556. c. 2. w. Ralf Pipard one of the barons summoned against the Scots, 26 Edward i. I. 655. c. 1. Walter Pipard his fees in Oxfordshire, 4 John, I. 666. c. 1. h. Walter and William his son, 11 Henry iii. II. 6. c. 1. z. Fermers of Hintlesdon, ibid.

Piperel, honor of, 19 Henry ii. I. 297. c. 2. k. See Pevrel. Honor of Piperel of Dovor, 18 Henry ii. I. 630. c. 1. d.

Pipewel,

INDEX

Pipewel, abbat of, receives Richard i. after his coronation, I. 22. Andrew abbat of Pypewel, 28 and 34 Edward i. I. 670. c. 2. *f.*

Pipin, his liberality to the church of S. Victor, I. 159. c. 2. *z.* And to the bishop of Marseilles, ibid. c. 2. *e.*

Pirariis, Henry de, accompts for Warr. and Legerc. 23 Henry ii. I. 210. c. 1. *f.* Henry and William de Pirariis contend for the terra de Saxeby, 21 Henry ii. I. 450. c. 1. *o.* William de, why amerced, 18 Henry ii. I. 560. c. 1. *q.*

Piratum, or Perry, I. 367. c. 2. *l.*

Piriford manor, granted by the Conqueror to Westminster abbey, I. 764.

Piro, William de, his seisure, 1 Richard i. II. 231. c. 2. *d.*

Pirot, Ralf, baron of the Exchequer early under Henry ii. I. 215. c. 1. *a.* His payment for his fees in Cambridge and Huntingdonsh. towards the king's ransom, 7 Richard i. I. 593. c. 1. *c.* Quit of scutage, 3 John, I. 665. c. 1. *e.*

Pirour, William de, dapifer of Henry i. I. 53. c. 1. *p.*

Pissebolle, terra de, I. 205. c. 1.

Pistorio, Andrew de, of the company of Friscobalds, committed to the Tower of London, 5 Edward ii. II. 239.

Piwelesdon, Mr Thomas de, 49 Henry iii. I. 76. c. 1. *u.* Present when Thomas de Cantelupe was chosen chancellor by the king and the magnates, ibid.

Planchis de Airel, the land of, William Semille, 2 John, I. 171. c. 1. *x.*

Planes, Roger de, fines for the daughter of Adam de Port and widow of Richard de Riveriis, 2 John, I. 520. c. 2. *h.* His plegius, ibid. Roger de Planes had the land of Huiam belonging to the barony of Dovor, before 10 Richard i. II. 226. c. 1. *w.*

Pleas of the crown and common Pleas how ancient, I. 142. Placitum signified primarily not a pecuniary mulct but a Plea, I. 210. Common Pleas when divided from the Exchequer, I. 213, 214. And how divided, II. 73, 74. Plea-Rolls in the Exchequer, II. 112. Pleas de vetito namio, II. 168.

Pleiford, Fulcher, his dependance on the earl of Moriton, I. 429. c. 1. *m.*

Pless, John de, earl of Warwick, his aid, 39 Henry iii. I. 617. c. 1. *f.* John de Pleissis earl of Warwick had not that earldom hereditarily, 40 Henry iii. I. 683. c. 2. *w.*

Plinton in Devonshire, I. 445. c. 2. *f.* The burgesses fine for an inquisition about their liberties, ibid.

Plugenoi, Hugh de, sherif of Kent, about 5 Henry ii. I. 365. c. 2. *x.* His claim in Hedendun, Oxfordshire, 2 Henry ii. II. 163. c. 1. *y.*

Plukenet, Alan, one of the barons called by writ to the Scotch war, 26 Edward i. I. 655. c. 2.

Plumland, town of, earl Richard in Devonshire, 24 Henry ii. I. 605. c. 2. *o.*

Plumton, sir Gilbert de, condemned to be hanged for committing a rape, an. 1184. 30 Henry ii. I. 20. But reprieved by the king's pity, ibid. c. 1. *o.* Plumton in Devonshire, that lordship the property of earl Richard, 24 Henry ii. I. 605. c. 1. *o.*

Pockelinton soke, Yorkshire, its donum to the Irish army, 33 Henry ii. I. 635. c. 2. *r.* and 3 Richard i. I. 698. c. 2. *q.*

Podio, Orlandini de, 7 Edward i. I.

INDEX.

662. c. 1. o. Cuſtos of the London mint, 7 Edward i. II. 90. c. 2. u. and II. 194. c. 2. k.

Poet of the king, 35 Henry iii. I. 391. c. 1. t. His ſtipend, II. 202. c. 1. w.

Poher, Ralf, ſherif of Herefordſhire in Wales, 23 Henry ii. I. 130. c. 1. q. William le Pohier, 6 Henry iii. I. 454. c. 2. h. Henry ſon of Ralf le Poher ſlain, before 4 Henry iii. I. 495. c. 2. f. Hugh le Poer's knights in Herefordſhire, 14 Henry iii. I. 677. c. 1. b.

Poictiers, archdeacon of, juſtice errant, 22 and 23 Henry ii. I. 131, &c. and I. 307. c. 1. y. Richard archdeacon of, fermer of the ſee of Wincheſter, 18 Henry ii. I. 366. See I. 585. c. 1. s.

Poictou, or Poictiers, Richard archdeacon of, the king's chief juſticier for many years, 20 Henry ii. I. 123, 124, &c. and I. 204. c. 2. k. See I. 215. c. 1. a. One of the fermers of the ſee of Lincoln, 18 Henry ii. I. 346. c. 1. i. Quere, If two of the name of Richard did not ſucceed to this dignity? Was cuſtos of the abbey of Glaſton and the ſee of Wincheſter, 18 Henry ii. I. 631. c. 1. f, g. Eſcuage of Poictou, I. 640. c. 1. s.

Poilton, Alured de, in miſericordia, 12 Henry ii. I. 541. c. 1. g.

Pole, Richard de la, has the commiſſion of array for Kyngeſton on Hull, 16 Edward ii. II. 112. c. 2.

Polhampton, Richard de, ſteward of Cornwal, 9 Edward ii. I. 624. c. 1. k.

Policy, I. 119.

Poll, men of York paid their donum by poll, 9 Richard i. I. 699.

Pollards, a ſpecies of coin, temp. Edward i. and Edward ii. I. 294. William Pollard, 11 Henry iii. II. 118. c. 2. i.

Polſtede, Hugh de, 9 John, I. 441. c. 2. y. Fines for a jury, ibid. Michael de Polſtede, the official of Norwich ordered to diſtrain him, 11 Henry iii. II. 249. c. 1. e.

Pomeray, Henry de la, 2 John, I. 172. c. 2. z. Geoffrey de la, Devonſh. 13 Henry iii. I. 347. c. 2. y. Henry de la Pomeray fines that the men of Exeter may have as good liberty as the men of Lidford, 9 John, I. 408. c. 2. t. Henry's grant of the land of Ar to H. Furnel, 9 Richard i. I. 790. c. 1. i. Maud widow of Henry de, 53 Henry iii. II. 304. c. 1. m.

Ponderatores of the Exchequer, II. 21. Again, II. 307. See Peſor. Ponderator Denariorum, II. 309. c. 2. g.

Pontanus's Origines Francicæ, Pref. xviii. c. 1. e, h, i. xix. and xxiv. c. 2. b.

Ponte, Robert de, ſells his half vavaſorſhip in Normandy on oath, I. 156. c. 1. h. Several London gilds de Ponte, 26 Henry ii. I. 562. c. 1. z. Henry de Ponte removed from being chamberlain of the Exchequer in Ireland, 22 Edward i. II. 136. c. 1. x.

Pontealcd, Henry de, 2 John, I. 523. c. 2. t.

Ponte Alerici, William ſon of Roger de, 5 Stephen, I. 497. c. 1. a.

Ponte arca, William de, chamberlain, 1 Stephen, I. 13. c. 2. s. Fined for the office and the daughter of Robert Mauduit, I. 58. c. 2. c. Oſbert brother of William, temp. Stephen, ibid. This family probably had the chamberlainſhip of Normandy, I. 58, 59. Cuſtos of the king's treaſures,

INDEX.

fures, I. 78, 79. Occurs, I. 165. William de Pontearch fherif of Hampfhire, temp. Stephen, I. 327. c. 1. *s*. And of Berkfhire, ibid. c. 2. *e*. William de Pontearch fines for feifin of his terra de Swindon, 9 Henry iii. I. 492. c. 1. *x*. Which had been arrefted for his non-appearance in the Welch army, ibid. William de Pontearch fines for a diftringas, 2 John, I. 519. c. 2. *z*.

Ponteburgh, William de, has a commiffion of array for the wapentak of Knarefburgh, 16 Edward ii. II. 112.

Pontefract, its tallage, 30 Henry iii. I. 710. c. 1. *w*. Richard de Ponte Fracto endures above three years imprifonment for fifhing in the king's ponds, 27 Edward i. II. 64. c. 2. *c*. Prior of Pomfret, 5 Edward i. II. 294. c. 2. *s*.

Pontibus, Reginald de, of Yorkfhire, 16 John, II. 211. c. 1. *b*. Pledge of Peter de Maillai for a thoufand marks, ibid.

Pontiniaco, William de, temp. Henry i. I. 56. c. 1. *o*. Earl of Pontiu has his danegeld remitted in Wiltfhire, 2 Henry ii. I. 687. c. 1. *i*.

Pope ufed to grant quintadecima's, vicefima's, &c. 4 Edward i. I. 353. c. 1. *m*. A triennial difme impofed by the Pope on the clergy, 5 Edward ii. II. 72. Pope's nuncio complains to the barons of the Exchequer againft the mayor of London, 12 Edward ii. II. 110. Pope had nine or ten thoufand annual marks from England, nomine cenfus, 9 Edward i. II. 137. c. 1. *a*. The Pope had a fourth referved, 5 Edward ii. II. 159. Has the fee of Canterbury kept vacant for his ufe, 35 Edward i. II. 224. Pope Boniface VIII. impofed a difme on the clergy for three years, II. 292. c. 1. *i*.

Porceftre, its tallage, 14 Henry iii. I. 703. c. 1. *o*. Again, 3 Henry iii. II. 118. c. 1. *g*.

Porfhore, William de, chamberlain of the Exchequer, 25 Edward i. II. 299. c. 1. *o*.

Porta Sueine de, his debet for the pleas of Ralf Baffet, Notingham, and Derbyfhire, 5 Stephen, I. 146. c. 2. *p*. Henry de Port holds pleas in Chent, 5 Stephen, I. 147. c. 1. *x*. Ingelram de Port had the honor of Spiney, before 3 John, I. 170. c. 2. *t*. Adam de Port fines for his lands in Normandy and Hampfhire, 26 Henry ii. I. 473. c. 1. *q*. Adam de Port, 22 Henry ii. I. 482. c. 2. *g*. Adam de Port marries his daughter fucceffively to Richard de Riveriis and Roger de Planes, 2 John, I. 520. c. 2. *g*, *h*. Adam de Port's knights fees in Herefordfhire, 7 Henry ii. I. 628. c. 2. *y*. John de Port's honor in Hampfhire, before 22 Henry ii. I. 642. c. 2. *c*. Adam de Port's fcutage for his Hampfhire fees, 2 Richard i. I. 667. c. 2. *p*. Was furety for Ralf de Cornhul, 9 Richard i. II. 198. c. 1. *r*. William chamberlain of the Exchequer, 18 Edward i. II. 298. c. 1. *n*.

Portejoye, John, his ftation in the chancery, 55 Henry iii. I. 60. c. 2. *y*.

Porter of Canterbury executioner for Kent, I. 373. c. 2. *c*.

Portefmuth fines for juftices to hold pleas there, 3 Henry iii. I. 444. c. 2. *w*.

Ports, a jufticiary of them, 7 John, I. 461. c. 2. *d*. Five Ports amerced for conveying corn to the king's enemies in Flanders, 1 John, I. 565. c. 2. *p*. Stephen de Peneceftre conftable

INDEX.

stable of Dovor receiver of the Cinque Ports in the close of Henry iii. I. 610. c. 2. The warden and barons of the five Ports, 33 Edward i. I. 613. c. 1. s. Five Ports quit by charter from paying the king recta prisa for their own wines, 6 Edward i. I. 770. c. 2. a. Enumeration of the several Ports of England, I. 772. c. 1. i. Ship arrested for putting in where was no Port, I. 773.

Portsoken ward in London, its tallage, 14 Henry iii. I. 709. c. 1. t. The tallage of Portsockene ward, 19 Henry iii. I. 738. c. 2. z. I. 739. c. 1. a.

Portyngton, Nicolas de, has the commission of array for Hoveden, 16 Edward ii. II. 212. c. 2.

Possession of thirty-one years adjudged a good prescription in private life, I. 90.

Poter, Walter le, sherif of London, 1 Edward i. II. 96. c. 1. w.

Poterne, James de, justice itinerant in Wiltshire, 9 John, I. 507. c. 2. g. The donum of the manor of Poterne while the bishop of Sarum's, 33 Henry ii. I. 634. c. 2. James accompts for the tallage of the see of York, 3 John, I. 706. c. 1. a.

Pourestok, its tallage, 14 Henry iii. I. 708. c. 1. o.

Poyntel, John, sherif of London, 12 Edward ii. II. 234. c. 1. o.

Poyntz, Hugh, one of the barons of Somerset or Dorsetshire, called by the king's writ to the war in Scotland, 26 Edward i. I. 655. c. 2. Nicolas Poyns, 52 Henry iii. II. 18. c. 2. p. John Poynz sherif of London, 12 Edward ii. II. 98. c. 2. d.

Poywick, Mr William de, 50 Henry iii. I. 101. c. 2. e. Extends some lands of Maud countess dowager of Clare, ibid.

Pratario, Robert de, his payment, an. 1184. I. 168. c. 2.

Pratellis, Maud de, fines, I. 167. c. 2. John de, 2 John, I. 175. c. 1. m. Peter de, I. 176. John and William de Pratellis of Normandy, 2 John, I. 523. c. 1. r. John de, 4 John, I. 537. c. 1. John de, 3 John, I. 766. c. 1. o.

Pratis, Hervey de, his fee at the Exchequer, 4 John, I. 176. c. 1. r. Peter de, ibid. c. 2. t.

Prato or Pree, prior de, his privilege in Normandy, I. 163. c. 2. x.

Preariis, Henry de, had the land of Turlaveston in custody, before 6 John, I. 151. c. 1. u. Fulk de Prees has the honor of Spiney, 3 John, I. 170. c. 2. t. Peter de Prees justicier of Normandy, I. 171. c. 1. u. Robert de Praeres, 18 Henry ii. I. 632. c. 2. n. His scutage in Sussex, ibid.

Prendelgast, Robert de, 30 Henry ii. I. 447. c. 2. a. Fines for dispatch, ibid.

Presentation of officers in the Exchequer, II. 87. Of mayors and sherifs, II. 92.

Presteton, belonged to the family of Montfort, 5 Stephen, I. 58. c. 2. b. Preston fines for the same liberties as Newcastle, 26 Henry ii. I. 398. c. 1. t. Has confirmation of liberties, 2 John, I. 402. c. 2. m. A plaint brought against them for their gibbet and goal, 3 John, I. 498. Preston Gileberti a town of the king of Scots, 14 Henry ii. I. 540. c. 1. z. Amerced, 31 Henry ii. I. 547. c. 1. z. Gilbert de, justicier, 39 Henry iii. II. 22. c. 1. r. and II. 202. c. 1. x.

Presthope,

INDEX.

Presthope, Roger de, of Middlesex, 15 Edward ii. II. 212. c. 2. *i.*

Preston, Walter, 10 John, I. 151. c. 2. *x.* Gilbert justice of the bank, 52 Henry iii. I. 236. Alexander de, disseized, 3 John, I. 487. c. 2. *t.* Its tallage, 11 Henry iii. I. 707. c. 1. *h.* Thomas de Preston contends for the advouson of Perham, 9 John, I. 791. Gilbert de Preston justice itinerant, 53 Henry iii. II. 71. c. 1. *i.* John customer in the port of London, 16 Edward ii. II. 91.

Prestwude, Thomas de, rewarded for bringing the head of an outlaw, 7 Richard i. I. 201. c. 2. *t.*

Pridias, Thomas, 1 Edward ii. II. 209. c. 2. *r.* Has a writ for the attermination of his debts, ibid.

Prin of queen's gold, I. 350. 360. c. 2. *s.*

Pringet, William, 5 Richard i. I. 564. c. 2. *f.* Amerced on his frankpledge, ibid.

Prior of Bath a lord, an. 1121. I. 109. Prior of Stutesbiri, I. 448. c. 2. *k.* Prior of Bernewell's right to Cestretun, II. 119. c. 1. *q.*

Prisa or recta Prisa, the custom or king's duty for wines, I. 765. Properly signifyed capture, ibid. The other senses of that word, ibid. Richard de Prisa accompts for the prise of the king's wines, 30 Henry iii. I. 768. c. 2. *w.*

Prison, fines for release out of it, I. 493, &c.

Pritewel, the aid of Reynold the provost and the men of it, 14 Henry ii. I. 586. c. 2. The manor of John de Warenne earl of Surrey, 2 Edward ii. I. 646. c. 1. *w.* The tallage or assise of Priterewell, 19 Henry ii. I. 701. c. 1. *z.*

Privilege not to be impleaded but in the king's court, I. 116, &c. Privileges granted to the king's debtors, II. 185, 186.

Privy Seal, as ancient as the time of king John, I. 86. See I. 265. c. 2. *e.* Privy Purse, I. 266. c. 1. *h.* Writs of Privy Seal, I. 358. Of Privy Seal and Liberate, I. 386, 387. Writs of Privy Seal granted for the recovery of debts, II. 76.

Prizes of woollen and linen cloth for the Exchequer, temp. Henry ii. &c. I. 191. Of several cattle and grain, 14 Henry iii. II. 152. c. 2. *z.*

Probitas, where it means prowess, Pref. xxiv, xxv.

Prodome, Elias and Isabel his wife, 12 Edward ii. II. 234. c. 1. *o.*

Profer, I. 267. c. 1. *o.* Was a prepayment made by sherifs twice a year, II. 153. The great penalties for a few days neglect of it, II. 154.

Professed in religion, a priest and his wife who became such, forfeited chattels to the king, 12 Henry ii. I. 346. c. 2. *l.*

Proprestures, I. 498. c. 1. *b.* ibid. c. 2. *n.* Ferm of the Proprestures, II. 284. c. 1. *x.*

Protections against being impleaded but before the king or his justicier, I. 116, &c. Protection to William de Merlai's effects, against the king intra septa ecclesiæ, 16 Henry ii. II. 182. c. 2. *w.*

Provers, I. 372, 373, 374.

Provinz, Theobald earl of, his merchants, 5 Stephen, I. 364. c. 1. *n.*

Provisors, statute of, I. 304.

Prudhume, Martin, 10 John, I. 442. c. 2. *e.* His liberum tenementum, ibid.

Prunhill or Primhill manor in Sussex, I. 107.

INDEX.

I. 107. c. 1. *b.* To whom it belonged, with its marsh, 4 John, ibid.

Puger, Elias, lieutenant of the constable of the Tower of London, 2 Edward ii. II. 49. c. 1. *i.* Baron of the Exchequer for surveying the king's castles and manors, 1 Edward ii. II. 67. c. 1. *q.* Mareschal of the Exchequer, 1 Edward ii. II. 286. c. 2. *g.*

Pugno, John cum, 16 Henry ii. I. 563. c. 1. *e.*

Puher, William le, fermer of the honor of William de Curci, 19 Henry ii. I. 297. c. 1. *i.* John le Puhier justicier about 6 Richard i. I. 592. c. 2. *y.* Robert Puhier custos of the land and heir of William de Curci dapifer, 33 Henry ii. I. 635, 636. c. 1. *s.* Walter le Puiher deputed sherif of Worcestershire, 10 John, II. 152. c. 2. *y.*

Puingnard, William, 2 John, I. 173. c. 2. *e, f.* I. 174. c. 1. *g.* Sherif of Caen, ibid.

Puintel, William, constable of the Tower of London, 2 Richard i. I. 387. c. 2. *y.* I. 388. c. 1. *z.*

Puinton, Alexander de, 4 John, I. 438. c. 1. *a.* Or Pointon tallager of Lincolnshire, 8 John, I. 734. c. 2. *b.*

Puisac, Henry del, of Yorkshire, fines for the daughter of Otho de Tilli, 31 Henry ii. I. 513. c. 1. *x.*

Pulain, John, his fee of Moreton, 14 Henry iii. I. 661. c. 1. *i.* Robert Pulein the bishop of Durham's sergeant, 8 Richard i. I. 715. c. 2.

Puletarii, I. 76. c. 2. *x.*

Puncard, Simon de, his serjeanty, 3 John, I. 650. c. 1. *l.*

Punchardon, Roger de, of Devonshire, 10 John, I. 169. c. 2. *p.*

Punnaunt, Alan, accompts for the profits of the see of Canterbury, 13 Henry iii. I. 718. c. 1. *n.*

Punninges, Michael, of Sussex, fines for a market at Crawley, 4 John, I. 404. c. 2. *i.*

Puntdeburc in Yorkshire have a confirmation of liberties, 6 Richard i. I. 400. c. 1. *m.*

Puntoise, John de, of London, 2 Edward ii. II. 31. c. 1. *i.* Held the same office in the coinage at the Tower that John le Porcher did, 2 Edward ii. II. 90.

Puntus, the point of a sword, I. 366. c. 1. *e.*

Purse or Bursa of each county, I. 287.

Puteaco, Henry de, wrongfully disseized of the land of Colingeham and Cumpton, temp. Henry ii. I. 483. c. 2. *q.* Amerced before the justiciers, 10 Richard i. I. 527. c. 2. *e.* One of Ralf de Cornhul's sureties, 9 Richard i. II. 198. c. 1. *r.*

Pykering soke, its tallage, 14 Henry iii. I. 708. c. 2. *p.* See Pikering. Pykering wapentake under a commission of array, 16 Edward ii. II. 112. c. 2.

Pyn, Thomas de, sherif of Devonshire, 8 Edward ii. II. 31. c. 2. *q.* Sherif, before 5 Edward i. II. 142. c. 2. *b.* Committed to the mareschal for a deficiency, 4 Edward i. II. 288. c. 1. *p.* See Pin.

Pyreu, William de, fines for the land of William de Tracey, 2 John, I. 522. c. 1. *n.*

Pyrie, Richard de la, of Cyrnecestre, 40 Henry iii. I. 746. c. 1. *c.* Thomas de Pirie committed for personating the bailif of Oxford, 9 Edward ii. II. 248.

Q.

INDEX.

Q.

Quachehaud, Godwin, accused of falsifying the coin, 5 Stephen, I. 497. c. 1. *x*.

Quadragesima granted, 17 Henry iii. I. 269. c. 2. *a*.

Quappelad and Holbech in Lincolnshire, whose, 35 Henry iii. I. 795. c. 2. *r*.

Quatremaris, William de, 2 Henry iii. I. 475. c. 2. *n*. Fines for the king's favour, ibid.

Quedic, Warin de, his amerciament affeered, 9 John, I. 528. c. 1. *g*.

Queen Ann's care of the records, Pref. v.

Queen consort had her chancellor, I. 60. Alienor sat in court and held pleas as custos regni, I. 102. Had a keeper of her gold, 52 Henry iii. I. 272. c. 2. *e*. The Queen had wardships, 39 Henry iii. II. 299. c. 2. *t*.

Queen's gold, I. 350, &c. payable especially, if not only, by the king's tenants in capite, ibid. Seems to amount to a tenth part of the fine paid to the king, I. 350 c. 2. *s*. Eleanor Queen-dowager had aurum reginæ, 7, 9, and 10 Edward i. I. 351. c. 2. *d, e*. Where the queen had no gold, I. 353. c. 1. *m*. Robe for the queen cost fourscore pounds six shillings and eight pence, 5 Hen. ii. I. 366. c. 1. *a*. Queen's cordubanarius, 2 Henry ii. I. 602. c. 1. *y*. Queen's-hith fermed, I. 781. Called ripa reginæ, & heda reginæ, ibid. Again, II. 228. c. 1. *f*. Liberty of London with the mayor and sherifs seiz'd for non-payment of Queen's gold, 38 Henry iii. II. 240. c. 1. *b, m*. c. 2. *n*.

Quenci, Saiher de, earl of Winchester, his dividend of earl Robert's estate, I. 51. Seher de Quency, an. 1184. I. 168. c. 2. His payment to the crown, for Leicester and Warwickshire, 9 John, I. 189. c. 2. *d*. His payment to the king how made, 12 John, I. 273. c. 2. *h*. Roger de Quency son and heir of Margaret countess of Winchester, 3 Henry iii. I. 302. c. 2. *a*. Seiher de Quenci fines for the mediety of the suburbs of Leicester, 10 John, I. 490. c. 1. *r*. Roger de Quency, or Margaret countess of Winchester to accompt for sixty knights fees in Warwick and Leicestershire, 30 Henry iii. I. 595. c. 1. *n*. Saier de Quency quit of scutage, 3 John, I. 665. c. 2. *e*. R. de Quency earl of Winchester pardon'd for a defalt of summons in Bedfordshire, 39 Henry iii. II. 11. c. 1. *a*. Colne Quency in Essex, II. 84.

Quenhul manor in Worcestershire the property of William de Kerdyff, 15 Edward ii. II. 103. c. 2. *b*.

Quietus, quit, free or discharged, Pref. xxiv. passim.

Quinzime paid for merchandise, 6 John, I. 468. c. 1. *o*. Again Quinzime for merchandise, I. 771, &c.

Qwelvetham, Geoffrey and Walter de, 9 Henry iii. I. 239. c. 2. *b*. Geoffrey seems to be chirographer, ibid.

R.

Rabayne, Elias de, of Lincolnshire, his fees, 1 Edward i. I. 678. c. 2. *b*. Exempted from pleas, because attending the king in his expedition against Lewellin son of Griffin, 5 Edward i. II. 218. c. 1. *a*.

Rackferms, no hundreds, wapentakes,

INDEX.

or bayliwicks to be so rented, II. 102.

Radduna, Richard de, sherif of Somersetshire, 5 Henry ii. I. 697. c. 2. d.

Radeclive, Glocestershire, accompts for a thousand marks for the king's passage into Ireland, 12 John, I. 606. c. 2. x. The men of the knights Templars here, ibid.

Radegund, St, near Dovor, the king's chapel there, 30 Edward i. I. 73. c. 1. q. Henry prior here was king's treasurer, 49 Henry iii. II. 36. c. 2. f.

Radenor, Mr. Peter de, archdeacon of Salop, and executor of John le Fraunceys, 52 Henry iii. II. 186. c. 1. q.

Radford, Notinghamshire, its tallage, 9 Richard i. I. 733. c. 1. p.

Rading monks discharg'd from scutage, 15 Henry iii. I. 674. c. 1. o. Their lands in Herefordshire, temp. Stephen, II. 138. c. 2. e. The foreign hundred of Rading, II. 166.

Radley, William de, his rolls, before 42 Henry iii. II. 257. c. 1. b.

Ragemer of Devonshire, his aid, 14 Henry ii. I. 588. c. 1. b.

Raimes, Robert de, of Suffolk, 5 Stephen, I. 476. c. 2. b. The eight knights fees of William de Raimis, 14 Henry ii. I. 573. c. 2. m. Richard de Reimis his fees, ibid. See Rames, Rannes.

Raley, Hugh de, sherif of Devonshire, 9 Henry ii. I. 691. c. 1. z. Accompts for the danegild of earl Reginald, ibid. Thomas de Ralegh sherif of Devonshire amerc'd, 35 Edward i. II. 237.

Ralf bishop of Chichester made chancellor of England by Henry iii. during his life, I. 63. With the power of assigning the seal, ibid. With the addition of the chancellorship of Ireland during life, I. 65. See Chichester.

Ralf or Rodolph translated from Rochester to Canterbury, I. 11. c. 2. k. His controversy with Turstein about precedence, I. 11. l.

Ralf [Langford] dean of St Paul's London, an. 1142. I. 198. c. 1. e.

Ralf archdeacon of Colchester accompts for the profits of the see of London, 1 Richard i. I. 311. c. 2. i.

Ralf abbat of Westminster, 9 John, I. 791. Contends for the advowson of Perham against Thomas de Preston, ibid. Fines that no forester shall come into the woods of Persore, 4 John, I. 253. c. 1. z.

Ramentona, Nigel de, Notinghamshire, 5 Stephen, I. 449. c. 1. a. Fines not to plead for his lands, ibid.

Ramesey, the compotus of that abbey, 14 John, I. 312. c. 1. q. Its charter of liberties, 4 John, I. 404. c. 2. h. Fine for a market of St Ives and Welles, ibid. Accompts for pleas, 21 Henry ii. I. 450. c. 2. r. Abbat fines for the removal of the archbishop of Nazareth, 5 John, I. 505. c. 1. i. Its scutage of Gannoc for four fees, 30 Henry iii. I. 667. c. 1. n. Claims Kings Kipton, I. 757. c. 1. u. Has the fairs of St Ives, II. 116. c. 1. q. In the king's hands, 26 Henry ii. II. 252. c. 2. w. Adam de Ramsey usher of the receipt, II. 299. and 26 Edward i. II. 302.

Rammesbiri, Mr John de, 11 John, I. 448. c. 2. k. That village in Wiltshire

INDEX.

shire amerc'd by G. Fitz-Peter, 31 Henry ii. I. 547. c. 1. y. The tallage of that manor as the bishop of Sarum's, 33 Henry ii. I. 634. c. 2.

Ramon, don Guillen de, steward of Catalunna, I. 54.

Randolph, John, executor of William de Braybeof, 13 Edward i. I. 231. c. 1. m. Commissioner for visiting the sea-ports on the concealment of customs, 27 Edward i. I. 784. c. 2. w.

Rannes, Roger de, of Essex, fined for making a park without licence, 5 Stephen, I. 557. c. 1. y.

Randulf perish'd by the tryal of water, 18 Henry ii. II. 131. c. 1. g.

Ransom of the king of Alemaign, 52 Henry iii. II. 276. Of king Richard i. I. 590.

Ranulph, chaplain of W. Rufus, made bishop of Durham, I. 9. c. 1. q. By whose advice Rufus had long govern'd, ibid.

Ranulph treasurer of Saresbiry and justicier, 10 Richard i. I. 565. c. 2. p. Again, I. 733. c. 2. s.

Rap of Hastings belong'd to the earl of Augi or Ou, temp. Henry ii. II. 577. c. 2. z. See Rappum.

Rape punishable with death, 30 Henry ii. I. 20. A Rape of Robert Fitz Askil punished by fine, 3 Richard i. I. 105. c. 1. q. Rape compounded, 7 Henry ii. I. 501. c. 2. u.

Rapeston in Kent, the land of Walter Amfr. 17 Henry ii. I. 429. c. 2. t.

Rappendon, Geoffrey de, one of the justices in Normandy, 2 John, I. 156. c. 2. i.

Rappum or Rape, I. 563. c. 2. l. Rapp of Hastinges part of the honor of earl Augi, 9 John, I. 790. c. 2. m. Its seneschalcy contended for by Robert de Hastinges and Simon de Ecchingham, ibid.

Rase, Thomas de, 8 John, I. 494. c. 1. q. Fines for a legal tryal, ibid.

Rastel, Roger, king's huntsman for Ireland, 31 Henry ii. II. 206. c. 1. y.

Ratyndon, John de, cousin and heir of Alice Mucegros, 35 Edward i. I. 321.

Raveneserode or Ravensore, near Kingston upon Hull, I. 422. Wapentake of Ravensere under a commission of array, 16 Edward ii. II. 112. c. 2.

Raygate, Robert de, commissioner of array for the wapentak of Barkeston, 16 Edward ii. II. 112. c. 2.

Raynger, the tallage of alderman Richard's ward in London, 14 Henry iii. I. 709. c. 1. t. Again, 19 and 20 Henry iii. I. 738. c. 2. z. I. 739. c. 1. a. Richard Reinger chamberlain of London, 8 Henry iii. I. 777. c. 2. w, &c. Richard fermer of Queen's hith, 11 Henry iii. I. 781. c. 2. p. Occurs, 18 Henry iii. II. 35. Richard Rengier sherif of London, 6 Henry iii. II. 94. c. 2. p. Richard Reinger ferms the mints of London and Canterbury, 13 Henry iii. II. 134. c. 1. r.

Realm, its defence, II. 102.

Receipt of the Exchequer, I. 262. David chamberlain made usher of the receipt of the Exchequer, 49 Henry iii. II. 296. c. 1. z. By William Mauduit earl of Warwick, ibid. David de la More made usher of the receipt of the Exchequer by William de Beauchamp, 52 Henry iii. II. 296. c. 2. c. Moiety of the ushery of

INDEX.

of the receipt of the Exchequer forfeited by the felony of Adam de Stratton, 30 Edward i. II. 299. c. 2. *r.*

Rech and Newbigging, villages in Northumberland, amerc'd, 17 Henry ii. I. 544. c. 1. *l.*

Recham, Robert de, his tenure of the church of Chichester, temp. Henry ii. I. 576. c. 1. *y.*

Recognitions in the Exchequer, II. 86.

Records or Rolls how ancient, I. 178, 179. London fines to make a Record within the city, I. 509. Records and judgments of the Exchequer, II. 112.

Recreancy, amerciaments for it, I. 549.

Rectum, law or legal right in glossaries, Pref. xxiv. passim.

Redderbrug hundred in Sussex, amerc'd for concealment, &c. I. 544. c. 2. *r.*

Rede, Roger de, one of the keepers of the mint of the abbey of St Edmund, I. 293. c. 1. *e.*

Redemere, frere John de, 15 Edward ii. II. 40. c. 2. *x.*

Redham, William de, sherif of Norfolk and Suffolk, before 9 Edward i. II. 28. c. 2. *p.*

Redlega in Glocestershire, its tallage, Richard i. I. 703. c. 2. *n.*

Redvers in Devonshire, the scutage for the knights fees of Baldwin de, 20 Henry ii. I. 633. c. 2. *p.*

Regency left by king Richard i. I. 34. By Henry iii. I. 68.

Reginæ ripa, or Queen's hith in London, I. 779. Styled also heda Reginæ, I. 781. c. 1. *m.*

Reginald goldsmith of St Alban, 38 Henry iii. I. 761. c. 1.

Reginald son of Reginald, Hampshire, 12 John, I. 454. c. 1. *z.*

Reginald, earl, 28 Henry ii. I. 104. c. 2. *n.* Earl Reginald in Devonshire holds of the fee of earl Richard, 14 Henry ii. I. 581. c. 1. *s.* Earl Reginald sherif of Devonshire, 20 Henry ii. I. 633. c. 2. *p.* His honor in the king's hand, 32 Henry ii. I. 642. c. 2. *d.* Earl Reginald's fees were those of Moreton, and paid in proportion of three for two, 6 Richard i. I. 649. c. 1. *d.* Sherif of Devonshire, 19 Henry ii. I. 701. c. 1. *b.* See Cornwal.

Reigni, William de, Dorf. 31 Henry ii. I. 97. c. 2. *a.* John de Reinni his lands in socage, Cumb. 3 John, I. 672. c. 2. *l.*

Reinelm chancellor of the queen, temp. Henry i. I. 60. c. 1. *t.*

Reiner, Henry de, amerc'd for a trespass, an. 1184. I. 167. c. 1. *k.* Walter son of, 15 John, I. 639. c. 1. *o.* Dapifer of Randulf de Glanvil accompts for Westmoreland, 23 Henry ii. II. 183. c. 1. *y.*

Reiner son of Berengar sherif or fermer of London, 11 Henry ii. I. 363. c. 1. *d.* Richard son of Reiner sherif of London, 1 Richard i. I. 369. c. 1. *x.* William son of Reiner sherif of Essex, 32 Henry iii. I. 376. c. 2. *z.* Reiner son of Berengaria, 16 Henry ii. I. 746. c. 2. *f.*

Reinervill, Adam de, fines, &c. 28 Henry ii. I. 104. c. 2. *o.*

Reines, William de, amerc'd for ill keeping a duel, 14 Henry ii. I. 545. c. 1. *y.* Richard de Reimes's scutage, 30 Henry ii. I. 676. c. 1. *s.*

Reliefs, I. 315. Every knight's fee paid an hundred shillings for Relief, I. 319. c. 1. *d.* Relief for a barony or knights fees, whether larger or less, was the same, I. 321, 322.

What

INDEX.

What paid for a barony and knight's fee, I. 537, 538. How improperly taken away if at all, I. 620. c. 1. *b*.

Religious houses could not purchase lands without the king's licence, 31 Henry iii. I. 320. c. 1. *l*. Nigel de Alebi fines to take the habit of religion, 5 John, I. 505. c. 1. *k*, *l*. c. 2. *m*. Religious holding land in frankalmoigne paid no scutage so long as the donor had any land in the county on which that service could be levied, I. 671. c. 2. *h*. I. 672. c. 1. *i*.

Remanens firmæ post terras datas, what, II. 163. Remanens firmæ & proficui, II. 169.

Remembrancer of the Exchequer, I. 75. Two of that denomination, II. 62. Their office, II. 114. The same person was Remembrancer and clerk of the Exchequer, II. 263. Anciently there were two Remembrancers, II. 264. Their chest, ibid. And a Remembrancer of the treasurer, II. 265. Remembrancers sent into the country to ascertain and hasten the king's debts, II. 268. Make out the summonces of the Exchequer, ibid. Three Remembrancers, 4 Edward i. II. 269. c. 2. *f*.

Renglas manor in Cumberland, belong'd to Richard de Luci, 10 John, I. 409. c. 2. *f*. Who obtain'd one fair and weekly market for it, ibid.

Replevin or bail, I. 493.

Repple, John de, clerk, controller of the mines of Byrlonde, Devonshire, 2 Edward ii. II. 8. c. 2. *m*.

Res, William le, of Somersetshire, distrain'd per terras, 45 Henry iii. II. 79. c. 1. *y*.

Resebelle, William de, the fine for a concordant with him, 29 Henry ii. I. 212. c. 1. *o*.

Respectus or respite, I. 223. Again more particularly, II. 213. passim.

Restormel castle in Devonshire, in whose custody, II. 145. c. 1. *p*.

Retford granted to the townsmen, with a reservation of its tallage, 4 Edward i. I. 729. c. 1. *r*.

Retontores Judæi, or clippers to be banish'd, 22 Henry iii. I. 245. c. 2. *z*. Fined, I. 775. c. 1. *q*.

Revel, Robert, claims Suineford, 31 Henry ii. I. 97. c. 1. *x*. Richard sherif of Devonshire, 9 Richard i. I. 276. c. 2. *w*. Robert Revel fermer of Northampton, 5 Stephen, I. 330. c. 2. *d*. Again, I. 362. c. 2. *c*. Richard occurs, 6 John, I. 441. c. 1. *t*. Mabel de, heiress of Walter de Effelega, I. 755. c. 2. *r*.

Revenue Royal center'd in the Exchequer, I. 208. Revenue of Judaism, I. 221. Under the controll of the treasurer and barons, I. 249. Species in which the ancient crown revenue was paid, I. 272.

Revenue of the crown how anciently and usually paid, ibid. Paid ad scalam, ad pensum or by combustion, I. 274. Paid in blank and numero, I. 283, 284. Notable branches of the crown Revenue, I. 295. The casual Revenue, I. 342. Alms usually charged on the Revenue, I. 348. The manner of levying it, I. 353. And of issuing it out, I. 362. Affairs relating to the Revenue, II. 63.

Rever, Richard de, justicier of Normandy, 2 John, I. 171. c. 1. *u*.

Reynald, Walter, treasurer of the Exchequer, 1 Edward ii. II. 38. c. 1. *l*.

INDEX.

See Bishop of Worcester. Again treasurer of the king, 1 Edward ii. II. 47. c. 1. *x*. Seems to protect those who reviled the king, 9 Edward ii. II. 84. c. 1. *p*. Reynald son of Henry moneyour of S. Edmunds, 42 Henry iii. II. 89. c. 1. *l*.

Reynham, Robert de, accompts for the hundred of Clavering under Robert Fitz-Roger, 5 Edward i. II. 178. c. 2. *p*.

Ria, Avelin de, amerced for making her son knight while in the king's custody, 22 Henry ii. I. 561. c. 1. *f*. The fee of Hubert de Ria, before 2 Richard i. I. 664. c. 1. *z*. Had thirty-five fees in Norfolk and Suffolk, I. 666. c. 2. *l*. And seems to have married his daughters to John Mareschal and Roger de Cressy, ibid. The quinzime of the merchandise for the port of Ria, 6 John, I. 772. c. 2. *i*.

Ribald, Fulk, in misericordia, 12 Henry ii. I. 541. c. 1. *g*. Amerced for adjudging a duel, 16 Henry ii. I. 545. c. 1. *e*.

Ribbeford, Simon de, 4 John, I. 505. c. 2. *o*. Fines not to accompt beyond sea, ibid.

Riburc, Agnes de, her plea, 12 Henry ii. I. 429. c. 1. *n*.

Rich, Mainer le, of Canterbury, tallaged, 1 John, I. 737. c. 2. *t*.

Richard son of Nigel bishop of Ely, &c. I. 78. See London.

Richard i. the order of his coronation, an. 1189. I. 21. Whom he disseises and impleads after his ransom and return, I. 22, 23. His charter to the church of Roan, I. 29. c. 2. *q*. His regency, I. 34. Raises five shillings on every carue or hyde of land in England, I. 205. c. 2. *m*. Account of the preparations for his coronation, 1 Richard i. I. 369. c. 1. *x*, *y*, *z*. c. 2. *a*, &c. His grant to the canons of S. Denys, I. 409. c. 1. *a*. The scutage collected for his ransom, 6 Richard i. I. 590. Took five shillings out of every hyde or carucat of land, I. 605. His escuage for Galwey and Wales, I. 637, &c.

Richard, earl, has the tertius denarius of Devonshire, 5 Henry ii. II. 164. c. 1. *b*. See Cornwal.

Richard de Warenne son of king John, 25 Henry iii. I. 233. c. 2. *y*. Sherif of Staffordshire and Berkshire, 5 Henry iii. I. 286. c. 1. *d*. Again of Berkshire, 4 and 5 Henry iii. I. 329. c. 1. *u*.

Richard treasurer, 28 Henry ii. I. 113. Richard the treasurer goes the iters, 26 Henry ii. I. 139. c. 1. *g*, *h*. Richard the treasurer one of the barons of the Exchequer, I. 213. c. 1. *p*. Richard [Fitz-Niel] dean of Lincoln king's treasurer, an. 1184. 30 Henry ii. I. 215. c. 2. *d*. See London.

Richard [Toclif] elect of Winchester, custos of the bishoprick of Lincoln, 19 Henry ii. I. 308. c. 1. *c*. And at the same time custos of the fees of Winchester and Bath, ibid. c. 2. *m*, *n*. Was archdeacon of Poictiers, and fermer of the see of Winchester, 18 Henry ii. I. 366.

Richard archdeacon of Sarum, employed by the crown at Ambresberi, about 31 Henry ii. I. 311. c. 1. *d*.

Richard archdeacon of Covintre. See Briton.

Richard son of Turstin fermer of Winchester city, 22 Henry ii. I. 331. c. 2. *o*.

Richard son of Gerard de Aplebi, sherif of Westmoreland, temp. Stephen, I. 328, c. 1. *i*.

Richemund,

INDEX.

Richemund, honor of, I. 406. c. 1. *u.* Richemunt castle, I. 499. c. 1. *r.* See I. 594. c. 2. *i.* John de Britannia earl of, taken by the Scots, I. 615. c. 2. *z.* Ransomed, ibid. Hospital and nunnery of Richemunt, 18 Henry ii. I. 631. c. 2. *l.* Countess charged with an hundred forty knights, 1 John, I. 638. c. 1. *i.* John de Bretagne earl of Richmund sat in the Exchequer, 2 Edward ii. II. 30. c. 2. *g.*

Richer, William brother of Adam, son of Adam son of, 31 Henry ii. I. 483. c. 1. *k.*

Ridale, Patrick, 5 Richard i. I. 98. c. 1. *l.* Fines for a writ of Mordancestor in the king's court, or that of S. Peter de Braebi, ibid.

Ridel, Stephen, chancellor of the earl of Moreton, temp. Richard i. I. 60. c. 1. *t.* To accompt to earl John, I. 205. c. 2. *l.* Geoffrey Ridel fines to remove the king's displeasure, 26 Henry ii. I. 473. c. 1. *p.* The town, I. 506. c. 2. *y.*

Rideware, William de, justicier, 9 Richard i. I. 733. c. 1. *p.*

Riefhope, Richard and William fermours of, 8 Richard i. I. 714. c. 2. In the bishopric were tallaged, 11 Edward i. I. 720. c. 2. *u.*

Rifletum, I. 472. c. 2. *i.*

Rihale, Margery countess has the terra de, 7 Richard i. I. 106. c. 1. *t.* Her sureties, ibid. Rihale adjudged to Henry earl of Hereford in right of his mother, temp. Richard i. I. 488. c. 2. *d.*

Rikeward, Geoffrey, assayer of the mint at Canterbury by mandate, 32 Henry iii. II. 88. c. 1. *d.*

Rindewell, Hertfordshire, in whose tenure, temp. Henry iii. II. 44. c. 1. *p.*

Ringeltone, Nicolas de, custos of S. Augustin's, Canterbury, 11 Edward i. I. 313. c. 1. *g.*

Ringsted, Herlewin presbyter of, 30 Henry ii. I. 116. c. 1. *a.*

Ripariis, Margaret de, countess de Insula, 42 Henry iii. I. 241. c. 1. *g.* Her fine, 14 Henry iii. I. 660. c. 1. *f.* Hugh de Riparia deputy warden of the sea-ports, 15 John, I. 774. c. 1. Margaret, 11 Henry iii. II. 21. c. 1. *n.* William de Ripariis his interest in Ireland, 30 Edward i. II. 180. c. 1. *y.* Richard de Ripariis one of the collectors of the aid in the Northreding of Yorkshire for the marriage of the king's sister, 22 Henry iii. II. 192. c. 2. *w.* Margaret de Ripariis seems to have the chamberlainship of England in fee, 25 Henry iii. II. 295. c. 2. *x.* Makes Thomas Esperun her deputy at the Exchequer, 29 Henry iii. ibid. c. 2. *y.*

Ripton, Reginald de, 14 Henry ii. I. 552. c. 1. *g.* King's Ripton, Hunt. granted, I. 757. c. 1. *u.* Men of Ripton, II. 122. c. 1. *o.*

Ripun, Yorkshire, fine for liberties, 3 John, I. 404. c. 2. *g.* The archbishop's freemen without Ripun tallaged, 9 Richard i. I. 699. c. 2. *r.* Wapentak of Rypoun, II. 112. c. 1.

Rischeton liberty in Northamptonshire, belonged to William de Goldingham, 18 Edward i. II. 248. c. 2. *y.*

Rival, Peter de, treasurer, 16 Henry iii. I. 64. c. 1. *m.* Occurs, 17 Henry iii. I. 65. c. 1. *n.* Abbat of Rival tenant to William de Molbrai, 11 John, I. 616. c. 2. *d.* Mabel Rivals held of the king in capite by barony under Henry iii. I. 622, 623. c. 1. *h.* Had the manors of Stok, Swell, and Peret, and seems to have been the wife of Robert de Beauchamp,

INDEX.

Beauchamp, I. 622, 623. c. 1. *h.* Peter de, 39 Henry iii. I. 712. c. 1. *a.* Peter de Rivalle baron of the Exchequer, 42 Henry iii. II. 17. c. 2. *h.* Peter de, treasurer of the Exchequer, 17 Henry iii. II. 34. c. 2. *y.* Peter discharged from accompting for the custody of the wardrobe, 35 Henry iii. II. 230. c. 1. *r.*

Rivere, Henry de la, 22 Henry ii. I. 96. c. 1. *n.* William de la Rivere, 13 Edward i. I. 361. c. 1. *u.* Peter de Riveria in Normandy, 2 John, I. 520. c. 2. *f.* Richard de Riveriis fines for the daughter of Adam de Port, 2 John, ibid. c. 2. *g.* Richard de la Rivere sherif of Glocestershire, 9 Edward ii. II. 216.

Roan, Walter [de Constantiis] archbishop of, an. 1189. I. 22. Authority of the archbishop and canons of Roan, I. 164. King John gives 2000 pounds of Anjou for the repair of this church, I. 172. c. 2. *a.* Was chief justicier under Richard i. I. 220. The assignment for that church on Killum in Yorkshire, I. 329. c. 1. *w.* William de, his claim, 15 Henry ii. I. 447. c. 1. *t.*

Robber burnt, 2 Henry ii. I. 372. c. 2. *s.*

Robe for the king's son, &c. 19 Henry ii. I. 363. c. 1. *e.* For the queen cost fourscore pounds, 5 Henry ii. I. 366. c. 1. *a.* See unto, I. 372.

Robert son of Sawin, fermer of Northampton, 19 Henry ii. I. 331. c. 2. *l.*

Robert son of Geoffrey, his fine in Hampshire, 5 Stephen, I. 457. c. 1. *h.*

Robert [Banastre] archdeacon of Essex, 1 Richard i. I. 311. c. 2. *i.*

Robert earl of Normandy came to visit his brother king Henry, an. 1104. I. 10. c. 1. *h.*

Robertsbridge contests with Battle abby, 4 John, I. 107. c. 1. *b.*

Roche abby in Yorkshire, 10 John, I. 152. c. 1. *z.* The village of, I. 554. c. 1. *n.* Thomas de la Roche summoned among the barons of Herefordshire, 26 Edward i. I. 655. c. 1.

Rochefolet, Robert, alderman of a London gild, 26 Henry ii. I. 562. c. 1. *z.*

Rochesford, Tomas, subsherif of Glocestreshire, 6 John, I. 192. c. 1. *t.* Payn de Rochefort, 2 John, I. 524. c. 1. *u.* The scutage of John de Rochesford for the king's ransom, 6 Richard i. I. 590. c. 2. *l.* G. de Rocheford seems to be justicier, 40 Henry iii. II. 22. c. 2. *s.* John de Rocheford, 27 Edward i. II. 228. c. 1. *h.* Rocheford hundred in Essex belonged to John de Burgh, 53 Henry iii. II. 248. c. 1. *u.*

Rochester, monks of, 29 Henry ii. I. 82. 155. 212. This see seized into the king's hands because Canterbury was, 31 Henry ii. I. 311. c. 1. *e.* B. [forte R.] bishop of, 32 Henry iii. I. 389. c. 2. *l.*

Rochingeham, a vineyard there, 5 Stephen, I. 364. c. 1. *l.* Adomar de Valencia custos of the castle of Rokyngham, 15 Edward ii. I. 383. c. 1. Rokyngham forest and castle accompted for by Alan la Zuche sherif of Northamptonshire, 52 Henry iii. II. 180. c. 2. *c.* Executors of Geoffrey de Rokyngham, 35 Henry iii. II. 185. c. 1. *k.*

Rode, Reynald de, to accompt for Hugh de Kynardele, 35 Henry iii. II. 289. c. 1. *u.*

Roderham,

INDEX.

Roderham, Yorkſhire, I. 534. c. 1.

Roderick king of Conaught, his concord with Henry ii. and his ſon, an. 1175. I. 18. c. 1. *f.*

Rodun manor, whoſe, I. 440. c. 1. *m.*

Roffa, William, Ralf and Robert de, 2 John, I. 175. c. 1. *o.* Prior of Roffa and S. Gregory, 31 Henry ii. I. 311. c. 1. *e.* What reception it gave to the cruce-ſignati in their paſſage to the ſea, I. 334. c. 1. *u.* Liberties of the archbiſhop there, ibid. Salomon de Roffa juſtice in Eire, 9 and 10 Edward i. I. 342, 343. c. 1. *e.* Rocheſter its aid, 14 Henry ii. I. 588. c. 2. *d.* Its donum, 5 Henry ii. I. 627. c. 2. *t.* Its aid, 2 Henry ii. I. 693. c. 2. *r.* Rocheſter tallaged, 34 Henry ii. I. 736. c. 1. *p.* and I. 739. c. 2. *b.* Ralf de Roueceſtre, 2 John, I. 790. c. 1. *k.* Allowance in Roffa's ferm for the Maltolt, II. 201. In the king's hands, 28 Henry iii. II. 246. c. 2. *f.* Salomon de Roffa juſticier, 14 Edward i. II. 257. c. 2. *c.*

Roſham, Richer de, alderman of the ward of Baſſieſhawe, 2 Edward ii. II. 235. c. 1. *t.*

Roger chaplain of the empreſs, quit of danegeld in Wiltſhire, 2 Henry ii. I. 687. c. 1. *i.*

Roger, king Stephen's nephew and chancellor ſeized by order, I. 14. c. 2. *t.*

Roger biſhop of Sareſbury chief juſticier to Henry i. I. 33.

Roger king of Naples and Sicily, an. 1144. I. 184.

Roger ſon of Folcher fermer of Hampſhire, 2 Henry ii. I. 331. c. 1. *f.* Peter ſon of Roger alderman of London, his tallage, 14 Henry iii. I. 709. c. 1. *t.*

Roger ſon of Geoffrey, fines, 5 Stephen, I. 425. c. 1. *c.* Again, 7 Richard i. I. 555. c. 2. *d.* Roger made conſtable of the Exchequer by the conſtable of England, 12 Henry iii. II. 281. c. 2. *g.*

Rogers, Lapine, maſter moneyour, and had been aſſayer, 12 Edward ii. II. 90. A ſecond Roger uſher of the Exchequer occurs, 28 Henry iii. II. 275. c. 2. *k.*

Rohham, Henry de, ſherif of London, 13 Henry iii. I. 283. c. 1. *o.* Alexander Fitz-William de Rogham, 26 Henry ii. I. 431. c. 1. *b.* Fines to implead the earl of Arundel and Robert de Mortemer, ibid. See Rugham.

Rokel, Humfrey de, a recognition againſt him, 12 John, I. 794. c. 2. *l.* forte Rokeſle.

Rokeſbi, Henry de, Warwickſh. 3 John, I. 106. c. 2. *a.* That town releaſed to the knights Templars, 4 Richard i. I. 155.

Rokeſle, Gregory de, principal of the aſſayers, 9 Edward i. I. 291. c. 1. *a.* A proceſs againſt Richard de Rokeſle for not going to the war in Scotland, 34 Edward i. I. 662. c. 1. *p.* Gregory de Rokeſle accompts for the chamberlainſhip of London, and the priſe of wines, 1 Edward i. I. 770. c. 1. *y.* and 5 Edward i. ibid. c. 2. *z.* Nicolas de Rokeſle ſeems to be proctor for the hoſpital of S. Bartholomew, London, 26 Edward i. II. 47. c. 2. *y.* Gregory de Rokeſle mayor of London and keeper of the mint, 7 Edward i. II. 90. c. 2. *u.* Was mayor, 4, 5, 6 and 7 Edward i. II. 94. c. 1. *l, m.* Sherif of London, 55 Henry iii. II. 96. c. 1. *u.* Occurs, 7 Edward i. II. 135. c. 1. *t.* Occurs, 4 and 5 Edward i. II. 180. The executors of Gregory

INDEX.

Gregory de Rokesle an accomptant, 27 Edward i. II. 229. G. occurs, 18 Edward i. II. 281. c. 1. *f*.

Rokingham, G. de, in execucia, 44 Henry iii. II. 260. c. 1. *n*. See Rochingeham.

Rolleston, William da, commissioner of the array for the wapentake of Beverle, 16 Edward ii. II. 112. c. 2.

Rolls, some account of them, I. 123. Rolls or records of the Jews, I. 231. The Rolls founded by Henry iii. for convert Jews, I. 259. Rolls of the pipe next in antiquity to Domesday book, I. 296. The several Rolls of the Exchequer, II. 112. Every county written by itself in the great Roll, II. 113. How it happened there were duplicates of the great Roll, ibid. Rolls dispersed called into the Exchequer, temp. Henry iii. II. 256, 257. Ingrosser of the great Roll, II. 269.

Roman empire, the declension of it, Pref. xvii. Languages deriving from the Roman, ibid. Richard king of the Romans, 54 Henry iii. II. 170. c. 1. *h*. See Cornwal.

Romance, or bastard Roman, the original of it, Pref. xxi.

Romayn, Robert, his writ of favour, 1 Edward ii. II. 123. c. 2. *a*.

Romenhal and Heth two of the five ports, I. 613. c. 1. *s*. Ports of Romenal and Hee, I. 718. c. 1. *n*.

Romesey, abbess of, I. 421. Nicolas de Romeley tallager of the see of Winchester, 52 Henry iii. I. 719. c. 1. *r*.

Romscot, surplusage of it in the see of Canterbury, 13 Henry iii. I. 718. c. 1. *n*.

Ropesley, Robert de, amerced for a default, 10 John, I. 553, 554. c. 1. *g*. Robert de Roppele, attests a charter, 16 John, II. 43. c. 1. *m*.

Ros, Robert de, 3 Henry iii. I. 67. c. 2. *x*. Robert de, respited by the king's writ de ultra mare, Yorkshire, 6 Henry ii. I. 85. c. 1. *o*. Robert de Ros was justiced, 9 John, I. 452. c. 2. *k*. William de Ros of Yorkshire fines for the king's goodwill, 31 Henry iii. I. 475. c. 2. *s*. The land of Jammes de Ros in Wuda, 6 Richard i. I. 483. c. 2. *p*. Jordan de Ros had the land of Lullingeston and Framehingham in Kent, 2 John, I. 486. c. 1. *k*. Robert de Ros had the lands of Walter Espec, 4 Henry ii. I. 511. c. 2. *n*. The scutage for the fees of William de Ros in Kent, 18 Henry ii. I. 630. c. 1. *d*. William de Ros in Kent held of the archbishop, 5 Henry iii. I. 670. c. 1. *d*. Peter de Ros one of the justiciers in settling the tallage, 8 Richard i. I. 704. c. 2. *s*. Robert de Ros of Cargave, 3 Edward i. II. 4. c. 2. *p*. Roger de Ros the king's taylor had lands in Hallingbury, Essex, 29 Henry iii. II. 101. c. 1. *s*. Richard Roce commissioner of the array for the wapentake of Beverle, 16 Edward ii. II. 112. c. 2. The tenure of Wichtone by Robert de Ros, 2 Henry iii. II. 116. c. 1. *r*. Geoffrey le Rus sherif of Bedeford and Bukinghamshire, 50 Henry iii. II. 174. The depredations on his manor of Hendon, ibid. c. 1. *r*.

Roscelin, William son of, his lands, 9 John, I. 489. c. 1. *o*. Robert son of Roscelin of Bradley, Linc. 3 John, I. 498. c. 2. *n*. William son of Roscelin has the manor of Heiford, 10 John, I. 499. c. 2. *z*.

Roteland, the ferm of it, I. 59. c. 2. *k*.

INDEX.

Its donum accompted for by Robert son of Goebold, 2 Henry ii. I. 695. c. 2. *a*.

Rothing, John de, his cafe, 1 Edward ii. II. 30. c. 1. *e*. W. de Rothing fherif of Norfolk, his repairs of the caftle of Norwich, about 26 Edward i. II. 67. c. 1. *p*. John's cafe, 1 Edward ii. II. 120.

Rotuli annales, or great Rolls of the pipe at Weftminfter, I. 179. paffim.

Roubiry, Gilbert de, juftice of the king's bench, 27 Edward i. II. 29.

Roucebi, Peter de, amerced, 17 Henry ii. I. 558. c. 1. *r*.

Rouceftre, the defcent of that family, in poffeffion of Erefwel, I. 623. See Erefwel.

Roven, Robert de, his debt, I. 166. See Roan. Robert of Roan pardoned for the death of Sewhall, 6 John, I. 505. c. 2. *q*.

Rougate, William de, late chamberlain of Weft-Wales, 1 Edward ii. II. 239. c. 1. *d*.

Rouille, William le, collector of the grand cuftumier of Normandy, I. 180. c. 1. *f*.

Roumara, William earl of, his knights fees in Lincolnfhire, 14 Henry ii. I. 584. c. 1. *p*.

Rowel manor belonged to the earl of Arundel, 1 Richard i. I. 229. c. 2. *e*. In Yorkfhire tallaged, 30 Henry iii. I. 710. c. 1. *w*. William de, clerk of the Exchequer, 56 Henry iii. II. 264. William de Rowel writer of the great rolls, 1 Edward i. II. 270. c. 2. *k*.

Roynges, John de, attorney of the bifhop of Norwich, 1 Edward i. II. 251. c. 2. *l*.

Royz, don Pedro, knight, his bequeft to the monaftery of Arlanza, Pref. xix.

Rualon fherif of Chent, about 5 Stephen, I. 327. c. 2. *z*.

Rucford abbey, 9 John, I. 472. c. 1. *b*.

Rudes, in Wiltfhire, its donum, 33 Henry ii. I. 634. c. 2. Its tallage, 20 Henry iii. I. 707. c. 1. *k*. Again, 30 Henry iii. I. 711. c. 1. *y*. William de Rude removed from being cuftomer in the port of London, 16 Edward ii. II. 91. c. 1. *a*. William de Rude concerned in the king's works, 12 Edward ii. II. 292. c. 2. *l*.

Rudge or Rugga, Nicolas, of Fenotri, Devonfhire, his aid, 23 Henry ii. I. 603. c. 2. *i*.

Rue, Richard de, 15 Henry ii. I. 447. c. 1. *u*. Fines for fpeeding his right, ibid.

Ruelent de Auvers, his terra, 33 Henry ii. I. 4. c. 1. *b*.

Ruffus, Jordan and David of Briftol, 5 John, I. 118. c. 2. *y*. and 451. c. 1. *z*. William Ruffus juftice errant in Devonfhire, 22 Henry ii. I. 128. c. 1. *y*. Was fherif of Devonfhire, 23 Henry ii. I. 129. c. 1. *h*. Fulcher Ruffus of Norfolk, temp. Stephen, I. 147. c. 2. *c*. Richard Ruffus archdeacon [of Effex] an. 1142. I. 198. c. 1. *e*. William Ruffus fherif of Devonfhire, 23 Henry ii. I. 211. c. 1. *h*. Walter Ruffus's grant to John Walenfis in Gyng-Mountney, 13 John, I. 218. c. 2. *u*. Nigel Ruffus accompts for the profits of the exchange of London, 9 John, I. 283. c. 2. *q*. The terra of Robert Ruffus in Navineby in the honor of Lancafter furrendered to Gilbert Cufin, 3 Henry iii. I. 300. c. 2. *w*. William Ruffus accompts for the ferm of Bukingehamfhire, 31 Henry ii. I. 330. c. 1. *a*. and 6 Richard i. I. 346. c. 1. *e*. Sherif of Devonfhire, 23 Henry ii. I. 363. c. 2. *f*.

Attefts

INDEX.

Attests the king's writ, 20 Henry ii. I. 370. c. 1. *f.* Fulk Ruffus, 31 Henry ii. I. 427. c. 1. *m.* Ralf Ruffus, 6 John I. 440. c. 2. *o.* Thomas Ruffus has the land of Ymmemere, 12 John, I. 490. c. 2. *u.* William Ruffus killed in the hundred of Redderbrug, Sussex, before 7 Richard i. I. 544. c. 2. *r.* Albric Ruffus amerced for exporting corn without licence, 23 Henry ii. I. 548. c. 1. *r.* Richard Ruffus king's chamberlain, 14 Henry ii. I. 581. c. 1. *a.* William Ruffus justicier for Devonshire, 23 Henry ii. I. 603. c. 2. *i.* Justice of the assise, 19 Henry ii. I. 701. c. 1. *b.* William Rufus justicier and king's tallager in Staffordshire, 7 Henry iii. I. 734. c. 2. *d.* David Ruffus and Amable his wife, 6 John, I. 790. c. 2. *n.*

Rufus, John, de Ipro, I. 452. c. 1. *g.* Richard Rufus clerk, belonged to the king's receipt, 29 Henry iii. II. 117. c. 1. *a.*

Rugemunt, Ralf de, who, 22 Henry ii. I. 103. c. 1. *b.* The county of York fines in an hundred pound for the record of a duel between him and Simon le Bret, ibid.

Rugham, Alexander de, son of William fines for his plea, 27 Henry ii. I. 97. c. 1. *s.*

Rumesie, Walter de, of Wiltshire, amerced for not making due payment at the Exchequer, II. 234. c. 2. *r.*

Runham in Norfolk, Robert de Bruweys interest in it, 56 Henry iii. II. 101. c. 1. *t.* Styled the manor of Ronneham, and in the possession of Ralf de Helebek, 9 Edward ii. ibid. c. 2. *w.*

Rupe, Richard de, fermer of the manors of the fee of Exeter, 31 Henry ii. I. 310. c. 2. *a.* Agnes de Rupe, 12 John, I. 795. c. 1. *p.*

Rupibus, William de, seneschal of Anjou, 2 John, I. 174. c. 2. *k.* Again, 4 John, I. 763. c. 1. *b.* Peter de Rupibus, 4 John, I. 176. c. 1. *s.* Peter de Rupibus, 8 John, I. 388. c. 2. *d.* Has two thousand marks given him by the king as bishop of Winchester, 8 John, ibid.

Russel, Robert, fines for ten virgats of land in Papworth, 10 John, I. 517. c. 2. *q.* Amerced for detaining Waleran's money, 14 Henry ii. I. 558. c. 2. *z.* Ralf de Russel seems to be sherif of Wiltshire, 47 and 48 Henry iii. II. 158. c. 2. *b.*

Russet at ten pence per ell, 14 Henry iii. I. 376. c. 1. *x.*

Russoc, Robert de, and his wife, fine that they may take the habit of religion, 5 John, I. 505. c. 1. *l.*

Russye, Richard de, alderman of London, the tallage of his ward, 14 Henry iii. I. 709. c. 1. *t.* and 19 Henry iii. I. 738. c. 2. *z.* I. 739. c. 1. *a.*

Rustics, juries ought not to be made up with them, I. 546. c. 2. *s, t.* Not to be distrained for their lords debts, II. 202.

Rustishal in Wiltshire, their donum, I. 697. c. 1. *w.*

Rutinton in Notinghamshire, 5 John, I. 438. c. 2. *e.* William and Agnes de, ibid.

Rydale wapentake under a commission of array, 16 Edward ii. II. 112. c. 2.

Rye amerced, 30 Henry iii. I. 568. c. 1. *r.*

Ryley's account of the sherif's oath, 5 Edward ii. II. 149. His account of the provision for tallies when lost, II. 260.

Rymer

INDEX.

Rymer corrected, Pref. xx. c. 1. *o*. Again corrected, I. 66. c. 2. *q*.

Ryngewode in Hampshire tallaged, 6 Edward ii. I. 744. c. 2. *y*.

Rythre, William de, of Yorkshire, his summonce to attend the Scotish expedition, 26 Edward i. I. 654. c. 2. *a*.

Ryvers, John de, one of the barons summoned against Scotland, 26 Edward i. I. 655. c. 2.

Ryves, Richard, his share of the manor of Borscombe, Wiltshire, held of Estgreenewich, 42 Elizabeth, I. 621. c. 2.

S.

Sabaudia, P. de, 37 Henry iii. I. 68. c. 2. *b*. Has the honor of Richmond, 31 Henry iii. I. 594. c. 1. *h*. His aid to make the king's eldest son a knight, 38 Henry iii. I. 596. c. 1. *t*. Wychard de Sabaudia, 29 Henry iii. II. 243. c. 1. *e*.

Saberge wapentac with Crec and Clive added to the fee of Durham by Philip, 1 John, I. 401. c. 1. *a*.

Sabloil, Peter de, his claim on the honor of Croyl and Scye in Normandy, 2 John, I. 518. c. 2. *x*.

Sabrictsworth, monks of their grant, I. 120. The tallage of Richard de Sabricthesworth of London, 19 Henry iii. I. 738. c. 1. *y*. Roger de la Grene de Sebrithwerth, 39 Henry iii. II. 14. c. 2. *q*.

Sabroil, I. 167. c. 1. *k*.

Sachevil. See Secchevil. Geoffrey fines for the king's good will, 9 John, II. 254. c. 2. *b*.

Sachibarones, sagibarones and salebarones, who, I. 198. c. 1. *d*.

Sacy, Emeric de, claims to be sherif of Hampshire for life, 25 Henry iii. I. 446. c. 1. *g*.

Saeck, a cause litigated, I. 198. c. 1. *d*.

Saford, the quinzime for the merchandise of this port, 6 John, I. 772. c. 2. *i*.

Saham, lands in Cambridgeshire in wasto, 2 Henry ii. I. 693. c. 1. *l*. The tallage of Saham in Norfolk, 9 Richard i. I. 705. c. 1. *u*. The rolls of William de Saham, 18 Edward i. II. 25. c. 2. *z*.

Saierus, Fitz-Henry, his executors in Surrey, 35 Henry iii. II. 185. c. 1. *k*. The pledges for his debts to the king, ibid.

S. Alban, Robert abbat of, 11 Henry ii. I. 44. W. abbat of, 3 Henry iii. I. 67. c. 2. *x*. Quit of carucage, &c. 2 John, I. 401. c. 2. *d*. Abbat of S. Alban amerced for defaults, 10 Edward ii. I. 530. c. 1. Its number of knights fees, 14 Henry ii. I. 573. c. 2. *m*. Occurs, I. 586. c. 1. *x*. Its scutage, 5 Henry ii. I. 627. c. 1. *r*. Accompts for its knights fees, 1 John, I. 659. c. 1. *s*. The donum of that abbey and its knights, 5 Henry ii. I. 697. c. 2. *c*. Strategem of the townsmen to defeat the abbat's power, I. 758. The abbat's claim examined, I. 759 c. 2. *x*. Its state after the dissolution of abbeys, I. 762. c. 2. Mr Nicolas S. Albans remembrancer of the Exchequer, 32 Henry iii. II. 52. c. 1. *t*. Fulk sherif of London, 17 Edward i. II. 96. c. 2. *z*.

S. Amando, Ralf de, married one of the daughters, and had a third of the barony of Robert de Albeniaco, Bedf. 21 Henry iii. I. 317. c. 2. *t*. Amauricus de, 16 Henry iii. II. 34. c. 1. *x*. Sherif of Herefordshire, 27 Henry iii. II. 176. Ralf, and the late Aumaric de S. Amando, 28 Henry iii. II. 184. c. 1. *f*. Ralf

de

INDEX.

de S. Amand heir of Almaric, 28 Henry iii. II. 190. c. 1. *k.*

S. Andrews, Roger bishop of, temp. John, I. 57. c. 1. *r.*

S. Augustin's, Canterbury, in custody of John de Burne and Nicolas de Ringeltone, 11 Edward i. I. 313. c. 1. *g.* See Thomas de Fyndon. Fine to have custody of their house on a vacancy, 14 John, I. 411. c. 2. *w.* Has a barony, 11 John, I. 506. c. 2. *x.* Their scutage, 14 Henry iii. I. 607. Held fifteen fees, I. 625, 626. c. 1. *p.*

S. Budoc, one of John Wak's seven churches in Exeter diocese, 29 Henry iii. II. 250. c. 2. *i.*

S. Claro, Hamon de, accompts for the honor of Eudo Dapifer, 5 Stephen, I. 297. c. 1. *e.* And for the ferm of Colchester, 5 Stephen, I. 330. c. 2. *e.* and I. 602. c. 1. *w.* S. Clare one of John Wak's seven churches in the diocese of Exeter, 29 Henry iii. II. 250. c. 2. *i.*

S. Clement, nuns of, I. 309. c. 1. *r.*

S. Denis, John de, archdeacon of Rochester, and custos of the house of converts, 11 Edward i. I. 259. c. 1. *m.*

S. Edmund, W. de, justice of the Jews, 29 Henry iii. I. 238. c. 1. *r.* An offering at S. Edmund's shrine for the king, queen, and their children, 42 Henry iii. I. 378. c. 1. *m.* Mr Roger of S. Edmund archdeacon of Richmond, 3 John, I. 515. c. 1. *i.* Sampson abbat of, temp. John, I. 517. c. 2. *r.* Knights fees belonging to the abbat of S. Edmund, 14 Henry ii. I. 573. c. 1. The donum of the abbat of S. Edmund, 5 Henry ii. I. 627. c. 1. *s.* Mr Roger one of the justiciers, who settled the tallage in Norfolk, 9 Richard i. I. 705. c. 1. *u.* The liberty of S. Edmund, 25 Henry iii. II. 193. c. 1. *a.* Seized into the king's hand with the liberties of Norwiz, Dunwiz, Ipswich and Yarmouth, 11 Henry iii. II. 244. c. 2. *n.*

S. Edward's day the vigil of the Epiphany, I. 69. c. 2. *e.* William de S. Edward and Roger— St Edward's abbey of Shaftbury in the king's hand, 31 Henry iii. I. 584. c. 2. *r.* S. Edward's town, I. 600. c. 2. *l.* Reginald de S. Edward clerk of the abbat of Hyde, 27 Henry iii. I. 609. c. 1. *d.* Abbess of S. Edward, her scutage, 33 Henry ii. I. 634. c. 1. *q.* Abbess of, 6 Henry iii. I. 676, 677. c. 1. *a.* Curators of S. Edward's shrine, 52 Henry iii. II. 91.

S. Gabriel in Normandy, prior of, contends for the land de Vileriis, 2 John, I. 519. c. 2. *b.*

S. George, Alan de, pleads for his lands because he had a son by the heiress of them, 3 John, I. 99. c. 1. *q.* Henry de S. George, 16 John, I. 274. c. 1. *k.* Alan of Sussex how he quits himself of a plea de foresta, 11 Henry iii. II. 227. c. 1. *b.*

S. Germano, Hugh de, sherif of Berks, 23 Henry ii. I. 130. c. 1. *o.* Accompts, 18 Henry ii. I. 580. c. 1. *o.*

S. Helen, Michael de, alderman of London, the tallage for his ward, 14 Henry iii. I. 709. c. 1. *t.* Again, 19 Henry iii. I. 738. c. 2. *z.* Reparator cuneorum for coinage, 6 Henry iii. II. 87. c. 2. *a.*

S. Helena, John de, Berkshire, 30 Henry ii. I. 452. c. 1. *b.*

S. Hilary, Stephen de, 9 John, I. 442. c. 1. *b.* Peter de, his claim of the land of Loges, 2 John, I. 523. c. 1. *q.*

S. John

INDEX.

S. John Port Latin, I. 70. Abbat of S. John of Derteford, II. 167. c. 2. *x*.

S. John, William de, 11 Henry iii. I. 63. c. 2. *l*. Richard de, king's chaplain, 16 Henry iii. I. 64. c. 1. *m*. Roger de, keeper of the king's seal, 49 Henry iii. I. 71. c. 1. *k*. Again, I. 71. c. 1. *u*. William de, quit of escuage for the king's ransom, 7 Richard i. I. 591. c. 2. *t*. John de, of Hampshire, one of the barons summoned by writ to the Scotch war, 26 Edward ii. I. 655. c. 2. Robert S. John fines ne transfretet, 7 Richard i. I. 658. c. 1. *l*. William de S. John, ult. John, and 6 Henry iii. his fees in Hampshire, I. 668. c. 1. *u*. Wine of S. John, I. 768. William seems to have been sherif of Yorkshire, 17 Henry iii. II. 118. c. 1. *f*. The ransom of John de S. John, 34 Edward i. II. 123. c. 1. *w*.

S. Ivone, John de, victualler for the army, 25 Edward i. I. 379. c. 1. Sherif of Lincolnshire, 26 Edward i. ibid. c. 2. *r*.

Sancto Laudo, or Lo, William de, 9 Henry iii. I. 252. c. 1. *t*. John de, late sherif of Somerset and Dorsetshire, 18 Edward i. II. 143. c. 2. *f*.

S. Laurence, Robert de, fermer of Hampshire, 22 Henry ii. I. 285. c. 1. *tt*. Osbert de, his fee, 12 Henry ii. I. 447. c. 1. *p*. Lazarus of Jerusalem, brothers of, in Sussex, 6 John, I. 206. c. 2. *r*. Ralf le Barre alderman of the gild of S. Lazarus, 26 Henry ii. I. 562. c. 1. *z*. That order occurs, 23 Henry ii. II. 200. c. 2. *g*.

S. Leodegario, Reginald de, Suff. 23 Henry ii. I. 450. c. 1. *n*. Emma de S. Leodegario mother to Geoffrey de Beauchamp, and wife of Walter de Baskervil, I. 513. c. 2. *b*. Her land descends to her son, ibid. William de S. Leodegario holds of the honor of Dunestor, Dorsetshire, 2 John, I. 659. c. 1. *w*.

S. Leonard the abbat, his day, II. 106. c. 2. *l*.

S. Maries Church, Peter de, chancellor's clerk, 2 Richard i. I. 388. c. 1. *z*.

S. Maries Church, William de, his payment in camera regis, 6 Richard i. I. 263. c. 2. *k*. Many of the small escheats committed to him, 6 and 7 Richard i. I. 299. Has the wardship of Robert son of Robert Fitz-harding, 6 Richard i. I. 323. c. 1. *y*. Attests the sherif's accompts, 1 Richard i. I. 370. c. 2. *i*. Abbey of S. Maria del Fiume, I. 571. William de S. Mary Church, 8 Richard i. I. 638. c. 1. *g*. William de S. Mary Church settled the scutage, 10 Richard i. ibid. And the tallage, I. 700. c. 1. *s*.

S. Martin, Alured de, dapifer of Normandy, 20 Henry ii. I. 51. See I. 167. c. 1. *k*. and I. 168. c. 1. *l*. Ralf de, accompts for the fee of Sarum, about 31 Henry ii. I. 311. c. 1. *d*. R. de S. Martino, king's tallager for Surrey, 10 Richard i. I. 733. c. 2. *s*.

S. Martin's London, Lucas Capellanus dean there, 11 Henry iii. I. 63. c. 1. *l*. The canons obtain an order for the restitution of their lands of Godicestra from G. earl of Essex, I. 108. c. 2. *k*. Quit of tallage, 9 Edward ii. I. 745. c. 1. *a*.

S. Mauro, William de, king's squire, 21 Henry ii. I. 367. c. 2. *m*. Ralf de, attached for not going to the Scotch war, 34 Edward i. I. 662. c. 1. *p*.

S. Mawen, one of John Wak's seven churches

INDEX.

churches in Exeter diocese, 29 Henry iii. II. 250. c. 2. *i.*

S. Medardo, Peter de, 22 Henry ii. I. 544. c. 1. *m.* Abbat of Burgh amerced two hundred marks for a man slain by Peter, ibid.

S. Michael, William de, the land he had in Aiwel, 12 John, I. 490. c. 2. *y.* Fined for the chamberlainship of London, 5 John, I. 777. c. 1. *t.*

S. Patric, William and Geoffrey de, 3 John, I. 436. c. 1. *s.* G. gave the church of Nutal to the prior of Lenton, ibid.

S. Pauls London, the land of Egburgheton given to it to find lights, before an. 1142. I. 198. c. 1. *e.* Dean and chapter quit of tallage, 9 Edward ii. I. 745. c. 2. *a.* Canons of, not to have amerciaments, 25 Henry iii. II. 10. c. 1. *w.* Armed men insult a Lombard in it, 12 Edward ii. II. 110. Liberties of the dean and chapter of S. Paul's, 38 Henry iii. II. 205. c. 1. *n.*

S. Paul's, earl of, about 23 Henry iii. had the manor of Derteford, I. 302. c. 1. *b.* Guy de Chastillon earl of S. Paul's, 4 Henry iii. I. 319. c. 2. *f.* And Isabel his countess, ibid. Robert de S. Paul king's tallager, 1 John, I. 433. c. 2. *g.*

S. Peter of Jumieges, abbat of, I. 108. A monk of S. Peter super Dinam, 11 John, I. 448. c. 2. *k.* Ysold widow of William de S. Peter, 10 John, I. 495. c. 1. *x.* Jocey son of Peter his tallage for his ward as alderman of London, 14 Henry iii. I. 709. c. 1. *t.* Church of S. Peter Oxford belonged to the scholars of Merton, 9 Edward ii. I. 745. c. 1. *a.* Atrium S. Petri, II. 287. c. 1. *l.*

S. Quintin, Hawisa de, her claim of the terra de Cherleton, Berkshire, 3 John, I. 106. c. 2. *z.* Herebert de, fines for a duel, 10 John, I. 107. c. 2. *c.* Walter de S. Quintin one of the justices, 20 Henry ii. I. 123. Herbert de S. Quintin, 9 John, I. 442. c. 1. *b.* Geoffrey de S. Quyntyn has a commission of array directed to him, 16 Edward ii. II. 111. c. 2. *c.*

S. Sepulchre, Lincoln, the friars of that hospital of the order of Simplingham, I. 218. c. 1. *s.*

S. Stephen, Robert de, 6 Richard i. I. 451. c. 1. *y.* Respite of payment for his lands in Devon, ibid.

S. Thomas the martyr, his chapel on Lincoln bridge, I. 745. c. 1. *a.*

S. Trinitate, Bartholomew de, amerced, 14 Henry ii. I. 545. c. 1. *a.*

S. Vedast, William de, I. 166. c. 1. *i.*

S. Victor, the provision made for that church, I. 159.

S. Waleric or Valery, Bernard de, who accompts for his fee, 18 Henry ii. I. 580. c. 1. *o.* Thomas de, his terra, &c. 4 John, I. 668. c. 1. *x.* Thomas de, grants the land of Chadeleswurthe in socage, I. 673. c. 1. *m.* Reginald de, 2 Henry ii. I. 686. c. 2. *f.* I. 687. c. 1. *h.* John de, baron of the Exchequer, 4 Edward i. II 112. c. 2. *f.* John sherif of Somerset and Dorsetshire, 1 Edward i. II. 195. c. 1. *m.* Baron, 4 Edward i. I. 269. c. 2. *f.* and II. 320. c. 2. *e.*

Sakenvill, Robert de, an. 1184. I. 167. c. 2. Jordan de Sakevil, fines, 16 John, I. 444. c. 1. *s.* See Secchevil.

Salcey, William de, his land, 1 Richard i. I. 213. c. 2. *u, w.* Ralf de Salcey's knights fees in Herefordshire, 7 Henry ii. I. 628. Hugh de, hanged before 2 Henry iii. I. 795. c. 2. *q.*

Saldeburn,

INDEX.

Saldeburn, a contention for the advocatus of it, about 31 Henry ii. I. 311. c. 1. *d*.

Sale, John de la, mayor of Dovor, 33 Edward i. I. 613. c. 1. *s*.

Saliis, Richard de, 2 John, I. 521. c. 2. *m*. His fine for his lands in England and Normandy, ibid.

Salkeld or Salukild, I. 596. c. 2. *w*.

Salley abbey had a right to the church of Tadcaster, 7 John, I. 488. c. 2. *e*.

Salmonets not to be taken at milldams, Pref. xxiv. c. 2. *d*.

Salmons put in pyes, I. 377.

Salmuneby, I. 555. c. 1. *c*.

Salmur, John de, 4 John, I. 176. c. 1. *s*. One of the king's receivers, ibid.

Salomon the queen's clerk, 2 Henry ii. II. 146. c. 1. *w*.

Saltmarsh, Ysilia widow of Adam de, fines to stand to right, touching the death of her husband, 1 John, I. 493. c. 2. *hh*.

Saltwude in Kent, its aid, 14 Henry ii. I. 588. c. 2. *d*.

Salveyn, Gerard, one of the king's council, 31 Edward i. II. 107. c. 1. *n*.

Sammarthani Gallia Christiana, I. 159. c. 2. and I. 162. c. 1. *r*.

Sampford, Gilbert son of John de, in Essex, amerced for not taking knighthood, 17 Henry iii. I. 510. c. 2. *e*.

Sampson abbat of Caen, and justicier, 2 John, I. 171. c. 2. *x*. I. 172, 173. Samson sellarius or sadler, 21 Henry ii. I. 546. c. 1. *n*. William Samson of Derbyshire summoned among the barons to the army in Scotland, 26 Edward i. I. 655. c. 1. John Sampson constable of the castle of Schipton for the earl of Albermarle, 52 Henry iii. II. 15. c. 1. *t*. Mr Henry Sampson, 14 Edward i. II. 260. c. 1. *n*. John Sampson owed the mareschal of the Exchequer two marks and a half for five days commitment, II. 289.

Sanctuary, Jeremy of London fined a hundred pounds for not coming out of one, 26 Henry ii. I. 104. c. 1. *l*.

Sandale, John de, chancellor of the Exchequer, I. 75. Styled the treasurer's lieutenant, 1 Edward ii. ibid. c. 1. *t*. and II. 279. c. 1. *y*. Chancellor and bishop of Winchester, 10 Edward ii. I. 76. c. 2. *x*. Locum tenens thesaurarii, 1 Edward ii. I. 314. c. 1. *k*. Again, 1 Edward ii. I. 380. c. 2. *w*. John de Sandale chancellor of the Exchequer, 2 Edward ii. II. 8. c. 2. *m*. Again, 1 Edward ii. II. 30. Succeeds Walter Reynald as treasurer of the Exchequer, 3 Edward ii. II. 38. c. 1. *m*. Displaced, 8 Edward ii. and restored when bishop of Winton, II. 39. c. 1. *o*. c. 2. *r*. Made lieutenant of the treasury of the Exchequer, 6 Edward ii. II. 50. and II. 51. c. 1. *p*. See II. 90. Was confirmed bishop of Winchester, 9 Edward ii. II. 92. See Winton.

Sandale, Yorkshire, tallaged, 30 Henry iii. I. 710. c. 1. *w*.

Sandee, Richard parson of, amerced, 3 Henry iii. I. 567. c. 1. *d*.

Sandhurst, Adam de, to accompt for Reginald de Acle sherif of Herefordshire, 56 Henry iii. II. 181. c. 1. *l*.

Sandoval, his history of Spain, Pref. xix. c. 1. *l*. Bishop of Pamplona, ibid.

Sandwich, Ralf de, keeper of the wardrobe, 49 Henry iii. I. 70. The manner of his keeping the great seal, I. 71. c. 1. *k*. Ralf de Sandwico constable of the Tower of London, 18 Edward i. I. 153. c. 1. *f*. Constable

INDEX

ffable and treasurer of the Tower, 14 Edward i. I. 270. c. 1. b. The port of Sandwich has Thomas de Schelming for its baron, 33 Edward i. I. 613. c. 1. s. The aulcagium at Sandwich, I. 768. c. 1. u. The quinzime for the merchandise of this port, 6 John, I. 772. c. 1. i. Stephen de, 49 Henry iii. II. 13. c. 2. l. Ralf constable of the Tower of London, 34 Edward i. II. 108, &c.

Sandwico, Ralf de, keeper of the wardrobe, 49 Henry iii. I. 71. c. 1. k. Ralf de Sandwyco, his inhibition, 5 Edward i. II. 77. c. 2. l.

Sandford, Thomas de, plegius, &c. 6 John, I. 471. c. 2. a.

Sanrige, William de, man of the abbat of S. Alban, 38 Henry iii. I. 761.

Sapy, Robert de, has the custody of Pevense castle, 15 Edward ii. I. 383. c. 2.

Saracenus, Petrus, his receipt from the Exchequer of Durham, 42 Henry iii. II. 4. c. 1. n.

Saresbery, burgesses of, their confirmation of liberties, 2 John, I. 402. c. 1. h. Its aid, 14 Henry ii. I. 589. Their aid, 23 Henry ii. I. 604. c. 1. l. Expences in building their castle, ibid. Its assise or tallage, 19 Henry ii. I. 702. c. 1. d. Again its tallage, 1 John, I. 705. c. 2. z. Villa of Saresbiry tallaged, 30 Henry iii. I. 711. c. 1. y. Old Sarum tallaged, 20 Henry iii. I. 743. c. 2. r. New Sarum, part of the temporalities of the bishopric, I. 762. c. 2. Adam de Sarum sherif of London, 17 Edward ii. II. 99. c. 1. f. Saresbery canons had tithes of paunage out of Windsor forest, II. 204.

Saresbury, Roger bishop of, temp. Henry i. I. 56. c. 1. o. Baron, &c. I. 179. Richard bishop of, 3 Henry iii. I. 67. c. 1. x. Seems to have been justicier and treasurer, if not chancellor too, I. 78. Dean of Sarum and fermer of that see, about 31 Henry ii. I. 311. c. 1. d. That church had a settled tith out of the king's forests, I. 348. The knights fees belonging to this see, I. 581. c. 2. a. Owned thirty-two fees, 33 Henry ii. I. 634. c. 1. p. Jordan dean of Saresbury, and custos of that see, 33 Henry ii. ibid. Roger bishop of, I. 745. c. 1. a. Its claim out of the forest of Windsor, II. 104. c. 2. l.

Sarresbiry, William earl of, 3 Henry iii. I. 67. c. 1. x. William earl of, justicier in Normandy, 3 John, I. 171. c. 1. u. Earl William's scutage in Wiltshire for the Welsh war, 2 Richard i. I. 664. c. 1. a. Accompts for the fee of Ely, 13 John, I. 666. c. 1. i. W. earl of Saresbery warden of the sea-ports, 15 John, I. 773. Earl William, 12 John, I. 795. c. 1. n. William de Montague earl of Saresbury, mareschal for life, temp. Edward iii. I. 797. c. 1. w. William earl of, 14 John, II. 201. c. 1. l. Earl William, 16 John, II. 211. c. 1. b.

Savage or Salvage, James, obtains liberties for his church of Ocham in Kent, and its chapels, 8 John, I. 408. c. 1. l. Henry le Salvage, 13 John, I. 444. c. 1. p. Geoffrey Savage amerced for a rescue, 31 Henry ii. I. 548. c. 2. u. Robert le Salvage, 7 Richard i. I. 789. c. 1. e. Roger le Sauwage justicier, dyed before 15 Edward ii. II. 40. c. 2. w. The mandate to Claritia his widow, ibid. Robert le Sauvage accompts

INDEX.

accompts as sherif for Norfolk and Suffolk, 35 Henry iii. II. 158. c. 1. z. Late sherif, II. 207. c. 1. f.

Savaric, Joldewin son of, 6 Henry ii. I. 471. c. 1. q. The clergiman, 18 Henry ii. I. 561. c. 2. o. Geldewin son of Savaric denies to hold his fee of the earl of Arundel, 14 Henry ii. I. 583. c. 1. i.

Savernac forest in Wiltshire, in the custody of Henry Esturmi, 2 Henry ii. I. 348. c. 2. e. The bailywick of the forest of Savernac in the custody of Henry the son, 1 John, I. 460. c. 1. w. In custody of Alan de Nevil, 9 Henry ii. II. 220. c. 1. o.

Savernestoke in Worcestershire, its tallage, 8 Richard i. I. 704. c. 2. q.

Saufordshire, the bailiwick of its serjeantery in Lancashire, 2 Henry iii. I. 462. c. 2. p.

Saviour, honour of S. late the possession of Roger the viscount, 3 John, I. 170. Assigned to Ralf de Tesson, I. 171.

Saukevill, Jordan de, 2 John, I. 174. c. 2. l. Repairs the Haia and castle of Arches and the forest of Awy, ibid.

Sawin, Robert son of, sherif of Northamptonshire, 2 Henry ii. I. 695. c. 1. z.

Saxeby, in the family de Pirariis, 23 Henry ii. I. 450. c. 1. o. A duel for it between William Fitz-Robert and Warner de Campanea, 18 Henry ii. I. 512. c. 1. r.

Saxons, how they expressed writings, Pref. xxviii. xxix. The expences of the crown for the duke of Saxony at Drincourt, I. 169. The duke's intertainment here, I. 368, 369. Wines of Saxony, I. 767. c. 1. s.

Say, Galfrid de, attests the first letters of the king's new seal, 3 Henry iii. I. 67. c. 2. x. Picot de Say one of the proceres under the earl of Shrewbury, an. 1082. I. 108. Hugh de Say quit of scutage for the king's ransom, 7 Richard i. I. 591. c. 2. t. Had twenty-three knights in Herefordshire, I. 594. c. 1. g William de Say's fees in Bedford and Buckinghamshire, 27 Henry iii. I. 677. c. 1. c. The executors of Henry de Say, 5 Edward ii. II. 187. Beatrice de Say married to Geoffrey Fitz-Pierre, 3 Richard i. II. 220 c. 2. q. II. 221. c. 1. r. She was heiress of earl William, ibid.

Scaccarium, the original signification of that word inquired into, I. 160, &c. Duo Scaccaria, I. 189. Scaccarium of Normandy changed into a parliament, I. 162. Other places had Scaccaria, I. 164, 165. Quatuor Scaccaria, I. 172. c. 2. a. No mention of a Scaccarium before the Conquest, I. 177. The inferius Scaccarium, or the receipt of it, I. 189. Scaccarium redemptionis, Aaronis, Hugonis de Nevill, Judæorum, I. 190, 191. See Exchequer. Andrew de Scaccario, his patent for water carriage from Abingdon to London, 5 John, I. 771. The two Scaccaria continued, II. 2. Kalendarium de Scaccario, II. 7.

Scaccis, Rogerius de, of Cornwal, his fees and aid, 23 Henry ii. I. 604. c. 2. m.

Scacia in the Exchequer, II. 258.

Scalam, ad, what that payment was, I. 274. Scale or trone, I. 782.

Scalariis, William de, executor of Roger de Kerdeston, 8 John, I. 441. c. 1. u. William de Scalariis, his relief for his half barony, 6 Henry iii. I. 317. William and Hugh de

Scalariis

INDEX.

Scalariis accompt for the scutage of Wales, 13 John, I. 666. c. 1. *i*.

Richard son of William de Scalariis his fees in Cambridge and Huntingdonshire, 6 Henry iii. I. 668. c. 1.*w*.

Scaldeford, the lord of that manor, 52 Henry iii. I. 101. c. 1. *d*.

Scales, Robert de, baron, and one of the courtiers, 26 Edward i. I. 655. c. 2.

Scalethwait, Andrew de, and Sarah his widow, 6 Henry iii. I. 496. c. 1. *m*.

Scallebi, Yorkshire, its donum for the army in Galwey, 33 Henry ii. I. 635. c. 2. Its donum, 3 Richard i. I. 698. c. 2. *q*. The tallage of the soke of Scallebi, 9 Richard i. I. 699. c. 1. *r*. Again, 30 Henry iii. I. 710. c. 1. *w*.

Scamna ad scaccarium baronum, I. 192. c. 1. *u*.

Scardeburg, monks of the Cistercian order, I. 118. The ferm of, I. 331. c. 2. *r*. Has a confirmation of liberties, 7 Richard i. I. 400. c. 1. *s*. and 2 John, I. 401. c. 2. *f*. Again have their liberties confirmed, I. 422. Its donum to the army in Galwey, 33 Henry ii. I. 635. c. 1. *r*. The donum of the men of Scardeburc, 3 Richard i. I. 698. c. 2. *q*. Again, 9 Richard i. I. 699. c. 1. *r*. Its tallage, 11 Henry iii. I. 707. c. 1.*i*. Scartheburg tallaged, 14 Henry iii. I. 708. c. 2. *p*. and 30 Henry iii. I. 710. c. 1. *w*. The villa of Scardeburc accompts for an hundred pounds, 8 Richard i. I. 737. c. 1. *s*. The quinzime for the merchandise of the port of Scardeburc, 6 John, I. 772. c. 1. *i*. Wapentak of Scardeburgh under a commission of array, 16 Edward ii. II. 112. c. 2.

Scardeclive, William de, 15 John, I. 773. Accompts in Yorkshire for the assise of woad, ibid.

Scarpe, Geoffrey, 5 Henry iii. I. 452. c. 1. *g*. Distrained, ibid.

Scavage, the duty of, I. 778.

Scheflega, William de, his land, 28 Henry ii. I. 113. c. 1. *r*. To whom his daughters married and his lands descended, ibid.

Schenlega, terra de, 29 Henry ii. I. 105. c. 1. *p*. William Mansel claims it against John de Caverton, ibid.

Schepwich or Chepwich, Somersetshire, the earl of Leicester's land, tallaged, 19 Henry ii. I. 713. c. 1. *b*. Had been lately burnt, ibid.

Schidimor, Peter de, sherif of Dorset and Somersetshire, 1 John, I. 202. c. 2. *a*. See Scudimor. Again, sherif of Dorset and Somersetshire, 1 John, II. 226. c. 1. *x*.

Schirai wapentak, its tallage, 9 Richard i. I. 699. c. 1. *r*. Ralf de Schirlegh sherif of Notinghamshire, 27 Edward i. II. 106. c. 2. *l*.

Scholastica the virgin, I. 71. c. 2. *l*.

Schorewel, William de, deputy sherif of Hampshire to Peter bishop of Winchester, 3 Henry iii. II. 140. c. 2. *p*.

Schornis, admiral Henry de, 30 Henry ii. I. 368. c. 1. *u*. The donum of Schornes, 33 Henry ii. I. 736. c. 1. *o*. See Shornes.

Schorteneftrete in Winchester, II. 314. c. 1. *d*.

Schotton in the bishopric tallaged, 11 Edward i. I. 720.

Scireburn abbey in the hand of Mr Thomas de Husseburn, 1 Richard i. I. 311. c. 2. *g*. In custody, 14 John, I. 312. c. 2. *d*. Manor belonged to the bishop of Sarum, 33 Henry ii. I. 634. c. 1. *q*. The ferm of the port Gabel and market of Schireburn

INDEX.

burn as belonging to the see of Sarum, 47 Henry iii. I. 719. c. 1. q.

Scirpenbec, Yorkshire, tallaged, 30 Henry iii. I. 710. c. 1. w. Parcel of the demeans of Robert de Cancy, ibid.

Scissor or Cissor, Hugh, was custos of the alnage or assise of cloth, before 26 Edward i. I. 785. c. 2. a.

Scneit in Yorkshire, its tallage, 30 Henry iii. I. 710. c. 1. w.

Scnide in Wiltshire, the burgh late of Wigan, its tallage, 1 John, I. 705. c. 2. z.

Scoperel, Hervey, 14 Henry ii. I. 559. c. 1. d. Amerced for using threatning before the justiciers, ibid.

Scopham, Ralf de, one of the heirs of Brian del Isle, 19 Henry iii. I. 492. c. 2. z.

Scoteigni, Lambert de, patron of Steinton, 30 Henry ii. I. 427. c. 1. l. Agnes de Scoteigni who had the esnecia married to William Fitz-Roger, before 6 John, I. 488. c. 1. c.

Scots, William king of, does homage and swears fealty to Henry ii. an. 1170. I. 17. c. 1. 2. Is in England, an. 1185. I. 20. Corrody for the king of Scots, 3 Henry ii. I. 207. c. 1. w. Alexander king of Scots has the wardship of earl David, 14 Henry iii. I. 325. c. 1. i. And of H. Bigod, ibid. k. Some account of the king of Scot's estate in England, 13 Henry ii. I. 539. c. 1. w. See I. 611. c. 1. l. c. 2. m. Scots styled rebels by the king, 17 Edward ii. I. 615. c. 1. z. Again, 15 Edward ii. I. 662. c. 2. q. Scutage for Scotland assized at twenty shillings, 13 John, I. 667. c. 2. r. Army against Scotland, 28, 31 and 34 Edward i. I. 671. c. 2. g.

Scovil, Humfrey de, brother of Richard de Cumb, I. 490. c. 2. a.

Scriptorii magister & scriptor Rotuli de Cancellaria, who, I. 194, 195.

Scrivelby manor, to whom it appertained, 9 Edward ii. I. 651.

Scroty, Richard, appealed Richard Muncelyn for a battery, &c. 25 Henry iii. I. 120. c. 1. g.

Scudimor, Peter de, amerced, 8 John, I. 566. c. 1. t. Godfrey de Scudemor held five fees of Robert Dewias, 14 Henry ii. I. 583. c. 1. h. See Schidimor. Godfrey de Skydemor assessor of the tallage of Shafton, 49 Henry iii. I. 742. c. 1. k. John de Escudemor of Berkshire, 26 Edward i. II. 260. c. 1. q.

Scurre, William, of Abendon, 26 Henry ii. I. 561. c. 2. r. Amerced as pleading in the chapter for a lay-fee, ibid.

Scutage or Escuage, the revenue arising from it, I. 619, &c. Bodin Scutarius, 21 Henry ii. I. 546. c. 1. n. Scutage of Ireland, 18 Henry ii. I. 580. Scutagium sometimes signifies any payment assessed on knights fees, as ad redemptionem, I. 619. The original of Scutage, I. 624, &c. For Galwey, Wales, Normandy, Scotland, I. 629, &c. Scutage of the Welch army, 2 Richard i. I. 664. c. 1. z, a. Form of inquisition about scutage, I. 681. c. 2. q. Scutage an aid arising out of knights fees, I. 694.

Scutelaria or Scullery, II. 130. c. 1. e.

Seal, great, profits of it, 55 Henry iii. I. 61. The king's seal, I. 62. The king's seal assignable, I. 64. What grants could pass the seal in the minority of Henry iii. I. 67. c. 1. x. Particular manners of enjoying it,

INDEX.

I. 70, 71. A fine paid for the king's seal, 5 Stephen, I. 457. c. 2. *q*. Edward de Westminstre has custody of the seal of the Exchequer, 32 Henry ii. II. 52. c. 1. *t*. Keeper of the seal of the Exchequer is chancellor, II. 52. A close writ of the great seal, II. 268. Patent under the great seal, 1 Edward ii. II. 286. c. 2. *g*. Great seal, 26 Edward i. II. 287. c. 2. *m*.

Sebrithwerth. See Sabricthswurth.

Secchevil, Robert, claims the right of presenting to the church of Twiford, 8 John, I. 99. c. 2. *w*. Has the custody of Branton in Devonshire, 13 John, I. 411. c. 1. *u*. The men of Branton oppose his impositions, 13 John, I. 507. c. 2. *f*. Henry de Secchevil, how his land of Foteston in Devonshire descended, 10 Richard i. I. 514. c. 1. *e*. See Sakenvill.

Seculer, Nicolas le, one of the esquires of the bishop of Hereford, 10 Edward i. I. 669. c. 1. *a*. One of the tallagers of Herefordshire, 19 Henry iii. I. 735. c. 1. *h*. Alexander le Seculer baron of the Exchequer, 49 Henry iii. II. 56. c. 2. *r*.

Sees, abbat of, 9 Edward ii. I. 599. c. 2. *g*.

Seffred, master, archdeacon and justicier, 20 and 22 Henry ii. I. 124. Sefred archdeacon of Chichester chief justicier, 19 Henry ii. I. 701. c. 1. *z*. Settles the assise or tallage, 22 Henry ii. I. 702. c. 2. *h*.

Sefoul, John, sherif of Norfolk and Suffolk, 12 Edward ii. II. 280. c. 1. *b*.

Seftbery in Devonshire, its aid, 14 Henry ii. I. 588. c. 1. *b*. Scheaffbery, its aid, 23 Henry ii. I. 603. The tallage of Schaftebiry, 19 Henry iii. I. 735. c. 1. *i*. By whom assessed, 49 Henry iii. I. 742. c. 1. *k*. Abbess of Shafton, II. 121.

Segrave, Stephen de, sets amerciaments, 14 Henry iii. I. 62. c. 1. *d*, *e*. Occurs again, 11 Henry iii. I. 63. c. 1. *l*. Justiciary of England, 17 Henry iii. I. 65. c. 1. *n*. Again, 10 Henry iii. I. 528. c. 2. *k*. Nicholas de Segrave summoned to the army in Scotland among the Northamptonshire barons, 26 Edward i. I. 655. c. 1. John de, baron and of the court, ibid. c. 2. S. de Segrave justicier, 17 Henry iii. II. 34. c. 2. *y*. Simon de Segrave convicted of trespasses, and fined in five hundred marks, 35 Edward i. II. 65. Sire Johan de Segrave, 25 Edward i. II. 105. c. 1. *i*. S. de Segrave, 14 Henry iii. II. 116. c. 1. *u*. Henry de Segrave sherif of Norfolk and Suffolk with the castle of Norwich, II. 144. c. 2. *o*. G. de Segrave justice itinerant de foresta, 27 Henry iii. II. 228. c. 1. *g*. Stephen de Segrave, 13 Henry iii. II. 253. c. 1. *b*. and 14 Henry iii. ibid. Nicolas de Segrave made mareschal of England by patent under the great seal, 1 Edward ii. II. 286. c. 2. *g*.

Seham manor, in Norfolk, whose, 5 Stephen, I. 482. c. 1. *c*. See Saham.

Seindiacre, Peter de, 1 John, I. 638. c. 2. *k*. Accompts for the scutage of Roger de Burun, ibid.

Seinesbery, Reginald de, fines for refusing Hascul Musard's daughter, 5 Richard i. I. 503. c. 2. *r*.

Seintier, Gerard le, 11 John, I. 470. c. 1. *l*. Fines to import a ship's cargo of wine, ibid.

Seizure of lands, arrests, and seisure of liberties, II. 234, &c.

Selden mistaken, I. 621. c. 1.

INDEX.

Sele de Bedford, terra de la, I. 85. c. 1. *q.*

Selebi abbey, I. 309. c. 2. *t.* Thomas de, 1 John, I. 434. c. 2. *l.* Abbat, I. 474. The village and William de Selebi amerc'd for the escape of the Flemings, 21 Henry ii. I. 560. c. 1. *w.* c. 2. *a.* Abbat has Crul in Lincolnshire, 33 Henry ii. I. 713. c. 1. *d.* The quinzime for the merchandise of the port of Selebi, 6 John, I. 772. c. 1. *i.* William and Andrew de, 53 Henry iii. II. 15. c. 1. *t.*

Seled of Cambridge, John son of, 7 Henry iii. I. 738. c. 1. *x.*

Selesia, William de, holds of the bishop of Chichester, temp. Henry ii. I. 576. c. 2.

Seleye, John de, mayor of York, 53 Henry iii. II. 15. c. 1. *t.* A venire facias against him, ibid.

Selfhanger, John de, seems successor of John de Gatesden sherif of Sussex, 42 Henry iii. II. 232. c. 1. *g.*

Selford, John de, of Cambridgeshire, kill'd by his son William, before 40 Henry iii. I. 446. c. 1. *k.*

Sellarius, See Sampson. Nicolas son of Sellarius, 7 Richard i. I. 555. c. 2. *d.* William Sellarius, 30 Henry ii. I. 563. c. 1. *h.*

Selvein, Osbert, 27 Henry ii. I. 427. c. 2. *b.* Claims a knight's fee in Lincolnshire, ibid.

Selveston, the king's manor and houses of, 56 Henry iii. II. 67. c. 2. *s.*

Semille, William de, has the fee of the land of Planchis de Airel, 2 John, I. 171.

Semplingham prior holds lands in Boleby, Linc. by frankalmoign, 29 Henry iii. I. 672. c. 1. *k.* Given by Nigel Fitz-Alexander, ibid.

Senehampton manor, part of the fee of the chamberlain of the Exchequer, II. 298.

Seneschal hereditary from the time of the Conquest, I. 48. See Dapifer. Earls of Leicester hereditary stewards, I. 51. An enquiry into what fees the Seneschal anciently enjoy'd, I. 53. Enquiry about their number, I. 63. c. 1. *l.*

Senior, with whom it denotes a lord or superior, Pref. xxii.

Sepeland, whose, 2 Henry iii. I. 491. c. 2. *m.*

Seranz, William de, 2 John, I. 172. c. 2. *z.* Makes an oblatum for right against Henry de Pomeray, ibid.

Serenic, Robert de, in Normandy, 2 John, I. 520. c. 1. *c.* I. 521. c. 1. *i.*

Sergenteria de magistra de Wapentacho, granted to Henry son of Gilbert, son of Waltheve, 18 Edward i. I. 57. c. 1. *r.*

Serjeanties of inheritance, I. 299. The Serjeanty of the hostiaria in the king's army, 15 Edward i. I. 321. c. 1. *q.* The Sergeanty of twenty flechiarum, 15 Henry iii. I. 326. c. 1. *l.* Several Sergeanties in capite, I. 326. Lands held by Serjeanty and knight-service too, I. 650. Never tallaged but by special precept, I. 721. Serjeanty of keeper of the palace of Westminster and of the Flete prison, taken into the king's hand, 9 Edward ii. II. 85. c. 1. *q.*

Serjeants, a tallage rais'd for the subsistence of those in the king's service, 10 Richard i. I. 705. c. 1. *w.* King John provides for five hundred, ib. c. 2. *y.* John le Serjaunt, 35 Henry iii. II. 17. c. 2. *i.* Serjeants of the sherifs how regulated, 42 Henry iii. II. 147.

Serlo,

INDEX.

Serlo, See Grendon. Son of Serlo, Devonshire, 5 Stephen, I. 449. c. 1. z. Serlo Francus, 7 Richard i. I. 555. c. 2. d.

Serres, Jordan de, 31 Henry ii. I. 548. c. 1. p. Amerc'd in Kent for stopping a watercourse, ibid.

Servat, William, 1 Edward ii. I. 385. c. 1. q. Keeper of the custom on wool, 2 Edward ii. I. 780. c. 1. i. William manucaptor to John de Lincoln, 9 Edward ii. II. 241. c. 1. q.

Setrinton, Yorkshire, the honor and knights of Albreda de Insula, 33 Henry ii. I. 635. c. 1. r. Its donum, 3 Richard i. I. 698. c. 2. q.

Setuans, Emma de, an enquiry of lawful matrons whether she had a son, 27 Henry ii. I. 430. c. 2. f. Robert de Setuans has the terra of Wiggeberg, Essex, but in ward, 1 Richard i. I. 703. c. 1. l.

Sevanz of Kent, Robert son of Robert de, his relief, 34 Henry iii. I. 320. c. 1. g.

Sevenhampton manor, was the countess of Albemarle's, 26 Edward i. I. 614. c. 2. w.

Severus in Normandy, prior of St, 2 John, I. 520. c. 1. c.

Sewalon, Henry son of, 5 Stephen, I. 497. c. 2. c. Fines to be quit of oaths, ibid.

Sewhale kill'd by Robert of Roan, 6 John, I. 505. c. 2. q. Sewhal de Neweton attach'd, 12 John, I. 794. c. 2. k. John Sewale, 42 Henry iii. II. 17. c. 2. h.

Sewin, Robert son of, fermer of Northamptonshire, 14 Henry ii. I. 587. c. 2. a.

Sewulf's aid in Devonshire, 14 Henry ii. I. 588. c. 1. h.

Sexlande, emperor of, I. 13. c. 1. q.

Sextenedal or Sezevals, William de, fines fourscore pounds for a rape, 7 Henry ii. I. 501. c. 2. u.

Shapestere, Isabel, an indictment for her death, 33 Edward i. II. 65.

Sheffield in Yorkshire, the manor of Thomas de Furnival senior, I. 534. c. 1. Sheffield or Sefeld castle belong'd to the manor of William de Luvetot, I. 535. c. 1. Styled Sedfeld and Saffeld, I. 536. c. 1. The accompts of John de Shefeld, 8 Edward ii. II. 124. c. 1. f.

Sheep valued at about nine pence halfpeny, 30 Henry ii. I. 535. c. 2. At twelve pence, 14 Henry iii. II. 152. c. 2. z.

Selfhangre, Walter de, sherif of Norfolk, 4 and 5 Edward i. II. 165. c. 1. i. II. 180. II. 232.

Shench, Johan, widow of John, forfeits the serjeanty of keeper of Westminster palace and the Flete, 9 Edward ii. II. 85. c. 2. q. For marrying Edmund de Cheny without the king's leave, ibid. John Shenche keeper of the king's palace at Westminster, 5 Edward ii. II. 278. c. 1. u. Richard Abbot his lieutenant, ibid.

Sherer, John le, accompts for the disme of Chichester, 9 Edward ii. II. 181. c. 2. o.

Sherifs of England, almost all deposed by Henry ii. an. 1170. I. 17. c. 1. d. Sherifs were justiciers, 20 Henry ii. I. 123. 125. 129, &c. Two sherifs for Northamptonshire, 23 Henry ii. I. 131. c. 1. x. The same person sheriff of several counties at the same time, I. 127, &c. Sherif's accompts, I. 204, 205. Again, I. 262. 276. Sherif of Devonshire, I. 276. Sheriffs of London, I. 282,

INDEX.

I. 282, 283. Sherifs answered for the small escheats, I. 300. Sherifs were indifferently fermours or custodes, I. 326. Richard Basset and Aubrey de Ver joint sherifs of eleven counties, about 5 Stephen, I. 327. c. 1. *t*. Sherif in each county the principal person in levying the king's money, I. 353. Sherifs to answer in their body, honor, land, and chattels, 53 Henry iii. I. 355. c. 2. *y*. A remarkable writ sent to a sherif, 39 Henry iii. I. 356. c. 1. *z*. Styled the king's bailif, ibid. The issues and accompts of Sherifs, I. 362. Sherifs to continue as long as they serv'd well, 6 John, I. 405. c. 2. *t*. Fines every man of twelve years old for not coming to his turn, 40 Henry iii. I. 446. c. 1. *k*. Sherifs often fined at coming in and going out of office, I. 458. c. 1. *y*, *z*, *a*, *b*. How it became necessary that scutage should be collected by the Sherifs, I. 680, 681. Four Sherifs of London accompt for its ferm, 5 Stephen, I. 686. c. 2. *d*. Sherif appointed by the king's chancellor, 8 Edward ii. II. 31. Removal of Sherif, II. 68. c. 2. *w*. Sherif of London displac'd for a transgression, 2 Edward i. II. 96. c. 2. *x*. Sherifs muster forces to march in the king's service, II. 103, 104. A discretional power in the barons of the Exchequer to remove Sherifs, 35 Edward i. II. 109. c. 1. *w*. Sherifs the chief accomptants to the crown for many reigns, II. 128, 129. Whether the Sherif took an oath to the king in the most ancient times, II. 147. Pledges to be given for Sherifs when required, II. 149. The duty of Sherifs reduc'd to heads, II. 151. Accompts of Sherifs consisted of a Profer, Visus compoti, and Summa, II. 153. Anciently made their profers in person, II. 156. The manner of the Sherif's accompt when he liquidated as firmarius, II. 162. Persons acquitted from Sherif's aid, II. 167. The difference between a sherif who was fermer and one who was custos, II. 168. The manner of their accompting by order of the king and council, 54 Henry iii. II. 171. c. 1. Hereditary Sherifs accompted as others, II. 175. Sherifs to be escheators, 5 Edward i. II. 157. c. 2. *u*, *w*, &c. Idonea de Leyburne one of the sherifs in fee of Westmoreland, 27 Edward i. II. 180. The method of bringing sherifs remov'd to accompt to the king, II. 195. c. 1. *m*. Sherif of Lincoln has forty marks allowed for his maintenance, 11 Henry iii. II. 207. c. 2. *e*. Not to depart from the Exchequer till they had balanced, 51 Henry iii. II. 231. c. 2. *b*. Sherifs attach'd by the coroners, 9 Edward ii. II. 138. c. 2. *y*. When they had levied the king's debt were to acquit the debtor, II. 194.

Shilling of Venice made eighteen pence of our money, 17 John, II. 261. c. 2. *t*.

Ships of the king, their commanders styled masters, 9 Edward ii. II. 381. c. 1. *y*. Owners of Ships amerced for lading and exporting corn without licence, 12 Henry ii. I. 558. c. 1. *n*, *o*. The bishop of Durham's great ship sailed by Robert de Stocton, temp. Richard i. I. 714. c. 1. *g*. Ship arrested for putting in at a place that was no port, I. 773.

Ship-

INDEX.

Shipload of firewood given yearly to the treasurer, 5 Edward ii. II. 48. The debate whether all ships laden with fish should land at Queenhith, 14 Henry iii. II. 228. c. 1. *f*.

Shirburn or Shyreburne, Richard de, king's tallager for Northampton, 52 Henry iii. I. 756. c. 1. *s*. The castle of Shyreburne, in whose custody, 18 Edward i. II. 143. c. 2. *f*.

Shirokes, Henry de, chamberlain of Northwales for several years, 15 Edward ii. II. 137.

Shirwode or Shyrewode forest in Notinghamshire, I. 754. c. 2. *p*. John de Shirewode attorney of the mayor, &c. of Notyngham, 15 Edward ii. II. 177. c. 1. *e*.

Shoreham, the regulation of it as a port, with regard to passengers, I. 410. c. 2. *m*. Alan de Sorhams junior, his ships, 5 John, I. 767. c. 1. *p*. The quinzime for the merchandise of the port of Schoram, 6 John, I. 772. c. 2. *i*.

Shornes, Henry de, of Kent, 29 Henry ii. I. 212. c. 1. *o*. See Schornis. Shoreness or Schornes, its aid, 14 Henry ii. I. 588. c. 2. *d*. Part of it belong'd to the king, ibid.

Shotbrok, Henry de, sherif, 13 Edward i. II. 209. c. 1. *n*.

Shrewsbury, Roger earl of, held a council of his proceres, an. 1082, 1083. I. 108. c. 1. *e*, *f*. Burghers of Shrewsbury occur, I. 277. c. 2. *c*. Burgenses of Salopebirie, 31 Henry ii. I. 332. c. 2. *g*. Fine in two marks of gold to have the ferm of their town, 16 Henry ii. I. 398. c. 1. *p*. None to buy raw hides and crude cloth here but in lots, I. 410. c. 1. *k*. Its aid, 2 Henry ii. I. 602.

c. 2. *a*. Its vintism by Alan Strawelove, 1 Edward i. I. 610. c. 2. That burgh tallaged, 1 John, I. 705. c. 2. *y*. The royal remittance to wall their town, 9 Henry iii. I. 706. c. 2. *g*. Its tallage, 8 John, I. 734. c. 1. *z*. Had a castle, 40 Henry iii. II. 141. c. 2. *u*. and II. 150. c. 2. *q*.

Shropshire, Guy Lestrange justice itinerant and sheriff there, 20 Henry ii. and 23 Henry ii. I. 124. Sherif of Shropshire, and custos of the honor of William Fitz-Alan, 19 Henry ii. I. 297. c. 2. *n*. Shropshire and Staffordshire abounded in horseshoes and nails, I. 382. See I. 407. c. 2. *i*. Tallaged by Hugh Bardolf, 9 Richard i. I. 773. c. 1. *r*. By Simon de Pateshul and Mr. Ralf de Stokes, 8 John, I. 734. c. 1. *z*.

Shrub, William le, keeper of the dye of S. Edmund, 52 Henry iii. II. 89.

Sibethorpe, Thomas de, commissioner to seise the office of mareschalcy, 18 Edward iii. I. 798. c. 1.

Sibri, Stephen, of Lincolnshire, 52 Henry iii. I. 241. c. 2. *s*.

Sicily, a judicier the most pre-eminent officer there, I. 38. Robert king of Sicily sentenced by the emperor Henry VII. an. 1311. I. 157.

Siffrewast, William de, his scutage for his lands in Berkshire, 18 Henry ii. I. 629. c. 2. *a*. Halenad de Sifrewast's scutage for his fee in Oxfordshire, 4 John, I. 666. c. 1. *h*. William Sifrewast his fees, 27 Henry iii. I. 679. c. 2. *l*.

Sigeston barony in the bishopric, 8 Richard i. I. 715. c. 2.

Sigillifer or chancellor, I. 66.

Sigillo, Robert de, temp. Henry i. I. 56.

INDEX.

56. c. 1. o. His salary rais'd as Magister Scriptorii in chancery, I. 195. Nicolas de Sigillo, 2 Henry ii. I. 273. c. 1. d. Nicolas [de Sigillo] archdeacon of Huntingdon, 16 Henry ii. I. 307. c. 2. z. Nicolas de Sigillo one of the judges of the assise or tallage, 19 Henry ii. I. 701. c. 1. a.

Silamsted, Berkshire, Bartholomew chaplain of, 52 Henry iii. II. 52. c. 2. z.

Silesdene manor in Skipton, I. 721. c. 1. w.

Silvani, Richard, an. 1184. I. 168. c. 2.

Siver, nine marks of it equal to one mark of gold, I. 277. c. 2. d. Silver mine at Byrlande in Devonshire, I. 291.

Silvester, John, had two shillings a day as keeper of the king's mint, 35 Henry iii. I. 204. c. 2. m.

Simia de Stappel, Adam, fines for having set calcatraps in his wood, 9 John, I. 499. c. 2. w.

Simon [Fitz-Robert] archdeacon of Wells, chancellor, 3 John, I. 171. c. 1. u. and I. 388. c. 1. a. Simon, earl, 23 Henry ii. II. 211. c. 1. k. Earl Simon's honors of Huntendon and Gant, in the king's hands, 31 Henry ii. I. 298. c. 1. c. Earl Simon's knights fees in Lincolnshire, 14 Henry ii. I. 584. c. 1. p. Earl Simon attests a charter of king Stephen, when Robert de Gant was chancellor, II. 138. c. 2. e. Earl Simon's lands given to Robert de Gant, 4 Richard i. II. 225. Earl Simon dead without heirs, 13 Henry iii. II. 227. c. 2. e. Simon son of Mary late sherif of London, 19 Henry iii. II. 234. c. 2. q.

Simpingeham, Gilbert de, Linc. 14 Henry ii. I. 303. c. 2. h.

Simpling, Adam de, his half fee in Oxfordshire, 4 John, I. 650. c. 1. m. Occurs, 15 Henry iii. I. 674. c. 1. o. His debet for the scutage of Kery, ibid.

Simplingham hospital, lands in Wellingour given to it, 12 John, I. 218. See Semplingham. Nuns of Simplingeham, 5 Richard i. II. 20. c. 2. z.

Sine Averio or Sanzaver, Albrede widow of Ralf, has licence to marry, 22 Henry ii. I. 464. c. 1. y.

Sivelisho pledged to Silvester de Brai, 21 Henry ii. I. 430. c. 1. a.

Siward, Robert son of, fines for the widow and office of Hugh Chivilli, 5 Stephen, I. 457. c. 2. w.

Skelton, the profits of that church challeng'd by the prior of Gisburn, 4 John, I. 487. c. 1. r.

Skepwich in Somersetshire, the land of the earl of Leicester, 19 Henry ii. I. 297. c. 2. l.

Skerton, Lancashire, its crementum, I. 333. c. 1. i.

Skipton honor, its scutage, 3 Richard i. I. 637. c. 2. f. Tallaged, 21 Edward i. I. 720. Skipton contains the manors of Skipdon, Seilesdene, Stratton, and Thornby or Thorleby, I. 721. c. 1. w. Roger de Schipton's tallage, 3 John, I. 722. c. 2. b. John Sampson constable of the castle of Schipton under James earl of Albermarle, 53 Henry iii. II. 15. c. 1. l.

Skyp, Walter, clerk of Richard de Luda, 16 Edward ii. II. 302.

Skyryk wapentake has a commission of array sent to it, 16 Edward ii. II. 112. c. 1.

Sleyt-

INDEX.

Sleytteburn, Yorkshire, its tallage, 30 Henry iii. I. 710. c. 1. *w*.

Sloctres, Glocestershire, tallaged, 7 Richard i. I. 703. c. 2. *n*.

Smalemanni in the bishopric of Durham, 5 Stephen, I. 694. c. 1. *s*.

Smethefeud, the profits of its field and bars, I. 779.

Snayton, the tenure of William de Vescy tallaged, 14 Henry iii. I. 708. c. 2. *p*.

Snchenefrith church, I. 480. c. 2. *b*.

Sneinton near Notingham, I. 472. c. 2. *i*.

Sneit in Yorkshire, the soch of, 28 Henry ii. I. 104. c. 2. *o*. Its donum, 3 Richard i. I. 698. c. 2. *q*.

Snetton, Ralf de, 31 Henry ii. I. 552. c. 2. *t*. Amerced for a retraxit, ibid.

Snyterton, sir Thomas de, 1 Edward ii. II. 151. c. 1. *r*. Manucaptor for Gilbert de Holm, ibid.

Socage, that tenure preferr'd to sergeanty in point of seignury, 15 Henry iii. I. 326. c. 1. *l*. A fine paid for foke and fake, I. 397. c. 2. *k*, *l*. Lands by this tenure excus'd from some aids, I. 599. c. 1. *f*. and I. 599. c. 2. *g*. Not chargeable with scutage, I. 672. c. 2. *l*. Socage or fee ferm, I. 673.

Sokele manor granted by the bishop of Bath to William de Calehull with a reservation of tallage, 8 Edward i. I. 729. c. 2. *t*.

Solariis, John de, alderman of London, the tallage for his ward, 14 Henry iii. I. 709. c. 1. *t*. Again, 19 Henry iii. I. 738. c. 2. *z*. I. 739. c. 1. *a*. Henry de Solariis custos of the county and castle of Hereford, 15 Edward i. II. 143. c. 1. *e*.

Solutaria, or hose for the ladies, II. 130. c. 1. *e*.

Somerfeld, William de, his money tender'd, 56 Henry iii. II. 87. c. 2. *y*.

Somerleton, John de, 52 Henry iii. II. 80. c. 1. *z*.

Somerlode, the manor of the bishop of Ely, 18 Edward i. I. 618. c. 1. *k*.

Somerset, John de, seems to be a wine merchant, 49 Henry iii. I. 769. c. 1. *x*. The executors of John de Somersete, 26 Edward i. II. 187.

Somersetshire, See Dorsete. Its donum, 4 Henry ii. I. 695. c. 2. *e*.

Somerton, in Lincolnshire, the constabulary of its castle, 15 Edward ii. I. 383. c. 2.

Someter or Sumeter, John le, of Somersetshire, attach'd, 45 Henry iii. II. 79. c. 1. *y*.

Somner's glossary on the word Scaccarium, I. 178. c. 1. *z*.

Sonday, judgment in pleas formerly given on that day, I. 108. See Sunday.

Sorewel, William de, accompts for the ferm of Hampshire, 5 Henry iii. I. 329. c. 1. *t*. And Somersetshire, 9 Henry iii. I. 329. c. 2. *y*.

Sotebroc, Berkshire, Robert son of Hugh de, his relief, 6 Henry iii. I. 318. c. 1. *w*.

Soureby, Walter de, surety of Nicolas de Stutevil, 5 Henry iii. II. 198. c. 2. *w*.

Southamptonshire, its ferm, I. 402. c. 2. *l*. Has Portum Mues included in it, ibid. 1 John, c. 2. The ferm of Southampton, 9 John, I. 409. c. 1. *a*. That village amerc'd for demolishing the castle, 30 Henry iii. I. 568. c. 1. *q*. Southampton tallaged, 10 Richard i. I. 705. c. 2. *x*. Again, 30 Henry iii. I. 711. c. 1. *x*. Again, 2 John, I. 734. c. 1.

INDEX.

c. 1. x. Again, 33 Henry ii. I. 736. c. 2. q. The quinzime for the merchandife of the port of Southampton, 6 John, I. 772. c. 1. i. Winchefter and Porchefter the only places tallaged in this county in the minority of Henry iii. II. 118. c. 1. g.

Spada, Ivo de, I. 166. c. 1. i.

Spalding, prior of, I. 405. c. 1. k. Prior of Spaulding and Pincebec fines for liberties, 3 Henry iii. I. 413. c. 1. i. Prior of Spalding, Pincebec, and Multon, 3 Henry iii. I. 508. c. 1. m.

Spanifh Æra reduced to our computation by deducting thirty-eight, Pref. xx. c. 1. o. Their language has a great mixture of Moorifh, Pref. xxi.

Spanneby, William, marefchal of the Exchequer, 34 Edward i. II. 286. c. 1. f.

Spanny, John de, merchant of R. earl of Leicefter, 5 John, I. 771. c. 1. e.

Sparewe, the fons of Richard, amerced, 14 Henry ii. I. 545. c. 1. b. John Sparrow bailif of Norwich, 35 Edward i. II. 82.

Species, in which the ancient revenue of the crown was paid, I. 272.

Speciarius, William, one of the fermours of the fee of Rochefter, about 31 Henry ii. I. 311. c. 1. e.

Speciofus, bifhop, Pref. xxvii. c. 2

Spelethorn hundred, Middlefex, I. 546. c. 2. s.

Spelman, fir Henry, I. 45. His account or folution of two dapifers, I. 49. c. 2. k. Of the chancery, I. 62. Does not diftinctly explain Tenant in capite, I. 621.

Spelfhot manor, Berks, from Robert Achard paffes to Robert fon of Elias de Colefhulle, 26 Edward i. II. 8. c. 1. f.

Spencer, fir John, has the fite of the priory of Tortington, Suffex, 42 Elizabeth, I. 621. c. 2.

Sperling, Ralf, alderman of London, his tallage, 14 Henry iii. I. 709. c. 1. t. Again, 19 Henry iii. I. 738. c. 2. z. I. 739. c. 1. a.

Sperun, Thomas, jufticier of the Jews, 42 Henry iii. I. 253. c. 1. z.

Spigurnell, Godfrey, his annual payment for lands in Sceggebi, 9 John, I. 189. c. 1. a. The Spigurnel or chafe wax, I. 194. Fee of the Spigurnels to the great feal, I. 386. I. 387. c. 1. w. Edmund Spygurnel fupported by the queen confort and queen mother, 1 and 4 Edward i. II. 233. c. 1. k, l. Spigurnel wax, 5 Richard i. II. 274. c. 2. d.

Spikefwic, Michael de, amerced, 14 Henry ii. I. 554. c. 2. r.

Spileman, William, amerced for a concord without the king or his juftices, 31 Henry ii. I. 548. c. 1. n.

Spiney honour, late the poffeffion of Ingelram du Port, affign'd to Fulk de Prees, 2 John, I. 170. Geoffrey de Spin. of Normandy, 2 John, I. 524. c. 1. u.

Spire, Conrad bifhop of, prefent at the figning the golden bull, I. 61. c. 2. a.

Spondon, G. de, Lanc. flain before 3 John, I. 504. c. 1. z.

Spotford, in Yorkfhire, its tallage, 30 Henry iii. I. 710. c. 2.

Spreuton, Wimund de, amerc'd for ill keeping a duel, 14 Henry ii. I. 545. c. 1. y.

Springefeld in Effex, tallaged as in the king's hand, 1 Richard i. I. 703. c. 1. l. Late the land of Ralf de Buefevil, ibid.

Spryng-

INDEX.

Spryngval, Benet, cuſtos of the Stagminaria, Wiltſhire, 26 Edward i. I. 655. c. 2.

Squier, Richard, his privy ſeal for a manor, 12 Edward ii. I. 265. c. 2. e. Was cuſtos of the manor of Fekenham, 12 Edward ii. II. 292.

Stable, Roger, juſticier, his grant, 2 John, I. 98. c. 2. o.

Stafford, Henry archdeacon of, his fine for king Richard's benevolence, 1 John, I. 190. c. 2. k. The aid of Stafford, 5 Stephen, I. 601. c. 2. u. Edmund baron of Stafford ſummon'd to the expedition againſt Scotland, 26 Edward i. I. 655. c. 1. Honor of Stafford, I. 680. c. 1. m. Miliſent de Stafford her ſhare in the honor, ibid. Robert de Stafford ſherif of that coonty, 2 Henry ii. I. 688. c. 2. o. Its donum, 5 Henry ii. I. 697. c. 1. s. Henry archdeacon, 1 John, I. 722. c. 2. a. Was the king's tallager, ibid. Its tallage, 7 Henry iii. I. 734. c. 2. d. Robert de Stafford has the ferm of that county, 2 Henry ii. II. 152. c. 1. t. John de Stafford mareſchal of the Exchequer, 27 Edward i. II. 187. c. 1. w. John de Stafford mareſchal of the Exchequer, 25 Edward i. II. 288. c. 2. q.

Stagminaria of Wiltſhire, Benet Spryngval cuſtos of it, 26 Edward i. II. 655. c. 2.

Stagnum for Stannum, I. 445. c. 1. c. and I. 775. c. 1. q. Stagnaria or Stannary, II. 145. c. 1. p.

Stainberg, Yorkſhire, its tallage, 30 Henry iii. I. 710. c. 2. Stayncros wapentake has a commiſſion of array ſent to it, 16 Edward ii. II. 112. c. 1.

Stalingburc, Lincolnſhire, the demeans of the ſee of York, 33 Henry ii. I. 713. c. 1. d.

Stanberg hundred in Devonſhire, I. 547. The king's ſergeanty of Stannebrugge, II. 78. c. 2. r.

Stanbrige in Huntingdonſhire, belong'd to the Giffards before 1 Richard i. I. 447. c. 2. b.

Stanes diſwarrened by the men of Middleſex, 11 Henry iii. I. 416. c. 1. w. Thomas de Stanes of London his tallage, 14 Henry iii. I. 709. c. 1. s. Ralf de Stanes chamberlain of the Exchequer in Ireland, 22 Edward i. II. 136. c. 1. x. Richard de Stanes juſticier, 55 Henry iii. II. 203. c. 1. b.

Stanford, Aluredus clericus præpoſitus de, 5 Stephen, I. 147. c. 1. t. Richard de Stanford, 10 Edward i. I. 266. c. 2. k. Gilbert de, 8 John, I. 494. c. 2. s. The town amerc'd, 49 Henry iii. I. 568. c. 2. t. In the king's hands, 27 Henry iii. I. 723. c. 1. c. An inquiſition about it, ibid. In Herefordſhire tallaged, 7 Richard i. I. 747. c. 1. k. Chuſe to be tallaged by the crown, not by inferior lords, 27 Henry iii. I. 757. c. 2. t. Prior of the hoſpital of S. Thomas de Stamford, 14 Henry iii. I. 48. c. 2. d. Richard de Stanford keeper of the prime roll, 4 Edward i. II. 112. c. 2. f. Bailifs of, 28 Henry iii. II. 203. c. 2. g. Richard de, 56 Henry iii. II. 264. & II. 269. c. 2. f, g. Richard de Stanford writer of the great roll, 3 Edward i. II. 320. c. 2. e.

Stanherſt, Hugh de, 6 Henry iii. I. 549. c. 1. c. Amerc'd pro impreſſione ſigilli, ibid.

Stanhol, the drengage of Uctred de, Lan-

INDEX.

Lancashire, 3 John, I. 333. c. 1. *i.* And the drengage of Gilbert clerk in Stanhol, ibid.

Stanlega near Chipeham, Wiltshire, N. abbat of, 3 John, I. 217. c. 1. *i.* Have the land of Childecnol, ibid. Manor of Stanley, Warwickshire, fines, I. 442. c. 1. *a.* Robert de Stanley sherif of Staffordshire, 5 Stephen, I. 457. c. 2. *p.*

Stanlowe, Richard de, seems to be king's attorney, 26 Edward i. II. 47. c. 2. *y.*

Stanstede manor in Suffolk, held of the honor of Hagenet by Gerard de Wachesham, 9 Edward ii. I. 652. c. 1. *u.* Stansted park in Sussex the earl of Arundel's, 2 Edward ii. II. 82.

Stanton, H. de, seems baron of the Exchequer, 9 Edward ii. I. 381. c. 1. *x.* Ulric de, his land, I. 426. c. 2. *a.* Adam de, 22 Henry ii. I. 482. c. 2. *g.* The town of John de Warenne, 33 Edward i. I. 741. c. 2. *i.* H [ervey] de Stanton teste, 9 Edward ii. I. 784. c. 1. *u.* Chancellor of the Exchequer, 9 Edward ii. II. 53. c. 2. *d.* King's chief justicier, 19 Edward ii. II. 53. c. 2. *e.* II. 54. c. 1. *f.* Was made chancellor of the Exchequer, 10 Edward ii. II. 59. c. 1. *e.* Geoffrey de Staynton has a commission of array, 16 Edward ii. II. 112. c. 1. Philip de Staunton late sherif of Cambridge and Huntingdonshire, 35 Henry iii. II. 238. c. 2. *z.*

Stapelford, Hugh de, sherif of Bedfordshire, 7 Edward i. II. 161. c. 1. *n.* His station, 56 Henry iii. II. 180. c. 2. *d.*

Stapleton, Robert de, 28 Henry ii. I. 104. Nicolas de, delivers an injunction, &c. 7 Edward i. II. 300. c. 1. *w.*

Stare, Hamun le, vanquished in combat and hang'd, I. 550.

Stargil, William de, commissioner of array for Skyryk wapentak, 16 Edward ii. II. 112. c. 1.

Starra, of Hebrew original, signifying the Jewish charters in our records, I. 237.

Staundon, Robert de, justicier of North Wales, 14 Edward i. II. 5. c. 1. *t.* Fishery of Staundon belong'd to Hugh de Clahale, 42 Henry iii. II. 18. c. 2. *n.*

Stebbinges, William de, resident in the Exchequer, 40 Henry iii. II. 22. c. 2. *s.*

Stebhee village in Middlesex, in arrears, 27 Henry iii. II. 193. c. 1. *z.*

Stede, Uchtrede de, king's fusor had salary, perquisites, and serjeanty, 26 Henry ii. I. 289. c. 2. *t.*

Steinton in Lincolnshire, a contest about the right of patronage, 30 Henry ii. I. 427. c. 1. *l.*

Stembia, to whom those lands were given, 21 Henry ii. II. 200. c. 1. *e.*

Stepering, alderman Ralf's tallage for his ward in London, 14 Henry iii. I. 709. c. 1. *t.* Again, 19 Henry iii. I. 738. c. 2. *z.* I. 739. c. 1. *a.*

Stephen, Ralf son and heir of Ralf son of, his relief, 6 Henry iii. I. 318. c. 1. *x.* Stephen bishop of Waterford was justicier and treasurer of Ireland, 13 Edward i. II. 8. c. 1. *k.* and 19 Edward i. II. 135. c. 1. *u.*

Stephen, king, seems to be the founder of Feversham abbey, I. 413. c. 2. *k.*

Sterling, one pound Sterling seems to make four of Anjou, I. 168. c. 2.

INDEX.

Steyngrine, John, brother and heir of Peter de, of Yorkshire, 52 Henry iii. II. 186.

Stichefwald, Maud, wife of Ralf de, 5 Stephen, I. 449. c. 1. y. The hyde-land of the prior of, 5 John, I. 605. c. 2. t.

Stillingfleet's account of our courts, I. 178. c. 1. a.

Stifted, Essex, tallaged, 1 Richard i. I. 703. c. 1. l.

Stivelingfeld, Norman de, amerced for false testimony, 17 Henry ii. I. 559. c. 2. l.

Stiviclea, Stiffeclay or Steucley, Walter de, 9 John, I. 478. c. 2. w. The king of Scots town, 13 Henry ii. I. 540. c. 1. x. Herbert de Stiveclai amerced for recreancy, 12 Henry ii. I. 549. c. 2. l.

Stocfeld, II. 45. c. 2. t.

Stoch, Michael clericus de, about temp. Henry ii. I. 3. c. 2. Safugel de Stoch of Dedham, his aid, 14 Henry ii. I. 586.

Stoclai, the tallage of Gerard parson of, 9 Richard i. I. 699. c. 2. r.

Stodham, Thomas de, his debt, 12 Edward ii. I. 234. c. 1. o.

Stoile, Alexander, I. 761. c. 1.

Stok or Stokes, Peter de, justicier of Normandy, 3 John, I. 171. c. 1. *n*. His widow Juliana married to Galfrid de Lucy, 9 John, I. 189. c. 1. b. Henry de Stok, who, 10 John, I. 489. c. 2. q. Peter de, 5 John, I. 525. c. 1. a. The ferm of Stok in Yorkshire, 25 Henry iii. II. 28. c. 1. k.

Stoke, Grenta de, his tenure from the bishop of Bath, temp. Henry i. I. 109. Terra de Stoke derained by the prior of Ely, 12 Henry ii. I. 82. c. 1. a.

Stoke manor the prior of Worcester's, I. 408. c. 2. w. The aid of the town of Stokes, Surrey, 14 Henry iii. I. 587. c. 1. y.

Stokeport, Robert de, 3 John, I. 397. c. 1. g. His lands, ibid.

Stokes, Owen de, 29 Henry ii. I. 105. c. 1. p. Richard Stokes forfeited his money for uttering it contrary to the assise, I. 280. c. 1. x. Peter de Stokes subsherif of Hantshire for Geoffrey Fitz-Peter, 5 John, I. 332. c. 2. e. Peter de, 4 John, I. 537. c. 1.

Stokes wood, in Bucks, turned into a park, 16 John, I. 472. c. 2. g. Stokes, Wiltshire, its donum, 33 Henry ii. I. 634. c. 2. Ralf de Stokes tallager of Shropshire, 8 John, I. 734. c. 1. z. Ralf de Stokes clerk of the great wardrobe, 12 Edward ii. II. 102. c. 1. z.

Stokesby, John de, hostiary of the Exchequer, 15 Edward ii. I. 359. c. 1. n. Again, 12 Edward ii. II. 102. c. 1. z. John de Stokesby one of the ushers of the Exchequer, 15 Edward ii. II. 280.

Stoketon or Stocton, Robert de, failed the bishop of Durham's great ship to London, temp. Richard i. I. 714. c. 1. g. The tallage of that villata, 8 Richard i. ibid. c. 2. Stoketon tallaged, 11 Edward i. I. 720. c. 2. u.

Stolde, Walter de, his duel, 6 Henry iii. I. 445. c. 1. c.

Stone, Stephen de, has a writ of prince Edward's in his favour, 35 Edward i. II. 125. c. 2. o.

Stonleye, Richard de, one of those appointed to take the office of mareschalcy into their hands, and to make inquiry, &c. 18 Edward iii. I. 798. c. 1. w.

Storteford, Richard de, master of the scholes of London, 30 Henry ii. I.

INDEX.

215. c. 2. d. Town of Storteford amerced, I. 568. c. 2. t.

Stoter, Roger, baron of the Exchequer, dyed, 5 Edward ii. II. 59. c. 1. c. Was succeeded by Walter de Norwich, ibid.

Stowe, frere William de, sacrist of the abbey of S. Edmond, and master moneyour, 12 Edward ii. I. 293. c. 1. e. The fairs of Stowe, I. 309. c. 2. w. The knights of the province of Stowe, ibid. The burning of Stow in Lincolnshire, before 23 Henry ii. I. 342. c. 1. b. Accompted for in the ferm of the fee of Lincoln, 18 Henry ii. I. 346. c. 1. i. Stow hundred in Norfolk, I. 545. c. 1. x. The tallage of the hundred of Stow, I. 706. c. 2. e.

Stradebroc advouson belonged to the honor of Eye, 9 John, II. 43. c. 1. k.

Strafford wapentake has a commission of array sent to it, 16 Edward ii. II. 112. c. 1. The abbat of Strafford, II. 201.

Strand, Walter le Brun mareschal or farrier of it, 19 Henry iii. II. 100. c. 2. n.

Strapeton, Robert de, 5 Stephen, I. 147. c. 2. b. Seems to be sherif of Northamptonshire, ibid.

Strata de Geldedon, that street in the north of Surrey, I. 399. c. 1. a.

Stratford, Yorkshire, tallaged, 9 Richard i. I. 699. c. 1. r.

Stratton, Ralf de Nevil as keeper signs his own presentation to it, 16 John, II. 43. c. 1. m. Stratton hamlet, whose, II. 298. Adam de Stratton's felony, 30 Edward i. II. 299. c. 2. r. His removal, 18 Edward i. II. 300.

Stratton, Hervey de, sheriff of Staffordshire, 23 Henry ii. II. 131. c. 2. c. Thomas de Stratton married Ysabella daughter and coheir of Philip de Ulecot, before 5 Henry iii. I. 463. c. 1. r. Richard de Stratton amerced for holding plea of a lay fee in court Christian, 1 Richard i. I. 561. c. 2. w. Stratton manor in Skipton, I. 721. c. 1. w. Adam's office in the Exchequer at Berwick, 6 Edward i. II. 5. c. 1. x. Adam de Stratton clerk of the Exchequer, 1 Edward i. II. 23. c. 1. w. Again, 56 Henry iii. II. 264. By autority of Isabel countess of Albemarle, Adam de Stratton presents Ralf de Stratton chamberlain, 49 Henry iii. II. 296. c. 1. a. Sir John de Windesor conveys to Adam de Stratton the office of ponderator, 49 Henry iii. II. 308. William del Palace made pesour instead of William de Stratton, 18 Edward i. ibid. c. 2. d.

Strawelove, Alan, receiver of the vintisme of Shrewsbury, 1 Edward i. I. 610. c. 2.

Striguil honour or barony in the king's hands, 31 Henry ii. I. 297. c. 2. p. Again was in the king's hands, 1 Richard i. I. 298. c. 2. q. Mentioned again, 33 Henry ii. I. 636. c. 2. y.

Stubelond, S. Michael, a fair granted to it, 2 John, I. 518. c. 1. s.

Stull, Geoffrey, has a commission of array for the wapentake of Buckros, 16 Edward ii. II. 111.

Stultiloquium, Richard fined ten pound for it, I. 167. c. 1. k. Many amerciaments for the like offence, I. 563. c. 2. I. 564. c. 1.

Stultus, Alan, 7 Richard i. I. 555. c. 2. d.

Sturmans, I. 387.

Sturmy,

INDEX.

Sturmy, Robert, oppressed by the Jews, 15 Edward i. I. 252. c. 1. *u.* John de Sturmy has the custody of Orford castle, 15 Edward ii. I. 383 c. 2.

Sturton Michel de, 1 John, I. 504. c. 1. *u.* His writ against a distringas, ibid.

Stutesbiri, prior of, his cause, 11 John, I. 448. c. 2. *k.*

Stutevil, Eustace and Nicolas de, 10 John, I. 100. c. 1. *z.* William de Stutevill custos of Yorkshire over the archbishop, temp. Richard i. I. 35, 36. Stutevill, a convention between him and Mubrai, I. 115. Nicolas de Stutevill his interest in Cumberland in the manors of Hukemannebi, Blenherset, Overic, Leventon, Lawefwater, Bikerenet and Stapleton, 3 Richard i. I. 116. c. 2. *b.* William de Stuttevil his contention with Pandulph, 4 Henry iii. I. 119. Roger de Stutevill sherif of Northumberland, 23 Henry ii. I. 130. c. 2. *u.* Robert de Stuttevill holds pleas at Carlisle, 17 Henry ii. I. 146. c. 1. *e.* Robert son and heir of William de Stuttevil in the wardship of archbishop Hubert, 6 John, I. 324. c. 2. *h.* Robert de Stuttevil sherif of Yorkshire, 21 Henry ii. I. 370. c. 2. *b.* William de Stutevil high sherif of the city and county of York and of Northumberland, 3 John, I. 461. c. 1. *a, b, c.* Helwise de Stutevil of Cumberland fines not to marry, 4 John, I. 465. c. 1. *o.* Nicolas son of Nicolas de Stutevil fines for a perambulation between the king and his forest, 11 John, I. 506. c. 2. *y.* William de Stutevil has the ferm of Cardvil or Carlisle, 3 John, I. 516. c. 1. *l.* Has the ferm of Penreth, Languadeby, Salkil and Scoteby, ibid. Henry de Stotevil of Normandy, 2 John, I. 520. c. 2. *h.* Robert de Stutevil's knights fees, 14 Henry ii. ibid. c. 2. *p.* William de Stutevil discharged from escuage in Yorkshire, because with the king, 6 Richard i. I. 591. c. 1. *r.* William de, accompts for the knights fees, late of Hugh de Say in Herefordshire, 29 Henry iii. I. 616. c. 1. *g.* William de, 11 John, ibid. c. 2. *d.* His scutage for his land in Yorkshire, 3 Richard i. I. 637. c. 2. *f.* Robert de Stuttevil sherif of Yorkshire, 21 Henry ii. I. 702. c. 2. *f.* The tenants of Eustace de Stotevil, Yorkshire, tallaged in Cropton and Barton, 14 Henry iii. I. 708. c. 2. *p.* Robert sherif of Yorkshire gave visum compoti, 21 Henry ii. II. 157. c. 2. *u.* William de Stutevil sherif of Yorkshire, before 22 Henry iii. II. 195. Nicolas and Robert de Stutevil, 5 Henry iii. II. 198. c. 2. *w.* Robert, 20 Henry ii. II. 200. c. 1. *d.* Nicholas de Stutevil pays a thousand marks for his ransom, 7 Henry iii. II. 222. c. 1. *w.*

Stutton in Sudfolch, whose, I. 113. c. 2.

Styntesford in Dorsetshire, whose fee, 2 Edward ii. I. 600. c. 1. *b.*

Suanewiz, Roger de Poles of, his men amerced for wrongfully seizing a royal fish, 31 Henry ii. I. 548. c. 2. *w.*

Suaveshee quit of tallage, 9 John, I. 748. c. 2. *t.*

Subery, Ralf de, his aid in Essex, 14 Henry ii. I. 586. c. 2. forte Sudbury.

Submission, the form of one for assaulting a judge in Westminster-hall, 52 Henry iii. I. 236. c. 2. *k.* Was tam de vita & membris, quam de terris, tenementis & omnibus bonis & catallis

INDEX X.

tallis fuis, ibid. The form of Robert de Ludham's, 14 Edward i. I. 254. c. 1. c.

Suburg, William de, of Northamptonshire, 6 Henry iii. I. 454. c. 2. k. Justices Berengar le Moine, ibid.

Succession, I. 183, &c.

Succheley in Worcestershire, its tallage, 8 Richard i. I. 704. c. 2. q.

Sudley, Otuel de, why his lands were seized, 9 Richard i. I. 39. c. 1. y. The visus of Richard de Sudlega, 20 Henry ii. I. 141. c. 1. x. William de Sudley his interest in Winchecumb, 1 John, I. 433. c. 2. h. Ralf de Sudley of Glocestershire his aid, and promissio, 14 Henry ii. I. 582. c. 2. f.

Sudton, Griffin de, and Maud his wife, their claim in Shropshire, 3 John, I. 213. c. 2. x.

Sudtwerch or Suthwerk, Edward de, his fine, 15 Henry ii. I. 99. c. 1. l. Prior of, 3 Richard i. I. 106. c. 1. s. Its aid, 14 Henry ii. I. 587. c. 1. y. See Suwic. Its aid, 5 Stephen, I. 601. c. 2. u. Again, 2 Henry ii. I. 602. c. 2. b. and I. 690. Its donum, 5 Henry ii. I. 697. c. 1. t.

Sudwerch, Adam de, 1 Richard i. I. 427. c. 2. q. Robert de Briddingheft amerced for hindring the jurors verdict about the church of Sudwerc, 15 Henry ii. I. 545. c. 2. c.

Sueine de Porta accompts for the pleas of Ralf Basset, 5 Stephen, I. 146. c. 2. p. See Port.

Sueine the king's scutiger, 5 Stephen, I. 365. c. 1. o. Robert son of Sweyn predecessor of Hugh de Cancelles, his grant to the abbat of S. James of Northampton, before 35 Henry iii. I. 119. c. 2. r.

Suellard, his aid, 14 Henry ii. I. 488. c. 1. b.

Sueteluve, William, of Lutton, his donum, 9 Richard i. I. 699. c. 1. r.

Suffolk. See Norfolk. Alan de Suffolk collector of the king's duty on wines, 25 Edward i. I. 770. c. 2. b. Thomas de Suffolk sherif of London, 25 Edward i. II. 96. c. 2. a. Alexander de Suffolk, 53 Henry iii. II. 304. c. 1. m. His recognition, ibid.

Sugerius abbat of S. Denys, his history of their purchases, I. 159, 160. c. 1. d.

Suinecumbe manor belonged to the abbot of Bec, 5 John, I. 396. c. 1. c.

Suineford, William de, sherif of Norfolk and Suffolk, 42 Henry iii. I. 378. c. 1. m. John de Suineford accompts for the prise of the king's wines, 49 Henry iii. I. 769. c. 1. x.

Suithun, Andrew prior of S. elect of Winchester, 43 Henry iii. II. 3. c. 2. l. That prior's contention with the abbat of Cerne, 27 Henry iii. II. 78. c. 1. q.

Suleby, Robert son of Robert de, one of the Westmerland drengs, 2 John, I. 659. c. 1. x. Fines for a rehearing before the king, 12 John, I. 795. c. 1. o.

Suleye, Bartholomew de, sherif of Herefordsh. 55 Henry iii. I. 270. c. 2. d. Has an allowance of six pounds for conveying the vintiesme of his county to the New Temple, ibid. Ralf son of Ralf de Sullega, his relief, 6 Henry iii. I. 318. c. 1. y. Imayne de Sulleye of Gloucestershire has respite in paying queen's gold, 28 Henry iii. I. 352. c. 1. f. John de Sule of Worcestershire, is summoned among the barons to the war against Scotland, 26 Edward i. I. 655. c. 1.

Sully

INDEX.

Sully island belonged to Cornwal, I. 343. c. 2. *i*.

Sumburn in Hampshire, its assise, 22 Henry ii. I. 702. c. 2. *i*.

Sumer, Ralf, 41 Henry iii. II. 22. c. 2. *t*. Made one of the tellers of the Exchequer by William de Haverhul, 29 Henry iii. II. 307. c. 1. *u*.

Sumercotes, John de, one of the tallagers of Lincolnshire, 33 Henry iii. II. 215. c. 1. *y*.

Sumeresvil and the isle of Gerner, that land claimed by William de Kaneby, 2 John, I. 521. c. 1. *k*.

Sumeri, Adam de, his donation to S. Mary and S. Nicholas de Ledes, 10 John, I. 217. c. 2. *n*. Roger de Sumery has the honor of Duddelega in Worcestreshire, 17 Henry iii. I. 510. c. 2. *e*. Fined for not taking knighthood, ibid. Ralf de Sumeri seems to be sherif of Staffordshire, 6 Richard i. I. 591. c. 1. *q*. Accompts for the scutage of Gervase Painel for the king's ransom, ibid. And for his own scutage in Worcestershire, I. 592. c. 2. *y*. Roger de Sumery his interest in the shires of Cambridge and Huntingdon, 31 Henry iii. I. 594. c. 2. *k*. Ralf de Sumeri quit of his scutage in Worcestershire, 3 John, I. 665. c. 1. *f*. Margery de Sumery, 27 Henry iii. I. 682. c. 1. *r*. Sir Adam de Sumeri is pledge for the debts to the king of the late Saier Fitz Henry, 35 Henry iii. II. 185. c. 1. *k*. Roger de Sumery going with the king into Gascoign, has respite, 38 Henry iii. II. 217. c. 2. *t*.

Sumerton, Basilia de, Linc. 24 Henry ii. I. 211. c. 2. *l*. Ralf de Sumerton amerced for recreancy, 12 Henry ii. I. 549. c. 2. *k*. The aid of the men of Sumerton, 14 Henry ii. I. 588. c. 2. *c*. The tallage of Sumerton, 14 Henry iii. I. 708. c. 1. *o*. The hundred of Sumerton granted to Alienor consort of prince Edward, 52 Henry iii. II. 167. c. 1. *u*.

Sumerville, William, returned by the sherif of Yorkshire as gone into Scotland, 4 Henry ii. I. 3. c. 1. Roger de Sumerville his interest in Barneby, Yorkshire, 31 Henry ii. I. 431. c. 1. *k*. Gervase de Sumervil, fines, 6 Henry iii. I. 492. c. 1. *r*. Roger de Sumervil in the army against Scotland, 34 Edward i. I. 657. c. 1. *h*. Roger de Sumervil holds the manor of Alrewas by fee ferm, 27 Henry iii. I. 678. c. 2. *i*. Roger de Somervill has the wapentake of Herthill under a commission of array, 16 Edward ii. II. 112. c. 2.

Sumeter, William le, to find pledges, 18 Henry iii. II. 15. c. 2. *x*. See Someter.

Summarius, or sumpter horse, I. 365. c. 1. *s*.

Summonces, in several forms, I. 653, &c. Of the Exchequer made out by the remembrancers, II. 268. A clerk of the summonces appointed, 18 Edward ii. II. 293. c. 1. *p*.

Sunday, the market day of the men of Burgh, 3 John, I. 403. c. 2. *u*, &c. Barons of the Exchequer sat on Sundays, II. 5.

Sunning, Elyas de, justice of the Jews, 18 Henry iii. I. 234. c. 1. *a*. and 21 Henry iii. II. 317. c. 2. *e*.

Sunning, the land of the bishop of Sarum, its donum for the army in Galwey, 33 Henry ii. I. 634. c. 1. *q*.

Sunnynghul, John de, in Dorsetshire, held his fee and half in Styntesford in socage, 2 Edward ii. I. 600. c. 1. *h*.

Super-

INDEX.

Superhidage, I. 686. c. 2. *f.* Relating to danegeld, I. 693. c. 1. *m, n, o.*

Superplus, I. 167. Again, I. 285. c. 2. I. 286. c. 1, 2. In sherif's accompts, &c. ibid. When the accomptant's payment of the revenues was more than his receipts, II. 231.

Superfife, I. 552. c. 1. *i.*

Sureties, not to be diftrained while the principal had wherewith to anfwer, II. 192. Called plegii obfides & manucaptores, II. 197. The king's debtors to find fureties if required, ibid.

Surita, his account of the antiquity of the justicia of Aragon, I. 38. His account of the steward of Catalunna, I. 54.

Surrey knights, fine to be quit of pleas of the foreft, 2 Richard i. I. 399. c. 1. *a.* The county deafforefted, 5 John, I. 405. c. 2. *q.* The aid it paid for marrying the king's daughter, 14 Henry ii. I. 587. c. 1. *y.*

Sutherton, the manor of John de Burgh, 36 Henry iii. I. 752. c. 1. *g.*

Suttchirch, how that town belonged to the prior of Chrift's Church, Canterbury, 9 Richard i. I. 113.

Sutton, Robert de, clerk of the fherif of Yorkshire, 15 Edward i. I. 355. c. 1. *w.* Geoffrey de Sutton collector of the cuftoms in the port of S. Botulphs, 15 Edward ii. I. 360. c. 2. *r.* Robert de Sutton, plegius, &c. 10 Henry iii. I. 496. c. 1. *o.* Peter de Sutton his fhare in the terra of Ralf Fitz-Gerold, 29 Henry ii. I. 512. c. 1. *t.* Sutton in Gloceftershire belonged to the abbat of Weftminfter, 19 Henry ii. I. 701. c. 2. *c.* Thomas de Sutton clerk of Godfrey de Giffard chancellor of the Exchequer, 51 Henry iii. II. 52. c. 1. *w.* William de Sutton late fherif of Effex and Hertfordshire, 27 Edward i. II. 203. c. 1. *d.*

Suwic, feems to be one of the king's palaces, 37 Henry iii. I. 68. c. 2. *b.*

Sutwerch has a loquela againft the men of London, 2 Henry ii. I. 449. c. 2. *g.* See Sudwerch.

Swadefeld, Julian de, fines for a duel with William de Curton for the land of Elingeham, 9 John, I. 507. c. 1. *a.*

Swaneflond, S. has the privilege not to be made mayor, fherif, coroner, or alderman of London, 12 Edward ii. I. 750. c. 2. *a.* Simon de, the king's merchant, ibid.

Swerdefton, Roger fon of John de, his chirograph, 12 Henry iii. I. 239. c. 2. *a.*

Swereford, Alexander de, author of the red book, I. 179. and I. 624. Flourifhed in the time of king John and Henry iii. I. 179. His care, I. 195. A quotation out of him, I. 625. Says the donum of 5 Henry ii. was a fcutage, I. 627. Occurs, 29 Henry iii. I. 677. c. 2. *d.* and 27 Henry iii. I. 681. c. 2. *p.* His accompt of danegeld, I. 689. c. 1. *p.* and I. 745. c. 1. *z.* The trefpafs on his land of Andebury, though baron of the Exchequer, 29 Henry iii. II. 13. c. 2. *k.* Was baron, 18 Henry iii. II. 54. c. 2. *i.*

Swilington, fir Adam de, committed to the caftle of Dovor and Tower of London, for going to torneaments beyond feas without licence, 35 Edward i. II. 109.

Swindon, terra de, was William de Pontearch's, 9 Henry iii. I. 492. c. 1. *x.* Richard de Swindon marefchal of the Exchequer, 22 Henry iii. II. 285. c. 1. *a.*

Swyne-

INDEX.

Swyneford, William de, sherif of Norfolk and Suffolk, 40 Henry iii. II. 150. c. 2. *p.* Again, 42 Henry iii. II. 207. c. 1. *f.* See Suineford.

Swynnerton, Roger de, constable of the Tower, and receiver of the king's subsidy, 16 Edward ii. I. 611. c. 2. *m.*

Sykard, Eimeric de, merchant, has judgment against the sherifs of London, 48 Henry iii. II. 11. c. 1. *b.*

Sylva without inclosure near a river, I. 186. c. 2. *u.*

Synoth, burgess of Hertford, his aid, 14 Henry ii. I. 585, 586. c. 1. *x.*

Syward, Richard, one of the king's courtiers and a baron, summoned by writ to the war in Scotland, 26 Edward i. I. 655. c. 2.

T.

Tabor, Suein, amerced for his bow and arrows, 31 Henry ii. I. 562. c. 1. *x.*

Tachesbroch, David de, 23 Henry ii. I. 210. c. 1. *f.* Plegius of Robert de Munfort, ibid.

Tadcastre in Yorkshire, belonged to the monks of Salley, 7 John, I. 488. c. 2. *e.* The tallage of Tatcastre, 30 Henry iii. I. 710. c. 1. *w.*

Taddewel, Robert Fitz-Gilbert de, accompts for the pleas of the king's chancellor, 2 Henry ii. I. 62. c. 1. *c.* William provost of Taddewelle, Linc. 16 Henry ii. I. 545. c. 2. *h.*

Taillard, Gilbert, seems to have been sherif of Cambridgeshire, before 40 Henry iii. II. 79. c. 1. *t.*

Taillour, Perot le, forfeits the office of alnager of cloth, 26 Edward i. I. 785. c. 1. *z.* Hugh le Tailur, who, 11 Henry iii. II. 6. c. 1. *z.*

Philip le Taylur amerced for not attending at the Exchequer as sherif of London, before 26 Edward i. II. 99. c. 1. *g.*

Taisson, Ralf, has the men of Wnford, Devonshire, 5 Stephen, II. 220. c. 1. *l.* See Tesson, Teisun.

Talea in the Exchequer, I. 206. c. 1. *o.*

Talebot, baron Gaufrid, 1 Stephen, I. 13. c. 2. *s.* Geoffrey Tallebot held twenty knights fees of Henry i. I. 578. c. 2. *g.* To whom they descended, ibid. Peter son of Thomas Talbot holds Thorpe in Suffolk by socage, 9 Edward ii. I. 673. c. 2. *n.* William Talebot of Devonshire, his carucage, 14 Henry iii. I. 730. c. 1. *z.* William Talebot's legacy from Edmund archbishop of Canterbury, 28 Henry iii. II. 190. c. 1. *b.* Gilbert Talebot goes beyond sea on the king's service, 26 Edward i. II. 219.

Talemunt, Benet de, justice of the Jews, 10 Richard i. I. 235. c. 1. *e.* ibid. c. 2. *f.*

Talents and Besants equivalent, I. 277, 278.

Tallage or donum, I. 221. Of the Jews, I. 221, 222. A Tallage roll directed, I. 224. Tallage granted for the taking off an interdict, 6 Henry iii. I. 388. c. 2. *f.* Tallage what, I. 605. Tallage, an aid arising out of cities, towns and burghs, I. 693. The king's demeans tallaged, 3 and 9 Richard i. I. 698. Tallage to the king and subordinate lords, I. 694. Tallage to the king arising from his demeans, escheats and wardships, ibid. Manors and lands talliable, which were in the king's own hands, I. 700. A Tallage upon the king's demeans, escheats and wardships in Lincolnshire, 8 Richard i. I. 705.

INDEX.

I. 705. The Tallage for taking off the interdict, 16 John, I. 712. Tallage of escheats and wardships, ibid. Serjeanties never tallaged but by special precept, I. 721, 722. c. 1. z. Tallage heavier in the king's demeanes than on the county at large, I. 723. Merchandize subjected a man to Tallage, I. 725, 726, 727. Tallage called by the name of none, disme, &c. I. 730. Tallage of old settled by the justiciers in their iters, I. 732. Generally collected by the sherif or fermer, I. 736. In what cases Tallage was not demandable, I. 744. Not on frankalmoign, ibid. Nor on lands held by knight service, I. 745. Freedom from Tallage granted to particular persons, I. 746, &c. During life, I. 749. Where subordinate lords had Tallage, I. 751, &c. Statutum de Tallagio non concedendo, I. 763.

Tallages, how imposed, 21 Henry ii. I. 125.

Tallies, their use and antiquity in the Exchequer, II. 258. Comes from the French, which signifies cutting, ibid. Provision for them when lost, II. 260. Called countertallies, II. 301 Robert de la Feld late keeper of the Tallies, II. 302. Which office is committed to John de Vyene, ibid.

Talyefer, deputy usher of the Exchequer deceased, 52 Henry iii. II. 276.

Tamworth castle granted to Robert Marmiun junior, 2 Henry iii. I. 301. c. 2. y. The aid of Tameword, 5 Stephen, I. 601. c. 2. u. Its poverty, ibid. The aid of Tameworth, 2 Henry ii. I. 688. Its donum, I. 697. c. 1. s.

Tancia, Martel de, 5 Stephen, I. 557.

c. 2. f. Amerced for the breach of peace, ibid.

Tanctin, Adam de, his land at Caen granted to Robert de Lisieux, 2 John, I. 763.

Tanner, Herbert the, the liber hospes of the hospitallers, 14 and 16 Henry ii. I. 746. c. 2. f. I. 747. c. 1. g. Hugh le Tanur, 35 Henry iii. II. 78. c. 2. s. Thomas le Tannere of Oxford, 9 Edward ii. II. 85. c. 1. r.

Tanquarville, Ralf chamberlain de, 8 Richard i. I. 29. c. 2. q. William de Tancarvile chamberlain of Normandy, temp. Henry i. I. 58. Camerarius de Tankarvilla, 23 Henry ii. I. 450. c. 1. n.

Tanton, William archdeacon of, seems to belong to Peter de Rupibus, 7 John, I. 388. c. 2. c. Tauton hundred, I. 553. c. 1. u. Taunton and Farnham were the bishop of Winchester's, 52 Henry iii. I. 719. c. 1. r. William de Wroteham archdeacon of Tanton, 6 John, I. 772. c. 1. i. Tamton park inclosed by the bishop of Winchester without warant, 12 Henry iii. I. 255. c. 1. i.

Tany, Geoffrey de, 10 John, I. 442. c. 2. f. Has land in Fifhyde, Essex, ibid.

Tappelawe, how that town belonged to the monks of Merton, 8 Richard i. I. 106. c. 2. w.

Tarde returned on a writ of distringas, II. 278.

Tarente abbess held in frankalmoign, I. 671. c. 1. g. William de Tarente, who, 32 Henry iii. II. 284. c. 2. z.

Tateshal, Robert de, derained the town of Wutton against William Fitz-Hervey, 6 Richard i. I. 199, 200. c. 1. k. Belonged to the king's chamber, 3 John, I. 388. c. 1. a.

Fines

INDEX.

Fines for a Thursday market at Tateshal, 4 John, I. 405. c. 1. *l.* Robert de, of Yorkshire, his writ, 26 Edward i. I. 654. c. 1. *a.* Baron Robert, 41 Henry iii. II. 183. c. 2. *c.*

Tatholm meadow, whose, II. 119. c. 2. *r.*

Tatisden, Richard de, one of the tallagers of Yorkshire, 30 Henry iii. I. 710. c. 1. *w.*

Taverham hundred in custody of Nicolas Castle, 9 Edward i. II. 2. c. 2. *f.*

Taverner, Walter le, of Yorkshire, 22 Henry ii. I. 556. c. 1. *o.* One slain in his house, ibid. Roger le Taverner and his not to be impleaded before the Exchequer, 34 Edward i. II. 74. c. 2. *u.*

Tavistoch, abbat of, I. 309. c. 1. *p.* In custody, 31 Henry ii. I. 311. c. 1. *c.* Walter abbat discharges it from fifteen fees, 22 Henry ii. I. 648. c. 1. *b.*

Taurus of Eureux, church of S. how endowed, I. 167.

Taxo, R. seneschal of Normandy, 4 John, I. 175. c. 2. *q.* Again, I. 537. c. 1.

Taxours and collectors, I. 730, 731.

Taylefer huisher of the Exchequer, 49 Henry iii. II. 16. c. 1. *y.*

Tebovil, Robert de, whose plegius, 2 John, I. 520. c. 2. *b.*

Tedings or Tithings, Devonshire, I. 544. c. 2. *s.*

Tedmar, John, 2 Edward ii. II. 235. c. 1. *t.* Executor of John Darmenteres, ibid.

Teisun, Ralf, quit of sherif's aid, 4 John, II. 167. c. 1. *t.*

Teivill in Normandy, the land of William son of Stur, 22 Henry ii. I. 430. c. 2. *d.*

Telarii or Weavers, of London, what they paid the crown for their gild through several reigns, I. 338. c. 1. *m, n, o,* &c. What the Telarii of Oxford accompted for, ibid. c. 2. *t, u.* I. 339. c. 1. *w, x,* &c. None to practise that craft within five miles of that burgh, I. 339. c. 1. *z.* Their poverty, ibid. The Telarii of many other places pay for their gild, I. 340, &c. Citizens of London fine to extinguish this gild, 4 John, I. 405. c. 1. *m.* Textores of Oxford have a confirmation of privileges, 7 Henry iii. I. 414. c. 2. *q.* Telarii of Oxford rendred a mark of gold for their gild, 5 Stephen, I. 467. c. 1. *e.*

Telier, Thomas le, of Buckingham, his claim, I. 448. c. 1. *f.*

Tellers of the Exchequer, II. 303. Ten in number, 1 Richard i. ibid. c. 2. *l.* Four Tellers, 52 Henry iii. II. 307. c. 1. *uu.* Allowance to the four Tellers of the Exchequer, 9 Henry iii. II. 311.

Temantale, what, I. 24. c. 1. *y.*

Templar, Peter le, II. 193. c. 2. *d.* Seems to be sherif of Devonshire, 40 Henry iii. ibid.

Templars, knights, a new assignment to them, 2 Henry ii. I. 204. c. 1. *g.* Their lands seized, 1 Edward ii. I. 302. c. 2. *c.* Had an appointed alms out of most of the counties of England, I. 348. Pay a thousand marks for confirmation of their charters, 2 John, I. 402. c. 2. *k.* Not to be impleaded but before the king, 3 John, I. 478. c. 1. *p.* Their court, 17 Henry ii. I. 558. c. 1. *r.* Fine voluntarily in seven hundred marks, 26 Edward i. I. 612. c. 2. *r.* Their appointment styled Eleemosyna noviter instituta, 2 Henry ii. I. 695. c. 1. *z.* See I. 697. c. 2. *a, c.* Their

INDEX.

Their lands in the foke of Pikering, Yorkshire, 30 Henry iii. I. 710. c. 1. *w.* Their large tenures in Glocestershire, 1 John, I. 734. c. 1. *w.* Pay six hundred marks for an eleventh, 23 Edward i. I. 744. c. 1. *u.* Had the privilege of quitting one man from the common assises in every burgh, I. 746. William de la More master of the Temple imprisoned, 1 Edward ii. II. 30. c. 1. *f.* Their case, 1 Edward ii. II. 120. Their lands and tenements seized, 2 Edward ii. II. 279.

Tendwardene hundred, Kent, why amerced, I. 544. c. 2. *q.*

Teneford, Richard de, of Northamptonshire, hanged for the murder of his wife, 31 Henry ii. I. 345. c. 2. *d.*

Tenere, to hold in vassalage or demean, Pref. xxiv. Tenure in capite subject to all payments to the crown, I. 571, &c. Escuage no tenure, but a service incident to tenure by chivalry, I. 620. c. 1. *a.* Tenant in capite not always a baron or a reputed baron, I. 621. c. 1. Tenure of land by cornage in Cumberland, I. 658. Several sorts of rent-service, II. 100. c. 2. Tenants, an enquiry how great men carry themselves towards them, II. 102. Tenant or defendant to be discharged by the judgment of the court, II. 118.

Terms of the law, II. 5. Barons of the Exchequer sat without the limits of them, ibid. And even on Sundays, ibid.

Terra, what it imports in the old charters, I. 2. c. 2. *b.* Was a general name for any large seigneury, ibid. Of the same import with honor or baronia, I. 296. Terra de Briggham, whose, I. 329. c. 1. *w.*

Terræ datæ, what, II. 162, 163.

Terue, John de, alderman of Worgate, Canterbury, 32 Edward i. I. 741. c. 1. *g.*

Tesson or Taisson, Ralf, has the honor of S. Saviour, 3 John, I. 170, 171.

Tessy, Gervase, a fugitive of Normandy, his crimes, temp. Henry ii. Richard i. and 2 John, I. 519. c. 2. *a.*

Testa, William, received the fourth reserved for the pope, 5 Edward ii. II. 159. Archdeacon of Dran and administrator of the see of Canterbury for the pope's use, 35 Edward i. II. 224.

Testard, William, adjudged to be archdeacon [of Notingham] by the judges delegates, 9 Richard i. I. 485. c. 1. *c.*

Teste meipso, the style of Geoffrey Fitz-Peter, 1 John, I. 680. c. 2. *n.*

Tething, I. 546. c. 1. *m.*

Tettehale, frere William de, master of S. John of Jerusalem, 34 Edward i. I. 614. c. 1.

Teudiscan language, Pref. xviii.

Tewaden, Reginald de, of Cornwal, underwent the tryal of the hot iron, 6 Richard i. I. 484. c. 1. *r.* Fines to save his land and not abjure the realm, ibid.

Tewiton in Cornwal, its tallage, 1 John, I. 733. c. 2. *t.* Tamerton, ibid. c. 2. *u.*

Tewxbery abbey fine for their lands in Ireland, 6 John, I. 488. c. 1. *z.* Abbat of Theokesbiry was the king's tallager, 1 John, I. 722. c. 2. *a.* Bernard de Theokesbiri of London tallaged, 9 John, I. 749. c. 1. *u.* Nicolas de Teukesbury sherif of Devenisheyre, 2 Edward ii. II. 69. c. 2. *c.*

Textor, Walter, of Kent, 6 Henry iii. I. 549. c. 1. *c.* Amerced pro impressione sigilli, ibid.

Teyngre,

INDEX.

Teyngre, Thomas and Geoffrey sons of John le, 9 John, I. 494. c. 2. *t*. John's large fines with pledges to get out of prison, ibid.

Thalamus baronum scaccarii, I. 192.

Thames, a duty paid of old for trafficking along that river, I. 771, &c.

Thedingpeni, I. 311. c. 1. *d*.

Thetford, a bishop's see, I. 7. Nuns of Thefford, I. 47. c. 1. *y*. The grant of Henry i. to the church of Thetford, I. 58. c. 1. *u*. Tietford, Fulchard provost de, accompts, temp. Stephen, I. 147. c. 2. *d*. Moneyours of Thetford, 14 Henry ii. I. 590. c. 1. *k*. The aid of Tietford, 5 Stephen, I. 601. c. 1. *r*. The donum of Tetford, 5 Henry ii. I. 627. c. 1. *s*. Its donum, 7 Henry ii. I. 697. c. 1. *u*. Its assise, 22 Henry ii. I. 703. c. 1. *k*. Prior of Teford, II. 118. c. 2. *k*.

Theins placed before knights, I. 8. c. 1. *l*. Summoned to the council of the proceres at Glocester, an. 1123. I. 12. c. 1. *o*. Again under the title of the king's Theins, ibid. c. 2. *p*. Drengs and Theins in Northumberland, 23 Henry ii. I. 130. c. 2. *u*. Theins in Lancashire fine fifty marks to be free from tallage, 13 Henry iii. I. 417. c. 2. *d*. The Theinage of Thomas son of Liulf of Northumberland, 2 John, I. 659. c. 2. *y*. Theins, Drengs and Smalemanni in in Durham between Tine and Tey, 5 Stephen, I. 694. c. 1. *s*. The donum of the Theins of Northumberland, 5 Henry ii. I. 698. c. 1. *e*. The tallage of the Theins and Drengs of Northumberland, 1 Richard i. ibid. c. 2. *o*. Theinage of Lancashire, their tallage, 11 Henry iii. I. 707. c. 1. *h*.

Theobald, Walter, tallages Colchester, 9 Richard i. I. 733. c. 1. *n*. See Walter.

Therric or Theodorick son of Stephen, 2 John, I. 520. c. 1. *e*. The tallage of Terric the goldsmith of Canterbury, 1 John, I. 737. c. 2. *t*.

Theodorick king of the Franks, an. 680. I. 90.

Thieves escaping made the places obnoxious, I. 556, &c.

Thievespathe, William de, Cornwal, underwent the judgment of the hot iron, 9 Richard i. I. 484. c. 1. *s*.

Thoh. John Julius de saint, 18 Edward i. II. 281. c. 1. *f*. Attaches the sherif of Cornwal, ibid.

Thomas the king's son, 35 Edward i. II. 125. c. 1. *l*.

Thoresby, Alan de, his tallage, 19 Henry iii. I. 735. c. 1. *g*.

Thorgarton priory held in socage and frankalmoign, 1 Edward ii. I. 599. c. 1. *f*.

Thorleby or Thornby, I. 721. c. 1. *w*.

Thorne, Geoffrey de la, keeper of the tallies, 5 Edward ii. II. 302. c. 2. *g*.

Thorneton, John de, of Stowesby, has the wapentak of Bulmer in array, 16 Edward ii. II. 112. c. 1.

Thorney abbey, I. 277. c. 2. *d*. In the king's hands, about 16 Henry ii. I. 307. c. 1. *w*. and 19 Henry ii. I. 308. c. 1. *f*. Tallaged, I. 725. c. 2. *g*.

Thornoure, W. de, justice itinerant has five marks for his expences from London to Durham and back again, 13 Henry iii. I. 718. c. 1. *m*.

Thorp, a contest about land there, 7 Henry iii. I. 445. c. 2. *e*. Simon de, slain about 15 John, I. 490. c. 2. *w*. See Torp.

Thrikingham, Lambert de, the king's tallager, 33 Edward i. I. 741. c. 2. *i*. and I. 752. c. 1. *i*.

Thronholm

INDEX X.

Thronholm priory, 7 John, I. 448. c. 1. g.

Thurkelby, Roger de, of the king's court, 39 Henry iii. I. 712. c. 1. a.

Thurlaeston, William de, justicier of the Jews, about 56 Henry iii. I. 253. c. 1. x, y.

Thus, Richard le, 10 John, I. 280. c. 2. b. Accompts for the ferm of Benfenton instead of Thomas Basset, ibid.

Tibert, Hugh, his grant to Robert de Montgomeri in Normandy, 2 John, I. 156. c. 1. g.

Ticheham, Robert de, king's prover, 9 Henry ii. I. 201. c. 1. p.

Tichefei of Kent, the land of William de, in the king's hands, 13 Henry ii. I. 299. c. 2. l. Geoffrey and William de Tichefey heirs of Odo de, 10 Richard i. I. 498. c. 1. l.

Tiece, the lands of Guy fon of, 5 Richard i. I. 142. c. 1. b. and 4 Richard i. I. 451. c. 1. x. Those lands disputed by Nicolas Fitz-Robert and Reginald de Argentein, 4 Richard i. I. 483. c. 1. m.

Tikehill, William de, left Albreda his widow, 3 Richard i. I. 105. c. 1. q. Honor of Tikehill, Ralf de Novo Mercato holds of it in Notinghamshire, 2 John, I. 659. c. 1. w. Niel de Luvetot holds five fees of this honor, 1 John, I. 665. John son of Ernald chaplain of Tikehul in Yorkshire, his donum, 9 Richard i. I. 699. c. 1. r. This manor was prince Edward's, 37 Henry iii. I. 752. c. 1. h. That honor escheated, 26 Edward i. II. 45. c. 2. t. Robert de Viepont's claim to this castle and honour superseded, 6 Henry iii. and given to the earl Augi, II. 68. c. 1. t. See Tykhul.

Tikefoure in Rutland amerc'd, 12 Henry ii. I. 561. c. 1. m.

Tilbery, Gervase of, said by the mother to be descended from Henry ii. Diff. Epist. II. 338.

Tilia, William de, join'd in arms with Falkes de Breaute, temp. Henry iii. I. 475. c. 2. r.

Tillebrok, Mr Guy de, one of the executors of J. de Kirkeby bishop of Ely, 18 Edward i. II. 186. c. 2. r.

Tilli, Henry de, deforces G. de Mandevil of his inheritance, 7 Richard i. I. 98. c. 2. n. and I. 99. c. 1. r. Occurs, 6 John, I. 317. c. 1. n. Roger de Tilli his knights fees from Henry de Laci, 22 Henry ii. I. 427. c. 1. d. Henry de Tylli's descent and loss of the honor of Merfwude, 10 John, I. 489. c. 2. q. Otho de Tilli, 31 Henry ii. I. 513. c. 1. x. To whom Otho married his daughter, ibid. Henry de Tilli's charter, 2 John, I. 522. c. 2. p. Henry de Tilli's escuage for the king's ransom, 6 Richard i. I. 591. c. 2. s. Arnald de Tylye made mareschal of the Exchequer, 5 Edward ii. II. 286.

Tillol, Robert de, 2 John, I. 520. c. 2. f. Fines for the daughter of Peter de Riveria with her inheritance, ibid.

Tilmanston, Roger de, baron of the five ports, 33 Edward i. I. 613. c. 1. s.

Tilnea, Ralf de, 31 Henry ii. I. 452. c. 1. e.

Timerefberwe, the land of Henry de Waddone, temp. Henry iii. I. 622, 623. c. 1. h.

Tinctor or Dyer of Carlisle, David the, I. 404. c. 1. d.

Tindal,

INDEX.

Tindal, Helwife de, fines that she may not be forced by ecclesiastical censure, to take her steward for her husband, 6 John, I. 465. c. 1. *p*. Adam de, has the wood of Langel. alias Wiveteley on the borders, 10 John, I. 489. c. 2. *p*. Tindale belonged to the king of Scots, 15 Henry ii. I. 553. c. 2. *d*.

Tinemue, monks of, seem to be subject to S. Albans, I. 405. c. 1. *n*. Prior and monks have a charter of confirmation, 6 John, I. 405. c. 2. *s*. Have near four knights fees in Northumberland, 29 Henry iii. I. 569. c. 1. *r*. Was a cell of S. Albans, 10 Richard i. I. 760. c. 2.

Tingden manor ingaged to pray for the soul of king John, I. 393. c. 2. *g*.

Tingeric, Sibylla de, has the land of Maretot and Wandour, 1 John, I. 464. c. 2. *b*.

Tingwic manor assign'd to the monks of Holy Trinity on the mount of Roan, 10 John, I. 218. c. 1. *q*.

Tinn in Cornwal, the coinage and issuing of it under the direction of the steward, 9 Edward ii. I. 386. c. 1. *s*. Tinners of Cornwal to be quit of tallages and aids, I. 748. c. 2. *s*. The mines accompted for, 10 Richard i. and 14 John, II. 132. c. 2. *k*, *l*.

Tintagel castle in Cornwal, II. 144, 145. c. 1. *p*.

Tinterne, abbat of, his office, 50 Henry iii. I. 101. c. 2. *e*.

Tiretai, Maurice de, sherif of Essex and Hertfordshire, 6 Henry ii. II. 164. c. 1. *c*. and 9 Henry ii. II. 252. c. 1. *p*.

Tiscote and Wengrave, Bucks, 18 Henry iii. II. 15. c. 2. *x*. Whose, ibid.

Tisun, Adam, his judgment in Lincolnshire, 24 Henry ii. I. 211. c. 2. *l*. Adam Tisun of Yorkshire, 5 Stephen, I. 449. c. 1. *t*. Seises the land of Henry Fitz-Gerold in Geynesburg, 9 John, I. 451. c. 1. *a*.

Tith of bread granted, I. 3. c. 2.

Title to the crown, an undoubted one surpassing, I. 182. Title of viscount for sherif occurs, 1 Edward ii. I. 380. c. 1. *t*, *u*.

Tivil, Ralf de, had the terra de Cropestoft, 9 John, I. 448. c. 1. *i*. Simon de Tivil his tenure by cornage in Cumberland, 3 John, I. 658. c. 2. *n*.

Tiwa Magna in Oxfordshire, its tallage or assise, 19 Henry ii. I. 701. c. 1. *a*.

Tiwondetun, that meadow or holm conveyed to the church of S. Paul's, London, 30 Henry ii. I. 215. c. 2. *d*.

Tocgie , her fate, I. 498. c. 2. *p*. See Grayhangre, Wreng.

Toddenham in Glocestershire, belong'd to the abbat of Westminster, 19 Henry ii. I. 701. c. 2. *c*.

Toeni, Roger de, his assignment from Holcham, Norf. 30 Henry ii. I. 328. c. 1. *n*. See Tooni. Ralf de Toeni, 18 Henry ii. I. 632. c. 2. *n*. His knights fees in his balliage, ibid.

Tolebu, Jordan, his land of Chainesbery, 24 Henry ii. I. 211. c. 2. *l*. Has judgment for and against him, ib.

Tolesan, John de, mayor of London, committed, 38 Henry iii. II. 240. c. 1. *k*.

Toli, Robert son of, 5 Stephen, I. 146. c. 2. *p*. Accomps for the pleas of G. de Clinton, ibid.

Toll,

INDEX.

Toll, not to be paid by persons in the Exchequer, for things bought to their proper use, II. 19, &c.

Tollard, Brian, in the service of king John, while earl of Moreton, I. 99. c. 1. *q.*

Tolosanus, Michael, his tallage, 12 Henry iii. I. 708. c. 1. *n.*

Tooni, Roger de, seems to be sherif of Norfolk, 10 John, I. 472. c. 1. *c.* Roger de Toni, who, 4 John, I. 505. c. 2. *o.* See Toeni. Michael Tony one of the manucaptors for the community of the city of London, 39 Henry iii. II. 240. c. 2. *n.*

Topeloverd, Richard de, of Bramton, Devonshire, 14 Henry ii. I. 588. c. 1. *b.*

Topesham in Devonshire, the town of Richard earl of Devon, 24 Henry ii. I. 605. c. 1. *o.*

Toppeclive, Yorkshire, its tallage, 30 Henry iii. I. 710. c. 1. *w.*

Torchard, Geoffrey, fined for non-appearance, 12 Henry ii. I. 201. c. 1. *m.* Amerced in Notinghamshire again, 14 Henry ii. I. 554. c. 1. *k.*

Toreby, the town of Guy de Vals, 14 Henry ii. I. 555. c. 1. *c.*

Torel, William, has the office of the king's napery, 9 John, I. 461. c. 2. *b.* Had the town of Yle, 31 Henry ii. I. 556. c. 2. *s.*

Torini, Ralf de, 10 John, I. 489. c. 2. *q.* One of the knights in the case of Robert de Mandevil, ibid.

Torinton abbat, I. 448. c. 1. *g.* Abbat of Torenton in Lincolnshire, his hydelands, 5 John, I. 605. c. 2. *t.*

Torkesey, Linc. prior and canons of, 3 John, I. 118. c. 1. *s.* The tenants of Thorkesey tallaged, 34 Edward i. I. 752. c. 1. *i.*

Torlaveston, Roger, his tenure from Wigan the mareschal, temp. Henry i. I. 44. c. 2. *f.*

Torneberg, by and to whom that church was granted about Henry ii. I. 3. c. 2.

Torneham, Robert de, steward of Anjou, 8 Richard i. I. 29. c. 2. *q.* Seneschal of Anjou, 9 Richard i. I. 53. c. 1. *s.*

Tornour, Adam de, pleas before him, 3 Richard i. I. 544. c. 1. *p.*

Torp, Ralf de, and Amice his wife, their interest in Multon, 4 John, I. 437. c. 2. *y.* The manor of Torp given to the canons of Wroxton by John de Mountague, I. 672. c. 1. *i.* Torp and Hesington in the bishopric, their tallage, 8 Richard i. I. 714. c. 2. Robert de Thorp clerk, warden of the mine in Byrland, Devonshire, 2 Edward ii. II. 8. c. 2. *m.* John de Thorpe, 33 Edward i. II. 122. c. 1. *n.* Robert de Thorpe examines the works of Clarendon, 12 Edward ii. II. 292. c. 2. *l.*

Torpel, the land and children of Roger de, 22 Henry ii. II. 322. c. 1. *t.* Roger Torpel's land seems to descend to Ralf de Kameis, 31 Henry iii. I. 594. c. 2. *k.*

Torre in Devonshire, the abbat of, challenged for holding the market of Wlinberge, 14 Henry iii. II. 216. c. 2. *k.*

Tortington priory, in Sussex, convey'd to sir John Spencer, 42 Elizabeth, I. 621. c. 2.

Toteneis, amerc'd for a gild without warrant, 26 Henry ii. I. 562. c. 2. *b.* See Tanton. Gilbert Basset archdeacon of Tottenesia, 8 John, II. 42. c. 2. *i.*

Totenham, II. 18. c. 1. *l.* Its visnue summon'd about an assault, ibid.

Totentrie

INDEX.

Totentrie hundred in Kent, I. 544. c. 2. *q*.

Tothil, Thomas de, has a commission of array for the wapentake of Agbrig, 16 Edward ii. II. 112. c. 1. Richard Tottell animadverted upon for his collection of the statutes, II. 172. c. 2. *n*.

Totingwich, the terra of the prior and brethren of Jerusalem, 3 John, I. 404. c. 1. *b*.

Tounstal in the bishopric tallaged, 11 Edward i. I. 720. c. 2. *u*.

Touny, Robert de, a baron call'd by writ to the Scotch war, 26 Edward i. I. 655. c. 2. And in the king's court, ibid.

Tower of London one of the king's treasuries, I. 267. 270. Four pence a day allowed for the white bear and keeper in the Tower, 36 Henry iii. I. 376. c. 2. *a*. The elephant, I. 377. c. 1. *c*. Tower ward assess'd by William de Coumbemartyn its alderman, 32 Edward i. I. 741. c. 1. *b*. The keepers of the king's works in the Tower of London, II. 123, 124. Tower in custody of earl William de Mandevil, before 8 Richard i. II. 176. c. 1. *y*. Sherifs and others committed to the Tower for non-payment to the king, II. 238.

Towns amerc'd for not making hue and cry, I. 556.

Traci, Oliver de, collected the scutage in Devonshire, before 4 John, I. 206. c. 1. *p*. His grant for life from William de Braiosa, 7 Richard i. I. 266. Robert de Traci and Dionysia his daughter, 31 Henry ii. I. 431. c. 2. *p*. Oliver de Traci, 5 John, I. 438. c. 1. *c*. William de Traci's land in Normandy passes to William de Pyreu, 2 John, I. 522. c. 1. *n*. Henry de Tracy's fees in Somersetshire, 31 Henry iii. I. 677. c. 2. *e*. Oliver de Tracey how to be distrein'd, 1 Edward i. II. 250. c. 1. *h*.

Traer, Ralf, 32 Henry iii. II. 192. c. 1. *s*. Not to be distrain'd while the principal debtor could answer, ibid.

Trailli, Walter de, of Bucks, fines in an hundred marks for a concord on a breach of peace, 5 John, I. 471. c. 2. *z*. See Treili.

Travers, John, alderman of London, the tallage for his ward, 14 Henry iii. I. 709. c. 1. *t*. and 19 Henry iii. I. 738. c. 2. *z*. I. 739. c. 1. *a*. Was chamberlain, 8 Henry iii. I. 777. c. 2. *w*, &c. John fermer of Queen's hith, 11 Henry iii. I. 781. c. 1. *o*. Sherif of London, 8 Henry iii. II. 95. c. 1. *q*. and II. 228. c. 1. *f*.

Treason, its punishment in William Rufus's time, I. 8.

Treasure trove, belonged to the king, I. 342. Under this head gold and silver found after fires accrued to the king, I. 342. c. 1. *b*. See Trovure.

Treasurer, Peter de Rival, 16 Henry iii. I. 64. c. 1. *m*. Treasurer was for the most part an ecclesiastick, I. 78. Styled Apotecarius regis, I. 79. c. 2. *u*. Formerly acted with the other barons at the Exchequer, I. 80. See I. 267. c. 1. *o*. Richard the treasurer settles the assise in Oxfordshire, 19 Henry ii. I. 701. c. 1. *a*. Treasurer of the king had the privilege of suing and being sued only in the Exchequer, II. 13. Sat in the Exchequer, II. 26. King's Treasurer has an hundred marks yearly for support till provided for,

18

INDEX.

18 Henry iii. II. 35. The Treasurer's salary, II. 41. His shipload of firewood, II. 48.

Treasuries, the king had several, I. 267. Treasury of the Tower of London, I. 269. Gervase de Thesauro has his danegeld remitted, 2 Henry ii. I. 687. c. 1. *h.* Philip de Wileghby keeper of the fourth key of the treasury, 7 Edward i. II. 321. c. 1. *p.*

Trebuchet or vantage money, used in French payments, I. 274.

Treili, Nicolas de, baron of the Exchequer in the beginning of Henry ii. I. 215. c. 1. *a.* Walter de Trailli, his concordat, I. 471. c. 2. *z.* Geoffrey de Traili fines for a partition of Walter Espec's lands, 4 Henry ii. I. 511. c. 2. *n.* See Trailli.

Trekarl, Richerius de, his feofment from Henry de Heriz, Cornwal, 3 John, I. 217. c. 1. *k.*

Trekemer, William de, of Cornwal, amerc'd by the king, 10 John, I. 151. c. 2. *y.*

Tremeldon barony in the bishopric, 8 Richard i. I. 715. c. 2.

Tremeton castle in Cornwal, II. 144. c. 1. *p.* II. 145.

Trencardus, Pain, for several years accompts for the danegeld of the Isle of Wicht, 5 Stephen, I. 686. c. 1. *c.*

Trenchemere, Alan, has the villages of Gumeelve and Potesdon in Surry, 6 John, I. 440. c. 2. *p.*

Trenchepais of Devonshire, his aid, 14 Henry ii. I. 588. c. 1. *b.*

Trente, W. sworn custos cambii for London, 8 Edward ii. II. 90. c. 2. *y.* William de Trent's executor, viz. John de Wengrave, 12 Edward ii. II. 234. c. 1. *o.* Was the king's pincerna, 35 Edward i. II. 261. c. 1. *r.*

Trentham in Staffordshire, fermed at ten pounds by Walter Hose, 15 Henry ii. I. 279. c. 1. *s.* Paid to the knights Templars, ibid.

Tresgoz, Robert de, his wardship of G. Hose, 1 John, I. 202. c. 1. *z.* William de Tresgoz custos of the honor of William Pevrel of London, 5 Stephen, I. 297. c. 1. *c.* Robert de Tresgoz plegius, 2 John, I. 518. c. 1. *t.* Robert's escuage for the king's ransom, 6 Richard i. I. 590. c. 2. *l.* Robert de Tresgoz has the fee of Hubert de Ria, 2 Richard i. I. 664. c. 1. *z.* John Tregoz a knight of the bishop of Hereford, 10 Edward i. I. 669. c. 1. *a.*

Trespasses and misdemeanours amerc'd, I. 544.

Tresport, Robert abbat of, compounded, an. 1376. for the alternative of the patronage of Euvreville, I. 164. c. 1. *b.*

Trevet, Thomas, tallager of Shafton, 49 Henry iii. I. 742. c. 1. *k.*

Trichet, Ralf, 5 Stephen, I. 482. c. 1. *b.* Fines for his father's land, Middlesex, ibid.

Trihanton, Roger de, his petition, 6 John, I. 480. c. 1. *i.*

Trikingham, L. de, justice, 5 Edward ii. II. 31. Baron of the Exchequer, 15 Edward ii. II. 182. c. 1. *t.*

Trillet, Robert de, to accompt for the sherif of Herefordshire, 35 Henry iii. II. 289. c. 1. *u.*

Trinity, abbat of holy, Roan, 5 Stephen, I. 685. c. 2. *b.*

Trinity, prior of holy, Canterbury, his aid, a third more than S. Augustin's,

INDEX.

14 Henry iii. I. 607. c. 2. *a.* Trinity priory, Norwich, I. 748. c. 1. *p.*

Triple, John de, 3 Edward ii. I. 750. c. 1. *z.* His liberties in London by patent, ibid.

Tronages with strandages accompted for, I. 778. Yet no profits to be accompted for, I. 780.

Trovure or treasure found, I. 342. See Treasure-trove.

Truan, Philip le, 13 John, I. 443. c. 2. *o.* Indicted of homicide, Linc. ibid.

Truite of Cumberland, I. 433. c. 2. *f.* His descent and claim, ibid. Richard son of Truite fines for his lands in the balliage of the sherif of Cumberland because he had attended John de Curcy into Ireland, 9 John, I. 489. c. 1. *m.*

Truitel, John, son of Walter and Juliana, 1 John, I. 433. c. 2. *g.* Claim, the leaded house in Northampton, ibid.

Trubeville, Henry de, his allocatio for his debt, 28 Henry iii. I. 224. c. 2. *t.* William de Trublevil, I. 520. c. 2. *b.*

Trussebut, Simon, escheatour of Lincolnshire, 2 Henry iii. I. 300. c. 2. *w.* Albrede Trussebut contends for her share of the land of Maud de Doura, 31 Henry ii. I. 512. c. 2. *u.* Richard Trussebut, 14 Henry ii. I. 559. c. 1. *d.* Geoffrey, 38 Henry ii. I. 635. c. 1. *r.* Roger, 2 Henry iii. I. 706. c. 2. *e.*

Trussel, William, sherif of Warwick and Leicestershire, 9 Edward ii. II. 31. c. 2. *p.* And of Kent, before 25 Edward i. II. 44. c. 2. *r.* and II. 258. c. 1. *f.*

Tuchet, William, summon'd with the Northamptonshire barons against the Scots, 26 Edward i. I. 655. c. 1.

Tudenham, Robert and Eve de, tenants of Ereswel manor, temp. Henry iii. I. 623. c. 1. *h.*

Tudewurde, Wiltshire, its donum, 33 Henry ii. I. 634. c. 2.

Tuit, Lambert de, 17 Henry ii. I. 502. c. 2. *f.* Disseiz'd without judgment, ibid.

Tumbrel, a punishment, 2 John, I. 504. c. 1. *y.*

Tunebrigge, Richard de, in the Conqueror's time, I. 32.

Tunstede hundred, I. 462. c. 1. *m.*

Turbert of Godelming in Surrey, amerc'd, 15 Henry ii. I. 545. c. 2. *c.*

Turbervil, Walter de, fines, 6 Hen. iii. I. 445. c. 1. *b.* Occurs, 12 John, I. 474. c. 2. *f.* Fines in a thousand marks, ibid. Amerc'd forty marks for bows and arrows found in his house, 10 John, I. 566. c. 2. *y.* See Trubeville.

Turcus, Peter, of Chent, 2 Henry ii. I. 277. c. 2. *e.* Accompts in six pound for one mark of gold, ibid.

Turgarston and Autingham belong'd to the abbat of Hulm, 12 John, I. 462. c. 1. *m.*

Turgis, Walter son of, fined for a retraxit, 3 Richard i. I. 105. c. 1. *q.* Adam son of Turgis, 1 Richard i. I. 563. c. 1. *f.* Turgis collector of the aid from the city of York, 5 Stephen, I. 601. c. 1. *n.*

Turketil, Ailwin son of, in misericordia, 12 Henry ii. I. 541. c. 1. *g.*

Turlaveston, Richard and William de, whose land they had in custody, before 6 John, I. 151. c. 2. *u.* Serlo de, 12 Henry ii. I. 429. c. 1. *o.* Fines to defend himself if he was appeal'd for homicide, ibid.

Turneham, Robert de, attests the charter of the Jews liberties, 2 John, I. 256.

INDEX.

256. c. 2. Married the daughter of William Foſſard, before 14 John, I. 299. c. 1. *d.* Had the manor of Doncaſter with Joan his wife, 9 Richard i. 484. c. 2. *z.* Stephen de, juſticier, 10 Richard i. I. 565. c. 2. *p.* Robert, 1 John, I. 644. c. 1. *m.* Stephen and his heirs, I. 677. c. 1. *c.* Was juſticier and king's tallager for Surrey, 10 Richard i. I. 733. c. 2. *s.* And for Wincheſter, 3 John, I. 734. c. 1. *y.* Stephen de Turneham juſticier and tallager in Kent, 1 John, I. 737. c. 2. *t.* And Wincheſter, 4 John, I. 743. c. 1. *m.* Robert de Turneham, 15 John, I. 774. c. 2. *m.* Robert ſeems to be dead, 25 Henry iii. II. 28. c. 1. *k.* Robert was dead, 16 John, II. 211. c. 1. *b.* And his heireſs Iſabel married to Peter de Maillai, ibid. Stephen de Turneham had a mark a day for the cuſtody of the king's niece, 2 John, II. 221. Robert de Turneham had married the daughter and heireſs of William Foſſard, before 10 Richard i. II. 225. c. 2. *u.*

Turnur, Warner le, alderman of the gild of Strangers, 26 Henry ii. I. 562. c. 1. *z.*

Turpin, William, 1 John, I. 486. c. 1. *h.* Matthew, 1 John, I. 663. c. 2. *u.* Has Winteſlawe, ibid.

Turre, Stephen de, ſeneſchal of Anjou in the time of Maud, I. 53. Nicolas de, juſticiary, 51 Henry iii. I. 236. c. 1. *i.* Richard de, keeper of the king's horſes, 2 John, I. 174. c. 1. *i.* Jordan de Turri, 1 Richard i. I. 370. c. 2. *i.* Gilbert de, baſtardizes Hamon de Maſci, 1 John, I. 434. c. 1. *k.*

Turſtin ſherif of Hantſhire, 2 Henry ii. I. 204. c. 1. *g.* Again has his danegeld remitted, 2 Henry ii. I. 687. c. 1. *h.*

Turvey and Braham granted to Lambert de Bedeford, temp. Henry ii. I. 722. c. 1. *z.*

Turvil, G. de, archdeacon of Dublin, and vice-chancellor of Ireland, 18 Henry iii. I. 66. c. 1. *p.* William and Yſabel de, 8 Richard i. I. 106. c. 2. *w.* Robert de Tureville ſherif of Oxinefordſhire, 23 Henry ii. I. 129. c. 1. *k.* Simon de Turevil his grant to the abbey of Feverſham, before temp. Henry iii. I. 413. c. 2. *k.* Robert de Turevil fines for not going beyond ſea with the king, 1 John, I. 659. c. 1. *t.* Robert de Turvil married Maud the widow of Roger de Beauchamp, II. 191. Dyed before, 22 Henry iii. II. 191. c. 2. *q.*

Tuſan, Wido, his fine of ten marks, 10 Richard i. I. 776. c. 2.

Tuttebury honour, Derbyſhire, in the crown, 14 Edward ii. I. 534. c. 1.

Twenge, Marmeduc de, appeal'd for homicide, 6 John, I. 494. c. 1. *p.* Marmeduc de Twenge ſummon'd on the king's council, 31 Edward i. II. 107. c. 1. *n.*

Twiford, to whoſe patronage it belonged, 8 John, I. 99. c. 2. *w.* Roger de Twiford, 3 John, I. 436. c. 2. *u.* His flight into Ireland on killing a man, ibid.

Twuverton, Litle, its aid, 14 Henry ii. I. 588. c. 1. *b.* Tuiverton, the lordſhip of earl Richard in Devonſhire, 24 Henry ii. I. 605. c. 1. *o.*

Twyer, William, one of the commiſſioners of array for the wapentake of Holderneſs, 16 Edward ii. II. 112. c. 1.

Tychefeld abbat and manor, II. 118. c. 2. *m.*

Tyche-

INDEX.

Tycheburn, John de, sherif of Wilts, 15 Edward ii. II. 160. c. 1. *h.*

Tydeswel manor in Derbyshire, granted by king John to John Danyel, I. 723. c. 1. *d.*

Tyeis, Henry, one of the barons to go with the king against Scotland, 26 Edward i. I. 655. c. 1. Sire Henry de, 25 Edward i. II. 105. c. 1. *i.* Richard de Tyeis keeper of the tallies, 16 Edward ii. II. 302. c. 1. *f.*

Tykul honor, Notinghamshire, devolv'd to the king, 14 Edward ii. I. 534. c. 1. Tickhil castle belonged to the barony of Luvetot, I. 535. c. 2. Wapentak, II. 112. c. 1. Nicolas de Tykehul, 15 Edward ii. II. 240. See Tikehil.

Tykingcot, William de, has his amerciaments attermined, 40 Henry iii. II. 208. c. 2. *b.*

Tyllebroc, William de, 14 Henry iii. II. 78. c. 1. *o.*

Tynwel, Thomas de, prosecuted for irreverent speech of the king, 9 Edward ii. II. 85. c. 1. *r.* Charged with questioning the king's legitimacy, ibid.

Tyrel, Hugh, convicted of divers conspiracies and fined, 34 Edward i. II. 65.

Tywe, John and Hugh de la, had belonged to S. de Montfort, 3 Henry iii. I. 496. c. 2. *s.* Walter de Teye one of those called by writ to the war in Scotland, 26 Edward i. I. 655. c. 2.

Tywing, Maurice de, man of Richard de Hereford clerk of the Exchequer, 35 Henry iii. II. 18. c. 1. *l.*

V

Val. Peter de, his donum for his knights fees, Norfolk or Suffolk, 5 Henry ii. I. 627. c. 1. *s.*

Valanis, Alan de, fined seventy marks for killing the king's servant, 5 Stephen, I. 557. c. 1. *a.* Theobald de Valaniis or Valoignes amerced for breach of peace, ibid. c. 2. *e.* Geoffrey and Robert de Valoniis their knights fees, 14 Henry ii. I. 573. c. 2. *m.* Again, Robert's knight's fee in Hertfordshire, I. 586. c. 1. *x.* Geoffrey de Valoniis had some relation to the honor of Lancaster, before 16 Henry ii. II. 253. c. 1. *z.*

Vale royal in Cheshire, abbat of, 27 Edward i. II. 228.

Valeines, William de, the lands given him, 1 Richard i. I. 205. c. 2. *l.* Theobald de Valeines his relief for six knights fees, 24 Henry ii. I. 316. c. 1. *c.* Jordan and Robert de Valeines his son have the wardship of the heir of Rueland de Auvers, 8 Richard i. I. 323. c. 2. *c.* Alan de Valeines sherif of Ghent, 1 Richard i. I. 369. c. 2. *b.* Sibylla de Valeines fines, 9 John, I. 489. c. 1. *b.* Alan de Valeines accompts for the ferm of Kent, 32 Henry ii. II. 152. c. 1. *w.* Sherif of Kent, 1 Richard i. II. 235. c. 2. *y.*

Valence, Adomar de, earl of Pembroc, 1 Edward ii. I. 75. c. 2. Custos of the castle of Rokyngham, 15 Edward ii. I. 383. c. 1. Has two thousand marks for his expedition against Scotland, 12 Edw. ii. I. 392. c. 2. *b.* William de Valencia the king's uncle, 18 Edward i. I. 598. c. 2. *e.* Eymer de Valencia one of the barons summon'd to the Scotch war, 26 Edward i. I. 655. c. 1. Reiner de Valencia, 5 Henry ii. I. 696. c. 2. *n.* Aymer de Valence has

INDEX.

has a privy feal to export wool cuftom-free, 25 Edward i. I. 785. c. 1. *y*. William de Valencia the king's brother, and one of his council, 54 Henry iii. II. 171. c. 1.

Valle, Ralf de, an ufurer, his chatels forfeited to the crown, 17 Henry ii. I. 346. c. 2. *p*.

Valle Dei or Valdey, abbat de, impleaded, 18 Henry ii. I. 430. c. 1. *y*.

Valle Torta, Reginald de, his large fhare for de-afforefting Cornwal, 11 Henry iii. I. 414. c. 1. *n*.

Vallibus, Robert de, one of the juftices errant, temp. Henry ii. I. 83. c. 2. *h*. Occurs, 4 John, I. 404. c. 2 *i*. Ralf and William de Vallibus, 10 John, I. 489. c. 2. *q*.

Vals, Robert de, one of the juftices errant in Yorkfhire, 22 Henry ii. I. 128. Called de Vaux, I. 130. Robert de Vallibus fherif of Cumberland, 23 Henry ii. I. 130. c. 2. *a*. Adam de Vallibus citizen of Canterbury fines for the liberties there, 27 Edward i. I. 421. c. 1. *w*. Robert fon of Robert de Vallibus has the land of Wilmundecot in Warwickfhire, 6 John, I. 441. c. 1. *r*. Robert de Vallibus occurs, 12 and 13 John, I. 474. c. 1. *e*. Robert de Vallibus fines for the efcape of prifoners while fherif, and for fuffering the currency of old coin, 5 Richard i. I. 503. c. 2. *q*. Robert de Vallibus criminal with regard to the wife of Henry Pinel, 12 John, I. 507. c. 2. *e*. Ralf de Vallibus, 7 Richard i. I. 513. c. 1. *a*. John de Vaux jufticier, 10 Richard i. I. 531. Guy de Valle has the town of Toreby, 14 Henry ii. I. 555. c. 1. *c*. Guy de Valle's fcutage for his Yorkfhire fees towards the Irifh expedition, 18 Henry ii. I. 629. c. 1. *z*. John fon and heir of William de Vallibus accompts for the caftle and honor of Knarefburg in right of his father, 9 Edward ii. II. 117. c. 2. *e*. William died in the king's fervice, and made Burga his wife joint executrix with his fon, ibid. Robert de Vals keeper of the caftle of Carlifle, 19 Henry ii. II. 205. c. 2. *r*.

Vafci, Walter de, 1 John, I. 494. c. 1. *n*. Fines for a replevin, if he fhould be appealed for homicide in Devonfhire, ibid. See Vefci.

Vafconick French, Pref. xx.

Vaffal anciently imported the moft honourable tenure, I. 4. c. 1. *d*. Even kings fo ftyled, ibid. In what cafes a vaffal might *infeftare* his lord, I. 182. c. 1. *b*. Vaffalli majores were barons, I. 198.

Vavaffors in Normandy, I. 156. William le Vavaffur accompts for the profits of the manors of the fee of York, 31 Henry ii. I. 309. c. 1. *r*. Again, 1 Richard i. I. 311. c. 2. *h*. Robert le Vavaffur his plea for the manor of Edinton, 12 John, I. 448. c. 2. *l*. William le, settles the tallage in Yorkfhire, 33 Henry ii. I. 635. c. 1. *r*. William Vavaceours, 26 Edward i. I. 654. c. 1. *a*. Malger le, fines, 12 John, I. 663. c. 2. *y*. William, 33 Henry ii. I. 713. c. 1. *d*. William and John le Vavaffour seem to be fherifs of counties, 31 Edward i. II. 107. c. 1. *n*. Malger Wawafor, 3 Henry iii. II. 113. c. 1. *f*.

Uctred fon of Walleof, fined for foke and fake, 5 Stephen, I. 397. c. 2. *k*. The burgeffes of Uctred, 10 Richard i. I. 452. c. 1. *i*. Uctred fon of Aftin his donum in Yorkfhire,

INDEX.

shire, 9 Richard i. I. 699. c. 1. *r.* See Ughtred.

Venatione or Venaison, Herbert de, 2 John, II. 179. c. 2. *x.* His oblatum for right against Richard le Avener, ibid.

Venecia, John de, gives three hundred marks for fine and relief, 3 John, I. 317. c. 1. *l.* Venecian shilling eighteen pence of our money, 17 John, I. 261. c. 2. *t.*

Venjons, Ralf, his benefaction to S. Mary Mealdon in or before the reign of king Stephen, I. 33. c. 2. *r.*

Venison, pleas of, I. 417.

Venour, Robert le, one of the esquires of Thomas de Cantilupe bishop of Hereford, 10 Edward i. I. 669. c. 1. *a.*

Venuz, Venuis and Venois, several of that denomination, 4 and 8 Richard i. I. 44. That family, though defeated of the mareschalcy, yet retained some insignia of it, I. 45, 46. William de Venuiz forester of Alshiesholt, Hampshire, and king's mareschal, 4 Richard i. I. 427. c. 2. *s.*

Ver, Henry de, temp. Henry ii. Pref. xxii. c. 1. *q.*

Ver, Alberic or Aubrey de, chamberlain, 1 Stephen, I. 13. c. 2. *s.* Again, temp. Henry i. I. 56. c. 1. *o.* Aubrey de Ver sherif of Essex and Hertfordshire, 5 Stephen, I. 164. and I. 187. William de Ver, builds Waltham church, 23 Henry ii. I. 226. c. 1. *a.* Geoffrey de Ver has the custody of Lindebery castle, 16 Henry ii. I. 306. c. 2. *s.* Alberic de Ver sherif of Surrey, Cambridgeshire, Huntingdonshire, Essex, Hertfordshire, Northamptonshire, Leicestershire, Northfolk, Suffolk, Bucks, Bedefordshire, on or about 5 Stephen, I. 327. c. 1. *t, u, w.* ibid. c. 2. *x, y,* and I. 364. c. 1. *l.* Aubrey de Ver fines to be quit as sherif of Essex and Hertfordshire, 5 Stephen, I. 458. c. 1. *b.* Aubrey de Ver sherif of Cambridge and Huntingdonshire, 5 Stephen, I. 541. c. 2. *h.* Geoffrey de Ver his nine knights fees, temp. Hen ii. I. 579. c. 2. *k.* H. de Ver earl of Oxford, 3 Henry iii. I. 593. c. 2. *f.* Hugh de Ver earl of Oxford has aid from his tenants for the discharge of his debts, 18 Henry iii. I. 617. c. 2. *h.* Earl Hugh de Ver, 22 Henry iii. I. 648. c. 1. *c.* Earl of Oxford and Hugh de Veer two of the barons summoned by writ to the expedition against Scotland, 26 Edward i. I. 655. c. 1, 2. William [de Veer] bishop of Hereford, justicier, and settled the tallage, 7 Richard i. I. 546. c. 1. *m.* and I. 703. c. 2. *n.* R. and A. de Ver, temp. Henry i. I. 757. c. 1. *u.* Hugh de Veer, 35 Edward i. II. 122. c. 2. *p, s.* That great lord Alberic de Ver one of the sherifs of Essex and Hertfordshire, 5 Stephen, II. 145. And justice errant of many of the counties of England, ibid. Geoffrey de Ver accompts for the honor of the constabulary, 15 Henry ii. II. 157. The executors of Robert de Ver late earl of Oxford, 25 Edward i. II. 187. c. 1. *s.* Alberic, 5 Stephen, and 9 Richard i. II. 197. c. 1. *q.* II. 198. c. 1. *r.* Geoffrey de Ver sherif of Shropshire, 14 Henry ii. II. 216. c. 1. *i.*

Ver, Rodbert de, king's constabulary, 1 Stephen, I. 13. c. 2. *s.* Was Stephen's chancellor, I. 33. c. 2. *r.* Was constabulary, temp. Henry i. I. 40, 41. Again, temp. Henry i. I. 56. c. 1. *o.* Rodbert de Ver seems to be king Stephen's chancellor, I. 112. c. 1. *m.*

428.

INDEX.

Ver, Walter le, his soke, 4 John, I. 428. c. 1. b. His scutage for the king's ransom, 6 Richard i. I. 590. c. 2. l.

Verdict or Verumdictum dapiferi, I. 630. c. 2. e. Verdict or verumdictum, II. 182.

Verdun, Bertram de, one of the justices errant, temp. Henry ii. I. 83. c. 2. h. Holds pleas for the king, 22 Henry ii. I. 94. c. 1. c. Again, 22 Henry ii. I. 103. Is chief, 24 Henry ii. ibid. c. 2. k. Occurs, 22 Henry ii. I. 128. c. 1. u. and 24 Henry ii. I. 133. c. 1. m. Sherif of Leicestershire, 23 Henry ii. I. 129. c. 2. m. Again, I. 139. c. 1. i. Chief justicier in Glocestershire, 23 Henry ii. I. 211. c. 1. i. Sherif of Warwick and Leicestershire, 22 Henry ii. I. 300. c. 1. q. Again, 20 Henry ii. I. 370. c. 1. f. Bertram de Verdun contends with the earl of Leicester, 18 Henry ii. I. 430. c. 1. x. Theobald de Verdun, 6 and 11 Edward i. I. 529. c. 2. p. Nicolas de Verdun accompts for the honor of Leicester, 11 John, I. 606. c. 1. w. Theobald de Verdun senior and junior summoned among the barons to the Scotch war, 26 Edward i. I. 655. c. 1. Thomas and Nicolas de Verdun sons of the sherif, II. 26. c. 1. a. Theobald de Verdoun's respite, 22 Edward i. II. 216. c. 1. d. Nicolas, to accompt for the aid of the knights of the honor of Leicester, 2 Henry iii. II. 227. c. 1. a. Bertram de Verdun guardian of Stephen de Beauchamp, 1 Richard i. II. 228. c. 2. k. Walter de Verdun, 3 Henry iii. II. 241. c. 2. r.

Verli, Hugh de, his donum, Yorkshire, 29 Henry ii. I. 278. c. 2. p. Again, 31 Henry ii. I. 477. c. 1. e. Again occurs, 30 Henry ii. I. 497. c. 2. h. Roger de, accompts, 20 Henry ii. I. 630. c. 1. c. Roger's scutage, 21 Henry ii. I. 675. c. 2. r.

Vernun, Richard de, 1 John, I. 401. c. 1. a. Sherif of Lancashire, 8 John, I. 461. c. 2. f. Matthew de Vernun, 5 Stephen, I. 470. c. 2. o. Earl William de Vernun, Berkshire, 3 John, I. 659. c. 2. a. William de Vernone, 2 Henry iii. I. 795. c. 2. q. Earl William de Vernun has the tertius denarius of Devon, 5 John, II. 165. c. 1. h.

Verrier, Nicolas, of Canterbury, his tallage, 1 John, I. 737. c. 2. t.

Versificator, Henry, the king's poet, 35 Henry iii. I. 391. c. 1. t. and II. 202. c. 1. w.

Versona, Michael de, his claim of Colemer, Hampshire, I. 431. c. 2. r.

Verun, Robert de, late sherif of Wiltshire amerced, 1 Edward i. II. 270. c. 2. k.

Vesano, Geoffrey de, the pope's nuncio in England, 9 Edward i. II. 137. c. 1. a.

Vesci, the honor of William de, 33 Henry ii. I. 4. c. 1. His barony or honor in the king's hands, 31 Henry ii. I. 297. c. 2. q. In the king's hands, 1 Richard i. I. 298. c. 1. k. The court of Eustace de Vescy in Yorkshire, 7 Richard i. I. 432. c. 2. a. Eustace de Vesci's contention with Richard de Unfranvill adjusted, 9 John, I. 507. c. 2. g. The tallage of the tenants of William de Vescy in Snayton and Brumton, Yorkshire, 14 Henry iii. I. 708. c. 2. p. William de, chief justice in Ireland, 22 Edward i. II. 136. William son of Eustace de Vesci, temp. John, II. 217. c. 1. r. The rescript of William de Vesci, 16 Henry ii. I. 253. c. 1. z.

Vessels

INDEX.

Veffels dedicated to the fervice of the altar not to be taken in pledge, I. 226. c. 1. d.

Veteri Ponte or Viepont, Robert de, 6 Henry iii. I. 86. c. 1. u.

Uggeford of Shropfhire, Philip and Nicolas brothers, 9 Henry iii. I. 496. c. 1. n. Fine in Shropfhire to be difcharged from prifon, ibid.

Ughelli's Italia Sacra, I. 5. c. 1. Again, I. 571. c. 1. f.

Ughtred, Roger, impleads Walter de Kelk, 2 Edward ii. II. 83. See Uctred.

Vicechancellor, an officer of the king's court, I. 77.

Viel, John, alderman of London, the tallage for his ward, 14 Henry iii. I. 709. c. 1. t. and 19 Henry iii. I. 738. c. 2. z. and 31 Henry iii. I. 739. c. 2. c.

Viepont, Robert de, 10 John, I. 263. Robert de Veteri Ponte's claim of the caftle and honor of Tikehul, 6 Henry iii. II. 68. c. 1. t. But has the county of Cumberland inftead of it, ibid. Robert de Viepont has refpite for his debts, 11 Henry iii. II. 214. c. 2. s.

Vilain, Warner and Ralf le, fermers of the city of Lincoln, 19 Henry ii. I. 331. c. 1. b. Walter and Ernald Villanus, 18 Henry ii. I. 430. c. 1. w. Walter Vilain amerced for not appearing againft Reimbald, 19 Henry ii. I. 554. c. 1. o.

Vilers, Gilbert de, his grant from Simon Peilleve, 2 John, I. 156. c. 2. i.

Villanus, its claffical and Romanick fignification, Pref. xxiii.

Vineyards in the fee of Lincoln, 15 Henry iii. I. 419. c. 1. o.

Vintry ward, London, affeffed by John le Corouner, its alderman, 32 Edward i. I. 741. c. 1. b.

Viroler, Philip le, of Newenton, profecutes Robert le Meffager for irreverent words againft the king, 9 Edward ii. II. 84. c. 1. p.

Vis de Lu, Roger, about temp. Henry ii. I. 3. c. 2. Humfrey Vis de Lu his fcutage for lands in Effex or Hertfordfhire, 18 Henry ii. I. 580. c. 2. q.

Vifcount, Guarin le, I. 108. Roger the Vifcount had the honor of S. Saviours, I. 170. c. 2. t.

Vifneto, inquifitio de, 6 Richard i. I. 432. c. 2. y. paffim.

Vifus or views in the Exchequer, II. 114. Vifus compoti, II. 153.

Vitalis, Ordericus, II. 32, 33.

Vivoniis, Hugh de, his gift from the king, 14 Henry iii. I. 661. c. 2. k. Held nine fees of the abbat of Glafton, 13 Henry iii. I. 670. c. 1. e. Has refpite for his debts while in the king's fervice, 14 Henry iii. II. 217. c. 1. r.

Ulecot, John de, deputy fherif to Falk de Breaut, 6 Henry iii. I. 286. c. 2. g. Philip de Ulecot accompts for the bifhoprick of Durham, 14 John, I. 312. c. 2. b. Again, 11 John, I. 384. c. 1. l. Some account of his fortune and five daughters, coheirs, 5 Henry iii. I. 463. c. 1. r. The coronerfhip in Northumberland and forefterfhip belonged to that family, ibid. Accompts for the fee of Durham, 13 John, I. 644. c. 1. o.

Ulfreton in Hampfhire, the king's domaine, 2 Henry ii. I. 687. c. 1. b.

Ulger, William fon of, 23 Henry ii. I. 430. c. 2. e. Hugh, Walter and Guy fons of Ulger, 5 Stephen, II. 197. c. 1. q.

Ulnaria, or alnage of cloth, I. 785. c. 2. a.

Ulri,

INDEX.

Ulri, John son of, whose plegius, 5 Stephen, II. 197. c. 1. q.
Ultra Usam, Edric de, 21 Henry ii. I. 560. c. 2. b. Amerced for screening the Flemings, ibid.
Umframvill, Odinel de, his claim, 26 Henry ii. I. 104. c. 1. l. Simon de Montfort paid a fine of ten thousand marks to have the wardship of the heir of Gilbert de Umfranville, 31 Henry iii. I. 326. c. 2. o. Richard Unfrancvil, 5 Henry iii. I. 452. c. 2. m. Richard de Umfranvil, 6 John, I. 480. c. 1. i. His quarrel with Eustace de Vesci accorded, 9 John, I. 507. c. 2. g. Richard de Umfranvil fines for his lands in Northumberland and not passing the seas, 6 Richard i. I. 658. c. 2. r. Gilbert son of Richard de Umfranvil, temp. John, II. 217. c. 1. r.
Umiliard hundred in Norfolk, II. 20. c. 2. b.
Undel in Northamptonshire, Henry dean of, amerced pro stultiloquio, 7 John, I. 563. c. 2. p.
Volt, John le, of Canterbury tallaged, 1 John, I. 737. c. 2. t.
Vou, Nicolas, cousin of Guy de, 10 Richard i. I. 776. c. 1. r. Guy ferms the mint, 4 John, II. 133. c. 2. o. Upton mill belonged to the abbat of S. James without Northampton, II. 119. c. 2. r. That liberty belonged to Hugh de Cancellis, 18 Edward i. II. 248. c. 2. z.
Urric, Master, maker of the king's engins, 2 John, I. 174. c. 2. k.
Ursus, Theodoric, his land in Oxfordshire, 5 Stephen, I. 426. c. 2. t.
Urteley, Henry, fines, 1 John, I. 428. c. 1. yy.
Usedemar, Antony and John de, king's receivour, &c. 12 Edward ii. I. 611. c. 1. l.

Ushers of the Exchequer. See Ostiary. That office in the Exchequer was ancient and hereditary, II. 271. The succession of them, II. 273, &c. Had two deputies, II. 276. Moiety of the ushery of the receipt of the Exchequer forfeited by the felony of Adam de Stratton, II. 299. c. 2. r.
Usurers, forfeited their chattels to the king, I. 342. 346. c. 2. o, p. I. 347. c. 1. q, r, s, t.
Uta's of Easter, I. 266.
Utime, a tallage, II. 104.
Uttefwurda, Elias de, 3 Richard i. I. 105. c. 2. r. Fines for the land of Cnaveherst, Surry, ibid.
Uvedal, Richard de, clerk, 5 John, I. 777. c. 1. t.
Vulperets or fox-dogs, I. 274. c. 1. k. ibid. c. 2. m. and I. 444. c. 1. r.
Vyene, John de, keeper of the tallies, 9 Edward ii. II. 302.

W.

Wach, Baldwin, fined in 850 marks, 26 Henry ii. I. 211. c. 2. l. Geoffrey Wac fines in 200 marks for his relief for the lands of his brother Simon, 9 John, I. 317. c. 1. m. The summonce of Baldwin de Wach, 26 Henry ii. I. 431. c. 1. i. Agnes de Wac daughter of William de Humez has the land of Wichenden in marriage, before 9 John, I. 451. c. 2. b. Odo Vigil or Wake alderman of a London gild, 26 Henry ii. I. 562. c. 1. z. The scutage of Baldwin de Wac of Lincolnshire, 5 John, I. 650. c. 1. n. John Wake baron and courtier, 26 Edward i. I. 655. c. 2. Joan de Wake dame de Lydel, 33 Edward i. II. 123. c. 1. w. The visus of Baldwin Wach, 3 Richard i. II. 133. c. 1. m. John Wac punished

INDEX.

nished in his pledge for not observing his attermination, 12 John, II. 235. c. 2. *w.* John Wak how to be distrained, having no lay fee, 28 Henry iii. II. 250. Baldwin's scutage, 5 John, II. 253. c. 1. *z.*

Wachesham, Gerard de, holds Stansted, Suffolk, of the honor of Hagenet, 9 Edward ii. I. 652. c. 1. *u.* His particular tenure, ibid.

Wade, Richard son of, 7 Richard i. I. 555. c. 2. *d.* Henry Wade committee of the manor of Selveston, 56 Henry iii. II. 67. c. 2. *s.* John de la Wade late sherif of Lincolnshire, removed from the Mareschal's to the Flete prison, 26 Edward i. II. 288. c. 2. *q.*

Wadenhal, Maurice de, 29 Henry ii. I. 212. c. 1. *o.* Employed in repairing Dovor castle, ibid. Fines for his land in Holewude, Kent, 27 Henry ii. I. 430. c. 2. *f.*

Waddon, William de, his relation to William de Novo Mercato, 5 Stephen, I. 482. c. 1. *z.* Alexander de Waddon, 10 John, I. 489. c. 2. *q.* Henry de Waddone has the villenage of Timeresberwe, about 36 Henry iii. I. 623. c. 1. *h.*

Wahul, Simon de, with Robert de Parentin his seneschal, 5 Richard i. I. 342. c. 2. *c.* Walter de Wahul surety of Fulk Fitz-Warin, 9 John, II. 198. c. 2. *s.*

Waia, that Water in Surrey opposite to the Kentish side, I. 399. c. 1. *a.*

Waidarii of London, I. 779. c. 1. *e.*

Waigneria, II. 200. c. 2. *g.*

Waineford hundred, its tallage, 2 Henry iii. I. 706. c. 2. *e.*

Waisdia or Woad, the assise or duty upon it in Kent and Sussex, &c. I. 773.

Waite, Robert la, 2 Henry iii. I. 44. c. 1. *p.* Stephen le Wayte's tenure in Rindewell, Hertfordshire, 29 Henry iii. ibid.

Waives, several amerced for harbouring them, I. 545. c. 1. *z,* &c.

Walchelin, clerk, son of Cheping, pays for his release, 5 Stephen, I. 493. c. 1. *c.* Richard son of Walchelin his manour from the abbat of S. Edmund, 5 Stephen, I. 501. c. 1. *n.*

Waldeive belonged to Trentham, 15 Henry ii. I. 279. c. 1. *s.* Son of Edmund, 22 Henry ii. I. 343. c. 1. *g.* William son of Waldef amerced for refusing to help the works of Baenburc castle, 16 Henry ii. I. 559. c. 1. *h, i.*

Waldin, Hugh son of, Glouc. 23 Henry ii. I. 211. c. 1. *i.* Occurs his knight's fee, 12 Henry ii. I. 447. c. 1. *o.* Alfwin de Waledene, his aid, 14 Henry ii. I. 586. c. 1. *x.* Abbat of, 18 Henry iii. I. 617. c. 2. *h.* Humfrey de Waleden baron of the Exchequer, 35 Edward i. II. 46. c. 1. *u.* II. 49. c. 2. *m.* and II. 57. Humfrey, 2 Edward ii. II. 224. c. 2. *n.*

Walensis, John de, his tenure, 13 John, I. 218. c. 2. *u.* Robert, his scutage in Yorkshire, 33 Henry ii. I. 635. c. 1. *r.* Again, 7 Richard i. I. 643. c. 2. *h.*

Waleran, bishop of Rochester, his executors, 31 Henry ii. I. 311. c. 1. *e.* Osmund amerced, 12 Henry ii. I. 558. c. 1. *n.* John, alderman of London, 14 Henry iii. I. 709. c. 1. *t.* and 19 Henry iii. I. 738. c. 2. *z.* I. 739. c. 1. *a.* Robert, 54 Henry iii. II. 170. c. 1. *h.*

Wales, scutage of Wales assized at ten shillings per fee, 2 Richard i. I. 664. c. 1. *z.* Assized at two marks per fee, 1 John, ibid. c. 2. *c.*

Walescroft

INDEX.

Walefcroft wapentac in Lincolnfhire, I. 502. c. 2. *b.*

Walefgrave, Yorkfhire, its tallage, 30 Henry iii. I. 710. c. 1. *w.*

Waleton and Wavetree, &c. I. 57. c. 1. *r.* Waleton hundred amerced, 29 Henry ii. I. 556. c. 1. *i.* Waleton in Surrey, its aid, 14 Henry ii. I. 587. c. 1. *y.* William de Waleton attorney of Walter de Gatelyn, 12 Edward ii. II. 292. c. 2. *l.*

Waleweyn, Mr John, furety, 12 Edward ii. I. 292. c. 1. *c.* William Walwein amerced for homicide, 14 Henry ii. I. 554. c. 1. *i.* ibid. c. 2. *s.* John de, treafurer, and one of the king's council, 12 Edward ii. II. 32. c. 1. *s.* Vicechancellor of the Exchequer, II. 39. c. 1. *q.* Occurs, II. 110. Again, 12 Edward ii. II. 327. c. 1. *z.*

Waleys, John le, a Scot, hanged and beheaded, 35 Edward i. I. 375. c. 1. *u.* Henry le Waleys fherif of London, 55 Henry iii. II. 96. c. 1. *u.* Ingeram le Waleys fherif of Southamptonfhire, with the caftle of Winton, 18 Edward i. II. 143.

Walford, John de, one of the efquires of the bifhop of Hereford, 10 Edward i. I. 669. c. 1. *a.* Robert de Walmesford writer of the great roll, 3 Edward i. II. 320. c. 2. *e.*

Walingford honor held by Turftan Baffet, 2 John, I. 659. c. 1. *u.* Why feized, II. 244. Robert de Meleburn mayor of, 35 Edward i. II. 247. c. 2. *p.*

Walkyngham, John de, charged with a commiffion of array, 16 Edward ii. II. 112. c. 1.

Walmesford, Robert de, writer of the great roll, 4 Richard i. II. 269. c. 2. *f.*

Walo the legate had the cuftody of the fee of Chichefter, 2 Henry iii. I. 578. c. 2. *e.*

Walfham hundred, in cuftody of Nicolas Caftle, 9 Edward i. II. 2. c. 2. *f.*

Walter chamberlain of Normandy, an. 1208. I. 163. c. 2. *y.* Hubertus Walteri, I. 215. c. 2. *d.*

Walter [de Conftantiis] archbifhop of Roan, one of the jufticiers in the Exchequer, 6 Richard i. I. 200. c. 1. *k.* Walter bifhop of Carlifle, treafurer, 14 Henry iii. I. 376. c. 1. *x.*

Walter, Theobald, an account of his barony, 8 John, I. 298. c. 2. *z.* Brings a plaint againft the men of Prefton, I. 498. c. 2. *o.* Fermer of the honor of Lancafter, 6 Richard i. I. 593. c. 1. *a.*

Walter fon of the bifhop of London contends for the church of Illing, 5 Stephen, I. 426. c. 1. *i.*

Waltervil, Jordan de, his plegius, 24 Henry ii. I. 211. c. 2. *l.* Ralf de Waltervil, his terra in the city of Lincoln efcheated, 24 Henry ii. I. 300. c. 1. *s.*

Waltervilla, Afcelin de, deraigned, 10 John, I. 107. c. 2. *c.*

Waltham church by whom built, 23 Henry ii. I. 226. c. 1. *a.*

Waltham S. Crofs, Richard abbat of, 9 Edward ii. II. 177. c. 1. *d.* Peter de Waltham, ibid. Hugh de Waltham deputy of John de Dalling, fherif of London, &c. 12 Edward ii. II. 181. c. 2. *r.*

Waltham, Wido dean of, 14 Henry ii. I. 44. c. 1. *c.* Terra de, to whom it belonged, 20 Henry ii. I. 96. c. 2. *p.* A grant to that church, I. 226. c. 1. *a.* John de Waltham treafurer's clerk, 2 Richard i. I. 388. c. 1. *z.* Abbat of Wautham amerced,

INDEX.

amerced, 3 Henry iii. I. 547. c. 2. *h*. The affife of Waltham, 19 Henry ii. I. 701. c. 1. *z*. Guy dean of, jufticier, 19 Henry ii. I. 701, 702. Waltham affifed in the king's hand, 1 Richard i. I. 703. c. 1. *l*. Ralf le Napier of Waltham, his aid, 14 Henry ii. I. 586. c. 1. *x*.

Waltheve, fome account of his eftate and defcendents, temp. John, I. 56. Earl Waltheve of Northumberland, I. 435. c. 1. *p*. ibid. c. 2. *q*.

Walton, the terra de, belong'd to Derham abby, Com. Norf. 8 Richard i. I. 106. c. 1. *u*. To whom it belonged, 28 Henry ii. I. 113. c. 1. *r*.

Waltringham manor, how far the prior's de Novo Loco, in Shyrewode, 34 Edward i. I. 754. c. 2. *p*.

Wam, Walter, 49 Henry iii. I. 16. c. 1. *y*. Why fued by Talyefer ufher of the Exchequer, ibid.

Wandard, William, his duel, 30 Henry ii. I. 67. c. 1. *u*.

Wanetir, Roger de, with Robert his fon, amerced in Cornwal, 10 John, I. 151. c. 2. *y*.

Wannervil, Adam de, has a commiffion of array, 16 Edward ii. II. 112. c. 1.

Wappinbiri, Richard de, and Juliana his wife, 3 John, I. 213. c. 2. *x*. Their land in Shropfhire, ibid.

Warblington, William de, his tenure, temp. Henry ii. I. 44. c. 2. *g*. Thomas de Warblinton fherif of Hantfhire, 20, 21, 22 Edward i. I. 354. c. 1. *q*. Sir Thomas de Warblington of Hantfhire, 26 Edward i. I. 466. c. 2. *d*. William de Warblinton acknowledges a knight's fee and quarter in Hantfhire, 29 Henry iii. I. 494. c. 2. *l*. Thomas de Warblington fherif of Hampfhire, 24 and 25 Edward i. II. 143.

Ward, a fine for marrying the king's Ward without licence, 3 Richard i. I. 105. c. 1. *q*. How irregularly abolifhed, I. 620. c. 2. Efcuage arofe from wardfhip, I. 642.

Ward, William de, his intereft in Burton, 24 Henry ii. I. 103. c. 2. *k*. Robert de la Warde fummoned amongft the barons by the king's letter to attend the Scotch war, 26 Edward i. I. 655. c. 1. Simon fherif of Yorkfhire, 15 Edward ii. II. 124. c. 1. *g*.

Wardens of the fea-ports and their deputies through England, 15 John, I. 772, 773, &c.

Wardon in the bifhopric tallaged, 11 Edward i. I. 720. c. 2. *u*. Abbat of Wardon, I. 722. c. 1. *z*. Abbat of, II. 217.

Wardrobe of the Jews near their Exchequer, I. 233. Whence their books and rolls were ftollen, 44 Henry iii. ibid. King's Wardrobe one of his treafuries, I. 267. Wardrobe of the king at Bafingeftok, 14 Henry iii. I. 418. c. 1. *h*.

Wardfilver, the manor of the bifhop of Ely, 18 Edward i. I. 618. c. 1. *k*.

Ware, William de, fines that his chatels and houfes be not burnt, 19 Henry ii. I. 503. c. 1. *k*. Roger la Ware, fummoned by writ among the barons to the Scotch war, 26 Edward i. I. 655. c. 2. And attended, I. 657. c. 1. *g*. Richard de Ware abbat of Weftminfter dyed treafurer of the Exchequer, 12 Edward i. II. 36. c. 2. *g*. The executors of Robert la Ware, 14 Edward i. II. 194. John de la Ware fenefchal of Ifabel de Fortibus, 1 Edward i. II. 297. c. 1. *g*.

Ware bridge broken down by the men of

INDEX.

of Hertford, 3 Richard i. I. 564. c. 1. z.

Warelvil, Hugh de, sherif of Sussex, about 5 Stephen, I. 327. c. 2. a. Hugh de Warelvil fined to be sherif of Northampton and Leicestershire, 5 Stephen, I. 458. c. 1. a. Warevil, Ustevil and Novil in Normandy, belonged to Thomas de Beaumont, 2 John, I. 518. c. 1. t.

Warengefort, Roger de, usher of the Exchequer to Henry ii. I. 56. and II. 272. c. 1. m. Brient Fitz-Count fermer of Warengefort, 5 Stephen, I. 330. c. 1. c. Fermers of Warengeforde, 30 Henry ii. I. 331. c. 2. t. Part of the land of Niel de Oilli, before 5 Stephen, I. 457. c. 2. s. William de Warengford and William de Witeham slew the father of Thomas Croc, 9 John, I. 499. c. 1. t. The barons of Warengeford, 2 Henry ii. I. 686. c. 2. f. I. 687. c. 1. i. and I. 696. c. 2. l. Wallingford priory a cell of S. Albans, 10 Richard i. I. 760. c. 2. Roger de Warenguefort or Walingford ostiary of the Exchequer, temp. Henry ii. II. 272. c. 1. m. ibid. c. 2. o. Was usher, 2, 7 and 12 Henry ii. ibid. c. 2. o, p, q, r. See Walingford.

Warenne, William earl of, 1 Stephen, I. 13. c. 2. s. Warenne or Guarenne, William de, chief justicier, an. 1073. I. 32. c. 2. f. Reginald de, an. 1162. I. 34. c. 1. u. William de, temp. Richard i. I. 35. S. earl of, I. 67. c. 1. x. William de, 7 Richard i. I. 106. c. 1. t. Reginald de, injoined to do justice to Robert de Mandevill, an. 1162. I. 112. Reginald one of the justiciers, 20 Henry ii. I. 123. 146. William de, 5 Stephen, ibid. c. 2. r. Richard de Warenne son of king John, 25 Henry iii. I. 233. c. 2. y. William earl of Warenne fines to be quit of the justiciary of the ports, 7 John, I. 461. c. 2. d. John de Warenne earl of Surry, 50 Henry iii. I. 476. c. 1. u. Milisent wife of William de Warenne, temp. Henry ii. I. 490. c. 1. s. Beatrice daughter of William de Warenne, and widow of Doun Bardolf, 11 John, ibid. Reginald has the honor of Wurmegai, 14 Henry ii. I. 572. c. 1. l. Justice itinerant, 14 Henry ii. I. 586. c. 1. x. and I. 590. c. 1. k. J. de Warenna earl of Surrey, 18 Edward i. I. 598. c. 2. e. John de Warenne earl of Surrey his escuage for the manor of Pritewel, 2 Edward ii. I. 646. c. 1. w. Earl of Warenne in the Scotch war, 26 Edward i. I. 655. c. 2. William de Warenne has the honor of Wermegai, 2 Richard i. I. 664. c. 1. z. See ibid. c. 2. c. Seems to have sixty fees of [earl Warenne] his barony in Sussex, 13 John, I. 666. c. 1. k. Reginald de Warenna sets the assise of Surrey, 22 Henry ii. I. 732. c. 2. l. John son of John de Warenne, 33 Edward i. I. 741. c. 2. i. His villes of Staunton and Grantham, Linc. ibid. The pleas of William de Warenne, 5 Richard i. II. 20. c. 2. a. W. earl Warenne sat in the Exchequer, 14 Henry iii. II. 27. c. 2. g. The executors of John earl of Warenne, 33 Edward i. II. 76. Earl William attests a charter of king Stephen, II. 138. c. 2. e. William earl of Warenne sherif of Surrey, 9 Henry iii. II. 163. John de Warenne son of William late earl of Surry, 48 Henry iii. II. 165. c. 1. l. William de, 9 Richard i. II. 198. c. 1. r. How William de Warenne's estate

INDEX.

estate descended to Hubert de Burgh, II. 214. c. 1. r.

Warham, men of, I. 410. c. 2. p. Alexander de Warham carries salt and hides into Normandy, 8 John, I. 470. c. 1. i. Belonged to the earl of Glocester, 22 Henry ii. I. 552. c. 2. o.

Warin, sheriff of Wiltshire, Dorset and Somersetshire, 5 Stephen, I. 327. c. 1. p. Again, 5 Stephen, I. 365. c. 1. o. William Warin, 18 Henry ii. II. 131. c. 1. g.

Warin prior of Locherons vicechancellor, an. 1198. I. 77. c. 2. e.

Warinus Vicecomes, in the time of Henry i. I. 112. c. 1. m.

Warle, Ingelard de, keeper of the wardrobe, 5 Edward ii. I. 385. c. 2. r. Baron of the Exchequer, 10 Edward ii. II. 59. c. 1. e. Is succeeded on his death by Robert de Wodehouse, 12 Edward ii. II. 60. c. 2. h.

Warner son of Turgar, fermer of Lincoln town, 14 Henry ii. I. 585. c. 1. s.

Warnest, Alan de, claims the land of Cecily de Abetot, 31 Henry ii. I. 447. c. 2. z.

Warnisture of the castle of Leicester, 20 Henry ii. I. 370. c. 1. f.

Warren, William de, one of the judges, 9 Richard i. I. 113.

Warrewick, Nicolas de, king's sergeant, 25 Edward i. II. 75. c. 1. z.

Warton, belonging to the honor of Lancaster, has a market granted, 1 John, I. 401. c. 1. a.

Wartre in Yorkshire, an escheat, 18 Henry ii. I. 631. c. 2. i.

Warwick, Roger earl of, 1 Stephen, I. 13. c. 2. s. William earl of, his grant of the land of Cota to Alan his cook, I. 57. c. 1. s. Earl of Warwick chamberlain in fee, 1 Edward ii. I. 75. Warwick castle kept by seven knights and ten sergeants, 20 Henry ii. I. 220. The mota and castle of Warwick, I. 370. c. 1. f. Maud countess of Warwick fines to marry to whom she will, 31 Henry ii. I. 464. c. 1. c. Earl of Warwick has above an hundred knights fees, 14 Henry ii. I. 574. c. 2. o. His escuage for the king's ransom, 7 Richard i. I. 591. c. 2. t. Has an hundred and two knights fees, 29 Henry iii. I. 595. c. 1. n. John de Pleff. earl of Warwick, 39 Henry iii. I. 617. c. 1. f. Earl of Warwick had seventy three fees, 5 Henry ii. I. 628. c. 1. w. Countess of Warwick's scutage in Yorkshire, 1 John, I. 638. c. 1. i. Earl has a hundred and two fees, 14 Henry iii. I. 640. c. 2. x. Earl one of the court, 26 Edward i. I. 655. c. 2. Maud countess of Warwick had fifteen fees, 7 Richard i. I. 676. c. 1. t. Thomas de Bellocamp earl of Warwick, earl mareschal during pleasure, 18 Edward iii. I. 798. c. 2. Guy earl of Warwick, 27 Edward i. II. 149. William Mauduit earl of Warwick, 49 Henry iii. II. 296. c. 1. z. William de Beauchamp earl of Warwick, 52 Henry iii. and 25 Edward i. II. 296, 297.

Wascelin, John, constabulary of Bamburc, 7 Henry iii. I. 329. c. 1. w.

Wascoil, Gilbert de, 3 Richard i. II. 220. c. 2. q. Seems to be paymaster for the foreign merchants, ibid.

Waspail, Ralf, 5 Henry ii. I. 696. c. 2. n.

Wassingeley, Reginald de, amerced for lying before a judge, 14 Henry ii. I. 559. c. 1. e.

Wastehose, Alan, fines, 3 Richard i. I. 105. c. 1. q.

Wastel,

INDEX.

Waftel, Ralf, 23 Henry ii. I. 548. c. 1. *r*. Why amerced, ibid.

Wafteneys, Edmund de, has a commiffion of array for the wapentake of Strafford, 16 Edward ii. II. 112. c. 1.

Wafthul, William de, his cafe, 18 Edward i. II. 44.

Waftum, what, I. 693.

Watefeld, Nicolas fon of Hugh de, 7 Richard i. I. 549. c. 1. *b*. Amerced for a falfe oath, ibid.

Water, thofe who dyed by judgment or tryal of it forfeited chattels, I. 344. c. 1. *n, o.* ibid. c. 2. *t*. Nicolas de Savigney has licenfe to exchange the tryal of water for a duel, 4 John, I. 525. c. 2. *b*. See I. 547. c. 1. *a, b, c*.

Waterford. See Stephen.

Watervill, Richard de, abbat of Whitebi, before 3 John, I. 99. c. 1. *p*. His charter of privileges to the townfmen difputed, ibid. Robert de Watervil has the wardfhip of the land and heir of Geoffrey de S. Martin, 1 John, I. 324. c. 1. *e*. Richard de Watervil's charter to Whiteby pronounced difhonourable, 2 John, I. 515. c. 1. *g*. Ralf had the fee of Birton, Linc. I. 713. c. 1. *d*. See Waltervil.

Watford, Mr William de, jufticier of the Jews, about 56 Henry iii. I. 253. c. 1. *x, y*. Euftace de Watford his efcuage in Northamptonfhire for the king's ranfom, 6 Richard i. I. 591. c. 1. *m*. Town and market of Watford were the abbat of S. Albans, 10 Richard i. I. 761. c. 1. Walter de Watford was dead, 7 Edward i. II. 194. c. 1. *h*.

Wathamftede and Harpedene hundred courts, the abbat of Weftminfter's, II. 23. c. 1. *w*. William de Wathamfted, deputy of William Hardel in the Exchequer, 33 Henry iii. II. 129. c. 2. *d*. Alured de Wathamfted, in mifericordia, 12 Henry ii. II. 213. c. 2. *o*.

Watteley, Walter de, the fherif fined for concealing his death, 21 Henry ii. I. 553. c. 1. *u*.

Waude, William de, jufticier in Normandy, 2 John, I. 171. c. 2. *x*.

Waverle abbey in Surrey held in frankalmoigne by the charter of king John, I. 671.

Wauncy, Nicolas de, fherif of Surry and Suffex, 35 Henry iii. I. 378. c. 1. *l*.

Waure, Robert de, poffeffed Suineford, 31 Henry ii. I. 97. c. 1. *x*.

Wauton, Adam de, fined in Yorkfhire, 7 Henry iii. I. 495. c. 2. *e*.

Wawayn, Robert, 16 Edward ii. II. 112. c. 2.

Wax ufed in fummonces of the Exchequer, 29 Henry ii. II. 273. c. 2. *x*.

Waxand, John, his commiffion of array in the wapentak of Brudeford, 16 Edward ii. II. 112. c. 1.

Waxtonefham, Warner de, his claim in Fifhide, 10 John, I. 442. c. 2. *f*.

Weavers. See Telarii.

Weden manor belonged to the abbat of Bec, I. 203. c. 1. *d*.

Wedding, Gilbert de Creffonerie fined feventy pound for being prefent at one, I. 167. c. 1. *k*.

Weighers, Pefours or Ponderatores of the Exchequer, II. 307. That ferjeanty conveyed by Sir John de Windefor to Adam de Stratton, 48 Henry iii. II. 308.

Weinfleet town amerced for taking toll illegally, 16 Henry ii. I. 545. c. 2. *g*.

Welbec abbey to be quit of aid, &c. 9 Edward ii. I. 599. c. 2. *g*.

Weleford, Rafe de, his claim on the

prior

INDEX.

prior of Derherſt, 31 Henry ii. I. 97. c. 1. *w.* Richard de, ſherif of London, 5 Edward ii. II. 251.

Welewe, the land of, to whom it belonged, 26 Henry ii. I. 431. c. 1. *i.* Welewa hundred amerced, Cambr. or Hunt. 1 Richard i. I. 558. c. 2. *a.*

Welhang, that land bordered upon, or belonged to the abbat of Rucford, 9 John, I. 472. c. 1. *b.*

Weliton, Shropſhire, tallaged, 1 John, I. 705. c. 2. *y.*

Welleboef, Robert de, fines for his diſcharge, 6 Henry iii. I. 495. c. 2. *i.*

Welleby, William de, diſcharged of ſcutage holding in ſocage, 9 Edward ii. I. 673. Occurs, 1 Edward ii. II. 122.

Welles, a market obtained for it, 4 John, I. 404. c. 2. *b.* Quere, Where. Welle wapentac in Lincolnſh. I. 502. c. 1. *b.* Dean of Welles, 18 Henry ii. I. 559. c. 2. *o.* Thomas archdeacon and Alexander dean of Welles juſticiers, aſſeſſed the hidage for the ranſom of Richard i. I. 592. c. 1. *x.* Adam de Welles a baron and courtier, 26 Edward i. I. 655. c. 2. Hugh de Welles, 4 John, I. 717. c. 1. *b.*

Wellewike, ſir Ralf de, committed to the Tower for non-payment, 34 Edward i. II. 239.

Welley, William de, II. 79. c. 1. *y.*

Wellingour, land there in frankalmoign given to the hoſpital of Simplingham, 12 John, I. 218.

Welton, Humfrey de, why amerced, 14 Henry ii. I. 554. c. 1. *m.* William de Welton of Northampton, 49 Henry iii. II. 17. c. 2. *f.*

Wenberge, Mr Thomas de, his office, 25 Edward i. I. 378. c. 2. *p.*

Wenge, Robert, for what amerced, 6 Henry iii. I. 564. c. 1. *s.*

Wengham, H. de, ſeems to have the ſeal, 37 Henry iii. I. 68. c. 2. *b.* Peter de Wingham his claim on the inheritance of Robert Baſſet, 10 Richard i. I. 114. c. 2. *t.* Henry de Wingeham king's tallager, 30 Henry iii. I. 735. c. 2. *k.*

Wengrave, John de, mayor of London, judicially proceeded againſt, 15 Edward ii. II. 85. Mayor, 12 Edward ii. II. 98. c. 2. *d.* Complained of by the pope's nuncio, 12 Edward ii. II. 110. Executor of William de Trente, 12 Edward ii. II. 234. c. 1. *o.*

Wenleſwurth, Laurence de, amerced, 29 Henry iii. II. 2. c. 2. *e.*

Wentale, Yorkſhire, its tallage, 30 Henry iii. I. 710. c. 1. *w.*

Wenunwen, Girfin ſon of, in Wales, 29 Henry iii. II. 215. c. 1. *w.*

Wepham, the fee of Rolland de Dinan, 14 Henry ii. I. 583. c. 1. *k.*

Weregrave, the manor of the biſhop of Wincheſter, I. 719. c. 1. *r.* and II. 146. c. 1. *x.*

Weremuth in the biſhopric, tallaged, 11 Edward i. I. 720. c. 2. *u.*

Wereſlea, the terra de, to whom it belonged, 15 Henry ii. I. 447. c. 1. *t.*

Werewel nunnery, 9 Edward i. I. 317. c. 1. *f.*

Werfeld, Shropſhire, tallaged, 1 John, I. 705. c. 2. *y.*

Werkeworde, I. 566.

Werkſop amerced, II. 259. c. 1. *i.*

Werres, Helewiſe, pays a fine not to marry though ſhe had vowed chaſtity, 10 Richard i. I. 464. c. 2. *f.*

Wermegai, the honor of William de Warenne, 2 Richard i. I. 664. c. 1. *z.*

Weſſinton in the biſhopric, I. 715. c. 1.

Weſtacre, canons of, 10 John, I. 472. c. 1. *c.* Fine for changing a road which

INDEX.

which lay through their court, Norfolk, ibid.

Weſtbery, Walter de, 29 Henry ii. I. 232. c. 2. *t.*

Weſtcour, Henry de, fines for his outlawry or abjuration, 4 John, I. 505. c. 1. *g.*

Weſt-Derby, tallaged, 11 Henry iii. I. 707. c. 1. *h.*

Weſtgate hundred occurs, I. 212. c. 1. *o.* Amerced for not purſuing the robbers of Hakinton chapel, Kent, 7 Richard i. I. 556. c. 2. *r.*

Weſtland, Theophania de, Kent, 6 Henry iii. I. 452. c. 1. *f.*

Weſtmarieland, I. 130. c. 2. *t.* Robert de Clifford and Idonea de Leyburn ſherifs in fee of Weſtmorland, 27 Edward i. II. 180. Accompted for three years ſucceſſively by Reinar, dapifer of Randulf de Glanvil, 23 Henry ii. II. 183. c. 1. *y.*

Weſtminſter, coronations, marriages and knighthoods of the royal family celebrated there, I. 2. How that church obtained the town of Benflet, I. 155. Its land in Becham, Kent, 14 Henry ii. I. 558. c. 2. *t.*

Weſtminſter, Laurence abbat of, 11 Henry ii. I. 44. W. abbat of, 3 Henry iii. I. 67. c. 2. Has fifteen knights fees in Worceſterſhire, 38 Henry iii. I. 596. c. 2. *u.* and 14 Henry iii. I. 660. c. 2. *g.* See his fine, I. 665. c. 1. *f.* Teſte R[ichard de Barking] abbat of Weſtminſter, 27 Henry iii. I. 682. c. 1. *s.* Some account of the abbat's eſtate in Gloceſterſhire, 19 Henry ii. I. 701. c. 2. *c.* The grant from Edward iii. for rebuilding this church, II. 3.

Weſtminſter, Edward de, of the treaſury, 37 Henry iii. I. 270. c. 2. *f.* One of the king's meſſengers which demanded tallage of London, 39 Henry iii. I. 712. c. 1. *a.* Edward de, treaſurer of the new Exchequer at Weſtminſter, 30 Henry iii. II. 3. c. 2. *k.* E. de Weſtminſtre clerk of the Exchequer, 42 Henry iii. II. 18. c. 2. *n.* Has cuſtody of the ſeal of the Exchequer, II. 52. c. 1. *t.* Commanded to ſeize on the city of London for treſpaſs of an aſſize, 39 Henry iii. II. 248. c. 1. *w.* Odo de Weſtminſtre remembrancer of the Exchequer, 14 Edward i. II. 265. c. 1. *l.* Simon de Weſtminſtre made teller of the Exchequer, 28 Henry iii. II. 307. c. 1. *t.* Edward de Weſtminſtre ſon of Odo the goldſmith purchaſes the office of fuſor, 24 Henry iii. II. 310. Odo de Weſtminſtre, who ſeems to be the ſon of Edward, makes a deputy, 51 Henry iii. ibid. c. 1. *k.* Edward de Weſtminſtre baron of the Exchequer, 48 Henry iii. II. 319. c. 1. *k.*

Weſtmylne, Richard de, of the county of Hereford, 55 Henry iii. I. 243. c. 1. *n.* The tallage or aſſiſe of Weſtmulna, 19 Henry ii. I. 701. c. 1. *z.*

Weſton, John de, juſtice of the Jews, 55 Henry iii. I. 240. c. 1. *d.* Geoffry de Weſton accompts for ſome late lands of the Templars, 9 Edward ii. I. 265. c. 1. *d.* The ſokemanni of Weſton, Norfolk, tallaged, 14 Henry iii. I. 725. c. 2. *g.* William de Weſton has a commiſſion of array for the wapentak of Morley, 16 Edward ii. II. 112. c. 1. And Robert de Weſton for Knareſburgh, ibid. Adam de Weſton committee of the lands of David ſon of Griffin a felon, 24 Edward i. II. 239. Committed to the Tower of London, 24 Edward i. II. 243. c. 2. *f.* Was of Northamptonſhire, ibid.

Weſtoure

INDEX.

Westoure community in Hampshire tallaged, 6 Edward ii. I. 744. c. 2. *y.*

Westwode, Richard le Later de la, a Venire facias against him, II. 14. c. 1. *p.*

Wetewong, Asketil de, of Yorkshire, his donum, 9 Richard i. I. 699. c. 1. *r.*

Wexcumb in Wiltshire, its aid, 14 Henry ii. I. 589.

Weyland, Thomas de, justice itinerant, 10 and 11 Edward i. II. 66. c. 1. *k.* Richard de Weylaund has respite of his debts while in the king's service beyond sea, 26 Edward i. II. 219. c. 1. *f.* Margery widow of Thomas de Weylond, 18 Edward i. II. 256. c. 2. *z.*

Whattele, John de, keeper of the queen-mother's gold, 7 Edward i. I. 351. c. 2. *d.*

Whita, William, 9 Edward ii. I. 650. c. 1. *k.* A writ in his favour, ibid.

Whitebi, abbat of, grants privileges to the townsmen, I. 99. c. 1. *p.* Which are contested, 1 John, I. 106. c. 2. *x.* The compotus of it, 14 John, I. 312. c. 1. *p.* The contest between the abbat and the town repeated more at large, 1 John, I. 514. c. 2. *f.* The quinzime for the merchandise of the port of Whitebi, 6 John, I. 772. c. 1. *i.* Wapentak of Whiteby under a commission of array, 16 Edward ii. II. 112. c. 2.

Whitefeld, Henry de, discharged of his scutage in Oxfordshire by the king's writ, 4 John, I. 666. c. 1. *b.* See Witefeld.

Whitewey, William de, parker of Stansted in Sussex, 2 Edward ii. II. 82.

Whystan manor in Yorkshire belonged to Thomas de Furnival senior, 14 Edward ii. I. 534. c. 1.

Whytewel, Asculf, had his purse cut in the court of the barons of the Exchequer at York, 26 Edward i. II. 82.

Wiard, Philip son of, 21 Henry ii. I. 546. c. 2. *u.* Amerced pro ferro Juisæ, ibid.

Wibert, prior of Christ's Church, Canterbury, I. 198. c. 2. *f.*

Wich, Worcestershire, tallaged, 8 Richard i. I. 704. c. 2. *q.* Tallaged again under the name of Wyz, 14 Henry ii. I. 708. c. 2. *r.* Walter de Wich elect of Sarum, 47 Henry iii. I. 719. c. 1. *q.* Instaurum de Wicha, II. 152. c. 1. *u.* Wich in Oxfordshire, II. 163. Wich in the king's hands, 22 Henry iii. II. 246. John de Wika usher of the Exchequer, 8 Richard i. II. 275. c. 1. *f.* Matthew usher, 33 Henry iii. II. 275.

Wichenden lands given in marriage to Agnes Wac by William de Humez her father, before 9 John, I. 451. c. 2. *b.* But claimed by the abbat of Nutley, ibid.

Wichenton, Henry de, his wardship reversed, 8 Richard i. I. 202. c. 1. *w.* Had the wardship of the daughter of Philip de Niwebote, 8 Richard i. I. 323. c. 2. *b.*

Wicht, the men of that island amerced for defalts, 16 and 18 Henry ii. I. 553. c. 1. *x.* The danegeld of that isle for several years, 5 Stephen, I. 686. c. 2. *c.* Thomas de Wyght's office in Kingeston on Hull, 6 Edward ii. I. 786. c. 2. *b.*

Wichtone, to whom it belonged, 2 Henry iii. II. 116. c. 1. *r.*

Wiclewood, William de, moneyour of Thetford, I. 590. c. 1. *k.*

Wicumb, belonged to the Fitz-Gerolds, temp. Henry ii. I. 59. c. 1. *g.* Men of Wicumb fine for a defect in their burels,

INDEX.

burels, 2 Henry iii. I. 479. c. 2. *c.* Twelve knights of Wicumb amerced, 5 Henry iii. I. 563. c. 2. *r.* Held by Alan Baffet, 1 John, I. 745. c. 2. *b.*

Widecot, Silvefter, 2 John, I. 175. c. 1. *o.*

Widemerepol, that land, I. 447. c. 2. *x.*

Widendon, Peter de, 1 John, I. 433. c. 2. *b.* His admiffion to land in Winchecumbe, whether from William de Sudley, whofe ward he had been, ibid.

Wider, William, his aid, 14 Henry ii. I. 588. c. 2. *c.*

Widerefdale or Witherdal, William de, his fees, 30 Henry ii. I. 116. c. 1. *a.* Alan de Witherfdal, 3 John, I. 447. c. 2. *d.*

Widermundesford tallaged, 1 Richard i. I. 703. c. 1. *l.* viz. in Effex.

Wido, or Guy the dean, juftice itinerant, 20, 21, 22, 23 Henry ii. I. 123. 131. Was jufticier and dean of Waltham, 15 Henry ii. I. 143. 150. c. 1. *r.* Wido dean of Gualtham, baron of the Exchequer in the beginning of Henry ii. I. 215. c. 1. *a.* Wido the fon of Tiece, how his lands defcended, 4 Richard i. I. 451. c. 1. *x.* Robert fon of Wido, 8 Richard i. I. 565. c. 1. *m.*

Widow, fines to marry whom fhe will, I. 323. c. 1. *w.* Another in wardfhip, ibid. c. 2. *a.* Another, I. 324. c. 2. *g.* Robert fon of Siward fines for the office and widow of Hugh Chivilli, 5 Stephen, I. 457. c. 2. *w.* Widows to have protection and fpeedy juftice, II. 102.

Widrigild, what, I. 92.

Widvil, Robert de, joined with Henry de Monfort as cuftos of the lands of Roger de Molbrai, 5 Stephen, I. 297. c. 1. *d.*

Wife of Hugh de Nevil fines to lye with her own hufband [probably in prifon] 6 John, I. 471. c. 2. *a.*

Wigan, marefchal of Henry i. I. 44. Ralf fon of Wigan quit of efcuage for the king's ranfom, 7 Richard i. I. 591. c. 2. *t.* Wigan had Scnide before 1 John, I. 705. c. 2. *z.*

Wigenhale, Peter de, and Simon his fon, &c. 24 Henry ii. I. 558. c. 1. *o.*

Wiggeberg in Effex, the terra of Robert de Setuans tallaged, 1 Richard i. I. 703. c. 1. *l.* Becaufe the heir was in ward, ibid.

Wiggemore abbey has two knights fees in Herefordfhire, 29 Henry ii. I. 596. c. 1. *s.*

Wight (Ifland of) and Herefordfhire granted to William Fitz-Ofbern dapifer, an. 1070. I. 49. c. 1. *g.* See Wicht.

Wiham hundred, I. 543. c. 1. *y.* Manor of Wyham in cuftody of Thomas de Camvill from Walter de Burgh, 28 Henry iii. II. 176. c. 1. *a.* One of the king's manors, ibid.

Wihtefeld, Robert de, one of king Richard's regency, I. 34.

Wikebout manor in Worcefterfhire amerced, 31 Henry ii. I. 563. c. 2. *i.*

Wikerlai, Roger and Jordan de, 22 Henry ii. I. 427. c. 1. *d.* Their two fees, ibid.

Wile, William de, faid to debauch his guard, 29 Henry ii. I. 483. c. 1. *i.*

Wileby, Philip de, baron of the Exchequer, 9 and 10 Edward i. I. 343. c. 1. *f.* and 4 Edward i. II. 60. c. 2. *k.* See Wylughby. Philip de Wyleby's falary as baron, 8 Edward i. II. 62. c. 1. *o.* Was chancellor of the Exchequer, 31 Edward i. ibid. c. 2. *p.* John de Wylughby was fherif of Northamptonfhire, 5 Edward ii. II. 69. c. 2. *d.* Philip de Wilugby

INDEX.

Wilugby chancellor of the Exchequer, 25 Edward i. II. 96. c. 2. *a.* P. de, who, 31 Edward i. II. 107. c. 1. *n.* and II. 188. c. 1. *e.* Occurs, 27 Edward i. II. 219. c. 2. *i.* Chancellor, 31 Edward i. II. 304. c. 1. *n.*

Wilinton, Ralf de, sherif of Devonshire, pledge of William de Lassebergh, 39 Henry iii. II. 150. c. 2. *o.*

William uncle of king John, a benefactor to Feversham abbey, I. 413. c. 2. *k.* Earl William brother of the king his knights fees, 14 Henry ii. I. 573. c. 2. *m.* Again, I. 586. c. 1. *x.* William the king's brother, 2 Henry ii. I. 602. c. 1. *y.* William the queen's brother, 2 Henry ii. I. 687. c. 1. *g.*

William i. raises six shillings on every hide of land here, I. 571. c. 2. *h.*

William the king's son [viz. of Henry i.] his writ to the bishop of Bath, an. 1121. I. 109.

Wilmundecot, in the family of Vaux, 6 John, I. 441. c. 1. *r.* Ralf de, amerced for recreancy, 14 Henry ii. I. 549. c. 2. *o.*

Wilton, Richard de, one of the justices, 20 Henry ii. I. 124. and I. 701. Sherif of Wiltshire, 23 Henry ii. I. 131. c. 1. *y.* Hubert de Wiltona, 5 Stephen, I. 146. c. 2. *q.* Peter de Wilton accompts for the profits of the fee of Exeter, 31 Henry ii. I. 310. c. 1. *a.* Richard de Wilton sherif of Wilts, 15 Henry ii. I. 373. c. 2. *e.* Alan de Wilton amerced for a duel, 7 Henry iii. I. 550. c. 2. *z.* Amerced for false measure, 5 Richard i. I. 564. c. 2. *e.* See I. 589. c. 2. *g.* Its aid, 23 Henry ii. I. 604. c. 1. *l.* That abbat's scutage, 33 Henry ii. I. 634. c. 1. *q.* The burgh's assise, 19 Henry ii. I. 702. c. 1. *d.* See II. 252.

Wiltshire, Richard archdeacon of, fermer of the manors of the see of Exeter, I. 310. c. 2. *a.* The aid of this shire, 14 Henry ii. I. 589. c. 1. *e.* Its donum, I. 695. c. 2. *c.* See II. 164. c. 1. *a.*

Wimar, capellanus, has custody of Hulm abbey, &c. 19 Henry ii. I. 308. c. 2. *k.* Fermer of Norfolk and Suffolk, 30 Henry ii. I. 328. c. 1. *n.* Fines to be quit as sherif of Norfolk and Suffolk, 1 Richard i. I. 458. c. 1. *d.* William Wymer, II. 79. c. 1. *u.* See II. 152. c. 1. *u.*

Wimbervil, Elias and Robert sons of Roger de, 25 Henry iii. II. 16. c. 2. *a, b.*

Wimund's fees, held of the honor of Glocester, not found, 15 John, I. 639. c. 1. *o.* Richard Wymund, his crime, 10 Henry iii. I. 793. c. 2. *g.*

Winchecumb, abbat in Glocestershire accompts for two fees, 29 Henry iii. I. 595. c. 1. *m.* The aid of the town, 23 Henry ii. I. 604. c. 1. *k.* The burgh tallaged, 7 Richard i. I. 703. c. 2. *n.*

Winchelse, barons and bailifs of, 6 Edward i. I. 335. c. 2. *b.* Its ferm how assigned, ibid. James de, his land, 1 John, I. 485. c. 2. *g.* That port amerced, I. 568. c. 1. *r.* See I. 772. c. 2.

Winchester, earl of. See Quenci. Abbess of, 25 Henry ii. I. 561. c. 1. *n.* Prior of Winchester amerced for having a bow in his house, 2 John, I. 566. c. 1. *u.* Soke of the bishop in the suburbs, I. 719.

Windsor, a royal chapel there, temp. Edward ii. I. 61. The fermer of Windsor, 21 Henry ii. I. 367. c. 2. *l.* Again, 14 Henry ii. I. 373. c. 2. *d.* William son of Richard de Windlesor

INDEX.

for amerces the men of Cambridge by command of the barons, 12 John, I. 528. c. 1. *i.* Edmund de Wyndesore the king's panetier distrained to accompt for the office of Gauge, 15 Edward ii. I. 770. c. 2. *c.* Osbert de Brai fermer of Windresore, 19 Henry ii. I. 774. c. 2. *n.* John and Thomas de, 6 and 25 Henry iii. II. 21. c. 1. *k.* c. 2. *l.* Thomas ponderator, 4 John, II. 307.

Wine, Nigel son of Osbert le, I. 495. c. 2. *g.* Imprisoned for the death of Gemian de la Yerd, 6 Henry iii. ibid.

Wine to wash the altar, I. 195. c. 1. *a.* A sextertium of wine sold for ten pence in Hereford, 14 Henry iii. I. 419. c. 1. *m.* Tonellum of red wine at fifteen shillings, 12 John, I. 766. c. 1. *n.* Several sorts of wine, I. 767.

Winesham, the land of Ralf de, in the king's hands, 14 John, I. 299.

Winestaneton, William de, 5 Richard i. I. 98. c. 2. *m.* His debet for the share of his wife Agnes's inheritance in Sussex, ibid.

Winferding, its aid, 14 Henry ii. I. 589. c. 2. *f.*

Winielton in Cornwal, its aid, 23 Henry ii. I. 604. c. 2. *m.*

Winterborne, Felicia and William de, 10 John, I. 453. c. 2. *x.* Her debet, ibid. That town belonged to Alured de Nicol, 11 John, I. 472. c. 1. *d.* The donum of the Winterburns, Wiltshire, 33 Henry ii. I. 634. c. 2. Its tallage, 1 John, I. 705. c. 2. *z.*

Winterhull, William de, held nothing of the king in capite in Surrey and Sussex, 41 Henry iii. I. 597. c. 2. *b.* John de Wintereshul of Hampshire, 42 Henry iii. I. 79. c. 1. *w.* See Wintreshul.

Winterlowe in Wiltshire, its tallage, 20 Henry iii. I. 707. c. 1. *k.*

Winteslawe, the terra of Matthew Turpin, 1 John, I. 663. c. 2. *u.* Of which he was disseized for not attending the king's army, ibid.

Winton, Peter bishop of, 11 Henry iii. I. 63. c. 1. *l.* Bishop of Winton (viz. Peter de Rupibus) made chancellor, 15 John, I. 67. c. 1. *w.* That bishoprick in the king's hands, 19 Henry ii. I. 308. c. 2. *m.* That See in the king's hands, 1 Richard i. I. 311. c. 2. *f.* Bishop Peter fermer of Hampshire, 5 Henry iii. I. 329. c. 1. *t.* T. J. bishop of Winchester, treasurer, 12 Edward ii. I. 381. c. 2. *a.* Bishop of Winton acknowledges sixty knights fees, 29 Henry iii. I. 594. c. 2. *l.* Richard archdeacon of Poictiers custos of this See, 18 Henry ii. I. 631. c. 1. *g.* Its aid for the marriage of the king's daughter, 31 Henry iii. I. 661. c. 2. *n.* Its scutage for Wales, 13 John, I. 667. c. 2. *p.* P. Winton excused from scutage, because he opposed the granting it, 5 Henry iii. I. 675. c. 1. *q.* Some accompt of the manors of this See, I. 719. c. 1. *r.* G[odfrey de Luci] bishop of Winton king's tallager in Cornwal, 1 John, I. 733. c. 2. *t.* Bishop Peter was justicier, 2 Henry iii. II. 26. c. 1. *a.* John de Winton clerk of the Wardrobe, 34 Edward i. II. 65. Nicolas de Winton sherif of London, 2 Edward i. II. 96. c. 2. *x.* Nicolas de Winton deputy usher of the Exchequer, 40 Henry iii. II. 276. c. 1. *m.*

Wintonia, Robert de, 2 John, I. 173. c. 2. *d.* Adam de Winton clerk, keeper

INDEX.

Wlethelesberwe, Adam de, collector of the vintisme, Leicest. 1 Edward i. II. 242. c. 1. *x*.

Wlinberge market belonged to the abbat of Torre, 14 Henry iii. II. 216. c. 2. *k*.

Wnford, Devonshire, was Ralf Taisson's, 5 Stephen, II. 220. c. 1. *l*.

Woburn abbey, I. 677. c. 2. *d*.

Wocking in Surrey, its aid, 14 Henry ii. I. 587. c. 1. *y*.

Woddetone, Robert de, sherif of Devonshire, 14 Edward i. II. 143. c. 1. *d*.

Wodeford, frere Lucas de, confessor to Edward i. and Edward ii. I. 393. c. 1. *e*.

Wodelowe, whose land, I. 57. c. 1. *s*.

Wokingeham, the bishop of Sarum's manor in Berkshire, 3 Henry iii. I. 415. c. 1. *r*. Has a Tuesday market settled, ibid.

Wollechirchehawe market in London, 52 Henry iii. I. 779. c. 1. *e*.

Wolleward, Walter, surety for William de Watford, 56 Henry iii. I. 253. c. 1. *x*.

Wolvesey at Winchester, the Exchequer of, 43 and 52 Henry iii. II. 3. c. 2. *l*.

Women married, their privileges and incapacities, I. 185, &c. Women had a right of tryal by duel, 31 Henry ii. I. 451. c. 1. *w*. Not to be distreined by their dower for the debts of the deceased, II. 191.

Woodhouse or Wodehouse, Robert de, made baron of the Exchequer in the room of Ingelard de Warle, 12 Edward ii. II 60. c. 2. *h*. Robert de Wodehouse baron of the Exchequer, 15 Edward ii. II. 182. c. 1. *t*. Robert de Wodehous baron of the Exchequer and auditor of the accompts, &c. 12 Edward ii. II. 292. c. 1. *k*.

Wool, fine for leave to export it out of England, 8 Richard i. I. 776. Tronage, or the office of weighing wool, or of the beam, I. 780. passim. Half a mark for every sack of wool exported from Len, 25 Edward i. I. 782, 783. Forty shillings for every sack in time of war, I. 783. c. 2. *t*.

Worcester, Godfrey Giffard bishop of, chancellor, 1 Edward ii. I. 76. That See in the king's hands, 31 Henry ii. I. 307. c. 1. *x*. Walter [Reynald] bishop and chancellor, 1 Edward ii. I. 380. c. 1. *t*. Accompt of the knights fees of this See, I. 581. c. 2. *y*. The scutage of this See for the ransom of Richard i. I. 592. c. 2. *y*. Has above forty-nine fees in that county, 38 Henry iii. I. 596. c. 2. *u*. The scutage for this See, 3 John, I. 665. c. 1. *f*. That burgh tallaged, 14 Henry iii. I. 708. c. 2. *r*. Walter bishop of, treasurer, 2 Edward ii. II. 8. c. 2. *m*. W. Reynald elect of Worcester, treasurer, 1 Edward ii. II. 30. Surrenders the treasurership of the Exchequer to John de Sandale, 3 Edward ii. II. 38. c. 1. *m*. Chancellor of England, 5 Edward ii. II. 48. c. 1. *a*. Godfrey bishop of Worcester one of the king's council, 54 Henry iii. II. 171. c. 1. Godfrey had the third part of a barony by inheritance, 20 Edward i. II. 223. Walter bishop of, treasurer, 2 Edward ii. II. 279. c. 2. *z*.

Worcester, their contention with Glocester, 6 Richard i. I. 400. c. 1. *p*. An account of the manors belonging to the prior and monks of Worcester, 9 John, I. 408. c. 2. *w*.
Prior

INDEX.

keeper of the rolls of Judaism, 7 Edward i. I. 244. c. 1. s. The town has an abatement of its ferm for twenty-one years by reason of its poverty, 49 Henry iii. I. 337. c. 1. k. c. 2. l. Its weavers fine for liberties, and to have an alderman, 12 Henry ii. I. 467. c. 2. i. The assise of the city, 22 Henry ii. I. 702. c. 2. i. Philip de Wintonia of London, 19 Henry iii. I. 738. c. 1. y. Tallaged, 4 John, I. 743. c. 1. m. Nicolas de Wintonia usher of the Exchequer, 5 Edward i. II. 165. c. 1. i. Why the town was in the king's hands, 56 Henry iii. II. 245. c. 1. s.

Wintreshul, William de, sherif of Hampshire, 55 Henry iii. II. 203. c. 1. b.

Wireceſtria, Ralf de, baron of the Exchequer, 30 Henry ii. I. 215. c. 2. d. See Worcester.

Wireton in Cornwal, its tallage, 1 John, I. 733. c. 2. t.

Wirkeburc in Yorkshire, its tallage, 9 Richard i. I. 699. c. 1. r.

Wisbech or Wysebech, the bishop of Ely's town, 18 Edward i. I. 618. c. 2.

Wischard, William, 6 Richard i. I. 432. c. 2. y.

Wistring, Oliver de, his tenure, temp. Henry ii. I. 576. c. 1. y.

Witacre, Jordan de, and Isouda his wife, their share in the honor of Stafford, 4 Henry iii. I. 680. c. 1. m.

Witefeld, Rodbert de, his pleas, 25 Henry ii. I. 79. c. 2. x. One of the barons of the Exchequer, 29 Henry ii. I. 82. c. 1. b. One of the justices itinerant, 26 Henry ii. I. 139. c. 1. g. One of the barons, 29 Henry ii. I. 213. c. 1. p. Fermer of Oxfordshire for several years past, 30 Henry ii. I. 328. c. 2. q. Ralf de Whitefeld killed by Hugh son of Emma, 8 John, I. 494. c. 2. r. Robert de, his pleas, 3 Richard i. I. 544. c. 1. p. Henry of Devonshire fines ne transfretet, 1 John, I. 676. c. 1. u. Walter de, his share of the honor of Stafford, 4 Henry iii. I. 680. c. 1. m. Robert tallager of Kent, 33 Henry ii. I. 736. c. 1. o.

Witeford in Devonshire, its tallage or assise, 19 Henry ii. I. 701. c. 1. b.

Witegrave, Ailric and Gilbert de, who in Staff. 7 Richard i. I. 552. c. 1. i.

Witeweia, William de, 5 Stephen, I. 457. c. 1. k. Held of the honor of Arundel, ibid.

Witewich, seems to have been the seat of the Grentemeisnils, I. 488. c. 1. b.

Witford in Devonshire their disme, I. 730. c. 2. a. See Witeford.

Witle in Surrey tallaged, 6 Edward ii. I. 744. c. 1. w.

Witlingham, that land by whom claim'd, 10 John, I. 100. c. 1. a.

Witney, Robert de, belonged to Eynsham abbey, 42 Henry iii. II. 251. c. 1. k.

Witso son of Leveſtan, 5 Stephen, I. 457. c. 1. l. His fine for his father, ibid.

Witton and Cave, I. 100. c. 1. z.

Wivelesthorp, Richard de, Yorkshire, amerced for a duel, 7 Henry iii. I. 550. c. 2. z.

Wivergate, Canterbury, I. 204. c. 2. k. Near the Tower ditch, ibid.

Wiverona, widow of Everwacer of Ipswich, fines to marry at her own choice, 5 Stephen, I. 464. c. 1. w.

Wives and children of the Jews to be seized for defalt, I. 225.

Wivil, Richard de, pays a hundred pounds for his donum in Yorkshire, 29 Henry ii. I. 278. c. 2. p.

Wlethelesberwe,

INDEX.

Prior of Worcester amerc'd for holding plea concerning a lay fee, 31 Henry ii. I. 561. c. 2. *u.* Scutage of Worcestershire for the ransom of Richard i. I. 592. c. 2. *y.* The villata of Worcester tallaged, 8 Richard i. I. 704. c. 2. *q.* Again, 18 Henry iii. I. 743. c. 2. *q.* Sir Richard de Worcester made sherif of Wilts, 51 Henry iii II. 68. c. 2. *x.* Guy earl of Warwick sherif in fee of Worcestershire, 27 Edward i. II. 149.

Worlegyan, one of John Wak's seven churches in Exeter diocese, 29 Henry iii. II. 250. c. 2. *i.*

Wormelawe hundred amerced, Herefordshire, 35 Henry iii. I. 567. c. 2. *k.*

Worth hamlet belonged to the chamberlainship of the Exchequer, II. 298. Worth under the sherif of Sussex was in part the prior of Boxgrave's, I. 599. c. 2. *g.*

Wotton in Warwickshire, prior of, 42 Henry iii. I. 268. c. 2. *s.*

Wrecks, several privileges relating to them, I. 66. c. 2. *q.* Belonged to the crown, I. 342, 343. Styled Werecs and Weregs, I. 343. c. 2. *h, i, k, l.* Not to be seised without warrant from the justicier, 14 Henry ii. I. 558. c. 2. *y.*

Wreng of Claihangre, Tocgieve wife of Osbert, slain before 7 John, I. 498. c. 2. *p.*

Writele, Essex, its aid with Joseph Clerk's and William Fitz Geoffrey's, 14 Henry ii. I. 586. c. 1. *x.* Its tallage, 19 Henry ii. I. 701. c. 1. *z.* and I. 703. c. 2. *m.* To whom the manor of Writele was granted out, 4 Richard i. II. 167. c. 1. *s.*

Writing, the manner of it in old membranes, Pref. xi.

Writs of course and precept, I. 70, 71. Writs de ultra mare, I. 85. and II. 221. c. 1. *s.* Original of writs, I. 86. Purchasing of a writ, ibid. c. 1. *t.* Writs of Liberate, I. 175. Writs of Liberate, Computate and de Perdono, I. 194. Writs of Allocate, I. 268, &c. Writ of Pone, I. 274. c. 1. *k.* Writ of restitution of temporalities, why, I. 306. Writs of privy seal to forward sherifs in their payments, I. 245, &c. Writs of Liberate of two sorts, I. 390. Of Assistance, I. 677. Writs of Duci facias, II. 65. Writs of privy seal, II. 73. Writs of the great and privy seal, II. 199. Writs of Allocate and Computate, II. 200, &c. Writ dormant, II. 222. A close Writ of the great seal, II. 268. Mareschal of the Exchequer keeper of the Writs, 10 Edward i. II. 286. c. 1. *e.* Clerk of the Writs of the Exchequer, II. 294. Writs of aid granted to king's debtors, II. 192.

Wroteham, William de, his grant from Richard i. I. 98. c. 2. *o.* William de Wroteham forester of Dorset and Somersetshire, 1 John, I. 460. c. 2. *y.* Has a confirmation of the land of Cathangre, 2 John, I. 477. c. 2. *m.* Richard de Wroteham hereditary forester of Sumersetshire, 9 Henry iii. I. 492. c. 2. *y.* Richard de Wrotham, his fine, 25 Henry iii. I. 527. c. 1. *b.* William fermed the quinzime of merchandise, 4 John, I. 771. c. 2. *g.* Again, being now archdeacon of Tanton, 6 John, I. 772. c. 1. *i.* William de Wrotham accompts for the mines of Cornwal and Devonshire, 10 Richard i. and 14 John, II. 132. c. 2. *k, l.*

Wroxhul, Hamon de, made deputy

INDEX.

fufor by Odo de Weftminftre, 51 Henry iii. II. 310. c. 1. *k*.

Wroxton canons pay no fcutage for the manor of Torp in Northamptonfhire, 27 Henry iii. I. 672. c. 1. *i*. Which manor was given them by John de Mountague, ibid.

Wuburne, John de, of London, tallaged, 19 Henry iii. I. 738. c. 1. *y*. See Woburn.

Wudeftoke, a council of the proceres fummoned hence to meet at Gloucefter, an. 1123. I. 12. c. 1. *o*. The repairs of that houfe with an Exchequer built there, 25 Henry iii. II. 3. c. 1. *i*.

Wudiete, fir Walter de, who, 10 John, I. 489. c. 2. *q*. William de, tallager of Dorfetfhire, 19 Henry iii. 1. 735. c. 1. *i*.

Wulfhal in Wiltfhire, its donum, 33 Henry ii. I. 634. c. 2.

Wulfie, Robert de, fines for his archdeaconry of Coventry, 1 John, I. 485. c. 1. *b*.

Wulfnoth, Henry fon of, de Pecham, Kent, 32 Henry ii. I. 549. c. 1. *z*.

Wulurunehampton tallaged, 7 Henry iii. I. 734. c. 2. *d*.

Wulwardefly manor, the prior of Worcefter's, I. 508. c. 2. *w*.

Wulwine accompts for the ferm of Chapmanfhal, 2 Henry ii. I. 341. c. 2. *o*.

Wulwinely in Yorkfhire, by whom that land was claimed, 3 John, I. 436. c. 2. *t*.

Wurmegai honor, in Reginald de Warenne, 14 Henry ii. I. 572. c. 1. *l*. See Warenne.

Wutton, that town belonged to Robert de Tattefhal, 6 Richard i. I. 200. c. 1. *k*. The church belonged to the abbot of Weftminfter, temp. Henry i. I. 209. c. 1. *a*. See Wotton.

Wuttorp, Thomas heir of Alan de, 11 John, I. 794. c. 2. *i*. His grant, ibid.

Wycheford hundred the bifhop of Ely's, 18 Edward i. I. 618. c. 2.

Wycumb, Simon de, keeper of the queen's gold, 52 Henry iii. I. 270. c. 2. *e*.

Wydepunt reed-ground, the bifhop of Ely's, 18 Edward i. I. 618. c. 2.

Wygeden, Richard de, his intereft in the manor of Haverhill, 40 Henry iii. I. 746. c. 1. *e*.

Wygetoft, the abbat of Croyland amerced for detaining that advowfon, 8 Edward ii. l. 529, 530.

Wygg, John, fherif of Devonfhire, before 5 Edward i. II. 142. c. 2. *b*.

Wykham, John de, arrays Whiteby, 16 Edward ii. II. 112. c. 2.

Wylburgham, Walter de, who, 1 Edward i. I. 610. c. 2.

Wyltonia, Peter goldfmith de, 42 Henry iii. I. 246. c. 2. *c*. William de Wiltonia holds pleas, 38 Henry iii. I. 761. c. 1.

Wylughby, Peter de, treafurer's lieutenant, chancellor of the Exchequer, 23 Edward i. I. 291. See I. 360. c. 1. *q*. Peter de Wylegby firft baron, &c. 25 Edward i. II. 44. c. 2. *q*. See II. 54. 60. See Wileby. Philip de Wyllughby chancellor of the Exchequer, 27 Edward i. II. 265. c. 1. *m*.

Wylwyth in Kent, II. 167. c. 2. *x*.

Wymundeham priory, II. 749. c. 2. *y*. A cell of S. Albans, 10 Richard i. I. 759. c. 2. *x*. Thomas de Wimundham king's treafurer, 50 Henry iii. II. 42. c. 2. *h*. Again, 51 Henry iii. II. 48. and II. 52. c. 2. *y*. Precentor of Lichfield, 52 Henry iii. II. 186. c. 1. *q*. Treafurer, 52 Henry iii. II. 307. c. 1. *uu*.

Wyne,

INDEX.

Wyne, Dionysia, held the manor of Penkeston, Derbyshire, of Thomas de Cadurcis, 2 Edward ii. I. 646. c. 1. *u.* Reynald de Wyme, 38 Henry iii. II. 190.

Wyngefeld, Roger de, clerk, 9 Edward ii. I. 265. c. 1. *d.* King's messenger to the Exchequer, 5 Edward ii. II. 7. c. 1. *f.*

Wynselver, the manor of the bishop of Ely, 18 Edward i. I. 618. c. 1. *k.*

Wynterburn, frier Walter de, 30 Edward i. I. 73. c. 1. *q.* Was one of the king's clerks, ibid.

Wyntonia, Adam de, removed from being justice of the Jews, 49 Henry iii. I. 234. c. 1. *c.* See Wintonia. Nicolas de Wynton usher of the Exchequer, 52 Henry iii. II. 280. c. 2. *d.*

Wyntrestok hundred the bishop of Bath's, 14 Henry iii. I. 418. c. 1. *h.*

Wyrksop and Gresthorp manors in Notinghamshire [f. Derb.] held by Thomas de Furnival of the king as part of the honor of Tykhul, 14 Edward ii. I. 533. c. 1. *t.* Terra de Werchessop, 30 Henry ii. ibid.

Wytene, Simon de, his tallage for his land in Fairmanneby, 30 Henry iii. I. 710.

Wytlesbury, Margery wife of Albric de, fined to the king to have the chattels of her husband who had drowned himself, I. 347. c. 2. *z.*

Y.

Yaie of Shropshire, the tallage of William la, 8 John, I. 734. c. 1. *z.*

Yarmouth paid custom three pence in the pound, 1 Edward ii. I. 385. c. 1. *q.*

Ybetoft, Lambert de, in Lincolnshire, his land, heir and widow in the custody of Bartholomew de Multon, 4 John, I. 324. c. 2. *g.*

Ycheburne, William de, 18 Henry iii. II. 15. c. 2. *x.* Has a pone per plegios against him, ibid.

Ydemeston, Wiltshire, the tallage of that town, 33 Henry ii. I. 634. c. 2.

Ydonea executed for clipping the denarii, 26 Henry ii. I. 279.

Ydonea brought the baronies of Hay and Kaunvile to the family of the Longespey's, before 40 Henry iii. I. 319. c. 1. *c.*

Yekand, William de, has the wapentake of Pykeryng under a commission of array, 16 Edward ii. II. 112. c. 2.

Yerd, Gemian de la, slain before 6 Henry iii. I. 495. c. 2. *g.*

Yffeld, Simon de, his fine and pledges, 10 Henry iii. I. 496. c. 1. *o.*

Ylaria wife of Robert de Budliers, 3 John, I. 790. c. 2. *l.*

Yle in the West, the town of William Torel, amerced with the provost for not making hue and cry, 31 Henry ii. I. 556. c. 2. *s.*

Ylger, Alured son of, why amerced, 23 Henry ii. I. 548. c. 2. *t.*

Ymmemere, the land of Thomas Ruffus, 12 John, I. 490. c. 2. *u.*

Ymmingham, the quinzime of the merchandise of this port, 6 John, I. 772. c. 1. *i.*

York, that county fined for recording a duel, I. 103. Gild of the merchants of York, 5 Stephen, I. 397. c. 2. *m.* Fine that they may not be impleaded out of the county, ibid. *n.* Has a confirmation of liberties, I. 399. c. 2. *h.* Burgesses and abbat of York, and abbat of S. Mary, York, have confirmation of liberties, 2 John, I. 401. c. 2. *f.* Again abbat of S. Mary, York, 19 Henry iii.

INDEX.

ibid. I. 420. c. 1. q. Judges and jurors of Yorkſhire fine to be no longer, I. 457. c. 2. u. The peculiar tenure of its ſherif, 3 John, I. 461. c. 1. a. Abbat of S. Mary, York, 3 John, I. 549. c. 2. i. Citizens of York amerced an hundred pound for not meeting the king, 3 John, I. 564. c. 2. c. Amerced, 55 Henry iii. I. 567. c. 2. n. The aid of the city, 5 Stephen, I. 601. c. 1. n. Its donum, 33 Henry ii. I. 635. c. 1. r. When Yorkſhire paid their danegeld, the city gave an aid, 2 Henry ii. I. 693. c. 2. q. York's tallage, 3 and 9 Richard i. I. 698. c. 2. q. I. 699. c. 1. r. The tallage of the men of S. Mary, York, 9 Richard i. I. 699. c. 1. r. The aſſiſe of York made by Richard de Luci, before 21 Henry ii. I. 702. c. 2. f. The tallage of York, 11 Henry iii. I. 707. c. 1. i. Its tallage by John de Kirkeby, 14 Henry iii. I. 708. c. 2. p. Again, 30 Henry iii. I. 710. c. 1. w. The tenants of S. Mary, York, tallaged by William Chimil their cuſtos, 10 Richard i. I. 714. c. 1. f. York tallaged, 3 John, I. 722. c. 2. b. The tallage of that city, 54 Henry iii. I. 743. c. 2. t. Quinzime for the port of York, 6 John, I. 772. c. 1. i. The Exchequer removed to the hall of the king's caſtle of York, 26 Edward i. II. 9. and 12 Edward ii. ibid. Its ſherifwick given to the higheſt bidder by Richard i. II. 138. Seized into the king's hands, 41 Henry iii. II. 154. c. 1. f. Several ſherifs of Yorkſhire, temp. Henry iii. II. 195, 196. Exchequer at York, 27 Edward i. II. 196. c. 1. n. Bailifs and citizens amerced for not making due payment at the Exchequer, 26 Edward i. II. 234. c. 2. s. The liberties of the canons of S. Peter and the city of York why ſeized, 38 and 40 Henry iii. II. 245. c. 1. q, r.

York, Turſtein the king's chaplain made archbiſhop of, about the year 1114. I. 11. c. 2. k. The archbiſhop diſſeiſed of all his manors except Ripon, temp. Richard i. I. 35 Had a houſe near Weſtminſter, 30 Edward i. I. 72. c. 1. o. Geoffrey archbiſhop of York, his controverſy with the dean and chapter, temp. Richard i. I. 87. The canons of York fined in an hundred pound for not attending at the king's ſummons, I. 103. The archbiſhoprick and abbey of York in the king's hands, 31 Henry ii. I. 309. c. 1. r. This See had a magiſter ſcolarum, ibid. Paid Peterpence, 31 Henry ii. ibid. Was in the king's hands, 1 Richard i. I. 311. c. 2. b. In the king's hands, 14 John, I. 312. c. 1. o. Lands held of that See by William de Paunton in the county of York, I. 320. c. 1. i. Geoffrey archbiſhop has the ſherifwick, 10 Richard i. I. 459. c. 2. r. Dean and chapter of York, 5 John, I. 478. c. 2. s. The archbiſhop's aid to marry the king's daughter, 14 Henry ii. I. 581. c. 1. w. His eſcuage for the king's ranſom, 6 Richard i. I. 591. c. 1. r. The archbiſhop has a writ to oblige his tenants in Leyceſterſhire to pay the proportion of the king's aid, 39 Henry iii. I. 598. c. 2. d. Walter archbiſhop, one of the receivers of the laſt vintiſm granted to Henry ii. I. 610. c. 1. i. Archbiſhop's ſcutage for the Iriſh xpedition, 18 Henry ii. I. 629. c. 1. z. Receives ſcutage from his tenants in proportion to their lands, 1 John, I. 680.

c. 2.

INDEX.

c. 2. *n.* The archbishop's freemen without Ripun tallaged, 9 Richard i. I. 699. c. 1. *r.* The tallage of the See of York accounted for, 3 John, I. 706. c. 1. *a.* Some accompt of lands belonging to this See in Lincolnshire, 33 Henry ii. I. 713. c. 1. *d.* William de Melton archbishop made treasurer of the Exchequer, 18 Edward ii. II. 41. c. 1. *y.* II. 51. c. 1. *q.* and II. 54. c. 1. *f.* Archbishop Geoffrey made sherif of Yorkshire as the highest bidder by Richard i. II. 139. c. 1. *f.* Walter archbishop one of the king's council, 54 Henry iii. II. 170. c. 1. *h.* Archbishop of York sherif of Notingham and Derbyshire, 5 Edward i. II. 180. Mr J. archdeacon of York, 42 Henry iii. II. 184. c. 2. *h.* The barony and regalia of the archbishop seized into the king's hand, 2 John, II. 237. c. 2. *p.*

Yrnham, Elias de, Dorset or Somersetshire, 5 Henry iii. I. 793. c. 1. *e.* How far Yrneham belonged to Robert de Gant, 9 Richard i. II. 225. c. 1. *t.*

Ysaac son of Bonefant of Bedford the the Jew, 7 Richard i. I. 216. c. 1. *e.* Ysaac the chirographer paid 5100 marks to his share of the tallage, 13 John, I. 223. c. 1. *k.*

Ysabel wife of William de Turevil her quit claim to the prior of Merton, 8 Richard i. I. 106. c. 2. *w.* Ysabel countess of S. Paul, I. 319. William son of Ysabel sherif of London, 19 Henry ii. I. 582. c. 2. *g.* William son of Ysabel sherif of London, 16 Henry ii. I. 746. c. 2. *f.* See Isabel.

Ysenbert, William de, had the mills and lands of Pockeford in fee in Wiltshire, I. 315. Was hanged about 42 Henry iii. ibid. c. 1. *n.*

Yseni, Adam de, 12 John, I. 218. c. 1. *s.* His grant to friars of the hospital of S. Sepulchre, Lincoln, ibid.

Ysilia widow of Adam de Saltmarsh, Glouc. in custody for the death of her late husband, 1 John, I. 493. c. 2. *bh.*

Ysolt. See Derebi.

Yvo husband of Emma, 3 Richard i. I. 105. c. 1. *q.* Richard son of Yvo, 10 John, I. 151. c. 2. *x.* Yvo husband of Emma amerced for withdrawing from a duel, 31 Henry ii. I. 550. c. 2. *c.* Yvo clerk constabulary, 10 Richard i. I. 776. c. 1. *r.*

Z.

Zatrichium, what, I. 160. c. 1. *g.*

Zuche, Roger la, sherif of Devonshire, 38 Henry iii. I. 277. c. 1. *y.* Alan la Zuche's fee in Northamptonshire, 18 Henry ii. I. 580. c. 1. *p.* Alan de la Zouche one of the Leicestershire barons summoned to the Scotch war, 26 Edward i. I. 655. c. 1. Elena de Zouche summoned to pay her scutage for the army in Wales, 10 Edward i. I. 656. c. 1. *e.* Roger la Zuche and Helena widow of Alan la Zuche, 5 Edward i. II. 77. c. 2. *l.* Sire Aleyn la Zouche, 25 Edward i. II. 105. c. 1. *i.* Alan la Zuche sherif of Northamptonshire, 52 Henry iii. II. 180. c. 2. *c.*

FINIS.